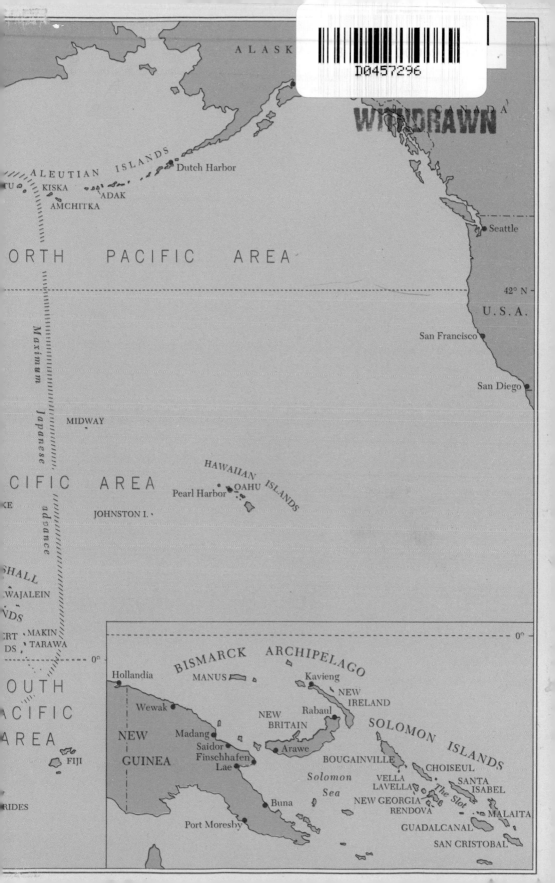

ALASKA

CANADA

ALEUTIAN ISLANDS
Dutch Harbor

TU
KISKA
ADAK
AMCHITKA

Seattle

ORTH   PACIFIC   AREA

42° N

Maximum Japanese

U.S.A.

San Francisco

San Diego

MIDWAY

HAWAIIAN ISLANDS

CIFIC   AREA

OAHU
Pearl Harbor

advance

KE
JOHNSTON I.

SHALL
WAJALEIN

NDS

RT
MAKIN
DS
TARAWA

0°

OUTH

BISMARCK   ARCHIPELAGO

0°

ACIFIC

Hollandia

MANUS

Kavieng

AREA

NEW
IRELAND

FIJI

Wewak

NEW
GUINEA

Madang

NEW
BRITAIN

Rabaul

SOLOMON   ISLANDS

Saidor
Finschhafen
Lae

Arawe

BOUGAINVILLE

CHOISEUL

RIDES

Buna

*Solomon
Sea*

VELLA
LAVELLA
NEW GEORGIA
RENDOVA

The Slot

SANTA
ISABEL

Port Moresby

MALAITA

GUADALCANAL

SAN CRISTOBAL

GEORGE C. MARSHALL

✳✳✳

ORGANIZER OF VICTORY

1943–1945

1880 - 1959

GEORGE C. MARSHALL:
ORGANIZER OF
VICTORY

☆ 1943 ☆

1945

☆   ☆

By FORREST C. POGUE

DIRECTOR OF THE RESEARCH CENTER
GEORGE C. MARSHALL RESEARCH FOUNDATION

Foreword by General Omar N. Bradley

NEW YORK: THE VIKING PRESS

First published in 1973 by The Viking Press, Inc.
625 Madison Avenue, New York, N.Y. 10022
Published simultaneously in Canada by
The Macmillan Company of Canada Limited
SBN 670-33694-7
Library of Congress catalog card number: 63-18373
Printed in U.S.A.
Unless otherwise credited, all photographs are
courtesy of U.S. Army Signal Corps
The following page constitutes an extension of this copyright page

ACKNOWLEDGMENTS

Harry C. Butcher: From *My Three Years with Eisenhower* by Harry C. Butcher.

The Devin Adair Co.: From *America's Retreat from Victory* by Joseph R. McCarthy and *The Untold Story of Douglas MacArthur* by Frazier Hunt.

Doubleday and Co., Inc. and William Collins Sons & Co. Ltd.: From *Turn of the Tide* by Sir Arthur Bryant, Copyright © 1957 by Arthur Bryant, and *Triumph in the West* by Sir Arthur Bryant, Copyright © 1959 by Arthur Bryant.

Harper and Row Publishers Inc.: From *Zhukov's Greatest Battles* edited by Harrison E. Salisbury, *Global Mission* by Henry H. Arnold, *The Blast of War* by Harold Macmillan, *Roosevelt and Hopkins* by Robert E. Sherwood, *On Active Service in Peace and War* by Henry L. Stimson and McGeorge Bundy, and *Soldier: The Memoirs of Matthew B. Ridgway* by Matthew B. Ridgway.

Her Majesty's Stationery Office: From *Grand Strategy*, Vol. VI, by John Ehrman and *Strategic Air Offensive Against Germany, 1939–1945*, Vol. III, by Sir Charles K. Webster and Noble Frankland.

Holt, Rinehart and Winston, Inc.: From *A Soldier's Story* by General Omar N. Bradley.

Houghton Mifflin Company: From *The Private Papers of Senator Vandenberg* by Arthur H. Vandenberg; *Closing The Ring, Hinge of Fate*, and *Triumph and Tragedy* by Winston S. Churchill; *War as I Knew It* by George S. Patton; and *Churchill: Taken from the Diaries of Lord Moran* by Lord Moran.

J. B. Lippincott Company: From the book *My Three Years in Moscow* by Walter Bedell Smith. Copyright, 1949, by Walter Bedell Smith. Reprinted by courtesy of J. B. Lippincott Company.

William Morrow & Co., Inc.: From *The Stilwell Papers* by Joseph W. Stilwell, Copyright 1948 by Winifred A. Stilwell, *The Business of War* by Sir John Kennedy, Copyright © 1957 by Sir John Kennedy.

W. W. Norton & Company, Inc.: From *Fleet Admiral King: A Naval Record* by Ernest J. King and Walter M. Whitehill.

Praeger Publishers, Inc.: From *The Mediterranean Strategy in the Second World War* by Michael Howard.

Random House, Inc.: From *The Politics of War* by Gabriel Kolko, Copyright © 1968 by Gabriel Kolko.

Simon & Schuster, Inc.: From *The Last Battle* by Cornelius Ryan, Copyright © 1966 by Cornelius Ryan, and *The War Memoirs of Charles de Gaulle, Unity 1942–1944*, Copyright © 1959 by Simon and Schuster, Inc.

Time Inc.: From *Reminiscences* by Douglas MacArthur, Copyright General MacArthur, *Life* Magazine, © 1964 Time Inc.

The Viking Press, Inc.: From *The Strange Alliance* by John R. Deane, Copyright 1946, 1947 by John R. Deane. Reprinted by permission of The Viking Press, Inc.

A. C. Wedemeyer: From *Wedemeyer Reports* by Albert C. Wedemeyer.

TO SECOND LIEUTENANT ALLEN TUPPER BROWN

WHO WAS KILLED MAY 29, 1944,

ON THE ROAD TO ROME

AND

TO ALL HIS COMRADES WHO PAID

A SIMILAR PRICE FOR VICTORY

Foreword

BY GENERAL OF THE ARMY OMAR N. BRADLEY

IN JANUARY 1943, as this book opens, the course of World War II gave the first signs of shifting in favor of the Allies. This was the critical period when United States forces, recovering from sharp setbacks in the Pacific, began to advance on the sure road to ultimate victory.

A large share in that final triumph belongs to the wise leadership of General of the Army George C. Marshall and to the Army and Army Air Forces that he had been building since his appointment as Chief of Staff in 1939. And tribute must go in equal measure to Fleet Admiral Ernest J. King's naval forces, including the Marines, which made their impact felt in the Pacific islands and on the sea lanes of the world.

In the choice of his commanders General Marshall evidenced his almost unerring judgment of men. Only one of his top commanders was relieved, and even on lower levels few were removed. From General Eisenhower to the division commanders, Marshall had sent to the combat theaters men whose work was well known to him. In the Pacific his theater commander was General Douglas MacArthur, whom he had urged President Roosevelt to summon back from retirement. For the China-Burma-India Theater he strongly recommended to Secretary of War Henry Stimson—Lieutenant General Joseph Stilwell. Now in 1943 he called on these officers to provide outstanding leadership, and they performed magnificently.

In my own case, after I had looked forward to being offered the post of superintendent of the U.S. Military Academy, General Marshall had favored me for command of the Infantry School at Fort Benning, where I had served under him in the stimulating years when he was in charge of instruction. The Chief of Staff then gave me two divisions to train, telling me that he had turned down recommendations that I have a corps command until I had completed this work. I trusted his judgment, and my patience was rewarded by rapid advancement to army and army group command.

My case typifies Marshall's rigor in testing his commanders for the critical tasks that lay ahead. He placed us in jobs where we could use our special training and experience. If we did our work well, he quickly entrusted us with a more demanding role. To his subordinates he always gave strong support and great freedom in carrying out their assignments.

His keen and perceptive concern, not only with strategic decisions, but with the well-being of the fighting man, was never more evident than on the visits he and the other Chiefs of Staff made to the invasion beaches less than a week after D day, in June 1944, and again to the whole Allied front in October of that year.

At a time when the Army is under criticism for its waging of an unpopular war, it is well for us to study the career of General of the Army George C. Marshall, whose roots were deeply embedded in the Army that he led. Dr. Pogue's volume performs an essential service in emphasizing, along with the historic triumphs to which the General contributed, the patience and understanding that he brought to the day-to-day operations of the Army in this unprecedented emergency. His penetrating and illuminating chronicle of Marshall's fifty years of service in the Army, where he spent most of his adult life, documents the quality of man the Army has produced and the self-sacrificing efforts of its officers and men. Those who are troubled about the future of the Army should consider the leadership and vision of General Marshall in times of danger and despair. General Marshall knew a time when the Army was neglected and generally spurned by the public, but he fought staunchly to preserve the nation's military strength. He recognized a need for this strength as a deterrent to aggression. The prevention of war was and is just as vital a mission for the military as the winning of it. Our indebtedness to General George C. Marshall, soldier and statesman, will become more clearly defined as history continues to chronicle his contributions to mankind.

Preface

THE CROSSING OF THE RHINE by United States troops in March 1945 prompted Prime Minister Winston Churchill to send warm congratulations to General George C. Marshall, whom he called "the true organizer of victory." Churchill thus paid tribute to the Chief of Staff's achievement in building the Army and Army Air Forces from a combined strength of less than 200,000 men in the summer of 1939 to 8⅓ million in 1945. Equally important was the task of arming and equipping these forces, training them in realistic exercises, and selecting able commanders for the campaigns that lay ahead. In a sense the British leader was repeating *Time* magazine's accolade at the end of 1943 when it named him "Man of the Year." George Marshall, it declared, "had armed the Republic."

Marshall not only helped to name or personally did name the key commanders of the Army and Army Air Forces in World War II, but he also carried the primary role in deliberations of the Combined Chiefs of Staff and the Joint Chiefs of Staff councils. He was sworn in as Chief of Staff of the U.S. Army on the date that Hitler invaded Poland and remained in that post until some months after the surrender of Japan. His leadership of the Army and Army Air Forces thus spanned the most tremendous six years of their history. As a leading representative of the Joint Chiefs of Staff in their dealings with Congress, the press, leaders of industry, and the general public, he played a more influential role than any other American or any British Chief of Staff. In the councils of the Allied Chiefs of Staff it was clear, as one British official historian put it, that he was *primus inter pares.* In those meetings, he was the chief American advocate of the cross-Channel strategy that was ultimately followed to victory in Europe.

The period 1943–1945 was marked by the growing recognition of Marshall by both President Roosevelt and Prime Minister Churchill. Increasingly he drafted messages concerning strategy and operations for the President's signature. At each Allied conference he was the American whose assent Churchill rated most vital for any strategic decisions.

In these years Marshall also won unparalleled respect from the President, the Congress, and the general public because of his absolute refusal to be considered as a possible presidential candidate. His nonpolitical position led him to avoid appearing before congressional committees or at news conferences in defense of administration proposals unless they specifically concerned the Army. Like Stimson, he resisted pressures to lend the War Department's or the Army's prestige to promote enactment of party measures. To an amazing degree he was able to prevent opponents of the President from attacking the Army and Air Forces for involvement in administration politics.

General Marshall and his associates have been severely criticized for their failure to think "politically" about military decisions in Europe. But as I shall show, their action was motivated not by disregard for political matters but by their belief that such matters belong to political chiefs of state. Marshall in particular maintained that only the political leaders could know all the factors affecting major strategic decisions, and he felt that they should be closely involved in decisions entailing the risk of substantial casualties.

Along with his conviction that political chiefs should make political decisions involving military forces went Marshall's equally strong conviction that the details of military operations should be left to military commanders in the field. He limited his own interference in combat operations, and he rejoiced that President Roosevelt refrained from intervention in these matters.

Marshall pursued an even-handed relationship with his subordinates. Although he believed that a commander should select good men and then give them his confidence, he was also prepared to proffer assistance when he thought it might be of value. Often a commander facing crises in the field found a steadying message from the Pentagon promising complete support in whatever decision he had to make.

The Chief of Staff had been notably successful in naming his field commanders. Drawing on his years of teaching officers at the Infantry School at Fort Benning, his own vast knowledge of leaders in World War I and the years between the wars, and the reports he had received from his advisers, such as the Chief of the Army Ground Forces, Lieutenant General Lesley J. McNair, and the Commanding General of the Army Air Forces, General H. H. Arnold, he had played a crucial role in choosing the key commanders of the Army and Air Forces in World War II. He had recommended that General Douglas MacArthur be recalled to active duty and made head of the U.S. Army forces in the Far East, had proposed that he be sent to Australia when it appeared certain that he could not hold the Philippines, and then had selected him as commander of U.S. Forces in the Southwest Pacific.

Marshall had called Brigadier General Dwight D. Eisenhower to Washington almost immediately after the attack by the Japanese on Pearl Harbor, had made him Chief of War Plans a few months later, and before spring had ended had sent him to the United Kingdom as commanding general of U.S. forces in that theater. Eisenhower's key position and his own abilities had brought him the post of Allied Commander-in-Chief in the Mediterranean and had prepared the way for his appointment as Supreme Commander. General Omar N. Bradley had been a protégé of Marshall's since the days at the Infantry School at Fort Benning, when, under Marshall's leadership, he had been a favorite instructor. In addition to advancing Bradley to division and corps command, the Chief of Staff had proposed him to Eisenhower for a special "eyes and ears" assignment in North Africa and later named him for army and then army group command in northwest Europe. Courtney Hodges, Mark Clark, Walter Bedell Smith, William H. Simpson, J. Lawton Collins, Alexander Patch, Lucian Truscott, and Matthew B. Ridgway were other outstanding commanders whose careers Marshall fostered. In the CBI, General Stilwell owed his selection by Secretary of War Stimson indirectly to Marshall's recommendation, and General Albert C. Wedemeyer could trace his position as Deputy to Lord Louis Mountbatten in the Southeast Asia Command and as Chief of the China theater to Marshall's warm endorsement. Although General Arnold had a major hand in naming his chief subordinates in the Army Air Forces, General Marshall had given his support to Kuter and Norstad. Among the officers who remained in Washington, he had given strong backing to the commander of Army Service Forces, Lieutenant General Brehon B. Somervell, to the Deputy Chief of Staff, Lieutenant General Joseph T. McNarney, and to the two chief assistants in the Operations Division, Lieutenant General Thomas T. Handy and Lieutenant General John E. Hull.

In the effort to show Marshall's role in World War II history, I have striven constantly to find the man. Reticent about his personal life, he submitted reluctantly to probings of his private thoughts and emotions. For this reason, I have had to depend heavily on the recollections of those who worked most closely with him during the world conflict.

During these years Marshall experienced one major personal disappointment and one major personal tragedy: He did not get the role of Supreme Commander to lead the cross-Channel invasion of Europe—to which, in some senses, his entire Army career had pointed and for which he had argued tenaciously, in the face of British doubts, at conference after conference. And shortly before the Normandy landing, his favorite stepson was killed in action in Italy. But on neither of these events did Marshall dwell—at least so far as the record goes.

I have grasped at many personal notes and comments—much more numerous than is generally supposed—which show his concern for good friends, such as Arnold and Hopkins, in times of illness, his constant vigilance on the welfare of troops, his intuitive skill in dealing with those under his command, and his recognition that men fight better who understand why they are in conflict. Especially in this present era with its strong distrust of the Army, its leaders, and its goals, I have felt it imperative to give a full portrait of a great commander, who loved his profession, who honored it for its service to the Republic, and who attempted to build a postwar force that would be acceptable to the American public.

Marshall had recognized the dangers faced by the Army in peacetime. He had seen that it was the special task of the Army to win the trust of the Congress and of the nation at large. He had sought their approbation by frank discussions with the committees before which he appeared, expert briefings of congressional representatives and of the press, candid revelations to investigating committees, and his determination to find and punish derelictions and failures in the Army before the problems reached the floors of the Senate and the House of Representatives or appeared in a newspaper column.

Aware of the costs of waging war and the great price of success, Marshall never forgot that the ultimate cost of victory lay in the loss of men's lives. In one of his last recorded interviews he said that he saw to it that the President was reminded weekly of casualties with the losses listed in vivid colors. It was essential, he declared, to remember the sacrifices. Because it is easy to get hardened to them.

In Marshall's war service we find the perfect blend of soldier and civilian. He was aware of the importance of the profession of arms that he had followed since the turn of the century and of the Army's contributions to the nation. He was equally aware that he was a servant of the Republic and that he was accountable for his actions in war as well as in peace.

Perhaps only at the close of the Civil War did the fighting men of North and South have as high a standing in the minds of the public as the fighting forces enjoyed in 1945. It was not only for their deeds in action against the enemy but for the spirit in which the battle had been waged that they were esteemed. As much as any other commander, George Marshall represented that spirit at its best.

I have selected the months from the Casablanca Conference in January 1943 to the end of the war in Europe as the period during which General Marshall exerted his maximum influence on world strategy and operations. Although important decisions had been made at Allied meetings between December 1941 and the end of 1942, it was at Casablanca that decisions were made opening the way to 1943–1945 strategy in Europe and the Pacific, including the proposal for the Combined Bomber Offensive and acceptance at least in principle of the commitment for a future date of the cross-Channel attack. May 8, 1945, is therefore a proper ending for the strategic arguments and decisions that began more than two years before at the Anfa conference.

Although General Marshall played an important role in the closing months of the war in the Pacific, the controversies and projected operations in the China-Burma-India Theater, and the decision to drop the atomic bomb on Japan, these matters actually provide a proper background for a volume on his mission to China, which followed the close of World War II. Therefore, I have retained only such material on these matters as is required to furnish a backdrop for the over-all development of strategy.

In any biography, it is necessary to focus the main attention on the author's subject. For this reason, I have sometimes failed to develop fully everyone's role at certain conferences and in certain decisions, and I have occasionally given only limited space to contributions of some of Marshall's colleagues. I have given scant attention to some matters that affected Marshall only peripherally or that show little of his character and leadership. I have been forced to conclude that biography is not the same as history and that one may sometimes better grasp the nature of one's subject by subordinating the details of historical narrative to the impact of the individual on a given conference or on a precise event. Such focus on a specific character—keeping the limelight on one performer throughout the entire drama—may lead at times to upstaging equally prominent or even more prominent performers. But any neglect of Roosevelt and Churchill has long since been corrected either by their admirers or by themselves; Leahy, Arnold, King, Alanbrooke, and Cunningham have told their stories. The excellent British and U.S. official histories have also helped redress any imbalance. As for Eisenhower, MacArthur, Montgomery, de Lattre de Tassigny, Bradley, Truscott, Krueger, Clark, Ridgway, de Gaulle, Brereton, Eden, Slim, Stilwell, Bedell Smith, we have detailed personal accounts to fill any gaps or correct any omissions in this account. Inasmuch as I have lived with General Marshall's papers since 1956 (and indeed with many of them since 1946, when I began writing the Army's official volume on Eisenhower's Supreme Command), I am of course more cognizant of his services and his explanations for his actions than I am of those of any other World War II leader—save General Eisenhower for the 1944–1945 period. As a result I have a bias in favor of my subject. This I can mitigate only by a presentation of the evidence that led me to my conclusions. I can only cite my healthy regard for the careful eye of critical theses writers of a later era—a breed whose latent threat and severe accounting makes more honest men of all of us who deal with history.

This volume owes much to the generosity of many friends whose gifts helped to pay for the over-all program of building the collection of documents, periodicals, and books at the George C. Marshall Research Library, Lexington, Virginia, and the writing of the biography with all the costs of research, interviewing, writing, and editing that such an effort entails. It also owes much to hundreds of people who have furnished material in various forms for our collection and the writing project. On pages 587–90 I have listed the names of many of the major contributors of money and material. It has not been possible to list all those whose assistance and good wishes have helped our program. At least we can say that our activities would not have been possible without them and that they have the eternal gratitude of all of us who work with the George C. Marshall Research Foundation.

It is proper to recall the crucial early efforts of the late John C. Hagan, Jr., as the original President of the George C. Marshall Research Foundation, the great contributions of General of the Army Omar N.

Bradley, who served as president of the Foundation, 1959–1969, and since as chairman of our board, and the current energetic leadership of Lieutenant General Marshall S. Carter. In the 1961–1964 period our fundraising efforts were headed by Joseph D. Neikirk, the executive vice president of the Virginia Military Institute Foundation. Since 1965 these efforts have been in the highly capable hands of Royster Lyle, Jr., whose assumption of many of the administrative tasks associated with the running of the Foundation has made it possible for me to devote much of my time to writing and research.

A special word must be said about the great contributions made by the late Miss Eugenia Lejeune, Archivist-Librarian of the Marshall library, whose work in collecting and organizing the collection of documents and books in the period 1957–1971 left a permanent imprint of excellence on our research program. The assistance of other members of the staff in Arlington and Lexington, is acknowledged on page 589.

In the editing of the initial drafts of this book I was aided by Joseph R. Friedman, Editor-in-Chief of the Office of Military History. Working on the chapters in his spare time, he continued the fine craftsmanship he had expended on earlier volumes of mine on which he worked. His knowledge of the period covered by this volume, which he gained as editor of numerous books in the "U.S. Army in World War II" series, as well as his sound advice, has been of great benefit in many ways.

For the final drafts of the book, The Viking Press secured the services of Phyllis Freeman, a skilled editor who brought a questioning eye to the manuscript. She has suggested means of improving organization and style, has caught some embarrassing errors, and in various ways has helped to produce a better book.

For the general editorship, I wish to thank Alan D. Williams, of The Viking Press, whose cogent suggestions for improving the book have been gratefully incorporated. His understanding of the problems of an author who has other duties to perform has been most helpful in a period of great pressures.

I hope that all those closely associated with me at the Marshall Foundation and Marshall Library, who have helped make this book possible by their understanding and their shouldering of some of the burdens I would have otherwise had to carry, will feel compensated—at least in part—by this volume, in which they had an important share. I wish to close with a special word of thanks to my wife, Christine, my severest critic and strongest well-wisher, whose longsuffering patience and rugged common sense have sustained me during the writing of this book.

FORREST C. POGUE

Lexington, Va.

Contents

xvii

Contents

Illustrations follow page 334

Maps

GEORGE C. MARSHALL

✶✶✶

ORGANIZER OF VICTORY

1943–1945

☆

☆ I ☆

☆   ☆

A Time for Decision

A YEAR of disaster that had ended with the glimmer of hope in a successful North African landing had tested the Americans and had seasoned the British even further since their political and military chiefs had sat down in Washington in late December 1941 to sketch desperate measures for dealing with chaos in the Pacific and with the Axis advance in Europe, Africa, and the Middle East. At Casablanca, in January of 1943, the emphasis had shifted toward the offensive in all theaters.

There was also a decisive change in the stature of General George C. Marshall. Now finishing his third year as Army Chief of Staff, Marshall was more than ever the pre-eminent figure on the military scene at home and abroad. Not by bluster or by push, but by agreement, he was fast becoming first among equals in Joint Chiefs and Combined Chiefs of Staff meetings.[1]* Several factors favored Marshall. With the exception of Admiral of the Fleet Sir Dudley Pound, who would die before the year ended, he was the only one of the Combined Chiefs of Staff to have held his position since the day war began in Europe. Although the British had been at war longer, he had more experience than any other military leader in finding resources for his own forces and America's allies, for dealing with members of Congress, the President, and the general public. As Chief of both the U.S. Army and the U.S. Army Air Forces, he had more men under his direction than any other British or American Chief of Staff.

But very special qualities reinforced Marshall's dominance: self-confidence, inner strength, will, character. To his opponents his firmness in debate often appeared to be stubbornness, even rudeness. To those, like Secretary of War Henry L. Stimson and Lieutenant General Dwight D. Eisenhower, who saw in him the element of indomitability, he was a rock in an age of uncertainty. At the forthcoming conference in Casablanca, Marshall would have to tax all these resources to the maximum.

* Numbered reference notes begin on page 611.

Many of the political and military leaders who had met in Washington in the dark hours of December 1941 were reunited at Casablanca. But they were joined now by others whose names had first become familiar in Allied circles during the intervening twelve months.

There was Churchill, dogged as he had been since he was summoned to the premiership in May 1940, more than ever the darling of destiny, determined to defeat the Hun, smash Italy, re-establish British mastery in the Mediterranean, open the sea lanes to India, avenge the setbacks in North Africa, and keep for Britain at least her prewar status in world affairs. He shared with the Americans a determined opposition to Japan, but he was not as convinced as they of the importance of speeding the attack against Germany in order to keep the Soviet Union in the fight. Now that the Russians seeemed to be able to hold their own against the Germans, he tried to avoid risking heavy British casualties. Ever conscious of his country's ebbing manpower, the Prime Minister preferred to exhaust other means of sapping Germany's strength before attempting a direct attack across the Channel.

Confident of the rightness of his views, Churchill was a difficult superior and a formidable opponent. He had worn down one Chief of the Imperial General Staff, Field Marshal Sir John Dill, and often reduced his successor, the much tougher General Sir Alan Brooke, to anger and frustration. Operating on the theory that he and his staff "were not paid to be polite to each other," the Prime Minister upbraided high subordinates in the presence of outsiders. "He berated me like a pickpocket in front of U.S. Ambassador John Winant," his wartime Chief of the Air Staff, Sir Charles Portal, said, recalling one embarrassing session. Churchill's saving grace was that he allowed those at whom he lashed out to be rude in return. But he took unfair advantage with sulking rages, tearful displays, and bland denials that his conduct had been outrageous. "Can't I ever get any commanders who will fight? You don't care if we lose the war. You just want to draw your pay and eat your rations," was a typical rebuke to a member of the Chiefs of Staff Committee who opposed his views. His British colleagues were brutally tried by his sudden shifts and by his tendency at international conferences to disrupt carefully negotiated accords with the Americans. Frequently Churchill's military chiefs doubted the soundness of his strategy and deplored his imperfect appreciation of logistical problems or of advances in weapons and tactics developed since World War I, but they never forgot his firm leadership in crisis, his great courage, and his shrewd intuition. Effectively exploiting the British practice of speaking with one voice in council after intramural differences had been resolved, Churchill was a formidable opponent of the more free-wheeling Americans in Allied meetings.[2]

Beginning the third year of his third term, President Franklin D. Roosevelt still remained buoyant despite the heavy burdens imposed by the Depression years and by the blows inflicted by the Japanese at Pearl Harbor and throughout the Pacific. Long proud of creating a new political coalition in the United States by the force of his personality and the play of circumstances, he had been slow to assume a major role in international affairs. Once committed, he had enjoyed his relationship with Churchill, his opportunity to balance the scales in the world conflict, and finally his growing leadership in the battle against the Axis.

In the first year of the conflict the President had followed Churchill's lead. But as he approached the Casablanca meeting, he increasingly took a more independent line. Never forcing the pace, he nonetheless showed great delight in turning from domestic politics to global developments. By the time of Casablanca he was looking beyond the war to playing a leading role in establishing a lasting peace. Unfortunately he had not constructed a grand design to implement it.

The Argentia conference in August 1941—a secret meeting in an isolated port, with the Prime Minister of Great Britain journeying across the Atlantic to meet him and ask his counsel—had stirred the President's imagination. But the meeting at Casablanca—with a somewhat risky flight across the Atlantic and the opportunity to sit down thousands of miles from home to help decide the strategy of the world—excited him even more. After World War I his onetime chief, Woodrow Wilson, had traveled to Europe to help plan the peace—something new for an American President. Roosevelt's was an even greater adventure. His historical allusion—"I prefer a comfortable oasis to the raft at Tilsit"—made it clear that he savored his role in the current international drama.

Although less susceptible to Churchill's influence now than he had been during the Prime Minister's U.S. visit in the summer of 1942, Roosevelt was still something of an enigma to his American advisers as the Casablanca conference opened. Seeing less of his Chiefs of Staff than Churchill did of his military advisers, Roosevelt imposed no unified plan, although he still seemed of half a mind to go along with the British drive in the Mediterranean if they declined to mount a cross-Channel operation in 1943. Assuming that victory was near at hand in North Africa, he wanted to press the attack. In addition he was deeply concerned over the claims of rival French factions and Allied acceptance of the unconditional-surrender formula he had proposed for the Axis.

General Marshall was more certain than he had been a year earlier of where he stood with the President. But the Chief of Staff still had twinges of doubt about Roosevelt's backing of the Army. And he constantly had to contend with Roosevelt's lack of administrative order, his failure to keep the Chiefs of Staff informed of private high-level discussions, and his tendency to ignore War Department advice in favor of suggestions from officials in other departments. Marshall knew that the President could be decisive if he chose, that he was wise in the ways of Congress, and that he was turning increasingly to the Chief of Staff for key presentations of plans—to meet problems at home or abroad. Marshall and his colleagues were frustrated more by Roosevelt's procrastination than by his browbeating.

Both the British and United States Chiefs of Staff had their work laid out for them as the conference, with its budget of disputed plans, approached. More irascible than ever as the pressure on him mounted, Marshall's British counterpart, General Sir Alan Brooke, now had to shoulder the double task of preventing the Americans from launching the cross-Channel attack before he was ready and of dissuading Churchill from proposing adventures in Norway, the eastern Mediterranean, or some other spot liable to frighten the Americans or prevent orderly development of his own plans. Highly voluble, speaking overrapidly to keep up with his racing thoughts, Brooke drove ahead impatiently in discussion, offending colleagues and Allies by his brusqueness and short temper. Portal once remarked that Brooke "clashed at times with the Americans—his bark was worse than his bite, although he could bite."

Happily for the Americans, the other members of the British delegation, although no less vigorous in debate than Brooke, were smoother in approach. The First Sea Lord, Sir Dudley Pound, grew less and less alert as the brain tumor that was to claim his life in October increased in deadliness. Often he dozed or seemed to sleep, only to spring awake when his beloved Navy was involved.[3]

Air Chief Marshal Portal, commander of the Bomber Command during the trying months in 1940 before he became Chief of the Air Staff, was more influential. He had won the admiration of the Americans at their first meeting in December 1941 and steadily gained their confidence. Marshall, who thought that Portal had the best brain in the British Chiefs of Staff organization, greatly preferred dealing with him on touchy subjects rather than with the other British Chiefs.

Everyone's favorite was Lieutenant General Sir Hastings Ismay, who had made a career out of reducing friction and keeping administrative wheels turning smoothly at staff meetings and conferences. As personal Chief of Staff for Churchill, who held the post of Minister of Defence, Ismay had the difficult task of presenting the Prime Minister's views to the British Chiefs of Staff and of making certain that the Prime Minister was fully informed of theirs. Undoubtedly Ismay's great gift of humor played a large part in enabling him to survive his punishing assignment.

If Churchill had drafted an insulting note, Ismay would suggest that there was no point in angering the addressee. Then Churchill, with fine scorn, would shout, "Appeaser!" To Ismay's reply, "Well, at least, let me check the facts," the Prime Minister would rejoin, "Check the facts, but don't change the tenor of the note." Ismay would cut out the insults and bring the revised note to Chiefs of Staff meetings. When Churchill heard criticisms of the draft, he would shout to the Chiefs of Staff, "Why do you let the man write notes like that?" [4]

Although loyal to Churchill, Ismay often amused his colleagues with imitations of his chief. One friend recalled that the General sometimes did "a good show on the way Winston would demand the impossible." The narrator reconstructed Ismay's dialogue: "Winston said, 'Give everybody at the table a biscuit!' There were three at the table and only two biscuits, so I said, 'But there are only two biscuits.' He replied, 'I said give everybody a biscuit.' Then I asked, 'Shall I give the first two one each and the third none?' And he answered, 'No, no, give them each a biscuit.' Then I asked, 'Shall I break them up and give part to each?' and he very angrily roared, 'No, I tell you, give each man a biscuit.' It was a perfect example of his habit of insisting on various plans when he didn't have enough to do them with." [5]

On the American side Admiral Ernest J. King, Chief of Naval Operations, often angered the British as Brooke did the Americans. A stubborn, dedicated sailor, proud of his reputation for toughness and ruthlessness, he was said to have remarked, "When the going gets rough, they call on the sons of bitches." He usually backed Marshall in European matters, but he never neglected the Navy's cause in the Pacific. His capacity for mean infighting, which Marshall knew all too well, sometimes shocked his opponents. British Rear Admiral C. E. Lambe, who observed him at conferences, remarked, "King is said to have had his eye on the Pacific. That is his Eastern policy. Occasionally he throws a rock over his shoulder. That is his Western policy." Lord Portal said of him: "King was fiery but in the long run cooperated beautifully. He usually delivered what he promised to deliver ahead of time. However, unless you tied him down, he felt it was quite all right to run off to the Pacific with his craft. Several arguments came over the meaning of words. Once when King said U.S. public opinion wouldn't accept certain things, Brooke said, 'Then you will have to educate them'—meaning to propagandize. King said, 'I thank you [to remember that] the Americans are as well educated as the British.' " [6]

Lieutenant General Henry H. Arnold, commanding general of the Army Air Forces, although given increasingly greater freedom by Marshall to control air operations, was content for the most part to remain in the Chief of Staff's shadow. Portal, the airman's British opposite number, later said of him: "General Arnold had trouble following the strategic arguments; he never talked except on air. He had trouble holding the interest of the group. He was a grand fellow; never had any trouble with him." The American battled effectively but quietly for his Air Forces, often relying on the affability that had won him the nickname "Hap" to get his way.

Admiral William D. Leahy was the one member of the current Combined Chiefs of Staff who had not held his position at the time of the December 1941 conference in Washington. He had retired as Chief of Naval Operations before the beginning of the war in Europe and then served as President Roosevelt's ambassador to the Vichy French government after the defeat of France. In mid-July 1942 he was appointed Chief of Staff to the Commander-in-Chief, at Marshall's suggestion. The two collaborated frequently in drafting messages for the President's signature, and Leahy often supported the Army Chief of Staff in debates between the Army and Navy.

As the North African conference approached, General Marshall considered the course to which the American effort could most consistently be held. Because of the problems of getting sufficient manpower to provide food and arms, as well as the fighting men needed for victory, the Chief of Staff believed it essential to focus on actions that were most clearly in the American interest. It was also vital to choose the strategy that led most directly to Germany and Japan.

Before Pearl Harbor the United States made available, first for cash and then under Lend-Lease arrangements, a considerable share of American industrial production for the British to use in accordance with their own strategic plans and needs. Concerned with safeguarding the United Kingdom and the sea lanes of the Atlantic, the Americans simply assumed that the British would use the equipment and supplies to best advantage. They accepted the view that whatever was good for the British Empire in this desperate situation was also good for the United States. To a marked degree Washington adjusted its output to fill British requirements while also supplying American naval and military needs. When the Germans invaded the Soviet Union, the United States extended aid to the Russians on much the same basis.

Once Pearl Harbor jolted the United States into war, the stock assumptions about the identity of American and British goals had to be re-examined. Clearly a prime necessity was to protect American interests in the Pacific and the Far East—interests that did not necessarily coincide with those of Great Britain.

From a narrow nationalistic point of view the United States could have justified utilizing its military manpower solely in the Pacific and turning the bulk of its resources in that direction, giving perhaps a fourth of its production to the British and Russians to press the fight in Europe while American forces finished with the Japanese. Indeed this was the course strongly favored by General Douglas MacArthur, U.S. Southwest Pacific commander, and many of his supporters in the United States. As the war continued, it became impossible to avoid strengthening the Pacific commitment.

However, because the United States Chiefs of Staff agreed with President Roosevelt that it was best to defeat Germany first, and then turn all efforts toward Japan, the United States continued to give the European conflict top priority. This policy was implemented at the direct expense of American forces in the Pacific and at the possible cost of paramount Japanese control over an area rich in natural resources. Without effective challenge to the enemy, former colonies of Britain, France, or the Netherlands might become integrated into the Japanese-dominated Co-Prosperity Sphere. This possibility, long dreaded by the United States and other Western powers, could not be ruled out.

For Britain the return to its prewar position was vital. Thus its priorities were: first, the security of the home islands; second, the protection of the lifelines through the Mediterranean and the Suez and the shortened sea voyage to India; and third, the fight to end German domination of Europe—all at the greatest saving possible in scarce resources and disappearing manpower. Particularly the British welcomed a chance to improve their situation in the Mediterranean. This was a reasonable approach, completely acceptable to the United States, so long as Churchill stuck to his pre-Pearl Harbor proposal to let the United States furnish the tools while Britain finished the job, and so long as American forces were not hard pressed in another corner of the globe.

Once the United States entered the war, the situation changed. Weary and weakened from the years in which they had fought almost alone, the British found it difficult to meet continually mounting demands for forces and equipment. They would be helped immensely if the Americans accepted British strategy and allotted increased manpower and supplies to the operations the British deemed most vital for the Allied cause. As a result they advocated a vigorous follow-up of the North African operations with assaults in the Mediterranean while building up in the United Kingdom as large a force as possible for a future cross-Channel operation. Such a policy left only limited resources for offensive operations in the Pacific.

In the eyes of the American Chiefs of Staff, whose views did not necessarily coincide with the President's, the ideal course for the United States was one that would bring the quickest end possible to the European war so that forces in the Pacific, largely American in make-up, would suffer minimal losses. Clearly it was necessary to prevent the Japanese from digging in. Although no one doubted Churchill's repeated assurances of full British support in the Pacific after the end of the war in Europe, Britain's growing weakness was evident. The American Chiefs, therefore, increasingly demanded operations in Europe where American troops and materiel could be used to maximum effect without committing the United States to additional operations that contributed only indirectly to German defeat. At Casablanca the American Chiefs would try to ascertain if the 1942 attack in North Africa represented for the British a temporary diversion or a way of life.

For these reasons, more than because of any inherent difference in the strategic viewpoints of insular and continental powers, the United States Chiefs of Staff, led by General Marshall, demanded a major operation that could be planned for a definite date with specific requirements. They were willing to risk the possibility of heavier initial losses to avoid accept-ance of commitments that meant further delays and the loss of American lives in operations not directly concerned with United States policy.

The nearest build-up point the United States could employ for opera-tions in Europe was the United Kingdom. The point from which maxi-mum airpower could be exerted in support of a landing against German-held territory was the United Kingdom. With the exception of the Iberian Peninsula, the point at which the enemy would be required to stretch his forces at a maximum distance from the Russian front was again the cross-Channel area. The operation least likely to involve the United States in the sticky pitch of the Middle East, the eastern Mediterranean, or possibly the Balkans (all areas where even the British Chief of Staff, General Brooke, dreaded the Prime Minister's improvisations) was the cross-Channel project. In short the most clearly defined, least complicated, most decisive effort for the United States in Europe was a thrust from the south and west of England across the English Channel. So ran the Ameri-can argument as formulated in Washington.

Accompanying this analysis was another that carefully outlined the di-vergences in British and American approaches to strategy. It was prepared by the long-range planners from the Army and Air Forces on the Joint Strategic Survey Committee, Lieutenant General Stanley D. Embick and Major General Muir Fairchild.

Embick, whose son-in-law, Brigadier General Albert C. Wedemeyer, was one of the strongest advocates of the cross-Channel attack, had devel-oped an unfavorable view of British imperial policies in World War I. In the spring of 1942 Embick had protested vigorously that American inter-vention in the Middle East or North Africa principally served British interests. And the JSSC report to General Marshall reflected Embick's long-standing fear that Churchill, whose military ability he discounted, would drag the United States into affairs irrelevant to its own interests.

Recalling that the British had not deviated in more than a century from the effort to maintain the balance of power in Europe, Embick and Fairchild noted that they still advanced this aim. The outright defeat of Germany, leaving the Soviet Union in a dominant position on the Conti-nent, was not in accord with Britain's historic position. "It would be in strict accord with that policy, however, to delay Germany's defeat until military attrition and civilian famine had materially reduced Russia's po-tential toward dominance in Europe." It seems likely, they reasoned, "that the purpose behind the British proposal is not primarily military but is political. It is therefore recommended that the Joint Chiefs of Staff do not compromise but insist upon acceptance of our military concept which was arrived at from the purely military viewpoint." [7]

The strong influence of these views on Wedemeyer, Chief of the Strat-egy and Policy Group of the Operations Division, can be seen in his ad-vice to Marshall at Casablanca and in the comments accompanying his request a few months later for a study on proper Allied strategy after the occupation of Sicily. In a statement that could have been written equally well before the Casablanca conference, Wedemeyer declared: "One of the most difficult arguments advanced by the British for me to counter includes the fact that our present operations in the Mediterranean have given us to a degree the initiative in that area and have gained us a certain momentum, both of which should be exploited to the fullest. My feeling about such line of reason is that *the British mind is not projected militarily to the future, but politically, and strategy is strongly influenced thereby."* He noted that sound military thinkers agreed with "overtop" operations as opposed to "underbelly." "They have also recognized," he went on, "that the continuation of operations which are prompted by political and economic considerations may postpone if not entirely remove our chances for a decisive victory. The United States cannot afford to follow the British strategy for many reasons. . . ." [8]

General Wedemeyer weighed American and British viewpoints and found the latter defective. The "militarily aggressive" Americans, faced with difficult tasks, wanted them to be "quickly and effectively done." The British, on the other hand, played for time so that with both Russia and Germany drained, he continued, ". . . the British [will be able] to enjoy their historic role of arbiter in the balance of power within continental Europe. Associated with this idea however is the possibility that a rapprochement may be effected between Russia and Germany. (There were 4,000,000 Communists in Germany when Hitler seized power in 1933.) There are reports that Russia is strained seriously in her economy and another year at the present war-making pace may swing the balance to our enemy." [9]

These pronouncements, which left some mark on Marshall and the other Chiefs, reflected a sector of American thinking that would later be attacked as lacking in political realism. Perhaps the trouble lay in the fact that the stress on "military" in American statements was misleading. The Americans saw clearly enough the political advantages Churchill might gain for Britain by his policies. But if these did not serve American interests, the U.S. Chiefs of Staff preferred to deal in terms of military advantages.

American military opposition to British policy was prompted not by a desire to support Soviet expansion but by a belief that the Soviet problem had to be handled by Britain and the countries of Western Europe rather than by the United States. The failure to see that a weakened Russia might be more to be desired than a weakened Germany arose, first, from an inability to believe that a country brought near defeat by Nazi armies in recent months could soon threaten the West and, second, from the assumption that Russian expansion would continue, as in the past, to be directed toward the Balkans and the Dardanelles. In the end the miscalculation lay less in underestimating Russian capacity to recover rapidly than in failing to foresee the virtual collapse of British military power at the close of the war. Churchill's brusque refusal to preside over the liquidation of the British Empire obscured the fact that, unaided, Britain could no longer maintain the balance of power in Europe.

General Marshall's thinking was also influenced by the fear that the United States lacked the means to meet demands for increased food and armament production and the manpower needs of the armed services. Only a few weeks before the Casablanca conference opened, the Chief of Staff had struggled with the President and various White House civilian advisers over the allocation of men and equipment to the Army and Army Air Forces for 1943 and 1944. He was particularly concerned that continued press emphasis on strengthening the naval and air forces, as opposed to ground units, would impress the President. It seemed likely that the Army's larger requirements would be slighted as the three services, industry, and agriculture scrambled for their shares of American manpower.

Responding to the demands of industry and agriculture, the director of the War Manpower Commission, former Governor Paul McNutt of Indiana, in September 1942 attempted to persuade the Joint Chiefs of Staff to set a ceiling on their demands. When the various services proposed a total of close to 11,000,000 men by the end of 1943—of which the Army and Army Air Forces would require 8,200,000 officers and men—the President provisionally approved the estimate. But he made clear his objection "to such a radical increase in the authorized strength at one time." Members of the War Production Board, which had been thinking in terms of a total force of 7,600,000, called the 11,000,000 figure unrealistic. General Marshall strongly disagreed. "We cannot make any cuts in our requirements for combat units if we expect to win the war," he insisted.[10]

The next day the Director of the Budget sent a statement to the War Department that seemed to expect just such cuts from the Army. The new recommendations, which Marshall assumed reflected the President's views, seemed designed to hold the Army and Army Air Forces until mid-1944 to the allocation of men and officers that the President had provisionally approved for the period terminating at the end of 1943. They represented a heavy blow to the Chief of Staff's future plans, and he decided on a swift and vigorous response.[11]

On November 9, 1942, the morning after the landings in North Africa, Marshall made his rebuttal to the figures from the Director of the Budget. He declared that the proposed ceiling meant that fourteen fewer transportable divisions than planned would be available in the spring of 1944. The Army would have to break up divisions in training or reduce the air program in order to maintain the divisions overseas.[12]

"The morale of the hostile world must be broken," the Chief of Staff maintained, "not only by aggressive fighting but as in 1918 by the vision of an overwhelming force of fresh young Americans being *rapidly* developed in this country." Reminding the President that in February 1942 he had given the Chief of Staff special responsibilities in matters pertaining to "strategy, tactics, and operations," Marshall declared: "It is my considered opinion that the instruction of the Bureau of the Budget referred to jeopardizes our success in this war and should be revoked immediately." [13] It was as firm a statement as the Chief of Staff had made to the White House thus far in the war. The strong language of a draft message that Marshall discarded was an even more significant indication of Army fears: "I am greatly disturbed by the obvious campaign in a large number of newspapers directed against the increase of the Army and in some instances contending for the principle of our providing the munitions while other troops do the fighting. The success in the Middle East has given impetus to this fallacious and humiliating proposition. A successful TORCH operation [code name for the Allied invasion of North Africa] will further strengthen this fatal psychology." [14]

Irked, the President sought to put matters right. In part he blamed the disagreement on confusing bookkeeping terminology: "I wish the Government as a whole would talk in terms either of calendar year or fiscal year but not both!" His recent directions to the Director of the Budget, he insisted, were not at variance with his approval of the Joint Chiefs of Staff estimates of late September. If both the Bureau of the Budget and the War Department followed his instructions, he concluded, there would be no disagreement. [15]

Marshall questioned the President's estimate. In a two-week period filled with conferences and extensive correspondence he and his colleagues persuaded Roosevelt to reaffirm his approval of a figure of 7,500,000 officers and men for the end of 1943. With this concession, however, the President warned that this figure would probably not be exceeded later. [16]

Aware that the armed forces had in mind still larger proposals, the War Production Board and the War Manpower Commission insisted on having some control over their future manpower quotas. Members of Congress echoed these views. In October the Senate Special Committee to Investigate the National Defense Program, headed by Senator Harry S. Truman, complained that the armed services had not consulted the manpower and production officials in setting up requirements; in November the House Select Committee Investigating National Defense Migration, headed by Representative John H. Tolan, asked that the President establish an authority to fix the size of the armed forces and to allocate manpower between them and industry and agriculture.

It seems likely that some of these pressures prompted General Marshall to reconsider an invitation to appear before the National Association of Manufacturers in New York City in early December. On November 12 he declined to talk; twelve days later he reversed his decision. He took the occasion of addressing the huge dinner audience of nearly four thousand to reply to critics of the Army.

He particularly stressed the importance of long-range planning, which he considered as important to the Army as to manufacturers. There was, he said, uneasiness in some quarters that the War Department leaders were building too large an Army and that they could not transport it to active theaters once they had it—"in short, the belief that we do not know what we are doing or where we are going." But the plans had been formulated after a year or more of intensive study and research. "The Army has only one concern—one purpose—the destruction of German and Japanese military power. The assumption that we have not even calculated our ways and means necessarily implies a serious doubt as to our competence to direct military operations."

> A democracy [he continued] demands effective military leadership, which is a good guarantee for efficiency. The trouble arises, not from the condemnation of leaders, but from the effort to dictate or influence the strategical employment of our forces without knowledge of the logistical requirements or of the various military situations and the world of international relationships involved. . . .

In his concluding argument, he underscored the importance of the Army manpower program:

> Finally I wish to emphasize one point. It is a comparatively simple thing to cut a program, to check the development of the Army, if the happy day comes when that is found permissible, but I assure you that it is utterly impossible to improvise military organizations, and it requires more than a year to build them. Therefore, it is our opinion that no more tragic mistake could be made than to ignore the great mass of enemy divisions and expect us to win this war on a shoestring or by some specialized process.[17]

Repeatedly he warned against eager acceptance of particular panaceas purporting to guarantee a quick ending to the conflict. Three days before leaving for Casablanca he wrote a World War I general who had become a powerful figure in the American Legion: "The public is continually impressed with the argument that victory through airpower alone is the proper course. They are told that this will give us a somewhat painless victory, and a speedy one." But, he countered, these advocates overlooked the fact that "the only limitation which our plans put on the expansion of our airpower is its ability to turn out planes and pilots, technicians and other necessary highly trained combat and supporting personnel. Victory through airpower alone is but one example."

The way to victory, he believed, was still distant, and it was essential to prepare the public for the necessary long pull. "The most important job for the Legion (in my opinion) is to fight down, everywhere and every day, the dangerous illusion that because we have won some successes the

war is 'in the bag.' . . . I am not so much worried over possible reverses
. . . as I am of its effect in the impeding of the war effort." [18]

As the Casablanca conference neared, the U.S. chiefs were all sharply
aware of these severe shortages in many areas. And perhaps their rivalry
over men and supplies was partly responsible for their failure to have a
common plan to present the President on January 7, at the only meeting
Roosevelt held with his advisers to establish an American position for the
forthcoming conference. General Marshall then stated candidly that
"there was not a united front on the subject [cross-Channel], particularly
among our planners." He noted that while the U.S. Chiefs of Staff preferred an operation in the north to one in the Mediterranean, the question was still an open one.[19]

Marshall had never favored sending forces eastward beyond Gibraltar
into the Mediterranean. Now he warned that heavy shipping losses would
follow operations there. Future Allied landings in the Mediterranean
could be hit by air from Italy, southern France, Corsica, and probably
Sicily, and by concentrated submarine attacks at sea. He also feared a
German thrust through Franco's Spain.

Thus far in his presentation the Chief of Staff was restating old arguments to Roosevelt. Then he shifted from the immediate Channel area as
the proposed landing site in the north. Perhaps to forestall British warnings of well-guarded coasts in the Cotentin Peninsula or to offer a target
area into which troops from North Africa could be more easily transported by sea, he suggested the Brest Peninsula as a possible landing place
once North Africa was free. He conceded that the losses there might be
greater in men than in shipping, but he was prepared to take that risk:
"To state it cruelly, we could replace troops whereas a heavy loss in shipping, which could result from the BRIMSTONE operation [proposed for Sar-
dinia], might completely destroy any opportunity for successful operations against the enemy in the near future."

Seeming dubious, Roosevelt closely questioned the Chief of Staff about
the proposed landing area. Marshall argued that there would be "no narrow straits on our lines of operations, and we could operate with fighter
protection from the United Kingdom." He insisted that a landing could
be made, although he granted that German armor could give trouble.

Rather than accepting Marshall's views that the question of the next
operation "had resolved itself into one thing or the other with no alternatives in sight," the President asked if the build-up in the United Kingdom
could not continue while the final decision was held in abeyance for a
month or two. He hinted at his ultimate choice by noting that of the
800,000 or 900,000 Allied troops then in North Africa, only some 300,000
would be required to maintain order there after Tunisia was cleared of
the enemy. What use, he asked, could be made of the remaining half-
million men? Apparently sensing that Roosevelt was set on a Mediterranean target, Marshall said that of the possibilities there Sicily seemed a

more desirable objective for a landing than Sardinia. The latter, closer to Italy and to occupied France, would be in range of German bombers, while the former was closer to the North African embarkation points.

Thus the White House meeting ended on a note of indecision. Although Roosevelt had said that the British would have a plan and stick to it, he failed to state a specific goal for the Americans to pursue or to require the Joint Chiefs of Staff to establish a common line for the conference. As an overall course the American Chiefs of Staff held at the meeting to the proposal they had circulated to the British Chiefs of Staff twelve days earlier: "To conduct a strategic offensive in the Atlantic–Western European Theater directly against Germany, employing the maximum forces consistent with maintaining the accepted strategic concept in other theaters." They also called for continued offensive and defensive operations in the Pacific and in Burma to break the Japanese hold on areas that threatened the security of Allied communications and positions.[20]

Marshall had not been won to Mediterranean targets by President Roosevelt's arguments at the White House conclave. As he explained to Secretary of War Stimson the same day, he preferred to attack the north coast of France, preferably the Brest or Cherbourg Peninsula, in 1943. He thought that the Allies could hold a lodgment area, and even if driven out, they would still cripple German resistance for 1944. The British, he warned, wanted to attack islands in the Mediterranean, hoping to draw the Germans into a costly defense of Italy. Not only would such operations result in heavy shipping losses, but they would bring a successful landing in the north no nearer.[21] Consequently Marshall planned to fight these British views at the North African meeting.

The Casablanca conference was held largely at the urging of the Prime Minister. As soon as the first footholds had been secured in North Africa by Eisenhower's forces, Churchill proposed a conference of representatives from Great Britain, the United States, and the Soviet Union to consider the next move against the Axis. The Americans suspected that he planned to propose scrapping BOLERO—the plan for the build-up of resources in the United Kingdom for a cross-Channel attack. Actually he was concerned lest the United States abandon that program in favor of operations in some other part of the world.[22]

Although President Roosevelt had even earlier suggested sending a small military delegation to Moscow to discuss future Mediterranean operations with the Russians, he thought that such a conference should await completion of operations in Tunisia. When he received Churchill's proposal for a three-power meeting, Roosevelt replied, in a message drafted by General Marshall, that he hoped that his proposed conference on military strategy could be held within four to six weeks and added that he would "probably send Marshall to head up our group. . . ."[23]

Churchill was clearly fearful of a Russo-American meeting without prior Anglo-American discussions. He hoped that if Marshall were sent, "he would not bypass this country." He suggested, instead, a meeting of the heads of government, including Stalin, and mentioned Iceland as a possible site.

After numerous exchanges in which it became clear that the Russian Field Marshal could not or would not leave his battle front, Churchill proposed a high-level conference with the President. Ruling out Iceland, Roosevelt spoke of Algiers or Khartoum and then, asserting that it might still criticism of his absence from the country in wartime if he inspected troops in North Africa, suggested a spot in Morocco north of Casablanca. When Churchill assented, Marshall asked Eisenhower to make suitable arrangements.

To ensure security for the visiting dignitaries, representatives of the British and Americans looked for quarters that could be shut off from a nearby town and surrounded with armed guards. Centering their search on the Casablanca area, they decided at the end of December on Anfa, a suburb about five miles south of Casablanca and one mile inland. The modern three-story Anfa Hotel and eighteen adjoining villas were requisitioned for the visiting officials. Barbed wire was strung around the area, and contingents of soldiers and plain-clothesmen were installed.[24] The hotel, set on a ridge, looked beyond the city to the sea. Its beguiling tropical resort atmosphere of palm and bougainvillaea made an incongruous setting for warlike planning, but regular pacing of armed sentries and the presence of bodyguards represented martial reality.[25]

Marshall and his colleagues were airborne by 8:30 a.m., January 9, from Gravelly Point, National Airport, Washington, in two C-54s, the four-engined work horses of the Air Forces. General Marshall, General Arnold, and Field Marshal Sir John Dill were among those in the first plane. Admiral King; Lieutenant General Brehon B. Somervell, head of the Services of Supply; Rear Admiral Charles M. Cooke, Navy planner; General Wedemeyer, and several others were in the second. Their course led from Washington to Miami and Puerto Rico, from there to Belém and Natal in Brazil, and then across the South Atlantic to Bathurst, Marrakech, and Casablanca. That evening around 10:30 p.m. Roosevelt, Harry L. Hopkins, and Admiral Leahy left by train for Florida, where they boarded the presidential plane for the overseas trip. At Trinidad, Leahy fell ill and was left behind.[26]

"Elaborate preparations" were made for General Marshall's trip to Casablanca and a possible postconference visit to Moscow, proposed by the President to Stalin but ultimately canceled at the latter's request. The equipment gathered by Marshall's assistant, Lieutenant Colonel Frank McCarthy, included one set of clothing for the heat of North Africa, another for Russia's midwinter cold. Life rafts, portable radios, survival kits —all standard equipment for long overwater flights—headed the list.

Much more was added. McCarthy recalled: "We must have had six or eight trunks in the plane. I had all the things that we would need in case the plane should go down in the desert on the way up to Africa. I had all sorts of tents which had been prepared for desert warfare and trinkets for the Arabs. I had beads, everything I imagined you could use, and every kind of ration, cooking equipment, and such a collection of stuff you have never seen. And then, having got all that laid in, I began to think what would happen if we got set down in the Russian steppes. So, I went to the other extreme and we wound up with cold-weather clothing, snowshoes, and everything else." [27]

Eager to be of help, members of the Office of the Quartermaster General urged McCarthy to prepare for mosquitoes in North Africa. As a result he requisitioned mosquito boots, mosquito gloves, and mosquito headgear—rather floppy, resembling a beekeeper's hat, with a net veil that came down in front.

When they approached Bathurst, McCarthy solemnly asked for attention and explained to members of the party how they must dress to beat the mosquitoes. First off the plane was General Marshall, garbed, according to McCarthy's instructions, in veiled hat and gloves and boots. Too late to salvage his dignity, Marshall saw that members of the welcoming party were dressed in shorts. Years later McCarthy recalled the Chief of Staff's look of disgust: "He just gave me the one look and took the hat off his head and the gloves off and handed them to me and said, 'Here you take these.' We never heard any more about that." [28]

After breakfasting with U.S. Brigadier General C. R. Smith, the Americans flew on to Marrakech to spend the evening. Next morning they completed the last leg of the trip. At Casablanca they were welcomed by Lieutenant General Mark W. Clark and Brigadier General Alfred M. Gruenther of Eisenhower's staff and taken to their quarters in the Anfa Hotel. They had just finished unpacking when the Prime Minister and his party arrived from the United Kingdom.

To the chagrin of the Americans, who had kept their party small at the President's behest, the British had brought a large delegation. And they had also provided themselves with a communications ship, anchored in the nearby harbor, that permitted a free flow of information between Casablanca and London. General Wedemeyer and Rear Admiral Cooke were the only two planning members of the original American delegation. Near the end of the fourth day of the conference Brigadier General John E. Hull and Colonel Charles K. Gailey turned up and were put to work. For the shortage of planners the President had to accept much of the blame. For any future conference Wedemeyer resolved to suggest changes in preparations and personnel "in order to relieve the Chief [Marshall] of part of the burden which he carried practically alone this time." [29]

The British left little to chance. Both Churchill and Brooke agreed that Marshall was the man they had to convince or to circumvent, and it was his views to which the British Chiefs of Staff turned their attention in preconference briefings on the afternoon of January 13. A month earlier Marshall's good friend Field Marshal Sir John Dill, head of the British mission in Washington, had warned the Chiefs in London that the United States Army Chief of Staff intended if possible to curtail operations in the Mediterranean after Africa was won. Soon after he arrived, Churchill and the British Chiefs of Staff invited the Field Marshal to explain General Marshall's position. Dill repeated the now-familiar views: the Chief of Staff's dread of being tied down in the Mediterranean, the possibility of provoking a German drive into Spain, and the likelihood that the Allies would suffer heavy shipping losses at the enemy's hands. Marshall believed firmly that something could be done in northern France in the fall of 1943 to open the way for a full-scale assault on the Continent in 1944.[30]

That evening, after hearing Dill's report, the Prime Minister reiterated the points on which the British sought American assent. Less wedded than Brooke to purely Mediterranean strategy at this time, he asked that a program for 1943 include an operation against Sicily, a campaign to recapture Burma, and a preliminary invasion of France. "Only in this way," Churchill declared, "should we be taking our fair share of the burden of the war." [31]

Churchill also outlined for his advisers the proper approach to their American cousins: they were to proceed carefully, never forcing the argument and always allowing full discussion. His listeners agreed. In the words of Brigadier Ian Jacob, Military Assistant Secretary to the War Cabinet, "They also felt that 'Uncle Ernie' [Admiral King] would take a less jaundiced view of the rest of the world if he had been able to shoot his line about the Pacific and really get it off his chest." For the same reason they were prepared for General Marshall, with his "strong feeling for China," to have his say about the situation in Burma.[32] The British jointly underlined their belief that Marshall was the key member of the U.S. Chiefs of Staff to be won over if American agreement was to be obtained.

Thus at Casablanca the representatives of Great Britain and the United States prepared to debate anew the strategy of cross-Channel versus the Mediterranean, returning to the arguments of the previous spring and summer, laying down the points that would be repeated, seemingly endlessly, but with variations on the theme, in the conferences that would follow in Washington, Quebec, and Cairo-Tehran before the year's end and the acceptance of the cross-Channel approach.

II

The Debate Opens

I N setting the Casablanca meeting Roosevelt had directed his Chiefs of
Staff to come to North Africa early so that they could discuss alternative military plans with their British counterparts before he arrived. As a
result Marshall and Brooke and their colleagues were deep in debate by
the time the President set foot in Morocco.

The SYMBOL, or Anfa, conference, as the Casablanca conclave was
called, followed a pattern common to most of the high-level Allied meetings. British and American staff planners drew up separate papers on various phases of strategy and submitted them to their opposite numbers
either in advance of their formal meetings or at the sessions themselves. If
there was general agreement, the Combined Planners were asked to prepare a final draft. If they could not agree, the British and U.S. Chiefs of
Staff then attempted to work out a compromise or sent the papers back to
the planners for further study. If there was no meeting of minds at this
stage, the question was then handed to the political chiefs for settlement.

Too often commentators on these sessions have incorrectly likened
them to congressional or parliamentary debates, in which the principals
deliver orations in support of their proposals. In practice the Combined
Chiefs of Staff sat around a large table, accompanied by their advisers,
who remained with or near them to furnish documents or additional ammunition in the course of the debate. From their seats the principals presented their arguments almost face to face. While free of the oratorical
flourishes of parliamentary encounters and appeals to the galleries, this
procedure often led to more heated personal exchanges than might have
been the case if there had been a succession of somewhat formal speeches.
This friction is not always reflected in the minutes, where cold paraphrases often mask stormy passions that could never be generated by the
shuffling of dry papers at a drowsy board meeting.

In the summer of 1942 the British had insisted on opening a front
somewhere during the next twelve months to aid the Soviet Union. Since

northern France was ruled out for the moment, they had proposed going into North Africa while planning a cross-Channel attack for 1943. At Casablanca they changed this formula.

Opening the Combined Chiefs' debate on January 14, General Brooke stressed the bombing of Germany and the encouragement of resistance in Nazi-dominated countries as a possible means of cracking enemy morale. With extravagant optimism he suggested that the Allies might need to launch only mopping-up operations on the Continent. If this convenient premise was true, the Allies already had enough troops in the United Kingdom. He proposed, therefore, that they make their immediate objectives knocking out Italy and bringing Turkey into the conflict.

To Marshall the arguments were tired variations on the 1942 theme of not launching a frontal assault on Germany. He attacked Britain's case for expanded efforts in the Mediterranean and pressed for an operation in 1943 that could be strongly supported by air from the United Kingdom and more easily supplied from the United States.[1]

His temper tightly reined and his demeanor icily correct, Brooke resumed the discussion the following day. Rapidly he reduced the alternatives to (1) concentration on the build-up in the United Kingdom or (2) operations in the Mediterranean, aided by a maximum air offensive from Great Britain against Germany, plus a small operation against Cherbourg. The second obviously offered the greater flexibility. As possible targets he held out Sardinia, Sicily, Crete, and the Dodecanese islands. Sicily was the biggest prize, but it would take longer to grasp than some of the others.[2]

After two days of argument on these proposals both Marshall and Brooke became weary. Although Brooke's temper was now growing thin, he resigned himself to the "slow and tiring business" of making the Americans gradually "assimilate our proposed policy." [3] Increasingly edgy, Marshall realized that he again faced the dilemma of the previous summer. Clearly there had to be an operation somewhere in 1943, but the British, who still had the bulk of the men and ships in the European Theater, wanted no part of a cross-Channel attack for that year. If they persisted, they could win over the President. All the U.S. Chiefs of Staff could hope for at Casablanca was to save the concept of the cross-Channel attack for 1943.

On January 16 Marshall challenged the British to state their plan for the best way to defeat Germany. They had listed aid to the Soviet forces, he said, as one of the keys to victory. If they meant it, they should invade the Continent. If the enemy was ultimately to be defeated there, they must face the fact that further involvement in the Mediterranean definitely limited the landing craft available for the northern operation.

The General was convinced that he had logic on his side. But aware that his cause was at the mercy of the flow of events, he was prepared to go one step further with the British in the Mediterranean if he could be assured that it would be the last. If an assault on Sicily was the only effective means of using the surplus troops that would become available in North Africa after the Axis forces were defeated there, he was prepared to approve it. But was the operation a means to an end or an end in itself? It was vital, he believed, to determine the part it played in overall Allied strategy. If he yielded on the Sicilian invasion, what were the British ready to do to assure him on future activities in northwest Europe? More important, what was the principal operation to be? "Every diversion or side issue from the main plot," he insisted, "acts as a suction pump." [4]

Because the "main plot" included Pacific and Far Eastern as well as European strategy, Marshall was almost as positive as King in proposing greater efforts against Japan. In the opening session with the British on January 14, he stressed the difficulties of apportioning resources between the Atlantic and Pacific areas. As a basis for planning he suggested allocating "70 per cent in the Atlantic Theater and 30 per cent in the Pacific Theater." Admiral King cheerfully concurred in this apportionment. Only 15 per cent of the Allied effort was currently engaged in the Pacific, the Indian Ocean, and Burma, he said. In his opinion this was not sufficient to prevent the Japanese from consolidating their gains. Even now the enemy was waging a delaying action and "digging in" along the whole line of the Netherlands East Indies and the Philippines.

General Brooke quickly broke in to emphasize the trials and opportunities of the European Theater. As reasons for moving slowly on Pacific commitments, he sketched the European situation: the submarine menace, the need for an expanded air offensive to hit Germany's material and psychological weak points, the chance to knock Italy out of the war, and the possibility of persuading Turkey to enter the conflict on the side of the Allies. [5]

Marshall readily agreed that the U-boat threat was the paramount problem faced by the Allies. But he did not want to allow the Japanese to continue unscathed in their efforts to build a defensive front—particularly with their air forces—from the Solomons through New Guinea and Timor. In the Pacific and the Far East the American Chiefs of Staff sought means of striking in the rear and against the flank of enemy defenses. Operations to retake Burma would weaken the Japanese front, lessen pressure on the Allies in the South Pacific, and open the way for stronger Allied support to China. Marshall said that the United States was "most anxious" to undertake Operation RAVENOUS. (This was a limited operation for reoccupying northern Burma. A plan for reconquering the whole of Burma—Operation ANAKIM—was under consideration for a somewhat later time.)

After lunch, continuing his appeal for operations in the Pacific and in Burma, General Marshall insisted that "We must not allow the Japanese any pause." General Brooke inquired politely how far the Americans proposed to go to prevent the Japanese from "digging themselves in." He saw a danger in overextending operations that would "inevitably lead to an all-out war against Japan." Was it possible, he queried, for existing Allied forces in the Pacific to stem the Japanese drive without draining further Allied strength? [6]

The debate took on a new dimension. Seconding the arguments of King —and of MacArthur as well—Marshall recalled that the United States had found it essential to act offensively to stop the Japanese. Americans had been forced to intervene in New Guinea to block the enemy advance. In this kind of fighting "it was very difficult to pause: the process of whittling away Japan had to be continuous."

Challenging Air Marshal Portal's suggestion that it might be possible to stand firmly on a line and inflict heavy losses on the Japanese when they tried to break through it, General Arnold explained that in the South Pacific the Allies had to operate from the tips of two narrow salients. With greater width in his line, the enemy could operate on a larger scale than could the Allies. Marshall further spelled out the problem. In Papua the Allies could gain additional airfields alongside the existing ones, but in Guadalcanal, where only a small strip of suitable territory was available, they could broaden their base only by moving north and west to seize New Britain and New Ireland.[7]

At American urging the Combined Chiefs of Staff attacked the problem of a campaign to recapture Burma, which had been overrun by the Japanese in the late spring of 1942. For several months Lieutenant General Joseph W. Stilwell, head of the U.S. Mission to China and adviser to Generalissimo Chiang Kai-shek, had been working with the India Command and with the Generalissimo on operations to achieve this goal. Their plans involved use of Chinese troops who had escaped into India and were being trained under Stilwell's supervision, Chinese forces in Yunnan, and troops of the India Command. The Commander in Chief of the India Command, General Sir Archibald Wavell, who had reverted to his Indian assignment after heading the short-lived American-British-Dutch-Australian Command in the Pacific, was skeptical of the possibilities of a full-fledged offensive in the immediate future. Planning was also complicated by the fact that the Generalissimo insisted on British amphibious operations in the Bay of Bengal as a prerequisite to his attack from China. After being told by Stilwell in late December that Wavell had decided that only a limited attack in northern Burma, beginning March 1, could be made, Chiang Kai-shek sent two despairing messages, one in late December and another in early January, to Roosevelt, who was preparing to leave Washington for the Casablanca conference.

In addition to the discouraging news from Wavell, the Generalissimo was upset to learn from the commander of the British Far Eastern Fleet, Admiral Sir James Somerville, that the formidable concentration of battleships, carriers, and other vessels in the Indian Ocean that Churchill supposedly had promised had now shrunk to a few destroyers and submarines. Chiang emphasized that his troops in Yunnan and India would be ready for an offensive in March, but that it would be impossible for them to move unless the British carried out their undertakings. He "earnestly" besought the President to urge the British "to engage sufficient naval, air, and land forces on their part to ensure the recapture of Burma." [8]

The President sought to mollify the Chinese leader on January 2 by stressing the importance of the efforts to reopen the Burma Road in north China and the fact that British vessels in the Bay of Bengal were needed at the moment to hunt Japanese ships around the Cape of Good Hope. To the U.S. Chiefs of Staff Roosevelt indicated his doubt that an operation to retake Rangoon was necessary at the moment. General Marshall at this point supported Chiang's views since the proposed limited operation (RAVENOUS) across northern Burma would have to be carried out over difficult terrain. If southern Burma could be retaken and the port of Rangoon opened, the flow of supplies into Burma would be greatly increased.[9]

During the same early period in January, General Marshall was pressing Sir John Dill to persuade the British Chiefs of the importance of supporting Chiang Kai-shek's requests. The likelihood of any such reassurance practically disappeared when Dill received a message from Wavell stating that he had "made it clear to Stilwell that naval cooperation could not be expected." [10] Prospects for a spring offensive in northern Burma were therefore doubtful when Marshall started for Casablanca in the early morning of January 9.[11]

Apprised of Chiang's second message shortly after he arrived, Marshall made a vigorous effort to save some form of Burma campaign for 1943. On January 14 he reminded his British colleagues of the importance of a new land route to China. If clearing the enemy from northern Burma yielded only a small increase in tonnage for Chinese forces, in addition to supplies brought in by air, it would nevertheless produce important benefits. First of all, Chinese ground forces required only about half the maintenance tonnage required by foreign troops. Second, Chennault had "done wonderful work" with only 12 bombers; with 50 he might produce "very great" results. (Arnold noted at this point that Chennault believed that with 175 bombers he could drive the Japanese Air Force out of China.) "It should also be remembered," Marshall stressed, "that any help given to China which would threaten Japan would have a most favorable effect on Stalin." [12]

On January 17 General Marshall again brought the subject of Burma to the attention of the Combined Chiefs of Staff. He deplored the British belief that ANAKIM could not be carried out during the dry season of 1943–44. He and his American colleagues were "particularly concerned about the timing of this operation because of the serious situation regarding China."

Brooke saw "two stumbling blocks" to mounting ANAKIM in 1943: the lack of naval cover and the time required to assemble landing craft for adequate training after the assault on Sicily. Admiral Pound explained that a considerable force had been withdrawn from the Eastern Fleet for operations in North Africa, and it was probable that other operations in 1943 would adversely affect the Eastern theater.

Admiral King and Rear Admiral Cooke promptly tried to remove these stumbling blocks. ANAKIM would not be undertaken for at least ten months; it could be started in November or December with the actual landings in January 1944. American production of landing craft would be considerable between April and January, and some would be available for Burma in October. As for the naval force, said Cooke, only carriers, destroyers, and cruisers would be needed. The over-age battleships, which Dill had told Marshall the British hesitated to send into the Bay of Bengal, would be compensated for if the United States Fleet contained the Japanese in the Pacific.

King could foresee that in ten months' time the American destroyer program should be well along, the submarine menace reduced, and the shipping situation much improved through increased production and the opening of the Mediterranean. King believed as firmly as Marshall that ANAKIM must not be postponed. To do so would put the Allies in a critical position and make it impossible to undertake the conquest of Burma for almost two years. King considered ANAKIM important to Allied strategy for defeating Japan. Moreover it was "absolutely essential" that China's geographical position and manpower be utilized.

At the request of Marshall the American planners came up with firm estimates on the following day, saying that the required landing craft could be made available in Burma by November 1, 1943, and would be over and above those needed for all other 1943 operations, including ROUNDUP in the European Theater. This satisfied Brooke, but Lord Louis Mountbatten, Chief of Combined Operations, pointed out that the British lacked crews to man additional landing craft beyond those requested. King was willing to commit himself to supplying British deficiencies. After the Rabaul operation was over, he could send some landing craft together with crews to Burma. As for necessary naval coverage, he would either dispatch United States naval units to the Bay of Bengal to take part in the Burma operation, or the United States would relieve the British from naval missions elsewhere. That promise of help from the Pacific, commented Mountbatten, altered the whole situation as far as the British were concerned. Brooke ended the discussion by saying "ANAKIM is now definitely on the books, is being planned, and should be put to the front. With the assistance of the United States Navy in providing landing craft, the operation would be feasible."

These optimistic conclusions of course depended upon the timing and success of the coming operations in the Southwest Pacific and upon the outcome of operations in the Mediterranean. The Combined Chiefs prudently agreed that they would determine the actual date for mounting ANAKIM in the summer of 1943, preferably not later than July.[13]

An effort to settle the broader goals had been made by the Combined Staff Planners since January 14, when their superiors had asked them to come up with an answer to the question: "What situation do we wish to establish in the Eastern Theater (i.e., the Pacific and Burma) in 1943 and what forces will be necessary to establish this situation." The American staff planners concluded that "efforts must be made toward the destruction of the economic and military power of all our adversaries at a rate exceeding their power of replacement." Then, recognizing that Germany was "the primary, or most powerful and pressing enemy," and that the major portion of the Allied forces was to be directed against Germany, the U.S. planners added, "insofar as it is consistent with the overall objective of bringing the war to an early conclusion at the earliest possible date." [14]

Here was the core of the argument. At the Combined Chiefs of Staff meeting on January 17 King tried to allay British fears. The American Chiefs of Staff, he assured the British, did recognize Germany as "our prime enemy," and their strategy did not envisage a complete Japanese defeat before the overthrow of Hitler. But, he continued, "every effort must be applied which will put us in a position of readiness" for the final assault against Japan upon Germany's defeat. Brooke seemed willing to accept this formula if it did not delay or jeopardize the effort against Germany. General Marshall at this point seemed disinclined to compromise. He felt that the problem involved "creating more than conditions of readiness." In one of his strongest statements on the necessity of maintaining the initiative against Japan "by offensive moves on our part," the United States Chief of Staff declared:

> The present operations in the South Pacific are tremendously expensive in merchant vessels, naval vessels, and escorts. The situation is also fraught with the possibility of a sudden reverse and the consequent loss of sea power. He . . . [was] most anxious to open the Burma Road, not so much for the morale effect on China as for the need to provide air support to China for operations against Japan and Japanese shipping. [The] . . . expensive operations in which we are now engaged in the South Pacific react on everything else the United Nations attempt to do whether it be in the Mediterranean, the United Kingdom, or elsewhere. . . . unless Operation ANAKIM could be undertaken . . . a situation might arise in the Pacific at any time that would necessitate the United States regretfully withdrawing from commitments in the European Theater.[15]

Brooke was seriously disturbed by this line of reasoning. After talking with his planners, he recorded in his diary: "We found that the main difficulty rested in the fact that the U. S. A. Joint Planners did not agree with Germany being the primary enemy and were wishing to defeat Japan first." Marshall and King had made no such statement, but the

American arguments were disquieting. Next day the British planners asked for a stronger statement of German priority with a recognition of Marshall's proposals: "The quickest way of achieving this [the end of the war "at the earliest practicable date"] will be to concentrate on defeating Germany first and then to concentrate our combined resources against Japan. Meanwhile such pressure must be maintained in [sic] Japan as will prevent her from damaging interests vital to the Allies, and will hinder her from consolidating her conquests." [16]

At a long afterdinner meeting on the seventeenth, the British Chiefs had checked further with their staffs. With a proviso that Brooke was to insist on next day, the British planners accepted the American position, declaring: "We agree in principle with this expression of the strategy required, provided always that its application does not prejudice the earliest possible defeat of Germany."

"Agreement in principle" did not aid the American timetable for Pacific operations for 1943. The British agreed that operations were "certainly required in 1943" to continue occupation of the Solomons and eastern New Guinea, culminating in the consolidation of the New Britain–New Ireland (Rabaul) area. But the timing of operations for occupation of the Gilbert, Marshall, and Caroline Islands, up to and including Truk, as well as for a further westward advance in New Guinea, would have to depend upon the speed with which the campaign for Rabaul was completed. A new offensive in the Central Pacific and in New Guinea up to the Dutch border would then be necessary to retain the initiative and contain Japanese strength. For this offensive the British paper urged detailed planning, with the decision on launching operations to await further developments.[17]

This was the kind of concession that unsettled the Americans. At least one of the British Chiefs, Portal, had recognized since the beginning of the conference that some of the American demands must be met. Always capable of seeing the position of the other side, he had stated the problem to his British colleagues: "We are in the position of a testator who wishes to leave the bulk of his fortune to his mistress. He must, however, leave something to his wife, and his problem is to decide how little he can in decency leave apart for her." The situation was complicated because the "fortune" belonged to the wife from the beginning. With King already in the mood of the aggrieved wife and Marshall in the role of a sympathetic relative, the Americans could not be ignored. But Brooke, the canny advocate, looked for the smallest amount for which the "wife" would settle. The British were certain that operations against Truk and a full offensive in Burma could not be carried out without interfering with the early defeat of Germany. The major debate on January 17 and 18 revolved around what was left over from the wife's dowry in Burma and the Pacific.[18]

On the eighteenth Marshall took the offensive in the controversy con-

cerning emphasis on future operations in the European Theater. Stung
by Brooke's complaint that the Americans had failed to emphasize that
Germany must be defeated first, Marshall retorted that the British seemed
satisfied with keeping the enemy engaged in the Mediterranean while
gathering a force in the United Kingdom sufficiently large to take advantage of a crack in Germany's military position. Apparently, Marshall said,
the British would prefer to leave such a force "dormant" in the United
Kingdom "awaiting an opportunity [rather than to] . . . keep the force
engaged in an active offensive in the Pacific." [19]

Brooke expected this viewpoint from King but was alarmed to hear
Marshall taking a similar tack. The British General warned somberly that
the Allies could not defeat Japan first, and if they tried to do so, "we shall
lose the war." Instead they must defeat Germany first, and therefore the
immediate question was whether to go to northern France or to exploit
the success in North Africa. The British believed that they should go all
out in the Mediterranean. Unless they maintained constant pressure on
the Germans, the enemy would be able "to recover and thus prolong the
war."

Marshall replied that the United States Chiefs of Staff "do not propose
doing nothing in the Mediterranean or in France." But the war must be
terminated as quickly as possible. That end could not be achieved "if we
neglect the Pacific Theater entirely and leave the Japanese to consolidate
their gains and unnecessarily strengthen their position." It was also essential that commanders in the Pacific not have to continue to conduct operations on a shoestring.

Brooke broke in to say that the British agreed in principle with the
United States strategy in the Pacific, "provided always that its application
does not prejudice the earliest possible defeat of Germany." It was a big
if, and King observed bitingly that the proviso could be interpreted "as
meaning that *anything* which was done in the Pacific interfered" with this
"and that the Pacific Theater should therefore remain totally inactive." [20]

As the debate continued, King charged that the British were trying to
dictate details of operations in the Pacific. Such matters, he declared, were
to be determined not by the Combined Chiefs of Staff but by the United
States Chiefs of Staff, who had been given the strategic responsibility in
the Pacific theater. He demanded sufficient resources to permit the Allied
forces to retain the initiative in the Pacific. Repeating his thought of the
last meeting, he stipulated that the "United States intentions were not to
plan for anything beyond gaining positions in readiness for the final
offensive against Japan." Holding that there were sufficient forces in the
Mediterranean Theater for pending operations, he concluded, as Marshall had, that neither future action there nor the build-up in the United
Kingdom would be affected by further operations in the Pacific.

Finding some hope in King's last statement, Portal interjected that the
British would be satisfied if they could be properly assured on that point.

They feared that extended operations in the Pacific would prevent the Allies from taking advantage of a crack in German resistance.

It was an all-too-familiar argument, and Marshall employed a tested rebuttal. Continued "hand-to-mouth" operations in the Pacific, he declared, might upset Allied strategy entirely. A disaster in the Pacific would require diversion of troops and weapons from other theaters to restore the situation. Marshall held that the Allies must secure their position in the Pacific "so that we knew where we were." The reconquest of Burma would be an enormous contribution to that end.

The mention of the Pacific and Burma reopened doors the British had thought closed. Brooke argued that they should stop with the taking of Rabaul and with preparations for ANAKIM. But just as Portal had recently insisted that the Allies might have to advance into Italy after taking Sicily, King suggested that once Rabaul was seized, the same forces might have to be moved against the Marshalls. He did not insist on this point, observing that such a movement might be stopped at any time. It might well be, he also conceded, that Truk, the key Japanese base in the Carolines, "would, after all, be found impossible to capture this year." [21]

Seeing in his colleague's concession a possible basis for compromise, General Marshall asked the British if they could agree that operations would continue northward as far as Truk if no additional forces were required. Fearing what King would do with such a loophole, Brooke held firm to his views. At this point the American Admiral declared that the British were trying to limit action in the Pacific while they apparently "contemplated an unlimited commitment in the European Theater."

Marshall then sketched a possible revision in the American demands. He suggested adding to the proposals for "seizure and occupation of Gilbert Islands, Marshall Islands, Caroline Islands up to and including Truk" the words *with the resources available in the theater.*" [22]

On this note the conferees recessed for lunch. Still thinking of King's argument rather than Marshall's later amendment, Brooke remarked to Dill as they walked upstairs from the conference room, "It is no use, we shall never get agreement with them." But Dill retorted: "On the contrary, you have already got agreement to most of the points, and it only remains to settle the rest. Let's come to your room after lunch and discuss it." [23]

Dill also told Air Marshal John Slessor, who was an aide to Portal, that the two groups were not as far apart as they seemed. His words prompted Slessor to seek a quiet spot on the roof of the hotel, where he rapidly sketched an agreement on operations that Portal decided that the British could accept.

After lunch Dill discussed with Brooke the points on which the Allies were agreed and those on which they were at odds and asked how far he would go to get complete accord. When Brooke declined to budge an inch, Dill warned that the dispute would then have to go to Roosevelt and Churchill. "You know as well as I do," he said, "what a mess they would make of it." He noted several points on which concessions could be made and asked if he might discuss them with General Marshall. Just as Brooke gave his assent, Portal brought in Slessor's proposed draft. They decided to accept it, and Dill set out to clear it with Marshall before the afternoon session convened. Their talk, another example of the effectiveness of the exceptionally warm Marshall-Dill relationship, smoothed the way for American acceptance of the compromise.[24]

As the British and Americans returned to the conference room, Marshall called King aside and showed him the British paper. Reading through the draft together, they discussed it in an undertone while their British colleagues awaited their decision. Finally, seeing their basic position accepted, the Americans agreed to approve the statement with minor changes. A revised memorandum was formally adopted on the morning of the nineteenth. The draft ultimately reported by the Combined Chiefs of Staff called for continuance of operations in the Pacific and Far East with the forces allocated, provided that they were kept within such limits "as will not, in the opinion of the Combined Chiefs of Staff, jeopardize the capacity of the United Nations to take advantage of any favorable opportunity . . . for the decisive defeat of Germany in 1943." Subject to these reservations, plans and preparations were to be made for (1) the recapture of Burma (ANAKIM) beginning in 1943 and (2) operations after the capture of Rabaul against the Marshalls and Carolines "if time and resources allow without prejudice to ANAKIM." [25]

With the acceptance of this compromise other military issues of the conference fell more easily into place. In the late afternoon of January 18 the Combined Chiefs of Staff met with Roosevelt and Churchill in the President's villa. Marshall presided and first called on Brooke to explain the agreements that had been reached. Speaking deliberately, lest he somehow upset the delicate balance, the British Chief summarized the main points. To his relief nothing was changed, and the heads of government gave their approval.[26]

The Allies confirmed that their overall objective was the defeat of Germany. The smashing of the U-boat campaign was given first priority. After North Africa had been cleared of the enemy, their next operation would be the invasion of Sicily. Later they would attempt to bring Turkey into the war.[27]

The Allied representatives were heartily united in issuing a directive for a Combined Bomber Offensive, to be known as POINTBLANK, whose primary purpose would be "the progressive destruction and dislocation of the German military, industrial and economic system, and the undermining of the morale of the German people to a point where their capacity for armed resistance is fatally weakened." The directive, addressed to the British Bomber Command, headed by Air Chief Marshal Sir Arthur Harris, and to Lieutenant General Ira Eaker, United States Eighth Air Force, reflected Air Chief Marshal Portal's view that defeat of Germany would require maximum pressure by land operations and that air bombardment alone would not be sufficient. Marshall agreed that control of Allied bombing operations from the United Kingdom would be under the British, but he specifically reserved for the commander of the Eighth Air Force decisions on technique and tactics for American bombers. Subject to weather and tactical feasibility, the following priorities for primary objectives in Germany were set up: (1) submarine-construction yards, (2) aircraft plants, (3) transportation, (4) oil installations, and (5) other targets in enemy war industry. The directive also listed enemy submarine bases on the Bay of Biscay and targets in Berlin as major objectives.[28]

Since further large-scale operations had been agreed on for the Mediterranean, Marshall realized that his hoped-for cross-Channel attack was ruled out for the coming year. After reviewing the resources available and problems to be overcome, he and his colleagues agreed to continue a build-up in the United Kingdom in 1943. A step was taken toward invasion by an agreement to appoint a British Chief of Staff to a Supreme Allied Commander, not yet chosen, with an independent U.S.–British staff, to begin planning for landings on the Continent under the terms of a directive then in preparation. The final terms of the directive specified the planning of small-scale raids and a return to the Continent in case of German collapse in 1943; failing this, a limited operation on the Continent in 1943 and a major invasion in 1944.

Marshall got much less than he had wanted. However he had been fairly certain before he came to Casablanca that he must accept a campaign against Sardinia or Sicily. To a disappointed Stimson, positive that the cross-Channel operation was still in jeopardy, Marshall later explained that he had accepted the operation against Sicily because (1) there were sufficient troops in the Mediterranean for the attack, (2) British Intelligence believed that the Luftwaffe had been severely depleted and that this was the best way to prevent its recovery, and (3) the British refused to go along with the cross-Channel operation for the present.[29]

General Eisenhower agreed with the British. He wrote Major General Thomas T. Handy, who had succeeded him as head of the Operations Division, that he did not see how the "big bosses" could have deviated from what they adopted. The cross-Channel attack, he declared, "could not possibly be staged before August of 1944, because our original conceptions of the strength required were too low. Inaction in 1943 could not be tolerated and, unfortunately, distances are so great that we could not devote 1943 to one enemy and 1944 to another." [30]

The British had every reason to be satisfied with the outcome of the conference. Indeed, Brooke concluded, "we had got practically all we hoped to get when we came here." [31] Brigadier Ian Jacob of Brooke's staff noted at the time "that if I had written down before I came what I hoped that the conclusions would be I could never have written anything so sweeping, so comprehensive, and so favourable to our ideas as in the end I found myself putting down [in the final record"].[32]

The British were disposed to give credit for their success to their advance preparations, to the logic of military events, to Dill's success in smoothing over disagreements, and at least in part to Marshall's own willingness to seek an understanding. Major General Sir John Kennedy, Director of Military Operations on Brooke's staff, was especially "impressed by Marshall's friendliness and honesty of purpose." "We could see," he recalled later, "he required time to consider all the arguments which were put to him, and that he would need to be thoroughly convinced before changing his mind. It was a relief to find that he was not obstinate or rigid in his strategic views." [33]

On one point Brooke and Marshall were in agreement. The British General had no doubt that Dill, more than anyone else, was responsible for the American acceptance of the compromise. After the conference Marshall pointed this out to President Roosevelt and asked that he write the Field Marshal a letter of appreciation. Dill's presence at Casablanca, Marshall wrote, "was of a vital importance and at one time practically prevented a complete stalemate regarding the differences between Admiral King and Sir Alan Brooke over the Pacific–European Theater issue." After each meeting, he explained, "It was apparent that . . . a great deal was done by Dill to translate the American point of view into terms understandable to the British, also the fact that in certain matters there could be no compromise [by the Americans]." [34]

In one of the most controversial acts of the conference—the announcement of the unconditional-surrender formula—Marshall and his fellow Chiefs of Staff had little part although it influenced and perhaps hampered their later actions. Apparently the idea had come out of meetings in 1942 of a group with a long name, a Subcommittee on Security Problems of the State Department's Advisory Committee on Postwar Policy, whose members included representatives of the Army and Navy. Early in the year the group concluded that "nothing short of unconditional surrender by the principal enemies, Germany and Japan, could be accepted, though negotiation might be possible in the case of Italy." The chairman, Norman Davis, passed these views on to the President. Although no recommendation was made to Roosevelt by the committee, the concept seems to have stuck in his mind. He had no study made of the proposal by the Joint Chiefs of Staff before the Casablanca conference, but it was to be listed as one of the most important announcements of that meeting.[35]

Significantly Roosevelt first mentioned the formula to his military advisers, at the White House meeting of January 7, 1943, as a means of reassuring Marshal Stalin. The President there asked General Marshall what he thought of going to Moscow from Casablanca. Somewhat surprised, the Chief of Staff asked, "What would I be expected to accomplish there?" Roosevelt replied, "The visit would be particularly for the purpose of giving impetus to the Russian morale." He supposed that "Stalin probably felt out of the picture as far as Great Britain and the United States were concerned and also that he has a feeling of loneliness." He added that he intended to speak to Churchill about the advisability of telling the Russian leader that the United Nations planned to continue on to Berlin and "that their only terms would be unconditional surrender." Also he wanted to discuss postwar disarmament with Churchill and possibly hold a meeting with the Prime Minister, Stalin, and Chiang Kai-shek the following summer. If the discussion with Churchill proved favorable, Marshall could tell Stalin what had been decided. Seen in this context, unconditional surrender was intended to bolster up the hard-pressed Soviet ally at a time when the much-promised second front in Western Europe still seemed in the distant future.[36]

During the Casablanca meeting Roosevelt mentioned the formula to the Prime Minister. Churchill, in turn, queried members of the British War Cabinet by wire on January 20 concerning inclusion in the final statement to the press of "a declaration of the firm intention of the United States and the British Empire to continue the war relentlessly until we have brought about the 'unconditional surrender' of Germany and Japan." The omission of Italy would encourage a break-up there, he thought. The War Cabinet's principal comment in replying to Churchill was that Italy should not be excluded. In view of these exchanges it is odd that the Prime Minister seemed startled when Roosevelt announced the formula in the final meeting with the press on the twenty-fourth.

Curiously nearly everyone who had anything to do with the formula recalled its history incorrectly. Roosevelt claimed to have thought of it on the spur of the moment in the press conference, although it was included in the notes he used. Ernest Bevin, a member of the War Cabinet, failed to raise any objection when Churchill submitted the matter in 1943 but later denied that the cabinet had ever been consulted. Churchill himself retorted that he had not heard of the formula until Roosevelt mentioned it at the final press conference.[37] Even General Marshall, who had been present when the words were at least mentioned on January 7, later declared that he thought he first heard of it at Casablanca.[38] Stranger still is General Wedemeyer's account that he recalls making an earnest plea against the formula at a Joint Chiefs of Staff meeting at the North African conference. Neither Arnold nor King, both of whom left accounts of the Casablanca meeting, referred to any such statement by Wedemeyer. When his colleagues discussed the matter with Admiral Leahy on their return, he noted that it apparently was not mentioned until the famous press conference. General Wedemeyer concedes that there are no records of the discussion and that the only reference to the statement consists of his notes. There is no other record of any such discussion at Casablanca, although rather full minutes were kept by Brigadier General John R. Deane, Secretary to the Joint Chiefs of Staff. Deane, who attended the

January 7 meeting at the White House, recorded that "unconditional surrender" was brought up there but very briefly, and he says flatly that the matter was not discussed at all by the Joint Chiefs of Staff or the Combined Chiefs of Staff at Casablanca.[39] In view of General Deane's testimony a possible explanation is that Wedemeyer prepared his talk for a later session of the Joint Chiefs of Staff.

Although the various disclaimers may have been prompted by the postwar criticisms of the formula, it appears likely that confusion arose from the fact that when first mentioned on January 7 and again at Casablanca, the concept was intended as a wide umbrella under which to rally the foes of the Axis rather than the rather rigid condition for peace that it later became. If so, everyone concerned could say truthfully that he had not heard this formula discussed in this sense before the end of the conference.

Because of postwar disputes over the effects of this principle Roosevelt has been blamed for not seeking further counsel from his military advisers and from the State Department. It is fair to assume that had General Marshall been consulted, he would have probably given his general agreement within the broad framework outlined by the President. At the close of World War I, Marshall had been given the task of drawing up a plan for occupying Germany should it prove necessary. His view then was that the advance to the heart of Germany should not be handled in a way that might encourage the spread of radicalism. But in retrospect he was impressed, as were Roosevelt and many other Americans, by the successful use Hitler had made in his rise to power of the argument that the Germans had been tricked into surrendering by Wilson in 1918 and had not really been defeated. As a result Marshall concluded that it might be well next time to require the Germans to acknowledge that they had been beaten in the field.

Marshall apparently reasoned that in January 1943, when the outcome of the Allied endeavor was far from certain, when the Russians were still unhappy over the failure to open a second front, and when there was no possibility of holding out prospects of quick liberation to the French and other conquered peoples, it was useful to make clear that the Allies remained set on the defeat of the Axis powers. Later he declared: "I think there was quite a possibility that the Germans and Japanese might have conceded the war a little earlier if it had not been for the unconditional-surrender formula. However, I think it had a great psychological effect on our people, on the British people, and on the Allied people generally, as well as on the Germans when it was made . . . because we had been going through a period of defeats and now this came out as a declaration that we were going into this thing to the finish." [40]

In 1944, when growing enemy weakness offered a reasonable basis for propaganda appeals, Marshall and his colleagues backed Eisenhower's appeal for a modification of the unconditional-surrender principle. But at

Casablanca the Chief of Staff did not—any more than did Churchill—oppose the formula.

The main meetings of the conference were concluded late on the evening of January 23, when the Combined Chiefs of Staff worked out their final agreements.

Since Marshall, Arnold, and King were interested in talking with Eisenhower before returning home, they flew on the morning of January 24 to Eisenhower's headquarters in Algiers and were warmly received.[41] Marshall inspected the headquarters and visited some of the barracks, impressing Eisenhower's naval aide, Commander Harry C. Butcher, by his lack of fussiness. Relaxed in the "homelike" atmosphere of his host's quarters, Marshall talked at length. Butcher found his phraseology "entrancingly superb, his thoughts . . . well put and frequently pointed up by a pat illustration."

On the second morning of his two-day visit to Algiers, Marshall revealed his paternal side to Eisenhower's aide. Over breakfast, after the Allied commander had gone to his office, the Chief of Staff "ordered" Commander Butcher to take care of Eisenhower's health by getting him outdoors as much as possible ("four or four and a half hours with the staff ought to be enough"), getting him home early, finding a masseur who would give him a rubdown before dinner, arranging for regular horseback rides or other forms of relaxation. Then he glanced back to Eisenhower's troubled negotiations with the Vichy government's Commander-in-Chief, Admiral Jean Darlan, whose collaboration with the Allies in North Africa brought a coupling of military advantages and political denunciations that was not stilled with Darlan's assassination on Christmas Eve of 1942. And Marshall forecast: "He may think he has had troubles so far, including Darlan, but he will have so many before the war is over that Darlan will be nothing."

Continuing to behave, Butcher thought, wholly like a father toward a son, Marshall confided to the naval aide his earlier views on Eisenhower. "When I brought him to head the Operations Division after Pearl Harbor, I put him in the place of a good officer, who had been in that job two years," he said. "I felt he was growing stale from overwork, and I don't like to keep any man on a job so long that his ideas and forethoughts go no further than mine. . . . General Eisenhower had a refreshing approach to problems. He was most helpful. But he began to work sixteen to eighteen hours a day and before he left I was beginning to worry about him. . . . You must keep him refreshed. . . . It is your job in the war to make him take care of his health and keep that alert brain from overworking, particularly on things his staff can do for him. . . ."[42]

Marshall's stopover proved to be a tonic in itself. Eisenhower wrote General Handy shortly after his Chief's departure, "The short visits that I had with him were more than stimulating, and I feel better able than ever to carry my own little burdens when I realize how cheerfully and effect-tively he is marching along under the heavy load he is carrying." [43]

Winding up his pleasant pause in Algiers on the morning of January 26, Marshall began his flight homeward, stopping overnight in Casablanca. On the twenty-ninth he wrote Mrs. T. B. Coles, aunt of his first wife: "I had a long trip home but made it in a remarkably short time; left Casablanca Tuesday morning and spent six hours in Dakar, flew from there direct to Trinidad, some 3400 miles I believe; spent a night in Trinidad and left there yesterday, landing in Washington at 6:30 last night." [44]

On the flight homeward Marshall read Arthur Bryant's *Years of Endurance, 1793–1802,* one volume of a trilogy on the Napoleonic Wars that Air Marshal Slessor had handed him before he left Casablanca. The lively story of William Pitt's efforts to rally England and her allies for a stand against France recalled to Marshall many of his own experiences in preparing the Army for battle. On his return he wrote the British airman: "I had finished it by the time we reached Trinidad and re-read some portions on the flight from there to Washington. It is a fascinating projection of that period into the present day and certainly gave me a better perspective." He had also read *This Was Cicero,* a volume on Roman history by J. H. Haskell, publisher of the Kansas City *Star,* and concluded that the two books gave him ground for consolation that grave problems of leadership were neither new nor insoluble.[45]

At the close of the conference Eisenhower wrote proudly of his Chief's role to General Handy: "In every contact between the British and General Marshall, his stature grows. The confidence reposed in him by British commanders of all services, by the Prime Minister and the British Chiefs of Staff would be amazing to anyone who does not know and appreciate his great qualities like you and I do." And to Marshall's old friend Major General Charles D. Herron he wrote on the same day: "[General Marshall] is unquestionably the great military leader of this war, a fact which the world will recognize before the affair is over." [46]

General Wedemeyer similarly voiced his admiration for Marshall's contribution in a letter to General Handy as the conference neared its close: "General Marshall did a magnificent job for the Americans. He was logical and again his candor was disarming. He received very little effective assistance from his colleagues. General Arnold is not a negotiator although a lovable character and striving in a cumbersome way to help. Admiral King was all Pacific and I must admit did make the British at least Pacific conscious, which is highly desirable. He contributed very little when other matters were being considered." [47]

Obviously the American generals did not reflect the thinking of everyone present. In a moment of frustration General Brooke set down in his diary the view that Marshall's thoughts "revolve around the creation of forces and not on their employment." [48]

More in keeping with the American estimates was the postwar judgment by Lord Portal, then Chief of the Air Staff, who declared: "Marshall was the big man of the delegation. . . . I suppose it is an open secret that Marshall had difficulty in concentrating for a while after a meal. During that period others would talk. But Marshall was always there when it mattered." [49]

III

Marshall at His Command Post

ONLY a few weeks before the Casablanca conference, which determined a new phase of war strategy, Washington acquired a new visual symbol for the might of the armed forces in American and world affairs. It was to this oddly shaped building in Arlington, Virginia, that the General returned after the conference. On November 15, 1942, when the landings in North Africa were a few days old, the Chief of Staff opened his office in the Pentagon. This transfer from the old Munitions Building in Washington, a few hours after that of the Secretary of War's staff, was the last step in a shift that had been in progress since the previous April and marked the real opening of the Pentagon. Although most of the Navy and important elements of the Army and Army Air Forces remained scattered throughout Washington, the new five-sided structure, vast, sprawling, almost intentionally ugly, at once became the center of American military power. Unmistakably marked for potential enemies from the air, it seemed to invite attack as well as to radiate resistance to the foes of the United States.[1]

Before Marshall and his advisers had crossed the Potomac to their new quarters, Capitol Hill and the White House had been the principal sites of power in Washington. From November 1942 the Pentagon had to be reckoned with. "The Pentagon thinks" and "The Pentagon says" soon became familiar in by-lined stories and "inside" columns. Baffling visitors with its seven and a half million square feet of space, its miles of long corridors, narrow stairways that seemed to end in No Exit passageways suitable for disappearances of Alice's white rabbit, and a vast Concourse filled with specialty shops and ticket counters that in bustle and confusion rivaled Grand Central Station at Christmas, the building overwhelmed tourists. Here some thirty thousand military and civilian personnel worked day and night, shuttling carloads of secret archives, brewing thousands of gallons of coffee, eating truckloads of sandwiches, and cluttering the air with hundreds of thousands of messages. Perhaps the flat sprawl and size of the building modified its grim fortresslike aspect. Armed sentries were kept at a minimum, and there was limited surveillance from civilian guards. Enlisted men, secretaries, and field-grade officers found common ground in the cafeteria lines. In a building where privates were a novelty and lieutenant colonels—according to current folklore—were assigned to answer telephones, it was sometimes difficult to discern a rigid military complex.

Yet there was an air of excitement. Unseen by most of the workers, mysterious couriers departed or returned from distant destinations with locked brief cases containing plans too secret to trust to channels of communication that might be tapped by the enemy. Important and self-important officials dashed off to international conferences, tests of new weapons, inspections of divisions being readied for overseas shipment, or interminable meetings set up at service commands, replacement-training centers, air bases, materiel commands, and dozens of other locations where Washington's best military brains could carry word of the latest instructions and most recent changes in doctrine formulated for the edification of the lower echelons. Back again to the Pentagon flowed reports—of lessons learned, failures or successes in training methods, requirements for modifications in weapons, pressing needs for scarce equipment—piling up new problems demanding more conferences and thousands more papers. Within a short time the massive, functional pile of reinforced concrete dwarfed other fortresses of bureaucracy in bigness and in drama. Of course Roosevelt, the Commander-in-Chief, met his advisers at the White House; the Joint Chiefs of Staff held their own meetings and conferred with their British colleagues in the Public Health Building on Constitution Avenue in Washington. Ultimate decisions were reached in these deliberations, but increasingly the execution of plans, so far as the Army and Army Air Forces were concerned, came from the Pentagon.

Directing this part of the war machinery was General George C. Marshall. Three weeks after he had moved into the new building, he described the far-flung boundaries of his command: "Officers of the War Department General Staff are always en route between Washington and the various theaters. In a single morning a few days ago, I interviewed two General Staff officers just in from Kokoda Pass and Milne Bay in New Guinea and from Guadalcanal; another from Chungking, China, and New Delhi in India; and still another from Moscow, Basra, and way points. London, Iceland, Greenland, Labrador and Alaska are frequently visited by officers of the War Department." [2]

Had there been no Pearl Harbor, a new War Department building—probably less gigantic, but certainly of imposing proportions—would still have been necessary. Even the staff needed to direct the force of 197,000 soldiers and airmen that Marshall had taken over in 1939 strained the office space available in Washington.

In 1941 an effort had been made to ease the pressure by earmarking a nearly completed federal office building for the Army. On April 25 when

Stimson saw the new building in Foggy Bottom, he thought it wonderful, "with 500,000 square feet and 260,000 square feet of office." Four weeks later he told the President he had changed his mind. It could not hold the segments of the Army and Army Air Forces scattered in seventeen different buildings in Washington and Arlington. By this time the draft Army was more than six months old, and National Guard units were in training. Although extension of the Selective Service commitment was still in doubt, the fall of France, the passage of the first billion-dollar defense bill, and fears of an aggressive Japan all pointed toward growing armed forces that would require a greatly enlarged administrative staff in the nation's capital.

Clearly something bigger than the Foggy Bottom building was needed. Possible War Department sites included one in the area now known as Fort Lesley J. McNair. General Marshall vetoed this location as already overcrowded. His idea that the work force could escape traffic jams by going to Virginia suggests that his prophetic vision may have been clouded by the mists that arose along the Potomac as he took his solitary rides along the horseback trails close to the site of the present Pentagon.

Near the end of July, Brigadier General Brehon B. Somervell and members of his staff in the Services of Supply proposed a new War Department building near the main entrance to Arlington National Cemetery on part of the former Government Experimental Farm. The Department of Agriculture had transferred the land to the War Department in 1940, and some temporary structures had been erected there. A mile to the southeast of the proposed site, on parts of the farm and the old Hoover Airport (soon to be superseded by the National Airport, farther down the river), the Quartermaster General had set aside an area on which he hoped to build a huge supply depot. But after the National Capital Park and Planning Commission had protested erection of a three-story office building near the cemetery entrance, the Army agreed to erect the warehouses elsewhere and use the onetime farm site for the new Pentagon. The substitute proposal was accepted by Congress as a means of reducing severe housing pressure in the District of Columbia. Unfortunately for the Army's later peace of mind, General Somervell submitted a construction estimate of $35 million, which proved as unrealistic in a period of rising costs as Marshall's vision of uncluttered lanes of traffic.[3] Oblivious at times to the necessity of cultivating members of Congress, Somervell neglected to keep key congressmen informed of essential changes in the plans that legitimately increased the costs. The inevitable consequence was that he was later accused of extravagance and bad management by critics who charged that politics was involved in the expenditures.

Happily Colonel Leslie R. Groves, the Engineer officer who supervised the construction of the building, was more successful in his relations with members of Congress. Knowing that one representative, Albert Engel of

Michigan, a vociferous critic of the War Department and the President, was proud of his skill as an amateur bricklayer, Groves instructed his foreman to take Engel on a tour through the scaffolding and clutter of the building. As a result Groves escaped the attacks that Engel later made on Somervell and Roosevelt; instead he was praised for the work being done.[4]

Paring expenditures, the planners decided on reinforced concrete for the building material and rigorously ruled out marble, flowing fountains, and artistic landscaping. Members of Congress, unable to comprehend the necessity for such a huge War Department building in peacetime, were assured that it need not be occupied permanently by the armed services. After the emergency the military departments could move back to Washington, freeing the building in Virginia for storage of documents or for use by another government agency.

Soon after construction began in the summer of 1941, it became evident that the architects were departing sharply from the neo-Roman pattern of downtown Washington. At the end of August the President told a horrified Stimson that they were going to have "a cubic block of a house for the War Department—a building without windows and lighted and ventilated artificially." Accustomed to spacious office buildings cooled by open windows and ceiling fans and heated by coal and wood fires laid in fireplaces, Stimson found the description so repugnant that he made no reply to Roosevelt but afterward told Somervell that he would not move into such a place. Perhaps the Secretary's protest was responsible for the installation of windows in outside offices, where he, Marshall, and other high-ranking officials could look out toward Washington. But thousands would work under electric light, unaware of sunshine or snow or rain until they left for home, and all would work in air-conditioned spaces—a procedure so novel in 1941 that congressmen attacked it as needless.

Employing a work force that at times reached fifteen thousand, building contractors rushed completion of the new building. By the time of Pearl Harbor some of the five concentric rings of the building had been carried up to the planned height of four floors, and construction of the roofs had begun. With the coming of war an additional floor was decided on.[5] This added expense, plus heavy costs for cloverleaf approaches, changes of roadways, and other items not included in the initial plans, soon pushed the figure well above the estimate. Since congressional elections were approaching, opponents of the administration revived old charges of Roosevelt's extravagance, Somervell's political activity (again Colonel Groves was not brought into line of fire), and gross overruns of estimates.[6]

The shock of Pearl Harbor and the growing demands of a rapidly increasing Army made it evident to everyone how essential the new space was. By the end of 1942 "the largest office building in the world" was not big enough to handle the tenants who wanted to use it. Except for one or two watchdogs, such as Representative Engel, who sent over detailed questions on every phase of the project, its critics held their fire until early in 1944—only a few months before the presidential election. But that spring government leaders from the President down were accused of waste, failure to heed congressional instructions, and using money from "expediting production" funds to evade the will of Congress.

Shortly before the Army completed its move to the Pentagon in late 1942, General Marshall exhibited his usual desire to promote closer unity among the services by urging that all their top operating echelons be assembled in the new building. One million square feet of space were offered to the Navy for a substantial portion of its staff. Some of the bureau chiefs demanded larger footage if they were to move. Stimson replied that if the demands were granted, 40 per cent of the Navy staffs in the Washington area would be in the new building as opposed to 30 per cent of the Army's personnel. He and Marshall found Secretary of the Navy Frank Knox willing to work out an agreement along lines proposed by the Army, but they were irritated to learn that one or two bureau chiefs were exerting pressure on Knox to turn down the arrangement. After several days of wrangling Marshall told the Secretary of War that he was disgusted and ready to withdraw his offer. When Knox brought the subject up a few days later, Stimson said that it was probably better to call the whole thing off.[7]

At times Stimson and Marshall doubted that the Navy leaders seriously wanted service unity. The Navy argued with considerable justice that it had to have sufficient space to install its intricate communications system, and the proposed move waited until after the end of the war. The Army had revenge of a sort, for the public assumed that all the services were operating from the Pentagon. The building became so identified with the direction of the war that many later writers had difficulty realizing that it was not there from the beginning. As a result occasional subsequent accounts of the attack at Pearl Harbor had officers rushing up and down in confusion in the fabled—and then uncompleted—Pentagon maze.

Had the Chief of Staff changed to keep pace with the great new building that symbolized the Army's new-found power? Not in reverence for pomp and circumstance and martial display. He still retained the instinct that had prompted him before Pearl Harbor to suggest that officers in the Washington area wear civilian clothes on duty. He soft-pedaled parades and military ceremonies, stressing always the great role of the civilian soldier in the armed forces. It was Stimson, the civilian head of the War Department, rather than General Marshall, who favored the wearing of uniforms. Stimson also loved a parade, although, to Marshall's amusement, he complained that it was disgusting to see scantily clad drum majorettes leading bands in a military procession.

The losses of war, and its strains and confusions, had strengthened

Marshall's already solid character. His old discipline of mind and body seemed tightened a notch. Except for infrequent bursts of fury, which may on occasion have been staged for effect, he was in control of his emotions. More than ever the General possessed the gift of being able to relax. His former commanding officer in China, Colonel Isaac Newell, summed it up in 1943: "I remember your philosophy; once you have made a decision that is done after best thought, [then] no further worry can affect the result." [8] Marshall had reached that conclusion after two physical collapses from overwork, and he preached it to all who would hear.

The General still struggled to lay aside his worries when he left his office, to snatch a thirty-minute nap after lunch, to continue his horseback rides or his walks with Mrs. Marshall in Arlington Cemetery, a short distance from their quarters, or to slip away for a weekend to the quiet of Dodona Manor, their house in Leesburg. These opportunities grew fewer as his trips around the country and to major conferences abroad increased.

Gone were the quiet canoe trips on the Potomac and most of the undisturbed afternoons working in the garden at Dodona Manor. However, he went down to the home whenever he could, and he reported in June 1943 to Mrs. Marshall's daughter, Molly Brown Winn: "The place looks very lovely, an immense improvement over last year. She has an attractive brick walk out to the tool house and a pergola there; also a small brick walk through the trees to the stone court off the dining room." But because she had been working in localities where the General had warned her not to go, Mrs. Marshall had another touch of poison ivy.[9]

The General made it a practice to share the news of the weather and garden with his stepsons once they were overseas. In the spring of 1945 he wrote Clifton Brown:

The place at Leesburg looks lovely now, with a riot of blooms, roses, peonies, hundreds of flags, poppies, etc. . . .

The vegetable garden is coming along very well and on a pretty large scale, possibly too large to successfully combat the weeds but it does no harm to plant and we have a considerable shortage of vegetables this summer just as there are now coming into force heavy cuts in sugar and meat allowances.

The spring has been very wet and cold since the unseasonable warmth in early March. Today, however, is bright and sunny and I think the warm weather is here.[10]

He grudged the hours that had to be spent in travel and sorely missed the moments he could spend alone with Mrs. Marshall. Once war began, the General's wife was involved in many extra duties. One month after Pearl Harbor, Marshall wrote his younger stepson, Allen Brown: "She had forty Army and Navy women and wives of heads of Departments for Tea yesterday afternoon in connection with the Soldiers and Sailors Club. Later she went to the Club to participate in a reception to newspaper women, so her day was pretty strenuous and mine was too, and we turned in at nine o'clock. After we breakfast at seven and the office at seven forty-five, that is not so 'early' after all." [11]

Mrs. Marshall's efforts in various war-relief activities taxed her constitution, which had been somewhat frail since a serious operation in the 1930s. Marshall often admonished her about her health and insisted that she go away for a few days of rest. But like many other wartime travelers, Mrs. Marshall ran into difficulties when she did try to get away. Upon her return from one visit the General wrote Allen: "Your mother got back last night after a rather confused trip on the train. She could not reach the ticket window in New York to buy a ticket; could not get a porter for almost a half hour; did not have a seat on the train; could not get a telegram off to me; could not find a taxi in Washington; arrived home safely by 9:30. She did get a seat on the train after all but had quite a time about it." [12]

In a typical letter filled with proper concern and the sense of helplessness a husband shows when he has reached the limit of his authority, the Chief of Staff wrote Admiral Harold R. Stark late in 1944 that he had recently sent Mrs. Marshall to Pinehurst, North Carolina, to recover from pleurisy and a mild attack of pneumonia but that she had returned sooner than he had expected, still quite vulnerable to a Washington winter. "But whatever I may be able to do in command and control within the Army," he lamented, "I seem to be quite impotent on the home front." [13] To other friends he wrote shortly afterward that she had used some of her spare time to buy a house in Pinehurst—much smaller than the Leesburg place—set off in the pine woods.

Despite his busy schedule the General tried to find time to write to various members of the family—sometimes asking his secretary to fill them in on his activities—placing personal matters lightly against a backdrop of affairs of state. Until Molly Winn came to live at Leesburg in 1943, after her husband, Major James J. Winn, was assigned to a post where housing was short, he wrote her often, displaying a grandfatherly concern about her children, Jimmy and Kitty, and passing on word about Mrs. Marshall's health, which she herself did not divulge.

His letters to Clifton, the older stepson, were warm and full of interest in his activities but less intimate than his correspondence with Mrs. Marshall's other two children. Old enough to share his mother's grief over his father's tragic death, Clifton had adopted a head-of-the-family attitude in the months before his mother's remarriage. Justly proud of the Brown family's high standing in the Baltimore community, where his father, son of a noted expert on admiralty law, was recognized as an able attorney, Clifton never established a really close relationship with Marshall. There remained between them a certain reserve that each tried to overcome but never quite succeeded in doing.

Allen Brown, who remembered his own father but was young enough to adapt himself to another, was especially close to his stepfather. Marshall—always "Colonel" to the two older children and "George" to Allen —worked hard at the task of giving fatherly guidance to this youngest of the stepchildren.

Allen was affectionate, but he had no intention of being babied. And he served notice that he wanted no favors. He also made clear that he did not always agree with the President and the Chief of Staff. He upset his mother and Molly, when Selective Service was being imposed, by saying that he saw no real "cause" for it. When they accused him of being ignorant of the facts, he appealed to the General:

> But what they both fail to realize is that there are millions who know even less than I do and who are therefore quite naturally against conscription since they know no real direct reason for it and at the same time will be directly affected by conscription. Why in the name of God doesn't the Government tell the people what is going on. . . . I am afraid that the opposition to this conscription bill is going to grow even stronger unless the government takes the people more into its confidence. Secret diplomacy will never get anyplace in a government where the people can bring direct pressure on the lawmakers. . . . These are dangerous times and certainly no time to keep the people "pitifully ignorant" about matters over which they have pressure control.[14]

The younger Brown continued to use his family connection to inform his stepfather of public opinion as the months passed. From all the evidence General Marshall neither resented his advice nor brushed it aside. He gently read Allen lessons on patience—at times Polonius-like but usually without preaching, and always with the saving grace of humor. Noting Allen's tendency to have a chip on his shoulder as he assumed the duties of head of a family and cast about for a job, Marshall wrote frankly —and yet with sensitive reticence. Once after warning Allen rather formally and being reassured that he was not offended, Marshall replied: "The incidents seemed to me to indicate a state of mind that I know from long experience is very unfortunate in this world and is not the way to get across in the long run. You have to save your ammunition for the big fights and avoid a constant drain of little ones." [15]

With the start of war the men of the family became heavily involved. Jim Winn, a Regular Army officer, was shifted back to the United States from Panama, but his wife, Molly, and the rest of the family were delayed in moving because of transportation problems. General Marshall thought that Winn, recovering from fever, should be assigned to a post where he could recoup his strength but hesitated to intervene unless Jim so requested. When the officer expressed no preference, his routine assignment to Fort Bragg was allowed to stand.[16]

Having no family responsibilities, Clifton volunteered shortly after Pearl Harbor and reported to the Reception Center at Fort Meade, Maryland, on January 8, 1942. From there he was sent to the antiaircraft-training center at Camp Eustis, Virginia, where he went through basic instruction and then, in accordance with existing procedure, to officers' school and a commission.[17]

In 1943 when Clifton was sent overseas, Eisenhower's Chief of Staff, Major General Walter Bedell Smith, was reminded of General Marshall's stand on special treatment for his relatives. Soon after Clifton received his orders, Colonel McCarthy, knowing that Marshall wanted no favors for his stepson, got in touch with Carter Burgess of Smith's staff and asked that the young officer be assigned to a post outside Eisenhower's headquarters. Not realizing that Clifton Brown was a relative of Marshall's, Smith had already placed him in Allied headquarters when he saw the exchange of messages between McCarthy and Burgess. In the sharp tone he customarily used to intimidate subordinates he asked McCarthy by what authority he undertook to interfere with assignments in Eisenhower's theater. His outburst was squelched by an equally positive George Marshall. "By my authority," he declared, making clear that he had not allowed his stepson—who was on limited duty due to a bad foot —to come overseas to be in a choice headquarters post.

Allen Brown, with a wife and young son, did not immediately decide on military duty, but he soon began "stewing" about the matter. Mrs. Marshall thought that he might enter service with a direct commission. Almost harshly Allen said that he wanted to go in as a private and make his own way. General Marshall then replied for himself and his wife:

> She showed me your letter to her, written before her arrival at Poughkeepsie, asking her to follow a complete hands off policy in connection with your enlistment. Whether or not she will scrupulously carry out what you request I do not know, but you made it pretty plain and I think you were very wise. . . .
>
> I would like to get you in the Tank Corps because I think you would find your interest greatly stimulated there and a fertile field for the future as a commissioned officer. However, I shall keep hands off. But should you find yourself assigned to the Hospital Corps or one of the other non-combatant branches, in that case tip me off personally and I shall arrange without anyone knowing how it is done to transfer you to a combatant branch. Otherwise I know you would be brooding and bleeding and raising general hell.[18]

Seeing that her brother, Tristram Tupper, an officer in World War I, a journalist, and a highly successful script-writer in Hollywood in the 1930s, was getting no special consideration for a post in the Army, Mrs. Marshall quietly furnished a division commander with documents indicating his background and experience. In due time Tupper was brought into the division and assigned to a post for which his background eminently fitted him. The division commander assumed that Marshall had been involved, and hoping that his action would not go unnoticed, he wrote the Chief of Staff that he was glad that he could use his brother-in-law. Marshall coldly replied that he had done him no favor by the action. Later when Tupper, on the basis of his own ability, became public-relations officer to Lieutenant General Jacob L. Devers, commanding general of the 6th Army

Group, Marshall turned down the General's initial recommendation for Tupper's promotion to one-star rank. Only after Devers renewed the proposal, noting that the position in other headquarters was filled by an officer of brigadier-general rank, did Marshall relent.[19]

Aware that officers under his control were likely to accept any suggestion as a command, the Chief of Staff attempted to avoid requests for favors to his family that might in any way impose on subordinates. He startled one post commander by apologizing because a member of the Pentagon staff had personally called him to get an urgent message through to Mrs. Marshall's daughter.[20]

Marshall's continued resistance to giving favors to his family persisted to the point that Mrs. Marshall at last burst out: "At least don't penalize them for being relatives."

Outside the family there was little time for social visits, but Marshall kept in touch with a few old Army friends in Washington and tried to find time on trips to renew old acquaintanceships. On a visit to London he was reminded by Lady Astor that he had attended the Virginia Military Institute with her brother "Buck" Langhorne. And her sister, wife of the famous illustrator Charles Dana Gibson, recalling that she had met Marshall at a ball at the Institute, wrote to say that she was sure he would not remember her. Marshall replied gallantly: "I still recall my excitement and pleasure over being invited to dinner by you at the old Lexington Hotel. I was a cadet captain and I think Buck was in trouble. Anyway I was included in the dinner by the beauty of the day." [21]

One of the younger friends with whom he corresponded and tried to find time to visit was his goddaughter, Rose Page, who had first met him in the Washington apartment building where the Pages, as well as Marshall and his first wife, Lily, lived in the early 1920s. Rose had introduced herself to Colonel Marshall when she was eight, and at eleven she asked him to be her godfather. She soon became a favorite of the childless Marshalls, and when they moved to nearby Fort Myer, she was allowed to claim a spare bedroom as her own whenever she visited. Over the years she had kept in touch with him, and he had taken comfort in writing and talking to her in the months following Lily's death. During his first year as Chief of Staff, when Rose lived in Washington, he invited her from time to time to accompany him on his daily ride, a diversion that his stepdaughter, Molly, also shared. After Rose married John Wilson in 1941 and moved to New York, the General took a lively interest in the young couple, giving them both fatherly advice. When their oldest son was born, he gladly agreed to act as godfather. On trips to New York City he tried to find time to drop by and delighted in inspecting the new household. Despite his busy schedule he found time to send the Wilsons brief notes on his activities. The eight-year-old he had met nearly a quarter-century earlier remained a link with a half-forgotten part of his past. Years later Mrs. Wilson wrote that she thought that the second Mrs. Marshall resented the memory they shared of Lily—a recollection from which she was excluded. Nonetheless when friends asked Rose if the General preferred the first wife to the second, she angrily made it clear that both were equally dear to him.[22]

Marshall found, as does every individual in high place, that it was difficult to resist the pressure of old friends for favors. In addition to requests for commissions, assignments to special advanced courses for officers, recall to duty of men in retirement, he was set upon for pettier favors, such as passes to the Army-Navy game or the installation of a private telephone in a period when instruments were being reserved almost wholly for the armed services. Inevitably he was called on for financial contributions to various government drives. In 1943 when an old friend from his birthplace, Uniontown, Pennsylvania, asked him to buy a government bond through the local sales committee, he was slightly embarrassed at having to explain that he lacked the $1000 to make the purchase. Only after reexamining some meager stock holdings he had inherited from his mother did he find some shares that he could sell for enough to buy the certificate.

Friendship with the General gained its possessors few advantages. Acquaintances—some digging up fancied intimacy from boyhood days— wrote him in behalf of sons or nephews. One lady reprimanded him because the Army had sent her son to bakers' school, when his background and education obviously fitted him for something better. Another indicated that her son was not prepared for the harshness of Army life. Still another asked for a direct commission to avoid the rigors of Officer Candidate School. Marshall urged all these petitioners to help their protégés by suggesting that they do their work well. Some he angered by observing that the writers of such letters needed to ponder their duties to the Republic.

Demands on his time became almost overwhelming. Among the many things that he found he had to give up to a considerable degree were the hunting trips that had once been a favorite diversion. Not only were his opportunities to accept invitations lessened, but he discovered that unless he weighed his acceptances with care, his weekend outings became the basis for an approach by someone wishing a favor. On one occasion he yielded to the importunings of his first wife's brother to accept the invitation of a wealthy friend who promised good shooting on his estate. On his return the General was uncharacteristically curt in his thank-you note. Later when the brother-in-law forwarded another invitation from his friend, the General was uncommunicative. At last when Lily's brother, hurt and puzzled, pushed the matter, Marshall wrote a sharp letter in the cutting tone with which he sometimes rebuked close friends when they pressed too hard, saying that he had not accepted because he did not want to be exploited. He had scarcely returned to Washington before his recent host wrote him asking for a favor. Marshall's brother-in-law, deeply embarrassed, apologized and the matter was forgiven. But it made the General more wary.

Marshall's rigorous refusal to extend even deserved favors strained some formerly close friendships and darkened others. One who presumed too far too often on his former association with the Chief of Staff was Major General Roy Keehn, commanding general of the 33d Division of the Illinois National Guard when Marshall was the unit's senior instructor, from 1933 to 1936. Keehn, once a powerful force in the state as attorney for Hearst interests in the Middle West, was a man accustomed to having his way. He liked to remind Marshall that he had been the first senior officer to propose publicly that the General be named Chief of Staff.

At first Marshall attempted to make clear that there were things he could not do in his position even for friends. When Governor Henry Horner of Illinois replaced Keehn as head of the division with Major General Samuel T. Lawton, and the Chief of Staff declined to express an opinion about the situation, Keehn was obviously unhappy. Marshall patiently bore numerous requests for transfers or promotions of Keehn's old friends in the division and listened attentively when the former Illinois commander expressed his views as a member of the National Guard Executive Council.

After several months during which Marshall turned aside a number of Keehn's recommendations or referred them to the proper authorities, he brought matters to a head by pressing Marshall to allow a Chicago firm to have control of concessions in the post exchanges of the 33d Division when it was called into federal service. Keehn explained that the firm was one of his legal clients. The Chief of Staff made it clear that the granting of concessions for the sale of certain items or installation of certain vending machines was a matter he left to the post commanders. Keehn, seemingly unable to understand that his old friend did not agree that some regulations were not meant to be enforced, apparently telephoned Marshall in an angry mood. The next letter from the Illinois General showed that the Chief of Staff had replied even more hotly. "Frankly, George Marshall," Keehn began, "I am a little worried about your nervousness and high tension." He went on to report the National Guard's objection to War Department policy on post-exchange concessions and warned against what he considered to be the Roosevelt administration's disregard of the rights of the states. But, he reiterated, his main worry was about Marshall's health.

In no mood for this approach, Marshall replied:

I appreciate your concern over my physical condition, but I do not think you need worry about it. I blew off a little steam on you, but considering the fact that this is the first time I have allowed myself that privilege in a year and a half, I think the explosion was mild. I must confess to the necessity for tremendous restraint of feeling in the light of irritating pettiness of continued pressures on me and unjustified criticisms of the War Department, at a time when we have leaned over backward in an effort to do at least the right thing, if not, I think more than we should. We are trying to organize an army, and we are still struggling with political aspects; given enough of the latter and we are wasting our money and gravely risking the security of the United States—to put it plainly. If everything pertaining to the Army has to be put on a town meeting basis, we might as well quit before we start.

I am writing rather frankly; however, you have written with extreme frankness and if I chose to, I could be much more offended but I have ignored all that, knowing you and feeling confident of your friendship for me and your genuine desire to see me make the grade.

I think if you were to occupy my chair for thirty minutes and struggle with things of vast importance to this country, and at the same time struggle with a wide variety of superficial, irritating, and prejudicial reactions, you would marvel that we could go ahead as smoothly as we do.[23]

There matters remained for several months with occasional exchanges on minor items. In August 1941 another storm seemed imminent. Keehn again sought Marshall's ear on behalf of a client who sold a freezer that might be used in Army kitchens. The request that the Army take a look at the freezer was reasonable and could have been made through normal channels. The problem arose when Keehn suggested that a model might be installed in Marshall's quarters so that he could see its value for himself. A week after receiving Keehn's letter he replied: "The Secretary General Staff [Brigadier General Orlando Ward, who had already made a polite estimate of Marshall's probable answer] was correct in his statement that I would not feel free to accept such installation in my own quarters and if I did so it would practically bar your freeze for Government contract." [24]

The Chief of Staff then sent the information about the product to the Quartermaster General. Several weeks later Keehn wrote off the matter by informing Marshall that they did not seem to have made much progress but that he had certainly had a cordial hearing from the Office of the Quartermaster General.

Other pleas for consideration of his clients' products flowed from Keehn's pen, but not until December 1942 did Marshall firmly tell his old friend that he must not try to do business at the War Department. Marshall wrote: "I simply cannot become involved in matters of personal intervention for individuals. Every day I receive requests of this kind and, as I have told you before, the moment I interfere with established policies or overrule our agencies who have thoroughly studied the matter, I am lost. . . . I enjoyed our little visit together the other day and hope you will understand why my friendship for you must not be permitted to interfere with the normal action taken in the War Department." [25]

This exchange did not greatly decrease a heavy correspondence—which resumed a warm tone in regard to personal relationships and polite exchanges about policy after the war. General Keehn also continued to give advice, to which the Chief of Staff responded, but there was a falling off in pressure for clients.

In 1944 the illness of Keehn's eldest son, an officer in the European Theater of Operations, brought renewed appeals from the Illinois General, but always as an anguished father asking the Chief of Staff's advice. Perhaps in memory of their service together, or in recognition of Keehn's bitterness in losing out in the National Guard unit he had helped develop, the Chief of Staff went further than was his custom in having inquiries made about the young officer's health, his return to the United States for treatment, and his later reassignment. Although Marshall still made clear that these measures had to be taken through normal channels, his kindnesses helped to restore the cordiality of the early relationship.

Keehn's last letter, after a minor stroke a few months before his death, expressed the desire that Marshall, now Secretary of State, would return to Chicago and relate what had happened in the world since he had left. Speaking of his hopes for a memorial armory on the lakefront to house some Illinois units, Keehn observed: "This is certainly a petty, minor matter compared to the big things you have been called upon to do. How I reflect back on our early ideas together and how curious I am from day to day remembering how that great mind of our old senior instructor struggles with these tremendous world problems you now have to deal with." [26]

Occasionally when Marshall was hounded for a letter of reference, even plain speaking did not prove effective. A man whose friendship Marshall prized wrote concerning his son-in-law: "If you will inquire of his commanding officer and state your interest I will be obliged to you." In the closemouthed terms he used for such requests, Marshall spelled out the reasons why he could not lend his name and office to such proposals. Back came the reply, "I agree with all your arguments. I am at a complete loss to understand just why you wrote me this homily." From such friends there was no escape.

However he managed to an astonishing degree to stay clear of entanglements, and he enjoined others similarly to avoid favoritism, insisting that commanding officers not use their sons or nephews as aides. Sometimes he would bend his rule a little but never for long. When, shortly after D day, sore beset by the pressures of the invasion, Eisenhower asked that his son, just graduated from West Point, be allowed to join him for a short visit, Marshall acceded. Warned by the Supreme Commander that the young officer would not want to come if he knew that the trip had been especially arranged, Marshall carefully concealed the fact from young John. In utter innocence he came to his father's headquarters and accompanied him for a short time on tours to the front in Normandy. Soon afterward John insisted that he be allowed to return to troop duty, and his father agreed.[27]

As announcements of losses mounted, Marshall became increasingly reluctant to accept special honors for himself. In addition to being naturally averse to publicity, he felt it unseemly for the Chief of Staff to be given special recognition while soldiers were being killed or wounded in foreign assignments. Marshall's memoranda to his press-relations officer asking if something might be done quietly to prevent publication of a book or an article on himself multiplied in the files of the secretariat. His old friend Major General Johnson Hagood, who had embarrassed him with a highly laudatory article in the late 1930s, drew a strong negative when he asked permission to write another Marshall story. William Chenery, publisher of *Collier's*, failing to get permission for a special article, sought to get around the War Department injunction by proposing an open letter to the President lauding Marshall. The Chief of Staff complained of inaccuracies and of extravagant praise, and managed to stop its publication.

When Marshall Andrews, military columnist on the Washington *Post*, submitted early chapters of a biography of the General, the Chief of Staff successfully appealed to the writer through Brigadier General Alexander D. Surles, director of Public Relations, to scrap it. Somewhat different action was taken in the case of a book by William Frye, which had been submitted to the Bobbs-Merrill Publishing Company. Marshall directed Colonel McCarthy, then Secretary General Staff, to contact the company's president. In a letter that set the pattern for all later wartime appeals, McCarthy made clear that General Marshall had no intention of suppressing the book. But he believed that his relations with the Army were "far more apt to be unfavorably prejudiced by such publicity rather than benefited. The Regular Army personnel in particular is suspicious of the basis of inspiration for write-ups of this character, and he feels, or rather realizes, that their confidence is essential to the successful leadership of the Army." Thus couched, the appeal was enough to get Frye's book postponed until after the close of the war. Andrews dropped his book completely, later graciously making his notes available to the author of this volume.[28]

The General's ban included personal decorations, honorary degrees, and other awards during the war. In early March 1943 he directed that all military attachés be informed: "General Marshall feels that such awards [from foreign governments] would constitute an embarrassment to him at this time, especially when he is desirous of lending specific assistance to the country concerned. The matter of a personal award to him raises the possibility of political attacks which would tend to limit his efforts to lend the desired assistance." A few months later he extended the policy to all senior officers to whom foreign governments might wish to give awards. "You are enjoined to see to it that neither you nor any person under your control intimates by word or deed or permits the impression to be gained that any high-ranking officer of the U.S. Army might welcome the offer of a foreign decoration." All such matters, he noted, should be held in abeyance until the conclusion of hostilities.[29]

In a few instances the General had no choice. The Sultan of Morocco included him with other officers decorated during the Casablanca meeting, the Defense Minister of Chile pleaded that he would be personally discomfited if Marshall did not accept an award, and President Roosevelt himself suggested that he accept the Order of Suvarov from the Soviet Union on the eve of D day 1944.[30]

Despite his air of aloofness, which seemed to increase as the pressure of duties grew heavier, Marshall still found time for a gracious gesture toward subordinates, but as more than one assistant observed, he did not like to be caught at it. Grateful officers, quick to express their appreciation for a promotion, were told almost brusquely, "Don't thank me. If you hadn't earned it you would not have gotten it."

Marshall's seeming lack of easy informality with many who served him daily did not mean that he was unobservant of people about him. Washington newspapers of the war period contain a clutch of stories about his kindness to strangers who asked directions, unaware of who he was, or about enlisted personnel or civilian secretaries he sometimes astounded by the invitation to "Get in" as he passed them waiting at a bus stop for their usual ride to the office. A retired officer, shivering in the intense cold of a wintry day during an Arlington burial, recalled that Marshall had insisted that he go to his car and get out of the killing chill.

He even retained the capacity to deal gently with a sleepy sentry. General John E. Hull of his staff recalled this incident: "One day in going to Fort Myer he passed the sentry in front of his house and the boy didn't present arms. He went over to him and asked if they didn't teach them to salute general officers any more. He [the boy] said he didn't see him. General Marshall said he had driven right by him. The boy then said he had been asleep. General Marshall said, 'All right.' (The boy was just a kid.) General Marshall then ordered that the guard post be abolished. He said he didn't see any use of it anyway." [31]

Although the General was frugal by habit and continued the practice, set early in his career, of making certain that he always had something ahead at the end of each month, he had never been able to accumulate large savings. He and Mrs. Marshall had pooled their resources, part of hers coming from proceeds of the sale of a cottage on Fire Island, to buy Dodona Manor, in Leesburg. In the early days of his service as Chief of Staff he had drawn on his personal means to supplement his meager entertainment allowance in order to furnish refreshments to visiting officials. Only after the coming of war did he receive a large enough fund to cover these necessary expenses. But the habits of years persisted. His private papers show that he required a strict accounting for the expenditures from government funds for entertainment and that he carefully checked with his aides on the lavishness of food and liquor.

Now sixty-two, Marshall seemed to have been affected physically very little by the year that the United States had been a participant in the war. The reddish tinge in his hair was giving way to gray, the reduction in the time that he could devote to exercise was showing up in the gain of a few pounds. There was, perhaps, a slight impairment of hearing. He wore his glasses more often, but he needed only slight magnification. Like most men who use spectacles for reading only, he was able to do without expensive prescription types, which he could have requisitioned from the Army. Instead his orderly regularly stocked several pairs from local five-and-ten-cent stores, keeping them where he could produce them on demand when a pair was suddenly missing.

Marshall's step was still brisk and assured, his gestures simple but determined, his face perhaps a little grimmer, his manner a touch more aloof. He did tire somewhat more easily, and he found opportunities, on the eve of great conferences or in periods of stress, to slip away from Washington for an inspection trip that would leave him a day for relaxation without being completely out of touch with the White House or the War Department. A number of these trips were taken to South Carolina, to the estates of Bernard Baruch, whose large holdings provided privacy.

Never a glad-hander, Marshall used the hearty approach even less now. Never one to overpraise, he was more sparing than ever in saying well done. And yet he encouraged top-quality work without quick compliments or easy approaches. Men strove to do their best in his presence because it was expected. They dreaded less his marked disapproval than a certain sense that they had failed him. His stinted expressions of approbation produced, of course, a whole new currency of rewards. "Not bad" was a suitable payment for a good position paper; "Very good" almost the ultimate in plaudits.

At the end of 1942 Marshall could look back on more than three years of preparations and solid accomplishment. His staff had shaken down and his routines were well established. Men he had carefully picked were at work at home and abroad organizing American efforts for victory.

IV

Marshall and His Staff

GENERAL Marshall's day started at six at Quarters One, Fort Myer, home of all the Army Chiefs of Staff, save the widower Pershing, since Marshall's old chief Major General J. Franklin Bell, had moved into it in 1908. Built in 1899 at a cost of $15,000, the three-story red-brick building stood near the corner of Arlington National Cemetery, on Arlington Heights, overlooking the city of Washington. In accordance with custom the house had been redecorated for the new Chief of Staff before he moved into it in 1939.[1] Only Marshall's own bedroom, simple in its arrangements, remained much as it had been. His main personal addition to the building had been a pen for chickens since he wanted to indulge his farmer's instincts by having his own flock. Inasmuch as this was not a normal fixture for the home of the Chief of Staff, he had insisted on paying the bill for the material needed. The chickens flourished under his care, and some were still there when he moved from Fort Myer near the end of 1945—to be left under the watchful eye of the new Chief of Staff, General Eisenhower, who dutifully reported on their welfare to his former boss after the latter's departure for China.

When the General rode in the morning, he had one of his two horses brought from nearby government stables and spent thirty to fifty minutes in the saddle before his shower and breakfast. Usually he followed an old practice that extended back at least to Fort Benning days, when he had forsworn the company of officers for fear that they would talk business, and had either ridden with some of their wives or alone. In his early tenancy of Fort Myer, before Molly Brown's marriage, he had sometimes ridden with her or with his goddaughter, Rose Page, but he preferred solitary outings, which allowed him time to think.

Breakfast was usually a substantial meal, prepared and cooked by Army personnel under the supervision of Staff Sergeant William Farr, a onetime hotel employee in Savannah, Georgia, where Marshall had spotted him while he was stationed at Fort Screven. The General, Farr

recalled, had a hearty appetite and liked simple food. He ate almost anything except shrimp, to which he was so allergic that standing instructions
were routinely forwarded to unwary hostesses or banquet arrangers to
omit shrimp in planning menus for him.

Over breakfast the General glanced at the morning newspapers. In all,
he said, "I scanned nine papers every day." [2] For a long time, the New
York *Times,* which he felt he should read regularly, was not at his breakfast table. Finally he complained to Arthur Krock, head of the paper's
Washington bureau, that there was no early delivery of the paper in the
Fort Myer area and that he often lacked time to read it at the office. When
soon afterward a vehicle appeared each morning with his paper, the General wrote Krock that he hoped that the delivery did not involve "a single
truck trip into that neighborhood." Krock graciously replied that "Even
if it required two trucks for the sole purpose of getting the New York
Times to you in the early morning it would be worth it to us and, I feel,
to the country." [3]

As the war's demands on him grew, General Marshall usually rose from
breakfast and went to his waiting car promptly at 7:15 A.M. In the early
days his two regular drivers were Sergeant James Powder and Sergeant
George Dumcke. In 1943 Powder, whose services as principal orderly to
the General had increased, was relieved of his driving assignment and a
WAC chauffeur, Sergeant Marjorie Payne, became the second regular
driver.

As the sergeant who served Marshall from the beginning to the end of
the war, not only as driver and personal orderly, but also as junior aide,
James Powder occupies a secure place in any account of Marshall's wartime service. Six feet four and three-quarter inches tall, then in his early
forties, this shrewd bear of a man was devoted to the General. Powder,
who bore a shortened version of a name with Polish origins, was descended from a great-great-grandfather who had gone to Russia with Napoleon. The sergeant, burning to equal the record of an older brother in
the Navy, entered the Army in 1914 by lying about his age. In the 1930s
after services in the Philippines and in various posts in France and the
United States, he was assigned to duty in Washington and detailed to
drive the Deputy Chief of Staff. General Marshall inherited him on assuming that position. When the General moved up to the post of Chief of
Staff, Powder went along. With the legerdemain that sagacious sergeants
command, he picked up information on units to be visited and generally
smoothed the details of Marshall's trips. More than once Marshall offered
to make him a captain or a major in the Reserve, but Powder demurred.
Since he had left school at the age of twelve, he felt handicapped by lack
of formal education, and he turned away the proffered commissions, saying that he did not want his chief to be ashamed of him. In fact Powder
could hardly have been expected to exercise greater authority as an officer
than he did as Marshall's orderly-aide. When distinguished generals

came to Washington, the Chief of Staff put them in Powder's keeping, and he managed their affairs as skillfully as he did Marshall's.

On trips Powder took care of the General's wardrobe, saw that there was an adequate stock of five-and-ten-cent-store spectacles, put copies of the Army's series of paperback books near his seat on the plane, and placed a candy bar or two by his bedside at night. If the Chief of Staff was unable to sleep, the sergeant doubled as masseur, using his powerful hands or a vibrator to help the General relax. Wise in the ways of repaying service on trips abroad, Powder loaded his luggage with inexpensive items difficult to find in wartime and had them available for his chief to distribute. On his return the sergeant brought back souvenirs, which he spread around the Pentagon or in shops where he bought supplies for the Chief of Staff, building a reservoir of goodwill he could draw on later.

During his travels Marshall liked Powder to be quartered near him so that he could call on him day or night. Once on a trip to Europe, however, a major, shocked at the notion that Powder should expect to stay in the area reserved for officers, insisted that he go to a distant part of the chateau with the other sergeants of the headquarters. The major waved away Powder's explanation that the General would not like it. At last Powder went quietly and deliberately remained in the room assigned to him until Marshall, wanting something from his luggage, sent the major, stammering and red-faced, to find the sergeant and move his belongings to a room nearer the Chief of Staff's.[4]

The WAC driver, Sergeant Payne, was assigned to General Marshall in the fall of 1943, when he asked for several members of the Women's Army Corps to serve on his personal staff. "You have the highest spot of any WAC," Colonel Oveta Culp Hobby, the Corps' director, impressed on her in making the assignment. "He will see the WAC through you."

Born in Michigan, daughter of a truck driver, pretty, blonde Marjorie Payne was a beauty-shop operator when she decided to enter the Women's Army Corps. After learning to drive and maintain trucks, jeeps, and limousines, she came to Washington, where she drove for several War Department generals before being assigned to the Chief of Staff. She idolized her boss, finding him stern but kind, flatteringly expecting the same performance from her as he would from a male chauffeur. And she proved her worth. Alternating the driving assignment with George Dumcke, a forty-nine-year-old tough Regular Army sergeant "who was issued, not born," she asked no quarter. She pleased Marshall by asking if she could use his car from time to time to give rides to wounded veterans, delighting them as she drove the Cadillac grandly through Rock Creek Park.

She found that Marshall did not want to attract attention to himself as they drove through traffic. He instructed her to leave the stars off his car and preferred most of the time to use the smaller official car, a Plymouth, or, for personal business, his own Oldsmobile. He took the official Cadillac only if he went to the White House or some ceremonial affair, since people were likely to recognize him in it. He dreaded halts in traffic as passersby sometimes stuck their heads into the car to speak to him. She remembered that when they had a vapor lock one hot day, the General, not wishing to be peered at by the curious, fled from the car while she tinkered with it. Sometimes when traffic was heavy and she had a plane to meet, she regretted his insistence on remaining inconspicuous. On the way to the airport to greet Eisenhower after the war, Marshall declined as usual to have a motorcycle escort, and the driver had heavy going until she was able to get in behind the Secretary of War's car. Stimson, equally opposed to attracting the attention of a crowd, was even more impatient of delays in traffic, so he had an escort.

At ease with Sergeant Payne's driving, Marshall gave her few instructions. She recalled that once when taking him to Capitol Hill for a speech to members of Congress, she approached a crosswalk where a number of men were passing, and he called out—good humoredly—"Don't hit them, I want to talk to them." After she had been in a collision with a bus, she was not sure how he would react but knew she had retained his confidence when he asked her to drive the new Cadillac. Years later she was still full of memories as she talked about the trips the General had made with her behind the wheel—once to Berryville, Virginia, to appear at Harry Byrd's Apple Festival, where he sat with dignity on the reviewing stand, inspecting the trucks and farm equipment passing before him as if he were on a drill field. She mentioned some of her interesting passengers—Madame Chiang Kai-shek, "intelligent, delicate, Oriental, beautifully dressed"; Bernard Baruch, who liked to lean over to the front seat and ask questions about the WAC; General de Gaulle, whom she brought from the Mayflower Hotel to the Pentagon on an occasion of which she had saved a treasured photograph with Marshall standing rigid while the Frenchman kissed him on the cheek; and Stilwell, Ridgway, Mark Clark as they came back to report on their various theaters of war.

She remembered also some of the people Marshall met frequently— General "Hap" Arnold (who at first had not liked WAC drivers but then changed his mind—at least as far as she was concerned), "a lovely man and jovial"; Admiral King, "severe and stern"; and Admiral Leahy, who seemed "somewhat warmer" in nature. She recalled an occasion when Admiral King's driver in leaving the White House had confused directions and was proceeding along the narrow driveway on a collision course with Marshall's car, departing correctly. Although protocol demanded that the General's car go out first, he directed that she back up and let the Admiral's car proceed. But the Navy driver recognized her passenger and retreated. A newspaperman who saw the incident wrote, "The Navy backs down." Marshall, she recalled, made no comment.

Ex-Sergeant Payne—now Mrs. Lunger—has always treasured an incident involving her two favorite Generals, Marshall and Arnold. During a long ceremony at the Tomb of the Unknown Soldier, a hulking Marine fainted after standing at attention for a prolonged period. She was startled to see the two officers rush to his side and the Army Chief of Staff push the man's head down to force the blood to flow back into it. Then the two Generals took the Marine into the car and asked to be driven to the hospital.[5]

On weekday mornings Marshall's chauffeur drove him from Quarters One along the road north of Arlington Cemetery to Fort Myer Drive or to one of the new approaches to the Pentagon. On the west, along Columbia Pike, temporary barracks, part of South Post, Fort Myer, were beginning to spread out toward the cemetery; northeastward were temporary housing units for government girls who had difficulty finding living quarters in the District of Columbia; westward, along Columbia Pike, the Navy Annex and barracks for sailors and Marines would soon take shape. To the southeast, on George Washington Memorial Highway, the National Airport neared completion, and at its north end Gravelly Point served for take-offs of Army transports bound overseas. To the east and west of the building traffic swelled as the military payrolls grew and as supplies were dispatched in ever-increasing volume.

Near the Pentagon's River Entrance, the General's driver would usually take the ramp into the garage beneath the building, stopping at a door leading to the elevator that opened directly inside the Chief of Staff's office. Unless Marshall took a rare trip to the huge Concourse to visit one of the shops or passed through the corridors to one of the conference rooms or to the theater to watch a training film, he would be seen by only a few members of his staff. Except for the weekly luncheons with members of the Joint Chiefs of Staff in their dining room across the river or with an occasional visitor in his private dining room in the Pentagon, the General ate his meals at his Fort Myer quarters. Aware that a trip to the Pentagon's barbershop would create a gathering of onlookers, he usually had his favorite barber, Joseph Abbate, the shop's manager, come to a small anteroom outside his office.

Some members of Marshall's staff felt that his sudden arrivals and departures by private elevator deprived him of a close rapport with officers and enlisted personnel on duty, in contrast to the happy effects of the warm "Good morning" delivered by other high-ranking officers striding down the corridors and through the anterooms leading to the main office. Members of Marshall's immediate staff had no such concern. They were more disturbed by the fact that he might be settled in his office before they knew he was there. As a result there was much opening and closing of doors to see if he had arrived until finally his assistants arranged to have a signal system installed that would indicate his progress from the moment that he stepped in the elevator until he closed the door at the office. Staff members soon learned that the General had a curious phobia about being peered at by people who pushed his door partly open and then darted back again when they saw that he was busy. To their great discomfiture he usually yelled out, "Come on in," and at length directed that no one should ever open a door to the office without entering it fully no matter who else was present or what was in progress. For the uninitiated it was an unnerving experience.

The Chief of Staff's morning routine began with an examination of the logbook containing important messages that had come in during the previous evening. In case of an extremely urgent communication demanding immediate attention, he would have been informed that very night. Otherwise papers that key aides thought he should see were put at once on his desk or discussed with him by top members of his staff. Since Army communications were used for some of the traffic between the White House and headquarters abroad, copies of messages just then reaching the President might also be included in the Chief of Staff's basket, particularly if it seemed likely that he would be expected to help draft a reply.

In addition the twenty to twenty-five personal letters the General received daily would be opened for his inspection. He quickly ran through them, wrote quick notes instructing how they should be disposed of, whether information was required, or whether a staff member could draft a suitable letter. He dictated about a third of the replies himself. On letters asking special action by the Chief of Staff, he would often pencil "Help him if you can" or "Write him a polite No" and sent them on to a member of the secretariat to draft answers. These would often be redrafted by the Secretary General Staff and then were subject to final editing by the General.[6]

At the staff Message Center many communications relating to plans or operations overseas would automatically be sent to the Operations Division or to proper offices of the General Staff for drafts of replies for the Chief of Staff's signature. In some cases these accompanied the messages to the Chief's office. His action regarding any paper was nearly always the same. As he picked it up, he reached for a pen from the holder on his desk and, as he read, began to make suggestions or to scrawl changes, leaving his definite imprint on each paper he handed back. One of his staff assistants, Colonel William T. Sexton, preserved hundreds of memoranda and drafts that show the steps in the education of a staff officer as Marshall slashed and cut verbiage from suggested replies and stressed the need for condensation and direct and simple writing. By the time Sexton became Secretary General Staff, in March 1943, he was an expert on Marshall's requirements. General Eisenhower, who had his share of Marshall's editing, recalled that once after he had taken in a number of papers that Marshall rewrote on the spot, he suddenly was handed an unmarked one. As Ike left the Chief of Staff's office, he whooped, "By God, I finally wrote one he didn't change!"

Since, except for key members of the Operations Division, the Secretaries General Staff were the individuals in closest contact with the Chief of Staff, their notes for record, interoffice communications, and reports to the Chief of Staff constitute a fascinating collection of the information handed General Marshall daily, as well as his reactions. One morning he picked up a note from Colonel McCarthy about a hurried request late the afternoon before from the Legislative Liaison Officer. A Midwestern congressman wanted a telegram from the Chief of Staff to read at a dinner honoring a prominent figure in a war industry. One of McCarthy's assistants, Major H. Merrill Pasco, had written the statement requested. Appreciating initiative on the part of his subordinates in this kind of situation, Marshall approved it. But he added a guide for the future: "OK. But next time see that the style is mine and not so ponderous." [7]

Handling a heavy volume of correspondence, the office of the Secretary General Staff channeled incoming messages to proper individuals for action or comment, called requests and replies to Marshall's attention, and promptly provided information he asked for. The office kept track of directives, appointments, and the whereabouts and future activities of the Chief of Staff. Through much of the war his secretarial staff included Miss Cora Thomas, assigned to him in 1939; Mrs. Sallie Garlington Chamberlin, niece of Mrs. J. Franklin Bell; and Miss Mona Nason, who became his personal secretary in 1940 and remained with his successors until her retirement a quarter-century later. Miss Thomas, in a little room across the hall from the General's office, acted as receptionist. Mrs. Chamberlin handled personal correspondence, becoming an authority on information required to answer Marshall's boyhood friends from Uniontown, inquiries on the family tree, or men who had served with him in the Philippines, at Leavenworth, or in World War I.

Miss Nason typed all the classified correspondence. A model of discretion and closemouthed dependability, she became the bane of newsmen and historians seeking inside information. Gracious but positive, she insisted that the General's secrets remain with him. While properly respectful, she was not in awe of the Chief of Staff, as is evident in a story she sometimes repeated about him. Despite a prodigious memory for statistics and dates, Marshall often forgot or confused the names of people who worked with him. He annoyed his secretary by calling her "Miss Mason." One day when he had asked for the third or fourth time that she send "Colonel McCartney" to him, she corrected him: "General, his name is McCarthy not McCartney and I am Nason not Mason." When she related the story to Colonel Robert N. Young of the secretariat, he retorted, "While you were at it, I wish you had told him that I am Young and not Maxwell Taylor." Even her pointed reminder was not enough to get the matter straight, and she became accustomed to a boss who after five years still called her "Mason" or who would direct her to telephone that "redheaded fellow" down the hall. [8]

Before General Marshall's tour of duty and even in his earlier years as Chief of Staff, the post of Secretary General Staff normally went to a senior colonel and was considered an important steppingstone to a higher staff job or field command. Colonel Orlando Ward, who held the post when General Marshall arrived, later commanded the 1st Armored Division in North Africa. His successor, Colonel Walter Bedell Smith, became Secretary to the Combined Chiefs of Staff organization shortly after it was established. Later he served General Eisenhower as Chief of Staff in North Africa, in the Mediterranean Command, and at Supreme Headquarters, Allied Expeditionary Force. After the war Smith was ambassador to the Soviet Union, commander of the First Army, director of the Central Intelligence Agency, and Undersecretary of State. Associated with these earlier incumbents were numerous other officers—including Omar N. Bradley, J. Lawton Collins, and Maxwell Taylor, plus Eisenhower and Ridgway, all later Chiefs of Staff—who served under Marshall before going on to high commands.

Bedell Smith was succeeded by Colonel John R. Deane, who became Secretary of the Combined Chiefs of Staff before reaching two-star rank as head of the United States Military Mission to the Soviet Union in the fall of 1943. Next in line, Colonel Robert N. Young, a student at Fort Benning under Marshall, occupied the post of Secretary General Staff for a few months before going to the 70th Division as assistant division commander and then to a similar position with 3d Division in France. He was to reach three-star rank before retirement.

The last Regular Army officer to serve as Secretary General Staff under Marshall was Colonel Sexton, one of the younger officers personally recruited by the Chief of Staff. Impressed by Sexton's book, *Soldiers in the Sun*, a volume on the Philippine Insurrection published in 1939, Marshall invited the young officer to join his staff. Sexton served his apprenticeship by drafting letters for the General's signature.

As the demand for older and more experienced officers of combat age became acute, General Marshall called on the commander of Ground Forces, Lieutenant General Lesley J. McNair, and field commanders to send him young men who could profit from training on his staff before going up to higher assignments. Feeling that his own advancement had been delayed by overlong tours of duty as an aide or as a staff officer, he attempted wherever possible to give Regular Army officers an opportunity to command. In time he brought in reservists or Officer Candidate School graduates to handle much of his staff work. The letter he wrote Lieutenant General Jacob L. Devers when Colonel Sexton was released to him was a typical expression of his solicitude for Regular Army officers in these matters: "I want him attached to a United States division in the line in Italy not as liaison or observer but a member on duty with artillery. What I want is to give him the experience in fighting as a final step to offset his long service to me here in this office. Thereafter he is on his own. You can keep him or we will assign him to a division training in the United States." [9] Devers kept him, assigning him as artillery officer of the 3d Division.

After 1943 General Marshall filled the main slots in the office of the Secretary General Staff with Reserve officers or with Regular Army officers who had been wounded in action. Sexton's replacement was Reservist Colonel Frank McCarthy, who remained with the General until the spring of 1945. When McCarthy was appointed an assistant secretary of State, he handed over his post to another Reserve officer, a fellow graduate of Virginia Military Institute, four years behind him, H. Merrill Pasco of Richmond.[10]

Marshall was worried sufficiently lest he be accused of favoritism for having too many VMI graduates on his personal staff—and indeed on a few occasions wives of West Point graduates made that charge—that he warned the alumni secretary at his Alma Mater not to publicize their assignments. He often explained that Generals Gerow, Brett, and Handy —also of VMI—had been in the War Department when he came and that McCarthy and Pasco had been assigned to his office before he knew their background.

McCarthy was the officer who came closest to filling the post of officer-aide. Although he held various titles—Assistant Secretary, Secretary General Staff, Military Secretary to the General Staff, and SGS—he continued to organize details of most of the General's visits at home and abroad, becoming an invaluable member of his personal staff.

After being graduated from VMI in 1933, McCarthy returned to his Alma Mater as an instructor and then remained as alumni secretary. In the late 1930s, when *Brother Rat,* a comedy based rather loosely on life at VMI, became a Broadway success and a popular road show, he served for two years as a press agent for George Abbott productions in New York. When the play was made into a movie, with Ronald Reagan in one of the leading roles, McCarthy began a connection with Hollywood that was to lead to a postwar career in public relations and movie production. After the war began in Europe, he entered graduate school at the University of Virginia and received his master's degree at the famous commencement ceremony where President Roosevelt delivered his impassioned attack on Mussolini for sticking a dagger in the back of defeated France.

Knowing that McCarthy had a Reserve commission, a former commandant of cadets at VMI, Colonel John Magruder, then a member of the G-2 Division in the War Department, advised his former student to come on active duty. He asked that McCarthy be assigned to his office even as another former commandant, Colonel Withers Burress, in G-3, asked a few months later that Pasco be sent to his division.

McCarthy remained in his G-2 division until the following spring. In June 1941 Colonel Ward, then SGS, asked for a junior officer for his department, and McCarthy was recommended. For a time he must have assumed that he was merely an office boy who would have no chance of coming into contact with the Chief of Staff of the Army. His chance came one Saturday morning in the early fall of 1941, when General Marshall read that the VMI football team was to play in Washington. Idly wondering if it was still possible to get a ticket for the game, the Chief of Staff pressed the buzzer for McCarthy and asked him to check on the matter. The young officer at once called the visiting coach, who promptly produced a ticket on the fifty-yard line. "Is the team so bad," Marshall asked, "that no one is going to the game?" When McCarthy explained how his VMI background had helped, the Chief of Staff suggested he get another ticket and cheer with him for the cadets.

Better jobs quickly followed. McCarthy went with the General on most of his important trips abroad, stepping aside occasionally to give Pasco an opportunity to accompany the Chief of Staff. Pasco, whose father had been at VMI while Marshall was there, was to serve as the General's last SGS and to supervise the collection of material for Marshall's final report to the Secretary of War on the years 1943–45.

Although the Chief of Staff worked members of his staff hard and took for granted virtual perfection in performance, he occasionally made a gesture or wrote a note that showed his warm appreciation. At Christmas 1944, when he knew that most of his staff members would have no holiday plans, he sent word through McCarthy that they were to be invited to his quarters for dinner, adding thoughtfully that they were not to change any of their personal arrangements to accept.[11]

Colonel Pasco recalled his matter-of-fact, almost shy, innate kindliness that same Christmas after he had sat up late, helping Marshall with his staff Christmas list. Next morning, as the General reflected on their mutual efforts, he penned the sort of letter that subordinates keep to show their children:

> You have assisted me in drafting many letters of Christmas greetings and appreciation to various leaders in the war effort. Quite naturally you omitted your own name from the list of those to whom such letters should go. I have stirred my memory many times for lessons out of my past experience, particularly of the first World War period, and the parallel to your situation occurred to me yesterday in recalling that as the various members of General Pershing's GHQ Staff took their final leave of duty with him I prepared appropriate and rather generous statements of his appreciation for the services they had rendered. Being the last to go I was the only one not to receive such a letter, though lack of appreciation was far from General Pershing's intention—it was that the habit had been formed of receiving suggestions for such communications from me. Hence the omission.
>
> I want you to know that I am conscious of the heavy burden of duties that you carry, not only as Assistant Secretary and frequently Acting Secretary of the General Staff, but in relation to more personal services for me. I appreciate very much all that you have done and the highly efficient manner in which you have done it.
>
> With my Christmas greetings to Mrs. Pasco and you and with very best wishes for you both in the New Year . . .[12]

All these men performed their duties well. But there was an additional dimension. Their effort to deliver was an extra element that they felt that the Chief of Staff silently demanded. They assumed that it must be done as anonymously as possible. In rare photographs where one of the assistants is present, he is in the corner of the picture; even more infrequently does an assistant's name appear in a news account of the day. It is notable that almost none of the officers who served closely with the General during the war wrote memoirs or articles about service with him. His WAC chauffeur won his strong approval after the war by declining a lucrative offer for her recollections of her work with the General. In 1948 the New York *Daily News,* noting the publicity greeting the memoirs of General Eisenhower's wartime chauffeur, approached General Marshall, then Secretary of State, to secure his consent to the writing of a similar account by Sergeant Payne. The General, while not enthusiastic, said he would not formally object. Mrs. Marshall, who had written her own memoirs with no encouragement from her husband, offered her assistance. But the former WAC chauffeur decided against the project. When the story was told on a national radio program, she received many notes of congratulation on her decision. But the note she treasured most came from Secretary of State Marshall, recuperating from a serious operation at Walter Reed Hospital. After explaining why he had not been able to see her when she had come to visit him, he wrote: "I would like to have seen you. I appreciated your calling and I wanted to tell you of my respect and admiration for your judgment about the matter of the article. I did not want to limit you in any way and I am afraid you have denied yourself a fair sum. However, you have shown a great deal of character, for which I have high regard." [13]

With the aid of such a staff the General reduced many of his daily activities to an efficient routine. In the early years of his tour of duty he had called at 9 A.M. for the Chief and Deputy Chief of the Operations Division, the Chief of Intelligence, and certain other officers to give the morning briefing on operations throughout the world. By 1944, concluding that senior officers were far too busy to have time to gather all the material for early briefings, he had changed the procedure. In 1956 he described the revamped "morning show":

> We had gradually, although I admit too slowly, gotten to the point where the presentation of the world picture was of great importance to me and the principal staff—because we had so many different theaters operating at once and along with that the stormy times with things at home. We had available artists of some talent and plenty of them, so we gradually formed [a] morning show on the basis of presentation by young men who were chosen for their ability to speak in an attractive manner. They got up at four o'clock in the morning and worked on the cables of the night before . . . and were ready for the presentation at nine o'clock. They . . . weren't expected to know all about the details of the operation, except that the actual procedure was going on at the time. The charts were so made that all the divisions were represented on [them]—Japanese, Russians, British, German . . . —and one of the young men moved these when it was necessary . . . and the other conducted the pre-

sentation of the day, after which the G-2 people came forward with any special statements they wished to make. But the main [presentation] of the operations in the Far East and Europe and Africa came at nine o'clock.

Just prior to that hour, about five minutes [before], this special force came into my office no matter what I was doing or with whom I was talking and set up all the machinery and then they started at nine. . . . It just went off like a theatrical thing. They became very expert at it, and it was really a thrilling presentation. You saw the whole war up to the last minute—done in such a way it was easy, in a sense, to comprehend.

Marshall was very proud of this arrangement, and after a briefing at Versailles, he twitted Bedell Smith, suggesting that he come to Washington to see how a proper presentation was run. And he made a point of inviting others to it, occasionally by arranging early-morning interviews—sometimes with visitors who would be impressed by a private view of the world situation, sometimes with old friends, and especially with suppliants from an overseas theater who had the feeling that their particular area was being forgotten.

In connection with the last group he often related the account of a visit from Philip La Follette. The Wisconsin political leader, then on MacArthur's staff, had come back, Marshall assumed,

to see what he could root up for General MacArthur, who was always in dire need of everything because he [got] but very little and for a time got almost nothing. The only one [who] got less was Stilwell. . . . I had the appointment [with La Follette] made at half past eight, much earlier than I had appointments made [usually] because I kept that time free for my own private thinking. So he was in there while this scene-setting began, without anything being said on my part while we were talking. And then the deputy Chief of Staff [Major General Thomas T. Handy] and [Chief of War Plans John E.] Hull and the other principals came in, I think about ten in all. La Follette's time was up and he got up to go, and I said, "Would you like to see this?" Oh, yes, he would, and sat down. Then he saw this presentation of the world picture and after it was finished he left.

After the peace I saw him . . . and he asked me, "Did you keep me back there purposely to see that?" Because it changed his whole state of mind the minute he saw the enormity of what was going on and what [the] requirements were and what . . . the demands were [throughout the world]. He began to see the picture in the light of the real circumstances. . . . I was always amused at his question. . . . I did keep him for [that] purpose but I let it just fall into place without any particular move because [I found] if those fellows could see what the [whole situation] was, they would understand more [of the] impossibility of many things that they were talking about.[14]

Familiar faces at these meetings were those of the team of Handy and Hull, which was to dominate Army planning and operations in most of General Marshall's conferences from the spring of 1942, when General Eisenhower went to the United Kingdom, until the war's end. Well-described by one associate as a fine soldier with "a country, easygoing gloss," General Handy gave strangers the impression of a mild, unobtrusive, relaxed subordinate. Behind his casual manner and his friendly façade, this VMI-trained field artillery officer had a no-nonsense approach to military problems and a hard-working capacity that Marshall treasured. Handy had gone overseas in the summer of 1917 with the 1st Division and then had transferred to the 42d Division as aide to the commanding general. Later he won his DSC while commanding a field artillery battalion that supported General MacArthur's brigade. He succeeded General Eisenhower as Chief of the Operations Division in June 1942 and had a hand in every major planning paper from that time until he became Marshall's Deputy Chief of Staff, late in 1944. His experience as a planner was impressive. A student at both the Army and Naval War colleges, he had served from 1936 to 1940 in the War Plans Division, forerunner of the Operations Division. After a short tour as commander of a field artillery battalion, he returned to War Plans in August 1941.[15]

Hull, a premedical student at Miami University when he went into the Army in 1917, had, like Handy, fought in many of the campaigns in France in World War I and then served in the Army of Occupation in Germany. He had met Marshall, as well as Bradley and Stilwell, at the Infantry School at Fort Benning in the 1920s. Between troop-duty assignments, he attended the Command and General Staff College at Fort Leavenworth, the Army War College, and was an instructor at Fort Leavenworth until 1941. Then after several months as the supply officer of VII Corps, he was ordered to Washington. On his arrival in early December he was told to get settled and to report December 8 to the War Department for duty. Coming out of a movie theater with his wife on the afternoon of December 7, he heard of the Pearl Harbor attack. As soon as he had taken his wife home, he reported to the Munitions Building, where he remained for the next thirty-six hours.[16]

The daily routine of the Chief and Deputy Chief of the Operations Division began at 8 A.M., when they met with their assistants to organize queries and problems raised in messages that had come in the night before. Once they were presented to Marshall, he gave needed decisions quickly, handing back the papers to the deputy. If plans were required, he might raise a question, carefully stating no personal view, and send the assistants out to prepare an answer or assign it to one of the planning groups of the Operations Division. Usually not until he had seen a draft did he begin to make it his own by suggesting numerous changes or giving directions to take it back and restudy certain items. If the paper was intended for the President's signature, Marshall worked over it carefully, filling the margins or the triple spaces between lines with his changes. He worked rapidly, often while the chief assistant and, perhaps, a subordinate who had done most of the work on the plan stood nearby. When he had finished, he returned the paper to them. "He had a fetish for a clean desk," said one assistant. "Nothing remained at the end of a day." If a paper still required quick action, it went into his brief case for later study at his Fort Myer quarters.

For action on routine matters and for special study of numerous others General Marshall relied heavily on the judgment of his Deputy Chief of Staff—Lieutenant General Joseph T. McNarney from March 1942 until late 1944, and General Handy from then until the war's end. McNarney, who had proved his worth in pushing through the reorganization of the War Department in January and February 1942, provided Marshall the tough decisive deputy he had been seeking for many months. The deputy who preceded McNarney had too often told his subordinates, "Show it to the Chief," when the General wanted *him* to act. McNarney followed no such pattern.

A Pennsylvanian, West Point-trained, McNarney had been commissioned in the infantry in 1915. Two years later he transferred to the Aviation Section of the Signal Corps and performed important staff and command duties as an airman in France in 1917 and 1918. His special training for work as Deputy included study at the Command and General Staff School and the Army War College, a tour as instructor at the college, and three years in the intelligence area of the Air Section of the War Department. He was with the War Plans Division from June 1939 until April 1941, when he went to London as chief of staff of an Army observer group. He served there until shortly before Pearl Harbor. At the time of the Japanese attack he was en route to the United States, and on his arrival he was assigned to the Roberts Commission, investigating responsibility for that tragedy.

"Quiet," "unemotional," "cold," as he appeared to most of his associates, McNarney brought to his job the ruthlessness that wartime conditions required. He made decisions quickly, sparing his Chief many heavy demands on his time.

In addition to seeing McNarney, Handy, and Hull one or more times a day when he was in the War Department, General Marshall also consulted the Secretary of War almost daily. At times he sat in on conferences with Stimson's chief assistants, Robert P. Patterson, Robert A. Lovett, and John J. McCloy. As the war progressed, Patterson became increasingly involved in war-production matters, in which Marshall was represented by Somervell. Lovett became more and more occupied with Arnold's plans and activities. Therefore it was Assistant Secretary of War McCloy on whom the Chief of Staff depended increasingly in the spheres of civil affairs and military government. To his biographer Marshall later said that for information on Japanese relocation, relations with the French, and the occupation of Germany, "Ask Jack McCloy. I usually took his advice." Marshall paid warm tribute to this special relationship, writing McCloy in the spring of 1943: "Your recent trip to North Africa has borne fine fruit in many ways. You have been a tower of strength in many problems of the Japanese civilian situation both on the West Coast and in Hawaii, the racial problems and the current issue of civil relations. In all you have been my strong ally in our joint effort to organize . . . the Army." [17]

Marshall had been close to Stimson from mid-1940, when he was appointed Secretary of War, and the General tended to see him even more often in 1943. There were grounds for possible disagreement between them when the President in February 1942 had made Marshall directly responsible to him for "strategy, tactics, and operations," bypassing Stimson. But during the crucial year for the cross-Channel attack Marshall kept Stimson informed of his recommendations to the President, meetings at the White House, and the general problems affecting operations of the war.

After OVERLORD began in 1944, operational demands or necessary absences took so much of Marshall's time that he talked to Stimson less often than he had earlier, and the Secretary sometimes felt left out of military developments. But their common ability to see each other's problems helped them surmount their occasional frictions and difficulties.

As the war continued, Marshall's relations with the President improved greatly. Although at Casablanca, Roosevelt's course was not fully to the Chief of Staff's liking, he at least did not ignore Marshall's advice on the cross-Channel attack as he had in the summer of 1942. From January 1943 on he listened increasingly to Marshall and his colleagues. Marshall, in particular, felt that he had the President's trust.

Roosevelt's death before the war's end deprived historians of any final summation from him on Marshall's contributions. In a message in 1943 to the superintendent of VMI, the President declared: "The nation joins in tribute to an honored son of Virginia Military Institute. Soldier, statesman, patriot and chivalrous gentleman, General Marshall in high public service exemplifies the noble tradition of a great school. We all share the pride which his Alma Mater feels today." [18]

This statement, official prose tailored for a specific occasion, must stand as Roosevelt's major public pronouncement in praise of the General. The President's true evaluation is more genuinely reflected in the increasing trust and reliance he accorded Marshall's ideas during the war and in the slightly uncomfortable but respectful formality he accorded the General in their personal contacts.[19]

In one respect the Chief of Staff made no progress with the White House: neither he nor any of his colleagues was able to persuade Roosevelt to adopt an effective administrative arrangement with the military. "It was very difficult," Marshall recalled, "to deal with the President under these conditions. Mr. Roosevelt didn't want things on the record. He didn't want a recorder. I brought up Deane once to keep some notes.

He [had] a big notebook, and the President blew up. Next time Deane brought a book so little he couldn't use it. . . . Stimson came back from one Friday cabinet meeting with some notes. We worked until Sunday night on the idea. The Navy worked on the notes Knox brought back. Then we found they had taken [down] two different sets of ideas. Each one was trying to keep notes while listening and presenting his own views. Stimson was horrified at the loss of time." [20]

Admiring the British defense secretariat and the way in which Churchill dealt with the British Chiefs of Staff through Ismay, Marshall in 1943 asked the latter for a summary of the procedure they used. He then circulated copies in Washington hoping that something could be done. "Things were in a mess," Marshall bluntly said in later years. "We found that Donald Nelson's outfit [the War Production Board] was meeting with the British and [taking decisions] opposite to what we wanted. . . . I wanted all sections in on it to distribute the stuff to all the people concerned. The British met in a building which belonged to the control staff. We could have done the same thing. I had picked Harriman to be secretary of the cabinet. Harriman was made ambassador to Russia [in the fall of 1943] and that ended this." [21] As a result the fairly chaotic system encouraged by the President continued, exasperating Stimson and occasionally making the task of his military advisers a nightmare.

The situation was manageable mainly because Harry Hopkins and Admiral Leahy passed on to Marshall and his colleagues some idea of what the President had in mind. Stimson kept notes of his military discussions at cabinet meetings or in private sessions with the President, and Marshall circulated to Stimson and the War Department staff pertinent information on his own talks at the White House. In addition the Chief of Staff carefully informed Roosevelt of any off-the-record testimony that he gave to committees of Congress, in order to guard against the possibility of someone's charging that he had kept the President in the dark. But the arrangement was haphazard.

The Joint Chiefs of Staff system that Marshall had worked to strengthen continued to function well, although Admiral Leahy, selected at Marshall's suggestion as the group's chairman, did not fully serve the purpose Marshall originally had in mind—that he be a neutral spokesman for the Joint Chiefs to the President. Still the system was an improvement over the earlier system, which had exacerbated interservice rivalries.[22]

The Joint Chiefs met regularly on Tuesday of each week at the Public Health Building across Constitution Avenue from the Munitions Building, usually arranging to have lunch together in their special dining room. On Fridays the American Chiefs of Staff joined with members of the British Joint Staff Mission, headed by Field Marshal Dill, in meetings of the Combined Chiefs of Staff. In each case, depending on whether purely American or Allied matters were involved, they "formulated and supervised the execution of plans and policies relating to the following matters: the strategic conduct of the war; the determination of over-all requirements based on approved plans; the need, availability, and assignment of means of transportation; and the allocation of critical means such as munitions, food, raw materials and so forth." [23]

By 1943 there were striking shifts of power among the three major commanders of the Army. The increasing movement of units overseas from training areas found the role of the commanding general of the Army Ground Forces, General McNair, steadily decreasing. Marshall still depended on him for tightening training procedures, incorporating battle lessons in new directives, and recommending commanders to replace generals in the field, but by the time McNair was killed in France, in 1944, his power in the War Department had dwindled sharply. Meanwhile his opposite number in the Army Service Forces, General Somervell, expanded his influence. A ruthless, impatient man, controlling supply and transport, he developed ever-greater control over personnel, construction, and communications. Members of the General Staff divisions complained that he had whittled them down to transparencies. Somervell's growing power and his tendency to disregard the finer points of cultivating congressmen hurt him on Capitol Hill. His numerous opponents in the Pentagon were suspected of leaks to the press concerning reorganization plans —designed to increase his domain; his mistaken estimates or overblown expenditures on construction projects, such as the Pentagon or the Canol pipeline, brought him some painful moments before committees of Congress. Although Marshall admired Somervell's abilities, he sometimes had to curb his subordinate's sharp tongue.[24]

The third of the Army commanders to experience a realignment in power was Air Forces General Arnold. In 1943 and 1944 recurrent efforts were made to make the Army Air Forces an independent service. The Chief of Staff depended on Arnold and some of his assistants, who had served on Marshall's personal staff, to help block this move until after the war. To quiet the demands of strong congressional partisans of the independence move, Marshall gave Arnold increasing autonomy. The airman carefully followed the Army's line at Allied conferences and refrained from divisive statements to the press, and Marshall saw to it that Arnold got nearly all he wanted. Soldiers complained of preferential treatment given airmen—special pay, quick promotions, plush training centers, leaves at resort hotels—but Marshall backed the Air Forces commander. In return Marshall felt that he received Arnold's loyal support.

The tone of the unofficial correspondence between Arnold and Marshall is a reminder of the longevity of a friendship going back to the Philippines in 1914. Marshall's personal regard is revealed in an exchange of letters at the time of Arnold's heart attack in May 1943. On the eve of the TRIDENT conference in Washington, Arnold wrote: "This is one Hell of a time for this to happen. My engine started turning over at 160 when it should have been doing 74 to 76. For this I am sorry." Fearful that the Air Forces Chief might try to return to work too soon, Marshall replied:

> A note came in yesterday that you planned to leave Sunday for Oregon. I think this is fine, but I was concerned to learn that you plan to leave there at the end of the month in order to make an address at West Point. Please don't do the latter. Your Army future is at stake. . . . Get solidly on your feet and absolutely refrain from any inspections, interviews, speeches, or anything in the way of business. It is vastly important to you, and it certainly is to me, and to the Air Forces, that you make a full recovery, and you cannot do it if you overrun your own internal machinery.[25]

Later, when he saw a cartoon of a four-star general (Arnold on a prescribed vacation) hauling in fish, killing ducks, and the like, Marshall teased him: "You are shown as a hunter of great prowess but hasn't your artist friend drawn a pretty long bow, or perhaps given undue credit to the power of four stars in field and stream? Mine don't help me a damned bit!" [26]

Arnold failed to slow down. In the spring of 1945 he had trouble with his heart again, and once more Marshall scolded him. Not reassured by the airman's letter outlining his plans for recreation, the General wrote after a few weeks: "I have read of your presence and statements with various active commands. Where is the Bermuda rest, the lazy days at Cannes, the period of retirement at Capri? You are riding for a fall, doctor or no doctor." [27] Hearing a week later that the Air Forces commander was planning a round-the-world trip, he finally threw up his hands: "It may demonstrate to the Army and to the public that you are not on the retired list but it may result in your landing there. I will have to trust to your judgment though I have little hope that you can continue your wasteful expenditure of physical strength and nervous energy."

Marshall's active benignity toward the Air Forces was not a personal favor to Arnold but was based on an early recognition of airpower's great importance to the war. From the early days of the fighting in the Pacific, he sought to determine what men and planes the Air Forces needed. In addition to supporting Arnold's trips to the various theaters, he sent out other officers to interview fliers and determine their wishes. He liked to tell how the pilots reacted to his efforts:

> I had to get into some of this very personally. [In] the first fighting out of Australia and the great island just to the north of it, the Japanese were quite successfully using their Zero planes and our Air Corps said our planes there . . . were too slow. . . . So I sent an officer out there to see the young airmen personally. It wasn't Arnold on this trip, because I wanted to instill the feeling in these young fellows that just because I wasn't an airman or the staff weren't all air, [we] wouldn't disregard the interests and the necessities of the air service.
>
> These young fellows were having a terrible time. They had no prospect of

relief. They were flying much, much too much, and they were having casualties and the replacements were not available and wouldn't be for quite a long time, and they had a deep feeling that the Zero plane was far better than theirs. Well, the truth of the matter was—I found out by investigation and particularly by talking to manufacturers—our plane had a lot of equipment in it which was heavy—armored to protect [them]. . . .

So I sent this officer out to tell these young airmen that I would have these planes stripped so they would be as light and as easily handled as the Zero if they wanted that. . . . When the proposition was put up to the young fliers . . . "Just say the word and I will have the plane stripped" . . . they voted against it.28

As Marshall recalled the story in 1956, the clamor of the pilots ultimately "boiled down to one thing—they wanted girls." On this point he could not be helpful. "I sent word to the pilots that I couldn't supply the girls. I could be sympathetic but I couldn't supply them."

There were complications with the airmen in the European Theater as well: "We had to have replacements [available so that] the mess table was always full," Marshall recalled. "If they failed to come in, the other men had to take their place because to sit down and find half the table empty was a very depressing morale factor. Those things—those psychological reactions—have to be foreseen." 29

Marshall continued to send representatives to talk directly to men in the field on all fronts and in all theaters as the conflict grew. He used every possible opportunity to get out of the Pentagon for personal visits to training centers or to units on maneuvers. Nothing, he believed, substituted for the Chief of Staff's own quick look at units or his prompt efforts to correct abuses or to furnish items in short supply. Often making stops in several states in a two- or three-day trip, he had to depend on a special sense developed in the course of many inspections to help him judge the state of readiness of units he visited. Mrs. Oveta Culp Hobby, the WAC's first commandant, recalled that the General had told her once to check on the morale on a certain post. " 'General Marshall,' I said, 'I wouldn't know whether the morale was good or bad.' He looked at me and said, 'You will get to the point where you can walk on a post, camp, or base station and know whether the morale is good or bad.' Of course, this is true. I later learned during the war that this was true." 30

Marshall's own inspections were supplemented by those of top subordinates—Arnold, Somervell, McNair were often sent on extensive trips—and by War Department observers who looked for special problems or special lessons that should be studied in Washington.

Because he was particularly concerned about the medical care of the men, Marshall selected Brigadier General Howard McC. Snyder, later President Eisenhower's special physician, to check on the operations of the Army Medical Service.

I picked him up and sent him all over the world but particularly all over this country when the hospitals were being established, and he saw that the thing

ran—that these overwhelming numbers of recruits were attended. There was a
flu epidemic at the time and he saw that the proper steps were taken in advance in connection with that, and he had a very hard time because he never
had a good plane and flying was a little bit primitive . . . in some respects and
he had . . . some dreadful flights and very dangerous flights. But he was perfectly splendid in what he did and should have received great rewards for it.
However his work now is very much appreciated, I believe, [by] the President.
I made him, incidentally, Assistant Inspector General. I don't recall that I even
spoke to the Inspector General department—they were pretty much hidebound,
those fellows—so the first [they] knew about it, I think, was when Snyder was
made a brigadier general. . . . Then he was put in charge of all the inspections and everything of that sort relating in any way to medicine or health in
connection with the draft. . . . That gave me something to lean on which I
felt up to that time I didn't have at all.

I might say, that it is always very hard to act on these things from Washington, because quite naturally there is resentment of the Pentagon coming in and
telling you how to do your business. . . . Our trouble was that the commander
himself, as a rule, was so involved with considerations in front of him that he
was apt to be slack in his follow-up on conditions in rear of him.[31]

As an illustration General Marshall related the way in which his
inspectors helped to correct a serious situation in the Pacific where a problem arose because, in their efforts to get ammunition and fighting equipment for the combat areas, supply officers failed to ask for mosquito net-
ting and screening essential in combating malaria.

So I sent out one or two malarial experts . . . to investigate and I had to
caution them very carefully how tactful they must be about it, but I had the
screening banked up on the West Coast so it could be sent in a minute and
we . . . sent it the minute their reports came in. . . . As I recall, the 1st Marine Division was out of the line for over a year—thirteen months, I think. We
couldn't supply troops on any such basis as that. We had to take better care of
them. . . .

One of the complications . . . threw us completely off base. We had figured
out . . . that the first people that would have to be replaced . . . would be in
combat aviation, but we found that the first badly needed replacements were
ground [crewmen]. The trouble was they had to work at night and naturally
they had to have . . . electric lights and naturally the mosquitoes swarmed
and under the conditions [the crews] couldn't wear any [netting] and they
were soon so filled up with atabrine that they became unsteady. I remember
some pilots stating that they were unwilling to have these fellows work on their
planes because they thought they were too uncertain and they would leave
cotter pins [or other items] out of place. . . ." [32]

On trips to the fighting fronts Marshall made it a point to include
visits to base hospitals. He worked continually to improve the administration of hospitals and field care.

Reflecting on the fact that many men were wounded in actions whose
details or purposes they never understood, he proposed that a series of
pamphlets be prepared on various battles and distributed to the
wounded. This suggestion gave impetus to a program by the Historical

Section of the Intelligence Division of the War Department of sending out teams to secure material for a series of "U.S. Forces in Action" pamphlets. Although the task of gathering and preparing such material failed to produce the studies as quickly as Marshall hoped, the project did help the development of the Department of the Army history program, which is still continued by the Office of the Chief of Military History.[33]

Marshall also encouraged dissemination of battle lessons men were learning from combat in various theaters of war. One day he said that he wanted some new men for the War Department staff. "General Marshall is sick of what he calls 'the staff type,' " one of his assistants reported to a friend. "He said, 'Bring in some officers who know how to get soldiers out of the rain.' " Among those who met this criterion was a young red-haired lieutenant colonel, son of a retired officer, who was an excellent athlete and had proved his ability as an officer with troops in the field—Russell P. ("Red") Reeder, Jr. Marshall directed him to take certain messages to Lieutenant General Delos Emmons in Hawaii, to explain to certain groups in New Guinea why the European war had to be fought first, and, most important, to bring back from Major General A. A. Vandergrift of the Marines and Major General A. M. Patch of the Army reports on combat lessons learned on Guadalcanal.

In an early use of the oral-history technique Reeder talked to privates, noncommissioned officers, and officers, asking about their problems and how they met them, their tests of good leadership, and the like. On his return home he wrote up the material, retaining the slang and colloquialisms used by the men he had interviewed.[34]

Reviewing his material, Reeder worried over Marshall's opinion of his efforts. There was no need for his anxiety. The Chief of Staff told him that he had once written a report in his own style and his immediate superior had suppressed it. This one was to stand as it was, and he added that he would try anyone who changed so much as a comma. To Reeder's delight Marshall ordered a million copies printed, directed that the booklet be sent to every unit in training, suggested the name *Fighting in Guadalcanal,* and proposed that it be bound with a light-blue cover. Reeder especially liked these words from the foreword Marshall insisted on providing: "Soldiers and officers alike should read these notes and seek to apply their lessons. We *must* cash in on the experience which these and other brave men have paid for in blood." With its firsthand combat material and the backing of the Chief of Staff, the booklet was acclaimed by those who read it an instant success. Some weeks later Marshall proudly sent on to General McNair a comment Reeder treasured: "The British General Sir Harold Alexander told me that this brief pamphlet is the most impressive training instruction he has seen. Alexander referred to it two or three times as the sort of study soldiers will read—the ordinary instruction bores them." [35]

Reeder's experience encouraged others to write. Lessons were picked up from other theaters, and the information was passed on to training centers. A historian wrote up his trip to Attu, and a private's comments on lessons of North Africa were printed. After a time men returning from distant combat were interviewed on their experiences by skilled questioners.

All the programs had the Chief of Staff's strong patronage, but his emissaries were not always welcome abroad. Marshall was aware of the field commander's aversion to an observer looking over his shoulder, and he often prefaced a proposed change or a suggested dispatch of a War Department representative to an overseas theater with an acknowledgment that no one likes visiting firemen.

On one occasion Bedell Smith grinned wickedly at sight of a classified report on the shortcomings of the Allied Headquarters in the Mediterranean found in an unlocked drawer of a desk assigned to one of Marshall's War Department men. Aware that the enemy had been delivered into his hands, Smith wrote the culprit: "I refrain from commenting on what we do here to naughty boys who leave secret papers in the drawers of desks, but you might read through your para. on the criticism of discipline in this theater with the above in mind as you do so." [36]

Marshall's close follow-up on medical care, supply problems, and similar matters also extended to the post exchanges throughout the world. Initially these facilities were controlled by each post headquarters, division headquarters, or the like, with profits distributed among the headquarters company and lower units for entertainment and recreational purposes. As the Army grew rapidly and became heavily involved overseas, the Chief of Staff recognized the importance of having skilled advice and management for these enterprises. He therefore brought in men with relevant training and experience and had them set up a central base of operation and a central purchasing center and in addition continued to supervise their functioning carefully. In speaking of his precautions in such areas, he reached back in his early experience for a lesson that aided him in World War II:

"You have to check on things if you want them done. I remember when I was at Fort Benning, I stopped one day at a flower shop to get some flowers for Mrs. Marshall. The woman there said she couldn't get the officers' club [at the Fort] to pay its bill. It owed a large sum. I sent "Pinky" Bull [Harold R. Bull, then a lieutenant colonel, later Eisenhower's Chief of Operations] to check. He came back white-faced to say that there were a number of bills owing and a shortage. He found that the [officer in charge] kept two sets of books but let us see only the top set, which showed a balance."

Marshall's insistence on rigorous checking helped him to avoid many potential scandals. Going on the philosophy that the Army should find its own culprits and administer punishment before any malfeasance reached the attention of Congress or the press, he urged vigilance wherever large sums of money were involved. It was this policy that General Eisenhower was following in France in the winter of 1944–45 when a shortage of cigarettes developed at the front. An investigation showed that a railway battalion's staff was diverting carloads of cigarettes from normal channels to its own black-market outlets in Paris. Several noncommissioned officers were carrying on this activity either by hoodwinking some officers or by paying a share of the profits to one or two cooperative ones. The first notice the press had of these activities was accompanied by the announcement that the guilty parties had been punished. If dirty linen had to be washed in public, Marshall and his commanders preferred that they report the crime and the punishment at the same time.

In addition to sending representatives to overseas headquarters, Marshall kept up a steady effort through correspondence to learn their needs and to go as far as possible to meet their demands. The relationships between Washington and the commanders of distant theaters varied sharply, and naturally, in accordance with personalities. General MacArthur, a four-star general and Chief of Staff when Marshall was merely a colonel, never forgot that difference in their former statuses. Aware of his strong backing by the Australian Prime Minister and his special position as a commander of Allied forces, MacArthur displayed an attitude toward the War Department that has rightly been termed that of a proud proconsul. The Chief of Staff carefully watched official channels in sending out congratulations, making certain that any commendation to a subordinate of MacArthur's went through the theater commander. Exchanges, occasionally sharp, were usually stiff and proper.

With Eisenhower the situation was totally different. In a favored theater and a protégé of Marshall's, the Mediterranean commander could afford a relaxed approach. Indeed it was in his nature to do so. From his first assignment in Europe, Eisenhower adopted the practice of sending long, chatty letters about his problems and his needs to Marshall. Although the Chief of Staff seldom replied in kind, he kept careful note of Eisenhower's requirements, passing on portions of the letters to members of the War Department staff, to Stimson, and to the President. So well did the Chief of Staff and theater commander understand each other that Marshall was able to reply to a request for supplies by saying that filling the order would mean specific withholdings from other theaters. Usually the Chief of Staff would add that if Eisenhower still believed he should have the items in question, they would be sent. In most instances, as he anticipated, Eisenhower would drop his request.[37]

From the Far East, Stilwell, near Marshall's age and a friend of long standing, wrote candidly and often indiscreetly to the Chief of Staff. One of the few officers willing to test Marshall's sense of humor, he was the only theater commander who dared rib him occasionally. Aware of his

Chief's tremendous interest in the China Theater, Stilwell worked closely with Marshall to keep some footing both at the White House and in Chungking. As a friend of the entire Stilwell family from the 1920's in Tientsin and the somewhat later period at Fort Benning, the Chief of Staff maintained an affectionate correspondence with both the China commander and his wife. After the Cairo conference at the end of 1943, he wrote to Mrs. Stilwell:

Dear Win:

Upon my return from overseas I found your Christmas card with its note to Katherine and the news of the family, and what a charming family you have, too.

Joe, in Cairo, seemed to be looking better than when he was in Washington, also he had a little opportunity for rest and relaxation, if he could manage the mental detachment necessary for that purpose. . . .

Sometime back I arranged that a rajah should invite him up to the vale of Kashmir for a vacation but he declined, said he was too busy and that he had been there once before. It is a hard job to try to get him to lay off. All of the others are similarly resistant but most of them eventually break down. He seems to be made of iron.

With my best wishes for the New Year to all the family,

Affectionately,
George Marshall [38]

To his orderlies and chauffeurs, as to the commanders on distant fronts, Marshall turned the same face. To all of them he paid the compliment of assuming they knew their task and of trusting them to get on with the job. If they needed help, he attempted to give it. And if he peered over a commander's shoulder at times, he tried to put himself in that officer's place. On April 24, 1942, he distributed a memorandum to the War Department General Staff and to the three major commanders:

At a dinner for me in London, the head of the British Administrative Services read for our amusement a letter that had come to his attention, written by the Duke of Wellington from Spain about 1810 to the Secretary of State for War, Lord Bradford. I asked for a copy and quote it below for our guidance in the present struggle.

"My Lord,

"If I attempted to answer the mass of futile correspondence that surrounds me, I should be debarred from all serious business of campaigning.

"I must remind your Lordship—for the last time—that so long as I retain an independent position, I shall see that no officer under my Command is debarred by attending to the futile drivelling of mere quill driving in your Lordship's Office—from attending to his first duty—which is, and always has been, so to train the private men under his command that they may, without question, beat any force opposed to them in the field.

"I am,
    "My Lord,
        "Your obedient Servant,
            "Wellington."

The reaction to instructions from Washington of a troop commander far from home, in surroundings with which we are utterly unfamiliar, may be akin to those of the Great Duke, and we could well govern ourselves accordingly.

G. C. Marshall
Chief of Staff [39]

V

Marshall and the Fighting
Man . . . and Woman

ONCE when reminded that he was accused of coddling the fighting man, General Marshall replied that he welcomed the criticism. He added: "I remember my great pleasure when I went into Italy and got up right behind the firing line, and they brought a battalion out to go into the forward position. . . . Before the men had . . . their pup tents up, one sergeant opened up the post exchange from two barrels which had been delivered to him, and here . . . [were] the various things you want right away, and they sold them right over the barrel. . . . I never allowed them to have sales going on in the rear until they had begun up front. . . ." He was delighted when parents cited letters from their sons describing the turkey and dressing they had been served at the front at Thanksgiving and Christmas. He glowed when MacArthur reported that some of the men who went into the Philippines had ice cream within twenty-four hours. "Many of our people forget the importance of little things to morale," he once said. "I insisted when I got to the top that . . . things be set up quickly along this line, since the men think if there is candy up forward, things can't be so bad." [1]

Marshall knew that the American soldier did not relish spartan life. He also was keenly aware that the soldier thousands of miles from home lacked the immediate spur that foreign troops felt in defending their homes. In addition he believed that the foot soldier, obliged to endure more than his proper share of cold and hardship, deserved all the comfort it was possible to provide. Others might call it softness; he rated it an essential of morale.

Marshall said after the war:

> As to coddling the soldiers, I was responsible for as much of that abroad (not much of it back here) as anybody because I felt that we had to do every-

thing we could to make the men feel that we had the highest solicitude for their condition[s]. . . . They were being taken from home; they were being taken away from [their] plows and their wives and families . . . [and were] in a distant country where the fighting was quite desperate and . . . the reasons were a little bit remote from them. . . . I was for supplying everything we could and then requiring him to fight to the death when the time came. You had to put these two things together. If it were all solicitude, then you had no army. But you couldn't be severe in your demands unless [the soldier] was convinced that you were doing everything you could to make matters well for him. . . .

And I remember when we took over several breweries in France, I thought I would be investigated for that (that's about the only thing I wasn't investigated for). . . . I suppose now, if this came out, I will [likely] . . . be attacked again. I didn't go into the production of hard liquor but I did [of] all the beer that we could possibly manage. I was challenged once . . . to have orange juice for these men. Well, we couldn't have much orange juice—it is bulky and hard to ship—but we got some shipments through just like we did Thanksgiving turkeys to have them feel that we were trying to get them what they craved so much in this touch of home. . . . And they responded, I thought, magnificently to that. . . .

Now when they wanted to go home and get a rest and not stay in the fighting, then I was adamant. They couldn't go home; they had to stay right there. When the time came up when they wanted to be relieved from the line, we probably couldn't relieve them from the line. And I was adamant again so far as that was concerned. And they would respond because they felt that [we] were really trying to do for them. . . .

The question of coddling troops went along with Marshall's analysis of what made the American soldier tick. "I think the first thing [about him] is that he has to know what it is all about, much more than any other soldier. I think the next thing is there has to be time to get him trained. [And next] we have to have very competent instructors, which we lacked at the opening of the war because they were not available in any number at all. . . ."

Once the American soldier knew "what it is all about," once he saw the results of his training, he was ready for action. There was always the fact, Marshall noted, that the American soldier was fighting for a cause remote from his own affairs. "You take an Iowa farmer—you can't get a much stronger character than that man—yet all of this [fighting] was in a distant field from his home, among distant people, and for a cause that couldn't [be cut] down to something like an Indian shooting at you, or a local army fighting against you." [2]

These factors made Marshall reluctant to contrast the fighting qualities of the American soldier with those of other warring countries in the World War II conflict. At the author's insistence he finally agreed, reiterating some of the factors that made the position of the American GI unique:

The fighting quality of the American soldier has to be measured in several ways. In the first place a man's fighting quality, his stamina, his relentless

purpose, comes most strongly from the association with his home and his family, and any American fighting near his own doorsill will display exactly that
same spirit. Our great difficulty was that the men were all far from their home
. . . they were thousands of miles from home in the Southwest Pacific and
Italy, in Africa, in places they had hardly ever heard of. There was none of that
tremendous spirit that comes of defending your own home, your own wife and
children, such as would fall to the French soldier . . . and to the others in
somewhat the same way. . . .

   That was one of the reasons I thought it was so vitally important to have the
Army educated as to what we were fighting about. Because it was all done so
far from home and always will be—so far as we are able to carry out our policy
of keeping the fighting out of continental United States. That imposes a very
great difficulty, that imposes a great problem of morale because a little detachment up in the Pribilof Islands or in the Himalaya Mountains, in Burma, in
Africa . . . has to be handled with a certain spirit.

   However in all of this a great deal [of the problem arises] from the monotony of the thing. You know, fighting as a rule is a very monotonous thing
unless you are on a grand rush like Patton's move through France. That seldom
is the case. And it is the monotony that . . . has very evil effects on morale,
and particularly when you are very far from home—when you have been in the
affair a long time.

In contrast, Marshall observed, the British soldiers managed to accept
the separation from home and families. "I was always struck by the British troops that took the long indeterminate periods in Africa, the way
they accepted the very hard life they had to lead and the long time they
were away from home and the heavy fighting they had to [endure] and
the losses they had to accept." The British fighters were very stolid, he
added, "very determined and accepted discipline without questions as
far as I could see."

The Japanese had quite a different quality. "The Japanese," he declared, "were a more spiritual fighter, if you accept [their religion] as
being a spiritual basis for the fighting. They were all dedicated to the
thing. Their lives were involved and they expected to give them up. They
could not surrender. They were desperate in defense of their leader. And
they were very well trained, as there was plenty of time to train this army,
which was . . . a conscript army."

There was the inevitable contrast between the German and the American doughboy. "The Germans are natural fighters, we must accept that,
they [were] natural warriors. And they were very highly trained, very
ably trained, particularly in their noncommissioned officers. And the basis
of their discipline was unbending. The thing you would find most effective with the Germans was that if you left a sergeant with a few men, he
fought [as if] he had a lieutenant general in command. . . . Too often
our fellows, when they were new at the game, would think that somebody
else ought to come right away and reinforce them or take over. And they
would tell the press so accordingly."

But it did not remain always thus. "When the time came, such as the

Battle of the Bulge, when they got going in that—not in the first surprise [attack], which [hit] a new division—[the American soldier] displayed magnificent fighting characteristics. They always would, under proper conditions. But they were far from home and the ordinary military quality is not dominant in the American any more. It is no longer the question of taking the gun off the mantelpiece and fighting against the savages." But the newspapers, he noted, especially in World War I seemed to think that Americans were still natural woodsmen. "Well, many of them had never seen the woods except in the national park or city park."

The Russians, he felt, differed from all the others. "I wouldn't say that [the Russian] was an intelligent soldier in any way but he had the courage to go ahead though he didn't understand at all why he was going. He accepted the leadership if it was any way decent and took terrific losses and accepted blindly lots of mismanagement. . . ."

The stoical acceptance of orders by the Russian differed markedly from the questioning typical of the American soldier. "With us you had to feel that all of your soldiers were readers of *Time* magazine and editorials from other sources and had listened to all the newspapermen and all those they met in this army of democracy. But it was a magnificent army when it reached its full development. I remember Eisenhower asking me to come over before it began to demobilize in order to see it as it was. And I don't think you could have found a better, more powerful army in the world than we had in [Europe] in 1945."

But training had gotten off to a slow start: "It takes a long time to make such an army—it is a long way to get the necessary leaders because the subordinate leaders are so important. And so few of them were of Regular [Army] origin. But the whole Army . . . was imbued with a tremendous fighting spirit and was remarkably well led. We had some of the most efficient army commanders and corps and division commanders that we have ever heard of, except maybe in the last year of the Civil War." [3]

In 1943 and 1944 Marshall and Stimson increased morale-building efforts extensively. Brigadier General Frederick H. Osborn's Morale Branch was expanded into the Special Services Division and was instructed among other things to stimulate the United Service Organizations further in drawing on the services of entertainers and artists for visits to training camps in the United States and combat theaters abroad. In addition to using the talents of top composers and stars, such as Al Jolson, Joe E. Brown, Bob Hope, Bing Crosby, Fred Astaire, Dinah Shore, Marlene Dietrich, Andre Kostelanetz, and Maurice Evans, the Army drew on more youthful entertainers in uniform to form small jeep companies that went to units throughout the world. Remembering the effectiveness of such groups in World War I, the Chief of Staff did everything possible to encourage these activities. He was especially moved by Irving Berlin's writing of the show *This Is the Army,* which drew on show people in and out of uniform, and by Berlin's donation of some ten million dollars in profits to the USO. He was touched by Al Jolson's appeal for permission to wear the Seventh Army patch on his jacket. When members of the General's staff recommended that permission be denied, he reproved them gently: "Aren't we being a little sticky about this?" [4]

Once USO facilities had been established, they worked fairly well. But providing recreational facilities and entertainment involved Marshall and Stimson in a brand-new field with a brand-new set of thorny problems. Sometimes there were jurisdictional disputes, but the program for the most part worked and at relatively little cost to the armed forces.

Early in the war Marshall had been convinced by Elmo Roper, one of the pioneer public-opinion pollsters, of the value of public-opinion surveys, and he directed Osborn to employ the most modern polling methods, using professional agencies and Army personnel, to determine soldiers' likes and dislikes. In addition he had samplings made of soldiers' mail that passed through censorship in order to get some notion of their complaints. Although there was a tendency for a few of his staff and for commanders in the field to dismiss many of the items as ordinary belly-aching, Marshall insisted that complaints be investigated and reports be made on action taken. Repeatedly he stressed to commanders that citizen soldiers with bitter grievances later became civilian opponents of the Army. When he found soldiers grumbling about uncomfortable leave trains or unpalatable food, he directed that high-ranking officers, even a general or two, ride the train with the troops and see for themselves what the conditions actually were. He was sure that if they shared the discomforts, they would soon correct them.

The General found time to examine suggestions on apparently trivial matters from trainees in Officer Candidate School. Passing on to General McNair his observation that men in the Civilian Conservation Corps had become sleepy after a strenuous morning and a heavy lunch so that during the first class after eating "little or anything of the subject of the lecture penetrates the befogged brain," he wrote:

> I know that the heavy meal at noon is an Army tradition just as the over-cooking and too early cooking of the meat is another practice that seems impossible to change. . . . It might be better to give them a light luncheon and the heavy meal at night. I sometimes think it has been the Army cooks who have controlled this situation, because almost all laboring men eat a light luncheon. Yet when we got into the CCC we were forced to haul those boys sometimes fifteen or twenty miles in order to eat a heavy noon meal. This I believe was partly caused by the old mess sergeants that we brought in from the Army for the time being while the CCC was being launched.[5]

After large military forces started moving overseas, the task of providing recreational facilities became a much heavier charge on military resources and required a greater degree of control. General Marshall watched this situation carefully because, as his Deputy, General McNarney, wrote, "Our experience in France in 1917 and 1918 convinced us, particularly General Marshall, of the urgent necessity for a carefully devised system of providing some form of normal and healthful outlet for the soldiers' physical and mental energies. . . ."

Especially concerned about remote garrisons, Marshall alerted the Special Services Division to the fact that Secretary of War Stimson had found no Army Extension courses available to men at Goose Bay, Labrador, on a recent visit there. "This, like the Pribilof Islands, Ascension Island, and other isolated posts, is exactly the type of station which needs the Army Extension courses." [6]

A strong supporter of the American Red Cross, General Marshall had announced a few days after the outbreak of war that "The Red Cross is recognized as the sole nonmilitary agency to operate with the expeditionary force during war." This policy was sharply questioned by Harper Sibley, president of the United Service Organizations—which, in addition to its general contributions to entertainment of servicemen, represented the YMCA, the YWCA, the National Catholic Community Service, the Jewish Welfare Board, the Salvation Army, and the National Travelers Aid Association. The Chief of Staff replied that the decision had been reached after careful study by the War and Navy departments. He explained that nonmilitary personnel had to be kept at a minimum in overseas theaters, noting that the Red Cross was especially organized for and accustomed "to rendering to military personnel the particular type of service which it will furnish in theaters of operation." Its selection, he added, "was primarily influenced by the fact of its established position and international character." [7]

The Red Cross was soon under heavy attack similar to that sustained by the YMCA in World War I. Some of the assaults came about because soldiers in Europe were unaware that the War Department had required that charges be made for refreshments in order to match requirements laid down by the British for their recreational units, and, Marshall recalled heatedly, "The reporters were just vicious . . . and I just pushed them aside and I said, 'I have seen all this. You sicked [the dogs] on the YMCA in the First War and now you are sicking [them] on these people in this war. Well, I am not going to have it.'" He was not always successful in his defense. The organization became so unpopular with many troops that he found in 1950, as head of the American Red Cross, "one of my principal jobs . . . was to compose the press and all favorably to the Red Cross or at least abate this enmity. . . . It was wholly illogical, wholly illogical." [8]

Although General Osborn worked closely with Secretary Stimson, the Special Services director at times found that he could get active support in certain training centers and overseas theaters only by having the Chief of Staff's full power behind him. "Sometimes, when things just got too hot for me," Osborn recalled, "I would send word I wanted to see General

Marshall, and he would always see me, usually very quickly, and would always listen, and sometimes he would pack me off; sometimes a little parentally he would say, 'I don't want to listen to this,' but he would always listen, find out what it was, then he would tell me very clearly and definitely. Sometimes he would say . . . , 'This is great, I hope it works, but I can't back you on it.' "

In other matters General Marshall specifically directed Osborn to put into effect projects that he particularly favored. When it came to the organization of the soldiers' magazine, *Yank,* the Chief of Staff explained to General Osborn how he wanted it done. Osborn recalled, "It was he who advised us to set it up in such a way that Mr. Stimson would find nothing objectionable in it, and he said, 'Now you let me handle Mr. Stimson on this, don't you talk to him about it.' He told me very carefully who to work with. I was under General Surles [for press-relations matters] . . . and I was under General Somervell for the rest of my operation. [Knowing] I was a great friend of Bob Patterson's . . . General Marshall told me once, 'I want you never to talk to Patterson about your work. It is not in Patterson's field, and I want him to have nothing to do with it and I don't want you to talk with him about it. Talk to Jack McCloy about it and Lovett.' " [9]

Marshall continually felt that the role of the infantryman was overlooked by the press and by the War Department itself. Too often, he remarked, the pilot who flew airborne troops into action was decorated while the man who jumped from the planes and landed in the rear of the enemy remained unknown. Moreover he wrote in the fall of 1943 to his theater commanders, Eisenhower, MacArthur, and Harmon: "An aggressive skillful infantry is vital to our success and that the individual courage, stamina, pride and relentless purpose of the infantry soldier is essential for the infantry organization." [10] Consequently he encouraged the efforts of the *Infantry Journal* (later *Army* magazine) to play up the infantry and to make available popular-priced books on the foot soldier.

Nearly a half year later he was pursuing the same theme. In one of his frequent reminders to the press-relations chief, he asked that greater efforts be made to improve the morale of infantrymen and to keep their numbers up to strength. Only 11 per cent of the Army (air and ground) were infantrymen, but they suffered 60 per cent of the casualties. "Men will stand almost anything," he emphasized, "if their work receives public acknowledgment." He then declared: "I am wondering just how we should go about dignifying the infantry rifleman. . . . It might well be charged that we have made the mistake of having too much of air and tank and other special weapons and units and too little of the rifleman for whom all these other combat arms must concentrate to get him forward with the least punishment and losses. I don't want to discourage the rifleman and yet I want his role made clear and exalted. . . ." [11]

Marshall was dismayed in November 1944 when a public-opinion poll conducted by the J. Walter Thompson Company at the War Department's request showed that among groups of high-school boys and girls the Air Forces and Navy topped the Army in popularity, and when asked to pick their favorite branch of the ground forces, they put the infantry at the bottom of the list. Danger, discomfort, lack of promotion, lack of glamour were among the items stressed as counting against the infantry.[12] Marshall continued McNair's earlier campaign to get better publicity for infantry actions and make the foot soldiers feel that they were remembered at home. But it was a battle he could never entirely win.

Marshall especially stressed the proper handling of decorations and awards. Since World War I he had insisted that a man's performance in the field should be promptly commended. On his return from one journey abroad he asked that a kit of medals be assembled for his next trip containing more valuable ones than he had carried previously, so that he could personally recognize outstanding acts of heroism.

Before the United States had been at war a year, the Chief of Staff asked the President to establish special service medals for the American, European, African–Middle East, and Asiatic-Pacific theaters. Since troops had been in contact with the enemy for only a short time, Roosevelt suggested that they wait for six months. The Chief of Staff accepted the ruling but insisted that the work of men overseas be recognized. He wrote the President:

> I am personally responsible for presenting the matter at this time. We have isolated garrisons scattered throughout the Pacific from Alaska to Australia. We have them in Labrador, Greenland, Iceland and many other places. Many of the men on this duty have been in position for more than a year and will probably continue in their present positions until the end of the war. We hope there will be no fighting in most of these garrisons but we must be ready for action. Morale is therefore an important factor and the difficulty of maintaining morale increases with the length of stay without active operations.
>
> In the past the War Department has invariably been a year or more late in such matters and therefore lost all the favorable reaction that comes from the wearing of a ribbon. I had hoped that the more isolated the group the more immediate would be the recognition of such service for I know that the right to wear a ribbon, particularly by a wartime soldier, has a profound influence on the individual. It is rather pathetic how much importance they attach to this.[13]

It seems likely that this letter turned the trick. Two months later the President approved the ribbons, and they were handed out to men almost as soon as they stepped ashore in foreign stations. The British, less generous than Marshall in making awards, were amused to find freshly arrived troops in the United Kingdom wearing the ETO ribbon solely for physically being there.

On the importance of Marshall's arguments Lieutenant General George S. Patton's testimony is striking. In mid-1943 he wrote Mrs. Marshall: "The medals which General Marshall has insisted on have had a wonderful effect, and I am sure that when we get the Bronze Battle Stars this effect will be even further enhanced. The result of decorations works two ways. It makes the men who get them proud and determined to get more, and it makes the men who have not received them jealous and determined to get some in order to even up. It is the greatest thing we have for building a fighting heart." [14]

Desiring to reward members of the ground forces, the Chief of Staff proposed early in 1944 that a Bronze Star Medal be given "for heroic and meritorious achievement or service, not involving participation in aerial flight, in connection with military or naval operations against an enemy of the United States." The President was uncertain. He feared that the medal might end up being given for normal performance of duty. He cited the case of one young man who, after a few months of service, sported ribbons from the Southwest Pacific, Aleutians, and the North Atlantic. "After five or six months in uniform, he is beginning to look like a Christmas tree." [15]

Defending the medals, Marshall replied through the service secretaries: "The latter proposal was initiated by me personally after I had obtained the comments of overseas commanders and had observed firsthand the effect of the awards of the Air Medal upon combat personnel of the Air Forces. The prompt award of this medal has been of tremendous value in sustaining morale and fighting spirit. . . ." Returning to the theme he had emphasized since World War I, he declared that "Decorations and service ribbons are of real value to the war effort only if promptly bestowed." He granted that some men who were transferred from theater to theater or who served in numerous landings and bombing operations might fill up their chests with ribbons. "But these are a very few people, and I am concerned about the thousands who never see Pennsylvania Avenue and are doing their best in some difficult or dangerous or isolated post overseas." The argument was persuasive. Roosevelt approved the letter and issued an Executive Order February 4, 1944, establishing the Bronze Star Medal.[16]

In the minds of Marshall and McNair one thing more was still needed to reward the performance of men in the infantry—increased monthly pay—and they made a strong plea for it. Ultimately, in mid-1944, they won the fight to issue Expert Infantryman and Combat Infantryman badges with additional monthly pay of five dollars for the first and ten dollars for the second.[17]

The Chief of Staff also saw to it that the soldiers and civilians near the front were not overlooked. Hearing that the European Theater ribbon was being awarded to field directors of the American Red Cross in that area, he wrote Eisenhower's Chief of Staff: "I probably am entirely wrong but this would rather indicate that ribbons are being awarded to high rank rather than to the fellow who lives and works under shell fire. Isn't there some [Red Cross] girl somewhere there who has served under the hardships of an advanced post who might be added to such a list?" [18]

If shortages of men and materiel prevented the Chief of Staff from filling the requests of commanders on various fronts, he attempted to indicate the War Department's gratitude for their services by some award. Although he realized that men in the field would have preferred additional men or supplies, he wanted them made aware at least that they were not forgotten. Once at a difficult time for the Southwest Pacific commander, when the bulk of American supplies was being rushed to Britain for the D-day build-up, Marshall asked General Handy: "What do you think of a DSM citation for MacArthur on his birthday?" Normally, he continued, they should wait for the fall of Rabaul or Kavieng, but the "latter is more Halsey's show and Rabaul is a long way off maybe." [19]

Men thrive on praise and awards, Marshall realized, but even more they prize advancement for their efforts. In peacetime, as he knew, able men were not always properly recognized for their services because of the Army's rigid adherence to claims of seniority. When presidential adviser Marvin McIntyre passed on criticisms he had heard of the number of general officers in Washington, Marshall seized the opportunity to inform the White House of his views on the importance of promotion to morale in wartime. He explained the proliferation of staff by citing the greatly increased tasks of the War Department over World War I. In addition to dealing with the responsibilities that the War Department had overseen in the earlier conflict, plus most of those that Generals Pershing and Harbord had administered in France, the current staff coordinated activities of numerous overseas theaters, handled the colossal program of furnishing military support for the Allies, and supervised the vast and complicated expansion of the Air Forces. The generals were not in Washington from choice, Marshall emphasized; they would prefer to be in more active theaters of action.

His officers were willing to do their duty without promotions, he continued, but he needed the authority to advance juniors. Otherwise he had to use a senior officer who might be "on the side of mediocrity." When an officer is charged with responsibility for thousands of men and hundreds of millions of dollars of materiel, he added, "it is only human that the individual should feel that he is receiving very poor treatment when he is denied a promotion—usually that of brigadier general which would give him prestige and therefore assist him in his job, and which literally does not cost the government a nickel." [20]

The General labored to keep the scales properly balanced in the case of senior officers, carefully explaining to theater commanders his reasons for advancing men in the War Department and asking that promotions of officers in the European and Pacific theaters keep pace. He chafed under the belief that his efforts in these matters were hampered by the President's desire to appoint an admiral every time the War Department proposed the name of a new general, although the Army was much larger than the Navy. Periodically he insisted that the theater commanders review their lists and include the names of those whose recent feats of arms or special performance deserved recognition.

At the end of 1943, after his trip around the world, Marshall directed his chief of personnel to investigate inequities in the promotion system that permitted rapid advancement at home and slow promotion abroad. Everywhere he had found lieutenants in important positions, rendering conspicuous service, who were held back because no vacancy existed in their units, while men at home with less service had been advanced. He declared: "This matter must be corrected and immediately. I am inclined to think that the instructions in the case are so complicated that nobody can figure them all out, but my interest is in 'effect' and I am not interested in background." He noted that one of his stepsons, Clifton Brown, stationed with an antiaircraft unit in the United States, had been moved up automatically from second to first lieutenant in six months and then to captain in another six months. The other stepson, Allen Brown, reporting to an armored unit in North Africa, found four company commanders who were still first lieutenants. All had been in action, three had been wounded, and two had been cited for their actions.[21]

By constantly hammering at the need to promote fighting men first, Marshall solved some of the inequities in the cases of junior officers, although he was never completely satisfied with the results. When it came to three- and four-star generals, he found that until late in the war each promotion list had to be backed with all the persuasive arguments he and Stimson could muster. Acutely aware of congressional opposition to authorizing too many high-ranking officers, Roosevelt closely examined each proposed list. Thus as late as mid-March 1945, Marshall found it necessary to prepare a detailed defense of his proposals to promote from three-star rank a roster comprised of such distinguished names as McNarney, Bradley, Spaatz, Kenney, Clark, Krueger, Devers, Somervell, and Handy. In sending his recommendations to Stimson the Chief of Staff declared: "It is difficult to make 2 or 3 of these promotions without giving serious offense and hurting morale. It is almost a case of all or none." [22]

Along with rewarding those who served Marshall carefully scrutinized the record of those excused from military service. He made little complaint regarding men exempt because of employment in agriculture or war industries, but insisted that deferment on other grounds be carefully examined. In November 1943 he took time out from the Cairo conference to instruct his Deputy Chief of Staff to inquire into the cases of two prominent athletes who had been turned down by Army doctors and that of a baseball catcher placed on limited duty because he had once broken two fingers. He declared:

> I fear a serious scandal in this matter if this action was taken by Army doctors. It is ridiculous from my point of view to place on limited service a man who can catch with his broken fingers a fast ball. If he can't handle a machine gun, I am no soldier. What I have in mind is to check up on these

particular cases, having the Inspector General go into the matter with the doctors concerned, to see if we are guilty of a serious dereliction. If the rejections were carried out by local boards, that is another matter, but if an Army officer on active duty is a participant, then we are responsible and I don't want any damn nonsense about this thing. I have seen dozens of men with half a dozen serious complaints in addition to their years passed by their Army doctors—and now to find great athletes, football and baseball, exempted is not to be tolerated.[23]

Early in January 1945 he told his chief deputy that "The physical-exemption business [has] reached the point in some cases of almost a racket," adding that he frequently saw soldiers well up in years doing their jobs in the Army while others who engaged in strenuous sports at home were turned down for military service. He had already ordered that all exemptions of celebrities be reviewed; was it not possible also to examine the recommendations of doctors exempting athletes.[24]

Similarly he asked General McNarney to look into the fact that a well-known musician had been deferred because of a punctured eardrum. Since ears were "vital to a musician, vocal or instrumental," he could not understand the ruling. To make his intent plain he declared: "If an Army doctor deferred him I want to know just why." When Marshall received a full report on the doctor's action, he accepted it but continued to grumble about widespread deferments.[25]

Along with the special decorations, articles and books on fighting units, and booklets on branches of the Army, General Marshall also sponsored the famous documentary movie series "Why We Fight," made by Frank Capra. Designed to demonstrate the background of the war, the films showed simply but graphically the stories of the rise to power of Germany, Italy, and Japan; their attacks on France, the Soviet Union, China, and Great Britain; and the Allied efforts to fight back. Accompanied by lectures and lists of related readings, the films mixed solid history with pro-Allied propaganda aimed at strengthening the soldier's will to win.[26]

Marshall believed that few of the other Army information projects had as great an impact as the Capra series. But the role of a movie producer was not without its trials, as his account makes plain:

> I [insisted] that the soldier be informed of what he was fighting for. At first they prepared pamphlets—very well prepared by experts from colleges and the like—but I found as a rule that they were presented after lunch and the man was tired and he went to sleep and the company commander who was explaining the thing was a very poor actor or performer. So I called Frank Capra, the leading motion-picture director at that time, and had him prepare the films, which were a complete education, I think, on the war to civilians as well as to recruits in the Army. And I had to do it, you might say, on the q.t. I never allowed the Secretary of War to see it or the White House to see it until we had it [an individual film] finished.
>
> The President was thrilled by it, and he still had a great many ideas. We got [one] over to the White House . . . and I didn't get it away for months. I had

to get it out to the troops in two weeks. I was raising an Army and I required that every soldier see [the film] before he left the United States. I remember the reports they gave me of the millions that [later] saw it. Mr. Churchill got hold of them and showed them all over England and even prepared and delivered an introduction to the films. I think they are one of the best educational set-ups that I have ever seen, and they are very interesting and they were done very expertly. They were amusing, they were serious, they were tremendous in their scope.

I remember I took Mrs. Churchill over to see one that had not been released. And I remember I would only do it on the basis that she would not mention it to anyone at the White House. Field Marshal Dill [brought] her . . . and we went to the little War Department projection room in the Pentagon. . . . She cried, she laughed, and she was just thrilled to the last and begged me to let the Prime Minister see it. I said . . . "I don't want him to speak to the President because I am not ready for the President to see it yet. . . ." Frankly, I wanted to get it on the road, because I knew . . . we would fool around for a month or two trying to get the thing fixed up. And time was golden with me. . . .

Well, she promised me, and then she went [back to the White House] and got to talking with Harry Hopkins. Hopkins got [me] on the phone and said the Prime Minister wanted to see it. (Mr. Roosevelt was away at the time.) Mr. Churchill came to the telephone and said he wanted to see it right away. "Well," I said, "I'm sorry, Mr. Churchill, because I don't want that to get out until it's ready because I will have all sorts of trouble with it if it does." . . . "Well," he said, "I'm asking you, I'm asking you." And I said, "I know you are, Mr. Churchill, and I know you are the Prime Minister . . . and you are the guest of the President, but he hasn't seen it yet and you are not going to see it ahead of him." "Well," he said, "when are you going to show it to him?" I said, "When it is finished. It isn't finished." . . .

[At last] I sent it over and Churchill . . . immediately sent back word [that he] wanted to take it to England. "Well," I said, "you can't do that until the President sees it." "Well," he said, "I'm going to hurry it up." "Well," I said, "it's the last damn thing you are going to get from me if you try to hurry it up. I'm doing a job and you are interfering. . . ." "Well," he said, "you certainly are stubborn." I said, "I am not half as stubborn as you are. But I'm not going to get this out." I said, "I am very, very fond of Mrs. Churchill, but I will never forgive her for telling you, because I might have known this would happen."

I didn't send it over to Mr. Roosevelt for quite a long time. And they kept it for four months. Meanwhile three million troops had seen it. I wouldn't let it go until three million men had seen it. . . . And every moving-picture house in England showed it. And the English people got this education and were very crazy about it. And I always thought it was very tragic that our people didn't get the chance to see the pictures.[27]

Marshall also gave his strong support to the development of soldier publications. Since the early days of his service he had recognized the value of unit newspapers throughout the Army, and he was therefore pleased when Major General James E. Chaney, commanding general of U.S. Army Forces in the British Isles, requested permission to resurrect *Stars and Stripes,* the soldiers' newspaper of World War I, for distribution to his forces. In London in mid-April, Marshall welcomed the reborn journal. Asked to comment for the first edition of the newspaper, which had originally appeared in Paris from February 8, 1918, to June 13, 1919, he declared:

> Like any other veteran of the A.E.F. in France, I am delighted to welcome the new version of *The Stars and Stripes*. By a fortunate coincidence I happen to be in England as it comes off the press.
>
> "I do not believe that any one factor could have done more to sustain the morale of the A.E.F. than *The Stars and Stripes*," wrote General Pershing of this soldier newspaper. We have his authority for the statement that no official control was ever exercised over the matter which went into *The Stars and Stripes*. "It always was entirely for and by the soldier," he said. This policy is to govern the conduct of the new publication.
>
> From the start *The Stars and Stripes* existed primarily to furnish our officers and men with news about themselves, their comrades and the homes they had left behind across the sea. A soldiers' newspaper, in these grave times, is more than a morale venture. It is a symbol of the things we are fighting to preserve and spread in this threatened world. It represents the free thought and free expression of a free people.
>
> I wish the staff every success in this important venture. Their responsibility includes much more than the publication of a successful paper. The morale, in fact the military efficiency of the American soldiers in these Islands, will be directly affected by the character of *The Stars and Stripes* of 1942.[28]

A few weeks later the Chief of Staff gave his blessings to the publication of a weekly soldiers' magazine, *Yank*, to be sold at five cents a copy. The first issue, which appeared on June 17, 1942, created a furor by an unfortunate juxtaposition on the cover. The headline "WHY WE FIGHT: F.D.R." (pertaining to an inspirational statement inside) was accompanied by a picture showing a soldier with a handful of money—referring to the new pay raise that increased a private's pay from $21 to $50 a month. Other protests arose because of the photographs of pin-up girls—relatively unclad for the 1940s—which proved to be the favorite feature of the magazine. Yet Marshall continued to back *Yank* as an aid to soldier morale. He particularly stressed the importance of its distribution to isolated posts. In the fall of 1943, he wrote General Eisenhower: "Your theater [is] the only one in which the weekly newspaper—*Yank*—was not on [sale]. . . . It is exceedingly well done. . . ." Eisenhower attributed the absence of *Yank* to lack of shipping space for printer's ink but said that would soon be remedied.[29]

At times Marshall must have had to restrain himself when he saw the degree to which the new citizen soldier would go in his statements to and in the press. He sometimes longed for the oldtime soldier who would carry out orders without appealing the Army's decisions to the press or to members of Congress. In his own day, however, he went considerably further to condone dissent than the old Army would have. He understood General Patton's frustrations with cartoonists and writers of *The Stars and Stripes*, but he approved General Eisenhower's moderate approach. On censorship he said:

I think in a democratic army a paper such as [Stars and Stripes] is quite essential as long as you don't find some individuals who are rather brilliant [who] take particular joy in [taking] cracks at the officer corps or a particular commander. It is very difficult to control that because if you begin to restrain it, the paper loses its caste as the voice of the enlisted man. In an army of democracy that is pretty nearly a necessity, and for that reason I was in favor of the paper though it was very provoking to commanders and all who had responsibility for [it]. . . . I had seen it in the First World War. I knew General Pershing's problems with it. Some very famous writers came out of the [first] Stars and Stripes. And he had to uphold them against the strictures of the troop commanders who were violent over what Stars and Stripes used to write. . . .[30]

Marshall's constant interest in winning the confidence of the citizen soldier was demonstrated especially in his determination to prevent bitterness and confusion in the handling of demobilization at the close of the war. As early as the summer of 1943 he directed a special staff in the War Department to make certain that the redeployment and demobilization phases would proceed with as little friction and discomfort as possible and that every attempt be made to reduce inequities. Point systems for discharge, well-organized redeployment centers, special instruction centers, and leave centers were all on the drawing boards months before they were needed. He also looked beyond the war's end to the return home and to such matters as Reserve training after the war. Reminding his colleagues that they would then have to proceed differently with civilian soldiers, he warned them not to try to cram too much into the program of candidates for commissions. Remember "the peacetime state of mind," he urged.[31]

Informing his colleagues in the Joint Chiefs of Staff of his special task force on demobilization, General Marshall at the end of July 1943 declared that the time was swiftly approaching when the armed forces would have to integrate their programs with those of twenty-three civilian agencies, such as Selective Service and the War Manpower Commission. He noted that planning was proceeding on the assumptions that (1) the war in Europe would be terminated one year before the end of the war in the Pacific; (2) partial demobilization would begin with V-E Day; and (3) the United States would furnish a share of the interim emergency forces to keep order. The postwar force to be left in Europe was estimated at 400,000, and it was assumed that at the moment of victory in Europe the forces in the Pacific would total 2,200,000. Possible delay of demobilization to avoid economic dislocations in the United States would not be included in the assumptions but would be considered later.[32]

The General personally assumed the task of arranging suitable receptions for officers and men after the war. Top generals and highly decorated enlisted men were to be sent to key cities across the country, preferably near their home towns, so that the whole country could have a share in the tribute. All that would have to wait until V-E Day for fruition, but the effort was part of a grand design to which the Chief of Staff was committed. The basis of his thinking was a point that he made to General Eisenhower near the close of the war in Europe. Writing of the postwar period, Marshall remarked that men liked to get away from the regimentation and narrow confines of a system that gave them little initiative and would welcome a short holiday where they could arrange something for themselves. Was it not possible, he asked, that two or three men be allowed to take a jeep and some rations and go out on their own for a two-day trip. Naturally the plan could not be implemented fully in the period immediately after the war ended because it would involve hundreds of thousands of men at a time when transportation would be at a premium and food difficult to supply. The fact that Marshall thought of it and that Eisenhower undertook the experiment on even a small scale showed something of the humanness of the two generals.

Marshall, Eisenhower, and Bradley, accused at times of pampering soldiers, all believed that the individuality of the American soldier, however difficult it made his training, was a priceless element that must be preserved. Marshall could not understand Churchill's attitude toward the common soldier. In an interview in 1957 Marshall referred with evident disapproval to the fact that the Prime Minister sometimes spoke of privates as "the dull mass." [33]

Few men valued more than did Marshall, who had dealt with the militia, National Guard, and Reservists most of his adult life—after attending a military school whose graduates with few exceptions were intended to enter civilian life—the maintenance of individual spirit and the need for the individual soldier to know his job and its importance to the nation. He insisted on discipline and respect for leadership, but he never ceased to demand that the soldier be treated as a thinking human being.

As he would show in his final report as Chief of Staff near the end of 1945 and in his tour of duty as Secretary of Defense, in 1950 and 1951, he was opposed to a large standing army in time of peace and strongly in favor of universal military training to produce a citizen army, which he believed firmly was the safeguard of a democratic system. He had favored the Selective Service System as the fairest and most effective method of raising millions of men quickly for the task of fighting World War II.

Marshall accepted dissent and disagreement as an element of a democratic society and slowness in preparation for defense as a part of the American attitude toward war. He recognized the advantages that dictatorships enjoy in being able to control men and materiel and to choose the suitable time to strike. And yet he believed that in the long run fortune favored the democracies. He said further in 1957:

> As to dictatorships, I think they have a very easy time of it at the start. They very easily can get ahead of us—way ahead of democracies. I think that when they start to break down, they go to pieces completely. And then democracy gradually gets stronger as it goes along. . . . You can take our battle in the last

war, when time after time there would be threats against the strength of the Army, and these various groups in this country would fight successfully against it. And of course we have to remember that if we carry out our main policy of keeping the war out of the United States, we are always up against a very expensive proposition of transport overseas, which runs the costs into billions and billions, and the management of the Army and the character of the Army has to be very, very carefully considered because you are not at home—you are not guarding your own fireside.[34]

Among the serious soldier problems Marshall had to deal with was the question of the place the Negro should occupy in the armed forces, an issue that was not settled then, despite his efforts to gain equal treatment for all men in the Army. One must not claim too much for him. More than a decade before the first Supreme Court decision on segregation in schools, he did not expect to break down the powerful social barriers that existed in American society between whites and blacks. Like Stimson, Eisenhower, and most other military leaders of that era, Marshall did not propose—even if he had been able to do so—to use the Army to impose social reforms. As an instructor of the Illinois National Guard and as chief of instruction at the Infantry School, he demanded fair treatment for Negro officers. As Chief of Staff, he worked on the problem with his Chief of Personnel, Major General John H. Hilldring, who had been specifically directed by Secretary Stimson to assure equal opportunity for Negroes eligible for commissions.

Marshall agreed with General Hilldring that equality of opportunity did not require commissioning a number of Negro officers proportionate to the ratio of Negroes to white men and officers in the Army—if that involved giving officer rank to men unqualified for it. He asked his Chief of Personnel, before drawing up a statement of policy, to talk with Judge William R. Hastie, special adviser on Negro affairs to Secretary Stimson, and three or four black leaders outside the government.

Hilldring found Negro leaders willing to accept this position provided that true equality of opportunity for commissions existed for qualified Negroes. He believed that they were convinced of the Chief of Staff's fairness in this matter. "General Marshall's advocacy of this policy was eloquent and persuasive, magnificent. . . . We adopted the policy. Mr. Stimson watched it, McCloy watched it like an eagle for a year or so, and I think the remaining days I was in G-1, I worked harder on that than . . . anything else, to get the word across to every commanding general in the field that this was the law and that regardless of their attitude about it the colored man would be given an equal opportunity. Of course, the policy worked well, and probably nothing we did in the war helped the colored man more than this policy. We commissioned thousands and thousands of officers, colored officers, . . . they did very good jobs because they were qualified before they were commissioned." [35]

In recalling this period, Marshall particularly praised Eisenhower's use of Negro soldiers in the battle of the Ardennes: "In [this] fighting . . . with a special percentage—I believe it was about fifteen per cent—of Negroes in the company, they put up a very splendid show. All along it was quite evident that what they lacked was leadership. I know that was so clear in the Meuse-Argonne battle [in World War I]. And I had personally to deal with this, with the troops—in the reorganization and their movement—of the colored units that were on the left of the First Army in that fighting. It was lack of leadership—lack of confidence of the men in their noncommissioned officers and particularly in their officers—that they had not developed that far." [36]

Impressed by the work of Dr. F. D. Patterson, President of Tuskegee Institute, General Marshall made an effort to give full backing to a Reserve Officers' Training Corps program there. Later he added a preflight training course, of which both he and Patterson were especially proud. In 1942, in acknowledging Patterson's letter of appreciation for the War Department's policy on training Negro troops, General Marshall replied: "The War Department is doing its utmost, consistent with military interests, to treat all races, communities and states evenly and fairly in the assignment and training of troops. Your response is a refreshing indication that our efforts are meeting with public approval." [37]

A year later, in thanking Marshall for a personal cash contribution to Tuskegee's fund drive, Patterson wrote: "I am *almost* embarrassed by your generous contribution to Tuskegee Institute for I regard you as already one of our benefactors. I am constantly grateful for what you have done to make it possible for Tuskegee Institute to render a large measure of service to the war effort through its ROTC and its aviation programs, which now include preflight training. This further contribution to our work makes me more grateful than I can tell you. . . ." [38]

Marshall's interest in the programs at Tuskegee continued after the war's end. A few weeks before he left office, he discussed with Patterson the future training programs at the institute. Marshall treasured the letter in which Patterson expressed his appreciation:

> I am most grateful to you for the conference granted me in connection with the future plans for aviation and military training at Tuskegee Institute. I appreciate the interest shown not only by yourself but by other members of the Army to whom you directed me. I left with a feeling that the Army has done a superb job in the war effort in spite of numerous difficulties and the necessity for harmonizing the opinions and actions of every race and creed in America.
>
> Your sympathetic interest in Tuskegee Institute and your overall awareness of problems faced by Negroes in America and your desire to see practical constructive steps taken for a solution of these problems leave me profoundly grateful for your interest and friendship.[39]

Not only did Marshall push efforts to secure equality of treatment, but he personally advanced outstanding Negro leaders, such as the elder Benjamin O. Davis, the first black officer to gain a star and the father of an airman who would rise rapidly in the Air Force and retire as a lieutenant general. By current standards, Marshall's acts would be judged paternalistic, favoring so-called Uncle Tomism rather than black self-assertion. He later described some of the opposition he received from militant black leaders:

> It was a very trying thing to me with the political pressures—the political attitude generally in regard to a question of this kind—and the very unfortunate statements on the other side of the question by men who should have known better than to talk as they did. We had very splendid men, of course, just as we have now—men like Bunche and others. The President at Tuskegee Institute was quite a friend of mine. And yet he was very much criticized by his own [people]—criticized because in a sense he was what I would call an evolutionist while they were revolutionists. In order to give him status, I would turn over my plane as Chief of Staff so that he could move from place to place in connection with his duties to help us in these matters. . . . But it was a very difficult thing to do and he probably was more criticized than almost any of the people concerned with this business. Yet he was the one that was supporting me in trying in every way to do what he could in the way that Booker T. Washington would have done. . . .[40]

But there were militant black leaders who also found it possible to praise the Chief of Staff. Judge Hastie, a vigorous supporter of equal treatment for Negro officers and men, made this clear in 1943 when resigning his position as special adviser to Stimson. He wrote Marshall: "While I have avoided imposing upon you personally the details of various specific problems with which this office has been concerned, I have been aware at all times of your concern that the Negro be equitably treated in the armed services. Although I have come to the conclusion that the greater good is to be accomplished by my withdrawal from the War Department at this time, I am keenly aware that your good will has been an all important factor in those things which this office has been able to accomplish during the past two years." [41]

All this was the beginning of a slow process that was not to change sharply until after World War II. As Secretary of Defense, Marshall would help apply a policy of integration by which the Army made more effective use of the Negro soldier in combat than in the past. Several years later in reflecting on the handling of Negro troops in World War II, the General concluded that many Negroes had suffered by being sent to the South for training. He explained: "I wanted the camps kept largely in the South because they didn't have to have as much construction as they would in a northern climate, and in addition . . . they could train outdoors for more days in the year. . . . I completely overlooked the fact [of] the tragic part of having these Northern Negroes in a Southern community. We couldn't change the bus arrangement, we couldn't change any of the things of that nature, and they found themselves very much circumscribed—to them outrageously so—because they were in there to train to fight for their country and put their lives ostensibly on the line, and they were being denied . . . things that the white troops accepted as a matter of course. . . ." [42]

Aware of particular problems that the Negro divisions and special units had faced, Marshall was watchful of their first performance in battle. In early 1944 he wrote Major General Millard F. Harmon in the Pacific that he wished him to take special notice of the first commitment of the predominantly black 93d Division in action. "The Secretary of War and I both feel it essential that it not, repeat not, be committed prior to adequate preparation." The first reports, he added, would undoubtedly be headlined, and it was important that the news releases be "strictly factual." "The War Department has been under constant pressure for alleged failure to utilize Negro soldiers in a combat capacity." He wanted a report on their activity after they had gone into battle. What he learned was disappointing. Despite excellent work by some of the units, particularly the artillery, the division's combat activity was rated below that of other units in the area. In the end the division spent much of its time in mopping-up areas, handling thousands of prisoners and relieving units that went on to other combat assignments. Representatives of Negro organizations felt that, despite Marshall's statement that the men would be used when feasible and MacArthur's assurances that race would not affect future combat assignments, the division would not be used in battle to the extent white divisions would be.[43]

Like many of his colleagues, General Marshall believed that the chaplain plays a tremendously important role in maintaining soldier morale. Not only does the chaplain minister to religious needs, but his office provides a place to which a soldier can bring his personal problems without being considered a malingerer or troublemaker. Realizing that the chaplain might be at a disadvantage if he was regarded as an appendage to the command, General Marshall upgraded the Chief of Chaplains to the rank of major general and made him an officer of the line, while insisting that members of the corps be addressed as "chaplain" rather than as "lieutenant" or "colonel" or "major," an arrangement that kept the chaplain in the field from measuring rank with his superiors or with the men seeking his advice. To make certain that commanders recognized the importance of the chaplain, Marshall insisted that maintenance of proper chaplain service in units be regarded as a responsibility of command.

The Chief of Staff believed that he was singularly fortunate in having as Chief of Chaplains an experienced officer, Monsignor (later Bishop) William Arnold. Near the end of December 1944 a prominent attorney who was an old friend of Secretary Stimson's wrote the Secretary that some of the top men in the Regular Army chaplaincy were not as strong as the men they supervised and that some critics believed that under Arnold, the Catholic influence in the Chaplains' Corps had become too strong. He proposed that Arnold be replaced at the end of his tour of duty by a Methodist, Colonel Milton O. Beebe, Chief Chaplain of the Mediterranean Theater of Operations, or an Episcopalian, Colonel Luther Miller, Chief Chaplain of the Sixth Army in the Pacific.[44]

General Marshall accepted the first charge but reacted sharply against the second. He agreed that there was mediocrity in some of the senior chaplain ranks, which he had been unable to counter "in quite the same drastic fashion I followed with the troop commands. Chaplain Arnold is well aware of this and has been, I am quite certain, embarrassed by the fact that certain of his assistants were not up to the desired standard." But he would hear no criticism of Arnold. "He himself, in my opinion, has been splendid. I doubt if many realize the terrific pressures under which he has been forced to operate and the successful manner in which he has met these pressures and preserved a unified front in the Chaplain[s'] Corps. He is an excellent administrator and, in my opinion, a strong character, therefore I place great dependence on him."

Aware that a Protestant bishop had prompted Stimson's friend to complain, Marshall wrote scathingly that if Arnold leaned on Catholic chaplains in his office, it was because he could not get the proper men from Protestant ranks. "In my opinion, and speaking very frankly, the great weakness in the matter has been that of the Protestant churches in the selection of their ministry. The Catholic system [of assigning able young priests to the Chaplains' Corps] provides a much higher average of leadership, judging by my own experiences, and the Protestant churches are too kindhearted in their admission of lame ducks."

As to the successor, Marshall admitted that he had not known that Arnold was nearing the end of his tour. If there was to be a change, he would select Chaplain Luther Miller, who had been "rather a protégé of mine" in Tientsin in the 1920s, where "we ran the church [attendance] up from an attendance of eight men to standing room only." Meanwhile, he asked the head of G-1, Major General S. G. Henry, to look into the complaints discreetly, avoiding anything that "smacks of an investigation." [45]

The Chief of Personnel's inquiry upheld Marshall's contentions concerning Chaplain Arnold. He reported that there was no even flow of chaplains by denomination and that proper distribution among religions could not be made in wartime. He denied that Catholics predominated in Arnold's office and emphasized that supervisory jobs were assigned on the basis of experience rather than denomination. He found that Arnold had done an outstanding job but, unlike Marshall, saw no evidence that any one denominational group was considered stronger in intellect, character, and general effectiveness than any other group.[46]

Recognizing that criticism such as he had received could prove harmful to Arnold's efforts, Marshall took a way out that kept the Monsignor's strong leadership for the Army and at the same time removed the office of the Chief of Chaplains from attack. Instead of extending Arnold's tour of duty when it expired, as he had intended, he called Luther Miller back to

Washington. But on the day of the Chief of Chaplains' retirement, Marshall announced that Arnold would remain on active duty as a member of the Inspector General's Office with special authority to ensure that the chaplains throughout the world functioned properly.[47]

To all bereaved parents and wives General Marshall sought to offer a sign of personal condolence. Very early in the war he himself wrote each individual, but as casualties rose sharply, he was forced to rely on an engraved card, which followed the official telegram from the Adjutant General. Many recipients did not reply, but some were obviously deeply moved. A letter from one father, which brought a grateful reply from the Chief of Staff, said:

> My son was killed in action in Italy on February 21st. I have received the chaplain's letter, the letter confirming the telegram, the card from your office. It is astonishing to me that a procedure, which must of necessity be a matter of routine, can be handled with such tact, dignified simplicity, and, above all, with such a personal touch. I am told that you are the man who has breathed the spirit into this procedure; and I am deeply grateful to you.
> It has helped me to write this letter. I hope that you may see it and derive some gratification from the knowledge that you have achieved your purpose in conveying a very human spirit when that is the thing that is most needed.[48]

In cases where two or three members of the same family met death, Marshall promptly sent a personally signed letter. One such read:

> I have just learned that it has been determined that your twin sons Carl and Clarence were killed in action last December. . . . Please accept my deep sympathy in your overwhelming loss. While few American families have been completely spared from the tragic consequences of this terrible struggle, you have been called upon for a much greater sacrifice than most and I pray that you will find the faith and strength to endure your loss.[49]

In addition he sought, where possible, to shift other members of a bereaved family to safe assignments. At times members of his staff would point out that the serviceman involved had not asked for special treatment or that the arrangement was not in accord with regulations. Usually his reply was a curt demand that the man be given noncombatant duty if he so desired.

Never the cold and unemotional man he was reputed to be, Marshall revealed intense feeling in his letters and conversations as the casualty lists grew. He had been personally hit hard early in the war as he read the rosters of dead, wounded, and missing in the Philippines and at Pearl Harbor, because they included old friends and children of old friends. Guadalcanal extended the lists, and then North Africa and the battles that followed flooded his office with reminders of the war's staggering cost. The General was no Patton who could scream imprecations at a soldier one moment and sob brokenly over a fallen rifleman the next. But he was touched by bills of death regularly presented.

He was proud of the sons of high-placed officers who had served bravely

and sought no special treatment. To Major General Willis D. Crittenberger, then a corps commander in Italy, whose young son, a corporal, was
killed in tank action in Germany, he wrote: "I have just learned that
your boy was killed in action. . . . You have my full sympathy. I am
grateful for the large contribution which you and your sons have made to
the Allied victory over Germany. It is most distressing to me that Townsend was called upon for the highest sacrifice. I hope that your pride in
his great service will be an eternal solace to you." [50]

Marshall was moved by the concluding paragraphs of General Crittenberger's reply: "As an eighteen year old boy [Corporal Townsend W.
Crittenberger] saw his duty very clearly, and chose to do it all on his own,
asking no favors. Because of this and the fact that he went out shooting,
my pride knows no bounds." [51]

As the tempo of battle increased, Marshall had a growing number of
personal letters to sign. Colonel Hines, son of General J. L. Hines, Pershing's successor as Chief of Staff, was blinded in action; Colonel William
Draper of Stimson's staff lost a son; the son of General McNair followed
his father in death within a matter of days, two oceans away. Marshall's
note of sympathy to Harry Hopkins on the death of his son drew the
reply: "The blow was hard and biting but I am overwhelmingly proud of
Stephen. Then too I am sure he died as gallantly as he lived through a
short but happy life. As for Robert, I hope you will not send for him. The
last time I saw him in Tunis he told me he wanted to stay until we got to
Berlin—in fact we have both agreed to meet there." [52]

For some the sense of loss was too great to be assuaged by card or letter.
One anguished father wrote of the death of his son, graduate of two uni-
versities, married for several years, father of a young daughter. "Your card
of sympathy, received yesterday, to the widow," he said, "was about the
last straw." He blamed the death on inadequate training. "In exactly six
months from the date of his enlistment, he was landed in France, ill prepared and was immediately sent across France into Belgium and I pre-
sume with Hodges' First Army and no doubt ordered to take some position with his machine gun and was mowed down like rats. My family feels
that he was actually murdered for lack of sufficient training." [53]

In 1944, several months after the death of Mrs. Marshall's younger son,
the grieving mother of an infantry soldier killed in action wrote Secretary
Stimson, who had sent her a letter of condolence. The last paragraph
particularly struck the Chief of Staff: "I hope this letter is read by some
one more in authority than a teen age secretary. And I do thank you for
the wording of your letter. The reaction to it was better than to General
Marshall's engraved card. If I were he I would save the Government's
funds."

Marshall promptly drafted a letter explaining the impossibility of writing a personal letter to relatives of all men killed in action. Members of
his staff urged that he not send it. McCarthy pointed out that most people

who wrote had expressed appreciation for the card. General Handy, aware of his Chief's solicitude, put it even more bluntly: "I doubt the advisability of any reply. No explanation or apology for the cards is called for, many people do appreciate them. If [the writer] does not realize that you cannot take personal cognizance of the death of each soldier, if she believes you have no real feeling of distress at these tragedies, the letter will not change her. *I see your feeling in this matter, but it is another burden you will have to bear.*" [Italics supplied.]

Marshall desisted for a few days until an even more bitter letter prompted by the card arrived: "I have received word today that my husband . . . was killed in action. I hope that those who are responsible for his return to active duty are satisfied that four small children are left without their good father and I without my husband. God's curses on all of them."

This time no one attempted to stop the General. The burden was something he could not bear alone in silence. The earlier draft was amended to drop any defense of the sympathy card, since its use had not been called into question, and sent as initially penned:

> Your [recent] letter . . . expressing resentment over the death of your husband . . . has been brought to my attention. I much regret the bitterness you express toward the War Department and I wish to indicate to you something of the situation confronting the Army.
>
> The tragedy of the war has struck homes all over America. It has reached my family, Mrs. Marshall's younger son having been killed in a tank battle in Italy. Her other son and her son-in-law are fighting in Germany. The sons and husbands of many of our friends have been added to the casualty lists, and the losses suffered by the families of Regular Army officers have been exceptionally heavy. So I can well appreciate the depth of the blow that has struck at your happiness and your future, and I therefore regret all the more your present feeling of bitterness.
>
> I witnessed the same tragic aftermath of the battles in the last war and because of my position the daily casualty lists bring to me the full impact of the tragedy of war. I deplore the unfortunate policies this country has followed which [have] led us into unpreparedness and, I think, possibly have failed to avoid wars with their fearful cost to young Americans and to the progress and peaceful prosperity of the country.[54]

He had made his defense. But it brought no peace of mind. Casualty lists were one daily event to which he never became accustomed.

Determined to utilize the nation's resources to the fullest in waging the war, Marshall vigorously supported the long-unsuccessful efforts to authorize women to participate in the Army. His energetic efforts on behalf of this somewhat controversial policy went, of course, far beyond publicity, but he made shrewd use of that instrument on occasion—and demonstrated his pervading sense of fairness.

During the Tunisian fighting, the Chief of Staff sent a sharp note to his

Director of Public Relations on the handling of news pertaining to one of his favorite organizations, the Women's Army Auxiliary Corps. "It seems to me," he wrote, "that very poor use is being made of the best publicity possibilities in the WAAC organization." He pointed out that the first group of WAAC officers sent to North Africa in December 1942 had been on a ship that had been torpedoed and that they had been picked up by a destroyer after losing most of their personal belongings. (He did not mention that he himself, at his own expense, obtained replacement clothing for them.) [55] During the Casablanca conference they had been entertained at dinner by the President and the Prime Minister. They had been traveling in fairly high circles, he observed dryly, but apparently there had been no public comment.

Much more was involved in Marshall's memorandum than a lesson in public relations. The General was keenly interested in proclaiming the value of the Women's Corps that he had fought so hard to establish and to have accepted by the Army. His message was one of many steps he took to ensure proper recognition of women's role in wartime activities.

An attempt had been made in World War I to get Army status for women when General Pershing asked for women assistants, especially telephone operators who spoke French, for overseas service. Some women employees were sent but without military status. Toward the end of the war the commanding general of the Services of Supply asked for 5000 women clerks, but he was informed that limited-service males could do the work and that there was no necessity for "a radical departure" at that time. Less conservative in this respect, the Navy actually enlisted some 13,000 women in the Navy and Marine Corps, but the Army only talked about the idea.

In 1920 Secretary of War Newton D. Baker recognized the changing status of women in public affairs to the extent of appointing a Director of Women's Relations in the War Department with the task of selling women's organizations in the United States on the value of the United States military establishment. In a period when the Army was shrinking in size and interest in military affairs was becoming vestigial, the lady in charge of this office was virtually ignored. In 1931 the Chief of Staff, General MacArthur, informed the Secretary of War that the office was of no military value.

Between 1920 and 1939 little real effort was made to plan for the use of women in the Army in future emergencies. A proposal to raise a force of 170,000 in time of war was rejected in 1926. In 1928 a more detailed plan was set forth by Major Everett S. Hughes of the G-1 Division, but it was buried so deeply that it did not resurface until more than a decade later, after the WAAC had been in existence for six months. When a friendly chief of G-1, Brigadier General Albert J. Bowley, appeared on the scene in 1930, he got so little encouragement for the proposed use of women in the Army that he concluded that we "may as well suspend; no one seems willing to do anything about it."

In October 1939, a month after General Marshall became Chief of Staff, a serious study was made on the value of a women's corps in case of war. The growing use of women in war work in the United Kingdom spurred this planning. General Marshall's views were first expressed publicly in the spring of 1941 when he wrote an inquirer that while the United States did not have Britain's acute manpower shortage, "we must plan for every possible contingency, and certainly must provide some outlet for the patriotic desires of our women." A short time afterward Mrs. Edith Nourse Rogers, Republican representative from Massachusetts, who had served in the American Red Cross in France in World War I and who had been active in veterans' affairs after succeeding her husband in Congress in 1925, informed General Marshall that the time had come for legislation to permit the use of women in Army activities. The Chief of Staff asked for a short time—and then an extension—to help prepare legislation that would meet the Army's needs. The view of some Army officials was reflected in the statement of the Chief of Personnel in April 1941 that Mrs. Rogers had a bill and Mrs. Roosevelt had a plan and that the purpose of the G-1 study was to organize a women's force along the lines that met with War Department approval "so that when it is forced upon us, as it undoubtedly will be, we shall be able to run it our way." [56]

With White House encouragement and assistance from the War Department, Mrs. Rogers introduced her bill at the end of May 1941. Almost alone among War Department officials, General Marshall greeted the plan with enthusiasm rather than apprehension. Colonel Hilldring, soon to be G-1 of the War Department, said later that the Chief of Staff "was intensely interested" by the summer of 1941. Because Marshall foresaw that the great bottleneck of the future would be manpower, he pushed the legislation. War had become a complicated business requiring many civilian techniques, he told Hilldring, and many of these were in the hands of women. He saw no reason, for example, to train men as telephone operators or typists when most of those jobs in civilian life were handled by women. There was another point. Hilldring recalled: "The Chief of Staff was also influenced by the fact that the ladies wanted in; he literally has a passionate regard for democratic ideals." [57]

Several snags slowed passage of the legislation through Congress. One of the most serious developed in the Bureau of the Budget, whose director informed Secretary Stimson on October 7, 1941, that he did not believe that "the enactment of the proposed legislation, at least at the present time, should be considered as being in accord with the program of the President." [58] General Marshall asked that the report on the measure be rewritten for reconsideration by the Bureau of the Budget—but not submitted before he was personally notified. Meanwhile he set to work to reduce opposition to the measure. In addition to making a personal call to the Bureau of the Budget and helping to rewrite the report, he made use of all the allies he could find at hand. In one case he was more successful than he could have foreseen.

Earlier in the year the Bureau of Public Relations of the War Department had proposed the establishment of a Women's Interests Section in its Planning and Liaison Branch to help answer questions of wives and mothers of men in the service. As its chief the department had obtained Mrs. Oveta Culp Hobby, a Texan involved in various women's activities, who agreed to serve for a limited time. Mrs. Hobby, then only thirty-six, was the wife of a former governor of the state. In her twenties she had served as a parliamentarian of the Texas legislature. Shortly after she took on her new duties, she asked the Chief of Staff to stimulate interest in the new program by speaking at a meeting of the national presidents of the twenty-one largest women's organizations to be held in Washington in mid-October. It was at that meeting that the General met Mrs. Hobby for the first time. She subsequently sent him a cordial letter thanking him for his contribution, which "was of exceptional interest to the visiting national club leaders and certainly played a large part in making the meeting valuable, both to the Women's Section and to members of the Advisory Council." [59]

Although Mrs. Hobby's section had not been established as a headquarters to lobby for the Women's Corps bill, her knowledge of women's problems and her relations with women's organizations made her help invaluable to the bill's progress. In mid-November she attracted General Marshall's attention with a report of a conversation she had recently had with Mrs. Roosevelt, who wished to know if the bill was broad enough to permit the War Department to use women "in anti-air barrage activities and similar fields of endeavor in which women are now being used in England." Mrs. Hobby added in the report that she thought that all useful ways of using women were anticipated and included in the bill. Sensing that he had a skillful advocate, Marshall directed the G-1: "Please utilize Mrs. Hobby as your agent to smooth the way in this matter with Mrs. R[oosevelt], G. C. M." [60] Soon he was to make further demands on her services.

The Chief of Staff continued to prod his representatives for action. Shortly before leaving for a long Thanksgiving weekend, he called in Colonel Hilldring and checked on legislation he wanted passed. Hilldring later reported: "General Marshall shook his finger at me and said, 'I want a Women's Corps right away and I don't want any excuses!' " [61] Before he left, he also approved a draft of a letter to the Bureau of the Budget, which noted that an organization similar to the one proposed was then operating in Great Britain with great success and that experience in World War I showed that "such an Auxiliary Force will be needed in the event active military operations on a large scale by the Army of the

United States are again required." Although Marshall did not know how close war was, he added with the temperate firmness that was his hallmark: "In view of the obvious advantages to be gained by the organization and training of a small Women's Auxiliary Corps in an orderly and efficient manner for use under present conditions and to provide a going concern capable of rapid expansion if needed in the near future, and with the thought that perhaps the matter was not previously explained in sufficient detail, the War Department requests reconsideration of the proposed legislation." [62]

These arguments and preparations would probably have been enough to produce a favorable reaction. But in less than two weeks the Japanese ensured it. Four days after Pearl Harbor the director of the Bureau of the Budget saw "no objection to the submission of this revised draft to the Congress for its consideration." [63]

Having won the first round, Marshall made certain that no steps were omitted in the dealings with Congress. Mrs. Rogers reintroduced the bill to include War Department amendments assuring the Civil Service Commission that the measure could not be used to displace civilians from their jobs. When the committees of Congress began hearings on the bill in January and early February, Mrs. Hobby was selected to testify as one of the War Department representatives. Since she was the sole female representative of the department, General Marshall took special pains to coach her for the ordeal. Mrs. Hobby's account of that encounter illustrates graphically the thoroughness of the Chief of Staff's preparations:

> When the committee set the bill for a hearing, General Marshall asked me if I would testify and represent the War Department and express the War Department's views. Of course, I said I would and worked closely with G-1 and the Assistant Secretary of War, McCloy, . . . and General Marshall's liaison to the Hill. The testimony had all been prepared, and we had done a dry run, so to speak. The morning that I was supposed to go up General Marshall called for me. He sat down and we talked about a number of things. He asked me if I had ever testified before a congressional committee, and I told him I had not. He said, "Do you know what you are going to say?" and I said, "Yes." I told him all about the presentation of the testimony and the dry run. I had it [my statement] folded in my purse and I handed it to him.
>
> He looked it over, took it over to the wastebasket and tore it up, then sat down and said, "Now I want to give you a piece of advice. When you go to testify before a congressional committee, you say what you have to say." I said, "General, there are many questions they will ask me [concerning which] I do not know the attitude of the War Department. I am about as unmilitary a person as ever existed." He said, "When you do not know what the attitude is, that's what you have a staff for. . . ." Well, he kept talking and the hour kept getting near, and I was very embarrassed for fear that I would be late for the committee, but [I knew] . . . that I could not excuse myself from the Office of the Chief of Staff. The interview was finally terminated, and I got into the car . . . [where] a G-1 officer was waiting for me. I told him what had happened, that General Marshall had torn up my testimony and told me to make a

statement. I said, "What does he expect me to do, throw the mantle of the Chief of Staff around my shoulders when I testify?" He said, "That's exactly what he means for you to do and you had better do it." [64]

In telling of this briefing in later years, General Marshall laughed at his worry about Mrs. Hobby's ability to present an effective case before politicians. "That woman listened to me telling her how to behave before a group of legislators and never said a word to me about acting as a parliamentarian of the Texas legislature!"

Marshall recalled that she not only presented the testimony ably but was aided by the fact that the second-ranking Democrat on the committee, Representative R. Ewing Thomason of Texas, was a personal friend of her father's. But, he noted, this did not persuade Thomason to favor the rank of colonel for Mrs. Hobby when it was later proposed. Southern congressmen, he remarked, offered great opposition to him in this regard. They "would kiss a woman's hand and give her an orchid but not consent to military rank." [65]

Although the reception of the bill in the committee indicated likely passage by Congress, normal legislative routine delayed progress for a number of weeks. The General decided to proceed on the assumption that the measure would be approved and started the machinery moving for establishing a training center, recruitment, obtaining uniforms, and the like.

Most important he chose a director for the Women's Corps. First he asked Mrs. Hobby for her recommendations of women qualified to head it. For about two weeks after she had submitted her list, he made no response. One day he sent for her and announced: "Thank you for this list, but we want you to head the corps." Mrs. Hobby said: "General, I have no military knowledge, none." Neither did any other woman, he replied. "I told him I would talk to my husband about it and I did," Mrs. Hobby recalled. "My husband was the one who thought I should go [earlier] as a consultant, because he felt that war was inevitable and that no one should refuse to do anything. So I did agree to do it." Marshall wrote Stimson of his choice: "In all of these duties [in the Bureau of Public Relations], she displayed sound judgment and carried out her mission in a manner to be expected of a highly trained staff officer. She has won the complete confidence of the members of the War Department staff with whom she has come into contact and she made a most favorable impression before the committee of Congress." Without waiting for final approval of the bill, Marshall removed her from the jurisdiction of the Bureau of Public Relations and started her on Women's Army Auxiliary Corps preplanning programs. [66]

As plans were outlined, Marshall urged action on Congress, writing to House Majority Leader John McCormack, who carried the measure through the House of Representatives in March by the lopsided vote of 249–86. The Senate worked more leisurely and talked of the need of women at home and the necessity of sparing the gentler sex the hardships of military life. Not until May 14, 1942, a year after the first bill had been introduced and five months after the beginning of war, did the Senate approve the measure, by a vote of 38–27.

Once it was clear that the Senate would act favorably, Marshall moved swiftly. To prevent any political pressure for the selection of someone other than Mrs. Hobby, he had papers drawn up for her appointment. On the evening of May 14 he sent Colonel Robert N. Young of his staff to the Secretary of War's home to get Stimson's signature. Two days later this slender, quietly pretty, very feminine woman, a Southern lady with an aura of breeding and gentility, wearing a straw sailor hat and a stylishly plain suit, became the first head of the U.S. Women's Army Auxiliary Corps. The new director raised her hand as Major General Myron C. Cramer administered the oath while Marshall and Stimson, her sponsors, beamed approvingly. Stimson recorded: "At 11:30 Mrs. Hobby took the oath of office as director of the WAAC. There was such a crowd anxious to see her that the meeting took place in the General Counsel room where I held press conferences and all the photographers were there and representatives of all the women. General Marshall and General Surles were there and the Judge Advocate General swore in Mrs. Hobby and photographs were taken of [both of us] shaking hands with her. The photographers generally had a field day. Afterwards she brought her husband in to [my office] . . . a former governor . . . older than me." [67]

Mrs. Hobby, for whom the whole affair was overpowering and a bit frightening, gratefully remembered General Marshall's "understanding . . . of other people and of other people's problems." "My husband came up for the swearing-in ceremony and when it was over, General Marshall stepped over to where my husband was sitting and said, . . . 'Could you come into my office?' We all went in, and he said, 'I know that any man must have great trepidation about his wife's taking such an assignment, but I want to tell you this: that the Secretary of War and I mean to give her added support in doing what we know will be a very difficult job.' My husband said, 'General Marshall, I had intended to seek an appointment with you to discuss this very thing because I know that it will be a very difficult thing to form a Women's Corps and to make it acceptable to the Army and to the population not accustomed to the idea.' "

The Chief of Staff kept his promise. "General Marshall," Mrs. Hobby said, "had uncanny intelligence. He always seemed to know when people had problems and needed help. Someone may have told him, but often I would go down [to his office] and he would say, 'I want to see you at lunch today, come home and eat lunch with Katherine and me.' And we would have lunch and he would say, 'Well are there any problems?' This always happened at a time when I had problems! So I have always considered that either his intuition or his intelligence was very good. . . .

Many people in the War Department, to use the old expression, always believed that I made end runs to accomplish some objective. I am not saying that I wouldn't have if a principle had been involved. Actually, I never had to." She concluded that without his continued strong backing the women's group "would have been at best a very limited and crippled organization." [68]

In June, Mrs. Hobby's uniform arrived. Properly dressed, she reported to General Marshall, who pinned on her the silver eagles of a colonel. Although Congress had authorized pay equal only to that of a major, he made it clear that she was the top commander in the WAAC organization, which included male full colonels.

Marshall found that he and the new director agreed on many points, notably the matter of commissions. He had always believed that an officer should have had some previous experience—either as a cadet or an enlisted man—before receiving a commission. He insisted that WAAC officers come out of the enlisted corps. "The Chief of Staff was a great democrat," his wartime G-1, General Hilldring, said, "I told Mrs. Hobby how at his direction, I had made a fight to get more officers from the ranks of enlisted men. I told her that he might not object to appointing a few civilian women for the top jobs, but the rest of the officers must come from the ranks. They must be the best women in the ranks, even if . . . [they were not] necessarily the best in the nation."

Once the battle to organize the WAAC had been won, various branches of the Army demanded more women auxiliaries than could be trained for many months. As requests flowed in, General Marshall reported on June 13 that Army Ground Forces were short more than 160,000 men and that he wanted the WAAC to drive ahead on organizing and training. Four days later a plan was presented for increasing the Corps from 12,000 to 63,000. Three months later a greater expansion was asked. Eisenhower was soon stressing the need for increased numbers abroad. By September, G-3 had suggested training a million WAACs—a program that could not readily be implemented.[69]

Not that everyone wanted women in uniform. The difficulties of finding proper training centers multiplied; the disagreements over uniforms and supplies increased. Assured that Marshall was in her corner, Mrs. Hobby attacked her problems vigorously. When she arrived at the WAAC Training Center at Fort Des Moines, Iowa, in cold weather and found the women still in summer uniforms—while men on the post were in winter coats and jackets—she went at once to her quarters and changed to summer wear. A short time later she was asking the Office of the Quartermaster General in Washington for overcoats for her charges. When told that the clothing was unavailable, she asked for men's apparel—and with Marshall's aid she got it. Looking rather like children dressed in their papas' overcoats, her WAACs drilled in overlong outerwear, not smartly but warmly until something more fashionable could be provided.

Marshall nearly always backed her up. In retrospect the outstanding feature of their relationship was that he let no opportunity pass to show his high regard for her efforts. Unable to attend the first WAAC commissioning ceremonies at Fort Des Moines, he sent a strong statement of approval to be read to the group.

On another occasion, however, Marshall made his disapproval plain—as well as his sympathy. In Mrs. Hobby's words: "General Marshall, in my years in the Army, overruled me once. It is one of the dearest stories that I can imagine." General Eisenhower and Bedell Smith had asked her to make WAACs available for the invasion of North Africa, where French-speaking telephone operators would be needed. Mrs. Hobby recalled that she retorted:

> "I cannot agree to send them in submarine-infested waters, in battle conditions, as long as they are not members of the Army." He [Smith] said, "Well, of course, you know I am going to take this to the Old Man." . . . So I went up to talk to General Marshall. . . . He looked at me and said, "Hitler won't wait." . . . He called Frank [McCarthy] and said, "Get my plane ready. Mrs. Hobby is going to [the WAAC Training Center at] Daytona Beach." He said, "Are you unhappy?" I said, "No, sir, I am not unhappy, I have an order and I will carry it out." He said, "I know it troubles you to send these people over there and I want to tell you something. You call the officers and women together and [while] you cannot tell them where they are going . . . you can tell them that they are going over submarine-infested waters into hazardous conditions, and then you ask for volunteers, and tell them that the roster will be in the office in the morning, that you are not going to take them all, that you will have to pick, and that no one will know who didn't volunteer. They may have reasons, family reasons, or otherwise."
>
> I went off to Daytona Beach that afternoon and called them together that night . . . and told them the roster would be ready for them to sign, and as I walked out of that room, people were pulling tablets and pencils out, signing their names and giving them to the commanding officer, and before they left that room, every woman had volunteered. . . . It is something I will never forget. . . . He knew how I felt, he knew he was absolutely right, this should have been done, but he made it easy for me. That way I felt right about it.[70]

The problem of sending auxiliaries into war zones soon prompted a change in the women's organization. General Marshall concluded that the WAAC would not be fully accepted or completely effective until it was a full-fledged part of the Army. Several bills were introduced to create a Women's Army Corps—a move that stimulated attacks on the existing auxiliary corps.

The General felt that some of the unfavorable reactions of soldiers to the WAACs were in a class with similar criticism of women in the Red Cross. Much of the trouble, he believed, came from disgruntled soldiers who could not get dates with the WAACs. At the beginning, he noted, every girl had about a thousand suitors, "and all except one got sore." He was delighted one day with Mrs. Hobby's spirited defense of her group and chuckled as he recalled the story: "I was talking to an officer . . .

one of those Gradgrinds who not only gets at the things he is supposed to do but includes everything else that he can criticize at the same time. He was not . . . connected with the WAACs but when Mrs. Hobby was waiting there to talk with me, he came in and said, 'Do you know what I saw? . . . I saw a WAAC and a soldier going down the road hand in hand,' and he turned to Mrs. Hobby and said, 'What do you think of that? Mrs. Hobby said, 'Well, they have been doing that for about a thousand years, haven't they?' Which I thought was a complete re-tort. . . ." [71]

Slanderous tales started to plague the corps almost as soon as recruiting began. The official WAC historian, Mattie Treadwell, compiled the following list of prime talebearers: resentful officers and enlisted men, some officers' wives, jealous civilian women, male and female gossips, disgruntled WAACs and fanatics—a number of whom hated anything favored by the Roosevelt administration. Some of their "reports" were the adolescent variety of off-color stories and lavatory graffiti that produce uneasy tittering. More repugnant were the innuendoes of widespread immorality among the WAACs, as if their willingness to serve their country was merely a cover for rampant sexuality. Unfortunately publication of statistics showing that misbehavior in service differed little from that at home and that the venereal-disease rate was almost zero among women in the WAAC seemed, paradoxically, to suggest to certain readers that something was wrong with women who tried to serve their country. No wartime criticism infuriated Marshall more than these attacks.

One of Roosevelt's old enemies and targets, a columnist in the Washington *Times-Herald,* suggested in one of his more venomous musings that the Army was encouraging promiscuity among the WAACs by handing out contraceptives. It was a victory for New Deal thinking, the writer suggested. "Mrs. Roosevelt wants all the young ladies to have the same overseas rights as their brothers and fathers"—a neat, double-barreled smear. It was the kind of vicious campaign that Marshall and Stimson, with their Victorian notion that one did not discuss a woman's good name in public, were ill equipped to fight. But they finally struck back, Stimson in an effective press conference and Marshall in a letter of confidence to Mrs. Hobby. "I wish you would reassure your subordinates," the Chief of Staff wrote her, "of the confidence and high respect in which they are held by the Army." [72]

At the end of June 1943 Congress took the step Marshall had long favored: making the WAAC organization an integral part of the Army as the Women's Army Corps. The next move was to improve Mrs. Hobby's position vis-à-vis the Chief of Staff. Initially her office had been placed under Army Service Forces, where she had continual difficulty in getting the officers at pick-and-shovel level to carry out the policies that General Marshall had approved. Reluctant to appeal over the head of her superiors, she struggled with red tape until someone at last informed General Marshall. He ordered G-3 to study the situation and then acted upon its suggestion that the Director of the WAC be moved to G-1, where she would have direct access to the Chief of Staff.[73]

Even under extreme burdens the Chief of Staff was always ready to consider the needs of the Women's Army Corps. When Mrs. Hobby was criticized for failure to provide a uniform for the corps as attractive as that supplied for female Navy and Marine Corps personnel, her suggested changes got close attention from Marshall. He found time to approve chamois-colored scarves and gloves. After the Office of the Quartermaster General stated that it could not procure a tropical-worsted WAAC uniform in time for the summer, he personally intervened to change this opinion.[74]

In a few matters General Marshall failed to go along with Mrs. Hobby. Realizing that many enlisted women would like officer status, she opposed direct commissions in overseas theaters for foreign-born civilian workers. Three Australian women were commissioned in MacArthur's headquarters before Washington had a chance to intervene. When General Eisenhower asked that his British chauffeur and secretary, Kay Summersby, be commissioned as a WAC lieutenant, Mrs. Hobby and G-1 officials objected. In this case Marshall ordered that Eisenhower's wishes be carried out. This action, which unfriendly columnists later distorted—alleging that Marshall rebuked Eisenhower for commissioning his subordinate—had the Chief of Staff's specific approval. Not only did Marshall in his own handwriting overrule the opposition of his subordinates, but he spelled out his reasons. "He said," Mrs. Hobby, who was present, recalled, "he never felt like telling a man who was responsible for winning a war not to do little things that he thought would help him win the war." [75]

To Marshall the importance of the WACs was summed up in the work of Lieutenant Florence T. Newsome, who was to end her Army career as a lieutenant colonel in the Chief of Staff's office: "She was used to replace an officer in the anteoffice to meet people. Her work proved so valuable that she was gradually moved from job to job until now she is my personal secretary for all matters pertaining to the U.S. Chiefs of Staff and Combined Chiefs of Staff, briefing the papers, making contact with the interested parties, who include General Arnold, General Somervell, and General Handy, and apprising me of the pros and cons of all the various issues. That is certainly an important job. . . ." [76]

Marshall's praise of his personal WAC assistants, such as Colonel Newsome and his driver, Sergeant Payne, typified the esteem he had for the members of the WAC organization. No wartime project for whose existence and growth he took a great personal responsibility gave him keener pleasure. His admiration was reciprocated. Speaking later about Marshall and the Women's Army Corps, Mrs. Hobby pointed out that the General made his farewell in his last important government post, Secretary of Defense, in a review of a WAC group. She summed up his role simply: "He was one of the greatest friends we ever had." [77]

He would certainly have treasured the compliment. But with his customary disparagement of praise, he would probably have replied, "Support of one's own is what a commander's for."

Facets of Command

A COMMANDER, Marshall had long ago decided, must be many-sided. He must be fair and generous to those under him, yet ruthless if need be. Strict in his own conduct, he had to have a knack for public relations and master the art of winning the support of colleagues and subordinates. Keeping his commanders in line, working for congressional support, cultivating the men in charge of war production, gaining the backing of the press, and winning endorsement for his programs from the President, the Chief of Staff worked constantly to maintain his authority and to strengthen the position of the Army. Apart from occasional bitterness from those who could not accept his stern sense of justice, he kept the respect and often affection of most of those with whom he worked in the critical war years.

From the beginning of his tour of duty as Chief of Staff, Marshall demanded that his subordinates in Washington and in the field work harmoniously with members of the other services, and on the outbreak of war he extended that injunction to include their relationships with America's allies. Some well-publicized cases exemplify his ruthlessness when his wishes were ignored.

In 1942 Marshall had the disagreeable task of ordering home from Iran an old friend, Major General John N. Greely. Late in 1941 Greely had been selected to head a mission to assist with Lend-Lease shipments to the Soviet Union. Delayed in Iran while awaiting visas from Moscow, he spent several frustrating months as the status of his mission was being reviewed. Ultimately, as a result of poor coordination between the State and War departments and the reluctance of the Russians to admit the mission, the group was dissolved. Greely then proposed that he be made head of the Army Mission to Iran in the place of Brigadier General R. A. Wheeler, who had been sent to Stilwell's staff in India. He was again disappointed when Wheeler's second in command was selected to take his place.[1]

At the time of the dissolution of the mission the Iranian government was seeking an American officer to act as intendant general of its Army, and Greely was appointed. When the General was told to await further instructions, he radioed the War Department that if he remained in Iran, he expected to assume command of all U.S. personnel and activities there. Marshall promptly instructed Greely to take no such authority. Soon afterward the U.S. Minister to Iran complained to Secretary of State Cordell Hull that "Greely's activities have now departed from realm of harmless interference and entered field of international politics." Already under orders to return to Washington for consultation, Greely left Tehran August 2. Although War Department representatives discussed his return as head of a mission with State Department officials later in the month and won their agreement to accept him—if there was no one else available and provided he was carefully instructed as to the limitations on his functions—he did not go back. It seems likely that Marshall made the final decision. Of his recall the official Army historian, T. H. Vail Motter, has recorded: "His [Greely's] impatience in the face of what appeared to him to be indecision and fence-walking in time of national emergency disregarded the principle of due consultation with, and specific approval by, those whose business it was to view the war in global perspective. What Greely proposed to do in 1942 was judged by the policy-makers to be premature and impracticable under the co-operative conditions in existence in the Persian Corridor. Therefore, General Greely had to go, and events had to unroll more slowly." [2]

The second episode, which also occurred in 1942, concerned an appointment that was canceled when Marshall became convinced that his prospective appointee would work poorly with officers of another nationality. The question arose during the summer, when General MacArthur suggested that the time had probably come to form an American corps headquarters in the Southwest Pacific. General Marshall agreed and suggested for its commander Major General Robert C. Richardson, Jr., a senior officer who had handled War Department press relations and was then on a trip to the Southwest Pacific. Richardson, noted for his firm opinions, soon balked at the suggestion that he serve under Australian General Thomas A. Blamey, MacArthur's Allied Land Forces commander. Richardson indicated that Blamey was not capable of handling such an assignment and hinted that the arrangement would be unacceptable to the American public once it became known. Marshall retorted that under the circumstances Richardson was not the proper man for the command. When the officer showed signs of reconsidering, Marshall declined to listen and instead suggested to MacArthur the name of Major General Robert L. Eichelberger. Although Richardson later complained that Marshall refused to hear his arguments, he fared better than Greely, getting the important Hawaiian Command. [3]

These and other reliefs or reprimands were balanced by advancement and high praise for officers who worked well with other services and other nationalities. Taking to heart Marshall's insistence on cooperating closely with Allies, Eisenhower and Bradley were rewarded with new responsibilities and increased rank.

A third case history illustrates how Marshall kept his eye on those who demonstrated loyalty and capability. In 1941 Major General Daniel Van Voorhis, head of the Caribbean Defense Command, set up by General Marshall to provide greater unity in that area, irritated the Chief of Staff by his disagreements with the Air Forces commander, Major General Frank M. Andrews. Despite Marshall's earlier warning that coordination with the Army Air Forces was exceedingly important and required "very special treatment" and that he had sent Andrews so that "a very competent man" would be available for that purpose, Van Voorhis continued to differ with his colleague. When Andrews finally convinced the Chief of Staff that Van Voorhis was improperly handling air matters, Marshall shifted the Caribbean commander to the Fifth Corps Area and appointed Andrews as his successor.[4]

The death of General Andrews in May 1943 in an air crash near Iceland at a crucial period in the conflict was both a public and a personal tragedy for Marshall. When Marshall came to the War Department as Chief of War Plans, in the fall of 1938, Andrews was commander of General Headquarters Air Force, as a temporary major general. Marshall was deeply grateful to Andrews for his efforts to acquaint him with the role of airpower. On becoming Chief of Staff, in 1939, Marshall sent for Andrews, who had reverted to his permanent rank of colonel after completing his tour of duty at GHQ Air Force. He made Andrews a brigadier general and appointed him Chief of the G-3 Division. Andrews won Marshall's respect by his ability to work with ground-force officers. Following his tour in the Caribbean Defense Command, Andrews was sent, in turn, to the Middle East Command and then to the European Theater, where his death occurred.

In later years friends of Andrews speculated that Marshall, believing that the war in Europe would be largely fought in the air, had deliberately assigned the airman a number of difficult tasks with the aim of preparing him to lead the invasion of the Continent. But when asked in 1957 if he had been deliberately building Andrews up for the European command, Marshall denied that this had been his specific intention. Instead he had been testing him in many positions, promoting him as he showed that he could handle the responsibilities entrusted to him. "If he had not succeeded, he would not have advanced," the Chief of Staff declared.

Marshall's close personal interest in field commanders continued throughout the war. Although he relied heavily on Arnold, McNair, and Somervell for recommendations on commanders in their particular jurisdictions, he kept his own book on performances. In addition to officers such as Bradley, Patton, Stilwell, Collins, and Clark, with whose careers he had been familiar over the years, he watched others whom he saw on maneuvers or at special inspections. After a number of officers had gained experience in the field in the Pacific and North Africa, he agreed with the theater commanders that their top officers should be men who had proved their mettle in combat. In time he directed that no man should lead a corps in action who had not had battle experience. By 1944 Marshall was insisting that at least 50 per cent of the vacancies in junior-officer ranks should be filled by direct commissioning of outstanding noncommissioned officers.

As he went through the lists he had solicited, his sharp eye caught names of men of whose past records he disapproved. On one occasion he overruled promotion for a colonel who had disclosed details of an approaching attack in a letter to his wife. The officer had made retribution certain by saying that he hoped his letter would not be checked by the censor or he would be in trouble. In another case Marshall wrote caustically to Eisenhower that a colonel he had proposed for brigadier-general rank had once been relieved from regimental command for maltreatment of his men. Later the same officer, when reproved for giving classified information to civilians, had replied flamboyantly, "The redundant phrases of the administrative reprimand may be a delight to War Department clerks but they choke with disgust a field soldier." For this he received a reprimand, about which Marshall wrote: "Incidentally, this last did not come to my attention or it would have been something other than a reprimand. Do you still feel that this man should be honored with high command?" In both cases the sponsoring commanders reiterated the request for promotion. The first was never approved; the second ultimately was.

Two letters, taken at random, show General Marshall's sympathies with officers and men who had received less than their due. He wrote Bedell Smith in the spring of 1943 of the brother of an old friend—with distinguished family connections—who had enlisted in the Canadian Army at the age of forty and then had transferred to the United States Army in 1942. He asked Smith to check on the case, adding: "I do this because it is a blessed relief to find a man of his years and background who is apparently cheerfully serving in a lowly status and not stirring up pressures to win for himself preferential treatment." [5]

A few days earlier he had written feelingly of Major General George Grunert, who, because he was filling a secret assignment in connection with mobilization planning, appeared to his friends to have been demoted. At the moment there was nothing Marshall could say publicly, but at least he could set the record straight: "Grunert has had some very hard knocks and has taken them all in a most soldierly fashion; his being superseded in the Philippines by MacArthur and his return to the States; his relief from an Army Corps because of age; his withdrawal from a Corps Area Command and its independence because . . . his services were more important here . . . and now, so far as his friends can see, he is dropped out of a high level position into something else which he cannot even talk about." [6]

Critics sometimes charged that Marshall made snap judgments on officers who were lucky enough to impress him on one occasion and thereafter never measured up to his expectations. His personal files show that his views on subordinates were by no means static. One division commander whose rise was due to his adept handling of a particular situation that Marshall observed made the mistake of overpublicizing his activities. When he forwarded the third folder of unit newspapers devoted to his exploits, the Chief of Staff marked through a letter of congratulations drafted by his staff, grimly commenting that the man engaged in too much self-advertisement. The officer kept his command, but he never went higher. After learning that an officer whose advancement he had backed had been lobbying for promotion, Marshall curtly voiced his disenchantment: "Unfortunately after a time ambition set in and he became too much concerned with his own career." Still another drew disapproval because the man's wife had become demanding and dictatorial after her husband's promotion. "Unfortunately," he observed, "I had not seen her before I pushed him up and she caused a great deal of trouble with other wives."

In only a few cases did Marshall reject the recommendations of a theater commander. He queried Eisenhower when he listed Patton, Third Army commander, for an extra star ahead of the 6th Army Group commander, Devers. Marshall made clear that if this went through, he would have to relieve Devers since Patton's promotion under the circumstances would destroy the former's usefulness.

Roosevelt's personal dislike for certain officers sometimes embarrassed the War Department. Deeply angered by the strong isolationist campaign carried on before Pearl Harbor by Charles Lindbergh, a Reserve colonel in the Air Corps, the President opposed the flier's request to go on active duty after war was declared. General Arnold, head of the Army Air Forces, was convinced that he badly needed the airman's experience and advice, and with Marshall's knowledge he arranged to use Lindbergh as a consultant.

Indirectly tied to the Lindbergh episode was the case of Colonel Truman Smith. Smith, who had been an instructor under Marshall at Fort Benning, continued as military attaché in Berlin in the 1930s to keep in touch with the future Chief of Staff. He correctly forecast German preparations for war and German strength. But he fell afoul of the White House and American public opinion by arranging for Lindbergh to be received by German Air Marshal Hermann Göring and to inspect German airplane factories, on a visit culminating with the American flier's acceptance of a German decoration for his air exploits.[7]

Retired from active duty for health reasons not long before Pearl Harbor, Smith was called back by Marshall soon after the war began. Like most of the G-2 officers who dealt with European matters, Smith was strongly impressed by German power. He and his colleagues doubted the staying qualities of the Soviet Union. At a point when it appeared that Britain might lose the Middle East and Russia might be defeated, Stimson directed the Intelligence Division to cease circulation of its pessimistic reports. Marshall hotly defended his experts and in time persuaded Stimson to help him support Smith at the White House. Despite these efforts Marshall concluded that it would be impossible to get approval for general-officer rank for Smith. Completely confident of the G-2 officer's ability, Marshall told him in the fall of 1943 that if he went to London, he wanted him there on his staff. He kept the colonel in his War Department billet until the war's end and saw that he was decorated for his work. Learning that Smith could not earn proper retirement credit unless he served until the following year, the Chief of Staff arranged for him to be held on active duty until 1946.

Aware of Roosevelt's deep antipathy for members of the America First movement, which until Pearl Harbor had fiercely opposed the administration's aid to Britain and the Soviet Union, General Marshall usually kept the White House informed when he made use of men who had been active isolationists. Thus, when Major General Robert E. Wood, head of Sears, Roebuck and a leading figure in the America First Committee, was called on to handle major supply problems, the Chief of Staff informed Roosevelt, adding that Wood was doing an excellent job. There is no record of a reply.

Although fully cognizant of the important role played by National Guard officers and willing to make use of those whose experience had prepared them for high-level command, Marshall and Stimson were averse to placing units in the field under any National Guardsmen whose chief service had been in politics. One of Marshall's tasks during the war lay in finding posts for such commanders where they could contribute to the war effort without running the risk of failure in combat. He agonized over some reliefs, recognizing the terrible blow they inflicted on the officers involved. To a former major general who lost his divisional command, he wrote: "I can thoroughly understand, I think, your feelings in the matter and I regretted throughout the period of hostilities that such action had to be taken from time to time in the public interest. War is terrible at best and the battle losses can never be recovered, but sometimes I think it is harder to bear your particular loss than any other." [8]

The Chief of Staff was not always sympathetic. One Regular Army officer relieved in Europe undertook a fight for reinstatement, even forwarding letters from civilians abroad testifying to his ability. Marshall dismissed his plea, saying later, "Can you imagine him asking for references from local French officials?" Although he was often caustic in regard to those who pressed too hard for vindication, he had a soft place in his heart for those who survived reprimands. When George Patton, who had come near relief in the spring of 1944 for his ill-considered remarks at a meeting in Great Britain, drove forward to Bastogne near Christmas 1944, Marshall watched his progress with delight. "Don't you love to see a man come rushing out of a doghouse?" he asked Colonel Oveta Culp Hobby.[9]

In promoting and assigning officers Marshall usually had the sympathetic backing of the President. But occasionally, when personal or political factors were involved, both the Chief of Staff and the Secretary of War felt the pressure of the White House.

In one instance—concerning the appointment of the Surgeon General of the Army—Marshall felt that President Roosevelt's physician, Rear Admiral Ross T. McIntire, was interfering. "This I am determinedly opposed to," he wrote Pershing.[10] With Stimson's help Marshall was able to block the redetail of the officer favored by the White House.

A fantastic, and protracted, tug-of-war resulted when Roosevelt proposed to commission Mayor Fiorello H. La Guardia of New York a general and send him to Eisenhower's headquarters as an expert in the field of military government. The episode provides an instructive study of the means by which Stimson and Marshall could occasionally outmaneuver the President on a proposal that they considered unwise.

A member of the House of Representatives when World War I began, La Guardia had gone into the Aviation Service, finishing the conflict as a major in command of the small U.S. air force on the Italian front. Shortly after La Guardia returned to his seat in Congress and served there until his defeat in 1933. A year later he was elected mayor of New York, an office he filled with great energy and ability. A vigorous and vocal opponent of fascism, he served for a time as chairman of the U.S. Section of the Canada–U.S. Joint Board of Defense and then as director of the Office of Civilian Defense. In addition he was an effective antifascist propagandist, broadcasting numerous speeches to Italy. Once Eisenhower had gone into North Africa, the mayor made strenuous efforts to get an assignment to his headquarters.

There was no question of La Guardia's qualifications for a role in military government or psychological warfare. But the Army saw other factors to consider. His waspish tongue and hot temper had angered many. As one of the top political figures in the country, he could be difficult to hold in check in an Allied military command. In addition both Stimson and Marshall firmly opposed giving direct general-officer rank to civilians.

General Marshall was brought into the discussion late in 1942, when La Guardia proposed that he and a small staff be assigned to Eisenhower's headquarters to coordinate various groups currently engaged in propaganda and psychological warfare. Seeing La Guardia's point, the Chief of Staff suggested to Eisenhower that such a move "might be a decided asset to you and at the same time relieve other members of your staff of the annoyance, confusion and loss of time attendant upon the activities of a number of semi-independent civilian agencies now in your area or about to descend upon you, such as FCC [Federal Communications Commission], OWI [Office of War Information], BEW [Bureau of Economic Warfare], Red Cross, etc." However, before acting, he asked for Eisenhower's reaction to La Guardia and to the principle that all U.S. civilian agencies in the area be put under one man.[11]

The Allied commander was less than enthusiastic about the proposal. He considered it inadvisable to complicate his staff problems by bringing in the New York mayor. No one could serve as head of his civil-affairs section who had not lived through "the hectic experiences of the past few weeks," he wrote Marshall. Also he thought that the role of the State Department's Robert Murphy in the preinvasion negotiations and the period immediately following the landing made it unjustifiable to relegate him to a subordinate position. At the same time Eisenhower saw considerable merit in organizing the various propaganda and psychological-warfare units in the United States under one man. "The idea of a single staff authority over the whole gang is eminently sound and I want them all to understand it before coming over." [12]

The matter was additionally complicated because of the disagreement between the British and the Americans over the nature of control of civil affairs in operations that might be directed against Italian-held territories after the completion of operations in Tunisia. Even the President was not certain how far he wanted to go in this matter. When, near Christmas, the New York mayor submitted a plan for control of propaganda and civil affairs in the next phase of Mediterranean operations, the President replied that he would delay any action on the proposal (and apparently on the appointment of La Guardia) for a long time.[13]

La Guardia continued to press his cause, appealing to Harry Hopkins for assistance with the President. On March 16, 1943, the mayor saw Roosevelt, who indicated that he would be commissioned in April and assigned to Eisenhower's staff. But there was still the matter of a physical examination and a possible waiver of any physical disabilities. Not wishing to bring up these details with Stimson or Marshall, the President's Army aide, Major General Edwin M. ("Pa") Watson, tried one of his occasional "end run plays." Apparently hoping to flatter one of Marshall's aides into evading the technicalities without going through channels, Watson confided to Colonel McCarthy, Marshall's Secretary General Staff, that the President had personally asked that he handle La Guardia's induction into the service. He said that the affair had already been arranged with Eisenhower but should be kept very quiet. "P.S. I told President you would handle it." But McCarthy had learned earlier that attempts to bypass Marshall merely led eventually to greater difficulties. He checked with Leahy in an effort to get a more specific directive from Roosevelt. When the Admiral said that he did not want to raise the matter again, McCarthy suggested to Marshall that they draft a letter for Stimson to send the President asking exactly what he had in mind.[14] The White

House's hopes for an easy solution of the problem were shattered. Stimson and Marshall were now directly involved.

Soon after his return to Washington on March 24 Stimson grumbled because the President, knowing the Secretary's opposition to commissioning men from political life, had taken advantage of his absence to sound out Eisenhower on the appointment. The General, who obviously did not want the mayor on his staff at that time, agreed to take him in uniform. Although displeased by the action, Stimson recorded on the twenty-seventh that he felt less depressed than some of his colleagues because the mayor, despite his terrible tongue and temper, was "a pretty efficient little man." [15]

The President told Marshall shortly afterward that he had "cleared" the La Guardia business with Eisenhower and that he wanted the mayor given a physical examination with a view to commissioning him. To make certain that Roosevelt was aware of Eisenhower's real attitude toward such an appointment, the Chief of Staff reviewed the correspondence for the President in December. "Churned up" over the transaction, General Marshall discussed it at the White House on the twenty-sixth at "the tail end of an overtime interview." Next day he wrote Assistant Secretary of War John J. McCloy some of his objections:

> I felt that under present circumstances La Guardia would provide nothing but confusion to the situation in Africa. In the first place he cannot touch propaganda because that is definitely under OWI by a recent Executive Order. In the next place, we are in a discussion now with the British in which the President takes the stand that when we go into Sicily all matters of a civil nature will be handled by a Joint British-American group without chairmanship, but merely under Eisenhower. The British feel that this is, by the President's own proposal, a British sphere of influence, at least of military responsibility. The exception in the North African set-up was made for the purpose of reducing the probability of French resistance to the landing and to the establishment of control in Morocco and Algiers. In the forthcoming affair, there is no question involved of reducing resistance. The matter under discussion is the method of organization after we take over.[16]

Despite Roosevelt's wish to give La Guardia one-star rank, the Chief of Staff held firm to a colonelcy. The New York mayor, while vowing that the rank made no difference and that he was willing to go as a cook in a stevedore regiment, was soon "kicking like a steer" for general's rank, according to Stimson. At the month's end Marshall informed members of his staff that the President had approved a colonelcy for La Guardia, adding that he would go to the Military Government school at Charlottesville, Virginia, for six weeks. On being told of this decision, La Guardia asked how soon he could go to North Africa.[17] Clearly he saw no need for additional schooling. This reaction was to be expected of a man who had long headed one of the great cities of the world. It must have been apparent to Marshall and Stimson that if they made the school requirement stick and offered nothing more than the colonelcy, he was likely to change his mind.

Then Stimson tackled La Guardia on April 6 and hurt the Mayor's feelings—an outcome that Stimson blamed on "the weakness and happy-go-luckiness of the President." He told La Guardia that he could be a propagandist or a soldier but not both. He proposed that the New Yorker remain as mayor and continue to broadcast appeals to the Italians. When La Guardia insisted that Eisenhower had asked for him, Stimson told him that he was mistaken. He made clear that the matter of rank had been left up to the War Department and that Marshall had decided that the colonelcy was the top opening possible.[18]

Much upset over La Guardia's report of developments, the President called Marshall next day. A short time later he chided Stimson for being too hard on the "Little Flower." Marshall felt they should hold firm on a colonelcy and a short stay at Charlottesville.

Despite Stimson's arguments La Guardia again approached the White House in mid-April, leading Hopkins to ask the President to consult Stimson and Marshall once more. Roosevelt must have concluded that he had been outmaneuvered and decided for the moment to let the matter drop. At least it did not reappear during the ensuing campaign in Sicily and southern Italy. But the idea of a commission was not permanently shelved. In early September 1944 the President—probably at La Guardia's urging—suggested that the mayor be sent, in Army or Navy uniform, to the Pacific as an expert on civil affairs. It is uncertain whether the matter had been cleared with MacArthur. Marshall passed the proposal on to Stimson with the observation, "I share your belief that we now have no firm ground on which to oppose Mayor La Guardia's entry into the Army." He did suggest that it would make relations with Congress better if the mayor entered the service as an Army colonel or Navy captain rather than as brigadier general or admiral. Next day when the President suggested that a general's commission would be preferable, Stimson countered with a warning about the difficulties that might arise because of La Guardia's temper. Apparently Roosevelt gave up at this point; at least no commission was issued to the mayor. Months later he received an appointment dealing with civil affairs—but as director general of the United Nations Relief and Rehabilitation Administration.[19]

The question of rank was again raised when the well-known Broadway producer Billy Rose asked for an Army commission. He would have certainly been satisfied with a more modest rank than La Guardia wanted, but Marshall was less generous in his case. Writing General Osborn, the Chief of the Morale Branch, that Rose wanted major's rank, he said: "I directed he be given the commission of Captain . . . and I now understand that he has declined to accept that. . . . I have felt that with his talents he could . . . [help organize] entertainment. . . . If he places rank as of such importance . . . I have no further interest in the matter." [20]

Another embarrassing situation arose when Associate Justice Frank Murphy of the Supreme Court requested temporary Reserve duty outside the United States during the recess of the court. General Marshall was quite willing to arrange an assignment for a high ranking Reserve officer who had served as governor of Michigan, high commissioner of the Philippines, and attorney general of the United States before going on the Supreme Court. Assignment had been easier in 1942 when Murphy asked merely to go to maneuvers in the United States. In March 1943, however, he proposed that he go to the Pacific. Marshall suggested that Murphy consider Alaska, the Aleutians, or Hawaii but questioned a proposed assignment to Australia in view of "his feelings regarding MacArthur while he was High Commissioner." [21]

Marshall's reaction settled the question for several months, but Murphy renewed his request in September, saying that he would have "no inward peace until I am a soldier in action once more." Marshall expressed appreciation of the justice's feelings, but added: "One of the most difficult things I have had to do is to subordinate my personal desires to the impartial administration of the established War Department policies." [22]

In the spring of 1944 Murphy appealed again to the President and to Marshall. This time he suggested that he could be helpful in Mindanao in working with Philippine guerrillas. General Marshall objected to this since the MacArthur-Murphy relationship would still be involved, but he grounded his refusal on the basis of security. It would be impossible to keep the justice's presence a secret, he argued, and it would be unwise to focus Japanese attention on an area to which the United States did not wish to call attention.

At the same time Marshall turned down Murphy's alternative proposal for the Italian theater: "As a matter of protection to the theater commanders, who are actively engaged in combat with the enemy, I have firmly opposed the idea of high government officials, including one or two of the Secretary of War's assistants, making visits to the combat area. . . . Despite General Crittenberger's desire to have you, I must be consistent in my policy and tell you that from the point of view of the War Department it would be embarrassing to us for you to go Italy at this time." This settled the matter, as Murphy in his final request had anticipated Marshall's reply by saying, "I know full well that military considerations must come first and personal hopes of an old soldier, like myself, must yield to them." [23]

Other political figures sought to go back into military service as Reserve officers but on a different basis from Murphy's. Senator Harry S. Truman, of Missouri, a field-artillery captain in France in World War I, who had kept his Reserve commission up to date, beseeched Marshall early in the war to call him to active duty. President Truman later related with great delight that the Chief of Staff had told him that he was "too damned old." When Truman remonstrated that Marshall was several years older, the Chief of Staff insisted that the senator was of greater value to the Army in his post as chairman of the Special Committee to Investigate the National Defense Program. Rather than irritating Truman, the incident strengthened his admiration of Marshall.

In the case of Senator Henry Cabot Lodge of Massachusetts, also a Reserve officer, Marshall agreed early in 1942 that he might make a special tour of duty with a U.S. tank unit attached to British units in Libya. This arrangement, while not usual, required only a short absence from the Senate. Lodge's observations were helpful to the Army, and his experience proved valuable later in his dealings with Army measures in the upper house. Re-elected in November 1942, Lodge resigned his Senate seat in early 1944 and went on active duty. With his youthful schooling in France and his thorough knowledge of the French language, he performed invaluable services as the 6th Army Group's liaison officer with the First French Army.

Soon after the Selective Service Act came into effect, Dr. Douglas S. Freeman, editor of the Richmond *News Leader* and biographer of Lee, wrote Marshall "that if worse comes to worst, and if you need any one who could recall the experiences of the Union and Confederate Armies in planning or in administration, you have only to call on me." Marshall suggested in reply that he observe the reception of the first selectees at concentration centers and report his observations to the country in several radio addresses. Dr. Freeman did not show interest in the project, and nothing came of the proposal. However shortly after the war began, Freeman—then fifty-five—said that if Marshall ever needed him, "I will quit all my jobs at any time for military service in any capacity that I can be useful." Again officers in the War Department misunderstood, and it was suggested to Marshall that the famous biographer might be interested in helping the Historical Section of the Army "commence a current collation of source material on the present war" in order to avoid a repetition of the situation regarding World War I, on which that section was still compiling data! A commission of lieutenant colonel for Freeman was held out as a possibility. Marshall correctly foresaw that the writer might not find the prospect interesting.

It was not until the summer of 1943, however, that Marshall realized that the student of the campaigns of Lee and Jackson hoped for a staff position in a foreign theater of the war.[24] In August 1943 Freeman told him that he had been invited to London by the British and that he hoped while there to persuade General Devers to give him "a job in the Intelligence Office at General Headquarters, England," a proposal he asked Marshall to look on "leniently and favorably." The Chief of Staff was noncommittal although he promised to keep Freeman in mind if General

Devers needed him in the United Kingdom.[25] Perhaps Freeman knew that there was no chance of his getting a staff role in a combat theater. At all events he accepted Marshall's reaction graciously, saying only at the end of 1943, when Eisenhower's appointment as Supreme Commander was made known, that he had hoped that if Marshall took that command "you would find a place for me, over there."

In instances involving relatives of the President and General Pershing, the Chief of Staff was pleased that his advice against special favors was followed. When President Roosevelt proposed his son-in-law, John Boettiger, for a colonel's post in military government in Italy, Marshall suggested that he go in as a captain, the rank usually given to men of his age and background, and work his way up to the higher rank. Boettiger agreed and advanced in the Chief of Staff's estimation.

In contrast, in the summer of 1944 Marshall recoiled when Lieutenant General Carl Spaatz, commanding general of U.S. Air Forces, Europe, recommended Elliott Roosevelt for general-officer rank. Recalling the blast of criticism when the President's son was given a direct commission earlier in the war, Marshall declined to consider it "in view of the inevitable reactions on the eve of the presidential election." In mid-January 1945 the President personally made the request. Marshall sent the name forward to Stimson to place on the next promotion list, with a terse note: "His command justifies the rank." [26]

There was no problem concerning Warren Pershing, only son of the World War I American Expeditionary Force commander. Marshall had known Warren since 1919 when the boy of ten had joined his father in France at the end of the war. Marshall had kept in touch with Warren while serving as the elder Pershing's aide. In World War II, when Warren said that he wished to enter the Army, Marshall suggested that he enter under the volunteer program whereby married men could go into basic training and then to Officer Candidate School. He made clear that Warren, as son of the General of the Armies, could have a direct commission, but he was gratified to have the young man accept the course proposed. He offered to help Warren to get into an officers' school of his choice. That the younger Pershing chose the School of Combat Engineers, a branch equal to the infantry in toughness and in danger, strengthened the Chief of Staff's position in denying special favors to others.

At the beginning of Marshall's tour of duty, Army public-relations activities were still under the G-2 Division, as they had been since World War I. In July 1940 a Press Relations Bureau was set up under Major Ward Maris, who was directly responsible to the Deputy Chief of Staff for Operations, Major General William Bryden. This bureau controlled information for the War Department; information on units outside Washington still came under G-2. It became evident that something more elaborate than the old system was needed in the fall of 1940 when the passage of the Selective Service Act aroused great opposition in the United States. Secretary Stimson and General Marshall became convinced of the need for supplying more information on Army activities to the nation's newspapers. Secretary Stimson concluded that he must have a War Department Bureau of Public Relations directly under his control. On February 11, 1941, he named Major General Robert C. Richardson, Jr., commander of the 1st Cavalry Division, to head the bureau and authorized him to set up sections to deal with the press, radio, magazines, movies and photographs, press analysis, and the like. Stimson himself inaugurated a regular weekly news conference, held each Thursday.[27]

Richardson, a forceful personality, sought advice from public-relations experts in New York and recruited a number of experienced newsmen for his new bureau. At the beginning of August 1941 he returned to a field command, as he had requested when first assigned to the bureau, and was succeeded by Brigadier General Alexander Surles, who served in the post until the war's end.[28]

While press relations came directly under the Secretary of War and most of the regular press conferences were held by him, Marshall helped draft many of Stimson's statements or furnished copious material for his use. In addition he kept Surles's in-box filled with suggestions on ways to present the Army's story more effectively. Some days he behaved like the publisher of a large daily, sending down crisp memos on achievements by a courageous individual or brilliant performances by a particular division.

Marshall also kept the theater commanders alert to publicity topics, particularly if he had a specific project in mind. Deciding midway in the war that the Marine and Navy bands had too long dominated the martial-music scene in Washington and the nation, he directed the organization of a first-rank Army band and asked that a special effort be made to get it recognized in the press. After a time he sent the band to Europe, charging Bedell Smith with the task of advertising it by getting engagements for it in the United Kingdom and elsewhere, and he complained to him periodically that no one seemed to know that the band was there.[29]

At one point during the war in North Africa, Marshall became seriously concerned over the strong anti-British sentiment he perceived in the Army and among civilians in the United States. Near the end of February 1943, in a gesture that revealed a depth of sympathy and sense of justice far outweighing his own occasional antagonistic reactions, he wrote his Public Relations chief:

> There continues to be an insidious business of stirring up ill-feeling between the British and us. . . . I think we should take more positive measures to offset this. Merely disputing the justifications for this or that attack gets us nowhere because the poison spreads.
> It occurred to me that if you could arrange to have a short article written on the subject of, say, "Courage and Sacrifice," along the following lines it might

make a profound impression to offset the littleness of irritations and jealousies which destroy teamwork between the two nations:

A very brief summary of the British ordeal from Dunkirk through the Battle of Britain, the fall of Singapore and the disaster in Libya of last June.

Follow this with a generalization on the sacrifices that have been made by the high, the middle, and the low, particularly the families of the dock workers who were subjected to terrific bombing in London.

This work is a summary of the losses suffered by families in high places commencing with the Duke of Kent, elaborating on the case of Lord and Lady Halifax who had one son killed some time ago, another killed in the successful fighting on the Alamein line—where Lord Halifax had to appear at a dinner on the same day he received the news of the loss of his son and Lady Halifax also had to subject herself to official meetings within a few days of this tragic news. More recently a third son has lost both legs in an explosion of a mine during the pursuit of Rommel. Again you find Lord and Lady Halifax quietly doing their duty without a word. At the same time these attacks on Great Britain are in progress, and American soldiers in this country are being stirred to a contempt for the British.

Air Marshal Tedder who has just been put in charge of the Mediterranean Air Force under Eisenhower has lost a son and within the last three months lost his wife in an air crash at Bengasi—she had flown there from Cairo to organize relief work.

I feel certain that the British could give you other examples of losses suffered by families in high places and the whole certainly would make a most impressive story without the necessity of any reference to the critical attitude in this country towards the British and their fighting capacities.[30]

Perhaps prompted by Surles—after Marshall had asked him why more publicity had not been gained for outstanding actions overseas—the Chief of Staff on several occasions pointedly demanded of General Eisenhower or General MacArthur why they had not given greater play in press reports to certain units. His dissatisfaction with coverage in the Pacific came to a head in the fall of 1944 after he had asked *Time* magazine to do a special story on the fighting along the northern coast of New Guinea. Feeling that this sector was being neglected in favor of operations on Guam and Saipan, he had proposed an article describing the nature of the New Guinea campaign—the great distances covered, the domination established over the Japanese, and the small number of casualties suffered. "I could not get an article of the character desired," he declared to MacArthur. "All of which leads me to this suggestion, that your public relations people give us more names, otherwise you can expect much less of desirable credits for your command than would otherwise be the case." He commented that he had found it necessary to take the same line with commanders in France and Italy, where "the results have been quite remarkable but the releases were not given over there until I pressed them in the interest of general morale of the troops themselves who follow the accounts so carefully." [31]

Hand in hand with the selection and training of officers and men went the task of persuading Congress to pass legislation needed to get military manpower, production of arms and materiel, military facilities, and the like. Marshall was his own best advocate in dealing with Congress. He already had an assured reputation for persuasive presentations before congressional committees, particularly in the period before Pearl Harbor. His efforts were reinforced by a brilliant Legislative and Liaison Division staff that had developed. When Stimson succeeded Harry H. Woodring as Secretary of War in 1940, General Marshall transferred to his own office Colonel Wilton B. Persons, who had handled congressional liaison for the Assistant Secretary of War and then for Woodring since 1934. An Alabamian, Persons had a diplomat's skill and the ability to lose himself in his superior's cause, which made him highly effective in working both for General Marshall and, subsequently, for General Eisenhower, as it had in his earlier service.

"General Marshall's instructions to me were brief," General Persons recalled thirty years later. "I was to keep in mind that he was somewhat closed in by the four walls of his office and that he depended on me to bring directly to him everything of importance that occurred on Capitol Hill which might affect the Army." Persons was also expected to inform the Secretary of War and the Deputy Chief of Staff of matters that affected them. By reporting to Marshall each morning, unless a question had to go to him at once, Persons kept his chief thoroughly aware of the temper of Congress.[32] Careful biographical sheets were drawn up on key members of the two houses, and an analysis was made of their attitudes toward the Army, their pet projects, and their backgrounds. It was thus possible for Marshall and his staff to be aware of subtle undertones of opinion in approaching individual congressmen and committees.[33]

In obtaining appropriations the Chief of Staff was aided by a skilled Budget Division, headed throughout the war by Brigadier General George J. Richards, a classmate of Eisenhower and Bradley at West Point. Following General Marshall's practice of candor with members of Congress, Richards developed excellent relations with such key members of House and Senate appropriations committees as Clarence Cannon and George Mahon in the Lower House and Kenneth McKellar in the Senate.

Both the liaison and budget officers, while eager to satisfy the wishes of congressional leaders, did not sway with every political breeze. They were aware that General Marshall would not hand over secret documents on demand to powerful senators and that he would not reshape Army programs to suit the political pressures of leaders on the Hill. As a realist, Marshall was willing to bend to political requirements if the location of a camp was equally satisfactory in Arkansas or Tennessee, but he refused to shift an Army facility or a division simply because the move would aid a deserving Democrat over a Republican opponent. The War Department succeeded in this policy because it obviously refused to play politics and because members of Congress agreed with Marshall that the main objective was to win the war. In taking this determined stand, he nonetheless satisfied most congressmen that the Army was attentive to the wishes of Congress as a whole and that it recognized civilian control. But once given the task of carrying out a certain policy, Marshall believed that he had his own obligations to the state.[34]

In speaking later of the General's influence with Congress, Speaker Sam Rayburn declared: "He has the presence of a great man. He doesn't dissemble. (If a man dissembles before the House of Representatives, he is ruined. The committees have no respect for that kind of man.) Marshall was simple, able, candid. He laid it on the line. He would tell the truth even if it hurt his cause. Congress always respected him. They would give him things they would give no one else." [35]

Representative Emanuel Celler voiced a typical congressional reaction late in 1943 after General Marshall had given one of his periodic briefings to members of Congress. Celler wrote: "I was indeed much impressed with your statement this morning. . . . I am sure that I and my colleagues will back you to the hilt." Thanking him for his gracious note, the Chief of Staff replied: "It is very reassuring to me. My experience has been that where the opportunity was presented for expressing matters to the Congress invariably I receive strong backing. The difficulty of the past, particularly before we entered the war, was the fact that much of what we knew, for several sound reasons, could not be declared, all of which proved a great embarrassment in getting forward with our program." [36] Marshall had hit the salient point with his emphasis on freedom to explain fully. It was there that he stood out among all his military colleagues. Harvey H. Bundy, one of Stimson's special assistants, expressed it this way: "I think he [Marshall] had great analytical powers. . . . I think he had great clarity of expression. . . . He was a great Army officer. He knew his stuff. I don't know how to explain it, but when Marshall spoke, when Marshall decided, I had a strong feeling that men around him said, 'That's it.' . . . I have heard him talk . . . and he was a very great advocate, I thought, largely because he just knew his stuff. As a human being he was a most disarming man." [37]

Another staff member, General Osborn, who watched Marshall in action during the war and later in the State Department, put it even more strongly:

> I was at Princeton when Woodrow Wilson was President [there]. My family and I knew him quite well. And I knew Theodore Roosevelt, because he was a friend of the family since [I was] a small boy. . . . And I knew Franklin Roosevelt well, and I knew Grover Cleveland very well (his daughters were just my age and he had retired and lived in Princeton) . . . [but] I never had any such impression from any of them as I always had of General Marshall. I had always the sense that I was in the presence of a man who was altogether my superior [in character and intellect] . . . and in the clarity and lucidity of his mind and his tremendous control over himself, and his tremendous determination. When he came to the conclusion that something should be done, he said it with such a firmness and with such a solidity that you just agreed with him.

You knew he was right. . . . There was something that gave you a tremendous sense of loyalty to his purposes and a desire to help him fulfill his purposes and also gave you a standard of conduct to aim at, just as Mr. Stimson did. . . . General Marshall had not only that standard of character but an ability to express it that Mr. Stimson lacked entirely. General Marshall was a very, very powerful and moving speaker. I heard Woodrow Wilson at his best. I heard William Jennings Bryan at almost his best, but none of them could hold a candle to General Marshall when he wanted to make people do things.[38]

In 1956, speaking of his experiences with Congress, General Marshall observed that between wars the military committees of Congress were often severe in their criticism of the Army, and War Department officials didn't protect their representatives. "I felt that the War Department didn't show any backbone at all. This is rather embarrassing for me because it seems immodest but I swore when I got up there that I wasn't going to have any of that damn business, and I carried the flag when we went before the committees of Congress and I just wouldn't swallow the stuff they were trying to put out. . . . There is bound to be deterioration [in the staff] where there is no active responsibility." He contrasted his position as Chief of Staff with that of his successors in the postwar period: "He [the Chief of Staff] has so many over him—I don't know how many assistant secretaries he's got, undersecretaries and secretaries, and his power is so reduced that he is kept busy explaining things. He just isn't able to stride into Congress and defend himself." [39]

Marshall's skill in dealing with Congress was matched by his ability to win the respect of leading industrialists. In one sense the forging of the relationship between the armed forces and industry that a later generation came to know as the "military-industrial complex" developed to a great degree in World War II. One of the prominent leaders in this development in the 1939–40 period was General Marshall.[40]

The cooperation of business and military leaders goes back, of course, to the beginning of modern technology. Since the Civil War and the Franco-Prussian War, the steel manufacturer, the railroad manager, and the purveyor of armaments and materiel have had to work together in wartime. Adequate food supplies, arms, and transportation helped make victory possible for the North in the Civil War. Although U.S. industry fell below hoped-for rates of production of arms for the Army's use in World War I, it was instrumental in equipping a large expeditionary force. In the period between the two world wars there was sufficient activity by American shipbuilders and manufacturers of ammunition and rifles for several to be condemned along with Krupp, Skoda, and others as "merchants of death."

The Great Depression and its accompanying development of antibusiness sentiment, the prolabor policy of the Roosevelt administration, and a general antiwar feeling in the late 1930s all made business extremely reluctant to go into large-scale production of materiel for the armed forces.

Fear by Roosevelt-haters that he would use a war situation to gain strong government control over factories and profits drove many businessmen into the powerful America First movement as Europe drifted toward war.

Despite this deep distrust among some business leaders many others in the late 1930s and early 1940s were prepared to work with the armed forces. The first step in the War Department was apparently taken by Assistant Secretary of War Louis A. Johnson, who approached Charles R. Hook, head of the Armco Steel Corporation, of Middletown, Ohio, and president of the National Association of Manufacturers, with the suggestion that he appoint a small committee to discuss defense needs with the service secretaries, General Marshall, Admiral Harold R. Stark, and other officials in Washington. Hook appointed two friends, Frederick V. Geier of the Cincinnati Milling Machine Company and James Francis, president of the Island Creek Coal Company, Charleston, West Virginia, to work with him.

Years after the first meeting of the committee in Washington, on the morning of November 2, 1939, Geier described the impact of the Chief of Staff's personality:

> He had no work papers on the desk, his mind was apparently completely free and open to attack a new subject, completely uncluttered, unhurried, or unhastened, and he showed a very keen interest in the viewpoint that we expressed, that here was industry about to make itself available in whatever problems [were to come]. He took out of his desk some papers which showed on a large diagram . . . the forces of the Army on paper, and then by symbols and by colors it indicated the degree [to] which it was merely paper, or whether there was some skeleton staff organization, or some skeleton cadre of men, and in the same way it indicated the presence of or the lack of the basic weapons and supplies that would go with that kind of military unit.
>
> I remember very clearly he said, "My problem is to bring home to others in government and to Congress from the standpoint of appropriations that a military organization on paper is one thing and entirely different from an organization that has all supplies, equipment, and the things that are needed for an active organization." He said, "The Navy has been much more successful than we have, because when they, in the past, have gotten appropriations for a battleship, it had all the guns that went with it and all the ammunition, and was a complete operating unit capable of going into action. . . ." An authorization for a division didn't mean anything unless it was also accompanied by all the military equipment . . . required for it. He said in the past that had not been done. . . . As I recall, we merely [indicated whom] we represented, what kind of industry, and that industry was anxious to help if they would only tell us where and how and what we could do.[41]

After talking with Marshall and Secretary of the Navy Charles Edison, the visitors returned for a second discussion with Louis Johnson. He suggested that Hook now pick a larger group of business representatives and indicate to them privately that there would soon be demands on them and that they should be ready. He thought that once the members of the group had been picked, it would be well to have Edward R. Stettinius,

Jr., then chairman of the board of the United States Steel Corporation, come before them and impress on them the importance of planning for large-scale production and the need for secrecy.

Hook followed up this discussion in the spring of 1940 at a meeting of the Executive Committee of the National Association of Manufacturers. A debate developed over efforts to place the association on record against increased aid to the Allies. Despite a strong isolationist fight led by General Wood of Sears, Roebuck, Hook managed to poll almost an equal vote for the other side and to win a motion to table the proposal.[42]

Once the United States entered the war, General Marshall's role in increasing armaments production diminished. Undersecretary of War Patterson and General Somervell assumed the chief responsibilities in this field.[43] However Marshall went regularly to meetings of the Commerce Department's Business Advisory Council to brief industrial leaders on defense needs and to spur them to greater cooperation with the government. Hook's opinion, based on his experiences as head of the National Association of Manufacturers, was that Marshall enjoyed the "great confidence" of leading businessmen. "Because," he recalled, "when you [talked] to the General, you realized that his whole heart and soul was in what was best for the United States and what we had to do to protect our interests and to build up our security." Geier stressed another point: "What impressed me about General Marshall was that his mind did not run along purely military lines. He had an immediate grasp of the industrial and preparedness problems, which were not understood by some other people in Washington. They didn't realize that you just can't go out and buy something and have it overnight. In some cases you had to design machines to build things, and you had to tune those machines up and you had a long cycle. [For example] take the cycle of the Garand rifle—I think it was something like seven years from the time it was started until it got into real production. . . . General Marshall seemed to have a plastic mind where he could grasp some of those things that were completely foreign to the line of experience he had before." [44]

Both men recalled Marshall's total lack of arrogance. "He was a very humble sort of man. He was no stuffed shirt. He just treated us . . . in a very friendly and informal manner." After the end of the war he continued to attend the council's sessions. "He would go to a council meeting," one member said, marveling, "and he might sit down with anybody . . . for breakfast or lunch . . . or in the lobby or in the meetings just like any other member. He was a very approachable man." His accessibility and his ability to summarize the international situation impressed most who met him, and Geier spoke for other businessmen when he declared, "I was very much impressed by the fact that here is a man who has the capacity to take a complex problem and resolve it into its basic simple elements."

Years later, during the attack on his China Mission activities, Marshall kept the confidence of most of the business leaders with whom he had worked during the war. Hook expressed the view of many of his associates when he summed up what he considered to be Marshall's chief characteristics:

> First, of course, his supreme integrity. You couldn't know the man and talk with him without being impressed with the fact that what he said he believed was in the best interests of the country. . . . He had a personality that won confidence. He was so perfectly frank. You never felt that he was holding back. If there was some important secret military problem that he couldn't answer, he would say so frankly, but there were few occasions of that if he had confidence in the men he was talking to. He was a kindly man. You wouldn't think of him as a fellow who bulldozed his way through. In other words, I figured that he was a developer, that he encouraged, he gave leadership, and knew when to dispense authority and to delegate it. . . . There has never been any question in my mind [that] whatever move he made he had studied carefully first. He had gotten all the information he could, and then his decision was based on what was best for the country, irrespective of what it might do to him. I am absolutely confident in that respect. . . . In his meetings with the council and other groups that he briefed and talked to, he brought about an understanding of situations which couldn't be publicized, because you couldn't give the enemy the information. He was frank and he had confidence in those he had tried and tested, and with them there was no question. . . .
>
> He came to meetings of the Business Advisory Council . . . at great sacrifice of time. Here he was loaded with all this responsibility, but that to me meant that he recognized the need of keeping as many people [as possible] informed. It was part of his big job. . . .[45]

The task in Marshall's day was as clear-cut as it was difficult: to get sufficient arms and supplies to defeat the Axis. He did not expect or condone war profiteering, but he did not expect industry to produce its products at a loss. Like the business and labor leaders he met, he assumed that the end of the war would mean a tremendous reduction in contracts. Indeed his great concern in the summer and fall of 1944 would be that of persuading industry and labor to resist pressure for a return to "business as usual." It was not World War II, but the coming of the Korean war, the development of NATO, and the policy of containing Communism that were to consolidate the military-industrial-labor alliance that troubled President Eisenhower as he left office.

In cooperating with industry, as in the forging of military strategy, Marshall always pursued the same basic aim of winning the war as quickly as possible. Although he looked upon an adequate defense force, backed with essential production to sustain it, as the proper responsibility of the military services and the nation, he could see neither the desirability nor the likelihood of prolonged military struggle on a large scale.

Although Marshall left many of the details of weapons production to members of his staff or to other officials of the War Department, he found it necessary to put the full power of his office behind many important developments in the ordnance field. Particularly in the early months of his tour as Chief of Staff, he was appalled at how outdated the Army's inventories were. He recalled: "At this time it was dealing with a forty-year-old rifle . . . and had to be rearmed. . . . I was much criticized for continuing the 57- and 75-mm. guns. I did that because we had no ammunition for the new 105 guns and we had very few of these and it would take a long time to get them. . . . So the only way was to use the 75s and the large accumulation of ammunition which was left over from the First War.

"We had the 105; we had the new automatic rifle; and we had the new machine guns. The poorest product gotten out by Ordnance at this time . . . was the 37-mm. cannon as an antitank gun. . . . This was archaic when it was issued to the troops. Yet it was the [latest] Ordnance product. We had had very great difficulty with Ordnance Department in the past, but I think that had been largely washed out by the operations of the General Staff [indicating] what models should be manufactured."

Shortly after he became Deputy Chief of Staff, Marshall had gone to the Chief of Ordnance and his principal assistants and asked them to list everything they needed. He found that "while the big industries retooled almost completely every three years or more, [Ordnance] had some machines in the arsenals that had been there fifty years, and there was no money to get any replacement of any kind. And . . . there was so much required that only a little bit could be apportioned to educational orders. It was a very fine thing to have educational orders . . . but by gosh, we had to have something . . . that we could use immediately."

It was in direct interventions of this type that Marshall judged he made his chief contribution to the arming of the ground forces. "It is inherent in the Army, a large organization with a control like that of the War Department—General Staff and the chiefs of branches—that it should be conservative and when a man comes up with a new idea, unless he handles himself very carefully, he merely stirs up opposition.

"In the first place a great many new things are proposed—a great many out of Congress, a great many by outsiders, and a great many by individual Army officers—[of which] only a few are practical propositions, and yet you have to clear the air of all the impractical ones, each one of which is somebody's favorite son. I tried to make it a point to see the proponents . . . of any of these [ideas]. I remember one in which an officer was in rather bad odor, it seemed, [because] of his feelings about the artillery . . . that was being mounted in the tanks. The feeling against him was rather strong. When I heard this, I sent for him and I had him lay out for me all of his thoughts on the subject . . . and I told him at the time about half his trouble was that his presentation wasn't a coordinated affair but was a highly prejudiced and almost semi-insulting procedure. I thought he had good ideas. . . . But he had successfully antagonized practically the whole staff by getting out of temper with them all. It re-

quired a little more subtlety than that, because they were in a firm position and he was not." [46]

One program of which Marshall was especially proud was the adapta-
tion of weapons for use in jungle warfare. When the American forces were
fighting north of Guadalcanal above Russell Island, he decided "to see
what I could do to increase the support of the ground troops and to lessen
the casualty rates in the way of heavier gunfire." He called in Colonel
William A. Borden of his staff and instructed him to determine what
could be done with existing weapons. He did not want to hear about
"something that took a year to produce," Marshall told him.

One of the principal requirements was to shave ammunition for the 80-
mm. antiaircraft guns so that it could be used for a trench mortar then in
service. This development permitted the ground forces to bring heavy
artillery fire close to the front line. Once these and other ideas were acted
upon, the General sent Borden and his assistants to the Pacific. "I had
them bring in the principal officers and . . . the sergeants [who] could
indicate what they wanted right there. He [Borden] would take the order
and that would be shipped the next day from San Francisco. And we
followed that up. . . . First, it was something that could be done quickly,
just like shaving down the side of a shell, and the next was having it
available so that the man looked at it and said, 'I will take that.' . . .
[Later] we carried this to a great[er] extent in Italy. The high commanders there . . . came down to inspect and pick out what they thought
might be usable." [47]

Of all the developments in which he had a part, Marshall spoke most
frequently of the way that the vehicle that eventually became known as
the "jeep" was accepted. He attributed it to the intervention of a member
of his staff, Major Bedell Smith. Smith himself was inclined to give great
credit to the General's own farsightedness.

Early in 1940, as Smith recalled it, someone from Secretary of War
Woodring's office reported that at a party the night before the Secretary
had agreed to see an automobile salesman about a new vehicle he wanted
to sell the Army. When he arrived, Woodring, being busy, asked Smith to
talk with the visitor. Smith found that he was a representative of the
Bantam Motor Car Co., then manufacturing an American equivalent of
the British Austin. The company had developed "a small, low silhouette
truck, light enough to be manhandled by its passengers, capable of carrying four or five men." However the importunate salesman had received
no encouragement from the Motor Transport Division of the Quartermaster Department or from the G-4 Division because the Army had recently standardized the ton-and-a-half truck as its light transport vehicle.
He asked only that someone from the War Department come to look at
the models. Smith sometimes had his blind spots, but in this case his perception was alert. As an instructor at Fort Benning under General Mar-

shall, he had been interested in a carrier such as the one he was now asked
to examine. Recognizing that authority was needed to overcome the opposition or indifference of the services concerned, he went at once to the
man who could get action in the War Department.

Marshall subsequently described Smith's next move: "During a conference I was having [with] a number of generals, he [Smith] came into
my office, which was his privilege, and interrupted to say that there was a
man in his office who had just come in, who had invented a small vehicle
that he [Smith] thought was excellent, but he had been unable to get any
favorable observers. . . . Smith took about three minutes to state this,
and I said, 'Well, what do you think of it?' He said, 'I think it is good.'
'Well,' I said, 'do it.' The conversation was about that long. 'Well,' he
said, 'it isn't that simple. We couldn't get along unless we had several of
them.' [Marshall said 15, Smith 40, and a member of the staff who checked
said 72.] So I said, 'How much will it cost?' and he gave me the estimated
cost."

The General approved the expenditure from his special contingency
fund. Smith went out but returned a few minutes later. When Marshall
asked what the trouble was, the major replied: "I should have said it
before and I say it now—that's the first damn time we have been able to
get anything for this [salesman] in this whole War Department, and I
think it is worthy of special comment." [48]

Once the initial order had been filled and distributed to various
branches for special tests, reaction was unanimous. The infantry and cavalry, already interested, were enthusiastic, and demands soon spread. A
first order was issued for 1500; the second request was for several thousands. "All these people who had turned it down now all wanted some,"
recalled the Chief of Staff. As in so many other situations relating to
weapons and equipment during the war, it was a member of his staff who
had seen the possibilities of an invention or a proposal and brought it to
him. It was not that Marshall took the initiative in these matters, but he
encouraged his advisers to listen to new ideas and pass them on to him,
secure in the knowledge that he would give careful consideration to their
findings.

VII

Williwaws and Jitters

T H E attack on Pearl Harbor sent shock waves across the Pacific that were speedily felt on the West Coast of the United States and in Alaska. While the fires in Hawaii and the Philippines still burned that first week in December 1941, the War Department and the White House were confronted with two immediate problems: control of native-born and alien Japanese in California, Oregon, and Washington and the defense of Alaska.

The astounding success of the Japanese bombing of the Pacific Fleet threw West Coast citizens into a virtual state of hysteria. The sneak attack reawakened their latent suspicions of the Japanese, fed by decades of racial antagonism and economic competition. Within a short time, local officials infected military commanders in the area with their distrust and fears. As a result Stimson and Marshall were soon faced with the possibility that the Army would be called upon to carry out mass evacuations of Japanese aliens and American-born citizens of Japanese descent.

Both men were united in opposition to the possible use of the Army during the war to deal with railroad and mine strikes, shutdown of factories, and closing of businesses. Not only were they averse to involving the Army in matters that might be deemed political, but they also did not want to divert troops from training to local peacekeeping duties. Consequently in the first weeks after Pearl Harbor they resisted requests for the use of the Army in resettling Japanese families in the West Coast area.

The demands for Army action in this situation were based on the fact that many citizens of Japanese descent—foreign- or native-born—lived near important airplane plants and defense facilities. The clamor came at a time of great pressures for Marshall. He was simultaneously trying to get aid to MacArthur in the Philippines, to work out strategy and command arrangements with the British at the Arcadia conference, to establish and to shore up the short-lived ABDA Command in the Pacific, reorganize the War Department, and to arrange for the shift of MacArthur to the

Southwest Pacific. He thus had little time to deal with a question that, in any event, properly belonged to the President and to civilian officials in the War and Justice departments.

Although it has often been assumed that Marshall was closely involved in the major decisions by which the Army took over the evacuation of the Japanese, his role was largely peripheral. But to some degree he was associated with the final decisions of the President, the Secretary and Assistant Secretary of War, the Provost Marshal General, and the Army's commander of the Western Defense Command, Lieutenant General John L. DeWitt.

Possibly Marshall's close friendship with, and reliance on, DeWitt may have been a factor in the Army's final participation in the evacuation of the Japanese. DeWitt was one of Marshall's oldest friends in the service. The son of a former general, he entered the Army during the Spanish-American War, while a sophomore at Princeton, and was commissioned in 1898, three years before Marshall, and outranked him at the time the General was named Chief of Staff. A classmate of Marshall's at Fort Leavenworth in 1906–1907 and a colleague on the First Army staff in France in the closing months of World War I (Marshall was Chief of Operations and DeWitt Chief of Supply), DeWitt was one of the two men senior to Marshall who were considered serious contenders for the Chief of Staff position in the spring of 1939. This background aided DeWitt in dealing with Washington in the early months of the war.

DeWitt, one of the few officers who continued calling Marshall "George" after the latter became Chief of Staff, was commandant of the Army War College in Washington when, in December 1939, the Chief of Staff assigned him to command Fourth Army at the Presidio in San Francisco. Of medium height and mild appearance, DeWitt deceived observers who assumed that he could be pushed around. Once set on a course, he pursued his aims with tenacity. Marshall and Assistant Secretary of War McCloy often found him obdurate.

At the time of Pearl Harbor, DeWitt also headed the Western Defense Command, a headquarters created in March 1941. Less than a week after the attack he was commanding a theater of operations. Responsible for defending the Western coastal frontier and Alaska with an exceedingly small force, he was especially alarmed because of the proximity of many West Coast airplane plants to heavy concentrations of Japanese aliens or citizens. Soon he was relaying to Washington reports of large stores of arms in Japanese-owned warehouses, illegal radio activity by Japanese, and signaling by local Japanese to ships at sea. Although later investigations minimized the importance of arms caches and questioned the reports of signaling, DeWitt's information seriously disturbed the War Department.

From the first DeWitt combined commendable zeal with a tendency to exaggerate. Apprehensive about the activity of the enemy aliens on the long coastline, he was susceptible to pressures exerted by frantic civic leaders on anyone in authority and near at hand. He, in turn, reacted vigorously, calling on Washington for speedy action.

In the War Department the civilian most directly concerned was Assistant Secretary of War John J. McCloy. The military official charged with police matters was the Provost Marshal General, Major General Allen W. Gullion. Gullion, deciding early in the conflict to take a hard line toward aliens, sent Major Karl Bendetsen, Chairman of the Alien Control Branch of his office, to work with General DeWitt and Justice Department representatives. In so doing, he arranged for DeWitt to deal directly with the office of the Provost Marshal General on matters pertaining to aliens rather than following the usual command channel through General Headquarters (soon to become Army Ground Forces Headquarters). The result was that Bendetsen, able and energetic (he was rising rapidly from major to full colonel), played a key role in dealing with DeWitt, Gullion, and McCloy. In the process General Headquarters was not always kept fully abreast of developments.[1]

Toward the end of January, General Marshall sent Brigadier General Mark W. Clark of General Headquarters to California to discuss the problems there with General DeWitt. On Clark's report that DeWitt wanted authority to bar aliens from sensitive areas, General Marshall directed Clark to draw up a memorandum that could be presented to the President. Meanwhile Secretary Stimson was urging Attorney General Francis Biddle to set up the requested restricted areas.[2]

While plans for limited action were being discussed—an operation that local officials and an augmented FBI force could probably have handled —public sentiment coalesced on the more radical proposal for mass evacuation of Japanese aliens some three hundred miles east of the coast. Increasing panic led next to a suggestion for voluntary evacuation of American citizens of Japanese descent from the vicinity of military installations and then from the Pacific Coast area. It was a short step from this point to proposals for forced resettlement and internment. Faced by demands for movement of American citizens, the Department of Justice declined to act on constitutional grounds and because of lack of personnel.

In this confused period General DeWitt was appalled by the tasks involved in moving from their homes an estimated 117,000 Japanese, of whom 70,000 were American-born. As late as January 24, 1942, he thought that arrangements made by the Department of Justice and the FBI would be sufficient; five days later he indicated his willingness to assume responsibility for evacuating the Japanese. DeWitt's initial failure to recommend mass evacuation of aliens convinced General Gullion and members of his staff that he was weakening in his stand.[3] The Provost Marshal General was needlessly disturbed. In a memorandum for the record, on January 31, DeWitt had indicated that "sentiment was being given too much importance in total defense matters." On February 3 Stimson noted that DeWitt was "clamoring" for action.[4]

The civilian heads of the War Department were wary. Schooled in a great conservative tradition of law, Stimson believed that constitutional rights of American citizens won by generations of Anglo-Saxons should not be denied to any Americans. McCloy, also trained in law, was aware that the Department of Justice was skittish on mass evacuation. "I feel concerned," he told DeWitt in a phone call, "that the Army . . . should not take the position even in your conversations with the political figures out there that it favors a wholesale withdrawal of all Japanese citizens and aliens from the Coast, for the reason that it may get us into a number of complications which we have yet not seen the end of." [5]

DeWitt put up a strong argument: he was responsible for the security of the West Coast, and he did not intend to be a scapegoat, as General Short had been for Pearl Harbor, he told McCloy. He could not escape the impact of local hysteria, and he had reason to be jittery. Perhaps it was too much for him to distinguish between measures to protect the West Coast and those necessary to quiet the jangled nerves of the local inhabitants. Finally he warned McCloy that unless the Army took strong action against Japanese-American citizens, the local Anglo-Saxon citizenry would rise.

When Marshall discussed the question with DeWitt on February 3—the day of the DeWitt-McCloy conversation—the West Coast commander said that Governor Curlbert L. Olson was still considering the possibility of shifting Japanese from critical defense areas without moving them great distances. The Chief of Staff listened carefully, made a few comments, and then apparently discussed the matter with Secretary Stimson and General Gullion.[6] After this Marshall was almost completely out of the picture.

Actually the future of the Japanese for the next two years was substantially settled between February 2, when DeWitt began conferences with Governor Olson and state Attorney General Earl Warren, and February 11, when the President in effect turned the Japanese problem over to the Army. Thereafter the question was how and when measures would be taken.

At times during the discussions it was hard to be certain of the Army's views either in Washington or San Francisco. In summing up the situation February 4, Colonel Bendetsen concluded, "No one has justified fully the sheer military necessity for such action." DeWitt, however, showed the way the wind was blowing by predicting that no matter what the Department of Justice said, local citizens intended to take matters into their own hands. Agreeing with this analysis, General Gullion informed McCloy two days later that "no half-way measures based upon considerations of economic disturbance, humanitarianism, or fear of retaliation will suffice." [7]

There were also more moderate voices in Washington. General Clark thought that Californians were unduly alarmed. He saw no chance for the Japanese to make sustained attacks on the United States. Secretary Stimson continued to stress the Constitution. It would put "a tremendous hole in our constitutional system" to say we cannot trust our citizens, he told McCloy. But by now the Assistant Secretary of War had become uneasy over what the enemy might dare. If the Japanese could establish their dominance in the Pacific, he thought they might try an invasion.[8]

To make certain of the President's attitude on the Japanese question, Secretary Stimson and Assistant Secretary McCloy went to the White House on February 11 with four specific questions, the two most important being whether Roosevelt was willing to authorize the Army "to move Japanese citizens as well as aliens from restricted areas" and whether the Army should undertake withdrawal from the entire strip as DeWitt had initially recommended. Roosevelt instructed the War Department officials to do anything they thought necessary under the circumstances. McCloy promptly told Bendetsen, "We have *carte blanche* to do what we want to as far as the President's concerned." Here at last was specific authorization of evacuation at the highest level. Roosevelt recognized that there might be unfavorable repercussions but said that action was dictated by military necessity. He had qualified his statement by saying, "Be as reasonable as you can." [9]

On February 11 General DeWitt was asked to draft recommendations relative to the evacuation of the Japanese. At the last, having momentary qualms about Marshall's attitude, he telephoned General Clark to ask "whether GHQ and the Chief of Staff have been thoroughly informed." Obviously unfamiliar with recent discussions, Clark replied that he doubted if they were going to remove citizens. No longer dubious on this point, DeWitt declared: "They've just got to. We must get them away from vital areas." [10] The following day he produced his draft of proposals for the evacuation.

On the same morning that DeWitt checked with Clark, Marshall's attention was caught by Walter Lippmann's regular news column. The Chief of Staff found it sufficiently interesting to pass on to Stimson—who forwarded it to McCloy. Alarmed by the enemy alien problem, the columnist saw imminent danger for the Pacific Coast from both within and without. That coast, officially a combat zone, might at any moment become a battlefield. In his best pundit's style, Lippmann asserted, "Nobody's constitutional rights include the right to reside and do business on a battlefield. And nobody ought to be on a battlefield who has no good reason for being there. There is plenty of room elsewhere for him to exercise his rights." [11]

General Clark was not fully aware of West Coast pressure that continued to increase on DeWitt and the President. On February 13 members of Congress from the Pacific Coast states recommended "the immediate evacuation of all persons of Japanese lineage and all others, aliens and citizens alike, whose presence shall be deemed dangerous or inimical to the defense of the United States from all strategic areas." Manchester Boddy, publisher of the Los Angeles *Daily News,* wired Attorney General Biddle on February 16 that the local Japanese situation was deteriorating rapidly and that he feared "irresponsible" action on the part of local citizens. Significantly he added that the first job was to get aliens in a concentration camp and then decide later on their ultimate destination.[12]

Roosevelt was receiving similar advice. Talking to him on the seventeenth, Stimson found the President "all right" on necessary West Coast action. Later that day the Secretary met with McCloy, Bendetsen, Clark, and Gullion to discuss instructions for DeWitt. Although Mark Clark was prepared to implement any presidential directive, he opposed allowing the West Coast commander "to absorb, like a sponge, many divisions for this purpose, because by so doing it would sabotage our expansion of the Army for offensive purposes." Stimson did not like the proposed wholesale evacuation plan but finally decided that DeWitt should be authorized to move out Japanese aliens and citizens if their removal was essential to protect critical installations. After checking with the Army Ground Force commander, Clark proposed telling DeWitt that he could use such troops as he could make available from those currently assigned to his command —with the exception of the 27th Division and the 3d Division Reinforced, whose training GHQ did not want disrupted. Summarizing the discussion and proposed action, General Clark wrote for the record: "I then telephoned to General Marshall and gave him the report on the meeting, the instructions that were to be sent by the War Department and the troops we recommended General DeWitt be authorized to use. General Marshall said all right." The Chief of Staff was now committed with the rest.[13]

The next move was to ensure the legality of the action. On the sixteenth General Gullion asked the Attorney General for a formal authorization. The following day Stimson and the Attorney General met with their advisers to discuss the matter. By now the Secretary of War had gone a little further down the road "towards a solution of a very dangerous and vexing problem." He had "no illusions as to the magnitude of the task and the wails which will go up." [14]

The resultant draft of a proposed Executive Order was shown to the President on February 19. The Attorney General explained that it was based not on any legal theory but on the fact that the actions of certain groups might lead to serious disturbances. Later that day Roosevelt signed the directive, Executive Order 9066, which was then forwarded to DeWitt.[15]

Marshall did not initial the War Department order. During the day, however, he asked Gullion for a summary of developments and was informed that DeWitt's authority was now limited only by the restriction on the number of troops he could use. At this point DeWitt was still assuring Washington that he was not going to have any mass movement, since he had to be sparing with his troops and not divert too many of them for this purpose. But several developments were in progress that were to change his mind.[16]

The decisive factor may have been a report on February 21 from the commandant of the 11th Naval District to General DeWitt declaring that the situation of the Japanese in Southern California was critical. Many were being forced by local pressure to move before new housing or means of support were provided. Next day DeWitt was informed that the Governor of Washington was issuing orders for evacuation on his own authority. A wire to governors of all states west of the Mississippi revealed that the chief executives of twelve of them did not want Japanese and would accept them only as wards of the Federal Government and under armed guard.[17]

Secretary Stimson could not completely suppress his basic dislike of the proceedings. He instructed DeWitt to go ahead with the partial evacuation that had been ordered and to stop talking about broader action for a time. DeWitt, he added, already had enough to keep him busy.

The War Department was getting drawn in more deeply than its officials wanted to be. It was one thing to shift people to new jobs and new homes; it was another to have to keep them under guard—unemployed—and to furnish housing, food, and clothing. Secretary Stimson was pleased when Attorney General Biddle proposed that a single civilian head handle the problem of resettlement. Following this lead, the President set up a War Relocation Authority, with Milton Eisenhower as its chief, to supervise this task.[18]

Seriously concerned about the evacuation, Stimson sent McCloy out in mid-March to ensure that the movement was made "with all humanity possible." A week later the Assistant Secretary of War reported to the War Department Council, which included Marshall and Stimson, that the evacuation was being carried out in good order and that DeWitt had shown good judgment and common sense. He noted, perhaps without irony, that the situation in Hawaii was being handled differently. There, with a population half-Japanese, it was not practicable to undertake a shift because the number involved was too great. Not only was the remainder of the local population less apprehensive, but the Army and Navy, fearing a labor shortage, opposed evacuation to the mainland.[19]

Demands for mass evacuation of all enemy aliens continued to spread. The situation became ludicrous in April when Attorney General Biddle reported to the President that Lieutenant General Hugh A. Drum was trying to move Italian and German aliens from the East Coast. Although

Stimson fulminated about the foolishness of the rumor and said that Biddle should be ashamed to repeat such a story, it persisted. More sensitive to German and Italian counterpressures than to those of the Japanese, Roosevelt reacted promptly. On May 5 he directed Stimson to take no action without consulting the White House.[20]

While carrying out his assignment, General DeWitt made an effort to keep the evacuation movements humane. But the uprooting of families and their resettlement in camps created great hardships and bitter feelings. Now committed to this policy, DeWitt stubbornly declined to reconsider it. Nearly a year later he told a House of Representatives subcommittee that he disagreed with the false sentiment of those who wanted to return the Japanese to the West Coast. He said that he would oppose their return "with every proper means at my disposal." [21]

Like many other decent, fair-minded men, DeWitt had managed in a year to come full circle—from preferring to depend on civilian agencies to prevent sabotage of military installations, to suggesting a reasonable pullback from the West Coast, to advocating mass evacuation of all Japanese. In subsequent investigations he found it difficult to justify his actions on the basis of military necessity.

Throughout this affair General Marshall's position was atypical. Normally Marshall was consulted at every step by military and civilian authorities on broad problems in which the Army was deeply involved. Although the great pressure of other duties at the moment made it difficult for him to intervene regularly in discussions that were mainly political, it was still remarkable that he was consulted so little. Only the fact that the Secretary of War and the Assistant Secretary of War were fully involved in the decisions makes it understandable.

The time came when General DeWitt feared that he had lost the Chief of Staff's confidence. In the spring of 1943, when Marshall informed DeWitt that he would be shifted to another post, the Pacific Coast commander asked if he was being transferred—as rumor had it—because of his handling of the Japanese evacuation. The Chief of Staff positively denied this charge. Marshall explained that he had recently worked out with Admiral King the establishment of a Joint Army-Navy College. The Chief of Naval Operations had agreed to the proposal but had suggested that the college be located at Newport. Marshall pushed for a Washington site and the appointment of DeWitt, who had been a commandant of the Army War College and a graduate of the Naval War College, as its head.[22] It was to this command that DeWitt was being shifted.

In later years Marshall declared that the evacuations had been made to avoid violent West Coast reaction rather than because of military necessity. Asked for comments on the relocation controversy, he replied: "We were in very great difficulties there because there were large numbers of Japanese almost next door to the airplane factories, particularly in Los Angeles. . . . And the people out there . . . were just bitter in their feeling that the Japanese should not be allowed to stay there. They were suspicious . . . of everybody Japanese. Therefore it reached such a point that it seemed to be the only thing we could do short of a semiriot or terrible occurrence out in California to put these people in an internment camp. . . . It was a very trying duty and trying necessity." [23]

Despite Marshall's assertion that it was necessary to relocate the Japanese, he was equally convinced that men of Japanese ancestry who wished to fight for the United States should be allowed to do so. But he exercised tactfulness in their deployment:

> I knew that it was quite unwise and quite unfair to send them to the Southwest Pacific where they would be in contact with their own people. . . . So we sent messages to commanders in Europe and, as I recall, I may be wrong about this . . . Eisenhower's staff people declined them. Then I offered them to General [Mark] Clark and his reply was, "We will take anybody that will fight." So I sent this battalion [of Nisei from Hawaii] over to him. Then we organized another one in California, and we finally built this up into a regiment [442d Infantry]. The division [to which] we first attached this battalion in Italy was opposed to it . . . the prejudice was so deep against the Japanese. [But, later, when they] found I was going to take [the battalion away] and build it up into a regiment, I had political pressure from Congress not to take this battalion away. . . .
> I will say about the Japanese fighting then in these units we had: They were superb! That word correctly describes it: superb! They took terrific casualties. They showed rare courage and tremendous fighting spirit. Not too much can be said of the performance of those battalions in Europe and everybody wanted them . . . in the operations, and we used them quite dramatically in the great advance in Italy which led up to the termination of the fighting there.
> I thought the organization of the additional battalions was very essential because we felt that unless we did something about the Japanese in this country, we would have a very hard time afterwards. I don't mean [with] the Army, I mean the civil population. As a matter of fact, even with their brilliant performance, some communities rather blackballed the men when they came home as veterans.[24]

West Coast alarms over the Japanese danger in the closing days of 1941 soon extended from internal dangers in California, Oregon, and Washington to the external threat to Alaska and the Aleutian Islands. A half-forgotten Far Western frontier was thrust back into America's consciousness.

Before World War II Alaska for most Americans was a frozen mystery. Cold, distant, basically unromantic despite the efforts of Jack London and Robert Service to trumpet its charms in their writings, the far-off territory often seemed to offer Stateside Americans a remnant of stubborn truth in the old libel of "Seward's Folly." The services tended to think of it as a potentially crucial outpost, ill fortified because of the difficulty of persuading Congress to take seriously the defense of what appeared to be an icebound wasteland. Even the Army and Navy, hard put to get an adequate force for mainland United States and key Pacific bases, tended to neglect this isolated vastness where distances alone might suffice for protection.[25]

Marshall had become aware of the area's potential in the late 1930s, when he commanded at Vancouver Barracks, Washington State. After becoming Chief of Staff in 1939, he kept closely in touch with Alaskan defenses through General DeWitt, whose responsibilities for West Coast Army and Army Air Forces activities included Alaska. Their plans were carried out by Brigadier General Simon B. Buckner, Jr., a strapping, impetuous Kentuckian, son of a famous Confederate general and former Kentucky governor, appointed by Marshall commander of United States troops in Alaska in 1940 and chief of the new Alaskan Defense Command the following year.

The new Chief of Staff also discovered that the Army's only tactical force in Alaska consisted of 400 men near Skagway. The Navy, equally weak, had a seaplane base at Sitka and a radio station and Coast Guard base at Dutch Harbor in the Aleutians. At that time fog was the area's best defense. Before the year ended, the Navy had begun constructing bases at Sitka and Kodiak and the Army an air base at Fairbanks. Defense efforts were spurred by the vague fear that the Russians might be strengthening Siberian bases that could threaten the Aleutians and the Alaskan mainland. There had even been a flutter in the late summer and fall of 1939, after the conclusion of the Russo-German alliance, lest the two powers might act together against the United States. But there were so many pressing defense needs that General Marshall's efforts to build air and ground installations at Anchorage in the spring of 1940 were set back temporarily when a House of Representatives subcommittee dropped the item from the proposed budget.

Congressional reaction to the fall of France brought a hasty restoration of the Anchorage project. Meanwhile General Marshall had ordered the establishment of a permanent ground force in Alaska and directed that a temporary garrison force of 3100 be dispatched at once. In March 1941, as a result of increased tension in U.S.–Japanese relations, the Chief of Staff earmarked additional ground forces for Alaska. He increased the allotment for Buckner in July when the fear arose that Japan might take advantage of Germany's attack on Russia to send forces into Siberia.[26] By September, Marshall had assigned more than 20,000 men to the Alaskan Defense Command. In fact he had moved so rapidly that some of the men arrived before housing was ready. Critics in Congress complained that men were living in tents constantly blasted by icy winds.

Struggling to build up the defenses of the Philippines and Hawaii, Marshall was unable to ship the aircraft for which DeWitt and Buckner pleaded. In mid-1941 the Air Forces in Alaska had fewer than forty planes. Aircraft scheduled by Marshall for delivery in late 1941 and early 1942 had not arrived at the time of Pearl Harbor.[27]

For a short time after war began in the Pacific, it seemed that Alaska might play important offensive and defensive roles. Washington officials dug up available maps, ancient and full of uncharted areas, of the Aleutian Islands, lying like a hundred-odd pebbles scattered in the freezing wind from the mainland in a 1200-mile arc almost to the Japanese Kuriles. The fifteen larger islands might serve as additional outposts against the enemy, as links in the ferrying operations for American Lend-Lease aircraft to the Soviet Union, or as wayside stops to American bases in Siberia that could be used against Japanese targets in case Russia and Japan went to war.[28]

Both the energetic Buckner and his Navy opposite number, Captain R. C. Parker, commander of the Alaskan Section of the 13th Naval District, declared at the end of January 1942 that recent events pointed more significantly than ever to "the strategic importance of Alaska as a dominant influence in determining the eventual outcome of the conflict." To defeat Japan it would be necessary to strike at her home territory, but of the previous approaches only the one through Alaska had not yet been cut.[29] As Chief of War Plans, Eisenhower summarized for Marshall the wishes of the Alaskan commanders: (1) negotiations with the Russians for air bases, (2) reconnaissance of bases and air routes, (3) rapid completion of airfields under construction, (4) prompt reinforcement of the Alaskan area, (5) construction of seaplane bases westward, and (6) aggressive action without delay against Japan.[30]

The proposals were attractive. But at a desperate period in the Philippines and the South and Southwest Pacific, the demands for a quick offensive build-up in Alaska had little chance of acceptance. Admiral King believed that a Japanese attack on Alaska or the Canadian West Coast, except for minor submarine and air raids, was "highly improbable." Until the Soviet Union was willing to permit American aircraft to operate from bases in Siberia, extensive unoccupied air facilities in Alaska and Aleutians would, he thought, constitute more of a liability than an asset.[31]

In view of the cautious reactions to the Alaskan proposals, mounting Air Forces shortages, and lack of progress in negotiating with the Russians for air bases, General Eisenhower recommended in mid-March that General Marshall adopt a "watch and see" policy. For the present, he suggested, American forces in the area should limit their action to the strategic defensive.[32] In accepting Eisenhower's reasoning, Marshall insisted that the Alaskan commanders understand fully why he must disappoint them. "Otherwise," he warned, "there is considerable discouragement involved, which is unfortunate for people in isolated regions." [33]

For a time in March, Washington leaders uneasily speculated on steps they should take in the event the Japanese withdrew part of their forces from the Central and South Pacific to strike northward. Early in that month Marshall and Stark, at Roosevelt's request, began studies of (1) an allied offensive to pull the Japanese forces southward, (2) the use of Chinese territory by the Soviet Union and the United States for an offensive against Japan, and (3) the opening of the Aleutian Islands route to Kamchatka and Siberia.[34]

As there was no way to make useful proposals on Soviet-American collaboration without fuller information on Russian installations in Siberia, the Joint Planning Staff urged that the President intervene with Moscow to ensure greater military cooperation between the two powers. Receiving a discouraging report on these efforts at the end of March, the Joint Chiefs of Staff agreed that "the United States could not make any plans regarding possible action unless full and complete information were first forwarded by the Russians as to what facilities in Russia would be made available for U.S. forces." The President noted their statement and returned it without comment.[35]

Meanwhile Japan's forces fanned outward in triumphant sweeps. In late April, General Marshall alerted DeWitt that the Japanese were concentrating naval forces near Truk and that it seemed probable that they would strike at targets in the Central or Southwest Pacific.[36]

As part of a main attack against Midway the enemy bombed Dutch Harbor, Alaska, on June 3–4 but not heavily enough to knock it out as a base. As a defensive measure the Japanese occupied two of the westernmost islands of the Aleutians, putting troops ashore without opposition on June 7. Two American civilians were found on Attu; ten U.S. sailors at a weather station in Kiska were captured.

Despite the decisive defeat of the Japanese fleet by the U.S. Navy at Midway, the subsequent Japanese moves in the Aleutians stirred apprehension in the States. As a practical matter the distance from the nearest Japanese base in the Kuriles to Attu was 650 sea miles and to Kiska by sea another 378. It was another 2200 miles by air and 2600 miles by sea from Kiska to Seattle. Although not seriously concerned, Marshall as a matter of caution ordered some ground forces, antiaircraft guns, and field artillery from the West Coast and from some of the less exposed locations in Alaska to those such as Nome that were more open to attack. The air forces were also beefed up. Leaving the reinforcements for the moment on a defensive basis, the War Department now considered other possibilities.[37]

The next question was whether the Japanese planned to move northward against the Russians. This possibility, plus the President's recent talks with Molotov about the second front and the renewed vigor shown by United States naval and air power at Midway, favored closer collaboration with the Russians in Siberia. But the negotiations broke down after a few months. Besides suspecting American motives, the Soviet leaders opposed giving up their neutrality vis-à-vis Japan. For the Americans the failure meant that emphasis had to be shifted back to ground activity in Alaska.

In mid-June, Admiral King informed the Joint Chiefs of Staff that he had the President's permission to discuss the Japanese threat with Russian military representatives. General Marshall proposed that Roosevelt ask Stalin to permit Russian military officials in the United States to conduct staff conversations with American representatives. Also at the recommendation of the War Department the President suggested to Moscow that an air-ferry route be set up from Alaska to Siberia. He further asked that the Russians authorize a survey of Siberian air facilities by an American air party.[38]

Stalin's cooperation was restrained. He agreed to a survey so far as it would expedite delivery of Lend-Lease planes to Soviet crews in Alaska but was silent on possible air operations in Siberia. Taking this limited response for agreement, the President named Air Force Major General Follett Bradley as his representative to Moscow.

General DeWitt was intensely interested in driving the Japanese from their bases in the recently occupied Aleutian Islands. With the indefatigable zeal and excitability that had led him to ring the industrial cities of the West Coast with everything available in the early weeks after Pearl Harbor, DeWitt flooded Washington with proposals for retaking Kiska and for occupying and fortifying intermediate islands that had to be secured as a base for this attack.

Like most commanders, DeWitt saw the needs of his area outweighing those elsewhere. Therefore he brought to his proper role of securing his command a nagging urgency that Washington did not always welcome. He worked hard to organize close cooperation among Army, Navy, and Air Forces commanders in the Alaskan area and to get necessary resources for his attack. Admiral Cooke, admiring DeWitt's persistence, told General Handy that they should put him in charge of the cross-Channel planning if they wanted to get action.

Although Marshall and King meant to carry out DeWitt's plans eventually, they still gave higher priority to tasks in the South and Southwest Pacific. Aware that the problems of weather and terrain in the windswept, mist-shrouded islands of the North made naval and air actions extremely dangerous, they were less eager than DeWitt for the fray.

To block the enemy move eastward and set the stage for the capture of Kiska, DeWitt proposed in mid-July the occupation of the island of Tanaga, 160 miles east of Kiska. The Navy, which would have to support the landing, preferred Adak Island, some 50 miles further east, because it had a better harbor. The opposing arguments collected from commanders in Alaska and in California now went forward to Washington for a decision. Learning from Army representatives that it would take longer to build an airfield at Adak than at Tanaga, the Joint Chiefs of Staff decided on occupation of the latter. This decision, in turn, was reversed when Admiral King, on the advice of the commander of the North Pacific Force, Rear Admiral Robert A. Theobald, concluded that the navigational hazards in attacking Tanaga were too great. With no choice left him DeWitt went along with the Navy. Finding near the end of August that the island was unoccupied by the enemy, the Army put 4500 men ashore. Within a few weeks, Adak-based planes were raiding Kiska.

Unfortunately Army-Navy differences over command arrangements, handling of operations, and selection of targets resulted in a comic contretemps that threatened to disrupt the close interservice cooperation promoted by Marshall and King. Already at odds with the somewhat pompous, irascible Theobald, the irrepressible Buckner was moved by disagreement over Tanaga to precipitate an incident that enraged the Navy commander and deeply embarrassed General Marshall. Either seriously misjudging the Admiral's sense of humor (Theobald was once described as "having one of the best brains and worst dispositions in the Navy") or, more likely, out of sheer boyish exuberance, Buckner relaxing over a drink with Theobald and several other officers read a piece of doggerel poking fun at the Navy's fears of risking operations in the Alaskan mists—fears that the Army commander, now an old hand, would have been the first to agree were justified. In true Gridiron Dinner style, he had the Admiral saying:

> In far Alaska's icy spray, I stand beside my binnacle
> And scan the waters through the fog for fear some rocky pinnacle
> Projecting from unfathomed depths may break my hull asunder
> And place my name upon the list of those who made a blunder.
> . . . .
> The Bering Sea is not for me nor for my Fleet Headquarters.
> In mortal dread I look ahead in wild Aleutian waters
> Where hidden reefs and williwaws and terrifying critters
> Unnerve me quite with woeful fright and give me fits and jitters.[39]

After seething over the incident for two days, Admiral Theobald decided the matter was of major importance and fired off a letter to Buckner filled with nineteenth-century politesse, eschewing all future social relationships, and countenancing only contacts required by military duty. The whole exchange, complete with Buckner's poetry, was sent by the Admiral to his Chief in Washington. Marshall was disturbed when King placed the dossier on his desk. Although he admired Buckner, the Chief of Staff deplored his poor judgment. He directed DeWitt to investigate the affair at once with the view of replacing the Alaskan commander if necessary.[40]

Buckner was in greater jeopardy than he realized. He had violated one of Marshall's unswerving tenets—the necessity of cooperating with other services in outlying bases and distant theaters of operations. In recent months the Army Chief of Staff had either refused to name certain officers to posts or had relieved others because they could not work well with officers of other American services or of other nations.

DeWitt handled the case with great skill. At first inclined to agree with Marshall that the Alaskan commander should probably be relieved, he explored the matter carefully with Theobald. Despite his ruffled feelings, the Navy commander opposed a relief based on his protest. DeWitt then called the two men together and was able to report to Marshall afterward that their differences had been settled and no reliefs should be made at that time.[41]

Marshall was doubtful. Passing on the correspondence to Admiral King, he said that at the moment he was not in accord with DeWitt and that he thought Buckner should be transferred after pending operations were completed. He also believed that at some later date the Air and Navy commanders should also be shifted. King suspended the argument by saying that in view of DeWitt's recommendations, "it would seem that a 'wait and see' attitude is in order." Marshall commented to DeWitt, "My feeling . . . is that however much you have patched up affairs there is no escaping the fact that Buckner's reasons were based on lack of faith in Theobald's willingness to engage an enemy except under conditions so favorable to us that they were unlikely to develop. However much they have patched up their differences no man can forget such implications." [42] For the moment DeWitt allowed command arrangements to stand as they were.

When bickering began later in the year over future targets, General Marshall considered replacing Buckner and also looked into suggestions for a separate Alaskan Department. Partly as a means of restoring harmony, Admiral Nimitz in early January 1943 shifted Theobald to another command, sending in his place one of the great fighters of the Navy, a positive, decisive commander, whose reputation in the Pacific was as highly respected by the Army as by his colleagues of the sea—Rear Admiral Thomas C. Kinkaid.

Despite his distress over the feud Marshall still had high regard for Buckner's organizing abilities. In February when he was seeking a replacement for DeWitt, soon due for reassignment, he asked him whether he thought Buckner could fill his place. Pleased to find DeWitt in agreement with the idea, Marshall still feared that the Navy would find it hard to forget "the implications of his jocular assault on Theobald." [43] Ultimately Marshall selected Lieutenant General Delos C. Emmons for DeWitt's post. Since Buckner was working closely and with minimum friction with Kinkaid, Marshall left him in Alaska until September 1944, when he placed him at the head of the Tenth Army. As commander of Army and Marine divisions, cooperating smoothly with the Navy in Pacific operations, the Kentuckian directed the successful assault on Okinawa and met his death there in the closing days of the battle in June 1945.

By late September 1942 Buckner and Theobald had composed their differences sufficiently to resume planning for an attack on Tanaga. However Army and Navy planners in Washington were now mulling over the occupation of Amchitka, 200 miles west of Adak and some 90 miles east of

Kiska. General DeWitt again championed an attack on Tanaga. Replying to a query from Marshall whether it was practicable to substitute Amchitka for Tanaga, DeWitt cited a recent reconnaissance report that building an airfield on Amchitka was believed to be a major engineering task requiring at least two months. Unless directed otherwise, he would proceed with the occupation of Tanaga. Marshall, who also knew of the reconnaissance report, called DeWitt's attention to the fact that its author disclaimed his technical qualifications to judge the feasibility of an airbase on Amchitka and to his recommendation for another survey. "Would it not be worthwhile," Marshall asked, "to have another reconnaissance made by an officer who is qualified to give us a good estimate of the time and means required for such a project?" DeWitt promptly informed Marshall that Buckner had been directed to arrange with Theobald for a second reconnaissance. But still unconverted, he reiterated that Amchitka should not be occupied until after Kiska had been reduced.[44]

Early in December, DeWitt regretted having to report that the reconnaissance party had been waiting for a month for Theobald to move it to Amchitka. According to Buckner, the Admiral would not agree to the survey until Japanese intentions to the west were clarified. He was apprehensive about indications of a forthcoming attack on Adak or on certain other islands, including Amchitka. DeWitt appreciated Theobald's hesitation to undertake the survey on account of the reduced strength of his command; naturally he must hold his entire force of ships and seaplanes together to counter enemy action. In view of the dangers lurking in the Aleutians, DeWitt renewed pressure on Marshall to capture and occupy Kiska at once. Nimitz saw "eye to eye" with him on the necessity to remove the Japanese threat on Kiska. There was no question, continued DeWitt, that they would attempt to improve their position in the western Aleutians by a determined effort to seize other islands. Every day wasted would make it more difficult to gain control of the "entire Aleutians area." [45]

Far distant from Alaskan jitters, Marshall could reassure DeWitt that King and he were "fully alive" to the need of routing the Japanese from the Aleutians "at the earliest practicable moment." As a first step toward offensive operations, they had also agreed to the early occupation of Amchitka, if the new reconnaissance proved favorable for an airbase there. But the timing of the ouster of the Japanese must be fitted into the over-all Pacific picture. Due to serious logistical shortages, particularly in the South and Southwest Pacific, and in Burma, an offensive operation in the Aleutians could not be undertaken in the near future. An airbase on nearby Amchitka could be crucial; air forces based there would completely dominate Kiska. In the breathing space gained, Marshall asked DeWitt to draw up with Nimitz a joint plan for driving the Japanese from the Aleutians, so that the required troops and ships might be made available.[46]

Shortly afterward the reconnaissance party made a favorable report: a fighter strip could be built on Amchitka in two or three weeks, and a main airfield with a 5,000-foot runway in three to four months. The Chiefs of Staff issued a directive for the assault on Amchitka. Bad weather prevented the first efforts to land on January 9, but three days later a combat command went ashore without opposition. Despite numerous Japanese air attacks beginning near the end of January, the fighter strip on Amchitka was in operation by mid-February. A week later U.S. air patrols were over Kiska.[47]

The directive on Amchitka drafted by the Navy was revised by Marshall in order to avoid overcommitment to specific operations after the island's occupation. As redrafted, the directive stated that possession of Amchitka would "render Kiska untenable as an operating base" and provide an advanced base for a "possible operation" against Kiska. While understating what the future would hold, Marshall agreed with King that a start should be made on training a force to assault and occupy Kiska. Marshall's purpose throughout was to deflate the estimates of the Alaskan commanders regarding Japanese capabilities and their requirements to meet this threat. In the letter to DeWitt in which he pledged eventual ejection of the Japanese, he emphasized that in the light of desperate fighting in the Solomons, New Guinea, and Tunisia, "we cannot afford this continual increase in Alaska." But he intimated that whatever specific assignments DeWitt might desire could be made in the event that operations in the Alaskan area were expanded.[48]

By February 1943 it was clear that forces for an early attack on Kiska, now reinforced by the Japanese, could not be pulled away from other commitments. In early March, Admiral Kinkaid suggested that Attu, some 378 miles westward, but more weakly held, might be taken with less effort. In fact the island, once virtually stripped of troops, had also been reinforced. On the basis of this underestimation of the enemy, which De-Witt shared, the Joint Chiefs of Staff agreed to the Attu operation—provided no additional forces would be required. On March 22 they set early May for the attack. The assault, launched May 11 by a combined Army-Navy force under Admiral Kinkaid, proved to be "in proportion to the numbers of opposing troops, the second most costly battle of the war in the Pacific." In heavy fighting during which the 7th Infantry Division commander was relieved by Kinkaid for lack of aggressiveness, the Americans sustained 549 dead and 1150 wounded. Only 29 prisoners were taken of the some 2400 Japanese troops on the island.[49]

Once Attu was secure, Kinkaid proposed that the attack on Kiska proceed. Expecting heavy resistance, he assembled 34,500 troops, including 5300 Canadians, at the end of July for training. Despite some opposition to the operation in the War Department planning groups, the Joint Chiefs of Staff approved it and set August 15 for the attack.

In view of the severe losses in taking Attu, commanders ordered the

heaviest bombardments seen in the entire North Pacific fighting. Although little response was noted, some pilots reported antiaircraft fire.
Therefore the landing on Kiska was made in full force, and the attackers
proceeded warily. After hours of inching forward, peering anxiously behind every possible hiding place, the invaders faced the ultimate in military embarrassment: the enemy had gone. Worse still, they had left before
the bombardments of early August.

The epilogue could have been expected. Military campaigns have a
built-in momentum. The Aleutians followed the pattern. On the eve of
the landing on Kiska, DeWitt asked for an attack on Paramushiru and
Shimushu islands, in the Japanese Kuriles, arguing that their capture
would provide the Allies with airfields 650 miles from Hokkaido and Sakhalin and within 1300 miles of Tokyo. He believed that the troops from
the Kiska operation would be sufficient for the attack.[50]

The War Department was less certain of the advantages. Marshall's
advisers pointed out that planes on Luzon would also be within reach of
key Japanese cities and that it offered "a far better base for operations."
General Emmons told the Chief of Staff that an attack on the Kuriles
would draw naval and air forces from the Southwest Pacific and wondered
if the Allies could take troops away from the main effort, "which is assumed to be towards the Philippine Islands." Can we, during the spring
of 1944, he asked, "divert the land, air and naval forces and the shipping
to make this secondary effort?" Obviously he did not think so.[51]

More important, once the islands were taken, they must be held or
there would be unfortunate psychological reactions at home and in
China. "To hold them may require serious commitments of all types of
combat and service forces," Emmons noted. Still he did not want to rule
out the operation. He suggested that the local commanders be permitted
to continue with their plans and with training but that Washington withhold final approval until the situation in Europe and the Pacific was clarified.

After the fall of Kiska the Joint Chiefs of Staff approached the next
move cautiously. King was willing to consider DeWitt's proposal regarding
the Kuriles. Marshall said he had considered such an operation but thought
it a rather formidable undertaking for the Navy. In addition the problem
of continued support after getting into Paramushiru would constitute an
extremely heavy responsibility for all concerned. However he would not
stand in the way. General Arnold intervened to say that anything that
would advance the Allied drive westward without interfering with the
South Pacific would be desirable. Having left themselves flexible, the
Joint Chiefs proposed waiting until they knew how operations in the Central Pacific were progressing before making a final decision.[52]

In effect, active operations in the Aleutians were at an end. After leaving the decision open, King said what was really in his mind: that Attu
was overgarrisoned and that if the Japanese had really given up on the

Aleutians, fewer troops were needed there. Above all, it was necessary to push operations in the Central Pacific as fast as possible. Falling into line with his argument, Marshall suggested that the 7th Division might be shifted from Kiska to the Central Pacific.

Before the end of August, the War Department acted on these suggestions. On the twenty-sixth Marshall directed that the Alaskan garrison, now at 150,000 air and ground personnel, be reduced to 80,000 as soon as shipping would permit. His move had been influenced by apprehension lest public opinion condemn him for keeping men idle under extremely trying circumstances. His view was confirmed a few days later when Assistant Secretary of War McCloy returned from an inspection tour to Alaska with "a rather disturbing report of morale conditions in the Aleutians." Some of the enlisted men, he reported on August 31, feared that they might be held in Alaska for the duration of the war with no prospects for combat service and no opportunity to return to the United States on leave.[53]

For Marshall the episode was typical of the problems he often faced in trying to forestall unfavorable public reactions. It stuck so forcibly in his memory that he was inclined later to exaggerate the promptness with which he had removed many of the troops:

> I remember when we discovered that the Japanese had retreated from that island . . . I sent for Somervell . . . and said, "You have to get a couple of transports right away . . . up to the Aleutians or Alaska . . . and start the movement of troops from that command." . . . He said, "I haven't got any transports. Every one is scheduled for these other operations and I just can't do it." I said, "Somervell, you've got to do it because if you don't do that instanter [sic], there is going to be set up a tremendous demand from these men to get out of the Aleutians and out of Alaska and it is going to come with an impact that will get political very, very quickly." He said, "I don't know where in the world I am going to get them." I said, "I certainly don't, but get them, by God, get them, and get them up there right away. If you could put them there tomorrow, I would say get them there tomorrow." Well, of course, it took some time to move a transport up. Within three days the impact on the whole command was that the fighting was over. They had put up with terrific conditions there in the Aleutians, now they wanted to come home and they wanted to come home fast, and I had a congressional committee on my hands the fourth day. When I got the transports up there . . . that took off the heat. . . . Somervell couldn't see that. I wanted to get it [redeployment] started immediately. I wanted the orders to be gotten out in twenty-four hours but I couldn't beat the punch on it. The instant fighting was over, the reaction was to come home. . . .[54]

The Chief of Staff's earlier decision to reduce the forces in Alaska had already brought anguished protests from his old friend General DeWitt, who seemed to feel that the decision was connected in some way with criticism of his own record. He complained that everyone seemed to know about his future assignment "except myself." In late August when DeWitt sought to delay the shift in order to continue Aleutian operations, Marshall ruled that no forces were available for the proposed expedition against the Kuriles. In early September the Chief of Staff directed that activities of the Alaskan Defense Command be diminished.[55]

Marshall defended his action at the Joint Chiefs of Staff meeting on September 7, characterizing retention of large forces in the Aleutians as "a great burden, a heavy morale problem, and a naval problem rather than an air problem." After considerable discussion Marshall proposed that Buckner be brought to Washington for consultation. King requested that Rear Admiral John W. Reeves, commander of Alaskan naval forces under Kinkaid, be summoned as well.

Supported by Reeves, Buckner made a strong plea for an Alaska-based operation against the Kuriles. However he made clear that they could not stop at Paramushiru but must go on to Hokkaido if they were to avoid the Japanese fate at Kiska. He estimated that two Alaska-trained divisions plus two others brought in from outside would be sufficient. This action, he argued, would influence the Russians to move against Japan. He believed that the Soviets, not wanting the United States to hold the Kuriles after the war, would rush to help. The Allies should go full blast to break the present Russo-Japanese neutrality, he insisted.[56]

The prospect was enticing, but Washington now saw the main battle elsewhere. King spoke for his colleagues in late September when he said that the Allies, currently preparing to open a ninth front, lacked the tools for the Kuriles operation. Perhaps they could make such an effort the following summer. He too emphasized the importance of encouraging the Russians to move. "We should be more ready than we are now with 'ways and means,' " he said, "not only to aid Russia but to exploit the availability of Russian territory to strike at Japan proper which will have to be done chiefly by air from air bases within air striking distance." [57]

In retrospect, one may envisage that a drive through the Kuriles to Japan proper—an operation supported by land, sea, and air forces from American bases—would have been successful. In the matter of miles the narrow arc, despite fog and cold winds and ice, had its attractions. But the whole affair turned on Russian entry into the war against Japan. For Buckner two additional divisions plus the two he had, four heavy-bombardment squadrons, and a chain of air bases would have sufficed for an offensive against Paramushiru. But it would not have been enough to sustain the drive against the Japanese home islands or to hold the base if the enemy had attempted a major counterattack. At that time American forces were already engaged heavily in the South, Southwest, and Central Pacific. Only if the effort in the north were accompanied by an active Russian effort against Japan would it have been practicable to try it. And it became quite clear that the Russians did not want to break the fragile neutrality that existed there. In addition they were unwilling to permit the surveys of air bases, preparatory to establishment of airfields in Siberia, that would have made American participation realistic. Later they charged—inaccurately—that the Americans had sought fields to use against the Soviet Union. Such a suspicion existed in 1943, and it was obviously powerful enough to prevent cooperation.

In view of these factors, long-range and current planners in Washington reached much the same conclusions as General Marshall had: that the garrisons then maintained in Alaska were too large from the standpoint of both the danger involved and their possible use against the Japanese before the spring of 1945.

Admiral King was not convinced that the area was yet free from a Japanese attack. But the other Chiefs agreed with Marshall and his advisers that keeping a large force tied up in the islands would be "a concession of superhuman power to the Japanese." After further discussion the Joint Chiefs of Staff in early October 1943 voted to reduce the garrisons in the Aleutians while authorizing the construction of air-base facilities for possible attacks against Paramushiru in the spring of 1945. The 7th Division and the First Special Service Force were already earmarked for a shift to other theaters.

Although theoretically some preparations were still to be made for further attacks in early 1945, the speed-up of operations in the Central Pacific and MacArthur's drive for the Philippines markedly eroded Alaska's potential role. By the end of 1943 Army forces there had been reduced to 110,000, and Buckner was directed to cut them to half that number, which was accomplished by the end of 1944. In early 1944 General Hull of Marshall's Operations Division pointed out that later attacks on such targets as the Kuriles could be mounted from the United States without keeping large garrisons in the Aleutians. Although the possibility of an offensive by way of the Aleutians and Kuriles remained, the proposal was never seriously revived. Advances by the forces of MacArthur and Nimitz and the continued neutrality of Russia toward Japan ruled it out. Perhaps the most important feature of this continued discussion was in fixing the minds of the Joint Chiefs of Staff on the importance of Russia's entry into the war to defeat Japan.[58]

VIII

Not So Peaceful Pacific

I N Pacific matters, as in those relating to Europe, the Casablanca participants left more questions unsettled than they resolved. The general
statement that future advances in the Pacific must not be allowed to
weaken the "Europe first" concept—a declaration purposely left vague to
win agreement between the British and the Americans—opened the way
for future sharp debate between the Allies, as well as within the American
services.

Knowing that the decisions at Casablanca would be especially painful
for MacArthur, both President Roosevelt and General Marshall promptly
made special efforts to have him briefed. They directed General Wedemeyer, already under orders to accompany Generals Arnold and Somervell to New Delhi and Chungking for briefings of officials in India and
China, to continue on to Australia to give the Southwest Pacific commander the background of determinations affecting his area.

Both the President and the Chief of Staff had warned Wedemeyer that
he would have to listen to the Southwest Pacific commander's own views
on global strategy before delivering his message. Living up to advance
billing, MacArthur launched into an hour-long lecture in which he declared that the United States would lose its traditional influence in Asia
unless it quickly built up its strength and restored the confidence of the
Filipinos and Chinese.

When his host paused, Wedemeyer politely explained that European
strategy still had first priority. MacArthur was interested in knowing
Churchill's strategic views and asked his visitor to tell Marshall that "the
momentum which appeared to be the Prime Minister's major point about
continued operations in the Mediterranean had an even greater application in the Southwest Pacific." [1]

Implicit in MacArthur's reactions was the thesis he was to restate vocif-
erously after the war's end. In later conversations and writings he insisted
that if the Allies had concentrated their forces in the Pacific in 1943—es-

pecially if they had diverted U.S. naval power from the Mediterranean—they would have quickly overpowered Japan. To arguments that the enemy was still dangerous at that time in Europe, he countered that the Axis's European fleets no longer had more than nuisance value, that the German threat to the Middle East had been deflected by the victory at El Alamein, that the German offensive had been stopped at Stalingrad, and that the Russians were preparing their counteroffensive.[2]

Even when aided by the advantages of hindsight, MacArthur's basic argument is hard to substantiate. With a bitter fight still to be won in North Africa, with Montgomery's forces not yet finished with Rommel, and with the Russians aware that the German Army, although badly shaken, was still deadly, the time was not ripe for halting advances in the European and Mediterranean theaters. The great Allied armies there were at last on the move; by MacArthur's own logic it would have been folly to stop the impetus of victory. More to the point, the British would not have agreed to it.

Had Wedemeyer questioned MacArthur on his current problems, he would probably have received a more lengthy lecture. For in early February the Southwest Pacific commander was deeply agitated over the command set-up in the Pacific, the next stage of operations, and resources available for it. Writing of this period in his *Reminiscences,* General MacArthur complained:

> Of all the faulty decisions of war perhaps the most unexplainable one was the failure to unify the command in the Pacific. The principle involved is the most fundamental one in the doctrine and tradition of command. In this instance it did not involve choosing one individual out of a number of Allied officers, although it was an accepted and entirely successful practice in the other great theaters. The failure to do so in the Pacific cannot be defended in logic, in theory, or in common sense. Other motives must be ascribed. It resulted in divided effort, the waste, diffusion, and duplication of force, and the consequent extension of the war, with added casualties and cost. . . .[3]

The principle of unity of command was widely accepted in Washington, and General Marshall in the first weeks of war had pushed for its adoption. However in 1942, when the time came to establish one or more American theaters of operation in the Pacific, it became clear that as a practical matter of implementation, the establishment of overall command in that area was virtually impossible. Instead of one theater, the Joint Chiefs of Staff settled for the establishment of the Southwest Pacific Theater under MacArthur and the Pacific Ocean Areas under Nimitz, with three subdivisions: South, Central, and North Pacific areas, the first commanded by Vice Admiral Robert L. Ghormley and later by Admiral William F. Halsey, and the other two by Admiral Nimitz. The situation was difficult because Nimitz made the allocation of ships for MacArthur's operations, and he insisted on keeping firm control over his naval units. As long as the Army and Navy conducted campaigns in fairly separate areas, the command problem did not become acute. Thus it was possible in August 1942, when MacArthur's forces pushed westward in New Guinea and the task forces under Halsey advanced on Guadalcanal, to have an arrangement by which the Southwest and South Pacific commanders coordinated their campaigns, giving mutual support where possible. It was also agreed that when later operations were started, greater unity would be essential. Inasmuch as Halsey's forces from the South Pacific would have to cross into the Southwest Pacific area, Marshall supported MacArthur's request for control of the later operations.

The Chief of Staff raised the command question at the beginning of December 1942, in sending Admiral King a draft directive proposing the seizure and occupation of Rabaul and the adjacent areas, involving basically Task Three (spelled out in the original directive of July 2, 1942). Still remaining was Task Two—the campaigns to secure the northeast coast of New Guinea (as far west as Madang) and to take New Britain and New Ireland and the continued march northwestward up the slanting ladder of the Solomons running from Guadalcanal to Bougainville.[4]

Thus shortly before Guadalcanal was cleared of the Japanese and the fight for Buna ended, Marshall returned to the strategic concept that the Joint Chiefs of Staff had laid down when the Japanese were still threatening to swing down into Australia and to islands south of the Solomons. The battle for Guadalcanal and the heavy fighting in eastern New Guinea, accompanied by massive sea and air attacks, had blunted the Japanese advance and prepared the way for offensives toward the north and west.

With the Japanese still on Wake Island, well to the north of the Solomons, and in the Gilberts and Marshalls to the northeast, the Allies faced several difficult tasks. They had to push the enemy out of New Georgia and Bougainville in the Solomons before establishing bases from which to attack islands to the northeast that threatened communications from Pearl Harbor to the South and Southwest Pacific and menaced the flank of attacks to the north. Before MacArthur could move westward on the road back to the Philippines, he had to destroy Japanese resistance as far west as Madang, on New Guinea, and eliminate the threat of sea and air attacks from Rabaul. In his opinion it was necessary to take New Britain and New Ireland. Marshall agreed.

Meanwhile the Navy was re-examining the plans and command arrangements for the Pacific set down in the July 2, 1942, directive. Marshall at the same time was proposing continuance of the earlier directive with strategic control of task forces under the Commander-in-Chief, Southwest Pacific—MacArthur.

Disliking the slow process of taking the Solomons one by one, which might drag on for two years, Admiral King sounded out Admiral Nimitz on the possibility of bypassing the Japanese there and seizing the Admiralty Islands northwest of Rabaul. Nimitz was wary. He returned a cautious reply almost at once and amplified it a week later (December 8) with a long qualified letter. Both he and Halsey recognized the necessity of "getting along with the war" and not becoming "bogged down," as King insisted. But though every possible short cut was being investigated, certain conditions caused delay. Task One, making the Guadalcanal-Tulagi area secure, was not yet completed, and the Allies still had to establish superiority in ground troops, aircraft, and naval forces before undertaking Task Two. Although they had some grounds for confidence, there was still much to be done. Nimitz estimated that Allied superiority in naval surface forces could be attained in the late spring of 1943. Parity in aircraft had now been reached, and increased allotment of new production would quickly bring superiority. "We should capitalize on the ready availability of superior air forces to overcome our weakness in other respects," Nimitz advised.[5]

The ground picture was much less favorable. Surveying the Marines available for an offensive, Nimitz cited the shortage of troops trained for amphibious operations as a serious drawback in preparing an offensive. He brushed aside possible use of Army divisions: "none in training, or even assigned, therefore none can be ready in less than three months." [6]

Nimitz seriously doubted the wisdom of outflanking the Japanese positions in the Solomons. While the prospect of bypassing some of the targets offered a strong temptation, the lines of communication of any base being seized would be left at the mercy of the bypassed forces. Moreover the Japanese position in the New Britain area was thought to be the most difficult to outflank. With the forces he had at hand, Nimitz narrowed his choice of objectives to Buin (on the southwest coast of Bougainville, 300 miles from Guadalcanal) or one or more intervening positions.

Marshall agreed basically with Nimitz. But when the Admiral discussed command relationships in the Southwest and South Pacific, the General raised a questioning eyebrow. In the July directive, the Joint Chiefs of Staff had agreed that while Task One was under way, MacArthur and Halsey would proceed separately to achieve their ends and that Tasks Two and Three would be under the control of General MacArthur. The Joint Chiefs reserved the right to decide when this shift should take place. Nimitz now saw a new solution in which "practically the whole of the Pacific Fleet," concentrated to meet the Japanese reaction to American seizure of Guadalcanal, would have to be retained for the operation of Task Two. Halsey had built up this organization with great difficulty, and Nimitz felt that it was "vital" that the same command set-up continue in the South Pacific.[7]

Marshall did not need the threat of an explosion from MacArthur to lead him to question the Navy proposal. Inviting Admiral King to inspect the map of the area, the Chief of Staff likened the disposition of forces in the South and Southwest Pacific to an inverted V, with the Japanese at the northern point at Rabaul and "a heavy, well organized Allied force" at the extremity of each leg. In this situation the enemy had all the advantages of position with the option of operating on interior lines and with central control of all his forces. It was essential for the Allies to oppose those forces under a unified command, instead of the present situation in which MacArthur's forces, some 450 miles from Rabaul, were attempting to cooperate with Halsey's forces, which were strategically controlled by Nimitz in Hawaii, some 3500 miles from the Japanese base.

If the battle had depended solely on ships and ship-based planes, Marshall could not have held to his basic argument. But he was aware that MacArthur's air component—consisting of about 1300 land-based planes, of which 500 were bombers—was essential to the success of Task Two. He also felt that Nimitz was slighting the ground forces under MacArthur's command. In opposing the Japanese, Marshall insisted, the Allies must deal with the enemy's advantage of position and direction by combinations of flanking and frontal actions in an "elbowing-forward" movement. In such an operation, unified direction could immediately exploit successes on either flank and effectively employ the strategic mobility of Allied bombers. He recommended that "a single strategic control for the South Pacific and Southwest Pacific Forces should be made at once." [8]

Admiral King, who was completely in favor of unified command for the whole Pacific if he could have a Navy officer in control, sounded out Marshall informally before submitting his official reply. Shortly before Christmas 1942 a Navy planner, Captain Richard L. Conolly, presented the Navy's preliminary draft to Marshall's Chief of War Plans, now General Handy. This draft and Handy's reply, which he carefully noted represented only his own thinking, actually constituted a rehearsal for the formal exchange of letters in early January.[9]

On January 6 Admiral King firmly stated the need for unified command throughout the Pacific. Flexibility in the use of naval resources, he urged, was essential to a commander with Nimitz's heavy and far-flung responsibilities—for the naval part of the current campaign in the South and Southwest Pacific, operations in Alaska, the protection of Hawaii and the West Coast of the United States, and maintaining the security of lines of communication to the South and Southwest Pacific—"tasks . . . so vital and so compelling I feel that they must be given precedence over lesser considerations that may be in conflict."

For the completion of current operations in the South and Southwest Pacific, King thought it might be possible for MacArthur and Halsey to continue on the basis of "mutually supporting coordination." However, once joint efforts were directed against Rabaul, it would be necessary to set up an integrated command. Thus far, he might have been echoing Marshall's earlier view on the need for unified command for Tasks Two and Three. But it was evident that they did not have the same commander in mind. "For this purpose," continued King, "my proposal is that Nimitz's command as Commander-in-Chief, Pacific Ocean Areas, be extended to include the Southwest Pacific Ocean (or Sea) area." If this were done, it would be feasible "to give to MacArthur strategic direction of operations against Rabaul—if the forces involved remain under the general command of Nimitz, and he is always kept in a position to meet enemy threats against other points. . . ."[10]

Underlying King's concern over command in the South Pacific, which led to this proposal, was the prospect that most of the Pacific Fleet might come under MacArthur's control. It had not been "visualized," wrote King, that most of the Pacific Fleet would have to be deployed in the South Pacific–Solomons area for the coming Task Two operations.

Marshall was now eager to settle the immediate question of unified command in the South and Southwest Pacific during current operations without getting involved in the stickier problem of unified command throughout the Pacific. Adopting the line already sketched out by Handy, he separated the long-range and the immediate problems, agreeing that "there should be a single commander of the entire Pacific and that he should be charged with all defensive and offensive operations therein" and that "all forces in the Pacific should be under his control." But the solution of this problem, he observed, would require careful study of international command structure and extensive organizational implications. He proposed that such a study be launched at once. Significantly he added that "it must be based fundamentally more upon the selection of the commander as an individual rather than upon his specific military or naval qualifications." He seemed to be hinting that MacArthur would have to be the choice.

Meanwhile there were operations against Rabaul that could—and should—be set on foot immediately. But in order to direct a maximum effort against the enemy at Rabaul, it would not be feasible to continue to depend on mutually supporting attacks between Halsey in the Solomons and MacArthur in New Guinea. Marshall therefore proposed that MacArthur at once be given strategic direction of all forces in the operations against Rabaul. In exchange for the Navy's acceptance of this fundamental Army position, Marshall was willing to grant Nimitz "sufficient general control" of all elements of the Pacific Fleet involved in these operations to permit him to shift naval units to meet any emergency in the entire area. Further, Admiral Halsey as commander of the South Pacific forces would exercise direct command of naval forces under MacArthur. Recognizing that flexibility was as important in the use of air elements as in the employment of naval strength, Marshall concluded by saying that Joint Chiefs of Staff control of the air forces could be exercised to meet emergencies.[11]

Sensing that Marshall would not give way on the command question as it affected MacArthur, Admiral King apparently thought it prudent to postpone a final settlement. He replied that he did not think "we should commit ourselves *at this time* . . . as we do not know much, if anything, about MacArthur's views as to how he plans to carry out Tasks 2 and 3." The Southwest Pacific commander could exchange views with Nimitz and Halsey and then forward plans for Tasks Two and Three to the Joint Chiefs of Staff.[12]

On January 7 Marshall informed MacArthur that King had proposed attacking the Admiralty Islands instead of assaulting Rabaul. At the same time he asked MacArthur for a brief summary of his concept "of the successive steps to be taken in the capture of Rabaul." A day later he told him that King had requested a copy of MacArthur's detailed plans for Tasks Two and Three of the joint directive of July 2 "or modifications thereof with corresponding plans to carry out." The Chief of Staff "strongly suggested" that MacArthur exchange views with Admiral Halsey or arrange for their representatives to meet for this purpose.[13]

MacArthur reacted promptly. He strongly opposed King's suggestion of an Admiralty Islands attack that lacked land-based air support. Regarding the other operations, he fell back on proposals much like those that he and his Navy opposite had submitted in July 1942. He still talked in terms of a five-phase advance for Tasks Two and Three.[14]

When he made this preliminary reply to Marshall's January 7 message, MacArthur had not yet seen the Chief of Staff's second message requesting a detailed plan. When MacArthur's second reply was received in Washington, still lacking desired details, Marshall had already departed for the Casablanca conference. In his name staff officers directed MacArthur to execute the directive of the Joint Chiefs of Staff set forth in the message of the eighth. They urged "early coordination" with Halsey and Nimitz, emphasizing that much time could be saved by a personal conference among the three.[15]

MacArthur's plans were not immediately forthcoming. He could argue that he was awaiting information from Halsey and Nimitz, but he failed to help his cause in Washington. Had he spelled out his reasons earlier, he could have strengthened Marshall in the debate over future command arrangements in the Pacific. Until King knew MacArthur's plans, he continued to postpone a decision on the command of Tasks Two and Three. Shortly before Marshall and King returned from Casablanca, War Department officials asked MacArthur for a report on his progress in coordinating with Halsey and Nimitz the plans asked for earlier in the month. Conceding that more time might be needed for a reply, Washington asked merely for his estimate as to the probable date of the answer.[16]

MacArthur answered at once, but strangely enough did little more than repeat his initial statements, which had also been sent three days later (on January 13) to Halsey and Nimitz. He explained that he had not heard from the two Navy commanders and could not predict when their replies would be forthcoming. Meanwhile he was developing his plans.[17]

Nettled at this response, King protested to Marshall. If MacArthur had no specific proposal, the Admiral suggested that the Joint Chiefs of Staff ask Nimitz and Halsey for their plans to support MacArthur's operations.[18]

Admiral King was further disturbed that Halsey lacked sufficient aircraft to meet emergencies in the South Pacific. In early February 1943 he reminded Marshall that the Joint Chiefs of Staff had not met the commitment made late in the previous October to bring Army Air Forces strength in the South Pacific up to 70 heavy bombers, 52 medium bombers, and 150 fighters.

To some extent the Admiral misread the agreement. General Arnold had returned from an inspection trip to the Pacific in early October believing that the South Pacific had sufficient Army aircraft to carry out planned operations. Later in the month he agreed with the Joint Chiefs of Staff decision to make the additional aircraft mentioned by King available for deployment in the South Pacific by January 1, 1943. In November 1942 Arnold expressly directed that planes to fill this commitment be allocated to Guadalcanal and five other island bases.[19] However the Army was thinking in terms of deployment from the United States rather than of the time of arrival in the South Pacific.

The information King most desired was supplied by General Handy on February 15. By February 24, the Army planner declared, all heavy and medium bombers that had been allocated to Halsey were scheduled to leave the United States for the South Pacific.[20]

Halsey's pleas for air support from MacArthur had been prompted by a belief that a major enemy attack on Guadalcanal was then in the making. MacArthur replied that his bomber resources were so limited that he would risk disaster on his own front if he detached planes to Halsey's command; from their present bases they could protect both their operations. When, as MacArthur had anticipated, the emergency in the Solomons failed to develop, Halsey asked for all practicable assistance in striking Japanese shipping in the Buin area on Bougainville. The Southwest Pacific commander, who had been trying to get a statement of intentions from Halsey, said that he could not dislocate his own plans without knowing what operations the Admiral contemplated for the future. Halsey acted swiftly; on February 11 MacArthur was able to inform Marshall that the Admiral's representative had arrived in Brisbane with information on his projected operations.[21]

In the end the Pacific commanders shifted responsibility for plans, allocations of resources, and the command question back into the laps of the Joint Chiefs of Staff. Pressed by Washington for his future plans, General MacArthur proposed sending his Chief of Staff and a small group of staff officers to explain to Marshall and King what he had in mind. After checking with his colleagues, Marshall wired approval in midmonth, enlarging the proposal to include representatives of Halsey and Nimitz and senior air officers from the South and Southwest Pacific. Such a conference, Marshall felt, would facilitate final decisions on future operations.[22]

Marshall also hoped to promote better relations between Army and Navy commanders in the Pacific. His earlier fears of friction had been confirmed by General Wedemeyer's report of March 11, which Stimson described as "disquieting on the subject of cooperation between the Army and the Navy." It was a problem that continued into 1944 until Marshall at one Joint Chiefs of Staff meeting told King that he would not remain further unless the Navy Chief ceased his criticism of MacArthur.[23]

After the war Marshall observed that both sides had been at fault. "On the matter of the respective attitudes of the Navy and MacArthur," he said, "the feeling was so bitter and the prejudice was so great that the main thing was to get an agreement. . . . Because you were in a war of personalities—a very vicious war." In these arguments, Marshall insisted, he supported the Southwest Pacific commander "through thick and thin on most of the questions." But his role as peacemaker was not easy. "All of this was arrangeable if the two commanders wanted to get together. But their approaches, particularly on MacArthur's side, were so filled with deep prejudices that it was very hard to go about it. . . ." [24]

Marshall did not blame the chief naval commander in the Pacific for this state of affairs. "Nimitz himself was not a quarrelsome man, but I think his staff was very much embittered because they were being criticized continuously by MacArthur's outfit." For this General Marshall held Major General Richard K. Sutherland, MacArthur's Chief of Staff, largely responsible. Although conceding that the sharp-tongued Sutherland was an able soldier, Marshall characterized him as the "chief insulter of the Navy."

Sutherland had already ruffled the feelings of ground and air officers in the Southwest Pacific. Postwar accounts by Eichelberger and other generals convey their irritation at his handling of MacArthur's directives. Lieutenant General George C. Kenney, the able Pacific Air Forces commander who gained deserved recognition for his striking contributions to victory, described vividly the way in which he promptly and permanently settled the question of who was to run the air battles in his part of the Pacific. Early in his relationship with Sutherland, Kenney informed him forcefully that he did not know anything about running air operations and that he was not to interfere in such matters. Sutherland withdrew quickly from that hot corner, but he continued to remain unyielding in regard to the Navy.[25]

To what degree Sutherland's truculence reflected his chief's attitudes is not clear. General Marshall thought that MacArthur himself disliked the Navy because he feared that its victories might detract from his own feats of arms. "He just took a decided stand on anything that affected his command. There were no concessions on his part whatsoever. Well, the war . . . is made up of concessions, and adjustable one way or the other. But Nimitz's staff had become . . . so bitter towards General MacArthur and MacArthur's staff so bitterly [disposed] towards Nimitz that it was almost impossible to get them together on anything. They would come in to see me, and I could find some of them notably desirous of reaching adjustments, but the suspicion was just profound. . . . The personal thing was getting into it deeply—the personal thing more on MacArthur's side. . . ." [26]

In all the quarrels over resources, personal interests became strongly intermingled with proper strategy. Each service found cogent arguments for developing the fight in the area where its forces were the strongest. As chief protagonist of the Central Pacific strategy, Admiral King led the Navy's fight against MacArthur. Absorbed in the European, Mediterranean, and China-Burma theaters, General Marshall left much of the Army's battle with the Navy to his Southwest Pacific commander.

Marshall recognized General MacArthur's natural disappointment at being relegated to a secondary theater. In a characteristic gesture he suggested near the end of February that the President send an encouraging message to MacArthur. Noting that Churchill had recently complimented MacArthur on the Buna campaign, at the end of 1942—a triumph already praised by Roosevelt and Marshall—and that it was clearly the Prime Minister's intention to set at rest any doubts about British appreciation of the war in the Pacific, he proposed that the President send congratulations on subsequent successes. Since MacArthur in the last few days had been reporting "truly remarkable bombing operations against Rabaul and other points in the Solomons," Marshall suggested this text:

> The President directs me to transmit the following message to you: "The tremendous and remarkably efficient bombardments launched by your air forces during the past few weeks and especially in the last few days in support of the situation in the Solomons and in furtherance of your own operations command our enthusiastic admiration. The arduous and difficult land campaign along the Papuan coast which has decimated the enemy and now threatens him at Salamaua has made a great impression on our people and must have a demoralizing effect on Japanese confidence in the fighting efficiency of their ground troops.
>
> "My thanks go to you and your leaders and to the officers and men of the Australian and United States forces who carried the fight to the enemy on all levels and over great distances and even greater difficulties." [27]

Obviously MacArthur was touched. He replied:

> Please convey to the President my grateful appreciation for his generous and inspiring message regarding the modesty [sic] of the forces in this area in furtherance of the great cause he leads and epitomizes. Its effect will be electrical and cannot fail to strengthen the determination and resolution of all ranks and grades. As a former member of his official family please express to him my personal thanks and give him my affectionate greetings. May God preserve and protect him in the almost overwhelming responsibilities that are his.[28]

MacArthur listed this first in an almost page-long footnote in his *Reminiscences* containing the texts of numerous congratulatory statements.

One notes the absence of any statement from Marshall in the midst of all this glowing praise from America and abroad. Apparently MacArthur never knew that the Chief of Staff was responsible for Roosevelt's message.

On March 12 representatives of the chief Pacific commanders gathered in Washington at the conference Marshall had organized. MacArthur had sent General Sutherland, his Chief of Staff, and General Kenney, commanding general of Allied Air Forces, Southwest Pacific; Halsey had likewise sent his Chief of Staff, Captain Miles R. Browning. Rear Admiral Raymond A. Spruance, Deputy and Chief of Staff to Nimitz, was also present. In addition there were Lieutenant General Millard F. Harmon, commander of Army and Army Air Forces in the South Pacific; Major General Nathan F. Twining, commander of the Thirteenth Air Force, which was under Harmon; and General Emmons, commanding general of the Hawaiian Department.

The imposing delegation was able to report hard-won victories in the Pacific. At the end of January, MacArthur's forces had cleared the enemy from New Guinea east of Gona; February 9 marked the end of hostilities on Guadalcanal; and between March 1 and 3 in a brilliant fight in the Bismarck Sea, General Kenney's bombers had virtually destroyed a convoy attempting to take a division from Rabaul to Lae, as well as annihilating much of the division.

Now the question was what the commanders could get for the next round. To determine that, the visitors sat down almost at once with the chief planners of the Navy, Army, and Air Forces. In the opinion of General Wedemeyer, the Army representative, who briefed Marshall on the early phases, all of them had come with the intent of getting everything possible for their areas of the Pacific. "For obvious reasons," he added, "they have been urged on and strongly supported by the Navy." [29]

Since Marshall's presence was not required in the early meetings, he spent part of the next ten days in Florida. After several strenuous days in late February working for passage of a manpower bill, he had become ill with a cold that forced him to miss an engagement at the White House on March 4 and to stay at home for the remainder of the week. To recuperate from the cold and get some rest for strenuous tasks to follow, he departed for Florida on March 7.

He and Mrs. Marshall took a cottage near the ocean on Miami Beach, in the hope of getting some sunshine and remaining inconspicuous. The General's efforts to remain incognito were at first successful. One evening near dark, as he lay on the beach dressed in civilian clothes, a Coast Guard official warned him that everyone had to be inside. Assuming that the rule did not apply to individuals in front of their own cottages, he mumbled that he thought it would be all right. A few minutes later he was startled by the appearance of a fat petty officer and a detail of men. The General was ordered inside. As he slowly walked toward the door, the grim upholder of regulations followed him, asking firmly if he didn't know there was a war on. The General remained silent until he reached the door, where the light fell on his face. Then he quietly stated: "That is enough. What is the reason for this ridiculous display? Does it take you and a patrol of six men to tell me that we are at war?" The guard quickly disappeared into the night.[30]

But he did not long remain unidentified. The day after his encounter with the Coast Guard and the Navy he went into the city. Two soldiers driving by stopped their jeep and asked if he was not General Marshall. The General replied, "Yes I am; but you haven't seen me." They agreed, saluted, and left. He was not so fortunate a short time later when he accompanied Mrs. Marshall to a store where she wanted to buy beach shoes. Recognizing him despite his dark glasses, the clerk whispered his secret to the cashier. She in turn called the manager. He casually strolled by the General, then turned, and in a loud voice greeted his eminent customer by name. The quiet crowd of shoppers turned into a noisy welcoming committee. A lady in a red hat pursued the Marshalls to a nearby taxi and hung onto the door as they started to drive away. Thereafter they remained close to their cottage, swimming early and then enjoying the air from their balcony. The irrepressible Mrs. Marshall teased her husband: "Your Dr. Jekyll and Mr. Hyde disguise is certainly working beautifully!" [31]

While Marshall soaked up sunshine to cure his cold, a hot debate flared in the Pacific Military Conference at Washington over the Army's allocations of air and ground forces to the Pacific for coming operations. The chronicle of this conference illustrates the problems faced by the Joint Chiefs of Staff and their subordinates each time a major campaign was planned. At this stage of the war, when shipping, planes, and equipment were in short supply, the success of an impending attack seemed to ride on allocations made almost casually by planners bending over their charts and inventories in Washington. Often fights for resources and personnel were carried on over great distances with bristling telegrams and letters substituting for verbal tiffs. But the Pacific Military Conference was especially noteworthy because the top-level representatives of MacArthur and Nimitz were on hand to present their cases and to rebut the arguments advanced by Washington planners in favor of coming European campaigns.

The Joint Chiefs of Staff had hoped to carry out offensives in the Southwest and South Pacific with planes and divisions already allotted. To their surprise General MacArthur's revised plan—ELKTON II, leading eventually to the capture of Rabaul—required a sharp increase in men and planes. This was disclosed at the opening meeting, March 12, when MacArthur's Chief of Staff, General Sutherland, made his presentation. For the tasks assigned MacArthur and Halsey—which the former was expected to direct—the Southwest Pacific commander wanted 22⅔ divisions and 45 air groups. This was unwelcome news for the Army and Air planners, whose estimates called for 5⅔ fewer divisions and 24 fewer air groups.[32]

Thus at the outset of the conference the planners were faced with the choices of finding additional forces, persuading MacArthur to reduce his requirements, or accepting a considerably restricted offensive in the Pacific for the remainder of 1943. The second possibility, getting the Pacific representatives to scale down their requests, seemed unlikely. So far as the additional divisions were concerned, there was nothing that could be done beyond sending the 3 divisions already allocated—2 to the Southwest Pacific and 1 to the South Pacific. From the start Marshall and his staff made clear that, although more divisions were available, shipping shortages made it impossible to send them for the proposed campaign. When it came to air groups, the problem was more complicated. These could be supplied only at the expense of projected operations in Europe. It was soon evident that the big controversy of the conference would come over the question of how to interpret the Casablanca decision providing for "the heaviest possible bomber offensive against the German war effort."

Admiral Cooke, described by some of Marshall's planners as "meaner than King" in his stout support of Pacific strategy, gave the Navy's interpretation. He had already made clear to his Army opposites that since the Pacific was the only area where the Navy had a chance to show what it could do, it intended to hold firmly to command there and push operations in that area. He never missed an opportunity to advance the latter— an attitude that made him popular with Pacific command representatives from all the services. He denied that the Casablanca agreement had ruled out vigorous campaigning in the Pacific, saying that the Allies had committed themselves only "to employing the maximum means against Germany which will not jeopardize our position in the Pacific." At his suggestion a subcommittee was appointed to "re-explore the various aspects of the ELKTON plan with a view to determining any readjustment of forces available and needed that might effect a change in the estimate of forces required for the execution of the plan." [33]

Further study did nothing to shake the Pacific representatives. After conferring through the weekend, they were ready to inform the Joint Staff Planners that they were unable to reduce the estimate. Admiral Cooke made a point at the next conference meeting, on Monday, March 15, of putting their view on the record. The various factors involved, Cooke argued, must be clarified so that the Joint Chiefs of Staff would have a comprehensive statement showing in particular the major difference: "that of the air forces required versus the air forces tentatively allocated." He called special attention to the primary consideration being given to air force deployment in Great Britain and North Africa.[34]

Cooke's charge of discrimination against the Pacific in the allocation of air forces precipitated a spirited argument. When the Air Forces planner, Brigadier General Orval Anderson, undertook to argue that the allotments had been made in the spirit of Casablanca and in the light of the decisions of the Combined Chiefs of Staff, Cooke opened fire.

Reporting the argument to Marshall, General Wedemeyer, who was far less rigid in his views on the overriding priority of Europe than was Anderson, said that the Navy had attacked the Army Air Forces' interpretation of the Casablanca agreement on the air offensive in Europe. "In the course of the proceedings," he noted, "Admiral Cooke asked General Anderson many questions which I felt were irrelevant; for example, What had the air units in the U.K. contributed toward the accomplishment of our overall war objective?" [35]

With the Navy supporting the Pacific representatives in their demands for more air groups and the Air Forces demanding that nothing be done to weaken the air offensive against Germany, the conference headed toward stalemate. It was up to Marshall and King to search for a compromise solution.

Marshall, who had returned to Washington from Miami on March 14, attended the Joint Chiefs of Staff meeting two days later. At once he and his colleagues learned from General Wedemeyer and Admiral Cooke that there were sufficient resources to increase allocations to the Pacific but not enough to meet General MacArthur's requirements. Although they agreed that unless the demands were met, Rabaul could not be taken in 1943, the officers recommended that the future operations in the Pacific this year be fitted to resources available. [36]

Predictably the members of the Joint Chiefs of Staff disagreed. Taking a practical approach, Marshall observed that they must first decide how the forces now allotted could be used and then investigate how much more was needed. His Chief of War Plans, General Handy, added that an attempt to meet the demands for air groups in the Pacific would significantly reduce those available for the United Kingdom and end by changing the strategy of the war. [37]

General Arnold's representative at the meeting, Major General George E. Stratemeyer, took the straight "Europe first" line already set forth by Anderson; he insisted that every heavy and medium bomber taken from United Kingdom allotments weakened by that much the bomber offensive against Germany—an action contrary to the intent of the Casablanca agreement. When King and Cooke muttered against these arguments, General Marshall intervened to say that the Army Air Forces had been conducting their operations in Europe with too few planes. If they could double the number of their planes for each strike, they could increase the effectiveness of the attack while reducing the percentage of losses.

The Joint Chiefs of Staff concluded by asking for alternative plans for the Pacific that would take into account forces above those already allocated that could be sent to the Pacific (1) by using all shipping then there or to be made available later and (2) by determining where additional forces, particularly air, could be obtained. Three days later the planners brought forward two proposals: the first allocated three divisions (two to MacArthur and one to Halsey), four air-combat groups, and ten air-support groups. Under the second plan the one division initially allocated to Halsey would be held back and the shipping thus saved would be used to take additional air groups—five and one-half combat groups and six additional maintenance groups—to both the South and Southwest Pacific.[38]

The Army planners sided with the Army Air Forces in favoring the first plan. They believed that the additional air groups envisaged in the second plan would be insufficient to capture Rabaul and would materially damage the air effort in Europe. Thus the problem, still unresolved, was back in the hands of the Joint Chiefs of Staff. In that body Marshall helped to decide the issue by joining Admirals King and Leahy in voting for the second plan. Marshall's vote for the extra air groups showed that he was not insensible to the needs of the commanders in the Pacific. Just before the final decision he had asked Wedemeyer what the preference of the commanders would be. Wedemeyer replied that while the Pacific commanders would like more ground divisions, "if a choice had to be made they all gave air forces priority over ground forces." [39]

The planners were right in saying that the additional air groups would not increase chances of capturing Rabaul in 1943. But the Pacific delegates were able to report that with the increased forces, they could carry out the first three steps of the ELKTON plan (Task Two). Harmon had gained inclusion of the southern end of Bougainville Island, for without it, he emphasized, the occupation of New Georgia would be hazardous. MacArthur could advance as far as Madang on New Guinea and, crossing the Vitiaz Strait, open airfields on the southern tip of New Britain.

General Marshall was particularly concerned about the sequence of proposed operations. General Sutherland explained that inasmuch as there were insufficient resources for simultaneous attacks in New Guinea and the Solomons, he thought it best to secure the Huon Peninsula first and defer operations in the Solomons until Lae and Salamaua were secured. He added that it might be decided to delay projected attacks in the Solomons against New Georgia and Bougainville until after Cape Gloucester had been occupied. Sutherland's opinions were promptly confirmed by General MacArthur when Marshall asked him for his views.[40]

Admiral King was not pleased at the prospect of Admiral Halsey's ships remaining idle during the New Guinea fighting, and Marshall and his staff worked hard to still his fears in the week preceding the issuance of the final directive. The conference discussions of coming operations had also revived the issue of command. The problem remained what it had been in January, when it had been postponed. Admiral King continued to insist that firm control of the Navy's resources be kept in the hands of the Commander-in-Chief, Pacific Ocean Areas—Admiral Nimitz. Although the Army's representatives debated the issue warmly with their

Navy opposite numbers, they understood King's concern. Since Nimitz was required to provide ships to every part of the Pacific, he might at any time have to call on any one of the Navy areas—North, South, and Central Pacific—for ships to meet a threat in some other area. King did not want to assign ships permanently to specified areas or theaters of operations. While he was willing to make certain ships available for MacArthur's operations in the Southwest Pacific area, he wanted to ensure that these would be assigned for specific objectives and then be withdrawn. But when MacArthur was put in charge of operations involving forces from the South Pacific, with Halsey and his ships under the Army commander's general direction, there was danger of freezing units under Army control that Nimitz might need elsewhere.

To meet the problem, King and his staff over a period of a week examined several alternatives. One suggestion that died almost at once was to move the demarcation line between the Southwest and South Pacific areas westward so that Halsey's operations in the Solomons would be in his own theater—with MacArthur and Halsey coordinating operations as they did earlier. Another was to extend Nimitz's control to the Southwest Pacific. By placing the whole Pacific under Nimitz, it would be possible to ensure greater flexibility for the Navy. This solution had no chance of acceptance in view of MacArthur's seniority to Nimitz, the importance of the Army Air Forces to operations in the South and Southwest Pacific operations, and the differing views of the Army and Navy commanders on future strategy. King returned to the idea from time to time, and Admiral Cooke, his formidable representative, asked that the Army play fair and give the Navy the same control of overall command in the Pacific that it had granted the Army for the invasion of North Africa and coming operations in France. But the Army did not agree.

When it became apparent that the drafts and counterdrafts were producing no results, the chief Army planner, General Handy, produced a proposal that Marshall presented to the Joint Chiefs of Staff on March 28; it put all the planned operations in the South and Southwest Pacific under MacArthur's direction. To quiet the Navy's fears, the Army proposed that "Naval units of the Pacific Fleet assigned as task forces engaged in these operations will remain under the control of the Commander-in-Chief, Pacific." King still feared that the language would perpetuate divided control. General Marshall explained that the Navy had wished "to avoid a situation in which a large Naval force would be controlled by an Army officer, General MacArthur. . . . Halsey commands a large area containing certain troop commands and certain air units, other than those to be used in these operations. These should not be under General MacArthur's control." [41]

In the end Admiral Leahy, who thought "that MacArthur should be given full command and full responsibility for results," [42] brought the Navy around. He observed that the proposed draft was ambiguous and would make it difficult to reconcile differences of opinion between MacArthur and Nimitz. At this point King outlined a formula by which units of the Pacific Ocean Areas other than those assigned to the task forces would remain under Nimitz. Leahy agreed, if the units were clearly specified and if it was stipulated that units once assigned to MacArthur for an operation would not be removed. Since this was basically what he had sought in the beginning, Marshall gave his assent.

One other point remained to be settled in the closing days of the conference. Still concerned about postponement of the Solomons campaign, King sought assurance in the directive that Halsey's operations would not have to await completion of MacArthur's battles in New Guinea. Soothingly Marshall pointed out that MacArthur's chief fear was that large-scale operations in the South Pacific area might compel him to dispatch forces, especially air, to Halsey at a critical point in the New Guinea fight. Marshall cited a message from Halsey pledging to continue pressure on the Japanese by land-based air and to move into New Georgia and southern Bougainville if the Japanese weakened their defenses sufficiently in those areas to make the operations feasible. This common-sense suggestion seemed to satisfy King, and the directive was allowed to stand as written.

On March 28 the Joint Chiefs of Staff directive was at last sent to Army and Navy commanders in the Pacific. They were to establish airfields on the tiny islands of Kiriwina and Woodlark, east of New Guinea and south of New Britain, from which medium bombers and fighters could reach Rabaul and the northern Solomons—a provision suggested early in the year, dropped in the ELKTON II plan, and now restored because the airfields would permit an interchange of planes between the South and Southwest Pacific areas. Also, they were to seize Lae, Salamaua, Finschhafen, and Madang in New Guinea; Cape Gloucester in western New Britain; and the islands of the Solomons up to the southern portion of Bougainville. The directive was less than MacArthur had wanted, but Marshall had made it possible for him to continue his fight and, equally important, had won him the control of operations that he deemed essential.[43]

While the military commanders argued over future strategy in the Pacific and the part to be played in it by MacArthur, there were signs that he was emerging as a possible presidential candidate for the following year. Some of the proposals affecting him were known to Roosevelt and the Chiefs of Staff; some were merely suspected.

As early as February 1942 Senator Arthur Vandenberg of Michigan, Republican leader and former strong isolationist, had thought of the General as a possible opponent for Roosevelt if the latter stood for a fourth term. By late 1942 sufficient speculation had appeared in print on MacArthur's availability in 1944 to compel him to repudiate the stories and say that his only desire was to do his duty and then retire. Undoubtedly much was done and said without his knowledge by political leaders and members of his own staff, but the record indicates that by the spring of 1943 he was aware that a political movement was forming around him, and he appeared more receptive to the idea. Like many other hopeful candidates, he allowed conversations to continue. Although not a politician, he handled himself with diplomatic correctness. He did not become involved to the point where he could not disavow developments, but he issued no unequivocal refusal.

While in Washington in 1943 to present their superior's case for greater assistance to the Southwest Pacific, Generals Sutherland and Kenney were invited by Representative Clare Boothe Luce, Republican member of Congress from Connecticut and wife of the powerful publisher of *Time* and *Life,* to meet Senator Vandenberg. There is no evidence that they sought the interview or that they did anything more than speak well of their commander. But MacArthur's candidacy was mentioned.[44]

As to MacArthur's viewpoint, his longtime aide, Colonel Sid Huff, later wrote in *My Fifteen Years with MacArthur* that the "idea wasn't unpleasant to MacArthur." In 1943 when he was making a trip back to the United States, the General told the aide, "Have a good time, Sid, . . . and while you're there—keep your ear to the ground," a reference that Huff was certain pertained to the MacArthur boom for President. On his return, Huff reported the one piece of pertinent information he had picked up. Recalling that MacArthur had a habit of carrying a small cane or swagger stick, he declared rather bluntly, "One of the things people asked me," I said, "was this: 'Why does MacArthur carry that cane around all the time? Is he feeble?" MacArthur, says Huff, "never carried the stick again."

Carefully grooming his candidate, Vandenberg was shortly afterward outraged when Secretary Stimson restated existing Army regulations banning political activities by Regular Army officers. After a "red hot" War Department press conference in which Stimson was asked by newsmen if he had MacArthur in mind, Senator Vandenberg sharply attacked the Secretary's action. Despite Stimson's declaration that he was merely reminding Army officers of existing regulations and his denial that he was hitting at MacArthur, the issue remained alive. In mid-May, according to *Time,* "Representative [Hamilton] Fish, who shares with the McCormick-Patterson family his enthusiasm for MacArthur as an anti-New Deal candidate, has introduced a bill to repeal the Army ban on the political candidacies of men in active service." [45]

Shortly after Vandenberg had intervened, he received a personal message from MacArthur via a member of his staff who had just flown in from Australia. Unlike some letters that the General wrote to politicians in later years, this was discreetly handled. After thanking Vandenberg for his confidence, MacArthur said: "I am most grateful to you for your complete attitude of friendship. I only hope that I can some day reciprocate. There is much I would like to say to you which circumstances prevent. In the meanwhile I want you to know the absolute confidence I would feel in your experienced and wise mentorship." Vandenberg, writing in his diaries that the message *"might* be supremely historic," was not certain whether it was his vigorous statement to Sutherland and Kenney or his repudiation of the recent War Department order that brought the response. "At any rate," he noted, " 'Mac' certainly is not running away from *anything*. It is typical of his forthright courage." [46]

Marshall and Stimson did not know what was in Vandenberg's diaries, but they were aware of whispers that a MacArthur ticket was in the making. In mid-April, Admiral Leahy heard from the well-known columnist Constantine Brown that Alfred Landon and Herbert Hoover had asked him about the prospects of "an anti-Roosevelt attack led by General Douglas MacArthur as candidate for President and Senator Harry Byrd as candidate for Vice-President." [47]

Even though Vandenberg's public reaction had been relatively mild, the War Department was once more put on notice that its actions affecting the Southwest Pacific were being carefully scrutinized in Congress. *Time,* whose publisher did not share his wife's apparent enthusiasm for MacArthur as the nominee, spoke of the recent "virulent" manifestation of "localitis" in the Southwest Pacific, where, "in conjunction with subordinate commanders and Australian politicians, he [MacArthur] waged a public campaign, through the press, to compel a major and immediate change in U.S. strategy." [48]

A few weeks later in an article illustrated with photographs of MacArthur and Vandenberg, *Time* published a scene straight out of *Alice in Wonderland.* In it the Senator fell asleep and dreamed of a procession in a great hall in 1944 led by Representative Hamilton Fish, "magnificent in khaki and gold braid," on a white horse. Over the noise of the crowd the Senator could at last make out the haunting tune: "There's something about a soldier." A columnist friend of Vandenberg, *Time* declared, had recently revealed that an active movement to make MacArthur the presidential nominee in 1944 was now under way and that the unofficial headquarters was the Senator's office. Vandenberg's argument was simple. No Republican wheelhorse could beat Franklin Roosevelt. "But the people will really be voting for a Commander in Chief rather than for a President, and there are no credentials equal to MacArthur's upon that score." [49]

For Marshall that spring the story was one more reminder that there is more to war than defeating the enemy.

IX

Winding Up in Tunisia

B EYOND the future planning that constituted the main business of the conference at Casablanca, it proved necessary to deal with British uneasiness about the current campaign in Tunisia. Somewhat dubious about Eisenhower's leadership and the readiness of American troops for battle, the British pressed for command changes designed both to give the Allied commander top-grade advisers and to increase the role of the British in the direction of fighting. The result was a reorganization of the Mediterranean Command, as well as a vigorous effort by General Marshall to remedy conditions that had raised doubts and criticisms.

At British urging an experienced and able team was assembled to assist Eisenhower. General Sir Harold Alexander was brought from the Middle East Command to serve as his deputy, and Admiral Andrew B. Cunningham and Air Chief Marshal Sir Arthur Tedder were placed in charge of Allied naval and air forces. General Brooke, Chief of the Imperial General Staff, believed that by the gesture of placing their senior commanders under Eisenhower, the British had flattered the Americans into agreeing to an arrangement favorable to the British. At the same time, he boasted, they "were pushing Eisenhower up into the stratosphere and rarefied atmosphere of a Supreme Commander, where he would be free to devote his time to political and inter-Allied problems, whilst we inserted under him one of our own commanders to deal with the military situations and to restore the necessary drive and coordination which had been so seriously lacking." [1]

General Marshall saw the changes in another light. Speaking in 1957 of the command arrangement, he cited the appointments as examples of Anglo-American ability to work out solutions to common problems:

> . . . while these sessions of lively arguments came up—and they were lively and they were very frank—we always came to a harmonious conclusion. We Americans must keep in mind that the British made tremendous concessions that posed for them a very difficult situation regarding public opinion.

They gave Supreme Command to General Eisenhower in Africa when we had very few troops there and they had the dominant armies. They gave the Supreme Command to General Eisenhower when General Montgomery's famous Eighth Army came up along the northern rim of Africa after its triumphant career from the initial fight near Alexandria to the final fights in Tunisia. The British public would undoubtedly [expect Montgomery to have] Supreme Command. And yet the Prime Minister was able to manage that Eisenhower continue as Supreme Commander . . . at the time the two armies came together.[2]

The Prime Minister's action was all the more courageous, Marshall thought, because the battle on Eisenhower's front was going slowly at the time Montgomery was driving into Tunisia. In addition Eisenhower was outranked by Alexander and Montgomery and by the air and navy commanders who would be put under him.

On his return from Casablanca, Marshall explained to his staff that the command question had been settled satisfactorily although it would be difficult for the British leaders to justify to their public placing Alexander and Montgomery under a junior commander with less fighting experience than they had. "The utter selflessness of the principal commanders was stressed in subordinating relative rank to command. This should be an example for all of us," he said.[3]

Marshall speedily set about relieving one of Eisenhower's problems— his having only three-star rank while his British subordinates had four. At lunch with the President near the end of the Casablanca meeting, the Chief of Staff spoke of Eisenhower's need for a fourth star, although he conceded that it might be difficult to give it to him at a time when his armies were stuck in the mud. According to Harry Hopkins, who came in at the end of the conversation, the President replied that "he would not promote Eisenhower until there was some damn good reason for doing it, that he was going to make it a rule that promotions should go to people who had done some fighting, that while Eisenhower had done a good job he hadn't knocked the Germans out of Tunisia." [4]

If the President was accurately reported, he was talking merely for effect, or he soon thereafter came up with a "damn good reason." Marshall was able to tell Eisenhower shortly before he left for the United States that his nomination for a fourth star would soon be submitted. He promptly made good on his promise; the name went forward on February 11. True to another promise, the Chief of Staff personally called Mrs. Eisenhower in Washington to give her the good news. Eisenhower was irritated at getting the announcement, as did thousands of others, second-hand from a BBC broadcast. "I'm made a full general, the tops of my profession, and I'm not told officially," he complained to Commander Butcher, his naval aide. But as he was still "grousing," he got the word from Mrs. Eisenhower—not an official announcement but close to it. Next day came the formal notification from the War Department and "a warm personal" message from General Marshall.[5]

On the political front British and American leaders had moved even before Casablanca to give Eisenhower expert civilian advice. Aware that factional bickering among the French took Eisenhower away from the battle at a time when things were not going well for the Allies, General Marshall had stanchly backed this move. On December 15, 1943, Roosevelt designated Robert Murphy as his personal representative in North Africa with the rank of minister. "He will continue on General Eisenhower's staff in his present capacity as Civil Affairs Officer until such time as consultation with the War Department suggests a change." In late December, Churchill selected Harold Macmillan, Undersecretary of State for Colonies, to serve as one of Eisenhower's political advisers, with the rank of resident minister. His appointment was announced on December 30, and he arrived in Algiers on January 2.[6]

At the same time Marshall strongly recommended to Eisenhower that he seek State Department help in solving some of his political and economic problems. A day or two later Marshall wrote Eisenhower's Chief of Staff, Bedell Smith, that his boss "must be given a chance to put his time and energy on the Tunisian battle." Eisenhower was not averse to the suggestion, acknowledging that "The sooner I can get rid of all these questions that are outside the military in scope, the happier I will be. Sometimes I think I live ten years each week, of which at least nine are absorbed in political and economic matters." [7]

Marshall was reacting to Churchill's demand that Eisenhower be given assistance in political matters. Roosevelt conceded this when he wrote the Prime Minister on New Year's Day: "I agree that Eisenhower has had to spend too much time on political affairs but Marshall has sent him very explicit instructions on this point. I don't know whether Eisenhower can hold Giraud in line with another Frenchman running the civil affairs but I shall find out. Why doesn't de Gaulle go to war? Why doesn't he start north by west half west from Brazenville [sic]. It would take him a long time to get to the Oasis of Somewhere." [8]

Nevertheless political complications continued to bedevil Eisenhower. Marshall too wrote on New Year's Day—to warn Smith that American civilians in North Africa were saying that Frenchmen favorable to the Allies "are all washed up" and that Frenchmen formerly in the anti-Allied camp "had put it all over on our Army and political authorities." [9]

While the British and American Chiefs of Staff were considering their next step in the Mediterranean, the enemy in North Africa—although no longer free to think beyond the pressing problem of the moment—did an effective job in sending in reinforcements. Between November 1942 and the end of the following January more than 110,000 troops, the major part Germans, arrived in Tunisia.[10] Meanwhile Rommel was retiring through Tripoli before Montgomery's Eighth Army, hoping to link up with the forces of General Juergen von Arnim to the west. Although his strength had been reduced by half since the previous October and his tanks to one-third their earlier number, he was falling back on Axis-held ports and he was still dangerous. Thus although the Combined Chiefs of Staff at Casablanca had proceeded on the assumption that victory in North Africa would soon be won, the toughest fight still lay ahead. To Marshall and to Eisenhower the possibility loomed larger that American troops and commanders would be considered unprepared to handle their share of the battle.

Carefully watching the developments, General Marshall continued to search for ways in which he could help Eisenhower cope more effectively with the mounting political and military problems. At the end of January 1943 he told Stimson that the Allied commander needed an effective civil-affairs organization in North Africa. He was not certain that Murphy, despite his diplomatic talents, had sufficient administrative skill for the job. Both he and the Secretary of War concluded that they should send over their favorite trouble shooter, Assistant Secretary of War McCloy, already busy with other civil-affairs problems in the War Department.

Stimson was especially concerned that the State Department was seeking too strong a hand in Eisenhower's civil-affairs organization. So long as military operations were in progress in North Africa, he wanted Eisenhower to retain control of civil affairs, reporting on these matters to the President through the Secretary of War.[11]

At the beginning of February, Stimson talked over McCloy's proposed trip with Marshall. For once he complained that he was receiving no help from the Chief of Staff, who, while hammering on the need to help Eisenhower, gave no helpful suggestions. Marshall temporized. He explained to Stimson that he was not yet prepared to tell the President that Murphy lacked the organizing ability to handle the civil-affairs problems at Eisenhower's headquarters. Engaged in winning the White House to a French policy helpful to Eisenhower's campaign, Marshall also sought to avoid upsetting Roosevelt. Noting that Stimson in his draft memorandum to the President on the North African situation referred to the "Imperial Council" in Algiers, he remarked: "The President disavows any acceptance of an 'Imperial Council.' This will irritate him and divert his thoughts from the proposal of your paper." It was for Eisenhower to speak for himself if he saw fit, Marshall concluded.[12]

At Casablanca, Marshall had suggested that Eisenhower appoint a military deputy, mentioning General Patton as a possibility. On the plane, while returning from the conference to Algiers, the Allied commander mulled over the matter, writing Marshall shortly afterward that he had in mind appointing Patton as "Deputy Commander for Ground Forces, giving him the necessary authority, and making use of his great mental and physical energy in helping me through a critical period." [13]

In mid-February, Eisenhower finally decided to use Patton for planning the projected invasion of Sicily. Marshall then proposed sending an outstanding officer from the United States to act as Eisenhower's "eyes and ears." The American commander reacted with enthusiasm, listing a dozen generals, including his former classmate Major General Omar N. Bradley, as suitable for the assignment. Marshall had been keeping Bradley in mind for a key appointment for many months. Since the late 1920s when the tall, calm Missourian, then a lieutenant colonel, had been head of the Weapons Section at Fort Benning, Marshall had entrusted him with increasingly important posts. Shortly after he became Chief of Staff, Marshall moved Bradley from the G-1 Division to his own secretariat. As the Army grew, the Chief of Staff picked the colonel as one of the officers to advance rapidly. In February 1941, he had him jumped from lieutenant colonel to brigadier general and made him commandant of the Infantry School. Before the end of the year he gave Bradley the newly activated 82d Division and saw to it that he received a second star. Six months later he assigned him to the 28th Division with instructions to whip it into shape. Later Marshall said that he had passed over Bradley for corps command only because he desperately needed his services as a division commander. Bradley did not complain, and he benefited from his quiet acceptance of the situation. Marshall had him marked down for the next corps opening when Eisenhower listed him as an officer he would be glad to have for the post suggested by the Chief of Staff. Promptly Marshall replied, "I propose Bradley for detail in question. If agreeable, he will be sent immediately. He would remain as long as you desire him." Bradley was thus started on the road to army group command in northwest Europe.[14]

In early February the American position in North Africa became seriously threatened by Rommel's arrival in Tunisia. Montgomery, methodically advancing after his recent victory at El Alamein, was not close enough to prevent the German commander from menacing the Allied front. For some weeks now Marshall's advisers had feared that Eisenhower's forces had pushed too far toward the south. In addition the French units between the British in the north and the Americans in the south were ill prepared to meet a heavy attack. The enemy could also see the possibilities. Realizing that Eisenhower might concentrate his forces for a drive to the coast near Gabès to prevent the link-up of General von Arnim and Field Marshal Rommel, the enemy decided that the II U.S. Corps must be shoved back. Von Arnim's Valentine present to the Americans was an attack that drove them out of their positions near Sidi Bou Zid.[15]

Eisenhower carefully briefed Marshall on the threatening development. It was a needless precaution. Marshall replied that while he appreciated Eisenhower's lengthy report on current fighting, "I am disturbed that you feel under the necessity in such a trying situation to give so much personal time to us." Operations reports and special summaries were necessary, he agreed, but "you can concentrate on this battle with the feeling that it is our business to support you and not to harass you and that I'll use all my influence to see that you are supported." [16]

It was a familiar note—one that Marshall had sounded in the early clamor over the Darlan affair—and one that he would repeat as late as the crisis in the Ardennes near the end of 1944. But his brave words hid the fact that he was more worried than he appeared. On February 17 he told Stimson that Rommel was concentrating his forces, and on the following day he expressed anxiety because the German commander still had two uncommitted divisions.[17]

There was worse to come, but the usual time lag in reports prevented him from knowing immediately of the setbacks of the next few days. He did not learn of the enemy seizure of Sbeitla and Thlepte and the later widely heralded penetration of the Kasserine Pass until spirited steps had been taken by Eisenhower to counterattack. American forces had rallied sufficiently by February 21 to convince Rommel that he could not gain victory on that front. By the time the extent of the German drive was fully known in Washington, enemy forces had withdrawn to the edge of Kasserine Pass and were turning eastward to meet Montgomery's forces assembling in southern Tunisia below the Mareth Line.[18]

The Americans regained their lost ground at a considerable loss in men, materiel, self-esteem, and reputation. When he came from the Middle East on February 19 to take tactical command of Allied ground forces, General Alexander was unfavorably impressed by II Corps' performance in particular. His reaction would influence him in his assignment of roles for the remainder of the campaign in Tunisia and in the early stages of the Sicilian campaign.

The enemy's mauling of United States forces provoked ruthless soul-searching in Washington. Put on his guard at the time of the Casablanca conference by Eisenhower's comments on the fighting qualities of American troops in North Africa, Marshall was not taken by surprise. On his return from North Africa at the end of January, he had informed General McNair of Eisenhower's anxiety about laxness of discipline, failure to salute, needless eating of reserve rations, and the like. "Some way or other," Marshall insisted, "we must immediately enforce a more exacting discipline and bring all of these men to understand what it means and why it must be done. I don't know that we can accomplish this through a mimeographed order, but it must be done." [19]

Shortly after the Kasserine Pass attack Eisenhower informed his Chief that the troops had learned that they were in a tough battle. "They are now mad and ready to fight. A certain softness or complacent attitude that was characteristic of all units only a few days ago has disappeared." Marshall passed these views on to his division commanders, making the point that they must prepare troops to meet the most highly experienced veterans in their first encounters. He quoted Eisenhower as saying: "Our people from the very highest to the very lowest have learned that this is not a child's game, and are ready and eager to get down to the fundamental business of profiting by the lessons they have learned. . . . I am going to make it a fixed rule that no unit from the time it reaches this theater until the war is won will ever stop training." [20]

Commenting later on the reactions of troops in North Africa, Marshall spoke sympathetically of their "ordeal by fire" and of the training pamphlet he released on it:

> I published an article by a private in a regiment in Africa who was writing up the duties of a reconnaissance platoon. And he went on to explain some of the tragedies that were happening. And he likened it to the fact that the men didn't realize what they were getting into. They didn't realize the brutality of the war. They didn't realize the determination and ruthlessness of the Germans. And he went [on] to say that these men had probably seen the ruins in London but they were other people's ruins and they didn't make much impression on [them]. . . .
>
> There had been a lot of bombing and [they] knew there had been a lot of lives lost, but not until the thing landed in [their] lap did [they] fully comprehend how ruthless war was and how ruthless the Germans were, and [they] had behaved very badly in some of the earlier encounters in Africa. Their training was only partially completed and Rommel's people came at them in a very vicious way and rather surprised them, it seemed. They walked around and displayed themselves, looking at souvenirs they could get out of a village while the Germans observed them in their performance and in due time came down on them with ruthless force and savagery. But they quickly got over this, and as the trained divisions arrived—it takes a long time to complete this training—that disappeared and they became magnificent fighting men. . . .[21]

The bitter fact was that in something like a week, Allied losses (mainly American) ran to an estimated 300 killed, 3000 wounded, and 3000 missing—casualties amounting to more than 20 per cent of the men engaged. Losses in materiel and supplies were also especially heavy; they were estimated at more than the combined stocks in depots in Algiers and Morocco.[22]

As was his custom Marshall said little to the commander in the field, since he had acted quickly to re-establish his position. But he began a careful re-examination at home of training doctrine and directed Army Ground Forces to take a closer look at recent fighting performances. In time he included the conclusions of General Bradley, who thought that overall the American troops did well but that the leadership was not as aggressive as it should have been initially—a situation partially remedied toward the end of the fighting. Bradley found nothing wrong with training doctrine as it applied to infantry and field artillery and the coordination of these branches. He asked for more training in the handling of mines and stressed that tank destroyers must hereafter be considered as totally defensive, a view that required a complete re-examination of that weapon. Air-ground cooperation, he noted, had not been completely and satisfactorily developed. He saw the influence of maneuvers in the case of some troops who, although hard pressed, had surrendered needlessly. They had reacted as if an umpire had ruled that they were defeated, forgetting that—in actual combat—a greatly outnumbered force could often accomplish miracles by "vigorous and aggressive action." [23]

Bradley's comments were strengthened by a detailed report by General Marshall's old friend Major General Walton H. Walker, now commanding IV Armored Corps, who visited North Africa shortly after the end of operations. He concluded that air-ground cooperation as envisaged in training in the United States did not exist. He praised highly the use of artillery, but declared that the infantry lacked aggressive junior leadership and often proper discipline. He blamed this on the fact that many of the younger officers were just out of Officer Candidate School and forced to depend on their noncommissioned officers for aid. The tank destroyer he found disappointing. Like Bradley, he believed that part of the problem arose from the misconception in training by which men had been taught that they could offensively engage tanks and defeat them on their own ground. The result was heavy casualties.[24]

Convinced earlier that the supply system in North Africa was not working well, Marshall passed on to Eisenhower details on the effective manner in which MacArthur handled the supply of a division. Aware that such advice could be unwelcome, he was extremely tactful: "I offer this in a purely personal manner and wish you to feel no necessity for explanation of why you do not consider it practical." [25]

Far more important than the supply system, in Marshall's view, was the performance of American leaders and troops under pressure. Eisenhower, equally concerned, began delving into these matters before the Chief of Staff could make inquiries or suggestions. On March 3 he reported his serious reservations about the II Corps commander, Major General Lloyd R. Fredendall, who had difficulty either in picking good subordinates or in getting the best out of them. It was therefore necessary "to find a good substitute for him or place in his command a number of assistants who are not disturbed by his idiosyncrasies." Alexander, Eisenhower said, doubted Fredendall's ability to develop a team.[26]

The Allied commander had been disturbed for some weeks by reports of disagreements between Fredendall and his division commanders. Several officers sent forward by Eisenhower as observers—Bedell Smith, Bradley, Major General Lucian K. Truscott, Jr., and Major General Ernest N. Harmon—all indicated that Fredendall constituted the main problem in command. When Alexander suggested that it would be helpful to have a new corps commander, Eisenhower heartily agreed.

Eisenhower would probably have relieved Fredendall earlier but for his hesitancy on removing a senior officer first proposed by the Chief of Staff. In early March, however, he recommended to Marshall that

Fredendall be returned to the United States for a new assignment. This was the first relief since Pearl Harbor of a field commander above division level, and General Marshall decided against demotion. Agreeing with Eisenhower that Fredendall's field experience could be profitably used in the training of future combat soldiers, he made him deputy to the commanding general of the Second Army, Lieutenant General Ben Lear, with the understanding that he would succeed Lear on the latter's retirement several weeks later.[27]

Eisenhower offered the II Corps command to General Harmon, who had served ably during the closing days of the Kasserine fight as a special commander in charge of tactical forces under Fredendall—handling both Major General Orlando Ward's 1st Armored Division and the British 26th Armoured Division. Harmon declined on the ground that it would not be proper for him to benefit from Fredendall's relief and suggested instead that Patton be named. Eisenhower promptly accepted this proposal.[28]

Since Marshall had earlier suggested Patton to Eisenhower for a special role, he was pleased with the suggestion and promptly approved it. He may have been influenced unduly and prematurely by Patton's enthusiastic report on his recent meeting with top British leaders in Tripoli. Praising a refresher course that Montgomery had conducted for officers there—"most instructive, I learned a great deal"—he singled out several of those he met at the gathering: Generals Alexander and Montgomery; Lieutenant General Oliver Leese, commander of the 30th Corps; and Lieutenant B. C. Freyberg, commander of the New Zealand Corps. "They are bound to impress anyone as truly great leaders. All were exceptionally courteous and helpful to me, and I did my uttermost to express my sincere and honest appreciation." [29] Patton's bubbling camaraderie, never again to be expressed, was welcomed by General Marshall, who was becoming disturbed by recurrent accounts of ill feeling between the British and Americans.

Patton assumed command in early March. It was understood that as soon as he could put II Corps back into effective fighting shape, he would begin active preparation for the proposed assault on Sicily. With this prospect in mind Patton named General Bradley, who had been sent to his command by Eisenhower, as his deputy, with the understanding that he would succeed to corps command around mid-April. Mindful of Marshall's interest in the new deputy, Eisenhower radioed the Chief of Staff: "I cannot tell you how fortunate it was for me that Bradley arrived here at the time he did. He has been a godsend in every way and his utter frankness and complete loyalty are things I count on tremendously." [30]

Contrary to widespread belief, Patton was not called in to revive a shattered force. More than a week before his arrival, the ground lost at Kasserine had been regained, and the Americans were once again on the attack. They had received a bloody nose and they had lost prestige, but they had fought back. His job—an all-important one—was to reorganize the troops and give them a shot in the arm. This job he did extremely well. Among his changes—shortly before he handed over command of the corps to his successor—was the replacement of General Ward by General Harmon, whose Patton-style cockiness contrasted strongly with the quiet demeanor of his predecessor. Ward, Marshall's first Secretary General Staff, was recognized as an able officer who was a victim of circumstances. The Chief of Staff felt that Ward was somewhat inclined to overestimate the fighting qualities of the Germans, but on the whole he thought well of his abilities. Initially he made him chief of the Tank Destroyer Center at Camp Hood, Texas, and then commander of the 20th Armored Division, which returned to Europe in the final months of the war. With his usual thoughtfulness Marshall told the press-relations chief to announce that Ward had been wounded and decorated before telling of his relief.

Patton's regime improved the morale of the American units, but it failed at the time to change Alexander's views of the fighting abilities of the American forces. Confident of the combat qualities of the experienced British Eighth Army and believing that the main battle should be fought on its front, Alexander assigned a secondary role to General Patton's troops in the last half of March and early April. When he learned that plans for the next campaign against the Germans in Tunisia left the Americans with only a subordinate task to perform, Patton insisted that his corps be used aggressively and not be pinched out of the line in any later rearrangement of the fighting forces. He was hotly backed by General Bradley, who stressed the importance of upholding American prestige. A misunderstanding of the limited tactical role assigned to the Americans in Tunisia had already led to criticisms in the United States of II Corps' failure to break through to the sea and to cut the enemy off in the south. General Marshall emphasized to Eisenhower the importance of removing this impression. As a result, shortly before the last campaign began, the Allied Commander-in-Chief urged Bradley, who had just succeeded Patton, to "prove to the world that the four American divisions now on the front can perform in a way that will at least do full credit to the material we have and the quality of our leadership." [31] The new II Corps commander was troubled at the British request that his 34th Division be withdrawn from the line for more training. Promising that if he were allowed to keep the unit in the line, he would see that it did its part, General Bradley persuaded Alexander to change his instructions. The division, thus spared, was to prove its worth, spending six hundred five consecutive days in the line in the course of the war.

As the 34th Division awaited its chance, American newspapers reported British dissatisfaction with the unit. At once Marshall warned Eisenhower that it had been a dispatch cleared by his headquarters that had reflected adversely on the unit. He was also disturbed by references to United States troops being left behind to clean up battlefields, which had "created further unfortunate impressions to our national disadvantage." Patton, he noted, had written him in late March of an inspiring action by the 1st Division but little of this positive reporting had come through. However Marshall was philosophic: "The problem of censorship is a delicate one and frankness has its eventual reward and in this particular matter the harm has already been done." [32]

Eisenhower was dismayed at Marshall's estimate of the damage resulting from uncensored press reports. He traced the trouble to an overzealous subordinate. Recently he had issued a directive that stories criticizing him were not to be censored. The officer involved had applied this liberal rule to any criticism of United States units and had passed the damaging dispatch.[33]

Marshall was equally uneasy over recent correspondence he had seen between Eisenhower and Alexander. Although Eisenhower had asked for continued use of American units in action, the Chief of Staff feared that he might not emphasize the request sufficiently. More insistent than usual, he directed, "Please watch this very closely. General Surles [War Department press chief] reports marked fall in prestige of American troops in minds of pressmen and in reaction of public." [34]

Marshall's warning reached Eisenhower at a time when he was already harassed by disagreements between British and American officers. Less than a week earlier Patton's headquarters had unwisely issued a situation report complaining of the inadequate support given him by Allied air forces. Air Marshal Arthur Coningham, who commanded the air-support units in Tunisia, had already shown his spirit by feuding with Montgomery. Now he retorted that Patton was trying to use air support as an alibi for poor performance by the ground troops. The reply was widely circulated before Eisenhower knew of its existence. In reporting the incident to Marshall, the Allied commander said, "I realize that the seeds for discord between ourselves and our British allies were sown, on our side, as far back as when we read our little red school history books." But he was trying to combat it. "My method is to drag all these matters squarely into the open, discuss them frankly, and insist upon positive rather than negative actions in furthering the purpose of Allied unity. . . . Admiral Cunningham, Tedder and Alexander are able lieutenants in developing and extending this policy." [35]

Now that the battle had begun to go the Allied way, the incidents were annoying but not really serious. Rommel's drive against Montgomery had failed completely in early March. As his last attempt to hurl back the Eighth Army ground to a halt, he was called back to Germany. He bade good-by to the remnants of the command he had once led victoriously in the Western Desert and departed for Germany on March 9, leaving to General von Arnim the task of dealing with the coming Allied attack.

Near the end of April, Alexander launched a combined offensive with the British First Army in the north and the British Eighth Army along the Mareth Line in the south. Montgomery's forces had unsettled the Germans with a left hook, and the First Army was in position to drive for the kill in the north. After the heaviest Allied air attack hitherto unleashed in Africa, the British struck toward Tunis on May 6. By midafternoon, Lieutenant General Kenneth A. N. Anderson's units had the city. Meanwhile to the northwest, General Bradley, given his chance to show what the Americans could do, drove forward from Mateur. At four-fifteen the following afternoon, shortly after the British entered Tunis, Americans went into Bizerte. Enemy hopes of staging a desperate stand in the Cap Bon Peninsula east of Tunis, and perhaps of organizing another Dunkirk evacuation, were dashed when British troops drove north to block the passage of retreating Axis troops into the area. Those racing toward the tip of the peninsula were soon overrun. By May 13 resistance was at an end. Nearly a quarter of a million enemy troops, half of them German, were captured in the last week of fighting; the proud Axis force that eight months before had controlled much of Africa no longer existed. The Germans alone had lost 155,000.[36]

The Allies had won a reasonably free passage through the Mediterranean and the opportunity to threaten the enemy in Sicily, Sardinia, Corsica, and southern Italy. The initiative at last shifted from the Axis, and the will of the Italians to fight was severely shaken. But the cost to the Allies was not light. Total casualties ran to 70,341, of which the British suffered 36,000, the Americans 18,000, and the French 16,000.[37] Churchill and Brooke obviously felt that the campaign had vindicated their decision to drop the build-up for a cross-Channel operation. General Marshall, although still convinced that the campaign had made operations in northern Europe impossible in 1943, was pleased at the successful outcome of a fight he had feared might turn into disaster.

Marshall's letter of May 6 to Eisenhower, filled with pride and pledges of support, told better than his later formal message of congratulation how he felt about the performance of the Allied commander and American troops in North Africa: "They have called on me for anything I might wish to get off to you by [courier]. At the moment there seems to be nothing for me to say except to express deep satisfaction in the progress of affairs under your direction. . . . My interest is to give you what you need, support you in every way possible, and protect you against the ravages of ideologies and special pleaders of democracies, to leave you free to go about the business of crushing the Germans and gaining us great victories."

In a lighter vein Marshall passed on the advice of a correspondent from upstate New York who said that he had just learned that Eisenhower drank cold water with his meals. Earnestly he asked the Chief of Staff to warn the Allied commander to take better care of his stomach. Marshall added: "After you have cut out the cold water I expect to see modified

HUSKY go through with a bang and the Germans left in the desperate plight of the Cap Bon Peninsula." [38]

The Chief of Staff's obvious relief now that the worst of the battle had passed underlined the great concern he had felt over the performances of American commanders and troops. His preinvasion fears that the assault might end in disaster had changed to worry lest Americans fail to do well in battle. At stake was not only his deep interest in a force that he had helped to produce but the crucial effect British evaluation of American fighting ability would have on future Allied strategy.

Running through all his thinking was a burning desire, retained from World War I, to prove to European commanders that the American soldier was equal to any in the field. He and Pershing and their World War I colleagues were never quite sure that their British and French comrades-in-arms sufficiently respected the American soldier as an effective fighter. The Chief of Staff was equally determined that they recognize American ability to command.

He relished General Patton's comment on May 8 on leadership. Discussing the problems, such as lack of proper reserves, that Eisenhower had been forced to face, the prickly American wrote:

> Indeed, I feel that hardly anyone realized on what a shoe string General Eisenhower has had to operate. Had it not been for his magnificent moral courage, self confidence and driving energy, the truly great victory which the Allies—mostly the Americans—gained yesterday, would never have come off. Ever since November he has been driving relentlessly, and in so doing, has had to assume tremendous risks, incident, first, to the ever present danger of a German eruption in Spain, and, second, to the necessity of maintaining in Tunisia an impossibly attenuated line. Further, he has had to add a great deal of starch to the somewhat flexible spines of most of the Allied Commanders. The results prove that, as ever, leadership and audacity bring success.
>
> Every once in a while I am completely overcome with gratitude and appreciation to you for the opportunities you have given me. As I said when I went to Morocco, the only way I can repay you is to promise that when I get my feet on the next historic beach, I shall not leave it except as a conqueror or a corpse.[39]

Marshall's own views were well expressed in several letters to friends shortly after the victory in North Africa. In reply to a well-wisher's letter of congratulations on the victory in Tunisia, he wrote: "There is little that we in Washington can do except to pick the right man for the job and back him up with every resource at our disposal. Eisenhower, Bradley, and Patton have done a grand job. Above all, General Eisenhower's control and coordination of the troops of three nations in simultaneous ground, air, and naval operations constitutes the great contribution to the war effort to date." [40]

In thanking an old friend of World War I, former Chief of Staff General John L. Hines, he spoke of another commander: "From all reports Bradley did us all proud and made an immense impression on the British.

Quiet, forcible, with a complete understanding of the requirements of the situation, he dominated the Second Corps and inspired them to splendid action." And in a thank-you note to Lieutenant General Embick, he returned to his praise of the Allied Commander-in-Chief: ". . . credit for this victory must go to Eisenhower. He is solely responsible for the complete unity of effort obtained among the armies of three nations which was the secret of our success. Through his untiring efforts, while remaining quietly and unselfishly in the background, this pattern of United Nations' cooperation was developed which spells the ultimate defeat of the Axis Powers." [41]

In his great pride in the work of his protégé, General Marshall worked hard to make the importance of Eisenhower's achievements known. Irritated at the frequent assumption that the General was an amiable figurehead who sat by smiling as the British commanders won the battles, the Chief of Staff boiled over on the morning after Tunis and Bizerte were captured when this line was taken by much of the press. Consequently he was especially impressed by an editorial in the Washington *Post* praising the close-knit Allied cooperation in the Tunisian victory, and he directed his Public Relations Chief, General Surles, to make use of this tribute as a means of persuading American newsmen and radio commentators to show proper "appreciation of the magnificent job Eisenhower has done and the great contribution he has made to the Allied cause in demonstrating, under the most inconceivably complicated circumstances, a successful unity of command." "You can tell some of these newsmen from me," he fumed in the memorandum, "that I think it is a damned outrage that because he is self-effacing and not self-advertising that they ignore him completely when, as a matter of fact, he is responsible for the coordination of forces and events which brought about the successful assaults of yesterday." [42]

There was more in his statement than simple pride in an officer he had chosen. Prime Minister Churchill and his military advisers were then on the high seas bound for Washington and the conference that would go into the record books under the name TRIDENT. He wanted them to know that the American commander was given just recognition at home. It would help block any suggestion that a British commander head the next operation in the Mediterranean.

Trident

CURRENT battles occupied only a limited part of the deliberations of the Combined Chiefs of Staff. Although the individual members were charged with providing manpower and supplies to their forces fighting in distant theaters and were ever alert to the effectiveness and needs of their commanders in the field, their corporate gaze was centered beyond the action at hand. Thus in January 1943 while the battle in North Africa remained at a standstill, they had looked toward further advances in the Mediterranean, with Sicily as the probable point of assault. Before that attack, HUSKY had been launched; they met again to discuss where they would go after Sicily was won.

Churchill had proposed this meeting to the Americans almost as soon as the final offensive began in Tunisia, in the early spring of 1943. Time was short for making the final decision on Sicily (Sardinia still remained as an unlikely alternative) and for deciding if the next victory should take the Allies to the Italian mainland. In the Far East, Chiang Kai-shek was again asking pointedly about future operations in Burma. Roosevelt agreed that a meeting was due, and Washington was chosen as the site. The conference, first in a series with nautical names, was christened TRIDENT.

Still weak from a recent bout with pneumonia, Churchill acceded to his doctor's urging that he come by ship rather than by plane. On the afternoon of May 5 he and a party of nearly a hundred set sail on the *Queen Mary,* which also carried a large bag of prisoners from North Africa being brought to the United States for safekeeping. Landing in New York six days later, the British leaders took the train to Washington, where they were met by the President.[1]

Aboard the British liner Churchill and his advisers employed their time in preparing for their coming confrontation with the Americans. There were some misgivings among the British. Inclined to be depressed by conferences, Brooke shuddered over the anticipated clashes with Marshall and King and the impossible duty of keeping the Prime Minister on the right course. "It is all so maddening," he wrote.[2]

In Washington the Americans had also been busy attempting to establish a common front. As a first step, the Joint Chiefs of Staff directed their advisers to consider plans for all reasonable courses of action that might follow victory in Sicily. In addition Marshall asked Eisenhower to draft plans for a full-scale invasion of Italy and an offensive effort in the direction of Crete and the Dodecanese islands with the object of encouraging Turkey to enter the war on the side of the Allies—recommendations that he expected the Prime Minister to make. But it was only an exercise. "You will understand that the operations outlined above are not in keeping with my ideas of what our strategy should be," the Chief of Staff wrote. "The decisive effort must be made against the Continent from the United Kingdom sooner or later." [3]

The big question of course remained: was it practical for 1943? Politically, as Marshall now realized, Roosevelt and Churchill could not allow their forces to stand still for a number of months. For operations in the immediate future, the central Mediterranean lay ready at hand. Clearing the Axis from the Mediterranean would assure the British of the shortest sea route to India, saving an estimated two million tons of shipping annually. It would provide a needed shot in the arm for Allied morale and would hearten the Russians and the people under German occupation. And it would weaken the Italians' will to fight while increasing pressure on the Germans. These arguments were conceded, sometimes grudgingly, by Marshall and his colleagues.

At the same time the Americans demanded a firm agreement on long-range strategy. They needed to set goals for military production and allot men and supplies for the various theaters. Even now Marshall did not know how many divisions and air groups would be needed to finish the job. More to the point, he feared that lack of a firm commitment on a 1944 invasion of the Continent would mean its postponement until 1945. And long postponement might bring new diversions of operations.

In March 1943 the U.S. Chief of Staff for the first time spoke of the political importance of going across the Channel. He suggested that serious problems might arise if the Allied drive from the west into Germany fell behind Russian advances from the east. If the Allies "were involved at the last in Western France and the Russian Army was approaching German soil," he warned, "there would be a most unfortunate diplomatic situation immediately involved with the possibility of a chaotic condition quickly following." [4]

Despite his fears over delays in the cross-Channel invasion, Marshall kept an open mind about the next phase of operations. He was willing to consider limited moves on the Italian mainland after attacks on Sicily or Sardinia. During the Casablanca meeting he had even suggested to Eisenhower that if they could advance into Sicily from Tunisia on the heels of withdrawing Axis forces, they might cash in on the resulting confusion to gain a great success very cheaply.[5] He was equally receptive to exploiting a Sicilian victory. In his willingness to grasp a sudden advantage, the Chief of Staff showed that he was not wedded exclusively to an early cross-Channel attack.

Although Marshall's experience was as a staff planner rather than as a field commander, he favored a bold approach to operations. Several times in the course of the war he urged Eisenhower and other commanders in the field to consider the unorthodox and the unexpected—a lesson he had taught long before at Fort Benning to officers now applying some of his teachings. But he respected the problems of the man on the spot. Unlike the much bolder Churchill, he recognized fully the logistical barriers to grand designs, and he declined to override planning groups merely because they were cautious. It was the duty of planners, he once declared, to outline for their chief the problems in his path and the steps needed to overcome them. But it was the commander's duty to decide, within the limits of his capabilities, how far he dared go. In 1956 he commented on the difficulties the commanders faced: "Staffs are very cautious. Eisenhower was largely influenced by his staff and particularly by [Bedell] Smith. He had a huge responsibility. With a mixed staff he was almost certain to have a group opposed to nearly any action. [His staff] proceeded on a very conservative basis in Italy in contrast to the chance they [took] in TORCH. The British were conservative, with the exception of Churchill. . . . You couldn't do dashing things with an Allied command set-up for national or international reasons. Very probably Eisenhower's procedure was a sound one." [6]

Eisenhower, aware of Marshall's views on cautious staffs, tried to reassure him. In early May he wrote him that "the products of group planners always tend toward the orthodox and the mediocre and that commanders must at times kick the planners out the window and decide on these things for themselves." [7]

So far as future strategic planning was concerned, Marshall was firmly set on the cross-Channel attack. He told Roosevelt on May 2 that the Joint Chiefs of Staff opposed following the invasion of Sicily with an attack on the Italian mainland. Marshall did not go into all the reasoning that lay behind this conclusion at his meeting with the President. But it was the consensus of Marshall and his colleagues that in all future operations in the Mediterranean they wanted to emphasize aid to Russia and, except for air attacks, exclude operations east of Sicily.

In talking with Stimson the day following his discussion with Marshall, the President said that the Allies should go to Sicily but not be drawn into Italy. To Stimson's amusement the President added that he hoped that the Chief of Staff would go along with his views.

Stimson attempted to limit the extent of Mediterranean operations. Warned by Marshall that the President was toying with the idea of bringing Turkey into the war, Stimson carefully reminded Roosevelt of the dangerous tensions created between Britain and Russia over Turkish policy in the late nineteenth century.[8]

On May 9, while the British party was still at sea, the Joint Chiefs of Staff outlined their strategic views in greater detail for the President and won his agreement that their principal objective would be "to pin down the British to a cross-Channel invasion of Europe at the earliest practicable date and to make full preparations for such an operation by the spring of 1944." Although pleased that the President accepted the proposals "in principle," Marshall admitted to Stimson that he was not certain exactly what this entailed. The Secretary of War agreed that they might have a repetition of 1942, when the Prime Minister had managed to sell the President on TORCH.[9]

Stimson even confessed in his diary some uncharacteristic doubts about Marshall's effectiveness in dealing with the Prime Minister. Depressed by General Arnold's heart attack on May 10, which would keep him out of the approaching conference, the Secretary of War recorded that he would miss him in arguments with the British since he was less diplomatic and less cautious than Marshall in dealing with them and was therefore a valuable counterpoise to the Chief of Staff.[10] In this judgment, which amazingly disregarded Admiral King's caustic powers in battling the British, Stimson was apparently impressed by Arnold's performances in recent Joint Chiefs of Staff meetings rather than in sessions with Churchill and his advisers. The minutes of the earlier Combined Chiefs of Staff conferences, which Stimson did not attend, gave no impression of Arnold's taking the ball away from Marshall. On matters concerned solely with air Marshall allowed Arnold to speak for the American delegation, but there is no indication that he was more outspoken than Marshall.

Stimson's concern about British influence on American policy was fully shared on Capitol Hill. In particular certain members of the Senate Foreign Relations Committee were troubled about possible political commitments at Casablanca. On May 8 Admiral King told his colleagues that Senator Tom Connally, the committee chairman, had questioned him on this point. King in turn had alerted Admiral Leahy, who informed the President of the query. Roosevelt blandly reminded Leahy that there were no political discussions at Casablanca of which the Joint Chiefs of Staff had knowledge. While conceding that this was correct, Leahy felt that they would have to appear on the Hill if summoned.[11] General Marshall then disclosed that General Wedemeyer had been asked to appear before a subcommittee of the Foreign Relations group, but that he personally did not believe questioning should begin at the planners' level. Instead Marshall himself offered—if they agreed—to go before the committee on the following Monday as the representative of the Joint Chiefs of Staff.

For some time General Marshall had been worried about increasing investigative activities in Congress. A few weeks earlier, in a letter to a friend, drafted but not sent, he complained that "Upwards of thirty committees have concerned themselves with duplicated and overlapping inquiry into War Department activities since January 1943 resulting in tremendous loss of time and effort and diversion from our military responsibilities." He feared that the Army and Navy would be deprived of control over procurement of military supplies and weapons. "Such involvement of civilian authorities directly in military decisions is based, by way of plausible argument," he continued, "upon the thesis that the Army and Navy have an inordinate ambition to control the civilian economy, this being the red herring which beclouds the basic issue." [12] He had just seen a new book on the Special Committee set up by Congress during the U.S. Civil War to inquire into military affairs, he told the Joint Chiefs. The author revealed that before they realized where their course was leading, the members of Congress had become deeply involved in military matters.

Somewhat apprehensively, therefore, Marshall appeared before the Senate subcommittee on the morning of May 10. He assured the senators that the Joint Chiefs of Staff did not discuss political matters at Casablanca. This did not mean that they were unaware of political implications, he added, since these were always in their minds. He pointed out that Washington was full of wartime agencies and committees and that the charge was continually being made that the Army was trying to get control of things. In fact this was one of his "most besetting problems and a very annoying one. He had very definitely informed the subcommittee that the needs of military strategy must dominate the situation as regards running the war . . . the attitude of the subcommittee was definitely in concurrence with this idea. He said the subcommittee was extremely cordial and seemed appreciative of his discussion with them." [13]

Apparently tipped off on disagreement between the Americans and the British, Senator Vandenberg pressed Marshall on that point. The Chief of Staff revealed that he and his colleagues had worked at some disadvantage at the January conference with the British because of "the completely integrated support of the British from Churchill down." Vandenberg said that he and some of his fellow senators were disturbed by the fact that the United States spokesmen were not similarly united and that the British usually ended up "on top." While the committee members were filled with pride about what Marshall had told them of the achievements of American troops and commanders, Vandenberg said, they were uneasy "about *who* makes our decisions and *how*, and about the British domin[at]ion."

When Senator Guy M. Gillette of Iowa attempted to ascertain the all-out military objectives of the Chiefs of Staff, Marshall declined to answer on the ground that they were so secret he could not tell "anybody" outside of a few of his own staff members. In view of the guarded nature of his answers and his insistence that planners not be called, Marshall would have been disturbed had he known of Vandenberg's comment on the hearing in his diary. Noting Marshall's replies on the relations between the Chiefs of Staff and the President, Vandenberg wrote: "It remains to be seen whether one of his general officers (General Wedemeyer), who heretofore has sought a chance to testify, will still come and still say that our *military* leaders totally disagreed with the commitments made by F.D.R. to Churchill at Casablanca, and that they have little or nothing to say about grand strategy—their function being solely to work out the achievement of the military plans upon which F.D.R. and Churchill agree." [14]

The divergent British and American positions appeared clear cut at the first meeting of the TRIDENT conference, convoked at the White House on May 12. The Prime Minister reaffirmed his loyalty to the cross-Channel attack—ultimately—but pressed first for further efforts in the Mediterranean. Holding that the "collapse of Italy would cause a chill of loneliness [to settle] over the German people, and might be the beginning of their doom," he set the defeat of Italy as the main prize to be sought after the taking of Sicily. Taking a leaf out of the American book, he stressed the need to aid the Soviet Union that summer and fall. This could best be done, he added, by knocking out Italy and forcing the Germans to send divisions from the eastern front to replace Italian units in the Balkans.[15]

In one breath the Prime Minister assured the Americans that his government favored a full-scale invasion of the Continent from the United Kingdom as soon as possible. In the next he added—provided a "plan offering reasonable prospects of success could be made." The qualification alarmed Marshall and Stimson, for Churchill predicated reasonable success on the virtual internal collapse of Germany. The Americans feared that his approach meant a lengthy pecking away at the fringes of Europe, while Allied airmen and Russian ground forces destroyed German will to resist. Marshall firmly believed that the Combined Bomber Offensive (devised at Casablanca "to [disrupt] the German military, industrial and economic system, and [for] undermining . . . morale") made an early invasion of the Continent possible, but he doubted if it alone could defeat the Germans.

For once the President took the lead in arguing the case of his military advisers. He insisted on a definite decision in favor of a return to the Continent in the spring of 1944, and he requested that this commitment be made promptly. Sir Charles Wilson (later Lord Moran), Churchill's physician, after discussing the Prime Minister's reaction with Hopkins, recorded that Churchill seemed surprised since he had been certain that he could again win Roosevelt to his point of view. Moran later wrote: "The Americans had done some very hard thinking, and Marshall was at the President's elbow to keep in his mind the high urgency of a second front. The results, according to Hopkins, were very satisfactory. The

President could now, Harry felt, be safely left alone with the Prime Minister." [16]

Not only was Marshall at the President's elbow in this conference, he was in fact floor manager for much of the American case. At the Chief of Staff's urging, Admiral Leahy presented the memorandum giving the views of the American Chiefs of Staff on the global strategy of the war at the first regular meeting of the Combined Chiefs, but Marshall assumed responsibility for the debate on the cross-Channel and Mediterranean operations that followed.[17]

The Chief of Staff had been impressed in recent weeks by the emphasis placed on air potentialities by members of the Joint Strategic Survey Committee. He was especially interested in the belief of Major General Muir S. Fairchild, Air Forces member of the committee, that decisive operations could be mounted against Germany in 1944. The Allies could best support Russia in 1944, Fairchild added, by avoiding future commitments in the Mediterranean and by building up reserves in the United Kingdom.[18] Unraveling the broad thread of this argument, Marshall urged that the Allies depend on air power as the principal means of harassing enemy forces in Italy. Allied air could contain the enemy in the Mediterranean and from that area direct crippling blows against Axis oil supplies in Rumania. A raid on Ploesti, he declared, seemed "well worth the gamble."

British opposition came promptly. General Brooke had made similar suggestions in connection with operations from the United Kingdom, and he was to do so again in regard to American activities in the Pacific, but he did not like the direction the discussion was taking where the Mediterranean was concerned. He emphasized the inexperience of Allied troops, the smallness of the forces, and the lack of other conditions favorable to a cross-Channel success.

Marshall saw in the British arguments a continuation of the old strategy. He feared that the proposed Mediterranean operations would, as always, ultimately far exceed initial estimates. He cited a current example: "The Tunisian campaign had sucked in more and more troops. . . . Once undertaken the [suggested] operation must be backed to the limit." He felt that the landing of troops in Italy "would establish a vacuum in the Mediterranean which would preclude . . . a successful cross-Channel operation and Germany would not collapse unless this occurred from air bombardment alone." He feared that continued expansion in the Mediterranean meant that Allied operations during the remainder of 1943 and virtually all of 1944 would be committed to that theater. This would mean stringing out the war in Europe and delaying the defeat of Japan. If they "were committed to the Mediterranean, except for air alone, it meant a prolonged struggle and one which was not acceptable to the United States."

Leahy joined Marshall in insisting that the Pacific was vital to the United States and that immediate action must be taken to keep China in the war. The conflict in Europe had to be brought rapidly to a decisive close.

Brooke took on both Americans. While agreeing on the need of a speedy termination to fighting in Europe, he denied that suggested operations in the Brest Peninsula would hasten Germany's defeat. He froze Marshall's hopes for a quick victory in Europe by declaring: "No major operations would be possible until 1945 or 1946, since it must be remembered that in previous wars there had always been some 80 French divisions available on our side."

Marshall could not believe this proposition. Assuming that this meant that the planned 1943 crossing—ROUNDUP—was still viewed as a vague concept, he asked, "Did this mean that the British Chiefs of Staff regarded Mediterranean operations as the key to a successful termination of the European war?

Despite Air Chief Marshal Portal's efforts to be reassuring, the delays envisioned by the British seemed to be interminable. Marshall thought that the way to begin was to begin. If the Allies proposed to re-enter the Continent by way of the Channel in 1944, then there must be a substantial build-up in the United Kingdom in 1943. Further adventures in the eastern Mediterranean would neither speed German defeat nor hasten a cross-Channel attack.[19]

At their meeting on the morning of the fourteenth the Joint Chiefs of Staff asked themselves where they stood. Admiral King felt that they had to get on with preparations for ROUNDUP or they would "fiddle-fuddle" along as before. He also saw a British disposition to "drift toward an incidental ROUNDUP." Marshall repeated his warning of the previous day against a vacuum in the Mediterranean. If the Mediterranean operation was "the proper way to defeat Germany, he wanted to do it that way." But he doubted that it was the proper way. On this point the Chief of Staff asked General Embick, who was present, for the views of the Joint Strategic Survey Committee. Still as suspicious of the British as he had been when he briefed Marshall in the spring of 1942, Embick asserted that adoption of the contemplated Mediterranean strategy would continue the war indefinitely. "He felt that the British proposals were predicated upon their desire to obtain a permanent control of the Mediterranean Sea. In this way the war would end in a manner favorable to the British." In passing, he warned that recent British proposals for operations in Sumatra might result in the early recapture of Singapore, "at which time they would probably let the United States conduct the remaining operations in the Pacific."

These views were always hotly denied by the British, and some British historians in recent years have chided the Americans for being men of little faith. At the moment the seeming reluctance of the British to come to grips with the cross-Channel concept for 1944 made the Americans more determined than ever to make their fighting position in the Pacific and the Far East secure.

Dismayed by Brooke's uncompromising attitude toward the cross-Channel operation, Leahy, Marshall, and King were agreed that, as King said, "we ought to convert our forces into the Pacific" if the British will give no "firm commitment" about ROUNDUP. As they left to meet the British that morning at ten-thirty, Marshall summed up the matter: the only way to handle global strategy was to outline American alternative action in the Pacific "unless the British Chiefs propose to do something concrete and effectual in Europe." [20]

As matters worked out, Marshall got no chance to give this warning. At the outset of the meeting Brooke told the Americans that it was the "firm intention" of the British Chiefs of Staff to carry out ROUNDUP at the first moment conditions warranted that the operation would contribute to the decisive defeat of Germany. These conditions might possibly arise in 1943, but it was the "firm belief" of the British that they would definitely arise in 1944. The conditions Brooke had in mind were familiar; they depended upon the success or failure of the Russian Army on the eastern front. The Western Allies therefore must intensify their bombardment of Germany and draw off as many forces as possible from the Russian front. This was hardly a firm commitment, but it blunted any American warning.[21]

Clearly it was time for a pause to examine differing viewpoints rather than a time for a showdown. For the British, the crucial decision to be made was whether a German defeat would be brought nearer by pushing Mediterranean operations at some expense to BOLERO, or by shutting down future operations in the Mediterranean for a maximum build-up for the cross-Channel attack. The Americans would continue to stress a full-scale assault from the United Kingdom against the Continent in the spring of 1944.

The Joint Chiefs recognized that the still-untested potential of intensive air bombardment in support of land operations in France might prove to be decisive in bringing the British back from the Mediterranean to the English Channel. Should General Eaker's plan for the build-up of the Eighth Air Force—SICKLE—be accepted as fundamental to Allied strategy? Discussion brought general agreement that it was too early to accept SICKLE as fundamental, though its possibilities were so obvious that it should not be reduced without critical examination. "Great faith," said Marshall, "was being pinned to the results of the bomber offensive." A delay in the build-up of forces in the United Kingdom, he added, would leave the Allies unready to take advantage of these results.[22]

Sir Charles Portal, the British Chief of Staff for Air, later praised Marshall's foresight regarding the importance of Allied air power. Portal said in 1947: "Marshall emphasized the fact that Anglo-American air superiority could offset German air power, and we could go into the Continent with less divisions than otherwise needed. He deserves great credit for seeing this early and pushing it." [23] Conceding that it might have been suicidal to land Allied troops in an emergency assault on France in 1942, for which he had once argued, Marshall asserted that Allied air domination of the lodgment area would eliminate the high degree of risk by 1944. With a successful cross-Channel assault in prospect he warned against committing the men and landing craft needed for it to further Mediterranean operations. Without additional forces in Great Britain, General Morgan's careful plans were useless; unless the Allies concentrated now on a build-up in the United Kingdom, they would lack the winning "punch" in the coming spring.

The Allied Chiefs of Staff had reached a good point for a break in their deliberations. As they adjourned at midday Saturday, the fifteenth, they gave their planners a taxing assignment: two plans for the defeat of Germany were to be ready for the meeting on Monday morning. The American plan would concentrate on assembling the biggest possible invasion force in the United Kingdom as soon as possible, while the British plan would be predicated upon the elimination of Italy as a necessary preliminary. And, significantly, the planners were directed to take "cognizance . . . of the effects of a full-scale SICKLE." [24]

The weekend gave Roosevelt and Hopkins a chance to whisk the Prime Minister away to the presidential cottage, Shangri-La, in the Catoctin Hills of Maryland. Marshall took the American Chiefs of Staff and their British counterparts to Williamsburg for a respite from the war.

Before the British arrived in Washington, Marshall had thought of the brief diversion and had worked out details with Kenneth Chorley, president of Colonial Williamsburg, and Frank McCarthy. In addition to mobilizing his own staff, Chorley enlisted the aid of John D. Rockefeller, Jr., who was responsible for the city's restoration. Rockefeller did his substantial best to make Marshall's party a success. He helped draw up the wholly American menu, which included terrapin à la Maryland, cooked in his club in New York City, crabmeat, fried chicken, and Virginia ham. Special fruits and cheeses were sent down from New York shops, and the rich cream needed for some of the dishes was hand-carried from his farm at Pocantico Hills by his New York butler. In the end to Marshall's embarrassment, Rockefeller declined to permit the Army to pick up the check.[25]

Marshall entered with great zest into planning the entertainment. The visitors were met at Langley Field, twenty miles from Williamsburg, by members of the Colonial Williamsburg staff and local dignitaries and brought to the former colonial capital of Virginia by way of Yorktown. Marshall urged his guests to forget the current war for the moment and turn their minds toward the earlier Anglo-American meeting in the area. Bearing no grudges over the remote unpleasantness at Yorktown, the Americans and their British guests reviewed the battle. In a spirit of levity—for he had served many years in India, where, as Governor-General, Lord Cornwallis retrieved some of the prestige he had lost in Virginia—General Sir Hastings Ismay minimized the defeat by exclaiming, "Let's see, what was the name of that chap who did so badly here?"

General Brooke began at once to engage in his favorite pastime, birdwatching; Field Marshal Wavell took hundreds of photographs. Other visitors set out for long walks, some played croquet, and several took a dip in the pool. The most frequently recounted tale of the holiday concerned Sir Charles Portal. Furnished an overlarge bathing suit for a swim, he emerged from the pool, after making a spectacular dive, without the garment.[26]

In the quiet and peace of Williamsburg, a city more English than American, the Chief of Staff relaxed. While Brooke watched a robin, Marshall jokingly reproved Chorley for failing to provide an oriole for the British Chief's inspection. Later Marshall regaled the visitors with his account of his poor showing in pronouncing the names of the churches of Asia Minor when he had read the scripture lesson at church in Bermuda the year before.

The guests had tea at Raleigh Tavern and a little later drank juleps, served in handsome goblets fashioned at the local silvercraft shop and made with "the finest bourbon," which Marshall's assistant, Major Pasco, had brought down from Washington. Dinner was served by candlelight in the great dining room of the Williamsburg Inn.

After dinner, despite the late hour, the guests set out for the Governor's Palace, brilliantly lighted with hundreds of candles. As they moved about the grounds, Admiral Sir Dudley Pound got lost in the Maze, was rescued temporarily by other members of the party, who in their turn got lost and had to be led out by local guides. The timeless atmosphere of the palace impressed the visitors; Brooke imagined that the colonial governor might walk in at any moment.

As Marshall wandered about the palace, he noticed a small spinet. In a rare moment of relaxation he sat down and played one of the few selections in his extremely limited musical repertoire—"Poor Butterfly," a plaintive ballad he had heard in World War I.

In later years the participants recalled the magic of this outing in the midst of war in one of the early British colonial capitals, a few miles from the first permanent British settlement in the United States, a short drive from the spot where the British, in effect, had been forced to grant America independence. Actually aware of the part that the former colony was playing in the survival of Britain in the current war, they could better appreciate why Lord Bryce had once described Yorktown as "the greatest British victory."

The brief hiatus, which ended on Sunday afternoon, had seen an adjournment of debate—nothing more. The Chiefs of Staff had enjoyed a truce; the familiar arguments on strategy soon resumed. General Marshall, late the boon companion, reminded his American colleagues "that the pressure would be terrific upon us to carry out operations in the Mediterranean." But perhaps, after all, the spirit of Williamsburg was still at work. In a statement indicating that he would take something less than he was demanding formally, Marshall suggested that "we shoot for something more than SLEDGEHAMMER and less than ROUNDUP." [27]

The discussion about how to defeat the Axis in Europe was slow in getting under way. Neither the British nor the American planning paper was ready (understandably perhaps) for the Monday morning meeting of the Combined Chiefs of Staff. To save time the Combined Chiefs directed that the papers be circulated when finished without prior approval of the Joint and British Chiefs of Staff. The next morning, May 18, Marshall told his colleagues that he was unwilling to commit himself when they met with the British Chiefs. He was unsure whether they had yet accepted their planning paper. He said that the Americans must not give the British a "stepping stone" by a lack of "absolute unity" in everything they said.

Returning to cross-Channel operations, Marshall explained that since ROUNDUP would require an American force of one million men, which would take a considerable time to assemble, it was important to examine a smaller-scale operation—a "glorified" SLEDGEHAMMER—more carefully. "Then we would be in a position to maneuver." While willing to consider such an operation, Admiral King wanted to require a firm British commitment on the number of men to be in the United Kingdom by April 1, 1944. Marshall agreed but urged that members of the American delegation stick to agreed-on priorities—getting the British to accede to a cross-Channel operation. If the Americans would act as a unit, he argued, they could win and the President would back them.[28]

An hour later, talking with the British, the Americans did not focus on a build-up in the United Kingdom at the expense of the Mediterranean; instead they tried to obtain a firm commitment on ROUNDUP for the spring of 1944. Early in the session Marshall remarked that the British proposals just prepared by the planners seemed to indicate the belief that a cross-Channel attack would be impossible in the spring of 1944. On reading further in the British paper, with which Brooke had assured him the British Chiefs were in general agreement, he gathered that if additional Mediterranean operations were undertaken in the interval, a target date of April 1944 could be agreed upon for cross-Channel. The Americans were almost ready for horse-trading.[29]

Brooke nimbly countered that an attack in the spring of 1944 was not possible unless the Mediterranean operations were undertaken first. These would divert German reinforcements from the landing area and permit a successful assault in France. Knocking Italy out of the war would be "the greatest factor" in using up German reserves and enabling the Allied build-up to outnumber enemy forces. Marshall was aware of the

British view that continuation of the bomber offensive in northern Europe and operations in the Mediterranean would best create the situation permitting a successful cross-Channel operation the next spring. But he could not help being extremely doubtful, if Mediterranean operations exceeded those then foreseen, whether enough forces would be left in Britain to exploit any favorable situation created.

Brooke assured him that the estimated cost of Mediterranean operations on the United Kingdom build-up would be no more than three and a half to four divisions. Moreover the various Mediterranean operations that might develop were not interdependent and the merits of each one could be appraised as it came along. And as if to underline his commitment to the bomber offensive, he added that none of the calculations affected the SICKLE build-up.

Marshall remained doubtful; the cost of Mediterranean operations could have been underestimated since "the wish might have been father to the thought." Both Leahy and Marshall wished to defer expressing definite opinions until the next day, when the American planning paper would also be available.[30]

Wednesday, the nineteenth, was the day of decision. In the end both sides sought a compromise on future action in Europe. The British agreed on the target date of May 1, 1944, for a cross-Channel assault on a basis of twenty-nine divisions. The Americans accepted such operations to follow the conquest of Sicily as were best calculated to eliminate Italy from the war and to contain the greatest number of German forces. But they retained a strong negative: "Each specific operation will be subject to the approval of the Combined Chiefs of Staff." More important from his standpoint perhaps, Marshall had wrung from his reluctant British colleagues the promise of seven divisions (four American and three British) to be ready for transfer from the Mediterranean to the United Kingdom from November 1 onward.[31]

Later some British critics charged Marshall with obstinacy on the Mediterranean. Reading the minutes, Secretary of War Stimson reached a different conclusion. The old lawyer had handled too many cases to assume that a firm statement of position closed the door to working out an agreement. Besides he knew Marshall. Through the verbiage of the reports he saw a line of reasonableness. Everything depended on the Chief of Staff's calm hand. Clearly "it is taking all Marshall's tact and adroitness to steer the conference through to a result which will not be a surrender but which will not be an open clash. The President seems to be helping us." [32] Stimson's judgment, though biased in Marshall's favor, was prescient.

For Lieutenant General Frederick E. Morgan, who had been appointed on April 1 as head of a planning staff for the cross-Channel attack (Morgan and his group were known as Chief of Staff to the Supreme Allied Commander, or COSSAC), there was at least now something on which to

work. The Combined Bomber Offensive was now also on a firmer foundation. The British Chiefs of Staff accepted an American proposal for a four-
phase bombing attack from the United Kingdom to be completed by
April 1944.[33]

In stormy passages at TRIDENT, Admiral King recorded in his memoirs,
he faced the opposition not only of the British but of the Americans as
well when he insisted on greater action in the Pacific and a greater share
of resources. It was a case, he wrote, of "King contra mundum." While the
official record indicates far less opposition to the Admiral by Leahy and
Marshall than the phrase would suggest, King did take the lead in the
fight for stepped-up operations in the Pacific, particularly in the Central
Pacific area. By no means opposed to increased Navy efforts there, General Marshall, however, continued to strive to prevent MacArthur from
being crowded out of the picture. Only in this sense could he be described as being against King. His attempts to strike a reasonable balance,
in fact, brought him criticism from the Southwest Pacific, where, it
seemed, the world was against MacArthur.[34]

The history of Allied conferences would be simpler if one could speak
of an American case and a British case. In actuality one finds the Americans against the British, the Army and Air Forces against the Navy, and
the Navy against MacArthur, with Marshall attempting to find a solution
somewhere between. In the long run no one remained in isolation, and in
the case cited in King's memoirs the official record shows that King's soli-
tariness was exaggerated. As a literary device stressing his individualism
and his basic concern for advancing the Navy position, especially against
the British, "King contra mundum" sums up a fact of life with which
Marshall, as well as his American and British colleagues, often had to
struggle.

King was in a strong position because United States naval production
was beginning to hit its stride. Six of the ten battleships authorized in
1940 were to be in service before the end of 1943. Carrier strength promised to increase even more dramatically: at the time of Pearl Harbor, the
Navy had one escort and seven line carriers; by the end of 1943 there
would be fifty of all types.[35] General Marshall, who often argued that it
was hazardous to risk everything on naval power in the Pacific, was
equally persuaded that the Joint Chiefs of Staff could not allow naval
strength in the Pacific to remain idle.

At the Casablanca conference the British had reluctantly accepted the
Americans' determination to maintain pressure on the Japanese, to keep
the initiative, and to get into "positions of readiness" for the final assault
on Japan. Now King would ask for a larger role. The American paper on
global strategy, which Leahy read at the first meeting of the Combined
Chiefs of Staff at TRIDENT, contained this clause: "2b. Simultaneously
[with compelling the surrender of the Axis in Europe], in cooperation

with our Allies, to maintain *and extend* unremitting pressure against Japan in the Pacific and from China." [36]

Probably at Leahy's insistence that he wanted only a short paper, "somewhat less than a page," to read at the first meeting, the Casablanca phrases limiting the objectives of pressure in the Pacific were dropped, leaving an apparently open-ended extension of pressure. Brooke was ready with a preliminary statement of the British viewpoint the next morning. The extension of pressure against Japan, he said, went beyond the views expressed at Casablanca, to which the British still adhered, and it might well cause a vacuum into which forces would have to be poured. Action in the Pacific must not be allowed to prejudice the defeat of Germany, which, as the American paper also asserted, came first in the strategic concept of the war. Before the meeting on the fourteenth ended, Leahy read the longer paper prepared by the U.S. Joint Staff Planners on the conduct of the war in 1943–44. The abbreviated paragraph 2b now included a restatement of the Casablanca objectives: "to maintain and extend unremitting pressure against Japan with the purpose of continually reducing her military power and attaining positions from which her ultimate unconditional surrender can be forced." [37]

On the Monday after the Williamsburg bird-watching, Brooke and his colleagues offered an amendment that, in effect, would subordinate extended efforts in the Pacific to commitments in Europe. Rather awkwardly expressed, the British formula would alter the proposal to "extend" pressure against Japan to make it "consistent" with the preceding clause (2a) that the unconditional surrender of the Axis in Europe would be brought about "at the earliest possible date." [38]

Although Marshall and his colleagues had always carefully avoided any minimizing of the "Europe first" strategy, the talk of extended operations frightened Brooke. Although not wishing to upset the British still further, Admiral Leahy reminded them that the defeat of Japan was a matter of vital importance to the United States. A situation might arise in the Pacific that would require the United States to increase its efforts to maintain the integrity of this nation and its Pacific interests, even at the expense of the European Theater. The British amendment, Leahy believed, would therefore be unacceptable to the American Chiefs of Staff. Undoubtedly Brooke realized that in an acute emergency, the United States would protect its national interests in the Pacific, but he wanted to keep operations there within bounds. The Allies, he warned, could not defeat Germany and Japan at the same time. It was essential to deal with Hitler's forces first. His statement made clear that they were back where they had started months earlier. It would be another week before the conferees returned to Pacific strategy. [39]

Brooke wrote sadly after this meeting: "The trouble is that the American mind likes proceeding from the general to the particular, whilst in

the problems we have to solve we cannot evolve any form of general doctrine until we have carefully examined the particular details of each
problem. The background really rests on King's desire to find every loophole he possibly can to divert strength to the Pacific." He was restating
the old clash of a rigid versus an opportunistic strategy. But the Americans felt that the British had a well-established general rule against coming to grips with the principal enemy. All the talk about general and
particular—worthy of a scholastic disputation on the One and the Many
—obscured the fact that each side wanted a loophole permitting it to
carry on its own favorite sideshow while talking of the major effort
against Germany.

The Americans found the British more likely to approve specific offensive operations than broad strategic intentions. King, who was often at his
disarming best in describing the operations he had in mind, did so in some
detail a few days later. By explaining away the frightening connotations
of the word "extend," King reduced much of the British opposition.
When he included Central Pacific operations to seize the Marshall and
Caroline Island groups, and "thence to the Marianas," the British made
no objection. For the Marianas were the key to the situation, King
pointed out, as they lay athwart the Japanese lines of communication.
Brooke wrote after the May 21 session: "The work was easier and there
was less controversy. We dealt with the Pacific and accepted what was put
forward." [40]

The drafts of the final report to the President and Prime Minister were
now ready for consideration, but the American Chiefs of Staff had still
made no decision on the British amendment that would make extension
of action in the Pacific "consistent" with the early defeat of the Axis in
Europe. Before meeting with the British on the twenty-fourth, the American Chiefs at last reached a verdict. After a "prolonged" discussion they
agreed to adhere "firmly" to their wording of the disputed paragraph 2b,
"carrying the question to the highest level if necessary." The British
amendment was, actually, as King noted apprehensively, "a lever which
could be used to stress European action at the expense of our Pacific
effort." [41]

The meeting with the British that followed was somewhat of an anticlimax. In low key Leahy explained why the British amendment was "in
his opinion" unacceptable. The British did not demur at the decision. Air
Chief Marshal Portal explained that he and his colleagues were not attempting to impose restrictions upon Pacific operations; they wished
merely to ensure that any surplus resources that might become available
would be concentrated on the early defeat of Germany. Marshall reminded him that the United States had already agreed to put in the
United Kingdom the maximum number of air groups the British were
willing to maintain there. If there was a surplus of air forces, they should
be sent to the Southwest Pacific, which was operating "on a shoestring"

and where great results could be achieved by relatively small additions to the forces.

The session ended harmoniously with the acceptance of "certain words" offered by Admiral Pound amending the disputed paragraph 2b. The added sentence read: "The effect of any such extension on the overall objective to be given consideration by the Combined Chiefs of Staff before action is taken." This was a much weaker restriction than the British had initially sought. Clearly Admiral King, whether he had to stand against the world or not, was still holding his own in the Pacific.[42]

Sensing that they had found a basis for agreement, Marshall added that he believed that all the decisions of the conference must be reviewed at the next meeting—or earlier, should events make it necessary. If Russia should fall or make a separate peace with Germany, they might not be able to launch a cross-Channel attack but would find it necessary to reorient Allied strategy toward defeating Japan first. Brooke agreed that they must have a future review, but he had a different area in mind. The time was approaching, he suggested, when they should consider exploiting the situation in southern Europe.

Less amenable to accommodation was the vexing problem of Burma. After much contention at Casablanca, the operation to retake the whole of Burma (ANAKIM) had been, in Brooke's phrase, placed "definitely on the books." What operations could be carried out in the China-Burma-India Theater dominated the second day at TRIDENT, both at the morning session of the Combined Chiefs on May 14 and at a White House session in the afternoon. Field Marshal Wavell, who had been charged with planning and carrying out this operation, was obliged to report that preliminary operations for an amphibious attack on Rangoon had failed. The success of the amphibious attack depended upon air cover from airfields on the Arakan coast to the west of Rangoon, but the Akyab airfields had not been captured. The lesson of the Arakan advance, Wavell said, was that the British troops were no match for the Japanese and would require careful and lengthy training. And as Chiang had warned before Casablanca, the Chinese divisions had not marched from Yunnan for a diversionary attack in north Burma.

Alternative operations in the rugged, wet, and nearly roadless country of northern Burma looked equally bleak to Wavell. Road, rail, and river communications in eastern India and Assam, which must support the bases at Imphal and Ledo and the airfields, were "very poor." Before leaving India he had requested another administrative survey; the report was that facilities were not available both to establish communications to maintain the large force necessary to invade Burma and to provide sufficient airfields for China's support. Wavell had left instructions to give top priority to airfield construction. At the end of his presentation to the Combined Chiefs, Leahy asked what he considered to be the best practicable action to keep China in the war. Wavell answered unhesitatingly that the best way to help China was to increase the strength of Chennault's air forces and the volume of airborne supplies.[43]

Before Wavell could repeat his tale of difficulties at the White House, Churchill gave him an unexpected assist. He had looked at Wavell's plan for the capture of Burma and did not like what he saw. He did not like the idea of making four attacks from the sea, "to say nothing of the advance up the Rangoon River to Rangoon, subject to attack from shore defenses of various kinds." And he personally had little inclination to go into swampy, malaria-infested jungles when he could not see how such operations would help the Chinese. Would not the construction and defense of airfields be sufficient to ensure a flow of supplies into China? Churchill felt "that there should be a *passionate* development of air transport into China, and the build-up of air forces in China, as the objectives for 1943." [44]

Stilwell, who was presenting the case for opening land communications across northern Burma to China, felt by the time his turn came at the White House session "that the weight of opinion was apparently against him." The China-Burma-India theater commander said China was a base that the United Nations needed both for its geographic position and for its use of Chinese manpower. Stilwell declared that "ultimately the United Nations must meet the Japanese Army on the mainland of Asia." (Variations of this belief that the Chinese Army would play a key role in the defeat of Japan were held in Washington at this time, even by King, whose Pacific Fleet had not yet had a chance to show its decisive power.) Control of the province of Yunnan, Stilwell continued, was vital to keep China in the war. He had been worried for a long time about the possibility of a Japanese attack on Kunming—particularly one from Indochina. The Chinese divisions now in training there, numbering well over 200,000 men, would be capable of defending Yunnan when trained and equipped. But he would need to use the full capacity of the air-transport route between now and September to provide sufficient equipment. It was "absolutely essential" to open alternative land communications to China. As Marshall had said at the end of the morning session, "the whole problem of maintaining China in the war was one of logistic difficulties which must be linked to our capabilities of overcoming them." [45]

When Stilwell made his bid for the entire tonnage of the air route to China, he was fully aware that Chennault was to be allotted the bulk of that tonnage. Less than two weeks before Roosevelt had at last yielded to the importunities of Chennault, Chiang, and Soong to give priority to Chennault's air operations. As the Chinese would not be informed of this decision for several more days, the President's apparent conversion to air power did not figure in these discussions. While the debate on Burma was edging toward a compromise between land and air, Roosevelt suggested that "a possible alternative solution would be to make use of the forces designed for ANAKIM for an advance towards China, opening the Road as the advance progressed." Even Wavell insisted that he had never intended to give the impression that limited ground operations and full-scale air operations could not be carried out at the same time. Churchill saw no reason openly to abandon the operation at present. Preparations could go on if they did not hamper the development of the air route. The President summed up the consensus thus for the staff planners: "the two objectives should be to get 7,000 tons a month by air into China by July; and secondly, to open land communication with China." It was for the military advisers to suggest the best way to carry out the second objective.[46]

A week later the Combined Chiefs of Staff met with Churchill and Roosevelt to go over their approved first draft of the final conference report. The secretaries had drafted well for the China-Burma-India Theater. As the President had directed, first priority was given to air operations. The air route to China was to be built up to a monthly capacity of 10,000 tons by early fall. Air facilities in Assam would be developed to intensify air operations against the Japanese in Burma and to maintain increased American Air Forces in China and the flow of air-borne supplies to support them. The provision for land operations read: "Vigorous and aggressive land and air operations from Assam into Burma via Ledo and Imphal, in step with an advance by Chinese forces from Yunnan, with the object of containing as many Japanese forces as possible, covering the air route to China, and as an essential step towards the opening of the Burma Road." A fixed date for the operations, felt essential by the Americans, was inserted in a later draft: land and air operations would start "at the end of the 1943 monsoon."[47]

Scanning the draft, Roosevelt noted an omission: Rangoon had not been mentioned. He felt that the Chinese would be much happier if Rangoon was included; it would be wise to do so if only for political reasons. Churchill quickly spotted a place for Rangoon. He would add to the section on "The capture of Akyab and Ramree Island by amphibious operations" the phrase "with possible exploitation toward Rangoon." Someone suggested that the Chinese would interpret this statement as a promise to take Rangoon; therefore the words "toward Rangoon" were deleted.

If Rangoon was unmentionable, operation ANAKIM could be inserted under another guise. The final report provided for the "continuance of administrative preparations in India for the eventual launching of an overseas operation of about the size of ANAKIM."[48]

In the end, while the meetings were marked by a number of stiff-necked sessions, the British were agreeably surprised at the concessions made by the Americans. Brooke counted it a triumph that the Americans had agreed to continue in the Mediterranean at all—a judgment that reveals a serious lack of understanding of United States strategy at the conference. From the beginning Marshall and his colleagues were prepared to make concessions if they could get positive assurances on the cross-Channel assault for 1944.

Brooke also showed that he misread Marshall by his comments on an off-the-record meeting on May 19. On this, "the most difficult day of the conference," the British Chief wrote, Marshall proposed to ease the acrimony of the meeting by chasing out the large crowd of advisers and turning the meeting into a small conclave of the Chiefs of Staff plus Dill. In the ensuing conversations they managed to build "a bridge across which we could meet." Brooke believed that the atmosphere had been cleared principally by the removal of Marshall's advisers since it seemed that "frequently Marshall did not like shifting from some policy he had been briefed in by his staff lest they should think he was lacking in determination." [49] In none of these conferences were Marshall's views imposed on him by his staff. He made the concessions that he and his staff had already agreed must be made. In fact some of his advisers at TRIDENT were prepared to go further than he had gone.

The chief impediment to final agreement at TRIDENT, in the opinion of both British and American observers, was Prime Minister Churchill. After accepting the statement of strategy presented by the military leaders on the twenty-first, he changed his mind on the twenty-fourth and, in Brooke's words, "repudiated" the paper to which they had agreed. In exasperation the British Chief burst out peevishly in his diary against Churchill's changeability. "And Winston? Thinks one thing at one moment and another the next moment." [50] Brooke was likely to be strongly upset at times and to imagine that most of the burden of Atlas rested on him unduly, but there was considerable truth in his complaint that the Prime Minister pushed strategic flexibility virtually to the point of chaos.

It was not the best time for disturbing an agreement drawn up after great difficulty. Current opinion polls in the United States showed that Americans were now interested in beating the Japanese more than the Germans and Italians, an attitude clearly reflected on Capitol Hill. Only after considerable effort were the Combined Chiefs of Staff, with Hopkins's aid, able to persuade Churchill to withdraw his main objections. Brooke believed that he had done "untold harm" by raising American suspicions "as regards ventures in the Balkans, which we have been endeavoring to suppress." [51]

The Prime Minister made temporary concessions on the agreed statement, but he was not finished with the fight. As he talked with the President about some final undecided items, he suddenly proposed that Marshall come with him to Algiers, where they could discuss future strategy with General Eisenhower. Churchill thought he could sell his views on the coming campaign to Eisenhower, and he wanted protection against U.S. charges that he had overinfluenced the American general. Therefore he asked that his chief antagonist at the conference be sent along. Marshall, who had been planning for some weeks to accompany Admiral King on a long-deferred visit to the Pacific, was staggered by the suggestion that he should depart instead for North Africa. But he put up a brave front and agreed to the radical change in his plans. Stimson did enough grumbling for both of them: "To think of picking out the strongest man there is in America, and Marshall is surely that today, the one on whom the fate of the war depends, and then to deprive him in a gamble of a much needed opportunity to recoup his strength . . . and send him off on a difficult and rather dangerous trip across the Atlantic Ocean where he is not needed except for Churchill's purposes is I think going pretty far. . . ." [52]

XI

Journey to Algiers

THE reluctant voyager set off for Europe on the morning of May 26 on the flying boat *Bristol* along with the Prime Minister, Brooke, and Ismay. The President, Hopkins, and Harriman came down to the Potomac to wish them well on their long journey.

During the first leg of the trip from Washington to Botwood, Newfoundland, General Marshall worked over various drafts of the message Churchill and Roosevelt planned to send Stalin on the results of the conference just ended. Faced by the necessity of explaining to Stalin exactly how their current strategy would aid him, the two heads of government had made several drafts from which Marshall was now trying to produce a coherent statement. Perhaps unaware of the Chief of Staff's skill at drafting and improving staff papers, the Prime Minister was agreeably surprised two hours after the flight began when Marshall appeared with a typed, clear copy that "exactly expressed" the political as well as the military issues involved. In his *Hinge of Fate*, Churchill wrote: "Hitherto I had thought of Marshall as a rugged soldier and a magnificent organizer and builder of armies—the American Carnot. But now I saw he was a statesman with a penetrating and commanding view of the whole scene." Possibly he read too much back into his wartime thinking, but he clearly was impressed. Churchill sent the message unchanged back to Washington as reflecting his views. He recalled later that the President—also capable of penning an effective statement—sent it off to Moscow just as Marshall had drafted it.[1]

The travelers had left Washington on a hot day; they landed at Botwood in chilly weather, amid great banks of snow on the airfield. After dinner they set out for Gibraltar, a hop of some three thousand miles. The weary VIPs were asleep almost before they were airborne.[2]

Next morning as they flew well past mid-ocean, the Prime Minister busied himself with accumulated dispatches while Marshall read. On trips a curious lassitude sometimes settled over the usually energetic soldier, and he then postponed his customary chores in favor of general reading or discursive conversation. During his travels he often dipped into volumes of the "Everyman" series that someone had given him for his plane. Later he stuffed into his pocket volumes of the U.S. Army's paperback series, which he passed on to others after he had finished them. Biography, westerns, history—all supplied enjoyment in these infrequent interludes.

Sometime before leaving Washington, the Chief of Staff had asked the British ambassador, Lord Halifax, onetime Viceroy of India, for something to read on that country since U.S. airmen and soldiers were stationed from Karachi to Ledo. "My knowledge of India was a boy's knowledge," he said later. "I had not read . . . with discretion and penetration. Now I needed to know." In a revealing gesture Halifax selected an account of the trial of Warren Hastings. Marshall was soon immersed in the details of the impeachment and the long-drawn-out trial that ended after several years in acquittal for the former Governor-General of India. Marshall became engrossed in the parliamentary procedures followed during the trial and was curious as to whether it had resulted in any reforms.

As lunchtime approached, Churchill finished his writing and came over to Marshall, intending, the Chief of Staff feared, to reopen the matter of future strategy in the Mediterranean before he had a chance to discuss the matter with Eisenhower. To postpone a showdown he decided to keep the Prime Minister occupied with other matters at least until after lunch. In desperation he grasped at the matter of the impeachment proceedings against Hastings, stringing out the process by questions on the bill of attainder. Always a historian and lecturer at heart, Churchill rose to the bait. Marshall was amazed by his erudition and delighted by the exposition. After about twenty minutes, however, even this source of information seemed to "run out of soap." The Chief of Staff then steered him to Rudolf Hess's flight to Scotland in May 1941. Again he had chosen well since Churchill had a personal interest in the incident.

Marshall was so caught up in the story that he forgot to think ahead for a third topic to keep the Prime Minister off the undesired subject. When the General realized that another diversion was needed, he frantically "made a grab and in the most impolitic way" asked Churchill about his role in Edward VIII's abdication. It was the perfect red herring. The Prime Minister reviewed the various legal and political ramifications of the affair, adding that the King's mistake lay in not marrying Mrs. Simpson first and presenting the party leaders and Parliament with a *fait accompli*. This disquisition proved lengthy enough to serve Marshall's purpose; the talk was interrupted by a call to lunch and the showdown was postponed.[3]

At 5 p.m. the travelers put down at Gibraltar, where they remained until the following afternoon. As Marshall had not visited the fortress before, the Governor-General, Sir Frank Noel Mason-MacFarlane, took special care in showing him around, proudly pointing out the new gallery cut in the rock, which had eight quick-firing guns for protection against an attack from the Spanish side of the fortifications. The Prime Minister believed that any threat from the mainland had now been eliminated. Before leaving Gibraltar, Marshall hesitantly told his host that while he admired the tremendous work that had been done, he recalled that a similar gallery had been cut at Corregidor. Unfortunately the Japanese had found the point of weakness. By firing their guns at the rock above, they were able in two or three days to block off the area by filling it with immense piles of rubble. The Governor of Gibraltar was thunderstruck, Churchill reported. "All the smiles vanished from his face." [4]

On this slightly somber note the travelers set out on the last leg of their flight. Now flying in the Prime Minister's new plane, a converted Lancaster, called a York, and escorted by a dozen fighters, they reached Algiers in the evening, where they were greeted by Eisenhower, General Sir Harold Alexander, Admiral Andrew B. Cunningham, Bedell Smith, and others.

The Prime Minister may have been diverted from his Mediterranean obsessions during the trip, but once he landed in Algiers he lost no time in getting back to them. As soon as he had seen his baggage set down at Admiral Cunningham's villa, he headed for Eisenhower's quarters nearby, where Marshall and Brooke were installed. At once he began to outline arguments for going on into Italy, interrupting his plea only long enough to get ready for dinner. Later that evening at Cunningham's, he continued his talk with Marshall, while Brooke concentrated on Eisenhower, who seemed to respond more favorably than did the Chief of Staff to the British proposals.[5]

Realizing that it was essential to win Marshall to his side, the Prime Minister made every effort to conciliate him and graciously included him in any honors intended for himself. He addressed his arguments principally to the American Chief at the meeting in Eisenhower's villa the following afternoon, stressing the importance he attached to the build-up for the cross-Channel attack and emphasizing the desire of the British people and the British Army to fight across the Channel. General Marshall was guarded in his comment, neither rejecting nor accepting an operation on the mainland of Italy after the Sicilian invasion. He stuck to his suggestion of setting up two planning groups, one to study an operation against Corsica and Sardinia and the other to consider moves against the mainland of Italy. When it was clear which should be attempted, all resources would be shifted to that attack. The Prime Minister would have preferred a more specific commitment from the Americans but was satisfied when Eisenhower indicated that if Sicily were polished off easily, he would be willing to go straight into Italy proper.[6]

The Prime Minister next trained his heavy guns on Eisenhower. On the evening of the thirtieth, while General Marshall and Colonel McCarthy were visiting Eisenhower's forward headquarters between Tunis and Bizerte, Churchill sought to allay American fears that the British were attempting to delay a cross-Channel attack. Sensing that Churchill's real purpose was to press for further action against Italy, Eisenhower explained that his opportunity for exploitation was somewhat limited by the string the Chief of Staff had placed on seven divisions, which were to be shifted to Britain by November.[7]

The projected shift of troops by no means denuded the Mediterranean fighting forces. As Brooke pointed out in his summary of resources for future operations, there were 27 British, 9 American, and 4 French divisions. Even allowing for casualties, there would be 36 divisions left. After the 7 were sent to the United Kingdom in November, with 2 to cover British commitments to Turkey, there would still remain 27—a force only slightly smaller than the total that the Combined Chiefs of Staff were allotting General Morgan for the opening phases of the cross-Channel attack.[8]

In the second meeting the Chief of Staff asked what additional forces would be needed if the Allies moved to the mainland from Sicily. General Smith estimated that they would require 33,000 American and 30,000 British troops from outside the North African Theater of Operations for action in the toe and ball, but not the heel, of the Italian boot. General Marshall thought that transporting this number of men would require extra shipping.

Foreign Secretary Anthony Eden, who had flown in from London, linked the knocking out of the Italians with successful Allied efforts to bring the Turks into the war. He thought that they would become much more friendly once Allied troops reached the Balkan area. Familiar with American antipathy to talk of eastern Mediterranean operations, the Prime Minister declared emphatically that he was not advocating or "sending an army into the Balkans now or in the near future." Eden hastened to assure the group that an invasion would not be necessary since the Turks would react favorably as soon as the Allies could threaten the Balkans.[9]

The final meeting of the conference came on June 3. Its early portion was dominated by General Sir Bernard Montgomery, newly arrived from the United Kingdom. The Eighth Army commander, enjoying great popularity in the United States as well as Britain as a result of his African victories, was observed closely by General Marshall as he outlined the projected HUSKY attack, in which he was slated to command Allied forces. The Chief of Staff was not impressed by his manner. This reaction may have been influenced by Eisenhower's unfavorable comments on him.[10] Marshall would have agreed with much that Brooke entered in his diary that day on Montgomery: "He requires a lot of educating to make him see the whole situation and the war as a whole outside the Eighth Army orbit. A difficult mixture to handle, brilliant commander in action and trainer of men, but liable to commit untold errors, due to lack of tact, lack of appreciation of other people's outlook. It is most distressing that the Americans do not like him, and it will always be a difficult matter to have him fighting in close proximity to them. . . ." [11] In a sense it was a judgment that might well have been applied to Patton. But Marshall knew the American better and made allowances for him that he declined to make for Montgomery.

The discussion of future operations went smoothly. Churchill, who had praised the fine cooperation of all hands and expressed his full confidence in General Eisenhower's leadership, ended by saying that post-HUSKY operations would be up to the Allied commander. He would recommend to the Combined Chiefs of Staff the course he considered best. Obviously the Prime Minister thought the battle won, because he added that he felt everyone was agreed that Italy should be put out of the war as soon as possible. If there were any difficulties about specifics of future operations, then the matter could be settled by the two governments.[12]

In fact the degree of agreement was minimal. For one thing Marshall had decided not to continue arguing with Churchill. For another the Prime Minister was simply deceiving himself. Lord Moran has made this point clear. Shortly after the meeting Churchill told his physician that he was happier than he had been for some time. To the doctor's query whether the American Chief of Staff had at last accepted his point of view, the Prime Minister replied, "He doesn't for the moment want to make up his mind. . . . But he is ready to accept my plan. He is not opposed to the invasion of Italy now." [13]

Later at the Combined Chiefs of Staff meeting in Quebec, when it became obvious that Marshall had not agreed on Italy, Moran pursued the question with the General. Marshall made clear that at the Algiers meeting he had not conceded the necessity of going into Italy. He preferred waiting until the attack on Sicily was well under way before deciding. "I wanted more facts," Moran quoted him as saying, "I wanted to ask Winston [it is doubtful if Marshall, who rarely used first names, referred to Churchill in this fashion] a dozen questions, but he gave me no chance. He kept telling me what was going to happen. All wishing and guessing." The General was certain that he had carefully explained his position on Italy: "Winston heard all right, but he kept telling me what was going to happen." In his diary entry Churchill's doctor agreed: "Winston is so taken up with his own ideas that he is not interested in what other people think. It is as if he had lived for years in a foreign country without picking up the language. . . ." [14]

The conference at Algiers produced two revealing stories about Marshall, one widely quoted in the press and another that he himself liked to tell. The first concerned the press conference that he consented to hold at the close of the meeting. Following his usual practice of emphasizing the great difficulties of other theaters in an effort to make the correspondents aware of the broad problems facing the Allies, he spent much of his time talking of the fighting in the South and Southwest Pacific. As he shifted his gaze around the room, asking for questions, he impressed the group by the careful attention he gave each questioner and his query. Then he amazed them by taking up each query in order and addressing his reply to the man who asked the question. In later years the General deprecated the feat, saying that he was merely discussing matters in which he was deeply immersed and that it was no trick to remember who had asked for the information.[15]

The General's own cherished anecdote was based on an incident during his trip to Tunisia and frequently thereafter related by Marshall with relish:

After the surrender of Tunisia and the Italian-Rommel forces [in May 1943], I found myself visiting in an olive grove where a battalion, I think, of the 34th Infantry was bivouacked following the battle, and this was on a portion of the battleground and it happened to be Decoration Day. So they planned a ceremony for which they asked me to delay my departure in order that I might witness it.

. . . in the late afternoon I went with the division commander, General Ryder [Charles W. Ryder, then a brigadier general], out on a field where the troops were assembled. The ceremony was conducted by the chaplain. His remarks were largely a repetition of the Order of the Day, which was a historical reminder of how the Decoration Day affair was organized shortly after the Civil War. So his remarks were not very interesting.

But more to the point was that when it came to the singing . . . he led and he was tone deaf. And they started to sing with him, but they quit. It was a very agonizingly pathetic performance. Added to which the men were in deep column, so that only a few were close enough to hear anything. Above all, they were facing the setting sun—it was square in their eyes—and it was not a cool day.

Now I had issued an order, against the advice of the Chief of Chaplains, Bishop Arnold, charging commanders with the same responsibility for the conduct of a chaplain as the regimental or battalion commander had for the training of his unit. We were not interested in denominational matters of religious procedure but intensely interested in the effectiveness of the chaplain. Was he carrying his weight? Or was he more or less innocuous? Bishop Arnold was very doubtful about this, particularly as he was the presiding judge, in effect. However, I went ahead with it.

So this particular chaplain in Tunisia came to my forcible attention on account of the miserable procedure. While the ceremony was going on, I taxed General Ryder with this state of affairs. He replied by saying that this was the battalion chaplain and that they had a perfectly splendid division chaplain. I replied that I wasn't talking about the division chaplain—I was talking about this battalion, which was his battalion, and that chaplain. He again tried to tell me about the division chaplain and I refused to hear.

At the end of the ceremony, I took over and faced the men away from the setting sun and had them sit down. And then gave them a talk describing what was going on with the American forces in the various portions of the world, trying to take the curse off this miscast ceremony. And when we got into the car to leave, General Ryder asked my permission to tell me about this division chaplain. "Well," I said, "all right, you tell me, but don't forget this battalion chaplain."

He said that the division chaplain drove up . . . at the time of the surrendering of the [enemy] troops. And on the plain right out there by us were thousands of prisoners. They were moving in from every division and . . . in some places the Germans were controlling the movements, just automatically taking control. Our fellows were busy fighting at some other point. This chaplain came up in his car and a German major attacked him on the failure of the Americans to organize this affair, leaving it to the Germans, and was very, very caustic and exceedingly arrogant. The chaplain explained that they didn't have any experience in this and would probably do better next time—implying in a gentle way that there would be a next time—which went over the arrogant German's head. [Finally] . . . the chaplain pointed to his [branch insignia] and asked, "Do you know what these are?" The German said that he didn't know at all what they were but he did not see any relation to this situation. The Chaplain said, "That means I am a chaplain. I have nothing to do with this affair at all." He said, "As a matter of fact, I came over here to bury one of you bastards."

Marshall then appended an epilogue in which he showed his admiration for Churchill:

Now when I returned to Algiers . . . I told the story to Mr. Churchill and he was much amused. But the next day after the review of all the troops—the victory parade as it were [apparently June 1]—he said to me, "You have got that story wrong." I asked, "Was General Ryder telling it to you?" He said, "Yes," and I said, "What was wrong with it?" He replied, "You said 'bury' that bastard and the chaplain said 'plant.'" [16]

The Chief of Staff returned to Washington on June 7, coming back across the South Atlantic.[17] With considerable pride he reported to Secretary Stimson, who had been apprehensive over the outcome of the journey, that he thought he had kept all the gains that had been made at TRIDENT.[18] And he had done it without jeopardizing his cordial relations with the Prime Minister. Marshall made this clear on the eighth in thanking Churchill for his "thoughtful consideration," which had made the Algiers meetings "much easier and more pleasant than they otherwise might have been." The Chief of Staff recalled to Churchill that during one of the last sessions, "I had occasion to express my views that the ability which our two nations had developed to work and fight as a team constituted a more severe blow to the enemy than the losses of personnel and materiel which we inflicted upon him in Tunisia.

"This happy situation had its origin in the friendly spirit of understanding and cooperation which you and your commanders have always shown us. The situation is maintained and heightened by your continuing kindness in personal matters, as well as by your broad view in official matters." [19]

Stimson was delighted to have Marshall back. In addition to facing a threatened railroad strike, the Secretary was being questioned by his one-time boss, former President Herbert Hoover, who was angry over criticism of him based on material leaked to the press by the War Department. When Hoover charged on May 31 that the United States food economy could not support the force of seven and a half million men being requested by the Army, someone in Undersecretary Patterson's office dug up from Colonel House's papers a prediction by Hoover in 1917 that the American economy could not support one and a half million men. This first estimate, which was no less erroneous than the second, was handed to the newspapers and promptly roused the former President's ire.[20]

Marshall returned just as his stepson Allen Brown was about to complete the officer-training course at the Armored Forces Center, Fort Knox, Kentucky. The commandant of the school, assuming that General Marshall would be pleased, invited him to attend his stepson's graduation. He got a chilly reply:

> The fact of the matter is, I had very much hoped that Allen could get through the school without his identity being disclosed, and I ask you now to see that his graduation bears no comment on his connection with me. The fact that it is known that he is my stepson denies him a good bit of the credit for earning his own way and I am disturbed that it has become public.
>
> Please ask General Holly to do his best to see that there is no public comment regarding Allen's connection with me. I hope you do not misunderstand my feelings in this matter.[21]

Marshall was not wholly disinterested. He knew that it was sometimes possible for enlisted men and officers to get rides on partly filled government planes on a stand-by basis—and he asked Frank McCarthy to help see that, after graduation, Allen could fly to Washington to visit the Marshalls. He also wrote Allen: "If you would care to get an immediate assignment to an Armored Division in Africa I possibly could arrange that." Even this intervention bothered him and he added a few days later: "I hope that McCarthy can arrange things in an unobtrusive manner, but I feel quite differently . . . when it is a move to the front rather than the opposite, or favoritism in gaining an appointment. However, with this start the rest of the course will entirely lie with you." [22]

McCarthy was discreet and prompt. Before many weeks Allen was ready to go to Africa as a replacement in the 1st Armored Division. And before very much longer, his older brother, Clifton, who had a bad foot, which normally would have kept him out of overseas service, had prevailed on the General to help have that restriction waived. Again Marshall said that he was always willing to intervene to get men duty overseas.

The farewell party for Allen brought the whole family together in Leesburg for the last time. Major and Mrs. Winn were there with their two young children, Jimmy and Kitty; Mrs. Marshall's sister, Allene, had come down from New York, as had Allen, his wife, Madge, and young

Tupper; and Clifton, a lieutenant with an antiaircraft unit, had come up from Richmond.

They had a gay reunion. Sometimes when the young officers of the family saw the General, they had a habit of telling him how to run the Army and he had remarked dryly several times on his unofficial advisers. Inevitably on this occasion, with officers present from several branches, an amiable argument arose as to their respective merits. Allen thought it fitting that he be the first of the group to go overseas, since the "tanks lead the fight." Clifton asked where the tanks could go without antiaircraft to protect them, and Major Winn, a Regular Army artillery officer, recalled that the field artillery had to clear the way for the tanks. Incautiously they decided to submit their argument to the Chief of Staff to referee. Although as an aspirant for a second-lieutenant's bars, young George Marshall had opted for the artillery, he had served forty-two years in the infantry. They found him as partisan as they had imagined. With mock humility he declared that he was a lowly foot soldier, not in a class with such august company. But he ventured an observation: "When the fighting is at its fiercest, it is invariably the Infantry that carries the ball over for the touchdown." The young officers laughed uproariously at his bias and on that happy note went in to dinner.[23]

Mrs. Marshall had produced a meal with a special regard for the dishes Allen liked best. The whole was topped off by a bottle of champagne that someone had given General Marshall on his last trip to Africa. Its history was like that of many other bottles of champagne drunk in the course of the war—French in origin, German by conquest, and then in turn British or American by "liberation."

At the dinner's close Mrs. Marshall brought in an old horseshoe that she had found in a nearby field. The group watched as Allen hung it up on the garage. When he had finished, and they had again drunk his health, they noticed that the shoe pointed downward. Protesting that all his luck would run out, the company persuaded him to put it up properly. With Madge's help he replaced it. Next day he flew off for England and Africa.

The question of Allen's future had come up in late June as the General gave his main attention to the coming invasion of Sicily. He and other War Department officials became concerned over the peace terms to be presented to the Italians in the event that an Allied victory in Sicily and a threat to the mainland led to a speedy collapse of the Italian government. Most of the American officials, Stimson found, believed that they should avoid direct negotiations with the Italians, while the British believed they should recognize some regime and deal with it.

Secretary Stimson and General Marshall disagreed on the use of the unconditional-surrender formula in the case of Italy. The former warned the President against strict application of this demand, maintaining that it was important to remind the Italian people that the Allies were merely trying to bring them the freedom for which Garibaldi had fought more than half a century earlier. Marshall told Stimson that he was afraid the American people were getting mushy and sentimental about Italy and that he was surprised to find the Secretary siding with this group. Stimson replied with some warmth that he was merely trying to divide and conquer. Marshall, as he explained later, was not opposed to a modification of harsh demands, but he did believe that the warring parties should not be left free to rearm again within a few years.[24]

On July 10, before this issue was settled, General Eisenhower sent the British and American forces under Alexander ashore against light opposition in the south and southeastern corners of Sicily. Strongly backed by naval and air support and large numbers of airborne troops, elements of more than nine divisions swarmed onto the beaches in the largest amphibious invasion yet launched. Marshall had followed final preparations with some concern as the weather turned bad, leaving the attack in doubt. "Is the attack on or off?" Marshall queried on the ninth. Eisenhower himself was waiting for additional weather information. When toward evening predictions gave some hope of improvement in the weather, he informed General Marshall that the assault would proceed.[25]

While greatly interested in the progress of the battle in Sicily, Marshall no longer focused his whole attention on the fighting, as he had in the North African campaign. He had other major problems in July. General Giraud had arrived in Washington shortly before the HUSKY operation began. Crucial discussions were also in progress on the Pacific, China-Burma-India, and Alaskan theaters. The question of manpower and the number of divisions required for the winning of the war pressed in on Marshall. Instead of asking Eisenhower what more he could do for him, the Chief of Staff at times had to ask him for possible support in sending troops to the Azores or to admonish him for asking for more troops than were absolutely necessary.

Accustomed to Marshall's earlier solicitous queries, Eisenhower was taken aback when the Chief of Staff radioed not long before the attack:

> In going over the request of your planners for additional antiaircraft, service troops and so forth, I am wondering whether or not the figures submitted have not been somewhat based on a policy of getting whatever it is possible to obtain rather than being conservative in order to assist us in the over-all problem with which we are now confronted. Also I am in doubt as to whether or not careful thought has been given to the possibilities of using French troops for many of the duties involved. . . .
>
> . . . During the battle of Tunisia and in preparation for HUSKY we have strained every resource to meet your requirements. We cannot continue to sacrifice all other theaters on such a basis of priority.

As he did so often in his exchanges with Eisenhower, Marshall still left the door open, adding: "You may be completely frank with me in expressing your reactions. . . ."[26]

Among the first difficulties that early came to General Marshall's attention in the HUSKY operation was the performance of the airborne units. Both British and American elements, widely scattered by contrary winds, landed shortly after midnight on July 10. Major General Matthew B. Ridgway, commander of the 82d Airborne Division, who had sent Brigadier General James M. Gavin's 505th Parachute Regiment into battle, noted that the drop was later called "the best executed snafu in the history of military operations" but that he preferred General Gavin's description of it as "a safu—a self-adjusting foul up." [27]

Although General Ridgway and others argued cogently that the scattered drop confused the enemy, it also raised questions about the future use of airborne units. Marshall and the field commanders pondered this lesson seriously before the cross-Channel operation in 1944. [28]

Unflaggingly watchful of the performance of American troops, General Marshall was cheered by a report from General Patton on July 18: "Thus far things have gone better than we had a right to expect and the troops have fought extremely well. The Navy landed the several units at the selected beaches with great accuracy and nearly exactly on time." Patton also praised the Air Forces for having softened up the defense. He had been amazed by the enemy positions back of the beaches and felt that the invaders would have had a much harder time "had these entrenchments been defended with half the energy used in their construction." He attributed American success in forcing the positions to this defensive mentality on the enemy's part, as well as to the vigor and speed of the attack. The Chief of Staff, highly pleased, promptly passed on the news to the President. [29]

The victories led Marshall to prod his press-relations officers to give proper credit to American troops and commanders. He objected to a proposed War Department release on July 19 because it failed to note that the commander of the 45th Division, Major General Troy Middleton, had been twice promoted in World War I on the same battlefield and that "Following his last promotion, he became the youngest regimental commander of a so-called Regular Army unit." Marshall recommended that references to Major General Lucian Truscott, commander of the 3d Infantry Division, should include the fact that he had served on Vice Admiral Lord Louis Mountbatten's staff in early planning and that he had participated in the Dieppe raid with the Canadians. He was not satisfied that his own World War I division, the 1st, had been properly recognized, since no mention had been made of its successful work at El Guettar in North Africa and its repulse, without assistance, of one hundred tanks. [30]

Meanwhile the Allied forces continued to advance in Sicily. The Chief of Staff watched the map in his morning briefings as Patton turned toward the center of the island and then northwestward toward Palermo and Montgomery slowly pushed toward the northeast corner of the island.

Looking ahead to possible operations after Sicily was occupied, Marshall near midmonth proposed to the British a landing near Naples rather than one being considered farther south.

On hearing this, an unduly optimistic Churchill assumed that the General had accepted his design for an all-out effort to knock Italy out of the war. But the Prime Minister was premature in his celebration. Almost at once, he spent his enthusiasm on the barren rock of Stimson's objections. The Secretary had left Washington for a visit to Europe at the beginning of the Sicilian invasion. He was startled to find Churchill talking of additional drives on the Italian mainland and Foreign Secretary Eden speaking of operations in the Balkans. (Eden's views may have been the same that he had expressed at Algiers and may have been more qualified than Stimson suggests.) The Secretary hastened to place Marshall's views in true perspective. He explained that the Chief of Staff had proposed the northern landing only to speed the capture of Rome and thus clear the deck for the cross-Channel assault. To set the matter straight, he called Marshall by transatlantic telephone. Although the scrambling noise over the wire distorted the General's voice so that it was almost unrecognizable, Stimson got the clarification that he wanted. As Stimson repeated the explanation he had given Churchill, the Chief of Staff interrupted to say, "That was exactly right; you were quite right; that was what I meant." [31]

In an earlier conversation with Churchill, the Secretary of War stressed his and Marshall's conviction that it was essential to launch a cross-Channel attack in 1944. Seizing on the Prime Minister's interest in the 1944 presidential election and the change of administration that might result, Stimson said there was a danger that by getting United States involved in the eastern Mediterranean in which Americans were not interested Britain might raise an issue that "would be used against the Administration in the campaign." Only by an intellectual effort had the Americans been convinced that Germany and not Japan was the most dangerous enemy that must be eliminated first: ". . . the enemy whom the American people really hated, if they hated anyone, was Japan which had dealt them a foul blow." If they got so involved in the Balkans, Greece, and the Middle East that they could not carry out the cross-Channel assault in 1944, "that would be a serious blow to the prestige of the President's war policy." [32]

The Prime Minister knew a telling political argument when he heard one, and he tried to offset it with an emotional reference to a Channel filled with corpses, an allusion he made to Stimson several times. The Secretary went at him "hammer and tongs," charging that he continued to oppose the cross-Channel venture and was "hitting us in the eye." Churchill admitted that if he were Commander-in-Chief he "would not figure the [cross-Channel] operation," yet having made his pledge he would go through with it loyally. He said he was not insisting on going farther than Rome "unless we should by good luck obtain a complete

Italian capitulation throwing open the whole of Italy as far as the northern boundary." Although he had no desire to send troops into the Balkans, he indicated that munitions and supplies would be sent to the foes of the Germans in that area. Stimson feared that Eden wanted to carry the war into Greece and the Balkans generally and that Field Marshal Jan Christiaan Smuts, Prime Minister of South Africa and Empire elder statesman whose advice was often sought by the British leader and the War Cabinet, was encouraging Churchill against the cross-Channel operation. Stimson reminded Roosevelt and Marshall that the Prime Minister "was looking so constantly and vigorously for an easy way of ending the war without a trans-Channel assault, we must be constantly on the lookout against Mediterranean diversions."

Stimson also explained to Marshall that his request for boldness in a landing near Naples had not been greeted with enthusiasm by Eisenhower's chief subordinates. They feared that they would be going beyond the range of adequate air cover and that the operation would cause a drain on available landing craft. To get a full report on Eisenhower's views regarding this plan and recent British Mediterranean proposals, Marshall urged Stimson to go to Algiers and talk with the Allied Commander: "Then you will have all sides and I think it is very important to go." [33]

Once at Eisenhower's headquarters, the Secretary again expressed concern that Churchill might not carry out the cross-Channel operation the following spring. He feared that the Prime Minister was trying to justify his World War I Balkan policy by carrying World War II operations farther East. After explaining Marshall's views, Stimson asked Eisenhower's ideas on future strategy so that he could brief the Chief of Staff, who would soon be leaving for the Allied conference to be held in Quebec.

Eisenhower was in a quandary about the next move after the conquest of Sicily. As Marshall's representative, he wanted to go ahead with cross-Channel; as commander of a winning team, he was receptive to the Prime Minister's arguments for continuing the drive into Italy. He told Stimson that he had always favored the OVERLORD concept, provided that the British would support it wholeheartedly, but that he could also see the advantages in exploiting the Allied victory in Italy. Eisenhower's aide, Butcher, probably expressed it best by writing that if Eisenhower failed to exploit his victory, he would be charged by history with missing the boat, "yet our own government seems to want to slam on the brake just when the going gets good!" [34]

Eisenhower stressed the importance of gaining airfields in Italy from which to attack factories and air installations in southern Germany. Bombing raids from the United Kingdom, he noted, were limited by distance, bad weather, and increased German air defenses. Forces in the south could operate daily, and their casualties would be lower. Stimson agreed, but insisted that the Italian operation should be finished quickly and should be confined to gaining air bases.[35]

Persuaded from his talks with Churchill and Eisenhower that the British were wavering in their commitment to OVERLORD, Secretary Stimson returned to the United States convinced that the operation would be carried out only if an American was named Supreme Commander and if that American was George Marshall. He was not downgrading Eisenhower. His visit to Algiers had convinced him that while the Mediterranean commander lacked Marshall's poise, he had grown in maturity. Stimson's main desire was to reverse the earlier decision—made by Roosevelt and Churchill when it appeared that the British would furnish a majority of the forces in a cross-Channel attack—to give the command to a British officer. He put these views—including his recommendation that Marshall be given the post—in a message to the President. When he showed a copy of the letter to Marshall, the General made it clear that he was unwilling to have any hand in it. Stimson replied that he had purposely signed it before showing it to him. He had no doubt, however, that his proposal was acceptable to the Chief of Staff.[36]

On August 10 Stimson went over his letter point by point with the President and was delighted to find him in a favorable mood. The Secretary had said that the "shadows of Passchendaele and Dunkerque" still hung too heavily over Churchill and Brooke to make it reasonable to expect from a British commander the vigor needed to carry through such an enterprise. He reminded the President that he was fortunate in being able to avoid the trials faced by Lincoln in finding a general in the Civil War. In General Marshall, he continued, Roosevelt had a man with "a towering eminence of reputation as a tried soldier and as a broad-minded and skillful administrator." As much as eighteen months earlier, the British had recognized this fact by suggesting him for this command. Stimson concluded: ". . . I believe that he is the man who most surely can now by his character and skill furnish the military leadership which is necessary to bring our two nations together in confident joint action in this great operation. No one knows better than I the loss in the problems of organization and world-wide strategy centered in Washington which such a solution would cause, but I see no other alternative to which we can turn in the great effort which confronts us." [37]

Roosevelt read through the statement approvingly, "saying finally that [Stimson] had announced the conclusions which he had just come to himself," Stimson recalled. From that time until early December, the Secretary believed that the search for a Supreme Commander was at an end. The chief problem now seemed to be to persuade the British to accept a solution whereby Marshall's services as a member of the Combined Chiefs of Staff would not be lost.

Oddly enough, when the prize he coveted seemed definitely within reach, Marshall refused to put forth his hand to grasp it. It was not Hamlet-like indecision that held him back, but strong pride. In the days when he was being considered for the Chief of Staff appointment, he had deliberately insisted on avoiding all publicity as the most politic way of handling the situation. His silence now was not due to any such calculated reticence. If this appointment was to be his, he wanted it without any effort on his part. Perhaps with the years he had concluded that he must be above any question of personal preferment. When the matter was discussed with him, he became nervous and ill at ease. Stimson was annoyed that he could not thresh out the best course of action with him. Once the press disclosed the possibility of his appointment, Marshall became even more aloof. Stimson noted that "he has been so upset and shy . . . that the President complained to me . . . he couldn't get any advice out of him on those subjects." [38] It was an attitude that ultimately—indirectly— was to be decisive in the final choice of the Supreme Commander.

XII

France Again
to the Battle

MARSHALL'S stay in Algiers forced him to give renewed attention to American policy on rearming the French, a matter that, involving strong political as well as military elements, had troubled him since the late fall of 1942. In dealing with the warring French factions, Marshall bowed to numerous strategic demands. At Casablanca he had refused to permit his personal distaste for General de Gaulle's arrogance and General Giraud's unrealistic demands to deflect him from the swiftest course to victory. And in Algiers top priority went to arrangements that would best complement Eisenhower's successes in the field in North Africa and implement the Combined Chiefs of Staff directive to defeat the Axis in the Mediterranean. In this, as in many other cases, the Chief of Staff outlined no special policy for Eisenhower to follow. However, as Eisenhower's immediate superior in U.S. Army matters, he gave first consideration to gaining the support of their mutual Commander-in-Chief. In keeping the President aware of the Allied commander's special problems with the French, Marshall was indispensable to Eisenhower.

Marshall's task was made harder by the growing divergence between British and American policies toward de Gaulle. At the beginning of 1943 General Marshall forwarded to Secretary Stimson a State Department report from London that the Foreign Office was continuing its course of building up de Gaulle as the French strong man. Impressed by evidence of support for de Gaulle in occupied France and more interested than the United States in the French postwar government, the British wanted a transitional regime friendly to Great Britain. Secretary of State Hull's efforts to get the Foreign Office to persuade British newspapers to soften their continuing criticism of Eisenhower's early policy in North Africa met no success. Not only did a British Embassy spokesman remark, with obvious relish, that the prevalent London view was that "a brilliant military episode had been tarnished and tainted by the Darlan affair," he also added: "The Prime Minister can no more embark on an effective muzzling of press and Parliament than the State Department could gag Willkie, Luce and Company when they say things that give offence here." [1] Marshall saw that the President was piling up special problems for Eisenhower in London as well as Algiers when he insisted that the Allied commander set an anti-Gaullist course in North Africa.

Eisenhower hinted strongly of trouble shortly after New Year's Day when he complained to Marshall that there appeared to be a conviction in the United States that the Allies were in North Africa "as an occupying, powerful, conquering army capable of giving orders and compelling compliance." He urged the Chief of Staff to do everything possible to soften or correct this view, "at least to the extent that during the ensuing weeks we do not receive any arbitrary instructions which might precipitate a military crisis." General Marshall forwarded the plea to the President, thereby endorsing it, after crossing out Eisenhower's tribute to Marshall's own activities: "I want to say again that my appreciation of your own understanding and support knows no bounds. I realize that you personally have saved us much anguish and worry." [2]

The joint efforts of Marshall and Eisenhower did not convince the President. On January 7 at his pre-Casablanca meeting with Marshall and his colleagues, Roosevelt had ruled out sovereignty for either the Gaullist or Giraudist faction. In a strong anticolonial—or, as de Gaulle would later have it, anti-French—mood, the President declared that Eisenhower could empower anyone he chose to have "a try" at organizing a local government, but that the grant of authority could be rescinded at any time. He criticized Eisenhower's recent actions in North Africa, saying that the Allied commander should not have recognized the French Council's selection of Giraud to succeed the assassinated Darlan and that Murphy had exceeded his authority in assuring the French on the nature of postwar settlements. Roosevelt was certain that some of the former colonial possessions "would not be restored to France, and he had grave doubts as to whether French Indo-China should be." As for British attempts to organize a government under de Gaulle, Roosevelt declared that he had the whip hand and would tell Churchill that the French leader was merely a military man with no authority regarding the sovereignty of France.[3]

Holding no brief for either French faction, Marshall fervently seconded Eisenhower's strong desire to end political infighting, however it could be done. He thus welcomed the feeble gesture toward reconciliation that Roosevelt and Churchill would prompt de Gaulle and Giraud to make at the end of the Casablanca conference.

On a military level General Marshall was especially interested in the forthcoming discussion with Giraud at Casablanca relative to implementing promises made before the North African invasion to rearm French units. Again the matter was complicated because of the warring French factions. The forces that had answered de Gaulle's rallying call after his flight from France to London in June 1940 had been equipped largely by the British. Shortly before Pearl Harbor, Roosevelt had declared these units eligible for Lend-Lease supplies but arranged for this aid to be channeled through the British. By the eve of the North African invasion 35,000 men were enrolled in far-flung units that gave allegiance to de Gaulle's French National Committee.[4]

The Allies meanwhile coveted French units in North Africa that might aid their future invasion efforts. Since the Germans had allowed the initial force of 100,000 men permitted under the 1940 Armistice to be increased to 137,000, it was a prize worth having. In the name of the President, General Marshall had authorized General Eisenhower to assure pro-Allied French representatives at Cherchel prior to the November landings that the United States would provide equipment for French forces "that will operate against the Axis."[5]

Consequently before TORCH the French had drawn up plans for the Allies to equip ten or more French divisions. The best known of the schemes, one outlined by General Charles Emanuel Mast, Giraud's representative, projected eight infantry and two armored divisions plus supporting tank, artillery, air, and service units. It was to obtain equipment for this force that General Giraud, named Commander-in-Chief of French ground and air forces in Africa by Admiral Darlan in mid-November 1942, sent a mission to Washington to talk with Roosevelt and Marshall before the end of the year.

By the end of November 1942 there were 265,000 French troops in North Africa, nearly twice the number of the Armistice army. The agreement by the French government in West Africa to place its troops under Giraud raised his military strength to more than 300,000 men. Unfortunately it was largely on paper. Lacking technicians, modern equipment, and transport, Giraud had only a few thousand men ready to go into the line.

Although skeptical of the practicality of Giraud's demands, General Eisenhower told Marshall that it was important as a political gesture to send at least a small shipment to the French. In order to get basic items for the 7000 men under General Alphonse Juin in Tunisia, Eisenhower had to ask his American units to lend them some of their vital stores.

On the day after Christmas 1942 Lieutenant General Emile Béthouart, head of the French mission in Washington, handed the War Department a revised version of General Mast's plan asking equipment for eight infantry and three armored divisions. Knowing Eisenhower's current shortages, Marshall asked him to estimate the effect on his military situation if the requests were filled. Struggling to get his advance started again, Eisenhower set first priority on the logistical build-up of British and American forces and the rehabilitation of the North African economy. The sequence of shipments, therefore, would have to depend on the military situation.

Marshall directed General Somervell, the Army Service Forces Chief, to examine the French requests. His planners reported that the United States could equip 272,000 French troops while also outfitting and maintaining the American forces scheduled for shipment in 1943. But these efforts would delay the equipping of units remaining in the United States, and the diversion of shipping to French supply would postpone the movement of some 250,000 to 275,000 Americans to the Mediterranean and interfere with maintenance of American forces already in North Africa. It would be a high price to pay for future French aid.[6]

Giraud, always inclined to underestimate such logistical difficulties, demanded prompt compliance with his requests. Eisenhower's expounder of grim realities, General Smith, accompanied by the British and American political representatives, dropped in on the French General on January 12, 1943, in an effort to explain Allied difficulties. Giraud was not swayed. He listed merchant ships turned over by the French to the Allied shipping pool and suggested that part of this tonnage be used to carry equipment for his forces. This was the situation when the Allied leaders met at Casablanca in mid-January 1943.

Hoping to get French aid, General Eisenhower appealed to the Combined Chiefs of Staff on January 15 for immediate military assistance for the French. He made clear that he was no Giraudist; he characterized the General as lacking in administrative ability, "dictatorial by nature," very sensitive and quick to take offense—in short seemingly not "a big enough man to carry the burden of civil government in any way." [7] But he saw the need to have the French divisions in action. General Marshall firmly backed the program for French rearmament. He quickly ran into British opposition. General Brooke was prepared to use French forces in North Africa to the maximum for garrison duties, but he thought that their usefulness in the field depended on the establishment of a suitable French government. Too many Frenchmen, he felt, were passively waiting for the end of the war, and leadership was required to rekindle their will to fight.

At a meeting attended by Roosevelt and Churchill and their military advisers two days later, the President asked that every effort be made to equip the 250,000 troops Giraud proposed to raise. General Marshall firmly agreed, asking that they be given the best equipment available. This aid would be furnished by the United States subject only to other shipping commitments.[8]

In a new appeal the next day the Chief of Staff argued that they must trust the French completely or not at all. He pledged to equip the French forces even at the expense of American units being formed in the United States.[9]

Giraud was next invited to explain his needs and prospects. Excessively hopeful, he talked of building 3 armored and 10 motorized divisions on existing cadres. He also believed that he could raise a respectable air force. He suggested 50 fighter squadrons with 500 planes, 30 light-bomber squadrons with 300 planes, and transport squadrons with 200 planes. He was confident that the French Army, if properly equipped, could make an important contribution to the Allied cause.[10]

Although he was less optimistic than Giraud, Marshall agreed with the General's main objective. "It was in the interests of the U.S.A. to bring the French forces to a high state of efficiency," the Chief of Staff said later in the meeting, "and everything possible would be done to obviate the difficulties. . . . It was not a question of whether to equip the French army, but rather of how to carry it out. Availability of equipment was not the limiting factor, but transport." [11] Unfortunately this reservation was overlooked by the French general.

In private talks with Giraud at Casablanca, Marshall and Somervell also stressed shipping as a serious limiting factor. However when President Roosevelt spoke alone with the French leader on January 24, just before leaving, he gave the impression that difficulties mentioned by his advisers would be swept away. Worse still, when Giraud handed him a summary of the equipment he wanted, Roosevelt wrote opposite the most important commitment, "Yes, in principle." Marshall, who had learned to his sorrow in World War I that "en principe" was a stronger phrase than "in principle," was not there to make certain that Giraud knew exactly what the President meant to convey. As a result Giraud went away from the conference convinced that the equipment for which he asked would soon be on the way.[12]

General Marshall left Casablanca for Algiers on the morning of January 24 without knowing the details of Roosevelt's crucial discussion with the French leader. Not until a few days later in Washington when General Béthouart handed him a copy of a memorandum that the President had purportedly approved did he know what Giraud assumed that he had won. Somewhat surprised, the Chief of Staff replied that he had no information from the President of any specific arrangements beyond a confirmation of the assurance that Marshall himself had given the French leader: that "we would proceed now with the greatest possible speed to equip his troops, and that the matter of cargo space, character of equipment as to priorities of shipment, etc., would be determined later." [13]

Appalled at this latest indication of poor administration, Secretary Stimson chided the President for failing to consult his advisers before approving Giraud's requests. When Stimson added that Secretary Hull thought the agreement was something that the President had signed over a drink, Roosevelt laughed and "virtually admitted," according to Stimson, that other parts of the understanding had probably been reached the same way.[14]

The haphazard but happy arrangement soon turned sour. Giraud was disturbed in early February when Prime Minister Churchill insisted on a three-power agreement to supersede the understanding between Roosevelt and Giraud. Not only did the new language seem to dilute the promise of American support, but there were unseemly delays in the arrival of supplies. On February 18 Ambassador Murphy warned Washington that a belief was growing in both the administration and Army in Algiers that "the United Nations have no intention of supporting a French Army except as a defensive force; that the military effort here is being held back, as a matter of policy; and that as a result French troops will have no share in the conquest of France and France will not be present at the victory." [15]

Roosevelt stoutly denied making any flat promises to Giraud. He radioed Murphy: "I wish our good friends in North Africa would get their feet on the ground. You can tell them at no time did I or General Marshall promise equipment for the French divisions on any given date. What was agreed on was the principle of rearming them—to be done as soon as we found it practicable from a shipping point of view." [16]

It was too late to calm the storm blowing up in Algiers. Murphy reported that Giraud believed that in his conversations with Marshall and Somervell at Casablanca "a far more substantial program was indicated." In addition the Giraudists were disturbed because de Gaulle's forces were continuing to receive supplies from the British. As a result the French in Algiers were giving some credence to a current report that the United States did not favor the creation of a French Army and was proposing, "with Great Britain and Soviet Russia, to exclude France from real participation in the peace settlement." [17]

A bitter and suspicious Giraud had told Eisenhower that he had lost interest in continuing the battle. He had joined the fight in North Africa to help in the liberation of France. If that opportunity were to be denied him, he wished to quit now. "He has every confidence in your sincerity and that of Generals Marshall and Somervell and Eisenhower," said Murphy, "but he feels that somewhere along the line there is opposition if not deception."

General Marshall had already sketched for Eisenhower the nature of the American agreement with Giraud. With Roosevelt's approval he had assured the Allied commander that the United States intended and desired that French North African forces take part in the liberation of France.[18]

In setting matters straight, the Chief of Staff dealt severely—some observers thought unfairly—with Giraud. Marshall firmly declared that Roosevelt's agreement "in principle" was based on "General Giraud's statement of a detailed arrangement with General Somervell and me which had not been reached. Furthermore, the President considered that his agreement 'in principle' did not involve detailed commitments."

Although nettled by Giraud's suspicions, the Americans remained set on the French rearmament program. Marshall had already directed General Somervell to explore the shipping problem. He continued with plans

even when the British asked for a Combined Chiefs of Staff agreement
before sending supplies to North Africa. Before the end of February the
Chief of Staff had marked for shipment sufficient supplies to equip three
infantry divisions, two armored regiments, four tank-destroyer battalions,
three reconnaissance battalions, as well as antiaircraft artillery battalions
and truck companies.[19]

Happily General Marshall was able to inform Eisenhower of the departure of a special convoy with the promised items just as the latter was
bracing himself to inform Giraud of the President's limited interpretation
of the Casablanca agreements. These deliveries eased the situation temporarily, but the French rearmament problem remained to plague Allied
relations with both Giraud and de Gaulle for many months more.

At TRIDENT the Combined Chiefs of Staff re-examined the role they
expected the French to play in future operations. During the meeting on
May 18 Admiral Leahy announced that some equipment was moving to
the French in North Africa. General Brooke urged that it not be supplied
at the expense of other Allied forces. The correct current policy, he suggested, was to equip the French units for a static role, thereby releasing
Allied troops for offensive operations. Later something could be done
about a French expeditionary force. To mollify the French, Marshall proposed that a United States division scheduled to move to the United
Kingdom from North Africa turn over its equipment there to French
units and pick up new materiel on arrival at its new station.[20]

In the end the Combined Chiefs of Staff settled on a formula satisfactory to the British: "The rearming and re-equipping of the French Forces
in North Africa should be proceeded with as rapidly as the availability of
shipping and equipment will allow, but as a secondary commitment to
the requirements of British and U.S. forces in the various theaters." It was
less than the Americans wanted. As Marcel Vigneras, the U.S. Army's official historian on French rearmament, remarked: "The Americans were
convinced that neither shortage of equipment nor shortage of supplies
would interfere with the arming of the eleven divisions as agreed. They
were equally convinced that the North African troops had proved their
usefulness and that therefore it would be militarily justifiable, if necessary, to arm those at the expense of American units." [21] On this point
Marshall and Eisenhower were fully agreed.

General Marshall's trip to Algiers in late May and early June coincided
with the effort by both the de Gaulle and Giraud factions to form a single
committee to control all French areas and forces outside Axis control. On
June 3 the establishment of a seven-man French Committee of National
Liberation (later enlarged to fourteen members), with de Gaulle and
Giraud as co-presidents, was announced in Algiers. Giraud also retained
the post of Commander-in-Chief of the armed forces.[22]

To some degree General Marshall shared Roosevelt's dislike of de
Gaulle's posturing and his rough handling of Giraud. But his primary

interest in the political situation in North Africa was still the effect of the factional quarrel on Eisenhower's battle against the Axis. In his dealings with Roosevelt and Secretary Hull on the French question, Marshall continually stressed the fact that the Allied Commander-in-Chief must have political stability in his rear areas and must be able to make maximum use of the French troops and leadership in later fighting. And increasingly Eisenhower and Bedell Smith found Giraud ineffective in organizing support among all the French factions.

Less than a week after the formation of the Committee of Seven, de Gaulle raised a storm by insisting on the creation of the post of Commissioner of National Defense, which he would control, and on the removal of several officeholders with former ties to Vichy. Among these was Pierre Boisson, Governor-General of French West Africa, who had incurred de Gaulle's undying enmity by defending Dakar against the latter's forces. However Roosevelt liked Boisson because he had declared for the Allies shortly after the landings in North Africa, and he had supported him strongly to prevent de Gaulle from getting control of Dakar. The President promptly instructed Eisenhower to tell Giraud and de Gaulle that he hoped "reports as to General Boisson's future are indeed unfounded." [23] At the same time he informed Churchill that he could not "feel happy unless Giraud has complete control of the French Army in North Africa" and that he could not consider "any de Gaulle domination of French West Africa." "This is so serious," he added, "that I should have to consider sending several regiments to Dakar and also naval vessels if there were any signs that de Gaulle proposes to take things over in French West Africa." [24]

Meanwhile a comic interlude had started in which de Gaulle resigned as co-president of the committee and Giraud showed signs of bowing out. The comedy became farce when de Gaulle handed Giraud a number of decrees, including one doubling the size of the committee by the addition of enough de Gaulle backers to assure him a majority and got the required signature. With control in his hands de Gaulle withdrew his resignation. Murphy explained to a bewildered Giraud the enormity of his indiscretion and suggested to Secretary Hull that Eisenhower call in the warring French leaders and explain the American position in regard to their military establishment.[25]

Murphy's messages fanned the vehement anti-Gaullism of both Secretary Hull and the President. They in turn hammered at Marshall. Told by Hull that much "vital ground" had been lost and that the Allies might soon be confronted "by a tragic situation in relation to French forces in North Africa," the Chief of Staff proposed to Roosevelt the following action: "That General Eisenhower should be directed by the President to exercise his direct influence as Commander-in-Chief in Africa, over the developments on the French Committee; that he be authorized to inform the Committee, if he sees fit, that in view of its action or proposed actions the United States will reconsider the matter of the armament, equipment, payment, etc., to the French Forces; that the President consult with the Prime Minister with a view to authorizing General Eisenhower to use the necessary pressure to prevent the control of the French army from falling into the hands of de Gaulle." In sending this to Eisenhower, Marshall added: "Meanwhile I wish you to know of our attitude here, particularly Mr. Hull's, who is extremely worried that you are not now in Algiers." [26]

Roosevelt, of course, needed no coaching on his lines. That afternoon he notified Eisenhower that "during our military occupation of North Africa, we will not tolerate the control of the French Army by any agency which is not subject to the Allied Supreme Commander's direction." It must be absolutely clear, he went on, that a further condition of the military occupation is that "without your full approval no independent civil decision can be made." Lest there be any doubt as to the target of his displeasure, he declared: "I want to state for your exclusive information that at this time we will not permit de Gaulle to direct himself or to control through partisans on any committee, the African French army, either in the field of supplies, training, or operations."

Passing this message on to Churchill, the President explained that he was "fed up with de Gaulle" and that he saw no possibility of working with him. He was "absolutely convinced that he has been and is now injuring our war effort and that he is a very dangerous threat to us. I agree with you that he likes neither the British nor the Americans. . . . I agree with you that the time has arrived when we must break with him." Roosevelt was convinced that de Gaulle was far more interested in "political machinations" than in prosecuting the war. As a result Eisenhower had been forced to give half of his time to purely local political matters. Roosevelt reminded Churchill that Britain and the United States had pledged to liberate France and return that country to control of the French people. Meanwhile he wanted to create a committee of Frenchmen "who really want to fight the war and are not thinking too much about politics." He asked Churchill to instruct Macmillan to aid Eisenhower in postponing any further meeting of the French Committee in North Africa.[27]

Roosevelt's distaste for de Gaulle had, of course, led him beyond a point that Churchill could persuade his pro-Gaullist Foreign Office to accept. The Prime Minister agreed that the French Army should be in hands completely friendly to the Allied cause and that no confidence could be placed in de Gaulle's friendship for the Allies. But he did not favor disbanding the Committee of Seven or forbidding it to meet, nor did he feel that he could say that it was time to break with de Gaulle. Nevertheless it was clear that he wanted Giraud to remain in command of French military forces.[28]

Apparently influenced by Macmillan, who, like Eden, was far less skeptical than the Prime Minister of de Gaulle, Eisenhower pursued a less belligerent approach to de Gaulle than the President had outlined.[29] He asked de Gaulle and Giraud to meet him at his villa on June 19 for an interview that, Macmillan recalls, "was naturally cold and unfriendly." The Allied commander sought assurances that the Commander-in-Chief of French Forces would have effective control of his troops, that no reorganization scheme would weaken his control, and that for the present Giraud was to be Commander-in-Chief. Thus he maintained the point that Roosevelt and Churchill, as well as Marshall, wanted most. But he issued no ultimatum.

For his pains at diplomacy he got a sharp sample of de Gaulle's famed hauteur. De Gaulle's own account makes clear that in his reply he lost no time putting the Allied Commander-in-Chief in his place. Pre-empting Giraud's share of authority and speaking as co-president of a committee scarcely ten days old, he jolted Eisenhower by proclaiming, "I am here in my capacity as President of the French Government. For it is customary that during operations the chiefs of state and of the government should come in person to the headquarters of the officer in command of the armies they have entrusted to him. If you wish to address a request to me concerning your province, be assured that I am disposed beforehand to give you satisfaction, on condition, of course, that it is compatible with the interests in my charge." [30]

After delivering this lecture, de Gaulle withdrew. It is doubtful that he was ever more magnificently insufferable.

De Gaulle wrote later that he and members of the committee decided to ignore the Allied demands. In fact they agreed to a compromise that, while not fully satisfactory to anyone concerned, was acceptable. A Permanent Military Committee, composed of Giraud and de Gaulle and their Chiefs of Staff for the various services, was to have responsibility for the unification, organization, and training of the armed forces. General Giraud was to be Commander-in-Chief in North and West Africa and General de Gaulle was to have control of forces in all other overseas territories.

Murphy was none too hopeful that the affair was settled: "We should have no illusions over the continuing determination of General de Gaulle to dominate the situation." He was aware, as were Eisenhower and Bedell Smith, that Giraud was no match for his opponent. Discounting the importance of the political side of his position, Giraud tended to make concessions in an effort to get unity. "The de Gaulle group have repeatedly taken advantage of this susceptibility," Murphy observed.[31]

Almost at once there was another flare-up—this time over the resignation of Pierre Boisson as Governor-General of French West Africa. The President was already on record as strongly opposing his removal when Boisson, presumably under pressure from de Gaulle's supporters, offered his resignation. Unaware of this background, Giraud at first accepted it and then attempted to cancel his action. Eisenhower and Murphy felt it best to go along with the resignation. In their efforts to calm the President they asked General Marshall's assistance.

The President was mollified when the French Committee put forth the name of Pierre Cournarie, French Governor of the Cameroons. But he was determined to ensure that Dakar, which he regarded as critical to the defense of the Western Hemisphere, remained free of de Gaulle's control. Consequently he drafted a message to Eisenhower indicating his desire to send a large United States force to Dakar to defend airfields there. Marshall sharply opposed this proposal. Such action, he warned, might give the Gaullists grounds for charging the Americans with attempts to dominate French affairs. With HUSKY near at hand nothing should be done to aid Axis propagandists. Roosevelt finally contented himself with the requirement that if at any time during the remainder of the war the United States requested a change in Cournarie's command, "such a change will be effected by putting in his place a man totally agreeable to the United States." [32]

Some time ago Roosevelt had invited Giraud to the White House, and he was now on his way. As Roosevelt wanted the French leader received solely in his military capacity, he asked that General Marshall make the principal arrangements for the reception. It made for a busy week. After it was over, the General wrote Molly Winn, now with her husband and children at Fort Blanding, something of how he spent his time: "Giraud's visit here of course involved me in a great many engagements. I met him Wednesday morning, took him to the White House for tea Wednesday afternoon, gave him a dinner for forty at the Mayflower Wednesday night, had an official meeting with Giraud Thursday morning and luncheon with him and the President and two others Thursday noon. Friday there was another luncheon for him here at the Pentagon followed by a staff meeting in the afternoon and a dinner for him at the White House Friday night." [33]

In between meals there were meetings. On the morning after the dinner at the Mayflower, Giraud appeared at a special session of the Combined Chiefs of Staff to discuss implementation of the program discussed at Casablanca and at TRIDENT. In addition to pressing for speedy shipment of equipment, he asked for a French expeditionary force large and powerful enough "to seize the opportunity of waging war on French soil." Marshall assured him that the American Chiefs of Staff fully sympathized with his views and that their planners were carefully studying French requirements. In order to make certain that materiel would be available to meet current French requests, he proposed to suspend the activation of several United States divisions previously planned between August and the first of the year.[34]

This meeting was followed by an exploration of French needs by Giraud and Somervell. Shortly afterward the Army Services Forces Chief told Marshall that he was confident the French requests could be filled.

Both he and the Chief of Staff continued to warn that shipping and the capacity of ports in North Africa constituted possible delaying factors. As a result they reminded Giraud that he must work out details with General Eisenhower. General Marshall added that it was the urgent desire of the American Chiefs of Staff that General Eisenhower use French troops wherever possible in preference to bringing in more troops from the United States.[35]

French rearmament was discussed to some degree on July 11 when Giraud journeyed down to Leesburg for lunch with General and Mrs. Marshall. Knowing that Giraud would have an interest in Civil War history, Marshall arranged with the officer who brought him down to show him some of the Civil War defenses of Washington. He wrote out a statement about General Stuart's failure to keep in touch with Lee and the possible decisive effects of his actions. In a remarkable aside he advised Giraud's guide not to "imply . . . that I am condemning Stuart but rather that here was the point where a decision of the moment had a very tragic result on the operations of an Army." [36]

The visit to Leesburg apparently was a success. Marshall wrote his stepdaughter: "We had a pleasant weekend at Leesburg except that your mother was heavily involved in arrangements for Giraud's luncheon. I did my usual work up to a half hour beforehand. He arrived at 12:00 and left at 3:30. The place was filled with FBI men who occupied Fleet [the Dalmatian who often accompanied Marshall on his rides and who had recently brought the Marshalls into disgrace by flunking out of the Canine Corps] and kept him out of the house." [37]

A few days later, while the French leader was in Canada for a brief visit, General Marshall informed him that Eisenhower was prepared to handle 3 convoys (9 ships per convoy) for French units during August. Instructions were being issued for shipment of clothing and accouterments for 200,000 French troops as filler cargo on regular United States convoys during July and August, plus munitions at an average rate of 25,000 tons a month. "This represents," said Marshall, "an immediate substantial compliance with your requests. I have also taken up with Eisenhower the question of placing your troops on the same status as American troops in regard to weapons and personal equipment." [38]

Giraud returned to Africa bolstered by the belief that he had strengthened his position. He soon found that during his absence de Gaulle had moved rapidly to fashion a new organization in which he would have the principal role in controlling French affairs. The French have a phrase for it: "The more things change, the more they remain the same."

XIII

The Goal in Sight

SINCE June, General Marshall had seen in every proposal from London the counsel of further delay. Even a plan for the peaceful occupation of the Azores, intended to protect the Portuguese islands from possible German attack, contained a whiff of diversionary tactics. The Chief of Staff strongly urged Roosevelt not to give the British an opportunity "to get out of doing OVERLORD." OVERLORD was the latest designation for a cross-Channel attack, replacing earlier code names such as ROUNDUP, SLEDGEHAMMER, and ROUNDHAMMER. The build-up for cross-Channel activities continued under the name BOLERO.[1]

For at least six weeks before Roosevelt and Churchill and their staffs met at Quebec (the QUADRANT conference) in August 1943, General Marshall's advisers searched for a formula that would—in General Wedemeyer's words—"stir the imagination and win the support of the Prime Minister if not that of his recalcitrant planners and chiefs of staff."[2]

In a memo to General Handy, Wedemeyer reviewed the three possible approaches: cross-Channel or Mediterranean operations or the use of air bombardment and blockade, "and of course there could be various combinations and permutations of these." Marshall himself still strongly favored the cross-Channel approach as the one most likely to result in victory over Germany in 1944.

London had no monopoly on shifting views. As the Allies became deeply immersed in Mediterranean operations, even some of Marshall's close advisers despaired of mounting a cross-Channel attack the following spring—among them Brigadier General John E. Hull, Chief of the Operations Division's Theater Group. One of the original authors of the cross-Channel approach, Hull developed doubts as he saw the resources intended for the build-up in the United Kingdom drained away southward. He reluctantly concluded that the Allies must seek a final decision in the Mediterranean.[3]

Hull won some support for shelving OVERLORD from the Navy representative on the Joint Planners Staff, Admiral Cooke. Seeing an opportunity to push Pacific operations, Cooke, who never slept when there was a chance to aid that area, suggested that OVERLORD might be reduced to an emergency effort. The bulk of the remaining resources could then go to the Mediterranean and Pacific. His Army and Air Forces opposite numbers, Wedemeyer and Kuter, disagreed with Cooke; they insisted that conditions had not changed sufficiently to justify reversing the earlier concept.[4]

Consequently the move to downgrade OVERLORD gained little headway in Washington. Moreover, even as faith in the operation seemed to flicker in certain American quarters, it flared up in London. Under General Morgan, the COSSAC staff at Norfolk House was now hard at work on plans for a cross-Channel invasion to be undertaken in the spring. After TRIDENT the Chief of Staff to the Supreme Allied Commander had received a supplementary directive to prepare an operation with a target date of May 1, 1944, in order to secure a lodgment on the Continent from which the Allies could launch further operations against Germany. In addition Morgan was to plan on the assumption that he would have in the United Kingdom twenty-nine divisions, nine of them to be used in the assault. He was directed to start expansion of logistical facilities in the United Kingdom and have an outline plan ready for submission by August 1.[5]

The presence in London of this active planning staff, strongly British in make-up, gave an OVERLORD operation for 1944 an immediacy that it had hitherto lacked. Although at times a frustrated General Morgan felt that his headquarters was being used by his own people as window dressing for an operation that they did not intend to carry out, he worked at his mission faithfully. He convinced Secretary Stimson of his sincerity during the latter's visit to the United Kingdom in July and earned the warm approval of General Marshall, who considered making Morgan his Chief of Staff if he commanded the invasion forces.[6]

Examination of General Morgan's plan was one of the chief purposes of the QUADRANT conference at Quebec convoked by Roosevelt and Churchill. At TRIDENT they had agreed that the next meeting of the Combined Chiefs of Staff would be in London, but in July, President Roosevelt requested that the August meeting be held in Canada. A railroad strike and noisy quarrels in his administration over the control of war-mobilization measures made it mandatory that the President remain close at hand.[7]

By early August, when the British prepared to leave for Quebec, they had before them COSSAC's list of conditions under which the OVERLORD operation could be made, the area where a landing would be feasible, and the phases in which the attack could be developed. At last it was possible for discussion to proceed on the basis of a specific plan for a specific invasion. Although lacking almost everything except the paper on which it was written, the plan had been made. General Marshall was encouraged to learn from Major General Ray W. Barker, Morgan's American second in command, who came to brief the Chief of Staff before the Quebec meeting, that OVERLORD was strongly backed by the British planners, as well as by General Sir Bernard Paget, commander of 21 Army Group, whose forces would furnish British troops for the operation. But Barker conveyed a word of caution: the Prime Minister was still keenly interested in further expansion in the Mediterranean and the Aegean, and when the British Chiefs of Staff came under his "sun lamp," they were likely to warm to his designs.[8]

To counter the Prime Minister's seductive fluency, Marshall since early July had been impressing his views on the President. On July 25 he explained to him that Churchill's strategy was based on the belief that continued Allied pressure would be sufficient to force political and economic collapse of German rule in the occupied countries. If the Prime Minister's analysis was wrong, his strategy led to a war of blockade and attrition that the American people would not support. Confronted with such a protracted struggle, they would prefer to seek a decision in the Pacific. Although Marshall made no reference to the possible reaction of the American public in the November presidential election, his implication was clear. The President expressed his general agreement with the Chief of Staff.

But even as Marshall promoted the northern campaign, events in Sicily made it almost impossible for the Allies to turn away from Italy. Weeks earlier they had hoped that a victory in the HUSKY assault, following hard on the debacle in North Africa, would topple Mussolini's tawdry empire. On July 25 the Italian Grand Council formally recognized the bankruptcy of the regime of the "Sawdust Caesar" and deposed the petulant Duce. Shortly afterward diminutive Victor Emmanuel III, enjoying a brief return to center stage, charged Marshal Pietro Badoglio, once Il Duce's henchman, to form a government that could deal with the victorious Allies. More than a week earlier General Marshall had given his blessings to a rapid transfer of the Allied forces to the mainland of Italy in case of the collapse of enemy resistance on Sicily. Now he urged that the Allies move quickly to take advantage of this new development, but he asked that they carry out the operations with the forces already allocated.[9]

Thus before the meeting at Quebec, the Chief of Staff demonstrated his willingness to remain flexible about operations in the Mediterranean. But there were limits to his willingness and that of the other Chiefs of Staff to postpone OVERLORD. Lest their British cousins misunderstand their course, the U.S. Chiefs put themselves on record as ready to consider (1) the elimination of Italy from the war and establishment of bases up to the Ancona area, (2) the capture of Corsica and Sardinia, and (3) the landing of American and French forces in southern France as a diversionary plan to aid OVERLORD. Beyond this they were willing to send supplies to guerrillas in the Balkans and to bomb Central European objectives from Italian bases. But there had to be an end to continued expansion of activities in Italy. Further operations in the Mediterranean must depend on resources already there, and OVERLORD henceforth was to have overriding priority.[10]

But the Americans were set on a cross-Channel attack. They argued that (1) the United Kingdom bristled with sea, air, and land bases from which a concentrated attack could be launched against Germany; (2) Allied forces from Britain could mount an air offensive that would effectively reduce the strength of the German Air Force; (3) attacks from the north would bring, as a bonus, the capture and destruction of enemy submarine bases in France; (4) and the Allied forces would bring the German armies to battle in an area where British and American strength would be effective and decisive. Hitler would either have to withdraw from France or reinforce his beleaguered troops with men from the Russian and other fronts.[11]

With their tidy plans tucked away in their brief cases, the American Chiefs of Staff left Washington for Quebec on August 13. Drizzling rain and heavy overcast forced the plane carrying Marshall, Leahy, and Deane to land at Montreal. Fortunately local Canadian officials hastily summoned limousines that brought them to Quebec on time. Although the old French city was "cold and bleak" when they arrived, Prime Minister William L. Mackenzie King provided a warm welcome at their hotel, the Château Frontenac.[12]

The Château Frontenac, which looks down on the old city and the winding St. Lawrence like a proud castle, had been cleared of its regular clients and turned over to the British and American delegations for their meetings. The Prime Minister and President were to be installed in the Governor-General's summer residence in the nearby fortress the Citadel.[13]

The British party, which crossed the Atlantic on the *Queen Mary,* had arrived in Halifax on the evening of the ninth. The trip added the usual quota of encrustations to the Churchill legend. British planners, armed with the details of the OVERLORD offensive, told of being summoned to the Prime Minister's stateroom to present the high points of the plan. Still in pajamas, he jumped out of bed excitedly to look at objectives on the maps thumbtacked to a display board. As he padded barefoot across the floor, his subordinates shuddered lest he step on a fallen thumbtack.

As usual he was full of guile. One day he invited key members of the planning staff to dine with him. He served choice food with vintage wine and, at the end, offered them a splendid brandy. With the officers mellowly off guard he got to the point close to his heart. "Now, be good [to me] and write me a nice plan [for liberating Norway]," he said, thus neatly resurrecting Operation JUPITER, which the Chiefs of Staff thought they had effectively buried.[14]

The British planners knew that Brooke and his colleagues had no sympathy with the Norwegian scheme. Nevertheless they sketched out a plan, to which they appended a negative recommendation. "The Joint Planners are suspended," Churchill informed them. In some bewilderment they sought out General Ismay and asked what the Prime Minister meant. "Continue to do what you are doing," Ismay advised. "But remember you are suspended." And so they went on as usual.

On August 12, shortly after arriving in Canada, Churchill left with his daughter Mary for Hyde Park to meet the President for talks before the opening of the plenary conference. He went to Quebec on the fourteenth, while Roosevelt returned to Washington for talks with his advisers on the morning of the sixteenth. To make certain that the President was aware of views expressed by the British Chiefs of Staff in preliminary talks and, perhaps, also to make sure that he had not been won over by the Prime Minister, General Marshall sent the Chief of the Operations Division, General Handy, from Quebec to Washington to brief Roosevelt. With the aid of Harry Hopkins, General Handy was placed aboard the President's train as it started north on the evening of the sixteenth. Over lunch the next day Marshall's adviser outlined the American case. As a result the United States Chiefs of Staff were less concerned than they had been on Churchill's visit the year before about his influence on Roosevelt.[15]

As students of history, the Combined Chiefs of Staff were naturally conscious of Quebec's military past. Looking out from the battlements of the Citadel or from the towers of their hotel, they were almost directly above the site of the critical battle that decided whether New Britain or France would prevail in Canada. In a setting fitted for plotting martial designs the successors of Chatham could boast even more than Canning that they had brought in the New World to redress the balance of the Old.

But the New World could be stubborn about the redressing. Sir John Dill had warned the British Chiefs of Staff that Marshall and his colleagues were in a very positive mood about future strategy. At Hyde Park the Prime Minister discovered that the President, formerly receptive to alternative suggestions, was firmly set on OVERLORD.

Appreciating that General Marshall had done his work well, the Prime Minister realized that he had to focus his campaign upon Marshall. The first evening in Quebec, as at the dinner given by the Canadian Prime Minister two nights later, Churchill gave most of his attention to the Chief of Staff.

Marshall had made his determination crystal clear at the preliminary meetings of the Combined Chiefs of Staff, and the first hours in Quebec had been stormy. The antiseptic pages of the official minutes leave little hint of the sparks struck off in the discussions on August 14. But other sources indicate that Marshall forcefully opposed further Mediterranean commitments and that Admiral King employed "very undiplomatic language, to use a mild term," in objecting to British pleas.[16]

Actually the Americans were less adamant than they appeared. Indeed

Brooke indicated on August 15 that there appeared to be no fundamental divergence in their positions. He supported OVERLORD as the chief operation for 1944, suggesting that the Italian offensive be planned with this in mind. Thus far there was no wide disagreement. But in restating COSSAC's requirements for a viable OVERLORD plan—(1) reducing enemy fighter strength, (2) holding down German strength in France and the Low Countries to manageable proportions, and (3) solving the problem of maintenance over the beaches—Brooke seemed to list them in a way that led straight to the Mediterranean.[17]

Brooke habitually blamed Churchill for frightening the Americans by talking of greater commitments elsewhere, but in this instance, even before the Prime Minister appeared on the scene, it was the Chief of the Imperial General Staff who roused their fears. Brooke suggested that the offensive lines across the neck of Italy, currently considered the northern limit of Allied advance, be regarded merely as the first stage of future operations and that they should try to seize areas to the north as well. From this vantage point it might be possible to drive into southern France. (This route had been proposed earlier by Admiral Leahy in a meeting of the American Chiefs of Staff, but Marshall had ruled it out since the advance would be through extremely rough terrain.)[18]

The Americans had anticipated that the visitors might force a postponement of OVERLORD by continued expansion in Italy. To King it seemed that Brooke had confirmed that suspicion. Rejecting the assumption that *only* Italian operations could pave the way to cross-Channel success, the Admiral declared that the required preconditions could be met by gains on the Russian front or by the air offensive then in progress from the United Kingdom. A little less rigid, Marshall was willing to take as much of Italy as weak opposition permitted. He agreed with Portal that it would be better for the Allies if they, rather than the Germans, held the airfields in the north, but he shared Arnold's belief that the same aerial results could probably be gained from fields in the area of Florence. He was willing to capitalize on enemy weakness but not to build a major front on the Italian mainland.

Having conceded something to Brooke, Marshall insisted that if OVERLORD was not given overriding priority, the slippage already evident in planning would continue and the operation would not take place. His bite was in the conclusion: if OVERLORD was out for 1944, then the whole strategy might have to be recast and the United States effort in Great Britain reduced to providing a reinforced corps for a return to the Continent in case of German weakness or collapse.[19]

Predictably Marshall's attitude irked Brooke. The morning had been a bitter one for the British Chief. Almost abruptly the Prime Minister had informed him that the Supreme Command, promised to him earlier, was not to be his; now a painful day became intolerable. Finding Marshall unyielding on OVERLORD, Brooke hastily assumed that the General had not even read Morgan's plan and was unaware of the relation between cross-Channel and the Italian campaign. He apparently was unaware that Morgan's American Deputy, General Barker, had earlier briefed Marshall and his colleagues on the plan and that they had carefully considered the part Italian operations might play in aiding landings in the north. He had heard from Dill that on this point the American Chief of Staff was adamant and had even threatened to resign if the British pressed for major operations in Italy.[20]

How much of Marshall's conversation he had staged for the benefit of the British is not clear. Perhaps the nervous excitability that Stimson had noted in him several days before was momentarily gaining the upper hand with the reopening of old arguments and exposing of raw nerves. What is more likely, since Marshall knew that Roosevelt intended to claim the Supreme Command of OVERLORD for an American, was that he was determined to ensure the operation's success.

Amid this prevailing tension it was not surprising that the British and the Americans continued to strike sparks from each other. On the sixteenth, after chasing all planners and secretaries from their conference, the Combined Chiefs explored their differences with brutal frankness. Brooke pleaded with the Americans for a greater show of mutual confidence. The Americans thought the British were not wholehearted about the cross-Channel attack, he noted, while he and his colleagues feared that the Americans would demand that OVERLORD be carried out even if the strategic situation in Europe changed. He conceded that he and his colleagues had continued to withhold final acceptance from the cross-Channel effort while the Americans, despite their strong arguments, had adjusted to every strategic change in the Mediterranean.[21]

Brooke laid the blame for the misunderstanding squarely on Churchill. With the Prime Minister constantly dredging up alternatives, Brooke complained, the Americans believed that he would continue to wander far afield in the hope that the German question could somehow be settled without a direct confrontation on the Continent. This was indeed what they believed. It was not failure to understand the possible value to OVERLORD of victories in Italy that caused Marshall to question British aims, but the obvious ill effects on the build-up in the United Kingdom that would result from a long-drawn-out fight in the Mediterranean.

The British were undoubtedly right in favoring the capture of airfields far enough north in Italy to support attacks on critical German industry in southern Germany. The Americans also acknowledged the importance of clearing the Mediterranean of enemy ships and removing the danger of bombing from Italian bases. They also favored exploiting Italy's loss of the will to fight by invading the mainland. The Germans would be compelled to commit forces in the south of Italy and to replace Italian forces no longer available for the Balkans. To some degree they would have to shift troops from the Russian front and draw on reserves that otherwise would be sent against a Normandy landing. The Americans accepted all these arguments in their private discussions. But the strength of the British argument was diminished once the Allies moved north of Rome. As the Germans fell back on their own bases and frontiers into areas where the terrain permitted them to make maximum use of their defenses and to benefit from shortened lines of communications, the question arose whether it was justifiable to tie up Allied forces in holding actions instead of employing them offensively. If the Germans had to contend with the problems of feeding or, at least, policing a hungry population in central and southern Italy—a responsibility that the Allies would have to assume if they went into the area—their forces would be effectively engaged far from Normandy. Consequently it was arguable that continuation of the advance up the boot hardly constituted the logical preparation for OVERLORD. Instead it appeared to be an attempt to avoid coming to grips with the main enemy in the spring of 1944.

As the sessions dragged on, the Allies in Sicily were hastening to conclude their conquest of the enemy. On August 17, thirty-eight days after the landings, the Allied armies completed their victory over a German-Italian force of nearly a quarter-million men. Although part of this force escaped to the mainland, Eisenhower was preparing landings in the toe of Italy across the Strait of Messina, and another assault, almost beyond the reach of air cover, was set farther north, on the beaches of Salerno. While the Chiefs of Staff talked in Quebec, an unofficial report came from Italy that the Badoglio government was at last ready to discuss surrender terms.[22]

Brooke's biographer suggests that the chance of overrunning the long Italian coastline, which he describes as virtually undefended in this period, was lost only because the Americans had callously sent off all the landing craft to the Pacific. In fact the restriction of the early assaults to the toe of Italy was imposed in large part by the lack of airfields in the Mediterranean close enough to cover more far-ranging attacks. The Salerno operation itself was widely questioned because it lay at the extreme point of fighter range from Sicily. The decision to attack north of the toe owed as much to Marshall and Brooke's insistence that bolder measures be attempted as to the proposals of the Mediterranean headquarters planners. Rather than holding back on these operations, the U.S. Chief of Staff did everything possible to aid this phase of Eisenhower's Italian venture.

At Quebec discussions also explored Russia's role in diverting German units away from the Normandy invasion area. General Brooke pointed out that the daily improvement in Russia's position would require the enemy to retain his forces on the eastern front and perhaps send more there. Brooke had traveled far since spring, when he trumpeted that the Sicily operation was needed to keep pressure off the Soviet Union.

Other aspects of Russia's future course were more worrisome. General

Marshall noted that the Soviets, once eager to get Allied help, were developing an increasingly hostile view toward the capitalistic countries. Under the changed circumstances he wondered if the Germans would be likely to facilitate the entry of the Allies as a means of escaping a Russian advance. For only a moment the curtain was raised on a question that was later to loom large in Western thinking. But the point was not explored. Brooke replied that he had often thought of the danger that the Russians might seize on international chaos to further their ideals. But Eduard Beneš of Czechoslovakia had assured him that Russia would need a period of recovery in which she would require a peaceful Europe as a market for exports. He had predicted that the Soviets would put a damper on activities of the international Communist organization for this purpose. Casually Brooke listed a part of Poland, areas of the Baltic states, and concessions in the Balkans as likely demands of the Russians. In a mood like Churchill's at Tehran a few months later, he concluded that Stalin under these circumstances would be anxious to aid the Western powers in maintaining the peace of Europe.[23] One day Brooke would call the Americans politically naïve for their wartime views toward the Russians.

The Russian question also figured briefly at the conference on August 23, when the President asked if measures had been considered for an emergency entry into the Continent and said that he wanted Allied troops to enter Berlin at the same time as the Russians. Brooke assured him that General Morgan's staff had prepared for prompt Allied entry into German-occupied territory in case it appeared that Nazi control in the West had collapsed.[24]

The British made no mention at this point of any special fear of the Soviet menace. General Wedemeyer of Marshall's staff, however, pursued the question with his Chief later, asking him if he thought Roosevelt was beginning to be concerned about Communist influence in Central Europe. Marshall said that he did not think so. In Wedemeyer's words: "He felt that it was just a question of prestige and ability to carry out the reorganization of Europe on an equal status with the Soviet Union. Marshall said Roosevelt recognized the importance of capturing Berlin as both a political and psychological factor." [25] The President's attitude toward Stalin in the coming months—especially at the Tehran conference—confirmed Marshall's interpretation.

In the final dissection of OVERLORD the Prime Minister reiterated that the British would accept the operation only if certain conditions as to the limits of German strength had been met. If it appeared that the enemy's ground or air strength was greater than the acceptable maximum, the launching of OVERLORD must be reviewed by the Combined Chiefs of Staff. Despite the opposition of his advisers he suggested that JUPITER, his perennial favorite, be developed as a second string to their bow. Brooke winced at the effect this alternative might have on the Americans. Churchill and his advisers stipulated that, as agreed at TRIDENT, seven divisions would be returned from the Mediterranean to the United Kingdom unless the strategic situation required a review of that provision. In addition he insisted that the invasion force for OVERLORD be increased by 25 per cent. In this requirement, at least, Marshall and his colleagues were in accord with the British.

The debate over Mediterranean operations was resumed in Washington shortly after the end of the Quebec conference. After its adjournment Churchill remained in Canada with most of his advisers for a short rest. Then, as most of his party returned to the United Kingdom, he went down to Washington to discuss the rapidly changing situation in Italy. General Montgomery's forces crossed the Strait of Messina on September 3 while preparations were made for troops under General Clark to attack farther north a short time later.

On September 9, as Clark's force landed at Salerno, the Prime Minister resumed his effort to win the Chief of Staff's support. Churchill showed Marshall and the other Chiefs a paper he proposed to submit to the President at a White House conference later in the day in which he outlined action to follow the expected surrender of Italy. If the fighting went well in the south of Italy, the British leader wanted Allied forces to march northward until they reached the main German positions. Once there they might construct a strong fortified line. Churchill firmly believed that "we should be very chary of advancing northward beyond the narrow part of the Italian Peninsula"—i.e., the Pisa-Ancona line. This limited objective was most acceptable to the Americans as was his assurance that "There can be no question of whittling down OVERLORD." [26]

Reading on, the Chiefs of Staff understood why he was willing to stop at the narrow waist.[27] This pause Churchill felt, would release forces "to emphasise a movement north and northeastward from the Dalmatian ports." Far-reaching reactions in Bulgaria, Rumania, and Hungary, he predicted, might spark a movement from Turkey without any Allied request. And then there were the islands of the Mediterranean. The occupation of Sardinia, partly through local Italian efforts, and of Corsica, by use of French forces, appealed to the Americans. But they were skeptical about his insistence on greater efforts to gain the eastern Mediterranean islands.

Admiral King thought that the Prime Minister was taking a short-term view in stopping with Sardinia and Corsica and ignoring the value of landing in southern France in support of OVERLORD. General Marshall strongly opposed diversions from OVERLORD, particularly those looking toward the east. His comment on the proposed northeastward march from Dalmatian ports was diluted in the record to read: It "did not look so good." [28]

Churchill's views were studied again by the Combined Chiefs of Staff on September 10. As for operations in the islands of the eastern Mediterranean, the Chiefs approved steps being taken by the Middle East commander, General Sir Henry Maitland Wilson, to occupy Rhodes and the neighboring islands. The Americans were willing, provided the operations were conducted with resources already at Wilson's disposal. They opposed any large-scale effort that would interfere with operations on the Italian mainland or the build-up in the British Isles. Nor did they see great value in operations designed to encourage Turkey to enter the war, believing that the Turks would be influenced more by developments on the German-Russian front than by attacks on the Mediterranean islands. The Prime Minister's enthusiasm for new possibilities opened up by recent developments in Italy got no takers. The Americans remained set on preparations for the cross-Channel attack.

The prior clash on Mediterranean policy had been accompanied by the inevitable debate over the steady increase of American activity in the Pacific. Earlier in the year General MacArthur, in pushing preparations for the opening phases of his CARTWHEEL operations (the combined attack toward Rabaul) in the Southwest Pacific, had obtained Marshall's approval for the establishment of an army headquarters in that theater. More important he had the Chief of Staff's agreement to assign Lieutenant General Walter Krueger, commander of the Third Army, to head a new unit, which would be designated as the Sixth Army. Born in Prussia in 1881, Krueger was brought to the United States at the age of eight. He enlisted in the Army at seventeen, on the outbreak of the Spanish-American War, and served in the ranks through both that conflict and the Philippine Insurrection before winning a commission in 1901. He met Marshall, his senior by a month, in 1902, when the young VMI lieutenant came out to the Philippines, and they were instructors together at Fort Leavenworth before World War I. Between wars Krueger served as instructor at both the Army and Navy War colleges and had two tours of duty in the War Plans Division. Brought back as a member of that division by MacArthur, he became its Chief under General Malin Craig, holding the post until 1938, when he was succeeded by Marshall.

While MacArthur attempted to organize further advances in the Southwest Pacific, the Navy looked north of Guadalcanal. As early as February 1943 Admiral King suggested an attack on the Gilbert Islands; in early June he proposed an operation against the Marshalls, farther north. Looking still farther, King felt it "imperative" to set up firmly timed operations for the Central Pacific area and to give Nimitz responsibility for timing offensive operations in the whole Pacific theater.[29]

Quick to catch the implications of the proposal, the Army planners dissented. Even if Nimitz was given authority to coordinate the timing of major amphibious operations in the Pacific theater, he could not implement his decisions unless he also had authority to direct the operations, and to allocate resources. "Since timing is a prerogative of command," the argument of the Army planners concluded, "this would be tantamount to giving CincPac supreme command of the entire Pacific Theater." Only the Joint Chiefs of Staff, they reasoned, possessed the overall knowledge of the global situation required to coordinate operations.[30]

On June 15 when the Joint Chiefs of Staff considered King's proposal, Marshall agreed with the objections of the Army planners. "The Navy proposal, if accepted," he said, "would place General MacArthur under the command of the Commander, Pacific Ocean Areas." The timing of operations, he believed, "should remain a function of the Chiefs of Staff acting on advice from commanders in the field." [31] Firmness had averted another round in the play for the supreme command role in the Pacific.

His suspicions deepened by distance, General MacArthur doubted if General Marshall and his staff were properly defending his interests. In reality the War Department planners had not only kept MacArthur's command role intact but had promptly gone on record against operations "in the Marshalls at the cost of planned operations in the Southwest Pacific." Admittedly, communication between Washington and Brisbane could be improved. A brusque request to MacArthur on June 11 for firm or tentative dates of specific operations other than those already given for the initial attacks brought a brief and somewhat offhand reply. The tentative date for the second operation, said MacArthur, would be September 1, but after the Lae-Finschhafen-Salamaua area on New Guinea had been captured, the sequence of other operations depended so much on the success attained and the enemy reaction that "an estimate of dates is pure guesswork." [32]

There was obvious need to bring MacArthur closer to Washington's thinking. At the meeting of the Joint Chiefs of Staff on the fifteenth, Marshall read a telegram from them to MacArthur that had been sent urgently without waiting for their approval. He noted that this message fully explained the reasons why dates and specific plans of MacArthur's operations were necessary. It would also bring the planned operations against the mandated islands "into the picture," and MacArthur could understand why his information was needed for the timing of the Central Pacific operations.[33]

The picture MacArthur received was disturbing. It showed what he regarded as a "diversionary attack" against the Marshalls pushing the "main effort" in the South and Southwest Pacific into the background. He would lose the First Marine Division—his only amphibiously trained division, which was scheduled to make the attack on New Britain. Over in the Solomons, Admiral Halsey would lose the Second Marine Division, all combat loaders, and the major part of his naval forces in the South Pacific for the attack on the Marshalls.[34]

Indignantly MacArthur fired a message back to Marshall, attacking the concept of returning to the Philippines by way of the mandated islands (Marshalls, Carolines, and Marianas). He warned that the shift of the two Marine divisions earmarked for his forthcoming operations would prevent the capture of Rabaul. He spoke darkly of the unfavorable political repercussions that would follow withdrawal of ground forces from his campaign. From a strategic viewpoint the withdrawal of these troops "would seem to indicate a complete reorientation." "I am completely in ignorance," he concluded, "regarding the discussions and decisions of the recent Washington conference and request that I be advised in this respect insofar as it affects the broad concept of operations in this theater." [35]

With MacArthur's angry response at hand, Marshall could answer a memorandum from King that had been on his desk for more than a week. Justifying the reassignment of the First Marine Division to the Central Pacific, King reminded Marshall that the planned operations for the Central Pacific presented at TRIDENT called for amphibious divisions with battle experience. The First Marines, he said, now rehabilitated from the fighting on Guadalcanal, would meet that requirement. Moreover, he understood that this division would be used only for shore-to-shore operations in the Southwest Pacific. Marshall replied on June 23 that the First Marine Division would indeed be used amphibiously in ship-to-shore as well as in shore-to-shore operations in the attack on New Britain. It was now being specially equipped and trained for its amphibious role in the CARTWHEEL operations. He did not believe that its withdrawal for employment in the Central Pacific would be "justified," as the removal of the First Marines would seriously interrupt the pending joint operations in the Southwest Pacific.[36]

King would be heard from again, this time with the strong support of a report made by the new Joint Strategic Survey Committee. Observing the Pacific scene with fresh eyes, the JSSC did not look upon MacArthur's "main effort" in the advance toward Japan as sacrosanct. The committee preferred to give strategic priority to the Central Pacific advance through the Marshalls and Carolines as the primary offensive, rather than currently conceived operations in the South and Southwest Pacific. When this report was considered at the meeting of the Joint Chiefs of Staff on June 29, King observed that the JSSC had done "great service by presenting this paper." [37]

On July 20, with King's assurance that Nimitz's operations would not interfere with MacArthur's, but rather would help them, Marshall joined the other Chiefs in directing Nimitz to prepare and carry out amphibious operations against the Gilbert and Ellice islands and Nauru around mid-November. Nimitz also was to make ready for operations to follow in the Marshalls about the first of January 1944. Offensive forces assigned to him were Halsey's Second Marine Division and an Army division, not yet designated. Marshall sympathized with King in his eagerness to begin the Central Pacific offensive. He felt that King's great carrier forces should not be left idle, and he, too, agreed that King's operations would help CARTWHEEL.[38]

Two days later another King memorandum arrived, which he did not think would wholly surprise Marshall. King's worry now was the lack of effectiveness of "mixed forces" in amphibious operations against the small islands of the Central Pacific, for which Marine divisions were so "eminently suited." He knew it would be difficult to disengage the Third Marine Division from the Solomons "and/or" the First Marine Division, still training in Australia. But "we both know much can be done where the will to do it prevails." Marshall could only again refuse the First Marines for the reasons already given. He could not take the Third Marines away from Halsey, who was depending upon using it for operations in the Buin-Faisi area by October 15.

But Marshall was prepared to make his "no" acceptable with a possible alternative. For a year there had been a well-trained division in Hawaii with excellent leaders—the 27th Army Division. All the advanced facilities for amphibious training were present on Oahu and with the minimum of three months available for concentrated training, this division could become a "well coordinated amphibious unit in the peak of condition." Admiral King accepted Marshall's offer.[39]

Throughout this period the Army planners reflected the desire of Stimson and Marshall that full consideration be given to MacArthur's operations. Despite the Joint Strategic Survey Committee's views in late June, the Army representatives held out against the premature selection of one route over another. With the exception of King, the members of the Joint Chiefs of Staff agreed. The brilliant progress of Nimitz's naval forces across the Pacific might be dazzling, but it would not eclipse MacArthur's dogged advance to Manila.

As debate continued over future strategy, offensives proceeded in the Southwest and the North Pacific. On the last day of June 1943 MacArthur launched an amphibious attack against New Guinea. Naval forces under Rear Admiral Daniel Barbey and air forces under General Kenney supported General Krueger's occupation of Woodlark and Kiriwina islands off the northeast coast. Along the north coast another force landed in Nassau Bay.

These landings were unopposed and operations went smoothly. The story was far different for the simultaneous assault in the Solomons—on the New Georgia group, northwest of Guadalcanal. Rear Admiral Kelly Turner's amphibious force, which included the 43d Infantry Division and a Marine Raider regiment, supported by Halsey's forces, landed on Rendova Island against initial light opposition. A furious Japanese counterattack compelled the task force commander to order Army reinforcements from Guadalcanal. Angered, Admiral Turner blamed the Army commander and reorganized the ground-force command before securing his objectives on August 5.[40]

Despite strong differences between Nimitz and MacArthur and disputes over command, the Joint Chiefs of Staff were more sanguine than their British colleagues about advances in the Pacific when they met at Quebec. The Joint Staff Planners assumed that Italy would be out of the war in

1943 and Germany by the fall of 1944. They saw the separate MacArthur and Nimitz drives reaching the line northward from Vogelkop (the bird's-head peninsula of western New Guinea) to the Palau Islands (part of the western Carolines), some 1100 miles southeast of Manila, by the end of 1944. Less hopeful, the Combined Planners were ready to assume that by the end of the year American forces would be in the Palaus and the Allied forces in control of the greater part of Burma, but objectives such as the Philippines, Formosa, the Ryukyus, and Malaya were set for 1945 and 1946. They estimated that final operations against the Japanese home islands would not begin until 1947 and would extend until the following year.[41]

Dissatisfied with this timetable, Navy representatives warned that failure to distribute Allied resources properly could indeed result in the protracted pace projected by the Combined Planners. Admiral Cooke suggested that by the proper balancing of forces in both the Atlantic and Pacific areas, the Allies could bring the defeat of Germany *and* Japan by 1945; otherwise Germany would be defeated in 1944 and Japan in 1948.

Neither General Marshall nor Admiral King took a 1947 or 1948 prognostication seriously, but they did fear delays. At the August 14 meeting in Quebec, Marshall asked that European and Pacific strategies be linked and a plan adopted to defeat Japan within twelve months after Germany's fall. This objective required greater emphasis on the Pacific and a shift of resources from Europe before the end of operations there.

Apparently assuming that current Pacific operations would not draw very heavily on troops earmarked for the build-up in Europe, the British accepted the broad outlines of his plan. The capture of distant islands in the Pacific, Brooke believed, could be accomplished by picked assault troops rather than by large masses of ground troops. The great battalions would be left for Europe.[42]

The British also supported some measure of greater naval pressure on the Japanese but not equal billing for both the Central and Southwest Pacific offensives. Later to hail MacArthur as the greatest strategist of the war, Brooke now declined to accept the Southwest Pacific commander's argument for a main drive by way of New Guinea. He suggested instead that activities in that area be restricted to a holding operation and resources earmarked for use there be sent to OVERLORD. Brooke was mistaken if he hoped by this means to win additional support for Europe from King. The tough-talking Admiral retorted that a two-pronged approach was better than a one-pronged. If the allocation to MacArthur was cut back, the forces thus saved should go to the Central Pacific. Marshall agreed. Since reinforcements were already on their way to the Southwest Pacific, slowing operations there would not aid efforts in Europe.

The British ended by accepting the American proposals. Near the close of the conference the Combined Chiefs of Staff agreed to Nimitz's advance through the Gilberts, the Marshalls, Ponape, Truk, and the Palaus to the

Marianas in 1943–44. In his area MacArthur was authorized to go as far as Wewak in northern New Guinea, the Admiralty Islands, and the Bismarck Archipelago. He was to neutralize rather than to invade Rabaul.[43]

But the major new developments in the Pacific and Far East concerned the proposed operations in the China-Burma-India Theater and the establishment of the Southeast Asia Command. Marshall and his colleagues continued to urge action in Burma—as they had done at the TRIDENT conference—proposing that Rangoon be taken after the area to the north had been cleared. The British Chiefs preferred to bypass South Burma in favor of an attempt to regain Singapore. Churchill had still another target —a recent favorite—the tip of Sumatra, whose seizure the Americans opposed as a diversion from main operations. Churchill swept aside their protests. Sumatra, he argued, would be a great diplomatic coup. The only alternative to such an operation would be "to toil through the swamps of South Burma." He made quite clear that he opposed such an arduous advance merely to please Chiang Kai-shek.

In the end the usual formula for settling problems in the Far East was adopted—the final decision on Rangoon and Singapore was left to another time. General Marshall was able to inform Stilwell that the Combined Chiefs of Staff had agreed to his campaign to recapture north Burma in order to establish overland communications to China. The Allies were to take Myitkyina and expand the air route to China and continue preparations for amphibious operations in the spring of 1944. The air route over the Hump was to be built up in order to permit intensified operations against Japan, keep China in the war, enlarge the Fourteenth Air Force, and equip and train Chinese forces.[44]

A new face and a new approach to China operations lightened the sessions with the arrival of the brilliant young Brigadier Orde Wingate, who had stirred up controversy in Palestine and Ethiopia. In the mold of the great eccentrics of battle, many of whom had been noted for their devotion to the Old Testament and for their conviction that they were, in Christopher Sykes's phrase, "instruments of fate," Wingate had a fanatic's aversion for military and political leaders who opposed his plans.[45]

In campaigning against the Italians in Ethiopia early in the war, Wingate had effectively used a special force of irregular troops. Later, in Burma, he developed the idea of flying in long-range penetration groups behind Japanese lines to disorganize and harass larger forces. Always welcoming new approaches to battle, Churchill ordered Wingate home on the eve of his departure for Quebec. The brigadier arrived in London only a few hours before the Prime Minister's departure for Scotland, where he was to board the *Queen Mary*. Impulsively he invited Wingate to come along and arranged even more suddenly for the brigadier's wife to join them on their special train. The startled officer had with him only the clothes that he was wearing; he had to be outfitted on board ship.

At Quebec, Wingate quickly won the backing of the American delegation for his proposals. Eager to get operations under way against the Japanese, General Marshall strongly supported the British officer's schemes. And, Marshall recalled later, "I . . . warned everybody that if they took anything from the operations (Stilwell, the British, and the Chinese all wanted some of the stuff I had allotted for Wingate), I would take it back."

From Quebec, Wingate journeyed to Washington for talks with Arnold and Marshall. To Wingate's delight the American Air Chief made every effort possible to furnish necessary air support for his operations, and General Marshall took a close interest in the arrangements. When Wingate explained special morale problems that arose in his operations because men feared that they would be left behind if wounded, Marshall asked Arnold if he could design an air-rescue project. The Air Forces Chief could and did, devising the forerunner of methods later perfected and used with great success in Korea and Vietnam.[46]

General Marshall developed a great fondness for Wingate. He said of him in 1956: "Wingate was strong for me, because I printed over here his report on what was needed when the British staff suppressed it. I wouldn't go for that a damned bit. They didn't want him [down] here but I asked for him, and I pushed his project." Of Wingate's talent he had no doubt: "Wingate would have been in the class of Lawrence of Arabia but for his death."

The fiery officer had only a few months more in which to demonstrate his genius. After some initial exploits in Burma that showed what his units could do, he was tragically killed. In late March 1944, while flying between Imphal and Lalaghat, his plane crashed and burst into flames. After the war his remains and those of his fellow victims were brought to Arlington National Cemetery.[47] In this snuffing-out of a victorious career, Marshall must have seen a parallel to the sudden end of an American military eccentric, the onetime mathematics professor whose exploits were religiously studied by Marshall and a host of VMI cadets—"Stonewall" Jackson.

General Marshall was pleased that the Quebec conference saw the final establishment of the Southeast Asia Command. Churchill had advanced the idea in June 1943, saying that the Allies could use either the Eisenhower or the MacArthur model in establishing a headquarters. He preferred the latter type, with the British Chiefs of Staff exercising the same supervision of operational strategy that the U.S. Chiefs of Staff exerted in the Southwest Pacific. He suggested Air Chief Marshal Sir Sholto Douglas, former Fighter Command leader, then commanding general in the Middle East, as head of the new command. Stilwell, he added, with a nod toward Marshall, might be the man for Deputy.[48]

General Marshall showed an American bias in recommending that the new command follow Eisenhower's model, in which the Combined Chiefs of Staff exercised control. He could not accept subordination to the British Chiefs of Staff of "any supreme command which embraces the means of our aid to China." Influenced by Stilwell's unfavorable impression of British leadership in India, the Chief of Staff believed it essential "that we provide American leadership for an American effort, as well as the Chinese troops concerned, rather than permitting those components to be placed under British command." [49] Further, the Americans foresaw that as the attack against Japan developed, operations from the Southwest Pacific and from Southeast Asia would have to be coordinated. In that case they believed that the Combined Chiefs of Staff organization, acting from Washington, was more suitable than the British Chiefs of Staff acting from London.[50]

General Marshall firmly opposed the nomination of Sholto Douglas. "I said," he recalled, "I would take every American out from under him if he was [put] in command. He didn't like Americans and was very frank in saying it. To me it was out of the question to have a man like that in supreme command where there were both forces involved." [51] Marshall's papers do not reveal the source of his information on Douglas, and he admitted that the "prejudices against him" might not be "justified," but he was adamant on the subject. In a letter he prepared for Roosevelt to send Churchill, the Chief of Staff wrote: "I have been advised that a number of general officers who have been thrown in contact with Douglas all have gotten the same reaction which is unfavorable to the prospect of success in Allied command." The Burma problem, one of great complications, required "a man of unusual breadth of vision, moral courage, and personal characteristics that lend themselves to coordinating actions of diverse peoples." For this task the Americans proposed Admiral Sir Andrew B. Cunningham, who not only understood the complications of Allied command but who had as well "an unusual understanding of Americans." Cunningham had served as a member of the British Mission in Washington early in the war, where he won American friendship as he did later as commander of Allied naval forces in the Mediterranean under Eisenhower. Marshall spoke for himself, as well as for his colleagues, when he wrote, "He enjoys our complete confidence." [52] The U.S. Chiefs also listed Air Chief Marshal Sir Arthur Tedder as a possibility. The British felt that neither man could be spared from European assignments. Before many months Cunningham succeeded the dying Sir Dudley Pound as First Sea Lord, and Tedder became Deputy Supreme Commander under General Eisenhower.

By refusing to accept Douglas, the Chief of Staff possibly influenced the final choice of a commander. In his memoirs Churchill indicates that his own first choice for the command had been Admiral Mountbatten. Knowing that Marshall shared his admiration for the young officer, he was probably not surprised when the Chief of Staff welcomed this nomination at Quebec. Brooke, who was surprised at the proposal, pointed out that Mountbatten had never commanded anything except destroyers, but he agreed that what the Admiral lacked in experience, he made up in self-confidence.[53]

The Combined Chiefs of Staff handed Lord Louis a sprawling empire to command—Burma, Ceylon, Thailand, Sumatra, Malaya. (India was put under India Command, and China was to have its own theater, headed by Generalissimo Chiang Kai-shek.) Because of personalities and politics and special problems of nationalities, an astonishing administrative organization was devised. The China-Burma-India Theater (U.S.) was not subordinated to the Southeast Asia Command but brought into close association with it because the theater commander, Stilwell, would be (or act as) Deputy Supreme Commander under Mountbatten. Chiang Kai-shek, with his own theater, did not deal directly with SEAC but established liaison through Stilwell, who continued to act as Chief of the Joint Staff under Chiang while commanding China's forces in India and Burma. SEAC's logistical support came from India Command, an arrangement bound to lead to contests for supplies, which were decided by the Viceroy, Field Marshal Sir Archibald Wavell. Stilwell's position was particularly confusing. The Chinese Army in India, commanded by Stilwell, was to fight in SEAC's area under its overall command. But the American commander had strong ideas about which British officer he was willing to accept. Stilwell would also have problems because the Fourteenth Air Force, based in China, would get its supplies from India and be under the Generalissimo. Informing the CBI commander of the complex arrangements, Marshall vastly understated the case when he said that they were "not sound administratively." [54]

The other major command change arranged at Quebec was the assignment to Mountbatten of an American Deputy Chief of Staff, General Wedemeyer, able member of Marshall's Operations Division and one of the chief proponents of cross-Channel strategy. According to Stilwell, tart as ever about anyone who nettled him, Wedemeyer reported that "General Marshall told me to go over there and get that operation put on. He said to me that he was giving me a good commander—Louis—and that he expected results. And if they wouldn't fight, he would pull me out and put [me] somewhere else." [55]

Stilwell's diary entry at the time suggests that when Wedemeyer was appointed, he saw his assignment as one of great importance entrusted to him by an admiring superior. Years later, bitter at the British who had delayed the cross-Channel operation and disenchanted with Marshall's handling of negotiations with Chiang Kai-shek, Wedemeyer wrote that both he and Mountbatten had been "eased out to Asia." Colleagues gathered that he thought that it had been the British who persuaded Marshall to send him to SEAC. Apparently, like Hugh Drum in 1942, when he was being considered for the post Stilwell ultimately got, Wedemeyer in retrospect saw China as a backwater of the war. Although Wedemeyer's assignment led to theater command and a third star, it seemed to him nothing more than the result of high-level machinations in London and Washington. In 1958 he wrote that he would have preferred a combat command or the Chief of Mission post in Moscow, which Harriman had offered him.[56] However, many of his contemporaries who had combat assignments won only two stars. General Deane, who was given the Moscow Mission at Wedemeyer's suggestion, retired with two stars; Wedemeyer retired with four. In 1944 when Stilwell was recalled from China, it was to Wedemeyer that Marshall turned for a successor. General Marshall's own records and recollections give no indication that he considered the Southeast Asia assignment as anything less than what Stilwell reported it to be—a special opportunity for a good soldier to be of great service in a difficult theater.

The final report of the Combined Chiefs of Staff at Quebec, approved by the President and Prime Minister, reiterated in language similar to final reports of earlier conferences that the Allies' overall objective was "to bring about at the earliest possible date the unconditional surrender of the Axis powers." At the same time they would maintain and extend unremitting pressure against Japan in order to reduce her military power and attain positions from which her ultimate surrender could be forced.

A major frustration for the Quebec conferees was their inability to influence the great events occurring across the Atlantic in Italy. While Eisenhower was laboring under earlier instructions to neutralize Italy's warmaking powers, he could not exploit the sudden collapse of the Italian government for a more far-reaching victory. To forestall a similar lack of effective planning in the future, the conference directed formation of a psychological-warfare committee to help commanders in the field devise means of hastening enemy surrender, as well as formulation of a precise civil-affairs policy governing areas occupied by Allied forces. Neither proposal could be implemented in time to help the present critical situation, and neither was fully operable a year later when the Allies reached the German frontier.

For Marshall a significant development of the August meeting was Churchill's offer, while at Hyde Park, to let the President name the Supreme Commander for the cross-Channel attack. It was soon clear that both leaders had Marshall in mind for the post.[57]

In offering the command to an American officer, Churchill anticipated Roosevelt's request for such an arrangement. In earlier discussions of a cross-Channel attack the two had agreed that the nation furnishing the bulk of the troops in a campaign should have the Supreme Command. Roosevelt obviously had this fact in mind when, shortly before the Quebec meeting, he asked Marshall for an estimate of the relative size of the British and American forces that would be available in the United Kingdom at the possible time of a landing in 1944. Marshall reported two days before departing for Canada that American forces would be preponderant by spring of the following year.[58]

Having announced his welcome news to Roosevelt, Churchill had the painful task of informing Brooke that he was not to have the command. The Prime Minister did this rather bluntly as he walked with the British Army Chief on the terrace outside the Citadel, looking down on the Plains of Abraham. Serene as a historical print in the cool light of late August, the scene of Wolfe's great victory was fixed forever in Brooke's mind by the almost brutal matter-of-factness with which his expectations of the thrice-promised prize were dispatched. Beneath his mask of impassivity bitter disappointment churned. "It was a crushing blow," he recalled, "to hear from him that he was handing over this appointment to the Americans, and had in exchange received the agreement of the President to Mountbatten's appointment as Supreme Commander for South-East Asia." [59]

Still later his deep-rooted fairness had somewhat mitigated the keenness of his disappointment: "With the matters as they stood and with this American preponderance, it should be an American commander, but I never received from him the slightest sympathy on losing what I had looked forward to as being something of a climax. I had planned everything to lead up to this re-entry into France. I had been told I was going to command it, then just to be told offhand like that, it was a little bit of a shock, but it wasn't really a bad shock because I felt it was a correct move, really." [60]

Oddly enough Brooke's deep feeling did not emerge in his diary entry for the day, nor did Churchill seem to be aware of it. Not until later, when he prepared autobiographical notes for a chronicle of his life, did the Field Marshal write of the pain of the blow and complain that Churchill "offered no sympathy, no regret at having to change his mind, and dealt with the matter as if it were of minor importance."

In 1961 he put the story of the command in a different context for the author:

> Winston approached me six months before the operation and said he wanted me to take over the command of that operation and I was to prepare myself and fit myself for it. Until the time came, he wanted me to remain on. . . . Not very long after that, he happened to have a sherry party at 10 Downing Street, and my wife happened to be there, and we both went up to say something to him, and he said to her, "How do you like having your husband taking command of the operations across the Channel?" She said that she had heard nothing about this. I said, "You did mention that it was entirely secret, you know, and I had not told her about it," and he said, "Oh, well, you are quite right about that." He told her all, and on several occasions he kept on referring to this, and it wasn't until we got to the big conference [that I found out]. . . . He was just back from stopping at Hyde Park for a visit with Roosevelt where he had been discussing the high command and he told me then: "I

see now the way the war is . . . [going], and there is no doubt that the preponderance of American forces in this operation will be such that really it
would be infinitely better to have an American commander, and therefore I
feel we ought to, in spite of what I have said to you, hand the command over,
and I suggested that to Roosevelt, and at the same time he agreed that we
could have command in the Mediterranean." [61]

Although Brooke resented later accusations that he was jealous of the
man who ultimately received the Supreme Command, in his hour of disappointment he must have felt especially bitter that the leader of the
cross-Channel expedition would be one he believed deficient in strategic
understanding and inferior to him in command experience.

It is less clear when and by whom Marshall was told that he was to have
the command. In later years he was certain that he had never received a
promise of the position from the President. Perhaps he got the news from
Secretary Stimson, who was told by Roosevelt that the Prime Minister had
volunteered Marshall's name for the command, thus sparing the President
the embarrassment of having to ask for it. Shortly afterward Churchill
confirmed to the Secretary that he had suggested Marshall, although it
embarrassed him because of his earlier promise to Brooke.[62]

For Stimson the announcement seemed the fulfillment of the dream he
had outlined in August to the President. From his standpoint the British
had ceded much to give the command to the American Chief of Staff. But
he had misjudged a segment of the American public. Within a few days
the nation's capital would be rocked by charges that enemies of Marshall
in London and Washington were conspiring to ease him out of the Pentagon.

A Season of Rumors

WASHINGTON at any season is awhirl with gossip, but the stress of war and garbled reports from the Quebec conference stirred clouds of dangerous chatter with the coming of fall in 1943. Stringent security controls and the reticence necessary to protect delicate negotiations invited the most honest columnists and the least responsible prognosticators to test the atmosphere by sending up trial balloons filled with the hottest of hot air. Add to the situation a growing suspicion of the designs of the occupant of the White House, a distrust of the Allies in general, the approach of a presidential election, nasty infighting in some corridors of the Pentagon, and one had the makings of a storm. All of this was exacerbated because, as Stimson observed, "the White House has not got a great reputation for truth in these matters of publicity." [1] The "credibility gap" is nothing new.

Such was the atmosphere in the nation's capital after the conference at Quebec. The rumors centered on Marshall's future role in the Allied offensive against Germany, few episodes were to cause him greater embarrassment. Indirectly, in the end, the furor may have cost him the Supreme Command. The affair constitutes a case study of the way in which lack of information, and the heat of politics and personal ambitions, can twist a well-meant action into a sinister shape, transforming a proposed appointment—ardently desired by Marshall—into a plot by the President or men near him to kick the Chief of Staff upstairs. The only beneficial result of the uproar may have been that it demonstrated the high esteem in which General Marshall was held by the country.

The suggestion that Marshall might lead the cross-Channel attack was not new. Indeed his name had been put forward in the press when preparations for a possible attack in 1942 were first considered. This idea was soon dropped as attention shifted to the North African attack, but the notion remained that Marshall would be the Pershing of World War II. The day after the opening of the Casablanca conference, news columnist

Constantine Brown reported persistent rumors that Marshall would soon take active command in Europe and Africa. The Washington correspondent of the London *Daily Mail* repeated them a few days later. The rumors quieted down after a few days but were revived the following month when a premature announcement was made that five-star rank would soon be established for Leahy, Marshall, and King. Misreading a plan started in the Navy for increased rank as a move to qualify Marshall for the Supreme Allied Command, the International News Service suggested that the Chief of Staff would soon become "commander of all United Nations armies with the rank of Field Marshal." [2]

The arrival of Lieutenant General Jacob L. Devers in London in May to succeed the late Lieutenant General Frank M. Andrews as commanding general of the European Theater prompted Harrison Salisbury of the New York *Times* to speculate that Marshall would soon come over to command the European and Mediterranean theaters, with General Sir Harold L. Alexander succeeding Eisenhower in the south and Eisenhower returning to Washington. A few weeks later the conclusion of the Allied meeting in Washington and Marshall's trip with Churchill to North Africa brought another flurry of excitement. The London *Herald*'s view that Marshall might head the forthcoming invasion of Europe was followed by other predictions that Eisenhower might head a force in the Mediterranean and Alexander one in the north.[3]

These early rumors were correctly treated by most commentators as pure speculation, and virtually none of the press stories implied that such an appointment was improper or unexpected. Certainly there was no suggestion that the White House was involved in a plot to kick the Chief of Staff upstairs. Instead the attitude seemed to be that Marshall was the logical choice for the post.

Had the President been inclined to remove Marshall from the Chief of Staff's position, he had his opportunity near the end of the summer when the General informed his Commander-in-Chief that his tour of duty would come to an end on September 1. Roosevelt promptly announced that Marshall would be continued in office indefinitely because of the outstanding service he had rendered the nation.[4] The action was hailed editorially throughout the country, and the press noted that Marshall was the first Chief of Staff to have his tour of office extended in wartime and that only one other officer—Douglas MacArthur—had served in the post longer than four years.

Yet within two weeks members of Congress were hammering at Stimson's door to know why Marshall was being eased out of Washington. This surprising reaction came in part from a leak to the press of the fact that Roosevelt and Churchill had agreed in Quebec on an American, presumably Marshall, as commander of the invasion forces. It seems likely that the chief sources of the great uproar in Washington were administration critics and alarmed Army officers who hoped to block Lieutenant

General Brehon B. Somervell's recently unveiled plan to reorganize the Army Service Forces.

Somervell had reached his position as commanding general of the Army Service Forces as the result of a reorganization of the War Department in 1942 that had transferred the functions and authority of the chiefs of Infantry, Cavalry, Field Artillery, and Coast Artillery to Lieutenant General Lesley J. McNair, the head of the Army Ground Forces. At the same time the various chiefs of supply and administrative services were directed to report to the head of the Army Service Forces rather than to the Chief of Staff, but they still kept considerable authority. In an effort to bring these various groups under a more integrated command, Somervell threatened to shake up some of the existing sections and divisions.[5]

Somervell had an excellent record as an engineer in France in World War I and in special service overseas in the 1920s and 1930s, but he was best known before World War II for his work on the Florida Ship Canal and as head of the New York City Works Progress Administration from 1936 to 1940. Inasmuch as the latter position had brought him into contact with Harry Hopkins, the national head of the WPA, he was a natural object of suspicion for critics of the administration. A hard driver and a man of quick temper, Somervell easily made enemies inside and outside the Army. He was regarded as an indefatigable empire builder. As a result his plan for reorganization was dreaded by agencies that he proposed to bring more closely under his control.

Somervell's timing was bad. He produced his recommendations in August 1943, just as he was preparing to leave for the Quebec conference, after which he made a world-wide inspection trip. Consequently he was out of Washington at a critical time for the fate of his plan. His sweeping proposal embraced a reduction in the powers of the technical services and consolidation of some of the service commands in order to achieve greater integration of functions and cut down the size of Army Service Forces headquarters in Washington.[6] Somervell showed the outlines of the plan to Marshall and his Deputy Chief of Staff, Lieutenant General Joseph T. McNarney, before leaving for the Pacific. They welcomed it as a move toward greater efficiency. It followed the lines of McNarney's reorganization of 1942 and answered in part his continued demand that Somervell trim the size of his staff in Washington—a force that numbered more than 30,000 soldiers and civilians before the end of the war.

Somervell's departure before discussing the proposal with either Stimson or his key undersecretary, Robert Patterson, also meant trouble. Although Somervell stopped in Hawaii to see Patterson, he failed to win his assent to all the provisions.[7] Since members of the Staffs were at odds on some aspects of the reorganization, the problem came back to Stimson. The Secretary of War was cautious in his response. He favored efficiency, but he also wanted no further division in the Army. He recalled the battles during his term as Secretary of War under President Taft when the Chief of Staff, General Leonard Wood, a strong personality like Somervell, had provoked such violent reactions in the War Department that an effort was made in Congress to eliminate the office of Chief of Staff. Knowing that bureau chiefs, jealous of their power, were prepared to carry their cases to Congress and the press, Stimson urged discretion. He feared that whatever benefits could result from the reorganization— and he was not certain that all the proposed changes were valuable— would not justify risking the controversy that might follow.[8]

Early in 1942 Marshall had won his reorganization fight by sudden, ruthless moves, carried out almost without warning by General McNarney, acting under his direction. Perhaps he could have done the same now if he had been directly concerned. For Somervell, who had earned many powerful enemies and was now away on the opposite side of the world, the feat was impossible. In 1942 Marshall had moved almost without the knowledge of the President, and it was easy to prove that the reorganization was not dictated by the White House. The delay in action in 1943 made it possible for the opponents of the plan to blame it on Roosevelt's advisers and to suggest that Somervell was in some way to be elevated at the expense of Marshall.

Although discussions on reorganization continued until November, the question was actually settled by early October. On October 6, when Stimson and Marshall were talking to several senators who had recently returned from a trip to the Pacific, Senator Richard Russell expressed his anxiety over the proposal. At this point Marshall waved his hands—in evident surrender—and Stimson announced that the plan was not going through.[9]

Unfortunately the reorganization plan became linked with Roosevelt's proposal to appoint General Marshall as Supreme Commander. In Washington it is often difficult for individuals to respect the thin line that divides personal interest and the public good. Few higher loyalties bar a frightened bureaucrat or a frustrated subordinate from leaking information to the press that he believes will save the nation or his own promotion. And it may have been friends of Marshall who, preferring his regime to Somervell's, alerted columnists and congressmen to the plans for his future and Somervell's reorganization. Whether the rumormongers knew or cared that Marshall earnestly desired the appointment is not clear. What is certain is that the story began to circulate that the Chief of Staff was being sent out of the country in order to make way for the promotion of an officer more responsive to Roosevelt's political plans.

Just where—in divisions of the technical services, in newspaper offices, or in Congress—the campaign was planned cannot be determined, but there is no doubt that it was planned. A study of the early speculations in news reports, editorials, and columns and of statements in Congress indicates that certain releases were carefully timed. A columnist's prediction that Pershing would protest to Roosevelt—using arguments that were shortly to be repeated in a service journal—was too close to the mark to be sheer coincidence. In 1963 the well-known military commentator Brigadier General S. L. A. Marshall suggested in his column that a group of young colonels in the Army Ground Forces, aspiring to rapid promotion, feared that their starry hopes would be lost if Marshall left Washington and was succeeded by Somervell or Arnold. "So they leaked the story to the press and also peddled the editorial line: 'Marshall in his present post is the indispensable man.' " [10] Perhaps this was the beginning of the hullabaloo. But once the story broke, other interests were soon involved, and what may have begun as a military squabble became more frankly political.

Word soon spread that Harry Hopkins (often referred to as the Rasputin of the Roosevelt regime), Justice Felix Frankfurter, and other New Dealers were engaged in a scheme to replace Marshall with Somervell.[11] No one seemed to realize that Stimson, who more than any other person hammered at the President for weeks to get the Supreme Command for Marshall, was nevertheless opposed to the adoption of the main features of the reorganization plan or that Marshall favored many of its provisions.

So violent did indirect attacks on Somervell become that Senator Truman felt it essential to warn General Marshall that there were plots against him in the War Department. The Chief of Staff assured the senator that he had full confidence in his subordinate's loyalty. It was next the turn of the ranking Republican members of the Senate Military Affairs Committee to voice their anxieties about Marshall's position. On September 15 Senators Warren Austin, H. Styles Bridges, and Chan Gurney called at Secretary Stimson's home to declare that they relied heavily on General Marshall's prestige in winning support from their colleagues for controversial measures to aid the Army. Finally they got to the nub of their argument: they doubted if Somervell would be able to fill Marshall's place. Stimson made it clear that Marshall was not being pushed out and that the appointment instead "would fill one of the deepest hopes of his heart." Recognizing, however, the force of their argument concerning the Chief of Staff's influence with Congress, he suggested that if Marshall were made General of the Armies, he might be able to continue to hold his place as Chief of Staff, while commanding troops abroad.[12]

In making this proposal the Secretary of War showed the extent to which he was prepared to go to get the cross-Channel command for Marshall. Stimson had earlier strongly opposed the Navy-backed measure for five-star rank for Marshall and the other Chiefs of Staff. He knew that the Army Chief was, if possible, even more adamantly opposed to the idea than he himself was and that he would take the title "General of the Armies," now borne by Pershing alone, only if the World War I leader consented.

Stimson made some progress with his visitors, but he merely stilled a part of the uproar. Greatly troubled, Hopkins called the Secretary on the twentieth to report that the matter was being used to attack the President. Assistant Secretary of War McCloy attempted to smooth matters over by talking to Senator Austin. The latter explained that he was satisfied with Stimson's reassurances, but his colleagues on Capitol Hill were still upset. On the twenty-first, Representative James Wadsworth—an old friend of Stimson's and Marshall's—came to see the Secretary. After twelve years in the Senate and nearly ten years in the House, Wadsworth was accustomed to partisan clamor. He predicted to Stimson that since the issue was "wholly artificial," it would run its course in a week.[13]

As the newspapers continued to fan the rumors, another element was injected into the charge of plots against Marshall. Columnist Drew Pearson reported on September 19 that friends of the Chief of Staff were "indignant over his forthcoming transfer, and he himself is none too happy. Senatorial friends attribute the shift to the British, who are reported to have had some stiff altercations with Marshall over a western front." On the same day Frank C. Waldrop of the Washington *Times-Herald* announced that he had been informed, and had excellent grounds to believe, that "General Marshall right today is out as Chief of Staff, because he won't further subordinate his 'technical' views on global strategy to Messrs. Roosevelt and Churchill."[14] These and other bits of "inside" misinformation prompted an editorial two days later in the influential *Army and Navy Journal,* an unofficial service publication that reflected the views of many Army officers. Professing its disbelief in the rumors, the *Journal* said that such a move, while heralded as a reward for the General, would be a demotion. It feared that he had "come into conflict with powerful interests which would like to eliminate him from the Washington picture and place in his stead an officer more amenable to their will." Walter Trohan of the Chicago *Tribune,* who later was cited by Senator Joseph McCarthy of Wisconsin as a source for some of his vitriolic attacks on General Marshall, reported Washington views that the British wanted someone more pliant in the Chief of Staff's post and that Army officers believed that Marshall should continue the job "for which he is best qualified by experience and ability."[15]

The most vehement statement on the British theme was made by Republican Representative Jessie Sumner, an Illinois isolationist, who assaulted the administration for trying to make the President head of a future world government. She assailed the British for trying to pull the United States into a world alliance and into "every war they fight." They had used their influence at Quebec, she hinted darkly, to get General Marshall kicked upstairs because he had stood up for American rights and had also opposed Admiral Leahy and General MacArthur. Warning moderate members of her party, she predicted that if they continued to support the President, the people would have no choice but to demand an

American Party, which would spread like wildfire through the United States.[16]

She climaxed her remarkably ill-informed attack by claiming that British propaganda for a permanent tie with the United States had "already caused Russia to come out for a strong post-war Germany." In fact, she declared, the talk aided Germany by tempting the Soviet Union to make a separate peace with Germany, "which would leave our American soldiers trapped in the Balkans."

Calmer voices attempted to restore an element of reason to the discussion. Columnist Arthur Krock of the New York *Times*, who thought it unwise to break up a successful Marshall-King team in Washington, argued that it would be possible to get another capable invasion commander but not a Chief of Staff of Marshall's caliber. Instead of a British plot against the Army Chief, David Lawrence of *U.S. News & World Report* saw in Churchill's offer of the command a fitting compliment to a great soldier. Even the Washington *Times-Herald*, which ran columns by John O'Donnell and Walter Trohan strongly attacking the President, recalled editorially that Roosevelt had recently paid high tribute to Marshall by reappointing him Chief of Staff. It concluded: "Mr. Roosevelt will do his duty as he sees it, just as Mr. Wilson and Mr. Lincoln did." [17]

Walter Lippmann and Ernest K. Lindley were even more soothing in their reactions. Lippmann found grounds for honest disagreement over the wisdom of such a move but none for sniffing out a conspiracy. Certainly, he chided, it was hardly logical to view the command of the invasion as a demotion. Referring apparently to continuing calls for MacArthur to become a candidate for President, he wrote: "It has been bad enough to drag the name of one eminent American general into partisan and factional politics during this war, and . . . any attempt to drag General Marshall's name into politics also will be strongly resented and resolutely resisted." [18]

One of the sanest views was that expounded by columnist Ernest Lindley. He pointed to the factors favoring the field command for Marshall, but noted the dread of the General's colleagues that the Joint Chiefs would be deprived of his counsel as well as of his prestige in Congress, "now almost without precedent." "It is a staggering tribute to one man that he is regarded by so many diverse but competent judges as, if not indispensable, at least the best equipped to administer the American Army, to represent it before Congress, and the public, to represent it on the highest Allied strategy-making body, and to command not only it but all the Allied forces in what may well prove to be the most intricate and hazardous but most powerful offensive campaigns in the history of warfare." [19]

Embarrassed by the furor, Marshall decided to take a hand to prevent the War Department's being seriously hurt by careless talk. He told Representative Walter G. Andrews of New York, ranking Republican member of the House Military Affairs Committee, that he resented deeply the accusations against a key subordinate, General Somervell. Marshall declared that he had the greatest confidence in Somervell and that he considered the rumors being circulated damaging to the Army. He repeated the same arguments to Representative Robert E. Thomason, Democrat of Texas. The chairman of the House Military Affairs Committee, Representative Andrew J. May of Kentucky, reviewed the whole affair with the General so that he could assure the House that everything being done about the command had Marshall's approval. Secretary Stimson also took a hand when William K. Hutchinson of the International News Service wrote that Marshall was being shifted in a "domestic coup d'état" designed to put Somervell in charge of funds to ensure that Roosevelt would win the 1944 election.[20]

When Representative John McCormack, Majority Leader of the House, warned Stimson that Representative Paul Shafer was primed to follow up the Hutchinson article with a scathing attack on the administration, the Secretary of War helped McCormack prepare an effective answer. True to advance billing, the Michigan Republican took the floor to declare that he had seen a blueprint of a plan that would purportedly streamline the War Department but would actually turn it into an organ of the New Deal. "In my opinion," he continued, "the activities of the men behind this plot are nothing less than treasonous." [21] At once McCormack rose and quoted Stimson's assurance that Roosevelt had "absolutely refrained from interfering in any way with the choice of any generals of the War Department and in the United States Army and in their assignment to duty." [22] In turn other representatives prompted by Marshall issued denials.

Stung by these unwarranted charges, Somervell later replied heatedly in a private letter to Marshall: "I was much disgusted with the . . . reference to the unfavorable publicity which was given to the rumor of your appointment as supreme commander. How such swine can exist is beyond me. I am, of course, distressed that my name was mixed up in it in any way, and that you had this stupid thing to contend with in addition to your other burdens." [23]

Meanwhile newspapers across the country called for an end to political attacks. Administration supporters insisted that the President should use Marshall where he could render the greatest service. The Detroit *Free Press* chided Republicans for playing politics with the names of both MacArthur and Marshall.[24] The Republican New York *Herald Tribune,* a supporter of the President in foreign affairs, lashed out against the opposition newspapers for the "mixture of unauthenticated 'news,' rumor, guesswork and innuendo which has exploded a teapot tempest around the figure of General Marshall." It charged that "the worst and most irresponsible deliberately exploit it—as the Patterson and McCormick news-

papers are constantly doing—to create the maximum of division and ob-
struction and baseless suspicion in the conduct of war and of affairs."
When Roosevelt used the *Herald Tribune* editorial to answer his critics,
the publishers in question struck back. In his usual rare form Robert R.
McCormick of the Chicago *Tribune* denounced the *Herald Tribune* as "a
foreign propaganda sheet devoted to returning the United States to the
status of a foreign colony" and Roosevelt as "devoting all his powers to
trying to destroy the republican form of government." [25] For the moment
the Patterson-McCormick press praised Marshall and sympathized with
him as the victim of a plot. In a later day they would portray him as a
simpleton.

Despite efforts by the War Department to allay congressional suspicions, Representative Shafer continued to ferret out New Deal plots. He
urged Congress to investigate a reported plan to remove Marshall and
other important generals and replace them with political appointees.
Reading the worst into the details of the Army Service Forces reorganization plan, he said that the "palace guard" was planning to remove some
sixteen generals and replace them with brain trusters. Anti-Semitic overtones were added as White House adviser Samuel Rosenman, presidential
assistant David K. Niles, and Justice Felix Frankfurter were listed with
Hopkins as instigators of the plan. Though Hopkins was not Jewish, he
was considered the ringleader. Among the civilians being considered to
replace experienced soldiers were Dr. Eli Ginzberg and James P. Mitchell,
one a statistician and the other the director of the Industrial Personnel
Division of the ASF.[26] This was political rumormongering at its most irresponsible, and it ignored the fact the Marshall shared many of Somervell's
beliefs in the value of the reorganization plan. It seems likely that the
President was as little aware of this plan as he had been of the reorganization efforts early in 1942. The difference was that newspapers in 1942 did
not bother to ask who made the proposal. In the fall of 1943 the parties
were girding for the 1944 presidential campaign.

Marshall managed to keep his sense of humor during some of the more
ridiculous phases of the debate. When a Nazi-controlled radio station in
Paris announced that he had been demoted and Roosevelt was now acting
as Chief of Staff, the General wrote Hopkins: "Dear Harry, Are you responsible for pulling this fast one on me? GCM." Hopkins passed the note
on to the President, who penned the comment, "Dear George—Only true
in part—I am now Chief of Staff *but* you are President. FDR." [27]

Unwittingly a helpful soul at the White House (Stimson and Marshall
thought it was Press Secretary Stephen Early) created new problems
abroad. Hoping to still the shrill debate, an "informant" told newsman
Kirke Simpson that Marshall was to be given world-wide command of
Anglo-American forces battling the Axis. Although this reflected current
thinking in administration circles, the idea had not been cleared with
Churchill. The Prime Minister, who had "a constituency" of his own to

consider, at once inquired of Roosevelt if there had been an alteration in the understanding reached at Quebec for Marshall to command OVER-LORD.[28] Hopkins replied for Roosevelt that he knew of no basic change. He thought that the public outburst was quieting down and blamed it on the McCormick-Patterson press, which, he added, had "inspired it for their own nefarious purposes." [29]

To Marshall one of the most distressing aspects was the effort to involve General Pershing made by some who opposed his getting the invasion command. The Chief of Staff believed that John Callan O'Laughlin, one-time treasurer of the Republican National Committee and owner and publisher of the *Army and Navy Journal,* which had just come out editorially against "demoting" Marshall, had prompted the eighty-three-year-old general to protest to Roosevelt.[30] Over Pershing's signature the following message went to the President:

> I am so deeply disturbed by the repeated newspaper reports that General Marshall is to be transferred to a tactical command in England, that I am writing to express my fervent hope that these reports are unfounded.
>
> We are engaged in a global war of which the end is still far distant and for the wise and strategical guidance of which we need our most accomplished officer as Chief of Staff. I voice the consensus of informed military opinion in saying that officer is General Marshall. To transfer him to a tactical command in a limited area, no matter how seemingly important, is to deprive ourselves of the benefit of his outstanding strategical ability and experience. I know of no one at all comparable to replace him as Chief of Staff.
>
> I have written this, Mr. President, because of my deep conviction that the suggested transfer of General Marshall would be a fundamental and very grave error in our military policy.[31]

Pershing had obviously acted on the supposition that his former aide needed assistance without any awareness of the fact that Marshall wanted the command very much. Although Roosevelt still resolved to go ahead with the appointment, it seems likely that Pershing had at least raised a question in his mind. In any case he could not lightly disregard the advice of the venerable leader of the American Expeditionary Force. With great diplomatic skill Roosevelt replied:

> My dear General:
>
> You are absolutely right about George Marshall—and yet, I think, you are wrong too! He is, as you say, far and away the most available man as Chief of Staff. But, as you know, the operations for which we are considering him are the biggest that we will conduct in this war. And, when the time comes, it will not be a mere limited area proposition, but I think the command will include the whole European theatre—and, in addition to that, the British want to have him sit with their own Joint Staff in all matters that do not pertain to purely British island affairs.
>
> More than that, I think it is only a fair thing to give George a chance in the field—and because of the nature of the job we shall still have the benefit of his strategical ability.

The best way I can express it is to tell you that I want George to be the Pershing of the second World War—and he cannot be that if we keep him here. I know you will understand.[32]

In writing thus to Pershing, the President was trying not only to still the doubts of Marshall's colleagues in the Joint Chiefs of Staff and of troubled members of Congress, but to deal with another fundamental problem. Secretary Stimson shared the President's desire to ensure that the overseas post would in no way—imagined or actual—constitute a diminution of Marshall's power. In a sense both of them tied the appointment of Marshall as Supreme Commander to British acceptance of a larger command than that of the cross-Channel forces.

After assuring a senatorial delegation on September 15 that Marshall wanted the European command, the Secretary of War discussed with Hopkins means of getting it for him. He next proposed—to Roosevelt— that the European and Mediterranean theaters be united under Marshall and that he assume the command no later than November 1. After writing this, he asked Marshall for comments. The latter expressed his gratitude but doubted if Churchill would agree since he would be under pressure from his own electorate.[33] A few days later Stimson again called in Marshall, who maintained his great reluctance to discuss his future role, and said he must help decide what position they should adhere to in discussions with the British and what compromise they could accept. Stimson spoke, for example, of a demand for unifying the two theaters and the need of having an American deputy as battlefield director for the cross-Channel attack. The Chief of Staff thought that the first problem was more important.[34]

Despite his embarrassment the Chief of Staff discussed the matter with the President, apparently on September 28. Next day he summoned Arnold and Handy and told them that the entire business "was getting into more and more of a mess" and directed them to work out a solution based on their own ideas without being influenced "in any way whatsoever [by the fact] that he was involved personally in the matter." [35]

Other key War Department leaders also tried their hands at a formula. Assistant Secretary of War Lovett and Colonel George A. Lincoln and General Hull of the Operations Division all submitted ideas. Lovett thought it possible to have an American officer serve as representative of the President and the Prime Minister in European operations. Marshall could handle this assignment as General of the Armies, while continuing as a member of the Combined Chiefs of Staff organization. In his absence a deputy would carry on the functions of the Chief of Staff.

Like his fellow Chiefs of Staff, Arnold did not want to lose Marshall's services in Washington. In his view, "leaving all personalities out of the problem, the Chief of Staff . . . has been a tower of strength to the President. . . . He, more than any other one man, has been able to give the President . . . advice and counsel in strict accordance with military conditions as they exist, and requirements for the future . . . for the Chief of Staff to be appointed as Commanding General of OVERLORD, makes him just another Theater Commander. He loses the value of his long years of experience. . . ."

Concluding that it looked to him "as if the whole thing is in one hell of a mess," Arnold proposed a solution that would permit Marshall to remain as Chief of Staff and yet be in a position to make certain that OVERLORD was carried out: the General would remain as Chief of Staff but assume the task of implementing the OVERLORD operation, taking Eisenhower as his Deputy. On completing this task he would revert to his original functions as Chief of Staff.[36]

General Handy and his assistants disagreed. Insisting that there must be a single, hard-driving operational commander for OVERLORD, they concluded that the logical nominee for the post was General Marshall, "who has been most instrumental in the preparation of the over-all strategic plan." For Deputy they proposed Air Marshal Portal. Handy conceded that Marshall's position must not be inferior to the one he now held and that American public opinion must be satisfied by permitting Marshall to keep the title of Chief of Staff and appear to be on "temporary leave of absence." [37]

Marshall had a realistic notion of his own worth, but these discussions embarrassed him when conducted outside his own office by the most intimate members of his staff. Nevertheless he finally agreed to review the various proposals. At the outset he stressed the need for a British deputy if he became Supreme Commander and proposed Sir John Dill as the logical appointee. Although he was not certain if this would be considered a proper position for a field marshal, he believed him ideal "from the standpoint of the personal relationship, trust and compatibility which must exist between a commander and his deputy." Dill, he added, "possesses a knowledge of both British and U.S. forces which is probably unequaled by any other high commander."

Handy proposed that since it was imperative to ensure that Marshall have an assignment equal in importance to his current post, the President should be able to recall him if necessary. Handy reasoned that if Germany collapsed suddenly, no assignment of importance would remain for Marshall in the European Theater. It was also possible that his availability in the future "might offer a solution, which would not be highly controversial, for an over-all Pacific commander." [38]

So far as Europe was concerned, the U.S. Chiefs held that the Combined Command was necessary to coordinate attacks from the south and west. They hoped this requirement could be worked out without upsetting the Combined Chiefs of Staff structure or raising the question of an overall commander in the Pacific. They proposed that Marshall at once assume operational control of the forces against Germany. They believed that he, as Supreme Commander, would need only a small staff and would rely mainly on the staffs of his operational commanders.

After reading the proposed drafts for Churchill, Marshall suggested several amendments to make them more palatable to the British leader. He urged Portal's immediate assignment as commander of the strategic air forces: "He is known and highly respected by the American people who, with their acute appreciation of airpower, will certainly expect that some well-known and highly capable air officer will be included in the high command." He assumed that General Alexander would be Churchill's choice for the Mediterranean Command. If there were to be a separate commander for OVERLORD, Eisenhower would likely be made available. Otherwise he would be made commander of American field forces. Marshall would give up his position on the Combined Chiefs of Staff but remain a member of the U.S. Chiefs of Staff, concentrating for the time on the duties of Supreme Commander.

The proposals constituted wishful thinking in the extreme. To a considerable degree they amounted mainly to a blueprint of the conditions that must be met if Marshall were to be spared from Washington. Like Roosevelt and Stimson, the planners were pinning the final selection of the Supreme Commander on British acceptance of the complete command package. Stimson at that time seems to have believed that they would grant nearly anything the Americans asked if they could have Marshall in charge of the invasion. Others were not so sure. Admiral Leahy, seeing the final draft, doubted if the British would accept it. Hopkins agreed that they were unlikely to make concessions of such magnitude.

In early October, before Leahy had a chance to present the various proposals to the President, the head of the COSSAC planning staff, General Morgan, arrived from London. His wholehearted sharing of American views on the importance of the cross-Channel attack and his obvious readiness to participate in plans for transatlantic cooperation stilled many War Department doubts about ultimate British acceptance of their proposals.

Like Ismay, Morgan had spent much of his early career in India. During the early months of World War II he served as a brigadier in charge of a support group with the 1st Armoured Division in France. On his return to England he formed and commanded the Devon and Cornwall County Division and later headed the 55th Division and the 1st Corps District Command of Lincolnshire and Yorkshire. From the latter command he went to a corps and was instructed to prepare for a possible landing in the Mediterranean in case the Germans attempted to strike through Spain at Gibraltar. When that threat decreased, he was told to plan for an invasion of Sardinia. It was not surprising that when the Casablanca conference decided to establish a planning staff for a cross-Channel attack, Morgan was picked to act as Chief of Staff to the Supreme

Allied Commander (COSSAC) who would be appointed at some later time. He had organized a staff with U.S. General Barker as Deputy during the late spring, and by the time of the Quebec conference COSSAC had a plan—restricted though it was by limited resources—ready for examination. General Marshall thought Morgan was highly capable of filling the Chief of Staff position in the permanent headquarters.[39]

General Morgan had come to Washington for a brief visit, but Marshall soon persuaded him to extend it to six weeks. Recalling from World War I that British and French officers he had met had known little of the United States and the American soldier, the Chief of Staff resolved that Morgan and his chief administrative officer, Major General N. C. D. Brownjohn, should meet key American leaders and see something of the country. Assuming that Morgan would be his Chief of Staff in case he took the Supreme Command, Marshall personally arranged the visit, inviting his guests to attend staff briefings, talk with principal officials in the Army, Navy, and Air Forces, travel to various camps and posts to observe amphibious training, airborne exercises, and the handling of supplies in the New York Port of Embarkation. In addition to having them out to Fort Myer and Leesburg for long talks, he proposed a busman's holiday to whatever historical areas near Washington they would like to see. He was pleased when they asked to visit the area covered by the Valley campaign in Virginia and to visit the battlefield at Gettysburg. Mindful of his own ride by horseback over this area at the end of his first year at Fort Leavenworth, he personally outlined an itinerary for their sightseeing exercise.[40]

General Marshall was attracted to Morgan from the beginning. Indeed most Americans liked him. Possessed of a fine sense of humor and great patience, he displayed a special aptitude for getting along with American cousins. Having served with Canadians in France, Morgan had picked up many North American expressions that made him at home in an American officers' mess. He liked to claim that by developing an understanding of the finer points of good bourbon and branchwater, he had endeared himself to members of Eisenhower's staff, and he was even elected to honorary membership in the Democratic Party by some of the Southerners. He developed an extravagant admiration for Marshall and Eisenhower that did not set well with some of his British colleagues—notably Montgomery.[41]

So well did Marshall hit it off with Morgan that he cited his experience to Admiral King as a model for Allied liaison in future planning: "I am certain at the present time we are going through an illuminating experience over here with General Morgan. He is in the Operations section. He is present at our daily operational meetings with Arnold, Handy, and me. We discuss all these matters with complete frankness and my impression is that he is so heavily on our side now as a result of such procedure that it may be embarrassing in his relation to the British Chiefs of Staff in London—though I am not unduly concerned over this phase of the matter." [42]

Morgan was equally well received at the White House. As soon as he heard that the COSSAC chief had arrived, Roosevelt asked to see him. At their first meeting Morgan requested three things of the President: "Your Army, your General Marshall, and your Ambassador Biddle [ambassador to the European governments in exile]." The President agreed that he could have the Army under proper conditions but that he could not at the moment make the other two available. In fact he hinted that for political reasons he might not be able to spare Marshall for the invasion.[43]

Having received a copy of Roosevelt's letter to Pershing, the Chief of Staff assumed that the matter of the Supreme Command was settled. In November he began to pick a staff for his future overseas headquarters. Not only did he continue to forward his views on command to the theater commander in London, General Devers, but he sent Major General Harold R. Bull, formerly an instructor on his staff at Fort Benning and later G-3 of the War Department, to London as the future Chief of Operations of Supreme Headquarters. As we have seen, he also indicated to Colonel Truman Smith of War Department G-2 that if he went to Europe, he wanted him on his staff there.[44]

Marshall also considered possible field commanders, placing General Bradley high on his list; he considered Devers, Eisenhower, Mark Clark, and Patton for other possible slots. Dreading to leave the field for the post in the Pentagon for which he was prominently mentioned, Eisenhower made clear his desire to remain possibly as an army group commander under Marshall. Betting in the Pentagon favored Eisenhower's return, but the Chief of Staff kept him on his list of potential key commanders in the invasion.

As he worked quietly to prepare his command for the invasion, Marshall hoped that the earlier storm over his appointment would subside. To his chagrin his name made the headlines in a different context in November, when Senator Edwin Johnson, Democrat of Colorado, often a critic of the administration and opponent of a fourth term for the incumbent, proposed General Marshall as the Democratic nominee for the presidency in 1944. Aghast at this proposal, especially since it seemed designed mainly to head off Roosevelt or provide a military counterfoil to MacArthur in case he became the Republican candidate, General Marshall pleaded with Stimson to squelch it as thoroughly and as quickly as possible. He wrote him on November 8:

> Attached are clippings of some of the recent newspaper articles regarding my presidential possibilities.
>
> My proposal is that at your next press conference, Thursday, you refer to this matter in some such manner as follows:
>
> "I regret very much the recent references to General Marshall of a political nature. Such discussions cannot be otherwise than harmful to our war effort on

which everything must be concentrated. I know they are embarrassing to General Marshall and furthermore, I feel that they make his present task more difficult.

"I can speak with authority stating that there has been no discussion of this nature with General Marshall by anyone. Further, that he will never permit himself to be considered as a possible Presidential candidate. His training and ambitions are not political." [45]

Stimson did as Marshall requested and succeeded in blocking further discussions of his candidacy. Apparently this did not stop Roosevelt from considering it. After the President's death Justice William O. Douglas told the General that Roosevelt had at one time mentioned him favorably for the 1944 nomination. Douglas's statement must be viewed in light of the fact that in private conversations in the months before Roosevelt made his decision to seek a fourth term, he threw out many names of possible candidates to those around him. And it is conceivable that the idea of a Marshall candidacy might have been revived by the White House had MacArthur been put into the race.[46]

However Roosevelt may have assessed Marshall's political prospects, he must have been impressed by the recent insistence in the press and in Congress that Marshall remain at his post in Washington. Marshall himself acknowledged that "Roosevelt resented . . . [it] when his own people would ask that I go [over on the Hill]." The President may also have been aware that, when a group of reporters were asked in December 1943 to name the men who had contributed most to the war effort, Marshall received one vote more than the President.[47]

The President had still other reasons to want to keep Marshall in Washington. There were rumblings of discontent from the Southwest Pacific, from the Far East, from London and Moscow that Marshall could probably handle better than any likely successor. All these developments undoubtedly figured in the President's thinking as he approached a final decision on the Supreme Command. Despite pressure from the Prime Minister and from Stimson in the fall of 1943 to send Marshall at once to London, the President continued to delay.[48] Conditions in Washington and around the world made it essential for him, in order to carry out his duties as well as to neutralize issues in the coming campaign, to have the backing of a powerful Chief of Staff. Increasingly Roosevelt would see that he could not give Marshall up unless the British accepted an arrangement that would permit the Chief of Staff to retain his status at home while commanding abroad.

Marshall's Dilemmas

U N D E R different conditions September would have been a satisfying month for General Marshall. Instead, as arguments over his appointment mounted, it became troubled and unsettled. Rather than looking confidently toward his future command, the Chief of Staff faced painful dilemmas.

The month had started well. At its opening Montgomery's troops had moved across the Strait of Messina into the toe of Italy, less than a week before General Clark's Anglo-American force landed at Salerno. On the day before the second landing, September 8, General Eisenhower announced the Italian armistice, arranged by members of his staff with the Badoglio government.

Recent weeks had also gone well for the Soviet Union. At the beginning of February 1943 the final remnant of German resistance around Stalingrad had ended to complete what Sir Basil Liddell Hart called "the most long-drawn-out battle of the Second World War." Then in July, after the greatest armored battle of the war, near Kursk, the Red Army beat back the powerful panzer forces of the enemy. On July 12 the Soviet forces opened their offensive against the Orel salient, retaking the city three weeks later and ending the possibility of any later attack on Moscow. Before the month ended, the Russians had clearly seized the initiative from the enemy and opened the drive that although slowed at times, would not be completely halted. By the end of August, Soviet forces had regained Kharkov, crossed the Donets, and were driving hard for the Dnieper.[1]

At home Marshall in his biennial report, issued on the day of the Italian surrender, had just reviewed his work since 1941 in preparing the Army and the Army Air Forces for war. Intended, as the Chief of Staff stated, to eliminate "various rumors and beliefs regarding the progress of the war and . . . to prepare the people for the heavy fighting and heavy casualties which must be endured prior to [the] victory," the report made clear the tremendous advances of the past two years.[2]

Since mid-1941, Marshall revealed, the enlisted strength of the Army had been "increased by 5,000,000 men" and "the officer corps had grown from 93,000 to 521,000." The gains included 182,000 officers and nearly 2,000,000 enlisted men in the Air Forces. Unprecedented growth included a 3500 percent increase in the Air Forces proper, 4000 percent in the Corps of Engineers, and 12,000 percent in the service personnel of the Air Forces.

Global war [reported Marshall] has introduced lines of communication encircling the earth (a rough check indicates that present protected supply lines extend over 56,000 miles). It has made necessary harbor improvements with depots and railroad management, as in the Persian Gulf for the transportation of supplies to Russia, and in the region of the Suez Canal and the Red Sea. It has required construction of bases in Australia and throughout the Pacific and air bases at Karachi and Calcutta on the west and east coasts of India; pipe lines and pumping plants to facilitate movement of gasoline, and a multiplicity of requirements to support our fighting forces and permit them to devote their undivided attention to the enemy.

Marshall called special attention to the assistance given Soviet Russia since the German invasion. "Over 3,000 airplanes, 2,400 tanks, 109,000 submachine guns, 16,000 Jeeps, 80,000 trucks, 7,000 motorcycles, 130,000 field telephones, and 75,000 tons of explosives" had actually arrived in Russia in addition to many other items of munitions, foodstuffs, and raw materials.

He ended by painting a rosy picture for the future:

July 1, 1943, finds the United States Army and Navy united against the Axis powers in purpose and in operations, a unity shared when the occasion demands by the British Commonwealth of Nations, the Chinese, Dutch, French, and other fighting elements among our friends and supporters. Across the Atlantic the enemy had been driven from North Africa, and Europe has been encircled by a constantly growing military power. The Russian Army, engaging two-thirds of the German ground forces and one-third of the German air fleet in deadly and exhausting combat, has dispelled the legend of the invincibility of the German Panzer divisions.[3]

The reactions of the former Chief of Imperial General Staff, Field Marshal Sir John Dill, were given wide publicity. He commented:

The tale of the orderly though nonetheless rapid development of the mighty strength of the United States Army is of itself a most impressive one, and one can gather how immense must have been the effort involved to ensure a proper balance and co-ordination. . . .

Every American citizen who reads this report will, I am confident, be filled with pride and thankfulness. Pride in the wisdom of the Commander in Chief, pride in what has been achieved, and thankfulness to the Chief of Staff and those working under his direction who made this vast achievement possible. Victory is not yet, but in this report we see how much the seeds of sure victory have been sown.[4]

And indeed almost without exception the chief newspapers of the nation applauded Marshall's achievements.

Paradoxically the tremendous growth of the Army under Marshall's leadership constituted one important reason why he found it difficult to take the overseas command. It was one of the manifold reasons that his continued presence in Washington seemed so important to his fellow Chiefs of Staff, leading members of Congress, and old friends, such as Pershing, and why he now faced a dilemma that he found increasingly difficult to resolve. Although he knew and characterized as "ridiculous" charges that he was being eased out of Washington, he could see daily evidence that a strong hand such as his, strengthened by a prestige slowly gained in Allied councils, would be needed to deal with pressing problems in theaters around the world and at home.[5]

First of all, old suspicions in the Pacific resurfaced. There had been a warning in the sharp reactions from the Southwest Pacific to the announcement that Lord Louis Mountbatten would head a new Southeast Asia Command. The significance of Mountbatten's appointment was widely misinterpreted and nowhere more than in MacArthur's theater. On the evening of September 21, in a statement described by one newsman at Southwest Pacific Theater headquarters as "mysterious and unexpected," the American General implied that his plans for winning the war in the Pacific had been scrapped at Quebec and that he had been relegated to a third-rate role in favor of the campaigns of Lord Louis Mountbatten and the island-hopping strategy of the Navy.[6]

In his criticism of the Navy strategy MacArthur explained that his own concept was only to use massive strokes against major strategic objectives, taking advantage of surprise and air-ground striking power, supported and aided by the fleet. "Island-hopping, with extravagant losses and slow progress," he continued, "is not my idea of how to end the war as soon and as cheaply as possible." "It is typical of MacArthur's humility," wrote one newsman from New Guinea, "that the man Roosevelt drafted out of retirement added: 'I have no personal military ambition whatever, and am perfectly content with such a role as may be prescribed for me.' "[7]

If MacArthur had no ambitions for a larger role, his friends did not share that view. One or more members of a five-man senatorial team just back from the Pacific had other ends in mind. Senator Albert B. ("Happy") Chandler of Kentucky announced on his return that he would urge in the Senate that MacArthur be given Supreme Command of Allied Forces in the war against Japan. In reporting Chandler's statement the *Army and Navy Journal* agreed that the Southwest Pacific commander should be "destined for direction of a far larger sphere in the Pacific than he now commands." The Washington *Times-Herald* polled several members of Congress and came up with "typical comments" by six members, three Democrats and three Republicans, praising MacArthur. Although Senator Rufus Holman of Oregon thought that MacArthur's plans had been discouraged possibly because the President feared him as a political rival, and Representative James W. Mott of the same state saw Mountbatten's appointment as the first step in easing MacArthur out, none of the men interviewed mentioned the plan suggested by Chandler.[8]

One of MacArthur's stanchest newspaper supporters, the *Times-Herald*, hailed his challenge to the plans made at Quebec. It continued:

> President Roosevelt, according to New Dealers, regards MacArthur as his McClellan. General George Briton [*sic*] McClellan, commander and organizer of the Army of the Potomac, ran against President Lincoln in the Civil War.
> MacArthur's blast was regarded in some quarters as a bid for the presidential nomination. Friends of the General dismissed this suggestion as absurd, declaring that he was making a bid for recognition of the proper conduct of the war. They insist that MacArthur's soldier's heart cherishes no presidential aspirations.[9]

There had been earlier straws in the wind that summer. Colonel McCormick said in an interview in New York: "Roosevelt's in a hell of a position. If MacArthur wins a great victory, he will be President. If he doesn't win one, it will be because Roosevelt has not given him sufficient support." In late August, Representative Hamilton Fish, a well-known Republican isolationist from Roosevelt's congressional district, spoke of the opposition being built by Republicans and anti-New Deal Democrats against "the power-hungry bureaucrats and left-wing New Dealers in Washington." He proposed drafting General MacArthur on "a win-the-war platform and on a one-term plank, as opposed to a fourth term and military dictatorship." A short time later Senator Arthur Capper, Republican of Kansas, expanded the slate by saying that he believed MacArthur or Eisenhower would be the Republican presidential candidate in 1944. To those who doubted the effectiveness of the MacArthur boom, a Gallup poll in mid-September gave some interesting data. In answer to the question of how they would vote if an election were being held at that time between Roosevelt on the Democratic ticket and MacArthur on the Republican, 58 per cent of those expressing an opinion favored the President and 42 per cent the General. But among Middle Western farmers the vote was Roosevelt, 44 per cent; MacArthur, 56 per cent.[10]

No matter how much MacArthur's friends then or later denied his political aspirations, the private record of one of his chief supporters for the presidency, Senator Vandenberg of Michigan, revealed irrefutably after his death what had been suspected earlier, that the Southwest Pacific commander was willing to be a presidential stalking horse. Although MacArthur carefully remained aloof from any overt political move, he was cognizant through one or more of his personal staff that efforts were being made to get the nomination for him. Possibly he wanted only to ensure that he got what he wanted in the Southwest Pacific, but it is difficult to doubt that he knew that an attempt was being made to take advantage of public resentment against the administration's policies. Throughout the summer of 1943 Vandenberg continued the efforts that he had begun earlier in the year to win support for a MacArthur candidacy by conferring with such potential backers as General Wood of Sears, Roebuck, former president of the America First movement, and newspaper publishers such as Frank Gannett and Roy Howard. Lest he precipitate a premature boom, Vandenberg warned his intermediary with the Southwest Pacific commander, Major General Charles A. Willoughby (MacArthur's chief of intelligence), to tell "my friend to just 'get on with the war' and to forget this whole political business back here in the States." In mid-September the senator wrote General Wood: "I have heard from General Willoughby that the 'situation is satisfactory' (which is all I care to put on paper) and that the guidance of friends like you and Edgar Queeny and Frank Gannett and Roy Howard and myself will be satisfactory. Roy Howard seems to be in doubt about the whole matter (although not through any lack of total loyalty to the General)." [11]

By the end of September public reaction against recent strategic decisions emphasizing the war against Europe and leaving MacArthur short of supplies encouraged Vandenberg to hope that an effort to cash in on American public opinion could succeed. "These people," he wrote, "can easily *martyrize* him into a completely irresistible figure. So it seems to me more important than ever that we should give our own 'commander-in-chief' [Roosevelt] no possible excuse upon which to hang his own political reprisals. It is obvious on every hand that the movement [for MacArthur] is making solid headway in all directions. . . ." [12]

Not all MacArthur's supporters were as discreet as Vandenberg. John O'Donnell, whose column faithfully reflected the Patterson-McCormick opposition to the administration, implied that campaign politics was involved in recent presidential decisions. He declared: The tart comment of General MacArthur from his Australian headquarters had only one meaning: "The American hero issued the statement and cleared through his censorship the blunt interpretations of correspondents so that the people back home shall know that higher-ups in Washington have been starving him for men and supplies to fight the Japs and that now he has been told to play second fiddle to Lord Louis Mountbatten, who will launch the spectacular main attack on Japan while the Hero of Bataan fights a third rate holding war in the islands north of Australia." He predicted that the real story would break within a few days as Senator Chandler led the fight for a larger role for MacArthur with support from Senators Lodge and Brewster. [13] O'Donnell had once goaded Roosevelt to the extreme of presenting him with a German Iron Cross for service to the enemy, and it is not unlikely that Roosevelt felt tempted at this point to send him another.

O'Donnell's speculation met strong rebuke from Republican and Democratic papers alike. The pro-Republican New York *World-Telegram* reacted heatedly:

When General MacArthur publicly challenges the strategic decisions of his superiors, that is news. But it is dangerous news, revealing a split so serious that the General feels justified, in the most unusual military course of carrying a highly technical strategy dispute to the public.

When this coincides with semiofficially inspired stories about a shift of General Marshall [to overseas] command, the whole thing becomes too explosive for safety.

We have too much admiration for MacArthur as a man and a great soldier and too much sympathy with his desire to press the war against Japan, to condemn him for this risky action without knowing all the facts. Nevertheless, the burden of proof certainly is on him to justify a course which, if followed by commanders on other fronts, might destroy public confidence and service confidence in the global conduct of the war.

Of course MacArthur has nothing to do with attempts to make political capital out of military disputes—those misguided efforts of some of his supporters in this country are hurting him more than are his critics.[14]

Roosevelt and his military advisers could not believe that the Pacific commander was opposed to what was being done in his name. Even if the presidency was not involved, it appeared that a challenge to the President and the high command might be thrown into Congress—where an expanded command or a different strategy for MacArthur would be demanded. Perhaps Roosevelt took the matter too seriously. But the fact that a few weeks later he told General Morgan of COSSAC that he might not be able to spare Marshall for political reasons may have meant that he feared a serious challenge in Congress in 1944. Further the question was whether, as Chief of Staff, Eisenhower, who had once served as a major and lieutenant colonel on MacArthur's staff in Washington and Manila, would be as capable of coping with the prestigious Southwest Pacific commander as would Marshall, who stood well with Congress and had the venerable Pershing as champion.

Equally important to the President and the War Department was the careful handling of Stilwell and the rancorous situation in the Far East. The relative calm that had prevailed in that area during the Quebec conference ended in early September. On the fifth Chennault took advantage of his authorized channel to the President to send a message of discouragement: he was not getting promised supplies. While he did not name Stilwell as the guilty party, he left Roosevelt free to draw only one conclusion.[15]

General Marshall discussed the Stilwell problem with Stimson on September 6, blaming the Generalissimo and Madame Chiang Kai-shek for much of the difficulty. Apprehensively both men awaited new complaints that would certainly be forthcoming.

They did not have long to wait. In mid-September, Dr. T. V. Soong, Chinese Foreign Minister, made a number of proposals designed to improve Chiang Kai-shek's position and to curb General Stilwell's power.

His first requests were totally unrealistic. He proposed Chinese representation on the Combined Chiefs of Staff and the Munitions Assignment Board, recommendations that the British would not accept and that the United States—despite its greater respect for Chiang's role—was not even prepared to transmit. He also asked for a Chinese Supreme Commander and a Chinese Chief of Staff for the China Theater with American deputies and urged that all military units of whatever nationality be under the Supreme Commander.[16]

Soong next attacked the multiplicity of jobs held by Stilwell, aiming at any job held by the CBI commander instead of at his absurd conglomeration of hats. Stilwell was the Generalissimo's Joint (Allied) Chief of Staff, China Theater, and commander of the U.S. Forces (including Air) in the CBI. A particular sore point to the Chinese was the fact that under him came Major General R. A. Wheeler's Services of Supply in India and China. In addition to these assignments Stilwell had command of Chinese divisions in India and exercised an undefined authority over Chinese forces in Yunnan Province. Worst of all, from Chungking's standpoint, he could influence the flow of Lend-Lease supplies.

Exasperated by the continual bickering and countercharges, Roosevelt asked Marshall to talk with Soong. The Chief of Staff conferred politely with the Chinese representative but firmly declined to make requested changes in the command structure. When near the end of the month Soong complained to the President that Chennault was not getting planes that had been promised, Roosevelt spoke more pointedly to Marshall, asking that he "get behind this again and vigorously push our agreed plans."[17]

As the Chinese situation continued to deteriorate, the Secretary of War attempted to take a hand. In talking with Roosevelt on October 18, he found him seemingly determined to recall Stilwell. Stimson hastened to inform Marshall of his conversation and to reiterate that he still believed Stilwell to be the best man for the job, even though he could not get along with the Generalissimo.[18]

"Marshall [was troubled] over it, being tired and worried himself, and I could see that it was a blow to him," Stimson wrote. The Chief of Staff told Stimson that he was now sorry that he had not brought Stilwell back earlier when the shift would not have appeared to be a dismissal. On the following day Marshall actually had a draft cable prepared ordering Stilwell's relief. Apparently he thought briefly of Somervell, then on a trip to the Far East, as a replacement. For a moment it seemed that Stilwell had lost.[19]

But he was to hold on for another year. In an intriguing episode Stilwell was saved in part because of the intervention of the Soong sisters, Madame Chiang and Madame Kung, and partly through the efforts of General Somervell.

Shortly before this development Mountbatten and Somervell had set out from Quebec to explain the QUADRANT conference decisions to Chiang Kai-shek. Enroute, at New Delhi, they met Dr. Soong, who informed Somervell that Roosevelt had agreed to withdraw Stilwell. Somervell had heard nothing of this before he had left Washington, a few days earlier. Marshall apparently got his first word on the nineteenth, when Stimson did. Soong then either had prior information from Roosevelt, which was not passed on to Marshall, or drew unwarranted conclusions from conversations with the President.

The Chinese diplomat also warned Mountbatten that any attempt to name Stilwell as his Deputy would be disastrous.[20] Mountbatten was startled by the idea, fearing not only the effect of command changes on his operations but also an unfavorable American reaction. "He felt," Somervell reported to Marshall, "that the same group that claimed that he was attempting to supplant MacArthur would claim that no sooner had he arrived than he had successfully ousted the one possible contestant for fame and glory in South East Asia." [21]

While Mountbatten remained briefly in New Delhi, Somervell flew on to Chungking. There the Generalissimo, using Soong as interpreter, indicated that he wanted Stilwell recalled. Knowing that Marshall's backing still held, Somervell urged Chiang Kai-shek to reconsider.

At this crucial moment Madame Chiang Kai-shek and her sister came to Stilwell's aid. In an atmosphere of "medieval court intrigue," as Somervell described it, the ladies upset the plans of the Generalissimo and of their brother. An "unholy family row" developed over Stilwell, and "the Madame was overheard telling Soong that thenceforth he would be sick, to go home, and not to reappear at the conference." Calling Stilwell away from a party that he was giving for Mountbatten, Madame Chiang urged him to seek an interview with her husband. She reminded him of the deference due Chiang's position, suggesting he explain that if he had made mistakes he had done so from misunderstanding and not intent and that he was ready to cooperate fully. The truculent commander's first reaction was to tell everybody to "go to hell," but he finally yielded to reason. He submitted resignedly to a lecture by the Generalissimo on the duties of a Chief of Staff and an admonition to avoid "a superiority complex." The talk, he noted, seemed to clear the air.[22]

Actually the rifts in Stilwell's relationships with the Generalissimo had only been papered over. A truce had been proclaimed, but Stilwell thereafter gave less and less attention to his activities as an adviser to Chiang Kai-shek. He stressed increasingly his duties as acting Deputy Supreme Allied Commander of the Southeast Asia Command and Commander of U.S. Forces, CBI.[23] So far as Chinese forces in India were concerned, he was a necessary link between the Generalissimo and SEAC. The British refused to place their troops under Chiang Kai-shek, and the Generalissimo insisted that his forces fight under Stilwell rather than under British command. This solution was further complicated because Stilwell did not wish to be under General Sir George Giffard, Commander-in-Chief, 11th Army Group, slated for command of Allied Ground Forces, SEAC. He proposed instead that he serve as a corps commander under Lieutenant General William J. Slim, commander of the British Fourteenth Army. With that Mountbatten had to be content. But the strange arrangement worked. Despite some snide remarks in his diary, where neither friend nor foe was completely safe from entries that apparently eased Stilwell's mind, "Vinegar Joe" held Slim in high esteem.[24]

Initially Stilwell seemed pleased at the appointment of Mountbatten, recording that Lord Louis was "a good egg." Within three weeks he was convinced that the Admiral was "after my scalp." According to Stilwell, Major General Patrick Hurley, in China to arrange for Chinese participation in the approaching Allied conference at Cairo, had tipped him off. "Louis is working up the 'controversy' between me and Chennault and spoke of it to Hurley," he wrote. "Apparently the idea is to judge me, take the part of my subordinate, and kick me out. Hurley asked him right out if he were by any chance following the old British game of 'divide and rule.' "[25]

If trouble was brewing between Stilwell and Mountbatten, the Chiang Kai-shek–Stilwell relationship seemed momentarily on the mend. On November 6, designated by the U.S. commander as "Love Feast Day," the Generalissimo "was affable as hell." He asked Stilwell to make China's report at Cairo. Marshall was informed of the improved state of affairs but not that it was more apparent than real. Stilwell's current addition to his diary read: "Ella [Madame Kung] had told me he [Chiang] was in a jubilant state of mind and ready to be very friendly. Well if I hadn't heard him rattle his tail I might have been taken in. Mistake! Last time he didn't rattle at all—just struck."[26] Had Marshall been looking over the General's shoulder, he would have been more certain than ever that the best time for Stilwell's recall had passed.

Neither the old arguments nor the new command tangles in the Far East had been settled when Marshall's attention was diverted to the task of helping to attain closer coordination of American and Soviet military efforts in Europe. This aim had been spelled out after Russian acceptance during the Quebec conference of an Allied proposal for a foreign ministers' meeting in Moscow in October, hopefully in preparation for a conference of the leaders of the three great powers and their staffs later in the year.

Before this coordination with the Russians could be achieved, Marshall found that the United States had to send to Moscow a team of military and diplomatic representatives who would concentrate on working with the Soviet leaders rather than quarreling among themselves. He knew that the American diplomatic-military set-up in Russia had been marked by dissension for many months.

Part of the trouble dated from the fall of 1941 when Lend-Lease arrangements with the Soviet Union were concluded by the Beaverbrook-Harriman Mission. To expedite the President's "hurry, hurry, hurry" directive to rush assistance to the Soviets, Hopkins had arranged that an American member of the mission, Colonel Philip R. Faymonville, be left behind as his Lend-Lease representative. A highly competent West Pointer, Faymonville had held the post of military attaché in Russia from 1934 to 1939. Despite Faymonville's obvious acceptability to the Russians and fluency in their language, General Marshall was disturbed by reports that he had been overfriendly to the Russians during his tour as military attaché. When Hopkins asked that Faymonville be assigned to the new position and promoted, the Chief of Staff passed on word that onetime associates of the colonel, including former Ambassador to the Soviet Union William C. Bullitt and Loy Henderson, assistant chief of the Division of European Affairs of the State Department, questioned the Lend-Lease officer's judgment and impartiality where the Russians were concerned. When Hopkins insisted that the Lend-Lease Administration must have the confidence of the Russians, Marshall did not argue further. Knowing that the President was depending on Hopkins to get supplies to the heavily pressed Soviet forces, Marshall agreed to a star for the colonel.[27]

To balance the harsh judgments on Faymonville, there is the private report to Marshall by Major General John R. Deane after he had worked with Faymonville at the Moscow conference in the fall of 1943: "Now as to the set-up here. We found the place seething with cliques, gossip, etc. . . . Perhaps it was unfortunate that Faymonville was returned here for a few days but I do not think so. . . . Despite everything that has been said, he impressed me more favorably than any of the old regime. He did his job well and was the only one who didn't think everyone else in Russia both Russian and American was an S.O.B. I think his trouble lay in a too literal interpretation of his instructions and a stubborn persistence in refusing to depart from his interpretation." [28]

Faymonville's cause was aided at the White House because of his predictions as early as the summer of 1941 that Russia would hold out—at a time when U.S. intelligence officers in the Soviet Union and in the War Department expected her defeat within a few weeks. But the accuracy that won him the title of "General Who Called the Turn" did not make him popular with the U.S. military attaché who was sending back contrary prophecies. Further the military attaché, Colonel Joseph A. Michela, found that Faymonville, with the use of Lend-Lease leverage, was getting information from the Soviets that was not available to the embassy staff. Michela complained to his superior in the War Department,

Major General George V. Strong, who passed the messages on to General Marshall. Faymonville was even less popular with the diplomatic representatives because he had asked for and received from the White House an understanding that he would not be answerable to the U.S. ambassador or the embassy staff.

General Marshall was embarrassed by the complaints and charges against the newly made general but because of Faymonville's special relationship with the White House, he did nothing. Later, in discussing Faymonville, he mused over the fact that representatives of a country who remain abroad for an extended period tend to see issues through the eyes of the people to whom they are accredited. Even Ambassador Joseph Kennedy, he recalled, although no wholehearted admirer of British policy, ended by supporting British Mediterranean strategy.[29]

An attempt was made to change the situation in 1942 with the arrival of the new U.S. ambassador, Admiral William H. Standley, former Chief of Naval Operations and a friend of Roosevelt's. Like Marshall and most other Army and Navy officers, the Admiral liked clear-cut lines of authority. It was repugnant to him to find that as the President's chief representative in the Soviet Union, he did not have control over an Army officer he far outranked. Standley became especially incensed when he found that Faymonville had far greater access to Russian officials than did the ambassador and his staff and that, as Michela had reported, he received information from the Russians and from the White House that he would not share with the embassy.

In addition Standley was infuriated by actions of some of the President's special representatives who also bypassed the ambassador, on their own arranged conferences with Russian officials to which he was not invited and of whose nature he was not informed, and without his advice made statements that sometimes caused considerable embarrassment. In the fall of 1942 he was particularly outraged by the visit of Wendell Willkie, Roosevelt's Republican opponent in the 1940 presidential election. To quote Standley, "his daily and hourly actions had served to by-pass me and undermine the prestige and respect due the American Ambassador."

Finally Standley, deciding that he must make clear to the Russians and the President that he could not remain unless his position was respected, asked to be brought back to Washington for consultation. After a frank talk with Roosevelt in which he felt that he had gained a promise that the situation would improve, he agreed to go back to Moscow. Among Standley's specific requests to which Roosevelt assented were that his naval and military attachés be made rear admiral and brigadier general respectively and that Faymonville be instructed to report to him for duty and be under his administrative control. The Lend-Lease Administrator, Edward R. Stettinius, Jr., issued the necessary orders concerning Faymonville. King agreed at once to promote the naval attaché. Marshall, when asked about the military attaché, replied, "Brigadier General is not the usual rank of an officer who has duty as Military Attaché, but if that is the way you want it, Bill, Michella [sic] will be promoted."

Within a short time after his return to the Soviet Union, Standley found that the promotions were almost all that he had gained. Faymonville continued to go his independent way, and as the weeks passed, other special representatives arrived who paid as little heed to Standley as had the earlier ones. Seven months after he returned, he became completely fed up. On May 3, 1943, the announcement that former Ambassador Joseph E. Davies was being sent by the President with a secret message for Stalin proved to be "too much." The Admiral asked to be relieved of his duties and brought back home not later than October 10.

Standley's request was still awaiting action in August when the President at Quebec decided to send Secretary Hull with a staff to meet in Moscow with Foreign Ministers Eden and Molotov and their respective delegations. Since this appeared to be a good time to reshuffle the staff in Moscow, he asked Standley to come to the United States in September in time to brief Hull before his departure. It was clear that the ambassador was not to return to Moscow.[30]

In one of his happier choices of the war Roosevelt named as Standley's successor Averell Harriman, an old friend and trusted representative, then serving in London as the President's Lend-Lease chief and member of the Combined Shipping Adjustment Board and of the Combined Production and Resources Board. Son of the great railroad builder E. H. Harriman, manager of part of the empire built by his father, Harriman had entered the first Roosevelt administration with a post in the National Recovery Administration and then had served as director of the raw-materials division in the Office of Production Management before being sent to London on his Lend-Lease assignment. He headed the American delegation in the Joint Mission to Russia on Lend-Lease in the fall of 1941 and was back again in Moscow the following August for the conferences between Churchill and Stalin. No admirer of the Soviet system, he had proved his interest in helping the Russians defeat the common enemy. The services he had already rendered the Soviets in their fight deserved and won from them a sympathetic reception.

From his visits to Russia, Harriman was aware—even without being warned by others—that a successful tour of duty in the Soviet Union required a changed administrative arrangement. For assistance he turned at once to General Marshall.

The Chief of Staff had been attending conferences with the new ambassador since the meeting at Argentia and was aware of his contributions as a trouble shooter for the President. But it was more than admiration for a gifted public servant that led him to agree heartily with the new ambassador's proposals. Detesting confused command channels, he accepted fully Ambassador Harriman's views that the Military Mission, which included the Supply Division, should work directly under him. The change was made easier because one of Marshall's bright young officers was selected as head of the Military Mission—Brigadier General John R. Deane, for whom the Chief of Staff at once recommended an additional star. Deane had served as Secretary General Staff and then had succeeded Bedell Smith in 1942 as Secretary of the Joint Chiefs of Staff. Later he was U.S. Secretary of the Combined Chiefs of Staff.

In a comprehensive discussion on September 22 Marshall and Harriman agreed on measures to end the era of divided responsibility and control. The small Military Mission was to be sent to Moscow under the ambassador's direction. Brigadier General Sidney P. Spalding, head of the Supply Division of the Mission, was made responsible for the handling of Lend-Lease matters in conformity with policies established by the Lend-Lease Administration but under the coordination and supervision of the ambassador and the chief of the Military Mission. The warring brigadiers, Michela and Faymonville, were to be recalled, and no military attaché was to be named until Harriman decided that such action was desirable.[31]

Marshall's directive, incorporating Harriman's thinking, defined Deane's objective as the promotion of "the closest possible coordination of the military efforts of the United States and the U.S.S.R." To achieve this goal Deane was authorized to discuss with Soviet authorities all information concerning United States military strategy, plans, and operations that, in his judgment, was appropriate. But he was "to make no commitments which cause an increased deployment of U.S. Army supplies or troops without War Department approval." [32]

Not included in the directive itself was a statement on primary objectives for the ambassador and the head of the Military Mission that had been agreed on by the President, General Marshall, and Admiral King. According to Harriman, he and his staff were "to break down Soviet suspicion and win their confidence that we might eventually obtain better knowledge of Soviet plans and establish a basis for closer cooperation in carrying out operational plans. We should also look toward the Pacific war not only to obtain Russian participation but to have them give us the right kind of help and enough time to prepare to make their help effective." [33]

As Deane observed after the war in his book, *The Strange Alliance,* the Russians were extremely suspicious of all foreigners. Recognizing that military and naval attachés, by definition, were engaged in getting information on the country to which they were assigned, the Soviet officials avoided seeing them. "It was partly to overcome this attitude," Deane noted, "that the United States withdrew its Attachés and substituted the Military Mission." In view of this situation Marshall instructed Deane shortly before his departure "to avoid seeking information about the Russians." This suggestion, reported by General Deane in his book, was cited in June 1951 by Senator Joseph R. McCarthy of Wisconsin as evidence that Marshall was pro-Russian. He overlooked the points italicized below from Deane's paragraph, which read in full:

> General Marshall took the view that even though the Soviet authorities turned over to us the blueprints of all their weapons, their tables of organization, and their complete tactical doctrine, the information would not change by one iota American production lines, organization, or tactics. He was convinced that a quest for such information was not only unnecessary but would irritate the Russians and make operational collaboration impossible. *His attitude made my task in Russia much easier and accounted in large measure for whatever success the Mission enjoyed.* Consequently we studiously refrained from seeking information about Soviet equipment, weapons, and tactical methods *unless we could present a strong case to show that such information was of value in our fight against Germany.* We did ask for and received some information about Russian cold-weather equipment, tactical methods in river crossings, and their organization to discover German agents operating in the rear of Soviet lines.[34]

In writing of his problems Deane contrasted Soviet secrecy with American openness in regard to tactics, production, and weapons. From a key statement in the book McCarthy chose to quote: "Our policy was to make any of our new inventions in electronics and other fields available to Russia" and then replaced with asterisks the following qualifying words, which apparently few of his admirers have bothered to read: "once we had used such equipment ourselves, had exploited the element of surprise, and were satisfied that the enemy had probably gained knowledge of the equipment as the result of its having fallen into his hands." Thus a number of important items were not passed on to the Soviets. The senator did quote Deane's later statement, "We never lost an opportunity to give the Russians equipment, weapons, or information which we thought might help our combined war effort," but the omission of the earlier passages—deliberate or not—gave a sinister overtone to Marshall's instructions.[35]

Deane was appointed by the American Chiefs of Staff to sit in on the forthcoming Foreign Ministers' conference in Moscow, October 19–30, as a military observer. The instructions the Chiefs gave him were guarded. He was authorized to reveal to the Russian representatives details on Allied operations in Europe not already given them, if developments in the conference warranted; if the target date for the cross-Channel operation was divulged, he was to explain the importance of coordinating Russian action with that attack; and in giving the general outlines of the offensive against Japan, he was to stress the advantages to the Soviet Union in joining with the Allies.[36]

At the meeting Deane and General Ismay were required at the start to assure the Russians that the Allies were at last firmly set on the cross-Channel operation for the spring of 1944. The Soviet representatives seemed pleased. As Deane reported to General Marshall:

> The Russians had only one subject to put on the Agenda—"Ways of hastening the conclusion of the War." This was divided into three parts: (a) Intensive measures in 1943 to ensure invasion of Northern France, (b) Get Turkey into the war now, (c) Get use of Swedish air bases now. Of course the British and we looked on this as a political conference but they had to agree to discussions which our politicos turned over to "Pug" Ismay and me. . . . The minutes . . . I think, will indicate that we were quite frank both as to our intentions and as to what conditions would have to exist for OVERLORD. We gave a brief indication of the preparations now underway and tried to impress on them the part that the bomber offensive is playing. The Soviet delegates appeared to be completely satisfied but reserved the right for further questioning. This was a great relief.[37]

In the course of the briefing both Eden and Ismay objected to the full presentation that the Americans wanted to give. Apparently on the strength of the British complaint to London and, in turn, to Washington, the U.S. Chiefs of Staff instructed Deane to go along with the British and limit the information that he gave the Russians. Ambassador Harriman forcefully complained to General Marshall that this restraint was not in accord with arrangements made with him before he left Washington. The new instructions, he said, "make it impossible to fulfill the commitments to the Soviets taken by Secretary Hull at the conference, on the advice of Deane and myself that the Soviet Military Authorities would be completely informed of the progress of our OVERLORD preparations."[38]

Although Harriman agreed on the importance of working as a team with the British, he did not expect that the Americans "would be compelled to go into double harness with them." Citing Deane's knowledge of security matters, gained from his experience as Secretary of the Combined Chiefs of Staff, Harriman asked that the Joint Chiefs of Staff's latest instructions be modified to allow Deane to use his judgment as to what should be told the Soviet authorities.[39]

Despite his initial elation at the Russian reaction to the report on OVERLORD, Deane soon had ominous news for Marshall. A gloomy report by Alexander on progress in Italy contained, in Deane's opinion, the inference "that OVERLORD will be delayed or possibly abandoned because of the Italian situation."[40] Foreseeing that "we may lose the OVERLORD fight in Moscow even before it is discussed at the coming conference" (Cairo-Tehran), Marshall recommended that the Joint Chiefs of Staff inform Deane that they felt that Alexander had failed to give sufficient weight to Allied naval superiority and complete dominance of the air in the Mediterranean. In his proposed statement, which was approved and dispatched, Marshall and his colleagues declared that they did not believe "the situation in Italy is such that it would cause a delay, much less an abandonment of OVERLORD." [41]

"Dirty baseball" Secretary Stimson termed what he believed to be British conniving. The Prime Minister, he feared, despite his lip service to the cross-Channel operation, was prepared "to stick a knife in the back of OVERLORD and I feel more bitterly about it than I have ever done before." This was not completely fair to the Prime Minister, because Stimson assumed incorrectly that Eisenhower disagreed wholly with Alexander and that Churchill had withheld this fact from the Russians. Actually the Allied Commander-in-Chief, in forwarding Alexander's statement, had described it as a clear and accurate picture of the battle situation in Italy. What he had added, and what General Marshall quickly sent to Moscow, was the statement: "the estimates of our buildup and availability of landing craft as given by General Alexander are not quite in line with my own understanding, as the allocation of craft were firmly made at the Quebec Conference and the only changes have been in our favor. Our buildup so far has at least equalled our estimates." [42]

Both the Prime Minister and the Secretary of War had spoken too quickly. Churchill had overreacted to the opportunity to lay the ground for further action in the Mediterranean; Stimson had lashed out in haste. In the future the British leader would press harder for delays in shifting landing craft and divisions to the United Kingdom from Italy, and Stimson would insist all the harder on the need of a firm hand in charge of operations against the Germans. More than ever, he was convinced that Marshall must be Supreme Commander.[43] Viewed in a different light, a light that perhaps both Roosevelt and Marshall were beginning imperfectly to perceive, the episode was one more excellent reason that fall why the Chief of Staff should remain at his vantage point at the seat of power.

General Marshall watched warily the Prime Minister's attempts to promote landings in the eastern Mediterranean. After the early September meetings in Washington, Churchill deluged the Middle East commander, General Wilson, with wires from Washington and, a few days later, from shipboard. The Prime Minister could argue that the Combined Chiefs of Staff had approved an attempt by Wilson to seize Rhodes and other islands of the Mediterranean. But they had stipulated that the effort should be made with the resources available to the Middle East commander. In the end Churchill's doggedness created what he himself described as "the most acute difference I ever had with General Eisenhower." Throughout the controversy Marshall steadfastly supported the Allied Commander.

Churchill's frenzied attempts to get additional shipping and men foundered as the battle slowed in Italy. The Salerno operation had started well on September 9 with word coming, as the forces neared the beaches the night before, that the Italians had signed an armistice.

Strongly backed by the Allied naval forces, General Clark's Fifth Army, with British and American corps, landed against fairly heavy fire put down by the Germans, who had taken over the defenses from the Italians. Salerno was taken, and the Allies were managing to push inland when the Germans rushed in reinforcements from the north and east. Meanwhile the enemy units that had been slowing Montgomery's Eighth Army as it inched up from the toe of Italy shifted northward. British warships moved forward off Salerno to give close support, and Allied air forces bombed columns of troops and attempted to break up troop concentrations. In a series of counterattacks during a three-day period the Germans threatened to drive the Allies back into the sea and at one point seemed likely to cut in behind American forces on the beaches. Fortunately the line held until armored and airborne units could be brought in. By the fifteenth the main battle was won, and by the eighteenth the Fifth and Eighth armies joined up to secure the area.[44]

The crisis had passed, but General Marshall was afraid that the enemy would dig in while the Allies were moving slowly against Naples. On the twenty-third, as the Allied commander was enjoying Churchill's message of praise for taking risks, he received a query from Marshall asking if he could hold a line before Naples and make an end run for Rome. Grieved to think "that General Marshall does not give him credit for cracking the whip," Eisenhower skipped breakfast and lunch although Smith and Butcher tried to cheer him by facetious wisecracks about complaints while they helped draft a reply, citing lack of landing craft. In passing Butcher noted, "We have the paradox of the Prime Minister applauding Ike's willingness to take risks while General Marshall and Sir John Dill, from their global viewpoint in Washington, criticize him for failure to be bold."[45] He failed to recall the main point—the American Chief of Staff had agreed to the operation in southern Italy and a push toward Rome only as a means of getting a firm position at which to hold while men and landing craft were shifted from the Mediterranean to cross-Channel preparations.

The situation improved near the end of September, and on October 1 the Allies entered Naples. It was soon evident that the next phases of the advance would be more difficult. As Clark met enemy resistance along the Volturno, Montgomery—engaged in moving his supply base from the toe to the heel of the boot—was slowed, and additional demands were laid on Allied shipping. There was little to spare in the way of men and ships at a time when the Prime Minister revived his scheme for securing the islands of the eastern Mediterranean.

Hoping to induce Italian garrisons in some of the islands to resist the Germans, the Middle East Command in September had set small forces ashore on Rhodes, Leros, Samos, and Cos. The Germans on Rhodes reacted quickly, seizing control shortly after the surrender of the Italian government. In October, German parachutists captured Cos, goading the

Prime Minister to enjoin fresh miracles on his Chiefs of Staff and on Ei-senhower. His demands startled both his own Army Chief and the Allied commander. General Brooke was convinced that "with the commitments we have in Italy we should not undertake serious operations in the Aegean." Unmoved by his adviser, Churchill soon "worked himself into a frenzy of excitement about the Rhodes attack . . . and has set his heart on capturing this one island even at the expense of endangering his rela-tions with the President and Americans and the future of the Italian cam-paign." [46]

Unwilling to concede that he could not push a campaign for Rome and grasp for the Dodecanese islands at the same time, Churchill thought that he merely had to persuade the Americans to see reason. When his appeal of October 7 to President Roosevelt for landing craft and assault craft was turned down, he tried another tack. Recalling that "far-reaching favour-able results" had followed his journey from Washington to Algiers with General Marshall in June, he asked Roosevelt to send the General or some other representative to Eisenhower's headquarters for another meet-ing. But the situation had changed. Replies for the President's signature, prepared in the War Department, reflected Marshall's firm intention not to make further concessions. The reply of October 9, ruling out a meeting, supported only such action in the Dodecanese as required no heavy com-mitments. The Americans were unwilling to divert forces from Italy that would "jeopardize the security of the Allied armies" there. More impor-tant, they were opposed to entering on another campaign that might bring greater involvement in the area east of Italy. "The problem then is," the President declared, "are we now to enter into a Balkan campaign starting with the southern tip or is there more to be gained, and with security, by pushing rapidly to the agreed upon position north of Rome . . . ? Strategically, if we get the Aegean Islands, I ask myself, where do we go from there and vice-versa where would the Germans go if for some time they retained possession of the islands?" [47]

At Churchill's insistence the President agreed not to bar Eisenhower's staff from further examination of the British case. Before they could reach a final decision, however, they had evidence that the Germans were pre-paring for a major battle south of Rome, which ended any prospect of diverting further strength to the battle for the islands. It spelled the end of the Prime Minister's hope. Although some assistance was given the gar-rison at Leros, it fell on November 16 to an assault by the Germans.[48]

Marshall's strong opposition to Churchill's pressure for operations in the eastern Mediterranean was the type of action he could take as a senior member of the Combined Chiefs of Staff, but one that would be scarcely possible for him as commander of the invasion force. This thought may have been in his mind as well as in Roosevelt's when the time came nearer for the final decision on the Supreme Commander.

XVI

An Exercise in Self-Denial

O N a cold and rainy morning, twenty-five years to the day since the end of World War I, the United States Chiefs of Staff sailed from the Washington Navy Yard aboard Admiral King's flagship, the *Dauntless*, going down the Potomac to a point near its mouth where they went aboard the *Iowa*, one of the nation's largest warships, there to await the arrival of President Roosevelt before departing for Allied conferences in Cairo and Tehran. Unlike the earlier wartime meetings, which had involved only U.S. and British officials, these were to include sessions between the British and Americans and Chinese in Cairo (SEXTANT) and between the two Western Allies and the Russians at Tehran (EUREKA). These discussions, which were to give General Marshall the firm agreement he sought on operations in Northwest Europe and to settle finally the question of the Supreme Command, also looked beyond the strategy of defeating Germany to postwar goals in Europe and the Far East.

Roosevelt had long been trying to arrange a conference with Stalin. Soon after the entry of the United States into the war he had suggested to the Soviet Marshal that the two meet in Alaska; shortly before the Casablanca conference he proposed a three-power meeting in the Aegean. In May 1943 he renewed the suggestion of a two-power talk, possibly in the Bering Strait. Stalin showed a polite interest but pleaded that demands of current campaigns prevented him leaving the fighting front.[1]

Not until September did Stalin indicate that he might be able to get away for a meeting with Churchill and Roosevelt. Ruling out previous suggestions for Alaska; Scapa Flow, off the coast of Northern Scotland; and North Africa, he named Iran as a possible site. In a remarkable two-month sequence the Western leaders suggested Cairo, Iraq, Asmara, Beirut, or aboard ships in the eastern Mediterranean. Stalin turned them all down. Roosevelt's argument that he could not get too far away from Washington while Congress was in session was neatly parried by Stalin's reminder that he was currently responsible for a battle in which 500 enemy and Soviet divisions were engaged. Tehran was especially suitable, he said, because the three powers not only had legations there but also had troops employed in shipping Lend-Lease materiel to the Soviet Union.

Roosevelt's efforts to entice Stalin to Basra, if the Western leaders could go that far, also failed. Harriman radioed from Moscow that the Russians feared that at this site they could not exercise the same degree of control and security "against Iranians, German spies known to be in the area, and possibly ourselves, as they do in North Persia." Suspicions submerged during the most trying months of German victories were beginning to reappear now that victory seemed in sight. The recent meetings in Moscow, although exhibiting an element of solidarity, had apparently left many doubts on both sides. Some of the Western leaders were disturbed by indications of Soviet intent to control the Baltic states, to ensure strong buffer states on their western frontiers, and to have a hand in the disposition of Japanese-held territory once belonging to China. They were encouraged to hear that the Russians intended to aid the West against Japan after the defeat of Germany, but they were worried by the determination of Soviet leaders to seek spoils of war on every front.[2]

By late October, Churchill and Roosevelt had almost given up hope of getting agreement from Stalin on a meeting place and decided that they would have to be content with another two-power meeting—possibly at Cairo. Bent on preserving whatever spirit of cooperation had been evinced at the Moscow conference, the President suggested inviting a Russian military representative to sit in on meetings of the British and American Chiefs of Staff. At first General Marshall objected that the Russians would assume that the Western Allies were trying "to penetrate their strategical and operational plans" and that it would be difficult to reach decisions with the enlarged group. He ended, however, by forwarding the President's proposal to Churchill.[3]

The Prime Minister objected on a different basis. He was willing to have a formal Soviet delegation at a three-power meeting, but he feared that a Russian representative at a two-power conclave might weaken an "intimacy and friendship" established between the Americans and British. Thus before the three leaders had met, the Russian presence had introduced a disturbing element into the Anglo-American relationship.[4]

Refusing to abandon the prospect of a talk among the three heads of state, Churchill attempted in early November to persuade Roosevelt to go to Tehran. At length the President gave in and announced that he would extend his journey, already long, from Cairo to Tehran.

With the Russian phase of the conference settled, final touches were given to arrangements, now well advanced, for a preliminary meeting with Chiang Kai-shek at Cairo. Although Churchill was not pleased when Roosevelt suggested China's participation, he joined the President in inviting the Generalissimo and Madame Chiang Kai-shek to attend.

Soon Churchill was further dismayed when the President seemed to be postponing Anglo-American talks. The Prime Minister proposed that they schedule several sessions before anyone else arrived in Cairo and jealously pointed out that he had learned from the British ambassador rather than from Roosevelt of the President's decision to go to Tehran. He was not reassured by Roosevelt's statement that it would be a terrible mistake if "Uncle Joe" thought they had "ganged up" on him on military action. Since previous meetings had been marked by discussions of Anglo-American assistance to the Soviet Union, this sudden zeal to reassure the Russians of Anglo-American good faith began to worry the British.[5]

Oddly enough at a time when Churchill fretted over the sudden *rapprochement* between the United States and Russia, the Secretary of War became disturbed at reports from General Deane in Moscow that Stalin might be joining the British in favoring an eastern Mediterranean operation over a cross-Channel attack. Always apprehensive about what the President might decide in a conference with Churchill, Stimson hurried to Harry Hopkins. Shortly before the delegation departed for Cairo, the Secretary drafted a strong letter for the Presidential confidant to follow in advising his chief. Since it concerned Marshall, Stimson showed it to him —only to find him still determined "to duck" comments on anything involving his future command status.

More convinced than ever that Allied success depended on Marshall's assumption of the Supreme Command, Stimson spelled out his arguments:

> 1. . . . The task [for the Supreme Commander] is to hold the situation firmly to the straight road which has been agreed to and which it is now on. He should tolerate no departures from the program. . . .
>
> 2. . . . I believe that Marshall's command of OVERLORD is imperative for its success. To make it effective he should be there very soon. The success of OVERLORD is so much the most important thing in the world horizon that Marshall should take up that command in spite of all counter reasons which I can envisage. He should do this even if no joint command with the Italian operation is yet achieved. I anticipate that his European command will be extended in future to all auxiliary movements in western Europe even if that is not now agreed upon.
>
> 3. No successor Chief of Staff should be appointed for the present but that post should be carried on by an acting chief. I anticipate that Marshall's presence in London will strongly tend to prevent any interferences with OVERLORD even if they were attempted, and as to other theaters of operation we shall have to take our chances of carrying on along the present plans which have been pretty well laid out. Certainly they are in far better situation than they were two or three months ago.[6]

The Secretary had done all he could, but he felt tense and knew that he showed the strain of worry over OVERLORD. Even Marshall's parting comments had created fresh anxiety. In a mood to accept any arrangement that would save the cross-Channel operation, the Chief of Staff informed Stimson that he was thinking of offering to serve as Deputy Supreme

Commander under Sir John Dill if this would lessen Churchill's opposition to the operation.

"I told him," wrote the weary Secretary, "that I wasn't prepared to think that was wise on account of the opposite reaction that it would have here. Our people's faith in Marshall is one of the things that will carry through the tragedies that may go with OVERLORD." [7]

Across the Atlantic other diarists were setting down their anxieties about the coming conference. Particularly revealing is the diary, less well known than Alanbrooke's or Stimson's, kept by Major General Sir John Kennedy, Director of Military Operations under Dill and Brooke from 1940 to 1943, and from the fall of 1943 until late 1944 Assistant Chief of the Imperial General Staff under Brooke. In late October, Kennedy noted: "there is still a very distinct cleavage of opinion between us and the Americans as to the correct strategy in Europe."

In mid-November, as the Americans were starting their voyage, Kennedy wrote: "We have now crystallized our ideas as to the strategy to be advocated in the coming conference. The main points are—to continue the offensive in Italy, to increase the flow of supplies to partisans in the Balkans, to bring about an upheaval by inducing the Balkan powers to break away from Germany, to induce Turkey to enter the war, and to accept a postponement of OVERLORD. . . ."

On November 18, as Brooke left for Cairo, Kennedy recorded: "The conference will be a difficult one. The Americans seem to think we have acted in an almost underhand way over the Mediterranean. . . . This is curious because we have felt almost the same about them. Brooke feels that the war may have been lengthened by as much as six months by the American failure to realize the value of exploiting the whole Mediterranean situation. . . . The time has come for plain speaking on both sides." [8]

"I wish," General Brooke wrote in his diary on the twentieth, "our conference was over. I despair of getting our American friends to have any strategic vision. Their drag on us has seriously affected our Mediterranean strategy and the whole conduct of the war. I blame myself for having failed to overcome their short-sighted views and to have allowed my better judgment to be affected by them. It would have been better to have resigned my appointment than to agree to any form of compromise. And yet I wonder whether such action would have borne any fruit." Fortunately Brooke's biographer included with this tragic interpretation a corrective in the form of a letter sent by Dill to Brooke a few weeks earlier. "I do not believe it was ever possible to make the Americans more Mediterranean-minded than they are today," Dill declared. "The American Chiefs of Staff have given way to our views a thousand times more than we have given way to theirs. Of course, this has led to compromises which are always dangerous, but inevitable when one is dealing with a strong ally.

But after all, things have gone well and I still think the defeat of Germany next year is a good bet." [9]

A British official historian of World War II, Michael Howard, has also helped rectify Brooke's overwrought account. In a forerunner of his official volume Howard concluded: "These comments were neither accurate nor fair." [10]

Although General Brooke later denied any British intention to renege on their pledge to launch the cross-Channel attack, he admitted that the Prime Minister worried the Americans by some of his extreme proposals. In view of Marshall's argument at Cairo-Tehran that the British approach was not one calculated to ensure OVERLORD in 1944, Sir John Kennedy's straightforward statement is highly revealing: "Had we had our way, I think there can be little doubt that the invasion of France would not have been done in 1944." [11] This admission casts strong doubt on Sir Arthur Bryant's thesis that events from North Africa to Sicily to the toe of Italy to Rome to cross-Channel went exactly as Brooke had planned. The point is crucial. It was on this issue, spun out during the remainder of 1943 and the early months of 1944, that the American demands for rigid adherence to earlier plans were based.

Having made clear to the Secretary of War that OVERLORD's importance outweighed any personal concern as to command, Marshall said farewell to him. Next morning he joined King for the trip to the *Iowa* to await the President. That evening General Marshall's mind turned toward the conference earlier in the year at Algiers. He entertained his friends by recalling that at the end of a rather heated session at which a closely debated point had been decided in the Prime Minister's favor, he had remarked to Churchill, "Well, you certainly fixed my clock." To his amusement a British officer who had overheard him asked him later, "Did the Prime Minister really repair one of your clocks so it would run?" [12]

Except for heavy seas the first day's voyage was uneventful. The next day sizzled with excitement. During a special exhibition of gunnery arranged for the President and his party by the *Iowa* and its escort ships, an alarm sounded, accompanied by the shouted warning, "This is not a drill," and the announcement that a torpedo was on its way toward them. Perhaps General Marshall had time to wonder if this was to be a repetition of his experience in 1917 aboard a transport bound for France, when a porpoise had been mistaken for a torpedo. If he thought so, he was soon aware that this time the seafarers faced the real thing—and from a friendly ship. The *William D. Porter,* one of the escorting destroyers, had accidentally loosed a torpedo, which headed straight for the *Iowa.* Successful evasive tactics left the missile well astern. (Arnold says 20 yards but the log read 1200.) Indignant and embarrassed at this reception for the Commander-in-Chief and the Chiefs of the sister services, Admiral King ordered an immediate investigation. He was prepared to relieve the destroyer commander at once but desisted when the President, as Commander-in-Chief, told him to forget it.[13]

The 3800-mile sea leg of the journey from Hampton Roads ended with their arrival at Mers-el-Kebir, near Oran, Algeria, early on November 20. The President and his party were met there by a group headed by General Eisenhower and Admiral Cunningham. From La Senia Airport, 50 miles away, they flew to Tunis. Here outside the city on the Gulf of Tunis, near the ruins of Carthage, General Eisenhower had a villa, which he turned over to the President. Realizing the attraction of a quiet evening to tired men, the Allied commander invited General Marshall and Admiral King to stay at the small cottage he used at La Mersa, near Carthage. The two commanders also welcomed his suggestion that they go sightseeing in the nearby ruins. As a boy, Marshall had become familiar with the story of Hamilcar Barca and Hannibal in G. A. Henty's *The Young Carthaginian*. Although he knew of Scipio Africanus, who had carried out Cato's demand "Delenda est Carthago," he hoped to see some remains of the Phoenician city. He and King were disappointed. At a local museum they found numerous Roman objects but little to recall the city that had once threatened the rule of Rome. More in evidence were the remainders of medieval history in Tunis, where the cathedral displayed relics of St. Louis (Louis IX), who had died there in 1270 while on his second crusade.

Eisenhower, who had been invited to dinner with the President on the evening of his arrival, arranged for Marshall and King to eat alone at their cottage. Stopping there for a brief visit before leaving for the President's villa, Eisenhower was startled to learn the Admiral's views on the suggested command arrangements for OVERLORD. He had known of proposed changes since the first of October, when Secretary of the Navy Knox had told Butcher while visiting Salerno that Marshall would have the Supreme Command and Eisenhower would probably be brought back home as Chief of Staff. Later that month Harriman on his way to Moscow had told Eisenhower that the President had Marshall in mind for the Supreme Command spot, but that he was not certain that it would come to pass. Shortly after Harry Hopkins arrived in November, he had told Commander Butcher that it was proper for Marshall to have the command, although the naval aide argued vigorously that it would take the Chief of Staff at least six months to learn Eisenhower's job and a similar length of time for the latter to pick up the reins in Washington. Eisenhower had also received a hint of the Quebec decision from Churchill at Malta, but as yet he had heard nothing definite from the Chief of Staff.

As Marshall listened in evident embarrassment, Admiral King explained that the President at Quebec had decided that the Army Chief should have the Supreme Command. He said that he and the other Joint Chiefs had protested against the serious consequences of taking Marshall from the Combined Chiefs of Staff organization. Marshall sat silently by as

King added that only because Eisenhower was to be Chief of Staff was he able to view the situation with equanimity. Nevertheless, King went on, he viewed the shift as a mistake and planned to argue the matter further with the President. Perhaps King was merely filling in Eisenhower on developments, but he may well have been hoping to persuade Marshall to reconsider.[14]

On the following morning the President brought up the matter with Eisenhower during a tour of recent battlefields near Tunis. As if trying to persuade himself of the necessity of going through with the appointment, the President explained that while he dreaded losing Marshall from Washington, he thought that the General should have the command. "Ike, you and I know who was Chief of Staff during the last years of the Civil War but practically no one else knows, although the names of the field generals—Grant, of course, and Lee, and Jackson, Sherman, Sheridan and the others—every schoolboy knows them. I hate to think that 50 years from now practically nobody will know who George Marshall was. That is one of the reasons I want George to have the big command—he is entitled to establish his place in history as a great General." [15] Although knowing that the President's decision probably meant that he was destined to return to take on the difficult Chief of Staff's post, Eisenhower made no effort to argue the question.

Thus as Marshall and his associates ended their stay in Tunis, most indications pointed to his appointment as commander of the OVERLORD invasion. At least a week later the General wired Stimson that he probably was going to assume the new post very soon.[16]

After leaving Tunis on Sunday morning, November 21, the Chief of Staff and his party arrived in Cairo in the late afternoon.[17] To permit their passengers some sightseeing en route, the pilots flew low over the desert battlefields of Libya and Egypt. Shifting sands had covered many tracks, and the relentless wind had piled great drifts over disabled vehicles and the wreckage and spoilage of conflict, but there was still ample evidence of carnage in the barren wastes. Burned-out tanks, trucks, and planes marked the route of battle across the vast spaces of Africa. Flying over Benghazi and Tobruk, the cities already linked with legend in a land where scars still bled from recent fighting, the travelers tired at last of the monotony of sand and debris and desolation. It was with relief that they welcomed the first sight of the greenness along the Nile Valley. Within minutes the sight of the Pyramids and the Sphinx indicated journey's end.

Near sunset such early arrivals as Ambassadors Winant and Harriman welcomed the visitors to Cairo. Australian Minister Richard Casey and United States Ambassador Alexander Kirk had made their villas near the Pyramids available for the President and the Prime Minister, but Marshall, Arnold, and six others had to share a small villa, and King and his party had a similar tight squeeze. The conference itself was held at Mena

House Hotel, almost at the base of the Pyramids, which seemed to impel every visitor to reflect on Napoleon's address to his men there nearly a century and a half before: "Soldiers, from these pyramids forty centuries look down on you."

Generalissimo and Madame Chiang Kai-shek arrived slightly ahead of the American Chiefs of Staff.[18] Their premature presence annoyed the Prime Minister, who believed that an agreement should be reached between the two Western powers on the European phase of their operations before they considered activities in the Far East. In any event he felt that the Chinese had little to contribute to the winning of the war. Roosevelt viewed the question in another way. Having watched sympathetically Chiang's struggle with the Japanese during most of his administration, he was convinced that the Generalissimo was important to keep alive the spirit of resistance in China and to carry out the reconstruction of the country after the war. He determined to boost China's morale by offering stepped-up operations in the Far East and by increased assistance in materiel supplies. Marshall shared his chief's desire to aid China, but not his confidence in the leadership of Chiang Kai-shek.

Marshall had met Madame Chiang Kai-shek on her trip to Washington months before, but he knew the Generalissimo mainly through Stilwell's acid reports. His first personal encounter with the Generalissimo came shortly after the arrival of the Americans in Cairo, at the President's tea in honor of the Chinese leader and his wife. Impassive, his skin stretched tautly over prominent facial bones, giving him an almost ascetic look, Chiang Kai-shek appeared to Westerners more like a traditional Chinese scholar than a powerful, ruthless military and political leader, controlling the destinies of millions of his countrymen. At first sight he seemed unobtrusive and colorless in contrast to his beautiful, American-educated wife, who spoke excellent English and appeared to be the more decisive of the two. Stunningly dressed, with charm compounded of femininity and forcefulness, she kept a watchful eye on proceedings, correcting her interpreter from time to time and adding clarifications that some of her hearers suspected were improvements on the original.

Earlier, on the basis of Stilwell's reports, Marshall had decided that no one could ever persuade the Generalissimo to attack. Recent indications of a changing attitude in Chungking led him to view the situation in the Far East more hopefully. Looking back, he was inclined to be charitable: "During the war Chiang had a terrible problem getting good men. . . . It took me a whole year to get rid of the bad [commanders in our forces]. Chiang didn't have any competent people to put in for his incompetents. He had a lot of terrible grafters and he couldn't [make the necessary changes] in a short enough time. He couldn't find out what the devil was going on. He was constantly sold down the river by his advisers. I don't believe that he was personally corrupt, but there were many corrupt people around him." [19]

The Chinese leader was invited to attend the first plenary session of the conference on November 23, at which Admiral Lord Mountbatten outlined his plans for Southeast Asia. The Admiral suggested a seven-stage operation in January. Salient points were that a British-Indian force was to move down along the southwest coast of Burma, while the Chinese Ledo Road forces moved eastward toward a meeting at Bhamo with Yunnan forces advancing westward from China. These efforts were to be supported by a display of British naval strength in the Indian Ocean and by an amphibious operation, possibly against the Andaman Islands, southwest of Rangoon.[20]

Suspicious of British intentions, Chiang Kai-shek reiterated his earlier statements that Chinese operations in Burma depended not only on the strength of Allied naval forces in the Indian Ocean but also on the coordination of naval and ground actions. Churchill—whose opinion of the Chinese "story" was summed up in his postwar quip that it was "lengthy, complicated and minor"—insisted that he could not guarantee fulfillment of the Generalissimo's requests. The fleet, he declared, could not be ready by January, and full strength would have to await spring or early summer of 1944. Nevertheless he saw little basis for the Generalissimo's fears, for he sincerely doubted that the Japanese could send a naval force in great strength to the Bay of Bengal.[21]

Seeing the whole Far East program in danger, General Marshall emphasized the importance of encouraging the Generalissimo. Where once Chiang had been reluctant to form ground units or to organize the Yunnan forces properly, preferring to rely almost exclusively on air activities, he was now taking an energetic interest in ground action. Urging careful and considerate attention to Chiang's demands, the Chief of Staff described the key role China could play once Germany collapsed and supplies began to flow to the Far East.[22]

The British, their eyes still fixed on the Mediterranean, were unmoved by Marshall's plea. When the Americans proposed an attack on the Andaman Islands (BUCCANEER) as a means of supporting the battle in Burma, General Brooke moved postponement of the discussion. His purpose became quite clear when he asked if it would be possible to divert landing craft from the proposed BUCCANEER attack to operations in the Aegean. At this latest effort to expand operations in the eastern Mediterranean, the U.S. Chiefs of Staff exploded. Although the official record is bland, the discussions steamed. Arnold recalled, "Before we finished, it became quite an open talk with everybody throwing his cards on the table, face up." The irrepressible Stilwell, happy to see the "limeys" put in their place, gave a brisker version: "Brooke got nasty and King got good and sore. King almost climbed over the table at Brooke. God, he was mad. I wished he had socked him." [23]

Marshall heard the Generalissimo's case firsthand when he lunched with the Chiangs and Stilwell on November 24. Chiang disapproved current plans for CBI operations because they seemed likely to lead to heavy casualties. Instead he asked for an amphibious operation launched simultaneously with the land attack in Burma and the advance of British and Indian units to a line running east and west through Mandalay. He thought that his Yunnan forces attacking westward should not go beyond Lashio. Marshall explained that Mountbatten's plan was only the first stage of operations to recapture Burma and was much less costly than Chiang Kai-shek imagined. Reporting this conversation to the Combined Chiefs of Staff, Marshall proposed that Chiang be informed as soon as possible of the nature of the naval build-up in the Bay of Bengal. In an attempt to win sympathy for the Generalissimo's position, he pointed out that the Chinese leader would have genuine cause for concern if support seemed insufficient. The British brushed this point aside. Brooke thought Chiang should realize that once the British had taken the first step in Burma, they were committed to its final recapture.

As both proponent and mediator, General Marshall took a major role in the discussions over China, as in those that followed over the Mediterranean. Watching him present the American case, General Arnold thought that the Chief of Staff "was increasing in stature, in comparison with his fellows, as the days went by. He had more mature judgment, could see further into the future. What he said was said in a way that carried conviction. I am sure that the President and the Prime Minister both felt the same, because each one called on him for advice and counsel at all hours of the day or night." As they looked at the Sphinx on the twenty-fourth, Roosevelt carefully sounded out Arnold about the Chief of Staff's future role. Arnold replied that he thought Marshall was the best man for the command in the European Theater, but he made the familiar objections: he would hate to see him go because of his important role in Combined Chiefs of Staff meetings and as adviser to the President. Roosevelt listened thoughtfully and agreed.[24]

At Cairo, Churchill made a last effort to reawaken American interest in an attack on Rhodes. Following his customary practice, he asked Marshall shortly after his arrival to have dinner with him. On the evening of November 23, as Roosevelt entertained Chiang Kai-shek and the British Chiefs of Staff gave a dinner for their American colleagues, the Prime Minister and the Chief of Staff discussed the Dodecanese, Italy, aid to the partisans in the Balkans, OVERLORD, and air operations.[25] Marshall recalled that they met at Churchill's villa, talking first in the courtyard, and then continuing their discussions through dinner until two in the morning. He was impressed as always by the great range of the Prime Minister's interests and his astonishing memory. When Marshall mentioned that while flying he had been reading the addresses of William Pitt, Churchill picked up the cue at once "and quoted whole speeches [that Pitt had made] before Parliament, word for word, got very intense about it, and strode about the room making these quotes." [26] In time he returned to the main business at hand.

Next day Churchill called in the Combined Chiefs of Staff. Almost at once he turned the conversation to the Rhodes operation, on which he had again been unable to sell Marshall the previous evening. Although not strong for the operation, the British Chiefs of Staff supported their leader. As Marshall remembered the discussion: "All the British were against me. It got hotter and hotter. Finally Churchill grabbed his lapels, his spit curls hung down, and he said, 'His Majesty's Government can't have its troops standing idle. Muskets must flame' (and more fine English like that). I said, 'God forbid if I should try to dictate but . . . not one American soldier is going to die on [that] goddamned beach.' The others were horrified, but they didn't want the operation and were willing for me to say it. Churchill never held this against me, but Ismay had to stay up with him all night." [27]

On Thanksgiving the conferees suspended their serious arguments to invite the Americans to celebrate their special holiday. The British Chiefs of Staff even arranged for a special religious service in the cathedral at Cairo. As the President entertained that evening for Churchill, Eden, and other special guests, the Chiefs of Staff met separately for "a merry party" from which the earlier heated topics were banished.

After the one-day truce tempers flared again over the eastern Mediterranean. The meeting on the twenty-sixth began peaceably with General Eisenhower's views on command in the Mediterranean and the best ways and means of prosecuting the war in that area. As expected, he favored centralized command in the Mediterranean. For the future he projected alternative plans based on an all-out effort during the winter or an attack using limited means. Under the first set of conditions he thought the objective should be the line of the Po. Outside of Italy the best targets lay in the Aegean. If action could be postponed there until the line of the Po had been reached, he thought he could find sufficient resources in the Mediterranean to mount such attacks. If means were limited, Eisenhower calculated that his forces would be able to reach only the line north of Rome and then be forced to go on the strategic defensive. Once their position was well established, they could then turn to the Aegean.

To General Brooke's question regarding Yugoslavia the Allied commander replied that if he advanced to the line of the Po, he would propose the establishment of small garrisons "in the islands on the eastern coast of the Adriatic from which thrusts as far north as possible could be made into Yugoslavia and the Patriots furnished with arms and equipment." He believed that all possible equipment should be sent to groups under Tito, inasmuch as Mikhailovitch's forces were "of relatively little value."

General Wilson, the Middle East commander, arrived next to emphasize the importance of further Aegean operations, maintaining that seizure of Rhodes held the key to success. He asked support from the western Mediterranean for this attack but said he could manage the remainder of the campaign with available resources. He believed that these actions would assure Turkey's entrance into the war.

Gun-shy after previous American explosions over eastern Mediterranean proposals, the British were agreeably surprised at the mildness of the Joint Chiefs of Staff's response. The Americans did not insist on a May 1 date for the Normandy landings, and they agreed that the opening of the Dardanelles and the capture of Rhodes, for which landing craft would have to be retained in the Mediterranean, could be discussed with the Russians. Both Admiral Leahy and General Marshall made clear, however, that they did not expect these operations to interfere with the attack on the Andaman Islands. General Brooke quickly interrupted to say that, if Rhodes and Rome were to be captured and BUCCANEER carried out, the date for OVERLORD would certainly have to be postponed. Marshall was willing to accept the delay but insisted that BUCCANEER proceed since the forces were available, the attack was vital to operations in the Pacific, and for political reasons it could not be interfered with.

Then suddenly in the midst of rather polite agreement Brooke precipitated what he described as "the mother and father of a row" with General Marshall by saying that perhaps they should consider postponing BUCCANEER since if they put all available resources into the battle against Germany, the war might be ended sooner. His reluctance to consider the requirements of the Far Eastern theater outraged the Americans. The Chief of Staff raised his voice to remind the British General of American contributions to the war against Germany. He doubted that postponement of BUCCANEER would shorten the war. The United States Chiefs of Staff, he reminded Brooke, had already gone far to meet British views, "but the postponement of BUCCANEER they could not accept." [28]

With storm signals flying the members of the Combined Chiefs of Staff now called for an executive session of the Chiefs with most of the staffs excluded so that problems could be thoroughly threshed out. After heated arguments, the U.S. Chiefs decided that they could not accept the abandonment of BUCCANEER and that any decision to postpone it would have to be made by the President and Prime Minister.

The vehemence with which Marshall and the other U.S. Chiefs defended BUCCANEER seemed surprising in view of their earlier milder statements on the twenty-third and twenty-fourth. Apparently the sudden change was precipitated by the President's action on the twenty-fourth when, wanting to give the Generalissimo something to show for his trip to Cairo, he promised generally to complete the equipping of ninety Chinese divisions and specifically to back the BUCCANEER operation. After that the U.S. Chiefs of Staff held stubbornly to the operation, retreating finally only after the President himself threw in the towel.

Having settled almost nothing, the Allied officials suspended their discussions at Cairo in order to keep their rendezvous with Stalin at Tehran. On the morning of November 27 General Marshall and the members of his party departed. Their course took a slight detour to enable them to peer down at an outline of biblical geography and history, as their plane flew low over Bethlehem, Jerusalem, Jericho, the Dead Sea, and the Garden of Gethsemane. Much of the six-and-one-half-hour flight was tedious, with nothing but barren desert to see until they reached the valleys of the Euphrates and the Tigris, described by historians since before the time of Christ. Shortly after three in the afternoon, they touched down at the airfield five miles south of Tehran. Then a city of some 600,000, the capital of Iran lies in a valley surrounded by mountains soaring 17,000 to 19,000 feet. Troops from Great Britain, the Soviet Union, and the United States, handling the Lend-Lease goods passing from Basra through Tehran on the way to Russia, went about their duties in this old-modern city as if they were extras in a Middle Eastern spy movie. The members of the delegations saw little of the city because a leak about the conference before they left for Tehran, and recent rumors of assassination plots, led to the imposition of stringent security measures.

Billeted at the United States Persian Gulf Command, five or six miles northwest of the city, Marshall and his colleagues found their quarters inadequately heated for the wintry nights, although the days were mild and comfortable. The President and his immediate party spent their first evening at the American Legation, some distance from the British and Soviet embassies, where Churchill and Stalin were staying, but at the urging of the Russian leader and the U.S. Secret Service, they moved next day to the Soviet Embassy as a security precaution.

In preparation for the tripartite conference the President on the morning of November 28 reviewed the United States strategic position with his advisers. Still concerned about the possibility raised by General Deane a few days earlier that the Russians might support British proposals for further operations in the Mediterranean, Marshall suggested that if the Soviet leaders wanted an operation before OVERLORD, the Americans might suggest increased pressure in Italy to expedite Eisenhower's move northward. "The British," he noted, "propose to undertake Rhodes in lieu of the Andaman operation. The means which would be sucked in for the accomplishment of the Rhodes operation would be considerable." He warned that an advance in Italy to the Ancona line, plus an attack on Rhodes, would force postponement of OVERLORD until mid-June or even July. If the Russians did not require immediate help, then it might be possible to finish the operation north of Rome, undertake the Rhodes operation, and postpone OVERLORD until mid-June. But he was convinced that a delay would be necessary if they accepted further commitments in the Mediterranean.

"What," asked the President, "should we say if the Soviets inform us that they will be in Rumania soon, and inquire what can the United States and Britain do to help them?" Marshall thought they could open small ports along the east coast of the Adriatic and send supplies to the Yugoslav partisan forces led by Tito. The Chief of Staff and Admiral Leahy also believed that once into northern Italy, Eisenhower would be in a position to push troops toward Austria as well as toward southern France. In conjunction with limited operations along the Adriatic coast, these threats could contain several German divisions.

The President foresaw possible complications in an attack on Rhodes. After that island was taken, the British would probably say, "Now we will have to take Greece." He preferred operations from the Adriatic rather than in the Dodecanese, suggesting that small commando groups be sent along the Adriatic coast to aid Tito's partisans, and a small force dispatched northward from Trieste and Fiume. He was cool to further pressure on the Turks, explaining that he did not have "the conscience" to insist that they enter the war. Still assuming that the Russians were backing British plans for the eastern Mediterranean, Marshall suggested that the Americans make an effort to find out exactly what the Russians had in mind.

In trying to satisfy Russian demands for operations to take pressure off the eastern front, as well as British insistence on action in the eastern Mediterranean, the Americans had a busy day. At its end Marshall talked to the President about Allied differences on command. The British, the General explained, "were wedded to committeeism." He preferred unity of command, which he believed would expedite operations. Conceding that the United States probably did not do committee work as well as the British, he added, "nevertheless they [the British] have certainly had a very serious time in the Middle East due to the lack of unity of command." On this note he closed his argument.[29]

To his chagrin the usually punctual Chief of Staff missed the first plenary session of the conference on the afternoon of the twenty-eighth. Told by the President at the end of the morning meeting that nothing was planned for the afternoon, the Chief of Staff and General Arnold arranged to take an automobile trip through the mountains north of Tehran. During lunch with Stalin and Churchill, the President changed his mind and decided that the three heads of state should hold a formal session. He then sent messengers to recall the Chiefs of Staff. King and Leahy hastened to the meeting, but Arnold and Marshall could not be reached in time.

Admiral King filled the absentees in on what had been an interesting session. As Roosevelt and Churchill attempted to impress Stalin with their points of view, the Russian leader had impatiently cut through their oratorical flourishes to say, "Now let us get down to business."

Roosevelt and Churchill, the Admiral related, had each taken familiar stands in their play for Stalin's approval—the President extolling cross-Channel and the Pacific campaigns and the Prime Minister pointing out that the Mediterranean activities, though secondary, were vital to Russia. To the delighted surprise of the Americans, Stalin had made quick work of the Prime Minister's arguments. He declared that the Western Allies must concentrate on OVERLORD and, as a diversionary action, make a landing in southern France, preferably well in advance of the landings in the north. He had disappointed Churchill by dismissing the likelihood of Turkey's entrance into the war and ruling out proposed operations in the eastern Mediterranean. Nor had he been interested in further campaigns in Italy, citing Marshal Suvorov, who had fought French revolutionary armies there in 1799 and 1800, on the difficulties of fighting in the Alps. The British were appalled to find the Russians backing United States strategy for the future.

The degree to which the Soviet representatives would reinforce the American position became clear on November 29 at the first meeting of the Combined Chiefs of Staff with Marshal Kliment E. Voroshilov, who represented the Russian armed forces. Brooke had crossed swords with him at the Moscow foreign ministers' meeting in October. Complaining that Voroshilov's questions were childish, Brooke concluded that his abilities were limited. At the Tehran meeting Voroshilov's interruptions were annoying, but anything but infantile, as he pressed for specific replies to his queries on Allied strategy.[30]

Brooke drew the Russian's fire by arguments against landings in southern France prior to OVERLORD. Voroshilov observed that General Marshall's remarks indicated that the United States considered OVERLORD of the first importance. "He wished to know if General Brooke also considered the operation of first importance. He wished to ask both Allies whether they think that OVERLORD must be carried out or whether they consider that it may be possible to replace it by some other suitable operation when Turkey has entered the war."[31]

Pleased at this unexpected support, General Marshall declared that the Allies already had more than a million tons of supplies in England, and that where there had been one division in August, there were now nine with a constant flow of reinforcements. Having explained earlier that the problem was not lack of troops (there were fifty divisions in the United States to be deployed) or supplies, the Chief of Staff said that their current difficulty lay in the lack of landing craft to carry out operations in the Mediterranean. He spoke of the recent decision to delay the shift from the Mediterranean to OVERLORD of earmarked landing craft so that General Eisenhower could expedite his operations. The United States was making a tremendous effort to increase output so as to augment the forces in OVERLORD and undertake additional operations in the Mediterranean.

Brooke brusquely replied that the British had always considered OVER-

LORD an essential part of the fight against Germany but were determined that it should be launched when it had the best chance of success. He thought that these conditions existed for 1944. Forces were currently being brought back to mount the operation, but efforts to keep a May 1 date would bring operations to a halt in the Mediterranean.

Concluding that Brooke was stalling, Voroshilov cannily apologized for his failure to understand but persisted that "he was interested to know whether General Brooke . . . considered OVERLORD as important an operation as General Marshall had indicated that he did." The British commander bristled at his pressure, replying that he deemed it of vital importance but that he was familiar with the defenses of northern France, and he did not wish to see the operation fail.

Voroshilov pursued his advantage. Agreeing that diversionary operations in the Mediterranean would be valuable, he insisted that the Allies should decide that OVERLORD was the key operation and that all the other operations "must be planned to secure OVERLORD . . . and not to hurt it."

Then the Russian tactlessly undertook to lecture the Allied leaders on the Channel crossing. While acknowledging that the Channel was wider than a river, he suggested that the Allies study Russian experiences in crossing the Dnieper and other large rivers. Marshall picked up the challenge. "The difference between a river crossing, however wide, and a landing from the ocean," he declared, "is that the failure of a river crossing is a reverse while the failure of a landing operation from the sea . . . means the almost utter destruction of the landing craft and personnel involved." He told the Russian that his own military education had been based on "roads, rivers and railroads" but that during the last two years he had been acquiring an education on the ocean: "prior to the present war he had never heard of any landing craft except a rubber boat. Now he [thought] about little else." Voroshilov replied, "If you think about it, you will do it." Pleased, Marshall responded, "That is a very good reply. I understand thoroughly."

Having missed the earlier meeting with Stalin, Marshall had to wait for his first glimpse of the Russian leader until the afternoon of the twenty-ninth. After the Chief of Staff and Brooke had briefly reviewed their discussions of the morning, the Soviet Marshal pointedly asked, "Who will command OVERLORD?" When the President replied that no decision had been made, Stalin bluntly countered: "Nothing will come out of the operation unless one man is made responsible." Churchill quickly interjected that he had indicated his willingness for an American to command, and the President added that their decisions at the conference would affect the selection. The Russian leader carefully denied any desire to take a hand in the choice itself but insisted that he should be selected at once.

Knowing that the Chief of Staff was a powerful champion of OVERLORD,

Stalin openly showed his high regard for him when he learned that he was being considered for the post. Marshall recalled:

> He pressed for me all the time. And [he] made it quite a point, and I could take it or leave it as to whether it was just because he thought I was the man or whether he was trying to precipitate the second front. He was very insistent. . . . He was [also] insistent about the date. He was insistent about the operation in southern France and played quite a part in those [decisions].
>
> I found the Generalissimo [Stalin] a very astute negotiator. He had a dry wit. He was agreeable, and in regard to me he made sort of semiaffectionate gesture. When we were in opposition, he would stand with his hands on my shoulders. He was arguing for an immediate second front. . . . He recognized the great effort then was to get us to do these things.
>
> When it came to the exact discussion of the military phases, Stalin was reasonably precise and, as later evidenced, very sincere, because he carried out his agreements to the day. (I am referring now to the matter of his moving his armies to Manchuria.) In contrast to this [I have] Stalin's [action] in the political field, where I met him as Secretary of State in Moscow in 1947. There he was completely evasive. . . .

In negotiating with the Russian leader the General found that it paid to speak bluntly. He remarked: "I always thought they made a mistake of treating Stalin [as if he were] a product of the Foreign Service. He was a rough SOB who made his way by murder and everything else and should be talked to that way." The Chief of Staff added that he was "surprised to find seemingly none of our people had read his early history, and I thought that was quite essential when you are dealing with a fellow who had done the things he did in the early days (such as robbing banks)— getting money for the Communist Party."

The Russian showed his tough side to the Prime Minister in the discussions over the eastern Mediterranean. As Marshall described it: "He was turning the hose on Churchill all the time, and Mr. Roosevelt, in a sense, was helping him. He [Roosevelt] used to take a little delight in embarrassing Churchill. . . . Stalin was very free in probing Churchill but did not follow this course at all with Mr. Roosevelt." [32]

However Stalin challenged both Allies by saying that if they were there to discuss military questions, he considered OVERLORD important and decisive. He doubted the value of the ad hoc committee set up the day before to explore plans but said that it should be given certain specific instructions to decide that (1) OVERLORD should not be postponed but carried through by a given date; (2) OVERLORD must be reinforced by landings in southern France a month or two before OVERLORD if possible or, if not, at the same time or a little later; and (3) a Supreme Commander should be named at once.

Now that Russian desires had been spelled out, the Combined Chiefs of Staff next day reconsidered Allied strategy. Marshall was unwilling to accept the Soviet timetable for an assault on southern France far in advance of the northern invasion; he declared that it should come not more than two to three weeks before the main thrust and preferably should coincide with it. Admiral King agreed.

Turning to the cross-Channel attack, the Chief of Staff said that the sixty-eight LSTs in the Mediterranean had to be released by March 1 if they were to be ready for an OVERLORD D day of May 15. Aware of the delays met in shifting landing craft, Admiral Sir Andrew Cunningham at once put in that February 15 was a much more realistic release date.

Marshall, already on record against the proposed Rhodes operation, predicted that it would probably delay the landings in southern France until mid-July. The British countered with several suggestions. Brooke referred to Eisenhower's message saying that an assault on northern Italy might be more valuable to OVERLORD than an attack in southern France and that the landings in the south of France should be considered as only one of several means of aiding OVERLORD. Air Marshal Portal proposed that lift for one division be left in Italy until Rome fell and lift for one division be left in the Middle East until mid-February, when it would be known if Turkey would come into the conflict. If she did not, the craft could be sent to OVERLORD. General Marshall disagreed. This arrangement, he feared, would divide the reserve of landing craft so that there would be no real strength anywhere. In the end a new operation—outlined by Churchill—would delay the shift of landing craft beyond the point Cunningham had considered wise.

From landing craft the Chiefs turned to the question of a date for OVERLORD. General Brooke conceded that unless a firm answer was given to the Russians, there was no point in continuing with the conference. But some embarrassment arose because the Western Allies had just promised the Russians that the operation would take place in May—the tentative date having been set at TRIDENT by splitting the difference between April 1, suggested by the Americans, and June 1, proposed by the British. After long discussion the Chiefs shifted toward the end of May or "by June 1," agreeing that if this were met, Stalin could not protest that they had not honored their pledge to attack in May. In a rare concert of opinion the Combined Chiefs of Staff recommended that (1) they continue to advance to the Pisa-Rimini line, which meant a further delay in the release of the sixty-eight LSTs for OVERLORD; (2) they mount an operation against the south of France; and (3) they inform Marshal Stalin that OVERLORD would be launched in May in conjunction with a supporting operation against southern France on the largest scale permitted by available landing craft.[33]

At the plenary session on the afternoon of November 30 General Brooke formally presented the Combined Chiefs of Staff's recommendations. When he had finished, Prime Minister Churchill turned dramatically to Stalin to ask his support so that "in closing on the wild beast all parts of the narrowing circle should be aflame with battle." To make certain that the operations were coordinated, the British and American leaders agreed to keep Moscow informed of any changes in the invasion date.[34]

In the political questions examined at Tehran—such as the dismemberment of Germany, the Polish frontier, and the like—the military commanders had no part. They were, of course, aware of many of the political implications, but the division was kept quite clear cut.

In the postwar period, when Marshall and other military leaders were attacked for having failed to take proper account of political factors in their decisions, the General explained their position very precisely: "We probably devoted more time in our discussions, our intimate discussions, to such matters [than] to any one [other] subject, because we were very fearful that we might find our whole campaign upset by some political gesture. I frankly was fearful of Mr. Roosevelt introducing political methods, of which he was a genius, into a military thing which had to be on a fixed basis." [35]

In pursuing this theme Marshall said:

["Diplomatic factors" were] . . . Mr. Roosevelt's [responsibility] and our problem was to be on guard that the military picture—meaning Army, Navy, and Air—was not completely disjointed by what I will call some irrelevant political gestures which were made without due thought to what was going on at the time. Of course, Mr. Churchill and the President were the dominant factors in all arrangements and all guidance. And they were the great political leaders of their country but they were also the military leaders, and it was quite a delicate issue back and forth, particularly in matters like the Mediterranean, the soft [under]belly of Europe, the Balkan states, the marches on Berlin and things of that sort. . . .

I repeat again that I doubt if there was any one thing except the shortage in LSTs that came to our minds more frequently than the political factors. But we were very careful, exceedingly careful, never to discuss them with the British, and from that they took the [view] that we didn't observe those things at all. But we observed them constantly, with great frequency, and particular solicitude, so that there is no foundation in that. We didn't discuss it with them because we were not in any way putting our necks out as to political factors which were the business of the head of the state—the President—who happened also to be the Commander-in-Chief.

. . . When the final considerations came, the President . . . called the meeting and we discussed the [issue]. You take, for example, the [occupation zones] of Western Europe. . . . I think we discussed halfway across the South Atlantic the various factors, you might say, of a political nature which were the President's deep concern in these matters, and which affected vitally the decisions which were made—which now may seem military decisions but they were very decidedly political [ones].

In some respects these arguments could be brushed aside by foreign critics of the American military leaders as oversimplifications of the problem. Indeed within the American military establishment a tendency developed after the war to insist on closer military participation in political decisions. On this point General Marshall never had any doubt. He stated in 1957:

> I do not think the military authorities should make any political decisions unless they are instructed accordingly, because the effects are too wide-reaching, there are too many influences involved, and it is quite a question of how much of this would be familiar to the military participants. Also it must be remembered the military responsibility in operations is very, very large, and it has with it a terrible measure of casualties. I know I was very careful to send Mr. Roosevelt every few days a statement of our casualties and it was done in a very effective way, graphically and . . . in colors, so it would be quite clear to him when he had only a moment or two to consider. [Therefore] I tried to keep before him all the time the casualty results *because you get hardened to these things and you have to be very careful to keep them always in the forefront of your mind.*[36]

The case for resting with the chief political authority the final decision as to actions that cost heavily in human lives has not been stated more succinctly.

For Marshall and his military associates the Tehran meeting terminated on the evening of the thirtieth with Churchill's dinner celebrating his sixty-ninth birthday. Since the heads of state had further business to discuss the following day, the British Chiefs of Staff invited the Americans to break their return trip to Cairo with a stopover at Jerusalem. They would be able to remain there overnight and still reach Egypt before the President and Prime Minister.[37]

General Marshall and the other Chiefs of Staff left Tehran in the early morning of December 1 and were in Jerusalem in time for lunch. In the afternoon they were taken by their hosts on a tour of the time-honored sights of the ancient city.[38] On the following morning, Marshall, an inveterate sightseer, managed to sandwich in visits to further landmarks before leaving at noon for the hour flight from Lydda back to Cairo.

The agreements sketched at Tehran began to fall apart at the first meeting of the Chiefs of Staff after they returned to Cairo. On taking a close look at the commitment for southern France, the British held out for enough landing craft to lift two divisions simultaneously. King recalled that the decision at Tehran merely stipulated that the assault be made in the greatest strength permitted by available craft. Marshall suggested that the planners be directed to determine the number of landing craft necessary for the attack to succeed without affecting OVERLORD adversely. The Chiefs of Staff finally decided to examine the plan on the assumption that there would be at least two assault divisions and that the resources would not be found at the expense of the cross-Channel operation.

Almost at once it became clear that if OVERLORD and the landings in southern France were to be mounted on a proper scale, something would have to give—and it would be BUCCANEER. The Prime Minister had never supported the Asian venture and had hoped he could shift the craft ear-marked for it to the Rhodes operation. Now that the eastern Mediterranean attack seemed less and less likely to materialize, he wanted some diversion in the Mediterranean that would aid the Italian campaign or OVERLORD.

Churchill cleverly argued that the Tehran discussions had changed the conditions under which Roosevelt had promised Chiang Kai-shek to launch BUCCANEER. The Russians had now indicated their willingness to go to war against Japan as soon as Germany collapsed; the Allies had told Stalin they would launch OVERLORD in May; and there was now a firm agreement to land in southern France. The President, chagrined at the prospect of having to disappoint the Generalissimo, urged that Mountbatten be instructed to stage the best operation he could with the resources he had at hand. Brooke tried to make the decision more palatable by arguing that it might be wise to divert the landing craft from BUCCANEER to provide a three-division lift for the operation in southern France. Before many months he and his colleagues would argue that a one-division diversionary attack would be sufficient. This was an instance of the opportunism that made the Americans suspicious of Brooke.

Both Admiral Leahy and General Marshall agreed that the prospects of strengthening OVERLORD and ANVIL (the assault on southern France) were appealing. But they warned of the serious issues at stake in dropping BUCCANEER. Marshall spelled out the problem in detail: "If BUCCANEER was cancelled, the Generalissimo would not allow Chinese forces to take part in TARZAN. There would be no campaign in Upper Burma, and this would have its repercussion on the operations in the Pacific. There would be a revulsion of feeling in China; the effect on Japan would be bad, and the line of communication between Indochina [India and China?] would be at hazard." [39] (TARZAN was the India-based portion of the proposed offensive in Burma.)

On the afternoon of December 5 the Combined Chiefs of Staff asked the Southeast Asia commander for his recommendations. Mountbatten's reply next day confirmed Marshall's recent warnings. Cancellation of BUCCANEER must inevitably lead to the collapse of TARZAN "since Generalissimo has only agreed to reduction in 'hump' tonnage and cooperation on [of] Yunnan force if amphibious operation is staged at the same time." [40]

Before Mountbatten's message arrived, the President had settled the matter. After four days of being "stubborn as a mule," Roosevelt perceived on the afternoon of December 5 that he could not budge the Prime Minister and his advisers. Probably he sensed that his own Chiefs of Staff would be pleased to have additional landing craft from the Far East. Reluctantly he decided to inform Chiang Kai-shek of his reversal of the promise made less than two weeks earlier.[41]

Although BUCCANEER was dropped, General Marshall could feel gratified that he had pinned down the British to a May date for the invasion of northern France and to an assault on southern France. He was not opposed to further advances in Italy or even in the eastern Mediterranean if they did not use resources earmarked for OVERLORD and ANVIL. But he wanted no further diversions from other theaters to Mediterranean "sideshows."

During the protracted debate over BUCCANEER the President at last made the decision that affected Marshall most personally—the selection of a Supreme Commander for Operation OVERLORD. After the exhaustive discussions in the early fall the command question had again been thoroughly explored by Roosevelt and his military advisers on board the *Iowa* en route to Tehran. On November 15 the President advanced the idea that Marshall should command all Western Allied forces in action against the Germans. Two days later Admiral Leahy outlined the formal arguments of the Joint Chiefs of Staff for the proposed supercommand.

Aware that the British would probably not accept the President's suggestion, the Chiefs examined two courses of action. The preferred solution was to designate a Supreme Commander who would command all United Nations operations against Germany from the Mediterranean and the Atlantic under direction from the Combined Chiefs of Staff. Under him would come a commander for operations in northwestern Europe, the Allied commander in the Mediterranean, and a strategic air forces commander who would exercise command over the U.S. Eighth and Fifteenth Air Forces and British Bomber Command.[42]

Leahy suggested that the President stress to the Prime Minister the importance of unified command. He then set forth the suggestion that Marshall had mentioned to Stimson as he prepared to leave Washington for the conference: "The necessity for unified command . . . is so urgent and compelling . . . we are willing to accept a British officer as over-all commander for European operations provided that man is Sir John Dill. . . . We have the highest opinion of his integrity of character and singleness of purpose. He understands our organization, our characteristics, our viewpoint on many subjects, and our way of doing business." [43]

If the British would not consider the overall command, the Joint Chiefs of Staff proposed that British suggestions for creating a unified command in the Mediterranean be accepted with the proviso that operational command of the U.S. Fifteenth Air Force be exempted from the Mediterranean Command and that a single strategic air forces commander be designated for the U.S. Eighth and Fifteenth Air Forces and the British Bomber Command.[44]

The President wanted the Chiefs to push the first suggestion even though the Prime Minister might not like it. As a bargaining point Admiral Leahy suggested that they withhold approval on the Mediterranean command, which the British wanted, until the overall command issue was settled. General Marshall dissented at once. A unified command in the

Mediterranean was logical, he argued, and American agreement would show good faith. Admiral King supported him on his insistence that the question "should be dealt with on its merits forthwith."

Marshall saw that the British could claim that they had suffered in the past in the Mediterranean through lack of unified command. Showing an awareness of British problems for which he seldom received credit from Brooke, Marshall said "that a commander, in a position such as General Eisenhower's, was always conservative regarding the sending of reinforcements to another command that was not his own responsibility. On the other hand, an over-all commander who had responsibility for an enlarged theater would feel differently toward bolstering up any weakened position in the theater for which he was responsible. . . ." If at the time of the Aegean operations Eisenhower had been in charge of the Middle East, as well as of Italy, "the British doubtless feel, and perhaps rightly so, he would have influenced the attitude of . . . Tedder and Spaatz towards additional air support in the Dodecanese and the situation might have been different."

As the session concluded, the President decided that before any change was made in the effort to get the overall Allied command for Marshall, there should be further discussions. He added that "we could agree to a unified command in the Mediterranean but not at the same time as we took up the matter of the Supreme Allied Commander." [45]

Before they left the United States, the Americans had made known to London their proposal for an arrangement to put all operations against the Germans under one commander. This was submitted formally on November 25.[46] On the following day the British Chiefs of Staff replied as the Americans had expected. The Prime Minister had already made clear that he would not agree to such an arrangement. General Marshall's strong opposition to the attack on Rhodes and his coolness to broad involvement in Italy were unlikely to gain Churchill's backing for an overall command. This was particularly true at a time when the Prime Minister saw the chance to have the Mediterranean Command under a British officer. Naturally he did not state that this was the basis for his opposition. Instead it was argued logically that the proposed arrangement had the effect of putting the Supreme Commander at a level above the Combined Chiefs of Staff.[47]

It is not certain at what point all parties concerned recognized that there could be no mutually acceptable command arrangement that would have made the selection of General Marshall as Supreme Commander feasible. The American Chiefs of Staff must have known that the proposition was completely dead by the time they left for Tehran. Yet the President's reply to Stalin that the decision as to the commander would depend on the results of the second Cairo meeting suggests that he may have yet hoped to win over the British.

When it was clear that the Supreme Commander's role would be limited to the cross-Channel attack, Roosevelt foresaw the revival of all the September arguments against Marshall's appointment. To the old charge that he would be downgrading the Chief of Staff by making him comman-der of OVERLORD, there was no effective answer save the one he had given Pershing: Marshall's standing in history depended on his leading the as-sault. If that was the sole issue, the President could not avoid reassessing his position. Should Marshall's reputation in the history books (a point never raised by Marshall himself) be considered against his worth in Washington in dealing with Congress, the general public, MacArthur, Stilwell, and the British? The prominent part taken by the Chief of Staff in current meetings, carrying the battle against Brooke and, in some cases, the Prime Minister, must have made the President realize anew the neces-sity of retaining him in the Allied councils. Weighed against this was Stimson's fierce insistence that only Marshall in command could carry through OVERLORD against the mercurial inconstancy of the Prime Minis-ter. But Tehran had brought a new force into negotiations in the person of Marshal Stalin, who strongly supported the OVERLORD concept. Sure of the Russian's determined advocacy, the President could put Eisenhower in London, keep Marshall in Washington, and still have the cross-Channel strategy safe. So Roosevelt must have reasoned.

There remained an implied promise to Marshall, an understanding so generally accepted in the United States and in European circles that Mar-shall and Eisenhower were already making their plans for the change. A short time earlier Marshall had even indicated to Colonel McCarthy that they might go to London shortly. A typically Rooseveltian solution to the dilemma was found, with the least damage to all concerned. Unlike Churchill, who had left Brooke bruised and bleeding, Roosevelt let Mar-shall make the crucial decision. It is possible that he sought a genuine expression of Marshall's preference and was prepared to accept any deci-sion the General might make, confident that he would consider all the arguments pro and con. If Roosevelt knew his man at all, and usually he was canny in such matters, he knew what the General's answer would be. For Marshall the command was the culmination of all his efforts between 1939 and 1944 and, in a sense, the climax to which all his career had been directed. But he would not have the command if he had to ask for it or even to reach out his hand. This too Roosevelt must have foreseen. But the drama had to be played out to the end.

On December 4 Roosevelt sent Harry Hopkins to see the Chief of Staff. Marshall recalled his saying that the President was "in some concern of mind over my appointment as Supreme Commander." It was the tip-off that the President was wavering in his original design. Marshall had been kept in suspense for many weeks. In September, after the Quebec confer-ence, he had expected an announcement.[48] Then had come the furor in the press. Although he heard from others that Roosevelt planned to select him, there was never any statement. Now he must have sensed that the President, bedeviled by many problems, had decided against the appointment. For several days at Cairo and Tehran he had expected to be offered the command formally. Surely he realized when Hopkins—so often the intermediary in delicate negotiations—appeared to sound him out that the President did not want to take responsibility for the final decision. From Hopkins's statement Marshall could not be absolutely certain what Roosevelt wanted. He sent back word that he would "go along wholeheartedly with whatever decision the President made." The choice must be Roosevelt's and not his own.[49]

Since this was not the answer that Roosevelt desired, he invited the Chief of Staff to his villa next day near lunchtime to settle the matter. As he went to meet the President, Marshall was aware that Roosevelt had been upset by political charges that he was trying to get him out of Washington. He may have known that the President's recent questions to other advisers during the conference had shown that he dreaded increasingly the prospect of losing Marshall's assistance in Washington. "I was determined," the General said later, "that I should not embarrass the President one way or the other—that he must be able to deal in this matter with a perfectly free hand in whatever he felt was the best interests [of the country]. . . . I was utterly sincere in the desire to avoid what had happened so much in other wars—the consideration of the feelings of the individual rather than the good of the country."

Marshall's account a dozen years later showed no emotion, and yet it dealt with the greatest drama of his life: the voluntary renunciation of his enduring ambition and the handing over of the Supreme Command to General Eisenhower, whose way to the Presidency it then made possible:

> As I recall, [Mr. Roosevelt] . . . asked me after a great deal of beating about the bush just what I wanted to do. Evidently it was left up to me. Well, having in mind all this business that had occurred in Washington and what Hopkins had told me, I just repeated again in as convincing language as I could that I wanted him to feel free to act in whatever way he felt was to the best interest of the country and to his satisfaction and not in any way to consider my feelings. I would cheerfully go whatever way he wanted me to go and I didn't express any desire one way or the other. . . . Then he evidently assumed that concluded the affair and that I would not command in Europe. Because he said, "Well I didn't feel I could sleep at ease if you were out of Washington." [50]

Once Marshall was eliminated from the running, there was only one other American possible for the Supreme Commander's post: Eisenhower was on the ground, had worked well with the British for two years, had helped develop the cross-Channel concept in the beginning, and had Marshall's full confidence. Furthermore he had made clear that he did not want to take the job in Washington. Through Bedell Smith and other friends who had gone back to Washington he had indicated his desire to stay in the Mediterranean or to lead an army group under Marshall in Normandy.

After Marshall declined to decide, Roosevelt presumably said, "Then it will be Eisenhower." If he did not say it at once, he said it shortly afterward. There was in fact, no need for a recommendation from Marshall. Roosevelt was aware that Eisenhower had been the Chief of Staff's choice for the U.S. theater command in Great Britain, that he had backed him for the North Africa command, and had strongly pushed his advancement to four-star rank in the Mediterranean. Although it was true that Marshall had not selected Eisenhower in the beginning for the Supreme Commander's post, he had certainly put him on the way to that position, and he as much as any other man was responsible for his reaching that goal.

Since the TRIDENT meeting Roosevelt and Churchill had entrusted Marshall with the task of writing reports to Stalin of their decisions at great conferences. This time the situation was the same. Besides drafting the message to Stalin saying that OVERLORD and ANVIL would be the first order of business, and a message to Chiang Kai-shek on the decisions at Tehran, he wrote out the following for the President's signature: "The immediate appointment of General Eisenhower to command of OVERLORD operation has been decided on." [51]

After the message had been signed by Roosevelt and the radio sent, Marshall in a characteristically kind act retrieved his handwritten draft and wrote at the bottom of the historic souvenir: "Dear Eisenhower: I thought you might like to have this as a memento. It was written very hurriedly by me as the final meeting broke up yesterday, the President signing it immediately. G.C.M." [52] This thoughtful gesture constituted the real passing of the torch to Eisenhower, and with it Marshall reassured the Mediterranean commander of his backing. Renouncing his great ambition, Marshall delivered the charge he had most coveted into the safekeeping of the officer he had been grooming for a key role since the beginning of the war. The Army that the Chief of Staff had prepared would go to victory under the command of an officer of Marshall's own choosing.

With the Supreme Command settled, Marshall turned back to a project that he had been considering since the first day he arrived in Cairo— nearly two weeks before he knew Roosevelt's decision on the command—a trip home by way of the Pacific. On November 22 he had written his Secretary General Staff, Colonel Sexton, that he was now "giving superficial consideration" to a visit to the Pacific Theater. He added: "Have the returning courier bring me a summer cap and my khaki kepi, also a waist belt—none were included in my baggage." He concluded in the laconic fashion that is the despair of biographers seeking human touches in the great conferences: "Tell Mrs. Marshall I am well and the weather has been fine and the scenery magnificent. I cannot say more for reasons of secrecy." [53]

Marshall's travel plans were kept secret, and he departed so quietly that not even the President knew of his destination. At least twice before the Chief of Staff had planned trips to MacArthur's theater only to be diverted from his trip by the President or Prime Minister. This time he wanted no slip-ups. His change of itinerary had one result that he later intensely regretted. When he left Washington, he had intended to stop off on his way home to see his stepsons, Clifton and Allen. This part of the trip had to be dropped. He was never to see the younger boy again.[54]

General Marshall, accompanied by General Handy, Admiral Cooke, and Frank McCarthy, flew in General Sutherland's C-54 to the Pacific. Not wishing to get involved with the military situation in India, he stopped only briefly in Ceylon and then set off on the long and dangerous overwater trip to Australia (all the landing fields short of Australia and eastern New Guinea were held by the enemy). It was some seventeen hours before they reached Port Moresby.

Now that his tasks were completely global, Marshall thought it highly important that he see the Pacific situation for himself. He also wanted to show MacArthur that he had not been forgotten. The Chief of Staff had been reminded just before the Cairo conference that while press agitation for his own presidential candidacy had quieted down, there was still political speculation about the Southwest Pacific commander. Sexton had written Marshall on November 20: "The *Times-Herald* in editorial yesterday demoted General MacArthur to Secretary of War and proposes that if any other Republican candidate for President carried the promise that MacArthur would be appointed Secretary of War upon his election, Republicans would win." [55]

In this first meeting between the two Generals in at least eight years there was a hint of the theatrical. Word of Marshall's coming was received by the Southwest Pacific commander as he was preparing to leave his forward headquarters at Port Moresby for General Krueger's headquarters on Goodenough Island. There plans were under way for landings at Port Gloucester. According to MacArthur's biographer Frazier Hunt, the General felt that a meeting might be embarrassing to the Chief of Staff. As a result he "seriously considered conducting the Gloucester operations in person, thus relieving Marshall of his presence." At last he decided to remain, but he prophesied that the Chief of Staff would never see him alone. And again according to Hunt, never for a moment did Marshall seek "to be alone with him. Nor did he evince any desire to confide in MacArthur or to give him his own inner thoughts and ideas on the global struggle." [56]

Marshall and his party were flown by General Kenney from Port Moresby to Goodenough Island. Following his usual practice, the Chief of

Staff joined General Krueger for an inspection trip, taking time out to
drive with him in a heavy downpour to some of the troop units and installations, where he inquired after the men's welfare and sought their
reactions.[57]

At last the two Generals met. No account was left by Marshall, but
MacArthur in his *Reminiscences* declared, "We had a long and frank
discussion."

In 1964 MacArthur recalled that when he spoke of the small number of
men and limited resources that he was getting in comparison with commanders of other theaters of war, Marshall had said that he regretted it
but that he could do little to correct the situation. According to MacArthur, the Chief of Staff was inclined to put the blame on Admirals King
and Leahy and on their influence on Roosevelt.[58]

The Southwest Pacific commander said that he reminded Marshall that
all the disasters in the Pacific had come about under Navy commanders;
that in his area there had been no naval losses of such magnitude; that he
was a supporter of both the Navy and Air Forces; that he felt that interservice rivalry should not be allowed to interfere with winning the war;
and that to get unity of command he had been willing to take a subordinate position.

Marshall seemed to agree, MacArthur wrote. However, having been
Chief of Staff himself, MacArthur realized "how impossible it was to have
professional and objective matters decided on the basis of merit and common sense." But there were some good results: "Upon his return to Washington he informed me that he had spoken to General Arnold, who promised greater air support. From that time on Washington became more
generous to the SWPA." [59]

In view of MacArthur's own statement Hunt was apparently misin-
formed by members of the Pacific commander's staff about the nature of
the meeting. The statement also points up the glaring error in Field Marshal Brooke's account of his visit to General MacArthur in Tokyo in 1945.
The British officer recorded that as he was leaving, the American General
thanked him for the visit, "especially as it was the first time during the
war that he had ever been visited by any of the Chiefs of Staff." "I am
certain," added Brooke, "he was referring to the fact that the American
Chiefs of Staff had not visited him." [60]

On the sixteenth Marshall left the Southwest Pacific, and after a stopover in Los Angeles because of "a front in the Cascades," he arrived in
Washington on the evening of December 22.

Next day the Winns came in from Arkansas, where Major Winn was
now stationed. They were on hand for Christmas dinner at Leesburg,
which was punctuated by a toast to Mrs. Marshall's absent boys, Allen
and Clifton. The weather, Marshall wrote his stepsons in Christmas letters, was completely seasonal: "It snowed and then sleeted—and to an
extent which began to break down limbs." [61]

From the letters as well as his reactions since the December 5 meeting with Roosevelt, one could not guess that Marshall had just made a major sacrifice. General Handy and Colonel McCarthy, who had accompanied him to the recent conferences and were with him during the long trip back to Washington, got no inkling of disappointment. Before Cairo he had shown no excitement over getting the command; now there was no indication of despair. Some who talked to him soon after the decision was made assumed from his calm demeanor that he did not want the post.[62]

In Secretary Stimson's mind there was no question of what Marshall had wanted. Bitter at the President's failure to appoint him, the Secretary wrote admiringly that only Marshall's "matchless power of self-sacrifice and of self-control" permitted him to give the appearance that it did not matter. The President tried to argue that Marshall had preferred to remain as Chief of Staff, but Stimson would not be quieted. As if voicing some strong inner grief of the General's, he replied firmly, "I said that I knew that in the bottom of his heart it was Marshall's secret desire above all things to command this invasion force into Europe." And then he noted that he had feared weeks earlier that this renunciation might take place: "I had begged him not to sacrifice what I considered the interests of the country to the undue sensitiveness of his own conscience in seeming to seek a post." [63]

In time the Secretary became reconciled to the arrangement. As for Marshall, he seemed to have dropped the matter from his mind once he had concluded his talk with the President at Cairo. The concept of duty in the code imposed on cadets at the Virginia Military Institute in Marshall's day had made the act of self-denial easier. "This institution," he once said, "gave me not only a standard for my daily conduct among men, but it endowed me with a military heritage of honor and self-sacrifice."

The personal prize went elsewhere. Marshall's self-imposed task thereafter was to make certain that Eisenhower achieved victory.

☆ XVII ☆

Italy Versus Anvil

"NOW come on home and see your wife and trust somebody else for twenty minutes in England." Still benignly protective toward the new OVERLORD commander, General Marshall summoned Dwight D. Eisenhower home in late December 1943 for a short rest in the midst of preparations to shift his headquarters from the Mediterranean to London. Marshall had long insisted that his commanders have a chance for relaxation before taking up new and crushing tasks, and he was determined that Eisenhower should pause for a rest before tackling the invasion of northwest Europe. "Things have been going ahead in the UK for a long time and under a wise and aggressive man [COSSAC Chief Morgan] and [Bedell] Smith has already been there. You will be under terrific strain from now on. I am interested in that you are fully prepared to bear the strain and I am not interested in the usual rejoinder that you can take it. It is of vast importance that you be fresh mentally and you certainly will not be if you go straight from one great problem to another." Marshall's paternal admonitions set the tone for the special relationship that would continue for the remainder of the war.[1]

Understandably Eisenhower was impatient to get to England, so much so that he growled to his naval aide, Commander Butcher, a few weeks after that there had been nothing he could do in Washington and that he had gone only at Marshall's insistence. He wrote later in *Crusade in Europe,* "Strictly speaking, my commanders were the Combined Chiefs of Staff but, realizing General Marshall's earnestness in the matter, I quickly cleared the point with the British side of the house and made ready to leave for the United States." He planned to return to Africa to turn over the United States forces to General Devers, who was being transferred from London, and to hand over the Allied Command to General Wilson.[2] As it turned out, Devers by then was already in his new command, and Wilson was planning the Anzio operation in the Mediterranean before Eisenhower's return to Europe.

Eisenhower's remarks to Butcher reflected possible worry over the shortness of time to prepare for OVERLORD, still set for the first of May, all too close at hand. Marshall had suggested the American interlude out of the conviction that Eisenhower needed the rest. Perhaps he thought that the General should renew his contact with Washington's thinking before being intensively subjected to the Prime Minister's pressures.

Great secrecy surrounded Eisenhower's arrival in Washington on January 2. Secretary Stimson learned of his presence only when Marshall called hastily that Sunday afternoon to say that the General's plane had landed. The Chief of Staff had given Colonel McCarthy the task of arranging for a few days of relaxation, and the aide followed a pattern that was to become standard in welcoming commanders from overseas in the months to come.

Some months earlier the Army's Ashford General Hospital had taken over the Greenbrier Hotel at White Sulphur Springs, West Virginia, as a convalescent home for its patients. General Marshall had requested that cottages on its grounds be used for commanders home on short vacations between assignments or for briefings. There the officers and their wives could escape from the social demands of Washington or, in cases such as Eisenhower's, have their presence in the country concealed. In General Eisenhower's case secret arrangements were also made for him to visit his son, John, at West Point and his mother and brothers at Manhattan, Kansas, before going to White Sulphur Springs and returning to Washington for conversations.

General and Mrs. Eisenhower left Washington by train—in a special car, which was picked up on a lonely siding—for the U.S. Military Academy, where John joined them aboard the car. The plans for Eisenhower's visit with members of his family in Kansas were no less elaborate. Since his brother Milton was president of Kansas State College, in Manhattan, it was decided to take the General there and have his mother and other members of his family join him. Despite all precautions, there were always complications. Frank McCarthy, who had been sent out to help with preparations, was uncomfortable at the Officers Club at nearby Fort Riley when an elderly colonel asked prying questions. A few members of the faculty and the local newspaper editor in Manhattan were let in on the secret, and they helped keep it quiet.[3]

Through careful arrangements and the cooperation of the press the visit to the States remained amazingly private despite the fact that General Eisenhower saw a number of people. As a part of a regular plan to give his commanders a firm build-up with congressional leaders, General Marshall on the evening of January 3 gave a party for the General and several other visiting commanders at the Alibi Club at 1806 I Street in Washington. For several years Marshall had made effective use of the old house, which had been bought years before by seven members of the Metropolitan Club as a place where "they [could] cook oysters, lobsters, and ducks to suit themselves, play poker, and put away a lethal sort of drink based on Medford Rum. . . ." It developed into a social club of fifty members. Through Robert Woods Bliss, Marshall was invited to entertain small groups there.[4]

The evening of January 3 brought out some of the top Democratic and Republican congressional leaders as guests. To meet them Marshall had invited, in addition to Eisenhower, Admiral Stark, back from London, and Lieutenant General George C. Kenney and Major General J. Lawton Collins, just back from the Southwest Pacific. Marshall saw to it that each of them had a chance to explain his recent activities. Collins told of his experience at Rendova and at Guadalcanal, Kenney spoke of parachute landings in the Markham Valley and operations in New Britain, and Stark talked of naval problems in the North Atlantic. Then Marshall called on Eisenhower to describe the latest Mediterranean operations. Given a chance to show to advantage, Eisenhower won friends for his program with his talk.[5]

In the eleven days he spent in the United States, Eisenhower was filled in on recent weapons development by Marshall and others. The Chief of Staff was especially concerned at the moment with development of rockets for use by the ground forces. As early as January 3 Stimson observed that Marshall had taken up "the whole subject of rockets replacing artillery and is having it studied and is even contemplating changes in the staff of the Ground Forces because he feels that they have been slow in giving this new rocket innovation proper attention. . . ." Stimson passed these new plans on to Eisenhower, noting a rocket attachment for tanks. Vannevar Bush was called in to warn of a possible German offensive combining the use of rockets and poison gas. All this was new to Eisenhower, who said finally, "You make me scared." [6]

As Eisenhower had anticipated, there was little possibility for realistic examination of the problems he would face in the cross-Channel attack. He had lacked an opportunity to study the COSSAC plan fully and had sent on to London his subordinates Montgomery and Bedell Smith, who were now looking into its particulars. He knew that his dissatisfaction with the limited scope of the earlier plan was shared by men who now would have to implement the operation.

There were many reasons for Eisenhower to hasten to London. From late December, when his representatives had arrived in the United Kingdom, demands had mounted for more resources for the cross-Channel landing than had been provided at recent conferences. As early as January 3, 1944, Montgomery, who was to lead the Allied ground forces in the initial stages of the invasion, asked for an expansion of the assault area. And the troops were on hand but not the landing craft; competitive demands around the world had reduced their availability. In part the blame lay at the door of planners in the United States who had failed to provide for an adequate increase in production of this essential craft. Critics of

Admiral King blamed him for contributing to the problem by retaining a large share of the vessels in the Pacific for operations that the British held to be secondary to the main theater in Europe. In this situation it was natural to seek support for OVERLORD at the expense of the secondary operation in the European Theater—ANVIL.

Montgomery had sensed his advantage on examining the COSSAC plan. If the Americans wanted to succeed in the operation for which they had argued so eloquently, they would have to give way on the landings in southern France or force King to disgorge part of his landing craft in the Pacific. Montgomery opened the game with a bid that ANVIL be dropped at once, and the southern operation reduced to a threat only. In transmitting this word to Eisenhower, still in Washington, General Smith strongly agreed.[7]

To General Marshall this argument was another British device aimed against cross-Channel itself. The attack in southern France was closely linked, he believed, to the success of OVERLORD. He was prepared to see the northern front broadened, but he wanted to be certain that everything had been done to find the landing craft elsewhere before abandoning the ANVIL assault.

The Chief of Staff's view was reflected in Eisenhower's reply from Washington on January 5, 1944. Although strongly favoring a broader-based OVERLORD—a view he had expressed before leaving the Mediterranean—he agreed with Marshall that ANVIL could not be merely a threat. He left the door open to the acceptance of Montgomery's proposal, however, by saying that only if OVERLORD could not be broadened without abandoning the landings in southern France would he consider it.[8]

The British Chiefs of Staff quickly sided with Montgomery; they notified the Prime Minister on January 14 that the proposed reduction of ANVIL to a one-division threat would not run counter to the Allied commitment at Tehran: "OVERLORD will be launched in May, in conjunction with a supporting operation against the south of France on the largest scale that is permitted by the landing craft available at that time." [9]

It was this seemingly constant search by the British for a loophole that upset the Americans, who saw carefully wrought compromises dissolving into meaninglessness. Eisenhower was clear about Marshall's viewpoint before he left for London on the evening of January 13. Four days later he assured the Chief of Staff that while most people there, including Montgomery and Smith, wanted a major reduction in ANVIL, he would not favor that except as a last resort. His resolve seemed fairly firm, but this last statement appeared to open the door to acceptance of London's views. He conceded that the Allies must keep in mind the promise to the Russians and the Allied investment in the French army that was to be used in southern France. But he added, "It is with such reasons as these in mind that I am determined to uncover every single expedient for increasing the initial weight of the OVERLORD attack before I am willing to recommend any great weakening of the ANVIL project." It was a dilemma that he could not resolve.[10]

The situation had been made worse by recent developments in Italy. While Eisenhower and Marshall talked of cross-Channel preparations, plans had been readied for an attack at Anzio that was to affect profoundly their ideas for landings in southern France simultaneously with OVERLORD. Churchill had set the Mediterranean pot to boiling again.

Recuperating at Marrakech from his second bout of pneumonia in a year, the Prime Minister had lightened his convalescence by reviving a plan for getting the Allies on the move again in Italy by a landing near Rome at Anzio (SHINGLE)—an operation on which Eisenhower and his Mediterranean headquarters staff had worked in mid-November and then shelved in December for lack of resources.[11] Thwarted in his plans for the Aegean, Churchill was determined that the fight for Italy would not flag. With the Mediterranean now firmly under British Generals Wilson and Alexander, he kept pressure on for expansion there. One day after Lieutenant General Mark Clark, in charge of planning for the operation, recommended that Anzio be dropped, Churchill got on the telephone to General Brooke, in London, about means of reviving it. He angrily reminded his Chiefs of Staff that stagnation on the Italian front was scandalous and that it was well-nigh criminal to leave landing craft idle for three months.

Reminded by his advisers that withdrawal of landing craft for Eisenhower's operations would not leave enough for Anzio, he asked Smith why the transfer of LSTs could not be delayed. To Smith's uncharacteristically mild reply that he had been granted two delays and could not bear to ask for a third extension, Churchill retorted that he had no such compunction. He thereupon informed the British Chiefs of Staff that the triumph or ruin of the Italian campaign depended on keeping the LSTs three weeks longer. The British Chiefs, caught between a probable Churchill eruption and another bruising round with Marshall and King, decided to risk the more familiar peril. "We feel we should not conceal from you," they wrote the Prime Minister in Marrakech, "the difficulty we expect with the United States Chiefs of Staff, if we tell them frankly the true position as we see it."

On Christmas Day, Churchill appealed to Roosevelt. Perhaps the spirit of the season won the requested delay in the shift of landing craft, but it was not enough to get everything the rugged invalid of Marrakech desired. In addition to stipulating that this action must not delay the launching of OVERLORD, Roosevelt specified that activities in Rhodes and in the Aegean must be sidetracked. In view of their recent promises to Stalin at Tehran, he warned that they must not hazard the success of OVERLORD and ANVIL.[12]

The views were undoubtedly Roosevelt's, but they reflected Marshall's determination not to let the Italian situation get out of hand. Later the

Chief of Staff said of this period: "I doubt if I did anything better in the war than to keep Churchill on the main point (he always wanted to take the side shots). I was furious when he wanted to push us further in the Mediterranean." [13]

Having secured the landing craft from Roosevelt, Churchill still found a good word for Marshall. In giving credit, he wrote, "I am sure I owed it not only to his [Roosevelt's] good will, but to Marshall's balance of mind, to Eisenhower's loyalty to the show he was about to quit, and to Bedell Smith's active, knowledgeable, fact-armed diplomacy." [14]

Clark, who had once outlined an operation at Anzio, had recommended that it be dropped. Anzio, in the end, was a British project. Marshall, beyond assenting to the President's concessions, had no part in it. Eisenhower, preparing to leave the theater, felt he should not interfere. He told his superiors in Washington in early January that the Prime Minister was "dead set upon making this offensive for political reasons." He thought that the old fighter did not want to go back to the United Kingdom with the Italian offensive stalled and lips sealed about prospects in the Channel, thus being without something to announce to the public. Bedell Smith, writing Eisenhower after the final decision for Anzio had been made, said that the operation was risky and a gamble on weather but if it worked it was worth the effort.[15]

As word came to Britain of Churchill's activities, Brooke suggested that he should fly to Marrakech. He was dissuaded by Portal and Cunningham, who argued with great discernment that unless General Marshall was also present, the Americans might accuse the British of running away with operations in the Mediterranean. Considering what the Prime Minister might do with available troops and landing craft, Brooke wrote next day, "I wish to God he would come home and get under control." Marshall, who found more than once that he and Brooke shared common views, would have fervently agreed.[16]

At length the Anzio attack was set for January 22. As a preliminary Alexander's main forces in Italy were to attack on January 17 in the hope of forcing the Germans from positions on the Garigliano and the Rapido. Alexander, Allied Ground commander in the Mediterranean, assigned the task of commanding forces in the landings to General Clark, Marshall's protégé. Clark in turn placed the actual assault operations in the hands of the commander of VI U.S. Corps, Major General John P. Lucas, a fifty-four-year-old officer who had won Marshall's approval as a division commander in the United States. Judging him a man of "military stature, prestige, and experience," the Chief of Staff had sent him to Eisenhower's theater in 1943 as an observer. On his return to the United States the Chief of Staff gave him a corps command. Later when Marshall sent him back to aid General Eisenhower, Lucas served in the Sicilian campaign as the Allied commander's representative with combat troops. When Bradley left Sicily for the United Kingdom in the fall of 1943,

Lucas succeeded him as head of II Corps. Shortly afterward during the Salerno fighting, he was brought to the VI Corps on the relief of Major General Ernest J. Dawley. Marshall thus had reasons for particular interest in the battle.

From the start Lucas was unhappy with the Anzio operation. Feeling his years and convinced that he lacked sufficient resources for the venture, he went into the fight with foreboding. A diarist, whose private musings frequently did not bolster his reputation for resoluteness, he summed up his state of nerves by writing, "They will end up by putting me ashore with inadequate forces and get me in a serious jam. Then, who will take the blame?"

Suffering, as one observer put it, from a "Salerno complex," Lucas was determined, once ashore at Anzio, to guard against a German counterattack. As a result this time, despite definite surprise and a landing in force without successful opposition, he did not strike boldly inland. His troops organized quickly, but dug in against an expected enemy attack. In the next three days he continued to bring in more men and supplies, watching for possible enemy reaction and delaying his main attack until he had more troops ashore. Not until January 30, more than a week after the start of the assault, did Lucas feel ready to act. When he did, Field Marshal Albert Kesselring was prepared to strike.[17]

By the end of the first week in February it was apparent that the gamble to get Rome quickly had failed. Churchill demanded of the Mediterranean Supreme Commander, General Wilson, why the U.S. parachute regiment that Marshall had made available had not been dropped; why no attempt had been made to occupy the high ground and key towns twelve to twenty-four hours after landing; and why no heavily mounted offensive on the main front had been made to coincide with the German movements from that front against the landings.

Defending his commanders, Wilson replied that both Alexander and Clark had urged action. Churchill thought the argument lame. On February 8, when Churchill learned that General Marshall shared his disappointment over the slowness of the attack, he sent Wilson's report to Dill, authorizing him to show the message to the American Chief of Staff at his discretion. "My comment," the Prime Minister declared, "is that senior commanders should not 'urge' but 'order.' "

Two days later he radioed Alexander, "I have a feeling that you may have hesitated to assert your authority because you were dealing so largely with Americans and therefore *urged* an advance instead of *ordering* it." He added that he had it from the highest American authorities that they wanted their troops to receive orders. "The Americans are very good to work with, and quite prepared to take the rough with the smooth." [18]

Soon Alexander was complaining to Brooke that Lucas lacked drive. Informed of his dissatisfaction, General Marshall radioed General Devers, the chief American commander in the Mediterranean, on February 18

that Washington estimates also indicated that the drive and leadership of
the corps and its commanders appeared below the stern standard required in the existing situation. "Let nothing stand in the way of procuring the leadership of the quality necessary," he added. "We comprehend
fatigue of troops but that is normal to every hard battle and the Germans
must be worse off than our men." On February 22 General Clark told
Lucas that he could no longer resist pressure from Alexander and Devers
and relieved him of his command.[19]

Later General Marshall was somewhat more lenient. He explained to
interviewers after the war that while Lucas could have reached the Alban
Hills soon after landing, he was wise to refrain from doing so. "For every
mile of advance, there were seven or more miles [to be] added to the
perimeter." Part of the trouble, he believed, had been due to lack of resources available. Apparently feeling that Lucas might have been the victim of a situation not wholly his fault, Marshall decided to give him another chance. On March 1 he wrote Eisenhower that McNair wanted
Lucas for a corps command, and ultimately he got the Fourth Army.[20]

Marshall may have felt sorry for Lucas, but he, as well as the British
and American leaders, could only rejoice at his successor. Major General
Lucian K. Truscott, Jr., who had caught Marshall's eye early in the war,
had made his reputation as an able fighter in the Mediterranean.
He had repeatedly showed a flair for bold and decisive action. He would
lead the VI Corps into southern France, and then return to Italy to head
the Fifth U.S. Army.

Anzio's delays added daily to the problems of OVERLORD and increased
the likelihood of ANVIL's postponement. Rather than speeding the larger
operation, Churchill's gamble, in which Marshall and Eisenhower had
acquiesced, became a serious drain. The effect of the Italian battle was
studied anxiously in London and Washington.

Pressure had continued to build up in the United Kingdom through
January for a reduction in the size of ANVIL. Still struggling to preserve
the operation as more than a threat, Eisenhower acknowledged that
Montgomery was justified in demanding a broader invasion front and a
five-division assault loaded for the cross-Channel attack. Casting about for
means of salvaging the assault in southern France, he was prepared to
delay the launch of OVERLORD and ANVIL until the end of May, thus bene-
fiting from an extra month of British production of LSTs at the cost of a
month of good campaigning weather.[21] To this proposal the Joint Chiefs
of Staff agreed within the week.

On the broader issues Eisenhower outlined his views formally to the
Combined Chiefs of Staff on January 23. "OVERLORD and ANVIL," he insisted, "must be viewed as one whole," and he described the ideal as being
a five-division OVERLORD and a three- or, at worst, two-division ANVIL. It
was becoming clear that if there were not enough resources for both, he
was prepared to accept a one-division ANVIL—but not without a nervous

glance in Marshall's direction. He assured the Chief of Staff that his recommendations were based on consultations with "my commanders and my own staff, but with no outside agencies." [22] He had already noted, however, to Marshall that both Montgomery, his chief subordinate for the invasion, and Smith, his Chief of Staff, were agreed on cutting ANVIL down.

As late as February 6 Eisenhower assured Marshall that he hoped to carry out the larger OVERLORD operation without giving up ANVIL. But he could not have been very hopeful. Bedell Smith was closer to the mark two days earlier when he telephoned Marshall's assistants, Handy and Hull, that the Anzio fighting might have severe repercussions and lead to the abandonment of ANVIL. Eisenhower admitted as much on the seventh to Butcher, his naval aide; with a stalemated Anzio the Americans must recognize the need to keep landing craft in Italy after the end of January no matter how much they shouted "principle and agreements." It was an end that Marshall had feared when he first was told of Churchill's plans for the new landing in Italy.[23]

In his anxiety Eisenhower became increasingly critical of American policy in the Pacific. He felt that the fighting there was taking too many of the Allied landing craft, an error that might prove serious. That the Allies were fighting two wars at once seemed wrong to him.[24]

Marshall did not know how completely Eisenhower was swinging to the London view, but he sensed that pressure was building up on the Supreme Commander and that Eisenhower was responding—as could be expected—to the situation closest at hand. In the past when Marshall had found commanders sore beset, he sought to bolster them by a firm statement of the American position. Now he did so by commenting dryly that the British and U.S. Chiefs of Staff seemed to have reversed themselves recently, with the Americans becoming Mediterraneanites and the British pro–cross-Channel.

The U.S. Chiefs also believed that the British were exaggerating the alleged shortage of LSTs in Europe. They suspected that estimates on the serviceability of craft and the number of men that could be transported were far too low—a point on which the British agreed in later years. Acting for the Joint Chiefs, Marshall asked Eisenhower on what basis London planners were making their predictions.

Failing to get the information he desired, Marshall wrote Eisenhower unequivocally: "OVERLORD of course is paramount and it must be launched on a reasonably secure basis of which you are the best judge. Our difficulties in reaching a decision have been complicated by a battle of numbers, that is, a failure to reach a common ground as to what would be the actual facilities. As to this the British and American planners here yesterday afternoon agreed that there is sufficient lift to stage at least a 7-division OVERLORD and at the same time a 2-division ANVIL on the basis of May 31st." But they found no such view in London where there "is an

oosevelt and Churchill at Casablanca in January 1943 with the Combined Chiefs of Staff and
eir advisers. *Seated:* Lieutenant General Henry H. Arnold, Admiral Ernest J. King, the P.M.,
D.R., General Sir Alan Brooke, Admiral Sir Dudley Pound, Marshall. *Standing:* Lieutenant
eneral Sir Hastings Ismay (behind Churchill), Vice Admiral Lord Louis Mountbatten, Brigadier
eneral John R. Deane, Field Marshal Sir John Dill, Air Marshal Charles Portal, Harry L. Hop-
ns.

Chief of Staff (*right foreground*) on one of his numerous visits to troop installations. At Fort
ing, Georgia, in March 1943, he was joined by British Foreign Secretary Anthony Eden,
ing through a new U.S. rifle. *Photo: George C. Marshall Research Library.*

The Women's Army Auxiliary Corps comes into being, May 14, 1942, as the Judge Advocate General, Major General Myron C. Cramer, swears in Mrs. Oveta Culp Hobby as its director. Marshall and Secretary of War Henry L. Stimson (*right*) had to buck stiff Army and Congressional opposition to establishment of the corps.

In Marshall's eyes, Captain Florence T. Newsome summed up why WACs were indispensable. He "She is my personal secretary all matters pertaining to the Chiefs of Staff and Combined of Staff . . . apprising me o pros and cons of all the va issues. That is certainly an in tant job."

Field Marshal Sir John Dill, Chief of the Joint Staff Mission in Washington, was credited by Marshall with the key role in minimizing Anglo-American frictions. When he died in November 1944—a year after this photograph at the Tehran conference—the Chief of Staff arranged for him to be buried at Arlington National Cemetery.

nksgiving Day, 1943, at Cairo. Behind the three heads of state are the Combined Chiefs of , with Chinese General Shang Chen at right.

As a result of the Cairo conference, U.S. aid to China was stepped up. To facilitate identification of American flyers who might be downed in China, they were issued insignia in Chinese script.

The Chief of Staff returned from the Cairo-Tehran conferences by way of the Southwest Pacific, to see the situation at first hand and to reassure the theater's men and commanders—particularly General Douglas MacArthur —that they would not be neglected in the preoccupation with Europe.

At the Chief of Staff's official residence, Quarters Number One, Fort Myer, Virginia, Mrs. Marshall strove to preserve an oasis where the General could walk, ride, and tend his chickens. Shortly after this picture was taken, her younger son was killed in the Italian campaign. *Photo: George C. Marshall Research Library.*

In 1944, at Dodona Manor, the Marshalls' retreat in Leesburg, Virginia, the General dandles Kitty Winn. She and brother Jimmy were the children of Mrs. Marshall's daughter, Molly, and Major James J. Winn. *Photo: George C. Marshall Research Library.*

At memorial services in the Fort Myer Chapel for Lieutenant General Frank M. Andrews, a protégé and close friend, the Chief of Staff is flanked by Secretary Stimson and the President's Military Aide, Major General Edwin M. Watson. In the second row are Mrs. Robert P. Patterson, wife of the Undersecretary of War; Mrs. Marshall; Robert A. Lovett, Assistant Secretary of War; and Lieutenant General Joseph R. McNarney, Deputy Chief of Staff.

Colonel Frank McCarthy, ASGS (*front right*), like his chief, was a VMI graduate. Among his duties was handling arrangements on inspection trips, such as this one in 1944 to the 81st Infantry Wildcat Division, commanded by Major General Paul J. Mueller (*at Marshall's left*), Camp Beale, California.

After years of Anglo-American wrangling over attack sites, and colossal troop and material build-ups, Operation Overlord was launched on June 6, 1944. A vast air and naval flotilla brought Allied troops across the English Channel to the Normandy coast of France to launch a second front against the Axis powers.

Within days of the Allied landings, Marshall and his fellow Chiefs set foot on Omaha Beach in Normandy. As Marshall straddles the edge of a DUKW, Supreme Allied Commander Dwight D. Eisenhower mounts, observed by General Arnold. Rear Admiral Alan G. Kirk, commander of U.S. naval forces, is at front left.

Two French children greet the Chief of Staff with a bouquet of flowers during his visit to a command post in October 1944. During the week-long trip he also toured posts in Belgium, Holland, and Luxembourg and carried home dozens of messages from officers and men. *Photo: George C. Marshall Research Library.*

In the thirties Marshall had spotted both Eisenhower and Omar N. Bradley (*right*) as top-caliber young officers. In France in the fall of 1944 he was proud that their performance—as Supreme Commander and commander of the Twelfth Army, respectively—more than validated his judgment.

At the headquarters of the 5th Infantry Division the commander, Major General S. Leroy Irwin, explains a model of the surrounding French terrain. *At left:* Lieutenant General Thomas T. Handy, Lieutenant General George S. Patton, Jr., and Major General Walton H. Walker (in dark jacket).

The battle for the Hürtgen Forest ended in December 1944 after weeks of grueling fighting. These American infantrymen are getting their first hot meal after the fifteen-day siege of the city of Hürtgen. In the foreground is Stephen Longstreth of Carnegie, Pennsylvania.

Despite massive Allied pressure in the Hürtgen Forest, the stubborn Nazi soldiers, some under age, some over age, were slow to surrender. This group at Jungersdorf held out until December 12.

Attending his last international conference, F.D.R. confers in Malta aboard the USS *Quincy* with Admiral Leahy, Admiral King, and General Marshall. After preliminary Anglo-American talks in Malta, the conferees went on to Yalta to meet with Stalin for discussions on Russia's entry into the war against Japan.

The first day of the Yalta conference, February 3, 1945, at Nicholas and Alexandra's Livadia Palace: At left, Andrei Gromyko talks with his chief, Soviet Foreign Affairs Commissar Vyacheslav Molotov. *Clockwise from Churchill's cigar:* Stalin, surrounded by generals; Major General Laurence S. Kuter; Admiral Leahy; behind him, General Deane; Roosevelt; Secretary of State Edward R. Stettinius, Jr.; and Admiral King.

Returning from Yalta, the Chief of Staff toured the Italian front. Against Marshall's orders, Lieutenant General Mark W. Clark, head of the 15th Army Group, held a review to show the unity and diversity of his forces. Clark's troops included Sikhs from India and numerous other British colonials.

Marshall relives the days of the Meuse-Argonne campaign of 1918 as he washes from a jerrican in an orchard near St. Pierre du Mont on his front-line visit to Normandy in June 1944. *Photo: International News.*

Carentan, shown here with entering American troops. As Marshall and his party approached the town, taken that same day by the Allies, the Germans continued to fire. The host, Lieutenant General Omar N. Bradley, fearing that a sniper's lucky shot might annihilate the Allied high command, abruptly terminated the tour. *Photo: Associated Press.*

In October 1944 War Mobilization Director James F. Byrnes accompanied the General on the first direct transatlantic flight to Paris since Lindbergh's 1927 feat. Eisenhower met them at the airport to discuss supply needs for the ending of the war in Europe—possibly before the end of the year.

With Lieutenant General Jacob L. Devers (*right*), commander of the 6th Army Group, Marshall visited General Jean de Lattre de Tassigny, head of the First French Army. Before a group of reporters de Lattre bitterly denounced an American colleague. Marshall held his tongue then, but years later he dressed the Frenchman down for that "most outrageous business."

Marshall toured extensively on foot during his Italian trip. Near Boccanello he slogs through slush behind Lieutenant General Lucian K. Truscott, Jr., commander of the Fifth Army. General Clark follows.

Marshall's February 1945 Italian trip was largely intended to show the troops that they were not fighting on a "forgotten front." A prime morale booster was the awarding of medals. Here Lieutenant Stephen Kosmyna of the Fifth Army receives the Distinguished Service Cross.

In April and May 1945 Russian and Anglo-American forces linked up in Germany along the Elbe and Mulde rivers. Here, an embrace between a soldier of the 82nd Airborne Division and a Russian, who shouted, "Americano! Americano!"

Despite his frequent choler at General Charles de Gaulle, and his distaste for personal honors, Marshall diplomatically accepted the Grande Croix of the Legion of Honor from the French leader after the war's end. *Photo: Associated Press.*

The triumphant Supreme Commander and Mrs. Eisenhower are greeted by cheering crowds as they arrive at Washington's National Airport, June 18, 1945. The beaming Marshall had written Eisenhower: "You have made history, great history for the good of mankind."

As victory came within grasp, Churchill cabled: "What a joy it must be to [General Marshall] to see how the armies he called into being by his own genius have won immortal renown. He is the true 'organizer of victory.'" The portrait is by Christine L. Pogue. *Photo: George C. Marshall Research Library.*

apparent disagreement with British planners . . . or Montgomery, I don't know which."

He added that if the Supreme Commander considered it "absolutely imperative" to send everything but one division lift to OVERLORD, "then it should be done that way." He warned, however, that before the decision was finally made, eight to nine divisions in the Mediterranean that could have been brought in through southern France would not be on hand to assist Eisenhower's main assault. Having dropped that shoe, he then asked, "Can you afford to lose this pressure, considering that we are almost certain to get an uprising in southern France to a far greater degree than in the north." [25]

Marshall remained reasonable about ANVIL in the event the Italian situation did not improve. If in early April the Allies were still unable to establish their lines north of Rome, "then ANVIL would of necessity be practically abandoned because we have a good and sufficient fight on our hands for a considerable number of troops and use of at least a divisional lift for end runs." However, if they were north of Rome by that time, they would not have a place for all the divisions available in the Mediterranean unless it appeared that an advance into the Po Valley was a profitable enterprise. He personally doubted that this latter alternative was feasible.

Finally Marshall appealed to Eisenhower to count up all the divisions that would be in the Mediterranean, including two newly arrived United States divisions. "Then consider the requirements in Italy in view of the mountain passes north of Rome and consider what influence on [your] problem a sizable number of divisions heavily equipped or advancing rapidly in southern France will have on OVERLORD."

As he often did in dealing with Eisenhower, Marshall promised his complete backing. But he ended with a hint that he thought the American commander was listening too sympathetically to British arguments. "I merely wish to be certain that localitis is not developing and that pressures on you have not warped your judgment." "Localitis" was a variant of "theateritis," which "Hap" Arnold defined as "a disease that theater commanders contracted, usually after they had been with their new commands for a short time." The symptoms, Arnold continued, were: "continued requests and demands for additional personnel and equipment of the latest type, regardless of the importance of the command in relation to others, regardless of the schedules worked out by the Joint or Combined Chiefs of Staff, regardless of production, and regardless of the effect upon other theaters. In addition, commanders with theateritis always suffered from the delusion that some mystic wave of the hand would bring about the impossible and secure thousands of airplanes overnight." [26]

To a degree there was an element of "theateritis" among Eisenhower's staff, and the form it took was a tendency to accept the British arguments that fitted into their particular problems. Marshall felt that he had detected it, first in Clark and Eaker in the Mediterranean, then in Bedell Smith in the United Kingdom, and now he saw signs that Eisenhower as well was succumbing.

If the Chief of Staff had hoped to get a reaction by using shock treatment, he was successful. Nettled that implied criticism had come from his strongest backer, General Eisenhower laid out a detailed defense of his views and actions in regard to OVERLORD and ANVIL. To remove any notion, hinted at earlier by Marshall, that he might be following the Montgomery line, he went back "a little bit into history" to "disabuse your mind about my own personal approach to this problem." When he had first seen the COSSAC plan, he had thought it was conceived on too narrow a front, and he had instructed Montgomery and Smith to go to London and press for increased lift for OVERLORD. "It was not," he argued, "until I had formed my own conclusions" and had submitted his views to the Combined Chiefs of Staff that he learned that the British Chiefs of Staff "more or less went along with my own views, except I believe that some of them have never attached the same importance to ANVIL as I have."

While at times he might have had to modify slightly his own concepts of strategy to achieve unity of purpose and effort, "I assure you that I have never yet failed to give you my own clear personal conviction about every project and plan in prospect." He did not think that anyone in London had urged him to present any particular project nor did he think he was afflicted particularly with "localitis." "I merely recognize that OVERLORD . . . represents for the United States and the United Kingdom a crisis in the European war. Real success should do much to hasten the end of this conflict but a reverse will have opposite repercussions from which we would recover with the utmost difficulty." [27]

Eisenhower had made a strong defense and Marshall accepted it. He left Eisenhower to do his best for ANVIL, while getting additional support for OVERLORD.

Long experience had taught Marshall that he could repose full confidence in Eisenhower; the same could never be said of Marshall's attitude toward his opposite number in London—Field Marshal Brooke. In these early months of 1944, with preinvasion problems becoming thornier and tempers shorter, Sir John Dill's liaison role in Washington became more crucial than ever. Always the honest broker, he tried unflaggingly to explain Brooke and Marshall to each other.

Dill earnestly tried to make clear to Brooke why the United States could not cast the Pacific aside. The recent successes in the Marshalls, he noted, had encouraged the Americans to take risks they would not have undertaken a month before. No one had anticipated, he wrote, that they could so flatten Japanese air forces in the Marshalls that the huge U.S. naval task forces could sail about almost unmolested. Brooke had also picked up gossip from the British liaison officer with the Southwest Pacific headquarters, who was back in London. He reported that Marshall and King were frightened of MacArthur's campaign for the presidency and that all military plans were overshadowed by political backgrounds. On this point Dill could not have given complete reassurance.

For his pains Dill veered perilously close in Churchill's eyes to the position Marshall had earlier obliquely charged Eisenhower with occupying —being overly sympathetic to his Allies' views. As a result, Marshall feared, Churchill was preparing to recall Dill to London. Convinced that this action would seriously damage Anglo-American relations at a crucial time of the war, he decided to build a backfire against it.

One day he went into the office of Harvey Bundy, Stimson's special assistant, and said: "I need help. I have word that Churchill is likely to throw out Sir John Dill and my relations with Dill are vital. I wish you would go up to Cambridge, to Harvard, and see if they can't give him a quick honorary degree." Bundy, a resident of Boston, spoke to Harvard authorities and was told that since the degree would require a special convocation it could not be done at the moment. When he reported this to Marshall, the General said, "Try Yale." As a Yale graduate, Bundy felt on somewhat stronger ground. Again he faced the problem of a special degree-awarding ceremony, but President Charles Seymour came up with an alternative solution. He had at his disposal the Charles P. Howland Prize for the individual who had contributed most to international relations. He agreed that the university would have an academic procession and a mace bearer and give the award ceremony full publicity. To make certain that the occasion received adequate press coverage, Marshall and Stimson and McCloy went along with Dill, Bundy, and Dill's aide, Major Reginald MacDonald-Buchanan. Seymour, Marshall, and Dill spoke and the affair, as Stimson put it, "made an awful splash" in the papers. Most uncharacteristically Marshall urged the photographers to take all the photographs they wanted. (He later apologized to Seymour for the exhibition.) The Yale prize was supplemented by degrees from William and Mary, Columbia, and other institutions.

Soon General Marshall jubilantly reported to Bundy that their efforts had succeeded. Through the underground he had learned that Churchill had said to a friend, "You know, Dill must be doing quite a job over there." So Dill remained.[28]

All Dill's tact was urgently needed as Washington and London neared a showdown on ANVIL. The old malady of split vision that had again and again plagued Anglo-American unity on plans for defeating the Axis had never been more troublesome as Churchill sought desperately to transmute the faltering Anzio campaign into an Allied victory, without undue concern that the stalemate there was delaying the essential shift of resources to ANVIL and OVERLORD. Indeed his energies were directed toward preventing the Americans from removing troops and ships that Alexander must have to win in Italy. All the Churchillian predilections for an overall strategy of bleeding Hitler's Reich to death by a lengthy nibbling at the fringes rather than risking dwindling British manpower in a now-or-never assault, apparently buried at Tehran, now were resuscitated. The Allied vision of strategy was virtually trifocal, for the Prime Minister frequently saw a campaign of his own—often as much to the dismay of Brooke and the other British Chiefs as to the Americans. His determination to edge past American watchfulness into the eastern Mediterranean, after Italy was secured, no longer counted heavily with Brooke. Once committed to OVERLORD the British General was determined it should succeed, but this, to London's thinking, did not necessarily require ANVIL.

So far as the British were concerned, General Hull informed his colleagues from London, "ANVIL might be an operation in the Marshalls." On February 19 General Eisenhower underlined this point by informing General Marshall that although he had just told the British Chiefs of Staff of his desire to keep a two-division ANVIL, he feared that developments in Italy would make this impossible.[29] Sympathetic to Eisenhower's problems, the Joint Chiefs of Staff decided to leave it up to him to reach a solution.

By this time Churchill had become sufficiently worried over the hotly contested questions of resources and priorities involved in OVERLORD/ANVIL to suggest another Combined Chiefs of Staff meeting—this time in London. General Marshall was not enthusiastic, and Admiral King was definitely opposed.[30] Marshall suggested that Eisenhower act as representative of the U.S. Chiefs in meetings with the British. The Americans sent along Admiral Cooke and General Hull to give technical advice. Field Marshal Brooke found in a long meeting between the British Chiefs of Staff and Eisenhower and Smith on the tenth that their views on cross-Channel requirements coincided with his, and he now felt that "all seems to be going well." [31]

In authorizing Eisenhower to act as their representative, the U.S. Joint Chiefs directed him to get an agreement or a carefully stated disagreement on future policy "and the Joint Chiefs of Staff will support your decision subject of course to approval of the President." The Joint Chiefs added that he was to continue planning for ANVIL, but if the campaign in Italy had not developed favorably by April, they would review the plan.[32]

The probability of the landings in southern France was now seriously compromised. On February 19 Eisenhower had written Marshall that ANVIL's chances were slim. A week later the Supreme Commander considered informing him that the operation was impossible, but he was deterred by Smith, who "feared it would give the impression of changing our minds too quickly." By March 9 Eisenhower felt he could wait no longer about telling Washington the bad news. He radioed Marshall that in its planning for OVERLORD, Supreme Headquarters had gone short fifteen LSTs to keep ANVIL alive. Now it believed it to be the "gravest possible mistake to allow demands for ANVIL to militate against the main effort even in the matter of time and certainty of planning." [33]

Brooke had foreseen the likelihood of winning his fight as soon as Eisenhower was appointed to represent the American Chiefs of Staff. Even before that directive had been issued, the British Chief congratulated himself on taking the Supreme Commander's measure. "I had a little difficulty with Eisenhower," he wrote on February 19, "but not much, to make him see sense, as all he required was a little pressure to go back to the plans he really liked best now that he had at least shown some attempt to support Marshall's idea. I think that matter is now all right."

The final concession had not yet been made. Eisenhower was back on February 22 to reargue the American case for ANVIL. Brooke grumbled that it was clear that Marshall did not "begin to understand" the Italian campaign and that while the Supreme Commander saw it a little more clearly, "he is too frightened of disagreeing with Marshall to be able to express his views freely." On reflection Brooke wrote next day, "We have got all we want but must word the wire to let the Americans 'save face' as much as possible. . . ." Brooke's biographer, Arthur Bryant, later spelled it out: By appointing Eisenhower as their representative, the Americans had enabled the British to resolve the deadlock. "Now, pressed by Montgomery and the British Prime Minister and the Chiefs of Staff, Eisenhower promised to recommend to Washington that the Italian campaign should for the present take precedence over all other Mediterranean operations, including ANVIL." [34]

Aware that Marshall viewed British efforts to push Italian operations as a deliberate blow at OVERLORD as well as ANVIL, Churchill hurriedly sent reassurances on March 11. He wrote Marshall that he was satisfied that everything was going well with the cross-Channel operation. Further, he was becoming a firm supporter. Using an expression that he was to employ more than once thereafter to American skeptics, he declared: "I am hardening very much on this operation as the time approaches, *in the sense of wishing to strike if humanly possible, even if the limiting conditions we laid down at Moscow are not exactly fulfilled.* I hope a chance may come for us to have a talk before long. Every good wish." [35]

Marshall recognized that kind words for OVERLORD meant almost certain death for ANVIL. He made one last effort to ensure that Eisenhower knew what he was doing if he consented to that decision. Brooke had deplored Marshall's lack of understanding of the Mediterranean situation and criticized his obstinacy. But the Chief of Staff's reply to Eisenhower in mid-March belied these interpretations. In a carefully reasoned statement he pointed out that if the Germans realized that there would be no attack in the Mediterranean, they would send reserves from southern France and elsewhere against an assault in northern France. "We know . . . the Germans are fearful of a landing in the North Adriatic or on the coast of southern France. However, if they once become aware of the fact that the facilities for such a landing are not available they could rearrange their forces to your great disadvantage."

So far as the Italian campaign was concerned, the Chief of Staff favored linking up the Anzio beachhead with the main front in Italy. But he wanted no major effort beyond that. "Under present conditions," he wrote, "I see no great purpose to be achieved in Italy aside from maintaining pressure on the enemy to prevent the transfer of his forces to your front."

Forthrightly recognizing that the basis for a final decision on ANVIL, seemed no more favorable than a month earlier, he conceded that "The only clearcut decision would be to cancel the ANVIL operation." In a broad gesture of trust and deep consideration Marshall concluded: "It is my intention with which Arnold agrees that we will support your desire regarding the ANVIL decision, whatever it may be. So the foregoing statement of my views is not to be accepted by you as a pressure from me to have matters arranged other than the way you would wish to see them set up." [36]

But his paternalism did not condone localitis. Marshall was not willing to give the British a bonus in landing craft for scratching ANVIL. He wrote Eisenhower: "We will not make this diversion which means a serious delay in the Pacific with the possibility of losing our momentum unless some sizeable operation of the nature of ANVIL is on the books." [37]

To Brooke the demands for firm commitments were maddening. "History" he wrote a short time later, "will never forgive them for bargaining equipment against strategy and for trying to blackmail us into agreeing with them by holding a pistol of withdrawing craft at our heads. . . ." [38]

The astute Dill agreed with Marshall on the danger of relieving the Germans of a real threat in the south of France. He informed the War Cabinet at the end of March: "It is a regrettable fact that Americans are not prepared to weaken their effort in the Pacific unless their proposal regarding Mediterranean strategy is broadly accepted." He explained carefully, as he had for Brooke in times past, what was needed: "It seems to us that the most important thing now is to get an agreed directive. . . . In preparing this directive we strongly recommend that it should order [the Mediterranean commander] to undertake operation ANVIL on 10th July and that preparations and plans should be pressed vigorously with this in view." [39]

Dill's knowing touch was present in the reminder to the British Chiefs of Staff on April 1: "U.S. Chiefs of Staff made the offer [of additional landing craft for ANVIL] . . . with a feeling of broadminded generosity and were shocked and pained to find how little we appreciated their magnanimity and how gaily we proposed to accept their legacy while disregarding the terms of the will."

In an effort to make Brooke see the problems faced by Marshall and

King, Dill added: "It is difficult to realise how hardly anything can be taken from the Pacific in view of the fact that the U.S. Chiefs of Staff are constantly being abused for neglecting [this] theatre." [40]

Marshall's Chief of War Plans, General Handy, also saw to it that General Eisenhower was reminded of his Chief's determined views. He radioed on March 1:

> . . . we cannot accept a diversion of landing craft from Pacific operations unless it is the firm intention of the Combined Chiefs of Staff now to mount ANVIL on a 2-division basis, target date, 10 July, in time to support OVERLORD. We state . . . such a decision must be taken to launch ANVIL on a specific date. Such a decision and preparations for the operation in no way preclude changing our plans should an undeniably better course of action be indicated by changing circumstances. In our opinion, the proposal of the British Chiefs of Staff that we postpone the issuance of a directive to General Wilson to proceed all-out along the line of a specific course of action amounts to admitting that the decision as to what happens next in the Mediterranean will continue to rest with the Germans.[41]

Continued acrimony over ANVIL suggested that another Allied meeting was needed to clear the air. Still opposed to Churchill's earlier suggestion for a formal conference, Roosevelt agreed with Stimson in March that General Marshall should go to London and seek a reversal on ANVIL. Stimson discussed the proposal with former Senator and Supreme Court Justice James Byrnes, now head of the Office of War Mobilization, who agreed that Marshall's mission would be the best substitute for a conference. "He dilated upon the confidence which the people of the country have in Marshall," Stimson recorded, "and thought it would have a very reassuring effect if it was known that he had done this before the invasion finally took off." [42]

Before they could set out, Eisenhower made an ardent appeal to the Chief of Staff: "I assumed . . . we could count upon the additional lift of 26 LSTs and 40 LCI (L)s becoming available in the Mediterranean. [I understand that] the views of [British and U.S. Chiefs] were so divergent that the U.S. Chiefs have decided to send this equipment on to the Pacific. I earnestly hope that this decision is not irrevocable and that . . . the British Chiefs of Staff may find it possible to accept the American viewpoint." Hoping somehow to lay his hands on these craft, he asked, "What would you think of committing the ANVIL assault to the French divisions still in Africa," with ground forces commanded by a good French general, under Wilson's supervision? [43]

Churchill also tried his hand with Marshall. It was painful to forgo the additional landing craft, but what he could not bear was "to agree beforehand to starve a battle [in Italy] or have to break it off just as the moment when success, after long efforts and heavy losses, may be in view." The point was well stated, but he knew that Marshall and King, having seen him torpedo an operation that they had thought certain, were wary.

He was never one to dodge an issue. "Dill tells me that you had expected me to support 'Anvil' more rigorously in view of my enthusiasm for it when it was first proposed by you at Teheran. Please do me the justice to remember that the situation is vastly changed." In November the Allies had expected to take Rome in January. Instead, despite their efforts on the main front and the Anzio operation, "we are stuck where we are, and the enemy has brought down to the battle south of Rome the eight mobile divisions we should have hoped a full-scale 'Anvil' would have contained."

But Churchill's arguments did not shake the American conviction that his enthusiasm for ANVIL at Tehran had been only for the additional landing craft and men that would be sent to the Mediterranean—resources that could later be shifted to Italy as well as to the landings in southern France. As if sensing that he had not sold his point, Churchill railed at the peculiarities of modern warfare rather than at the Americans. The whole problem, he concluded, arose out of the absurd shortage of LSTs.[44]

With D day rushing fast upon him, Eisenhower grew increasingly impatient with the War Department. He had a habit of telling his troubles to his naval aide at times when his worries mounted—a practice he regretted when the aide published many of the conversations. He told Butcher that he believed if he could talk with Harry Hopkins (a vain thought because Hopkins had become ill on New Year's Day and was out of action for seven months), he could get word back to the President that action must be kept going in the Mediterranean while OVERLORD was still in progress. He was also unhappy with the British because they would not make a deal with Marshall and his colleagues "on the Italian situation." He felt that he was caught between the two forces. Each side, he declared, thought he was for the other. Butcher reminded his boss that in a presidential year Roosevelt could not neglect the Pacific. Eisenhower, intent on his own campaign, retorted perhaps unrealistically that if OVERLORD failed, the President could not win. He added that he put no stock in glib phrases about the Pacific, such as the need "to keep operations going so as not to lose the weight of the momentum"—a suggestion Marshall had included in one of his recent messages.[45]

In a fretful mood, he wished he could fly home for a talk with Marshall and Roosevelt and was moved to grumble that if the Chief of Staff had not insisted that he go to Washington in January, he could go back now. Eisenhower's dark musings, which led him to ungenerous remarks about King that he did not publicly reveal, actually reflected Brooke's arguments for the British case.

Marshall had no inkling of these despairing comments, except as their spirit tinted some of the Supreme Commander's communications, but he was aware that Eisenhower shared the British desire for more landing craft. As if answering the doubts in the Supreme Commander's mind, he reported on March 25: "We proposed [yesterday] that once the beach-head and Fifth Army front have joined, the major concern in the Mediterranean is to prepare for a later ANVIL 10 July . . . and that Rome would not be considered a primary effort to the disadvantage of the proposed ANVIL. Dill indicated the British would view with concern because of the political importance of Rome." [46]

Rome—the latest source of Anglo-American disagreement—had vivid memories for Marshall. He had learned its historical importance first as a wide-eyed tourist—wandering through the ruins of the city and visiting the private dining room of Victor Emmanuel in 1910—then sitting in the same room as Pershing's aide at a state dinner in 1919. And he must have been stirred somewhat by the romantic appeal of raising the American flag in the Eternal City, but now he had had his fill of prestige items, and he was convinced that the prize was not enough. The United States would not divert resources from the Pacific unless something on the order of ANVIL was planned in the Mediterranean.

Marshall made his point. In the end both sides made concessions. Churchill, still anti-ANVIL, in mid-April revived an earlier proposal for a possible landing at Bordeaux. Near the end of the month the British Chiefs of Staff informed their American colleagues that they favored some form of operation in France to be launched three weeks or so after OVERLORD. Admiral King—often accused by the British of noncooperation—declared on April 28 that if the British would make a definite recommendation for an assault in southern *or* western France, he was prepared to send the shipping that he and Marshall had offered earlier for ANVIL. Still reluctant to bind themselves too rigidly, the British in early May suggested four alternative landings within the Mediterranean: one near Sète, west of Marseille, another near Toulon, another in the Gulf of Genoa, and still another north of Rome. On May 8, in another concession, the U.S. Chiefs of Staff accepted the proposals as satisfactory and said they would start sending additional LSTs in successive waves, the first group to arrive by June 20 and the last a month later.[47]

There was much to be said in favor of the flexibility of planning demanded by the British. But the Americans had seen too much of it. They feared it might mean sweeping additional resources into the Italian campaign in the summer. Even though they had to pin the British down on this, they felt that they had made some of their arguments stick.

Rome's status became academic before the Normandy landings. Despite preparations for OVERLORD and the shifting of landing craft and men northward, there were still resources—as Marshall had maintained—for the immediate tasks at hand. As the debate over ANVIL progressed, Allied bombers were striking heavily at German communications. Allied forces under Alexander and Clark regrouped; by May they had more than twenty-eight divisions to oppose twenty-three of the Germans.

On the evening of May 11 Alexander struck to the north and west between Cassino and the sea. His Polish and British troops moved around Cassino, and the town and monastery were cleared by May 18. To the south British, Canadian, French, and American troops pushed forward.

In the Anzio beachhead General Truscott began his move on May 23. Two days later his forces took his first main objective, Cisterna, and troops of his command also made contact with elements of the II U.S. Corps which had advanced from the southeast. Truscott now drove toward the Alban Hills in the face of heavy German fighting. Not until June 2 and 3 was resistance broken. American and British troops then raced toward Rome, which U.S. forces entered on the fourth.

The cost had not been light, and in the last days of heavy fighting General and Mrs. Marshall sustained their most tragic personal loss of the war. On May 29, as Lieutenant Allen Brown led his tank unit near Velletri, south of the Alban Hills, he stood up in the turret of his tank to observe the front through his field glasses. A German sniper fired and Allen died instantly.[48]

It was a blow no less bitter for Marshall than for Allen's mother. At the time of the General's second marriage Allen had been young enough to fill the place of a son. Often Allen wrote his stepfather to confide his problems and his successes, and the General responded frequently and warmly, however pressing his official duties were.

At Allen's request the General had hastened his transfer to North Africa the previous August. At first the young officer's luck had held. In the fall he was shifted with his unit, the 1st Armored Division, to Italy. Early in 1944 Allen complained of having little to do in his outfit and mentioned difficulties with his back. He was soon reporting that the physical problem had diminished and that he was in better shape than most men in his outfit. In February his comments on bad weather stirred the General to recall "that always appears to be the case in war, at least it was my experience in France; cold or rain and mud, high winds, or extreme heat and dust. We can but pray that this war will soon be over." Mrs. Marshall, he noted, was following the news of the Italian campaign on the radio. "She doesn't talk about it much but it is constantly on her mind." [49]

The severities of winter fighting—of which Italy had more than its share—were still in the General's thoughts a few days later as he wrote Allen of a dinner that he expected to attend that evening: "I wish you could join us and spread yourself in the warmth of a heated room and with the bountiful food I assume will be at hand. You could do much better by it than I shall be able to do, and with better results, too." Still there were consolations: "You are young. I had rather be young and in the mud than at my age and in an office chair, though it seems to me I spend a great deal of time in the air not to mention slogging over considerable muddy terrain. All good luck to you and may the good Lord watch over you." [50]

During the fighting around Cassino, Allen, then in a tank-maintenance assignment, was attached to a New Zealand armored regiment. He wrote his wife, Madge, that he was happy as he had been "slowly going crazy from inactivity." He was pleased to be with the New Zealanders although "I personally don't give a damn who I fight with, just so I can be part of the 'show' as these 'blokes' call it." [51]

The letter that followed disclosed that he was getting almost more activity than he had bargained for. Allen was sitting by a window in a peasant's house that he shared with eight other men, writing his wife, when German artillery shelled the house, killing two men and wounding three others. There was no time to get into a slit trench outside, so he stayed put until the firing was over and then finished his letter. "Don't let anybody ever tell you that they don't get scared under an artillery barrage," he wrote, "because believe me it scares the hell out of you. You get a split second's warning from the whistle of the shell and then she hits." [52]

The weather improved on March 7. "Today is a beautiful day," Allen wrote his wife. "It is warm out and the feel of spring is in the air. It is hard to believe that men are killing and being killed all around us. The noise of the artillery is a reminder, however, and no matter how beautiful it is, it is bound to be a sad day for many people as is every day of this war. . . ." [53]

Improved weather brought increased enemy air and artillery activity. In mid-March, Allen had a close call while on a reconnaissance mission with two companions. "We had finished and had almost gotten back to our jeep when a heavy artillery shell hit about twenty feet to my right. They were both on my left, and dove to the ground, but the blast of the shell just blew me over on my side like a pin in a bowling alley. . . . The effective range of a shell burst that size is fifty yards, so you can see how lucky we were. . . . Shell fragments have been known to cause casualties at a distance of a 200 yds., but ordinarily you are safe at 50 yds. if you hit the ground quick enough and darling am I quick. . . ."

A day later his group was not so fortunate. "I'm very tired and a little bit jangled this morning. We all had a tough night's work last night. Right in the middle of the fight for nine hours completely exposed to constant artillery, heavy mortar and sniper fire. We went out at 6 P.M. and did not get back until 3 A.M. Jeff Wiles, the New Zealand captain that I had been working with . . . was wounded around 2 A.M. We had been side by side all night, and although stuff had been dropping around us the whole time, neither one of us had gotten nicked. Just before 2 A.M. I pulled away, and he was to follow me shortly afterwards. I heard the shell coming which got him and one [of] his men plus nine Maori infantrymen. Fortunately, he was not badly injured, and should be out of the hospital in a month." [54]

Shelling continued for three more days, and one shell passed through the top of the house in which Allen was sleeping. But the fight was nearing its end. On March 22 he was able to report: "My men and I were relieved today after 28 days on the front." All his small group had come out safely and were soon back at the rear where shells no longer fell "in and around us." Two days later he visited his brother, Clifton, stationed nearby, and saw some friends at the base hospital.[55]

General Marshall found time for a note to his stepson every few days. When he learned where Allen was located, he searched for "some very interesting air photographs of the Cassino region and the connecting valleys up to the beachhead." He wrote him that he saw that it was difficult country and the type "where the defender always digs in." He hoped that there would be good weather in Italy soon to put an end to the mud and the poor flying conditions. Speaking of the weather in Washington, he wrote: "First signs of green are showing on some of the willow trees along the river and I think two or three warm days will bring everything out." He spoke of Poughkeepsie, where Allen had his home, and added, "I can imagine your longing to get back to those surroundings, not to mention the family." [56]

In April, Allen said that he had heard of the organization of a Army Combat Reporter Corps and wondered, in light of his newspaper experience, about the possibility of getting into it. Before Marshall could reply, the stepson wrote that he was inclined to think that the outfit did not exist and would forget about it. He had recently been shifted from maintenance officer to command of a platoon, "which I must admit is what I wanted." "We have moved again," he added, "but just where we are finally headed for nobody knows. One thing I feel certain about is that we will be going into action somewhere before long. If I have half the luck I had with the New Zealanders I will consider myself a very lucky guy. I don't know who was taking care of me up there, but whoever it was, I hope they are along the next time." [57]

Mrs. Marshall was still following news of the campaign carefully, and she had recently sent packages to Allen and Clifton by General Clark, who had visited Washington that spring. Marshall wrote Allen: "Your mother seems to take the situation with considerable calm, though I imagine it is largely a matter of repressing feelings. In any event she never refers to it." He encouraged him with the news of how the Allies were closing in on the Axis. "Altogether, however hard it is in any particular spot our enemies are in a dreadful dilemma." [58]

In mid-May, Mrs. Marshall was relieved to learn that Allen was no longer in the Cassino area. She knew that he had gone to the Anzio beachhead and apparently assumed that it was safer. The General decided not to enlighten her.[59] On May 29, the day before Memorial Day, she received letters from both Allen and Clifton saying that they had spent three wonderful days together just before Allen left for the beachhead.

In some of the most touching lines of her book, *Together,* Mrs. Marshall recalled that "Clifton said, 'The war looks good from here, both in Germany and Japan.' Allen wrote, 'I feel sorry for any German in Italy. The horseshoe has held my luck. I shall take it down this Christmas and keep it for the rest of my life.' George smiled at his 'this Christmas. . . .' " [60]

The General knew how much strain and death yet remained before the weary troops could return home. He went to the Capitol at 10:30 A.M. for a meeting with congressmen and then left shortly afterward with Admiral King for a Governors' Conference near Hershey, Pennsylvania.

As he left for the Pentagon the following morning, the General was pleased to see Mrs. Marshall still bubbling with happiness from the letters from her sons. His WAC chauffeur, Marjorie Payne, drove him to the Pentagon and then took her usual station in an outer room near the office, waiting until she was sure he was well settled before going for morning coffee. As she tarried, chatting with secretary Cora Thomas, the door opened suddenly and the General strode out. Something in his face alerted Miss Thomas, who had worked for him since his first days as Chief of Staff, and she said to Sergeant Payne, "You had better run. Something is up." [61]

A few minutes later, as Mrs. Marshall stood at the window in her room at Quarters One, she turned to see the General in the doorway. "He came in, closing the door behind him, and told me Allen was dead," she recalled. "He had given his life . . . in a tank battle on the road to Rome." [62]

☆

☆ XVIII ☆

☆   ☆

"Man of the Year"

T H E face on *Time*'s cover on January 3, 1944, as "Man of the Year" was that of George Catlett Marshall. The magazine, later severely critical of Marshall, said of him then: "The link between the biggest military establishment in U.S. history and the U.S. people, George C. Marshall was at year's end the closest thing to 'the indispensable man.' " "Never in U.S. history," it declared, "has a military man enjoyed such respect on Capitol Hill." One reason lay in the fact that he was completely free of political ambitions; the Congress knew that "this man is a trustee for the nation." [1]

"He had armed the Republic," *Time* continued. "In a general's uniform, he stood for the civilian substance of this democratic society. *Civis Americanus*, he had gained the world's undivided respect. In the name of the soldiers who had died, General George Catlett Marshall was entitled to accept his own nation's gratitude."

Among many complimentary letters he received was one from Douglas Freeman. The noted Virginia biographer and editor was delighted. Further he enclosed an editorial he had written on *Time*'s selection of him as "Man of the Year": "Had there been any other choice, informed Americans would have dissented. His friends always hesitate to express their true opinion of him, lest they embarrass him; but when they ask themselves what are his noblest qualities, [they] turn almost instinctively to [Jefferson's] characterization of George Washington. . . . Said Jefferson of the commander of the Revolution: '. . . as far as he saw, no judgment was ever sounder. . . . His integrity was most pure, his justice the most inflexible I have ever known, no motives of interest or consanguinity, of friendship or hatred being able to bias his decisions.' That is George Marshall—that and much besides." [2]

Shortly before, on December 22, Marshall had returned from a 35,000-mile trip around the world—journeying home from Cairo via the Pacific.

348

He talked with Stimson of the background of Eisenhower's selection as Supreme Commander, confirming the account the President had given the Secretary of War, and Stimson reported that he "showed his usual bigness about the whole darn thing." [3]

On the thirty-first Stimson gave his usual year-end birthday party for the Chief of Staff. Marshall, he said, was in a position to gain the unique distinction of being the only American leader of the United States to lead its armies through an entire war. In the pleasantries that followed Marshall called General Somervell into the center of the circle of friends and suddenly struck up "Now We're Working on the Railroad." [4] Marshall's jocularity, startling in itself, had a greater impact because of the events of the day.

That morning Marshall had risked his standing with Congress and the American people by delivering in an off-the-record press conference a withering blast at those workers he charged with playing into the hands of German propagandists by threatening to call crippling nation-wide strikes. In this step, as in others connected with manpower, production, propaganda, in which he was to be engaged for the next six months before D day, he used all the prestige that he had gained as Chief of Staff to see that every resource possible to aid Eisenhower was made available.

Stimson informed Marshall on his return from the Pacific that the President had told him that morning that the Railway Brotherhoods would probably strike on December 30 and that he wanted the Army to take over the railroads if no agreement was reached by that evening. Roosevelt was also ready to propose enactment of a National Service Bill dealing with civilian manpower, which Stimson had been advocating since 1942. On the twenty-seventh the President gave the War Department authority to take over the railroads, authority delegated by Stimson to Somervell and Major General Charles P. Gross, Chief of Transportation. The threat of action sufficed. On the twenty-ninth three of the brotherhoods indicated they would call off the strike. On the thirty-first the strike had been temporarily averted, but some noncooperating unions were still making trouble, and Stimson believed that they had only postponed a showdown. [5]

To Marshall, forty years a soldier, just back from American fighting fronts in the Mediterranean and in the Pacific, such a situation was monstrous. As Stimson confided his fears of future trouble, Marshall exploded at the thought of the lift in spirit the strike and government takeover would give the Germans. Heatedly he said he thought it would protract the war by six months, "and it came out for the first time," wrote Stimson, that he had hoped Germany might collapse in the spring "largely through our propaganda in the Balkans and the satellite Axis countries." Now he thought the chance "gone with the wind" as Goebbels pictured the United States on the brink of chaos. His emotions at a high pitch, the

Chief of Staff was quoting an oversanguine Intelligence report as well as an overimaginative statement of the possible effects of strike news on German resistance.

Normally Marshall was cautious to the point of invisibility about taking sides in labor disputes. Not many months before he had even declined to sign a statement congratulating business and labor on their cooperation, since he felt that it was not proper for the military to be drawn into such areas. Now he was very angry, and Stimson arranged for him to explode to James F. Byrnes, head of the Office of War Mobilization. Byrnes brought in a group of "trustworthy newsmen" to whom Marshall delivered his furious blast.[6]

Marshall's rage had only two temperatures—freezing or blazing. On this occasion it was the latter. "He banged his white-knuckled fist on the desk, and although not a blasphemous man, he swore bitterly," *Time* reported with some awe. He repeated the burden of his earlier remarks to Stimson. To bring German collapse more quickly, it was essential to lead the Nazi satellites to defect. That day would be hastened when they ceased to fear or to trust German might. Any suggestion that there was division in the United States would encourage them to remain in the enemy camp. The resultant prolongation of the war might cost the invading Allies hundreds of thousands of lives.

His remarks were promptly reprinted throughout the country, although attributed initially to "a personage high in the councils of the U.S. and the U.N." Shortly afterward the St. Petersburg, Florida, *Times* revealed that General Marshall was the speaker. Labor spokesmen at once hit back. President William Green of the American Federation of Labor challenged the General or anyone else to prove that labor's ranks had aided the enemy's propaganda effort.[7]

Most of the nation's press reacted favorably to Marshall. The Atlanta *Constitution* said that if the statement was by the Chief of Staff, as generally believed, it gained added force "because there is no man in America, not excepting President Roosevelt, who is better informed as to conditions inside Nazi Europe, as to the whole military strategy, than General Marshall." The *Christian Science Monitor* observed that, after all the critics had had their say, "the statement remains like a mountain when the storm passes. The fact is that labor disputes, whatever the provocation, do weaken the war effort." The Communist *Daily Worker,* which once would have been inclined to defend labor, obviously measured the effect on the Soviet Union. After arguing, with some effect, that Marshall had not attacked labor but merely had pointed to the results of strike threats, it added that he had spoken as a soldier "who had just returned from the battlefronts, charged with the task of rallying everything to make good that scheduled 1944 knockout." [8]

Unexpected and far more frightening to the Chief of Staff than anything opponents might say were the reactions of some of his friends.

Colonel "Eddie" Rickenbacker had announced that Marshall was the kind of man who should be President of the United States. "That's about all that's needed to start one of those 'Marshall for President' movements," declared the Memphis *Commercial Appeal*. Already wary of another general-for-president movement that was gaining some backing at the time, Marshall was aghast at this proposal.[9]

The striking laborers exhausted Marshall's patience because he saw with dismay that at all levels Americans were slipping into the comfortable belief that the war was nearing an end and that there could be a shift to business as usual. As a result he faced the problem of getting sufficient infantrymen and keeping armament plants in full production. He was in fact lashing out at the danger of America's letting down too soon at a crucial point in the war. Walter Lippmann in his column, "A Standard of Morality," echoed Marshall's deepening uneasiness: "Let no man think that the war can be so divorced from domestic issues that we can ask men to face death in battle and on the home front can have politics-as-usual, special-interests-as-usual."

Marshall amplified the same points in a short but intense plea that he made at an American Legion dinner at the Mayflower Hotel in Washington on February 3. After outlining recent gains in the Marianas, the success of bombing raids against Germany, and the build-up in the European Theater, he declared: "the Allied avalanche is at last in motion and it will gather headway in each succeeding month. . . . What is now required is the ardent support of our forces by the people at home."

He continued: "I speak with an emphasis that I believe is pardonable in one who has a terrible responsibility for the lives of many men, because I feel that here at home we are not yet facing the realities of war, the savage, desperate conditions of the battle fronts. Vehement protests I am receiving against our use of flame throwers do not indicate an understanding of the meaning of our dead on the beaches at Tarawa. Objections to this or that restriction are inconsistent with the devoted sacrifices of our troops."

In conclusion he turned to the point he had made in his statement on strikes: "Our soldiers must be keenly conscious that the full strength of the nation is behind them; they must not go into battle puzzled or embittered over disputes at home which adversely affect the war effort. Our small sacrifices should be personal even more than financial. They should be proof positive that we never forget for a moment that the soldier has been compelled to leave his family, to give up his business, and to hazard his life in our service." [10]

Marshall's earlier outburst reflected not only his anger at public failure to support the war effort, but his weariness after the long discussions at Cairo and Tehran and the journey back around the world. On January 7 he and Mrs. Marshall slipped out of Washington for a brief trip to Miami. The Army had taken over a number of hotels there for training purposes, and he was able to get a rest in a warm climate, far from the constant clamor for his ear or his counsel, and at the same time keep up with his mail, which was brought to him by courier every day. He returned to Washington on the sixteenth, before the President had known that he had gone, prepared for a heavy schedule of conferences and for a number of speeches that he had agreed to make in the spring.

Ten days later, in a birthday greeting to the President, he showed that his vacation had helped restore his optimism and confidence. A year earlier, he recalled:

> . . . we were treasuring our great hopes as a result of the recent Casablanca conference. It seems to me much more was realized than we anticipated then, and I have the feeling that the Lord will bless our efforts in the coming months, again beyond our expectations.
>
> I anticipate some very hard knocks but I think these will not be fatal to our hopes, rather the inevitable stumbles on a most difficult course.
>
> I wish to thank you for the strong support you have given me personally and to the entire Army in the past twelve months.[11]

Before the June 6 invasion and the heavy burdens he correctly foresaw would follow, Marshall seized every possible opportunity to catch a day or two of relaxation. Like the President, he was never off duty. The daily pouch of mail nearly always found him. Occasionally, however, he could hide away for an entire weekend. One favored retreat was Bernard Baruch's estate near Georgetown, South Carolina. There on the last Saturday and Sunday in February he escaped from the telephone. The trip was short but the hunting was good. "In two hours got 11 quail," he wrote Bedell Smith.[12] A month later he hitched a ride with "Hap" Arnold to Bermuda, taking along Field Marshal Dill, who was beginning to suffer from a bad hernia he had acquired early in 1943 while pigsticking in India. Dill and Marshall, who were guests of the Governor-General and his wife, Lord and Lady Burghley, leisurely inspected the military installations on the island, rested, and relaxed. From the weekend visit Marshall developed a pleasant relationship with his host and hostess, particularly with Lady Mary, which Mrs. Marshall was to share. He searched for a suitable gift to send and found it in a recording of *Oklahoma!*, whose "Surrey with a Fringe on Top" reminded him of Bermuda's carriages. Remembering the three children in the family and their ills, he also sent along a new serum for whooping cough recommended by his doctor.[13]

At times Marshall varied the capital routine by inspecting the troops. It was always a tonic for him, as he watched men being trained, to be reassured that the Army and Air Forces on which he had labored so long were at last measuring up to the standards he had established many months before.

One inspection trip took him to the South and Southwest in early March. The plans made by McCarthy and Pasco for this trip were typical of those for his tours of this period. The two officers sent detailed instructions to various base and division commanders, outlining specifically the things the General wanted to see and the way in which he wanted his trip handled.

He stopped first at Eglin Field, Florida, arranging ahead of time to have lunch on his plane and then to proceed at once on arrival to see demonstrations of new developments. Less than five hours after he had landed, he was off to Camp Shelby, Mississippi, where Major General Charles L. Bolté of the 69th Division and Major General S. E. Reinhart of the 65th Division were to meet him. The instructions sent by Pasco to Bolté vividly illustrate his method of operating:

> To be met by the two division commanders and no one else. . . . Visit is not to be advertised. No repeat no objection to photographs provided they are taken by Army personnel and also provided there will be absolutely no posing requested. . . .
>
> The visitor would like to have a simple dinner Saturday night . . . with the senior officers, generals and full colonels of the two divisions and to include the post commander. . . .
>
> Sunday he wishes to have breakfast at 7:15 am in his quarters, if convenient, and wishes to leave . . . at 8:00 to see a battery of 105's and a battery of 155's from each of the divisions do some firing. He wishes to have a rifle company from each division on a target range where he can call for such firing and grenade throwing as he may wish to have carried out. He will wish to see a section of engineers from each division plant and remove mines.[14]

After this he wanted to talk with the troops. He directed that some 600 men—junior officers and noncommissioned officers of the two divisions— be present for the talk. He spelled out that by junior officers he meant lieutenants and captains, although an occasional young major might be included. The ban on the usual crowding in of older officers who wished to talk to the Chief of Staff extended to nearby higher echelons: "It is expected that no officer from the Second Army Headquarters or the Ninth Corps will come to Shelby during this visit."

Marshall's stay would remain simple. "The visitor directs that there will be no guard of honor or ceremony of any kind at the air field or at the post. No escort is desired except when absolutely necessary to expedite travel through congested areas. . . . No *repeat* no aides or orderlies of any kind." [15]

As he proceeded to the Louisiana maneuver areas, he added the instruction that while he would like to see the senior sergeants or first sergeants of a number of companies, he did not "wish to hold them in over this Sunday for the purpose of his visit." In a statement that would have won the approval of the troops, he directed: "Cancel no leaves because of this visit except in the cases of senior commanders." [16]

From the maneuver areas Marshall flew to San Antonio to visit Randolph Field, where he had dinner with a number of retired officers who, he said, felt "left out of the war." From San Antonio, he went to Camp

Hood, Texas; Fort Sill, Oklahoma; and Fort Campbell, Kentucky, returning to Washington and work and worry on the evening of March 8. Although the long and crowded trip was physically tiring, it refreshed and calmed his mind for the increasingly demanding burdens of his office. He needed all his strength to deal with the problems that now crowded in on him as the invasion approached.

An especially acute problem was the pressure on the ground forces created by the national manpower shortage. After prolonged debate through much of 1943, with the Army finally paring down its demands by a half-million men, the Joint Chiefs of Staff won presidential approval for an overall armed-forces total of 11,264,000, to be reached at the end of 1944. Of this number the Army and Army Air Forces were allotted 7,700,000. The number of divisions was set at 90.[17]

Presidential authorization of increased armed-forces strength did not mean that more combat ground forces would be available during the coming year. Marshall and Stimson were still faced with the problem of getting these additional men from Selective Service or from those already inducted. The situation was especially serious because of the workings of the replacement system. General Marshall had decided early in the war that it was better to keep divisions with experienced staffs in battle and to fill vacancies from replacement pools as deaths, wounds, illness, rotation, created gaps in existing units. Finding these replacements in the spring of 1944 constituted his chief concern. At the beginning of the year General McNair had warned him that one or more divisions in the United States might have to be "cannibalized" to provide replacements for units in action. Although Marshall told McNair angrily that he was "damned tired" of these recurrent manpower crises, he heard the bitter truth in mid-January that Eisenhower's theater in the next two months would require 50,000 more infantry and artillery personnel than could be provided by the replacement-training centers to which draftees were sent.[18]

In late January, General Marshall took the problem to the War Manpower Commission chairman, Paul McNutt. The infantry and armored divisions were now short nearly 100,000 men, and it was almost impossible to keep the units at the battle fronts, constantly suffering casualties, at full strength. Replacements were also required for soldiers and airmen in the Pacific who had been stationed there for one and a half or two years, malaria-ridden and dulled by the monotony of jungle life.

The Army's problems had been intensified in recent months because the Navy, Marines, and Air Forces, formerly able to fill their quotas with volunteers, were now competing with the Army for draftees. Further the shifting nature of the fighting overseas had led to shortages in certain types of combat units. When Marshall began planning for cross-Channel operations in 1943, he had asked for the formation of additional infantry units. Then when the massive assault was postponed, the immediate need was for service forces to aid in the build-up of supplies and equipment in the United Kingdom. As a result the supply units drained off many able-bodied men. When Operation OVERLORD was scheduled for late May 1944, the Chief of Staff had many men assigned to units that could not be readily used in combat. Either he had to tear up these units, reassigning and retraining personnel, or he had to find men with basic infantry training who could be easily placed in replacement pools for shipment to divisions abroad.

By the spring of 1944 Marshall recognized that even if he could get more draftees, he was unlikely to meet the infantry's needs for the coming summer and fall from Selective Service alone. The additional men had to be found within existing units in the Army.

Although the process would be wasteful and basically unfair to men who had trained for their current duties, he had no alternative except to close out certain units, such as coast artillery and antiaircraft, that had been organized earlier in the war when it was assumed that the United States would engage mainly in defensive efforts. Tank-destroyer units, once very much in vogue, had proved to be less necessary than originally supposed, and it was decided that some of their personnel could be shifted. In addition there were men at training centers and supply bases who would become free of duties as divisions in training were sent overseas. Finally there was a quickly available body of men in the Army Specialized Training Program (ASTP), which had been started at the end of 1942 purportedly to train men in colleges for certain scarce specialties such as medicine, languages, and engineering. Since many enlisted men with degrees in these fields were actually being used by the Army as typists, public-relations assistants, mechanics, and the like, some cynics believed that the program existed more to help college administrators keep their schools in operation than to supply any serious need. As pressure for additional ground troops mounted in 1944—especially to fill shortages in units due for shipment before the end of August—General Marshall saw no alternative to phasing out the ASTP and transferring the men to divisions then in training.

On February 10 Marshall formally asked the Secretary of War to liquidate the program. To Stimson, who shared Roosevelt's special interest in the ASTP, Marshall put the matter bluntly: either reduce and finally abandon the ASTP or disband ten Army divisions and certain nondivisional units then in being to use for replacements. Reluctantly Stimson, citing Marshall's arguments, told the President on February 18 that the program must be scaled down. Orders were issued shortly afterward, and some 75,000 men from the program were shifted to divisions in training. The units to which they were assigned were pleased at receiving many potential specialists. On the other hand the former ASTP men complained of being shortchanged in the program.[19]

Marshall had never fully shared Stimson's enthusiasm for the ASTP. Like many other officers, he distrusted any program that drained off the best-educated men and natural leaders from the regular combat units. His reservations were based also on a feeling—shown in his general opposition to direct commissions for college men—that the Army should not discriminate between the college trained and those less well educated.

The manpower situation worsened in March. Although there were still 3,000,000 men in the Army and Air Forces within the United States, more than 2,500,000 of these were earmarked for shipment overseas or being trained, along with those doing the training. New sources had to be uncovered for replacements and for the coming big push in Europe.

On March 17 Marshall had a breakdown of U.S.–based Army and Air Forces manpower prepared for Stimson to use in a cabinet meeting to offset criticism of excessive demands.[20] The same day Marshall told Undersecretary of War Patterson that "no Army call has been completely filled in the past six months." He declared that "only the drastic economies we have effected over the past six months have enabled the Army to meet its program. What has actually happened has been a constantly increasing deficiency on the part of Selective Service which would have left us in a tragic position had we not been making tremendous economies ourselves, all of which have been eaten up in overcoming the deficiencies in meeting new demands for operations which were not on the books or conceived six months ago." The great difficulty was that however quickly the Selective Service System made up the deficits, the Army would be unable to provide the trained men when currently scheduled operations required their employment.[21]

To bolster his case, the Chief of Staff on March 23 outlined to James Byrnes plans for meeting the Army's needs. "This narrative," he declared in the memorandum, "should not be interpreted as an Army complaint concerning intolerable burdens. Instead, it should be considered as a record of the adjustments we have made." But there was a reminder for civilians: "As the war moves on, activities which are no longer necessary will be ruthlessly cut. The Army, I believe, has the right to expect similar action from the rest of the nation." [22]

Part of the trouble, the Army believed, continued to come from the War Manpower Commission's efforts to increase deferments. Stimson discussed the situation with Roosevelt on the twenty-second and came away blaming the President for picking weak men. The board's chief, Paul McNutt, the Secretary decided, was a failure. Stimson wrote sharply to the Selective Service Director, General Hershey, reminding him that he was responsible under the law for deferments and that he must not be swayed by McNutt and other civilian administrators. When the Secretary of War sent Byrnes the memorandum Marshall had prepared to "show our sacrifices made in our strength and how near the bare bones they were," the War Mobilization chief reminded Stimson that Congress had given Hershey control over deferments because it did not trust McNutt.[23]

Deferments alone did not constitute the major problem. There were millions of men exempt from the draft under 4-F classifications who were capable of doing work in industry. At the end of March, Undersecretary of War Patterson, fiery as ever, insisted that Stimson and Marshall ask Congress to force these men to work or fight. The two men demurred. "He [Marshall] was against it, just as I was sure he would be," wrote Stimson at the end of the conference. The Secretary reflected both their views when he recorded that the proposal "prostitutes the Army into a compulsory machine to compel men to work." He saw all sorts of dangers in the idea and tried to get Patterson to desist.[24]

When Patterson, now talking of going into the Army on active duty to offer an example of personal service, seemed set on pressing his case, Stimson arranged a presentation of his own. He set up a conference between two key members of the House Military Affairs Committee and Patterson and then called in Marshall to present the arguments against the plan. Seeing that he was outflanked, Patterson capitulated.[25]

Stimson and Marshall were not opposed to a measure to induce men to take jobs in critical war industries, but they felt Patterson's approach was insufficiently comprehensive. They favored a National Service Bill, which would regularize the entire civilian manpower situation. Recalling his sponsorship of such a measure many months before, Stimson in early January 1944 had persuaded the President to announce his public support for the Austin-Wadsworth bill, which stated that every person had an obligation to serve the war effort "as he or she may be deemed best fit to perform." In addition to registration of all men between the ages of eighteen and sixty-five, this measure would call for the listing of all women between twenty-one and fifty.

Aware of the bitter opposition the bill would encounter, the President tied to it a program of tougher taxation, renegotiation of war contracts, food subsidies, and enactment of price legislation. Despite appeals for strong national backing of the war effort and attempts to spread the burden of supporting the war, the measure did not prosper. It was in serious trouble when labor representatives joined the National Association of Manufacturers in opposing it. Determined to rush passage, Secretary Stimson asked Marshall to help him with a strong plea to Congress. But the opposition was too great and the push for enactment in 1944 failed.[26]

Of more immediate concern to Marshall was enrollment of a sufficient number of inductees to keep his current divisions up to strength. Months before he had decided to take a gamble. Instead of piling up large numbers of divisions, which might be understrength and understaffed, he decided to fix the number at 88 to 90 and keep them supplied with trained men to replace the dead and wounded and those rotated home. In that way he believed he could keep his divisions near full strength and preserve the experience and know-how of the older divisions.

Stimson was not totally in agreement. He had been impressed by the fears of his assistant Goldthwaite Dorr on the subject, and on April 12 he tackled Marshall. Prepared for an argument, the General recalled that the earlier 200-division planning figure had been reached at a time when it seemed that the United States might have to fight without the aid of the Soviet Union or the United Kingdom. As the situation had improved, the figure had been dropped to 100 divisions and below. He now wanted, as Stimson reported it, "a superlatively good Army" kept at present strength with "superlatively good replacements." He counted on the Air Forces to provide the extra punch for victory. If the Allies could once get securely placed in France with the Russians very close across the way, "No nation on earth could stand the punishment which we could give Germany with our Air Force from those close bases where even our medium bombers and our light bombers can reach every part of Germany." But Marshall's point was not clear to the general public or to the British, who were now beyond the peak of their strength and cannibalizing units to a degree that the United States never reached. The 90-division program, already seriously threatened by decreases in Selective Service returns, required Russian advances and continued Russian help. And, Marshall conceded, it gave no margin for any diversion from the main show.[27]

Stimson was somewhat skeptical, but he refrained from reopening the issue as he continued his fight for stronger public support of the war effort. The Secretary was impressed by the General's performance at a conference of key business and labor leaders arranged by Secretary of Navy Knox in April, a few days before his death. At the meeting Knox introduced representatives of the armed forces who sought to win support for the National Service Bill. Stimson, who had often seen Marshall save such a conference, wrote enthusiastically that after several poor presentations "they called on Marshall who always makes a good speech and Marshall, whom everybody respects and likes, won the applause of the audience." In this case applause did not mean that he had won the group's backing for the desired legislation. But it did mean general support for the Army's program.[28]

In the weeks before the invasion the General's calendar was filled with similar speaking engagements. At the luncheon of the American Society of Newspaper Editors at the new Statler in Washington on Friday, April 21, his candid off-the-record remarks were greeted with cheers. The following Tuesday he flew to New York to speak to the American Newspaper Publishers Association at the Waldorf and there again gained the plaudits of his hearers.

Roy W. Howard of the Scripps-Howard Newspaper chain spoke for many of his colleagues when he wrote after the first meeting: "It has been a long time since I have seen a group of newspapermen so deeply stirred or so favorably impressed as were those constituting the group to which you spoke at the Statler luncheon last Friday." [29]

As he had earlier with Congress, the Business Advisory Council, the American Legion and kindred veterans' organizations, Marshall won the confidence of the editors by his frankness and his realistic portrayal of the problems that faced the nation. In speeches and in private correspondence he attempted the sort of educational campaign with the press that he had carried on with members of Congress since he had become Chief of Staff. He had come slowly to the art of dealing with the press, first holding its members at arm's length, then delegating his press officers to explain the Army's policy patiently and openly, then instituting his off-the-record briefings for top Washington correspondents, and at last appearing at press meetings before key members of the profession. Shortly before he spoke to the American Society of Newspaper Editors, he tried still another tack—making direct appeals to influential editors. Endeavoring to offset the flood of unfavorable publicity about General Patton's slapping hospitalized soldiers, he had sent on to Roy Roberts of the Kansas City *Star*, president of the editors' group, a protest from General Wilson, chief of the Mediterranean Command, about press stories that had jeopardized a cover plan involving Patton. General Marshall seized on this situation to appeal to the editors through Roberts for understanding of the Army's problems in the preinvasion period. He wrote:

> I feel that we must depend on you and your most influential associates to protect us from this business of throwing pop bottles at the umpire in the hope of influencing his decisions, when the thrower of the bottle has not even played sand-lot baseball. I think we must all have clearly in mind that the American public, except through family relations in the armed services and from the very minor irritations of gas and food rationing and inability to buy certain things, is not aware of what war means as is the public in England where thousands have died and many more thousands have been injured. I am the more concerned in this matter because we are approaching the most difficult period in the war and in the midst of a presidential campaign. You men who are leaders of the Press have a very grave problem on your hands with a multitude of difficult people and ulterior motives to combat.[30]

He was asking a great deal of the press, but he was confident that it was equal to the challenge. He reported to General Devers, the American theater commander in the Mediterranean, that the War Department would try to block further references in the press and radio exposing Army plans. "This will give me a strong weapon to control OWI and the press," he added.[31] His confidence that he could persuade press leaders to stop their damaging comments was unjustified, but the major point that he had stressed to Roberts—for the press to stop firing random blasts at the Army—was heeded by most of the newspapers of the country. Strong opponents of the administration, such as the Chicago *Tribune*, were not likely to halt their attacks, especially where the President was concerned, but so far as the conduct of the war was involved, the tendency was to give the armed services the benefit of the doubt.

Less than a week after his New York speech the Chief of Staff made his last inspection of Army camps and bases before the invasion. Leaving

Washington on the afternoon of April 30, he visited the WAC Training Center at Fort Oglethorpe, Georgia, and then headed for the Southwest, where he saw infantry and armored divisions at Camp Bowie, Texas, and Fort Huachuca, Arizona. He visited other units at Fort Ord, Camp Cooke, and Camp Beale, California. Then he headed north to the Boeing Aircraft plant at Seattle and Camp Adair, Oregon.[32] His last stop brought him back to the familiar country of Vancouver Barracks and to old friends of those days.

Among these Erskine Wood, a Portland attorney who had learned his camping lore by spending a couple of seasons with Chief Joseph of the Nez Percé tribe, had a fishing camp on the Metolius. He invited Marshall and Frank McCarthy to join him there for a short vacation, almost completely cut off from radio messages and cablegrams and the thoughts of war. Mrs. Wood helped out by sending pheasant, country butter, and other delicacies to supplement the "rather routine Army rations" that the men prepared. "The rest in those surroundings was perfect but the trout were reluctant." But it was the rest that mattered—"four days . . . as carefree and restful as any I have spent since the war began." By the time Marshall reached the Pentagon again after a bumpy ride from Seattle, Washington, he was "already nostalgic for the Metolius." [33]

Another pleasurable memory was connected with this trip to the Metolius. The young officer at the airfield where the Chief of Staff landed who was responsible for arrangements regarding the trip told McCarthy that he was trying desperately to get transferred to Hawaii so that he could marry a Navy nurse stationed there. When the colonel reported this to Marshall, the Chief of Staff was moved to try the role of Cupid. Unwilling to interfere with the officer's permanent assignment, he asked McCarthy if the Army didn't need a courier to fly out with highly classified messages to Pearl Harbor for a couple of days. The Army did and the officer was dispatched. In a very short time the couple was married. Under Navy regulations the nurse was returned home. Marshall later told King with some relish that the Army had helped in the redeployment of Navy personnel.[34]

When Marshall returned to Washington, May 10, and plunged back into his problems, Stimson noted the gratifying change that the trip and a few days' relaxation had produced. The General began by examining the administration's seizure of Montgomery, Ward and Company plants after its president, Sewell Avery, refused to continue a closed-shop agreement with labor representatives. Secretary Stimson and his civilian assistants had opposed the action on the ground that the plants produced little or no war material and that it would be harmful for the Army to get involved. The argument appealed to Marshall. During his absence the Army had been ordered to act, however, and everything had been handled in a low key. The War Department had sent a lieutenant with a platoon of men to enforce its orders. When Undersecretary of Commerce Wayne Taylor suggested an officer of higher rank, Stimson and his advisers replied that a platoon was adequate for the job and that a lieutenant was the proper person to lead a unit of this size.

The few men dispatched were indeed sufficient. The lieutenant used only four enlisted men when he informed Avery that he was taking over the plant. When the executive refused to leave, a sergeant from Milwaukee and a private from Memphis carried him to the elevator and then out of the building. A few days later Attorney General Francis Biddle got a temporary injunction barring Avery and other company officials from the plant until a hearing could be held. Shortly after the Army withdrew. Members of Congress attacked the President for using Gestapo methods, and newspapers flailed the administration. In the minds of many the picture remained of soldiers carrying an old man in a chair out of the building. Stimson called it folly, and Marshall did not disagree.[35]

Then Secretary Stimson handed him a memorandum he had recently written on "Our Military Reserves." Fearing that the Allied divisions would barely match German units in France by summer, Stimson repeated his worries over the Army's strength. Once the troops allotted for OVERLORD left the United States, there would be only fourteen uncommitted divisions. This reserve was little more than that held by the Germans.

Stimson had less faith than Marshall in America's air strength. He saw the possibility of a stalemate in France by the following November, and he thought that the lack of overwhelming strength would prolong enemy resistance. As for the Russian counterbalance, he wondered if the Soviet forces—a long way from home and requiring long lines of communications—would be inclined to continue their drive once they had reached the limits of their former boundaries. It was unsound, he believed, to have the possibility of complete victory "entirely dependent" upon Russian decisions made at a time "when we were for all apparent purposes deadlocked." [36]

In the lengthy talk that followed Marshall firmly stuck by his ninety-division plan. The basic need, he argued, was an adequate supply of young and well-trained replacements. Such troops, placed into older units, were better than completely new divisions. He wanted the replacement system arranged so that it could not be killed off "by the pull and haul of the theater organization." He envisaged giving recruits seventeen weeks of training in the United States and then shipping them to the overseas theaters, where they would be further polished before being committed to action. Stimson was won over by the Chief of Staff's "powerfully marshaled" facts and the information he had gained from his recent inspection of twelve divisions then in training.[37]

Convinced of the necessity for tightened control over personnel, Marshall had recently lectured Eisenhower and Devers sternly about handling replacements in their theaters. He had told Eisenhower in mid-April that the replacement and general personnel situation was so bad that he was requiring General Devers to take prompt and drastic corrective action. Long dissatisfied with the way the personnel system had been handled in the Mediterranean Theater, he now scolded officers in the northern theater as well. He declared that they needed a single commander with the sole responsibility for operating the replacement system in conformity with War Department and theater policies. He wanted a vigorous and aggressive officer with sufficient rank and staff qualified to do the job. This officer would have control of all casual personnel and coordinate programs for the recovery and proper utilization of men coming out of hospitals and for the retraining of able-bodied men in the Communications Zone to make them available for duty in the combat zone. Above all he must take constant and forceful action to prevent the accumulation and stagnation of men in depots, such as had occurred and was still occurring in North Africa. He demanded rigid control of loss replacements to prevent their diversion to other theaters.[38]

Marshall's statements reflected more than his determination to stop wastage of manpower. It also was a reaction to his learning that deputies of Lieutenant General John C. H. Lee, Eisenhower's Services of Supply commander, strongly opposed these proposals. In an imperative tone that he almost never used toward Eisenhower, Marshall demanded immediate action in the European theater to forestall a repetition of the North African situation. He insisted: "I cannot accept a stiff necked attitude in opposition to essential change based on our experiences in the latter theater." [39]

Marshall's tough attitude toward Lee may have been prompted in part by his recent embarrassment over Lee's promotion to three-star rank without Eisenhower's knowledge. Lee, who had won Marshall's approval in a peacetime maneuver and was a friend of Somervell's, had been sent to the United Kingdom in the spring of 1942. He remained there in command of Services of Supply troops after Eisenhower left for Africa. On his return the Supreme Commander was unfavorably impressed by Lee's special train and his fondness for empire building. Aware that in the coming campaign Lee was slated not only to handle American supply but also to act as Deputy Commander of the American theater headquarters under him, Eisenhower was not certain that he was the man for the job. When Lee was made a three-star general a few weeks later, without a recommendation from him, Eisenhower wrote Marshall of his amazement at learning of the promotion from the newspapers. Marshall confessed that the fault was his. Seeing Lee's name on a recent list, he had assumed that Eisenhower had recommended him. Marshall blamed his undue haste in submitting the name to Congress on pressure from MacArthur for promotion of his Chief of Staff, General Sutherland. The Southwest Pacific commander had asked that his subordinate be advanced to keep step with Bedell Smith. Not wishing to send up one name, Marshall had added Wheeler of the CBI and Lee to the list.[40]

Having done Lee a favor, Marshall wanted cooperation from him. With unaccustomed tartness he observed to Eisenhower that the SOS commander should follow Washington's views on replacements: "Lee was not in North Africa, he has not had the benefit of that experience nor is he familiar with the situation that developed there." He added that he was not basing his judgment on reports by a few junior officers but on the mass of cumulative evidence. Recognizing that he was being severe, Marshall took some of the sting out by remarking quietly that he understood the "irritated resistance of staff officers to any adverse report or proposed change by people who have not borne the heat of the battle." [41]

Startled by Marshall's peremptory tone, Butcher asked Eisenhower for an explanation. The General admitted that replacements had been allowed to accumulate, and many of them had been used for noncombat duties. One hundred thousand service troops—including port labor battalions and antiaircraft units—had been held in North Africa in readiness for the off-again, on-again ANVIL landing. [42]

Wise in the ways of dealing with a determined superior, Eisenhower picked a line favored by Marshall: "Your latest suggestion that I set up a Commander with no other responsibility than that of handling replacement procedure is one that I have been contemplating. The real problem is finding the right man. He must be tough but understanding, and broadly experienced but full of energy. He must be able to get along with people." The Supreme Commander had Brigadier General Everett Hughes in mind, but he knew that Marshall felt that Hughes failed to meet the last requirement. So for the moment Eisenhower did his best to keep his eye on replacements and to search for someone to handle the job. [43]

In the Mediterranean, General Devers worked steadily to improve the replacement situation. In late May he praised the system to Secretary Stimson for keeping units fresh and vigorous. The Mediterranean commander's energetic efforts to solve this and other problems overcame any earlier reservations General Marshall had about his performance in his new post. Before D day Marshall passed on to Stimson with evident approval a statement by General Ira Eaker of the air command lauding Devers's contributions. [44]

Despite Marshall's efforts to strengthen the replacement system, Stimson was convinced that the National Service Bill was more essential than ever. Yet he found the Chief of Staff less pessimistic than he about the manpower situation. Although he believed the situation dangerous, Stimson resolved not to raise the issue with Marshall. "We differ a little on the shading," he wrote, "but not the essence." After reflecting on his conversation with Marshall—and reassured by the War Department G-1, Major General Miller White, that the Army would be safe for the rest of the year with the divisions already trained—Stimson remarked that it might be better to postpone the manpower proposals until they really had a disaster "which makes it more evident to these dumb-headed congressmen that it is necessary." Before the year ended, such a crisis seemed at hand.[45]

Shortages in manpower and in certain critical supplies led inevitably to congressional criticisms of wasteful practices. In addition to his efforts to find surplus fighting troops in various theaters of the world, Marshall now appealed to commanders for strenuous measures to reduce waste. A major fault, he found, lay in the duplication of many supply and procurement efforts and facilities by the Army and Navy. He had long favored some degree of service unification; now others began to express the same view.[46]

Charged with the task of improving mobilization of resources for the war effort, former Justice Byrnes asked Secretaries Knox and Stimson on March 15 to coordinate Navy and Army activities more closely. In Stimson's words, the War Mobilization Administrator was talking of an "old evil" that had long troubled him and Marshall. Indeed while aide to Pershing in the early 1920s Marshall had served on a special board with Assistant Secretary of the Navy Theodore Roosevelt, Jr., to investigate a unified Army-Navy purchasing system. He still favored unified efforts, but he was also a realist. At a time when he had gained a good working relationship with Admiral King, he feared that it would be disastrous "to raise the question now." He told Stimson that he was prepared to raise the devil with the Navy after the war "in the general final organization" but that he preferred to postpone the issue for the duration.[47]

The House of Representatives had become sufficiently interested in the issue to set up, on March 29, a Select Committee on Post-War Military Policy, under the chairmanship of Clifton A. Woodrum of Virginia. Alarmed at the prospect of a fight developing with the Navy before the committee, Secretary Stimson named Assistant Secretary of War Lovett to see if he could get a postponement of the hearings on a proposed defense-unification project.[48]

To Stimson's amazement Secretary Knox favored a single Department of Defense. On the same day that he made this discovery, the War Secretary discussed the question of unification with Marshall at some length. While he agreed with Marshall generally on the need for one department, he was concerned that the system recommended would diminish the authority of the civilian secretary. After some discussion Marshall's staff outlined a draft that Stimson could accept.

On the broader question cleavage developed between the War and Navy departments, especially after the death of Secretary Knox in late April. His Undersecretary, James Forrestal, who was soon to replace him, had opposed Knox on unification. Neither as Acting Secretary nor as Knox's successor was he inclined to fight the admirals.[49]

Shortly after Marshall's return from his trip to the South and West, he was irritated to find that the President opposed any proposal for consolidation. The General blamed it on the Navy, which he reported to Stimson was running wild. He was still smoldering several days later when the Secretary of War suggested that he stay out of the fight over unification before the Woodrum Committee and leave the matter to the civilian staff. Marshall growled wrathfully that he was holding himself in but that if Navy officials provoked him too much, he would blow them out of the water.[50]

In reality Marshall preferred to avoid a showdown at this point. However Representative Woodrum felt that since Navy representatives had already testified, it was essential for the Army case to be presented. Marshall followed Stimson's advice and the example of Leahy and King in refraining from appearing before the committee. In the end the matter was delayed for future consideration by Congress.[51]

Another proposal presented to Congress that spring was a highly controversial one providing five-star rank for top Army and Navy commanders. President Roosevelt had startled Admiral Leahy one morning in early January by announcing that he was going to promote him to higher rank, suggesting the title "Admiral of the Fleet." Leahy replied that similar rank should be given to the other members of the Joint Chiefs of Staff. A few days later, on January 13, a Navy captain informed the Army Chief of Personnel that Representative Carl Vinson, chairman of the House Naval Affairs Committee, would shortly introduce a bill prepared by the Navy Department to provide two new ranks, Admiral of the Navy (six-star rank) and Admiral of the Fleet (five-star). The plan was to give the higher rank to Leahy and King and the lower to Nimitz, Halsey, and Ingersoll. The President had approved the plan in part and had said that similar action to provide higher rank would be taken by the Army.[52]

Possibly the captain's statement was the first official notice the Army had of the President's move. Rumor soon had it that the President had been trying to get a promotion for his personal physician, a naval officer, and for some of the Navy bureau chiefs and that he had been told that it would first be necessary to elevate some of the men at the top.

General Marshall disliked the whole idea. Some Washington columnists suggested that he opposed the plan because his five-star rank would make him "Marshal Marshall." Already a household word, his name threatened to corrupt permanently the spelling of Field Marshal and Provost Marshal. Anything more would merely compound confusion.

Marshall later clarified his feelings: "I didn't want any promotion at all. I didn't need it. The Chiefs of Staff on the British side were already field marshals so they would be senior to me whatever I was made. I didn't think I needed that rank and I didn't want to be beholden to Congress for any rank or anything of that kind. I wanted to be able to go in there with my skirts clean and with no personal ambitions concerned in it in any way. I could get all I wanted with the rank I had. But that was twisted around, and somebody said I didn't like the term 'Marshal' because it was the same as my name. (I know Mr. Churchill twitted me about this in a rather scathing tone.) I don't recall that I ever made the expression." [53]

Marshall was convinced that a promotion at this stage of the war was unnecessary and embarrassing. Further five-star rank for Marshall and Arnold would take away the luster of the unique title "General of the Armies," borne by General Pershing—a fact that some of his World War I associates soon made clear. Retired Major General James G. Harbord, Pershing's wartime Chief of Staff, now chairman of the board of the Radio Corporation of America, worked diligently to kill the bill. Assuming incorrectly that General Marshall was backing the legislation, he wrote Representative Wadsworth of the House Military Affairs Committee that nothing justified the departure from the precedents in the cases of Grant, Sherman, Sheridan, and Pershing of withholding their final promotions until after the close of the conflicts in which they were involved. He went further in an attempt to persuade the editor of *The New Yorker* to attack the proposal, suggesting that the Chief of Staff was trying to advance his cause at the expense of his old chief.[54] General Marshall was already concerned lest Pershing, now aged and ailing, think that his former assistant was lacking in proper respect. Although he visited the AEF leader at Walter Reed Hospital as frequently as the pressure of duties would permit, he found at times that the General had forgotten some of his visits and was inclined to complain that Marshall did not come to see him any more. Under these circumstances Marshall shuddered at the possible reactions of his old chief to Harbord's allegations.

When Stimson heard of the proposal at the end of January, he felt that Congress would not approve the advances for the Navy unless similar arrangements were made for the Army since there would be great public resentment if Marshall was excluded. The Chief of Staff told Stimson that he preferred to have nothing to do with the scheme, but that it seemed inevitable that the President would insist on the legislation.[55]

Armed with a copy of the Navy proposal that the President had approved, Stimson scolded the Commander-in-Chief for his action. Roosevelt blandly informed him he had never advocated a six-star rank, even when the Secretary showed him a memorandum from Representative Vinson claiming that he had. Although Stimson was not strong for the legislation, he conceded that there was some justification for a one-jump promotion since the British had recently advanced all their Chiefs of Staff, who were thus generally one star above their American counterparts.[56]

Opposition to the proposal developed in the press and in Congress. Many newspapers deplored the tendency of the United States to copy other countries where high rank was hastily bestowed. The *Army and Navy Journal* called on Congress to go slow on the proposal and pigeonhole the pending bills until after the war, when the services of the top war leaders could be more truly evaluated and recognized. A few days later it disclosed that Marshall and Stimson opposed the measure and noted that the pressure for the bill had come from friends of the Navy. In view of the reluctance of the War Department, the *Journal* suggested that the Navy bill be returned to the committee or allowed to die.[57] This vigorous opposition from various quarters convinced sponsors of the measure to wait until a successful landing in Europe softened some of the opponents.

Settlement of one debatable topic merely freed the newspaper columns for other controversies. One mid-May morning Senator H. Styles Bridges, Republican of New Hampshire, a ranking member of the Military Affairs Committee, came to Stimson in great alarm to investigate reports that the War Department was burning vital intelligence records. According to rumors Army officials, acting on White House directives, were destroying files of subversives. Some senators thought they smelled a Democratic plot or at least a savory mess to serve up for the fall elections. Believing that Bridges was acting in good faith, with the intent of heading off his critical colleagues, Stimson made a diligent inquiry. "All that we were doing," he discovered, "was . . . cleaning up the old records of G-2, none of which were complete and which were greatly encumbering the work of the Bureau." Stimson asked Marshall's Deputy, General McNarney, to talk to the senator, "and he very soon satisfied Bridges that there was nothing doing." [58]

Bridges may have been satisfied, but some of his colleagues were not. He proposed, therefore, establishment of a military-affairs subcommittee to investigate the charges. He was selected as chairman with Senators Albert B. Chandler of Kentucky and Joseph C. O'Mahoney of Wyoming— both Democrats—as colleagues. General McNarney; Major General Virgil L. Petersen, the Inspector General; Brigadier General Philip Brown, the Deputy Inspector General; and Colonel Otto Nelson of the Deputy Chief of Staff's Office were appointed to work with the group.[59] Ultimately, as in so many cases of this type, the committee found the report to be greatly exaggerated and the matter was dropped.

Despite all the major worries and minor annoyances that calendared the Chief of Staff's days in early 1944, he kept a watchful eye on world strategy. In private and public appearances he tried to keep a proper focus on the victory still to be won. The degree of his success is shown by the fact that in mid-May the correspondents of *Look* picked Marshall "as the top useful official in Washington." [60]

Marshall's ability to impress the leaders of the nation was never shown more graphically than near the end of May 1944, the day of his stepson's death, when he accompanied Admiral King to Hershey, Pennsylvania, to speak at the annual conference of the nation's governors. Forty-four of the forty-eight state chief executives gathered to hear the two service Chiefs tell of the war's progress, what still remained to be done, and what was expected of the citizens and administrators of the country. These political leaders were experienced in public speaking and the arts of winning an audience. They were thoroughly immune to oratory and suspicious of spellbinding. They expected nothing spectacular from the two serious men of war. But they respected their leadership, and they listened.

King spoke first. Never at ease in public speaking, he found it difficult to talk to a sizable group without having the full text of his speech before him. He spoke dryly, briefly, matter-of-factly about the Navy's participation in the war. He had the polite attention of the audience and a ripple of applause at the end. He was conscious of the contrast with Marshall's easier delivery and observed later in his account of the meeting that the Chief of Staff was a trained speaker who used no notes and made his points easily.[61]

Brigadier General Robert Cutler, who was working on plans for absentee voting by soldiers, has given a graphic account of Marshall's impact on the governors:

> Sitting at the right of the Chairman . . . [the Chief of Staff] epitomized all that he was: calm, dignified, collected, quite at ease, instilling a sense of confidence in this troubled passage of the war by his own serenity and dispassion. He had no notes of any kind with him. His garrison cap, with his gloves neatly folded in it, rested on the table beside him. Except for his austere but gentle sense of command, it would have been thought he had just happened to drop by the meeting for a brief word.
> But when he spoke, it was different. In his low but clear voice, speaking carefully articulated and exactly formed sentences, he gave an accounting of the military activities in each theater of war all over the globe. No sentence was ever begun without being carefully and purposefully ended. No words were wasted. Each word fulfilled its special thought.[62]

The governors, expecting a repetition of King's routine, flat delivery, were stilled to attention by something completely different. The room was deathly quiet as Marshall, employing a technique that so often succeeded with Congress, kept his voice and the pace low pitched. He took up each theater in turn, lucidly stating the disposition of forces, the Allied objectives, the present risks, and the future hopes. He concluded his "general round the world situation summary" with the campaign in Italy and what he knew of Russia's plans. His speech was off the record, but notes prepared for background use emphasized the fact that success in operations had tended to create lethargy at home and stressed that the "critical period in production, like the critical period in operations, lies ahead." [63]

For an hour and a quarter Marshall continued, unhurried, unexaggerated, emotionless. "And when he had completed the exposition of America's might throughout the world, he stopped speaking just as he had begun—calm, unruffled, complete." For what seemed a half minute, the group sat quietly as if hesitant to break the spell. At length Governor Leverett Saltonstall of Massachusetts, whose impulses moved through generations of New England certainty (which was to impel him to rise in the Senate to Marshall's defense seven years later, after Senator McCarthy's attack), rose and asked his colleagues to give a standing vote of thanks to the speaker. Only after they had paid their silent tribute and then sat down did they break into applause.

Near the end of 1943 Marshall had stepped out of the leading role in the cross-Channel invasion. Now some six months later, on the eve of the attack, he was still proving in words and deeds that he was Man of the Year.

XIX

Overlord *at Last*

LONG before the final date of OVERLORD was set, the Chief of Staff had begun his search for the men who would lead it. By the late summer of 1943 Marshall, who assumed that he would command the assault, began reviewing names of likely key commanders and the nature of the headquarters that would direct the assault from the United Kingdom. Expecting to draw heavily on the Mediterranean for experienced commanders, he worked closely with Eisenhower, the Allied commander there, in making up his list. When the prize post went to Eisenhower, Marshall shifted his emphasis slightly but never his interest. He followed every development in the European Theater, giving high priority to the Supreme Commander's requests and continuing to suggest officers for various commands as Eisenhower had done when he had thought that Marshall would lead the invasion. With General McNair at hand to advise him on commanders in the United States and with his own knowledge of experienced officers in the early Pacific fighting, Marshall was primed to select a winning team. Although denied the chance to lead the invasion, he would not forgo the opportunity to help pick its commanders. He went about this task with a zest that he showed in few other phases of the preparations.

When Marshall had thought that he would lead OVERLORD, he had naturally sought as his chief field commander someone he could trust implicitly. He dispatched the following to Eisenhower at the end of August 1943: "Devers and Morgan have been pressing U.S. since early July to appoint an American Army Commander immediately to parallel activities of British Army Commander now building up in rather formidable fashion as to requisitions, requirements, etc. My choice had been Bradley. . . . Could you release Bradley for this command." [1]

It was Marshall who had sent Bradley to Eisenhower in North Africa. There, as Patton's successor in Tunisia, Bradley had won his first battles and had followed this up with a fine performance in Sicily. Patton, Bradley's superior in that campaign, might have seemed the likelier choice but Marshall was not certain about his judgment. Stressing the importance of balance and steadiness for command of the assault that he considered would be the great test of the war, Marshall concluded that Bradley was the man for the job. Since the days when Marshall had first known him at Fort Benning, Bradley had always measured up to the Chief of Staff's exacting standards. Every duty Marshall had given him had been well performed. Bradley, always patient, worked without friction, and his quiet assurance spread to his men. The Chief of Staff's judgment was confirmed by Eisenhower, who wrote of Bradley on August 24: "He has brains, a fine capacity for leadership and a thorough understanding of the requirements of modern battle. He has never caused me one moment of worry. He is perfectly capable of commanding an Army. He has the respect of all his associates, including all the British officers that have met him." [2]

On receiving Marshall's request for Bradley, Eisenhower contrasted him with his other top commanders, Patton and Clark, and reinforced his earlier recommendation: "Of the three, Bradley is the best rounded in all respects, counting experience, and he has the great characteristic of never giving his commander one moment of worry." While personally distressed at the thought of losing Bradley, since he had come to lean on him so heavily, he recognized that this "very reason probably makes him your obvious choice for the other job. . . ." [3] A week later, discussing the promotion list, Eisenhower wrote Marshall that he believed Bradley to be "the best rounded combat leader I have yet met in our service. While he probably lacks some of the extraordinary and ruthless driving power that Patton can exert at critical moments, he still has such force and determination that even in this characteristic he is among our best. In all other things he is a jewel to have around and I cannot tell you with what real distress I see him leave the theater." [4] Eisenhower's message only strengthened the decision Marshall had already made. And for Ike there was a happy ending. Unknowingly he had picked his own chief lieutenant for the invasion.

The next man Marshall considered for an army command was George Patton, and here Eisenhower's enthusiasm for that hell-for-leather fighter overrode Marshall's reservations. Although the Allied commander had extremely fresh and compelling reasons—probably not yet known to Marshall—for doubting whether he could give a clean bill of health to his Seventh Army commander, he believed that Patton had fighting qualities that "we cannot afford to lose unless he ruins himself." He added: "So he can be classed as an army commander that you can use with certainty that the troops will not be stopped by ordinary obstacles." [5]

But there were ugly facts to bother Eisenhower. On two occasions a week apart in early August, General Patton under the pressure of the Sicilian campaign had struck soldiers in evacuation hospitals, declaring that they should be shot for cowardice. When he learned of the outrages, Eisenhower warned Patton of possible serious consequences and ordered that he make a series of public apologies for his conduct. Patton complied, and the story was kept out of the press. From the veiled reference in Eisenhower's letter to Marshall September 6, it seems that he had not reported the matter to Washington. In fact in that letter Eisenhower expatiated on Patton's virtues as a commander; he explained that actions in which Patton "indulged his temper toward individual subordinates" were overbalanced by his tremendous achievements. "His job of rehabilitating II Corps in Tunisia was quickly and magnificently done. Beyond this, his leadership of the Seventh Army was close to the best of our classic examples." [6]

Indeed there is no evidence of a report on Patton's soldier slapping until November, when Drew Pearson broke the story that correspondents in Sicily had agreed to keep secret.[7] In the interim Eisenhower continued to push Patton for a command in the United Kingdom. As if consciously balancing his leadership against Montgomery's, Eisenhower wrote Marshall: "Many generals constantly think of battle in terms of, first, concentration, supply, maintenance, replacement, and, second, after all the above is arranged, a *conservative* advance." Important as such considerations are, occasions arise when "boldness is ten times as important as numbers." Patton's strength, he continued, "is that he thinks only in terms of attack as long as there is a single battalion that can keep advancing." He doubted if he would ever want Patton to head an army group, "but as an army commander under a man who is sound and solid, and who has sense enough to use Patton's good qualities without being blinded by his love of showmanship and histrionics, he should do as fine a job as he did in Sicily." [8]

Actually this analysis of Patton was not needed. Long before, Marshall had grasped the nature of the man's ferocious genius and intended to use it. By the end of the month the Chief of Staff was weighing Patton's ultimate transfer to the United Kingdom. Meanwhile he had other tasks for him in the Mediterranean. Knowing that the Germans would be watchful of any place where Patton was stationed, Marshall in late October directed Eisenhower to send the General and some of his staff to Corsica and other areas in the Mediterranean as decoys to deceive the enemy about the next Allied move.[9]

The third member of the American triumvirate that Eisenhower praised confidently to Marshall was Mark Clark. "He is the best organizer, planner, and trainer of troops I have met," ran his dispatch in 1943.

Among the British ground commanders he considered Alexander notable—broad gauged and skilled at working on an Allied basis.[10] Noting that Marshall would need a top airman who was "thoroughly schooled in all the phases of strategic bombing and more particularly in the job of *supporting ground armies in the field,"* Eisenhower strongly recommended Air Chief Marshal Tedder for this post.[11]

As the dialogue on commanders continued after Eisenhower knew that he, not Marshall, would have the cross-Channel assignment, both men changed their emphasis. Where once Eisenhower had mingled praise with regret over losing men from his theater, he now dangled the names of one after another of his trusted subordinates for invasion roles. Facing the greatest challenge of his career, Eisenhower naturally felt more secure with men who had served under or with him during the recent campaigns in North Africa and Italy.

Conversely, to replace himself in the Mediterranean Theater, Eisenhower suggested Devers, an officer more thoroughly Marshall's man than his. The Supreme Commander realized that Devers, three years his elder but untried in combat in World War II, would be difficult to pass over for a high command if he remained in the United Kingdom. Bradley had already gone from Italy to London. Patton, he added, should go to the United Kingdom for a command, and Clark should head the Seventh Army in its landings in southern France.[12]

The Mediterranean shift became even more apparent, as Eisenhower filled in other details. He wanted a single ground commander for the assault phases, and he saw Field Marshal Alexander in that role. He proposed to bring Air Chief Marshal Tedder along as his chief airman, with Spaatz, also in the Mediterranean, as the chief of the U.S. Strategic Air Forces. Bradley would serve first as army commander and then move up in time to army group. He also wanted Patton as an army commander but was willing to accept an army commander from the United States who would work alongside Bradley during the invasion and be prepared to succeed him when the former moved up.[13]

These proposals were disturbing to Marshall on several grounds. It appeared to him that the Supreme Commander's chief advisers were intent on shipping out of the United Kingdom all officers who would stand in the way of new arrivals. But Marshall was willing to accept this since he had high regard for many of the men Eisenhower wanted to bring along. Yet as his global responsibilities required, Marshall had to weigh also what Eisenhower's new command group would leave for the Mediterranean. Many tasks were still to be performed there, and Marshall feared that the current tendency "to gut the Mediterranean headquarters and leadership" left General Wilson, the Mediterranean Theater commander, with a most complex situation. He finally suggested that Eisenhower ease the transition by leaving Smith in the Mediterranean until mid-February, noting that General Morgan in London was a very capable officer "and almost seems more American than British." [14] Moreover both Churchill and Brooke indicated their disquiet at seeing the Italian theater of operations denuded of experienced leaders. Furthermore to the British and

American planners at COSSAC, Morgan's headquarters, who had worked unceasingly to find a workable plan—with limited resources and no supreme commander—it seemed that men "with sand in their boots," picked up in North Africa, along with some recent mud from Italy, intended to make a clean sweep of plans and staffs that had been built up in London.

To complicate the situation further, a slight misunderstanding arose at this juncture: Marshall, on his way back to the United States by way of the Pacific when Eisenhower's recommendations were sent, did not see them before he made his own suggestions. With no personal field headquarters to pick from Marshall tended to range over various theaters in selecting possible members of the OVERLORD staff. Moreover, wishing to give the senior officers some consideration, he listed as possible combinations General McNair, able head of Army Ground Forces, who had trained the fighting divisions, as army group commander with Bradley and Devers as army chiefs, or Devers as army group commander with Bradley and Hodges under him. He recognized the natural pull of the Mediterranean leaders on Eisenhower's affection; therefore he thought that the General might have Clark in mind for an assignment in the United Kingdom, and he added that if Truscott, continuing to perform brilliantly in Italy, was not to have a command in ANVIL, he should have a corps in the United Kingdom.[15]

Unaware that Marshall had not seen his earlier message, Eisenhower replied somewhat defensively that for the major command he profoundly hoped "to designate an officer who has had combat experience in this war." Bradley was his preference for the army group post with Patton as one of the army chiefs and perhaps Major General Courtney Hodges, then commanding the Third Army, or Major General William H. Simpson, a corps commander, for the other. Again he suggested Devers for Mediterranean Theater Command, Clark for ANVIL, Lucas for the Fifth Army, and Truscott for VI Corps. If circumstances permitted, he would like to have Truscott for OVERLORD "because he is the finest combat commander in the corps and divisional levels we now have on the front." [16]

This message was awaiting Marshall on his return to Washington shortly before Christmas, along with further intimations—apparently from Arnold—that Eisenhower and his staff were shifting out old-timers from London. At this point Marshall specifically questioned Eisenhower's desire to send Eaker and Devers to the Mediterranean. Eaker, who had commanded the Eighth Air Force in some of its greatest trials, resented being transferred to a quieter theater now that the show in the United Kingdom promised to be at its best. General Devers, who had replaced Eisenhower in May 1943 as commanding general of the European Theater, sadly faced the prospect of giving up his dream of heading an army group in the assault.

Distressed at the depth of General Marshall's displeasure over the proposal to shift Eaker to the Mediterranean, the Supreme Commander insisted that he would be glad to have Eaker but that orders had already been issued and that the appointment had been recommended by Arnold in a brief conversation in Sicily.[17]

Eisenhower reiterated that he was interested only in getting men accustomed to his views of combat. His main object, he declared, was "to have a few senior individuals that are experienced in the air support of ground troops." Unless a ground commander had men of some vision and understanding of the technique, he was "forever fighting with those air officers who, regardless of the ground situation, want to send big bombers on missions that have nothing to do with the critical effort."

Eisenhower seemed less at ease in discussing the case of General Devers. If the Chief of Staff wanted to leave him in England, Eisenhower said that he had no doubt that a useful job could be found for him—not a promising beginning for Devers, who felt that he could be "of most use" as an army group commander, a post Eisenhower had earmarked for Bradley. Rather than trying to downgrade Devers, the Supreme Commander continued, he thought he was recommending him for an important post, particularly as "I know that he would be acceptable to the British." [18]

On returning home, Marshall moved to clear up the contradictory proposals, observing apologetically, "I followed a confused trail while travelling the Pacific." He was not opposed to Eisenhower's selections, he wrote. To settle all doubts, he agreed that Devers should take the Mediterranean Command. Patton was to have an army in OVERLORD, Clark would command ANVIL, Lucas would take Clark's former command in Italy if his work as corps commander justified it (he was relieved a few weeks later of his corps), and Eaker would go to the Mediterranean. "In other words," the Chief of Staff concluded, with the gracious gesture often evident in his dealings with theater commanders, "you list your final desires and so far as I can see now they will be approved." [19]

His earlier alarm removed, Eisenhower with obvious pleasure said that everything was cleared up. He asked that Hodges, then in command of the Third Army, now earmarked for Patton's headquarters, be sent over, so that he could live at Bradley's side and be prepared to succeed him as First Army commander later in the year. McNair's chances were wrecked, as Marshall had feared, by his deafness, which Eisenhower thought would hamper him in an Allied command.[20]

In fact Marshall was more than satisfied with new arrangements. He had long favored picking young men and men with battle experience for key command posts. He would be even better pleased as the fighting continued. The fact that Bradley was extremely high on both Marshall's and Eisenhower's lists meant that the way was open for him to assume army group command. By D day it was clear that only complete failure in Normandy could prevent him from having the number-one place among American field commanders.

In addition the older men were not forgotten. Hodges would succeed
Bradley as commander of the First Army, Patton would lead the Third
Army, and Devers, after a time as commander of the U.S. Mediterranean
Theater, would return to northwest Europe by way of southern France as
Eisenhower's Sixth Army Group commander.

Lest there be any doubt about the points of agreement, Eisenhower
summarized them for Marshall on December 29. To the earlier appointments he added that Major General James H. Doolittle, then commanding the Fifteenth Air Force in the Mediterranean, would take over the
Eighth Air Force, which would be cut down to provide an overall headquarters for General Spaatz. This last suggestion disturbed the Chief of
Staff. A firm believer in small headquarters, Marshall noted that Portal
had objected to the Strategic Air Forces because it entailed the building
of another large headquarters, but he had been assured by Marshall and
Arnold that this would not be needed. "So I am disturbed if Spaatz is
going to aggrandize his job in an administrative manner. It would defeat
our purpose in placing the Strategic Air Forces under one command." He
added, "Tell him to follow Foch's method which is admirably suited to
his job and oppose this human reaction to build up a heavy overhead." [21]

Although Marshall gave Eisenhower nearly everything he asked for, he
could not ignore other calls. In mid-January the Chief of Staff informed
the Supreme Commander that Alexander and Devers both needed Clark
for the Italian campaign and Devers did not want to let Truscott go. [22]

With Clark held in Italy, Marshall raised the question of letting Patton
lead the Seventh Army in the assault on southern France. Eisenhower
obviously wanted this experienced commander for his own difficult battle,
but he did not oppose the assignment. He noted that Devers and Patton
were not congenial but on reflection decided that they were good enough
soldiers not to let this factor interfere. Favoring the appointment was the
fact that Patton was on the ground, was well liked by the French, and
knew many of the Seventh Army staff. [23]

Possibly aware of these transatlantic discussions, General Devers now
asked for Clark as the ANVIL commander. Since this would leave Patton
with no suitable assignment in the Mediterranean (there seems to have
been no request for him to take a command in Italy), Devers suggested
that new orders be issued for him. General Marshall considered briefly
bringing him to the United States for a short rest, then decided that his
return might occasion a raking over of old attacks. Eisenhower agreed,
saying that if he was not to be used for ANVIL, he needed him for an army
command. Thus when Patton assumed that he was wandering in a wil-
derness, the officers able to decide his future were debating only which of
two top assignments available he would handle best. Meanwhile Patton
spent some unhappy days and did not know until near the end of January,
when he was ordered to London, exactly what the future held for him. On
his arrival he was told that he was to have the Third Army. Historians

who like to discuss might-have-beens may find it interesting to speculate on the course of the war in France in the summer and fall of 1944 if instead of leading the Third Army in the pursuit across northern France, Patton had commanded the landings in the south that began fifteen days later.[24]

Ultimately the Seventh Army command went to Major General Alexander M. Patch, then commanding IV Corps in the United States, who had already been marked by General Marshall for an important post in Europe. Patch, whose work had come to Marshall's attention in France in World War I, had won his admiration for his outstanding leadership in the Pacific fighting as commander of the Americal Division and as successor in December 1942 to Major General Alexander A. Vandegrift, in charge of the Guadalcanal operations. With Clark unable to leave Italy, and Patton committed to OVERLORD, Marshall made Patch available for the ANVIL command.

As the weeks passed, General Marshall forwarded additional suggestions for Eisenhower's consideration, leaving his handprints over the command structure the Supreme Commander was building. In listing briefly the qualifications of the men selected, it is almost impossible to avoid giving the impression that these officers were standardized parts, valuable but mass-produced, almost interchangeable in the successful functioning of the machinery for winning the war. This one was high in his class at West Point, another was commissioned on the battlefield in France in World War I, another attracted Marshall's or McNair's attention in a successful maneuver, and so on. To an extent this concept of interchangeable parts is true. Not because these men went to West Point, VMI, the Citadel, Texas A & M, or came in by way of Reserve Officers' Training Corps, or fought the hard way up from enlistment, but because they had studied similar doctrine, sat out hard years of slow promotion in isolated posts, shared the same yarns in clubs in Manila, Fort Riley, or the Presidio, worked on the same problems at Fort Benning or the Army War College, enjoyed retelling the exploits of their particular regiments, they were parts of a whole. Yet there were no duplicate personalities. It was the uniqueness of his gifts that enabled each officer to use his training and experiences to great advantage in a common cause, to perform his duties in such a way that he stood out from his fellows and became a good—often a great—commander.[25]

The process of General Marshall's personal selection had been a long one. Of the corps commanders picked for northwest Europe in 1944, he had known the performances of Major Generals Manton S. Eddy, Troy H. Middleton, Walton H. Walker, and Clarence Huebner in France in World War I. Leonard T. Gerow, Wade H. Haislip, and E. H. Brooks had worked in the War Department before going to division and then corps commands.[26] J. Lawton Collins had been an instructor under Marshall at Fort Benning and then made his mark as a division commander in the Pacific. Charles H. Corlett had impressed him by brilliant work in Alaska and at Kwajalein. Matthew B. Ridgway had served with him in Tientsin, at Fort Benning, in Illinois maneuvers, and in the War Department before moving out as second to Bradley in the 82d Division.

Critics of Marshall saw in some of these appointments evidence of favoritism. Undoubtedly his acquaintanceship with some of these men played a part in their selection. But there were others he had known well who did not go up the promotion ladder when they failed to produce. It is a matter of record that he checked often and depended heavily on the lists kept by General McNair based on performance in the field.

The ground command had required mainly choices between alternatives. Since these were entirely American decisions—concerning command of American units only—the appointments were not unduly complicated. Neither was the selection of the commander of the invasion forces a matter of debate. Once he had been chosen Eisenhower had discarded General Devers's plan for separate U.S. and British commanders for D day. Rather he decided that a British officer should command all ground forces in the first phase of the invasion. He had preferred Alexander for this assignment—as apparently had Churchill. When Brooke picked Montgomery instead, and at a time when Alexander was fully engaged in planning for future operations in Italy, the question was settled so far as Marshall and Eisenhower were concerned.

Two appointments, the Allied Naval Commander-in-Chief and the Allied Air Commander-in-Chief, went to key members of the planning staff that had been set up provisionally to work with COSSAC. They were, respectively, Admiral Sir Bertram Ramsay and Air Chief Marshal Sir Trafford Leigh-Mallory. At Quebec the Combined Chiefs of Staff had accepted these two officers as the Supreme Commander's main naval and air subordinates. After Eisenhower's arrival he saw no reason to challenge the naval arrangement, but a debate soon started over the extent of Leigh-Mallory's authority.

The first problem arose because Eisenhower was bringing with him as Deputy Supreme Commander Air Chief Marshal Tedder, his chief airman in the Mediterranean. At the end of December the Supreme Commander asked Marshall to oppose a British proposal to select "a man named Mallory" as his chief airman, saying that it would virtually reduce Tedder to the position of air officer without portfolio. Although he understood that Leigh-Mallory, former chief of Fighter Command, was an airman of the highest caliber, "this tendency to freeze organization so that a commander may not use trusted and superior subordinates in their proper spheres disturbs me very much." [27]

Eisenhower complicated the problem by insisting that he control both bomber and fighter forces in the invasion. He knew that neither the British nor American bomber commanders wanted their planes under any other headquarters, particularly under Leigh-Mallory, whose main interest was in the tactical air forces.

The Supreme Commander raised the air command question with General Marshall during his visit to the United States in January 1944. The Chief of Staff agreed thoroughly with Eisenhower, saying that if he had been appointed to that command, he had intended to insist on air control to the extent of denouncing publicly any refusal of the British to integrate the air forces by charging them with failure to go "all out" for OVERLORD.[28]

Backed firmly by General Marshall, Eisenhower pressed his fight against the "bomber barons." After several weeks of discussions, and the intervention of Air Chief Marshal Portal, a compromise formula was worked out that gave Eisenhower the direction of all air forces out of the United Kingdom engaged in supporting the cross-Channel operation. It was understood that Eisenhower would exercise his control through Tedder and that the directive would be reviewed after the invasion forces were well established on the Continent.

In most of his interventions in European Theater planning that spring, General Marshall acted only after the Supreme Commander requested assistance. But in one case the Chief of Staff took the initiative to get Eisenhower's careful consideration of a War Department proposal.

An early believer in the use of airborne troops, General Marshall felt that they were not being properly utilized in European operations. He deplored the tendency of commanders to grasp at any new tactic or weapon as a means of advancing their current battles, often wasting valuable assets. Thus when tanks were first developed, ground commanders had thrown them into battle piecemeal, losing the effect that might have been gained by a massed attack. More recently ground commanders had called on air units to support minor operations without considering the greater role they might perform if properly committed. Now Marshall felt that airborne units were being frittered away merely as support troops instead of being used decisively in an assault.

The Chief of Staff had expressed his views on airborne forces to Eisenhower at Algiers in the summer of 1943. At that time he realized that the matter was academic since sufficient airlift was lacking for deployment of these forces in a massive attack. But with this deficiency removed, his air planners early in 1944 came up with new proposals that the Chief of Staff sent on to the Supreme Commander. Recognizing that one problem in dealing with new forces was the planners' "lack in conception," General Marshall took special care that Eisenhower understood that the plan was not to be easily brushed aside by an impatient subordinate. In sending two members of the air staff to explain the War Department's views, Marshall emphasized: "I might say that it was my determination in the event I went to England to do this, even to the extent that should the British be

in opposition I would carry it out exclusively with American troops."
Even so, Marshall still left Eisenhower an out: "I am not mentioning this
as pressure on you but merely to give you some idea of my own conclusions in the matter." [29]

Relishing his rare excursion into operational planning, he analyzed for
Eisenhower alternative plans prepared by General Arnold; Brigadier
General Frederick W. Evans, head of the Troop Carrier Command; and
Colonel Bruce W. Bidwell, the Operations Division airborne consultant.
Marshall's presentation, although certainly based on the work of others,
indicated a deep interest in operational details that he seldom had an
opportunity to indulge. His advocacy of the airborne proposals suggested
that had he commanded the Allied forces in northwest Europe, the planning might have been bolder.

Plan C contained a location "in keeping with my ideas on the subject, one that can be quickly established and developed to great strength
in forty-eight hours." This area lay south of Evreux, astride the road from
the beaches toward Paris. It had been selected because of four excellent
airfields that could be developed there. Instead of scattering airborne
units at Caen and in the Utah Beach area, he wanted to fly in and drop
several divisions around Evreux. "This plan appeals to me," he added,
"because I feel that it is a true vertical envelopment and would create
such a strategic threat to the Germans that it would call for a major revision of their defensive plans." He ticked off the advantages: "It should be
a complete surprise, an invaluable asset of any such plan. . . . It should
serve as a rallying point for considerable elements of the French underground." In a sense, he continued, "we would be opening another front
in France and your build-up would be tremendously increased in rapidity."

Foreseeing that the dismayed planners, already deep in more conven-
tional planning and already behind schedule, would fight the proposal,
Marshall urged Eisenhower to examine it personally. He sounded like the
innovative assistant commandant of the Infantry School asking for new
ways to achieve objectives: "The trouble with this plan is that we have
never done anything like this before, and frankly, that reaction makes me
tired. Therefore I should like you to give these young men an opportunity to present the matter to you personally before your staff tears it to
ribbons." Then, as if he had interfered too much with the man on the
ground, Marshall added: "Please believe that, as usual, I do not want to
embarrass you with undue pressure. I merely wish to be certain that you
have viewed this possibility on a definite planning basis."

Because of Marshall's deep interest in the proposition Eisenhower listened carefully to the War Department representatives. As soon as he had
heard them, he rushed off a tentative reply to the Chief of Staff. He recalled the Algiers conversation in 1943 when Marshall said that the
proper development of airborne operations gave the allies a field in which

they could get ahead of the enemy. "Since that time," Eisenhower declared, "this has been one of my favorite subjects for contemplation."

The concept outlined to him by Marshall's two emissaries was good, he wrote, but not the timing. He emphasized the degree to which the success of the landings depended on securing one good sheltered harbor. For this purpose he needed the airborne troops. But he feared the danger of putting units too far inland, where they could be isolated and defeated in detail. The Italian campaign, he noted, had failed to establish that Allied air superiority could prevent the enemy from concentrating forces for an attack. "An airborne landing carried out at too great a distance from other forces which will also be immobile for some time, will result in a much worse situation." Since he believed that his chief problem would be to neutralize the opposition at the beaches, which would be greater than anything yet met in the European war, he counted on dropping an airborne unit in the Cherbourg Peninsula to bar reinforcement by the enemy and to help the landing of Allied infantry in the area.[30]

He considered Marshall's proposal a possibility for the future, but for the moment airborne operations had to be visualized as "an immediate tactical rather than a long-range strategical adjunct of landing operations." Attempting to disabuse Marshall of any suspicion that he lacked daring, Eisenhower concluded: "I instinctively dislike ever to uphold the conservative as opposed to the bold. You may be sure that I will earnestly study the ideas presented by the two officers because on one point of your letter I am in almost fanatical agreement—I believe we can lick the Hun only by being ahead of him in ideas as well as in material resources."

Marshall could see the problems, but he clearly felt that his main point — the need of an imaginative and bold approach—had been overlooked. He did not press the argument, however, but replied: "I am sorry you do not see your way clear initially to commit the airborne effort en masse. I hope, however, that the visit of these two officers stimulated thought in the matter and served a useful purpose." [31]

Eisenhower worried over Marshall's reaction. More than a week later he asked the Chief of Staff to tell General Arnold that in spite of the glowing prospects he painted for his airborne plans, the ground situation in Normandy would yield only to stern fighting. "The fact is that against a German defense, fingers do not stab out rapidly and join up in the heart of enemy held territory unless there is present solid tactical power and overwhelming strength." He recalled that the ground action at Anzio resembled an airborne operation. The invaders were unable to augment their force quickly and would not have survived if access to the sea had been cut off. Yet the Germans had had little air strength and only nineteen divisions in the whole of Italy. "At the very best we are going to have here lively air opposition and a strong and well-organized ground defense." He thought that the airborne effort must be applied "after the beachhead forces gain the power to put on a sustained offensive." [32]

In the June landings the airborne forces, although scattered, did help win the foothold Eisenhower wanted in Normandy. But they achieved less than he wished. British airborne forces secured a bridgehead over the Orne near Caen but did not make possible the rapid seizure of the city. Although the two American airborne divisions aided the landings of the ground troops on Utah Beach and hastened the link-up at Carentan, they did not ensure the capture of Cherbourg as quickly as Eisenhower had planned. Indeed throughout the summer of 1944 he operated without the sheltered port that he thought essential to success.

If Marshall had chosen to re-examine the earlier arguments then, he would have been able to note that the Allied air forces succeeded in virtually blocking enemy reinforcement of the beachhead. He could have added that the bulk of the German strength in the first days of the attack was concentrated relatively close to the beaches and that an aerial landing in force might have created sufficient disorder in enemy ranks to aid a breakout.

But Eisenhower could have found support for his views in the outcome of the later airborne landings in and near Arnhem, where the enemy had responded quickly and where the ground forces that were supposed to link up with the airborne troops had reacted slowly. Montgomery's cautious approach in Normandy could have led to costly failure. To make such an operation work, it would have been necessary to change the plans for the landings. The emphasis would have had to be on a massed drop and support by air on a scale sufficient to meet any German attack from the Paris or Pas-de-Calais area and to disconcert an enemy braced for an attack from the sea.

General Marshall was averse to second guessing his commanders, especially when they were successful. But he always spoke wistfully of a possible lost opportunity. Despite the Arnhem experience he declared in 1957:

> The airborne unit was a collective enterprise. I was very strong for it. I opposed the way the air was used even to the last. The pressure, of course, is to give each person air. They used it very much like the Federal Army—until Grant came along with Sheridan—used its cavalry in the Civil War. They pieced it [out] all over the place.
>
> I've always felt, for instance, that in the final battle in Normandy that the plan they worked out in detail for the air, but which Eisenhower's people didn't think they could safely risk, was the quick way to end the battle—and that was to seize a field near Paris with glider planes, with parachute troops, and then fly in these small tractors and other things and then gather in all the motor transport of the surrounding country[side], and of course, all the French undercover units would have joined us and [have been] built up with ammunition—which of course we could do. We could put in these 105 guns and build up a force there right behind the German lines before they had time to get things together and make it almost impossible for them to do anything but to fight you with small groups.

But he was fair as always to the commander:

> However, that was a hazard. It was a brand-new thing and Eisenhower's staff and Eisenhower, himself, I guess, didn't feel it was proper to take the risk. But I always thought it was wrong to divide up the men into little groups everywhere.
>
> It was very natural for the commander[s] to want [the airborne support]. . . . It was very natural for them to want certain passes, certain crossings in connection with the first landing—going up on the right flank of the Utah Beach and with General Montgomery on his part of the front. But I believe the air could have been used with great effect in splitting up the Germans very quickly at the start. And the minute it was a little split up, the whole thing would fall because the continued reinforcement [by us] would have been a simple matter. . . .[33]

One can never be sure that the Germans would have responded in the same way to the landings or that the Allied air forces would have been as effective against the enemy if they had been supporting the airborne action Marshall wanted. But it was an idea worth extremely serious consideration. And had it worked, the bloody battle of the hedgerows would have been avoided.

Except for his intervention in the airborne operation General Marshall left planning details to Eisenhower and his subordinates. At the Supreme Commander's request, he phased forward troops and supplies, urged that the Navy give additional fire support in the landings, backed Eisenhower's efforts to get closer cooperation with the French Committee of National Liberation, and endorsed his plea to Roosevelt and Churchill for a modification of the unconditional-surrender formula that might make psychological-warfare appeals to the Germans for capitulation more effective. His role in these matters was a supporting one.

In one final episode before D day, however, Marshall played a major part. In April, as tension mounted and crises seemed to multiply, General Patton again made international headlines. Despite firm warnings from Eisenhower, mindful of Patton's past indiscretions in Morocco and Sicily, the irrepressible son of Mars added new burdens to those already carried by the Chief of Staff and the Supreme Commander. Childish or arrogant, the Third Army commander had sounded off at the opening of a Welcome Club for his soldiers at Knutsford near his headquarters. Apparently feeling the false sense of security that has misled many speakers at small luncheon meetings where they were assured that no reporters were present, he happily dropped a few improvised remarks, assuming that what he had to add to the occasion would not be long remembered. Instead he rattled windows not only in London, but at the White House and on Capitol Hill.[34]

Speaking of earlier welcome parties, he said that his practice had been to "welcome Germans and Italians to the 'infernal regions.' " He amused the dominant feminine contingent by saying that once his soldiers told the

American women how lovely the British women were, the jealous ladies at home would force the war to a conclusion. All this was harmless persiflage, but he got into difficulty with the suggestion that "since it seems to be the evident destiny of the British and Americans to rule the world, the better we know each other the better the job we will do."

To some in the United States and Britain who realized how long the Russians had been carrying on the fight against the Germans while their demands for a second front remained unanswered, Patton's boast seemed untimely. To those in the United States who still seethed at the memory of the slapping incidents, this new outburst represented a new high in irresponsibility.[35]

Marshall himself informed Eisenhower's headquarters—the Supreme Commander was away at a training exercise—of the uproar in Washington. On April 26 the Chief of Staff radioed: "Newspapers today carried glaring reports of General Patton's statements reference Britain and America's rule of the world. We were about to get [Senate] confirmation of the permanent makes [promotions]. This I fear has killed them all." [36]

The promotion lists were already in trouble, since some members of Congress felt that there were too many generals. Now others took up the cry. Patton had succeeded, declared Representative Karl Mundt, Republican of South Dakota, in "slapping the face of every one of the United Nations, except Great Britain." The Washington *Post,* in a scathing editorial forwarded by Marshall to Eisenhower, recalled an incident the Army was trying to forget: "General Patton has progressed from simple assaults on individuals to collective assault on entire nationalities." [37]

The *Post* editorial reflected what was being said in hundreds of letters that were being sent to the Pentagon. It referred to Patton's remarks "on welcoming the Germans and Italians into hell and also his reference to the 'English ladies' and 'American dames,'" with the comment: "This was intended no doubt as gallantry and perhaps as a rough sort of military humor. The truth is, however, that it is neither gracious nor amusing." Denying that its attitude was prissy, the *Post* declared, "Whatever his merits as a strategist or tactician he has revealed glaring defects as a leader of men. It is more than fortunate that these have become apparent before the Senate takes action to pass upon his recommended promotion in permanent rank from Colonel to Major General. All thought of such promotion should now be abandoned. That the War Department recommended it is one more evidence of the tendency on the part of members of the military to act as a clique or a club." The full danger of Patton's indiscretion was revealed in the observation that the incident raised the question whether permanent promotions should be made at all in wartime.[38]

General Marshall offered to share with Eisenhower the decision on Patton's future. He observed that the public did not take into consideration "the unmistakable fact that Patton is the only available Army commander for his present assignment who has actual experience in fighting

Rommel and in extensive landing operations followed by a rapid campaign of exploitation." Then he added with rare understanding, "You carry the burden of responsibility as to the success of OVERLORD. If you feel that the operation can be carried out with the same assurance of success with Hodges in command, for example, instead of Patton all well and good. If you doubt it then between us we can bear the burden of the present unfortunate reaction. I fear the harm has already been fatal to the confirmation of the permanent list." [39]

Before receiving Marshall's message Eisenhower indicated his intention to deal firmly with the Third Army commander. He declared with some heat, "Apparently he is unable to use reasonably good sense in all those matters where senior commanders must appreciate the effect of their own actions upon public opinion." He added that while the effect of Patton's remarks was exaggerated, he had "grown so weary of the trouble he constantly causes you and the War Department to say nothing of myself, that I am seriously contemplating the most [dramatic] action." Having expressed his full disapproval, the American commander shifted back to Washington part of the responsibility by asking the Chief of Staff whether Patton's "latest statements have caused such serious reaction at home as to prevent the War Department securing Congressional approval of any of its recommendations?" Did Marshall consider that retaining him in high command would tend to destroy or diminish public and government confidence in the War Department? "If the answer to either of the above is in the affirmative, then I am convinced that stern disciplinary action must be taken so as to restore the situation." [40]

Marshall's answer was already on the way. Meanwhile Eisenhower was putting the fear of SHAEF and the War Department into Patton with warnings of "drastic potentialities." Regretting that Patton would not be prudent despite "the most drastic instructions and orders," he declared: "I am thoroughly weary of your failure to control your tongue and have begun to doubt your all-round judgment, so essential in high military position." [41]

In reporting his dressing down to Marshall, Eisenhower added: "On all of the evidence available I will relieve him from command and send him home unless some new and unforeseen information should be developed in the case." But his next paragraph indicated a weakening of his resolution as he contrasted Patton and Hodges: "The big difference is that Patton has proved his ability to conduct a ruthless drive whereas Hodges has not." Later in the message he hedged further: "Moreover, there is always the possibility that this war, possibly even this theater, might yet develop a situation where this admittedly unbalanced but nevertheless aggressive fighting man should be rushed into the breach." [42]

Eisenhower was now on record for imposing the extreme penalty, but he dreaded to go the whole distance. Marshall had replied to his request for guidance by saying, "the decision is exclusively yours." Then, as so often happened in these matters, the Chief of Staff made the tough decision easier by urging, "Do not consider War Department position in the matter. Consider only OVERLORD and your own heavy burden of responsibility for its success. Everything else is of minor importance." He volunteered further support: "In any event, I do not want you at this time to be burdened with the responsibility of reducing him in rank. Send him home, if you see fit, and in grade, or hold him there as surplus if you so desire, or, as I have indicated above, continue him in command if that promises best for OVERLORD." To take all heat off Eisenhower, he added: "I fear my quotation from one editorial may have resulted in overemphasis in your mind of the necessity for drastic action to meet difficult resulting situation here at home." No one, he explained, had called for Patton's removal.[43]

With obvious relief Eisenhower replied that unquestionably Patton's removal would mean loss of important fighting experience and "his demonstrated ability of getting the utmost out of soldiers in offensive operations." He accepted Marshall's backing: "Because your telegram leaves the decision exclusively in my hands, to be decided solely upon my convictions as to the effect upon OVERLORD, I have decided to retain him in command."[44] To Patton he wrote, "I am once more taking the responsibility of retaining you in command in spite of damaging repercussions resulting from a personal indiscretion. I do this solely because of my faith in you as a battle leader and from no other motives."[45] Marshall and Eisenhower had made it possible for Patton to fight another day.

With the last major command problem settled the Supreme Commander could concentrate on fixing the day of landing. He informed the Chiefs of Staff on May 17 that the attack would be launched on Y day (June 1, given the code name HALCYON) plus 4. This notice of change, like those that came afterward, was duly passed on to Marshal Stalin, who had promised to follow the landings in Normandy within a week with an offensive of his own designed to put maximum pressure on Germany.[46]

Having named the date, Eisenhower characteristically fretted over the matters that might go wrong and the nature of the offensive that he would like to make. He reacted to the tension as he had on the eve of TORCH by putting his thoughts on paper. Sometimes he wrote a memorandum for the diary kept by his aide, Commander Butcher. At other times he appeared to gain confidence and relief by expressing his thoughts to General Marshall. The letters were seldom answered, since they usually called for no reply, but Eisenhower and Marshall each understood.

On May 21 the Supreme Commander reported a serious breach of security by a naval officer. This, coming on top of a grave indiscretion of an Air Forces major general concerning the date of the invasion and the temporary lapse of a fatigued sergeant, who had addressed copies of a highly classified operational plan to his home address in Chicago, irritated and upset Eisenhower more than it would have in less anxious hours. "Sometimes," he radioed Marshall, "I get so angry at the occurrence of such needless and additional hazards that I could cheerfully shoot the offender myself."

Often he wrote of pleasanter topics. He had recently made an effort to visit many of the invasion units in England, Scotland, and Wales. There was no question of the readiness of troops, he reported. They were well trained, fit, and impatient to get the job under way. To impress on Marshall his belief in bolder methods, he concluded, "I am trying to visualize an operation in which we would bring in behind the initial beachhead a great strength in armor and seek an opportunity to launch a big armored attack in conjunction with a deep and very heavy penetration by airborne troops. Such an operation might be accompanied also by an additional amphibious affair." [47]

If Marshall, in these closing days of May, allowed himself to ponder the role he might have had, he must have reflected sardonically at times over the petty annoyances he and the Secretary of War had to face at home. Judging from Stimson's diary, the most violent issue that moved the War Department in the last days before the landings was an ugly dispute, "dreadful and fruitless," that broke out between the Army Emergency Relief Organization and the American Red Cross. The Air Forces and the Army Service Forces, Stimson complained, had set up personnel-affairs branches that duplicated the work of the Red Cross. This situation was made worse by "complications of femininity and rank." Determined to have no more nonsense, Stimson sent Marshall a scorching paper on June 2—milder than the one he had initially drafted, but still hot. To the Secretary's dismay Marshall reacted out of character; he was moody and inclined prematurely to jump off on the wrong side. As sometimes happened, the two men resorted to some "pretty plain words" but ended by agreeing to think it over. A conference on June 4 reduced some of the heat so that by the time of the invasion the private war was on its way to settlement. [48]

Almost on the eve of the invasion the old troubles in China flared up again. On June 1, as Allied troops moved to the top of the Alban Hills on the way to Rome, word came that Chiang Kai-shek was threatening to seize Stilwell's stores of supplies. Inevitably Stimson and Marshall contrasted the relatively smooth workings of the teams in the Mediterranean and in the United Kingdom with the nasty split between Chennault and Stilwell and the dangerous quarrel between the Generalissimo and the American commander in China. [49]

On June 4 the news was good: General Clark was at last in Rome. Next morning a delighted Marshall gave full details of the capture to his associates. Churchill, who had fought hard for the campaign, could take the bows, but Marshall shared his hope that the end of the fight was a little nearer—the end of a war that had taken his stepson's life less than a week before. Rome's fall to the Allies was a bitter blow for Hitler on the eve of another landing. His propagandists were rudely embarrassed at being caught short by the pace of events. When American troops entered the towns of Normandy three days later, they found on the walls mocking posters that the Germans had put up on the eve of Rome's capture, depicting a snail painfully inching up the boot of Italy.

The snail was no longer a valid symbol of advances in Italy, but to leaders watching the calendar and the clock in London and in Washington it still seemed entirely too relevant. For Marshall, to whom the coming assault was Judgment Day, the waiting was made worse because the last-minute decisions had passed from his hands. When to invite de Gaulle to the United Kingdom, the nature of the D-day announcements, whether Eisenhower and Churchill could watch the battle, even the timing of D day were all questions being settled abroad. At times he must have felt himself a forgotten bystander.

In reality the Chief of Staff was often in the minds of his subordinates. Colonel Elliott Roosevelt, returning to London from Moscow in late May with a party that had been seeking Soviet bases for U.S. photographic-reconnaissance aircraft, played bridge one evening with Eisenhower, Butcher, and Brigadier General Ted Curtis. When the Supreme Commander spoke of his desire to visit the beachhead on D day, the President's son mentioned possible dangers and the controversy over a successor that might arise in case of Eisenhower's death. The Supreme Commander shrugged off the problem. General Marshall, he said, would be quickly shifted to the post. He disagreed with young Roosevelt's belief that Montgomery or Brooke would be selected, arguing that other British generals would not want a British Supreme Commander and that an American Supreme Commander had been set up to counterbalance the British commanders of ground, air, and naval forces in the invasion.[50]

Weather forecasts at the beginning of June were uncertain, and sailors who knew the Channel feared bad sailing for the invasion craft. Early on the morning of June 4 Eisenhower found the forecasts too threatening to permit him to carry out the plan for landing on June 5. Postponing the assault until the sixth, he scheduled meetings of the key commanders for the early morning of the fifth to see if the skies were more friendly. Rain and wind greeted him as he left his camp for Southwick House in Portsmouth. There he was advised by the meteorologist that bad weather would continue, but there might be several hours of improved conditions on June 6. In an hour of terribly difficult decision he weighed the costs of turning back, the possibility of losing surprise, the necessity of waiting another two weeks until tides were again suitable, and the small chance of improvement in the weather. His airmen were dubious, his ground commanders preferred to go ahead, and the sailors said that they could manage. After looking carefully at all angles, he gave the command to go. To Marshall he flashed the final message "HALCYON plus 5 finally and definitely confirmed." [51]

Shortly afterward General Marshall passed on to Secretary Stimson the welcome news that the invasion was on. The parachutists would leave the United Kingdom at 11 p.m. on June 5 and land two hours later. Forces from the sea would begin landing on June 6 at 6:30 a.m. London time.

Unlike Stimson, Marshall kept no account of D day or of his reactions. But like the Secretary of War, he could look back on the long arguments with Churchill and his advisers, and he shared Stimson's vision of "the thousands of young men who are keenly on their toes in Great Britain at this time facing the adventure of their lives and perhaps their deaths." Stimson spoke for the Chief of Staff and all those who now stood poised for the attack in saying that it was one of the great events of world history, "perhaps the greatest and sharpest crisis that the world has ever had, and it has all focused together on tonight." [52]

It was not Marshall's nature to brood over what might have been. There is temptation to assume that he carefully buried his disappointments—the greater they were, the deeper he thrust them—never permitting himself to call them by that name again. Whether this is true, everything on record repudiates any suggestion of regret that he was not leading the assault and shows that he was gratified by the realization that all his efforts at training and planning and selection of strong commanders had come together on this day. He remained self-contained as usual. Mrs. Marshall could recall nothing out of the ordinary in his demeanor. It appears that he was not prompted, as was Stimson, to rise early to turn on the first radio reports of the attack.[53]

We may be certain that the cost of victory was in his thoughts. His stepson's widow had come down to Leesburg for the weekend of June 3–4 before leaving on an assignment for *Life* magazine to Chicago and Wisconsin. The General found time on June 7 to thank her for some purchases she had made for the Marshalls and to add that her brief visit "gave a great deal of pleasure and I think had a highly beneficial effect on Katherine." [54] After this trip Madge was assigned to the Washington office of *Life* until Labor Day, and she spent much of that time at Fort Myer or Leesburg with the Marshalls.[55]

There was little to be learned of the attack in the early hours of June 6. Eisenhower, who had been on hand for the departure of the airborne forces, waited anxiously at Portsmouth for the first reports. He knew that Marshall was no less eager than he himself to get accurate details of the landings, and he asked impatiently for dispatches. Finally at 8 a.m., he radioed: "I have as yet no information concerning the actual landings nor of our progress through beach obstacles. Communiqué will not be issued until we have word that leading ground troops are actually ashore." However, preliminary reports were hopeful, and Leigh-Mallory, who had predicted heavy casualties in the airborne operation, announced that this phase of the operation was going well.[56]

As additional news came in, Marshall and his colleagues made ready to fly to Europe. They justified the trip, planned several days earlier, on the grounds that they would be able to make any quick decisions required in an emergency and to come to conclusions on later operations. What was left unstated was that these men who had fought so long for OVERLORD and had given the "go" sign for so many landings now wanted to see their greatest assault in progress.

Their departure was delayed until the morning of June 8 so that they could attend President Roosevelt's dinner the previous evening for Premier Stanislaw Mikolajczyk of Poland. As the guests lined up to go in to dinner, White House secretary William D. Hassett stopped to talk briefly with General Marshall. Although not a cynic, Hassett—who had been watching the Washington scene since 1909—was not easily impressed by capital personalities. But that evening, stirred perhaps by the long fight just starting in northwest Europe, Hassett whispered a tribute and a prayer for Marshall: "Wherever this man goes he inspires reverence—may God spare him." [57]

XX

Of de Gaulle and
the Ljubljana Gap

"I THINK we have these Huns at the top of the toboggan slide and the full crash of the Russian offensive should put the skids under them." So wrote a jubilant Marshall with uncharacteristic slanginess to President Roosevelt on June 14. He was still glowing after his visit to the American landing area in Normandy.[1]

Marshall, Arnold, and King had arrived over Scotland a few days earlier after an uneventful flight across the Atlantic, but heavy fog prevented their planes from landing at the intended destination, Prestwick. After an hour and a half of circling over the invisible airfield they were diverted to Valley, an Air Transport Command base in the northwest tip of Wales, where no preparations had been made to receive them. Colonel McCarthy, sent over several days before to help make arrangements, had gone on to Prestwick with the controversial special train furnished by the Services of Supply commander, General Lee. McCarthy had passed on Marshall's instructions that Lee was not to meet the party, since he undoubtedly had more important things to do in the first days of the landings in Normandy. To McCarthy's astonishment General Lee met the train, "booted, spurred, and replete with riding crop." But fog had spoiled his welcome. The fussy General, whose initials, JCHL, were sometimes interpreted as "John Court House Lee" or "Jesus Christ Himself Lee," stood lonely at the Prestwick station waiting for the VIPs who did not appear.

Bad weather, train delays, unforeseen changes in plans conspired in the first hours of arrival to remind the Chiefs of Staff that they, too, like ordinary soldiers, sailors, and airmen, could also "hurry up and wait." When they finally landed at Valley, they found that the best course of action was to flag down the Irish Mail, a London-bound express. McCarthy, who had

wangled a flight to Wales in a two-seater, managed with the aid of the
local officials to get an extra car hooked on. The car was unheated, but
the conductor provided a large tin container of strong, scalding tea, into
which each officer dipped his cup.[2]

The tired, cold passengers were warmly welcomed at Euston Station in
London by the British Chiefs of Staff. As cheering as their pleasant greeting was the appearance of blue skies and sunshine. Within a short time
the guests were on their way to their billet in Stanwell Place at Staines,
about twenty miles southwest of London.[3]

Meeting at the War Cabinet office on June 10, the Combined Chiefs of
Staff examined the progress of the war on all fronts. King outlined plans
for the Marianas and what would follow in the Palaus, and the Chiefs
considered operations in north Burma as well as flights over the Hump.
Arnold reported that the Air Transport Command had carried more than
11,000 tons into China in the past month and that he hoped to reach
16,000 in July. More important, he said that airplane production was
reaching a level at which "most of the theaters were becoming saturated,
and the demands for airplanes were being met everywhere." [4]

The reports on the Pacific and Burma, normally important items of
business, obviously were not now of overriding interest for the assembled
Chiefs of Staff. The big show then in progress and the plans for a new
front in the Mediterranean overshadowed everything else. Almost certainly the ANVIL operation was the main topic between Marshall and
Churchill when the Prime Minister invited the Chief of Staff out to
Chequers that evening. On the following day at Stanwell Place the Combined Chiefs of Staff moved at once to take up the landings in southern
France, postponed in April and now back at the head of the agenda.

In the euphoria produced by the success in Normandy the opening discussions were amiable. The British did not object when the Americans
suggested that the Italian advance stop at the Apennines or hold at the
Pisa-Rimini line, although Brooke noted other possibilities in Italy. The
Americans matched their colleagues' bonhomie when they learned that
the British were prepared at last to consider proceeding with landings in
southern France. They were momentarily startled when Brooke resur-
rected Churchill's plan for a landing at Bordeaux, in western France. But
he did not press the point, nor did he argue strongly for an Istrian Peninsula operation in northeastern Italy. Privately he commented that the
Chiefs had at last put the operation in southern France in proper perspective. By the time the Allied forces reached the Pisa-Rimini line, Brooke
thought they would have succeeded in diverting German resources from
northern France. They could then consider landings in the south to win a
beachhead where French troops from North Africa could be used.[5]

General Marshall argued for priority for the south of France, although
he was willing to consider a landing at Sète and an advance northwest
toward Bordeaux or northward up the Rhone Valley instead of in the

Toulon-Marseille area. He stressed the possibilities of extensive air transport, requiring bold decisions and fresh approaches to problems, particularly if the offensive that the Russians were about to open went well. Echoing this argument, General Arnold declared that the Allies could build up enough transport in three months to land four or five divisions with accompanying heavy guns in one night. This prospect, which Brooke said Montgomery had considered on a smaller scale, opened up opportunities of using long-range penetration groups, such as those employed in Burma, to foster and support the French underground.

While noting the role of air in weakening enemy resistance, Air Marshal Portal spoke of a possible amphibious operation, via the Istrian Peninsula, at the head of the Adriatic, if the Russian advance made such a move feasible. Although willing to consider such an operation, Admiral King reminded him that this move depended on Soviet ground operations. So far as Italy was concerned, he favored forcing the enemy to hold the Pisa-Rimini line in strength.[6] Marshall agreed that the Allies should keep "the options open as long as possible" but urged that they prepare for an operation in the not-too-distant future.

At last the Combined Chiefs of Staff agreed that an amphibious operation should be mounted from the Mediterranean with approximately a three-division lift. They directed the Mediterranean commander, General Sir Henry Maitland Wilson, to draw up alternative plans for the original ANVIL operation (Toulon-Marseille), a landing at Sète, and an operation on the Istrian Peninsula. General Eisenhower was to plan a landing in the Bay of Biscay, with special attention to the area between the mouth of the Loire and Bordeaux. The final decision on the actual place of landing was to be made later; July 25 was suggested as the target date. After the heated controversy of February and March southern France was back in the running, apparently without acrimony.

The Combined Chiefs of Staff reckoned, however, without the Prime Minister, who would subject ANVIL to fiery trials before the summer ended. At the moment Churchill's chief interest was in the battle in Normandy. Denied an opportunity to watch the landings by the united efforts of George VI and the Supreme Commander, the British leader was impatient to get a look at the fighting front and, if possible, a crack at the enemy. He invited the British and U.S. Chiefs of Staff to accompany him to the far shore.

There was the unmistakable air of an outing about the expedition to the battle front. The irrepressible Prime Minister was exuberant and the others excited at the prospect of seeing the results of their deliberations and debates.

Joining the Prime Minister and Field Marshal Jan Smuts on the former's private train for the overnight trip from London to Portsmouth, the Chiefs of Staff were invited to a convivial meal around a long banquet table set up in one of the cars. Everyone seemed in a mood for celebration except King. Finally after casting impish glances in the Admiral's direction, Churchill quipped, "Don't look so glum. I am not trying to take anything away from the United States Navy just now." [7]

A grinning Eisenhower met them at Portsmouth. There the party broke into two groups, the British boarding one of their destroyers for British-held beaches and the United States contingent going on the U.S. destroyer *Thompson* to their sector. They moved out of a crowded harbor, jammed with warships and landing craft, under skies filled with roaring planes, marveling at the Allied control of sea and air, which ensured the safety of the Channel and made possible the uninterrupted flow of supplies and men to the fighting area. The great charts and loading tables, the tables of organization, the vast build-up of supplies under Operation BOLERO, the lines of transportation that, in Marshall's words, "stretched all the way back to central United States"—all these suddenly came to life for the Chiefs who had visualized that these miracles could come to pass. For Marshall, who had never let this cross-Channel assault be forgotten, it was a day of fulfillment.[8]

Transferring to a submarine chaser, the Americans, now joined by Rear Admirals John L. Hall and Alan G. Kirk, took a look at the invasion area from the sea. Shifting to a DUKW, an awkward-looking amphibious vehicle that could swim and also run on land, they moved ashore. Photographers caught Marshall and his associates clambering awkwardly over the side of the DUKW as they prepared to set foot on the soil of France. They had come to "Easy Red" on hard-fought Omaha Beach, where throughout D day it had seemed that Major General Leonard T. Gerow's V Corps elements, under murderous fire from prepared positions along the hillside or from guns on the heights above, would not make it ashore.

General Bradley and many of his chief commanders greeted the visitors from Washington, showing them the points of enemy resistance, the ugly beach obstacles now bulldozed aside, the improvised ditches, the bunkers, uncompleted minefields. Clearly the battle was still near at hand. Cameramen posed the officers against the cliffs near St. Laurent sur Mer, where one could see in the same sweep dozens of small craft coming into shore, ships unloading with great barrage balloons floating overhead, and up the roadway the stream of trucks and jeeps and men on foot pouring through the gap to enlarge the force that the enemy could not long contain in the tangled hedgerows a few thousand yards beyond.

It was General Marshall's first return to France since September 1919, when, as General Pershing's aide, he had said good-by to Foch and his staff at Brest. That day was undoubtedly in his mind, as was the more vivid recollection of a June day in 1917 when he had been the second member of the 1st Division to come down the gangplank at St. Nazaire. On that earlier landing the Americans had arrived with a token force—so the French had viewed it—to raise morale. Marshall had been disturbed to find that so much was expected by a weary people and so little was ready for the fight. Twenty-seven years later he came with the forces that had provided much of the power already to break Hitler's control of northwest Europe. Liberation of nearly all France was only three months away.

The U.S. Chief of Staff thought first of the wounded. An airstrip had been set up just back of Omaha Beach on ground hotly disputed five days earlier. Here Marshall, Arnold, and King visited a plane loaded with men ready to be evacuated to the United Kingdom for further treatment. Nearby they could see where the first dead had been temporarily buried, close to the site at St. Laurent sur Mer later chosen for the permanent cemetery, on the peaceful cliff looking calmly out to sea.

True to his policy of rewarding valor promptly, Marshall had already directed that special recognition be made of bravery performed in the landings. Hours before his arrival officers went out from army and corps headquarters to the lower units to get information for citations in order that he might personally make some of the awards. The General had also asked for names of officers and men who would be promoted for their actions in the landings. Nor did he forget those who were killed while coming ashore, those who died at the water's edge, and those who were struck down making their way through the narrow exits from the beaches.

Shepherded by Bradley and members of his staff, the Americans went inland, visiting Grandcamp and Isigny, towns taken in the early fighting in the V Corps sector. As they drove along in three reconnaissance cars, on narrow roads being beaten into heavy dust by the trucks and tanks that moved in a continuous stream, meeting troops and hundreds of prisoners, stopped at times by confused traffic or occasional roadblocks, they came to grips with the flow of battle, which could never be envisaged by use of even the most sophisticated visual aids in the Pentagon. Of the visiting party perhaps only General Marshall, recalling his own task in moving hundreds of thousands of men in and out of the Meuse-Argonne area in late 1918, could fully appreciate the massiveness of the task being executed here.

At times General Bradley's aide, Major Chester B. Hansen, had to act as a traffic cop to disentangle the vehicles carrying the visitors from the crush. Besides the traffic a whiff of danger was added as the officers neared Carentan, through which the party would have to pass to reach Utah Beach. Taken that day, the town was now under harassing fire from the recently withdrawn enemy artillery. Reflecting, as he had at nearby Isigny, on the damage to the Allied high command one German sniper could inflict, General Bradley decided that they should run no more risks.

Calling a halt in the busy morning, the First Army commander took his guests to his headquarters, a tented command post located in an orchard near St. Pierre du Mont. The visitors were proudly welcomed by Bradley's principal field commanders, Hodges, Collins, and Gerow. But the amenities were limited, marked by all the simplicity of an army in the field. They washed up in the open, pouring water from a jerrican, sharing the primitive facilities. The food, C rations and crackers, more palatable than the K rations carried by soldiers on the move, tasted good as they sat under apple trees reclaimed for France.

At the close of a full day Arnold flew back to England from the airstrip near the sea while Marshall and King hastened aboard their destroyer to rejoin the Prime Minister at Portsmouth. They were much too early—their third delay of the trip. Hoping for an opportunity to shoot at the enemy, Churchill had waited until he could fire a gun. This done, he joined them aboard the train in high spirits to serve victory champagne and an excellent dinner.

During the meal Marshall composed a message. As he finished, he showed the Prime Minister a radiogram for Admiral Mountbatten that he asked all around the table to sign. To a commander with whom he had worked since early 1942 he had written:

> Today we visited the British and American armies on the soil of France. We sailed through vast fleets of ships, with landing craft of many types pouring more and more men, vehicles, and stores ashore. We saw clearly the maneuver in process of rapid development. We have shared our secrets in common and helped each other all we could. We wish to tell you at this moment in your arduous campaign that we realize that much of this remarkable technique and, therefore, the success of the venture, has its origin in developments effected by you and your staff of Combined Operations.
>
> ARNOLD, BROOKE, CHURCHILL,
> KING, MARSHALL, SMUTS [9]

Marshall's satisfaction with what he had seen was evident in the message he sent Roosevelt two days later. "Conditions on the beachhead are generally favorable . . ." he reported. "The Germans appear unable to muster a sizeable counterattack for some days to come. French Resistance good. Interruption of communications by air seems effective." Equally important, the morale of troops and commanders was excellent. The General was especially impressed "by the calm confidence of . . . Bradley and by the aggressive attitude of his corps commanders." In the midst of what appeared to be great confusion at the water's edge, he saw in the organization of the beaches "a remarkable scale of efficiency." [10]

As the visitors returned from the beaches, the Germans dropped their first robot bombs (V-1s; V for "vengeance") on London. Since the missiles hit at random, Stanwell Place, which had been selected for them because of its remoteness from a bombing target area, was rocked by explosions early on the thirteenth.[11] Although the war had been taken across the Channel, the enemy was still capable of striking back at London.

The fireworks created by the V-1s seemed mild in comparison to the emotional ones that flared up among the Chiefs of Staff when they learned of the actions of General de Gaulle, head of the French Committee of National Liberation. Their wrath was understandable, but they should not have been surprised at de Gaulle's behavior. The trouble had been brewing for months.

Since his arrival in London early in 1944 General Eisenhower had sought to clarify his relations with the French Committee of National Liberation. An old problem that had harassed him in the Mediterranean became worse as the day of landing on French soil approached—dealing with de Gaulle. In numerous requests to the War Department for instructions the Supreme Commander conceded the difficulties presented by le Général but insisted that "he is the best we have." Although unfavorably impressed by de Gaulle's aloof imperiousness and perhaps overly influenced by Admiral Leahy's anti-Gaullist attitude, Marshall was inclined to go along with Eisenhower. As he heard of situation after situation made worse for lack of an Anglo-American agreement with de Gaulle and the French Committee, he grew even more sympathetic to Eisenhower's pleas for an official *modus vivendi*.

In May the Supreme Commander himself added fat to the fire. As a security measure he asked the British government to bar the sending of messages in code from the United Kingdom except by British, American, and Russian diplomatic representatives. Seeing in this action one more slight to the French Committee, de Gaulle ordered his representative in London, General Pierre Koenig, to break off discussions with Eisenhower's headquarters. Marshall shared Eisenhower's relief when Koenig agreed that American and British officials could pass on the security of information in French messages before permitting him to send them in French code with his assurance that they had not been changed.

More serious was determination of the degree of recognition Eisenhower should give the French Committee of National Liberation once the invasion was launched. At issue were French cooperation with the Allies in liberated France and the nature of civil relations. The President insisted that Eisenhower hold his dealings with de Gaulle's group to a minimum and that he make no decision that might be interpreted as recognizing the special position of the French Committee. He regarded the French people as shell shocked and not yet prepared to think through their political future. "We, as the liberators of France," he declared, "have no right to color their views" or give any group the right to impose its rule on them. Self-determination for the French people should be the true aim of the Allies. His point was valid, but his failure to recognize that he must choose either Gaullists or the people of Vichy showed a curious blind spot.[12]

Churchill had planned to invite de Gaulle to London before the invasion, but after receiving this message from the President he told General Bedell Smith that he had now decided to do so only if the French leader would agree to remain in London until after the landings. Smith replied that de Gaulle would refuse any such invitation. He suggested instead that they issue the invitation just before D day.

Through long experience as a staff officer under Marshall, Smith had learned that he could depend on his Chief's careful consideration of an issue. On May 15 he therefore spelled out the difficulties confronting the Supreme Commander. "I am sure that nothing would suit General Eisenhower better," he radioed Marshall, "than to have his responsibility rigidly confined to matters of purely military concern, but no one who has dealt with a foreign government at close range, as we have, can fail to realize that when a military commander is operating on foreign soil there is no clear-cut line of demarcation between military and civil or political questions."

In the same message Smith detailed the delicate situation arising from lack of a formal directive from the Combined Chiefs of Staff to Eisenhower on the French problem. The Supreme Commander could not act on the basis of a unilateral statement from the President. Although the Prime Minister had stated, as recently as the night before, that he stood with the President on all questions concerning the French, "it must always be remembered that the one ministry which the Prime Minister does not control is the Foreign Office." As Smith had expected, the Chief of Staff promptly forwarded the message to Roosevelt. Marshall asked that the President not let the Prime Minister know of Smith's comments lest the disclosure "destroy his usefulness at a very vital moment." [13]

Eisenhower followed up Smith's careful preparations with a promise to Marshall to deal with the French Committee of National Liberation only in matters concerning military affairs and civil administration. Noting a choice of evils, he added that current information showed only two major groups in France—the Vichy "gang" and the group "with unreasoning admiration for de Gaulle." Since his was an Allied command, as he blandly phrased it, he hoped that he would receive Roosevelt's desires in the form of a joint directive from the two governments.[14]

The President had a habit of keeping unpleasant missives around for a time, perhaps believing that events would make a reply unnecessary. More than two weeks after receiving Eisenhower's message he instructed Marshall to inform the Supreme Commander "that I still think he does not quite get the point." More bluntly he laid it out: "He evidently believes the fool newspaper stories that I am anti–de Gaulle, even the kind of story that says I hate him, etc., etc. All this, of course, is utter nonsense. I am perfectly willing to have de Gaulle made President, or Emperor, or King or anything else so long as the action comes in an untrammeled and unforced way from the French people themselves." [15]

Roosevelt reminded the Chief of Staff that his fair-haired generals were not always as well informed as they thought. "I do not agree when Ike says that there are only two major groups in France today. . . . I wonder how he knows this because nobody else knows anything really about the internal situation in France." The President then hammered home a lesson: "It is awfully easy to be for de Gaulle . . . but I have a moral duty that transcends 'an easy way.' It is to see to it that the people of France have nothing foisted on them by outside powers. It must be a French choice—and that means, as far as possible, forty million people. Self-determination is not a word of expediency. It carries with it a very deep principle in human affairs."

The words were fair and did him honor. But Marshall and Eisenhower both knew from experience in North Africa that the President would cheerfully impose solutions if he felt they served American interests. They realized that he would have been less indulgent to French public opinion if de Gaulle had been his candidate.

Thus on his arrival in London, Marshall lacked the desired clear-cut directive, but he had firmly in mind presidential restrictions on dealing with de Gaulle. Already disturbed by reports of the French leader's actions in Algiers and his own unsatisfactory meeting with him months earlier in London, Marshall was not disposed to be charitable to de Gaulle.

There were of course strong reasons for de Gaulle's behavior in early June. Summoned to London at almost the last minute before an invasion in which his aid was solicited, he was asked to read a statement appealing to the French to obey the instructions of the Supreme Commander. Even had the contents been wholly acceptable, it is likely that one who considered himself—with justice—to be a master of the French language would have disdained a text prepared by other hands. The men in London who had written the words for him assumed mistakenly that gratitude for the liberation of France—a move that would cost American and British lives— would salve the pride of "the savior" of France. They had misread de Gaulle but not for lack of previous warnings.

Suspicious and hurt on his arrival in London, he grew icier by the hour as the plans were unfolded. Summoning all his natural hauteur and his resources of injured dignity, the French leader declined to participate. In an *opéra bouffe* routine, made tragic because of its implications for the future, de Gaulle debated his role with the Allied representatives until the early morning of D day. In the end he refused to speak until the evening of the landings. He refused to speak just after the Supreme Commander. He wrote a speech in which he mentioned Britain but not the United States and not the authority of the Supreme Commander. Making clear that he acted as a free agent, he called on Frenchmen to follow the instructions of the French provisional government and of the leaders authorized to give orders.[16]

Determined to bar any further action that implied an impediment to the sovereignty of France, as represented by him and the French Committee, de Gaulle challenged the Allies repeatedly in the week that followed. When he learned on the eve of D day that despite his previous disapproval the Allied commanders had issued invasion troops specially printed paper francs to be used in place of pounds and dollars, he ordered French officials in the liberated areas to treat the money as if it were counterfeit. For once he did not disturb Roosevelt. The President observed correctly that the currency had been devised to avoid the harmful effect on the franc of the circulation of American and British money in large quantities and that de Gaulle would bar it at his peril.

More maddening to the Allies was the French leader's handling of the French liaison officers. Realizing that there would be a shortage of officers with knowledge of the French language and with the administrative competence to handle liaison duties between local French officials and the liberating armies, the Allies trained more than 180 Frenchmen to accompany them to the Continent. To show his displeasure, worthy of the Sun King's wrath at those who insulted his ambassadors, de Gaulle stopped the transport of all but 20 of these officers in the early hours of the invasion. This act, again more likely to hurt him than the Allies, made his point even at the risk of poisoning relations with those who favored France's cause.

De Gaulle's highhandedness provoked one of Marshall's especially memorable explosions of anger. "I got hold of de Gaulle's chief officer [Lieutenant General Emile Béthouart, Chief of Staff of the General Staff of National Defense] and raised the devil," he recalled. To another French representative he raged that what the General had done was a "contemptible thing." He told Foreign Secretary Eden that de Gaulle's actions were "outrageous," and that "no sons of Iowa farmers would fight to put up statues of de Gaulle in France." [17] Shock waves of the explosion lapped at Washington, where Stimson noted that "when Marshall gets indignant it usually makes a profound impression." [18]

Marshall was still angry about de Gaulle's moves years later. He declared: "We didn't dare tell de Gaulle too far in advance about the invasion. His people leaked. De Gaulle was furious. We had trained French officers for civil affairs, and he canceled every damn thing. The first thing Bradley told me in Normandy was that he had messed up their arrangements. They had fixed things up well and then, by God, de Gaulle had canceled it all." [19]

Appalled at these developments, Eisenhower appealed to the United States Chiefs of Staff shortly after they arrived in London. He held no brief for de Gaulle, but he feared worsened relations at a moment when he most seriously needed French cooperation. He alarmed Marshall and his colleagues to the point that they urged the President to make some modication of his previous restrictions. Although the Prime Minister agreed with Roosevelt, they pointed out that foreign relations was one field in which Churchill could not dominate the War Cabinet—which favored de Gaulle. At best, the U.S. Chiefs of Staff said, the situation was unpleasant and, in view of the possible unfavorable effect on French Resistance efforts, potentially dangerous.

Roosevelt radioed Marshall in reply that "we should make full use of any organization or influence that de Gaulle may possess and that will be of advantage to our military effort provided that we do not by force of our arms impose him upon the French people as the government of France. . . ." [20]

Marshall knew that ten days before the invasion Roosevelt—under pressure from London—had arranged for Vice Admiral Raymond Fenard, head of the French Naval Mission in Washington, to extend an unofficial invitation to de Gaulle to visit the American capital later in the summer. Here it was hoped that some meeting of minds could be reached on the role of the French Committee.

The Chief of Staff did not know the full details of a heated session Churchill had held with de Gaulle near Portsmouth on June 4. His effort to convince the French General of the need for closer accord with the United States had been diluted by expressions of pro-Gaullist sentiments by Foreign Secretary Eden and other members of the War Cabinet. [21]

Without knowing all that had gone before Marshall had seen and heard enough to be deeply upset. In a transatlantic telephone conversation with Stimson on June 15 he outlined the disturbing situation. "And then he began to tell me," wrote Stimson, "of what he had observed of de Gaulle there and he was very hot; also of how violently Eden was fighting Churchill and the power that Eden had in the Cabinet and as leader of the House of Commons. The new thought that Marshall put into it was that all of this attack on the military effort, the troops, directly by de Gaulle, and indirectly by Eden's support of de Gaulle, was playing with the most dangerous kind of fire; that as soon as the American people learned that the cause which their boys were dying for was being obstructed by the French, there would be a tremendous explosive reaction against the French themselves which would play right into the hands of isolationism and make our people anxious to drop France altogether and drop her for good. . . ." If they could put this point across to the British, and to Eden in particular, it might do some good. [22]

After his return to Washington the Chief of Staff amplified his telephoned account. One evening at Chequers, Foreign Secretary Eden had urged that the Prime Minister grant full recognition to the French Committee of National Liberation as the provisional government of France. When Churchill raised objections, the Foreign Secretary pressed him harder. Marshall listened, growing angrier as the talk continued. Finally, as Stimson recorded the Chief of Staff's account, "Marshall broke loose. He said he couldn't talk politics but he said he knew more about the army and he knew more about the people of the United States than Eden did and that if Eden went on in this way and the things that had happened

from de Gaulle's course came out in the Press in full, how he had attacked
our money and how he had refused to send over men who had been
trained for the very purpose of helping us in the invasion it would make a
wave of indignation in the United States which would swamp the whole
damn British Foreign Office." Eden got very angry, his face flushed, and
he left the room and went upstairs.[23]

Marshall later explained that he had failed to realize that Eden was a
great deal more than an appointee of the Prime Minister. He emphasized,
as did Eisenhower, the special position that the Foreign Secretary had in
the cabinet. Eventually he conceded that Eden was a strong, shrewd man.
"I am ashamed to say that I was ignorant of his leadership in Parliament.
I didn't appreciate him at full value. We had some difficult scenes, especially over de Gaulle." [24]

Marshall's ire at de Gaulle was based on his disapproval of the French
leader's personal tactics rather than on agreement with Roosevelt's conclusion that de Gaulle had no backing among the French. Despite his fury
at the Frenchman's actions Marshall recognized the pointlessness of refusing to deal with the French Committee of National Liberation. For the
success of the invasion he and the other U.S. Chiefs of Staff urged Roosevelt to make some arrangement with de Gaulle—even though this would
involve a recognition of his special position as a representative of Free
France.

Unmoved by Stimson's presentation of the Joint Chiefs' arguments,
Roosevelt replied that de Gaulle's power would crumble if properly supervised elections could be held in France. Reflecting information that he
had received from London, Stimson disagreed. The view there was that de
Gaulle had become a symbol of deliverance to the French people. The
President was still dubious. Citing Brigadier General William Donovan
of the Office of Strategic Services as his source, Roosevelt asserted that
other parties would spring up as the Allied armies moved forward.[25]

In an effort to smooth out relations between the Foreign Office and the
American political and military leaders, Stimson talked to the British ambassador, Lord Halifax, about the problems Eisenhower and Marshall
faced at the moment in London. Halifax promised to advise Eden (1)
that Eisenhower wanted some compromise, (2) that the President was
willing to move toward some adjustment, and (3) that Marshall was worried over the dangers raised by de Gaulle's obstructionism.[26]

Impressed by the strength of Marshall's convictions, Stimson next em-
barked on two courses—one to moderate strong pro-Gaullist sentiment in
the American press and the other to moderate Secretary of State Hull's
bitter anti-Gaullist views. Indirectly he appears to have inspired a column
by David Lawrence and a Washington *Star* editorial criticizing de
Gaulle's recent actions.[27]

Stimson next tackled Secretary Hull directly. It was a matter of common sense, said the Secretary of War. Since de Gaulle had been invited to

Washington, they had the alternatives of "telling him he is a blank, blank, blank, or trying to get some working arrangement." [28] As one familiar with Hull's brand of Tennessee profanity and his hot-tempered distaste for de Gaulle, Stimson recognized that the chief difficulty would consist of knowing how many "blanks" would be involved if they came to name calling.

Within a few days the situation eased. Roosevelt arranged a friendly reception for the French leader, directing Marshall to handle many of the details. Marshall was far from enthusiastic. He wrote Sir John Dill after de Gaulle's visit: "After exceedingly rough action on my part while I was in England I now find myself in the embarrassing position of being made seemingly the principal intermediary in the expression of General de Gaulle's desires on a large number of points. I had rather supposed that I would be taboo after my emphatic language in London but it seems to have had the opposite effect. . . ." [29]

Marshall reacted to dealings with de Gaulle much the same as he had in regard to the 1942 accord with Darlan. He viewed the French problem solely in the light of its effect on Eisenhower's campaign and its effect on American public opinion. So far as the long-range political implications of recognition were concerned, he followed the President's lead.

Before Marshall's return to the U.S. in late June he had attempted to clear up disagreements over future operations in the Mediterranean by flying to Italy for talks with Field Marshal Wilson, General Alexander, General Clark, and others. On his arrival he first flew over the Salerno beaches and up to Anzio. Then, accompanied by General Devers, chief of the U.S. Mediterranean Theater, he went to the Fifth Army, where General Clark, the commander, met him for a tour of his area. Nearly a hundred miles northwest of Rome, he observed a division that was chasing the Germans toward Pisa. A newspaper reported that "Driving past Grosseto under sporadic Nazi artillery fire, Marshall visited the sector on the west, and then with Clark went to a company command post east of the town where he watched U.S. artillerymen hammer a mountain pass through which German troops were travelling." He was near enough to the front to have a feel of the battle, but far enough behind that a correspondent had to rely on such tepid reports as this: "As Marshall's jeep approached Grosseto, the windshield was lowered to avoid reflecting the sun which would have attracted the attention of the Germans." As an indication of the General's daring, a reporter noted: "Marshall wore khakis, forbidden G.I.s at the front because they offer less camouflage than woolens. However, as his jeep came within enemy range, he slipped on a leather jacket but continued to wear his officer's cap, disdaining a helmet." [30]

At Clark's Fifth Army command post near Tuscania, north of Rome, Marshall met the corps commanders, among them General Alphonse Juin, whose French units were achieving great success. Clark proposed that Marshall include the Frenchman among the officers to receive the

Distinguished Service Medal. When Marshall protested that he had no authority to decorate a foreigner, Clark persisted. Finally Marshall agreed and pinned on Juin the first DSM awarded a Frenchman in World War II. The Chief of Staff formed a lasting respect for Juin, who became his favorite among high-ranking French officials.

Clark recalled later that he tried to win Marshall to a continued drive in Italy as opposed to landings in southern France. The Chief of Staff emphasized Eisenhower's desire for ANVIL in order to open Marseille as a port of entry. If that decision was final, Clark replied, he would do everything possible to back it. But he feared that the Allies were passing up an opportunity to strike hard at the Germans in Italy and that they could not be certain how fast they could proceed after the team in Italy was broken up. Of this meeting Marshall said later: "When we got to Rome, Alexander wanted to go up in the Balkans where he would be in command. Clark said something about favoring it in his book. Like the others, he wanted something in his sphere. But he never said a word [publicly] at the time. He was a very good soldier and very loyal. . . ." [31]

Before he left Italy, General Marshall had a personal pilgrimage to perform. He wanted to be able to tell Mrs. Marshall and Madge Brown that he had seen Allen's grave at the Anzio beachhead. Accompanied by his brother-in-law, Colonel Tristram Tupper, now Public Relations Officer at Devers's headquarters, Marshall went through the cemetery on June 18. In the field of 7,000 graves, in which the last interments were then being made before a new cemetery was opened near Rome, he found the young officer's resting place. Allen's plot lay on the main pathway through the cemetery a short distance beyond the main flagpole. After a short stay Marshall returned to the beach area, where he joined General Arnold for a visit to a nearby airstrip. There they found twenty ambulances with wounded lined up waiting to load their patients on departing planes. The two Generals went from vehicle to vehicle speaking softly to the men.

Marshall had paid his respects to Allen, but he wanted to know more of the action to fix its details in his mind. He next flew north in a small plane toward Velletri, twenty miles southeast of Rome, coming down to 300 feet so that he could clearly see the terrain over which Allen's unit had advanced. Still he was not satisfied. Later at Clark's headquarters, north of Rome, he interviewed Lieutenant Druckenmiller of Nazareth, Pennsylvania, who had a tank in Allen's company and had been just behind him in the final fight, and his stepson's tank driver and gunner, Technician Clifford A. Doherty of Pittsfield, Maine, and Private Wallace Bobo of Spartanburg, South Carolina. The lieutenant had Allen's map, "a much rumpled paper with the various lines and objectives noted in crayon," which he used to describe the action as the two enlisted men added their personal details.

Now knowing what he sought, the General drove to the Alban Hills and again boarded a small plane, from which, with the aid of the map, he was able—as he told Madge Brown—"to identify the scene of Allen's last action." These facts, noted calmly and precisely, made his stepson's last hours a part of his own experience, softening the pain of his death.

With his mind full of Allen's final battle at the end of May, the General was attentive to the bearing and performance of other Americans he saw moving up into the current fighting. He wrote Madge: "These men looked in good shape and in high morale as they were engaged in a remarkably successful pursuit. The road north for forty or fifty miles was a litter of destroyed transportation, tanks, trucks, self-propelled artillery, etc., which the Air Corps had knocked out. Allen's division was moving towards the front at the time, to deliver an attack. . . ."

To cheer the recent widow—it was three weeks since Allen had been killed—Marshall noted wryly that his stay in Rome had brought him unfavorable attention in the press. "I see by the papers here that I am being criticized because they turned on the hot water [in the Grand Hotel] in honor of my arrival. Also they apparently moved one or two newspaper men out of their rooms to accommodate our party, which did not please."

After his journey to the scene of Allen's death the General spent a busy day visiting other units, returning to his starting point for dinner with senior American and British officers. Next morning after early breakfast he left for Casablanca, had lunch there, dined in the Azores, and breakfasted in Newfoundland at five the following morning. He relaxed there on a brief fishing trip arranged by local officials and was back at his office on June 22 for the renewal of the debate on Operation ANVIL.[32]

Stimson had avidly followed Marshall's activities in Europe. Hearing his account of the trip, the Secretary of War admitted to himself for the first time that it was probably best that Marshall had stayed at his Washington post. "He is as a matter of fact keeping his hand on the control of the whole thing and his influence in driving ahead the war fast in the Pacific as well as in the Atlantic is a unique power nobody else could render."[33] The Secretary's delayed reassessment came in part from his appreciation of Marshall's role in the renewed American effort to save the landings in southern France. Stimson now saw that Marshall, as a member of the Combined Chiefs of Staff, exercised an authority that he could never have mustered as Supreme Commander.

Determined finally to pin down Churchill and his staff on ANVIL, Marshall made that operation the main theme of his talks with General Wilson and members of the Mediterranean Theater staff on his visit to Italy in mid-June. The Chief of Staff had declared on June 17 that the activities of the Resistance forces in France exceeded expectations. Combined with the German need to be prepared for other possible landings in northern Europe, this factor seemed to have stretched enemy forces to the point where it was impossible for the Reich to move substantial reserves to the OVERLORD area. It would materially help Eisenhower if the Allies struck the overextended enemy forces from the south before autumn.

At the meeting with Wilson, the U.S. Chief of Staff questioned the alternative the British proposed—an attack at the head of the Adriatic. He insisted that the American Chiefs had no intention of going into the Balkans unless the Soviet Union did. General Eaker, U.S. Air Forces commander in the Mediterranean, replied that he gathered that the Russians had no current plans for going into the Balkans but that Allied penetration would bring them in. General Wilson stressed the importance of timing: ANVIL could not be mounted before August 7, but a drive northward from the Po Valley could be accomplished by that time.[34]

After showing his willingness to discuss other possibilities, Marshall played his trump card for ANVIL. Convinced of American dependence on the opening of ports in southern France, he told Wilson that he had thirty to forty divisions still in the United States that could not be introduced into France through the ports of northwest France as quickly as they were needed by Eisenhower.

After the war Lord Wilson said of his meetings with Marshall:

> We had a conference three days there. . . . We argued our case and General Marshall, in his masterly manner, argued the U.S. case. I must say, after he had finished, he convinced me that . . . our case . . . wouldn't stand up. The two points that struck me as the flaws in our case—the first one was that we in the Mediterranean had no idea how Eisenhower was hampered by not having the ports, you see, and the extreme importance that Marseille would be to his future campaign against Germany. . . . Another one was that the French wouldn't play on any operations across the Adriatic, and they were pressing, you might say, to go to France. . . . Once Marshall told me that, I knew that strategically [ANVIL] was the only way. We had to clear our sails and get those ports going. Alexander was visibly disappointed, because he said it was knocking the stuffing out of his offensive. None of us liked the offensive in Italy, really, against those mountains. It was a costly affair and we fought going that way instead of [the] way that was going to get us around it [apparently the Adriatic]. . . . Marshall I must say did impress me with the way he put his case, and I said, "Well General, after what you said, I agree. We will go for the landing on the south of France at the earliest possible date that we can do it."[35]

Nonetheless Wilson loyally argued Alexander's case. Although he recognized that in stressing the need for ports, Marshall had brought out clearly "for the first time a point which seems to be of paramount importance to the whole consideration of the strategic problem," Wilson thought the Allies must still decide whether to make a major effort to finish the war in 1944 or work to ensure German defeat in the first half of 1945. If it was considered essential to have another major port—a decision that he obviously thought pointed toward a long-range build-up rather than an attempt at a quick thrust—then "I am convinced our only course is to carry out Operation ANVIL on the lines already planned."

If landings were to be made elsewhere in France, Wilson considered Churchill's Bordeaux venture unsuitable. It was too late for this operation to succeed. He also argued that a landing at Toulon was preferable to one farther west at Sète, where the beaches were the worst in the Mediterranean and the most heavily defended. In his opinion it would be possible with a three-division assault force and three divisions preloaded to take Toulon by D plus 10, Marseille a month later, and to build up the force in southern France to ten divisions by D plus 60. In the operation's favor were (1) the strong French Resistance movement in the area, (2) the excellence of Marseille as a port, and (3) the fact that a successful attack would virtually end the submarine menace to the Mediterranean. Against it was the danger that it would be impossible to attack until August 15 without prejudicing operations planned to destroy German forces south of the Pisa-Rimini line. He feared that a switch of Allied units from Italy to ANVIL would enforce a six-week pause on Alexander's operations.[36]

In much of his report Wilson reflected Marshall's influence. But in deference to the Prime Minister's views he spelled out once more the case for a continued offensive in Italy. In the event of an effort to win the war in 1944, he considered it possible to gain decisive results in Italy by a drive across the Po and then an advance toward southern Hungary through the Ljubljana Gap. Later Sir John Kennedy, Assistant Chief of the Imperial General Staff, characterized this proposal as the "red herring" that was introduced "by Jumbo [Wilson] in his original project for the advance through the Julian Alps." [37]

Dismissing the Mediterranean commander's arguments, Eisenhower remarked to Marshall that Wilson "seems to discount the fact that the Combined Chiefs of Staff have long ago decided to make Western Europe the base from which to conduct decisive operations against Germany." The Supreme Commander felt that "to contemplate wandering off overland via Trieste to Ljubljana is to indulge in conjecture to an unwarrantable degree at the present time." Eisenhower saw no point in waiting until mid-August to act, emphasizing to Marshall that "time is the vital factor, and the overriding consideration must be . . . to launch an operation in France, and nowhere else . . . at the earliest possible date. It is imperative that we obtain and maintain superiority over . . . [the Germans] and this must be done in France as quickly as we can. We need big ports." Marshall agreed fully with Eisenhower's diagnosis. There must be no delay in getting a firm decision, he insisted.[38]

The question was far from settled, however. From Italy, General Devers warned Marshall on June 20 that Eisenhower's British political adviser, Harold Macmillan, had left hurriedly that morning for London "expressly to influence the Prime Minister to back the advance into the valley of the Po and then northeastward through the Ljubljana Gap, thence into Germany." [39]

Macmillan had indeed departed on an undertaking that he cheerfully conceded was "far outside even the most liberal interpretations of my functions"—somewhat to the annoyance of the Foreign Office, which was caught unawares. After a formal dinner party General Eaker had given for Marshall on June 17, Alexander had suggested that Macmillan fly to London with Wilson's Chief of Staff, Lieutenant General Sir James Gammell, to put his plan before the Prime Minister. They assumed mistakenly, although it is difficult to see why, that Marshall was not "as hostile as might have been supposed." Perhaps on this point Alexander had been unduly influenced by General Clark's strong support, in which he was backed by General Eaker, for a continued major offensive in Italy. Macmillan may even have assumed that he had won Marshall's tentative acquiescence. Macmillan relates in his memoirs that at dinner one night during the visit Marshall had said, " 'Say where is this Ljubljana? If it's in the Balkans we can't go there.' I told him it was practically in Austria and he seemed relieved." [40]

Actually, the General's views were unchanged. For Marshall, as for Roosevelt, Ljubljana—wherever it lay—was well east of the area to which he proposed to send American soldiers. Even then members of the Strategy Section of the Army's Operations Division were examining the implications of Alexander's proposal. They doubted if Wilson had troops to carry out his proposed operations against the Istrian Peninsula and the subsequent advance through northern Italy toward the Ljubljana Gap. Bad weather, poor lines of communication, French opposition to use of their troops for such an offensive, and the fact that the operation would not aid OVERLORD all constituted sound military arguments against these actions. On the political side the planners argued against movements that would involve the United States in Greece and Yugoslavia. The Chief of the Strategy Section noted: "Had we adopted a strategy to defeat Germany politically and economically then the suggested operation might be considered." But he warned, "Remember . . . the Austrians held off the Italians [in this area] for 4 years in World War I." [41]

Macmillan's trip to London was not necessary to win Churchill to Alexander's strategy. The Prime Minister warmly welcomed his guest, adding that while the Foreign Office was ruffled at his coming, he was very pleased. He invited Macmillan to present Alexander's proposals to the British Chiefs of Staff and the Foreign Secretary on June 22. The visitor found that Air Marshal Portal was attracted by the idea, that General Brooke seemed "more uncertain," and that Admiral Cunningham took little part in the proceedings.

Brooke was far more than "uncertain," and it is hard to understand why he failed to make his opposition clear to Macmillan. In his account of the meeting Brooke disparaged Churchill's support of Alexander's advance on Vienna: "I pointed out that, even on Alexander's optimistic reckoning, the advance beyond the Pisa-Rimini line would not start until after September; namely, we should embark on a campaign through the Alps in winter. It was hard to make him realize that, if we took the season of the year and the topography of the country in legion against us, we should have three enemies instead of one. . . ." [42] Brooke's assistant, General Kennedy, recorded at this time: "the right course seems to be to give Alexander a free hand *South* of the Alps, then he can threaten the Julian front with small forces." The surplus forces could be used for an amphibious operation against France and reinforcing Normandy.[43]

On these points Brooke and Kennedy were saying privately much of what Marshall and Eisenhower were thundering publicly against the Alpine operation. Brooke and Kennedy held to the earlier British strategy of intensifying the campaign in Italy to compel Hitler to reinforce his line there. Brooke was certain, Bryant wrote, "that so long as he was subjected to pressure in Italy, Hitler would reinforce his troops there. . . ." As always, Brooke was baffled by the American Chief of Staff's inability to see what a trap, given Hitler's congenital inability to yield ground, Italy constituted to the German Army. Marshall, on the other hand, continued to maintain that the Germans, if strongly attacked in the Apennines, would "withdraw to the Alps without contesting the Po Valley," and so leave Alexander "beating the air." [44]

American interest in additional ports in the south of France was intensified by the great Channel storm of June 19 that destroyed the American artificial harbor off Omaha Beach, wrecked hundreds of vessels, and prevented nearly all landing activity for a period of four days. As a result Eisenhower on the twenty-third stressed to the Combined Chiefs of Staff that his advance was slowing down and that he had been forced to postpone the second phase of his build-up. Fearing a stalemate, he urged the launching of ANVIL not later than the end of August and preferably by the middle of the month.[45]

The United States Chiefs of Staff of course agreed. On the twenty-fourth Marshall, in an informational memorandum to Eisenhower, ticked off the points in ANVIL's favor. After providing this reinforcement, the U.S. Chiefs of Staff asked that a directive be issued to General Wilson setting the date for the operation at August 1 at the latest.[46]

Divergences between the various British advisers and the Prime Minister now began to appear. Kennedy and Brooke returned to the argument that Alexander must finish off Field Marshal Albert Kesselring's forces south of the Alps, after which they would send their surplus forces either to ANVIL or around to the Channel coast to reinforce Eisenhower. They focused solely on Italy, while Churchill clung to a drive to Vienna by way of the Julian Alps as a thrust of a dagger "under the armpit." Kennedy wrote gloomily in his diary that these operations were impossible "unless the Germans are finished." Three days later as he worked with Brooke on the reply to Washington, he noted that the Prime Minister had produced a long memorandum on the Vienna operation. "This last, I think," he wrote, "should be kept to ourselves for the moment." Brooke was inclined to agree. "He said," Kennedy wrote, "we had led the Americans by the nose from Casablanca to Florence, and it would not be easy to put this policy over on top of all that. They are so inclined to regard fresh ideas, to match new situations, as breaches of contract." Neither man saw that it was not the fresh idea but the extremely old pattern—their holding something back—as old as the TORCH concept, that worried Marshall. As a result, although the Ljubljana Gap concept was muted, the Americans were anxious about what came next in Italy beyond the Alps.[47]

The British opponents of ANVIL now used growing concern over Eisenhower's need for ports as a basis for attacking the operation. They favored continued priority for OVERLORD and exploitation of its successes. Eisenhower, they argued, should retain all the landing craft he needed for further amphibious assaults and for developing port facilities along the coastline, as he captured it. The critical port area was along the Channel coast and not in the south. ANVIL's role of diverting the enemy from the OVERLORD area could be achieved by French Resistance forces in the Rhone Valley combined with a threat from Italy provided by Alexander's drive northward.[48]

The American Chiefs of Staff fired back a sharp reply: "British proposal to abandon ANVIL and commit everything to Italy is unacceptable." They denied that Alexander would lack sufficient troops for his operations. They slapped at the British statement on the lack of air resources for both operations: "The U.S. Chiefs of Staff consider this comment proposes a condition of war-making on the Allied side which is a most serious reflection on the fighting ability of our ground forces. . . . 5,500 Allied operational planes are at present opposed by 300 enemy planes in Italy." Conceding that the Italian campaign had profited the Allies, they held this must be attributed in part to Hitler's "ill advised determination to fight south of Rome."

Marshall had shown at times a considerable capacity for bluntness—or, in Brooke's opinion, rudeness. This quality, evident in the conclusion, indicates the Chief of Staff's hand: "It is deplorable that the British and U.S. disagree when time is pressing. The British statements concerning Italy are not sound or in keeping with the early end of the war. . . . There is no reason for discussing further except to delay a decision which must be made."

The Chiefs' reply may have also been intended to stiffen Eisenhower's resolve. But there was no danger that the Supreme Commander would repeat his April decision to postpone ANVIL or that Montgomery would press him as he had in the spring. In late June, Allied troops were still held up in the hedgerows; Eisenhower believed that the British Chiefs of Staff had about reached the point of accepting ANVIL. Explaining to Marshall that while the British were honestly convinced that they could best aid OVERLORD by a drive toward Trieste, Eisenhower noted that they were well aware of Washington's fixed intention to mount ANVIL and of his own firm sponsorship of that operation. He added: "I have the further impression that although the British Chiefs of Staff may make one more attempt to convince you of the value of the Trieste move, they will not permit an impasse to arise and will, consequently, agree to ANVIL." [49]

Events proved Eisenhower right. The British did make a strong final effort to scuttle ANVIL before capitulating. Impressed by a recent intelligence report that Hitler had decided to hold fast in the Apennines, thus proving the correctness of Alexander's estimate of probable enemy action, they demanded continuance of the Italian campaign. Allied strategy, the British Chiefs of Staff persisted, "should be the continued use of maximum forces, wherever the enemy may be induced to fight." Dramatically they warned of the consequences of American policy: "History will not forgive commitment of substantial forces to an operation which will not mature for three critical months and may pay small dividends for three more." Under the circumstances they did not see how they could advise His Majesty's government to accept the American views.[50]

His Majesty's government, as represented by the Prime Minister, needed no coaching. Churchill argued the British case with the President, Eisenhower, Marshall, and Hopkins. On June 28 he reminded Roosevelt that in choosing places to attack the Allies had to emphasize first the relation of the assault to the main effort and second the strain produced on the German high command.[51]

Then taking up specific proposals for southern France, Churchill knocked them down in turn. The proposed landing at Sète, directed toward Bordeaux, was a "heavy-footed method of approach." "We are therefore left," he lamented, with the "bleak and sterile" Toulon-Marseille operation. This landing, he warned, could not begin until the end of August.

Returning to the theme he had so consistently pursued, he declared that there was a grave question "Whether we should ruin all hopes of a major victory in Italy . . . and condemn ourselves to a passive role in that theater. . . ." He did not want to see Alexander deprived of much of his offensive strength in Italy for a march up the Rhone that the Combined Chiefs of Staff had described as unprofitable.

In a much debated passage the Prime Minister raised anew the argument of the project for an attack across the Adriatic and the possible capture of Trieste by September. He was looking toward political considerations, he noted, "such as revolt of populations against the enemy or the submission and coming over of his satellites. . . ."

Marshall and his associates, ready for this and the more familiar arguments, drafted a reply to which the President added two major paragraphs before sending it to London. Political considerations were important, the Chiefs conceded, "but military operations based thereon must be definitely secondary to the primary operations of striking at the heart of Germany."

Roosevelt agreed that Sète and Bordeaux were out of the picture but he was equally unconvinced by Alexander's advocacy of a drive toward Trieste. In talking of Istria the British disregarded "two vital considerations: the grand strategy firmly believed by us to be necessary to the early conclusion of the war and the time factor as involved in the probable duration of a campaign to debouch from the Ljubljana Gap into Slovenia and Hungary." The President could not see the French using their troops in that role.

Although Churchill called the Toulon area "sterile," it offered suitable beaches and communications. The Rhone corridor, Roosevelt added, "is better than the Ljubljana Gap and certainly a lot better than the terrain over which we have been fighting in Italy."

In another of the paragraphs added at the White House, the President declared: "At Tehran we agreed upon a plan. That plan has done well up till now. Nothing has occurred to require a change. History would never forgive us if precious lives and time are lost as the result of indecision and debate. My dear friend, I beg you to let us continue my plan." Roosevelt's closing statement has been much quoted since the war: "Finally, in addition to the military, there are political conditions here which must be considered. I would never survive even a minor set-back in Normandy if it were known that substantial troops were diverted to the Balkans." [52]

To Brooke the explanation for American opposition to British strategy lay in this final declaration. Misreading it, he wrote, "Owing to the coming Presidential Election it is impossible to contemplate any action with a Balkan flavour on its strategic merits." [53] The history of the drafting shows that the arguments were made first along the line that Marshall and his colleagues had consistently held and that Roosevelt had added an argument that he knew Churchill, as an old political campaigner, would understand.

Churchill next tried his hand with Eisenhower. In reply the Supreme Commander repeated Marshall's argument that ANVIL would open up additional ports through which to bring American divisions. By seizing Marseille the Allies might gain twelve more divisions than currently scheduled. It was a fateful decision, the Prime Minister said, but he left Eisenhower more hopeful than he had been earlier. "I have been informally advised," the Supreme Commander radioed Marshall, "that the Prime Minister will probably telegraph the President today agreeing to ANVIL." [54]

Ten days later Eisenhower discovered the full force of the Prime Minister's passion when he stopped by Chequers. At this encounter Churchill "gave him hell" for insisting on ANVIL when there were greater opportunities in Italy and the Balkans. [55]

In short no matter could be regarded as finally settled where the Prime Minister had been convinced against his will. On July 6, between his first and second talks with Eisenhower, he lashed out furiously. In a highly significant statement he told Sir Hastings Ismay, his personal representative on the British Chiefs of Staff Committee: "Let them take their seven divisions—three American and four French. Let them monopolise all the landing-craft they can reach. But let us at least have a chance to launch a decisive strategic stroke with what is entirely British and under British command. I am not going to give way about this for anybody. Alexander is to have his campaign." Although he later emphasized grand strategy and the need of a careful plan to stop the Russians, Churchill could never eradicate this evidence of his very human desire to do something purely British for a Britain already falling behind in the struggle. An extremely proud man, conscious of the Empire whose survival he was determined to preserve, the Prime Minister wrote resolutely to Ismay: "I hope you realise that an intense impression must be made upon the Americans that we have been ill-treated and are furious. Do not let any smoothings or smirchings cover up this fact. After a while we shall get together again; but if we take everything lying down there will be no end to what will be put upon us." [56]

Thus not in petulance but in pride he had proclaimed his challenge. Aware, as Brooke demonstrated, that the Americans were swinging the weight of a preponderance of men and materiel, Churchill still was defiant. He was repeating the claims of one who had borne the heat of battle. Later he and his advisers would suggest that he spoke as a prophet of the Russian menace; actually he spoke then for an all-British challenge.

However, on July 12 the Combined Chiefs of Staff directed Wilson to launch the operation at the earliest possible date. He was to make preparations for a three-division assault, an airborne lift of a strength yet to be determined, and a build-up to ten divisions. After months of struggling, the Prime Minister seemed to have capitulated at last [57]

On August 1 ANVIL was renamed DRAGOON for security reasons, lest the enemy finally light on the significance of the word. The American rose under another name smelled no sweeter to Churchill; sadly he spoke of being "dragooned." He continued to thrash about in frenzied efforts to divert, postpone, or strangle the operation. In early August he seized on a communication from Eisenhower that he interpreted as proposing a landing on the Brest Peninsula in preference to southern France. Whether he misunderstood or milked the statement for more than it was worth is not clear. Seeing one last chance to kill the operation, he telegraphed the President that he "backed up" the Supreme Commander's plan for a change in the landing place. Brooke also misinterpreted Eisenhower's proposal, calling it "by far the best solution" and "what we want." [58]

Eisenhower was uneasy over the British reaction. Knowing that Marshall had always felt that he had failed to stand firm on the earlier ANVIL, Eisenhower hurriedly assured his Chief: "I will not under any condition agree at this moment to a cancellation of DRAGOON." He explained that he believed that if there were sufficient port facilities elsewhere to support unlimited forces, troops should be brought in wherever possible. The Prime Minister might have misconstrued these views, but "I have never wavered." [59] There was no assurance that the Brittany ports could be working before several weeks. The main point was that he needed more troops and soon.

A week before the DRAGOON attack Churchill had one last try at the Supreme Commander. In this case, as in many others, it is a question how much of his performance represented deep conviction and how much was histrionics. Eisenhower apparently took him at face value on this occasion. Churchill raged that the United States was acting as "a big strong and dominating partner" rather than one trying to see the British viewpoint on the Italian campaign. Eisenhower, who for his part failed to see the importance attached to the drive toward Trieste, had never seen him "so obviously stirred, upset, and even despondent." In a final dramatic appeal the Prime Minister cried out that he might have to go to the King and "lay down the mantle of my high office." [60]

The familiar act was getting stale. Eisenhower assured him that the Americans had not disregarded British views nor had they used their strength as a bludgeon in conferences. In a kind understatement of the extent to which Churchill had used every means at his command to bulldoze the Combined Chiefs of Staff, Eisenhower recalled that British views had often prevailed and that he did not see why the Americans "should be considered intemperate in our long and persistent support of ANVIL." [61]

In last-minute efforts to stop DRAGOON Churchill next appealed to the President and to Harry Hopkins. Roosevelt, on his way to Hawaii to confer with MacArthur and Nimitz, merely confirmed his earlier decision. Hopkins, probably advised by Marshall, replied that it was too late to change.[62] The Prime Minister still fought until his own subordinate, General Wilson, ruled against the switch of the operation to Bordeaux by saying that forward units of the DRAGOON force had already sailed.

Once he had surrendered, the Prime Minister proved gracious. On the eighteenth he radioed Eisenhower that he had watched the landings on the fifteenth from afar. "All I have seen there makes me admire all the perfect precision with which the landing was arranged and intimate collaboration of British-American forces and organizations." Expressing a view strongly shared by Marshall, Eisenhower replied: "I am delighted to note in your last telegram to me that you have personally and legally adopted the DRAGOON. I am sure that he will grow fat and prosperous under your watchfulness." [63]

The landings went much more rapidly than predicted. Rather than influencing decisively the battle in Normandy, the southern landings were aided by developments on Eisenhower's front. Before the first troops had landed in the south, United States forces in northern France had broken out past St. Lô (July 25–August 1) and were sweeping into Brittany. Within a few days the bulk of the Allied forces had reversed direction and were driving eastward against the enemy. Operation DRAGOON came as the Allies were closing in on the Germans near Falaise.

Along the Loire, U.S. tactical air forces and French Resistance forces harassed German units withdrawing from western France. With U.S. and French units pouring across the DRAGOON beaches, the Germans in the Rhone Valley and southern France could not be spared to interfere with Eisenhower's advance on the north. After short delays the Allied forces liberated Toulon and Marseille and moved northward in what at times were little more than road marches. To the British the ease of the operation, forecast by the Americans, was proof that it was not needed. To the Americans it was evidence that the Prime Minister and his advisers had frivolously delayed what could have been an important contribution to OVERLORD.

If the rapid clearing of France was important and if the cross-Channel concept was valid, Operation DRAGOON, while no longer crucial to Eisenhower's victory, was still worth the effort. It hastened the ousting of the Germans from most of France, it brought French forces back onto French soil, it started the rehabilitation of French industry and transport, it threatened the Ruhr and the Rhineland, it freed excellent ports for the introduction and support of additional American units, it eliminated a number of German units, and it opened up new air bases for attacks on the German homeland.[64]

Yet Churchill then and many British writers since have viewed DRAGOON as a mistake of almost disastrous proportions for British and, perhaps, Allied arms. Intent on victory for Alexander in Italy, Churchill viewed any diversion from that effort as folly. In the years that followed General Marshall held firmly to his wartime views on ANVIL/DRAGOON. In 1956 he declared: "I don't agree with the Prime Minister on ANVIL at all. In fact, I am in almost complete disagreement on every phase of it. He was intent on one thing and he sways all his arguments to justify that one thing. . . . Almost everything he said to deter us from that operation down there went exactly the other way with a tremendous success."

In 1956 Marshall insisted strongly, as had Brooke on other occasions, that Churchill's concepts of military strategy were deplorably unrealistic: "The 'soft underbelly' had chrome-steel sideboards. That was mountainous country. There was no question in my mind that the West was the place to hit. If we had accepted the Balkan thing, it would have scattered our shots. They are letting political considerations after the fact dominate the whole concept." [65]

Again in 1956 Marshall demonstrated that his support of ANVIL derived from considerations of overall strategy and a sense of history that could give Churchill pause: "What we keep hearing about are aftermath performances. The operation in southern France is convincing on the basis of arithmetic and logic. Half of Patton's army was supplied from Marseille.

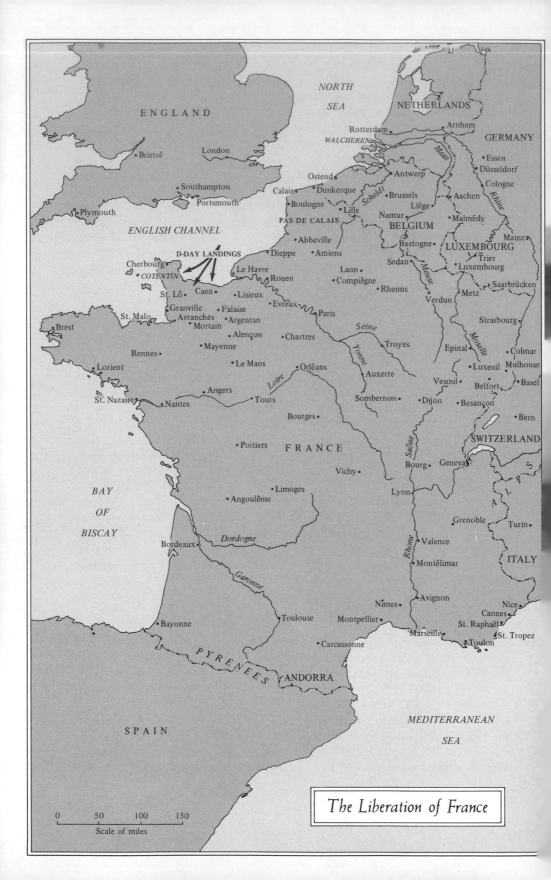

The Liberation of France

It was important in the Ardennes period. It helped to complete the Eisenhower operation in Normandy.

"We determined to go through with the big thing. We didn't want to have trouble like Haig did in the First World War. We wanted to keep to the main thing. The southern France operation was one of the most successful things we did." [66] General Marshall recalled that he later had a paper prepared for possible use at the Malta conference in which the dire warnings of Churchill, Wilson, and others were listed and then followed by a statement of the turn of events which proved the critics wrong. "The differences were so great that it was almost facetious," said Marshall. He found that the paper, referred to as "The Castigation of ANVIL," was so bitter that he couldn't use it. Preserved in his files, the original copy was carefully sealed with instructions not to let it be circulated.

To a considerable extent Marshall saw British insistence as an example of "localitis." He said: "If you take a commander, say Alexander, in that place, of course he wants it [the operation] there. MacArthur was just as much opposed to ANVIL as Alexander was, for the same reason. He wanted the things . . . out there where he was. If you followed every commander, you'd just be lost, we'd be sunk, you'd be all over the place. Our hardest [task] was trying to keep to the things that we could do. . . ." [67]

Against Marshall the British have argued that ANVIL deprived Alexander of possible victory in northern Italy over Kesselring's forces. Undoubtedly the shift of units from the British front to ANVIL hampered the advance in Italy. To the British commander, as to General Clark, this development after months of maddeningly slow advances seemed doubly tragic. Now that the battle was shifting in the Allies' favor, it seemed that all-out victory in Italy and a possible speedy drive to Vienna were blocked only by the wrongheadedness of the Americans. Some British writers placed the decision at the door of a mulishly obstinate Marshall.

The first strong charge against American "folly" was made by Australian newsman Chester Wilmot and has since become virtually an article of faith for opponents of the landings in southern France.[68] It has been made into a special myth by anti-Soviet writers, who continually shift further back into early 1944 or late 1943 the date at which Churchill began to consider an Italian victory as a means of forestalling the Russians in Central Europe. It is a fascinating theory, but it will not stand up against the facts.

For convincing refutations of these statements one need not go beyond the British official historians and two of the chief British officers involved —Brooke and Wilson. True, Churchill was an old antagonist of the Russian bear clawing its way toward India or the Eastern Mediterranean or the marches of the old German Empire. Certainly he became disquieted as he saw a badly mauled and heavily scarred Red Army recover magnificently for a drive on Budapest and Warsaw and threaten Vienna, which had stood against the Turks. A successor of Castlereagh and Disraeli, he feared the Eastern armies as they moved into Western preserves. Much as Metternich and Castlereagh had shivered as the horsemen of the steppes moved through Central Europe toward the streets of Paris, Churchill dreaded the coming of the Red Army. In later years it seemed to him and others that this fear, never fully dormant during the war, had been at the forefront of his insistence on Alexander's strategy.

John Ehrman, official British historian of this period, although wedded to some degree to the Italian campaign strategy, concedes that in the spring and summer of 1944 Churchill never presented his argument for pushing a drive toward Trieste as a means of forestalling the Russians. Unquestionably the Prime Minister and some members of the British Foreign Office became uneasy about the Russians in the summer of 1944. Churchill's physician, Lord Moran, records that one day in early August, Churchill burst out, "Good God, can't you see that the Russians are spreading across Europe like a tide; they have invaded Poland, and there is nothing to prevent them marching into Turkey and Greece." [69] Moran said that Churchill had got it into his head that Alexander might solve the problem by "breaking into the Balkans." Perhaps Russian power was behind his intense advocacy of the Italian campaign. If so, he made no mention of it in his arguments with Marshall; his main interest appeared to be ensuring that Alexander had his chance to score a major victory.

Whatever Churchill's intent, the question remains whether on tactical grounds he was right and Marshall wrong on the shifting of troops from Italy to southern France. Here there is no easy answer. If the Germans were ready to fold up—but one cannot forget their staying power around Antwerp and at Arnhem, in the step-by-step defense of the Roer Dam and the bridgeheads of the Rhine, and their counteroffensive in the Ardennes —then one could contend that a rapid drive to the northeast corner of Italy might conceivably have hastened the collapse of Germany.

In view of the rugged terrain beyond Florence, eloquently described by Alexander himself, there is considerable doubt that even if the British commander had been permitted to keep the seven American and French divisions that were taken from him, he could have made the drive to Trieste and through the Ljubljana Gap into the heart of Germany more quickly than Eisenhower ultimately pushed his forces eastward.[70]

Had Churchill now urged an anti-Russian crusade on Marshall, the Chief of Staff might well have asked some searching questions: (1) Is it in our interest to create possible clashes with the Russians when the Germans and the Japanese are still undefeated? (2) Is it possible to prevent the Russians from keeping what they already occupy? (3) If the British were so intent on forestalling the Russians, why hadn't they backed the cross-Channel attack a year earlier?

Although Field Marshal Brooke grumbled unceasingly over Marshall's lack of strategic insight and Eisenhower's lack of generalship, he never completely shared Churchill's fondness for the Ljubljana Gap and Trieste. In the postwar period he categorically denied that he had ever presented these measures to Marshall as a means of stopping the Russians. "I never supported Winston or Alex in that maneuver, because it didn't seem feasible . . ." he said in 1961. "There is no doubt," he continued, "that Winston had a Balkan liking . . . and he used to make matters rather difficult for me with Marshall with statements he would make, which Marshall would often think were inspired by me, and they were not inspired by me at all." [71]

Field Marshal Wilson also had his reservations about Churchill's infatuation with the Balkans. Wilson said after the war that the "weakness really in our going over the Adriatic was the logistic one, and what it came to [was] if we had a pushover we would do jolly well, but if we got stuck in heavy battle, the question of the supply and maintenance would have become very difficult then, and perhaps the further we got, the more difficult it would have become. In that I think our people in Italy and the Mediterranean were more optimistic than the planners here in London. But I did have a talk afterwards with one of our planners and [he] said, 'You know you are on very thin logistic ice as regards maintaining a large force if you went beyond the Ljubljana Gap.'" Wilson recalled how he had changed his mind and favored the landings in southern France after Marshall made his arguments about the need of a large port. He declined to do any second guessing about the decision. "As it happened, the way things worked in the south of France, the way we jumped the Germans in getting the road from the coast practically up to Lyons intact, really made all the difference in the world, and as it worked out, it [made] for the best. That really, I think, gives you the whole picture. . . . I have never altered my opinion. I gave it and I have never gone back on saying it." [72]

Lord Moran records that he once asked Alexander if Churchill would have made a good general. The Field Marshal remained silent so long that Moran interjected: "Winston is a gambler. Marshall would make a big decision, but only after he had carefully removed every possible source of error." To which Alexander, half to himself, replied: "Yes, that's true. Winston is a gambler." [73] The exchange may have some validity so far as the ANVIL operation was concerned. In the summer of 1944 the landings in southern France seemed to promise more certain advantages to Eisenhower's campaign than did Churchill's gamble, which might have brought the Allies to the gates of Vienna.

On this issue Marshall had no doubt of the rightness of his course. He had lost too many battles to Churchill and Brooke over Mediterranean operations to be broad-minded on this issue. He had happily carried home too many beribboned contracts only to find that there were serious reservations in the fine print. The Anzio landing, to which he reluctantly agreed, had brought grievous setbacks. In his grudging agreement to delay

ANVIL in the early spring of 1944, when he gave way to Eisenhower's arguments and the firm resistance of the British, he had made clear that it was
his last concession.

When summer came, he refused to go further with the Prime Minister.
He had commitments across the Pacific and he did not propose to put
them in jeopardy. Only a clear decision by the President and Churchill
that henceforth the main effort would be to forestall the Russians in Central Europe would have changed his view. And that decision not only was
not made; it was not then raised in the Allied councils by any member of
the Combined Chiefs of Staff or by Roosevelt or Churchill.

☆

☆ **XXI** ☆

☆ ☆

The Drive toward Germany

THE trouble started with Montgomery. Marshall had disliked the picture of the Eighth Army commander he had received from Eisenhower at Casablanca. "Conceited" and unwilling to attack until he had everything in sight were some of the descriptions Eisenhower had given. Now Marshall liked even less what he saw in the press about operations in Normandy. The name of the ground commander in the landings—the scrappy British General—led all the rest: "MONTGOMERY'S TROOPS DRIVE ON CHERBOURG," "MONTGOMERY'S FORCES ATTACK ST. LÔ." Although there were no British troops within miles of either objective, it was not surprising that the British press emphasized his role, but it grated on American nerves. General Marshall understood the problem. At the time of the Dieppe raid two years earlier British and Canadian newspapers had sizzled when journals in the United States had hailed the participation of some fifty Americans in the raid: "U.S. AND BRITISH INVADE FRANCE!" "TANKS AND U.S. TROOPS SMASH AT FRENCH COAST!" and "U.S. TROOPS LAND WITH COMMANDOS IN BIGGEST RAID!" Disturbed by these banner headlines, a scandalized Marshall had asked Eisenhower whether so much publicity should have been released about the American share in the attack. Now in July 1944 he urged Eisenhower to make public more information on American units and commanders.[1]

Irritation at Supreme Headquarters developed in the first weeks of the invasion as the initial Allied drives inland gave way to stalemate. Montgomery especially was accused of undue caution and refusal to attack unless he was sure he could win. In part the problem arose from his efforts to draw the German forces on to his front at the eastern sector of the invasion arc in order to enable Bradley to make a broad sweep from the west. That was the official argument, although the planners had initially assumed that the Americans might be slow in coming up to the Seine. More important was the fact that Montgomery dreaded to risk his thinning reserves without a chance to gain substantial results.

In his postwar judgment of the British commander Marshall reflected the comments he received from Eisenhower, Bradley, and others: "Montgomery when he got into the fight was, I think, excellent, but on the other hand if we had about three commanders like Montgomery, we would have never made any fights because they never would have settled who was to get everything to do it. Montgomery required, you might say . . . forces and supplies and everything of such [great quantity] . . . that we couldn't have conducted these campaigns if everybody had followed his procedure because there just wasn't enough to go around." [2]

Meanwhile American forces drove to Cherbourg, key port of the Cotentin Peninsula, in late June and forced the surrender of that city. Throughout early July, as Montgomery massed his forces against the ancient city of Caen, criticism mounted among both American and British officers at Supreme Headquarters because of his earlier failure to break out on his front. An American on Montgomery's staff made an effective defense of the British General to Eisenhower's naval aide near the end of the month, saying that he "felt that Monty, his British Army Commander, Dempsey, the British corps commanders and even those of divisions are so conscious of Britain's ebbing manpower that they hesitate to commit an attack where a division may be lost. To replace the division is practically impossible. When it's lost, it's done and finished. Even naval ratings, Air Force personnel and nondescripts are being 'cannibalized' for replacements." The commanders felt, he added, that the blood of the British Empire, and hence its future, was too precious for dash in battle. "In addition, the tank losses, including crews, which are even more precious, have been heavy." [3]

By late July there were mutterings in Washington that Marshall could not ignore. Critics spoke of the disproportionate losses by American troops. Of the more than 21,000 Allied dead in June and July nearly 14,000 were Americans; of the total casualties, now reaching nearly 100,000, two-thirds were from the United States. One could explain these as due to heavy losses in taking Omaha Beach and the cost of gaining hedgerows in the drive toward St. Lô, but the comparison continued to be made in men's minds and in the news columns.[4]

Washington was disturbed too because of the scant information on operations in Normandy. At the end of July, Marshall reported to Eisenhower that members of the British Staff Mission in Washington complained that they had no knowledge of his future plans. "It is true," said the Chief of Staff, "that until your [message] arrived Saturday we had not received recently any information on your thoughts concerning the situation and your probable course of action. . . ." Plaintively he added, "we received no information of Bradley's present offensive except unexplained reference in a radio from Mr. Stimson [then on a trip to Europe] referring to COBRA, whatever that was." The elusive COBRA, of course, was Bradley's plan for a breakout from the Cotentin Peninsula in the area west of

St. Lô to gain a base from which the First Army and the newly activated Third Army could drive westward toward Brest and eastward toward Paris.[5]

Marshall's plea brought more regular reports from Eisenhower on his current estimates and future intentions, but there frequently was a time lag in communications between Supreme Headquarters and the War Department. This fact provides the best answer to the often-repeated canard that Marshall had to give Eisenhower daily instructions on how to run the battle. Considering that it was War Department policy to give broad initiative to theater commanders, the suggestion is more a slap at Marshall than at the Supreme Commander. Indeed the Chief of Staff's entire philosophy of command was to pick good men, give them broad powers, and then support their efforts. He interfered far less in campaigns than did Churchill and Brooke.

In July and August he was more concerned with getting ANVIL under way to aid Eisenhower's attack than with the day-to-day dispositions of troops in Normandy. He kept track of broad plans and was prepared to make suggestions on strategy, alternate plans, and more effective use of men and supplies, but he did not interfere in the daily battle. If he could not trust a commander, his practice was to relieve him rather than continually peer over his shoulder. In this Marshall followed Army doctrine as well as his own well-established command philosophy.

However high-level command arrangements affecting British and United States forces required Marshall's intervention. To ensure the effective use of airborne troops, he had joined Arnold in the spring in suggesting the establishment of an allied airborne army. They considered it important that Eisenhower should have a headquarters under him that would control both troop-carrier units and the airborne units when committed to battle. The Supreme Commander agreed and suggested various officers for the command, among them Major General John Cannon, head of the Twelfth Air Force in the Mediterranean, and Major General Hoyt S. Vandenberg, the Deputy Commander-in-Chief, Allied Expeditionary Air Force. In the end the post went to Lieutenant General Lewis H. Brereton, then commander of the Ninth Air Force. On August 8 the first Allied Airborne Army was activated under Brereton with Lieutenant General F. A. M. Browning, commander of the British Airborne Corps, as his Deputy. Vandenberg then replaced Brereton as chief of the Ninth Air Force.[6]

Responding to General Marshall's pressure for use of the airborne forces, Eisenhower in mid-August outlined alternate plans for their commitment. He spoke of the possible use of these troops to force the passage of the Seine. Should this operation prove unnecessary, he proposed a large drop in the Pas-de-Calais area, an action designed to eliminate the launching sites for flying bombs and facilitate normal supply activities by the British.[7]

It is possible that persistent urging from Washington for more effective use of the airborne forces was a factor in Eisenhower's continued proposals for such drops despite General Bradley's belief that the ground forces would overrun the drop sites before the target dates for the air operations. However, in the hotly debated decision to stage a drop at Tournai in late August—a scheme finally abandoned after several critical days during which planes needed for transporting gasoline to ground units were withdrawn—both Eisenhower and Montgomery were responsible. As for the Arnhem operation in mid-September, which shifted the main effort in the north temporarily from the Antwerp area to Holland, General Eisenhower took the responsibility for backing Montgomery's plan.[8]

On one hotly debated point—that the time had come for Eisenhower to take over command in the field—Marshall was most positive. He definitely nudged the Supreme Commander on this question.

Badly strained nerves on both sides of the ocean almost reached the breaking point in late July and early August with the initial changes in command. In accordance with preinvasion arrangements, Eisenhower in late July moved to bring in an additional army—the Third—with an army group—the 12th—to control the First and Third U.S. armies. On August 1 Bradley became active as 12th Army Group commander with Hodges and Patton as First and Third Army commanders. It was agreed that on September 1 Eisenhower would assume command in the field. Until that time Montgomery continued as Ground Forces commander, a situation that irritated the American generals in the field and many of their countrymen at home. Patton's friends became especially annoyed when announcement of his entry on the scene was delayed. They reacted skeptically to SHAEF's truthful explanation that they wanted to keep his presence a secret as long as possible because of the deception plan.

In mid-August a censor's error resulted in premature publication of the statement that Bradley was now equal in authority with Montgomery. Since this arrangement was not slated to go into effect for several weeks, SHAEF officials denied the story. Newspapers in the United States and Britain had a field day. The London *Mirror,* never known for its pro-American sentiments, tartly demanded that the officer responsible for the error be punished and an apology made to Montgomery. In Washington the anti-British and anti-administration *Times-Herald*—taking a cue from Colonel Robert McCormick—fired a broadside at George III, charging that the *Mirror*'s attack had "served to emphasize British dominance of the command and conduct of the invasion." "It is generally recognized in congressional circles and common gossip in military circles that General Eisenhower is merely a figurehead," the newspaper declared, "and the actual command of the invasion is in the hands of the British General Staff and the British dominate the American War Department and Army." [9]

It was less this violent diatribe than the gentler chiding of a friendly paper that stirred the Chief of Staff. On August 17 he read in Hanson Baldwin's column in the New York *Times* that it was unfortunate that the recent announcement on organization still left Montgomery with tactical command of American and British ground forces. Baldwin reasoned thus:

"There are always many Americans who are ready to suspect the British of ulterior purposes; they will find recruits if the present arrangement is long continued. And it is human nature for the men of one army to blame any general not of their own nationality who exercises tactical control over them for the mistakes they and their own leaders may make.

"Each army in France should have its own commander, operating under one supreme command. This is a principle—one for which Gen. John J. Pershing fought—that is as old as the first World War. It should be honored today." [10]

Marshall had heard enough. He promptly declared to Eisenhower: "The recent statement from your headquarters that Montgomery continues in command of all ground forces has produced a severe reaction in the New York *Times* and many other papers and I feel is to be deplored. Just what lay behind the confusion in announcements I do not know, but the Secretary and I and apparently all America are strongly of the opinion that the time has come for you to assume direct exercise of command of the American contingent. I think you will have to consider this matter very carefully because the reaction here is serious and will be, I am afraid, injected into the debates in Congress within the next 24 hours." He concluded: "The astonishing success of the campaign up to the present moment has evoked emphatic expression of confidence in you and Bradley. The late announcement I have just referred to has cast a damper on public enthusiasm." [11]

Still as thin-skinned about certain types of criticism as he had been in North Africa, Eisenhower retorted that he and Bradley were somewhat taken aback that their plans for command assignments were not understood in the War Department. "It seems," he added, "that so far as the press and public are concerned a resounding victory is not sufficient; the question of 'how' is equally important." It would be a great pity, he said, if Bradley were deprived of full credit for his brilliant performance because general instructions and policies he had pursued had been channeled through Montgomery. He was indifferent as to what the New York *Times* or any other paper said of his conduct of the war, "but it is a matter of deep concern that you and the Secretary of War should be disturbed because I have as yet been unable to put into effect an arrangement which I fully agree is now logical and awaiting only the physical means for implementation."

With a degree of asperity he asked Marshall to inform General Surles, the War Department's Public Relations Director, who had recently radioed Smith for information, that "(a) no major effort takes place in this

Theater by ground, sea or air except with my approval and that no one in this Allied Command presumes to question my supreme authority and responsibility for the whole campaign; (b) the exact time at which my headquarters can be in position to deal directly and consistently with both Army groups, and soon with the DRAGOON group, must be determined by physical conditions, but will be at a reasonably early date." [12]

Despite communications problems Eisenhower decided that the time had come to act on field command. He conceded that his action would "cause some outcry and some uneasiness but I am sure that all things considered, it is absolutely sound. The principal argument that will be advanced against it is that Bradley has operated with a considerable degree of independence for a long time. He and I are in constant touch and the change is really more obvious than real." [13]

Anticipating criticism in the British press, Churchill announced that Montgomery—whose name, he proclaimed, "is a household word" with the British people—would have the rank of field marshal as of September 1. He would thus outrank not only Eisenhower and Bradley but Marshall as well. Both Brooke and Montgomery denounced Eisenhower's command change as a blunder and were convinced that the whole maneuver was a political one intended to aid Roosevelt in his presidential campaign. They were of course far off the mark.

The "political" angles came from the Pentagon instead of the White House. Now that the U.S. troops fighting on the Continent had come to outnumber the British forces, morale was likely to suffer if the Americans continued to serve under British command. Marshall's reservations about Montgomery's fighting spirit—a feeling that he shared with Bradley, Patton, and other American commanders—probably played a part in Eisenhower's decision. Brooke and Montgomery's judgment that Eisenhower lacked knowledge of strategy and ability to command troops in the field would, if it had been known to Marshall, have confirmed him in the belief that it was high time to change field commanders. But there was still another reason. At no period of the war did Marshall have a higher opinion of Bradley's leadership. His pressure on Eisenhower to take command in the field was intended not only to give the Supreme Commander an active role but to make certain that Bradley would have his chance to shine.

Two recent events in Normandy had brought personal grief to the Chief of Staff. Two friends he had known from World War I died within a few weeks of each other, one a victim of heart attack and the other of American bombing. The first, Theodore Roosevelt, Jr., died on July 12 just as he was being considered for division command. Marshall could remember the closing days of World War I when Roosevelt, badly wounded in the leg, chafed at confinement in the hospital and hungered to return to duty. Colonel Marshall, then at First Army, sympathized with his old friend from the 1st Division. When former President Roosevelt asked him to help get his son back into battle, Marshall covered for him when he went AWOL from the hospital in order to return to his regiment (the 26th). He recalled the younger Roosevelt, limping along at the head of his men, as they went headlong toward Sedan. It was to Marshall that Roosevelt's wife had appealed in the spring of 1944 after his relief as assistant division commander of the 1st Division in the Mediterranean. It was "all right to pull strings and favors if what you wanted was a more dangerous job than the one you had," he told her. Through Marshall's aid Roosevelt was sent back to the wars in February 1944. He went ashore with the 4th Division on D day at Utah Beach, rallying his men with nothing but a walking stick.[14]

After Roosevelt's death General Eisenhower at once proposed him for a Distinguished Service Cross, but Marshall and Stimson, two incorrigible romantics where World War I friends were concerned, overruled the Supreme Commander and awarded the Medal of Honor. For Stimson it was probably as much for the former Governor-General of the Philippines as for the soldier in Normandy; for Marshall it was given to the crippled officer hobbling along on the road to Sedan.[15]

Thirteen days later Lieutenant General Lesley J. McNair was killed near St. Lô as Allied bombs were released short of their target. The former Army Ground Forces chief had succeeded Patton in command of a paper army group for the purpose of deceiving the Germans. So long as a high-ranking general was still in the United Kingdom and several divisions were there, it was possible to make the enemy believe that the Normandy invasion was merely a diversionary attack and that a massive assault was being prepared against the Pas-de-Calais. In mid-July with Patton almost ready to go into action, General Marshall sent McNair to continue the deception. Before taking up his assignment in England, McNair went forward in Normandy to observe preparations for the attack. There he met his death—a few days before his only son died in battle against the Japanese on Guam. Marshall felt the General's loss keenly. He wrote his widow on July 26: "General McNair's death has taken from me one of the strongest supports I have had in this war. I am at a loss for words sufficient to describe the great contribution which he has made to the Army and to the war effort through the force of his character and wisdom in leadership. My official feelings, however, are more than equalled by the strong personal loss I feel. Our long association has given me a regard for him which amounted to deep affection." [16]

Shortly after the war ended in Europe, General Marshall paid public tribute to McNair in a ceremony at the Army War College, soon to be renamed Fort Lesley J. McNair. With a degree of emotion unusual for him, he said:

> It was General McNair's task to build an efficient ground army to defend the interests of this nation without sacrifice of the principles of the liberty of the individual to which we were dedicated. His task was made more difficult by the

many of that period who thought and proclaimed that the day of the ground army and especially of the infantry had passed, that wars would be won by tanks and planes alone.

The credit of much of our success in battle may be placed squarely on the type of training which our units have received. General McNair insisted on the thoroughness of this training and made it more and more realistic in character.

His influence and the touch of his genius will live on through every unit of the great fighting army which he organized and trained. History will commemorate the "quiet thoroughness of this outstanding soldier." [17]

Other changes in command followed the landings in southern France. Knowing of General Marshall's high opinion of General Devers and the latter's desire to lead an army group in Europe, General Eisenhower wrote Marshall in July that he considered that the U.S. Mediterranean commander, who already had the U.S. invasion forces under him, could handle the assignment satisfactorily. General Marshall then decided to give Devers the 6th Army Group, initially under British General Wilson, Mediterranean Theater commander, for the invasion and then, on its link-up with the forces in the north, under Eisenhower. This shift came on September 15. At that time the First French Army, headed by General Jean de Lattre de Tassigny, and Patch's U.S. Seventh Army, under 6th Army Group, passed to Eisenhower's command. [18]

With Devers's departure from the Mediterranean an American Deputy was required for General Wilson. For this assignment, Marshall in October sent his second in command, General McNarney, to Wilson's headquarters at Caserta. For some time the Chief of Staff had felt that Generals Clark and Eaker were coming too much under British influence, as evidenced by their support of the drive toward the Ljubljana Gap, and he made certain that the new American Deputy would be one who was acquainted with Washington's view. It meant giving up a forceful Deputy who had taken many details off his shoulders, but a highly capable replacement was readily available in the person of Lieutenant General Thomas T. Handy, who had been Marshall's Chief of the Operations Division since the late spring of 1942. Handy, although less abrasive in disposition than McNarney, had proved that he could also be forceful. Perhaps more important was the fact that he had worked as Eisenhower's Deputy Chief of War Plans in the early months of the war and that he had a long friendship with MacArthur, dating back to World War I. Handy's job as Chief of the Operations Division was taken over by Major General John E. Hull, who had served in that division since the day of Pearl Harbor. This combination was to remain together until the war's end.

When Eisenhower requested still one more senior commander to continue the deception in the United Kingdom, General Marshall called on another old friend, Lieutenant General John L. DeWitt, to succeed McNair as head of the paper army group. The elaborate pretense was worth the effort. German troops in the Pas-de-Calais, who could have strengthened enemy resistance in Normandy, waited too long to make their move.

Eisenhower's assumption of control in northwest Europe, long urged by Marshall, did not come at a wholly propitious time. Unfortunately his new headquarters at Jullouville, near Granville, at the base of the Cotentin Peninsula, had been picked when the battle seemed to be shifting toward Brest. Now it was swiftly isolated from the main body of troops, as the Allied armies suddenly turned eastward, sweeping toward the Seine and then toward Belgium and the German border.

Eisenhower was cut off from the main battle for about three days when he reinjured a knee (first damaged in West Point football days) while trying to help push his small plane, which had made an emergency landing along the beach. This incident and time lag between Normandy and Washington put Marshall and his colleagues almost completely out of touch with events for nearly a week. At one point Marshall and his fellow Chiefs of Staff thought Patton was at the German border, when he actually had been stopped in front of Metz.

The change of command and the decision to advance on a broad rather than a narrow front—made just as the momentum of the breakout was slowing—furnished Montgomery with the argument that he was deprived by the Americans of a chance to finish the war before the end of the year. He blamed not only Eisenhower but Marshall and the coming United States election. Montgomery was not alone in criticizing these moves. Patton's admirers also later added to confusion about the war by claiming that if Eisenhower had not sent most of the available supplies to Montgomery, the Third Army commander could have bounced across the Rhine and ended the fight months earlier than May of 1945.

In this debate General Marshall supported the Supreme Commander's strategy. He declared in an interview in 1957:

> As to General Patton at this time and the matter of gasoline, I think General Eisenhower's actions were normal to command in that period of the war. Of course he [Patton] wanted more gasoline; of course Montgomery wanted more gasoline and a larger freedom of action. That is just natural to commanders under these circumstances. What was going on was the First Army was making very rapid moves in a very positive manner and getting very little public credit for it in this country. The Third Army was getting far more credit because of Patton's dash and showmanship. General Hodges was very quiet, and some very remarkable actions took place here for which General Hodges was entitled to the credit. All these things are pressed by the press—twisted by various interests —so that it is quite hard to get the actual facts in the case. Montgomery wanted to get free and to go ahead on his part. Patton wanted to get free—with the great temptation of running right up to the Rhine—and there was almost no gasoline. . . . I think Eisenhower's control of the operations at that time was correct. And that all the others were yelling as they naturally would yell. There is nothing remarkable about that except one was the supreme commander of the British forces, which at that time was very small, and the other was a very high-powered dashing commander who had the press at his beck and call— General Patton.

In trying to judge what was the correct disposition of the available gasoline, one has to remember a great many subsidiary facts and prospects. For example, take the German operation in the Bulge later on. If it was successful, it was a grand thing. But it wasn't successful. . . . You can sometimes win a great victory by a very dashing action. But often or most frequently the very dashing action exposes you to a very fatal result if it is not successful. And you hazard everything in that way. For example, the control of the British Fleet in World War I . . . [The British Navy] could lose the war in one action of a few hours. They didn't dare risk that until the conditions were highly in their favor. But everyone wanted [Admiral] Jellicoe to commit the fleet immediately. It would have been very unwise, it seems to me. At the time it was committed, that was the proper time. But nobody pays any attention to that. They want the dash. In these dashing movements of Patton [across France] he was absolutely right. And Eisenhower gave him a very free hand [in that sweep]. But that is not always the case.[19]

Oddly enough, even as the Allied armies were slowing their pace, military leaders in the United States and Great Britain saw signs of victory before the year's end. As early as August 11 Major General Kenneth W. D. Strong, Eisenhower's Chief of Intelligence, thought the war would be over in three months. Most astounding, post-exchange officials distributed a memorandum saying that they were arranging to return Christmas presents—already in the mail—to the United States.[20]

So infected with enthusiasm did the intelligence agencies become that even Marshall and his colleagues in Washington were influenced by the talk. For once President Roosevelt and Prime Minister Churchill were less optimistic than their commanders. Churchill thought that the odds favored continuance of German resistance after the first of the year. Eisenhower, anxious lest the home front slow down its production of war materials, castigated those who predicted that the war would be over in a matter of weeks.

On the surface there was good ground for optimism. Bolstered by massive U.S. shipments of materiel, by growing German weakness and Hitlerian folly, and by their own effective handling of troops, tanks, and artillery, the Russians had continued to smash at the enemy since the summer of 1943. By the end of September 1943 the Soviet forces had driven to the Dnieper and by the first week of November had recaptured the key city of Kiev. Mobile columns moving southwestward across the river threatened to cut off the Germans in the Crimea. By early fall the Russians had taken back the most valuable parts of the Ukraine that had been lost to the Germans. Before the first week of January 1944 had passed, Soviet forces had crossed the old Polish frontier.[21]

In the early days of spring, as the Allies prepared to invade France and move on Rome, the Russians crossed the River Bug and then the Dniester. In April, Stalin's forces opened a Russian siege of Sevastopol, which ended with its recapture and the regaining of the Crimea in mid-month.

After a short lull the Russians opened their summer offensive on June

23. Caught between armies moving northward from Rome, westward from France, eastward from the long Russian front, which extended from Finland to the Black Sea, and constantly pounded from the air, the Germans found it difficult to establish a line that they could hold against their opponents.

By mid-July, Russian troops had overrun much of northeastern Poland. Near the month's end advanced elements were within a hundred miles of the Polish capital; on the thirty-first units were in the suburbs of Warsaw east of the Vistula.

As Hitler urged his commanders to stand and fight—not allowing them to retreat to a better position until too late—Red units forced Rumania to leave the war on August 23 and entered Bucharest at the month's end. Less than a week later they were on the Danube. On September 8 Bulgaria, under the threat of annihilation, declared war on Germany.

This tremendous push from the east accompanied the drives in Normandy and northern and southern France. After the Normandy breakout in late July, extending through early September, the Germans fell back as Allied armored columns swept across France, into Belgium, and across the Rhine. Montgomery's units cleared the Pas-de-Calais, destroying the V-bomb sites in that area, captured Antwerp virtually intact, and drove on toward Holland. While one American corps sped westward into the Brittany Peninsula, the bulk of Bradley's forces turned eastward, helping to close the Falaise Gap and bringing the capture of more than a quarter of a million Germans. First Army elements crossed the Seine and drove northward into Belgium and Luxembourg and penetrated Siegfried Line defenses in Germany before coming to a stop on September 11. The Third Army swung south of Paris and drove eastward to besiege Metz. The approach of the First and Third Armies to Paris encouraged the French to rise against the Germans on August 19. On August 23 the 2d French Armored Division, under U.S. V Corps, was given the honor of entering the city first. Paris was formally liberated by elements of the French division and the U.S. 4th Division on August 25. As a show of strength and to complete the capture of the city, General Bradley sent the 28th Division on a road march to the front through the center of Paris.

Premature announcements of the city's liberation reached Washington on August 22, prompting the chief of the French Naval Mission to the United States, Admiral Fenard, to write General Marshall:

> I cannot let this day go by without telling you my joy, my elation at the liberation of Paris. This great event made possible by the splendid surge forward of the American armies that rolled back the tottering forces of Germany across the French land, concretizes and foreshadows the complete liberation of France; a mighty step towards victory.
>
> There will be great rejoicing today in France, not only because freedom looms very near where it has not been actually achieved, but also because the whole country feels that it can at last take part in the final crushing of our

common enemies, in the East as well as in the West. The arms which have been taken up will not be laid down until victory is final, until the account with Germany and Japan has been settled.[22]

On his return from the West Coast on the thirtieth the Chief of Staff replied: ". . . I want you to know that the liberation of Paris was a source of great satisfaction to me as it was to all those who hold France in high esteem. The day is steadily approaching when your country will again enjoy complete freedom from the domination of the Nazis." [23]

With the war going well in Europe and the Pacific, General Marshall a week earlier had accepted General Arnold's proposal that they escape the pressures of Washington for a short vacation. Arnold picked a spot in the High Sierras near Bishop Air Base in California for a fishing trip. Knowing that they could not divest themselves of day-by-day responsibility for the conduct of the war, they made careful preparations to keep in touch with Washington. Colonel Carlisle Humelsine, who handled communications at the Pentagon Message Center, directed that a portable code machine be set up at the nearby air base. In addition the party took along a portable radio for unclassified messages and arranged for classified messages to be dropped daily by pouch.[24]

Flying out to Bishop Air Base on August 22 in the C-54 built for the President, the two generals proceeded by car and horseback to a camp in the mountains. Traveling by horseback, they moved to a different site each day, keeping up with the outside world by radio and signaling to their courier by flare from each new location.[25] The fishing was excellent and the recreation splendid for the two tired men, but the chief diversion consisted in getting the mail. On one occasion a courier dropped a pouch containing classified messages into woods some two miles from their camp, setting off a hectic search, enlivened by one of the party who accidentally set off a half-dozen fires in the forest while trying to signal to the rest of the group. To their intense relief the pouch was found, intact and still securely locked.[26] The Generals returned to Washington on August 30 to prepare for the next meeting with the British.

There had been no full-dress meeting of the Prime Minister and the President with the Combined Chiefs of Staff in nine months. It was time, Churchill thought, to sit down again in conference. Feeling that they should go back to a British site, he suggested Scotland, then Bermuda, and finally Quebec. The Canadian location was accepted, and the conclave was given the code name OCTAGON. In early September, General Marshall, accompanied by General Handy; Colonel Pasco, of the SGS; Miss Mona Nason, Marshall's personal secretary; and Sergeant Powder, his longtime orderly, set out for the old French Canadian city.

As they had a year earlier, Marshall and the other military advisers stayed at the Château Frontenac, while the President and Prime Minister were again at the Citadel. The Governor-General of Canada was their host at dinner on the first evening of their stay.

Midway through the meal Marshall and Arnold were called aside to deal with a serious emergency that had developed abroad. On August 1 as the Russian forces advanced near Warsaw, the Polish Home Army under General Tadeusz Bor-Komorowski had risen against the German occupation forces. At this point the Russians slowed their drive. Short of food and ammunition, the resistance forces were soon in a desperate state. The Allies attempted to answer their appeals for aid by dropping supplies, much of which fell into German hands. The Poles then appealed to the United States ambassador to Russia, Averell Harriman, for further Allied air supply. It was this plea, which he forwarded to Marshall, that Marshall and Arnold received in Quebec.

Although aware that additional supplies also would probably miss their target, Marshall and Arnold decided on one more drop. Before the dinner ended, Arnold radioed instructions to that effect to U.S. Air Forces in Europe. General Spaatz was told to contact General Deane of the U.S. Military Mission to Moscow and to coordinate his activities with the Russians. The Soviet authorities went along reluctantly with the air drop, leaving the impression that they were quite willing to abandon the Polish fighters to their unhappy fate. As Marshall and Arnold had feared, the effort was fruitless. On October 2 the Poles were forced to capitulate.[27]

Following their usual practice in foreign cities, the Chiefs of Staff spent some of their free time poking about the historic sections of old Quebec. They had come to Quebec almost exactly 185 years after the Anglo-French battle for the city. Wolfe had begun the attack in the late evening of September 12, 1759, and the city had fallen to the British in six days. Less than twenty years later American Revolutionary forces had attempted to take Quebec from the British. In a narrow street near the Château Frontenac the U.S. Chiefs saw markers noting the high point of the assault by troops under Brigadier General Richard Montgomery, Colonel Benedict Arnold, and Lieutenant Colonel Daniel Morgan.

The second Quebec conference was noteworthy for the general air of goodwill and agreement. This was the first of the meetings to be held when good news was coming in from almost every quarter, and the stresses and strains of the Arcadia, Casablanca, first Quebec, and Tehran conferences were missing. The great plan of invading northwest Europe was a success, and as the Chiefs of Staff gathered at Quebec, the Allied armies were still driving steadily eastward. In Eastern Europe the Russians were advancing on all fronts. In the Pacific, Nimitz and MacArthur continued their drives. Instead of discussing the familiar problems of getting additional forces, the Allies now debated whether the British could be employed in the Pacific campaigns.

Missing from the proceedings was General Marshall's old friend Harry Hopkins. There were signs that his state of health was pulling him down and indications that the President no longer depended on him to the extent that he once had. In sending Hopkins birthday greetings shortly

before the Quebec conference, the Chief of Staff had made clear the regard he held for the President's adviser:

> The conventional expression of the wish that you have "many more" does
> not meet the situation. Your good health is a matter of great and professional
> interest to me. I missed you much and sadly during the recent period of your
> indisposition and I am worried now, particularly with the Washington sultry
> heat, that you may again be overdoing. You have rendered a great service to
> the country in the past three years, one which will never be understood and
> therefore unappreciated, and given reasonable health—you always have the
> courage—you will be of great importance to what comes next in our interna-
> tional and war problems.
>
> I don't wish, I ask you to be careful, to conserve your energies and not to
> overdo and I am also prepared to damn you for your cigarettes, your drinks
> and your late hours. Confine your excesses to gin rummy.[28]

The changed tone in negotiations was evident at the first meeting of
the Combined Chiefs of Staff at the Château Frontenac on September 12.
Brooke suggested (1) that there had not been enough emphasis on securing sea communications and opening the ports of Rotterdam and Antwerp and (2) that it was important to make a strong attack on the northern flank. Since his stress on securing the approaches to Antwerp was in
line with Eisenhower's directives to Montgomery, Marshall readily agreed
with the first point. As to the means of securing the islands at the mouth
of the Scheldt, the Chief of Staff, usually a proponent of airborne attacks,
favored bombing rather than the air drop proposed by Brooke.[29]

The command of strategic bombers, lengthily debated in the spring of
1944, was brought up for review at Quebec in accordance with an earlier
agreement. Air Chief Marshal Portal suggested that with the shift of the
Supreme Commander's headquarters from Great Britain to France,
Eisenhower's control over the bombers was merely a formality. He cited
Air Chief Marshal Sir Arthur Tedder's small SHAEF air staff and his
separation from General Spaatz's headquarters and Harris's Bomber
Command as indications of the need to return to the former command
arrangements. He proposed that he and Arnold, working through their
representatives, Air Marshal Sir Norman Bottomley and Spaatz, should
control the use of the bomber forces.[30]

As a possible solution General Marshall suggested the assignment of a
small strategic force to the Supreme Commander with the remainder
being handled as Portal had suggested. Although Eisenhower thought
that the control might well be left as it was, he concluded that he could
get what he wanted under the proposed arrangement. Portal emphasized
the need for coordination with the Russians; the importance of drawing
on combined-bombing experience in London; the need to ensure that
priorities for POINTBLANK—the Combined Bomber Offensive against Germany—were properly observed, and the value of measuring the proper

psychological moment to hit the Germans. All these would be handled better if control reverted to the staffs in London.

Before an agreement was made at Quebec, Tedder conferred with Bottomley in London. They spelled out the means by which the strategic bombing forces would support Eisenhower's land battle in the final phases of the assault on Germany. First priority was to be given to oil targets and second to the German transportation systems—especially those leading to and through the Ruhr and the Saar—motor-transport and tractor factories, and ordnance plants and depots. Tedder, who had hoped for assignment of a third priority to the German Air Force, felt reasonably satisfied with the solution.

The debate over the status of strategic air forces persisted after the Quebec meeting. During a visit to Europe in early October, General Marshall proposed to Tedder that the Combined Chiefs of Staff decide whether they should try to end the war in Europe by the year's end or play it more cautiously until an all-out attack could be made in 1945. This earlier effort would require concentration of the air effort in the battle area instead of mounting a major bombing effort against strategic targets. It would be sufficient, he thought, to reduce the enemy output of critical items until the end of the year rather than trying to knock out production entirely. Such a course would require greater control over strategic air forces by General Eisenhower.

Portal disagreed. He believed that concentration of bombers against targets behind the front would be more effective than Marshall's plan to shorten the war. He feared that each division commander, desiring to save men, would demand bomber support, thus frittering away the whole air effort. In this argument he had Tedder's support. The Canadians, Tedder pointed out, had called for heavy bombers to attack a battery on Walcheren Island during the recent battle to secure the approaches to Antwerp—an excellent example of what a later generation would call "excessive overkill." The SHAEF Deputy also argued that while oil should continue to be the main target, a strong effort should be made to hit transportation, particularly in the Ruhr.

Near the end of October, General Eisenhower became concerned about current thinking in Washington. He told Tedder that General Marshall was backed by the other members of the Joint Chiefs of Staff in requesting that all the bomber effort be placed immediately in support of the land battle. The Supreme Commander agreed with Tedder that if such a directive as that suggested by General Marshall were issued, it should be along the lines proposed by Tedder. In the end the strategic air directive was amended to keep oil as the first target and transportation and rail centers as the second. Portal believed that this was the best reply to Marshall's arguments.[31]

General Marshall agreed with Brooke on the need for the early opening of Antwerp. At a time when support for the British and U.S. drives in northern Europe depended heavily on supply over the beaches and through the recently opened port of Cherbourg—operations requiring extremely long hauls by truck—the need for a large port nearer the front could scarcely be exaggerated. Despite the directive by the Combined Chiefs of Staff to clear the approaches to the Belgian port, Montgomery continued to delay action hoping for some opportunity to cross the lower Rhine. On October 6 Field Marshal Brooke commented: "I feel that Monty's strategy for once is at fault. Instead of carrying out the advance on Arnhem he ought to have made certain of Antwerp in the first place." Brooke was joined in his criticism by a fellow Englishman, Admiral Sir Bertram H. Ramsay, Commander-in-Chief of the Allied Naval Expeditionary Force, who "brought this out well in the discussion and criticized Monty freely. Ike nobly took all blame on himself as he approved Monty's suggestion to operate on Arnhem." 32

In reviewing the Italian campaign at Quebec, the British again raised the issue of the drive on Vienna. Although Brooke did not strongly favor the operation, he dutifully set forth the Churchill-Alexander proposal at the opening day's meeting. He said that there were great advantages in a swing toward Trieste and an advance from there to Vienna. But he conceded that if it encountered determined German opposition, there was little chance of reaching the Austrian capital that winter. Nonetheless there was the possibility of seizing the Istrian Peninsula as a base from which troops could be sent into Austria in case of German collapse. Such a move, he argued, would be not only of military value, but politically important in light of Russian advances into the Balkans.33

Once capable of arousing strong American opposition, the proposed drive to Vienna stirred little emotion at the conference. In an expansive mood Admiral King indicated that he was considering the possibility of an amphibious operation in the Istrian Peninsula. Equally amenable, General Marshall said that he had no immediate intention of withdrawing the U.S. Fifth Army, whose continued presence in Italy would be essential to continued action in the Mediterranean area. In the end the Combined Chiefs of Staff agreed that (1) they would not withdraw forces from Italy until they knew the results of Alexander's current offensive; (2) the final decision would be contingent on these results, German withdrawal in Italy, and Eisenhower's reactions; (3) if General Wilson wished to keep landing craft for an attack against the Istrian Peninsula, he should submit a plan not later than mid-October.34

Brooke had carefully kept his arguments on the military plane. Next day Churchill stressed the national and political elements involved. He now made clear publicly what he had often emphasized to his staff: Britain's greatest stake was in Italy. It was there, he reminded the group, that the largest British Empire army in existence—sixteen divisions in all: eight from the United Kingdom, two Canadian, one New Zealand, one

South African, and four British Indian—was committed to action. Under these circumstances he insisted that Alexander should not be deprived of the means to continue his campaign. Pondering future possibilities, he added that if the Germans were knocked out of Italy, the Allies should focus on Vienna. In passing they should think of capturing Istria and occupying Trieste and Fiume.

Thus far Churchill was merely reviewing arguments set forth by Wilson and the British Chiefs of Staff earlier in the summer. But now he emphasized a point raised by Brooke the day before. The encroachment of the Russians into the Balkan area and the consequent spread of Soviet influence into that sphere, the Prime Minister declared, called for Allied action. "He preferred to get into Vienna before the Russians did as he did not know what Russia's policy would be after she took it." [35]

In later years Marshall and his colleagues would be attacked for failure to see the Russian menace that Churchill supposedly had clearly advertised. In fact the Prime Minister had generalized about an operation that would have necessitated a change in basic Allied strategy—from defeating the Germans to forestalling the Russians—and the adoption of a project for which his own Chiefs of Staff clearly had no well-defined plans. Brooke wrote in his diary at the time: "According to him we have two main objectives, first an advance on Vienna; secondly the capture of Singapore!" In his postwar notes Brooke added pointedly: "Neither of them in our plans. We had no plans for Vienna, nor did I ever look at this operation as becoming possible. Nor had we any plans for the capture of Singapore. By mentioning these objectives, he was not assisting in our discussions with the American Chiefs." [36]

☆

☆ **XXII** ☆

☆ ☆

Roads to Tokyo

T HE issue of the main road to Tokyo had been left unresolved by the U.S. Joint Chiefs of Staff at the Cairo meeting in December 1943. They proposed, and the British Chiefs of Staff accepted, a general advance toward the Formosa-China-Philippines area, with Nimitz's forces proceeding by way of the Marshalls and the Carolines to the Marianas and MacArthur's forces taking the Vogelkop Peninsula at the western end of New Guinea and attacking Kavieng in New Ireland and Manus Island in the Admiralties.

MacArthur and Nimitz had been busily occupied since the late summer of 1943 in pressing their separate offensives against the Japanese. In New Guinea the Southwest Pacific commander had advanced on September 5–6 against Lae with an amphibious landing and an airborne drop, while an Australian force under his command moved against Salamaua. The latter position was evacuated by the enemy on September 11; Lae was taken four days later. An Australian brigade, landed by sea, seized Finschhafen later in the month.

On November 1 troops from the South Pacific landed in Empress Augusta Bay to secure the approaches to Bougainville, the westernmost and largest island of the Solomons. MacArthur also continued to move eastward in New Guinea with a series of amphibious end runs.

In the Central Pacific, Nimitz's forces pushed toward targets in the Gilbert Islands. Makin, lightly defended, and Tarawa, strongly fortified, were hit in separate attacks under Admiral Spruance on November 20. After four days the 27th Infantry Division took Makin. On Tarawa the 2d Marine Division, in some of the hardest fighting of the war, suffered 3300 casualties while killing nearly 4700 Japanese in a two-day fight. With the Gilberts secured, Nimitz prepared to send joint Army-Marine task forces into the Marshalls.

When General Marshall visited the Southwest Pacific in December

1943, MacArthur had strongly protested to him about developments in the Central Pacific. In addition to disapproving what he felt was a Navy effort to bypass the Philippines, MacArthur asked for greater resources to continue his advance in New Guinea.

Immediately on his return to Washington the Chief of Staff inquired into ways to assist the Southwest Pacific commander. He promptly informed General MacArthur: "I arrived in Washington late last night and on resuming business here this morning I wish first to express my appreciation for the reception you gave me in the Southwest Pacific and of the admirable organization and fighting force you have under development there. I was greatly impressed by all that I saw. Already this morning I have talked to Arnold about some of the air matters and probably will have a little encouraging news for you in a few days. All good things to you and your command in the New Year." [1] Within the week, General Marshall notified MacArthur that he was trying to get a carrier on the West Coast to bring fifty pursuit planes to him, which would be in addition to those already allotted. The pursuit-plane reserve was to be increased 20 per cent, and his Third Bomber Group was to be brought to full strength.[2]

Although MacArthur now had evidence of Marshall's backing, he remained uneasy over the Navy's intentions. Nor was the Southwest Pacific commander encouraged by the results of a conference of representatives of the Southwest, Central, and South Pacific commanders at Pearl Harbor near the end of January. At its conclusion MacArthur pressed the Chief of Staff to concentrate forces along the New Guinea route to the Philippines. He would welcome any British forces that could be assigned, saying that he would place them under Admiral Halsey as Allied Naval commander. Finally he proposed to send his Chief of Staff, General Sutherland, to Washington to present his views [3]

Soon afterward, Admiral Nimitz sent his Chief of Staff, Rear Admiral Forrest Sherman, to present the Central Pacific case. While Sherman talked with King, General Sutherland outlined MacArthur's views to the Secretary of War and the Chief of Staff, urging that strategy be changed to bring the United States forces into Mindanao quicker than planned. General Marshall told Sutherland that matters were going the way Mac-Arthur wanted them to and insisted that the Pacific commander's views were not being slighted.[4] Later in the Joint Chiefs of Staff meeting, King advocated continuance of a two-pronged advance but with emphasis on the Central Pacific drives. General Marshall parried by proposing that the Joint Staff Planners study the proper sequence of operations and the allotment of resources for future advances.

Shortly after the talks began, a personal appeal from MacArthur was placed before Stimson. The Southwest Pacific Commander had outlined his arguments to General Osborn of the War Department staff, while he was on a trip to his theater, for him to report to the Secretary of War. It was MacArthur's strongest bid thus far for his own strategy and for over-all control in the Pacific.

He buttressed his case by speaking of three current attacks—Arawe and Cape Gloucester in the New Britain area and Saidor on New Guinea—in which he had bottled up 20,000 Japanese. In future advances he proposed to follow the same procedure: cut off transport with air, destroy stores, move in with minimum losses, build airstrips, move up air, and repeat the sequence. Using the same tactics, and keeping the loss of American lives to the minimum, the Southwest Pacific commander planned to establish his forces firmly in Mindanao by the end of the year, provided he had strate-gic control of ships, men, and equipment in the Pacific. "I need only that," his message continued; "what is now in the Pacific is sufficient if properly directed. I do not have to call on men or supplies being sent to the European front. That decision is one for the Joint Chiefs of Staff. I do not want command of the Navy, but must control their strategy, be able to call on what little of the Navy is needed for the trek to the Philippines. The Navy's turn will come after that. These frontal attacks by the Navy, as at Tarawa, are tragic and unnecessary massacres of American lives."

The Navy operations proposed for the Marshall Islands would be the same, he predicted. "The Navy fails to understand the strategy of the Pacific, fails to recognize that the first phase is an Army phase to establish land-based air protection so the Navy can move in."

He then made clear why he had appealed to Stimson. "Mr. Roosevelt is Navy minded. Mr. Stimson must speak to him, must persuade him. Give me central direction of the war in the Pacific, and I will be in the Philip-pines in ten months. Time is against me." The Japanese, he warned, were fortifying their positions in New Guinea and Mindanao.

Knowing that some of his friends believed that Roosevelt was against his strategic proposals because their success might make him a presiden-tial contender, MacArthur sought Stimson's aid in disabusing the Presi-dent of that view. But there was a strange ambiguity in his approach. A short while before he replied warmly to a letter from a Nebraska rep-resentative attacking the President's policies, and a few days later he re-plied similarly to a second letter from the Nebraskan, who suggested that MacArthur was needed to block a march toward monarchy under the current administration. Between these two letters the General had said to Osborn: "Tell Mr. Stimson I have no political ambitions. I have but one ambition; to return to the Philippines, to save the Philippine people, who are a great people, from their present agony; to restore the prestige of the United States. That is all that is moving me."

He apparently thought that Stimson, a former Governor-General of the Philippines and a man who sometimes held serious reservations about the Navy's demands, would respond favorably. But he failed to realize that neither Stimson nor Marshall would react well to his concluding plea:

"Tell Mr. Stimson to talk to the President. Don't let the Navy's pride of position and ignorance continue this great tragedy to our country." [5]

In light of this attitude it is not surprising that MacArthur became disturbed in late February by what he considered to be a move by the Navy to put the entire Pacific under Admiral Nimitz. A message from Nimitz on February 23 recommending that the back areas of the South Pacific should be reduced as forward areas were developed, seemingly reasonable in itself, became an object of suspicion when it went on to suggest that these arrangements could best be handled by placing the commander of South Pacific forces under Nimitz. The Navy had mentioned only Manus Island in the initial proposal, but MacArthur feared that much more was involved. This island, located in his area and about to be recovered by forces under his command, was essential to his basic plan. Nimitz, he declared, "thus has proposed to project his own command into the Southwest Pacific by the artificiality of advancing South Pacific Forces into the area." [6]

Such a change when "the success of long and bitter labors were in sight" could not fail to be regarded as a serious reflection on his capacity to command, he declared. On the command issue he was backed by Australian Prime Minister John Curtin, who had said he would oppose any further modification in strategic boundaries. Since these had been agreed on in international conferences by the governments, they could not be redrawn without further consideration.

At stake was not merely the glory of taking one small island; on this hinged control of the entire campaign in the Pacific. MacArthur insisted that his personal integrity, "indeed my personal honor," was involved. If an attempt was made to change his control, he asked "that I be given early opportunity personally to present the case to the Secretary of War and to the President before finally determining my own personal action in the matter." Once more, as some months earlier when he had considered his control threatened, he called on Prime Minister Curtin for help and also hinted at a possible appeal to the American public.[7]

General Marshall hastened to quiet his fears: "I am in agreement with the reasons you advance against such a proposal. You should retain command of all base facilities in your area unless you yourself see fit to turn over control of them." But he saw some merit in Nimitz's request. The action of the fleet should not be restricted by limitation of facilities. There was no idea that control of the Pacific campaign should be taken from him, the Chief of Staff maintained. Lest there be any doubt of his meaning, Marshall concluded: "Your professional integrity and personal honor are in no way questioned. . . . However, if you so desire I will arrange for you to see the Secretary of War and the President at any time on this or any other matter." [8]

Fortunately high-level debates did not hinder the progress of operations now under way. South Pacific units landed on Green Island in the northern Solomons in mid-February just before planes from Nimitz's carriers smashed at the Japanese naval base at Truk. The Central Pacific forces were already striking heavily at the Marshall Islands. A Marine-Army task force hit Kwajalein on February 1, and a similar group went ashore on Eniwetok in mid-month. These objectives were soon taken, and a mop-up operation began in the smaller islands, which ended in either occupation or neutralization of the important ones in April.

At the end of February, General MacArthur ordered an assault on the Admiralty Islands in the Southwest Pacific. In mid-March, Marshall was able to congratulate him "on the skill and success with which the Manus Island operation has been carried through." He asked MacArthur to pass his message on "to Krueger, Kenney, Kinkaid and in particular to [General] Swift and his people who have evidently made a magnificent showing in their first fight." [9]

The Chief of Staff's warm words brought little consolation to General MacArthur, who felt that the recent Joint Chiefs of Staff directive of March 12, while attempting a compromise, had been weighted in Nimitz's favor. In the directive Hollandia was set as a mid-April target for MacArthur's forces, but Nimitz was to have his Marianas operation in mid-June and an assault in September against the Palaus. However, as Marshall had promised, MacArthur kept control of his Philippine campaign. His troops were to plan for a move against Mindanao in mid-November. A target date of mid-February 1945 was set for either Formosa or Luzon, with a decision to be made later.[10]

As the advances continued, Marshall and the other Chiefs of Staff sought additional men, planes, and supplies for the Pacific—while pushing ahead with the OVERLORD assault. On his departure for London shortly after the landings on the Normandy beaches, Marshall expressed his delight to MacArthur over his latest victories in the Southwest Pacific:

> On the Aitape–Hollandia–Maffin Bay–Biak Campaign which has completely disorganized the enemy plans for the security of Eastern Malaysia and has advanced the schedule of operations by many weeks. The succession of surprises effected and the small losses suffered, the great extent of territory conquered and the casualties inflicted on the enemy, together with the large Japanese forces which have been isolated, all combine to make your operations of the past one and a half months models of strategical and tactical maneuvers.
>
> We are now engaged in heavy battles all over the world which bid fair to bring the roof down on these international desperadoes. I am off this morning for England.[11]

These were exciting times as MacArthur continued his advance along the northern coast of New Guinea, the Admiralties passed into Allied control, and the Japanese were isolated in the Bismarcks. To the north Nimitz's forces were preparing to strike from the Marshalls toward the Marianas with the aim of isolating Truk, the enemy naval base from which most of the Japanese fleet had already fled and where merchant shipping had been heavily blasted by carrier planes in late February. Beyond also lay the Carolines.

On their visit to London the American Chiefs of Staff discussed with the British alternatives now open to the Allies in the Pacific. With the war stepped up in Europe they might contemplate accelerating the attack elsewhere. Possibly the Philippines and the Palaus could be bypassed and an attack made against Formosa. Or perhaps, ran the wild surmise, Formosa could be bypassed for a direct attack on Kyushu. The Chiefs of Staff voted to get the opinions of MacArthur and Nimitz on these alternatives.

Again General MacArthur opposed any plan to bypass the Philippines. He spelled out obvious drawbacks to a direct attack against Formosa: it would have to be launched without appreciable air support and based on the Hawaiian Islands 5000 miles away. On purely military grounds he considered it necessary to reoccupy the Philippine Islands in order to cut the enemy lines of communication to the south and to get air and naval bases. But beyond that was the need to go back to the Philippines "where our unsupported troops were destroyed by the enemy." He spoke of a moral issue: "We have a great national obligation to discharge. Moreover if the United States should deliberately bypass the Philippines, leaving our prisoners, nationals and loyal Filipinos in enemy hands without an effort to retrieve them at the earliest moment we would incur the greatest psychological reaction." It would prove the truth of Japanese propaganda, lose prestige for Americans in the Far East, and cause an extremely adverse reaction in the United States. As if to stress the last point, he said again that if bypassing the Philippines was seriously considered, he wanted the opportunity to return home to present his case to the President.[12]

Marshall and King were back from Europe at their offices in Washington on June 22. The Army Chief of Staff lost no time in briefing Stimson on the problems that had developed during his visit. In a morning meeting he spoke forcibly about his differences with de Gaulle. In the afternoon he discussed problems in the Pacific. He mentioned MacArthur's latest protest and asked the Secretary for his opinion. Stimson believed that the Pacific commander had a point in saying that in attacking the Chinese coast directly the Americans would lack land-based airpower. As for the rest he thought MacArthur was wrong.

Unwilling to grant even this point, General Marshall said that carrier-based planes could bring great force to bear against Formosa and they would be aided by the Chinese-American Air Force planes up from Chungking. To follow MacArthur's advice would mean that "we should be going the slow way; we should be butting into the large forces the Japanese have accumulated in the Philippines and in the Netherlands East Indies where they can't get away to go north . . . on account of the shortage of ships. We should have to fight our way through them and it would take a very much longer time than to make the cut across." [13]

Backed by Stimson, General Marshall returned a strong reply to Mac-Arthur. Intercepts of Japanese messages indicated a steady build-up of strength in the areas of Mindoro, Celebes, Halmahera, and Vogelkop, where the Southwest Pacific commander wanted to strike, and in the Palaus, which Nimitz was thinking of attacking. Possibly more forces would be needed to attack Formosa in 1945 than in the next few months; there was also the possibility of early collapse of resistance in China unless some move was made in the Far East. For these reasons an early attack on Formosa was being examined.[14]

Further studies might show, he continued, that a more economical operation could be carried out against the southern tip of Japan proper because the naval approach there would be somewhat easier than that toward Formosa. In addition Kyushu would have adequate harbor facilities and airfields.

Marshall carefully explained that plans for both Formosa and Kyushu were still in the study stage, "but neither operation in my opinion is unsound in the measure you indicate." Whether either could be attempted before a heavy blow was struck at the Japanese fleet, he conceded, was a serious consideration. There was little doubt in his mind, however, that once a crushing blow had been struck against the enemy fleet, the Americans should move as close to Japan as possible to shorten the war.

The attack on Japan, Marshall insisted, would ensure the reconquest of the Philippines. Certain of this position, he lectured MacArthur: "We must be careful not to allow our personal feelings and Philippine political considerations to override our great objective, which is the early conclusion of the war with Japan." Bypassing the Philippines was in no way synonymous with abandonment; on the contrary by defeating Japan they would expedite the liberation of the islands.

Anticipating that MacArthur would blame the Navy for converting him to its views, General Marshall made it plain that this was not the case. But it was important, he believed, to keep the great Pacific fleet with its thousands of planes in almost constant employment because of its mobility, the power to select objectives along a tremendous front, and the ability to increase rapidly the carrier force available for attack. Consequently, he explained, "I have been pressing for the full use of the fleet to expedite matters in the Pacific and also pressing specifically for a carrier assault on Japan."

In his conclusion Marshall softened somewhat. He had no objection to MacArthur's coming home to present his case. If the occasion arose, he himself would speak to the President. "I am sure he will be agreeable."

A few weeks earlier Marshall might have been doubtful about Roosevelt's desire to bring the General home on the eve of a national convention at which the President's name would be presented for a fourth-term nomination. As late as April 1944 newspapers still indicated that General

MacArthur was gaining support around the country as a Republican candidate. Senator Vandenberg attempted to keep his name out of primaries, but an enthusiastic backer entered the New Hampshire race as a MacArthur delegate and ran last. In Wisconsin, despite Vandenberg's wishes, backers of the General put him in the race against Thomas E. Dewey and Wendell Willkie. The New York governor won the primary, ending Willkie's chances for the nomination and supposedly knocking out any possibility of a nomination for MacArthur. Still MacArthur had been only "a ghost candidate" like Stassen, entered perhaps to make certain of knocking Willkie out. Vandenberg decided to wait until May 1 before deciding whether or not to join the Dewey parade.[15]

After running second in Wisconsin and picking up 3 delegates, MacArthur piled up 500,000 votes in an Illinois preferential primary against a political unknown. No delegates were involved, but the vote indicated increasing strength.

However, MacArthur's fate was sealed shortly afterward because he had selected the wrong politician to receive his written opinions on the state of the union. At this point Representative Albert L. Miller of Nebraska released to the press some of the letters he had earlier sent and received from the Southwest Pacific commander. Miller had written: "the New Deal, including President Roosevelt, is scared to death of the movement in this country for you. . . . I am certain that unless this New Deal can be stopped this time our American way of life is forever doomed. You owe it to civilization and the children yet unborn to accept the nomination. . . . You will be our next President." Some men would have suspected a trap in such rhetoric; others would have reasoned that it was the type of letter a theater commander in the midst of war should leave unanswered or have replied to with platitudes. MacArthur's second sentence in his two-sentence reply was sufficiently safe, but he invited trouble with his first: "I do not anticipate in any way your flattering predictions, but I do unreservedly agree with the complete wisdom and statesmanship of your comments." [16]

Encouraged by the response, Miller near the end of January 1944 had written a stronger statement speaking of "a tremendous revolution on in this country" and a "mass movement by the citizens who are displeased by the many mistakes now being made by the Administration." He concluded: "If this system of left-wingers and New Dealism is continued another four years, I am certain that this monarchy which is being established in America will destroy the rights of the common people."

Apparently pleased by the sentiments and seemingly persuaded that the representative would be as prudent as Vandenberg, MacArthur sent a second letter. Later he said that his letters were merely "amiable acknowledgments" to a congressman he scarcely knew. But for political purposes, while a candidacy was still budding, they were exceedingly naïve. In the second exchange the General wrote: "I appreciate very much your schol-

arly letter. Your description of conditions in the United States is a sober-
ing one indeed and is calculated to arouse the thoughtful consideration of
every true patriot." He added that "We must not inadvertently slip into
the same condition internally as the one which we fight externally." Read
without reference to Miller's vitriolic allegations, these letters would have
created no uproar. Released by a strong admirer of MacArthur, they
threatened, in Vandenberg's words, even "to hurt the General's military
status." Confused and angry, the Michigan senator wrote: "Miller, in one
inane moment, crucified the whole MacArthur movement and MacArthur
with it." [17]

A few backers still said that MacArthur would accept a draft, but Vandenberg knew better. As the hubbub mounted, the Pacific commander
cleared the air by saying: "I have on several occasions announced I was
not a candidate for the position. . . . I do not covet it, nor would I
accept it." The Washington *Times-Herald*'s "McClellan" had chosen
General Sherman's way out of the race. In bowing out MacArthur had
said that suggestions had been made "that it is detrimental to our war
effort to have an officer in high position on active service at the front
considered for President." But Vandenberg, who had nurtured great
hopes for many months, knew better. He wrote the obituary to the candidacy in frustration and bitterness. He had no doubt that MacArthur
would have been incomparably the best commander-in-chief the United
States could have had in the war and he did not regret supporting the
General, although it had cost Vandenberg himself the temporary chairmanship of the Republican National Convention. Saddened but realistic,
he recorded in his diary his skepticism of MacArthur's stated reason for
bowing out:

> That is not the *real* reason. If it were, he would have said it long ago. The
> *real* reason is (1) that the tragic mistake made by Congressman A. L. Miller
> (Nebraska Republican) in publishing his private and confidential correspond-
> ence with MacArthur made the latter's position untenable; (2) that the Dewey
> movement has such momentum that it is remotely likely that any other candi-
> date can overtake him and the General wishes to retire from the scene with
> dignity and honor. I agree to the statement on both counts. (On the latter
> count, I have advanced it through our mutual friend, Brigadier General C. A.
> Willoughby, who is G-2 at MacArthur's headquarters).

Later Vandenberg commented: "I shall never understand why . . .
[the letters] were written in the first place." [18] Had he written of the
consequence of MacArthur's correspondence with another Republican
representative, Speaker Joseph Martin, some years later, he might well
have marveled that the General still expected politicians to keep his letters confidential.

The Joint Chiefs of Staff understood General MacArthur's personal
commitment to return to the Philippines, but they also wanted to choose
the quickest way to end the war. Working in favor of the Navy's Central

Pacific drive was the growing Army Air Forces interest in the Marianas as a base for long-range bombers (B-29s) that would be able to hit the Japanese home islands. The amphibious attacks by Admiral Raymond A. Spruance's Fifth Fleet, then being readied against Guam, Saipan, and Tinian under the Joint Chiefs of Staff directive of March 12, would give the Navy and its attached forces the opportunity to seize the islands that King and others regarded as the key to the Central Pacific—unlocking the way for operations bypassing the Philippines. Troops assigned for the three landings included two Marine divisions, two Army divisions, and a reinforced Marine brigade under Major General Holland M. ("Howling Mad") Smith, a senior Marine commander known for his drive and fiery temper.

The first target, Saipan, where 30,000 Japanese were entrenched, was attacked on June 15. After heavy preliminary naval and air bombardment the two Marine divisions, the 2d and 4th, landed on the first day. Despite powerful naval support, American D-day losses were heavy, and the beachhead was not fully established for two days.

The attack succeeded in bringing out the Japanese fleet, which was reported headed for the American force on June 16. Spruance decided to land the 27th Infantry Division on Saipan and to postpone the Guam attack, set for the eighteenth, while turning his force at sea against the enemy.[19]

While the land operations continued, Spruance prepared for one of the major naval battles of the war. The Japanese opened the attack on June 19 with a tremendous air strike near Guam in which they lost more than 350 planes to a tenth that number for the Americans. Next day they again lost heavily in aircraft and ships (including three carriers) and were forced to withdraw. Still intent on his main mission of supporting the Marianas operation, Spruance did not pursue the retreating force and so lost an opportunity to destroy it. The action, however, ended the enemy's last possibility of saving his garrisons in the Marianas.

Although doomed, the Japanese Army decided to fight on. In desperate fighting they inflicted nearly 10,000 casualties on the American forces before Saipan was secured on July 9. Twelve days later the attack on Guam began with a Marine division, an Army division, and a Marine brigade committed to the action. Final resistance ended on August 10. Meanwhile Marine units had swarmed ashore on Tinian, a few miles from Saipan, on July 24 and in a textbook action completed the occupation on August 1.

The capture of the Marianas, coupled with the tremendous Battle of the Philippine Sea, were regarded by Admiral King and the men involved as the decisive actions of the war in the Pacific. For the enemy it was indeed a savage blow. General Tojo's cabinet fell on July 18, bringing in its wake the realization by the Japanese for the first time that the war would soon be brought to their shores.[20]

Unfortunately the victory was to be marred by one of the noisiest and bitterest controversies of the war, one that must have reminded General Marshall of the absurd uproar over the race for Sedan in 1918, which was to be fought over years afterward in bars and clubs throughout the world.

Difficulties began when Major General Holland Smith, commanding the ground forces in Saipan, decided after several days of costly fighting that Major General Ralph C. Smith, commander of the 27th Infantry Division, was not sufficiently aggressive. At issue was the fact that Marine and Army units were trained to use different tactics, the Marines stressing violent hand-to-hand battles for beachheads and the Army resorting to a more methodical approach, backed by stronger artillery support and air power. On Holland Smith's recommendation, the Army commander was relieved by Spruance, and Major General Sanderford Jarman, an Army officer, was placed at the head of the division until another Army commander, Major General G. W. Griner, could be sent out from the Hawaiian Command.

The Army commander in Hawaii, commanding army forces under Admiral Nimitz in the Central Pacific, Lieutenant General Robert C. Richardson, Jr., had a temper as quick-triggered as Holland Smith's and a low opinion of the ability of Marine officers to handle units above division level. Assuming that at least part of the 27th Division's problem had been due to the corps organization on Saipan and concluding that Holland Smith had reflected adversely on the fighting qualities of soldiers, he quickly appointed a board headed by Lieutenant General Simon B. Buckner, Jr., to investigate the relief. Smith and his naval superiors in the Marianas promptly condemned the inquiry as requiring a review of actions of officers outside Richardson's province and blasted its members for failing to get the views of the Marine officer mainly concerned. Shortly after naming the board, Richardson flew to Saipan, where, without calling on Holland Smith, he decorated members of the 27th Division. Going then to Smith's headquarters, he soon became involved in a heated argument. He ended this phase of the imbroglio by crossing verbal swords with Vice Admiral Kelly Turner, Smith's superior, who asked Nimitz to look into Richardson's activities.

The story of the warring Smiths (actually Ralph Smith stayed out of the fight) was soon taken up by the Hearst press, which used the incident as the basis not only for an attack on Holland Smith and the Marine Corps' type of fighting, which the newspapers alleged led to heavy casualties, but also for a demand that General MacArthur be given supreme command in the Pacific. A few weeks later knowledgeable articles in *Time* and *Life* upheld the Marines in the controversy.

Meanwhile General Richardson had sent Marshall findings of the Buckner Board, which, while upholding Holland Smith's authority to relieve Ralph Smith, concluded that it "was not justified by the facts." The Chief of Staff, not involved until this point, now entered the picture, fearful that the fight would soon make the earlier Buckner-Theobald incident in Alaska look like a parlor game. He turned the hot issue over to one of his chief deputies, General Handy. Handy reported that while there was some basis for the charge that the 27th Division's commander lacked aggressiveness, there was also ground for believing that Holland Smith's fitness to command in this situation was open to question because of his strong prejudice against the Army. He felt that "bad blood" had developed between the Marines and the Army to the point that it would infect future operations. A therapeutic move, he believed, was to get both Smiths out of the Pacific. The Army accepted its part of Handy's prescription, and Ralph Smith, by now commanding the 98th Division in Hawaii, was transferred to the European Theater. It was unrealistic, of course, to assume that the Navy would attempt to transfer one of its heroes out of the area where he had just won a great victory. However, a higher headquarters, Fleet Marine Force, Pacific, was being created and Holland Smith was put at its head. Although the change was not made for that purpose, it ensured that he would not again be in direct command of Army units.[21]

On publication of the *Time* and *Life* articles in late August and early September, General Richardson complained to Admiral Nimitz, suggesting that a rebuttal signed by General Griner, the current commander of the 27th Infantry Division, be published and that the accreditation of the offending *Time-Life* newsman (whose articles had been unsigned) revoked. Admiral Nimitz had already made a determined effort to keep the peace by deleting derogatory statements concerning the 27th Division from Spruance's official report. This action had angered some of Nimitz's Navy and Marine Corps friends, and they became even more irate when he forwarded Richardson's requests to Admiral King with a recommendation that they be approved.[22]

Although willing to make a vigorous effort to restore harmony, Admiral King was inclined to blame General Richardson for much of the dispute. However, the Admiral wrote Marshall that he would be willing to get General Holland Smith to issue a statement making clear that there was no question of the personal bravery of the soldiers of the 27th Division and that he was willing to have Griner's letter published if Marshall thought it advisable. He identified the author of the *Time* and *Life* articles as Robert Sherrod but declared that there were no grounds for requesting withdrawal of his credentials.[23]

Taking careful aim at Richardson, King slapped at his use of an all-Army board to judge a Marine Corps officer's action. He took strong exception to intemperate attacks on Holland Smith that had been made in testimony before that board. "General Richardson's unilateral handling of this problem of joint command by an ex parte investigation was, in my opinion, improper and prejudicial to inter-service relations."

There were elements here that could have produced a nasty quarrel, but Marshall, Nimitz, and King managed to avert that. Marshall undoubtedly recalled that King had kept his head in the Buckner-Theobald affair, actually suggesting that Buckner be kept on after the Army Chief of Staff had offered to transfer him. Although Marshall defended Richardson's right to set up an Army board—one that had no judicial authority and did nothing more than furnish advice to the commander naming the board—he made no statement about Holland Smith. He further suggested that harm rather than good might come of additional explanations to the press: "The 27th Division will have other opportunities to vindicate its record, and the Navy Department might then consider the desirability of expressing appreciation of the Division's efforts." [24]

Without mentioning Handy's recommendation that both Smiths be removed from the Pacific, General Marshall declared: "The information at hand indicates that relationships between the Marine and Army forces on Saipan deteriorated beyond mere healthy rivalry. Corrective measures are needed if we are to remove the potentiality of similar troubles in future operations. In order to obviate all possible embarrassment to the Joint Command, the War Department has transferred General Ralph Smith from the theater." Marshall suggested that the senior officer of each service in the Pacific Ocean Areas be told that "the prevention of such a state of affairs is squarely his own responsibility, as is also the task of promptly remedying it should it be found to exist." He enclosed a draft of a proposed message to this effect, inviting King's frank opinion.

The Navy Chief effectively ended the exchange by saying that, in accordance with Marshall's desire, he would take no further action about a press statement. As to Marshall's proposed letter, he feared that it might boomerang. "I can foresee no benefit in encouraging him [Richardson] to make a further investigation along the lines he considers appropriate." King would be seeing Nimitz shortly and would discuss the matter with him. He asked that Marshall withhold action until he returned.[25]

Apparently all agreed to let the matter stand thus for the remainder of the war. The outward appearance of restored good relations did not prevent the principals from seething inwardly. It was rumored that when General Marshall read Richardson's reports, he had angrily vowed that he would never permit another soldier to serve under Marine command. If Marshall was quoted correctly, he must have altered his views before the war was over: soldiers did again serve under Marine generals in the Pacific, as did Marines under Army commanders. More important the battle of the Smiths did not prevent the Army and Marines from cooperating in the closing campaigns of the war.

General Handy, who worked closely with Marshall, says that he never heard the Chief of Staff make the statement attributed to him. Admiral Nimitz thought that he had done so but believed that he had changed his mind after getting all the facts. If he made any such statement, it was probably to the effect that he would never allow soldiers to serve again under General Holland Smith. General Marshall was well aware of Richardson's temper and temperament, having declined to let him serve as a commander in the Southwest Pacific after he protested against having to be placed under an Australian commander. Nevertheless Marshall was inclined to accept at least some of Richardson's remarks about Holland Smith's prejudice against the Army. When asked by the author in 1959 for a statement on the Marine General's actions, Marshall replied: "I do not wish to comment about General Smith. My opinion of the matter was too fixed to let me get involved in this thing here." [26]

In 1949 the appearance of extracts from General Holland Smith's book, *Coral and Brass,* brought the controversy to the headlines again. The official historian of the 27th Division, Edmund Love, entered the fray and in several articles challenged Smith's views. The result was an extended airing of the old Army–Marine Corps debate. The situation was worsened because of a bitter argument at that time over unification and the role of the various services in the future defense set-up. Not until the Korean War made necessary the combined efforts of all the services did the controversies subside.

While the Smith versus Smith fight raged, General MacArthur was trying his considerable best to get his own disagreement with the Navy over future strategy settled in his favor. In early July he proposed to General Marshall that his forces advance by way of western New Guinea and Morotai to Mindanao toward the end of October and to Leyte in mid-November. An all-out effort would be made at Lingayen Gulf on Luzon in the early spring, requiring six divisions, including one armored and one airborne unit. When the Joint Planners received this proposal from Marshall, they questioned it seriously since it did not involve any planning for an advance from Mindanao to Formosa. [27]

Representatives of MacArthur and Nimitz met at Pearl Harbor in early July to discuss the possibility of speeding up planned operations. The Navy representative agreed to plans for taking the southern Philippines but was unwilling to accept the taking of Luzon in the north before an attack was made on Formosa. He felt that victories over the Japanese fleet might make it feasible to bypass Luzon. At this point President Roosevelt decided to take a hand. Looking back, Admiral King believed that politics was involved and that the President, whose name was then being presented to the Democratic convention for a fourth term, was interested in publicly exercising his authority as Commander-in-Chief. On July 21, the day Senator Truman was nominated as the vice-presidential candidate, Roosevelt and his party sailed for Hawaii on the *Baltimore* to confer with General MacArthur and Admiral Nimitz. [28]

King, who left Hawaii for Washington about the time Roosevelt started for Pearl Harbor, asked Nimitz to think carefully before expressing his views. The President arrived July 26 and shortly after received MacArthur and Nimitz aboard his cruiser. For the next two days he conferred ashore with the two commanders. The two officers explained their viewpoints in detail, with MacArthur making a strong plea based on American obligations to the Philippines. The President listened carefully to the conflicting presentations.

MacArthur, who had come without a staff and with no papers, felt that the Navy had an advantage, with many charts and maps and Nimitz's staff from nearby headquarters. However, Nimitz was soon convinced that it was the Army commander who had the edge. He had particular grounds for this conclusion one afternoon during the conference when the President decided to take the two of them through Honolulu on a visit to various naval and military establishments. Roosevelt's staff had called for an open car in which to ride and it was found that only two were available in the city: one, painted red, belonging to the fire chief, held five people; a larger one, more sedate in appearance, belonged to the madam of one of the city's better-known brothels. General Richardson, realizing that the latter car would be readily identified, chose the smaller though less chastely colored vehicle for his guest. As a result Nimitz was squeezed in between the President and MacArthur in the back seat. During the ride the Admiral soon felt that he was merely creating an obstacle in the conversation since it was carried on mainly between "Douglas" and "Franklin." Before the final conference he concluded that MacArthur had won his case. Whether Roosevelt was moved by MacArthur's strategic arguments, the importance of fulfilling a moral obligation, or the value of making certain the Army commander would bring no embarrassing issues into the fall campaign, he ended by favoring the return to Luzon.[29]

With this point settled, MacArthur brought up a recent development of which he had been apprised by a letter from Admiral King. King had passed on a British proposal to take over a large part of the Southwest Pacific area after American forces became established in the Philippines. As the Navy Chief probably expected and desired, MacArthur promptly replied: "I am completely opposed to this proposition." The Southwest Pacific Theater, he reminded both King and Marshall, was set up under an agreement among various powers interested in the area. "It was agreed by the nations concerned that the war would be fought with American leadership," he declared. "We are about to win that war. I can see no reason why the American command should be superseded by a British command at the moment of victory in order to reap the benefits of the peace." He feared that the British would want his Australian and New Zealand troops and would contribute no logistic support but would require Lend-Lease. The Dutch were opposed, the Australians did not want their support, and the whole idea was unjust. The Joint Chiefs should understand that a British command would damage American prestige in the Far East. He welcomed additional British contributions to the Southwest Pacific but under the previously established command structure. Besides there were ample opportunities for the British in the Far East—Burma, Malaya, Sumatra, the east coast of Asia, and India.[30]

Possibly King had in mind building a backfire against a second British plan that was in the making. Near the end of August, General Marshall passed on a proposal for sending British fleet units to the Pacific to take part in operations. The British said that if the Joint Chiefs did not wish to accept portions of the fleet for the main efforts, they were willing to propose an alternative scheme. This involved forming a British task force to operate in the Southwest Pacific under MacArthur's supreme command. Under such an arrangement the British units, if needed, could still be used in support of the United States Pacific Fleet. King suggested that in case the British offer was accepted, he would want to send Admiral Royal Ingersoll so that he could outrank a high-ranking British commander. MacArthur did not favor a change but said he would be willing to assign Ingersoll as Allied Naval Forces commander. He would still want to keep Vice Admiral Thomas Kinkaid as commander of the Seventh Fleet to handle operations in which MacArthur's forces were involved.[31]

Despite American reluctance to accept British assistance at this stage of operations, Prime Minister Churchill believed that it was tremendously important for the British to be represented to some degree in the final campaigns. At the second Quebec conference his eloquent request to be included in the battles against the Japanese was accepted by the President. An irreverent British observer, noting Admiral King's obvious displeasure, declared that the official minutes should read: "At this point Admiral King was carried out."

While the Combined Chiefs were engaged in Quebec in discussing Pacific and European strategy, they were suddenly called upon for a dramatic and sudden decision concerning the attack on the Philippines. This is General Marshall's official account of the episode:

> Toward the end of August Admiral Halsey's Third Fleet began a probing operation in the western Carolines and the Philippines. His carrier planes struck at Yap and the Palau Islands on 7 and 8 September, and the next two days bombed Mindanao. On the morning of the 12th, Admiral Halsey struck the central Philippines and arrived at a conclusion which stepped up the schedule by months.
>
> The OCTAGON Conference was then in progress at Quebec. The Joint Chiefs of Staff received a copy of a communication from Admiral Halsey to Admiral Nimitz on 13 September. He recommended that three projected intermediate operations against Yap, Mindanao, and Talaud and Sangihe Islands to the southward be canceled, and that our forces attack Leyte in the central Philippines as soon as possible. The same day Admiral Nimitz offered to place Vice Admiral Theodore S. Wilkinson and the 3d Amphibious Force, which included the XXIV Army Corps, then loading in Hawaii for the Yap operation, at General MacArthur's disposal for an attack on Leyte. General MacArthur's views were requested and 2 days later he advised us that he was already prepared to shift his plans to land on Leyte 20 October, instead of 20 December as previously intended. It was a remarkable administrative achievement.

The message from MacArthur arrived at Quebec at night, and Admiral

Leahy, Admiral King, General Arnold, and I were being entertained at a formal dinner by Canadian officers. It was read by the appropriate staff officers
who suggested an immediate affirmative answer. The message, with their recommendations, was rushed to us and we left the table for a conference. Having
the utmost confidence in General MacArthur, Admiral Nimitz, and Admiral
Halsey, it was not a difficult decision to make. Within 90 minutes after the
signal had been received in Quebec, General MacArthur and Admiral Nimitz
had received their instructions to execute the Leyte operation on the target
date 20 October, abandoning the three previously approved intermediary landings. General MacArthur's acknowledgment of his new instructions reached me
while en route from the dinner to my quarters in Quebec.[32]

The decision at Quebec was to have important consequences for the
debate on Formosa and Luzon. Since the Leyte attack had been advanced
to October 20, it was possible to set the Luzon landing forward to December 20. On October 3, after considerable debate, the Joint Chiefs of Staff
issued a directive to MacArthur to take Luzon after Leyte. They added
that during the Philippine operations Admiral Nimitz would support
MacArthur. The scene would then shift to Navy operations with Bonin
Islands operations scheduled for January 1945, and attacks on the Ryukyus in March. The two roads to Tokyo would then be opened for the
final phase.

☆

☆ **XXIII** ☆

☆　　☆

Soldiers as Governors

T H E second Quebec conference brought to a head the question of military government for Germany. The problems of civil and military government had been dealt with piecemeal in North Africa, Sicily, Italy, and northern Europe. It had been possible to improvise arrangements in liberated countries or in areas now friendly to the Allies. But when it came to the major Axis power, capable of great mischief unless properly governed, postwar policy was critically important. Some preparations had been made, but much remained to be done as Eisenhower's armies neared the German border. In late August the Supreme Commander and his Chief of Staff besieged the U.S. Chiefs of Staff for a clear-cut directive on future policy.[1]

Marshall had foreseen the problems early in the war. He vividly remembered the chaotic situation he had encountered serving in the U.S. occupation forces in the Philippines in 1902: "I had gone in myself as a second lieutenant with no instruction of any kind whatsoever—no schooling of any kind whatsoever—and not even an Army regulation. A storm had destroyed practically all the papers, and what I could find in a barrel [were] rain-soaked, and I had to make up my own returns—I was the only officer there—and [some] of my early returns for property I had to deal with and supplies I had to issue—were made up almost [wholly] out of my imagination. But I was given no instructions at all and I was practically governor in effect of quite a large territory, about half an island." The situation had improved little by 1917: "In the First World War it was not until after the actual fighting [began] that they started in to try to get officers that had been trained—some by [Major General Frederick] Funston in the [Mexican intervention]—and began circulating [requests] to get any copies of the regulations which had been [issued] at that time." [2]

Marshall was determined to avoid these pitfalls in World War II. In 1942 he and members of his staff recognized that officer-administrators must be trained for the tasks of military government. A School of Military

455

Government was consequently established in Charlottesville, Virginia. At its head was Reserve Brigadier General Cornelius Wickersham, whom Marshall described as "a very fine lawyer of New York, member of the firm Cadwalader, Wickersham and Taft, whose father had been, I think, Attorney General [under President Taft]."

Difficulties developed when division commanders, asked to nominate officers for the school, sometimes sent men they wanted to drop from their own staffs. "If they didn't want their chief of staff, and they didn't have the nerve to reduce him or get him transferred," General Marshall recalled, "they would send him to a school like that—kick him upstairs as it were—and I had to act very drastically with several of them for using this as a convenience to get rid of people [they didn't want]."

Before long the school ran into fire from administration liberals. Marshall's Provost Marshal General, Major General Allen Gullion, who was given the task of administering the school, was regarded in some circles as a personal empire builder and as an advance man for postwar imperialism. Secretary Ickes, Harry Hopkins, and other presidential advisers soon reported that the school was being filled with right-wing opponents of the President, and antidemocratic doctrines were being taught. Stimson recorded: "Other Departments have criticized it thinking that we were encroaching on their prerogatives. McCloy ran into feeling from State and Interior Departments. He had a talk with Dean Acheson [and] easily satisfied the latter of our innocence. But the cherubs around the White House still scented danger and, when they found that the school had enrolled a man by the name of Julius Klein (the same name as an old intimate friend and adviser of Herbert Hoover's), they thought the worst had happened and rushed to the President with the bad news. Apparently he swallowed the story and I found a rather sharp memo from him wanting to know what the Army was doing and by what authority it was doing it without going to him. . . ." [3]

Two days later the matter exploded in a cabinet meeting. Marshall, intent on the approaching landings in North Africa, was irritated when the Secretary of War told him what had happened. The Chief of Staff declared later: "There were some accusations that . . . we were trying to organize a new government [at the school]. . . . They didn't claim we were making glass, but I never heard of so many foolish cracks about it. Mr. Stimson came back from a cabinet meeting that lasted almost all afternoon and I discovered that they had been discussing entirely this particular officer whose name was the same as that of an intimate of a onetime Republican leader. And Mr. Roosevelt was very bitter about this matter and Mr. Stimson was very much stirred up over it. . . . I was shocked when I found out how long the cabinet spent—all afternoon— warring over this thing. And I expressed my surprise and incredulity that such a thing should happen and Mr. Stimson called up the President and explained that they were talking about the wrong man all the time. . . ." [4]

In the heated atmosphere of the time a number of wild charges were made. Marshall appointed Gullion to investigate and, when he did not report, pressed him for an answer. The Provost Marshal General replied that he had been embarrassed to find that one extreme rumor had indicated that there was actually a plot to establish a new government with a right-wing political leader as president and Marshall as vice president. Still managing to keep his sense of humor, the Chief of Staff retorted: "Well, I can tell you right now about the first part of it . . . I was going to be president. I was not going to be vice president. But the whole thing is utterly ridiculous." [5]

Although Stimson was furious at the charges in the cabinet, a friend, whom he obviously regarded as soundly conservative, told Stimson that he had also been alarmed at the character of some of the teaching. Stimson directed McCloy to look into the matter and report on the administration of the school and the attitudes of some of the professors. After a time Stimson was able to convince Roosevelt that his suspicions of the school were ill founded. The furor resulted in more careful selection of officers to study at the school and a more exact survey of the courses of study and the theories of government taught there.[6]

In the spring of 1943 Stimson and Marshall decided to establish a special Civil Affairs Division to give policy direction to the entire military-government program. The division was expected to act as adviser to the Secretary of War on "all matters within the purview of the War Department, other than those of a strictly military nature, in areas occupied as a result of military operations." The division was established on March 1, 1943, first on the General and then on the Special Staff.[7] Marshall chose as its head an officer who had served under him first at Fort Benning and later as chief of the G-1 Division of the War Department, Major General John Hilldring. Early in 1943 Hilldring had been sought by General MacArthur to command a division in New Guinea. Before he could assume that post, Hilldring had suffered a heart attack. Some weeks later in San Francisco, while awaiting a hospital board decision ordering his retirement, he asked General Marshall to intervene. Impressed by Hilldring's statement that his risk of death by continued duty should not be considered at a time when officers and men throughout the world were facing death in action, Marshall ordered him to Washington. Hilldring assumed his new position on April 7 and retained it until the end of the war.

In several sessions Marshall made clear to Hilldring the problems that awaited him and the policy he wanted him to pursue. Hilldring recalled that he warned him first of the nature of the task—"that it was a very treacherous job that I was taking, that there wasn't much chance that the reputation of the Army would be in any way enhanced by anything that I

might do, but [the danger] that the reputation of the Army might be
. . . damaged was enormous and I must have eyes in the back of my
head and on the sides of my head to watch for the formation of clouds in
the sky and unjust accusations." The civilian agencies of the government,
he continued, "were very unhappy about the fact that the Army, and not
they, were going to have this problem in the wake of battle, in the
dust of battle, to put in order the areas we had liberated, we had
conquered. . . ." Marshall added that it was "Eisenhower's disgust with
these seventeen civilian agencies roaming around areas in Africa, causing
him more trouble than the Germans, that . . . finally persuaded the
President that he would have to abandon the original concept of civilian
control by civilian agencies and turn it over to a new organization in the
Army." "The President himself," General Hilldring remembered Marshall's saying, "had come to this conclusion without any pressures at all by
the War Department because General Marshall didn't want this job at
all, but that nobody else in the cabinet, except perhaps Mr. Stimson and
Mr. Knox, had any sympathy with the President's decision, and that some
cabinet members, notably Mr. Ickes and to some extent Mr. Morgenthau
and . . . others, like Mr. Hopkins . . . had great doubts about the wisdom of giving to soldiers the amount of political power and influence to
be exerted by [the division] in the years ahead." [8]

Marshall's reluctance to take responsibility for military government did
not mean that he opposed it during the early period of occupation while
fighting was still in progress in overseas theaters. But he felt it important
for the military to stay clear of prolonged control of civil affairs. In 1943 he
carefully sketched his personal philosophy on this point. As recalled by
Hilldring, it was as vigorous a statement of his views on civilian control as
the one he was later to make in the hearings on the removal of General
MacArthur. Hilldring recounted that Marshall said:

"I'm turning over to you a sacred trust and I want you to bear that in mind
every day and every hour you preside over this military government and civil
affairs venture." He said, "Our people sometimes say that soldiers are stupid."
(Of course, he was then talking about professional soldiers.) He said, "I must
admit at times we are. Sometimes our people think we are extravagant with
public money, that we squander it, spend it recklessly. I don't agree that we do.
We are in a business where it's difficult always to administer your affairs as a
businessman can administer his affairs in a company, and good judgment sometimes requires us to build a tank that turns out not to be what we want, and we
scrap that and build another one, but that's part of the development of military weapons, expensive and regrettable, but sometimes unavoidable. But even
though people say we are extravagant, that in itself isn't too disastrous. . . .

"But," he said, "we have a great asset and that is that our people, our countrymen, do not distrust us and do not fear us. Our countrymen, our fellow
citizens, are not afraid of us. They don't harbor any ideas that we intend to
alter the government of the country or the nature of this government in any
way. This is a sacred trust that I turn over to you today. We are completely
devoted, we are a member of a priesthood really, the sole purpose of which is

to defend the republic. We concentrate our time and attention on that subject. That doesn't mean that we don't understand other things, but it simply means that we devote our time and attention exclusively to this. And I don't want you to do anything, and I don't want to permit the enormous corps of military governors that you are in the process of training and that you are going to dispatch all over the world, to damage this high regard in which the professional soldiers in the Army are held by our people, and it could happen, it could happen, Hilldring, if you don't understand what you are about, and how important it is that this reputation we have is of enormous importance, not only to the Army but to the country. This is my principal charge to you, this is the thing I never want you to forget in the dust of battle and when the pressures will be on you. . . ." [9]

General Marshall maintained a firm conviction of the need for close civilian-military rapport, which he demonstrated by his backing of the Standing Liaison Committee, consisting of representatives of the State, War, and Navy Departments, of which he was a member while Deputy Chief of Staff, 1938–40. In the summer of 1944 when he was trying to develop the Joint Army and Navy Staff College (forerunner of the National War College), he wrote Undersecretary of State Edward R. Stettinius, Jr., that after World War I an effort had been made to get representatives of the State Department to attend courses at the Army War College but that it was soon abandoned. "This to my mind," he commented, "was a very unfortunate business because political strategy must always have in the background military fundamentals or capabilities or else written history is a great misrepresentation of what has occurred in the past. When I came into the War Department I found practically no relationship between the War and State Departments except in minor irritating little matters, generally some Ambassador or Minister's difficulties with the Military Attaché or the desire of some Ambassador or Minister to have some portion of our poverty-stricken military equipment made available to some Latin-American country, to build up goodwill." [10] The Chief of Staff explained that an effort was being made to give the Army officers "a great deal that had to do with political matters concerning Latin-American, European and Far Eastern countries because unless there was an understanding of such involvements the individual would not be competent to advise as a General Staff officer when such complications arose." He hoped that the State Department would be able to detail a few men to take the entire four-and-one-half month course. "When the matter is brought to you, please give it careful attention. The usual answer is, no one is available." General Marshall was pleased when Stettinius replied promptly to say that his people would cooperate, although the State Department did have a manpower shortage. [11]

Assistant Secretary of War McCloy, who had worked closely with civilian authorities on matters pertaining to military government, wrote Marshall concerning the recommendation that Foreign Service Officers attend the embryo college: "In my judgment this is a most advisable, if not an essential step to take. I don't suppose that any war in history has more clearly shown the truth of Clausewitz's old dictum than this one. The politico-military aspects of the war are so apparent that they do not need any enumeration. Whether it is in China, [the] Southwest Pacific, the Mediterranean or E.T.O., the political side is all tied in with the military, and the soldiers have to do most of the political work." [12] McCloy felt that such an arrangement would result in greater realism in American diplomatic thinking. "Our foreign policy in the past," he said, "has had far too little relation to our military capacities."

The problem of Allied occupation of a defeated Germany was raised seriously early in 1943 when COSSAC headquarters was established to plan for a return to northwest Europe. One of Churchill's favorite dreams was that Germany's will to fight could be reduced by bombings, attacks from the Mediterranean, and risings in the occupied areas to the point that she might be easily occupied without a massive assault. Consequently he promptly asked the COSSAC staff to prepare plans to take advantage of several contingencies: (1) the collapse of Germany, (2) the lessening of German efforts, and (3) the surrender of German satellites.

During the summer of 1943 a British committee under Clement Attlee, Deputy Prime Minister, undertook to draw up a memorandum spelling out British views on zones of occupation in Germany. This furnished guidance for COSSAC and stated pretty much the boundaries ultimately recommended. Meanwhile, under his directive from the Combined Chiefs of Staff, General Morgan drew up the overall plans to take advantage of German collapse or surrender, called RANKIN, Cases A, B, and C. On the assumption that sudden German weakening or collapse would make an Allied assault unnecessary, the COSSAC planners envisaged the dispatch of picked troops to key centers—political, economic, communications—to speed surrender and ensure the formal takeover of the administration of government.

Considering speed essential to foster the process of dissolution opened by any sudden weakening in Germany, the Allies emphasized lightning movements. Roosevelt obviously had this in mind when he spoke of a race to Berlin in case of German collapse, a remark that has been interpreted as a desire to challenge the Russians. At the time he made the statement, 1943, he thought that all the warring troops from the east and the west would need to push toward Berlin as rapidly as possible. Perhaps prestige was involved but nothing in his conversations or plans at this period indicates that he was planning to forestall the Russians for political purposes. Nor does anything in General Marshall's papers or recollections support this view.

On board the *Iowa,* as they headed for the Cairo conference, the U.S. Chiefs of Staff queried Roosevelt on his reactions to the proposed occupation zones for the United States recommended by the COSSAC staff. In a lengthy discussion, confusingly recorded, the President indicated his reluctance to accept responsibility for the temporary occupation of southern Germany. He also said that the zones should probably correspond to the three postwar states into which Germany would be divided—one to be held by the British, one by the Russians, and one by the United States. Hamburg and Hanover should go to the Americans, Prussia and Pomerania to the Russians, and Baden, Württemberg, and Bavaria to the British. Taking up a recently issued *National Geographic* map of Europe, he quickly sketched out what he thought the United States zone should be.[13]

Considerable confusion later arose over what he intended. Apparently he called off some tick marks as he drew. At least General Marshall took notes—struggling to keep up and losing out part way through—of what he intended. The President began at the German-Danish border and then went west to take in the Netherlands thence east by south along the Rhine to Düsseldorf and thence southward along the Rhine to Mainz. Then he slashed eastward across Germany along the 50th parallel slightly north of Bayreuth to the Czech border near Eger. He then moved north just east of Leipzig and then east and northward through the approximate center of Berlin to Stettin. At the conclusion of the meeting, General Marshall gave the President's original map, his own rough notes—which read "Norway and Denmark, thence west and south along the north shore of the Rhine, then north [the words "or east" have been erased] to Berlin and the Baltic. (Easterly side of Hesse Darmstadt, thence north to the Baltic near Stettin)"—and oral instructions as to the President's wishes on RANKIN to General Handy, Chief of the Operations Division. Handy recorded on November 19 that it was General Marshall's understanding that the President planned to use one million men in Germany (in case of occupation) and that it was the "President's idea . . . that Berlin will be jointly occupied by U.S., British and Russian troops." In the same memorandum Handy spelled out the boundary which the President wanted. The boundary ran the same as the President's to Mainz. Then it was described as going to Bayreuth and to Leipzig, thus leaving an area from Bayreuth to the Czech border untouched, and swerving sharply to the east to take in Cottbus and then switching westward to Berlin. The German capital was specifically excluded from the American zone by Handy's statement obviously to indicate the joint occupation which Marshall had noted.[14]

The President's instructions and his map had an interesting subsequent history. In part because Dr. Philip Mosely, who later worked on occupation boundaries, was unaware of the background of the map and instructions, and in part because all the records were not available to Cornelius Ryan, George Kennan, and others when they wrote of the occupation zones, accounts have been circulated that do an injustice to the Joint Chiefs of Staff and, in particular, to the War Department.

Following earlier accounts, Ryan has written that Marshall's notations of Roosevelt's wishes and the map itself were filed away in the archives of the Operations Division and did not see the light for four months. He declares: "The shelving of the Roosevelt plan by his own military advisors was just one of a series of strange and costly blunders and errors of judgment that occurred among American officials in the days following the *Iowa* meeting. They were to have a profound influence on the future of Germany and Berlin." [15]

But the Roosevelt plan and map were not shelved. True, Handy did not pass the documents on to the State Department. But that was not the proper channel. Leahy should have passed them on if Roosevelt had wanted this done. In fact, as Stettinius explained later, the President had told him that Hopkins would keep notes of agreements and he would pass them to the State Department. Unfortunately, on his return Hopkins went into a hospital and was to remain on the sick list for the next six months.

Rather than being shelved or sat on for several months, the suggestions were quickly made known to the British. On December 4 General Handy's notes—which put Marshall's summary of Roosevelt's instructions into definite form—were incorporated into a Joint Chiefs of Staff memorandum that requested COSSAC to re-examine the proposed occupation boundaries in light of Roosevelt's views. The British Chiefs of Staff, while not in accord with the proposal, agreed that the new suggestions be forwarded for study.[16]

On the evening before Roosevelt's instructions were put into an official paper, he discussed his plans for the occupation zones at dinner with Churchill, Eden, and Leahy. Unfortunately he did not invite to that dinner Ambassador John G. Winant, then in Cairo, who would serve as the U.S. member on the European Advisory Commission in London, which had, among its duties, the drawing up of occupation zones.

The European Advisory Commission, set up at the Moscow conference to plan for the postwar period, had its first meeting on January 14, 1944, in London. Ambassador Winant found himself at a distinct disadvantage since he had not been made aware of the official American position. When he finally pressed Acting Secretary of State Stettinius for instructions, the latter asked President Roosevelt for guidance. Stettinius also sent queries to the War Department. General Hilldring, head of the Civil Affairs Division, forwarded a document that led Mosely, Ryan, and Kennan to conclude that the Army was rather highhanded in its action. The suggestion is that someone in the Army, without any solid basis of authority, issued instructions for the EAC representative. Perhaps the War Department representative who brought the document to the State Department was rude or lacking in perception. But the paper presented to Stettinius to send to EAC was the Combined Chiefs of Staff paper, containing the Joint Chiefs' memorandum, written by Handy on the basis of Marshall's statement of what Roosevelt wanted. None of the instructions that various State Department officials resented came from the Army; they came

from the President. A careful reading of Stettinius's letter also reveals
that the Army had sent the document for information and not as a directive. The Acting Secretary of State forwarded it for information and comment.

George Kennan, then working with Winant in London, had a shrewd
suspicion of the background of the directive. He correctly concluded that
the President was involved, but his later account is in error. He speaks of
the document forwarded by Stettinius as a military directive from the
Joint Chiefs of Staff, consisting—as he remembered it—of a single sentence describing the zone to be held by the United States. As we have
seen, it was not a directive to EAC but the Joint Chiefs' memorandum of
December 4 to the Combined Chiefs asking that COSSAC restudy the
boundaries. Faced by British and Russian agreement on Soviet zone
boundaries, Winant asked and got Roosevelt's acceptance of their proposals.[17]

In this matter as in many others the Joint Chiefs of Staff followed an
extremely careful line of action. Far from trying to lay down the rules, as
the critics suggest, they outlined exactly what the President had directed.
In fact the Joint Chiefs felt that the President was attaching undue importance to the assigned zones in declining to accept the southern zone of
Germany.

It is often forgotten that the early occupation arrangements dealt with
the liberation of territory occupied by the Germans and the disarmament
of German forces in case of collapse. At Tehran the discussion with Stalin
turned not on the zones but on the partition of Germany to prevent her
from threatening the peace of Europe again. At one point the question
seemed to be whether there would be three or five states created out of the
defeated Reich.

The failure to distinguish between early RANKIN planning that did not
look beyond a quick occupation of territory in the case of widespread
collapse, and later planning for an occupation in force following defeat of
the German army in the field, has led some writers to confuse the first
COSSAC proposals with those outlined by the European Advisory Commission some months later.

An article based on an interview conducted in 1961 by Henry Luce of
Time-Life with General Eisenhower, for example, had the General con-
tradicting the account he gave in Crusade in Europe of a talk he had with
the President while in Washington in January 1944 about post-hostilities
planning. In the book, published in 1948, Eisenhower said that he told
the President that he opposed a division of Germany into "national sec-
tors." He further urged that occupied territories be turned over as soon as
possible to civil authority. Roosevelt, the General said, "seemed impressed
but did not express himself." Luce quoted Eisenhower as saying that, disturbed by the possibility of trouble developing with Russia, he had flown
home to protest against the European Advisory Commission proposal for

dividing Germany into separate zones. In his later volume, *At Ease,* the General described a talk with the President in which he opposed such a division, proposing that "the military government . . . be conducted under a coalition of the Allied forces and the Russians." Roosevelt, he declared, said that the matter had already been settled and should be left to political authorities.[18]

Any discussion Eisenhower had with the President occurred before the members of the European Advisory Commission acted on the zones, since they did not have their first meeting until the day of his return to London from Washington. Apparently the Luce article was based on a misunderstanding of what Eisenhower said since, according to *At Ease* and *Crusade in Europe,* he heard of the plans from Roosevelt after his reluctant return to Washington at Marshall's urging. It seems likely that Roosevelt spoke of the zones that he had discussed in November 1943 on the *Iowa.*

But Eisenhower's views were not set forth formally until mid-February, after the European Advisory Committee had outlined proposed zones. At that time he wrote General Marshall:

> I have seen one or two of the telegrams passing back and forth on the political level, concerning so-called British and American areas or spheres of occupation in Europe after the Axis has been defeated. Naturally I well understand that our President wants nothing whatsoever to do with the policing of France, and more particularly Italy and the Balkans. If we were compelled to police any area separately I would quite agree that North Europe is the preferable area for us. However, as you know, because of the existence of German Naval Bases in that region, in which the British Navy will have a transcendent interest, and the natural tie-in between British, Belgian, and Dutch Air Services, we would be compelled to make many concessions and detailed arrangements that would be quite irksome.
>
> My proposition is this: refuse to take specific American responsibility for any area.
>
> Instead of this, why should we not place ourselves on record as saying we will retain responsibility, particularly military and relief responsibility in Europe, only so long as the Allied principle of unity of Command is observed, with orders and policies issued through the Combined Chiefs of Staff? Whenever, or if ever, Great Britain should decide that she wanted to control any specific major portion of Europe strictly from London, then we should simply withdraw U.S. physical occupational facilities, that is, military forces and large stocks of supplies.
>
> It seems to me this simple formula would do much to keep us out of unnecessary difficulties and would still give our President a major voice in the establishing of policy.
>
> An added consideration is the fact that the United States will have to furnish a good proportion of the products needed for European relief, and as long as that condition obtains we should be strongly represented in the whole controlling system.[19]

The discussion over zones continued through the first half of 1944 with Roosevelt insisting that he wanted no responsibility for France and for southern Europe and Churchill standing fast for the northwest zone. The Joint Chiefs of Staff loyally backed the President's views in conference but privately admitted that the matter was not of tremendous importance. Not until the second Quebec meeting, in September of 1944, did the President finally give way. There he agreed to the British proposals—only after winning some readjustments in the boundary and American enclaves at Bremen and Bremerhaven, with right of access for Americans between those ports and the American zone.[20]

While the President and the Prime Minister continued to disagree on the matter of zones, the European Advisory Commission drew up a tentative protocol, specifically defining the Soviet zone but making no division of the area to be occupied by the United States and Great Britain. Compromise provisions were finally agreed upon within the commission and signed in mid-November 1944. Although the final provisions relating to Bremerhaven and Bremen were not settled until January 1945, the British signified their approval of the agreement in December 1944. Final ratification by the United States held fire until the American delegation reached Malta en route to the Yalta conference. There at the urging of Winant, who felt it important that a decision be agreed on before the Russians reached the limit of their zone and kept on going, the Secretary of State authorized Winant to give American assent. Five days later the Soviet Union gave its formal approval to boundaries that corresponded generally to those outlined by the British and accepted by the Russians nearly a year earlier.[21]

The vexing problem of what to do about Germany's warmaking capacity in the future, which had been discussed by the Allies at Tehran and was then discussed at some length by the Americans in the spring and early summer of 1944, led in late August to bitter debates within the Roosevelt administration. In these wrangles Secretary of War Stimson became the strongest opponent of a peace of vengeance. Although he led the fight, his diary shows that he felt reassured because of Marshall's strong backing of his stand.

Between the two great world conflicts the United States had gradually retreated from the view held immediately after World War I that Pershing and Foch had been right in their wish to march to Berlin. A growing rift with an increasingly nationalistic France and evidence of French highhandedness in the Rhineland created sympathy for the Germans. Revisionist accounts of the background of World War I, pacifist literature on the war, and shocking revelations from the investigations into the munitions industry later convinced many Americans that Germany had been more sinned against than sinning. More important, they concluded that the heavy reparations, loss of German trade, and territorial demands had imposed on Germany ruinous conditions that had contributed heavily to the world-wide Depression.

Hitler's brutal rise to power helped reverse this trend of thinking. The

Nazi invasion of Austria and Czechoslovakia and the overrunning of Poland blotted out the once-favorable view of Germany and raised the suspicion that perhaps the war-guilt clause of the Treaty of Versailles had
been justified. As the Germans spread their domination over Western and
Eastern Europe, the Western Allies became convinced that Germany
would have to be policed and severely limited economically—perhaps by
partition into several states—if peace was to be kept in the future.

By 1943 plans were discussed not only for reparations from Germany
and limitations on her fighting forces but for regulation or banning of
industries that might aid war production. There was also growing support
for the territorial division of the Reich. This project was discussed briefly
at Tehran, where both Churchill and Roosevelt seemed convinced that
Prussia, at least, must be separated from the other German states and that
the rich areas of the Saar and the Ruhr should be put under international
control. Although some experts were disturbed over the possible economic
dislocations that such a peace might entail, the search for suitable punishment continued to be discussed.[22]

In the summer of 1944 sentiment toward Germany, as evidenced in
polls taken in Great Britain and the United States, showed that 81 per
cent of Americans wanted to enforce unconditional-surrender terms on
Hitler's Reich and to reduce Germany to the status of a third-rate power.[23]

In the spring and summer of 1944 several political and military leaders
in the United States and Europe turned their attention to America's future course with Germany. Among these Secretary of the Treasury Henry
Morgenthau was one of the most active. A close friend of the President
and personally dedicated to the destruction of Nazism, Morgenthau had
extended his activities well beyond the province of finance to problems
properly belonging to the Departments of State and War. In the summer
of 1944, he had journeyed to Europe, where from talks with Eden, Eisenhower and others he gained the impression that these leaders favored imposing a much sterner peace on Germany than was actually being drafted.
He was extremely upset to discover that a handbook then being developed at Supreme Headquarters for use by occupation officials in Germany
came down on the side of softness. Bearing a copy of the document given
him by a former member of his staff, Colonel Bernard Bernstein, now Chief
of the Finance Section of SHAEF's Civil Affairs Division, Morgenthau
returned to Washington to warn Roosevelt against permitting Eisenhower's staff to let down its guard. Terming it "pretty bad," Roosevelt at once
directed the War Department to stop circulation of the handbook.[24]

Morgenthau developed a plan for postwar Germany that would strip
that country so completely of economic power that it could not again
threaten the peace of Europe. Outlining his views to Secretary Stimson
and Assistant Secretary of War McCloy at lunch soon afterward, he found
that Stimson was firmly opposed to his more drastic proposals.[25]

Shortly before the Quebec meeting Stimson discussed with General

Marshall some of the coming problems with Germany. In particular he took up plans for a tribunal to deal with members of the Gestapo. Disturbed by suggestions that some top Nazis be shot out of hand on capture, the Chief of Staff backed Stimson's proposal for a properly constituted tribunal, consisting of civilian rather than military members so far as possible. Pleased by Marshall's calm and reasonable approach to the postwar treatment of Germany, Stimson wrote: "It was very interesting to find that Army officers have a better respect for the law in these matters than civilians who talk about them and who are anxious to go ahead and chop everybody's head off without trial or hearing." [26]

Stimson grew increasingly perturbed when Morgenthau appeared to be winning Secretary Hull to his proposals. On September 5 in a meeting of the committee set up by President Roosevelt to advise him on postwar policy for Germany, Stimson found Secretary Hull as bitter as Morgenthau against the enemy. Hull seemed to back Morgenthau's plan to wreck the Ruhr-Saar area industrially and turn it into a second-rate agricultural area. Hopkins, recently added to the committee, was willing only to bar the manufacture of steel in the area. Seeing his colleagues completely divided in their views, Stimson termed the meeting the most unpleasant he had attended in four years.

The troubled Stimson returned to his office to prepare a statement that would show that the whole administration had not run amuck. As he so often did, he called on Marshall for aid. Once again he found the General's sympathy a refreshing tonic. Marshall was amused when Stimson repeated the statement he had made earlier to members of the committee that he, the man in charge of the department that did the killing, was the only one with any mercy for the enemy. [27]

The committee met with the President the following day. Roosevelt's attitude was harsh; he reverted to his suggestion tossed out at a cabinet meeting a week or two earlier that the Germans could live on soup from soup kitchens if necessary. The President spoke of the spartan diet of American pioneers, which Stimson interpreted as a slap at him. Never one to give up a fight when his anger had been aroused, the Secretary retorted that he was opposed to the destruction of a gift of nature, something that he foresaw in the Roosevelt-Morgenthau approach to Germany's economy. [28]

Meanwhile Stimson had drawn up a memorandum opposing Morgenthau's views. He asked Marshall and Brigadier General Alexander Surles, the Army's public-relations chief, to read his arguments and give their opinions. Both thoroughly approved his moderate stand. He next showed them Morgenthau's memorandum saying that leaders of the Nazi Party should be shot on capture. As he expected, Marshall and Surles rejected absolutely "the notion that we should not give the men a fair trial." Marshall observed that this was the sort of reaction that followed every war and that bitterness after the current one was bound to be extreme. The

Secretary was heartened by their support, writing that their attitude "towards this wave of hysteria . . . symptomatic of what I have always found among good soldiers—they are in many respects the best educated men of the country in regard to [the] basic principles of our Constitution and traditional respect for freedom and law."

On September 9 Stimson went back to Roosevelt. Suffering from a cold, the President looked wretched and nearly exhausted. He worried Stimson by continuing to harp "on two obsessions": the feeding of Germans from soup kitchens and the desire to be protected from revolution in France. He feared that Roosevelt was not prepared for the meeting in Quebec.[30]

Stimson was more discouraged a few days later when he discovered that when the President reached Quebec, he had sent for Secretary Morgenthau. Roosevelt needed Morgenthau's advice on planning the second phase of the Lend-Lease program once the war had ended in Europe, but Stimson feared that he would prove a dangerous adviser on Germany.[31]

At dinner in Quebec on the fourteenth Churchill lashed out at Morgenthau, saying that he didn't want to be tied to the dead corpse of Germany. But the situation changed next day. Morgenthau managed to win over Lord Cherwell, Churchill's trusted adviser, who then converted the Prime Minister to the harsh line, despite Eden's protests. Cherwell's telling argument was that the crippling of German industry would aid British export trade.

The Prime Minister's switch led some observers to decide (incorrectly) that he had made a deal with Morgenthau on Lend-Lease in exchange for backing his plan for Germany. After Churchill had accepted the Morgenthau proposal, he actually dictated the formula and added the suggestion for the "pastoralization" of Germany. To Stimson this was totally irresponsible. He wrote that it was a terrible thing that the total power of Britain and the United States should be in the hands of two men, Roosevelt and Churchill, "both of whom are similar in their impulsiveness and their lack of systematic study." He deplored what he called the Carthaginian attitude of the Treasury, a case of Semitism gone wild for vengeance, which carried with it the seeds of another war.[32]

Foreign Secretary Eden had attempted to argue the matter with Churchill, reminding his superior that they had publicly taken an opposite stand. Stung all the worse by the realization that he was in the wrong, the Prime Minister retorted that he preferred the interest of his own people to that of the enemy and warned Eden not to go home and stir up opposition in the War Cabinet. The Foreign Secretary recorded in his diary that on only one other occasion had Churchill hit at him in front of foreign representatives.[33]

In time reason had its way. When word of the Morgenthau Plan leaked out through Drew Pearson's column, the press of the country condemned it. Governor Dewey, searching for an issue in his campaign against Roosevelt, attacked the Secretary of Treasury, charging that the proposal would frighten the Germans and thus prolong the war.

When taxed by Stimson for his part in the affair, Roosevelt at first said that he had not signed the paper and then indicated that he never intended anything so drastic. A short time later he told Ambassador Winant that he thought he had been mistaken in his action. In his repentance he apparently was more candid than Churchill. Writing after the war, Lord Moran indicated that the Prime Minister had been "got at" by Cherwell. He explained that Churchill had come to Quebec unprepared on Germany because he had become so engrossed in the conduct of the war that he had little time left to plan for the future. The manner in which the Prime Minister glided over his role in the affair when he came to write his memoirs, Moran said, was an example of the great man's inability to confess that he was wrong.[34]

Although Marshall had no part in Roosevelt's shift of opinion, he was pleased that Stimson had stood firm. In late April 1947, when the wartime Chief of Staff, now Secretary of State, faced the matter of aid to Germany, he recalled Stimson's arguments against the President's policy of harsh retribution. He asked for a copy of the memorandum and passed it on to Undersecretary of State Dean Acheson, who said that he had not seen its contents at the time, although it was prepared while he was Assistant Secretary of State for Economic Affairs. Acheson thought the action a striking illustration of Morgenthau's "irresponsible meddling" in international affairs. Informing Stimson of his action, Marshall wrote: "I found my recollection had not deceived me that you had displayed remarkable foresight and logic in your memoranda to the President on this subject." [35]

The great debate over occupation policy for Germany reflected a growing feeling that the defeat of Hitler might be near at hand. Events would soon prove otherwise.

XXIV

Victory Deferred

I T was the best of times, it was the worst of times." So Marshall, who knew his Dickens, must have thought that fall and early winter of 1944. The bright certainty of summer, fading in the weak sunlight of autumn's half promises, ended in chilled and darkening hopes at mid-December. Victory, so close at hand in August, seemed far away on the eve of Christmas.

The advances in northwest Europe and in Italy north of Florence stirred momentary optimism abroad while at home the politics of a presidential election emerged as a temporary embarrassment for the War Department. The siege of Metz, the drive on Aachen, the dreadful losses in the Hürtgen Forest were sometimes overshadowed by politics as New York's Republican governor, Thomas E. Dewey, sought to deny Franklin Roosevelt a fourth term in the White House.

The approach of victory abroad had brought to the surface old suspicions and divisions between the Western Allies and the Russians; it had also reawakened partisan hopes on the home front.

Silent temporarily in the face of foreign challenges, Roosevelt's opponents became active as Allied fortunes prospered. Mid-summer 1944 saw a renewal of interest in the background of the Pearl Harbor disaster, and Congress called for further investigations into the background of the attack. From late July until late October 1944 separate Army and Navy inquiries were made.[1]

Both the Army and Navy were especially disturbed because full answers to the questions raised would involve the disclosure that the Japanese diplomatic code, which they were still using, had been broken before Pearl Harbor. Although efforts were made to preserve secrecy, some information leaked out. Demanding an accounting from Roosevelt, Representative Forest A. Harness, Republican of Indiana, cited General Marshall's message on the morning of December 7, which indicated that it was thought that the Japanese would be presenting an ultimatum at 1 p.m. and that their embassy had been told to destroy their code machine.[2]

At this point Marshall was informed that Governor Dewey was in full possession of information concerning the diplomatic code and was planning to reveal it in a campaign speech. He was appalled at the possible consequences. He recognized that politically it was smart for the Republican nominee to say that the President knew of Japanese intentions prior to December 7 and failed to act. But to the Army and Navy, still crucially dependent on reading intercepted enemy messages, the revelation that they had broken Japanese codes would be tragic. Marshall later described the situation: "At this time the sinking of Japanese vessels was developing at a rapid rate. General MacArthur was then making his final preparations for the invasion of the Philippine Islands and getting vital information. We were [still] getting vital information. . . ."

Hearing that Mr. Dewey was in the Middle West on a campaign tour and fearing that he might divulge cryptographic secrets without realizing their continued imperativeness to the Army and Navy, Marshall asked his intelligence advisers to draft a message to the governor. He eliminated a paragraph from the letter asking Dewey to persuade the Republicans to stop their inquiries into the breaking of codes and then sent it to King for concurrence. Marshall explained: "This letter of course puts him [Governor Dewey] on the spot, and I hate to do it, but see no other way of avoiding what might well be a catastrophe to us." Just what Dewey could do without giving his reasons for not acting he did not know, "but at least he will understand what a deadly affair it really is." Anticipating that party leaders would probably oppose Dewey's dropping of the issue, Marshall considered calling in Republican House Floor Leader Joseph Martin and explaining the danger of the attack so he would understand Dewey's attitude. The whole thing, Marshall told Admiral King, "is loaded with dynamite but I very much feel that something has to be done or the fat will be in the fire to our great loss in the Pacific, and possibly also in Europe." [3] King heartily assented.

The letter was taken to Dewey in Tulsa by special courier, Colonel Carter Clarke of the War Department staff. After looking at the first paragraph the Republican candidate declined to go further. Marshall had asked him to stop before reading the reasons he was outlining unless he could agree in advance not to pass the information on. The request was unusual, and the governor said frankly to Clarke that he would make no such pledge since (1) he already had considerable information on the subject, some of which he thought was probably enclosed, and (2) he could not believe that such a letter would be written by Marshall and King without the President's knowledge.

Having taken the plunge, General Marshall decided to go further on his own. In a slightly changed version, which he sent by Clarke to the governor, now back in Albany, he said he was willing that Dewey read the entire letter provided he communicated to others only facts that he then had or that he received from someone other than Marshall. Dewey replied that on an issue of this magnitude, he owed it to his party to seek the counsel of a major political adviser and proposed that he be allowed to discuss the information with Elliott Bell, a close personal friend and political strategist. Marshall agreed to the condition.[4]

This matter arranged, Dewey now read Marshall's assurance "that neither the Secretary of War nor the President has any indication whatsoever that such a letter has been addressed to you or that the preparation or sending of such a communication was being considered." The only persons who knew of the message were Admiral King, the seven key officers concerned with cryptographic matters, and the secretary who typed the letter. "I am trying my best to make plain to you," he explained, "that this letter is being addressed to you solely on my own initiative, Admiral King having been consulted only after the letter was drafted, and I am persisting in the matter because the military hazards involved are so serious that I feel some action is necessary to protect the interests of our armed forces."

Having set the stage, Marshall then outlined the tremendous advantage that the United States had gained from breaking the diplomatic code. He cited the successes at Midway, submarine activities in the Pacific, and Halsey's current raids. "Now the point to the present dilemma is that we have gone ahead with this business of deciphering their codes until we possess other codes, German as well as Japanese, but our main source of information regarding Hitler's intentions in Europe is obtained from Baron Oshima's messages from Berlin reporting his interviews with Hitler and other officials to the Japanese Government. These are still in the codes involved in the Pearl Harbor events.

"You will understand," he continued, "the utterly tragic consequences if the present political debates regarding Pearl Harbor disclose to the enemy, German or Jap, any suspicion of the vital sources of information we now possess." He then spelled out the possible consequences of partisan speeches in Congress. Revelations about American cryptographic activities could also prove embarrassing to America's allies. He told of difficulties that had arisen because various U.S. agencies failed to coordinate their actions. "Some of Donovan's people"—i.e., from the Office of Strategic Services—had raided Japanese Embassy offices in Portugal without telling U.S. military officials that they had such action in mind. As a result the Japanese had changed their military-attaché code, thus denying information to the Army and Navy that had earlier been available. The conduct of General Eisenhower's campaign and all operations in the Pacific, Marshall continued, were closely related in conception and timing to information secretly obtained. Such information contributed greatly to final victory and to the saving of American lives. "I am presenting this matter to you . . . in the hope that you will see your way clear to avoid the tragic results with which we are now threatened in the present political campaign," Marshall concluded.[5]

Dewey accepted the General's word that his action was not a political trick and that the diplomatic code should be kept out of the political campaign. It is possible that Dewey's action cost him thousands of votes that could have been garnered by the revelations. At any rate the matter was never mentioned publicly until shortly after the war's end. Then someone—Marshall assumed it was a member of Governor Dewey's staff— revealed to the Joint Congressional Committee the existence of the correspondence. Within a short time Marshall was under heavy pressure to release it to the committee.[6]

Not until the disclosures of 1945 did General Marshall inform the White House of what he had done. He explained to Truman, who had succeeded Roosevelt five months before, that only a part of his letter to Dewey should be released because some of the paragraphs affected other countries.[7]

The President reacted with his usual hearty approval of Marshall's initiative, writing at the bottom of the letter, "Dear General: As you know I have the utmost confidence in you and your judgment. I suggest you give both of these—memo and letter to Dewey—to the Press for tomorrow. It will stop all the demagogues." [8] Marshall appreciated the vote of confidence but still felt that the whole text should not be published. The Joint Chiefs of Staff now proposed that the entire correspondence be given to the Joint Congressional Committee in executive session with the warning that certain information involving foreign governments not be published. Shortly after discussing the matter with the Chiefs of Staff at Fort Myer on September 27, the President accepted their recommendation.[9]

In the broader context of global war the political stirrings of an American presidential campaign were fairly minor as millions of men risked their lives on the battlefields and in the battle fleets across the world. While Roosevelt labored to make American electoral history, his forces on many fronts continued their struggle against the enemy.

At Quebec it had appeared possible that the Allies could press northward rapidly in Italy and make a landing in Istria in mid-October. This was not to be. Shortly before the meeting Alexander had ordered an assault by the U.S. Fifth and the British Eighth Armies against the Gothic Line, whose 170 miles of fortifications ran from the west coast near Massa along the northern Apennines to the Adriatic near Pesaro. Rimini fell on September 21, but the advance slowed quickly as the tired soldiers, weakened by withdrawal of units for service in southern France, faced the nine rivers and "hundreds of minor watercourses" between the Adriatic and Bologna. Unusually bad weather, a staple in Italy during the war, brought the Allied armies to a standstill near the end of October. The

Fifth Army, battling for Bologna, was forced to go over to the defensive when it was less than 10 air miles from its objective. Not until the following April—on the twenty-first—did Bologna fall.[10]

Replacement shortages, lack of ammunition, and the withdrawal of troops for service in Greece strained Alexander's troops still further. On October 14 General Wilson examined the situation and decided that Italy was unlikely to contribute materially to Allied progress in the next few months. He believed that the Russian advance, still gathering momentum, was more likely to effect Kesselring's withdrawal than would Alexander's advance.[11]

Still refusing to countenance such an abortion of his Italian designs, Churchill asked Roosevelt for three divisions. But his own staff planners in London argued against him, insisting that Italy must now adapt to the steadily increasing needs of OVERLORD. Three courses were open in Italy: (1) a spring offensive accompanied by an assault on Istria or the Dalmatian coast; (2) withdrawal of the American portions of the Fifth Army (one armored and four infantry divisions and one equivalent division) for Eisenhower's theater; or (3) withdrawal of British and Empire troops to form a strategic reserve. The British planners estimated that the line of the Adige-Piave could be held by eight to ten infantry and four armored divisions, permitting the release of four or five armored and six to eight infantry divisions. Only the greatest necessity, they maintained, could justify Churchill's effort to commit one airborne and three infantry divisions in a December offensive. The British Chiefs of Staff agreed in general with their planners. However the subject proved academic on October 16, when Roosevelt, heeding the recommendations of his own military advisers, refused Churchill's request.[12]

Marshall's views on the Italian theater were undoubtedly influenced by his recent visit to American units in Europe. Accepting the Joint Intelligence Committee report that there was a possibility of finishing the war before the year's end, the Chief of Staff decided to go to Europe for conferences with Eisenhower and a close look at the divisions then in the line. He also thought it would be a good opportunity to indoctrinate former Justice Byrnes, director of War Mobilization, on the Army's needs. Specifically he urged Byrnes to go along to see what could be done to hasten unloading of ships at Cherbourg and to speed transport of ammunition to the front. Byrnes gladly accepted and the two men, accompanied by several members of the War Department staff, set off on October 5 in the presidential plane, the *Sacred Cow*. After a brief stop in Newfoundland they flew nonstop to Paris, the first such flight since Lindbergh had made it alone in a one-engine plane from Roosevelt Field, Long Island, to Le Bourget in 1927.[13]

Eisenhower, Bradley, and Bedell Smith met the party at the airport and talks with the Supreme Commander began at once. On October 7 Marshall set out for Verdun by plane, having the pilot fly low over the Argonne area so that he could view the terrain in which American forces had fought in World War I. Later he drove by car through the St. Mihiel sector and visited the billet where he had stayed in Souilly in the late summer of 1918. From Verdun, Marshall and Bradley traveled to Patton's headquarters at Étain near Metz. There, after lunch, the Third Army Commander presented his staff and his plans for taking Fort Driant. Marshall fired his usual "very incisive questions" on the details of the coming battle, which Patton promptly answered.[14]

On the eighth Marshall and Bradley flew to Eindhoven, Holland, to visit Montgomery's 21 Army Group headquarters. Their trip was marked by a dismaying performance by the fighter escort furnished by the Ninth Air Force. Of the four planes sent for this duty one became mired on the runway, where it was hit by a second when it attempted to fly over it. The third, after a poor landing on the airfield in Holland, burst into flames as it came to a halt near the wing tip of Bradley's plane. The pilot of the fourth plane was frightened away by the fire. When air headquarters offered four more fighters, Bradley's aide declined them, saying, "I'm sure the general couldn't take another day like this one." [15]

When he finally reached British headquarters, Marshall found the Field Marshal at odds with Eisenhower over his coming operations. In a private conference in his office caravan Montgomery presented his case. He complained that since Eisenhower had taken over direct control of operations, the armies had become separated geographically. As Montgomery recalled it later, he had said: "There was a lack of grip, and operational direction and control was lacking. Our operation had, in fact, become ragged and disjointed, and we had now got ourselves into a real mess." Marshall spoke little, but the Field Marshal was uncomfortably aware that he did not agree.[16]

Keeping quiet proved to be a chore. Marshall said in 1956: "I came pretty near to blowing off out of turn." Marshall recalled that "it was very hard for me to restrain myself because I didn't think there was any logic in what he said but overwhelming egotism." [17]

Marshall's restraint nearly failed him later in the day when he went with General Devers to Luxeuil in eastern France to visit General Jean de Lattre de Tassigny. De Lattre, noted for his histrionics and sharp tongue, seized the opportunity to denounce General Truscott bitterly. He charged that the latter's VI Corps had shown up well in recent fighting because it had taken the gasoline allocated to French troops.[18]

In an amazingly bland version de Lattre later wrote that he took advantage of Marshall's hurried visit to acquaint him with the inadequacy of his supplies: "General Marshall at once showed surprise at a complaint which he visibly had not expected, but he recognized it as being well founded and promised me that he would put the matter right." General de Lattre's attack was made not only in front of American and French officers but in the presence of Allied correspondents. The Chief of Staff was furious with de Lattre and with William Bullitt, then a major in the French Army, who stood by without saying anything. Marshall's temper flared, but he decided to avoid a scene by terminating the discussion. "I just stopped the thing right where it was and walked out." [19]

The matter still rankled years after. When the ground-force headquarters for NATO was being organized, de Lattre was proposed for the command. Knowing that Marshall, now Secretary of Defense, had been angry over several episodes during the war, the Frenchman asked him if he would oppose his selection. The anger that the Chief of Staff had banked that day at Luxeuil was paid out with interest. "I said," Marshall related later, " 'That was the most outrageous business of yours. I restrained myself very, very carefully from tearing you down to the ground. Because what you did was a most culpable performance for a man who had any idea of how Allied forces must get along. And in the next place you didn't have a leg to stand on. You celebrated all the way up the road. You were late on every damn thing and there weren't any [supplies] to divide and you were critical of Truscott, who is a fighter and not a talker. . . . I am not going to oppose you on this at all because as a matter of fact the command doesn't amount to much right now. It will, but doesn't right now. You are no man to command any Allied thing because you are a politico.' " Not wishing to be unjust, Marshall added to the biographer: "Actually he was a good fighter. He did a good job out there in Indo-China, where he died as a result of it. But the performance there [earlier] was terrible—right in front of all those reporters—but fortunately they didn't bring it up at all. I think they spared me because I was so outraged by it. I was outraged at my people . . . for standing there and letting it go on . . . [And] Bullitt didn't say a damn word. He just stood there and smirked. God knows what he told the reporters. I was out with him right then. . . ." [20]

Marshall spent the night of October 9 with Major General Manton Eddy of the XII Corps at Nancy. Next morning he breakfasted with Patton, who asked for promotions for several of his officers. On the tenth Marshall went with Patton and Eddy to the 35th Division, where he asked many questions, especially about the adequacy of winter clothing and the comfort of the troops. His pace unrelenting, he pushed on to the 80th Division and to meetings with the commanding generals of the 26th Infantry, the 4th and 6th Armored, the 5th, 90th, and 83d Infantry divisions and with his old friend General Walker of the XX Corps.

After spending the night at Arlon, Belgium, at the Ninth Army headquarters of General Simpson, he was up early on the eleventh to visit Corps Commanders Middleton (VIII), Gerow (V), and Collins (VII) and divisions under their commands, and he spent the evening with General Hodges at First Army headquarters at Verviers, Belgium. During the day he had gone by armored car into Germany in the vicinity of Aachen—on his first visit to German soil since 1919. On the twelfth he visited the 30th Division Command Post, where he was greeted by its commander and by the commanders of the XIX Corps, the 2d Armored Division, and the 29th Division. Thirty minutes later he went to XIX Corps headquarters at Maastricht, Holland. He flew to Versailles that afternoon and spent the following day at Eisenhower's headquarters, leaving Paris on Friday evening for Newfoundland. The flight back was comfortable save between Newfoundland and Maine, where headwinds reached sixty miles an hour, and the pilot found he had the lowest barometer recording he had ever seen. They stopped briefly in Newfoundland on the fourteenth and were back in Washington in the early evening.[21]

It had been a stirring experience for the Chief of Staff to visit front-line units and talk with the men who had fought their way eastward from the beaches. Photographs show him speaking earnestly to headquarters troops of the V Corps in a dark wooded area near Luxembourg, laughing with Major General Wade H. Haislip over a cup of coffee, and accepting flowers from a smiling boy and girl in France. In this mosaic we find him reaching out more closely than at any other time in the war to the men who fought and the people who were being aided. He promised dozens of the officers and men with whom he talked that he would send word to their families on his return to say that he had seen them and they were well. This practice, which he had begun as an aide to General Pershing, was carefully observed. He informed Mrs. Patton that "I saw George the second day after I arrived" and that he "looked in splendid health and in fine fettle and full of fight." To Mrs. Eisenhower he wrote: "I wanted to tell you that Eisenhower was looking very well and handling himself and his job beautifully. Of course he is under a very heavy strain but bears up under it wonderfully and has exhibited a store of patience to meet the various trying incidents of his position other than the direct conduct of the campaign." [22]

In another vein General Marshall summarized the high points of his trip for his old friend Major General Frank McCoy:

> I had an intensely interesting inspection trip in France, covering an immense amount of ground in a very short time. I was astonished at the repetition of situations and localities from the days when you and I were in that part of France. The right of Patton's Third Army was in the village and No Man's Land in the exact spot that I found in October 1917, when I arranged for the induction of separate battalions of the First Division into a French front. The coincidences of this sort were apparent all along the front and I even found in one place that our Fifth Division was deployed in its old World War sector with its same companion, the 90th Division, on its left and the commander of the Corps a former officer of the Fifth Division.
>
> During my hurried trip I started out after a night at Verdun, flew to Holland to see Montgomery and then immediately South the same morning to the Bel-

fort front. During the next four days, three of them a downpour of rain, I went through five Armies, eight Army Corps, sixteen divisions, and also saw the commanders and staffs of eight other Divisions.[23]

The General regretted being too rushed to see Madame Jouatte, in whose home at Gondrecourt he and several other officers of the 1st Division had been billeted in World War I. However he had instructed General Patton to inquire after her health and to leave some supplies for her when the Third Army swept through her area of France. The old lady had been sent away to a quiet sector, and she wrote from there to express her appreciation for the General's interest.

To Eisenhower, Marshall radioed on his return: "The trip was immensely profitable to me and to those with me because I do believe that in a very short time we learned a great deal about conditions with you and therefore are much better prepared to meet your requirements from this end." [24] Above everything else Marshall had received a better perspective on the pressing difficulties his commanders faced. General Bradley in particular had disputed the notion that the war could be ended in 1944. He and Eisenhower and their staffs had laid out for Marshall and Handy the various serious shortages in ammunition and personnel that must soon be remedied if they were to continue on the offensive. For his part the director of War Mobilization, James Byrnes, had received confirmation of the Army's argument that the time had not yet arrived to cut back war production.

The immediate problem on Marshall's desk when he came back to his Pentagon office was the Stilwell imbroglio. Since the previous year there had been continual difficulty between Chiang Kai-shek and Stilwell over strategy, the use of Chinese troops, the matter of supply, air versus ground priorities—in which General Chennault, with some aid from the White House, sided with the Generalissimo. The final showdown came in the late summer and fall over Stilwell's efforts to revise the command situation and to bring Chinese Communist forces into the fight against Japan. At Stilwell's urging War Department officers had prepared at Quebec a draft message for the President to send Chiang urging agreement with Stilwell's proposals. Although Roosevelt softened the message somewhat, its tone was still strong. Delivered by Stilwell personally, the communication was taken by Chiang as a personal affront. A few days later he notified Ambassador Patrick Hurley that he could not appoint Stilwell as field commander. Shortly before he left for Europe, Marshall had helped draft two replies by the President, one disagreeing sharply on the question of firing Stilwell and the other suggesting that Stilwell be retained only as commander of Chinese troops in Yunnan and Burma. The President selected the milder version, but it failed to win a change of heart from the Generalissimo. Instead he made it clear that he did not want Stilwell in any post but was willing to have another American officer in his place.

It was at this point in the controversy that Marshall returned from his

European tour. His first impulse was to fight the issue, but he ended by accepting the President's decision to recall Stilwell. He managed to write into Roosevelt's reply the statement that no American could assume responsibility for the operations of Chinese forces in China. He agreed only that the War Department would furnish an officer to take Stilwell's post as one of Chiang's Chiefs of Staff.

Chiang Kai-shek had already suggested Generals Eisenhower, Patch, Krueger, and Wedemeyer as officers of the type he would like to have. At the War Department's suggestion the President proposed General Wedemeyer, who shortly afterward became commanding general of U.S. Forces in China.

Stilwell's return to Washington less than a week before the presidential election posed the possibility that he would lash out at Roosevelt and create a political uproar. Determined to prevent any controversial headlines, Stimson and Marshall devoted themselves to "trying to keep him out of reach of all newspaper men and not give them an opportunity to catch and distort any unwary word just before the election." [25] Marshall might well have given these instructions personally to Stilwell when he arrived at the National Airport on November 3, but in the course of the day he had learned that Field Marshal Dill was dying at Walter Reed Hospital, and he was there when Stilwell's plane touched down. However he himself penned instructions that the former CBI commander was to confine himself to the statement that he had been ordered home and make no other comment. He sent Colonel McCarthy to meet the plane with those instructions and had Generals Handy and Surles there to impress on him the need of discretion. Later that evening when General Marshall visited the Stilwells at the guest house at Fort Myer, he indicated that he had in mind giving him the Army Ground Forces command and subsequently a command in the Pacific or Europe. A few weeks later Stilwell succeeded Lieutenant General Ben Lear in the Ground Force command; in the spring of 1945, when General Buckner was killed, Marshall named Stilwell as Tenth Army commander. At the war's end the former CBI commander took over the Sixth Army at the Presidio at San Francisco. He was still serving in this post at the time of his death in October 1946.

Although deeply disappointed by the developments in the China Theater, Marshall could spend little time deploring what had happened in an area where the United States would take a less important role than it had initially planned. He had never been willing to commit large combat forces to the China-Burma-India Theater, and now it seemed more realistic to proceed by way of the Philippines and the islands of the Central Pacific. Immediately facing him was what came next in Europe.

In retrospect it seemed remarkable that as late as October 20, General Marshall discussed a quick ending of the war in Europe. Although General Bradley and others a few days before had poured cold water on his hopes for ending the war in 1944, he directed the attention of the Combined Chiefs of Staff to "an undecided question, that is, whether or not we should conduct the war in France during the next two and one-half months on the basis of playing everything for a conclusion." This would, he believed, have a bearing on the decision to permit use of the highly secret design for setting off projectiles near a target without explosion by contact (the proximity fuse), as well as the choice of air targets and the timetable for moving ground units. An effort to go all-out in 1944 would require concentration on battle areas, rather than a major effort against long-range strategic targets, and a release of strategic reserves and supplies from theater stockpiles.[26]

The replies from Europe were guarded. General Eisenhower believed that with more troops and supplies, he could hasten the end of the war, but he made no promises. At the end of October the British Chiefs of Staff accepted the view of their planners that the earliest date that could be suggested for the end of the war was January 31, 1945, and the latest was mid-May. To launch an all-out offensive before Antwerp had been opened to shipping, they argued, would be to court failure and perhaps prolong the war well in 1945. They also questioned Marshall's proposal for changing the main air effort. They therefore proposed that the United States Chiefs of Staff withhold the proposed directive for the time being. On November 1 Marshall directed that nothing be done until further notice.[27]

One gets the impression that the reply was not unexpected. General Marshall was aware that General Bradley felt the forces in Europe were in no position to end the war soon, and his firsthand knowledge of supply and manpower difficulties was reinforced by General Eisenhower's October 20 message reminding him that the shortage of artillery ammunition was becoming acute.[28]

General Marshall informed Eisenhower that ammunition was being shipped as fast as it could be produced but that he saw no prospects of increasing loadings of certain critical items in October or early November.[29] He was worried not only about production but about the fact that ammunition ships were awaiting discharge in French ports and that there was divided responsibility for supply in France.[30]

To complicate matters the Germans began to drop V-2 bombs on the port of Antwerp just as plans were being made to make major use of it. The Chief of Staff warned Eisenhower against putting everything in "the Antwerp basket." The Supreme Commander replied that he was avoiding that danger, although conceding that he could not receive in French ports "all the ammunition that we should have." He stressed the critical shortages in medium artillery calibers (105 mm. and 155 mm.). Despite the difficulties involved, he still felt that Antwerp was the *sine qua non* for the final attack against Germany.[31]

In late November, Eisenhower sent Marshall a chilling report on Bradley's situation. The 12th Army Group commander estimated that he had on hand only enough ammunition to permit him to continue the current offensive until December 15. He would then have to assume a static position indefinitely. "It would not be enough even for this if we were against an enemy capable of any offensive action." Unless German resistance collapsed, the crossing of the Rhine under these circumstances was out of the question.[32]

In early December, Churchill wrote gloomily to Roosevelt over lost opportunities. General Marshall helped draft the President's reply that Eisenhower's broad-front strategy was developing according to plan.[33] Marshall's current state of mind emerges more clearly in his letter of December 8 to Admiral Stark in London: "We are engaged in a good many heavy battles now, with the great problem of munition deficiencies here at home to meet the tremendously increased demands. However, I am decidedly optimistic rather than pessimistic about the progress of the war and I think anyone is bound to be who analyzes for a moment the predicament of the enemy. By comparison our situation is a rosy one in contrast to the desperate plight of the Germans and the clear evidence of disaster facing the Japanese." [34]

Yet in writing his old friend, General Marshall expressed greater cheerfulness than he probably in truth felt. In November he had suffered one of his severest personal losses of the war with the death of Field Marshal Dill. The British officer had not been well for some months, but the Chief of Staff was disturbed on his return from Europe in mid-October to find him on the critical list at Walter Reed. He had seen signs that Dill was slowing up a year earlier at the first Quebec conference, when Brooke noted that the Field Marshal was suffering from the effects of an operation for an old hernia. In the spring of 1944 Dill was weakened by anemia, and during the summer he was so ill that Marshall directed that arguments over ANVIL be kept off his desk. At the second Quebec meeting in September, Brooke observed that Dill was showing evidence of serious physical deterioration. Churchill's physician examined the doctor's analysis shown him by Dill and thought: "I saw at a glance that he was not reacting to treatment, and I doubt if he will last long. I wonder if he knows?" [35]

Seriously concerned, Marshall sent Dill to Hot Springs under Sergeant Powder's watchful eye. Despite careful attention the Field Marshal's condition grew worse, and he was quickly transferred to Walter Reed Hospital. He was conscious on November 1, but apparently knew no one the following day. Marshall made his farewell call on the afternoon of the third, when Stilwell arrived in Washington and shortly before his own departure for a meeting of the Business Advisory Council. Next day the Field Marshal was dead.

Months earlier Marshall had done everything possible to prove to Prime Minister Churchill the importance of keeping Dill in Washington.

Now he was determined to show British and Americans alike what the Field Marshal had meant to Allied unity. At the services for Dill at the National Cathedral, Marshall read the lesson for his old friend. Learning from Lady Dill that her husband had expressed a wish to lie in Arlington National Cemetery, he moved at once to make this possible.

Stimson recorded that Dill "was a noble character and won the hearts of all of us in the War Department and the Army who came in contact with him." His death, he observed, would be especially hard on Marshall. A few days later the Secretary spoke of the elaborate preparations the Chief of Staff was making to honor Dill's memory. Stimson pleased him by citing as a precedent for special tribute the fact that the British government had arranged for a tablet to be erected in Westminster Abbey in World War I in memory of Ambassador Walter Hines Page.[36]

Armed with the Abbey precedent, Marshall found his way around regulations against burial of foreign soldiers in Arlington. Even more impressive, he succeeded in getting members of Congress to pass an unusual resolution of appreciation for Dill's services. Nor did he stop there. Deciding that an equestrian statue should be erected in his friend's memory, he moved after the war in the face of other regulations barring such memorials in Arlington Cemetery. At length he roused the opposition of some American Legion officials and barely managed to get tabled a resolution by one of the Legion's state conventions opposing his action. He also took a leading role in raising money for the monument, working closely with former Ambassador Robert Woods Bliss, who headed the drive. The statue, located near the Fort Myer Drive at the front of the cemetery, was unveiled by President Truman in 1950.[37]

Aware of Marshall's deep affection for Dill, Churchill in thanking him for the condolences sent by the U.S. Chiefs of Staff said, "He did all he could to make things go well and they went well." [38]

Mindful of Churchill's moves to recall Dill some months earlier, Marshall chided him gently: "Few will ever realize the debt our countries owe him for his unique and profound influence toward the cooperation of our forces. To be very frank and personal, I doubt if you or your cabinet associates fully realize the loss you have suffered and the U.S. also has suffered for that matter, in purely post-war adjustments by his death. I am hopeful that his interment in the American Valhalla of Arlington where his services may be memorialized will result in a continuation of his great and beneficent influence in the troubled years to come." [39]

On December 16, the day after Congress acted on its resolution of appreciation, Marshall wrote Lady Burghley, who had been his and Dill's hostess in Bermuda the previous spring: "With all the bickerings that are going on and are inevitable in the future it is to me most refreshing to have his wonderful example of a great service not restricted solely to his own country but extended to the United States and the world in general." [40]

Marshall's deep friendship had been reciprocated by the Field Marshal, as Lady Dill made clear in her letters to him: "He really loved you, George," she wrote on December 22, "and your mutual affection meant a great deal to him—he always trusted you implicitly." A few weeks later she wrote again:

> Thinking back on that time, it seems that yours was such a lovable, kindly presence, never obstructing, yet always there to share our joys and sorrows and give us both your very precious friendship.
>
> Your thoughts for us, with lovely invitations to relax in beautiful places, dinners to meet interesting people—ball game seats—Thanksgiving lunch with the hunting folk, then the great honour of the Howland Memorial Prize at Yale, ending in that last invitation of all—that Jack should rest in Arlington, and his work and ideals should be cherished in the resolution which has been passed by both Houses—for all that I can never thank you adequately— George. . . .[41]

Dill's post was taken a few weeks later by Field Marshal Wilson, the Supreme Commander in the Mediterranean. "Jumbo" Wilson, renowned for his affability, tried extremely hard to fill Dill's place with Marshall. But he never succeeded. It was almost as if the Chief of Staff resented anyone else's trying to replace his old friend. Marshall could never find again the casual touch that marked his relationship with Dill. Wilson apparently sensed that the close ties could never be reknit and was somewhat ill at ease. Often he could do little more than forward and answer messages. Possibly the sharp tone that appeared at times in Anglo-American correspondence after November might have been moderated had Dill lived. Or again, perhaps the memory of his lighter touch still had some magic. Fortunately the biggest differences on operations had been settled. There were still sharp issues to be settled but not dangerously divisive matters requiring the close friendship and personal skill that had been supplied by Dill.[42]

The question of the five-star promotion that Stimson thought he and Marshall had buried in the spring of 1944 returned to plague them in mid-September. From Quebec came word that Roosevelt wanted the bill passed by Congress. Informed by Marshall of the President's directive, the Secretary gave way on September 13. And he managed an ingenious solution that would make the measure less distasteful to Pershing's friends. He and McNarney arranged for adoption of the title "General of the Army" for the five-star Army rank, so that Pershing would continue to be alone in bearing the title "General of the Armies." Having made that gesture, Stimson went to Walter Reed Hospital to congratulate the World War I leader on his eighty-fourth birthday. Next day he announced his concurrence with the new five-star bill but added in his diary that the Navy had insisted its chiefs needed five-star rank to deal with the British. He grumbled, "Nobody has had more to do with the British than Marshall and he has seen no need [for more rank]." [43]

As Congress continued to delay action on the bill into late November, Marshall was blamed by some columnists for holding up the legislation. Stimson was disgusted and indicated that he would be glad if the whole matter was stuck in Congress. On the twelfth General Handy brought word that the bill would be passed and that he had worked out seniority arrangements with the Navy. Admiral Leahy ranked first, then Marshall, and then Admiral King, MacArthur, Nimitz, Eisenhower, Arnold, and Halsey were to be the other five-star officers.[44] The legislation and approval of the new generals went through on December 15. Marshall, who had returned from a two-day inspection trip, was in the Pentagon shortly after noon when word came of the approval of the nominations to the new rank. He had just finished talking with General Stilwell about his new assignment as chief of the Army Ground Forces when he was summoned to Stimson's office. As he and Arnold went in one door, more than a score of the top commanders of the Pentagon came in the other. They joined in toasts to the new Generals of the Army.[45]

December also saw another milestone for Marshall. The last day of the year marked his sixty-fourth birthday, an age at which he normally would be required to retire. Stimson noted this in mid-November, adding that the President could extend the term, but that he thought it would be better for Congress to act. With his cooperation this was done.[46]

Notification of Eisenhower's nomination for new rank did not reach the Supreme Commander until December 16 (he actually ranked from December 20). It was almost the last good news he was to hear for the next ten days. In a final gamble Hitler struck suddenly that day in the Ardennes. His surprise stroke ended Allied hopes for a quick termination of the war.

Despite the optimism Marshall had expressed ten days earlier to Admiral Stark, there were reasons why he and his colleagues in Washington and Europe should have been worried. During his recent visit to the western front, the Chief of Staff had traveled along the widely stretched VIII Corps Sector in the Ardennes, where three divisions—two relatively inexperienced and one exhausted from long and strenuous fighting—held a ninety-mile forested front in Belgium. His commanders told him that they were taking a calculated risk and were not perturbed. The terrain and the road net in the area did not seem favorable for an attack. Besides the Germans were in a desperate state and barely able to hold on.[47]

Since his visit there had been many signs of a German build-up in the Ardennes. Later intelligence chiefs could point to statements that showed the possibility of attack. The enemy's intentions were hidden by the fact that the German Army, hard pressed on all fronts, was calling on semi-invalids, the old, and the very young to fill its ranks. Bombing attacks on the oil supply of the Reich had produced serious fuel shortages. True, there was evidence of enemy troop movement along the Allied front, but since the Germans were probably aware of American preparations for an offensive on December 13, it seemed reasonable to assume that they were getting set to meet the attack.

Above all there was a misreading of the German mind. After a period of rustication Field Marshal Gerd von Rundstedt had been returned in the fall to command the enemy forces in the West. He was known to be a cautious commander. Montgomery's Chief of Intelligence went so far as to say that if Hitler were running the show, the Allies could expect some surprises. But since von Rundstedt was now in charge, there need be no fear.[48]

From an Allied viewpoint it seemed absurd that the Germans, already badly hurt, would leave their protected positions for an area less suited to defense. But Hitler, whose troops were in desperate conditions on all fronts, could not afford to play it safe. As matters stood, he had two choices. If he could catch the Americans off balance in the Ardennes, perhaps he could sweep through to Antwerp, knocking out the timetable for the offensive and seizing and destroying vital stocks. At best a smashing success might slow Allied preparations until there might be a chance for a negotiated peace. At worst time might be gained to develop some miracle weapon—the jet fighter, for example, against which the Allies, as Bedell Smith recently noted, had no effective counterweapon. The gamble was extreme, but earlier risks had worked for Hitler. All in all it seemed better to hazard loss than to wait for certain disaster.

Carefully the Führer gathered his armored units, hoarded precious gasoline, trained special troops who would spread disorder by dressing in American uniforms and driving American jeeps in the Allied rear areas, and guarded the secrecy of his plans. When his weather experts were able to predict five days of bad weather, sufficient to ground the feared Allied bombers, Hitler unleashed his attack in the Ardennes.

On the front held by the VIII Corps the German attack went well. Two regiments of the green 106th Division were overrun, the 99th Division fell back, and the 28th Division was hard hit.[49]

But the north flank held. The seasoned 2d Division dug in; elements of the 1st Division stood firm on the Elsenborn Ridge at Dom Butgenbach. As V Corps brought up reinforcements, the attackers were forced to sideslip southward. Thrown off schedule, they lost the opportunity for a real breakthrough in the first twenty-four hours. It meant that time was gained for the defenders of the road net farther south.

The first reports were not alarming. As late as the morning of December 18 Marshall and Stimson agreed that the Germans could not get very far. Recalling the last desperate German counterattack of 1918, the Secretary of War and the Chief of Staff were still not worried.[50] In a sense they were reflecting the attitude of the commanders in the field. However, developments on December 19 put matters in a different light. Eisenhower had already ordered forward his last American reserve—the 82d and the 101st Airborne divisions. That evening, explaining that General Bradley's headquarters in Luxembourg was almost out of touch with the First Army in the north, General Eisenhower shifted command of the First Army temporarily to Field Marshal Montgomery. General Patton was ordered to break off his attack and send troops to the relief of Bastogne. It now became clear to Washington that the Germans might be able to delay the day of European victory.

Knowing that the enemy breakthrough meant that shortages in manpower and ammunition would soon become critical, Marshall moved at once to reduce the deficits. The Chief of Staff informed Eisenhower that he had given orders that he was to be left free to give his complete concentration to the fighting. "I shall merely say now that you have our complete confidence." He explained later: "I kept down the messages to Eisenhower; I made them recall one they sent during the Bulge; I said, 'Don't bother him.'" Marshall was heartened by the President's attitude. Through all the crisis, "Roosevelt didn't send a word to Eisenhower nor ask a question. In great stress Roosevelt was a strong man." [51]

The worst of the German attack was over by Christmas. In the end it was the quick recovery of ground units, the digging in of the seasoned divisions, the prompt shift of units from other fronts, and the lifting of the mists, which permitted tremendous air strikes against the enemy, that turned the trick.

Later, two episodes would be recalled in the Battle of the Bulge. One was General Patton's suddenly breaking off an attack in the Third Army sector and turning his units in a 90-degree shift toward Bastogne to make the dramatic drive that ensured the holding of that keypoint in the Allied road net. The other was the spirited defense of the threatened Belgian town by the 101st Airborne Division, supported by elements of the 10th Armored Division. When the Germans struck, the 101st Division commander, Major General Maxwell D. Taylor, was in the United States, at General Ridgway's request, for discussions with General Marshall. He did not leave Washington until December 22 after a final talk with the Chief of Staff—and then chafed at delays that prevented him from rejoining his unit. He need not have worried. On that date his second in command, Brigadier General A. C. McAuliffe, having looked at the best the Germans had to offer, had replied to their polite invitation to surrender with the famous rejoinder, "Nuts." [52]

Other than supporting Eisenhower with supplies and men, Marshall intervened chiefly by his sharp reactions to British pressure for a change in command. Since early fall Montgomery had pushed for the appointment of a ground commander between Eisenhower and the army groups. Although he declared his willingness to serve under Bradley if the Supreme Commander so decided, it seemed unlikely that this arrangement would be acceptable to the British. Believing such a move unwise, Eisenhower continued his personal command of the Allied forces.

Eisenhower's action on December 19 giving Montgomery command of all Allied troops north of the Bulge seemed to the British to justify a reopening of their demand for either a ground commander or two ground commanders of equal power, controlling forces north and south of the Bulge. The latter arrangement, which would leave the U.S. First and Ninth armies under Montgomery, was not acceptable to General Bradley.

Marshall was willing to go along with Eisenhower's move as a temporary expedient, but he was irritated at Montgomery's use of the incident to force the appointment of a permanent ground commander. Fearing that under the pressure of events Eisenhower might feel inclined to make some concession to British demands, the Chief of Staff radioed him near the end of December: "My feeling is this: under no circumstances make any concessions of any kind whatsoever. You not only have our confidence but there would be a terrific resentment in this country following such action. I am not assuming that you had in mind such a concession. I just wish you to be certain of our attitude on this side."

Once more Marshall had acted to strengthen his subordinate's position before he was asked for support. Proclaiming his full backing and his confidence for the success of future operations, the Chief of Staff concluded with a New Year's thought: "You are doing a fine job and go on and give them hell." [53]

XXV

Crisis in Manpower

SECRETARY Stimson faced his regular Thursday press conference on December 21 with the knowledge that news from Europe was bad. General Marshall had anticipated his problem and had prepared an encouraging appraisal of the situation for his use. Although the news from the Ardennes front was still bad, Marshall, like Stimson, could remember the final German offensive in the late summer of 1918—a sputtering flare-up before the final collapse. His suggested statement radiated hope. But when Stimson repeated the optimistic announcement, many newsmen found it misleading.[1]

The Philadelphia *Record* spoke for many critics in recalling boasts two months earlier that the Germans lacked reserves for a counterattack and that an Allied victory was possible before the end of the year. Eisenhower had termed the attack a last desperate gamble of the Nazis, and Stimson had compared it to the final German surge in 1918. The editor was not so sure. It was high time for people in high places to quit making predictions. The need was to "fight, fight, fight . . . [and] stop talk, talk, talk."[2] Columnist Constantine Brown noted caustically that for months the public had been told that the Germans were on their last legs. "The propaganda menu served to the American people," he declared, "has become somewhat indigestible."[3]

When Stimson the following week used later Marshall notes describing the news from the Ardennes as "distinctly favorable," even members of the War Department staff complained. Intent on spurring war production, General Somervell thought the optimistic talk unwise and sent a tart message to the Chief of Staff. Possibly he knew that Marshall had supplied Stimson with his information and chose this means to reprove the Chief of Staff though seeming to chide the Secretary. He wrote sharply: "So the Army thinks the country is complacent and acts as though the war were won. . . . What's to make a man think otherwise? Listen to the highest authority in the War Department: 'I am confident we are winning. . . .

Time will reveal that this German throw of the dice will have disastrous consequences for him. . . . The news today is distinctly favorable'!" [4]

The effect of such talk, Somervell continued, was to encourage complacency on the part of defense-plant workers. "Let's knock off next week at the plant. . . . The German drive is surely over now. . . . To hell with waiting, let's duck out of town tonight."

To rub in the point Somervell continued, "What do you think of this as an appraisal of reaction to this? Especially in view of the fact we have to get results on the basis of public opinion without any sanctions to enforce our requirements."

Marshall kept silent on the fact that Stimson's statement closely resembled the memorandum forwarded by his office. Repaying tartness with acid, he penned: "I note the emphatically antagonistic review of S/Ws comment, but just what do you think he said that should not have been said or modified?" [5]

Somervell was not to be lightly brushed aside. With a toughness he often used to subordinates he replied to his boss: "You hold me responsible for production. Our material requirements for E.T.O. [European Theater of Operations] have been increased since last September. I have no mandatory authority by which I can command people to produce more. I can only get that production through leadership and a common understanding of our problems." [6]

Marshall and Stimson had spoken in an optimistic vein in order to reassure the public that Eisenhower was on top of the situation abroad. But they recognized the justice of Somervell's remarks. For weeks now there had been evidence of a general letdown on the production front. At a time when more workers were needed in war jobs, thousands were leaving plants to seek permanent peacetime jobs. Pay was good at the moment, but peace would bring massive layoffs. The end of the war would mean millions of discharged servicemen competing for jobs; it was wise to get well entrenched in a permanent job while there was still time. It was hard to keep the public at fever pitch when the country was prosperous, the war far from American shores, and events seeming to point toward speedy victory.

With some bitterness General Somervell cited a recent walkout of 1400 men, stopping production on ball turrets for bombers, which had occurred in protest against the transfer of an inspector. When he had recently called for a study of increased manpower requirements for a small-arms ammunition program to reach its peak in June 1945, both management and labor had been skeptical of the need for the increase. "Again I am not fighting the same war as is in the minds of the people on whom we depend for voluntary cooperation." As a starter he asked that all press conferences, press releases from the theaters of operations, and official statements be pitched at a tone more conducive to public awareness of a long tough war ahead. [7]

Somervell had a strong point. A few days later Stimson described the dilemma he and Marshall faced when the news from the Ardennes finally sounded more favorable. "It seems funny . . . I should be distressed by . . . good fortune," he wrote, "but the true fact is these things are going to make it more difficult than it would have been to get necessary legislation through our Congress. Just as soon as the news of our victories comes, everybody wants to put on his coat and stop working. The curious characteristic of our noble people in the U.S. is that they have no more notion that they are in a war or the sacrifices which are involved or needed—just so many children." [8]

The manpower problem, already serious before the Ardennes attack, became daily more critical. The questions the War Department faced were: whether it had underestimated the size of the needed Army, whether it had been premature in shifting strength to the Pacific, and whether the present Selective Service was providing enough men for the Army's needs. Shortly after V-E Day, General Marshall explained:

The final manpower crisis occurred during the prolonged and very heavy fighting in the fall of 1944 and the winter of 1944–45, both in Europe and in the Philippines. However, our own tribulations of this nature were much less serious, it is believed, than those of our Allies and certainly of the German enemy, whose divisions at times were reduced below 5,000.

In the Siegfried Line fighting prior to the final advance to the Rhine, the weather was atrocious and most of the troops had been continuously engaged since the landing in Normandy in June. The lack of port facilities prior to the opening of Antwerp to Allied shipping made it impossible to maintain divisions in normal corps reserve and thus permit the rotation of units between the fighting line and comfortable billets in rear areas. Divisions for this purpose were available in England and in northwestern France, but the state of the railroads and the flow of supplies made it impossible to maintain them at the front. All this resulted in a great strain on the fighting troops, and when a shortage in replacements was added, the situation grew very serious. It was just at this moment that the Germans launched their final offensive effort in the Ardennes.

This shortage in replacements at such a vital moment was the final effect of long-accumulating circumstances. The Army's manpower balance had been disturbed in the fall of 1943 by shortages in deliveries of inductees by the Selective Service System, which amounted during one 3-month period to about 100,000 men. A second factor was the miscalculation after North Africa that resulted in too many men being trained for the armored forces, the artillery and special troops, and too few by far for the infantry. Another factor was failure in the early phases of the war to compensate in the over-all strength ceiling for the number of men who would be required to fill the long overseas pipelines and the time involved between the completion of the training of the individual in the United States and his final arrival in the division. Still another was the heavy pressure brought to bear on the War Department to hold down or reduce its demands for manpower. It will be recalled that for more than a year a rather vigorous attack was maintained against the War Department's estimates of manpower requirements.[9]

Although many of these points had been evident to Marshall and Stimson when they discussed the manpower problem on December 27, 1944, they were inclined to blame part of it on the Selective Service System, and they actually considered replacing Major General Lewis B. Hershey, its head. The Hoosier-born, free-speaking, red-haired gamecock had been dealing with recruitment problems since 1936 when he became secretary and executive officer of the Joint Army-Navy Selective Service Committee, a position he held for four years. During his tenure he had been sent by Marshall along with several colleagues to aid in drafting the measure that was passed by Congress in 1940. Shortly afterward he was made Deputy Selective Service Director under Clarence A. Dykstra, who was on leave from the University of Wisconsin. In July 1941 Hershey became head of Selective Service. Now there seemed to be some doubt that he was sufficiently effective in getting the men the Army needed into the service.

Among those considered as his replacement were Brigadier General Frank J. McSherry, formerly G-5 under General Eisenhower in the Mediterranean and Deputy to the G-5 in SHAEF; Colonel Kenneth Royall, a special assistant to the Secretary of War; and Brigadier General William H. Wilbur, who had won distinction in North Africa.[10] In the end General Hershey held onto his position for some twenty-five years more.

Hershey had his faults, but there were many problems beyond his control. As he later pointed out unflinchingly to the Chief of Staff, shifts in Army policy that depended on political and military matters compelled the Selective Service System to deal with the burden of stop-and-go induction calls. Further it had been unrealistic to maintain peacetime physical and mental standards in such periods of critical manpower need as July–September 1943, when nearly one-third of the men called for induction had been rejected for minor ailments.[11]

On the last day of the year Stimson filled Roosevelt in on the situation in Europe. Like Marshall the Secretary of War was grateful that the President "has not asked any questions or sought to interfere in any way with either Marshall or myself while the crisis of the German counterattack had been going on." Now on December 31 the Secretary was pleased to announce that Bastogne was safe. He also took along Marshall's telegram to Eisenhower of the previous day in which he had sought to buck him up and to strengthen his determination not to yield on the matter of a British ground commander.

Stimson talked of the manpower problems that he and Marshall were confronting. He reassured Roosevelt that they were "satisfied" that the French were fighting well and spoke of proposals to equip and train more French troops. The Secretary also presented statistics, furnished by Marshall, showing the number of British and American divisions in being. Noting the scattered nature of Britain's force dispositions, Roosevelt remarked: "Churchill always is a disperser." Stimson said that it was not unnatural for the Prime Minister to scatter his troops since he had to distribute his forces to protect the Empire, but such a policy was not suitable for the United States: "We have to win this war. Nobody else can." [12]

General Marshall was pleased with Stimson's successful session with the President. It was gratifying to hear that at last Roosevelt had agreed to come out strongly for a National Service Bill in his forthcoming State of the Union speech. Seeing the possibility of prying the measure out of congressional committees where it had been lying for many months, the Secretary asked Marshall to examine the draft of a letter that Undersecretary of War Patterson had proposed that Stimson and Navy Secretary Forrestal sign in support of the bill. Marshall agreed to help put it in final shape.[13]

Stimson also asked Marshall for information to answer the President's query: Why were there only 500,000 men fighting out of 1,500,000 men in Europe? Armed with material furnished by Marshall's staff, Stimson stayed behind after the next cabinet meeting to explain that in ground combat on the Continent outside of Italy the Army had more than 1,750,-000 U.S. ground troops plus 193,476 airmen in France and another 218,-727 in the British Isles. In addition there were more than 90,000 ground-force replacements on the Continent and some 117,000 in the British Isles. Thus the number of men in the ground forces overseas was at least 500,-000 more than Roosevelt had supposed and the fighting men more than twice as many as he had estimated. The number of service of supply and nonoperational troops was about 800,000 instead of 1,000,000 he had indicated.[14] General Marshall also indicated the location of units under Eisenhower's command or scheduled to come under it. On the Continent outside Italy were forty-seven divisions plus nine infantry regiments (the infantry of three divisions) and in the British Isles two divisions. Still waiting in the United States for shipment to Eisenhower were seven divisions plus three divisional headquarters. By spring Eisenhower was scheduled to have fifty-nine U.S. divisions or roughly two-thirds of all U.S. divisions in being.[15] At this time the British had eleven divisions plus three Canadian and one Polish division; the French had eight.

The statistics gathered to satisfy the President failed to reassure Stimson. He was disturbed at Russian slowness to attack and had become convinced, Marshall recalled, "that they were going back on us." Realizing that the last ground resources in the United States were now committed and due to sail by spring, the Secretary of War insisted on new divisions. He tackled Marshall on the subject in early January: "I have an uneasy feeling that we ought to make some more divisions and begin to do it now and have them ready by next summer or next autumn. . . ." He believed that ten new divisions were needed.[16]

It was, as Stimson said later, "an old difference between us." Marshall repeated his arguments of the previous May and December: he still relied on Allied air superiority and the American replacement system to see the war through. However he conceded that if the Germans defeated the Allies in the counterattack or particularly if the Russians failed to act, it would be necessary to "recast the war." The Army would have to go on the defensive and have the people of the United States decide whether they wanted to raise new armies. But he did not expect that problem to arise.[17]

Stimson was less inclined than ever to agree. The Air Forces, he argued, had not been able to prevent the Germans from continuing to fight. Despite terrific punishment, the enemy had managed to reorganize new units out of the "depths of the barrel" and had put nearly as many divisions on the western front as the Allies had. While conceding that these were smaller than American divisions and less well equipped in weapons and air support, he still felt that "it is too close for my comfort."

Marshall once said that the lawyer in Stimson made him seize on one case at a time and stay with it until he had seen it through. The Secretary had given way momentarily twice before on the need for new divisions. This time he was determined to make a stronger fight for his idea. Strongly convinced that there must be more ground units, he "had it out with Marshall in a perfectly friendly but very firm way." He was careful in his arguments since he wanted to avoid "joggling his elbow, so to speak, when he is under such great strain." [18]

To strengthen his case Stimson brought in McCloy on the ninth. In a lengthy session beginning at lunch and continuing until 5:30, they discussed the situation. Finally, Marshall said later, "I opposed this [the ten divisions] to the point where I [said I] would resign and asked him to tell the President this." He conceded that it was unusual for an officer to make such a threat in wartime. But "it would mean robbing us terribly and the [units] wouldn't be [ready] before a year. It took us almost twenty-two months to get a division ready to go overseas and our early-replacement system was not good. . . . With every man we took away we were ruining divisions. The final climax was Stimson's proposal for ten divisions. I told him I had to stop it if I could. Then he dropped it." [19]

The General "was very stormy" at first, Stimson noted in his diary, but he and McCloy calmed him with their assurance that they did not want to interfere with his replacement system or the bringing of maximum forces against the Germans in the current battle. Their plans, they added, could not go into effect until the following summer or fall, but if announced earlier might help in the passage of the National Service Bill.

Marshall agreed that he would think it over. Stimson was pleased at this concession, writing in his diary, "He is always reasonable after he gets over his explosives, and this time was no exception." In fact Marshall assumed that Stimson had given up his main proposal. A Russian offensive eased the problem. "About that time," as Marshall recalled, "the Russians showed up. The Russians did not turn us down on the plans they were committed to." [20]

Marshall was by no means opposed to more troops. As he explained:

"The feeling we had about large bodies of troops was that we had to meet a very tremendously large force, and that the British power was vanishing. The Eighth Army is the last thing they showed up in [at full strength]." But the U.S. trouble lay, he felt, in the inability to keep units up to strength, and it was this that worried him.[21]

Meanwhile efforts to get more men into the manpower pool both for the armed forces and for industrial production were gaining speed. The War Department turned again for assistance to the National Service Bill introduced in Congress more than a year before by Senator Warren Austin and Representative James W. Wadsworth.

Backed by Stimson and Forrestal, and by Marshall and King, whose support he cited, Roosevelt on January 6 called for the passage of the measure. The closer "we come to the end of the war," he declared, "the more pressing becomes the need for sustained war production." Such legislation would ensure that "we have the right number of workers in the right places at the right time." In addition to the general-service legislation, he asked again for the drafting of nurses for the Army and Navy, the drafting of 4-Fs (men deferred for disabilities), and universal military service after the war—"a pretty good stiff dose," as Stimson called it.[22]

Despite the momentary scare of the Ardennes breakthrough, Congress was no more prepared than before to agree to the whole measure. Roosevelt had indicated that he would accept something less than the entire package by suggesting that while the broader bill was pending, Congress pass a bill to make available for service some 4,000,000 men from the 4-F group. The war industries needed 300,000 workers, and the armed forces needed 1,200,000 for replacements and expansion. Only 700,000 of the latter could be found from the current eighteen-year-old group newly ready for drafting. The remainder had to come from men previously deferred or from agricultural workers. The new legislation proposed reexamination of men previously deferred for failure to meet minimum physical standards.

To handle the stopgap measure asked by the President, Representative Andrew J. May of Kentucky and Senator Josiah W Bailey of North Carolina proposed to require men in the eighteen to forty-five group to stay on war jobs or transfer to them. The Army, however, balked at proposals to induct men who refused war jobs into an Army labor corps.[23]

To gain the lower chamber's backing for the bill, Stimson, Patterson, and Marshall urged the House Select Committee on Postwar Military Affairs to postpone its pending measure on universal military training for a "Win the War Now" theme. They managed to obtain the cooperation of the representatives, who asked, however, that the measure not be too long delayed.[24]

A few days later the above members of the War Department team met with Chairman May and two other members of his House Military Affairs Committee to push passage of the National Service Bill. When General

Marshall was called on to speak, Stimson reported that he made "a good talk on the immediate importance of help and told what an uprising of public opinion we are going to have when the needs of our Army become understood by the people, and I think he made an impression on them." [25]

Stimson was wrong in his optimism. It was the Army that had to give way. Part of the change in its attitude came from War Mobilization Director Byrnes, who, as a former Senate leader, was trying to put together a measure that would win congressional support. At length Byrnes persuaded the War and Navy representatives that the Bailey-May bill was the best they could get. Stimson ended by telling the President that if he couldn't get the Austin-Wadsworth bill, "this would be a pretty good thing after all." [26]

With the decks cleared the President on January 15 staged a meeting with General Marshall, Admiral King, Byrnes, and key members of the Senate and House military committees. Roosevelt read a report from Stimson, Byrnes spoke for industry, and King responded briefly for the Navy. Then, reported *Time*, "George Marshall made the strongest appeal of all." He carried his point by picturing men half-sick and half-frozen forced to fight on without rest in France and Italy. He spoke of 431,000 men in hospitals and the hard and costly fighting that was to come. "Scrupulously staying in his place as a military leader," the Chief of Staff said that he was not trying to tell the congressmen what to do. But "they had given him a job of fighting a war and it was his job to tell them what he needed." It was a fine performance. At the end of the session the President sent a message to Representative May with the joint blessing of Marshall and King. While avoiding endorsement of any specific legislation, the two made clear that they needed 900,000 troops in the next six months plus 700,000 additional workers in war industry. The Navy's rocket and ship-repair programs were jeopardized for lack of workers, and the merchant-shipping situation was critical. The Army cited problems with small-arms ammunition, tanks, tires, cotton duck, mines, smelters, and basic-metal fabrications—all involving hard and dirty work with low pay.[27]

To win congressional approval for the armed services program and to explain the situation in the various theaters, the War and Navy departments arranged a briefing for members of Congress in the Coolidge Memorial Auditorium at the Library of Congress on January 23. This procedure had worked well before, and Marshall had been effective in his previous appearance. This time, however, Stimson feared he would be unprepared. "Poor Marshall," the Secretary wrote, "hasn't had much time on what he has to say and that is going to be the main thing, but he came in and talked with me a little about it." [28]

Stimson had worried unnecessarily. Although the full turnout of congressmen presented a challenge, there was no problem for the Chief of Staff. Stimson recorded: "King made a very good statement but he spoke from notes and was not as impressive as Marshall who made his extemporaneously. Both, however, were extremely good and it was very evident that the Congress, who listened with rapt attention, were much impressed." [29]

The careful preparations by the White House, War and Navy departments, and congressional leaders paid dividends initially when, on February 1, the House passed the May bill by a vote of 246 to 165. The Senate presented a tougher challenge. Marshall's representatives again made contact with friends in Congress. But there were disconcerting reactions. As the official historians have noted: "When Marshall and Patterson claimed that they needed 900,000 draftees, no one could say them nay, though the figures were not held above suspicion. But the demand for 700,000 additional workers because of manpower shortage was greeted with general disbelief." [30]

A change in the Army's fortunes in Europe and MacArthur's concurrent triumphs in the Philippines "sent optimism soaring like a balloon." "Good news," wrote *Time* in mid-February, ". . . flooded Washington like spring sunshine." While Marshall and King were overseas at Yalta, it added, the Senate put up its feet and relaxed.[31]

The unlikely coalition that had defeated National Service legislation in 1943 and 1944 worked again. Labor-union leaders teamed up with representatives of the National Association of Manufacturers and the National Chamber of Commerce to argue that additional workers would not be needed—if wastage were eliminated—and that the legislation would lead to increased government regimentation of labor and industry.

In the absence of the President and the military chiefs Secretary Stimson went on the air on February 18 with a strong speech in favor of the National Service measure. Of its effect he wrote: "Poor Jerry [Colonel Wilton B.] Persons who is our liaison officer with the Senate Military Committee is shivering in his boots over the violence of my language and its effect upon the gentlemen he has to work with. But . . . I have concluded that it is time to speak out." [32]

Persons's fears were justified. The War Department was attacked for trying to "dictate legislation" and for misusing statistics. Critics of the bill insisted that voluntary measures were sufficient to get needed manpower.[33] The Army, just bouncing back from its hard knock in the Ardennes, was not certain that such means would produce the needed manpower. But it found the public set against stringent legislation. An uproar resulted over Justice Byrnes's proposal to shut bars, night clubs, and other places of entertainment by midnight in order to discourage loss of man-hours at plants. Critics retorted that early closing would deprive workers on swing shifts of their proper relaxation and would actually delay production. Soon mayors, who had initially indicated they would go along with the proposal, began to renege on their agreement. The reaction was such that when Marshall in late February passed on some optimistic items that

Stimson might include in his next news conference, the Secretary said he feared they might throw cold water on the chances of the National Service Bill.[34]

Despite the strong War Department efforts, the Senate committee reported out a weakened substitute measure instead of the legislation originally proposed. Despite further efforts from the White House the Senate passed the substitute by almost four to one. An attempt to incorporate some of the stronger features adopted in a conference meeting with House representatives also failed of Senate passage.[35]

The good news in late February and in March further undercut the Army's efforts. The capture of Manila, the pounding of Tokyo by bombers from the Marianas, the continued advances in the Central Pacific, and the capture of the Remagen bridge across the Rhine all seemed to point to the early ending of the war. Members of Congress, who since Pearl Harbor had almost automatically approved all demands for men and money, were now becoming restive at continued military requests. There was also growing resentment against the President and a yearning to get back to business as usual.

Marshall had recognized the change in public opinion near the end of 1944. He directed a search for men suited for combat from installations in the United States, the Canal Zone, and Alaska. In late December he ordered Eisenhower to seek replacements from his own rear echelons. On January 6, 1945, the Chief of Staff took stronger action. He directed General Somervell to look into the personnel and supply situation in the European Theater of Operations. Marshall explained to Eisenhower that "with your attention centered on the battle, with Major General Ray Barker the G 1 of an Allied Force and not a pugnacious character and with Lee in command of affairs in England and many in France I am fearful that too much of a delay will occur in bringing about the changes that appear imperative.

"It seems absolutely clear to me," he continued, "that little has been done in Lee's command or in the 8th Air Force Command for that matter, vaguely approximating the drastic measures we have taken back here to obtain Infantry replacements." He proposed, therefore, to send Major General Lorenzo D. Gasser to survey the situation. "We must get immediate action since we can no longer bleed ourselves much more on this side of the Atlantic to meet deficiencies on yours." The Chief of Staff added that Gasser could only "point the finger" and that Eisenhower needed a tough soldier to see to it that drastic measures were put into effect.[36]

Next day mentioning British uneasiness about the command situation in Europe, General Marshall returned to his argument: "I see one weak point in our position which I should like you to think over and that refers to the command of the rear areas. Whether or not Lee is the right man does not answer the question. The trouble is, he is involved in both sup-

plying the Front and supplying himself. While the troops on the Front
suffer heavily and work with reduced numbers he has continued apparently to operate with plenty of fat meat. This awakens suspicion in the
minds of front line commanders as to the adequacy of the support they
are receiving. We had exactly the same thing here, still have, though to a
very mild degree at present, the continued suspicion by the Air Corps and
the Ground Forces of Somervell's people because the ASF is performing
two functions, one for the Army at large and . . . one . . . for itself. . . ."

To carry out the job in Europe the Chief of Staff had in mind the
retiring Army Ground Forces commander, General Lear. "The more I
think of this the more it impresses me and Handy is of the same opinion,
that Lear who is loyal, stern and drastic, and very soldierly, be made a
deputy of yours for command of the rear areas with the head of the supply
service subordinate to him." [37]

Recognizing the determined tone in Marshall's message, Eisenhower replied, "Please send Lear on at once. While I know him only slightly his
rank, experience and the qualities you describe should be useful to us."
Not all Eisenhower's staff agreed. Bedell Smith, who resented visiting firemen, later complained that the War Department had the bad habit of
dumping garbage on them from the States. When told of this, Marshall
replied, "Well, we did dump some, but Gasser and Lear were not part of
it." The Supreme Commander welcomed the arrival of both men. He
proposed to make Lear deputy U.S. theater commander with responsibilities chiefly for those matters "that are currently giving us so much
trouble."

In one respect Eisenhower limited Lear's usefulness by deciding that
"While he will use existing staffs rather than to establish a new and large
headquarters, his detached position directly under me will give him
ample authority with respect to all senior subdivisions of the U.S.
Theater." In fact Lee still controlled the office space, the staff, and the
rear echelon. Although Lear and Gasser pried loose thousands of men,
they fell short of what Marshall—and possibly Eisenhower—had in mind.
Marshall said later that he was disappointed in Somervell's measures to
straighten out the Communications Zone set-up; this was one of the few
jobs that the Army Services Forces commander failed to handle satisfactorily.[38]

In dealing with the troop shortage Eisenhower listed points on which
he needed assurance: (1) the assumption that the Russians were going to
begin a sustained major offensive that would force the Germans to reverse their flow of troops; (2) the possibility of getting additional divisions from the Italian front; (3) the immediate and drastic comb-out of
able-bodied men; (4) the increase in the Army ceiling for the Continent,
if possible, to permit him to subtract hospital patients from the total allowed; (5) a continuous effort to expedite the flow of critical ammunition

types and tires; and (6) the speed-up of the development of French divisions.

Looking about for new sources of manpower, Eisenhower suggested that the Marines might be willing to let him have 100,000 men—an idea that seems not to have been discussed further. He then added that a large number of able-bodied soldiers, mostly black, were engaged at work on docks, in depots, and on roads in back-breaking jobs. Although men were needed for the heavy jobs, he felt that "in existing circumstances I cannot deny the Negro volunteer a chance to serve in battle. If volunteers are received in numbers greater than needed by existing Negro combat units I will organize them into separate battalions for temporary attachment to divisions and rotation through front line positions. This will preserve the principle for which I understand the War Department stands and will still have a beneficial effect in meeting our infantry needs." General Marshall enthusiastically agreed.[39]

Back of Eisenhower's message lay earlier discussions at his headquarters concerning the basis on which Negroes were to be used in battle. The Army, following an established principle that the services could not be used as an instrument for social reform, had concluded that Negro troops should be used in Negro units rather than being integrated in small units. Now under the pressure of battle losses the Army accepted the idea of attaching smaller black groups to white units.[40]

Another result of the search for more men was the increased use of eighteen-year-olds in combat—a move that was to provoke congressional criticism of the Chief of Staff. In fact Marshall and his advisers had worried over the problem for months. When legislation was passed late in 1942 extending the draft to eighteen- and nineteen-year-olds and to pre–Pearl Harbor fathers, War Department spokesmen indicated that there was no intention to send younger recruits overseas without a year of training. Apparently no binding promise was made, but General Marshall's reiterated view that twelve months or more of training were necessary before combat was taken as a guarantee.

Desiring to put more youth and vigor into infantry units, General Marshall had directed that 75 per cent of the teen-age men were to be assigned to divisions activated after January 1, 1943. Under normal conditions they would receive a minimum of one year's training with their unit before going into action. However, many of the recent young recruits went to replacement-training centers from which they were sent overseas with as little as thirteen weeks' training. Fearing possible adverse public reaction, planners in the Army Ground Forces raised the question as to whether or not all eighteen- and nineteen-year-old inductees should be assigned to units and older men to replacement-training centers. Since activation of new units was declining, this action did not appear feasible, and the practice continued of assigning men to replacement-training centers without regard to age.[41]

The situation disturbed Major General Milton A. Reckord, chief of the Third Service Command, Baltimore. As early as June 1943 he warned General Somervell that "many young men are being shipped overseas who are not properly trained, some of them having been in the service only a few weeks." If this fact became known to the press, he warned, it might "bring discredit upon General Marshall." Reckord added that the Chief of Staff had repeatedly emphasized to congressional committees that men needed "perhaps 18 months training and certainly not less than a year." He believed it important for Somervell to present this problem to General McNair, who, as commanding general of the Army Ground Forces, was responsible for infantry and armored training, since he knew that McNair would do nothing that would reflect adversely on General Marshall.[42]

There is no evidence that this warning was ever passed on to General McNair or General Marshall, but McNair was already aware of the generally unsatisfactory situation in regard to replacements of all ages being received overseas. Two days before Reckord's letter was sent, the Army Ground Forces commander had been reminded by General Marshall's G-1 that "Rapidly accumulating reports from the theaters of operation invariably indicate that enlisted loss replacements received to date in the theaters have been unsatisfactory as to physical standards, discipline and training" and that officer replacements who had not had some command experience after being commissioned at Officer Candidate Schools were unsatisfactory. Less than two weeks later the Army Ground Forces proposed extending the existing thirteen-week basic-training course to seventeen weeks.[43]

Rising demands for replacements from the Mediterranean, where casualties were rapidly increasing, created a mounting source of worry for McNair. In September 1943 Marshall wrote to the Ground Forces commander of "the impact on me of a number of . . . reports which, in summation, do not present a favorable impression." He cited particularly a recent observer's comment on a replacement center in North Africa where he had been unimpressed "with the flabby, ill-trained look of these men." They were not young, the average age being reported as twenty-eight, but they were still raw recruits, most of them "fresh from basic training—13 weeks—although some had as much as 4 to 5 months training behind them." The "frightened and unsure look in their eyes and in their manner was not heartening." The Chief of Staff asked for a report on the situation.[44]

Fortunately for McNair some changes in the replacement-center system, discussed in June, had been put into effect before Marshall's letter. He was able to report three days later that the situation was improving at the centers in the United States. Currently all replacements sent overseas had complete individual training. However, to provide for current demands it would be necessary to take part of the loss replacements from divisions in training in the United States. "Apparently," he remarked with an eye cocked toward Marshall's immediate staff, "the War Department has been unable to predict the needs accurately." [45]

Despite these efforts General Eisenhower was moved at the end of 1943 to ask General Marshall to send men from divisions rather than from replacement-training centers because of the extreme youth— and consequent inexperience—of many replacements coming to his theater. His suggestion undoubtedly reinforced earlier proposals for drawing on the divisions for experienced replacements. At the end of February 1944 the War Department directed that men from the units were to have at least six months' service and that the men with longest service were to be taken first. Eighteen-year-olds and pre–Pearl Harbor fathers were not to be shipped as long as men could be found from other sources. [46]

After a brief period during which divisions were stripped of older men, by June the requirements for replacements abroad made it necessary to dip again into the replacement-training centers for men with seventeen weeks' training. To protect the younger recruits the War Department in late June banned the shipment overseas of any man under nineteen as an infantry or armored replacement. It was soon clear that the administrative problems of "storing" men until they were nineteen or of assigning them to special nondivisional units were becoming almost insurmountable. In addition the deprivation of younger and more vigorous replacements for the fighting units meant a falling off in the quality of their replacements. Within less than a month and a half the War Department rescinded its ban and eighteen-year-olds were again assigned to infantry and armored replacement-training centers. [47]

Marshall thus faced an almost classic example of the difficulty of holding to a cautious policy in the face of demands from the fighting fronts. It was similar to the situation in 1940 when he hoped not to have to send draftees and National Guard members outside the continental United States. But military demands made it necessary to use such forces or virtually to dismantle units to which they had been assigned. He was caught again in the same dilemma. While the ban on early shipment of eighteen-year-olds lasted, the quotas of replacements were filled by stripping some twenty-two divisions in the United States of an average of approximately 4000 enlisted men per division. Because of the Ardennes losses the War Department found that it had to shorten the training period for replacements to fifteen weeks. With the youngest recruits now assigned to infantry and armored replacement centers, it was inevitable that some were killed or wounded only a few months after entering the service. Strong protests welled up in Congress, whose members were already aroused over the shipment of pre–Pearl Harbor fathers to the front. Marshall attempted to explain that the youngsters assigned to seasoned units became combat ready far more rapidly than they would have in the United States. Thus they could do with less training than he had previously proposed. But his arguments did not go down well with the critics.[48]

Dissatisfaction over the use of eighteen-year-olds abroad with less than a year's training led to a Senate debate in February 1945 and again in April. Although the discussion still lay in the future when General Marshall prepared to leave in late January for the Allied conferences at Malta and Yalta, he was fully aware of the thin margin the American forces had in manpower and the problems he faced in getting more men and new divisions. He did not need reports from his planners to remind him that Russian manpower was required to bring the final defeat of Japan. What did need emphasis was that it seemed likely that Russian cooperation would be essential to victory in Europe. And more to the point, the Allies had left the impression on Stalin that they needed his assistance against Germany.

Nearly two weeks before the Ardennes attack General Eisenhower had expressed to Marshall his worry over the lack of Russian activity on the eastern front, which was permitting the Germans to shift units to the West. Of his future plans he declared, "Much now depends on the date and scale of the anticipated winter offensive of the Russians. I say 'anticipated,' as we have nothing except conjecture on which to base our ideas as to Russian intentions." He reported that enemy reinforcements were arriving from Hungary and East Prussia. The Supreme Commander was not informed when Ambassador Harriman discussed Russian intentions with Stalin about ten days later, on December 14. The Russian Marshal indicated to Harriman that a winter offensive would be launched but was vague about the situation because of bad weather. Although Stalin indicated that he might be able to give some further information within a week, nothing had been passed on to Eisenhower by the time of the Ardennes attack.[49]

The unexpected Ardennes counteroffensive, staggering in its force, increased the Supreme Commander's anxiety. Four days before Christmas he informed Marshall of new shifts of German troops from the eastern front. He declared: "The arrival of these divisions obviously influences the events in my area and if this trend continues it will affect the decisions which I have to make regarding future strategy in the west." Again he requested that he be given information to permit his "coordination" with Russian plans. He offered to send to Moscow a high-ranking officer from the SHAEF staff and to give details of his forthcoming plans in return for Russian information.[50]

Eisenhower's appeal, endorsed by Marshall, prompted Roosevelt to contact Stalin. The message was carefully worded to avoid any hint that the Supreme Commander was seeking help. As if he were initiating the action, the President said that he would like to tell Eisenhower to send a staff officer "to discuss with you the situation in the West and its relation to the Russian front in order that information essential to our efforts may be available to all of us." He played down threats on the western front: "The Belgian situation is not bad; necessary to see what comes next. Hope you will see Eisenhower's representative and arrange exchange of information of mutual value. Complete secrecy will be maintained." Stalin soon replied that he would be willing to receive the SHAEF representative.[51]

In informing Eisenhower of Roosevelt's message and Stalin's reaction, Marshall passed along some rather puzzling statements that the Marshal had made in past weeks about Allied-Russian cooperation. In his October meeting with Churchill, Stalin had spoken of the possibility of outflanking the Siegfried Line by an Allied move through Switzerland and the withdrawal of some of the Allied forces from Italy and their transfer to the Balkans with a view to joining up with the Russians near Vienna. In the more recent talks with Harriman he had spoken of the possibility of transferring up to eight divisions from Italy to Dalmatia for an advance on Zagreb to join up with the Russians in southeast Austria.[52]

Anticipating that Stalin might raise these points with the SHAEF party in Moscow, the Combined Chiefs of Staff on December 29 suggested that, if queried, the Allied representatives should reply that the outflanking of the Siegfried Line by going through Switzerland involved violation of Swiss neutrality—a decision that would have to be made by the heads of government. On the possibility of transferring units from Italy to Dalmatia they were to say that they were not empowered to deal with this matter but that the point could be raised with Alexander.[53] Churchill was sufficiently interested in this possibility to consider sending Alexander with the SHAEF party to Moscow. This suggestion was soon dropped, and the entire proposal seems to have been ruled out shortly afterward when Field Marshal Wilson informed the Combined Chiefs of Staff that he might soon have to go on the defensive in Italy.

On January 1, 1945, the SHAEF party, consisting of Air Chief Marshal Sir Arthur Tedder, Deputy Supreme Commander; General Harold Bull, SHAEF G-3; and Brigadier General Thomas J. Betts, SHAEF Deputy G-2, set out from London for Moscow. Because of bad weather they had not progressed beyond Naples five days later. At this point the Prime Minister offered to try his hand at getting information about Russian plans by a direct approach to Stalin. He wired the Soviet leader that "It is Eisenhower's great desire and need to know in outline what you plan to do, as this obviously affects all his and our major decisions." He added that Tedder had been held up. "In case he has not reached you yet, I shall be grateful if you can tell me whether we can count on a major Russian offensive on the Vistula front, or elsewhere during January, with any other points you may care to mention."[54]

The reply was all that he could have wished. Stalin replied almost at once that while the weather was bad, he was preparing an offensive. "You may rest assured that we shall do everything possible to render assistance to the glorious forces of our Allies." [55]

In an unusually friendly mood Stalin received the belated SHAEF mission on January 14 with the announcement that the Russian offensive against Germany was already under way. Casting aside the secretiveness that he and his subordinates had shown for months, he now laid out for the delighted visitors the details of his coming campaign. Tedder was fully equal to the occasion, apparently winning the Russian's respect by his candor and his compliments on the Soviet Union's fighting record.[56]

Tedder, Eisenhower, Roosevelt, and Churchill all expressed pleasure at the Russian reaction. But Stalin was even more delighted. Although the Ardennes problem was well on its way to solution before Tedder's party left for Moscow, the fact that Roosevelt and Churchill had sought Stalin's help gave him a basis for claiming later that he had saved the Western Allies from a defeat at German hands. While he was entirely wrong on that score, he was encouraged in his belief that in the coming months—in Central Europe no less than against Japan—the Western Allies needed his assistance more than he needed theirs. By the end of January, Marshal Konstantin K. Rokossovsky had moved northward from Warsaw to the Baltic and isolated East Prussia from the Reich. Marshal Ivan S. Konev, striking across the south of Poland, reached the Oder and established bridgeheads across it in several places in time for his feats to be announced at the Yalta conference in February. Between these two forces the armies of Marshal Georgi K. Zhukov drove toward Berlin. Advance units of his armor were within a hundred miles of the German capital at a time when the American and British forces, licking their wounds and rebuilding units mauled in the Ardennes, were planning to drive toward the Roer. Even before this drive the Germans had retreated from Albania and France and part of Yugoslavia, and Russian troops held all of Bulgaria and Rumania, more than half of Poland and Hungary, and most of the Baltic States. Thus Stalin approached the February meeting with Roosevelt and Churchill in a mood of confidence. The high cards seemed to be in his hands.[57]

XXVI

The Great Myth

IN late December a noted reporter of the American scene, Frederick Lewis Allen, visiting the Army, Navy, and Air Force Chiefs of Staff at their offices, found General Marshall "unhurried, relaxed . . . and unaffected." [1] He characterized King as distant and aloof and Arnold and his staff as overeager to sell their case. Marshall was a man at ease, sure of himself, "one expounding a complex situation to a group of people he respected."

Allen described the Army Chief of Staff as he was usually seen by his associates and by many visitors to the War Department. In a large office, later to be transformed by Secretary of Defense Louis Johnson, Marshall sat behind an antique mahogany desk, largest of six bought by Lieutenant General Philip Sheridan in the 1880s, when he was commanding general of the Army. Across the room was a large table also from the Sheridan era. On one wall hung an oil painting of the Meuse-Argonne fighting borrowed from the Smithsonian Institution and opposite it a portrait of General Pershing. In one corner stood a grandfather clock flanked by an American flag and the General's personal four-star flag (his new one with the added star had not yet been designed). Somewhere in the room (although Allen did not mention it) was a painting done a few months before by a sergeant from a World War I photograph. Aware that the General treasured a shot of a group of soldiers in a damaged church in France, standing around an organ as they sang just as the sun came through the window, Colonel McCarthy of his staff arranged for a soldier-artist to do a picture in oils. Marshall liked to explain to visitors then and after the war that he kept it because it was a pleasant contrast to the more usual picture of soldiers drinking and carousing. However he found one fault in the painting. As he explained to an aide, one figure in the picture had been portrayed too accurately—his stomach was too large. Running his thumb along the offending bulge he indicated the proper military lines. More quickly than the most drastic diet could do it, the artist slimmed his subject.[2]

Allen was startled by Marshall's double chin—a roll of fat between his "not-so aggressive jaw" and his collar. The drooping was due less to good food—since Marshall's weight had increased very little despite a cut in his exercise time—than to the old thyroid problem from which he had long suffered. Those who mentioned his so-called receding chin misread their man and betrayed their own careless observation. Although there was no jutting point of rock, there was hard steel in the lines of the mouth. Allen found that he had "rounded features, blue eyes, sandy-brown hair (a full head of it) graying, especially at the temples, and fine hands, smallish, a little loose-skinned and freckled, which he used expressively in quiet gestures."

Marshall's voice was rich and full, his accent cultured, with hints of the South and the Midwest. "He spoke quietly, not in any sense speechmaking, not talking down to us. . . ." Allen was impressed, as many others had been, by his ability to speak without notes and to convey "a coherent and unconfused sense of the overall situation, and also by his ability to recite exact figures on such matters as the amount of tonnage handled by the invasion ports." His delivery seemed effortless, but it had precision. "By contrast with Arnold and King, whom we heard later, he was clearly a word-minded man, an intellectual with something of the artist in his sense of language. At times he was amusing in his turns of phrase. . . . At times . . . his voice rose in power. . . . The main impression he made on us was of an absolutely first-class mind, in grasp, range, and judgment. . . ."[3]

The Chief of Staff would need all this and more to deal with the problems that were approaching in the wake of the Ardennes attack, the manpower crisis, and especially the meetings at Malta and Yalta that were at hand. Now the final phase of the European battle was to be resolved.

Near daybreak on January 26, 1945, General Marshall's C-54 put down at Terceira in the Azores. Just ahead of him a plane landed bearing the recently appointed Secretary of State, Edward R. Stettinius, Jr., son of an old friend from World War I, and another with Admiral King. Hours earlier they had left Washington, traveling by way of Bermuda, headed for meetings with the British at Malta and with the British and Russians in one of the great conferences of the war at Yalta in the Crimea. For Marshall there was to be a highly important intervening stop—at Marseille—to discuss future plans with General Eisenhower.

With the war against Germany entering its final stage and with crucial plans for the defeat of Japan now being formulated, Marshall and his associates were fully aware that they were helping to make history. The Chief of Staff had grave issues to review with the Secretary of State when he joined him after breakfast on the terrace overlooking the airfield. "As we watched the sun come up over the hills on this lonely island we dis-

cussed our hopes for the future and for the new age that was dawning,"
Stettinius later wrote. They spoke particularly of the atomic bomb, of
whose existence Stettinius had only recently been informed. He thought
the Russians might ask about progress in this field and wanted to know
what he should say if questioned. Pragmatic as always, General Marshall,
who had played an important role in its development, said that they
could not prepare for such an eventuality and must handle the matter in
accordance with "the circumstances and the conditions, as and if it
arose." [4]

Even had he become suddenly garrulous, there was not too much that
Marshall could tell. At the end of December he, Stimson, and the President had been informed by General Groves that one atomic bomb, with
great destructive potential, would be available by August 1, 1945, and
another by the year's end. But this tremendous weapon had still to be
tested, and there were those, Admiral Leahy among them, who doubted if
the monstrous engine of destruction would work. At this stage there was
not sufficient evidence of its power to justify refusal of Russian aid or
active discouragement of Soviet action against Japan.[5]

Roosevelt had sought over a number of weeks to hold the conference to
ensure Marshal Stalin's help in the Far East and his backing of the
United Nations Organization. Stalin's military commitments had interfered in the beginning, and then Roosevelt wished to postpone the conference until his inauguration on January 20. Possibly because of the lack
of novelty, wartime austerity, or his own failing health, the President decided to hold this fourth ceremony on the south portico of the White
House instead of at the Capitol. On a cold January day with Marshall
and the other Chiefs of Staff dutifully in attendance, he was sworn in for a
new record-breaking term. Three days later Roosevelt left on the cruiser
Quincy for the Mediterranean, accompanied by Admiral Leahy, James
Byrnes, and other advisers. The Joint Chiefs of Staff and Stettinius, wishing to talk in Malta with their British counterparts before Roosevelt arrived, flew from Washington on January 25. King and Marshall traveled
separately in accordance with the understanding that the country should
not be deprived of both their services in case of accident. Flying with
Marshall, in the place of the ailing General Arnold, who had been hospitalized a few days earlier in Miami with a heart attack, was Major General Laurence S. Kuter, representing the Army Air Forces.

"No more let us falter! From Malta to Yalta!" Churchill had wired
Roosevelt in January 1945, when the site of Czar Nicholas II's Crimean
home was selected for their meeting place. The Prime Minister's rollick-
ing doggerel hid his apprehensions about the site ("We could not have
found a worse place for a meeting if we had spent ten years on research,"
he told Hopkins) and about the coming encounter with the Russians. The
President had not supported him strongly in the recent British intervention against the Communist faction in Greece, and there had been dis-

agreements over future policy in Italy. Churchill was disturbed over the battle and command situations in Western Europe, and he saw threatening portents in the attitude of Marshal Stalin. The President and his advisers were more sanguine about future prospects. In time they would find themselves described as bunglers or worse by critics of the Crimean conference.[6]

After the Azores, Marshall made an overnight stop at Casablanca. Next morning he and his party left at eight, flying by way of Algiers and east of Majorca to the Allied air base twenty miles west of Marseille. Here they were met by a fleet of automobiles and taken to the Château Valmonte par Ste. Marguerite, until recently the headquarters of the German naval commander of the area. Marshall and his party were welcomed by Brigadier General John P. Ratay, whose fierce mustache reminded Marshall of Field Marshal von Hindenburg's. Ratay, noted for his appreciation of good living, had done himself proud.

Marshall recalled less about the château—"a monstrosity" in the opinion of General Kuter—than he did about members of the staff. Asking for a barber, the Chief of Staff was furnished the services of an Italian prisoner of war. Reminded that he might soon be met by British officers demanding an attack through the Ljubljana Gap, Marshall asked the Italian if he knew the area. He was pleased when the barber said that he had been born near one of its exits. When Marshall questioned him closely, the barber called in as interpreter a compatriot who had been born near its other exit. By the time he had finished with his haircut, the General—like many other barbershop patrons—had a firm grasp of the subject in question. He recalled later that at Malta the British Chiefs of Staff were amazed at his knowledge of the area.[7]

Marshall had arranged his stop in the south of France in order to discuss future plans with General Eisenhower. Realizing that the Supreme Commander hesitated to leave the current battle for a meeting in the Crimea, the Chief of Staff had suggested that he make the shorter trip to Marseille.

In most respects Marshall knew the problems facing the Supreme Commander. Not only had Eisenhower urged him in late December to find out what the Russians were going to do, but on January 15 he had also gone over the details of his coming campaign. "The worst conditions in Europe," he wrote, ". . . would be: (a) Weak and ineffectual Russian offensive. (*I do not even mention a lack of Russian offensive, for without this a quick decision cannot be obtained.* We would have to mobilize much French manpower and additional U.S. Divisions.) (b) Partial enemy withdrawal from Italy without compensatory reinforcement here. (c) Continued enemy withdrawal from Norway to reinforce here."

Careful coordination with the Soviet offensive was essential. He went on:

Should the Russian offensives be strong and sustained, I estimate that with the forces we will have, when the good weather starts, it may well be possible to defeat the enemy on our front, but we would be justified in expecting quick success only after we have closed the Rhine throughout its length, concentrated heavily in the north, and staged a definite supporting secondary attack somewhere to the south of the Ruhr.

If the Russian attack proves ineffectual, we may be restricted by the enemy's strength to limited operations in the meanwhile. With our present forces, and the build-up outlined above, I do not consider we shall meet with any serious reverse. However, in these circumstances we may be faced, initially at least, with some 100 divisions, although later the resumed Russian offensive may develop great power and draw back some forces over to that front. Moreover, the Germans will have obtained a respite during the intervening period of restricted operations to recoup their losses, rehabilitate their forces and strengthen their defenses, our own defensive problem would be greater. In this event, *to insure quick success*, I should have to have the additional 20 Divisions and definitely close the Rhine throughout as a preliminary to the great invasion. The alternative would be time and attrition.[8]

Clearly a Soviet offensive was important to Eisenhower's spring attack.

In Marshall's eyes second only to this forthcoming offensive was the quashing of British agitation for the appointment of a ground commander. It was an old issue and one on which he had made up his mind. Marshall indicated to Stimson afterward that he had not been certain of Eisenhower's ability to stand up to the British. "This time I also found," Stimson wrote, "that Marshall thought that Eisenhower had been over-conciliatory in his dealings with the British in this matter. I have always been afraid of this. Eisenhower has been extraordinarily successful in his diplomacy in keeping the composite command of which he is at the head in full effect and in preserving the cordial feeling between the two armies. . . . I myself have been worried lest he lose sight of the necessity of supporting sufficiently our national views where they were at variance with the British. That was the reason why I favored the appointment of Marshall for this European command a year and a half ago. But with Marshall's vigorous interposition at this conference he seems to have readjusted the balance and given a healthy boost."[9]

Montgomery and the British had never fully accepted Eisenhower's taking over field command at the beginning of September 1944. The Field Marshal continued to allude to problems that had arisen after the Supreme Commander changed the earlier arrangement. The Prime Minister had brought up the matter in a message to Roosevelt shortly before the Ardennes, and the counterattack there seemed to provide a chance to install a British ground commander. When Eisenhower, seeking reserves to put into the battle, had committed the two U.S. airborne divisions, he had to look to Montgomery for additional troops. Then finding Bradley's headquarters at Luxembourg out of contact with the U.S. First Army, he had transferred the First Army, under Lieutenant General Courtney

Hodges, to the British commander. Shortly afterward Montgomery had appeared, as one writer put it, "like Christ coming to cleanse the temple." The Field Marshal told Eisenhower that Hodges was shaken and received permission to relieve him if necessary. In the circumstances it was easy for Montgomery to assume that he was back again as ground commander of the Allied forces.

During the first bad days of the counterattack some evidence of anti-Eisenhower feeling appeared in segments of the British press. Then when Montgomery took over, suggestions were made that the Supreme Commander had been forced to call on the Field Marshal to save the situation. As this impression spread, Montgomery decided that he must hold a press conference to "help Ike." He could scarcely have done worse for his own and the Allied cause. Later he would admit that it was a mistake.[10]

It was not for lack of warning. His Chief of Staff, Major General Francis de Guingand, and Alan Moorehead, his favorite correspondent, tried to dissuade him. At the conference he praised the performance of American troops, but his tone was unfortunate. He left the impression that the American commanders had fallen down in performance. Later he blamed the Germans for broadcasting a distorted account of the affair.

His words were exaggerated by the Germans, but the reports of his Sir Galahad attitude in the press conference were enough to infuriate the normally placid Bradley. Already sensitive because the First Army had been shifted from his command to Montgomery's, Bradley promptly made clear in a news conference of his own that the arrangement was temporary. This set off angry reactions in the British press, involving aspersions on American leadership. Eisenhower had already tried to smother such innuendoes by praising General Bradley to the press, by assuring Washington that "there was no disposition to blame" the 12th Army Group commander, by recommending that he be made a four-star general at once, and by warm personal letters to Bradley and Hodges for their handling of the enemy counterattack. But as long as Montgomery remained in command, the battle would rage. Eisenhower later called it the most difficult problem he had to face in the war. When the British argued for a ground commander, which meant a return to the arrangement at the time of the invasion, Bradley flatly stated that he would resign rather than serve under Montgomery. Patton fervently backed him. In Washington, General Marshall declared that there would be no commander between Eisenhower and his army group leaders.

Greatly dismayed, Churchill hastened to apply unguents to bruised feelings. In a handsome statement in Parliament he praised the efforts of the Americans and graciously contrasted their heavy losses to the lighter ones suffered by the British units. His poultices removed some of the sting but did nothing to make the Americans welcome a British ground commander. General Marshall had gone on record against such an appointment in his message to Eisenhower at the end of December—a fact that the Field Marshal knew—and Churchill's statement did nothing to change his mind.

Marshall's determination had stiffened Eisenhower's own resolve in this matter. When Montgomery renewed his criticisms of command arrangements, Eisenhower retorted bluntly that they had reached a point where he would have to ask the Combined Chiefs of Staff to choose between them. On December 30 Bedell Smith and Major General J. F. M. Whiteley, the British Deputy G-3 at SHAEF, made clear to Montgomery's Chief of Staff, General de Guingand, that there was no turning back on the issue. Unwell, de Guingand returned to his chief's headquarters to lay out the grim details for him. After fortifying himself with a stiff drink, he told his superior that in a showdown someone would have to go, and "it would not be Ike."

By this time Montgomery—apparently unknown to Eisenhower—had seen Marshall's message. The Field Marshal wrote later: "That telegram finished the issue of operational control so far as I was concerned and I knew it would be useless to open it again." Brooke too was thoroughly acquainted with Marshall's views, and he had already warned Montgomery against trying to get the ground command. Montgomery grasped the nettle bravely. Asking de Guingand to help prepare a statement, he made a graceful surrender: "You have stated your views and I have stated mine. We will now go on with your proposals. Your obedient subordinate. Monty." [11]

This would have ended the matter for anyone but Churchill. The Prime Minister had always preferred Alexander to Montgomery for the European Command, but he indulged Brooke in his contrary preference. Churchill was aware that Eisenhower had wanted Alexander at the time of the cross-Channel attack, so he ingeniously refurbished the idea, suggesting that Alexander, now the Italian commander, come to France as Eisenhower's Deputy in place of Air Chief Marshal Tedder, who was needed for the Far East. A few months earlier the proposal might have been accepted, but the time had now come when Marshall and the American commanders, holding the whip hand, intended to stand firm against a British ground commander—who would in effect supersede Eisenhower in the field.

It was partly to scotch the Prime Minister's action completely that the Chief of Staff had stopped at Marseille. He scented some weakening in Eisenhower's reply that he would be willing to have Alexander as Deputy. Marshall came immediately to the point when he and Eisenhower sat down to talk. And he left no doubt that there would be no concessions on command. Eisenhower later dictated notes on Marshall's position: "a. General Marshall will not agree to any proposal to set up a Ground Commander-in-Chief for this theater. If this is done he says he will not remain as Chief of Staff. He recognized the necessity of giving Montgomery an American Army." [12] So far as Eisenhower and Montgomery were concerned, the issue was dead. But it was to be raised twice more by Churchill.

Next in order was Eisenhower's plan for "closing the Rhine." Although the exact meaning of this concept became a point of argument at Malta a few days later, Eisenhower's dictated account of his understanding with Marshall was explicit: "He [Marshall] agrees that crossing in force should be preceded by well-conducted campaigns to eliminate the German forces west of the Rhine." This did not mean, as the British said in opposing the plan, that the divisions should be spread thinly along the whole front. Rather Marshall thought that the attack should be "so conducted as to employ in the front lines the fewest possible number of divisions so as to have well-rested and re-fitted the greatest number of divisions when the time comes for the all-out attack." [13]

To reinforce Eisenhower's effort, Marshall would bring up several divisions from Italy. These should be mainly British, he thought, in order to strengthen Montgomery's 21 Army Group. However he held out hopes of getting at least one American division—an idea that was dropped soon afterward at Malta. Marshall was amused at this point when Eisenhower asked if he could have the 10th Mountain Division, recently assigned to General Clark. The unit, organized over some War Department doubts through General Marshall's intervention, had been turned down by members of the SHAEF staff who may have felt that a unit trained for possible fighting in the frozen north would not meet their current needs. The Chief of Staff said, "You had your chance, and you turned them down as not being trained for your area. Clark said he would take anyone who would fight. . . ." Eisenhower, apparently hearing this explanation for the first time, looked at his G-3, General Bull, who in some embarrassment tried to elaborate on SHAEF's reasons for declining the unit.[14]

General Eisenhower also raised the possibility of promoting Generals Bradley and Spaatz to four-star rank—a suggestion that he had made in the case of the former as a sign of confidence shortly after the Ardennes attack began. Marshall was especially willing to advance Bradley and recognized the importance of giving both officers rank more nearly comparable to that held by their British opposite numbers. Montgomery, who commanded two armies, was a field marshal while Bradley, with four armies totaling a million men under his command, was a three-star general; Spaatz, in charge of all U.S. strategic bombing in Europe, was at least one star behind the British airmen with whom he had to deal. But Marshall faced serious problems in regard to these promotions. He pointed to the claims of McNarney, Devers, Clark, Eaker, and Krueger, all senior commanders with important commands. And if Krueger were elevated, the question of four stars for Patton would arise. And his name might still produce trouble in Congress. Marshall decided to take a little more time before settling this point.

Eisenhower's presentation had stilled any possible doubts the Chief of

Staff might have had about American performance in the Ardennes. He also left for Malta with the realization that all available reinforcements—whether they came from the Italian front, the United States, or Russia—were needed to ensure the success of the planned offensive. If he had needed any encouragement to present the strongest possible case for Eisenhower at the forthcoming conferences, he had gained it from his talks.

On January 29 after a trip of some 20 miles through numerous small villages unscarred by war, Marshall and his party came to Marseille, where rail centers and other targets showed the signs of Allied bombing. In bright sunshine they took off for the 750-mile trip to Malta by way of Sardinia and Sicily. Below them snow-covered hills served notice that the balmy Mediterranean could be freezing in winter. As they landed at Malta, a "cold, blowing mist" confirmed that fact. They found that the stone buildings in which they were quartered had stored up the dank chill of centuries. Billeted in the Royal Artillery barracks, the Americans took their meals in the Union Club, which hundreds of years earlier had been the palace of the Grand Commander of the Order of St. John, the ruler of Malta. As the ranking American military officer until Admiral Leahy arrived, Marshall was given preferred VIP treatment. But as he told his associates next morning, such rank sometimes had its disadvantages. Shortly after their arrival important envelopes marked "Most Urgent" had been handed over to proper authorities for delivery to the guests. As Marshall was the senior officer in quarters, an efficient sergeant awakened him at 4 a.m. to deliver the weighty message. Opening it, the General found an invitation from the Governor to have dinner at the palace the following evening.[15]

Sleepily joking about his early reveille, Marshall opened the first meeting of the Joint Chiefs of Staff at Montgomery House on the morning of the thirtieth with a statement of Eisenhower's strategy, which he proposed to back in their conference with the British Chiefs that afternoon. The Supreme Commander had explained at the Château Valmonte that the principal objective was still Berlin and the main attack was to be made by Montgomery north of the Ruhr. However a strong secondary offensive between Frankfurt and Kassel under Bradley seemed essential.

Marshall, already in agreement with Eisenhower's strategy, was prepared to back it vigorously when the British and U.S. Chiefs of Staff met. He invited the Chief of SHAEF's Operations Division, General Bull, to give the details of operations and the SHAEF Chief of Staff, Smith, to defend the overall concept. For Generals Smith and Bull, who had served with Marshall at Fort Benning in the late twenties and early thirties and more recently in Washington, it seemed a familiar exercise.

The SHAEF Chief of Staff first sketched the plans that Eisenhower had outlined to Marshall two days earlier. Smith affirmed that the main effort was to be north of the Ruhr, emphasizing that Eisenhower had gone beyond Montgomery's proposal in insisting that thirty to thirty-six divisions be used in the area rather than the twenty to twenty-one suggested by the 21 Army Group commander. Like Montgomery, Eisenhower wanted a secondary effort, but he preferred the Frankfurt-Kassel area to the Cologne-Bonn thrust suggested by the Field Marshal. With considerable force Smith argued that the latter area was too close to the main assault to draw off German forces, that the crossing points were not good, and that the nature of the terrain across the Rhine would make advances in that area difficult.

Bull explained two pending operations, which might be launched within a few days. According to the first, VERITABLE, Montgomery would strike with the First Canadian Army in a southeasterly direction to the Rhine between February 8 and 10. If it then seemed feasible, he would make a thrust northeastward (GRENADE) with the U.S. Ninth Army, still under his control, to link up with the Canadians at the Rhine. Within a short time, Bull added, it would be necessary to decide if Bradley should continue his proposed drive in the Ardennes or remain static while the main effort was made in the north.

General Smith then followed with an exposition of the importance of the time factor as a result of the recent Russian advances. The German Sixth Panzer Army, recently on the Ardennes front, was thought to be in the process of withdrawing from the west. It was thus necessary to get to the Rhine in the north as rapidly as possible to take advantage of this shift.

As Smith and Marshall already knew, the British were seriously disturbed about some phases of the plan. Several days before Eisenhower had alarmed Brooke and his colleagues with his proposal to close the Rhine along its whole length, an action they feared would blunt the main northern attack. On his own Smith emphasized that the Supreme Commander did not intend to carry out this plan if it would delay the main attack until midsummer or hinder an opportunity to seize a bridgehead and cross in strength in the north.

Smith's response had defused much of Brooke's objection. Though reassured, the Field Marshal still stressed the need for concentrating on the northern thrust and subordinated everything else to this attack. Seeing Brooke waver, General Marshall added his own interpretations:

> In his view the considerations involved in the plan were as follows: the most favorable spot logistically, that is, in the North; . . . the number of divisions required to maintain security in the non-active parts of the line; the assessment of the number of divisions which could be logistically supported in the northern thrust. He considered it essential that there should be more than one possible line of advance. The strategic reserve should be fed into either advance in the light of how well that advance was succeeding. If extremely heavy casualties were sustained in the northern attack there were the alternatives of either battling through or switching the weight of the attack elsewhere. . . . It was likely that the Germans would put up a heavy resistance in the North and,

with the aid of jet-propelled reconnaissance aircraft, would assess the likelihood of our attacking in that area.

The Chief of Staff's statements, influenced by his recent talks with Eisenhower, proved less reassuring than Smith's. Brooke insisted on a more specific commitment to the action on Montgomery's front. At his request
discussion was put over until the following day.

Almost equally disquieting to the British were American efforts to
move the Fifteenth Air Force and its heavy bombers from the Mediterranean to the United Kingdom. Although it was an American force, Alexander wanted it to support the ground units of a diminishing Anglo-
American force in Italy. Anticipating Alexander's needs, Air Chief
Marshal Portal insisted that any proposed shift of the Fifteenth Air Force
must be approved by the Combined Chiefs of Staff. At once Marshall
reminded him that the initial agreement regarding the Fifteenth had permitted the Strategic Air Forces commander, General Spaatz, flexibility in
employing his forces when conditions were not favorable to the existing
arrangements. Having made his point, he added that there was no intention of making a permanent shift of these forces. This pledge satisfied
Portal.

Marshall's conciliatory attitude in the discussions over Italy at this
point reflected the general understanding that the British Chiefs of Staff
did not intend to stress further Mediterranean operations. Their effort to
hold U.S. air units in Italy was based on a desire to increase defensive
strength rather than to launch further offensive action. On the thirty-first
Brooke—in a pronouncement that must have saddened Churchill—
agreed that the Allies should reinforce the western front at the expense of
the Italian battle. Trieste, Istria, the plains of Hungary were no longer set
forth as possible goals. The Field Marshal declared: "There was now no
question of operations aimed at the Ljubljana Gap and in any event the
advance of the left wing of the Russian army made such an operation no
longer necessary."

In a generous mood Marshall agreed with Brooke that the American
units in the U.S. Fifth Army, a mixed force, should not be disturbed and
that the number of divisions transferred from the Mediterranean to
Eisenhower should be reduced from six to five. Marshall suggested that
two of the divisions should be Canadian (thus placing all the Canadian
units on the same front) and the remaining three British. Two of the
British units would have to come from forces in Greece.

The Chief of Staff met British resistance with his further proposal to
withdraw part of the Twelfth Tactical Air Force from Italy to aid the
French First Army and U.S. Seventh Army in southern France. Field Marshal Alexander felt that in view of the impending loss of five divisions, he
would especially need Allied medium and light bombers for his defense.
General Smith, whose requests Marshall was backing, replied that SHAEF

had no desire to reduce the security of the Italian front and that he was willing to leave the final decision to Alexander.[16]

Thus far the tone of the meetings was mild. But there was to be one turbulent session before the Chiefs of Staff left Malta. As if they were sundials, counting only unclouded hours, the conference secretaries recorded nothing of the thunderstorms that followed when Brooke continued to question Eisenhower's plans. Marshall later recounted: "At Malta we had a very acid meeting [as] Smith came on and the British put great pressure on him. They were opposing the previously agreed-upon plan and General Eisenhower's procedure and in particular his advance to the Rhine. In describing the advance, the Americans on the Combined Staff had let themselves in for a British term, 'closing the Rhine,' which [the British] seized [on] and whipped the whole [plan] with. Smith [tried] to explain it was a British expression, but to me it was the sort of Gettysburg [speech] stuff [instead of] a simple statement of what [was] wanted."

As the argument intensified, Marshall asked for a closed session. With only the top advisers remaining and with no record kept, the discussions crackled with heat. The Chief of Staff vigorously opposed any orders to Eisenhower that would "cramp" his action. Insisting on pinning the Supreme Commander down to Smith's interpretation, Brooke asked for a specific directive.

Marshall recalled that "Brooke said the British Chiefs of Staff were much worried by the influence on General Eisenhower by General Bradley and I think he mentioned General Patton. And I said, 'Well, Brooke, they are not nearly as much worried as the American Chiefs of Staff are about the immediate pressures . . . of Mr. Churchill on General Eisenhower. The President practically never sees Eisenhower, never writes to him—that is at my advice because he is an Allied commander—and we are deeply concerned by the pressures of the Prime Minister and of the . . . British Chiefs of Staff, so I think your worries are on the wrong foot.' We had a terrible meeting." [17]

Convinced that Brooke's distrust of the Eisenhower plan stemmed from Montgomery, Marshall at last took up the 21 Army Group commander, allowing himself, in Brooke's words, "to express his full dislike and antipathy for Monty." In telling Stimson two weeks later of the affair, Marshall still snorted angrily. The Secretary of War recorded: "[He] had some sharp issues with the British who have been trying to push Montgomery forward in respect to Eisenhower. Marshall who is always very tolerant in . . . dealing with the British was finally quite aroused by this situation and evidently 'lit out' in the conference so vigorously that he carried everything before him. Montgomery . . . wants everything in the way of help and preparation of command [and] then is rather overcautious in his advances." [18]

Brooke misjudged Marshall in concluding that the American Chief of Staff was engaging in a personal vendetta with Montgomery. Perhaps Marshall had been overstimulated by reports from his commanders in Europe, by headlines in the British press concerning Montgomery's recent press conference, or by his own unfavorable impression of the 21 Army Group commander the previous October. But his ire against Montgomery —like his anger in his dealings with Chennault and de Lattre—was roused because he felt that the 21 Army Group commander was unwilling to be a member of a team. He remarked later that Montgomery had never gone to Eisenhower's headquarters for a conference, but always made the Supreme Commander come to him. Marshall had always been willing to excuse eccentric and stubborn behavior in commanders; what he could not accept was what he believed to be open contempt of an officer for his superiors.

Having expressed himself fully, Marshall relaxed thereafter. It was the last tempestuous conference he was to have with the British Chiefs of Staff. There would be an exchange of sharp telegrams in March and early April when the British Chiefs undertook to reprimand Eisenhower over his correspondence with Stalin, but there were no more stormy sessions of the Combined Chiefs of Staff.

Churchill was reluctant to accept the recommendations of his military advisers on Italy. Shortly after the President's arrival Churchill made his position clear to him: "He felt it was essential that we should occupy as much of Austria as possible as it was undesirable that more of Western Europe than necessary should be occupied by the Russians." Here was a new element in the epic Churchillian argument for the Mediterranean area. Not many months before he had declared that Alexander "shall have his battle" and had pleaded with the Americans not to withdraw victory from the forces in Italy. Now at last he said flatly that he wanted to forestall the Russians. Although Lord Moran and others have recorded that he had mentioned such a strategy before, this was the first time he had made it his major point in talking to the American representatives. Again and again in the weeks that followed, he was to return to the argument, and in time he and some of his colleagues would push further back in time the date at which they urged on the Americans the need to out-race the Russians.[19]

In addition the Prime Minister was still dissatisfied with the handling of the war in China and Southeast Asia. He asked the President if he too was not disappointed at the results achieved by the Chinese in view of the tremendous American efforts made in their behalf. In a remarkable shift in attitude the President conceded that "three generations of education and training would be required before China could become a serious factor."

The U.S. Chief of Staff was less pessimistic than the two heads of state.

Stilwell's able successor, General Wedemeyer, was getting the Chinese on the move again, Marshall reported. And he scraped up hope from the recent transfer of well-trained Chinese troops from Burma to China, the even more recent opening of the Burma Road, which permitted supplies and reinforcements for the Chinese Army to go through from the west, and the possibility that gains in Burma would release additional Chinese units for their home front.

The Prime Minister would not be comforted. American and British operations in Asia now seemed to be diverging, with the Americans turning toward China as the British turned southward. He wondered if the planners had considered sending British and Indian divisions from Burma into China. Both Brooke and Marshall agreed that it was not practicable to maintain British troops in China, and the American Chief of Staff suggested instead giving American aid to Mountbatten in Southeast Asia. Sticking to his argument, Churchill repeated for the record that if the United States requested the dispatch of British troops to China, he would certainly be prepared to consider it. Admiral Leahy discounted this possibility by pointing out that all transportation available was now required for forces currently in China or earmarked for that country. Marshall agreed, adding that it was impracticable to increase forces in China until a port was secured.[20]

Clearly there had been drastic changes in the Far East in six months. Where once the Americans had begged the British for action in Burma, Mountbatten now sought assurance that the Americans would back his actions there. He further suggested that all American, British, and native forces be made available to him to clear the Japanese out of Burma and then perhaps drive them from the Malay Peninsula up through French Indochina and then apparently through China to Japan. But the Americans now wanted to bypass much of Burma and Southeast Asia. President Roosevelt inveighed against helping the French return to Indochina. Marshall and the other American Chiefs now preferred to put the bulk of the forces under Wedemeyer in China to work with Chiang Kai-shek's armies in striking toward the Japanese mainland. At the first opportunity they proposed to open a port on the China coast.

On this theme the Western Allies concluded their preliminary meeting at Malta and prepared to fly to the Crimea for their more crucial conference with the Russians. The transport of the two heads of state and their chief diplomatic and military advisers to Yalta created considerable anxiety. The 1500-mile trip—across the Mediterranean from Malta, across Greece and the Macedonian Peninsula, and then across the Black Sea to Saki, the airfield near Sevastopol on the west side of the Crimean Peninsula, which would be their terminus—would normally have not been considered risky. But they had to fly over airfields controlled by the Germans or only recently evacuated by them, in absolute radio silence, and, save for the planes of the President and Prime Minister, without air escort. To forestall trouble, they prepared to make much of the trip in darkness. Even then they ran the chance of being fired on accidentally by Turkish antiaircraft batteries and of being held up by fog and lack of instrument-landing facilities at Saki. In order to take maximum advantage of darkness, the dispatchers routed the voyagers out of bed soon after midnight on February 3 and took them through a light, cold rain to their aircraft. In a well-organized exercise the planes were sent out at ten-minute intervals.

Exactly on time Marshall's plane set down at Saki on the morning of the third. Here he was greeted by a delegation headed by General Alexei I. Antonov, First Deputy Chief of Staff of the Red Army, who led the visitors at once to a large oval tent in which a long table, attractively set with fine crystal and silver and laden with food, awaited them. A member of Marshall's party, General Kuter, opened his book on the conference with his recollection of the Chief of Staff's reaction: "General of the Army George C. Marshall . . . was invariably dignified, controlled, and composed in public. Even [he] looked surprised at a big breakfast on February 3, 1945, when a tumbler which appeared to contain fruit juice proved to be full of Crimean brandy." [21]

The feast was completely à la russe. After the opening toasts the guests were served vodka and caviar. This substitute for orange juice, bacon, and eggs was followed by cold cuts of ham, tongue, and bologna, washed down with wine. Then a curd cake and more wine and finally apples and champagne and glasses of hot tea followed.

The heavy repast was in preparation for the long trip by car on to Yalta and the nearby villas, where they were to stay. Some eighty-five miles had to be covered by way of Simferopol before they reached their destination. The railroad would have been more direct, but the trip by automobile gave the travelers a view of the surroundings and of the impressive damage inflicted by the Germans. Although the Crimea had been cleared of the enemy, the rolling, snow-covered countryside was still strewn with shells of burnt-out buildings, wrecked tanks, and smashed railroad equipment.

From Simferopol they proceeded southeast to Alushta, on the east coast of the peninsula, and then followed a high, winding road that curved around the highest mountain in the Crimea to Yalta. Even more intriguing than the changing scenery were the thousands of young guards, many of them girls, who lined the road from Saki.[22]

At the time of the conference the name Yalta meant little to most Americans. The names of other Crimean cities—Balaclava, Sevastopol, Alma—were more likely to be recognized. Yet as *Time* reminded its readers after the meeting, Mark Twain had made the area familiar in the United States nearly eighty years earlier. His description of Yalta and the nearby homes of the czar and Russian nobles as they appeared in 1867 when the "Innocents" from the *Quaker City* were received by Czar Alexander II was still found useful by the news magazine in 1945:

> To me the place was a vision of the Sierras. The tall, gray mountains that back it, their sides bristling with pines—cloven with ravines—here and there a heavy rock towering into view—long, straight streaks sweeping down from the summit to the sea, marking the passage of some avalanche of former times—all these were as like one sees in the Sierras as if the one were a portrait of the other. The little village of Yalta nestles at the foot of an amphitheater which slopes backward and upward to the wall of hills, and looks as if it might have sunk quietly down to its present position from a higher elevation. This depression is covered with great parks and gardens of noblemen, and through the mass of green foliage the bright colors of their palaces bud out here and there like flowers. It is a beautiful spot.[23]

The later visitors were reminded of a small resort town on the Riviera. The czars and dukes who had built their villas there had kept the town small by design, even barring the railroad from coming too near. After the 1917 Revolution, the homes of the nobility had been turned into rest homes to join the sanatoria that had been built there in the days of the Romanovs.

Livadia Palace, which provided quarters for the Americans and the meeting place for the conference, was a fifty-room stone building that had replaced the earlier wooden structure occupied by Czar Alexander II at the time of Mark Twain's visit. Czar Alexander III had died in the earlier building in 1891. It was in Yalta that Nicholas II succeeded to the czardom and that his fiancée, the future Czarina Alexandra, became a member of the Orthodox Church shortly before their marriage. Since Yalta was a favorite resort of Nicholas and his wife, he built the new palace in 1911 and visited it as often as possible, particularly at Easter.[24]

The palace and two adjoining buildings were crowded by an American party of more than two hundred. The senior members of the delegation did not fare badly, but General Arnold's representative, General Kuter, shared a room with three other generals, and a similar bedroom housed eleven colonels. The junior members of the party were less lavishly accommodated. But some of the senior members mixed exclamations of delight at the beauty of the palace, the landscape, and the sea with groans of dismay at the paucity of bathrooms—built in a simple age for a more limited clientele. "Excepting only the war," said one writer, "the bathrooms were the most generally discussed subject at the Crimean Conference." [25]

The President's party did quite well. Roosevelt had the czar's first-floor apartment, and Leahy, Stettinius, and Byrnes occupied ample quarters on the same floor. The conferences were held in the banquet hall and in the grand ballroom, where the young Grand Duchess Olga had danced at her first ball.[26]

The second floor, formerly occupied by the czarina and her four daughters, supplied bedrooms for Hopkins and most of the military representatives. General Marshall had the imperial bedroom and King the czarina's boudoir. "General Marshall," Kuter recalled, "made sure that everyone understood that it was not his bedroom but Admiral King's that was reached by the concealed outside circular staircase rumored to have been built by the mad monk, Rasputin." [27]

The Livadia Palace, like the two nearby estates where the British and Russian delegations were housed, had been occupied until April 1944 by the Germans. All three had been thoroughly looted and virtually wrecked by the retreating enemy. General Deane, who had gone to Yalta from Moscow prior to the meeting, found the Livadia Palace without chairs, tables, beds, sheets, curtains—nearly everything needed for comfort. He wired General Marshall to be prepared to "rough it" in a palace devoid of heat and every item of furnishings. But in a few days the Russian hosts had changed all that. Marshall's Operations Division Chief, General Hull, reported: "When we arrived we found beds, curtains on the windows, bedsheets, pillow cases, heat, and a complete complement of maids, butlers, etc. They really did a magnificent job. The Hotel Metropol and possibly other hotels had been stripped of everything needed, including service personnel required. . . ."

As usual the Russians took no chances in protecting the Big Three. "I have never lived under such total security," Hull recalled. On one occasion when they were lining up in the grand ballroom for picture taking, he saw a demonstration he was never to forget:

> First to arrive was the President accompanied by a few secret service men in civilian clothes; next, in came Churchill with a small coterie of uniformed guards; then in came Stalin completely surrounded by so large a contingent of uniformed guards—each with an automatic Russian rifle carried in front of his chest—that it was very difficult to see Stalin.
>
> About half way between the floor and the ceiling of the room a balcony ran all the way around. As the various contingents of guards arrived, some of them placed themselves on this balcony with their guns at the ready, glaring at each other. I thought at the time that if somebody set off a fire cracker in that room all Hell would break loose.[28]

The imperial trappings, the tragedy of the Romanovs, the contrast of the old and new regimes, the gamy overtones of Rasputin's relationship with the royal family—all impressed the visitors. But there was something more, as the banter about the bathroom facilities and King's occupancy of the czarina's boudoir showed. Despite the recent setback in the Ardennes the smell of victory was in the air and it made for excitement. An atmosphere that stimulated Marshall and Leahy to twit King about the private staircase to his boudoir and that enabled the frosty naval chief to enjoy the joke reflected the passage to a new phase of the war. This light mood contrasted sharply with the sinister overtones later associated with the meeting.

Oddly enough Marshall was to be roundly condemned for his role in the major political decisions at the Yalta conference, although it was in these that he took the least part. Since many of the key and most criticized decisions—such as those dealing with German reparations, Poland, concessions in the Far East, and the three Soviet votes in the U.N.—concerned political matters, Marshall, King, and Kuter were not present when they were considered by Roosevelt, Churchill, and Stalin. Even military matters seemed less important at Yalta than at Malta. At the earlier meetings where Marshall had led the American delegation in discussing future military strategy, he had played a major role. At Yalta the military emphasis was on measures to aid the Russian advance, on demarcation of bombing areas, on exchange of intelligence information, on mutual use of air bases, and on planning dates for the end of the war. All these were important, but not crucial in the sense of the Malta decisions, and did not depend on Marshall's personal guidance.

For all his limited role Marshall was later accused of having dominated an ailing Roosevelt at the Crimean conference. Purporting to quote accurately from Admiral Leahy, Stettinius, Hanson Baldwin, and others, Senator Joseph McCarthy in his famous attack on Marshall pictured the Chief of Staff as sitting by Roosevelt's right hand in the key political meetings, pressing the President to make concessions to Russia. With total inaccuracy McCarthy charged: ". . . at Yalta, General Marshall redoubled his endeavors for Russia's entrance with all the indomitable persistence he had applied to the 'second front now' and to blocking Mark Clark and the British over the eastern European strategy." [29]

One of the few cases where the Chief of Staff took any notice of the Wisconsin senator was in regard to this statement: "I was somewhat amused . . . with the political heights [I reached] in which apparently I was king at Yalta. . . . As a matter of fact when they had the final dinner at Yalta—and it was organized by the Russians and the Americans submitted their guest lists—the U.S. Chiefs of Staff weren't even invited. The Senior Chairman, Leahy, was invited. The British Chiefs of Staff were in attendance, but the American Chiefs were left out. So that was the dominant position I occupied at that . . . time. But to read the [later] debates in Congress one would have thought I was cock of the walk all the way through. I remember Mr. Byrnes was very critical of the fact that the British Chiefs of Staff were present and King and I [and Kuter] were not." [30]

Of course the failure to invite the U.S. Chiefs was the result of an oversight or misunderstanding on the part of Roosevelt's staff; it made no difference in decisions at the conference. But beneath the wry humor Marshall hit on the important point that in the major decisions—largely political in nature—the Joint Chiefs of Staff were not consulted.

McCarthy's mention of Marshall's efforts to get Russia into the war against Japan is the least inaccurate of his accusations. Yalta saw the culmination of the long effort by the United States to get the Soviet Union's aid against Japan. An analysis of that attempt helps to put this aspect of Yalta in better perspective.

Immediately after Pearl Harbor, American leaders in Washington and the Pacific urged Russian entry into the war against Japan.[31] Marshal Stalin, fully engaged with the German Army, declined to make any aggressive move. Marshall and his associates then turned their attention to possible moves they should make in the North Pacific to counter Japanese action against the Soviet Union in Siberia. By the time of the TRIDENT conference in the spring of 1943, the Allies had worked out a formula—to be reaffirmed at later conferences: upon the defeat of the Axis in Europe they would act in cooperation with other Pacific powers "and, if possible, with Russia to . . . bring about at the earliest possible date the unconditional surrender of Japan." [32]

Although the Soviet military position improved after the winter of 1942–43, the Russians remained vague about commitments to attack Japan. But the U.S. Chiefs of Staff believed that the Soviet Union would have to fight the Japanese. For planning purposes in the late summer of 1943, the Joint Chiefs of Staff assumed that a basic conflict of interests existed between Russia and Japan in the Far East. The Russians could assure their hold on eastern Siberia only by "the ultimate expulsion of Japan from the mainland of Asia and from southern Sakhalin." Sooner or later, the Chiefs believed, the Soviet leaders would act against Japan but only after the removal of the German threat. "After that, she (Russia) will make her decision in the light of her own interests and will intervene only when she reckons that Japan can be defeated at small cost to her." [33]

The planners proposed no steps for bringing the Soviet Union into the war against Japan, and Roosevelt and Churchill did not mention the subject in sending Moscow a summary of the decisions on future strategy taken at Quebec in August. In instructing General Deane, head of the U.S. Military Mission to Moscow, to attend the October 1943 conference of foreign ministers as their representative, the American Chiefs spoke very generally, of "the great importance of the Soviet Union's full participation in the war against Japan after the defeat of Germany as essential to the prompt and crushing defeat of Japan *at far less cost to the United States and Great Britain.*" [34]

To the surprised pleasure of the Americans at the October meeting, the Russians were willing to comment privately on their future action against Japan without being asked. Secretary Hull informed Roosevelt that he had received such assurance from Stalin, and Ambassador Harriman shortly afterward told General Marshall that he had received a similar statement from Molotov.[35]

A few weeks later at Tehran, Stalin declared that he could not intervene in the Far East until Germany was defeated but indicated that an offensive could be launched against Japan as soon after that time as he could build up his forces. Roosevelt then handed him a number of questions drawn up earlier by the Joint Chiefs of Staff, asking for information on intelligence, air bases, ports, and the like that could be used by the Allies in planning for future collaboration against Japan. The Soviet Marshal postponed his reply.

On returning from Tehran to Cairo, the British and U.S. Chiefs of Staff examined and approved in principle an overall plan for the defeat of Japan that had been drawn up earlier at their request by the Combined Staff Planners. They assumed (1) that the invasion of the principal Japanese islands might not be necessary and that Japan could be defeated by air blockade and intensive air bombardment, (2) that Germany might be defeated as early as the spring of 1944, and (3) that Russia might enter the Pacific war shortly after the defeat of Germany. On balance they wanted to be prepared in case invasion proved necessary.[36]

The planners stressed that the Soviet Union be urged to enter the war as soon as possible, suggesting that its leaders be asked what they proposed to do when they came in and the help they wanted from the United States.[37] In approving this recommendation more than a year before Yalta, the British and U.S. Chiefs of Staff added: "We are agreed that every effort should be exerted to bring the U.S.S.R. into the war against Japan at the earliest practicable date, and that plans should be prepared in that event." [38]

In unanimously supporting pressure on the Soviet Union to join the struggle against Japan, the Joint Chiefs of Staff did not take into consideration what Stalin might ask in return. Two assumptions underlay this seemingly naïve oversight: that Russian national interests would bring them in and that any question of territorial concessions was a political one to be settled by the heads of governments. At Tehran, Stalin made some of those interests clear to the political leaders. He wanted the Kurile Islands, to which Russia had surrendered its claims years before to Japan, and southern Sakhalin, ceded by Russia to Japan at the close of the Russo-Japanese War.[39]

Anticipating some such request, the President mentioned that possibility to Chiang Kai-shek at Cairo before he talked with Stalin at Tehran. Some months later when Vice President Henry Wallace talked with the Generalissimo, he reported that Stalin had expressed a desire for a warm-water outlet in the Far East and that Roosevelt had suggested that Dairen be made a free port. Chiang revealed that he had already discussed the matter with the President "and had indicated his agreement provided the U.S.S.R. cooperated with China in the Far East and provided there was no impairment of Chinese sovereignty." [40]

In view of Churchill's later suggestion that he had merely gone along with the President at Yalta in making concessions to Russia at China's expense, it is worth examining his reactions a year earlier at Tehran when Stalin hinted at some of his future demands.

In discussing the great size of the Soviet Union the Prime Minister said that he thought a land mass as great as Russia deserved access to warm-water ports—a question that would "form part of the peace settlement . . . [and] could be settled agreeably and as between friends." Seeing his opportunity, Stalin quickly retorted "that since Mr. Churchill had raised the question he would like to inquire as to the regime of the Dardanelles." Even here Churchill thought something could be worked out, although he frankly said that this had not always been his view. Roosevelt tactfully shifted the discussion to northern areas, saying that he had been examining the possibility of establishing the former Hanseatic cities of Bremen, Hamburg and Lübeck in some form of a free zone, with the Kiel Canal put under international control and guarantee. Marshal Stalin said "he thought that was a good idea, and then asked what could be done for Russia in the Far East." [41]

Diplomatic when he wanted to be, the gruff Soviet leader carefully avoided the appearance of haste or grasping in saying that "of course the Russians had their views, but that it would perhaps be better to await the time when the Russians would be taking an active representation in the Far Eastern war." He opened the door on his thinking, however, saying "that there was no port in the Far East that was not closed off, since Vladivostok was only partly ice-free, and besides covered by Japanese controlled Straits."

Foreseeing this argument, Roosevelt suggested that "the idea of a free port might be applied to the Far East besides, and mentioned Dairen as a possibility." Since this was not quite what Stalin had in mind, he replied that he doubted if "the Chinese would like such a scheme." Roosevelt, who had already sounded out Chiang Kai-shek on the subject, was sure that "he thought they would like the idea of a free port under international guaranty." That "would not be bad," Stalin observed, repeating that Russia had only one ice-free port, Murmansk.

Churchill, who had talked with Stalin in Moscow, a month before the Tehran meeting, recognized that a list of particulars for the Far East awaited the Allies. In a curious way the remarks with which he closed the discussion were likely to whet rather than curb the Russian's appetite. The Prime Minister declared "that it was important that the nations who would govern the world after the war, and also would be entrusted with the direction of the world after the war, should be satisfied and have no territorial or other ambitions. If that question could be settled in a manner agreeable to the great powers, he felt then that the world might indeed remain at peace. He said that the hungry nations and ambitious nations are dangerous, and he would like to see the leading nations of the world in the position of rich, happy men." [42]

At Tehran, without any military advisers present, both Roosevelt and

Churchill recognized the need of making considerable concessions to Stalin, not so much to induce him to enter the war against Japan, but as a means of associating him with them in keeping the peace. Although Roosevelt at the close of that conference did not know the full extent of Stalin's designs on Japanese-held territory and leaseholds, he was aware of many of the demands that would be made later at Yalta. More to the point, he announced them to members of the Pacific War Council in Washington on January 12, 1944. The council members—all the Allies involved in the joint effort in the Pacific—who heard him that day represented China, the Netherlands, Canada, New Zealand, Australia, the Philippines, and Great Britain. The summary of the council meeting includes these points:

> . . . President Roosevelt informed the Council that his discussions with Generalissimo Chiang Kai-shek and with Marshal Stalin were highly satisfactory—in that both had agreed that Japan should be stripped of her island possessions and that the civil control of the islands north of the equator should be taken over by the United Nations, while the policing of the Western Pacific and, therefore, the necessary air and naval bases should be taken over by those powers capable of exercising effective military control. Marshal Stalin had specifically agreed to the idea that Manchuria, Formosa and the Pescadores should be returned to China; that the Koreans are not yet capable of exercising and maintaining independent government and that they should be placed under a 40-year tutelage; that Russia, having no ice-free port in Siberia, is desirous of getting one and that Marshal Stalin looks with favor on making Dairen a free port for all the world, with the idea that Siberian exports and imports could be sent through the port of Dairen and carried to Siberian territory over the Manchurian railroad in bond. He agrees that the Manchurian Railway should become the property of the Chinese Government. He wishes all of Sakhalin to be returned to Russia and to have the Kurile Islands turned over to Russia in order that they may exercise control of the straits leading to Siberia.
>
> President Roosevelt stated that it was extremely gratifying to him to find that the Generalissimo and Marshal Stalin saw "eye to eye" with him on all major problems in the Pacific and that he felt that there would be no difficulty in reaching agreements about the control of the Pacific once Japan had been completely conquered.[43]

To the President the restoration to Russia of some of the possessions she had held in the Far East prior to the Russo-Japanese War did not mean that he was making the Soviet Union a Pacific power. Instead, he saw it as shoring up the Soviet Union against Japan's possible recovery of great strength in that area—and a Soviet bulwark there was much to be desired in January 1944. There is no evidence that he or Churchill ever sought a military opinion on the military advantages or disadvantages of these arrangements or that the members of the American or British Chiefs of Staff would have questioned the political aims of Churchill and Roosevelt had they been asked.

With the Allies steadily advancing in the Central and Southwest Pacific, War Department planners in the spring and summer of 1944 continued to search for means to end the war as speedily as possible. While they agreed that sea and air blockade and air bombardment could lower Japan's ability and will to resist, they saw no guarantee by these methods of achieving an early unconditional surrender. Consequently they observed that it might be necessary to invade the Japanese home islands. Admiral Leahy later stated that he doubted the need of an invasion and that he believed that naval action alone at length could have defeated the Japanese. This view, which perhaps all of the U.S. Chiefs of Staff shared, overlooks the stress on "early" defeat. Much of the case for invading Japan was based on the hope of hastening the end of the war with Japan and of reducing the number of American casualties.[44]

For planning purposes only, therefore, Marshall and his colleagues in early July 1944 approved advances through the Ryukyus, Bonins, and southeast China, with the objectives of intensifying the air bombardment of Japan and creating a situation favorable for an amphibious assault on Kyushu and a "decisive stroke against the industrial heart of Japan by an amphibious attack through the Tokyo Plain assisted by continued pressure from Kyushu." [45]

Opinions differed in the War Department over the need for pressing the speedy ending of the war. In response to General Marshall's request for arguments on this point, his principal long-range planner, General Embick, suggested that Russia, which would normally be expected to enter the war against Japan to protect her own interests, might delay this action until she could occupy Manchuria at a minimum effort if it appeared that the United States attached great importance to a speedy conclusion of the war.[46]

Embick was not proposing to keep Russia out of the war but attempting to make sure of her early entry. For he considered the proposed invasion of the home islands one of "unprecedented military magnitude," which should not be undertaken until the Japanese defense potential had been materially reduced. He suggested that once U.S. forces were securely established in the Bonins, the Ryukyus, and on the China coast, they should await the cooperation of the Soviet Union. Meanwhile they could make use of their great air and naval strength to cut down enemy resistance.

Marshall did not favor this kind of maneuver. Rather he leaned toward the views of the Chief of the Operations Division and of several members of his staff incorporated in a draft reply to Embick. Although for some reason Marshall decided against sending the message—preferring perhaps to discuss the matter with the strategic planner—it was clear that he wished to press the attack against Japan. "At first thought it seems to me that our bargaining position in this matter would be weakened rather than strengthened by slowing down the tempo of operations against Japan. On the Russian side they have to consider that their armies in Manchuria will be confronted by the largest concentrations of Japanese ground troops and therefore the fighting will be bitter in the extreme. . . . Should we adopt such a scheme as you suggest the Russians might reasonably think we are maneuvering to get them into the fight in such a manner that they will suffer the major losses."

"I agree with you," the Chief of Staff continued, "that we should exploit our sea and air power to the utmost during a rapid advance to the heart of Japan." But he drew the line at a deliberate slowdown: ". . . have you considered the political and economic acceptability of deliberately extending the length of the war with Japan?" Do you think, he asked, that ground opposition to divisions landing in Japan will be less under a plan delaying the landings, permitting the enemy to build up his forces, "or under a plan calling for a rapid movement against the heart of the Japanese homeland, taking full advantage of his increasing transportation difficulties in redeploying his troops due to the heavy sinkings of shipping we are carrying out day by day?" [47]

Marshall was aware of Russia's growing sensitivity about its role in the fight against Japan. Harriman had already reported Stalin's reaction to the report on the second Quebec conference. Noting that it contained no specific plan for Soviet cooperation, the Marshal asked if the Western Allies still wanted his aid in defeating Japan. Both sides were being coy about taking the first concrete step; if the Allies asked Stalin's help, they made it easier for him to state stiff demands. The President handled the matter as if it were completely settled. Blandly he wired Moscow that he had never doubted Stalin's intentions since the agreements were made concerning the Far East at Tehran; a week later he assured the Russian leader that he accepted his statement that he wanted to assist.[48]

Meanwhile the Joint Chiefs of Staff were outlining specific proposed missions for the Soviet Union, listing as priority tasks the destruction of the Japanese ground and air forces in Manchuria and the occupation of southern Sakhalin. In addition they asked for naval support and the use of a naval base at Petropavlovsk as well as the use of air bases on the Kamchatka Peninsula.[49] Without indicating any acceptance of earlier Russian requests, the act of specifying Russian missions in Manchuria and southern Sakhalin entailed as a concomitant that Stalin's victorious forces in these areas would be solidly emplaced to enforce his postwar demands. It was the logic of this arrangement, rather than any specific pressure by the Joint Chiefs of Staff at Yalta, that reinforced the President's willingness to make political concessions there.

Apparently satisfied with the role he was to play, Stalin was in an amiable mood in Moscow in mid-October 1944 when he discussed future operations with Churchill and Eden. The Marshal accepted the outlined objectives and the United States requests for air bases and a naval base and disclosed that the Soviet forces would begin an offensive against Japan within three months after the end of the war in Europe. In turn he requested equipment, food, and fuel for a build-up in Siberia.[50]

Six weeks before Yalta the U.S. Joint Staff Planners had presented a cautious report—accepted by Marshall and the other Chiefs—on assistance to the Russians:

> Throughout current war planning there is implicit conviction that the defeat of Japan may be accomplished without Russian participation in the war. As a corollary it has been considered that our main effort is a first charge against our forces and resources and that no support which would prejudice this effort could be afforded Russia. However, there is also general recognition of the desirability, from our standpoint, of Russia's early entry into the war in order to add to the weight of force which may be applied to obtaining the earliest possible Japanese defeat. Within limitations imposed by time, availability of forces and resources, and by lines of communication there will remain the capability for undertaking measures to encourage Russian entry into the war and to provide some degree of support prior to and after their entry. . . .
> *Russia's interests in the Far East and in post-war world politics will undoubtedly force her entry into the war against Japan. Unless Japan strikes first, the factors affecting the timing of Russia's entry will be predominately those of self-interest.* It is probable, however, that logistical and operational support from us would be significant in influencing the time of Russia's entry; specifically, assistance in building up her level of supplies in the Far East.[51]

Pre-Yalta discussion now turned not on the necessity of bringing the Soviet Union into the war, but on the means necessary to get the maximum possible help in *shortening* the conflict. Again the Joint Staff Planners were set to work. The memorandum they recommended be sent the President was approved by the Joint Chiefs of Staff on January 18, 1945:

> The Joint Chiefs of Staff have been guided by the following basic principles in working toward U.S.S.R. entry into the war against Japan:
> Russia's entry at as early a date as possible consistent with her ability to engage in offensive operations is necessary to provide maximum assistance to our Pacific operations. The U.S. will provide maximum support possible without interfering with our main effort against Japan.
> The objective of Russia's military effort against Japan in the Far East should be the defeat of the Japanese forces in Manchuria, air operations against Japan proper in collaboration with U.S. Air Forces based in eastern Siberia, and maximum interference with Japanese sea traffic between Japan and the mainland of Asia.[52]

In this declaration the planners and the Joint Chiefs of Staff exhibited a growing tendency to insist on more specific commitments from the Soviet Union and reflected explicit proposals made to Marshall by General Deane a few weeks before Yalta.

Months of negotiating with the Russians for the use of bases, for exchange of technical information, for handling of prisoners and the like had made General Deane extremely wary of handing over supplies without firm pledges in advance. At the beginning of December 1944 he proposed to General Marshall that the United States thereafter try a different approach in dealing with the Russians. Months earlier, when the Red

Army had been set "back on its heels," it had been proper for the United States to bolster Russian morale in every possible way. Now that the situation had improved, he said, the United States should change its approach.

In a careful analysis of the situation Deane explained that part of the trouble arose from Russian suspicions of foreigners. "They simply cannot understand giving without taking, and as a result even our giving is viewed with suspicion. Gratitude cannot be banked in the Soviet Union. Each transaction is complete in itself without regard to past favors. The party of the second part is either a shrewd trader to be admired or a sucker to be despised."

He made it clear that the picture was not all bad—the individual Russians were likable, and he thought that they would be friendly if they dared. "The Soviets have done an amazing job for their own people—both in the war and in the prewar period. One cannot help admire their war effort and the spirit with which it has been accomplished. We have few conflicting interests, and there is little reason why we should not be friendly now and in the foreseeable future."

Deane laid down a number of principles that should regulate future relations with the Soviet Union: (1) "Continue to assist the Soviet Union, provided they request such assistance, and we are satisfied that it contributes to winning the war; (2) insist that they justify their needs for assistance . . . (3) in all cases where our assistance does not contribute to winning the war, we should insist on a quid pro quo; (4) . . . present proposals for collaboration that would be mutually beneficial and then leave the next move to them; (5) when our proposals for collaboration are unanswered after a reasonable time, we should act as we think best and inform them of our actions; and (6) . . . stop pushing ourselves on them and make [them] come to us."

General Marshall was impressed by Deane's arguments, but when he prepared to send his letter to the President, Generals Handy and Hull suggested that it might prejudice the President against Deane and also embarrass Deane with Harriman. In forwarding the letter to Stimson, Marshall noted: "I agree with them [Handy and Hull], though I am sorry that we can't send the letter to the President because his ideas are very well expressed and I agree with them in toto." The Secretary obviously shared Marshall's views. Soon after the Chief of Staff asked Deane if Harriman had seen the letter and if there was any objection to sending it to the Secretary of State and perhaps the President. General Deane replied at once that Harriman had seen the letter and concurred in the proposal to send it to both the White House and the State Department. Marshall's acting Secretary General Staff, Colonel Pasco, drafted a note to Roosevelt for Stimson to sign describing the accompanying letter as "splendid and sound." It is not clear whether the letter had any influence on its recipients, but Marshall seemed to be reflecting some of the Deane doctrine when he advised Eisenhower in mid-January to use "simple Main Street Abilene style in talking to Stalin—he likes it." [53]

Despite his action Marshall's approval of Deane's views did not become generally known. After the war when Deane's letter was made public, Marshall was accused of withholding it from the President, and on the basis of this inaccurate charge there were further speculations that had he sent it to the White House, American policy would have been different at Yalta. The record is clear. Marshall and Stimson not only approved Deane's arguments; they made their approval evident to the President when they forwarded the letter to him.

From this evidence it is difficult to agree that Roosevelt was badgered by his Chiefs of Staff into making concessions to the Russians in the Far East at the expense of China. Indeed a striking change had taken place in the Joint Chiefs' position since Tehran. At the 1943 meeting the military leaders had seemed more intent than they were at Yalta on getting Soviet assistance, while Roosevelt had attempted to moderate Stalin's territorial demands.

Several explanations have been advanced for the President's final decision to honor Russia's demands near the end of the Yalta conference, even agreeing to points—subject to Chinese acceptance—that had not been raised earlier by Stalin. There is the view that he assumed that the Russians were in a position to move into Manchuria, the Kuriles, and Sakhalin at the close of the war and would thus be in a position to enforce their demands. It would therefore be pointless to oppose what would soon be a *fait accompli.*

Others suggest that he was mortally tired, or wanted desperately to secure Soviet aid for the United Nations Organization, or hoped to get better arrangements in Central Europe by concessions in the Far East. An alternative explanation is that he believed he could get peace between the Nationalists and Communists in China by promoting agreement between Chiang Kai-shek and Stalin or that, like Churchill, he felt that a sated Russia would be a peaceful Russia.

Whatever the reason, Roosevelt accepted the Soviet Union's demands and Churchill became co-signer. Since his feeling toward China was largely disgust, the Prime Minister's concessions must have bothered him less than those he had made a few months earlier to the Soviet Union in Bulgaria and Rumania in exchange for the chief role in Greece. Acquiescence of the two Allied leaders in Stalin's schemes opened the way to postwar charges of corrupt bargains. The Far Eastern agreements, revealed some months later when the Western Allies were accusing the Russians of failing to live up to their commitments on Poland and Germany, brought down harsh condemnation on everyone connected with the conference.

The early defenders of the President argued that he had given in to Russian demands only because of Joint Chiefs of Staff pressure for the

Soviet Union's entry into the war against Japan.[54] But as we shall see, the record does not support any such leverage by the Chiefs of Staff.

At their first meeting in Yalta—on the morning of February 4—the President and his military advisers talked briefly of the meeting the British and American military staffs were to hold with their Russian counterparts later in the day. Leahy said that it was necessary for Marshal Stalin to instruct his staff to participate in full and free discussions with the Allied staffs. He also thought it desirable to have coordination and exchange of information among Eisenhower, Alexander, and the Red Army Staff. General Marshall added that the direct liaison for day-to-day communication between the Allied commanders and the Russians was vital.[55]

Shortly before the military meeting broke up, Secretary of State Stettinius and Harriman joined the group.[56] Stettinius invited the military Chiefs to remain "in order that they might be fully informed of the diplomatic position of the State Department and thus be in a position to correlate this with the secret military conferences that were to take place with the Chiefs of Staff of the three countries."

The Secretary of State listed seven major topics on which the President should be prepared to talk with Marshal Stalin. These were: (1) postwar international organization; (2) an emergency European high commission to function during the interim period between the end of the war and the setting up of the permanent organization; (3) treatment of Germany, political and economic; (4) Poland; (5) Allied Control Commissions in Rumania, Bulgaria, and Hungary; (6) Iranian relations; and (7) China. It was clear that all these were political questions and the Chiefs of Staff were not asked for opinions, nor did they express any.[57]

Under the topic of China the question was raised of the desirability of seeking Soviet and British assistance in composing the relations between the Chiang Kai-shek government and the Chinese Communists. At mention of China, Ambassador Harriman spoke of Stalin's wishes in the Far East. The full account of the remainder of the meeting follows:

> Mr. Harriman stated that Marshal Stalin would very likely wish to raise the question of what the Russians would get out of the Pacific war. He stated that they would want the southern half of Sakhalin, and the Kuriles. They would wish to maintain the *status quo* in Outer Mongolia and to obtain control over the railroad running to Dairen.
>
> The President said he wished to have the views of Generalissimo Chiang Kai-shek before discussing the *status quo* in Mongolia but was ready to go ahead on the other questions.
>
> At this point Mr. Matthews and Mr. Hiss entered the meeting to discuss the papers prepared by the Department of State for the President.[58]

There is no official record of any discussion on these demands. If there was strong objection—and there were two State Department memoranda by George H. Blakeslee and Hugh Borton opposing concessions on the Kuriles and Sakhalin, which Roosevelt apparently did not see—this was the time dissent should have been voiced. But the official record shows no such disagreement.[59]

Subsequently Admiral King was quoted as saying that "the Joint Chiefs of Staff did not agree with the President's ideas of 'sweetening' Stalin in order to obtain his help against the Japanese, for it seemed to King and his military colleagues that the price asked was far too high. . . . The U.S. Chiefs felt that the southern part of Sakhalin would have been quite enough, but as the Joint Chiefs of Staff did not make political policy, their views did not prevail." [60]

Admiral Leahy mentions no discussion on concessions at Yalta. His first point—that he did not believe Russian entry into the war against Japan was necessary—is often quoted, while his statement that it seemed reasonable to him that Russia should have back what had been taken from her, "and no one was more surprised than I to see these conditions agreed to at Yalta labeled as some horrendous concessions made by President Roosevelt to an enemy" is usually forgotten.[61]

General Marshall, in discussing the concessions in 1957, was positive on the matter: "I did not talk to the President about the need of making concessions to Russia in order to get help against Japan. Stalin had been very specific as to what he could do if we gave him time in which to do it. He discussed with me how long it would take to move the troops they would have to move through Siberia to get ready for the attack in cooperation with us. . . . He went into the days required, the character of the attack, as I recall, and [ultimately] he followed out the schedule that he talked over—to the day—when the event finally developed in the opening of the war against Japan." Marshall was also quite certain that his colleagues did not oppose concessions at Yalta. "This was news to me when it came out in recent years." [62]

Perhaps the best witness is General Arnold's representative, General Kuter, since he had no personal position to defend in later years. His statement is worth quoting *in extenso:*

> During this general orientation session on United States military and United States diplomatic positions, views and objectives, no special point was made concerning the entry of Russia into the war with Japan. Ever since the subject had first been mentioned to Stalin at Teheran more than a year earlier, the United States planners had assumed that Russian entry into the war against Japan was a naturally assured fact. American plans and preparations had gone forward on that basis. After Guadalcanal and Tarawa, it had been apparent that, should an invasion of the main islands of the Japanese homeland be necessary, such an invasion would be very costly in American killed and wounded. Iwo Jima and Okinawa were shortly to provide bloody confirmation of those fears. At various times estimates went as high as half a million Americans required for such an invasion, with the expectation that one hundred thousand Americans might be casualties. The United States Joint Chiefs of Staff were on record that it would be desirable that Russia enter the war as quickly as she could do so without cost to the Allied efforts in Europe and the

Pacific or in other theaters of war. Additional Russian, air, ground, and sea pressure against the Japs in Manchuria and in their home island would hasten the surrender of Japan, and would surely make an invasion of the home island less costly in American lives if such an invasion had to be made. With the knowledge that their losses in the Russo-Japanese war still rankled in the Red minds, it was normal and natural to assume that Russia would sometime move the forces fighting the Germans and then retake the areas lost in the Russo-Japanese war. The United States military believed it desirable that the Russians enter the war against Japan quickly. All was a matter of time. All was believed generally settled at Teheran at the end of 1943.

And then he gives the lie to military pressure on Roosevelt:

Neither at this conference nor at any other military conference attended by General Arnold's representative was there any discussion of any "deal" or terms on which Russia should enter the war against Japan, although at this conference Mr. Harriman stated that Stalin would likely wish to raise the question of what the Russians would get out of the Pacific War, and observed that they would want the Kuriles and the southern half of Sakhalin.[63]

Marshall did not sit at the President's side when concessions in the Far East were made. There were seven sessions attended by the heads of state. The General was at the first, at which he summarized the military situation in Europe, and he was at one of the final meetings, where topics other than the Far East were discussed. At the intervening conferences attended by Roosevelt, Stalin and Churchill, Admiral Leahy represented the U.S. Chiefs of Staff. Although Marshall, more than any of the other Chiefs, wanted a quick end of the war—because he knew that the Army would suffer most of the casualties in a long-drawn-out conflict and because he knew intimately the precarious manpower situation—he did not dictate or materially influence the President's decision on the Far East at the Crimean conference.

Marshall's own reaction to the controversy over the Crimean conference was characteristically temperate:

I think Yalta has become so much a political factor, a political discussion, that it would be almost impossible to get the real reactions of the day and the time. I find in all these things when you go into . . . the historical discussions, and they get into Congress . . . they are so twisted that it is almost impossible to discuss them. And you find on the part of officers very frequently, tragically, I think, too frequently, that their later states of mind don't accord with what they had in mind at the time. [He was alluding to statements by Leahy and King indicating that they made more of a fight on concessions than he remembered or than the record showed.] Apparently they are sort of 'backed out' by the political recriminations and accusations. But this is to be expected though I think it was far too common except that we had a tremendous political war on. We had a Republican Party that had been out of power for a long time. They had built up a great deal of feeling towards Mr. Roosevelt and there was some Democratic assistance to it, I believe. And they were trying in every way to find a basis for defeating him in case he ran again for re-election. . . . But in all these matters I find that the minute [a question] gets into the political ring, it

[is] very difficult for the ordinary citizen to ever ferret out the truth of the matter.[64]

The President's decisions at Yalta flowed obviously from earlier agreements or concessions made as far back as Tehran. The fault at Yalta lay in concessions that legitimized Soviet spoils.[65] More important the American and British leaders failed to agree on political considerations marking the final phases of the military defeat of Germany. General Eisenhower was left to make his decisions purely on the basis of military factors.

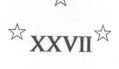

The Faltering Axis

GENERAL Marshall scowled as he got out of the car that had
brought him from the airport at Pisa to General Clark's headquarters near Florence. Clark had disregarded a message the Chief of Staff had
sent him a short time before. In announcing his proposed visit—on the
way back from Yalta to the United States—Marshall had stipulated: "Do
not meet me at the airport. I will come to your headquarters. No honors."
When the Army Group commander had attempted to argue these points,
the Chief of Staff had reiterated: "Don't meet me. No honors repeat no
honors." [1] Marshall's orders should have settled the matter, but Clark, in
keeping with the title of his postwar book, took a "calculated risk." When
Marshall reached the headquarters, there was a large honor guard to greet
him. Ready for his inspection were representatives of all the nationalities
then under the 15th Army Group, which Clark had commanded since the
previous November. [2]

Clark owed his escape from Marshall's legendary, though rarely unleashed, wrath to recent statements by Representative Clare Boothe Luce,
Republican of Connecticut, that had upset War Department officials. On
her return from a visit to the Italian theater with other members of the
House Committee on Military Affairs, Mrs. Luce had declared that
morale was extremely low in Italy because operations there were receiving
little attention in the American press. To her embarrassment and to the
dismay of Stimson and Marshall the press overemphasized the "forgotten
front" routine.

These reports, Marshall declared later, "hit morale a dreadful blow—a
really dreadful blow—and some of the corps commanders told me they
didn't know what to do about their troops. They had gotten obsessed with
the fact that we had forgotten them entirely. Well, of course, the semi-
amusing part of this was the troops in the Southwest Pacific [earlier] had
exactly that same feeling about the troops in Africa. All the writing was
about the troops in Africa and the troops in Sicily, and they felt they were

being ignored. Now they were into the fighting, and the troops in Italy were obsessed with the idea that they were forgotten. And this thing just rattled back and forth. . . . The battle to maintain morale under those conditions was very hard and it was quite amazing that we got through that as well as we did. But I think the battle in Italy, where they were told we had forgotten those divisions . . . was one of the hardest of all—was one of the most absurd . . . challenges that [we] could have gotten." [3]

Counterattacking, Marshall wrote into Roosevelt's 1945 State of the Union message to Congress a special tribute to the fighting men in Italy and directed commanders in that theater to circulate the statement widely.[4]

General Marshall and the War Department were further disconcerted a few weeks later when British Field Marshal Alexander invited Mrs. Luce to visit his troops at the Italian front. Since the War Department had just turned down Representative Everett Dirksen's request to visit the front there, Republican leader Joe Martin inquired bluntly why Dirksen was being excluded and Mrs. Luce admitted, and he threatened to attack the Army and administration on the House floor for playing politics. A War Department spokesman explained that Mrs. Luce was a guest of the British and that the Army had nothing to do with the invitation. Policy on visits to fighting fronts by congressmen who were not members of the military affairs committees, he added, was a Joint Chiefs of Staff decision. Martin retorted: "Come on now, everybody knows who runs the Joint Chiefs of Staff." [5]

Marshall's visit to Italy, intended to show the troops that the Chief of Staff remembered them and had their contributions vividly in mind, gave Clark his chance to parade representatives of the various units under his command. Ranged before Marshall's still somewhat disapproving gaze were soldiers from the United States, Scotland, Wales, Ireland, India, Brazil, Canada, South Africa, Poland, Italy (partisans as well as regulars), and nurses and women auxiliaries from the U.S., South Africa, Canada, and India. Of the groups that had served under Clark only the French and the Nisei, who had fought with great distinction, were missing. They had been shifted to the south of France the previous summer and now were fighting in Western Europe.[6]

The visitor's glacial displeasure melted as he reviewed the polyglot forces. Clark breathed easier when the Chief of Staff admitted that he was glad that the General had ignored his instructions.

Clark's demonstration succeeded because it emphasized the united effort being made to defeat the Axis. After a hard winter the Allied forces were making headway again. Stalin had made clear to Marshall at Yalta that the Russians were moving toward Central Europe. On the day that the Chief of Staff came to Clark's headquarters, Eisenhower's forces were launching their attack toward the Roer.

Halfway around the world the first convoy from Ledo—led by Major General Lewis Pick over the famous Ledo Road from India to China, won and built at great cost—had reached Kunming. And elements of Krueger's Sixth Army captured Manila after two weeks of bitter fighting. MacArthur's announcement had reached Yalta at a luncheon meeting of Foreign Ministers on February 5, and, the official record reports, "Mr. Molotov immediately proposed a toast to the victory of the Allied armies." [7] Soon afterward Marshall drafted a message to MacArthur for Roosevelt's signature. He wrote: "Congratulations to you personally and to your commanders and troops on the liberation of Manila. This is an historical moment in the re-establishment of freedom and decency in the Far East, and the celerity of movement and economy of force involved in this victory add immeasurably to our appreciation of your success. Please give the men of the guerrilla forces my thanks and congratulations on their gallant contribution to the campaign and especially for the years of suffering they have endured in preparation for this moment." [8]

After years of holding actions, of disasters, and disheartening setbacks, the Allies now moved confidently toward victory. Roadblocks still remained. The manpower situation in the U.S. forces in Europe was not completely solved, severe winter weather interfered with plans for attack on the western front and particularly in Italy, and in the Italian theater there was also the persistent morale problem.

Another problem in Italy especially disturbed Marshall: the performance of the 92d Division, made up of Negro enlisted men and Negro and white officers. He reluctantly described the division as untrustworthy under fire shortly after it had gone into the line.[9]

Writing Eisenhower to request the shift of the veteran Japanese-American 442 Infantry Regiment from France back to Italy to help retrieve the situation along the 92d Division front, General Marshall explained that the division, holding twenty-two miles on the Fifth Army left front in a final tryout during a three-day offensive, had been heavily supported by air and tanks. It had met little opposition on most parts of the front, "but the Infantry literally dissolved each night abandoning equipment and even clothing in some cases." He said that the artillery, engineers, and other divisional troops appeared excellent, and the command and staff were superior. "But as matters now stand, the division itself is not only of little value but weakens the front by necessitating the putting of other divisions in the rear to provide the necessary security against a local German thrust through to Leghorn and supply lines, divisions that should otherwise be disposed in the center of the army." [10]

Marshall's criticisms of the division reflected his great disappointment after the high hopes he had held for it. A strong advocate of protection of rights of black troops from his days as senior instructor of the 33d Division in Illinois and as the head of the Infantry School at Fort Benning, he had pressed hard for equable treatment for Negroes as Chief of the Staff of the

Army. Just as he had taken special pains to see that the 93d Division and other Negro units in the Pacific had special training and preparation before going into action in that theater, he insisted that the 92d Division be completely readied for its assignment in Italy. Since he had taken this course despite considerable reluctance among Army commanders to use Negro troops in combat roles, the poor performance of the unit not only angered him but made him fear that opposition to further use of black troops in combat would be strengthened.[11]

After changes had been made to increase the combat efficiency of the division, commanded by Major General Edward N. Almond, the War Department arranged for Secretary Stimson's civilian aide on Negro affairs, Truman Gibson, Jr., to visit Italy. After his trip Gibson issued a statement in which he blamed part of the difficulties on promotion policy in the division, on the large number of black troops from the two lowest categories of IQ scores, and on discrimination against Negro officers in the division. He was sharply attacked by some of the more militant Negro papers, which resented his remark on illiteracy in the division. He was also accused of being an "Uncle Tom" for agreeing in any way with any criticism of the fighting qualities of the troops.[12]

On his return from Italy General Marshall now had to grapple with the problems of winding up the war in Europe. It seemed likely that late spring would see the defeat of Germany. Since mid-1943 he had had members of his staff working on redeployment of units from the European Theater of Operations to the Pacific. Now directives went out to Eisenhower and McNarney to screen their units for men to go to the Pacific. Specific units were earmarked for later duty, and a search began for experienced officers to lead units in the invasion of Japan. In light of Washington's great stress on the speedy redeployment of one or more armies from Europe within a few days after the war's close there, Eisenhower's decision of mid-April to stop at the Elbe is more understandable.

As the defeat of Germany neared, dozens of questions—attainment of unconditional surrender, partition of Germany, establishment of military government, arrangement of occupation zones and lines of demarcation between advance units of the Allies and the Russians, and growing tension in relations with the Russians—became increasingly significant to the Chiefs of Staff and their political chiefs in Washington and London.

The story of the last three months in the European struggle, seen from Washington, consisted mainly of British efforts to have a larger share in the final victory, Churchill's desire to establish the greatest advantage possible over the Russians, and Western dismay—leading to stiffening attitudes toward the Russians—as Soviet suspicion and rudeness toward the Western Allies increased daily. At Yalta the Russians had served warning that they expected to make a hard peace with the Germans. Although acquiescing to a degree to Russian demands for reparations, Churchill favored moderation much more than he had in the past. He still was willing to discuss in principle the partition of Germany but was disposed to reduce Roosevelt's proposal for dividing Germany into five or seven states to somewhat fewer and to postpone to a later date the Russian proposal on dismemberment.[13]

In purely military matters the Russian Army representatives at Yalta seemed interested in cooperating with the Allies on the final stages of the battle.[14] Although General Alexei I. Antonov, First Deputy Chief of Staff, was reluctant to agree on specific liaison between Allied and Russian commanders on bombing arrangements, he expressed willingness to work closely with them on movement of ground troops, air operations in support of ground forces, and details of operations.[15]

Meeting with Russian military representatives on February 5, both Marshall and Brooke asked for continued Soviet operations to aid the offensive in the West. Brooke said that the actual crossing of the Rhine presented the greatest problems for the Western Allies and expressed the hope that operations on the eastern front, which he recognized would be difficult because of thaw and mud, would be continued. Aware from Eisenhower's recent statements that he critically needed Russian assistance, General Marshall pointed out that the Western forces were threatened by their insufficient ground superiority. Although they had air superiority, bad weather might neutralize this power at any time. If an enemy thrust came at such a period, the lack of ground superiority could prove serious. "Another restriction arose from the fact that there were only a small number of favorable locations for crossing the Rhine. It was therefore most important to insure that the enemy could not concentrate strongly at the point of attack." The Germans were operating behind the Rhine and the Siegfried Line and had freedom of maneuver, but, he concluded, they must not be allowed to concentrate against the Allies on the very narrow bridgehead available.[16]

Antonov replied that as Stalin had pointed out, "the Russians would continue the offensive in the East as long as the weather permitted." While there might be interruptions because of the weather, "The Soviet Army would . . . take measures to make such interruptions as short as possible and would continue the offensive to the limit of their ability." The Russians did not believe that the Germans could transfer large forces from the eastern front to the West, Antonov continued. The question was whether the Allies could prevent the Germans from shifting forces from the Italian front to the East.

Brooke made no effort to exaggerate the Allied potential in Italy. The Germans had certain advantages there because of terrain—notably a series of rivers that made it possible for them to conduct rearguard actions while withdrawing forces gradually. The enemy would have to retreat through the Ljubljana Gap or the passes of the Alps. "The coast in the Bay of Venice," he noted, "was not suitable for amphibious operations, and therefore outflanking operations in the Adriatic did not appear fruitful." There had been continuous offensive operations to drive the enemy out of the Apennine Line and into the valley of the Po, but winter weather and floods had brought operations almost to a standstill.[17] Since the Allies could do no more than hold down the rate of withdrawal, they had decided to switch five divisions to the western front.

Realizing that Brooke's explanation was not satisfying Antonov, General Marshall called attention to the importance of Allied airpower in Italy. Air Chief Marshal Portal divulged that there were a total of 14,000 U.S. and British aircraft on the western and Italian fronts. "Everything possible would be done," he said, "as General Marshall had stated, to bring the greatest possible air assistance to the vital points of attack in the land offensive. Such air assistance included the operations of a number of airborne divisions, for which the necessary transport was available." Portal added that, so far as requirements of the land battle permitted, the strategic bomber forces would concentrate on the enemy's oil supply. The Western Allies also proposed to continue their attacks on railway communications in order to stop troop movements, even though previous efforts had produced disappointing results because the enemy repaired the facilities with relative ease. Since the Allies knew that the Germans intended to assemble a strong force of jet-propelled fighters during the year, they had decided to hit jet-fighter plants. "It was an agreed principle that when the land offensive began," Portal said, "everything in the air that could contribute to its success should be so used."

Still the Russians were not reassured. At this point General Marshall stressed that the British and American Chiefs had agreed to implement the request Antonov had made at the session the previous day—that airpower be employed to prevent the Germans from withdrawing from the western front only to turn east and fight the Russians. For this purpose the Allies would set rail junctions as primary targets. Antonov had urged: "By air action on communications hinder the enemy from carrying out the shifting of his troops to the East from the Western Front, from Norway, and from Italy. In particular, to paralyze the junctions of Berlin and Leipzig." [18]

The exchange over Western Allied attacks to prevent movement of German forces from west to east was later to be subjected to close scrutiny by historians because of the British and American bombing on February 13/14 of the relatively undamaged baroque gem of Germany—Dresden— creating a fire storm and killing a large number of Germans.

General Marshall was brought into the controversy because of the misreading of a memorandum that credited him with an attempt—through misunderstanding or design—to excuse the bombing on the grounds that it had been requested by the Soviet Union. The raid in fact was not some improvised terrorist action or the result of a whim of a bomber commander, nor was it made at Russian request. Rather it grew out of plans, some considered as early as the previous summer, for hastening the end of the war by attacks on certain key cities in central and eastern Germany and by strikes against vital communications centers.

On August 1, 1944, as the Allied breakout from Normandy was getting under way and the invasion into the heart of France was about to begin, Portal, as Chief of the Air Staff, prepared a memorandum outlining the potential for a shattering attack against German morale by making a massive air strike against Berlin at a time when the ground offensive was going strongly against the Reich. He also stated that "Immense destruction could be produced if the entire attack was concentrated on a single big town other than Berlin and the effect would be especially greater if the town was one hitherto relatively undamaged." Portal had long advocated bombing specific strategic targets to weaken the German war effort rather than the area-bombing program favored by Air Chief Marshal Harris of the Bomber Command. The British Chiefs of Staff approved Portal's initial suggestion on August 5 and asked General Eisenhower to have a plan prepared for an attack on Berlin along the lines suggested. In their authoritative history of British strategic bombing Webster and Frankland commented on this action: "Though this did not take place until February, 1945, and though, as will also be presently seen, the Anglo-American desire to assist the Russian land campaign had by that time added a powerful motive for the selection of that particular time, it is necessary now to grasp the full implications of this air staff memorandum which may be regarded, indirectly, as the title deed of that controversial operation."

For months the various air chiefs had disagreed over the proper priorities for targets and the types of bombing that should be employed. General Spaatz had pushed continually for attacks against oil targets, Air Chief Marshal Harris wanted increased area bombing, Air Chief Marshal Tedder of SHAEF preferred attacks on communications. Air Chief Marshal Portal, who leaned more toward the Tedder and Spaatz views than to Harris's, found himself confronting a powerful opponent. Harris had the backing of Churchill and was popular with the general public. Thus in the fall of 1944 when Portal proposed a new directive reiterating basically the old priorities, Harris reminded him that the Bomber Command claimed the virtual destruction of forty-five of the sixty leading German cities in the past one and one-half years. The destruction of ten remaining important cities, including Dresden and Munich, and increased strikes on Berlin and Hanover would complete most of the plan.

The German attack in the Ardennes in mid-December raised Allied fears of renewed enemy air activities. In mid-January 1945 the air chiefs proposed that in addition to the priorities on oil and communications, attacks on German jet-aircraft production and on air-training and air-operational facilities also be assigned priority.

Meanwhile the success of a Russian offensive opened on January 12, 1945, led members of the British Air Staff and the Joint Intelligence

Committee to study means of aiding the Soviet advance. In a report of January 25 the latter group suggested that the earlier proposal for morale-shattering attacks on Berlin should now be considered in the light of the assistance that they would render to the Russian advance westward. Bombardments that forced massive departures of refugees from Berlin would create great confusion and "interfere with the orderly movement of troops to the front and hamper the German military and administrative machine." This would not only aid the Russians but might have a "political value in demonstrating to the Russians . . . a desire on the part of the British and Americans to assist them in the present battle." Attacks on marshaling yards and communications, the report noted, should "now be considered in addition to destroying the transfer of forces eastwards."

On the day the intelligence report was issued, Portal's Deputy, Air Marshal Bottomley, discussed it with Harris. The Bomber Command Chief now suggested that the main attacks be concentrated on Chemnitz, Leipzig, and Dresden, which, like Berlin, housed great numbers of refugees from the East and were key points in the German communications network through which troops might pass to the eastern front.

As usual Prime Minister Churchill was searching out new opportunities to hit the enemy. On the evening the report appeared he asked the Secretary of State for Air, Sir Archibald Sinclair, what plans the Royal Air Force had for hitting the retreating Germans. Cautiously Sinclair replied that there might be opportunities to bomb Berlin and other large cities, such as Leipzig, Dresden, and Chemnitz—repeating almost the exact language of the report regarding the military importance of these cities.

To this Churchill replied that he had not asked about attacks to harry the German retreat but whether Berlin and other cities in eastern Germany "should not now be considered especially attractive targets." Two months later he was to question the bombing of German cities "simply for increasing the terror, speaking particularly of Dresden," but at the moment he was speaking as Harris would have liked him to have done.[19]

The British air historians believe that Churchill's note was a key factor in persuading Bottomley to inform Harris that Portal was in favor of one big attack on Berlin and related operations against Dresden, Leipzig, Chemnitz, "and any other cities where a severe blitz will not only cause confusion in the evacuation from the East but will also hamper the movement of troops from the West." Harris needed no urging, but Bottomley requested that—subject to overriding claims of oil and other approved targets—as soon as moon and weather factors were right, "you will undertake such attacks with the particular objects of exploiting the confused conditions which are likely to exist in the above mentioned cities during the successful Russian advance." Churchill was informed of this proposal.

Thus as the Combined Chiefs of Staff were proceeding to Malta for preliminary talks before going to Yalta, a directive was being hammered out for the attack on major cities in eastern Germany. After talks among

Portal, Bottomley, and Spaatz and the latter two and Tedder, it was agreed on January 31 that first priority would still be given to oil targets but that second priority would go to the bombing of Berlin, Leipzig, Dresden, and associated cities for the reasons Bottomley had stressed.

Although these priorities were not reviewed by the Combined Chiefs of Staff at Yalta, they were accepted by the British Chiefs of Staff. Portal suggested that Bottomley get Spaatz's views and that if he approved, they issue a revised directive. No new directive was issued, but within the framework set forth in the January 12 directive, planning for bombing of communications went forward.

It was in this context that General Antonov at Yalta asked the Western representatives for bombings of rail centers to block the transfer of German troops from the western front to the eastern—citing as particular targets Berlin and Leipzig.[20]

At Yalta Marshall had already discussed with American representatives plans for hitting German communications. To a member of the U.S. Strategic Air Forces he "indicated general concurrence, but real concern that the Russians be notified of these attacks in accordance with present liaison procedure." He also referred to a proposed plan to use fighters to launch attacks all over Germany and was told that numerous enemy cities would be hit under Operation CLARION, when the situation was ripe. He then suggested that among the targets they should hit Munich "because it would show the people that are being evacuated to Munich that there is no hope." Aware of these various plans, Marshall informed Antonov of the thousand-bomber attack on Berlin that had been made on February 3 and a similar attack that was to be made against Leipzig. Obviously Dresden was not specifically in his mind, but clearly he was attempting to assure Antonov with these and other statements about current bombings that the Western Allies were bringing full pressure to bear to meet his request for a paralysis of German communications.[21]

On February 8, 1945, Eisenhower's air staff—on the basis of recommendations of the Combined Strategic Targets Committee—notified the RAF Bomber Command and the U.S. Strategic Air Forces that Dresden was among the targets slated to be hit because of their importance to the movement of military forces to the eastern front. In accordance with Marshall's wishes and established procedure Moscow was notified on the same day of this decision and specifically informed on February 12 that, weather permitting, U.S. air forces would attack the Dresden marshaling yards on February 13. Weather conditions did not permit, and the Soviet authorities were informed that the attack would be made the following day.[22]

Almost at once, as soon as the widespread damage on Dresden became known, there were questions about the necessity of the raid in the British press and in Parliament. British critics, who had already sharply attacked the bombings of cities, reacted sharply when a briefing officer at SHAEF indicated that the attack was part of a new terror-raid policy being adopted by the Allies. In Washington, General Arnold's Deputy, Brigadier General Barney Giles, asked Spaatz if a new policy had been instituted contrary to War Department knowledge and was told that he was acting under the previous directives. SHAEF made clear that the briefing officer's statement was incorrect.

Disturbed by what he had read, Secretary Stimson apparently asked General Marshall, after his return from Yalta, for further information on the Dresden raids. The Chief of Staff's office passed the request on to Arnold's staff. General Spaatz's headquarters in Europe replied to Washington early in March, giving the number of missions and total tonnage of bombs dropped and noting that much greater tonnage had been dropped by British than by American bombers. Brigadier General Joseph Loutzenheiser of Arnold's staff, who had been at Yalta, added a statement to the effect that Dresden was a communications center of major importance "through which reinforcements pass to reach the Russian front." [23]

This memorandum was forwarded to General Marshall's office, where a slightly different version was prepared. It opened with Loutzenheiser's comment on Dresden's importance as a communications center and then added that a press statement from London—given an incorrect date—indicated that Dresden, a "center of a railway network and a great industrial town, has become of the greatest value for conducting any defense the Germans may organize against Marshal Konev's armies. Dresden is closely related with the German potentialities for launching a counterattack against the southern wing of the great Russian Bulge." [24]

Neither Loutzenheiser's memorandum nor that forwarded by Marshall did more than point out why Dresden was a proper target for communications bombing. No mention was made of a Russian request. However the U.S. Air Forces official account of the incident (which was the only account available for many years) gave some grounds for confusion by saying that "The Secretary of War had to be apprised of Dresden's importance as a transportation center and the Russian request for its neutralization," citing "Memo for Stimson for Marshall (drafted by Loutzenheiser), 6 Mar 45." Had Marshall made such a statement, Stimson would probably have been satisfied. Instead he penciled a note on the memorandum reflecting his uneasiness about the bombings: "I doubt this report makes the case any better—on the face of it the British on February 13 bombed the city. While our bombing was said to be aimed at military objectives the results were practically unobserved. I think the city should be photographed carefully and the actual facts made known." With Marshall's approval his Secretary General Staff forwarded the message to Arnold's office for the necessary action.[25]

Two weeks later finding that no reply had been obtained, Colonel McCarthy reminded a member of Arnold's staff that Marshall and the Secretary were still waiting. On April 7 when McCarthy queried Stimson's office on the subject, he was told that a reply—which in fact repeated information on the relative damage inflicted by the U.S. and British bombers and included photographs of the destruction—had been sent directly from Spaatz's headquarters to the Secretary of War. Apparently this was satisfactory.

Ten days later the third Allied attack on Dresden (a second had been delivered in March after the initial heavy strikes)—this time by U.S. Eighth Air Force planes against the marshaling yards—was made after suitable notice had been given to Moscow, and the targets, with the exception of an objective in Prague, were accepted by Russian authorities.[26]

Churchill, who had earlier urged more punishing air strikes against the Germans, showed his uneasiness in late March in a memorandum to Portal that mentioned Dresden specifically and questioned the value of creating deserts in Germany. Portal, knowing that Churchill's backing had helped Harris's drive for expansion of area bombing, reminded the Prime Minister of his earlier views and got a toned-down memorandum in which Dresden was no longer mentioned.[27]

Oddly enough, there was little uneasiness or outcry over heavy bombings of Berlin and Leipzig, which came just before Dresden. The protests over Dresden arose from several sources. The chief charges of inhumanity spring possibly from exaggerations in the reported death toll—sometimes estimated as high as 250,000, then knocked down to 135,000—a figure still widely accepted but apparently in light of recent disclosures about 100,-000 too high. In fact the losses there rank below those in Berlin and Hamburg and in the prenuclear attacks on Japan.[28] (The toll in Dresden was actually higher than it would normally have been because of the influx of refugees who had fled there from other bombed areas.) Also there was outrage at the destruction of the heart of a relatively undamaged city known for its beauty and apparently of minimal military importance. In the years since the city has become a symbol for Allied brutality and mindless destructiveness.

Although Dresden had no great industrial plants of key importance to the German military efforts, its marshaling yards and location on main highways were of great military importance for the movement of reinforcements toward the East. In sober retrospect the question is not whether the bombing of Dresden was requested by the Russians, whether its destruction hastened the defeat of Germany, or even whether the attacks were necessary to bring victory. Certainly in mid-February the Germans were still resisting stoutly and were inflicting losses on the Allied armies on both the eastern and western fronts. There remain, however, two questions: whether these bombing attacks represented the best use of strategic airpower and whether bombings of cities were ever justified. If the attacks in February 1945 on Berlin and Hamburg—which were feebly protested if at all—were justified, then the bombings of Dresden—on a military basis—also were.

For the whole bombing policy in the last months of the war the heads of state and the Chiefs of Staff have to share the responsibility directly or indirectly. Churchill on the eve of Yalta was surely eager to see the Germans harried further, and Roosevelt did not object. The Russians, for all their later propaganda about not wanting Dresden hit, plainly showed no mercy for the cities and citizens of the Reich. The Chiefs of Staff did not so much direct the specific bombing as leave the choice of targets in the hands of subordinates who found it difficult to stop the momentum of attacks on a hated enemy. Once the policy of bombing cities as a means of hastening German defeat was accepted, it was difficult to maintain day-by-day control. It was easy for airmen to demonstrate as late as the beginning of April that the bombing of cities through which key communications linked eastern and western Germany could aid the Russian offensive. A policy talked about in the summer and fall of 1944 as a means of hastening the end of the war and changed to include assistance to the Russian advance gave signs at times of being an end in itself.

The Soviets at Yalta had finally approved the changed German zones of occupation. However they had been settled, so far as the Western Allies were concerned, in early December. In the light of this background, it is somewhat confusing to find General Eisenhower saying after the war that he always "felt that the Western Allies could probably have secured [at Yalta] an agreement to occupy more of Germany than we actually did" if the political heads had been convinced "as we were at SHAEF of the certainty of early victory in the West."

Several things are wrong with this statement. The zones had in effect been settled before the Allies had penetrated very far into Germany and at a time when the battle for the Reich had come to a complete halt, when the British were complaining bitterly of lost opportunities, and when advances in the Hürtgen Forest and on the Siegfried Line were reduced to inch-by-inch movements in the "bitter woods." The agreements had been to all intents reached before the Ardennes counterattack. They had been decided before the Supreme Commander had told General Marshall in mid-January, less than a month before Yalta, that the nature of his offensive in February or March depended on the scale of the Russian offensive.[29]

Quoting Eisenhower's statement, Henry Luce in a well-known article in *Life* in 1961 declared that the Supreme Commander had sent Bedell Smith to Malta "to intercept them [Roosevelt and Churchill] and urge that the Soviet zone be restricted."[30] It appears that Luce must have heard the General incorrectly, for Smith was sent to Malta specifically to discuss the coming offensive in the West. Before Marshall reached Malta, General Eisenhower had his own opportunity at Marseille to discuss the matter with him. In the minutes Eisenhower dictated of his conversation with the Chief of Staff, the zones were not mentioned. The point that impressed Marshall was Eisenhower's cautious statement in mid-January that he could not stage an early offensive unless the Russians attacked all along their front.

In view of Eisenhower's emphasis on the need for coordinating the Western Allied and Russian attacks and his earlier request to Roosevelt and Churchill to arrange for SHAEF representatives to go to Moscow to find out Stalin's offensive plans—they had been dispatched there in early January—it is not surprising that the Allied representatives at Yalta spoke not of what the Russians would give up but of what they could be persuaded to do to aid the advance in the West. Rather than begging the political leaders at Malta to stand firm against Stalin, Smith had said that timing was the main consideration: "As much as possible to occupy German forces should be accomplished while the Russian offensive is underway." Speaking of Rhine operations, he said, "If it becomes impossible to establish a firm bridgehead, it may be necessary to coordinate our operations with the Russians in June." In writing of this period in his volume, *My Three Years in Russia*, Smith made no allusion to any effort on his part to protest the arrangement of zones. Smith also wrote that when Churchill mentioned to him near the end of the war his worry that the Allies would pull back from zones that had been promised to the Russians, the British leader added: "two years ago if someone had told us that the Russian Army was approaching the Rhine we would have been happy about it." [31]

Zones or no zones, by the end of the Yalta conference Prime Minister Churchill was intent on sending Allied troops into one or more of the key cities of Central Europe. If he had controlled the troops needed for this purpose or if he could have persuaded the United States to furnish the necessary troops, he almost certainly would have raced the Russians for Berlin and Prague. Because Marshall, Eisenhower, and Bradley opposed such a race, they were severely criticized in the United States and Europe years after the war. British leaders, such as Montgomery and Brooke, who at the time showed the same desire to take their troops into the German capital as Clark had shown in driving for Rome, have insisted that their chief interest was forestalling the Russians. How many ills, they later suggested, the Western Allies could have avoided by going to Berlin, Vienna, and Prague.

Churchill, for whom the Russian menace now represented almost as great a challenge as the splendid prospect of raising the British flag in the German capital, did not stress the Red problem to Washington until the closing months of the war. Careful not to drift too far away from the President and aware of Roosevelt's desire to work closely with Stalin in the postwar era in the keeping of peace, the Prime Minister did not hammer home his point on Berlin at Malta and Yalta. His emphasis at these conferences was on a powerful single thrust on the northern flank by American and British forces commanded by Montgomery. Thus presented, Churchill's proposal aroused American opposition from the front-

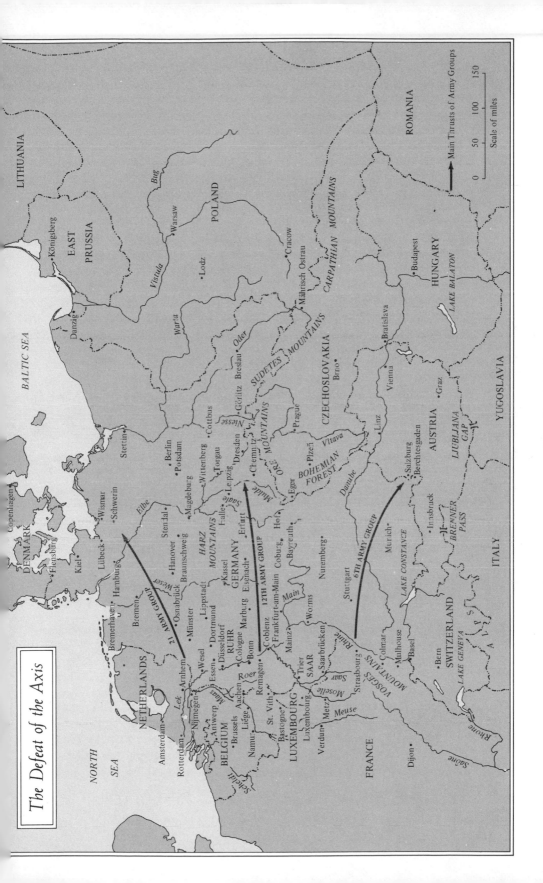

The Defeat of the Axis

LITHUANIA

BALTIC SEA

Copenlaqen
DENMARK
Flensburg
Kiel
Lübeck
Wismar
Schwerin

Königsberg
EAST
PRUSSIA

Danzig

Stettin

Warsaw

POLAND

Vistula

Bug

Lodz

Warta

Cracow

Mährisch Ostrau

NORTH
SEA

Bremerhaven
Bremen
Hamburg
21 ARMY GROUP
Weser
Osnabrück
Hanover
Braunschweig
Stendal
Magdeburg

Berlin
Potsdam

Witterberg
Torgau

Cottbus

Oder

Görlitz Breslau

Neisse

SUDETES MOUNTAINS

CARPATHIAN MOUNTAINS

Amsterdam
Rotterdam
NETHERLANDS
Lek
Arnhem
Nijmegen
Wesel
Münster
Lippstadt
Dortmund
Düsseldorf
RUHR
Essen
Cologne Marburg Eisenach
Bonn

HARZ
MOUNTAINS
Kassel

Elbe

Saale
Erfurt
Halle
Leipzig

Mulde

Dresden
Chemnitz

ORE MOUNTAINS

Prague

BOHEMIAN
FOREST

Vltava

Plzeň

CZECHOSLOVAKIA
Brno

Vienna

Bratislava

Budapest

HUNGARY

LAKE BALATON

Antwerp
Brussels
BELGIUM
Namur
Liège
St. Vith
Bastogne
Luxembourg
LUXEMBOURG
Verdun
Metz

Maas

Roer
Aachen
Remagen
Coblenz
Trier
SAAR
Saarbrücken
Saar
Mosell
Meuse

12TH ARMY GROUP
Frankfurt-am-Main
Mainz
Worms
Main

Coburg
Bayreuth
Hof
Eger

Nuremberg

Danube

Linz

AUSTRIA
Graz

Salzburg
Berchtesgaden

LJUBIJANA
GAP

YUGOSLAVIA

Scheldt

FRANCE

Dijon

Saône

Verdun

Strasbourg
VOSGES
MOUNTAINS
Colmar
Mulhouse
Basel

6TH ARMY GROUP

Stuttgart

Rhine

Munich

LAKE CONSTANCE

Innsbruck
BRENNER
PASS

ITALY

Bern
SWITZERLAND
LAKE GENEVA
A L P S

Rhône

GERMANY

Main Thrusts of Army Groups

Scale of miles
0   50   100   150

ROMANIA

line division commanders to the President. The only hope, admittedly small, of getting Roosevelt to agree to a race with the Russians to the capitals of Central Europe was to persuade him of an overpowering Soviet threat and the impossibility of working out postwar collaboration with the Soviet Union. Had the American leaders, blamed later for starting the cold war with the Russians, been intent on stopping the Soviet Union, they would have backed Churchill's strategy.

But many factors weighed against the Prime Minister in the final three months of the war in Europe. At this point Churchill was caught in the mesh of British history; widespread American distrust of Britain's imperialist designs (crusty American admirals and generals—conservative as any mustached British officer relaxing over past colonial victories in his London club—cast suspicious glances at the Empire's world-wide policies), was bolstered by Britain's World War II negotiations over the Mediterranean, which left even her stanch friends, such as Roosevelt and Marshall, feeling that they were being used to further British policy.

Churchill would also have had to convince the President and the U.S. Chiefs of Staff that the establishment of a Central European roadblock against a Russian advance was worth delaying the defeat of the Japanese in the Pacific. But he had frittered away his advantage in yearnings for Rhodes and Cos, which had no great relevance to stopping the Russians in Central Europe, by his insistence that "Alexander shall have his victory," and by agreements with Stalin on spheres of influence in Eastern Europe. His efforts at Christmas 1944 to forestall the Communists in Greece seemed too much like his earlier promonarchy stance in Italy to be reassuring.

The British plea at Malta for a thrust by Montgomery to Berlin seemed to Marshall and his Army colleagues less a hedge against Russian aggression than a maneuver for a British-led, American-supported, expedition to plant the flag in the German capital. This suspicion was fed when Churchill spoke of a pressing need for Tedder's services elsewhere and proposed that Alexander take his place in Eisenhower's headquarters. To the Supreme Commander, who had once favored Alexander for the command that Montgomery received, Churchill's proposal seemed a transparent effort to reinstate a British ground commander-in-chief in northwest Europe. Knowing that this idea was anathema to Marshall, Eisenhower opposed the suggestion vigorously.

Marshall had already pointed out that in the coming battles American forces, greater than ever before as new divisions were sent into the line from the United States and as units were transferred from Italy, could be expected to bear the major burden of Allied casualties thenceforth. They could be borne more easily if they occurred under American command.

The biting exchange between Marshall and Brooke at Malta should have settled the matter, but Churchill persisted. He revived the idea in

March, although a prudent man would have abandoned it after the discussion in February.

Not until March 2 when Montgomery, late a prime mover for the field command himself, informed Churchill that he had told Eisenhower the day before that the war was nearly won, and that he should leave Tedder and Alexander at their current posts, did Churchill admit final defeat.[32] The whole affair, endlessly revived under various guises, was exactly the sort of maneuver that made the Americans increasingly suspicious of the Prime Minister's grand designs.

Churchill's past also created doubts about his strategy for driving on Berlin, Vienna, and Prague in the spring of 1945. Just as the Americans fought grim ghosts of the Somme in arguing with him for a cross-Channel attack in 1942 and 1943, so did the Prime Minister face apparitions of World War I European and Middle Eastern misadventures in urging his Western Allies to forestall the Red armies in Central Europe. Later the Prime Minister deplored the American blindness that lost the fruits of victory—an interpretation happily seized on by American critics of Roosevelt, Marshall, and Eisenhower. But in that final spring of the war the President had no intention of keeping troops on the Rhine or the Danube or the North Sea for more than a year or two at most, and he was positive that the American public would clamor indignantly against lengthy and extended commitments in Europe. Knowing that the United States would have to bear the brunt of any showdown with the Russians, he preferred not to challenge them but to seek an understanding. The more he saw of reawakening British anti-Soviet policy, the more he insisted on dissociating himself from it.

Marshall remembered well the resurgence of American isolationism within months after the end of World War I and the almost immediate revulsion against keeping a large military force in being. He believed that the same reactions would recur and favored a strategy leading to disengagement rather than further involvement. Under these conditions the Supreme Commander followed a policy of doing only what was necessary to defeat the Germans. Thus he made minimum efforts to take areas assigned to the Soviet Union for occupation since they would have to be evacuated at the close of fighting.

The Roer proved to be a more difficult objective to win than the Rhine did later; swollen floods and stormy weather held up armor and infantry. Crossings were nevertheless forced all along the front in late February, and the Allied armies pushed forward to the Rhine. Strongly reinforced, Montgomery in the north prepared for a set-piece crossing of the German river. With elements of three armies led by two airborne divisions he prepared for a heavy blow. Before he could ready his attack for late March, the incredible happened. On March 8 armored units of the U.S. First Army, not daring to hope for an unblown bridge, surprised them-

selves and the Germans by seizing and crossing the Ludendorff Bridge at
Remagen—left intact through a combination of enemy delay, bad judgment, and poor explosives. It was neither the ideal area nor in accord
with the SHAEF plan, which gave the main show to Montgomery, but the
U.S. commanders at all echelons applauded the build-up over the bridge.
A few days later, on March 23, Patton was across the river to the south,
jeering at Montgomery who was still intent on his careful preparations in
the north. Not until the next day would the 21 Army Group commander's
beautifully planned and well-executed attack go off as scheduled. It went
according to the book and could be studied for those who wanted to see a
book solution. But it came too late for Montgomery's purposes.

The sensational Remagen crossing gave Marshall a needed shot in the
arm at a time when he felt especially harassed by criticism at home. Only
the day before in a somewhat weary letter to Eisenhower he had balanced
against the good news problems on the home front:

> Your people are certainly doing fine work and seem to be trembling on the
> verge of still greater things. With your successes in Europe and MacArthur's
> successes in the Philippines the public is greatly encouraged; however, there is
> a terrific drive on against the use of 18-year-old men in combat which has been
> fulminated by a speech by Senator Taft on the floor of the Senate, citing the
> case of the son of a friend of his. I was impressed yesterday with the difficulties
> of my position in the necessity of simultaneously answering attacks on the use
> of these young men and alleging the inadequacy of their training, and at the
> same time answering several radios, one in particular from MacArthur emphat-
> ically protesting against the shortage in replacement, and further, meeting the
> appeal of some of the commanders against further conversions of their men to
> individual replacements. The combined circumstances could hardly present a
> more illogical pressure.
>
> We are under attack of course for the inadequacy of our winter clothing and
> now for the charge that 75 per cent of our materiel is inferior to that of the
> Germans. They grant that the jeep and the Garand rifle are all right but
> everything else is all wrong. Making war in a democracy is not a bed of roses.

He closed with some complaining of his own. A few days earlier he had
protested because of what he felt was failure to publicize a spectacular
action of the 3d Division. He had received in reply a long list of press
releases on the 3d Division fighting. "My comment on this is that I am not
much interested in the explanation. What I am interested in is the result
and I go back to my usual comparison, that had it been a Marine Division
every phase of a rather dramatic incident would have been spread
throughout the United States. They get the result, we do not. Our technique therefore must be faulty." Might it not be good publicity, he
prodded Eisenhower, to release some mention of Generals Collins and
McLain and their work on the advance to Cologne and Düsseldorf? [33]

The Supreme Commander patiently answered the complaints. He was
working to improve public relations and to get publicity for the work of
outstanding commanders. He noted that in trying to compete with the

Marines the Army had fifty divisions on the European front as compared with one or two Marine divisions in an island battle. As for the inferiority of weapons he replied: "It is my opinion that when we have the new T-26 in sufficient numbers, and especially when we get the even newer model that has the souped-up 90 mm. gun, our tank force will be superior in slugging power as well as in maneuverability and in numbers. Our artillery, rifles, machine guns, airplanes (except for the jet airplane), and in general our clothing and equipage all outclass the enemy's. The jeep, the large trucks and the ducks are far ahead of him. The German 88 is a great all round gun and as a separate anti-tank weapon has caused us lots of trouble. But his artillery as a whole is far behind and the 90 mm. will match the 88."

These careful reassurances were garnished with a little sprig of Eisenhower's graceful humor. "Misery loves company," he declared. "Sometimes when I get tired of trying to arrange the blankets smoothly over several prima donnas in the same bed I think that no one person in the world can have so many illogical problems. I read about your struggles concerning the eighteen year old men in combat, and about the criticism of our equipment, and went right back to work with a grin." [34]

Eisenhower made a heroic effort to improve publicity by issuing a message to his army group commanders. He made clear that in seeking to present more vivid accounts of the American soldier, "we must be careful as always that there is no implication of disparagement of our allies." They were not fighting the war for headlines, "but proper publicity does have an effect on our troop efficiency. . . . Moreover, it will have an enduring effect on the future of American defense forces. . . ." He had caught the Chief of Staff's main point with his concluding statement: "General Marshall has frequently communicated with me on this general subject. He is vitally interested in it not only because of its postwar effects but because of its influence on his current problems of manpower, equipment, deployment and so on." [35] Pershing's former aide remembered how quickly the American public had forgotten all but a few battles and units of World War I, and he wanted to imprint the Army's great work on the public's postwar memory.

The hard knocks inflicted on Bradley and Hodges over the Ardennes attack prompted Marshall a few hours before Montgomery's drive across the Rhine to send his compliments to Bradley and his subordinates. Prefacing his communication, which was channeled through Eisenhower, with the reservation, "If you think it wise, that is without offense to Devers' group or to Simpson's [Ninth] army, and as a possible antidote for an overdose of Montgomery which is now coming into this country," he asked that Eisenhower send the following message to the 12th Army Group commander: "I am filled with admiration of your handling of the operations involved in the development of the Remagen bridgehead and the clearing of the Saar Basin. I want General Hodges and General Patton and their corps and division commanders to know that their great military successes of the past few weeks have registered a high point in American military achievement. Incidentally I am profoundly impressed with the remarkable logistic support of the Remagen bridgehead and the supply of Patton's forces which made possible the rapidity of their bold advances." [36]

Eager to make full use of the recent jump in morale, the Chief of Staff took another reading. As March neared its close, he noted that the 4th Armored Division was again carrying out a particularly brilliant operation. He wondered if this might not be the proper time to cite it for its drive to the Rhine and south of the Moselle. Later "a number of divisions [will be] spearheading advances all along the front and serious resentment would be engendered" by such action. "An immediate citation would act as a spur to all. If you have the same view this is your authority to act." [37]

Eisenhower agreed. No less than Marshall, he recognized the importance of spurring the pursuit against the Germans. With nearly two-thirds of the forces in the West under his direct command and with the supplies necessary to mount any final attacks in his firm control, the Supreme Commander by the end of March was in a position to develop the battle as he saw best with the full support of Marshall and the other U.S. Chiefs of Staff. The President stanchly backed his generals.[38]

The situation had changed remarkably in three weeks. On March 8 Eisenhower had told Marshall that Bradley was rushing troops to secure an adequate bridgehead "with the idea that this will constitute greatest possible threat as supporting effort for main attack." [39] By the end of the month his tone clearly implied that he and Bradley had other plans in mind for the remainder of the war.

It was in this strong flush of elation over victory infusing Eisenhower and his generals, and fully shared by Marshall and his Washington associates that the last vital decisions of the war in Europe were made. The unexpected developments on the central front had allowed a new approach. Aware of Marshall's great pride in the American forces and his fierce support of Bradley, Hodges, and Patton, Eisenhower moved more certainly than at any time during the war to exercise full command of Western Allied troops in the field. He was soon to come into collision with the Prime Minister and the British Chiefs of Staff. But Washington saw to it that his plans were not denied.

The change was obvious in Eisenhower's happy report to Marshall on March 26: "Naturally I am immensely pleased that the campaign west of the Rhine that Bradley and I planned last summer and insisted upon as a necessary preliminary to a deep penetration east of the Rhine, has been carried out so closely in accordance with conception. . . . I hope that this does not sound boastful, but I must admit to a great satisfaction that the things that Bradley and I have believed in from the beginning and have carried out in the face of some opposition both from within and without, have matured so splendidly." [40]

The unexpected crossing ended Montgomery's hope for a grand finale on his northern front. The disposition of troops, if nothing else, opened the way to Leipzig instead of to Berlin. Montgomery's road to the German capital lay over a low area crisscrossed by rivers sufficiently broad and difficult to permit hard-core SS units to make last-ditch stands. The Canadian Army was sorely beset in Holland, where flooded areas helped the desperate Nazis.

Montgomery's longed-for drive on Berlin required the continued control of at least one American army, U.S. supplies, and the close cooperation of another American army. The decision went against the British Field Marshal. In his capacity as commander of U.S. forces in Europe, Eisenhower shifted Simpson's Ninth Army back to Bradley and gave the 12th Army Group commander the mission of driving for Leipzig and the Elbe. These arrangements were made in Europe, but they were in line with Washington's thinking and had Marshall's complete approbation.

In late March, perturbed by Montgomery's order stressing the drive toward Berlin as the main Allied effort in the West, Eisenhower took the step of informing Stalin directly that he planned to drive toward Dresden and Leipzig. He explained that he wanted to encircle and destroy the Ruhr and to link up with the Russian forces. Taking a clear sight along Bradley's main front, he added that the best axis would be Erfurt-Leipzig-Dresden, with Regensburg-Linz as the secondary line of advance.[41]

Such a strategy would mean the end of further important gains by Field Marshal Montgomery. Just as American thinking had been influenced by the current drives of Bradley's armies and the natural lines of advance toward the East, so the 21 Army Group commander must have combined ruminations on the political importance of Berlin with his strong desire to lead the attack on the German capital. Even without Montgomery's prompting the British Chiefs of Staff buzzed angrily over Eisenhower's message, protesting to Marshall that they must make the main thrust across the open plains of northern Germany to take Berlin. They would open German ports, cut German communications to Holland, end the U-boat war, and liberate Swedish and Norwegian shipping.[42]

It was Churchill who saw the weakness of the British case. He had learned well by now what Marshall would say to such arguments, and with words that sounded almost like a paraphrase of the American position, he lectured the British commanders. The Americans would insist that they should not go off on tangents. It was important that they stick to the main issues. Grimly he set forth the facts of life for the British Chiefs of Staff. While agreeing that they should present their views to the U.S. Chiefs, he said, "I hope however we shall realise that we have only a quarter of the forces invading Germany, and that the situation has thus changed remarkably from the days of June 1944. . . ." He saw that one of the chief criticisms of the Eisenhower position was that "we might be condemned to an almost static role in the north and virtually prevented from crossing the Elbe until an altogether later stage in the operations has been reached. All prospect also of the British entering Berlin with the Americans is ruled out." He conceded what Montgomery had not been willing to do before—that if resistance was practically collapsing, there was no reason why the advances "should not take place on a broader front than hitherto. This is a point on which the Supreme Commander must have the final word." [43]

Despite his admonitions to his Chiefs, Churchill that same day continued to dispute Eisenhower over Berlin, writing him: ". . . I do not consider myself that Berlin has yet lost its military and certainly not its political significance. The fall of Berlin would have a profound psychological effect on German resistance in every part of the Reich. . . . The idea that the capture of Dresden and junction with the Russians there would be a superior gain does not commend itself to me. . . . But while Berlin remains under the German flag it cannot, in my opinion, fail to be the most decisive point in Germany."

Although Churchill would not entirely relinquish any stand, he saw that the Supreme Commander held all the cards. Continuing his lecture to the British Chiefs, he pointed out: "It must be remembered that Eisenhower's credit with them [the U.S. Chiefs] stands very high. He may claim to have correctly estimated so far the resisting strength of the enemy and to have established by deeds (1) the 'closing' of the Rhine along its whole length, (b) the power to make the double advance instead of staking all on the northern advance. . . . These events, combined with the continual arrival of American reinforcements, have greatly enhanced General Eisenhower's power and prestige, and the Americans will feel that, as the victorious Supreme Commander, he has a right, and indeed a vital need, to try to elicit from the Russians their views as to the best point for making contact by the armies of the West and of the East." He had correctly read Marshall's views.

As usual, when he felt that the gambit might work, Churchill mingled some wheedling with words of praise. Later he would argue with the U.S. Chiefs of Staff and then Roosevelt, but for the moment he told Eisenhower that he feared that if the main axis of advance was shifted to the south and the Ninth Army withdrawn from 21 Army Group, "the offensive role which was assigned to him [Montgomery] may peter out." Now he took a different tack on Berlin: he did not understand why Eisenhower felt that there was virtue in not crossing the Elbe. "If the enemy's resistance should weaken, as you evidently expect and which may well be fulfilled, why should we not cross the Elbe and advance as far eastward as possible?" This move, he declared, had an important political bearing, as the Russian army of the south seemed certain to enter Vienna and overrun Austria. "If we deliberately leave Berlin to them, even if it should be in our grasp, the double event may strengthen their conviction, already apparent, that they have done everything." [44]

The decision in April to turn the main attack toward Leipzig resulted to a great extent from Eisenhower's desire to give Bradley and Patton their chance, now that U.S. forces constituted the greater part of the troops on the western front. Marshall fully backed this desire.

On April 2 Marshall sent the President a War Department study of the situation in Europe. The report, if anything slightly pessimistic, said that Allied forces should reach the Elbe River between Magdeburg and Halle by April 20, and Stuttgart and Nuremberg should be in Allied hands by April 20 and Munich by May 1. The British were expected to advance more slowly in the north.

The Russians, if the Western Allied view proved correct, would be able to begin their general offensive by April 10 and by May 1 be in contact with American forces along the Elbe and Saale, south of Berlin. It was assumed that by May 1 no cohesive enemy front would exist, although pockets of resistance would undoubtedly remain.

There was much debate on whether the Nazis would set up a National Redoubt in southern Germany. However there was more definite agreement on this topic than generally believed. The April 2 study that Marshall had forwarded to the President concluded: "The many rumors as to German preparations for the defense of the 'Alpine Redoubt' are believed to lack substance. No reliable information has reached the War Department of unduly large storage of supplies in the 'redoubt area' and there are no indications that any fortifications are being constructed in Bavaria or Austria to prevent an Allied ingress into the 'redoubt area' from the north. . . ." Although several pockets might be established, including some in Bavaria, the report continued: "If Hitler is true to the character he has shown in past crises, he will make his exit bravely and dramatically and thus remain a psychological force for his enemies to reckon with for decades." [45]

The War Department was prophetic about Hitler's end. But the intelligence experts were not sending out similar prophecies about the approaching end of Franklin Roosevelt's life. Three weeks before Hitler and Mussolini he would pass from the scene suddenly at Warm Springs, Georgia.

General Marshall had left his office on April 12 and was sitting on the porch of Quarters One when Colonel McCarthy drove from the Pentagon to tell him that the President was dead. Mrs. Roosevelt's first thought had been of Harry S. Truman and after that of her children. Her messages to her four sons in uniform—"Daddy slept away. He would expect you to carry on and finish your jobs,"—sent to the Pentagon for transmittal, were the first announcement McCarthy had of the President's passing.[46]

Hurrying to the White House, General Marshall offered his condolences and assistance to the widow. Mrs. Roosevelt asked him to assume responsibility for all details of the journey north from Warm Springs, the funeral service at the White House, and the final trip to Hyde Park. At once the great machinery of the Pentagon was put into action. From Fort Benning two thousand men were ordered to Warm Springs, guards of honor were to be placed along the route the train would take northward, thousands more were to line the streets in Washington as the President's body was borne from Union Station to the White House. General Marshall put his chief orderly, Sergeant Powder, in charge of the bearers of the coffin, and it was the tall sergeant who walked behind the caisson.[47]

Next day as the train started northward from Warm Springs, General Marshall joined the other Chiefs of Staff (with General Barney Giles representing General Arnold, who was in Europe) and Secretaries Stimson and Forrestal for the first meeting of the service chiefs with the new Commander-in-Chief. President Truman explained at the outset that he was completely satisfied with the way the war was going and that he wanted them to go on as before. At Stimson's suggestion Marshall and King gave short summaries of the current war situation. Then the group left the President to grapple wtih the myriad problems that had suddenly become his.[48]

The new Chief Executive was a familiar figure to the service chiefs, particularly to Stimson and Marshall, who were, of course, fully aware of his work in the Senate as chairman of the special committee on the conduct of the war. Truman respected Marshall for his candor and leadership, according him a trust in his judgment that the Chief of Staff later said that he found almost frightening.

Roosevelt's successor impressed Stimson as "a man who is willing and anxious to learn and to do his best but who was necessarily laboring under the terrific handicap of coming into such an office where the threads of information were so multitudinous that only long previous familiarity could allow him to control them." Stimson knew that Truman had first learned of the atomic bomb from his own briefing a few hours before; it would be more than a week before James Byrnes could bring him up to date on the notes he had taken at Yalta. Still carefully locked up in Leahy's safe were the secret provisions of talks between the President and Stalin at Yalta. A few days away was the conference at San Francisco that would launch the United Nations Organization; some three weeks away was the end of the war in Europe, a victory that would bring so many trials for those in authority.

Some of these problems were discussed by Stimson and Marshall as they rode back from their first official meeting with the new President. The Secretary of War felt some reassurance. Marshall was cautious: "We shall not know what he is really like until the pressure really begins to be felt." He had not yet heard two slogans that the new occupant of the White House would inscribe in history: "If you can't take the heat, stay out of the kitchen" and "The buck stops here." This was the kind of reaction to pressure that Marshall and Stimson and their colleagues wanted. Within ten days they would be convinced of the staying power of the man from Missouri.

As the machinery of government readjusted to the sudden change in direction, the final ceremonies were being prepared for the fallen Commander-in-Chief. On the morning of the fourteenth the new President and his family, accompanied by members of the Cabinet, the Supreme Court, leaders of Congress, and the Chiefs of Staff met the dead President's train as it arrived from Georgia. A procession started from the railway station at 10 A.M. Preceded by the Marine Band and a squadron of forty-eight scout cars, an armed escort, consisting of a battalion of field artillery, a battalion of infantry, a battalion of Marines, a battalion of sailors, and a composite battalion of WACS, WAVES, and female Marines, marched from Union Station down to Constitution Avenue and headed for 15th Street, where they would turn to go to the White House. Following them were the horse-drawn caisson and the limousines with members of the family, the presidential party, and high government officials.[49]

At 4 P.M. in the East Room three hundred mourners heard Bishop Angus Dun of the National Cathedral, assisted by the pastors of St. Thomas and St. John's, conduct the simple service requested by Mrs. Roosevelt. The President's body remained in the East Room of the White House, guarded by four enlisted men, until time for the 10 A.M. departure for Hyde Park. Truman and members of his family, Mrs. Roosevelt and her family, and a number of friends went northward on two special trains. Stimson, Marshall, King and Giles decided instead to fly to Stewart Field near West Point, where they would spend the evening as the guests of the superintendent of the Military Academy, Major General Francis B. Wilby.[50]

The Chiefs of Staff were still at West Point as the train, which had traveled from New York City along the east bank of the Hudson, passed across the river. They then drove rapidly along the Hudson through Cornwall and Newburgh before crossing to Poughkeepsie and Hyde Park. There they joined members of the presidential party, who came from the railway at the bottom of the bluff on which Roosevelt's home stood. At the graveside in the rose garden of the estate, they waited as the caisson, escorted by cadets, wound its way up the hill. The dirgelike funeral march was heard as cannons fired the last twenty-one-gun salute for the dead President.

All the arrangements had gone perfectly, but when the eight servicemen moved from the caisson to the grave, it seemed, that they would be unable to support the weight of the heavy bronze casket. Two men in uniform standing nearby, one of them Sergeant Powder, sprang forward to steady the coffin as it was being placed in the grave. The elderly rector of St. James Episcopal Church of Hyde Park, where the Roosevelts had worshiped, read the service for the dead as the young cadets stood silent and erect. Then came the traditional three volleys and the sounds of *Taps*.[51]

Another long trip still lay ahead for the President and his family, Mrs. Roosevelt and her daughter and son, and other members of the funeral party, who started back to Washington by train shortly after the graveside service. Knowing that developments in Europe and the Pacific would not wait, the Chiefs of Staff flew back shortly afterward. There was no time for lingering thoughts of the leader who had fallen; too many problems awaited solution. On the afternoon after Roosevelt's death urgent calls had come from Europe in connection with proper procedures to be followed as German collapse approached. Growing difficulties with the Russians were clearly evident as the enemies of Hitler closed in from east and west.[52]

End in Europe

HITLER was on the ropes, but his dream of dividing his enemies seemed to be coming true at the beginning of April 1945. On the second General Marshall and Secretary Stimson discussed the disturbing state of relations with the Soviet Union, the General agreeing with Stimson that they could not allow "a rift to come between the two nations without endangering the entire peace of the world." Marshall was still hopeful. "He had anticipated these troubles," he told the Secretary of War, "and thought they would be pretty bad and irritating but thought that we must put up with them." [1]

On the following day after telling Marshall of a talk he had had with Secretary Stettinius the evening before, Stimson recorded: "I am keeping close with him [Marshall] in order to have my power in my elbow for the conference that may come up when we talk with the State Department and the Navy Department and with the President. There has been growing quite a strain of irritating feeling between our government and the Russians and it seems to me that it is a time for me to use all the restraint I can on these other people who have been apparently getting a little more irritated." It was not out of lack of toughness, he made clear. "I . . . feel the importance of firm dealing with the Russians, but as Marshall agrees, what we want is to state our facts with perfectly cold-blooded firmness and not show any temper." [2]

Firmness without temper was something Marshall could manage if he tried. He was to need both strength and patience to handle the next developments.

The division between the Western Allies and the Soviet Union had been papered over when Hitler invaded the U.S.S.R. in 1941, but little that had occurred since had made relations easier. The Russians had never been gracious allies, even when their homeland was being overrun by the Germans, and now that the enemy was being pushed back, they grew more truculent than ever. Moreover the advances from both east and west that promised to bring Anglo-American and Russian forces into contact on the ground instilled a new urgency into questions of postwar borders and governments. Where arguments on these points, however bitter, had once involved remote and theoretical goals, they now dealt with immediate and concrete stakes.

Some assert that the Anglo-American delay in launching a cross-Channel invasion laid the basis for Russian disenchantment that was to lead at last to a cold war. It is to be doubted that a canny negotiator such as Foreign Affairs Commissar Vyacheslav Molotov took too seriously President Roosevelt's exuberant offer in 1942 to return to the Continent that year—when it was apparent that the United States did not then have the means to mount such an offensive and that Churchill strongly opposed such a guarantee. It is far more likely that the Russians were reacting to prewar suggestions in the British and American press and in Parliament and Congress that Germany and the U.S.S.R. be allowed to destroy each other. An alarmed Stalin might see in each delay of the second front evidence that this was still the case.[3]

Russian suspicions, fed by the memory of Western Allied interventions against the Soviet government in 1917–21 and strengthened by Stalin's fear of invasion on every front and the belief—sometimes well founded—that the Western world would overthrow his regime if it could, surfaced all too plainly as the war in the West reached a climax, and Britain and the United States became less essential to Russia's safety. Stalin was never at ease with the idea of Allied bases on Soviet soil or the presence of Allied liaison parties for any purpose—whether it be laying out new airfields, arranging for shuttle bombing, exchanging information on weather or operations, or hastening the return of Allied prisoners of war to their own lines after rescue by Red Army forces—and he habitually delayed implementing agreements on such matters. Pleading that his mobile forces could not supply amenities for their own troops, he rejected American complaints that he was failing to care properly for recently liberated U.S. fliers. He angered the questioners by implying that the Allies, with less cause than he, had failed to give proper care to Russian prisoners overrun by Allied forces.

Suspicion operated in both directions throughout the weeks after the Yalta conference had closed in an atmosphere of cordiality and seeming accord, and it helped to exacerbate daily relations. There were many possible sources for disagreement—German partition, reparations, liaison arrangements, and the like—but the crucial issue was Poland. Churchill, whose country had gone to war to protect Poland, did not propose to hand that country over to the rule of a committee that had been set up with Russian backing. At Yalta, Roosevelt had candidly explained to Stalin—in a realistic exposition of the political facts of American life—that he must satisfy his large constituency of Polish-American voters that he wanted justice for the representatives of the former Polish government.

Attempting a compromise and not wishing to wreck the conference on this issue, the Western leaders had relied too heavily on an apparent Soviet concession. But Stalin was less moved than Churchill by Roosevelt's desire to conciliate minorities.

Within a few weeks after Stalin's forces swept through Poland the Russian-supported Lublin government entered the homeland in the Red Army's baggage. It became clear that Stalin had no intention of requiring free elections from this faction and that any poll taken would be arranged to give short shrift to the representatives of the Polish government-in-exile, backed by London. It was a bitter disappointment for Roosevelt and a constant reminder to Churchill of the growing areas of disagreement between Britain and the Soviet Union in Central and Eastern Europe. Recognizing, although not sufficiently, the growing weakness of the British position economically and militarily, the Prime Minister sought to involve the Americans in Europe indefinitely. And he sought to tie American support to an improvised policy, developed swiftly from mid-March onward, dedicated to holding back the Red forces as much as possible—or, as he put it, "we should shake hands with the Russians as far to the East as possible." At once this policy became mixed with pressure to push as hard as possible for Berlin—a goal tinged with a hope that troops under Montgomery might plant the Allied standard there.[4]

The basis was laid for a Churchillian reassessment of previously agreed-on Allied strategy for the defeat of Germany—now closely intertwined with the rapid conclusion of the fighting there and the prompt redeployment of Allied efforts to the Far East, where it was still assumed that Russian aid would be needed. Churchill's goal of re-establishing the balance of power in Central Europe, mainly with American help, required much more than running advice to Eisenhower and sudden pleas to Roosevelt and Marshall. The fact that a later generation would have preferred such a policy should not blind it to the fact that the Prime Minister could not sell it even to his own people and his own armed forces. John Ehrman warned in his British official history: ". . . attitudes and policy should not be confused. In the first place, even if the Prime Minister and Foreign Secretary . . . had decided in the spring of 1945 that action should be taken on the assumption that Russia might be a potential enemy, there was no likelihood of such action being adopted by their country or in the United States. But secondly, they did not so decide. Disappointed, distrustful and sometimes deeply alarmed as they were, their hopes, and British policy, rested on a continuing partnership of the three Powers expressed in and operating through the instrument of the United Nations. . . ." [5]

Rather than adopting a strategy designed for defense or attack against Russia, which could have been advanced by making a separate peace with Germany, the British proposed to finish quickly with Hitler's forces on all fronts in order to negotiate with the Russians from strength. "They [the

British] did not despair of a solution with the Russians: indeed they expected it. But they expected it as a result of firm and timely measures which would remind their ally of his obligations, and whose inception depended on the movements of the Western armies in the few weeks that remained." [6]

The Russian side of the story has not been completely told. Whether Stalin planned from 1944 on to seize the main capitals of Central Europe, or whether he merely attempted to shore up his positions against the unfriendly intentions of the Western Allies, is not clear. What is evident is that he feared that the Western Allies might come to terms with the Germans on the western front while leaving the Red forces heavily occupied in the East.

The first ugly round of recriminations came over German forces in Italy. Near the end of February certain German officials in Italy believed that the war had been definitely lost and that an effort must be made to initiate preliminaries to an armistice. Making use of Italian and Swiss intermediaries, representatives of General Karl Friedrich Wolff, SS commander in Italy, established contact with Allen W. Dulles, OSS representative in Berne. The extremely tentative approaches of early March, tainted with treason from a German standpoint and great suspicion from the Anglo-American viewpoint, risked a serious split with the Russians. The question arose as to whether or not the Soviets should be brought into the exploratory conversations. General McNarney, the American commander in the Mediterranean, felt that inviting the Russians in at that stage increased the danger of stopping negotiations entirely. The Russians were notified that Field Marshal Alexander was sending representatives to Ascona, Switzerland, to look into German proposals. Molotov indicated that his government did not object but wanted to send three representatives to the meeting.[7]

In this matter, as in those matters in which Eisenhower dealt directly with the Russians, the Americans stressed quick military success over long-range political considerations. The result was what Washington should have expected. Stalin and his advisers, deeply suspicious by nature, saw nothing but deception in the Swiss discussions. In mid-March, Molotov sent what Stimson called a "quarrelsome letter," insisting that since the United States refused to allow the Soviets to participate in the talks, negotiations should be broken off. Sure of American good intentions, Stimson said that the letter indicated a spirit "which bodes evil in the coming difficulties of the postwar scene." [8]

But Western persistence on continuing talks without Russian participation merely confirmed the darker doubts of Moscow. On March 23 Molotov accused both the British and Americans of negotiating with the Germans behind the backs of the Soviet government. The Commissar of Foreign Affairs took the occasion to announce that he would not attend the San Francisco conference then being planned to organize the machinery of the United Nations Organization.[9]

At the end of March, Stalin added his voice to Molotov's earlier protests to Roosevelt over exclusion of the Russians from the armistice negotiations. Marshall and his staff prepared the reply that the President sent, denying that there had been anything more than peace feelers and reassuring the Russians that they would have a part in any final negotiations —which would be based only on unconditional surrender.[10] The reply did not satisfy Stalin. Either as a device to soften mounting Allied indignation over Poland or as a symbolic warning shot across the Anglo-American bow, he sent Roosevelt a message filled with suspicion and recrimination. Those who knew his capacity for ugly speaking had no doubt that he had prepared much of the message himself.

The Russian leader bluntly accused Roosevelt's informants of misleading him. "It may be assumed," he wrote, "that you have not been fully informed. As regards my military colleagues, they, on the basis of the data which they have on hand, do not have any doubts, that the negotiations have taken place and that they have ended in an agreement with the Germans, on the basis of which the German commander on the Western Front, Marshal Kesselring, has agreed to open the front and permit the Anglo-American troops to advance to the East, and the Anglo-Americans have promised in return to ease for the Germans the peace terms." He could not understand why the British had remained silent on this affair, leaving to the Americans the task of informing the Russians of negotiations in which the British had taken the initiative. (He was incorrect in assuming that the British had started the talks.) He could see, he went on, the advantage to the British and Americans of being able to advance almost without resistance into the heart of Germany, but why conceal that fact from an ally, Russia? "It is understandable that such a situation can in no way serve the cause of preservation or the strengthening of trust between our countries." [11]

It was to deal with this situation, threatening Allied cooperation in the final offensive against the enemy, that Marshall and his aides sat down on April 4 to draft a reply that President Roosevelt—now at Warm Springs, Georgia, where he would die scarcely more than a week later—might send Marshal Stalin. In requesting the draft Leahy stressed the importance of disabusing the Russian leader of the misconception that the Allies were having easy going against the Germans: "This is a new statement of the Soviet suspicion which might be answered by telling U. J. [Uncle Joe] something about the difficulties that Eisenhower encountered in disorganizing the German armies on the Rhine." [12]

In their initial draft Marshall and his aides firmly rejected Stalin's accusations. They proposed that Roosevelt flash back indignant denials of the statements made by the Marshal and his informants. When the draft reached the White House, Admiral Leahy reiterated the assurances given in earlier messages: (1) there had been no negotiations with the Germans; (2) the preliminary meeting with Germans had no political implications; (3) if a surrender came in Italy, it would be on an unconditional basis; and (4) Soviet representatives were welcome at any meeting held to discuss final surrender.[13]

The firmest language of the message drafted by Marshall and his staff was retained. The advances of the Western armies, Stalin was reminded, came from the tremendous impact of Allied air power on German communications and the fact that Eisenhower had destroyed much of the German Army west of the Rhine. Turning to the question of reliable informants, the final reply suggested that Stalin's views on the state of negotiations in Italy must have come from German sources attempting to create dissension between the Western Allies and the Russians. "If that was Wolff's purpose in Berne your message proves that he has had some success." The closing paragraphs were those that Marshall had sent to the White House:

"Finally I would say this, it would be one of the great tragedies of history if at the very moment of the victory, now within our grasp, such distrust, such lack of faith should prejudice the entire undertaking after the colossal losses of life, material and treasure involved.

"Frankly I cannot avoid a feeling of bitter resentment toward your informers, whoever they are, for such vile misrepresentations of my actions or those of my trusted subordinates." [14]

Churchill fired off a reply to Stalin backing Roosevelt's statements and adding that in the interests of Anglo-Russian relations, "We thought it better to keep silent than to respond to such a message as was sent by M. Molotov, but you may be sure that we were astonished by it and affronted that M. Molotov should impute such conduct to us." [15]

Stalin replied to the President that he had never doubted his integrity or Churchill's. The question was "what is admissible and what is inadmissible as between one ally and another." If surrender was to be discussed with the Germans, then the Russians should be represented. He could not understand why the Germans were still putting up crazy resistance to the Russians for an insignificant railway station in Czechoslovakia, "which is as much use to them as hot poultices to a corpse," although in the West they gave up highly important centers. He reiterated his belief in his own informants.[16]

Stalin's reply shocked General Marshall because it sneered at American intelligence data on German intentions that Marshall had earlier furnished to the Russians. On February 20 the Chief of Staff had sent Deane for transmission to Stalin data from intercepts indicating that the Germans were preparing for counteroffensives in the general area of Pomerania and in the Vienna–Mährisch Ostrau region. A week later Marshall reported that these possibilities no longer obtained because of continued

German withdrawal and Allied air attacks on production facilities, principally oil and ammunition. In an angry mood Stalin rejoined that his own informants had brought him correct data that enabled him to meet the main blow in the neighborhood of Lake Balaton, southwest of Budapest.[17]

Another explanation was the fact that Hitler and some of his advisers were now talking wildly of various plans they had no possible capacity to put into effect. The German Foreign Minister, Joachim von Ribbentrop, had told Japanese Ambassador Hiroshi Oshima that Hitler intended to mount a great offensive in the East after May or June. In the West the Rhineland had collapsed and the Western Allies had been able to make unexpected advances into Thuringia. But the Germans still talked of new preparations.

The sharp rejoinders from Roosevelt and Churchill in early April moved Stalin to assure the British Prime Minister that neither he nor Molotov had any intention of "blackening" anyone. He pointed out that his messages were all personal and confidential, a fact that he felt made it possible to speak frankly. If these were to be regarded as offensive, it would make any kind of communication difficult. "I can assure you," he wrote, "that I had and have no intention of offending anyone." This was as close to an apology as Stalin could bring himself, and it evoked Roosevelt's final plea, the very day of his death, that the Western Allies minimize differences with the Russians.[18]

Stalin did not bother to moderate his rather brutal answer to Marshall concerning his intelligence information until after Potsdam. Talking with Eisenhower after the conference, he acknowledged that he had been unduly rude to the Chief of Staff and wanted to express his regret.[19]

Eisenhower's decision to telegraph Stalin about his future plans and his insistence on a clearly marked line of demarcation between the advancing Allies, such as the Elbe-Mulde river line, may have been influenced to some degree by the desire to keep friction with the Red Army to a minimum and to avoid any accidental clash. It was not so much the decision to stop on the Elbe that disturbed Churchill as it was the fact that Eisenhower had informed the Russians of this decision by going directly to Stalin rather than through high-level political and military channels. Both aspects disturbed the British Chiefs of Staff and they complained at once to General Marshall that the Supreme Commander had exceeded his powers and asked the Allied military missions in Moscow to hold up delivery of amplifications by Eisenhower of his earlier message.

Recognizing political overtones in the protest, Marshall and his colleagues insisted that the Yalta arrangements for liaison with the Russians to prevent incidents gave Eisenhower sufficient authority to communicate directly with Moscow. The Americans rejected any proposal that would lower Eisenhower's prestige, saying that if changes were to be made in his message to Moscow, he should make them. Not only did they defend his strategy, but they held that the battle for Germany had reached the point "where the commander in the field is the best judge of the measures which offer the earliest prospect of destroying the German armies or their power to resist." [20]

Thus challenged, the Prime Minister finally revealed what he had in mind. Would it not be better to proceed on to Berlin or as far east as circumstances permitted lest the Russians, who already had Vienna within their grasp, get the wrong idea from their conquests?

Confident of Marshall's backing, Eisenhower held to his position. He knew his Clausewitz, and it was not news to him that "war is waged in pursuance of political aims." However he regarded it as "militarily unsound at this stage of the proceedings to make Berlin a major objective, particularly in view of the fact that it is only 35 miles from the Russian lines." If the Combined Chiefs of Staff should decide that the Allied effort to take Berlin outweighed "purely military considerations in this theater," he was willing to readjust his planning and thinking to carry out such an operation. Unless they gave him such a directive, he preferred to stop at a well-defined line—along the Elbe-Mulde—and send his troops northward to establish the Allied left flank on the Baltic near Lübeck and to the south to clear out any German efforts to establish resistance in the National Redoubt. His move to cut off possible Russian occupation of Schleswig-Holstein represented, of course, a willingness to take a political action, which he had declined to take in the case of Berlin.[21]

Eisenhower's reference to the National Redoubt muddied the intelligence picture in later years, and it was widely assumed that until late April the Supreme Commander took seriously the threat of a well-prepared German attempt to hold out indefinitely in the Bavarian mountain area. Without doubt such a possibility had been considered. Ribbentrop told an acquaintance in early April: "Although it has been our policy to keep the German Supreme Commander and Government in Berlin, in view of the changes in the war situation the occasion may arise in which we would move the German Government temporarily to southern Germany." [22] But no real effort was made to implement the redoubt plan. Although Marshall warned Eisenhower to be on his guard against any build-up in southern Germany, there never was any positive evidence of a crucial problem in the area. Within a week after Marshall's warning his Chief of Intelligence reported that there was no information substantiating the threat. Perhaps the most authoritative statement about the real state of affairs was made after the war by Major General Sir Kenneth Strong, Eisenhower's wartime Chief of Intelligence: "My own expressed view about the National Redoubt was that it might not be there, but that we nevertheless had to take steps to prevent it being established. After the Ardennes, I was taking no more chances with the Germans. . . . Eisenhower shared this skepticism, but he agreed that the stories could not be ignored and therefore took full account of the possibilities in his planning." [23]

It seems, however, that Eisenhower's moves involved not only caution but also the willingness to use the possible threat of the National Redoubt to justify the decision to stop at the Elbe. Thus while making certain there would not be another Ardennes, the Supreme Commander was strengthening his case for not driving to Berlin.

The Combined Chiefs of Staff made no direct response to Eisenhower's pronouncement that he must have a specific directive if he were to drive for Berlin rather than toward other objectives he considered more important militarily. This lack of action by no means ruled out a thrust to the German capital by Western Allied units, but it meant that such an offensive would have low priority.[24]

The decision of the Joint Chiefs of Staff, sustained by President Roosevelt, that Eisenhower was in the best position as commander in the field to make military decisions in a time of great fluidity of operations was reaffirmed by President Truman little more than a week after he came into office. Replying to Churchill regarding the zones of occupation, in a message in which Leahy and Marshall likely had a hand, the new President declared: "The question of tactical deployment of American troops in Germany is a military one. It is my belief that General Eisenhower should be given certain latitude and that where time permits, he should consult the Combined Chiefs of Staff before any major withdrawal behind our zone frontiers." [25]

With the decisions left to him to make on military grounds Eisenhower held firm to a halt at the Elbe. Later he indicated that General Bradley had told him it might cost 100,000 casualties to fight his way into Berlin and that it seemed foolish to go forward merely to be told to pull back. In addition the American forces in many areas had outrun their supplies.[26]

Again it is difficult to doubt that the disposition of armies played some role in the decision. When Field Marshal Montgomery on April 6 asked for ten American divisions to aid his main thrust toward Berlin and the Baltic coast, the Supreme Commander made clear the vast change from a month before. Somewhat impatiently Eisenhower replied: "You must not lose sight of the fact that during the advance to Leipzig you have the role of protecting Bradley's northern flank. It is not his role to protect your southern flank. My directive is quite clear on this point. Naturally, if Bradley is delayed, and you feel strong enough to push out ahead of him in the advance to the Elbe, this will be all to the good." So far as the German capital was concerned, he declared: "As regards Berlin I am quite ready to admit that it has political and psychological significance but of far greater importance will be the location of the remaining German forces in relation to Berlin. It is on them that I am going to concentrate my attention. Naturally, if I get an opportunity to capture Berlin cheaply, I will take it." Montgomery, now convinced of the futility of arguing for a main drive on Berlin, replied: "It is quite clear to me what you want. I will crack along on the northern flank 100 per cent and will do all I can to draw the enemy forces away from the main effort being made by Bradley." [27]

General Simpson, commander of the Ninth Army, did not agree with Eisenhower. Reaching the bank of the Elbe on the day that Roosevelt died, he pushed two bridgeheads across the river, the closest only fifty-three miles from the German capital. Although his forces were thrown back at one point, he was convinced that his troops could have taken Berlin ahead of the Russians, who were only some thirty-five miles away. The well-known military historian Colonel S. L. A. Marshall, then acting Theater Historian and in the area at the time, believed that Simpson was oversanguine, but the question remains a subject of hot controversy.[28]

Brought into the main fighting in the early fall, Simpson had spent much of his time under command or control of Montgomery's 21 Army Group, where he had ably handled a number of work-horse assignments. In the late winter and early spring he and his staff believed that they were being slighted by Montgomery by being given minor assignments in the coming fight for the Rhine. This resentment helped convince the high command that Simpson's army should be shifted back to Bradley after the bridgehead over the Rhine had been well established. Thus for the great encircling movement of the Ruhr, the Ninth and First armies shared honors for trapping nearly a third of a million men under Field Marshal Walther Model. Now having contributed to the growing German collapse, Simpson wanted to be in on the kill. When he reached the Elbe, he urged Eisenhower to allow him to go on to Berlin. Eisenhower repeated his previous orders to stand fast and reiterated his instructions to clear positions west of the river in his area.

To General Marshall the Supreme Commander reported that not only were the other objectives more important than Berlin but it would be senseless to press on to the German capital in view of the relative positions of the Russians and the Western Allies. "While true that we have seized a small bridgehead over the Elbe, it must be remembered that only our spearheads are up to that river; our center of gravity is well back of there." [29]

His arguments satisfied the Chief of Staff. General Marshall at the time and more than a decade later supported the Supreme Commander. Speaking of the failure to drive for Berlin—in full knowledge of the Berlin blockade of 1948 with which he had had to deal as Secretary of State and with ample opportunity for reflection—the wartime Chief of Staff defended Eisenhower's decision. To the question "In retrospect do you feel that we should have tried to take Berlin and Prague as Churchill wanted us to?" General Marshall replied:

No, I do not think we should have gone into Berlin at that time. . . . However it must be remembered that all this time we were trying to do business with the Russians. We had been fighting with them. They were part of the armed forces—a very decided part. They had played a great part in the fighting, the wearing down of the German strength, and we had to take that all into careful regard. At that time, toward the close of the struggle, they were exceedingly sensitive, looking all the time for something that would indicate that the British and Americans were preparing to go off alone and to settle the thing . . . to their [British and American] satisfaction and to the disadvantage of the Russians. So we were very careful about this, the Americans more so than the British, because Mr. Churchill was quite positive in the matter, and events and time have rather proved that he was possibly more nearly right than the American position. But we were trying very hard to find a basis of negotiation to go along with the Russian government. Eisenhower was in a particularly trying position because in command of the troops he was brought into constant situations that had to be handled . . . in a way that displeased one party or the other and I thought he did extraordinarily well in this matter.

Now just what the effect would have been [in the] question of Prague is open to discussion. I might say in all this it is very much a Monday-quarterback business because all sorts of things have happened since those days, and our relations with Russia at that time were quite different.[30]

As early as March 22, 1945, General Marshall's Chief of Intelligence had noted the importance of having a clearly marked point of demarcation for the meeting between forces coming from east and west, and had suggested the line of the Elbe and Saale as one possibility. Although this precise memorandum apparently was not passed on to Eisenhower, Marshall in early April did note the value of a carefully marked line and indicated the need of a clear understanding with the Russians. There had already been incidents on both sides because airmen could not be certain whether they were in Russian or Allied zones.[31]

After careful consideration the Allied commanders concluded that it was not logical for the armies from the West to stop their advance at the edge of the zone allotted to the Russians—at the risk of leaving Germans free to operate in the area until the Red forces came up. Rather it became evident that armies from east and west should be permitted to advance at will until they reached some clearly defined point, such as a major waterway, shortly before a link-up was imminent. General Eisenhower suggested to Marshall and his colleagues in early April that either side should be allowed to advance freely until contact was made. After the link-up either the Red Army commander or Eisenhower could request the other to retire behind zonal boundaries set by the European Advisory Commission.[32]

The British Chiefs of Staff objected at once to any mention of the interzonal boundaries for the purpose of defining areas while hostilities were in progress. They suggested to Washington that the armies stand in place until their governments ordered them to withdraw.[33]

Officials of the State and War departments balked at the British argument. Brigadier General George A. Lincoln of Marshall's staff reported that the State Department believed that movements of troops should remain "*a military consideration* at least until SHAEF is dissolved and the ACC (Allied Control Commission) set up." State feared that the proposed British action would stir the Russians to a race for the remaining unoccupied German areas in order to gain as many miles of enemy territory as possible before an armistice was reached. To members of the War Department this meant that the State Department desired a straight military solution to the problem. That notion disturbed the Russians. General Antonov feared that such an arrangement would change the occupation zones already assigned. He asked for and got Eisenhower's assurance that upon completion of tactical operations, Anglo-American forces would withdraw from zones assigned previously to the Soviet Union.[34]

Mindful of the earlier arguments over political and military negotiations with the Russians, the Combined Chiefs of Staff on April 21 spelled out for Eisenhower the policy he was to follow. They suggested that the forces from east and west halt as and where they met, with the line being adjusted by local commanders to deal with enemy opposition. After hostilities ceased, forces were to be disposed in accordance with military requirements regardless of zonal boundaries. So far as he was able, Eisenhower was to obtain approval from the Combined Chiefs of Staff before making major adjustments in boundaries. Within these limits he was permitted to negotiate with the Red Army staff.[35]

On April 21 and 22 General Eisenhower moved within the framework of his instructions from Washington to avoid future clashes with the Russians. Once again he repeated his intention to stop at the Elbe and to turn his troops north and south to clear out enemy opposition. It was evident that his northern forces would cross the lower Elbe and strike at the enemy at the base of the Jutland Peninsula, and that the southern forces would drive through the Danube Valley into Austria. It was equally evident that the armies from east and west would continue to advance until they linked up. On the central front he had chosen the Elbe-Mulde line as a desirable stopping point. However it was possible after a first contact that a firm link might be made along some "well-defined geographical feature." Eisenhower proposed that the adjustments and definitions of operational boundaries be made between the Russian and Allied army group commanders most concerned.[36]

The Russians, seemingly disturbed at the Western armies' rate of advance, speedily seized on the Supreme Commander's proposal, accepting the line of the Elbe and Mulde as a common border. On April 24 they added that they expected to occupy Berlin and to clear enemy forces from areas east of the Elbe north and south of Berlin and also in the Czechoslovak region from the Vltava (Moldau) Valley.[37]

When the Russian forces met delays in driving to Prague, Churchill

and his colleagues pressed Eisenhower to force his way on to the Czechoslovak capital. Near the end of April the Prime Minister pointed out to
the Joint Chiefs of Staff that the Western powers could gain major advantages by liberating Prague and a large part of the Czechoslovak state.
General Marshall studied the proposal but reacted as he had earlier,
backing Eisenhower's military decisions. In forwarding the British proposal to the Supreme Commander, he declared in a statement that the
other Chiefs in Washington accepted, "Personally and aside from all logistic, tactical or strategical implications I would be loath to hazard
American lives for purely political purposes." [38]

Marshall was merely restating his earlier reasoning on the taking of
Berlin. Eisenhower was in accord. He replied that he proposed initially a
thrust toward Lübeck and Kiel, which he had already indicated was intended to forestall the Russians in that area, and a drive in the south
toward Linz and any Austrian Redoubt. If additional troops were available, he proposed to attack enemy forces still holding out in Czechoslovakia, Norway, and Denmark. However it appeared that the Russians were
in perfect position to clear the Germans from Czechoslovakia and that
they would probably reach Prague before U.S. forces. In the same sense in
which Marshall had written, Eisenhower replied: "I shall not attempt any
move I deem militarily unwise merely to gain a political prize unless I
receive specific orders from the Combined Chiefs of Staff." [39]

In the closing days of the campaign the Prime Minister repeatedly
voiced pleas to turn Eisenhower in the direction of Prague, pleas that in
the final hours of the fight were echoed by Undersecretary of State Joseph
Grew in communications to the War Department. On May 4, after Czech
officials in Prague and in London appealed to the Allies to advance to the
Czech capital to save leaders there from German reprisals, Eisenhower
notified Moscow that he was willing to move forward after the occupation
of České Budějovice, Plzeň, and Karlsbad (three points initially defining
a line of demarcation) to the line of the Elbe and the Moldau to clear the
west banks of those rivers. General Antonov dissented vigorously, asking
that Eisenhower avoid "a possible confusion of forces" by staying west of
the original line. Significantly the Russian General added that the Soviet
forces had stopped their advance to the lower Elbe east of the line of
Wismar-Schwerin-Dömitz at the Supreme Commander's request and that
he hoped General Eisenhower would comply with Russian wishes relative
to the advance of the U.S. forces into Czechoslovakia. The Supreme Commander assured the Soviet leader that he would not move beyond the
agreed-on line. His action left Prague and the rest of Czechoslovakia
to be liberated by the Red Army.[40]

This was the decision Marshall later said he was not certain that the
Western Allies should have made. He made it clear however that he was
thinking in terms of postwar developments in relations with the Russians.
And he repeated twelve years later that in early May 1945—in the closing

hours of the war—he and Eisenhower were trying to keep on good terms with the Russians: "They were always delicate; they were always jealous, and it was very, very hard to preserve a coordinated association with them. But we did it to a [considerable] extent at that time—which is unthinkable today in the knowledge of later events. Nobody but the Lord could foresee all that has happened since." [41]

Letters between Marshall and Eisenhower and memoranda between Stimson and Marshall about the approaching postwar situation reflected the fact that they thought in terms of 1919—that American public opinion would demand a recall of troops from abroad, that a demand would be made for a sharp cutback in the armed forces, that a resurgence of isolationism would bring a revulsion against stationing American troops abroad to be caught up in Europe's quarrels, and that final arrangements would be made at a peace conference. On the way to Cairo, Roosevelt had said that "he personally envisaged an occupation force of about one million United States troops." And to Marshall's query as to how long they would remain he replied, "for at least one year, maybe two." [42] Although Roosevelt had spoken fleetingly of wanting to take Berlin, the seriousness of that comment must be weighed against this prediction. If he meant it to be taken seriously, it was because he thought only a short occupation would be required. He himself waved the suggestion away lightly a few weeks later. No one at the White House, the State Department, or the higher levels of the Joint Chiefs of Staff contemplated a strong force glaring at the Russians across occupation lines for twenty-five years or a fifteen-month-long airlift to supply a beleaguered Western Sector of Berlin a few years after the war ended.

As early as mid-1943 Marshall, mindful of demobilization problems after World War I, had begun to draw up plans for an orderly return to peacetime conditions. He also stressed careful organization of the redeployment of troops from Europe to the Pacific. In accordance with an elaborate scheme he had sent Eisenhower instructions in the early spring of 1945 for screening his units to pick the men who would be shipped overseas. By April troops were taking physical-fitness tests to determine their assignments for further duty. In that same month, when decisions had to be made about driving for Berlin and Prague, Marshall and Eisenhower were discussing which commanders might go to the Far East. Patton, complaining pathetically that at his age this would be his last war, kept reminding Marshall as he had since the time of Casablanca that he was willing to serve in any capacity from division up. (Later when he knew that there was no place for him in the Far East, he fulminated because he had been stopped short of Prague and reproached Eisenhower for not permitting his Third Army to press on.) A half-dozen division and corps commanders were listed for advisory tasks in China, and a call went out for a couple of dozen field commanders to handle redeployment centers in the United States for troops being shifted back for later duty against Japan. In short the American concept of war in March and April of 1945 was not one of settling down to a long occupation and even less one of a prolonged confrontation with the Russians. The United States still cherished the idea of redeploying troops to restore order in the Far East and then returning them home, hoping to retain only a minimal peacetime army.

A number of later critics maintain that Roosevelt, Marshall and his colleagues, and the commanders in the field should have been more prescient. Berlin and Prague, they say, should have been seized to make certain that Allied prestige remained high in Europe. Of course Churchill urged such action. But to the military commanders there was no point in seizing territory they had no intention of holding or racing the Russians for areas they had already agreed to share. With their main interest centered on defeating Japan, the U.S. leaders believed it unwise and fruitless to make a move that might precipitate conflict by stringing out separate armies across an area that was due to be turned over to the Russians. The early plans to drop airborne troops into Berlin or to speed armored columns into that area had been designed to disarm a collapsing German government. Since German forces were not collapsing but remaining to be beaten in the field, it seemed logical to leave the job to the force nearest Berlin. Among many soldiers there was a feeling for a short time at least that the Germans would be more properly punished if left to the tender mercies of the Russians. Stimson, far from a bloodthirsty man, seemed for a time in the summer of 1944 to hold this view. In arguing in favor of a southern occupation zone for the United States, he said the United States would be "further away from the dirty work that the Russians might be doing with the Prussians in eastern Germany." [48]

From a military standpoint it made no sense to deploy a force—then being readied for shipment to the Far East or home—for a possible conflict with the Russians unless someone at high governmental level made a political decision to change the strategy of the war. Since the time of the first Berlin crisis there has been a tendency for critics to argue backward from that point. On the assumption that Berlin was essential to trip-wire strategy or to the protection of the West's position in Europe, they have held that the Western Allies should have established a stronger foothold in the former German capital. But this argument begs the question. If Marshall or Eisenhower, both seasoned military leaders, had started with the notion that they would later have to defend Western Europe from Communist attack, they would not have chosen to go to a zone in Berlin surrounded by Communist-occupied territory. A novice in such matters would not have deliberately chosen as a base for an outpost a position that could be supplied only by highways leading for a hundred miles through a Russian zone—even if right of access had been spelled out in the most careful treaty. From the day the Russians began the Berlin crisis, the former capital was a hostage, a source of potential weakness to the

Western Allies. Rather than reacting to definite threats to the security of the West, the United States has been required to react to every act of provocation there from the Soviet Union.

It is often asserted in Britain and the United States that Churchill had the right policy, with the corollary being that Marshall and Eisenhower prevented him from implementing it. But the brutal fact was that lack of military power, economic enfeeblement by long fighting and great destruction, the disintegration of the Empire, and lack of resources made it impossible for Britain to enforce the policy in Europe that the Prime Minister wanted. Although he still thought in terms of a reborn Empire —a view that Americans sometimes accepted—his dream of maintaining British ascendancy in the Middle East, in parts of the Balkans, in Central Europe could not be realized by British arms. In fact it had been French rather than British forces that had maintained the long occupation of Germany after World War I. If Russia was to be challenged in Central Europe, if Berlin was to be held as the symbol of Western intentions, then the United States would have to furnish the men and the machines and the money for much of that task. Further it would have to be demonstrated to an American public reluctant and slow to accept any commitment to Europe that it should assume burdens of indefinite length in an area difficult to defend—a ruined city, no longer the effective capital, of a beaten country—against a current ally whose armies dominated the government of the country on the eastern border of Germany and held an occupation zone completely surrounding the city.

From time to time long-range planners in Britain and the United States had noted that the total defeat of Germany and Japan would leave Russia supreme in Europe. But there was never a time when this possibility was put on the agenda of Anglo-American discussions, nor was it ever suggested until the final days of the war that the early intention to partition and punish Germany should be changed.

At Yalta the Prime Minister, together with Roosevelt and Stalin, examined the possible partition of Germany into three or perhaps five states— preferring less disruption than he had supported earlier but still not attempting to spare the Third Reich the consequences of Hitler's errors. As late as January 1945 Churchill had indicated to Stalin that Russian aid was still needed against Germany by pressing the Red leader to receive Eisenhower's representatives in order to coordinate plans. Through February, Western Allied troops still slogged through the mud and snow of the area west of the Roer, and some Westerners hoped that the Russians would meet the Western armies at the Rhine and shorten the agony. Not until the capture of the Remagen bridge in March did it at last seem that the Anglo-American forces might take the Ruhr before the Russians entered Berlin. Not until nearly mid-April did the Americans, their forces dangerously extended, reach the Elbe, and only then did the Prime Minister begin to demand a strong challenge to the Russians. But no groundwork for the sudden switch had been laid with Washington.

In the last two weeks of his life Roosevelt was too intent on working out postwar peace machinery with the Russians to risk an open break over Prague and Berlin. There was no time between his death and the end of the war in Europe—less than a month later—to work out a different strategic or diplomatic orientation. And despite growing apprehensions over Russian policy, later stressed heavily by Leahy and King, not one member of the Joint Chiefs of Staff attempted to change Roosevelt's views.

From Marshall's standpoint so long as American policy was to defeat Germany unconditionally, there was no basis for quarreling with a power that was helping to make Hitler's total defeat possible and that was in a position, even more than Britain, to contribute to the speedy and unconditional defeat of Japan. It was unlikely that the British people, weary of war and for the most part sympathetic to a country that had also borne much of the human cost of the conflict, would have strongly backed a challenge to the Soviet Union over Berlin or Prague in late April or early May. It was less likely that General de Gaulle, who had signed a security pact with Moscow the previous December, would approve such a move. Although American public opinion had once favored allowing Germany and the Soviet Union to fight to a draw, there was no widespread support for postponement of the showdown with Japan in order to make a vigorous challenge to the Soviet Union in Central Europe.

The crux of the argument lies in the charge that Marshall and Eisenhower failed to think politically. Marshall was well aware of the close relationship between political and military matters. In 1944 and 1945 when he was urging establishment of a true national war college, he vigorously encouraged State Department representation in order to achieve integration of political and military thinking.[44] Eisenhower made the point clear in discussing with Marshall the need to go to Berlin. He conceded the fact that wars were fought for political purposes, but he asked either to be given a political directive to go into Berlin or to be allowed to make a decision to stay out on military grounds.

The strongest deterrent to a shift in emphasis from a campaign to destroy Germany to one designed to halt Russia was the fervor with which the campaign against Germany had been carried on. The French had the physical presence of Germans on their soil and the British the memories of bombers over their cities to fire their hatreds. The Americans had responded to the preaching of a crusade against the Axis powers, and the emotional stimulation necessary to sustain the drive was maintained by the goal of total victory.

Strangely enough some of the fiercest opponents of American intervention in 1940 and 1941 became the fiercest proponents of a strong line in Central Europe against the Soviet Union. But in criticizing Eisenhower and Marshall for not racing the Russians to Berlin and Prague, they are attacking military leaders because they did not take Churchill's political advice. They confuse the issue. It was not failure by the military leaders to think of political consequences but their refusal to make political decisions that their critics apparently deplore. On that point the position of Marshall and Eisenhower was in the soundest political tradition of the Republic.

It has been argued that Marshall and his colleagues in Washington might have taken political actions with propriety in the interim between Roosevelt's death and Truman's assumption of firm control of the administration. With very little pressure they could have set policy for a new and untried President. In that confused period Marshall was consulted frequently by Truman, and it has been suggested that he was responsible for the crucial decisions of late April and early May. This view overlooks the fact that Truman, a student of military and political history, had been examining the conduct of the war as chairman of a major and active Senate committee since early in the conflict. He was not precisely untried in military matters. Moreover Marshall never attempted to make political decisions that went contrary to those laid down by Roosevelt and apparently accepted by Truman. In the absence of new directives he continued to follow the course set by the late President.

Those who seem startled that Marshall did not exercise greater control mistake their man. At the end of World War I, Marshall had seen his superior and mentor Pershing excoriated as a militarist because he, like Foch, urged a drive on to Berlin. Marshall's own view in 1919, as expressed in the plan he prepared for the occupation of Germany in case she failed to respect the armistice provisions, was to avoid involvement in German affairs beyond the point necessary to enforce compliance with the provisions and to keep order. Like Pershing and most of the other military leaders of his generation, Marshall held fast to the idea that political decisions must be made by the head of the state—a view in which he was stanchly supported by the other Chiefs of Staff.

In one respect the Chiefs of Staff could properly be criticized for their policy. By insisting that nothing be allowed to interfere with Eisenhower's control of the battle and that military rather than political considerations take precedence, they may have obscured full consideration of possible changes in political directions. But in this case political and military considerations were not contradictory. In late March and early April when the British criticized Eisenhower's purely military approach to the Berlin question, the U.S. Chiefs' rejoinders hewed strictly to Roosevelt's political desires. And it is clear enough from study of developments immediately after Roosevelt's death that President Truman was not dominated by his military advisers.

Political matters certainly dominated the discussions initiated by Truman with his political and military advisers on April 23 because he was infuriated by Soviet actions in regard to Poland. Russian Foreign Affairs Commissar Molotov, then in Washington en route to the approaching United Nations Conference at San Francisco (where he was at last being sent somewhat reluctantly by Stalin) angered the new President by insisting on a seat for the Russian-backed Lublin government of Poland at San Francisco. Secretary of State Stettinius considered this proposal, virtually installing a faction in Poland favorable to Russia, a direct violation of the Russian pledge at Yalta to sponsor free and democratic elections in the liberated Polish state. He did not believe that the Lublin government in any way represented the Polish people.[45]

President Truman, who had quickly assumed control within the ten days since the presidency had descended on him, called in his Secretaries of State, War, and Navy, plus Leahy, Marshall, King, Harriman, Deane, and Assistant Secretaries of State Charles E. Bohlen and James C. Dunn. "Without warning," Stimson wrote a few hours later, "I was plunged into one of the most difficult situations I have ever had since I have been here." [46]

Not yet known as "give-em-hell Harry," the new Chief Executive, outwardly usually mild and colorless, was in a tough mood. He said that he felt that so far American agreements with the Soviet Union "had been a one-way street and that could not continue; it was now or never. He intended to go on with the plans for San Francisco and if the Russians did not wish to join us they could go to hell. . . ." [47] Having stated his very pronounced views, he asked his advisers to state theirs.

Although capable of plain speaking, Secretary Stimson in this case asked for a moderate approach. He noted problems with the Russians in the past over minor matters, "and it was necessary in these cases to teach them manners." But he felt that it was important to find out what their motives were in regard to the lands on their borders. Without understanding fully how seriously they took the Polish question, the United States "might be heading into very dangerous water."

The argument seemed dubious to Secretary of the Navy Forrestal, already a hard-liner on Russia. He feared that the Russians believed that the United States would not object if they took all Eastern Europe under their control. If they were going to be rigid in their views, he thought, "we had better have a showdown with them now than later." [48]

Ambassador Harriman, who had explained to Undersecretary of State Joseph Grew and members of the Secretary of State's Staff Committee on April 20 and 21 the importance of standing firm on Poland, declared that the real issue "was whether we were to be a party to a program of Soviet domination of Poland." He recognized that if negotiations were properly handled with the Soviet Union, trouble might be avoided.

Stimson still stuck with his point that the United States needed to know how far the Russians would go on the Polish question. Without endorsing their actions he still felt that the Russians were "being more realistic than we were in regard to their own security." Admiral Leahy commented that he had left Yalta with the view that the Russians did not intend to permit a free government to operate in Poland and that he would have been surprised if they did. He believed that the Yalta agreement was subject to two interpretations. He thought it serious to break with the Russians but urged that they be told that the United States stood "for a free and independent Poland."

Marshall, who had been listening quietly to the discussion, now broke in. His political superior was giving the political views of the War Department. Now he wanted to talk of military considerations. Stimson, who had been disturbed that no one had supported his efforts to see if the two superpowers could get the situation ironed out without "a headon collision," was pleased. "Then to my relief a brave man and a wise man spoke and he said that he, like me, was troubled and urged caution." [49]

The Chief of Staff was not attempting to propound the broad Stimson position, which was to seek an understanding with the Russians in Central Europe. Stimson's approach was that of traditional diplomacy—similar to the one hinted at by Churchill at Tehran—that a satisfied power might be a peaceful power and that a great power freed of its major fears over insecure borders might be nonaggressive. Marshall's was a simpler and narrower approach. He said that he was not familiar with the Polish issue and its political aspects; he could speak only of the military aspects. "He said from the military point of view the situation in Europe was secure but that they hoped for Soviet participation in the war against Japan *at a time when it would be useful to us*. The Russians had it within their power to delay their entry into the Far Eastern war until we had done all the dirty work. He said the difficulties with the Russians such as in the case of CROSSWORD [the German peace feelers in Italy] usually straightened out. He agreed with Mr. Stimson that the possibility of a break with them was very serious." [50]

Stimson concurred wholeheartedly. The Russians' failure to back free elections made him pessimistic about relations with them in the future. But, he observed, outside the United States with the exception of the United Kingdom, there was no country that understood free elections—"the party in power always ran the elections. . . ." It was a judgment born of supervising balloting in Latin America and of observing Tammany Hall politics at first hand.

Ambassador Harriman did not support Stimson's view. While conceding that the Soviet Union had kept its big agreements on military matters, he noted "that those were decisions which it had already reached by itself but that on other military matters it was impossible to say they had lived up to their commitments." General Deane, scarred by many unsuccessful negotiations with the Soviet representatives, thought that the Soviet Union "would enter the Pacific War as soon as it was able, irrespective of what happened in other fields. He felt that the Russians must do this because they could not afford too long a period of letdown for their people who were tired. . . . [He] felt that we should be firm when we were right."

As the discussion ended, Truman thanked his military advisers for their views. From a military point of view, he said he was satisfied that there was no reason why the country should fail to stand up "to our understanding of the Crimean agreements." He then asked his diplomatic advisers to remain behind to help him prepare for his talk later that day with Molotov.

Stimson and Marshall had not won their argument for a cautious course, but they may have swayed Truman from the sharper approach he had outlined at the beginning of the meeting. Certainly, there is no basis for assuming, as Professor Gabriel Kolko has done, that by the time "the Cabinet adjourned Truman was in something of a rage." As the published record shows, the remark that he planned to tell Molotov to join us or "they could go to hell," which the author cites to illustrate the President's rage, was actually expressed at the beginning of the meeting. It ended on a much calmer note.[51]

Later in the afternoon the President stood up firmly to Molotov—talking in strong Independence, Missouri, vernacular. He declared that United States was prepared to carry out its agreements at Yalta, and it expected the Soviet Union to do the same. He desired friendship with the Soviet Union on the basis of mutual observation of agreements and not "on the basis of a one-way street."[52] One may see in the tough talk evidence of a bellicose Yankee spoiling for a fight or an anti-Red itching to use the atomic bomb, but the explanation was simpler than that. In fact the new President had reacted to the power politics of Moscow in the manner of a proud senator from Missouri accustomed to respond vigorously to provocation. But at this juncture at least, it was too early to discern a calculated anti-Russian line in Truman's moves.

It was in reality impossible for Truman to launch an anti-Soviet policy so long as he accepted the Marshall-Stimson argument that Russian aid was needed against Japan. And he did. As he later wrote, "I was anxious to get the Russians into the war against Japan as soon as possible, thus saving the lives of countless Americans."[53] Although strong messages continued to flow back and forth between Moscow and Washington and London, and there were serious disagreements at the United Nations meeting, there was a measure of Soviet cooperation with the Western Allies at San Francisco on the organization's charter. More important the final drives to victory in Germany brought a show of concerted action despite numerous flare-ups at the conflict's end.

As the debates on Russia's political actions proceeded in Washington in late April, Soviet troops closed in on Berlin from the east and the Western Allies sped for the Elbe-Mulde line and a link-up with the Russians. On April 25 Russian and American patrols met at the Elbe and at points east of the river. Next day the formal link-up occurred at Torgau between elements of the U.S. 69th Division and the Soviet 58th Guards Division. Other link-ups rapidly followed along the line. Only a few days would be required to bring the war to an end.

In northern Italy representatives of the United States and Britain were still engaged in the negotiations that had earlier outraged the Russians. That the melodrama did not turn into tragedy for the Germans concerned was due mainly to the fact that the final curtain in Central Europe was about to fall. General Wolff's masters and rivals in Italy and Germany recognized that the end was near. They were not prepared, as Hitler had been, to shoot officers who fell back on the ancient rule of "sauve qui peut." It did not make sense to act too boldly against the negotiators lest they betray their own doubts and, in some cases, secret overtures. So the cloak-and-dagger meetings proceeded with material enough for several thrilling "stranger than fiction" volumes and suspenseful Hollywood dramas.[54]

Despite the early start the surrender came only after Mussolini had been captured and hung up by his heels in Milan and after Hitler had died in his bunker—apparently by his own hand. Because of the need for secrecy, details of the careful negotiations in Italy were scarcely known in Washington. At a critical point the U.S. Chiefs of Staff ordered the negotiations broken off. But this anticlimax was avoided when General Wolff —at last—offered surrender.

The final capitulation in Italy, coming only shortly before the complete Axis collapse, paid some dividends. Allen Dulles, a key participant, maintained that the long negotiations were useful in pointing a way toward surrender in Germany. Shortly after Hitler's death, on April thirtieth— ten days after his fifty-sixth birthday and a little more than twelve years since he had taken the chancellorship of the Third Reich, Admiral Hans Georg von Friedeburg, an emissary of the new Reichsführer (Admiral Karl Doenitz), arrived at General Eisenhower's headquarters in Reims to discuss capitulation. Following the Italian format, troops facing Field Marshal Montgomery had already arranged for surrender of those troops on that front, just as German forces facing General Devers's 6th U.S. Army Group did to the south. Through his representative, General Bedell Smith, Eisenhower demanded unconditional surrender of all remaining German forces. Pleading that his instructions permitted no such arrangement, the emissary asked Doenitz at Flensburg for further instructions. General Alfred Jodl was now dispatched to assist Friedeburg in the discussions. When the two emissaries continued to delay, hoping for some arrangement whereby they could surrender on the western front while continuing to oppose the Russians, Eisenhower gave them forty-eight hours to accept his terms or take the alternative of his sealing the western front, leaving the Germans to the east at the mercy of the Soviet forces. In the face of this threat Jodl signed at 2:41 on the morning of May 7. It was agreed that hostilities would end at midnight on May 8. Although the war would then be over, the armistice stipulated that a ratification must be signed in the presence of Russian commanders in Berlin on May 9. This was arranged with Tedder acting for Eisenhower, Zhukov for the Russians, Spaatz for the Americans, and de Lattre for France.

For those who search the last weeks of fighting in Europe for signs that the Western Allies were even then preparing the cold war against the Soviet Union, no better proof of the groundlessness of this charge could be found than in Washington's strict observance of the unconditional-surrender formula in the case of Wolff's surrender in Italy and the stern refusal to enter into an arrangement with Doenitz for cessation of hostilities only against Western forces. It could be seen in Eisenhower's directive for representatives to inform all German commanders on his front of the unconditional surrender. It was further evident in his strict adherence to the arrangement by which Germans from the Prague garrison who had held out against the Russians, and then retreated westward after the Armistice, were held at his front line and handed over to the Soviet forces.

Marshall's supreme interest at the moment of victory in Europe was in getting on with the task of defeating Japan. For weeks planning had been under way for possible invasion of Japan and an operation—OLYMPIC—had been set for October 1945. General Hodges and his First Army headquarters were selected in April to participate in the attack. Shortly before the armistice they were ordered to start their shift to the United States in preparation for duty in the Far East.

Thus while in Europe and the United States, V-E Day brought a season of rejoicing and celebration, it was for Marshall the triumphant second act of a long drama. Before the final curtain he and his colleagues still had to set the stage and ready the cast for one more act.

In the brief time he had Marshall sent his heartfelt congratulations to the commander he had chosen and backed completely to carry through the operation on which they had worked together since the first weeks after war began. It was no mere formality when he signaled Eisenhower:

> You have completed your mission with the greatest victory in the history of warfare.
>
> You have commanded with outstanding success the most powerful military force that has ever been assembled.
>
> You have met and successfully disposed of every conceivable difficulty incident to varied national interests and international political problems of unprecedented complications.
>
> You have triumphed over inconceivable logistical problems and military obstacles and you have played a major role in the complete destruction of German military power.
>
> Through all this, since the day of your arrival in England three years ago, you have been selfless in your actions, always sound and tolerant and altogether admirable in the courage and wisdom of your military decisions.
>
> You have made history, great history for the good of mankind and you have

stood for all we hope for and admire in an officer of the United States Army. These are my tributes and my personal thanks.[55]

Like many other busy men of public affairs, Marshall sometimes used the services of gifted writers on his staff for his personal tributes. This one he wrote himself. He was repaid in kind. Writing before he received Marshall's praise, Eisenhower recognized that his victory owed an incalculable debt to the Army Chief of Staff:

> Since the day I first went to England, indeed since I first reported to you in the War Department, the strongest weapon that I have always had in my hand was a confident feeling that you trusted my judgment, believed in the objectivity of my approach to any problem and were ready to sustain to the full limit of your resources and your tremendous moral support, anything that we found necessary to undertake to accomplish the defeat of the enemy. This has had a tremendous effect on my staffs and principal subordinate commanders. This conviction that you had basic faith in this Headquarters and would invariably resist interference from any outside sources, has done far more to strengthen my personal position throughout the war than is realized even by those people who were affected by this circumstance. Your unparalleled place in the respect and affections of all military and political leaders with whom I have been associated, as well as with the mass of American fighting men, is so high and so assured that I deeply regret you could not have visited here after this army had attained its full growth and before the break-up necessarily begins. Our army and our people have never been so deeply indebted to any other soldier. . . .[56]

There would be many more tributes from around the world, and Marshall treasured them all. But the two he must have liked best had been sent him shortly before the war's end, as the Allied forces streamed across the Rhine into the Third Reich.

One of them came from an old comrade-at-arms who, as Chief of Naval Operations, had helped to arm the Navy and had early concluded that Germany must be defeated first. Admiral Harold R. Stark, who had been sent to London to head the U.S. Naval Mission there shortly after Pearl Harbor, wrote his friend on March 30:

> Back of all success in the war in Europe is George Marshall. God bless him. There isn't anything in the world I wouldn't do for you that I personally could.
>
> In my humble opinion . . . few realize the full extent of what you have meant and do mean to this old war-torn world.
>
> I simply thank God for you from the bottom of my heart. I don't know how we could have gotten along without you.
>
>   Faithfully and affectionately,
>
>   Betty.[57]

And there had been the accolade from the old lion, the Prime Minister, with whom he had argued endlessly over the timing of the cross-Channel attack. But Marshall liked a fighter, and he could forgive much in one who had dared his enemies to do their worst. Together they could savor the defeat of Hitler. Churchill did not wait for the final seal of triumph to send his praises. Instead as March came to a close, with its evidence of certain victory in Europe, he radioed to Field Marshal Wilson, now chief of the British Mission in Washington:

> Pray . . . give . . . [General Marshall] my warmest congratulations on the magnificent fighting and conduct of the American and Allied Armies under General Eisenhower, and say what a joy it must be to him to see how the armies he called into being by his own genius have won immortal renown. He is the true "organizer of victory." [58]

Churchill said it first. But when all the returns were in, History would say the same.

Acknowledgments

ON PAGES 591–95, I have listed the names of individuals who contributed directly to the book in the form of interviews or other materials pertinent to the biography. Noted below are the names of many others who helped make the book and overall program of the George C. Marshall Library possible by various types of contributions, financial and otherwise.

The largest financial contribution to this volume in the form of support for research, interviews, collection of material, payment of the salary of the author came from the Ford Foundation. Support was also received from the Scaife Fund, the Richard K. Mellon Fund, the Robert T. Stevens Fund, the Mary W. Harriman Foundation, the Rockefeller Brothers Fund, and the Oveta Culp Hobby Foundation. An advance by The Viking Press was added to these funds. As a private, nonprofit foundation, we continue to depend on the generosity of many loyal supporters throughout the nation for the overall operation of the Library, the purchase of books and materials, the operation of the museum, and the like.

During the period since the last volume appeared, the following have served as members or officers of the Board of Directors of the George C. Marshall Research Foundation, initially headed by the late John C. Hagan, Jr. Giving liberally of their time and efforts were the permanent members: General of the Army Omar N. Bradley, Lt Gen Marshall S. Carter, Robert A. Lovett, Maj Gen Richard L. Irby, Lt Gen George R. E. Shell, J. Clifford Miller, Jr, Maj Gen William M. Stokes, John C. Parker, Brig Gen Frank McCarthy, H. Merrill Pasco, Harry A. deButts, Lt Gen Milton G. Baker, Fred C. Cole, Carter Burgess, and Robert E. R. Huntley. This number also included ex officio members of the board who served during the period that they held the position of President of the Board of Visitors of the Virginia Military Institute: Elmon T. Gray, J. Randolph Tucker, Lt Gen Edward M. Almond, Gorham B. Walker, Jr, Clarence E. Thurston, Jr, and Sol W. Rawls, Jr. Royster Lyle, Jr, has served ably as secretary of the board since 1962.

The Foundation has been aided in great measure by the personal efforts and financial contributions of the members of the Advisory Board. Those who have served since the appearance of the last volume are: David K. E. Bruce, James Bruce, Ward M. Canaday, Lewis W. Douglas, William C. Foster, Gordon Gray, W. Averell Harriman, John H. Hilldring, Oveta Culp Hobby, Anna Rosenberg Hoffman, Paul G. Hoffman, Carlisle Humelsine, W. John Kenney, William McChesney Martin, John J. McCloy, Robert D. Murphy, Frank Pace, Jr, William D. Pawley, John Lee Pratt, Edward V. Rickenbacker, Matthew B. Ridgway, Mary G. Roebling, James R. Shepley, Robert T. Stevens, Lewis L. Strauss, Maxwell D. Taylor, Juan T. Trippe, Thomas J. Watson, Jr, Langbourne M. Williams, and Erskine Wood. Members of the board who died during that period are: Harrison Jones, George M. Humphrey, Dan A. Kimball, Spyros Skouras, Mrs Philip W. Pillsbury, and Charles E. Wilson.

Five Presidents of the United States—Harry S. Truman, Dwight D. Eisenhower, John F. Kennedy, Lyndon B. Johnson, and Richard M. Nixon—have granted access to official documents and have given their backing to our project. Dr Rudolph Winnacker, historian, Department of Defense, has served faithfully and effectively since 1955 as liaison between the Marshall Foundation and various government departments and agencies. At the National Archives, we have been aided in many ways by the General Services Administrator, Robert L. Kunzig, and by the late Wayne Grover, former archivist; Dr Robert Bahmer, his successor; and the incumbent, Dr James B. Rhoads. At the World War II Reference Branch of the National Archives, we are deeply indebted to the former heads, Sherrod East and Wilbur Nigh, and their successor, Thomas Hohmann, and to Hazel Ward, Garry Ryan, Lois Aldridge, Virginia Jezierski, Henry Williamson, William Cunliffe, Hildred Livingston, Camille Hannon, and Geneva Penley.

Others in the National Archives and the presidential libraries who have been of great assistance are Robert W. Krauskopf, Herman G. Goldbeck, and Miss Mabel E. Deutrich of the National Archives staff and Philip C. Brooks, longtime director of the Harry S. Truman Library; John Wickman, Dwight D. Eisenhower Library; Elizabeth Drury, James O'Neill, and William L. Stewart of the Franklin D. Roosevelt Library.

In the Department of the Army Library, I am indebted to Paul Burnette, former director; his successor, O. W. Holloway; the present director, Mrs Mary Shaffer; and indeed to most of the staff.

At the Office of the Chief of Military History, Department of the Army, we have benefited greatly from the generous aid of a number of friends of this project: in particular the former Chief of Military History, Brig Gen Hal C. Pattison, and his successor, Brig Gen James L. Collins, Jr, and the former Chief Historian, Stetson Conn, and his successor, Maurice Matloff, and Robert W. Coakley, Charles B. MacDonald, Charles F. Romanus, Detmar Finke, Royce L. Thompson, and James E. Hewes. In the Adjutant General's Office, I have received great cooperation from Ollon McCool, Seymour Pomrenze, Cyrus H. Fraker, and Paul L. Taborn.

In the Department of State, I wish to acknowledge especially the assistance and advice of William M. Franklin, historical officer, Bureau of Public Affairs, and his deputy, G. M. Richardson Dougall. In the Joint Chiefs of Staff Historical Section, I am indebted to Wilber Hoare, head of the section, and to Vernon Davis and Helen Bailey. Col George S. Pappas, director of the U.S. Army Military Records Collection, Carlisle Barracks, Pennsylvania, has made material available from his files.

I received access to the Henry L. Stimson papers, which included the invaluable Stimson Diary, from the director of the Historical Manuscripts and University Archives, Yale University. Miss Judith Schiff checked the quotations I have used from the diary.

Edgar F. Howell, Jr, curator of the Division of Military History, Smithsonian Institution, has been helpful to the Foundation in many ways.

Special thanks are due to the former superintendent of the Virginia Military Institute, Lt Gen George R. E. Shell, who served during most of the period when the first three volumes of this book were written and who cooperated in every conceivable way in making our program a success. We have also received the same kind of fine assistance from his successor, Maj Gen Richard L. Irby, since his assumption of the superintendency in July 1971. The Marshall Foundation has continued to benefit from earlier efforts of Joseph D. Neikirk, executive vice president, VMI Foundation, and from continued support by the VMI alumni. Many members of the institute staff have given generously of their time. Mention should be made of Brig Gen James Morgan, acting superintendent during the illness of General Shell, and currently dean of the faculty, who has been of great aid, and Lloyd Davidson, who has continued since 1956 to give advice and counsel on the development of the Library program.

The former president of the Washington and Lee University, Fred C. Cole, who remains on the Board of Directors as an elected member, and his successor, Robert E. R. Huntley, have continued to aid in projects for developing the work of the Marshall Library. Members of their staffs have cooperated gladly with their counterparts at VMI in advancing our program.

Mrs George C. Marshall has been most gracious in answering questions about General Marshall and herself and family. I have also received great assistance from her son-in-law and daughter, Col and Mrs J. J. Winn, and the widow of her son Allen Brown, Mrs Madge Brown Pendleton. I have benefited greatly from Mrs Marshall's book, *Together,* which has supplied me with information about the General's activities and furnished several excellent anecdotes for this volume.

Several members of General Marshall's wartime and peacetime staffs have been especially helpful: Gen Thomas T. Handy, Gen John E. Hull, Brig Gen Frank McCarthy, Maj Gen William T. Sexton, and Col C. J. George. I wish to express my special appreciation to Generals Bradley and Carter for their strong backing during the writing of this volume. I also wish to thank General Bradley's Pentagon secretary, Mrs Annie McGhee, for her aid.

I cannot speak too highly of my staffs in Arlington and Lexington during the years in question. The late Eugenia D. Lejeune, archivist-librarian, 1957-71, whose recent death left us sadly bereft, contributed heavily to this volume with the materials she gathered and organized and with the numerous suggestions she made for improving the book. Her former assistant, Mrs Juanita Pitts, continued the work she had begun under Miss Lejeune's direction and assumed additional duties in the Arlington office after Miss Lejeune assumed direction of the collection in Lexington. Mrs Pitts has continued to select documents for microfilming, and has checked meticulously quotations and footnotes for this book. Mrs Arline Van B. Pratt, who has worked as a research associate with me since 1957, did the basic research on the chapters dealing with the Pacific area, also checking the quotations and footnotes of those chapters on which she worked. Her work, as always, has been most careful and exact.

Mary Ann Knight, who began work under Miss Lejeune's direction shortly before Volume II was completed, continued working with Mrs Pitts for several years, contributing effectively to the overall project and assisting particularly in typing cards for the William F. Friedman collection. Mr Wilbur Nigh performed extremely valuable work for me during two periods after his retirement from the Archives staff. Myles Marken and John H. Gauntlett, who had completed most of their work before the beginning of this volume, left many valuable cards summarizing newspapers and periodicals. (An even larger collection of material for this volume was made at Lexington by Mrs Henry A. Wise, who did most of this work without pay.)

Mrs Dorothy Dean has contributed in many ways to this volume. In addition to her great ability to type accurately from messy typescript and barely legible handwritten corrections by the author, she has handled all my correspondence, telephone calls, and mounting irritation with problems in general in an admirable manner.

The daughters of Mrs Pitts and Mrs Dean, Susan and Dorothy, assisted their mothers for short periods of time. Mrs John K. Jennings, who had worked mainly in Lexington, gave effective aid to the author in Arlington during the next to the last summer of the writing of this book.

I am under great debt to members of the Marshall Foundation staff and of the Marshall Library staff in Lexington for their aid in the raising of funds, the splendid administration of the Library, research pertaining to the book, and continuing organization of the collection. I cannot speak too highly of the work of Royster Lyle, Jr, secretary to the board and assistant to the director of the Library, who has headed the fund-raising efforts of the Foundation and worked closely with the president of the Foundation in its various activities. In the fund-raising programs he has been assisted by Maj Chester W. Goolrick of the VMI faculty and by other members of the faculties and staffs of Washington and Lee and the Virginia Military Institute.

Mrs Boyd G. Stuart has handled myriad problems pertaining to administration and business management of the Foundation. Also aiding in these matters have been long-time staff members Mrs H. Blair Tolley and Jorge R. Piercy. Other assistants have included: Mrs Richard Abrams, Mrs Jeffrey Sheehan, Miss Virginia T. Dickinson, and Mrs William H. Oast. In the work of the Library I wish to note the efforts of Mrs D. C. Watkins, cataloguer, who has been with the Library since the publication of the last volume; former members of the staff, Mrs B. McCluer Gilliam, Mrs Charles C. Lewis, Mrs James D. Madewell, Miss Mary Jo DelVecchio, Mrs Hubert Young, Mrs John Hosey, Mrs Arnold Grandis, Mrs Benjamin Cummings, Mrs Fox Urquhart, and Mrs John K. Jennings; and current members, Mrs Henry A. Wise, Mrs William D. Elliot, Miss Kathy J. Moore, Mrs James F. Pascal, and Mrs W. Steven Coleman.

Bibliographical Note

MARSHALL INTERVIEWS

In 1956–57 General Marshall recorded on tape some forty hours of answers and comments in response to questions submitted by me. This material was recorded in sessions at the Pentagon, at Leesburg, and at Pinehurst. Some of the comments were recorded without my being present, with his orderly, Sergeant William Heffner, running the machine. In addition, General Marshall talked to me about fifteen hours without a tape recorder. Part of the comments in these sessions were recorded by his secretary, Miss Mary Louise Spilman, and part by me.

The interviews and this biography began with a project first suggested in 1951 by friends and admirers of General Marshall. In 1953 a group of graduates of his alma mater, the Virginia Military Institute, headed by the late John C. Hagan, Jr, established the George C. Marshall Research Foundation to collect material on the General's career that would furnish information for a definitive biography and for numerous special studies on the period in which Marshall served as soldier and statesmen. Earlier the group had been assured of the backing of President Harry S. Truman in the collection of documents and the development of a Research Center. Shortly before leaving office, Mr Truman issued a directive to the General Services Administrator, the Secretary of State, and the Secretary of Defense "to cooperate with Virginia Military Institute and the proposed George C. Marshall Research Foundation in procuring documentary material relating to the activities of General Marshall as a soldier, as Secretary of State, and as Secretary of Defense." In 1956 President Eisenhower wrote a similar letter, and this official support was reaffirmed by President Kennedy in 1962, President Johnson in 1965, and President Nixon in 1970.

In 1956 funds to start the collection of documents and the writing of a biography were provided by a generous personal gift from John D. Rockefeller, Jr. Impressed by the actions of President Truman and President Eisenhower and the urgings of many friends, General Marshall agreed in 1956 to cooperate with a biographer in recording, on tape, information on high points of his career.

I was aided by earlier research that I had conducted between 1946 and 1952 while preparing the Department of the Army's *The Supreme Command,* the official account of Eisenhower's command in northwest Europe, 1944–45. I had collected thousands of pages of notes from personal and official files, which I left with the Office of the Chief of Military History when I completed the volume. These papers were sent to the General's office for my use. Since the collection included my notes on Allied planning from January 1941 through Casablanca and Yalta to Potsdam, this phase of preparation was simplified.

Inasmuch as General Marshall had no opportunity to check the transcripts of his interviews and perform the careful editing at which he excelled, I have taken the liberty of making occasional slight corrections in the text without in any way altering the sense or flavor of the language. Exact transcriptions will be placed on file with the Marshall papers. (It should be noticed that in those cases where I have quoted from my handwritten notes, the quotation marks denote the language of my transcription of his remarks rather than an exact reproduction of his statements.) For a more detailed discussion of the method of conducting interviews see *George C. Marshall: Ordeal and Hope,* 442–44.

OTHER INTERVIEWS

More than three hundred friends and former associates of the General have granted interviews used in the preparation of my books. Individuals whose names are starred gave material for this volume both in interviews and in the form of letters, photographs, clippings, newspapers, and the like: Dean G. Acheson,* Gen Sir Ronald Adam, Brig Gen and Mrs Claude M. Adams,* Field Marshal Lord Alanbrooke, Lt Gen E. M. Almond,* Mrs H. H. Arnold,* Lord Attlee, Lord Avon, Helen Bailey, Maj Gen Ray W. Barker, Bernard M. Baruch,* Col William Baumer, Brig R. F. K. Belchem, Brig Gen T. J. Betts, Ambassador Charles E. Bohlen, Gen Charles Bolté, Gen of the Army Omar N. Bradley,* Lt Gen Lewis H. Brereton,* Lt Gen George H. Brett,* Rear Adm R. V. Brockman,* Lt Gen E. H. Brooks,* Lt Gen Harold R. Bull, Harvey Bundy, Lady Mary Burghley, Maj Gen James H. Burns, Brig Gen Frederic B. Butler, James F. Byrnes, Brig Gen B. F. Caffey, Lt Gen Marshall S. Carter,* Maj Gen James G. Christiansen, Gen Mark W. Clark,* Brig Gen Carter Clarke, Henry C. Clausen, Gen J. Lawton Collins, Brig Gen James L. Collins, Jr, Philip E. Connelly, Adm C. M. Cooke, Maj Gen Norman D. Cota, Maj Gen Frank L. Culin, Adm of the Fleet Lord Cunningham of Hyndhope, Gen John E. Dahlquist, Brig Gen T. J. Davis, Maj Gen John R. Deane, Gen Sir Miles Dempsey, Gen Jacob L. Devers,* Lady Dill, Lewis W. Douglas,* Sgt George E. Dumcke, Col R. E. Dupuy, Gen Ira C. Eaker, Gen of the Army Dwight D. Eisenhower,* Lt Gen Delos Emmons, Sgt William Farr, Brig Gen Louis J. Fortier,* Justice Felix Frankfurter, Col William F. Friedman, William Frye,* Maj Gen Philip E. Gallagher, Frederick V. Geier, Col C. J. George,* Gen Leonard T. Gerow,* Col Stanley Grogan, Lt Gen Leslie Groves, Maj Gen C. C. Haffner, Gen Wade H. Haislip,* Gen Thomas T. Handy, William D. Hassett, Maj Gen Charles D. Herron,* Lt Gen Lewis B. Hershey, Maj Gen John H. Hilldring, Mrs Oveta Culp Hobby, Gen Courtney Hodges, Gen William M. Hoge,* Gen Sir Leslie Hollis, Charles R. Hook,* Gen John E. Hull, Carlisle Humelsine, Gen Lord Ismay, Lt Gen Reuben E. Jenkins, George Kennan, Gen Walter Krueger, Gen Laurence S. Kuter, Sir Basil Liddell Hart, Col G. A. Lincoln, Robert A. Lovett,* Scott Lucas, Mrs Marjorie Payne Lunger,* Gen of the Army Douglas MacArthur, Col J. E. McCammon, Brig Gen Frank McCarthy,* John J. McCloy, Mrs Frank R. McCoy,* Maj Reginald Macdonald-Buchanan,* Gen Joseph T. McNarney, Donald Mace,* Mrs George C. Marshall,* Brig Gen S. L. A. Marshall, John Martyn, Maj Gen Sherman Miles, Francis Pickens Miller, J. Clifford Miller, Jr, Maj Gen Luther D. Miller, L. Arthur Minnich, Field Marshal Lord Montgomery of Alamein, Lt Gen Sir Frederick Morgan, Adm of the Fleet Lord Mountbatten of Burma, Miss Mona Nason, Brig Gen Arthur Nevins, Fleet Adm Chester W. Nimitz, Maj Gen Thomas North, Brig Gen Frederick Osborn, Arthur W. Page, Gen Sir Bernard Paget, H. Merrill Pasco,* William D. Pawley, Mrs Madge Brown Pendleton,* Maj Gen Wilton Persons, Marshal of the Royal Air Force Lord Portal, Sgt James Powder, John Lee Pratt,* Sam Rayburn,* Col

Russell P. Reeder,* Maj Gen George J. Richards, Gen Matthew B. Ridgway,*
Walter S. Robertson, Brig Gen Paul McD. Robinett,* Mrs Eleanor Roosevelt,
Dean Rusk, Maj Gen William T. Sexton,* James Shepley, Lt Gen William H.
Simpson, Gen George Simonds, Field Marshal Lord Slim, Col Truman Smith,*
Gen Walter Bedell Smith,* Maj Gen Howard M. Snyder, Mrs Brehon B. Somer-
vell, Gen Carl Spaatz, Col William Spencer,* Maj Gen M. C. Stayer, Adlai
Stevenson, Mrs Joseph Stilwell, Lt Gen Richard K. Sutherland, Charles P. Taft,
Gen Maxwell Taylor, Miss Cora Thomas, Maj Gen Thomas S. Timberman,
President Harry S. Truman, Gen L. K. Truscott,* Brig Gen H. A. Twitchell,
Maj Gen Fred L. Walker, Maj Gen Orlando Ward,* Mrs E. M. Watson,* Mark
S. Watson,* Gen A. C. Wedemeyer, Maj Gen Charles West, Field Marshal Lord
Wilson, Col and Mrs J. J. Winn, and W. Averell Harriman and Anna Rosen-
berg Hoffman.

For background I have used notes on interviews that I conducted in 1946 and
1947 while gathering material for *The Supreme Command*. In addition to Alanbrooke, Betts, Bradley, Cunningham, Eisenhower, Morgan, Mountbatten, Portal,
and Smith listed above among those I interviewed later, I received information
pertinent to this volume from Maj Gen Ray W. Barker, Maj Gen Robert W.
Crawford, Gen Charles de Gaulle, Brig Gen Thomas J. Davis, Maj Gen Julius
Holmes, Adm John Hughes-Hallett, Marshal Alphonse Juin, Fleet Adm Ernest
J. King, Capt C. E. Lambe, Fleet Adm William D. Leahy, Henry Cabot Lodge,
Brig Gen Arthur S. Nevins, Marshal Jean de Lattre de Tassigny and Brig
E. T. Williams.

LETTERS

The General's personal files contained copies of much of his correspondence
for the years 1939–42. I have supplemented these by papers from the official files.
I have also used my notes on General Eisenhower's correspondence with General Marshall, which I had taken from the former's files in 1946. Among other
letters I have used were those furnished by Bernard M. Baruch and Mrs Madge
Brown Pendleton and letters of General Arnold's furnished me by Murray
Green.

ADDITIONAL SOURCES OF INFORMATION

The following have supplied information in various forms, such as letters, photo-
graphs, clippings, speeches, articles, or general information pertaining to General
Marshall or the events covered by this volume: Lt Gen Edward M. Almond,
N. J. Anthony, Brig Gen Clifford Bluemel, Leo Cherne, Robert Coakley, Hugh
M. Cole, Brig Gen Robert Cutler, L. M. Dorsch, Col Trevor Dupuy, Sherrod
East, Rear Adm E. M. Eller, Stanley Falk, Detmar Finke, Kenneth Hechler, Sgt
William Heffner, Col R. D. Heinl, Jr, James E. Hewes, Lt Gen Thomas F.
Hickey, Wilber Hoare, Col Bertram Kalisch, Richard Leighton, Misses Eugenia
and Laura Lejeune, Ernest K. Lindley, Speaker John McCormack, Louis Mor-
ton, Col Homer C. Munson, Col R. V. Murphy, John C. Parker, Milton F. Perry,
Capt Edgar F. Puryear, Jr, Charles F. Romanus, R. G. Ruppenthal, Mel Ryder,
Jr, Robert Sherrod, John P. Spore, Rep Frank A. Stubblefield, Riley Sunderland,
Donna H. Traxler, Rudolph A. Winnacker and Milton Schreiber.

DIARIES

I have drawn heavily on the Diary of Secretary of War Henry L. Stimson, which is at the Yale University Library. Since Stimson saw General Marshall almost daily when the two men were at the War Department, and made frequent summaries of their conversations, it is an invaluable source on the wartime Chief of Staff. Unquestionably the Diary contains comments by both men made when they were tired or angry, which later they would have preferred to revise. In fact, Secretary Stimson omitted many of them from *On Active Service,* which he wrote in collaboration with McGeorge Bundy. I have included some of these on the ground that they reflected War Department thinking at the time. (Quotation marks around statements from the Stimson Diary may refer to the Secretary of War's paraphrase rather than to General Marshall's exact words.)

Material from the Morgenthau Diaries, to which I was directed by John Blum's *Years of Urgency,* was furnished me by the Franklin D. Roosevelt Library, Hyde Park, New York. For those portions of the Diary entries not open to the public, I have relied on Blum's book.

I have also made use of notes taken from the diary of the Commander-in-Chief that was kept by Capt. Butcher during the period 1942–45.

MEMOIRS, AUTOBIOGRAPHIES, AND BIOGRAPHIES

On this material see my note on pages 446–47 in *George C. Marshall: Ordeal and Hope.*

ARCHIVES AND LIBRARIES

General Marshall's personal papers were given to the George C. Marshall Research Library before his death, and title was confirmed by Mrs Marshall. Many of the papers are now deposited in the Marshall Library at Lexington, Virginia. Others are still in Washington. These files are not yet open to researchers.

The principal official records pertaining to the Chief of Staff's activities for the period 1943–45 are in the custody of the National Archives. Record collections that have been used for this volume include:

RECORD GROUP 165—*Records of the War Department General and Special Staff:* Office of the Chief of Staff (OCS)—to March 1942; War Department Chief of Staff (WDCSA)—after March 1942; War Plans Division (WPD)—to March 1942; Operations Division (OPD)—after March 1942; Personnel Division (G-1); Intelligence Division (G-2); Organization and Training Division (G-3); Civil Affairs Divson (G-5).

RECORD GROUP 107—*Records of the Secretary of War and Assistant Secretary of War.*

RECORD GROUP 160—*Records of Headquarters Army Service Forces (ASF).*

RECORD GROUP 218—*History of the Joint Chiefs of Staff* (Hayes).

RECORD GROUP 331—*Records of the Supreme Headquarters, Allied Expeditionary Force (SHAEF).*

RECORD GROUP 332—*Records of the United States Theaters of War.*

RECORD GROUP 337—*Records of Headquarters, Army Ground Forces (AGF).*

RECORD GROUP 338—*Records of Western Defense Command (WDC).*

RECORD GROUP 407—*Records of the Adjutant General's Office (TAG).*

RECORD GROUP 18—*Records of Army Air Forces (AAF).*

The author has drawn on material from the National Archives, Modern Military Branch; The Office of the Chief of Military History; The Department of the Army Library; The National War College Library; The Library of Congress; The Franklin D. Roosevelt Library; The Office of Naval Records and Library, U.S. Marine Corps Historical Section; The Yale University Library; the Air University Library and The Virginia Military Institute Library. I wish to thank their directors and staffs for their willing cooperation.

OFFICIAL HISTORIES

I am heavily indebted to the Department of the Army's official volumes in the "United States Army in World War II" series. Based on all the available official records and presented in great detail, they were invaluable for background information and for guides to the official sources. Although I have attempted to check the original sources wherever available to me, I have been influenced in my selection of material and in my interpretations in many cases by these volumes.

For the British side of the story I have relied heavily on *Grand Strategy* by John Ehrman.

Pertinent volumes by Samuel E. Morison on the operations at sea and the Air Force volumes edited by Craven and Cate, in the "Army Air Forces in World War II" series, were frequently consulted.

NEWSPAPERS AND PERIODICALS

Members of the staff have checked the files of the following newspapers and periodicals for the period 1943–45 for editorial and general comments: New York *Times;* Washington *Post;* Washington *Star;* Chicago *Tribune; The Times of London; Army and Navy Journal; Army and Navy Register; Time; Newsweek;* and *Life.* Several years ago the Marshall Library acquired the New York *Times'* own clipping file of its stories on World War II, arranged by topic. This collection, now at Lexington, fills some 164 boxes. The Library also has an extensive clipping collection on General Marshall from the UPI collections at the New York *World-Telegram & The Sun;* a collection made by Don Russell and presented to the Library; a collection made over a number of years by Arthur Webb, former U.S. correspondent for the London *Mail;* and an extensive collection presented to the Library by Mel Ryder, Jr, publisher of the Army Times Publishing Company.

Also of assistance was the annotated bibliography of articles, editorials, and books pertaining to General Marshall for the war years that was prepared by my wife, Christine Pogue, as her master's thesis at Catholic University. Copies are on file at the university, at the Department of Army Library, and at the George C. Marshall Library.

Selected Bibliography

Alexander, Field Marshal Earl. *The Alexander Memoirs, 1940–1945.* Edited by John North. New York: McGraw-Hill, 1963.

Ambrose, Stephen E. *Eisenhower and Berlin, 1945: The Decision to Halt at the Elbe.* New York: Norton, 1967.

———. *The Supreme Commander.* Garden City, N.Y.: Doubleday, 1970.

Armstrong, Anne. *Unconditional Surrender: The Impact of the Casablanca Policy upon World War II.* New Brunswick, N.J. Rutgers University, 1961.

Arnold, Henry H. *Global Mission.* New York: Harper, 1949.

Baldwin, Hanson W. *Battles Lost and Won.* New York: Harper & Row, 1966.

———. *Great Mistakes of the War.* New York: Harper, 1950.

Baruch, Bernard. *My Own Story.* Vol. II, *The Public Years.* New York: Holt, Rinehart & Winston, 1960.

Bath, Gerald H. "A Report on Visit of British High Command to Colonial Williamsburg May 15–16, 1943." Unpublished account.

Beaver, Daniel R., ed. *Some Pathways in Twentieth-Century History: Essays in Honor of Reginald Charles McGrane.* Detroit: Wayne State University, 1969.

Birse, A. H. *Memoirs of an Interpreter.* New York: Coward-McCann, 1967.

Blum, John M., ed. *From the Diaries of Henry Morgenthau, Jr. See* Morgenthau, Henry, Jr.

Blumenson, Martin. *Anzio: The Gamble That Failed.* Philadelphia: Lippincott, 1963.

———. *Breakout and Pursuit.* Washington: Department of the Army, 1961.

———. *The Duel for France, 1944.* Boston: Houghton Mifflin, 1963.

———. "General Lucas at Anzio." In *Command Decisions,* edited by Kent R. Greenfield. Washington: Department of the Army, 1960.

———. *Kasserine Pass.* Boston: Houghton Mifflin, 1967.

———. *Salerno to Cassino.* Washington: Department of the Army, 1969.

———. *Sicily: Whose Victory?* New York: Ballantine, 1969.

Bradley, Omar N. *A Soldier's Story.* New York: Henry Holt, 1951.

Brereton, Lewis H. *The Brereton Diaries; The War in the Air in the Pacific, Middle East and Europe, 3 October 1941–8 May 1945.* New York: Morrow, 1946.

Bryant, Sir Arthur. *Triumph in the West. Based on the Personal Diaries of Field Marshal Lord Alanbrooke.* Garden City, N.Y.: Doubleday, 1959.

———. *The Turn of the Tide: A History of the War Years Based on the Personal Diaries of Field Marshal Lord Alanbrooke, Chief of the British Forces.* Garden City, N.Y.: Doubleday, 1957.

Buchanan, Albert R. *The United States and World War II.* New York: Harper & Row, 1964. 2 v.

Bullock, Alan. *Hitler: A Study in Tyranny.* New York: Harper, 1962.

Burns, James M. *Roosevelt: The Soldier of Freedom, 1940–1945.* New York: Harcourt Brace Jovanovich, 1970.

Bush, Vannevar. *Modern Arms and Free Men.* New York: Simon and Schuster, 1949.

Butcher, Harry C. *My Three Years with Eisenhower: The Personal Diary of Captain*

Harry C. Butcher, USNR, Naval Aide to General Eisenhower, 1942 to 1945. New York: Simon and Schuster, 1946.

Bykofsky, Joseph, and Harold Larson. *The Transportation Corps: Operations Overseas.* Washington: Department of the Army, 1957.

Byrnes, James F. *All in One Lifetime.* New York: Harper, 1958.

———. *Speaking Frankly.* New York: Harper, 1947.

Cantril, Hadley. *Public Opinion, 1935–1946.* Princeton: Princeton University, 1951.

Capra, Frank. *Frank Capra: The Name Above the Title.* New York: Macmillan, 1971.

Caraley, Demetrios. *The Politics of Military Unification: A Study of Conflict and the Policy Process,* New York: Columbia University, 1966.

Casey, Richard G. C. *Personal Experience, 1939–1946.* New York: McKay, 1963.

Catton, Bruce. *The War Lords of Washington.* New York: Harcourt, Brace, 1948.

Chandler, Alfred D., Jr., and Stephen E. Ambrose, eds. *The Papers of Dwight D. Eisenhower: The War Years. See* Eisenhower, Dwight D.

Chaney, Otto. *Zhukov.* Norman: Univ. of Okla. Press, 1971.

Churchill, Winston S. *The Second World War.* Boston; Houghton Mifflin, 1948–53. 6 v. Vol. IV, *The Hinge of Fate;* Vol. V, *Closing the Ring;* Vol. VI, *Triumph and Tragedy.*

Clark, Mark W. *Calculated Risk.* New York: Harper, 1950.

Clemens, Diane S. *Yalta.* New York: Oxford University, 1970.

Cline, Ray S. *Washington Command Post: The Operations Division.* Washington: Department of the Army, 1951.

Coakley, Robert W. and Richard W. Leighton. *Global Logistics and Strategy, 1943–1945,* Washington, Dept. of the Army, 1968. [See under Leighton & Coakley]

Cole, Hugh M. *The Ardennes: Battle of the Bulge.* Washington: Department of the Army, 1965.

———. *The Lorraine Campaign.* Washington: Department of the Army, 1950.

Coles, Harry L., ed. *Total War and Cold War: Problems in Civilian Control of the Military.* Columbus: Ohio State University, 1962.

———, and Albert K. Weinberg. *Civil Affairs: Soldiers Become Governors.* Washington: Department of the Army, 1964.

Collier, Basil. *The Defence of the United Kingdom.* London: H.M. Stationery Office, 1957.

Conn, Stetson, and Byron Fairchild. *The Framework of Hemisphere Defense.* Washington: Department of the Army, 1960.

Conn, Stetson, Rose C. Engelman, and Byron Fairchild. *Guarding the United States and Its Outposts.* Washington: Department of the Army, 1964.

Craven, Wesley F., and James S. Cate. *The Army Air Forces in World War II. See* U.S. Air Force.

Crowl, Philip A. *Campaign in the Marianas.* Washington: Department of the Army, 1960.

Cunningham, Andrew B. *A Sailor's Odyssey: The Autobiography of Admiral of the Fleet Viscount Cunningham of Hyndhope.* New York: Dutton, 1951.

Current, Richard N. *Secretary Stimson: A Study in Statecraft.* New Brunswick, N.J.: Rutgers University, 1954.

Cutler, Robert. *No Time for Rest.* Boston: Little, Brown, 1965.

Davis, Kenneth S. *Experience of War.* Garden City, N.Y. Doubleday, 1965.

Davis, Vincent. *Postwar Defense Policy and the U.S. Navy, 1943–1946.* Chapel Hill: University of North Carolina, 1966.

Deane, John R. *The Strange Alliance.* New York: Viking, 1947.

De Conde, Alexander. *A History of American Foreign Policy.* New York: Scribner's, 1963.

de Gaulle, Charles. *The War Memoirs of Charles de Gaulle.* New York: Simon and Schuster, 1958–60. 3 v. Vol. II, *Unity, 1942–1944;* Vol. III, *Salvation, 1944–1946.*

de Guingand, Sir Francis. *Generals at War.* London: Hodder and Stoughton, 1964.

———. *Operation Victory.* New York: Scribner's, 1947.

de Lattre de Tassigny, Jean. *The History of the French First Army.* London: Allen and Unwin, 1952.

DeWeerd, H. A., ed. *Selected Speeches and Statements of General of the Army George C. Marshall*. *See* Marshall, George C.

Dennett, Raymond, and Joseph E. Johnson. *Negotiating with the Russians*. Boston: World Peace Foundation, 1951.

Divine, Robert A. *Causes and Consequences of World War II*. Chicago: Quadrangle, 1969.

——. *Roosevelt and World War II*. Baltimore: Johns Hopkins, 1969.

Dole, Minot. *Adventures in Skiing* [10th Mtn. Div.] New York: Watts, 1965.

Donnison, F. S. V. *Civil Affairs and Military Government, Northwest Europe, 1944–1946*. London: H.M. Stationery Office, 1947.

Douglas, Sholto. *Combat and Command: Memoirs of Lord Douglas*. New York: Simon and Schuster, 1966.

Dulles, Allen W. *Great True Spy Stories*. New York: Harper & Row, 1968.

——. *The Secret Surrender*. New York: Harper & Row, 1966.

Dulles, Foster R. *The American Red Cross: A History*. New York: Harper, 1950.

Dupuy, R. Ernest, and Trevor N. Dupuy. *Military Heritage of America*. New York: McGraw-Hill, 1956.

Dziuban, Stanley W. *Military Relations Between the United States and Canada, 1939–1945*. Washington: Department of the Army, 1959.

Eden, Anthony. *The Reckoning: The Memoirs of Anthony Eden, Earl of Avon*. Boston: Houghton Mifflin, 1965.

Ehrman, John. *Grand Strategy*. London: H.M. Stationery Office, 1956. Vols. V and VI.

Eichelberger, Robert L., and Milton Mackaye. *Our Jungle Road to Tokyo*. New York: Viking, 1950.

Eisenhower, Dwight D. *At Ease: Stories I Tell to Friends*. Garden City, N.Y.: Doubleday, 1967.

——. *Crusade in Europe*. Garden City, N.Y.: Doubleday, 1948.

——. *The Papers of Dwight D. Eisenhower: The War Years*. Edited by Alfred D. Chandler, Jr., and Stephen E. Ambrose. Baltimore: John Hopkins, 1970. 5 v.

——. *Report by the Supreme Commander to the Combined Chiefs of Staff on the Operations in Europe of the Allied Expeditionary Force. 6 June 1944–8 May 1944*. Washington: U.S. Government Printing Office, 1946.

Eisenhower Foundation. *D-Day: The Normandy Invasion in Retrospect*. Lawrence: University of Kansas, 1971.

Eisenhower, John S. D. *The Bitter Woods*. New York: Putnam's, 1969.

Ellis, L. F. *Victory in the West*. London: H.M. Stationery Office, 1962. 2 v.

Esposito, Vincent J., ed. *A Concise History of World War II*. New York: Praeger, 1964.

Fairchild, Byron, and Jonathan Grossman. *The Army and Industrial Manpower*. Washington: Department of the Army, 1959.

Falk, Stanley L. *Decisions at Leyte*. New York: Berkley, 1966.

Farago, Ladislas. *Patton: Ordeal and Triumph*. New York: Obolensky, 1964.

Feis, Herbert. *The China Tangle*. Princeton: Princeton University, 1953.

——. *Churchill—Roosevelt—Stalin: The War They Waged and the Peace They Sought*. Princeton: Princeton University, 1957.

Fergusson, Bernard. *The Watery Maze: The Story of Combined Operations*. New York: Holt, Rinehart & Winston, 1961.

Ferrell, Robert H. *American Diplomacy: A History*. New York: Norton, 1969.

Foot, M. R. D. *SOE in France: An Account of the Work of British Special Operations Executive in France, 1940–1944*. London: H.M. Stationery Office, 1966.

Forrestal, E. P. *Admiral Raymond A. Spruance, USN, A Study in Command*. Washington: U.S. Navy Historical Office, 1966.

Forrestal, James. *The Forrestal Diaries*. Edited by Walter Millis, New York: Viking, 1951.

Franklin, William M. "Yalta Viewed from Tehran." *In Some Pathways in Twentieth-Century History: Essays in Honor of Reginald Charles McGrane*, edited by Daniel R. Beaver. Detroit: Wayne State University, 1969. "Zonal Boundaries and Access to Berlin," *World Politics*, Oct. 1963.

Frye, William. *Marshall: Citizen Soldier*. Indianapolis: Bobbs-Merrill, 1947.

Fuller, John F. C. *The Second World War, 1939–1945: A Strategical and Tactical History*. New York: Duell, Sloan and Pearce, 1949.

Garfield, Brian. *The Thousand-Mile War: World War II in Alaska and the Aleutians*. New York: Ballantine, 1969.

Garland, Albert N., and Howard McGaw Smyth. *Sicily and the Surrender of Italy*. Washington: Department of the Army, 1965.

Girdner, Audrie, and Anne Loftis. *The Great Betrayal*. London: Collier-Macmillan, 1969.

Glennon, John P. "This Time Germany Is a Defeated Nation." In *Statesmen and Statecraft of the Modern West*, edited by Gerald N. Grob. Barre, Mass.: Barre, 1967.

Green, Constance M., Harry C. Thomson, and Peter C. Roots. *The Ordnance Department, Planning Munitions for War*. Washington: Department of the Army, 1955.

Greenfield, Kent R. *American Strategy in World War II: A Reconsideration*. Baltimore: Johns Hopkins, 1963.

———, ed. *Command Decisions*. Washington: Department of the Army, 1960.

———, Robert R. Palmer, and Bell I. Wiley. *The Organization of Ground Combat Troops*. Washington: Department of the Army, 1947.

Grew, Joseph C. *Turbulent Era: A Diplomatic Record of Forty Years, 1904–1945*. Boston: Houghton Mifflin, 1952. 2 v.

Grob, Gerald N., ed. *Statesmen and Statecraft of the Modern West*. Barre, Mass.: Barre, 1967.

Groves, Leslie R. *Now It Can Be Told*. New York: Harper, 1962.

Halifax, Lord. *Fullness of Days*. New York: Dodd, Mead, 1957.

Hall, Hessel D. *North American Supply*. London: H.M. Stationery Office, 1955.

Halsey, William F., and J. Bryan, III. *Admiral Halsey's Story*. New York: Whittlesey House, 1947.

Hammond, Paul Y. "Directives for the Occupation of Germany: The Washington Controversy." In *American Civil-Military Decisions: A Book of Case Studies*, edited by Harold Stein. Birmingham: University of Alabama, 1963.

———. *Organizing for Defense: The American Military Establishment in the Twentieth Century*. Princeton: Princeton University, 1961.

Harmon, Ernest N., Milton MacKaye, and William R. MacKaye. *Combat Commander*. Englewood Cliffs, N.J.: Prentice-Hall, 1970.

Harrison, Gordon A. *Cross-Channel Attack*. Washington: Department of the Army, 1951.

Hassett, William D. *Off the Record with F. D. R., 1942–1945*. New Brunswick, N.J.: Rutgers University, 1958.

Heinl, Robert D. *Soldiers of the Sea: The U.S. Marine Corps, 1775–1962*. Annapolis: U.S. Naval Institute, 1962.

Higgins, Trumbull. *Soft Underbelly*. New York: Macmillan, 1968.

Hobbs, Joseph P. *Dear General*. Baltimore: Johns Hopkins, 1971.

Holley, Irving B. *Buying Aircraft: Materiel Procurement for the Army Air Forces*. Washington: Department of the Army, 1964.

Howard, Michael. *The Mediterranean Strategy in the Second World War*. London: Weidenfeld and Nicolson, 1968.

———. *Studies in War and Peace*. New York: Viking, 1959.

Howe, George F. *Northwest Africa: Seizing the Initiative in the West*. Washington: Department of the Army, 1957.

Huff, Sid, and Joe A. Morris. *My Fifteen Years with MacArthur*. New York: Paperback Library, 1964.

Hull, Cordell. *The Memoirs of Cordell Hull*. New York: Macmillan, 1948. 2 v.

Hunt, Frazier, ed. *MacArthur and the War Against Japan*. New York: Scribner's, 1944.

———. *The Untold Story of Douglas MacArthur*. New York: Devin-Adair, 1954.

Huntington, Samuel P. *The Soldier and the State: The Theory and Politics of Civil-Military Relations*. Cambridge, Mass.: Harvard University, Belknap, 1957.

Huston, James A. *The Sinews of War: Army Logistics 1775–1953*. Washington: Department of the Army, 1966.

Irving, David. *The Destruction of Dresden.* New York: Ballantine, 1963 and 1964.

Ismay, General Lord. *The Memoirs of General Lord Ismay.* New York: Viking, 1960.

James, D. Clayton. *The Years of MacArthur, 1880–1941.* Boston: Houghton Mifflin, 1970.

Julian, Thomas Anthony. "Operation *Frantic* and the Search for American-Soviet Military Collaboration, 1941–44." Ph.D. dissertation, Syracuse University, 1967.

Kecskemeti, Paul. *Strategic Surrender: The Politics of Victory and Defeat.* Stanford: Stanford University, 1958.

Kennan, George F. *Memoirs, 1925–1950.* Boston: Little Brown, 1967.

Kennedy, Sir John. *The Business of War: The War Narrative of Major General Sir John Kennedy.* New York: Morrow, 1958.

Kenney, George C. *General Kenney Reports: A Personal History of the Pacific War.* New York: Duell, Sloan and Pearce, 1949.

King, Ernest J., and Walter M. Whitehill. *Fleet Admiral King: A Naval Record.* New York: Norton, 1952.

Kirby, Stanley W. *The War Against Japan.* London: H.M. Stationery Office, 1957–69. 5 v.

Kingston-McCloughry, E. J. *The Direction of War.* New York: Praeger, 1955.

Kolko, Gabriel. *The Politics of War: The World and United States Foreign Policy, 1943–1945.* New York: Random House, 1968.

Kreidberg, Marvin A., and Merton G. Henry. *History of Military Mobilization in the United States Army, 1775–1945.* Washington: Department of the Army, 1955.

Krueger, Walter. *From Down Under to Nippon.* Washington: Combat Forces, 1953.

Kuter, Laurence S. *Airman at Yalta.* New York: Duell, Sloan and Pearce, 1955.

Lane, Frederic C., Blanche D. Coll, Gerald J. Fischer, and David B. Tyler. *Ships For Victory.* Baltimore: Johns Hopkins, 1951.

Lash, Joseph P. *Eleanor and Franklin: The Story of Their Relationship Based on Eleanor Roosevelt's Private Papers.* New York: Norton, 1971.

———. *Eleanor Roosevelt: A Friend's Memoir.* New York: Doubleday, 1964.

Leahy, William D. *I Was There: The Personal Story of the Chief of Staff to Presidents Roosevelt and Truman. Based on His Notes and Diaries Made at the Time.* New York: Whittlesey House, 1950.

Leasor, James. *The Clock with Four Hands: Based on the Experiences of General Sir Leslie Hollis.* New York: Reynal, 1959.

Lee, Ulysses. *Employment of Negro Troops.* Washington: Department of the Army, 1966.

Leighton, Richard M., and Robert W. Coakley. *Global Logistics and Strategy, 1940–1943.* Washington: Department of the Army, 1955.

———. *Global Logistics and Strategy, 1943–1945.* Washington: Department of the Army, 1968.

LeMay, Curtis E., and McKinlay Kantor. *Mission with LeMay: My Story.* Garden City, N.Y.: Doubleday, 1965.

Leopold, Richard W. *The Growth of American Foreign Policy: A History.* New York: Knopf, 1962.

Liddell Hart, B. H. *The History of the Second World War.* New York: Putnam's, 1971.

Lincoln, George A. *Economics of National Security: Managing America's Resources for Defense.* New York: Prentice-Hall, 1954.

Linebarger, Paul M. A. *The China of Chiang K'ai-shek: A Political Study.* Boston: World Peace Foundation, 1941.

Lochner, Louis P., ed. *The Goebbels Diaries: 1942–1943.* Garden City, N.Y.: Doubleday, 1948.

Lohbeck, Don. *Patrick J. Hurley.* Chicago: Henry Regnery, 1956.

MacArthur, Douglas. *Reminiscences.* New York: McGraw-Hill, 1964.

———. *A Soldier Speaks: Public Papers and Speeches of General of the Army Douglas MacArthur.* New York: Praeger, 1965.

McCarthy, Joseph R. *America's Retreat from Victory: The Story of George Catlett Marshall.* New York: Devin-Adair, 1951.

MacDonald, Charles B. "The Decision to Launch Operation Market-Garden." In *Command Decisions*, edited by Kent R. Greenfield. Washington: Department of the Army, 1960.

———. *The Mighty Endeavor*. New York: Oxford University, 1969.

———. *The Siegfried Line Campaign*. Washington: Department of the Army, 1963.

Macmillan, Harold. *The Blast of War, 1939–1945*. New York: Harper & Row, 1967.

Marshall, George C. *Biennial Report of the Chief of Staff of the United States Army, July 1, 1941 to June 30, 1943 to the Secretary of War*. Washington: U.S. Government Printing Office, 1943.

———. *Biennial Report of the Chief of Staff of the United States Army, July 1, 1943 to June 30, 1945 to the Secretary of War*. Washington: U.S. Government Printing Office, 1945.

———. *Selected Speeches and Statements of General of the Army George C. Marshall*. Edited by H. A. DeWeerd. Washington: Infantry Journal, 1945.

———. Research Library. *Addresses Delivered at the Dedication Ceremonies of the George C. Marshall Research Library, May 23, 1964, Lexington, Va*. 1964.

Marshall, Katherine T. *Together: Annals of an Army Wife*. Atlanta: Tupper and Love, 1946.

Marshall, Samuel L. A. *Night Drop: the American Airborne Invasion of Normandy*. Boston: Little, Brown, 1962.

———. *Bastogne: The First Eight Days*. Washington: Infantry Journal Press, 1946.

Massie, Robert K. *Nicholas and Alexandra*. New York: Dell, 1967.

Matloff, Maurice. "The Anvil Decision: Crossroads of Strategy." In *Command Decisions*, edited by Kent R. Greenfield. Washington: Department of the Army, 1960.

———. "The 90-Division Gamble." In *Command Decisions*, edited by Kent R. Greenfield. Washington: Department of the Army, 1960.

———. *Strategic Planning for Coalition Warfare, 1943–1944*. Washington: Department of the Army, 1959.

———, and Edward M. Snell. *Strategic Planning for Coalition Warfare, 1941–1942*. Washington: Department of the Army, 1953.

May, Ernest R., ed. *The Ultimate Decision: The President as Commander in Chief*. New York: Braziller, 1960.

Miller, John, Jr. *Cartwheel: The Reduction of Rabaul*. Washington: Department of the Army, 1959.

———. *Guadalcanal: The First Offensive*. Washington: Department of the Army, 1949.

Millett, John D. *The Organization and Role of the Army Service Forces*. Washington: Department of the Army, 1954.

Millis, Walter, ed. *The Forrestal Diaries*. See Forrestal, James.

Milner, Samuel. *Victory in Papua*. Washington: Department of the Army, 1957.

Minott, Rodney G. *The Fortress That Never Was*. New York: Holt, Rinehart & Winston, 1964.

Moffat, Jay Pierrepont. *The Moffat Papers: Selections from the Diplomatic Journals of Jay Pierrepont Moffat, 1919–1943*. Edited by Nancy Lee Harvison Hooker. Cambridge, Mass.: Harvard University, 1956.

Montgomery of Alamein, Field Marshal the Viscount. *The Memoirs of Field Marshal Montgomery*. Cleveland: World, 1958.

Moran, Lord. *Churchill: Taken from the Diaries of Lord Moran*. Boston: Houghton Mifflin, 1966.

Morgan, Lt. Gen. Sir Frederick. *Overture to Overlord*. Garden City, N.Y.: Doubleday, 1950.

———. *Peace and War: A Soldier's Life*. London: Hodder and Stoughton, 1961.

Morgenthau, Henry, Jr. *From the Diaries of Henry Morgenthau, Jr*. Edited by John M. Blum. Boston: Houghton Mifflin, 1959–67. 3 v. Vol. II, *Years of Urgency*, 1965. Vol. III, *Years of War, 1941–1945*, 1967.

———. *Morgenthau Diary (Germany)*. Prepared by the Subcommittee to Investigate the Administration of the Internal Security Act and Other Internal Security Laws of the Committee on the Judiciary, United States Senate. Washington: U.S. Government Printing Office, 1967.

Morison, Elting E. *Turmoil and Tradition: A Study of the Life and Times of Henry L. Stimson.* Boston: Houghton Mifflin, 1960.

Morison, Samuel E. *History of United States Naval Operations in World War II.* Boston: Little, Brown, 1947–60. 15 v.

Morton, Louis. *Pacific Command: A Study in Interservice Relations.* The Harmon Memorial Lectures in Military History, No. 3. Colorado Springs: U.S. Air Force Academy, 1961.

———. *Strategy and Command: The First Two Years.* Washington: Department of the Army, 1962.

Motter, T. H. Vail. *The Persian Corridor and Aid to Russia.* Washington: Department of the Army, 1951.

Mountbatten, The Earl of Burma. *Report to the Combined Chiefs of Staff by the Supreme Allied Commander Southeast Asia 1943–1944, Vice Admiral the Earl Mountbatten of Burma.* London: H.M. Stationery Office, 1951.

Murphy, Robert D. *Diplomat Among Warriors.* Garden City, N.Y.: Doubleday, 1964.

Nelson, James, ed. *General Eisenhower on the Military Churchill: A Conversation with Alistair Cooke.* New York: Norton, 1970.

Nelson, Maj. Gen. Otto L. *National Security and the General Staff.* Washington: Infantry Journal, 1946.

Notter, Harley A. *Postwar Foreign Policy Preparation, 1939–1945.* Washington: Department of State, 1950.

O'Connor, Raymond G. *Diplomacy for Victory: FDR and Unconditional Surrender.* New York: W. W. Norton, 1971.

Palmer, Robert R., Bell I. Wiley, and William R. Keast. *The Procurement and Training of Ground Combat Troops.* Washington: Department of the Army, 1948.

Parker, Theodore W., and William J. Thompson. *Conquer: The Story of Ninth Army, 1944–1945.* Washington: Infantry Journal, 1947.

Patton, George S. *War as I Knew It.* Boston: Houghton Mifflin, 1947.

Payne, Robert. *Marshall Story.* New York: Prentice-Hall, 1951.

Playfair, I. S. O., and G. J. C. Molony. *The Mediterranean and Middle East.* London: H.M. Stationery Office, 1966. Vol. IV, *The Destruction of the Axis Forces in Africa.*

Pogue, Forrest C. *George C. Marshall: Education of a General, 1880–1939.* New York: Viking, 1963.

———. *George C. Marshall: Ordeal and Hope, 1939–1942.* New York: Viking, 1966.

———. *The Supreme Command.* Washington: Department of the Army, 1954.

Postan, Michael M. *British War Production.* London: H.M. Stationery Office, 1952.

Potter, Elmer B., and Chester W. Nimitz. *The Great Sea War: The Story of Naval Action in World War II.* Englewood Cliffs, N.J.: Prentice-Hall, 1960.

Pratt, Julius W. *A History of United States Foreign Policy.* New York: Prentice-Hall, 1955.

Puryear, Edgar F., Jr. *Nineteen Stars.* Washington: Coiner, 1971.

Reeder, Russell P., Jr. *Born at Reveille.* New York: Duell, Sloan and Pearce, 1966.

Riddle, Donald H. *The Truman Committee: A Study in Congressional Responsibility.* New Brunswick, N.J.: Rutgers University, 1964.

Ridgway, Matthew B. *Soldier: The Memoirs of Matthew B. Ridgway.* New York: Harper, 1956.

Robinett, Paul. *Armor Command.* Washington: McGregor and Werner, 1958.

Rogow, Arnold A. *James Forrestal.* New York: Macmillan, 1963.

Romanus, Charles F., and Riley Sunderland. *Stilwell's Command Problems.* Washington: Department of the Army, 1956.

———. *Stilwell's Mission to China.* Washington: Department of the Army, 1953.

———. *Time Runs Out in CBI.* Washington: Department of the Army, 1959.

Rumpf, Hans. *The Bombing of Germany.* New York: Holt, Rinehart & Winston, 1961.

Roosevelt, Eleanor. *This I Remember.* New York: Harper, 1949.

Roosevelt, Elliott. *As He Saw It.* New York: Duell, Sloan and Pearce, 1946.

Roosevelt, Franklin D. *F. D. R.: His Personal Letters.* Edited by Elliott Roosevelt. New York: Duell, Sloan and Pearce, 1947–50. 4 v.

————. *The Public Papers and Addresses of Franklin D. Roosevelt,* with a Special Introduction and Explanatory Note by President Roosevelt. Compiled by Samuel I. Rosenman. New York: Random House, 1938–50. 13 v.

Roosevelt, Mrs. Theodore, Jr. *Day Before Yesterday: The Reminiscences of Mrs. Theodore Roosevelt, Jr.* Garden City, N.Y.: Doubleday, 1959.

Roskill, S. W. *The War at Sea.* London: Her Majesty's Stationery Office, 1960.

Ruppenthal, Roland G. *Logistical Support of the Armies.* Washington: Department of the Army, 1953, 1959. 2 v. Vol. I, May 1941–Sept. 1944; Vol. II, Sept. 1944–May 1945.

Ryan, Cornelius. *The Last Battle.* New York: Simon and Schuster, 1966.

Seventh Army. *The Seventh United States Army in France and Germany, 1944–1945.* Heidelberg: Seventh Army, 1946. 3 v.

Shannon, David A. *Twentieth Century America; the United States since the 1890s.* Chicago: Rand McNally, 1963.

Sherwood, Robert E. *Roosevelt and Hopkins: An Intimate History.* New York: Harper, 1948.

Shugg, Roger W., and H. A. DeWeerd. *World War II: A Concise History.* Washington: Infantry Journal, 1946.

Slessor, Sir John C. *The Central Blue: Autobiography.* New York: Praeger, 1957.

Slim, William. *Defeat into Victory: The Magnificent Account of a Great Campaign of the Second World War.* New York: McKay, 1961.

Smith, Gaddis. *American Diplomacy During the Second World War, 1941–1945.* New York: Wiley, 1965.

Smith, Melden. "The Bombing of Dresden Reconsidered: A Study in Wartime Decision Making." Ph.D. dissertation, Boston University, 1971.

Smith, Ralph Elberton. *The Army and Economic Mobilization.* Washington: Department of the Army, 1959.

Smith, Robert R. *The Approach to the Philippines.* Washington: Department of the Army, 1953.

Smith, Lt. Gen. Walter Bedell. *My Three Years in Moscow.* Philadelphia: Lippincott, 1950.

Snell, John L. *Illusion and Necessity: The Diplomacy of Global War, 1939–1945.* Boston: Houghton Mifflin, 1963.

————, ed. *The Meaning of Yalta.* Baton Rouge: Louisiana State University, 1956.

Snyder, Louis L. *The War: A Concise History, 1939–1945.* New York: Julian Messner, 1960.

[Soviet Commission on Foreign Diplomatic Documents.] *Correspondence Between the Chairman of the Council of Ministers of the U.S.S.R. and the Presidents of the U.S.A. and the Prime Minister of Great Britain During the Great Patriotic War of 1941–1945.* Moscow: Foreign Languages Publishing House, 1957. 2 v.

Spanier, John W. *American Foreign Policy Since World War II.* Rev. ed. New York: Praeger, 1962.

Stalin, Iosif. *The Great Patriotic War of the Soviet Union.* New York: International, 1945.

Standley, Adm. William H., and Adm. Arthur A. Ageton. *Admiral Ambassador to Russia.* Chicago: Henry Regnery, 1955.

Starr, Chester G. *From Salerno to the Alps.* Washington: Infantry Journal, 1948.

Stein, Harold, ed. *American Civil-Military Decisions: A Book of Case Studies.* Birmingham: University of Alabama, 1963.

Stettinius, Edward R., Jr. *Lend-Lease Weapons for Victory.* New York: Macmillan, 1944.

————. *Roosevelt and the Russians.* Garden City, N.Y.: Doubleday, 1949.

Stilwell, Joseph W. *The Stilwell Papers.* Arranged and edited by Theodore H. White. New York: Sloane, 1948.

Stimson, Henry L., and McGeorge Bundy. *On Active Service in Peace and War.* New York: Harper, 1947.

Sykes, Christopher. *Orde Wingate: A Biography.* Cleveland: World, 1959.

Tedder, Lord. *With Prejudice*. Boston: Little, Brown, 1967.

Theoharis, Athan G. *The Yalta Myths: An Issue in U.S. Politics, 1945–1955*. Columbia: University of Missouri, 1970.

Toland, John. *The Last 100 Days*. New York: Random House, 1966.

Treadwell, Mattie. *The Women's Army Corps*. Washington: Department of the Army, 1954.

Trevor-Roper, H. R. *Blitzkrieg to Defeat*. New York: Holt, Rinehart and Winston, 1965.

Truman, Harry S *Memoirs*. Garden City, N.Y.: Doubleday, 1955. Vol. I, *Years of Decisions*.

Truscott, Lucian K. *Command Missions: A Personal Story*. New York: Dutton, 1954.

Tuchman, Barbara W. *Stilwell and the American Experience in China, 1911–1945*. New York: Macmillan, 1970.

Tunner, William H. *Over the Hump*. New York: Duell, Sloan and Pearce, 1964.

U.S. Air Force. *The Army Air Forces in World War II*. Prepared under the editorship of Wesley F. Craven and James S. Cate. Chicago: University of Chicago, 1948–58. 7 v.

U.S. Department of State. *Foreign Relations of the United States, Diplomatic Papers*. 1943: *Europe and China*, 6 v.; 1944: *Europe, China, and European Advisory Commission*, 7 v.; 1945: *Europe, China, and European Advisory Commission*, 8 v.; 1949: *United States Relations with China (With Special Reference to the Period 1944–1949)*; and conferences at Casablanca, Quebec, Trident, Cairo-Tehran, and Yalta.

Vandenberg, Arthur H. *The Private Papers of Senator Vandenberg*. Edited by Arthur H. Vandenberg, Jr., with the Collaboration of Joe Alex Morris. Boston: Houghton Mifflin, 1952.

Vansittart, Lord. *The Black Record of Germany, Past, Present, and Future*. New York: New Avon Library, 1944.

Verrier, Anthony. *The Bomber Offensive*. New York: Macmillan, 1968.

Vigneras, Marcel. *Rearming the French*. Washington: Department of the Army, 1957.

Webster, Sir Charles K., and Noble Frankland. *The Strategic Air Offensive Against Germany, 1939–1945*. London: H.M. Stationery Office, 1961. 4 v.

Wedemeyer, Albert C. *Wedemeyer Reports*. New York: Henry Holt, 1958.

Weigley, Russell F. *History of the United States Army*. New York: Macmillan, 1967.

Wheeler-Bennett, John W. *King George VI: His Life and Reign*. New York: St. Martin's, 1958.

———, ed. *Action This Day: Working with Churchill*. New York: St. Martin's, 1969.

Whitney, Courtney. *MacArthur: His Rendezvous with History*. New York: Knopf, 1956.

Williams, Mary H., comp. *Chronology, 1941–1945*. Washington: Department of the Army, 1960.

Willoughby, Charles A., and John Chamberlain. *MacArthur, 1941–1951*. New York: McGraw-Hill, 1954.

Wilmot, Chester. *The Struggle for Europe*. New York: Harper, 1952.

Wilson, General Maitland. *Reports by the Supreme Allied Commander, Mediterranean, to the Combined Chiefs of Staff on the Italian Campaign*. London: H.M. Stationery Office, 1946–48. 3 v. Part I, *8 January 1944–10 May 1944*. Part II, *10 May 1944–12 August 1944*. Part III, *13 August 1944–12 December 1944*.

———. *Report by the Supreme Allied Commander on the Operations in Southern France, August 1944*. London: H.M. Stationery Office, 1946.

Wilson, Rose P. *General Marshall Remembered*. Englewood Cliffs, N.J.: Prentice-Hall, 1968.

Woodward, Sir Ernest L. *British Foreign Policy in the Second World War*. London: H.M. Stationery Office, 1962.

Zhukov, Georgei K. *Marshal Zhukov's Greatest Battles*. Edited by Harrison E. Salisbury. New York: Harper & Row, 1969.

———. *Memoirs of Marshal Zhukov*. New York: Delacorte, 1971.

Ziemke, Earl F. *Stalingrad to Berlin: The German Defeat in the East*. Washington: Department of the Army, 1968.

Chronology 1943–45

Based on *Chronology, 1941–1945,* compiled by Mary H. Williams, (Department of the Army, 1960).

1943

12Jan	US force lands in Amchitka in Aleutians without opposition.
14–23Jan	British–US conference of political and military leaders in Casablanca.
12Feb	MacArthur's headquarters issues ELKTON plan.
4Mar	Battle of Bismarck Sea ends; decisive victory for Allies.
12–15Mar	Pacific Military Conference in Washington to plan operations against Japanese in Pacific in 1943.
23Apr	Allies issue directive for establishment of COSSAC (Chief of Staff Supreme Allied Commander) under Lt Gen Frederick E. Morgan to start planning for cross-Channel attack.
11–30May	US amphibious force attacks Attu in Aleutians.
12–25May	TRIDENT conference in Washington. Plan for HUSKY (invasion of Sicily) approved.
30Jun	Operation CARTWHEEL opened.
10Jul	Invasion of Sicily.
25Jul	Mussolini overthrown as Italian dictator.
14–24Aug	British–US conference (QUADRANT) in Quebec. Date for cross-Channel attack (OVERLORD) set for 1May44. Establishment of Southeast Asia Command (SEAC) under Lord Louis Mountbatten.
3Sep	Force under Montgomery lands in southern Italy. Italians sign short-term armistice to become effective 8Sep.
9Sep	US Fifth Army lands at Salerno.
12Sep	Australian force occupies Salamaua in New Guinea.
19Sep	Sardinia surrenders without fighting.
2Oct	Australian force takes Finschhafen.
19–30Oct	Conference of US, British, and Soviet foreign ministers in Moscow.

22Nov–7Dec	Allied conferences at Cairo, Tehran, Cairo.
28Nov	Marines secure Tarawa at heavy cost.
7Dec	Eisenhower named Supreme Commander for cross-Channel attack.
26Dec	Main attack on New Britain opens with assault on Cape Gloucester.

1944

22Jan	Fifth Army launches invasion of Italian mainland at Anzio (SHINGLE).
31Jan–4Feb	US amphibious force assaults and takes Kwajalein in Marshalls.
24Mar	Japanese counterattack on Bougainville repulsed; last enemy offensive in the Solomons.
22Apr	Allied forces began landings in Hollandia (New Guinea).
28Apr	Sec of Navy Frank Knox dies; succeeded by James V. Forrestal.
4Jun	Rome falls to Allies.
6Jun	Allied landings in Normandy.
15Jun	China-based B-29 bombers make first bombing attack on Japanese home islands, hitting targets on Kyushu.
	Amphibious landing on Saipan led by Marine Gen Holland Smith.
19–20Jun	Battle of Philippine Sea; major defeat for Japanese.
23Jun	Russians open offensive on central front.
27Jun	Cherbourg surrenders.
9Jul	Saipan secured.
18Jul	US forces take St. Lô.
	Gen Hideki Tojo's cabinet falls in Tokyo.
20Jul	Attempt to kill Hitler fails.
21Jul	US landings on Guam.
25Jul	Operation COBRA to break out of Cotentin Peninsula in Normandy launched.
30Jul	Landings on Japanese-held Vogelkop Peninsula in New Guinea.
10Aug	Japanese opposition on Guam ends.
15Aug	US Seventh Army and French naval, airborne, and ground elements begin landings in southern France (Operation DRAGOON).
19Aug	Resistance forces rise in Paris. Germans sign truce giving them until 23Aug to evacuate city.
25Aug	French 2d Armored Division under US V Corps command enters Paris.
4Sep	British forces drive into Antwerp.

8Sep	Maj Gen Patrick Hurley becomes special representative to Chiang Kai-shek.
9Sep	US units enter Holland.
10Sep	Forces from southern France link up with OVERLORD forces near Dijon.
11Sep	US patrol enters Germany from Luxembourg—first allied force to enter from west.
12–16Sep	OCTAGON conference of British and US leaders in Quebec.
14Sep	Russian troops enter suburbs of Warsaw.
18Oct	Stilwell relieved of command and returned to Washington. Lt Gen A. C. Wedemeyer subsequently assumes command of China theater.
20Oct	Belgrade falls to Russians and Marshal Tito's forces. US Sixth Army invades Leyte.
23–26Oct	Battle of Leyte Gulf; decisive defeat of Japanese fleet.
13Nov	Liberation of Greece completed.
10Dec	France and Soviet Union sign treaty of alliance.
16Dec	Germans counterattack in Ardennes.
18Dec	Soviet forces reach Hungarian-Czech border.
22Dec	Gen A. C. MacAuliffe rejects German demand for surrender of Bastogne.
26Dec	US Third Army armored units break through to Bastogne.

1945

1Jan	Germans attack US Seventh Army in Colmar area.
9Jan	Landings by Gen Krueger's Sixth Army in Lingayen Gulf in Luzon.
12Jan	Soviet forces open winter offensive.
15Jan	Initial convoy over Ledo Road reaches Myitkyina.
17Jan	Russians occupy Warsaw.
30Jan–9Feb	ARGONAUT conference of British, US, and Soviet leaders at Yalta. (Preliminary British–US conference at Malta—designated CRICKET—to 2Feb.)
4Feb	First Ledo convoy reaches Kunming. US Eighth Army begins attack on Manila.
5Feb	Russians reach Oder River within 30 miles of Berlin.
13Feb	Red forces capture Budapest.
19Feb	Marines land on Iwo Jima.
23Feb	US Ninth Army and First Army units cross Roer River.
3Mar	Japanese resistance in Manila ends.
7Mar	US forces capture Ludendorff Bridge over Rhine at Remagen.
11Mar	US Eighth Army forces land on Mindanao.
16Mar	Iwo Jima declared secure.

23 Mar	Montgomery's forces cross Rhine.
24 Mar	US Ninth Army crosses Rhine.
12 Apr	President Roosevelt dies; succeeded by President Truman.
18 Apr	German resistance ends in Ruhr.
22 Apr	Russians enter eastern suburbs of Berlin.
26 Apr	Formal meeting of US First Army units with Russians at Torgau.
28 Apr	Mussolini executed by Italian partisans.
29 Apr	Germans in Italy surrender effective May 2.
30 Apr	Hitler commits suicide. Adm Doenitz becomes Reichsführer.
2 May	Russians complete clearance of Berlin.
7 May	Representatives of Doenitz surrender to Allies at Reims.
8 May	Proclaimed as V-E Day by Truman.

Notes

Unless otherwise specified:

1. Interviews were conducted by the author, Forrest C. Pogue.
2. Citations of letters to and from General Marshall are to copies found in the General's Pentagon files. Originals or copies will ultimately be deposited in the Marshall Research Library.
3. General Marshall's speeches are from Marshall's typewritten reading copies of speeches, hereinafter cited as *Marshall Speech Book*. Secondary source is cited if available.

It should be remembered throughout that minutes made at the international conferences and Joint Chiefs of Staff meetings are not transcriptions of direct statements but edited paraphrases agreed on by the secretaries and sometimes corrected by the participants. Also classified messages sent in code had to be paraphrased when a copy was made. In citations of cable messages to and from the War Department the date before the CM-IN number refers to date of dispatch. If receipt date is different it is put after the CM-IN citation in parenthesis. (First msg date is date of dispatch. If date of arrival does not coincide, it is added in parentheses.)

ABBREVIATIONS*

AAF Army Air Forces

AAG Air Adjutant General

ABC American-British Conversations

ActACofS Acting Assistant Chief of Staff

ACofS Assistant Chief of Staff

AG Adjutant General (used for file location of documents)

AGF Army Ground Forces

ALUSNA US Naval Attaché

AMMISCA American Military Mission to China (code name for American headquarters at New Delhi)

ASF Army Service Forces

ASW Assistant Secretary of War

BRCOS British Chiefs of Staff

BPR Bureau of Public Relations

BurBud Bureau of Budget Director

CAD Civil Affairs Division

CBI China-Burma-India Theater

CCAC Command Civil Affairs Committee

CCS Combined Chiefs of Staff

CDC Caribbean Defense Command

CG Commanding General

CinCLant Commander-in-Chief, US Atlantic Fleet

CinCPac Commander-in-Chief, US Pacific Fleet

Cmdt Commandant

CM-IN (or -OUT) Cable Message, Incoming or Outgoing

CNO Chief of Naval Operations

CofS Chief of Staff

CsofS British and/or US Chiefs of Staff at conferences

* Documents have special nomenclature which does not always agree with approved abbreviations but it has been used for quick identification.

609

Cominch Commander-in-Chief, US Fleet
CO Commanding Officer
Conf Conference
COS Chiefs of Staff (British)
COSMED Chief of Staff, Mediterranean
CTO Chinese Theater of Operations

DCofS Deputy Chief of Staff
DefDept Defense Department
DSM Distinguished Service Medal

Exec Executive File (OPD) (used for file location of documents)

G-1 Personnel Division
G-2 Intelligence Division
G-3 Operations Division
G-4 Supply Division
GHQ General Headquarters
GHQ Air Forces US Air Forces, General Headquarters

HawDept Hawaiian Department
int interview

JAG Judge Advocate General
JB Joint Board
JCS Joint Chiefs of Staff
JPC Joint Planning Committee
JPS Joint Staff Planners
JRC Joint Rearmament Commission

OCMH Office of the Chief of Military History
OCS SGS Office of the Chief of Staff, Secretary General Staff
OPD Operations Division
OpNAV Office of the Chief of Naval Operations

PMC Pacific Military Conference

PMG Provost Marshal General
PMGO Provost Marshal General's Office
POA Pacific Ocean Area
PTO Pacific Theater of Operations

RG Record Group
ROTC Reserve Officers' Training Corps

SAC Supreme Allied Commander
SACMED Supreme Allied Commander, Mediterranean
SEAC Southeast Asia Command
SGS Secretary General Staff
So Pac South Pacific Area
SS Strategy Section
SWPA Southwest Pacific Area

TAG The Adjutant General of the Army
TS Top Secret

USA United States Army
USAAF United States Army Air Forces
USAFFE United States Army Forces in the Far East
USAFIA United States Army Forces in Australia
USN United States Navy
USSTAF United States Strategic Air Forces

VMI Virginia Military Institute

WD War Department (used for file location of documents)
WDC Western Defense Command
WDCSA War Department Chief of Staff Army (used for file location of documents)
WH White House

GLOSSARY OF CODE NAMES

ANAKIM Plan for recapture of Burma.
ANFA Site of Casablanca conference, 14–23Jan43; sometimes used by OPD officers as a code name for the meeting.
ANVIL Early plan for invasion of southern France.
ARGONAUT International conference at Yalta, Feb45.

BOLERO Build-up of U.S. forces and supplies in the United Kingdom for cross-Channel attack.

BRIMSTONE Plan for capture of Sardinia.
BUCCANEER Plan for amphibious operation in Andaman Islands.

CARTWHEEL Converging drives on Rabaul by South Pacific and SWPA forces.
CLARION Coordinated attack on transportation throughout Germany by combined air forces.
COBRA Operation launched by US First Army, 25Jul44, designed to effect breakout from the Normandy lodgment.

CRICKET British–US conference at Malta, preliminary to Yalta meeting with Soviets.

CROSSWORD Surrender of German and Italian land, sea, and air forces under German commander-in-chief, Southwest Mediterranean, May45. Also *Sunrise*.

DRAGOON Allied invasion of southern France, 15Aug44, planned under the code name ANVIL.

ELKTON MacArthur's 12Feb43 plan for recapture of Rabaul.

EUREKA International conference at Tehran, Nov43.

GRENADE Ninth Army supporting attack for Operation VERITABLE.

HALCYON Code name for 1Jun44, sometimes called Y day; the date when all preparations for the Normandy assault had to be completed.

HUSKY Allied invasion of Sicily, Jul43.

JUPITER Plans for operations in northern Norway.

NEPTUNE Special code name for initial phases of *Overlord* assault. Directives for these phases had a Bigot classification.

OCTAGON US–British conference in Quebec, Sep44.

OLYMPIC Plan for invasion of Kyushu, Mar46.

OVERLORD Allied cross-Channel invasion of northwest Europe, Jun44.

POINTBLANK Combined Bomber Offensive against Germany.

QUADRANT US–British conference in Quebec, Aug43.

RANKIN A-B-C Plans for Allied return to Europe in event of deterioration of German position.

RAVENOUS Plan for 4 Corps' advance into Burma.

ROUNDUP Plan for major US–British cross-Channel operation in 1943.

SEXTANT International conference in Cairo, Nov–Dec43.

SHINGLE Amphibious operation at Anzio, Italy.

SICKLE Build-up of US Eighth Air Force in the United Kingdom for bomber offensive against Germany.

SLEDGEHAMMER Plan for limited cross-Channel attack in 1942.

SYMBOL Casablanca conference, 14–23Jan-43.

TARZAN India-based portion of general offensive in Burma.

TORCH Allied invasion of north and northwest Africa, Nov42.

TRIDENT International conference in Washington, 12–25May43.

VERITABLE 21 Army Group plan for a Canadian attack between the Maas and the Rhine, Jan–Feb45.

I: A TIME FOR DECISION

For Chapters I and II, I have relied heavily on *US For Rels, Casablanca;* Maurice Matloff, *Strategic Planning for Coalition Warfare, 1943–1944;* John Ehrman, *Grand Strategy*, VI; and Arthur Bryant, *Turn of the Tide*. Initially I used the Army's own minutes of the great conferences, but in order to make citations easier for scholars to follow, I have keyed them to the *US For Rels* volumes. I have also drawn on interviews with the following: Gens Marshall, Wedemeyer, Hull, Ismay, Alanbrooke; Adms King and Mountbatten; Air Marshal Portal; and Frank McCarthy.

1. See view of British official historian, John Ehrman, *Grand Strategy*, VI, 342.
2. Lord Portal int, 7Feb47.
3. Sir Arthur Bryant, *The Turn of the Tide*, 246.
4. Gen Sir Hastings L. Ismay, Lt Gen Sir

Frederick E. Morgan, and Maj Gen Ray E. Barker ints, 17Dec46 (author's notes).
5. Rear Adm C. E. Lambe int, 26Feb47.
6. Portal int, 7Feb47.
7. Embick and Fairchild to Marshall,

sub: Comments on CCS 135/1 and 135/2, 4Jan43, *WDCSA 334 CCS (1–4–43)*.

8. Wedemeyer to Chief, Strategy Section, OPD, sub: Cross-Channel Operations, 10Apr43, *OPD 381 Security, Sec 1, Case 31* (italics in original).

9. Ibid. Cf Albert C. Wedemeyer, *Wedemeyer Reports*, 94–96, where he apparently changed his views to some extent: "To sum up, it is only too obvious today that our strategic planning should have been oriented toward denying to the Soviet Union the opportunities which she used so promptly and effectively to extend her frontiers and her power." Again, "Our failure to use political, economic and psychological means in co-ordination with military operations during the war also prolonged its duration. . . . The Western Allies, by refusing to use the political and psychological instruments of strategy, and by committing themselves to defeat Germany solely by military means, gave Soviet Russia the initiative which should all along have been ours." And finally, "It was only at the eleventh hour that Winston Churchill began to take cognizance of the postwar balance of power. . . ."

10. President's endorsement on memo, Leahy to Roosevelt, 30Sept42, cited Richard M. Leighton and Robert W. Coakley, *Global Logistics and Strategy, 1940–1943*, 604–605; Byron Fairchild and Jonathan Grossman, *The Army and Industrial Manpower*, 47–49.

11. BurBud to SecWar, 4Nov42, *WDCSA 020 (11–7–42) SW Open Files*; Leighton and Coakley, *Global Logistics, 1940–1943*, 605; Roosevelt to BurBud, 29Oct42, *F. D. R.: His Personal Letters*, II, 1358, shows Roosevelt's thinking.

12. Marshall to President, 9Nov42, *SecWar File Folder, WH Corres*.

13. Ibid. In *George C. Marshall: Ordeal and Hope*, 42, I mistakenly based my statement of Marshall's responsibilities on a directive of 5Jul39. These were not defined until 28Feb42. Cf Mark Watson, *Chief of Staff: Prewar Plans and Preparations*, 66.

14. Draft Marshall to President, 7Nov42, *Marshall Library Files*.

15. For budget purposes, he said, the strength of the Army was set for an average of 6,500,000 enlisted men for 1943. At the beginning of 1943 there would probably be 5,000,000 men and the Army would be lucky to get 7,000,000 by the end of the year. The average, he felt, could not possibly exceed 6,500,000. He agreed, however, that equipment should be provided for 7,500,000 by the end of 1943. Roosevelt to Marshall, 10Nov42, *Marshall Library Files*.

16. Fairchild and Grossman, *Army and Industrial Manpower*, 50; Leighton and Coakley, *Global Logistics, 1940–1943*, 605.

17. Speech to National Association of Manufacturers, 4Dec42, including carbon of reading copy of speech and earlier drafts, in speech folder, *Marshall Library Files*.

18. Marshall to Maj Gen Frank Parker, 6Jan43, *Marshall Library Files*.

19. Mins of WH conf with CsofS, 7Jan43, *OPD Exec 10, Item 45*. Also see *US For Rels, Casablanca*, 505–40.

20. From JCS 167/2, 23Dec42, circulated as CCS 135 on 26Dec42, cited Maurice Matloff and Edward M. Snell, *Strategic Planning for Coalition Warfare, 1941–1942*, 376.

21. Stimson Diary, 7Jan43.

22. Winston S. Churchill, *The Hinge of Fate*, 650–59. For the entire background see exchange of msgs *US For Rels, Confs at Washington, 1941–1942* and *US For Rels, Casablanca, 1943*, 488ff.

23. *US For Rels, Casablanca*, 488–89.

24. Marshall to Eisenhower, 23Dec42, *WDCSA 381 (SS) (1942)*; Eisenhower to Marshall, Cable 3501, 29Dec42, *The Papers of Dwight D. Eisenhower: The War Years*, ed Alfred D. Chandler, Jr, II, 875–76. For interesting description see Harold Macmillan, *The Blast of War*, 192–94; additional details in President's log in *US For Rels, Casablanca*, 522ff.

25. A valuable source for the conference is the diary of British Brig Ian Jacob, Military AsstSec to the War Cabinet, who had helped to pick the site and make arrangements for the meeting. He permitted me to examine excerpts from his diary, copies of which were furnished me by Dr Stephen Ambrose, assoc ed. *Papers of Eisenhower*.

26. Henry H. Arnold, *Global Mission*, 388, has the most detailed account of the party's leaving. William D. Leahy, *I Was There*, erroneously gives 10Jan as the date of the President's departure. See accounts of trip by Ernest J. King and Walter M. Whitehill, *Fleet Admiral King: A Naval Record*, 415, and Wedemeyer, *Wedemeyer Reports*, 171.

27. McCarthy int, 17Oct57. He went on: "I never went for those elaborate preparations again, because I realized that if General Marshall's plane went down, someone would know it and come rather quickly and we wouldn't be spending weeks trading with the Arabs. When he heard about this, he roared with laughter, and he asked me, when the trip was over, for a copy of the inventory of what we had taken. I think that was one of the best laughs he got during the war."

28. Ibid. The story is repeated in McCarthy memo, 18Jan61.

29. Wedemeyer to Maj Gen T. T. Handy, 22Jan43, *OPD Exec 3, Item 1a.*

30. Bryant, *Turn of the Tide*, 444.

31. Ibid, 444–45. (Bryant's paraphrase of Churchill's statement is: "Nothing less, he felt, would be worthy of two great powers and their obligations to Russia.") Jacob's Diary, 13Jan43; Sir John Kennedy, *The Business of War*, 280–81.

32. Jacob's Diary, 14Jan43.

II: THE DEBATE OPENS

1. Mins CCS 55th mtg, 14Jan43, 10:30 am, *US For Rels, Casablanca*, 545. Although I used Gen Marshall's own copy of the minutes of this conference in my research, I have cited page references in *US For Rels*, which will be easier of access for the researcher.

2. Mins CCS 57th mtg, 15Jan43, ibid, 570.

3. Bryant, *Turn of the Tide*, 448.

4. Mins CCS 58th mtg, 16Jan43, *US For Rels, Casablanca*, 583.

5. Mins CCS 55th mtg, 14Jan43, 10:30 am, ibid, 536–40.

6. Mins CCS 55th and 56th mtgs, 14Jan43, 10:30 am and 2:30 pm, ibid, 545, 550, 553.

7. Mins CCS 56th mtg, 2:30 pm, 14Jan43, ibid, 553.

8. Stilwell to Marshall, AMMISCA 1558, 28Dec42, CM-IN 12637 (30Dec), quoting Chiang Kai-shek to President. Repeated in msg Roosevelt to Churchill, 7Jan43, *US For Rels, Casablanca*, 514–15.

9. Mins JCS mtg at WH, 7Jan43, ibid, 505–514. Also see Mins, CCS mtg on 23Jan43, ibid, 707–719, where Roosevelt stressed the importance of air power in aiding China.

10. Dill to Marshall, 2Jan43, Marshall to Dill, 5Jan, *WDCSA Burma TS;* Marshall to Handy, 5Jan, *OPD Exec 10, Item 22;* Dill to Marshall, 6Jan, enc COS tel quoting Wavell, *OPD Exec 10, Item 65.* Marshall had acceded to Dill's wish to delete a passage implying that Roosevelt felt there was "some sense" in Chiang's demand for strong naval action and a seven-division drive by the British into Burma. Dill's phrasing was accepted: "I feel that we must do something to ensure that the Chinese put their full weight into the operations which are due to start in March. Can you suggest any assurances which will have this effect?" Dill to Marshall, 3Jan43, *WDCSA Burma TS;* Churchill's reply, 10Jan43, was wholly negative. *US For Rels, Casablanca*, 517–18.

11. Hours after Marshall had left, a warning message came in from Stilwell giving the gist of Chiang's reply. ActCofS McNarney sent the message to the WH with a draft reply at 8 pm. The full text of Chiang's message was not ready before the WH party had left by late train for Miami. McNarney to President, 9Jan43, *WDCSA Burma TS;* President to Chiang, 9Jan43, *US For Rels, Casablanca*, 516; Stilwell to Marshall, 30, 9Jan43, CM-IN 3875, *OPD Exec 10, Item 22;* Stilwell to Marshall, 31, 9Jan43, CM-IN 3980, in Charles F. Romanus and Riley Sunderland, *Stilwell's Mission to China*, 259–60.

12. Mins CCS 56th mtg, 14Jan43, 2:30 pm, *US For Rels, Casablanca*, 554.

13. Mins CCS 59th mtg, 17Jan43, ibid, 601–602; mins CCS 60th mtg, 18Jan43, ibid, 614–617; also references to CCS 154, 17Jan43, rpt by Br JPS "Operations in Burma, 1943," fns 5, 6, ibid, 614, 616.

14. CCS 153 (Rev), 17Jan43, rpt by US Joint Staff Planners, ibid, 755.
15. Mins CCS 59th mtg, 17Jan43, 10:30 am, ibid, 602–603. At this time the term "United Nations" referred to the states associated in the fight against the Axis powers through their adherence to the Atlantic Charter. When the world body bearing that name was being established in the spring of 1945, the word "organization" was added to distinguish it from the earlier group.
16. Bryant, *Turn of the Tide*, 449; memo by Br JPS, CCS 153/1, 17Jan43, *US For Rels, Casablanca*, 758.
17. Memo by Br JPS, CCS 153/1, 17Jan43, *US For Rels, Casablanca*, 758–60. See also 618–19.
18. Portal, quoted in Jacob's Diary, 14-Jan43.
19. Mins CCS 60th mtg, 18Jan43, *US For Rels, Casablanca*, 617.
20. Mins CCS 60th mtg, 18Jan43; CCS 153/1, para 2(c), 17Jan43, ibid, 618–19, 758.
21. Mins CCS 60th mtg, 18Jan43, ibid, 619–21.
22. Ibid; CCS 153/1, para 11(c), ibid, 621–22, 757 (italics in original).
23. Bryant, *Turn of the Tide*, 449–50.
24. See Pogue, *Ordeal and Hope* for Marshall-Dill relationship; Bryant, *Turn of the Tide*, 450. There is some discrepancy between the accounts in Brooke's diary and in Air Marshal John C. Slessor's *Central Blue*, 446, about this incident. Since Slessor had handed over the paper to Portal, it seems likely that he did bring it to Brooke and Dill without Slessor's knowledge and that Dill did discuss it with Marshall. Possibly Marshall did not see the paper until after the meeting reconvened, but the speed with which he and King accepted it suggests that Marshall, at least, had been told what was in the paper. The fact that Brooke suggested that the paper be read and that Marshall and King withdrew to discuss it does not necessarily mean that the US CofS had not been told of its contents.
25. For action of CCS, *US For Rels, Casablanca*, 622, 637; for changes, ibid, 760, 774–75.
26. Mtg of CCS with Roosevelt and Churchill, 18Jan43, 5 pm, ibid, 627–37; Bryant, *Turn of the Tide*, 449.
27. CCS 155/1, "Conduct of the War in 1943," 19Jan43, *US For Rels, Casablanca*, 774.
28. Mins CCS 65th mtg, 21Jan43, ibid, 667–79, contains discussions leading to agreement; see Combined Bomber Offensive directive, 21Jan43, ibid, 781–82; see also Sir Charles K. Webster and Noble Frankland, *The Strategic Air Offensive Against Germany, 1939–1945*, II, 10–21, on the Casablanca directive.
29. Stimson Diary, 30Jan43.
30. Eisenhower to Handy, 28Jan43, *OPD Exec 3, Item 1a*.
31. Bryant, *Turn of the Tide*, 454.
32. Jacob's Diary, 19Jan43.
33. Kennedy, *Business of War*, 283; Bryant, *Turn of the Tide*, 454.
34. Bryant, *Turn of the Tide*, 450; Marshall to Roosevelt, 20Feb43, with draft ltr to Dill, *Marshall Library Files*. Marshall noted the importance of Dill's trip to India and China with Somervell and Arnold after Casablanca. His presence at New Delhi, Marshall believed, "was the major factor in enabling us to reach an agreement with the British and to stimulate them to aggressive efforts toward mounting a Burma operation."
35. Maurice Matloff, *Strategic Planning for Coalition Warfare, 1943–1944*, 39–40; Harley A. Notter, *Postwar Foreign Policy Preparation, 1939–1945*, 125–27; John P. Glennon, "This Time Germany Is a Defeated Nation," in *Statesmen and Statecraft of the Modern West*, ed Gerald N. Grob, 112–13.
36. Mins of WH conf with CsofS, 7Jan43, *OPD Exec 10, Item 45*. See also *US For Rels, Casablanca*, 505–14.
37. Churchill, *Hinge of Fate*, 684–89; *US. For Rels Casablanca*, 506, 635, 704.
38. Marshall int, 29Oct56.
39. Wedemeyer, *Wedemeyer Reports*, 186–87; Deane to author, "Jul68," in answer to author's ltr of 28Jun68.
40. Marshall int, 11Feb57.
41. There is some uncertainty about the time of the departure. Some accounts indicate that Marshall and the other US CsofS left Casablanca before the conference was concluded. In fact the last session in which they were involved ended on the evening of 23Jan.

The next morning's activities consisted of conversations between Roosevelt and Churchill and the French leaders and of a press conference. The US CsofS seem not to have attended the historic conference where General Charles de Gaulle and General Henri Giraud shook hands. See Col McCarthy to Col Robert N. Young, 23Jan43, *OPD Exec 10, Item 45A, Pt 2*, which indicated that a Stratoliner with Dill, Marshall, King, Cooke, Hull, McCarthy, and others would leave at 0700 on the morning of Sunday, 24Jan, for Algiers. Arnold, Wedemeyer, and others departed at approximately the same time for Algiers in a B-17. All were scheduled to arrive at Algiers at approximately 1100. A message from McCarthy to Young, 26Jan43, same

file, said that members of the two parties had landed at 1100 as expected.

42. Harry C. Butcher, *My Three Years with Eisenhower*, 247–50.
43. Eisenhower to Handy, 28Jan43, *OPD Exec 3, Item 1a*.
44. Marshall to Mrs T. B. Coles, 30Jan43, *Marshall Library Files*.
45. Marshall to Slessor, 4Feb43; Marshall to Haskell, 4Feb43; *Marshall Library Files*.
46. Eisenhower to Handy, 28Jan43, *OPD Exec 3, Item 1a;* Eisenhower to Herron, 28Jan43, *Papers of Eisenhower,* II, 929–30.
47. Wedemeyer to Handy, 22Jan43, *OPD Exec 3, Item 1a.* Cf Wedemeyer, *Wedemeyer Reports,* 191–92.
48. Bryant, *Turn of the Tide,* 454.
49. Portal int, 7Feb47.

III: MARSHALL AT HIS COMMAND POST

Much of the material for Chapters III and IV comes from interviews. Among those who furnished material were Gen Marshall, Brig Gen Frank McCarthy, Maj Gen William T. Sexton, Gen Thomas T. Handy, Gen John E. Hull, Gen Maxwell Taylor, Maj Gen Orlando Ward, Gen of the Army Omar N. Bradley, H. Merrill Pasco, L. Arthur Minnich, Miss Mona Nason, Miss Cora E. Thomas, M/Sgt James Powder, Mrs Marjorie Payne Roberts Lunger, Maj Gen John H. Hilldring, M/Sgt George Dumcke (in interview by Dr E. M. Coffman for author), Col Russell P. Reeder, Jr, Lt Gen Leslie R. Groves, Brig Gen William A. Borden, Gen of the Army Dwight D. Eisenhower, Col Truman Smith, Gen Walter Bedell Smith, John J. McCloy, Brig Gen Paul M. Robinett. For the material pertaining to the Pentagon, I drew heavily on material gathered by Wilbur J. Nigh from the Chief of Staff's and Army Service Forces' files. Copies of all these can be found in the Pentagon Project Folder in the *Marshall Library Files.* Two of the most valuable sources are those collected in 1943 and 1944 by the Army Service Forces to be used in answering criticisms from Congress: Brig Gen C. F. Robinson to CG, ASF, subj: "The Pentagon Project," 25Jun44; Brig Gen Leslie R. Groves to CG, ASF, 3Apr42, with attached: "Basic Data on the Pentagon," 9Mar43, *ASF Pentagon Building, 1944.*

1. TAG memo W340–32–42, 13Nov42, *AG 029.21 (7–24–41) (1) Sec 1a.*
2. Reading copy of speech to National Association of Manufacturers, Waldorf Astoria, 4Dec42, *Marshall Library Files.* See also H. A. DeWeerd, *Selected Speeches and Statements of General of the Army George C. Marshall,* 220.
3. Stimson to President, 24Jul41, *AG 029.21 C/S Pentagon.*
4. Lt Gen Leslie R. Groves int, 7May70.
5. Although the contractors spoke of four floors, Pentagonians count the ground floor as one and speak of five. There is a subbasement and even a sub-subbasement under parts of the building.
6. For details of planning, costs, and

progress of construction, see *HQ ASF Pentagon Bldg, 1941, 1942, 1943, 1944; C/S Pentagon AG 029.21.*
7. Stimson Diary, 19–20, 24, and 27Nov42.
8. Newell to Marshall, 17Oct43, *Marshall Library Files.*
9. Marshall to Molly Winn, 29Jun43, *Marshall Library Files.*
10. Marshall to Maj Clifton S. Brown, 14May45, *Marshall Library Files.*
11. Marshall to Allen Brown, 7Jan42, *Marshall Library Files.*
12. Marshall to Allen Brown, 1Sept42, *Marshall Library Files.*
13. Marshall to Adm H. R. Stark ("Dear Betty"), 8Dec44, *Marshall Library Files.* Admiral Stark received the nick-

name "Betty" as a plebe at the U.S. Naval Academy in 1899 when there was a national ceremony honoring "Betty" Stark, wife of Revolutionary War General John Stark of the Battle of Bennington fame. Stark is usually quoted as having said at the battle that they would win it before night or "Molly" Stark would be a widow. Since his wife was named Elizabeth (Betty), the expression is confused. S. E. Morison, *Battle of the Atlantic*, 39n. The nickname became a term of affection for Stark. He was one of the few Marshall ever addressed so familiarly.

14. Allen Brown to Marshall, 19Aug40, *Marshall Library Files.*
15. Marshall to Allen Brown, 22Jan41, *Marshall Library Files.*
16. Marshall to Molly Winn, 8May42, *Marshall Library Files;* Col James J. Winn int, 4Apr66.
17. Marshall to Allen Brown, 7Jan42, *Marshall Library Files.*
18. Marshall to Allen Brown, 1Sept42, *Marshall Library Files.*
19. Devers int, 12Aug58.
20. Marshall to CO, Fort Benning, Georgia, 22Sept44, *Marshall Library Files.*
21. Marshall to Mrs Charles Dana Gibson, 29Jan42, *Marshall Library Files.*
22. Rose P. Wilson, *General Marshall Remembered*, contains a number of letters and postcards he sent over the years, including a poem he wrote for her when she was small and a description of a postcard that he had Gen Pershing and Marshal Foch autograph for her when Gen Marshall accompanied the two on a trip to St Louis in 1921. This book of reminiscence, interesting for its warm picture of the General, is marred by the attempt to recall exact conversations. The author attributes opinions to the General that sound more as if taken from the text of a speech than from colloquial conversation.
23. Keehn to Marshall, 11Nov40; Marshall to Keehn, 19Nov40, *Marshall Library Files.*

24. Keehn to Marshall, 12Aug41; SGS to Keehn, 15Aug41; Marshall to Keehn, 18Aug41, *Marshall Library Files.*
25. Marshall to Keehn, 2Dec42, *Marshall Library Files.*
26. Keehn to Marshall, 13Sept48, *Marshall Libarry Files.* Keehn died in Feb49.
27. Eisenhower to Marshall, 15Mar44; Marshall to Eisenhower, 23Mar44, *Marshall Library Files; Papers of Eisenhower*, III, 1769.
28. McCarthy to D. L. Chambers, President, Bobbs-Merrill, 14Apr44, *Marshall Library Files.* The letter relative to Andrews is in *Marshall Library Files.*
29. Circular ltr 222, 18Mar43, *WDCSA 201 Marshall;* Lt Col C. M. Adams to All Military Attachés, 17Jul43, *WDCSA 201 Marshall.*
30. On 18Mar44 Stimson wrote the President that Marshall had tried to block the Russian award and asked Roosevelt's view. The latter replied that he sympathized with the Chief of Staff but did not want to offend the Russians. He suggested that they check with Dill and if he said yes to go ahead. Dill, with whom Marshall had an agreement to decline exchange of decorations by the two governments during the war, agreed that under the circumstances the General should accept. Dill consulted the British Chiefs of Staff, who replied on March 20: "We entirely agree with you that General Marshall cannot refuse the Soviet decoration. To do so would almost certainly give offense to Marshal Stalin." In consenting Marshall made it clear that he considered that the award was being made to the Army— and he listed most of the top officers in the War Department as guests who should attend the presentation ceremony. President to SecWar, 14Mar44; SecWar to President, 18Mar44; Br CsofS to Dill, 20Mar44, *SecWar Safe File.* Gen Marshall also accepted an award from Cuba.
31. Hull int, 8Aug57 (author's notes).

IV: MARSHALL AND HIS STAFF

1. See Brian Kelly, "Quarters One," *Commonwealth Magazine*, Dec67, 32–35.
2. Marshall int, 15Feb57.

3. Marshall to Krock, 28Sept44; Krock to Marshall, 2Oct44, *Marshall Library Files.* Marshall did not list the other

papers he read. However, he once told the author that he particularly liked the *Christian Science Monitor.* He obviously glanced at the Washington papers, the *Post*, the *Star*, the often-critical *Times-Herald*, and the *News*.

4. Powder int, 19Oct59.
5. Marjorie Payne Roberts Lunger int. 20Jun69.
6. Much of the description of a day in the office is based on information from Maj Gen William T. Sexton, who served in the secretariat from 1940 to 1944, and from Gen John E. Hull, who served in the Operations Division, War Department, from 1941 to 1946.
7. McCarthy to Marshall, 1Oct43, with comments by CofS, *Marshall Library Files*.
8. I have heard the story from Miss Nason, Gen Taylor, and Gen McCarthy. At the farewell party for Miss Nason, Gen Ridgway repeated it.
9. Marshall to Devers, 25Mar44, *Marshall Library Files*.
10. Other Reserve officers on the staff included B. W. Davenport, who had taken his law degree at the University of Virginia with Pasco at the same time as McCarthy was in graduate school there; L. Arthur Minnich, a student of history who was picked by Col McCarthy from a group of convalescents at Walter Reed Hospital; Gordon Bell, who was badly wounded at Anzio; Charles Heitzberg, who aided Bell, Pasco, and Davenport in covering the White House; Frank Werneken, who was McCarthy's special assistant; and Randall Oulie.
11. McCarthy to Marshall, 24Dec44, *Marshall Library Files*.
12. Marshall to Pasco, 25Dec44, *Marshall Library Files*.
13. Ned Brooks to Mrs Richard Roberts, 6Dec48, enclosing script of his broadcast on the sergeant's decision not to write her story; Marshall to Mrs Richard Roberts (now Marjorie Payne Roberts Lunger), 27Dec48, *Marshall Library Files*.
14. Marshall int, 21Nov56.
15. Ray S. Cline, *Washington Command Post: The Operations Division*, 166; Gen T. T. Handy int, 9Jul70.
16. Gen John E. Hull int, 5May70.

17. Marshall to AsstSecWar McCloy, 31-Mar43, *Marshall Library Files*.
18. Roosevelt to Lt Gen C. E. Kilbourne, 21May43, *Marshall Library Files*.
19. Pogue, *Ordeal and Hope*, 22–23, 30–33, 131.
20. Quotations are in Marshall int, 13-Nov56 (author's notes).
21. Marshall to Byrnes, 10Jul43, *WDCSA 040 (10Jul43) SS*. Also see ltr with attachments Ismay to Marshall, 3Jul43, *Marshall Library Files*.
22. See Pogue, *Ordeal and Hope*, 298–300, on reorganization.
23. Maj Gen Otto N. Nelson, *National Security and the General Staff*, 397–404, has a valuable description of the Joint Chiefs and Combined Chiefs of Staff organizations as they functioned in Washington. It should be remembered that the Joint Staff Mission acted in accordance with directives from the British Chiefs of Staff in London, and that at international conferences the British group in Washington was supplanted personally by heads of the various services. See also Cline, *Washington Command Post*, 98–106.
24. Marshall int, 13Nov56.
25. Arnold to Marshall, 10May43; Marshall to Arnold, 14May43, *Marshall Library Files*.
26. Marshall to Arnold, 18Oct43, *Marshall Library Files*.
27. Arnold to Marshall, 22Mar45; Marshall to Arnold, 8Apr45, *Marshall Library Files*.
28. Marshall ints, 14Feb57, 21Nov56.
29. Ibid, 21Nov56.
30. Mrs Oveta Culp Hobby int, 28Aug63.
31. Marshall ints, 4 and 14Feb57.
32. Ibid, 4Feb57.
33. Bell I. Wiley, *Historical Program of the US Army 1939 to Present*, 44ff.
34. Col Russell P. Reeder, Jr, *Born at Reveille*, chaps 23–26, 182–224.
35. Ibid, 214–17. An autographed copy of *Fighting in Guadalcanal* is in the Marshall Library.
36. Memo by Bedell Smith from AFHQ file.
37. For Eisenhower corres with Gen Marshall, see Joseph P. Hobbs, *Dear General*. A typical reply is in Marshall to Eisenhower, 28Sept42, *Marshall Library Files:* "When you want some-

thing that you aren't getting tell me
and I will try to get it for you. I have
complete confidence in your management of the affair, and want to support you in every way practicable."

38. Marshall to Mrs Stilwell, 29Dec43,
Marshall Library Files.
39. Marshall to WD Chiefs and CG AGF,
AAF, SOS, 24Apr42, *ASF Styer Miscel-
laneous.*

V: MARSHALL AND THE FIGHTING MAN . . . AND WOMAN

I have drawn heavily on interviews with Mrs Oveta Culp Hobby and Maj Gen Frederick Osborn and on Mattie Treadwell, *The Women's Army Corps,* and Ulysses G. Lee,
Employment of Negro Troops.

1. Marshall ints, 28Sept56 (author's notes),
21Nov56.
2. Marshall int, 15Feb57.
3. Rearranged somewhat in order from
Marshall int, 15Feb57.
4. Jolson to Marshall, 26Oct43; Marshall
to Jolson, 10Nov43; Marshall to G-1,
9Nov43, *Marshall Library Files.*
5. Marshall to McNair, 28Jul43, *WDCSA
430 (1942–43).* The Civilian Conservation Corps was set up by President
Roosevelt early in his first term to
give employment to young men. Many
of the projects were devoted to for-
estry or to prevention of soil erosion.
6. McNarney to Sen Rufus Holman, 10-
Nov43, *Marshall Library Files;* Marshall to Special Services Division, 2Aug-
43, *WDCSA 325.01 (1942–43).*
7. Harper Sibley to Marshall, 27Feb42;
Marshall to Sibley, 6Mar42, *AG 353.8
(11–5–41).* Marshall emphasized that
soldiers constantly needed reports on
conditions in their homes, communications with relatives and friends, and
advice on personal matters—services
routinely provided by the Red Cross.
Marshall's reference to an expeditionary force apparently was influenced
by his World War I experience. Naturally the arrangements applied to
Red Cross activities with all American
forces sent to combat theaters.
8. Marshall int, 21Nov56.
9. Maj Gen Frederick Osborn int, 18Feb-
59.
10. Marshall to Theater Commanders,
5Oct43, *Marshall Library Files.*
11. Marshall to Surles, 6Feb44; see also
Marshall to Roosevelt, 6Feb44, *Marshall Library Files.*
12. Survey by J. Walter Thompson Co,
Nov44, *Marshall Library Files.*
13. Marshall to Roosevelt, 28Sept42, after
President turned down initial request
on 14Sept42, *Marshall Library Files.*
14. Patton to Mrs Marshall, n.d. but 1943,
after Sicilian campaign, in Harry H.
Semmes, *Portrait of Patton,* 173–74.
15. Roosevelt to SecWar and SecNavy, 11-
Jan44, *Marshall Library Files.*
16. Marshall to Roosevelt through channels, 3Feb44, *WDCSA 200.6, Sec 1;
Exec Order 9419,* 4Feb44.
17. See Robert R. Palmer, Bell I. Wiley,
and William R. Keast, *The Procurement and Training of Ground Combat Troops,* 62.
18. Marshall to W. B. Smith, 30Mar45,
Marshall Library Files.
19. Marshall to Handy, attached to draft
message Marshall to MacArthur, 24-
Jan44, *Marshall Library Files,* containing congratulations on his sixty-fourth
birthday and announcement of an additional Oak Leaf Cluster to his Distinguished Service Medal.
20. Marshall to Marvin McIntyre, 2Apr42,
Marshall Library Files.
21. Marshall to G-1, 24Dec43, *Marshall
Library Files.* Allen Brown, who had
always been quick to spot injustice,
had reported this state of affairs to his
stepfather on reaching North Africa.
22. Noting that Stilwell, head of Army
Ground Forces, now had four stars,
and Arnold, head of the Army Air
Forces, had five, he outlined the responsibilities of the nine men he now
proposed for four: McNarney, Deputy Supreme Allied Commander, Mediterranean, with half a million men;
Bradley, commander of 12th Army
Group, with nearly 1 million men;
Spaatz, head of U.S. Strategic Air
Forces in Europe with some 230,000;

Kenney, top air commander in the Pacific, with some 170,000; Clark with an army group of more than half a million; Krueger with Sixth Army; Devers with 6th Army Group and nearly 450,-000 men; Somervell, commander of Army Services Forces, with more than 1 million men; and Handy, Deputy Chief of Staff of the Army. Message drafted by Marshall's office with note by Marshall, sent by Stimson to President, 12Mar45, *Marshall Library Files.*

23. Marshall to Sexton, 22Nov43, *Marshall Library Files.*

24. Marshall to Handy, 3Jan45, *Marshall Library Files.*

25. GCM [Marshall] to Gen McNarney, 27Dec43; J. T. M[cNarney] to Marshall, containing report of examining doctor and opinion of Surgeon General, 29Dec43, *Marshall Library Files.*

26. Frank Capra, *Frank Capra: The Name Above the Title*, 325–67.

27. Marshall int, 14Feb57. A film consisting of extracts from the series was shown after the war in the United States.

28. *Stars and Stripes*, 18Apr42.

29. Washington *Star Magazine*, "5¢ Magazine for $180," 29Sept68; Marshall to Eisenhower, 29Oct43, *Marshall Library Files;* Eisenhower to Marshall, 1Nov-43, *Papers of Eisenhower*, III, 1548.

30. Marshall int, 15Feb57.

31. Marshall to Handy, 12Jan45, *Marshall Library Files.*

32. Marshall to JCS, 30Jul43, *WDCSA 370.9 (30Jul43) SS.*

33. Showing his own disapprobation of the term, he suggested that the statement should not be printed. I have quoted it because Lord Moran in his *Churchill: Taken from the Diaries of Lord Moran*, 392, cites a conversation between Marshall and Churchill in 1952 that indicates that the former agreed with the Prime Minister. Marshall's interview 15Feb57 would indicate that he did not. Marshall certainly believed strongly that there must be professional soldiers to stiffen units made up mainly of men brought in by the draft. But he did not denigrate the civilian soldier.

34. Marshall int, 14Feb57.

35. Hilldring int, 30Mar59.

36. Marshall int, 20Feb57.

37. Marshall to Patterson, 24Aug42, *Marshall Library Files.*

38. Patterson to Marshall, 18Oct43, *Marshall Library Files.*

39. Patterson to Marshall, 14Sept45, *Marshall Library Files.*

40. Marshall int, 20Feb57.

41. Hastie to Marshall, 30Jan43, *Marshall Library Files.*

42. Marshall int, 14Feb57.

43. Marshall to Harmon, 18Mar44, *Marshall Library Files.*

44. Stimson to Marshall, n.d., forwarding memo dated 5Dec44, *SecWar Safe File, Folder Chaplains.*

45. Marshall to Stimson, 18Dec44; Marshall to Maj Gen S. G. Henry, 19Dec-44, *Marshall Library Files.*

46. Henry to Marshall, 3Jan45, *Marshall Library Files.*

47. Henry to CofS, 30Mar and 5Jul45; Henry to Handy, 26Mar45, *WDCSA 201, Miller, L. D.*

48. George H. Day to Marshall, 17Mar45; Marshall to Day, 22Mar45, *Marshall Library Files.*

49. Marshall to Mr and Mrs A. J. Carlson, 14Mar45, *Marshall Library Files.*

50. Marshall to Crittenberger, 1Jun45, *Marshall Library Files.* Gen Crittenberger would lose another son in action in 1969.

51. Crittenberger to Marshall, 28Jun45, *Marshall Library Files.*

52. Hopkins to Marshall, 16Feb44, *Marshall Library Files.*

53. Ltr in *Marshall Library Files.*

54. The letters, authors purposely left anonymous, with comments are in files relating to letters of condolence in *Marshall Library Files.*

55. At Casablanca, Marshall got from the five secretaries a list of items they wanted replaced. Mattie Treadwell, the WAC historian, notes on the basis of interviews with the officers involved: "Finding that there was no legal means of free replacement, he personally paid for and forwarded new clothing, refusing to accept repayment." Treadwell, *The Women's Army Corps*, 361.

56. Ibid, 5–7, 11–12, 16–17.

57. Hilldring int, by Lt Col Treadwell, 17-Jan46, cited in ibid, 20.

58. BurBud to SecWar, 7Oct41, *AG 291.9 WAAC, Sec 1, Pt 1 (6-2-41).*

59. Brig Gen A. D. Surles to Marshall,

5Sept41; Surles to Marshall, 18Sept41; Mrs Hobby to Marshall, 20Oct41, *Marshall Library Files.*

60. Handwritten note to Gen Haislip on Mrs Hobby to CofS, 14Nov41, *AG 291.9 WAAC, Sec 1, Pt 1 (6–2–41).*
61. Hilldring int, by Treadwell, cited in Treadwell, *The WAC,* 22.
62. WD (signed by Gen Bryden in Marshall's absence) to BurBud, 25Nov41, *AG 291.9 WAAC, Sec 1, Pt 1 (6–2–41).*
63. Harold D. Smith to SecWar, 11Dec41, *AG 291.9 WAAC, Sec 1, Pt 1 (6–2–41).*
64. Mrs Hobby int, 28Aug63.
65. Marshall int, by R. A. Winnacker, 1Dec48.
66. Mrs Hobby int, 28Aug63; Treadwell, *The WAC,* 29.
67. Stimson Diary, 16May42.
68. Mrs Hobby int, 28Aug63.
69. Treadwell, *The WAC,* 50, 54, 62, 84, 91.
70. Mrs Hobby int, 28Aug63.
71. Marshall int, 21Nov56.
72. Treadwell, *The WAC,* 218, 203.
73. Marshall to Somervell, 17Sept42, *Marshall Library Files.*
74. Treadwell, *The WAC,* 531.
75. Mrs Hobby int, 28Aug63.
76. Marshall int, by R. A. Winnacker, 1Dec48. In an interview with author 15Nov56, Marshall said that he would have taken Col Newsome to conferences abroad "but King would have gone crazy."
77. Mrs Hobby int, 28Aug63.

VI: FACETS OF COMMAND

I have drawn in this chapter on interviews with Harvey Bundy, Col Stanley J. Grogan (by telephone), Speaker Sam Rayburn, Gen Osborn, Frederick V. Geier, and Charles R. Hook. I have made considerable use of Ralph Elberton Smith's *The Army and Economic Mobilization* and John Millett, *The Organization and Role of the Army Service Forces.*

1. T. H. Vail Motter, *The Persian Corridor and Aid to Russia,* 68–81.
2. Ibid, 165–69. See summary of Record Relative to Gen Greely's Mission in Iran, Brig Gen St Clair Streett to Marshall, 17Aug42, *OPD Exec 10, Item 56;* Greely to CofS, 7Sept42, sub: Report on duty as adviser, Iranian Army, 19-May–4Sept42, *OPD 210.684 Iran, Sec 1, Case 45;* WD to Greely, 16May42, *AG 210.31 (5–13–42);* Handy to CofS, 1Oct42, *Abstract PGF 261;* Summary attached to Welles to McNarney, 23-Sept42, *Dept State 891.20/175/MEL,* last three cited Motter, *Persian Corridor,* 165–66.
3. Richardson to CofS, 28Jul42; Marshall to MacArthur, 2Aug42; Handy to CofS, 8Aug42, *WDCSA SWPA 1942–43;* Marshall to McNair, 6Oct42, *WDCSA 201 Richardson.*
4. Stetson Conn, Rose C. Engelman, and Byron Fairchild, *Guarding the United States and Its Outposts,* 331–35. See Marshall to Van Voorhis, 4Jan41, *WPD 4440–1* and Marshall to Van Voorhis, 5Mar41 in *WPD 4440–51;* Marshall to Van Voorhis, 9Apr41, *OCS 17611–35.*
5. Marshall to Smith, 27Apr43, *Marshall Library Files.*
6. Marshall to Somervell, 12Apr43, *Marshall Library Files.*
7. *The Wartime Journals of Charles A. Lindbergh,* 94–130.
8. Marshall to Col ——, 22Oct45, *Marshall Library Files.*
9. Mrs Hobby int, 28Aug63.
10. Marshall to Pershing, 27Mar43, *Marshall Library Files.*
11. Marshall to Eisenhower, 3Dec42, *OPD Exec 10, Item 36a,* cited Harry L. Coles and Albert K. Weinberg, *Civil Affairs: Soldiers Become Governors,* 55.
12. Eisenhower to Marshall, 4Dec42, CM-IN 1675, *OPD Exec 10, Item 36a,* cited Coles and Weinberg, *Civil Affairs,* 55. A résumé of this exchange is given in Marshall to President, 22Mar43, *Marshall Library Files.*
13. La Guardia to Maj Gen George V. Strong, 23Dec42 (two memos); Strong to Marshall, 23Dec42, *WDCSA 386 Africa, 1942,* cited Coles and Weinberg, *Civil Affairs,* 56. See Marshall to President, 22Mar43, in *Marshall Library Files,* for résumé of proposal.
14. La Guardia to Hopkins, 17Mar43, cited in Robert E. Sherwood, *Roosevelt and Hopkins: An Intimate History,* 725;

E. M. W. [Maj Gen E. M. Watson] to McCarthy, 16Mar43; McCarthy to CofS, 19Mar43; and McCarthy to Marshall, 19Mar43, with Marshall note, "Call his [Leahy's] special attention to the portion of Eisenhower's message I have underlined," *Marshall Library Files.*

15. Stimson Diary, 27Mar43.

16. Marshall to President, 22Mar43; Marshall to McCloy, 27Mar43, *Marshall Library Files.*

17. Stimson Diary, 31Mar43; Marshall to McCarthy, 30Mar43, and McCloy to Marshall, 30Mar43, *WDCSA 201 La Guardia.*

18. Stimson Diary, 6Apr43.

19. Pasco memo for record, 6Sept44; Marshall to SecWar, enclosing draft ltr to President, 7Sept44, *Marshall Library Files;* Stimson Diary, 8Sept44.

20. Marshall to Osborn, 15Apr43, *Marshall Library Files.*

21. Murphy to Marshall, 25Mar43; Roosevelt to Stimson, 29Mar43; SecWar (drafted by Marshall's office) to President, 1Apr43; Marshall to Murphy, 1Apr43; Murphy to Marshall, 10May43; Marshall to Murphy, 11May43; Marshall to President, 1Apr43, *Marshall Library Files.*

22. Murphy to Marshall, 1[0]Sept43; Marshall to Murphy, 25Sept43, *Marshall Library Files.*

23. Murphy to President, 25May44; Murphy to Marshall, 26May44, with msg to President enc; Marshall to Murphy, 8Jun44, *Marshall Library Files.*

24. Freeman to Marshall, 4Oct40; Marshall to Freeman, 10Oct40; Freeman to Col Ward Maris, 15Jan41; Marshall to Freeman, 17Jan41; Freeman to Marshall, 18Jan41; Freeman to Marshall, 9Feb41; W. T. S[exton] to Marshall, 12Feb42, and Marshall comments, *Marshall Library Files.*

25. Freeman to Marshall, 6Aug43; Marshall to Freeman, 9Aug43, *Marshall Library Files.*

26. Marshall to Stimson, 18Jan45, *Marshall Library Files.*

27. The Press Section was headed by Lt Col Stanley J. Grogan, the Radio Section by Col Edward M. Kirby, the Magazine Section by Col Francis V. Fitzgerald, the Movie and Photograph Section by Col Mason Wright, and the Press Analysis Section by Lt Col Reg-

inald E. Looker. Memorandum by Maj Gen Robert C. Richardson, n.d. furnished by James Hewes.

28. Info from William J. Donohoe, Public Information Division, Pentagon, tel int, 26Oct71; Grogan tel int, 1Sept69; Richardson Memoir.

29. Marshall int, 20Feb57.

30. Marshall to Surles, 22Feb43.

31. Marshall to MacArthur, 8Sept44, *Marshall Library Files.*

32. Persons to author, 1Jul70.

33. The liaison chief gathered around him other skilled practitioners of the public-relations art, such as Lt Col Bryce Harlow, who later served Presidents Eisenhower and Nixon, and Brig Gen Robert Cutler, on duty part time from the SecWar's office. Other assistants included Maj Gen Edward Smith, later vice president and general counsel, Southern Bell Telephone Co; Lt Col Edward Crosland, vice president, American Telephone and Telegraph Co; Col Dillon Anderson, attorney in Houston; Cols John Dinsmore, Edward Walsh, and Kilbourne Johnson of the Judge Advocate General's Dept. Based on information from Gen Persons.

34. At Christmas 1942 Marshall wrote Persons a glowing tribute: "I am taking this rather formal method of giving you my Christmas greeting, for I wish to include my personal thanks for all that you have done with such conspicuous success to represent the interests of the War Department on the Hill. You are one of the few men in the Army whom I consider irreplaceable in your present job so please watch your health and when you need a vacation, take it." Two years later, also at Christmas, he wrote: "The cordial relations of the War Department with Congress are due largely to your political acumen and tactful handling of situations that might easily have been sources of considerable embarrassment." Marshall to Persons, Dec42 and Dec44, *Marshall Library Files.*

35. Speaker Sam Rayburn int, 6Nov57 (author's notes).

36. Celler to Marshall, 20Oct43; Marshall to Celler, 22Oct43, *Marshall Library Files.*

37. Bundy int, 7Oct59.

38. Osborn int, 18Feb59.

39. Marshall int, 19Nov56.
40. See Paul A. C. Koistinen, "The 'Industrial-Military Complex' in Historical Perspective: The Inter-War Years," *The Journal of American History*, Mar70, 819–39. Professor Koistinen outlines the steps by which the military and industrial leaders formulated plans for cooperation in industrial mobilization that bore fruit in World War II.
41. Geier int, 23Apr59. Hook told much the same story (int, 20Apr59), recalling that the chart showed what was needed in a white diagram with the small part available under the head of each item in a drab color. The spaces were almost solid white.
42. Hook int, 20Apr59.
43. See R. Elberton Smith, *The Army and Economic Mobilization*, chap 7; John D. Millett, *The Organization and Role of the Army Service Forces,* chap 12.
44. Hook int, 20Apr59; Geier int, 23Apr59.
45. Hook int, 20Apr59.
46. Marshall int, 7Dec56.
47. Ibid.
48. Marshall to Surles, 27Oct43, containing Smith to Marshall, 29Jul43, *WDCSA 451.1 (1942–43)*; Marshall int, 7Dec56. See also Gen Maxwell to Marshall, 30Oct43, *WDCSA 451.1 (1942–43)*.

VII: WILLIWAWS AND JITTERS

I have depended heavily on the Army's official volume pertaining to Alaska and the Aleutians, Conn, Engelman, and Fairchild, *Guarding the U.S. and Its Outposts.* Also of value have been Samuel E. Morison, *The Aleutians, Gilberts and Marshalls;* Brian Garfield, *The Thousand-Mile War: World War II in Alaska and the Aleutians;* and Stetson Conn's extensive notes on relocation and Alaska.

1. Stetson Conn, "The Decision to Evacuate the Japanese from the Pacific Coast," in *Command Decisions,* ed Kent R. Greenfield, 129.
2. Clark to JAG, GHQ, 24Jan42, cited Conn, *Guarding the U.S. and Its Outposts*, 121; Marshall to President, n.d. but apparently 25 or 26Jan42, prepared by Provost Marshal General for Clark; Stimson Diary, 25Jan42; Sec-War to Atty Gen, 25Jan42, *AG 381 (1–25–42).*
3. Gullion's deputy, Col Archer L. Lerch, who had lived in California and Hawaii for many years, was convinced that anything short of removal of Japanese aliens and strict surveillance of citizens of Japanese descent was inconsistent with national safety. He characterized DeWitt's approval of a meeting between Gov Curlbert L. Olson and representatives of the Japanese-Americans as savoring "too much of the spirit of Rotary and overlooking the necessary cold-bloodedness of war." Next day Gullion informed Sec McCloy that DeWitt seemed to be leaning toward a policy of voluntary cooperation, which he considered extremely dangerous. Dep PMG Col Archer L. Lerch to PMG Gullion and Bendetsen, 4Feb42, *PMGO 384.4 WDC;* Gullion to McCloy, 5Feb42, *ASW 014.311 WDC, Box 20.*
4. Stimson Diary, 3Feb42; DeWitt, Memo for record, 31Jan42, cited Conn, *Guarding the U.S. and Its Outposts,* 124.
5. He thought that the War Dept had about concluded that withdrawal of the Japanese should be restricted to certain protected areas. There were, he added, "so many legal questions involved in discrimination between the native-born Japanese . . ." and "so many that would be involved in a mass withdrawal, the social and economic disturbances would be so great that we would like to go a little slowly on it, and we are a little afraid that if it gets about out there that the Army is really taking the position on mass withdrawal, that it may stimulate [anti-Japanese feeling]. . . ." Tel conv DeWitt with McCloy, 3Feb42, *PMGO 384.4 WDC.* Transcript of the conversation from McCloy.
6. Gen J. R. Deane to SecWar, 3Feb42, *SecWar Safe File.*
7. Bendetsen to PMG, 4Feb42, *PMG 014.311 Gen P/W;* Gullion to McCloy, 6Feb42, *ASW 014.311 WDC, Box 20.*
8. Stimson Diary, 10Feb42.
9. Stimson Diary, 11Feb42; tel conv Mc-

Cloy to Bendetsen, 11Feb42, *WDC 384.4, Vol I, RG 338;* Conn, "The Decision to Evacuate the Japanese from the Pacific Coast," in *Command Decisions,* ed Greenfield, 103–104.

10. Tel conv DeWitt with Clark, 12Feb42, cited Conn, *Guarding the U.S. and Its Outposts,* 132.

11. Copy of Lippmann column, "The Fifth Column on the Coast," 12Feb42, forwarded to Stimson by Deane with note, "General Marshall wants you to see this." *ASW 014.311 WDC, Box 20.*

12. Ltr Boddy to Biddle, 16Feb42. On the same day he sent a wire in which he said that leaders of a local Japanese citizens' group were deeply worried and approaching a state of panic. Both in *ASW 014.311 WDC, Box 20.*

13. Stimson Diary, 17Feb42; Brig Gen Mark Clark, GHQ, Memo for record, 3:30 pm, 17Feb42, *GHQ file WDC: Enemy Aliens,* cited Conn, *Guarding the U.S. and Its Outposts,* 135; Conn, "The Decision to Evacuate the Japanese from the Pacific Coast," in *Command Decisions,* ed Greenfield, 146.

14. Stimson Diary, 18Feb42.

15. Ibid, 20Feb42.

16. Gullion to CofS, 20Feb42; *PMGO 014.311 WDC;* tel conv DeWitt with Bendetsen, 20Feb42; Bendetsen to SecWar, 21Feb42, *SecWar Safe File, Aliens.*

17. Knox to Biddle, 22Feb42, *ASW 014.311 WDC, Box 20;* tel conv DeWitt and Joyce, 23Feb42, *WDC 384.4, Vol I, RG 338;* Tolan Committee to Governors, 26Feb42.

18. Stimson Diary, 26Feb42; Stimson notes after cabinet meeting, 27Feb42, *WDCSA 334 Mtgs and Conf; Exec Order 9102,* 18Mar42; *Exec Order 9106,* 20Mar42; *Exec Order 9066,* 19Feb42.

19. Notes on War Council, 23Mar42, *OCS SGS.*

20. FDR to SecWar, 5May42, *ASW 014.311 Gen, WDC.* DeWitt strongly favored moving German and Italian aliens from the West Coast. Informed that the shift was not feasible in view of the President's attitude, the General declared that he thought someone was making a great mistake and that he would not change that view. His protests were in vain. McCloy advised that no other mass evacuations be undertaken. Tel conv DeWitt with Bendetsen, 11May42, *WDC CAD 311.2 Tel Convs,* cited Conn, *Guarding the U.S. and Its Outposts,* 146.

21. DeWitt testimony, House Subcommittee on Naval Affairs, 13Apr43.

22. DeWitt to Marshall, 31May43; Marshall to DeWitt, 8Jun43, *Marshall Library Files.*

23. Marshall int, 20Feb57.

24. Ibid, 15Feb57.

25. Conn, *Guarding the U.S. and Its Outposts,* 231–32.

26. Adams to DeWitt, 3229, 3Jul31, *Marshall Library Files.*

27. Wesley F. Craven and James S. Cate, *The Army Air Forces in World War II,* I, 166–70; Marshall to Buckner, 23-Sept41, cited Conn, *Guarding the U.S. and Its Outposts,* 249.

28. Conn, *Guarding the U.S. and Its Outposts,* 253–54.

29. Buckner to CG, Western Defense Command, 31Jan42; Parker to Cmdt 13th Naval Dist, 1Feb42, *OPD 381 ADC, Sec 1, Case 6.*

30. Eisenhower to Marshall, 13Mar42, *OPD 381 ADC, Sec 1, Case 6.*

31. King's second endorsement to Parker to Cmdt 13th Naval Dist, 1Feb42, comments on Buckner and Parker plans as given in ltr Buckner to DeWitt, 31-Jan42, with first endorsement by De-Witt, 21Feb42, *OPD 381 ADC, Sec 1, Case 6.*

32. Eisenhower to Marshall, 13Mar42, *OPD 381 ADC, Sec 1, Case 6.*

33. Marshall to WPD, 18Mar42; suggestions were part of third endorsement to Buckner ltr in Eisenhower to TAG, 24Mar42, *OPD 381 ADC, Sec 1, Case 6.*

34. Roosevelt to Stark and Marshall, 4Mar-42, *OPD 380.3.*

35. JCS 16/1, 29Mar42, "U.S. Action"; JCS 16/2, 19Jun42, "U.S. Aid to Russia," *ABC 381 (1–23–42);* Matloff and Snell, *Strategic Planning, 1941–1942,* 145.

36. Pogue, *Ordeal and Hope,* 324–25.

37. Morison, *Aleutians, Gilberts and Marshalls,* 4–5; Matloff and Snell, *Strategic Planning, 1941–1942,* 258; Conn, *Guarding the U.S. and Its Outposts,* 264–65.

38. Mins JCS 20th mtg, 15Jun42, *ABC 334 JCS Mins (2–14–42), Sec 1.*

39. Copy in *Marshall Library Files* and correspondence with King. Attached to Theobald to King, 19Aug42, forwarded by King to Marshall for comment, the poem—marked "Read to Rear Admiral Theobald by General Buckner,

Aug 18, 1942"—was quickly spread throughout the Alaskan Command and a copy or copies reached Marshall outside channels almost as quickly as it came to him through King. Samuel E. Morison, *Coral Sea, Midway and Submarine Action,* 171.

40. Theobald to Buckner, 20Aug42; Marshall to King, 3Sept42; Marshall to DeWitt, 3Sept42, *Marshall Library Files.*

41. Marshall to DeWitt, 3Sept42; DeWitt to Marshall, 5Sept42, 8Sept42, 9Sept42, and 23Sept42, *Marshall Library Files.*

42. Marshall to King, 28Sept42 with King to Marshall comment on bottom of msg; Marshall to DeWitt, 2Oct43, *Marshall Library Files.*

43. Marshall to DeWitt, 27Feb43; DeWitt to Marshall, 5Mar43; Marshall to DeWitt, 17Mar43, *Marshall Library Files.* DeWitt later said the rift was exaggerated. Marshall did not agree.

44. Marshall to DeWitt, 2062, 15Oct42; DeWitt to Marshall, from Comdt 13th Naval Dist, 17Oct42, Résumé of Procedure Resulting in Joint Directive for the Occupation of Amchitka, n.d., Tab A, rpt of Lt Col W. J. Verbeck, 4Oct42, *WDCSA Alaska (1942–43) SS;* Handy to Marshall, 29Oct42, Marshall to DeWitt, 29Oct42, *OPD 381 ADC, Sec 1, Case 36.*

45. DeWitt to Marshall, 5Dec42, *WDCSA Alaska (1942–43) SS.*

46. Marshall to DeWitt, 17Dec42, *WDCSA Alaska (1942–43) SS.*

47. DeWitt to Marshall, Rad 244, 20Dec42, *OPD Msg File;* Conn, *Guarding the U.S. and Its Outposts,* 275–76: Résumé of Procedure Resulting in Joint Directive.

48. King to Marshall, 15Dec42, Marshall to King, 16Dec42, *WDCSA Alaska (1942–43) SS;* Cominch to Cincpac, 17-Dec42 (sent 18Dec), *OPD 381 ADC, Sec 1, Case 38;* DeWitt to Marshall 5Dec42; Marshall to DeWitt, 17Dec42, *WDCSA Alaska (1942–43) SS.* Marshall was unable to grant DeWitt's request to reassign the 44th Division and the 184th Infantry Regiment from his command to Alaska. The 44th Division, as DeWitt now knew, had been detached from the Western Defense Command for assignment elsewhere. As for the 184th Infantry, there was no regiment available to take its place. Even if it could be spared, Marshall said that he would be "reluctant" to commit it to Alaska, "except in the course of additional offensive operations in that area."

49. See Garfield, *Thousand-Mile War,* 207, 238–52, for vivid account of battle, question of relief of Maj Gen Albert E. Brown, commander of the 7th Infantry Division, and casualties. For fuller discussion of the entire period see Conn, *Guarding the U.S. and Its Outposts,* chap 2, and Morison, *Aleutians, Gilberts and Marshalls,* 37–51.

50. DeWitt to Marshall, 30Jul43; DeWitt to Marshall, 2Aug43, *OPD 381 Security, Sec 7, Case 206.*

51. Emmons to Handy, 4Aug43; Handy to CofS, 23Sept43, *OPD 381, Sec 7, Case 206.*

52. Mins JCS 108th mtg, 19Aug43, *ABC 334 JCS Mins (2–14–42), Sec 5.*

53. Marshall to Handy, 26Aug43; McCloy to Marshall, 31Aug43; unsigned résumé of observations made in Alaska and the Aleutians, obviously by McCloy, 10Aug43; draft of ltr Col Paul Goode, OPD, to Brig Gen E. D. Post, n.d. but shortly after McCloy returned to Washington, *ASW 333.1 Alaska.*

54. Marshall int, 21Nov56.

55. DeWitt to Marshall, 31May43, 28Aug-43, *Marshall Library Files;* and 27Aug-43, *WDCSA Alaska (1942–43) SS;* Marshall to DeWitt, 7Sept43, *WDCSA 210.311 (5Sept43).*

56. JPS, 101st mtg, 15Sept43, *ABC 334 JSP Mins (2–13–42), Sec 5.*

57. Adm King to JCS, 21Sept43, *ABC 381 Japan (5–31–42), Sec 1.*

58. F. N. R. [Col Frank N. Roberts] in covering note to Handy, 23Jan44, on Strategy Section study, 21Jan44; Goode to AsstCofS, OPD, 22Dec43; Paul Carraway to Billo, 25Dec43; JEH[ull] to Handy, 26Jan44; Mins JCS 117th mtg, 5Oct43, *ABC 334 JCS Mins (2–14–42), Sec 5.*

VIII: NOT SO PEACEFUL PACIFIC

I have drawn heavily in this chapter on Louis Morton, *Strategy and Command: The First Two Years.*

1. Wedemeyer, *Wedemeyer Reports*, 193–94, 205–207.
2. MacArthur to Maj Gen Albert C. Smith, 7Jan55, cited Morton, *Strategy and Command*, 438–39.
3. Douglas MacArthur, *Reminiscences*, 172–73. Cf MacArthur to Smith, 5Mar-53, cited Morton, *Strategy and Command*, 250, with slightly different text.
4. Marshall to King, 1Dec42, *OPD 381 SWPA, Sec 2, Case 83*; Morton, *Strategy and Command*, 302–304, 619–20.
5. Morton, *Strategy and Command*, 370–71, citing King-Nimitz radios, 30Nov, 2Dec42; memo for Marshall et al, 15Dec42, enc ltr Nimitz to King, 8Dec-42, *OPD Exec 10, Item 67b.*
6. King had anticipated that a bolder strategy in the Solomons would require increased forces. In a memo of 3Dec42 he asked Marshall if Army ground troops could relieve 17,000 Marines on defense duty in the Hawaiian and Samoan areas. He also asked for relief of five air squadrons for offensive operations in other areas. On 24Dec Marshall said he did not see how he could manage the relief of the Marines because of the shortage of troopships and cargo ships. The critical need for air support in North Africa made it "practically impossible" to commit more units and planes to the Pacific. Marshall reminded King that the draft directive on Rabaul drawn up three weeks earlier provided that Nimitz and MacArthur jointly would determine the task forces to be used in offensives in the Southwest Pacific and the defense forces needed to protect lines of communications. "The decision in this matter would have a preliminary bearing on your memorandum of Dec 3d." *WDCSA SWPA 1942.*
7. Nimitz to King, 8Dec42, *OPD Exec 10, Item 67b.*
8. Marshall to King, 21Dec42, *OPD Exec 10, Item 67b.*
9. King to CofS, "Preliminary draft for staff study only," sent to Handy personally by Conolly, 12/23/42; Handy to Conolly, 29Dec43, *OPD Exec 10, Item 67b.*
10. King to Marshall, 6Jan43, *OPD Exec 10, Item 67b.*
11. Marshall to King, 8Jan43, *OPD 384 PTO, Sec 2, Case 43.*
12. King to Marshall, 8Jan43, *OPD Exec 10, Item 67b* (italics in original); Marshall to MacArthur, 8Jan43, CM-OUT 2833, contains King's proposals, *OPD Msg File.*
13. Marshall to MacArthur, 164, 7Jan43, CM-OUT 2273; Marshall to MacArthur, 192, 8Jan43, CM-OUT 2833, *OPD Exec 10, Item 23b.*
14. MacArthur to Marshall, C-82, 10Jan43, CM-IN 4574, *OPD Exec 10, Item 23a.*
15. Marshall to MacArthur, 249, 11Jan43, CM-OUT 3664, *OPD Exec 10, Item 23b.*
16. Marshall to MacArthur, 616, 26Jan43, CM-OUT 8822, *OPD Exec 10, Item 23b.* Marshall did not return to Washington from Casablanca until 28Jan. Although he may have directed that this be sent from Washington, it seems likely that his planners there requested information that they knew would be required when Marshall and King returned.
17. MacArthur to Marshall, C-251, 27Jan-43, CM-IN 12553, *OPD Exec 10, Item 23a.*
18. King to Marshall, 6Feb43, *OPD 381 PTO, Sec 3, Case 195.* Marshall on the same day sent a repeat of his 8Jan message to MacArthur.
19. See Pogue, *Ordeal and Hope*, chap 17; King to Marshall, 2Feb43, enc radios from Halsey to Nimitz and MacArthur, 1, 2Feb43, and Arnold memo to Stratemeyer, 11Nov42, *WDCSA SPA 1943.*
20. Handy to Cooke, 15Feb43, *WDCSA SPA 1943.*
21. King to Marshall, 2Feb43, enc radios from Halsey to Nimitz and MacArthur; MacArthur to Halsey, 3Feb43, enc with King to Marshall, 3Feb43, *WDCSA SPA 1943*; MacArthur to Marshall, C-390, 9Feb43, CM-IN 4496; MacArthur to Marshall, C-416, 11Feb43, CM-IN 5610, *OPD Exec 10, Item 23a.*

626 Notes

22. MacArthur to Marshall, C-447, 15Feb-
43, CM-IN 7418; Marshall to Mac-
Arthur (and to Emmons for Nimitz
and Harmon for Halsey), 1222, 16Feb-
43, CM-OUT 5656, *WDCSA 381 (16-
Feb43)*; Marshall to King, 17Feb43,
OPD 381 PTO, Sec 3, Case 125.
23. Stimson Diary, 11Mar43 and 22Nov44.
In the latter entry Stimson said: "He
[Marshall] was speaking of the hostility
which Admiral King has for General
MacArthur and how it crops out in
the meetings whenever they have to
deal with the southwestern Pacific. It
dates back to the rumpus which Mac-
Arthur had with the Navy at the outbreak of war when he could not get
on with Admiral Hart at all. King has
inherited that hostility and it has gotten so bad that Marshall finally said
to him, thumping the table, 'I will not
have the meetings of the Joint Chiefs
of Staff dominated by a policy of
hatred. I will not have any meetings
carried on with this hatred,' and with
that he shut up King."
24. Marshall int, 21Nov56.
25. Robert L. Eichelberger and Milton
MacKaye, *Our Jungle Road to Tokyo,*
14–16; George C. Kenney, *General
Kenney Reports: A Personal History
of the Pacific War,* 52–53. Kenney also
wrote (26–27): "While a brilliant, hard-
working officer, Sutherland had always
rubbed people the wrong way. He was
egotistic, like most people, but an unfortunate bit of arrogance combined
with his egotism had made him almost
universally disliked."
26. Marshall int, 21Nov56. Marshall spoke
when memories were still fresh of recent attacks on him and the Navy in
books written by members of Mac-
Arthur's staff. However the record
shows ample evidence of strong resentment of the Navy by the Southwest
Pacific commander and some members
of his staff.
27. Marshall to President, 21Feb43, *WDCSA
201.2 (21Feb43) SS;* White House to
CofS, 22Feb43, enc rev msg, *WDCSA
201 MacArthur, Douglas.* The words
"tremendous and remarkably," "enthusiastic," and "and difficult" were omitted from the message sent by the
President. However the phrase "and
your leaders and to the officers and

men of the Australian and United
States forces" was included in the
President's message but does not appear in the version quoted in Mac-
Arthur's book. Marshall to MacArthur,
1398, 22Feb43, CM-OUT 7781, *OPD
Msg File;* MacArthur, *Reminiscences,*
171–72.
28. MacArthur to Marshall, C-533, 23Feb-
43, CM-IN 11883, *OPD Msg File.*
29. Matloff, *Strategic Planning, 1943–1944,*
93.
30. Appointment book kept by Marshall's
secretary shows that he left the office
early on Wednesday, 3Mar, because of
a cold and that he was absent with a
cold the remainder of the week. He
left about noon of 7Mar for Miami
and returned from there on the afternoon of 14Mar in time to attend an
informal supper at the White House.
Katherine T. Marshall, *Together,* 141.
31. Ibid, 142.
32. Mins PMC 1st mtg, 12Mar43, 10:30 am,
ABC 370.26 (7–8–42), Sec 4; ELKTON
Plan II, 28Feb43, ibid, Sec 2; Matloff,
Strategic Planning, 1943–1944, 93–94;
Morton, *Strategy and Command,* 390–
91. It should be noted that the count
of divisions assigned MacArthur sometimes varied because only 3 of the 11
Australian divisions were prepared for
offensive operations.
33. Mins PMC 3d mtg, 13Mar43, *ABC
370.26 (7–8–42), Sec 4.* Gen Kenney and
Brig Gen L. R. Boyd, Emmons's Chief
of Staff, were ranking Army members
of the subcommittee.
34. Harmon and Sutherland as senior representatives to JPS, 14Mar43; Annex
"A," Mins PMC 4th mtg, 15Mar43,
ABC 370.26 (7–8–42), Sec 4.
35. Mins PMC 4th mtg, 15Mar43, *ABC
370.26 (7–8–42), Sec 4;* Wedemeyer to
Marshall, 16Mar43, *ABC 370.26 (7–8–
42), Sec 1.*
36. JCS 238, 16Mar43, *ABC 370.26 (7–
8–42), Sec 1;* Mins JCS 66th mtg, 16-
Mar43, *ABC 334 JCS Mins (2–14–42),
Sec 3.*
37. Mins JCS 66th mtg, 16Mar43, *ABC
334 JCS Mins (2–14–42), Sec 3.*
38. JCS 238/1, 18Mar43; Mins JCS 67th
mtg, 19Mar43, *ABC 334 JCS Mins
(2–14–42), Sec 3.*
39. Mins JCS 67th mtg, 19Mar43, *ABC 334
JCS Mins (2–14–42), Sec 3;* JCS 238/1,

18Mar43, *ABC 370.26 (7-8-42), Sec 1;* Matloff, *Strategic Planning, 1943-1944,* 95; Morton, *Strategy and Command,* 395. How the votes of the JCS are split is rarely a matter of record. Lt Grace P. Hayes, USN, of the Historical Section of the JCS, states in an unpublished study that Stratemeyer, representing Arnold, alone voted against added air groups for the Pacific. Hayes, "The War Against Japan," The History of the Joint Chiefs of Staff in World War II (1953), I, chap 13, 441. A copy of this study, declassified Nov71, is now in Record Group 218, National Archives.

40. Mins JCS 68th mtg, 21Mar43, *ABC 334 JCS Mins (2-14-42), Sec 3;* MacArthur to Marshall, C-1162, 25Mar43, *OPD Msg File.*

41. Mins JCS 70th mtg, 28Mar43, *ABC 334 JCS Mins (2-14-42), Sec 3.* Approved

directive JCS 238/5/D, cited Morton, *Strategy and Command,* 641, app K.

42. Leahy, *I Was There,* 153.

43. JCS to MacArthur, Nimitz, and Halsey, 29Mar43, CM-OUT 11091 through 11093, *OPD Msg File.*

44. Kenney, *General Kenney Reports,* 215-16, says that he kept telling all comers that if they would leave MacArthur alone, he would win the war for them. He wrote of political speculation about MacArthur but did not mention meeting with Mrs. Luce or with Senator Vandenberg. See Arthur H. Vandenberg, *The Private Papers of Senator Vandenberg,* 76-77.

45. *Time,* 17May43.

46. Vandenberg, *Private Papers,* 77-78, (italics in original).

47. Leahy, *I Was There,* 150.

48. *Time,* 26Apr43.

49. Ibid, 17May43.

IX: WINDING UP IN TUNISIA

I have drawn on interviews with Gens Eisenhower, Bradley, Alanbrooke, Ismay, de Gaulle, Robinett, Julius Holmes. I have made considerable use of George Howe, *Northwest Africa: Seizing the Initiative in the West,* Harold Macmillan, *The Blast of War;* Robert D. Murphy, *Diplomat Among Warriors;* and Dwight D. Eisenhower, *Crusade in Europe.*

1. Bryant, *Turn of the Tide,* 454-55.
2. Marshall int, 4Feb57.
3. Mins of General Council in ODCofS, 1Feb43, *WD General Council Mins.*
4. Sherwood, *Roosevelt and Hopkins,* 689.
5. Butcher, *My Three Years with Eisenhower,* 259-60. Eisenhower to Marshall, 27Jan43, in referring to the approaching promotion asked that Mrs Eisenhower be informed before public announcement was made. "As a matter of sentiment, I would like for her to be be first, outside of official circles, to hear." Butcher seems to have exaggerated Eisenhower's unawareness of the steps being taken in Washington—or the messages were delayed. On 9Feb. Marshall radioed that he would personally notify Mrs Eisenhower, adding "the probability is for Thursday though I have not yet secured formal commitment." On 11Feb he sent word: "I telephoned your friend at ten this morning. Your nomination went forward at noon." Marshall to Eisenhower, 9 and 11Feb43, *Marshall Library Files.*

6. WD to Eisenhower, 18Dec42, CM-OUT 6349, *OPD Msg File,* cited Coles and Weinberg, *Civil Affairs,* 40. Robert D. Murphy, *Diplomat Among Warriors,* chap 11; Macmillan, *Blast of War,* 168-74. Murphy, incorrectly designated in my *Ordeal and Hope* as consul general in Algiers, served in French North Africa from 1940 to 1942 as representative of the President although still designated as counselor to the embassy in France. He served as special adviser to Eisenhower in the fall preceding the invasion and shortly after the landings became head of the Civil Affairs Section of Allied Forces Headquarters. Roosevelt's action in 1943 merely regularized one phase of his work.

7. Eisenhower to Marshall, 30Nov42, forwarded by Marshall to SecState, 31Dec-42, in *US For Rels, Europe, 1942,* II, 501.

8. Roosevelt to Churchill, 250, 1Jan43, *US For Rels, Europe, 1943,* II, 23-24.

9. Marshall to Smith, 670, 1Jan43, *OPD Msg File.* Marshall noted that he was sending this message to Smith in order

not to worry Eisenhower, commenting that Milton Eisenhower had spoken to him that morning about his brother's problems.

10. George F. Howe, *Northwest Africa: Seizing the Initiative in the West,* 368.

11. Stimson Diary, 30 and 31Jan43. Stimson recalled that in Cuba during and just after the Spanish-American War the commanding general had been in charge of military government and had acted through the SecWar and not the SecState.

12. Marshall to SecWar, 1Feb43, *WDCSA Africa 1942–43;* Stimson Diary, 2Feb43.

13. Eisenhower to Marshall, 17Jan43, *Marshall Library Files.*

14. Eisenhower to Marshall, 187, 11Feb43, CM-OUT 5597, *OPD Exec 3, Item 1b;* Marshall to Eisenhower, 2312, 15Feb43, CM-OUT 5111, *OPD Exec 3, Item 2;* Eisenhower to Marshall, 1086, 16Feb43, CM-IN 8030, *OPD Msg File.* On Gen Bradley's relations with Gen Marshall at this time, see Omar N. Bradley, *A Soldier's Story,* 19–22.

15. Howe, *Northwest Africa,* 422.

16. Marshall to Eisenhower, 2362, 16Feb43, *OPD Exec 3, Item 2–13.*

17. Pogue, *Ordeal and Hope,* 415–16, 419–24; Stimson Diary, 17 and 18Feb43.

18. Howe, *Northwest Africa,* 439, 469–70.

19. Marshall to McNair, 1Feb43, *WDCSA 250 (1942–43).*

20. Eisenhower to Marshall, 2771, 24Feb43, CM-IN 12476, cited Howe, *Northwest Africa,* 481; Marshall to Brig Gen C. L. Bolté, 27Feb43, *Marshall Library Files;* Marshall to Devers, 25Feb43, *WDCSA 250 (1942–43).* Marshall also told McNair: "Where there is so much smoke there must be fire and whatever corrective measures are being taken I wish them to register a positive and marked change in procedure." Marshall to McNair, 31Mar43, *Marshall Library Files.*

21. Marshall int, 15Feb57.

22. Howe, *Northwest Africa,* 477; Martin Blumenson, *Kasserine Pass,* 303–304; Paul Robinett, *Armor Command,* 169–97.

23. Bradley to Marshall, 29May43, *Marshall Library Files.*

24. Walker to AGF, 12Jun43, *OPD 381 Africa, Sec 4.*

25. Marshall to Eisenhower, 3072, 1Mar43, *WDCSA 381 Husky, 1942–43.*

26. Eisenhower to Marshall, 3Mar43, *Marshall Library Files.*

27. Promoted soon afterward to the rank of lt gen, Fredendall served out the war as Second Army commander at Memphis. Offered first to MacArthur and then to Eisenhower for further field command, he was turned down. A large number of his headquarters personnel at Memphis furnished the staff for Eichelberger's Eighth Army in the Pacific.

28. Howe, *Northwest Africa,* 471; Ernest N. Harmon, Milton MacKaye, and William R. MacKaye, *Combat Commander,* 120.

29. Patton to Marshall, 22Feb43, *Marshall Library Files.*

30. Eisenhower to Marshall, 11Mar43, *Marshall Library Files.*

31. Bradley, *Soldier's Story,* 73–74.

32. Marshall to Eisenhower, 5940, 14Apr43, *OPD Exec 10, Item 36a.*

33. Eisenhower to Marshall, 16Apr43, *Marshall Library Files.*

34. Marshall to Eisenhower, 14Apr43; Eisenhower to Marshall, 29Mar43, enc Eisenhower to Alexander, 23Mar43, *Marshall Library Files.*

35. Eisenhower to Marshall, 5Apr43, *Marshall Library Files.* See views on Montgomery in latter.

36. Howe, *Northwest Africa,* 655–66, 676.

37. Ibid, 675–76.

38. Marshall to Eisenhower, 6May43, *Marshall Library Files.*

39. Patton to Marshall, 8May43, *Marshall Library Files.*

40. Marshall to Herbert Bayard Swope, 10May43, *Marshall Library Files.*

41. Marshall to Maj Gen John L. Hines, 14May43; Marshall to Embick, 20May43, *Marshall Library Files.*

42. Marshall to Surles, 8May43, enc editorial from Washington *Post* of that day, *Marshall Library Files.*

X: TRIDENT

I have drawn heavily on Matloff, *Strategic Planning for Coalition Warfare, 1943–1944; US For Rels, Washington and Quebec, 1943;* Romanus and Sunderland, *Stilwell's Mission to China.*

1. Churchill, *Hinge of Fate,* 783, 789; Leahy, *I Was There,* 158.
2. Bryant, *Turn of the Tide,* 500.
3. Mins JCS 76th mtg, 27Apr43, *ABC 334 JCS Mins (2–14–42), Sec 4;* Marshall to Eisenhower, 27Apr43, CM-OUT 11068, *Marshall Library Files.*
4. Marshall to Handy, 30Mar43, *WDCSA 381 (30Mar43) SS.*
5. Eisenhower to Marshall, 5May43, *Marshall Library Files,* reminded Marshall of his earlier statement.
6. Marshall int, 13Nov56 (author's notes).
7. Eisenhower to Marshall, 5May43, *Marshall Library Files.*
8. Stimson Diary, 3May43; Matloff, *Strategic Planning, 1943–1944,* 124.
9. There is some confusion on the date of the session. Leahy speaks of a meeting at the WH on Sunday, 8May. However Sunday was the ninth. Stimson in his diary entry for 10May refers to a meeting of the Joint Chiefs of Staff at the WH on the previous day. At a meeting on 8May the Joint Chiefs discussed points that would be raised with the President. They stressed the close relationship between the war in Europe and the fight against Japan and strongly opposed any action that would jeopardize the cross-Channel assault in 1944. They were willing to consider limited operations in the western Mediterranean after the Sicilian campaign, provided that they did not prevent the subsequent withdrawal of units from the area, supported the Combined Bomber Offensive, and left the cross-Channel operation intact. Matloff, *Strategic Planning, 1943–1944,* 124; Leahy, *I Was There,* 157–58; Stimson Diary, 10May43.
10. Stimson Diary, 10 and 12May43.
11. Mins JCS 78th mtg, 8May43, *ABC 334 JCS Mins (2–14–42), Sec 4.*
12. Marshall to Maj Gen Frank Parker, 12Apr43, marked "not used," *Marshall Library Files.*
13. Marshall rpt to colleagues on appearance before Senate subcommittee, Mins JCS 79th mtg, 10May43, *ABC 334 JCS Mins (2–14–42), Sec 4.*
14. Vandenberg, *Private Papers,* 48–50 (italics in original).
15. Mins CCS mtg with Roosevelt and Churchill, 12May43, 2:30 pm, WH, *US For Rels, Washington and Quebec, 1943,* 24–33.
16. Moran, *Churchill,* 102–103.
17. Mins CCS 83d mtg, 13May43, Annex A, Global Strategy of the War, *US For Rels, Washington and Quebec, 1943,* 35, 222–23; Mins JCS 78th mtg, 8May43, *ABC 334 JCS Mins (2–14–42), Sec 4.*
18. JSSC Embick to S&P Gp OPD, 1May43: Global Estimates of the Situation, 28-Apr43; M. S. F[airchild] to Embick, 1May43, *ABC 381 (9–25–41), Sec 7.*
19. Mins CCS 83d mtg, 13May43, *US For Rels, Washington and Quebec, 1943,* 34–48.
20. Mins JCS 81st mtg, 14May43, *ABC 334 JCS Mins (2–14–42), Sec 4.*
21. Mins CCS 84th mtg, 14May43, *US For Rels, Washington and Quebec, 1943,* 53.
22. Mins JCS 81st mtg, 14May43, *ABC 334 JCS Mins (2–14–42), Sec 4;* Mins CCS 85th mtg, 15May43, *US For Rels, Washington and Quebec, 1943,* 80–85.
23. Portal added: "Marshall from 1943 on believed and emphasized that with ten-to-one air superiority (and we just about had that) we could do the job in Normandy." Portal didn't believe that it could be done in 1943, but he did in 1944. Portal int, 7Feb47. (author's notes).
24. Mins CCS 85th mtg, 15May43, *US For Rels, Washington and Quebec, 1943,* 81, 83, 84.
25. See 53-page account of the visit, plus letters of thanks, by Gerald Horton Bath, "A Report on the Visit of the British High Command to Colonial Williamsburg, May 15th and 16th, 1943." I have also drawn on McCarthy int, 29Sept58.
26. The Portal incident was related by several of the participants. Marshall to Mrs M. C. Long, quoted in Bryant,

Turn of the Tide, 506–507, mentions Brooke's bird-watching.

27. Mins JCS 83rd mtg, 17May43, *ABC 334 JCS Mins (2–14–42), Sec 4.*

28. Mins CCS 86th mtg, 17May43, *US For Rels, Washington and Quebec, 1943*, 95; Mins JCS 84th mtg, 18May43, *ABC 334 JCS Mins (2–14–42), Sec 4.*

29. Mins CCS 87th mtg, 18May43, *US For Rels, Washington and Quebec, 1943*, 97–108.

30. British conversion to the efficacy of air power is also underlined in their planning paper prepared over the weekend. The first of three necessary prerequisites for a re-entry on the Continent across the Channel is an "intensified combined bomber offensive." Mins CCS 87th mtg, 18May43, CCS 234, 17May43, *US For Rels, Washington and Quebec, 1943*, 97–108, 261.

31. Mins CCS 88th and 89th mtgs, 19May43; Mins CCS mtg with Roosevelt and Churchill, WH, 19May43, 6 pm; CCS 237/1, Resolutions by the CCS, 20May43; ibid, 112–22, 281–82.

32. Stimson Diary, 19May43.

33. Craven and Cate, *Army Air Forces in World War II*, II, 305; Webster and Frankland, *Strategic Air Offensive Against Germany, 1939–1945*, I, 309–13.

34. King and Whitehill, *Fleet Admiral King*, 441.

35. Morton, *Strategy and Command*, 449.

36. Mins CCS 83d mtg, 13May43, Annex A, Global Strategy of the War, *US For Rels, Washington and Quebec, 1943*, 35–36, 222–23 (italics added).

37. Mins JCS 78th mtg, 8May43; Mins JCS 81st mtg, 14May43; *ABC 334 JCS Mins (2–14–42), Sec 4;* Mins CCS 84th mtg, 14May43; CCS 219, 14May43; *US For Rels, Washington and Quebec, 1943*, 52–54, 227–29. While this paper was drafted by the US Joint Staff Planners, the short memo read by Leahy 13May had been drafted by the Joint Strategic Survey Committee at the Joint Chiefs' request.

38. Mins CCS 86th mtg, 17May43; CCS 232/1, Agreed Essentials in the Conduct of the War, 18May43; *US For Rels, Washington and Quebec, 1943*, 93–94, 231–32.

39. Mins CCS 86th mtg, 17May43, *US For Rels, Washington and Quebec, 1943*, 93–94.

40. Bryant, *Turn of the Tide*, 507, 510; Mins CCS 92d mtg, 21May43, *US For Rels, Washington and Quebec, 1943*, 145–48.

41. Mins JCS 90th mtg, 24May43, 9:30 am, *ABC 334 JCS Mins (2–14–42), Sec 4.* The report of this discussion goes no further than my text indicates. See King and Whitehill, *Fleet Admiral King*, 441, for King's recollection in later years.

42. Mins CCS 95th mtg, 24May43, 11:30 am; CCS 242/6, rpt of CCS to Roosevelt and Churchill, 25May43, Overall Strategic Concept, II, 2, *US For Rels, Washington and Quebec, 1943*, 184–86, 364–65.

43. Mins CCS 84th mtg, 14May43, 10:30 am, *US For Rels, Washington and Quebec, 1943*, 57–62.

44. Mins CCS mtg with Roosevelt and Churchill, 14May43, 2:00 pm, WH, ibid, 67–68 (italics in original).

45. Ibid, 72ff. See also Stilwell's presentation at the morning CCS mtg, ibid, 62–64.

46. Ibid, 75–76; Mins CCS 84th mtg, 14May43, ibid, 64. See Romanus and Sunderland, *Stilwell's Mission to China*, 320–27, for the Washington conf and Roosevelt's decision.

47. Mins CCS 91st mtg, 20May43, 3:30 pm, *US For Rels, Washington and Quebec, 1943*, 142; CCS 242/3, 24May43, Draft rpt, CCS to President and Prime Minister, ibid, 362 (Opns in Burma-China Theater).

48. Mins CCS mtg with Roosevelt and Churchill, 21May43, 5:00 pm, WH, ibid, 155–56; CCS 242/2, 23May43, ibid, 356 (Opns in Burma-China Theater); CCS 242/6, 25May43, Final rpt, CCS to President and Prime Minister, ibid, 369.

49. Bryant, *Turn of the Tide*, 508–509.

50. Brooke went on: "At times the war may be won by bombing, and all must be sacrificed to it. At others it becomes necessary for us to bleed ourselves dry on the Continent because Russia is doing the same. At others our main effort must be in the Mediterranean directed against Italy or the Balkans alternately, with sporadic desires to invade Norway and 'roll up the map in the opposite direction Hitler did.' But more often

than all he wants to carry out all operations simultaneously, irrespective of shortage of shipping." Ibid, 513.

51. Stimson Diary, 19May43; Bryant, *Turn of the Tide*, 514.
52. Stimson Diary, 25May43.

XI: JOURNEY TO ALGIERS

I have drawn heavily on Leighton and Coakley, *Global Logistics and Strategy;* Churchill, *The Hinge of Fate;* and interviews with Col John J. Winn.

1. Churchill, *Hinge of Fate*, 812–13; Roosevelt to Stalin, 2Jun43, *OPD 300.6 (OCS Papers), 1943–44.*
2. During the night they were shaken awake briefly by some sudden bumps that were explained either as electrical discharges or an actual crash of lightning. Churchill, *Hinge of Fate*, 813; Bryant, *Turn of the Tide*, 516–18.
3. Marshall int, 20Nov56; Churchill, *Hinge of Fate*, 814, refers to Marshall's interest in the questions of attainder and impeachment.
4. Churchill, *Hinge of Fate*, 815.
5. Butcher, *My Three Years with Eisenhower*, 316; Bryant, *Turn of the Tide*, 518–19.
6. Churchill, *Hinge of Fate*, 817–19; Mins Algiers conf, 1st mtg, 29May43, *Trident Conf Bk, May43*, 467–75; Butcher, *My Three Years with Eisenhower*, 317–19.
7. Butcher, *My Three Years with Eisenhower*, 317–19.
8. Churchill, *Hinge of Fate*, 821; Leighton and Coakley, *Global Logistics and Strategy, 1940–1943*, 65.
9. Mins Algiers conf, 2d mtg, 31May43, *Trident Conf Bk, May43*, 477–95.
10. Eisenhower to Marshall, 5Apr43, *OPD Exec 3, Item 1a.*
11. Bryant, *Turn of the Tide*, 525.
12. Mins Algiers conf, 3d mtg, 3Jun43, *Trident Conf Bk, May43*, 497–505.
13. See the perceptive chapter in Lord Moran's *Churchill*, "The Conversion of Marshall," especially 109.
14. Ibid, 110–11. Marshall told the doctor, "He is a very wonderful man, but he won't look at things like a man who has been all his life a soldier. I must have facts." Note comments on Moran by John Colville and others in *Action This Day: Working with Churchill*, ed John Wheeler-Bennett.
15. Thomas M. Johnson, "America's No. 1 Soldier," *Reader's Digest*, 17Feb44; Butcher, *My Three Years with Eisenhower*, 324; Marshall int, 21Nov56.
16. After allowing time for the story to be savored, Marshall added: "He got on the word right away—'plant' was very much better." To the author's suggestion that there probably had not been anyone like Churchill as a "master of language in our time" and that perhaps Woodrow Wilson was closest to him in the United States in this era, General Marshall agreed that the former President was a great master of words. "But the trouble with Mr. Wilson," he added, "I would say by comparison, was his very perfect English, but it didn't arouse you." In contrast "Churchill's was calculated to put everybody on their feeling. The fact is that he defended England at its weakest by his statements. He rallied the whole nation." Marshall int, 15-Nov56.
17. In a letter of 8Jun43 to Brig Gen O. E. Walsh, he spoke of enjoying lunch with him "last Saturday" in Recife. As a result of possible engine trouble, he had paid a surprise visit to Belém. In a letter to Col John Mullenix he said that he had heard so much about Ascension Island that he was glad to be able to visit it on his way home from Algiers. To the pilot, Capt S. T. Stanton, he wrote 8Jun43: "Again I wish to thank you for a very pleasant and comfortable trip across the Atlantic. I remember very well the skill you displayed when you took me to England and back a year ago in a Stratoliner. It is easy to see that you are equally artful with a C-54."
18. Stimson Diary, 8Jun43.
19. Marshall to Churchill, 8Jun43, *Marshall Library Files.*
20. Stimson Diary, 31May and 3Jun43.
21. Marshall to Maj Gen A. C. Gillem, CG Hq Armored Forces, 11Jun43, *Marshall Library Files.*
22. Marshall to Lt Allen Brown, 16 and 29Jun43, *Marshall Library Files.*

23. Mrs Marshall, *Together,* 153–54; Col J. J. Winn int, 4Apr66.
24. Stimson Diary, 1Jul43; Marshall int, 11Feb57.
25. Dwight D. Eisenhower, *Crusade in Europe,* 172; Eisenhower to Marshall, 123, 9Jul43, CM-IN 6408; Marshall to Eisenhower, 419 3Jul43, CM-OUT 1760 (4Jul), *OPD Msg File.*
26. Marshall to Eisenhower, 1759, 5Jul43, CM-OUT 1894, *OPD Msg File.*
27. Matthew B. Ridgway, *Soldier: The Memoirs of Matthew B. Ridgway,* 68–70.
28. See ibid, 71, for view of Gen Karl Student and contrary views cited in Albert N. Garland and Howard McGaw Smyth, *Sicily and the Surrender of Italy,* 422–25.

29. Patton to Marshall, 18Jul43, *Marshall Library Files.*
30. Marshall to Col Stanley J. Grogan of Press Relations, 19Jul43, *Marshall Library Files.*
31. Stimson Diary, 19Jul43.
32. Ibid, 12Jul43 and rpt to President filed with entry under 10Aug43; Henry L. Stimson and McGeorge Bundy, *On Active Service in Peace and War,* 429–35.
33. Stimson Diary, 19Jul43.
34. Butcher, *My Three Years with Eisenhower,* 373–74.
35. Stimson Diary, 10Aug43, rpt to President.
36. Ibid, 28Jul, 9Aug43.
37. Stimson to Roosevelt, 10Aug43, Stimson and Bundy, *On Active Service,* 436–38.
38. Stimson Diary, 1Nov43.

XII: FRANCE AGAIN TO THE BATTLE

I am especially indebted to Marcel Vigneras, *Rearming the French;* Murphy, *Diplomat Among Warriors;* and *US For Rels, Europe, 1943.*

1. Marshall to SecWar, enc Matthews to SecState, 1Jan43; memo by SecState, 5Jan43; Hull to Matthews, 6Jan43; Br Embassy to State Dept, with aide-mémoire and attached statement, 7Jan43, *US For Rels, Europe, 1943,* II, 27–33.
2. Eisenhower to Marshall, 4367, 5Jan43, *OPD Exec 5, Item 13.*
3. Mins of WH conf with CsofS, 7Jan43, *OPD Exec 10, Item 45.*
4. Marcel Vigneras, *Rearming the French,* prol and chap 1.
5. Marshall to Eisenhower, R-2080, 17-Oct42, CM-OUT 5682, *OPD Exec 5, Item 8,* passing on presidential directive that Gen Clark conveyed to French representatives.
6. Vigneras, *Rearming the French,* 31; rpt Logistics Div SOS, 9Jan43, *ASF Planning Div, Logistical Study 6.*
7. Mins CCS 57th mtg, 15Jan43, *US For Rels, Casablanca, 1943,* 569.
8. Mins CCS mtg with Roosevelt and Churchill, 18Jan43, 5:00 pm, at President's villa, ibid, 636.
9. Mins CCS 61st mtg, 19Jan43, 10:00 am, ibid, 639.
10. Mins CCS 62d mtg, 19Jan43, at 4:00 pm, ibid, 652.
11. Ibid, 653.
12. Vigneras, *Rearming the French,* 38;

Sherwood, *Roosevelt and Hopkins,* 683, 693; Murphy, *Diplomat Among Warriors,* 193.
13. Marshall to McCloy, 4Feb43, *WDCSA France (SS).*
14. Stimson Diary, 3Feb43. Roosevelt asked Stimson to give Marshall his views since there had been no time to see him since his return.
15. Samuel H. Wiley (from Murphy) to SecState, 1Feb43; Wiley (from Murphy) to Sec and UndSecState, 6Feb43; Wiley (from Murphy) to President and SecState, 18Feb43, *US For Rels, Europe, 1943,* II, 44–46, 48–51, 55–56.
16. President to Murphy, 20Feb43, *OPD Exec 1, Item 13.*
17. Murphy to President and SecState, 20-Feb43, *OPD Exec 1, Item 13.*
18. Marshall to President, 20Feb43, enc proposed msg to Eisenhower. Approved by President. *WDCSA France (SS).*
19. Marshall for Béthouart, 24Feb43, *WDCSA France (SS).*
20. Mins Trident conf, CCS 87th mtg, 18-May43, *US For Rels, Washington, 1943,* 97–108.
21. Vigneras, *Rearming the French,* 57.
22. Wiley (from Murphy) to Hull, 3Jun43, *US For Rels, Europe, 1943,* II, 134–35.
23. Hull to Wiley (for Murphy), 7Jun43;

Roosevelt to Eisenhower, 10Jun43, ibid, 138, 145.

24. Roosevelt to Churchill, 281, 10Jun43, ibid, 146, n 53.

25. Wiley (from Murphy) to SecState, 13-Jun43; Wiley (from Murphy) to Sec-State, 16Jun43, (2msgs), ibid, 151–55.

26. Marshall to Eisenhower, 492, 17Jun43, CM-OUT 7060, No. 492, *OPD Exec 10, Item 47*. Murphy's message of June 16 had helped prompt this action by suggesting that it should be made abundantly clear to the French that in light of the recent developments it was necessary for the United States to review its current policy of rearming the French forces.

27. Roosevelt to Churchill, 17Jun43, *US For Rels, Europe, 1943*, II, 155–57.

28. Churchill to Roosevelt, 18Jun43 (2 msgs), ibid, 159–61.

29. Macmillan, *Blast of War*, 282–83. Murphy in *Diplomat Among Warriors* is far less informative on this phase of activities.

30. Charles de Gaulle, *The War Memoirs of Charles de Gaulle*, II, 129.

31. Wiley (from Murphy) to SecState, 23-Jun43, *US For Rels, Europe, 1943*, II, 163–64; cf de Gaulle, *Memoirs*, II, 133.

32. CofS to Leahy, 4Jul43, *WDCSA 676.3 (2Jul43)*. Clear copy sent WH, 4Jul43, 10:00 am. Apparently this was in reply to memo by Rear Adm Wilson Brown, naval aide to President Roosevelt, to Marshall and other CsofS, 3Jul43, asking comments on the proposed message. Draft Roosevelt to Eisenhower and Murphy, reply to: Wiley (from Murphy) to SecState, 1195, 30-Jun43. However the message in *US For Rels, Europe, 1943*, II, 168–69, does not include the suggestion to which Marshall objected.

33. Marshall to Molly Winn, 13Jul43, *Marshall Library Files*.

34. Mins CCS spec mtg, 8Jul43, *ABC 334 CCS Mins (1–23–42), Sec 5*.

35. Somervell to Marshall, 10Jul43, *JRC 902/II Rearmament Plan*, cited Vigneras, *Rearming the French*, 84, and Marshall to Arnold, Somervell, et al, 12Jul43, *WDCSA France (SS)*.

36. Marshall to Brig Gen Louis Fortier, 10Jul43, *Marshall Library Files*.

37. Marshall to Molly Winn, 13Jul43, *Marshall Library Files*.

38. Marshall to Giraud, 16Jul43, *JRC SHAEF Mission to France 902/II, RG 331, Box 217*.

XIII: THE GOAL IN SIGHT

I drew heavily in this chapter on volumes by Matloff, Morton, Bryant, and *US For Rels, Washington and Quebec, 1943*. Interviews include those with Gens Handy, Morgan, Alanbrooke, Kenneth McLean, Baeker and Adm C. E. Lambe.

1. Memo to President and appended msg, drafted by OPD, approved by Marshall, sent to Leahy 30Jun43; notes by CofS on JCS 377 (rev) Opns to Assist Portugal, *OPD Exec 1, Item 26, Paper 2*.

2. Wedemeyer to Handy, 4Jul43, *ABC 381 Husky (1943), Sec 1-B*.

3. Hull to Handy, 17Jul43, *ABC 381 SS Papers (7Jan43), Nos 96–126/3*; Matloff, *Strategic Planning, 1943–1944*, 165–66.

4. Matloff, *Strategic Planning, 1943–1944*, 167.

5. CCS rpt to Roosevelt and PM Churchill, 25May43, *US For Rels, Washington, 1943*, 367–68; Forrest C. Pogue, *The Supreme Command*, 103.

6. Lt Gen Sir Frederick Morgan, *Overture to Overlord*, 73; Morgan int, 2Apr-

46. Gen Morgan also showed me his "Diary of an Underdog in Chief," in which he complained of the scapegoat role that he believed was being wished on him. Marshall int, 15Nov56.

7. His request to Churchill to change the place of the meeting was sent the same day as he dissolved the Board of Economic Warfare headed by Henry Wallace and put its functions and others that had been handled by the Sec of Commerce under James F. Byrnes, now director of the Office of War Mobilization. Sherwood, *Roosevelt and Hopkins*, 740–41.

8. Mins JCS 100th mtg, 6Aug43, *ABC 334 JCS Mins (2–14–42), Sec 4*. See Marshall remark that Handy had said that in the Mediterranean political consequences were the goal while in

OVERLORD they had an offensive action that would accomplish military results by itself.

9. Lt Col Walter E. Todd to OPD, 26Jul-43, gives account of Marshall's reasoning, *OPD Exec 5, Item 11, Paper 2,* cited Matloff, *Strategic Planning, 1943–1944,* 174–75.

10. CCS 303, 9Aug43, *US For Rels, Quebec, 1943,* 472–82; Mins JCS 102d mtg, 9Aug43, *ABC 334 JCS Mins (2–14–42), Sec 5,* cited Matloff, *Strategic Planning, 1943–1944,* 175. In view of Gen Marshall's acceptance in mid-July of an attack on the mainland of Italy and his statement to the President on 25Jul, it is difficult to understand Sir Arthur Bryant's charge that peace feelers on 16Aug (the first tentative one is mentioned by Churchill several days later) came just in time to prevent the Americans from throwing over Brooke's Mediterranean strategy. Bryant, *Turn of the Tide,* 580.

11. SS 90, 8Aug43, "Conduct of the War in Europe," *ABC 381 SS Papers (7Jan-43), Nos 2–95,* cited Matloff, *Strategic Planning, 1943–1944,* 177–78.

12. King and Whitehill, *Fleet Admiral King,* 482; Leahy, *I Was There,* 174.

13. The log of the President's visit to Canada, 16–26Aug43, personal copy furnished by Gen T. T. Handy to author.

14. Maj Gen Kenneth R. McLean int, 13-Mar47, and Adm C. E. Lambe int, 26-Feb47.

15. Handy int, 9Jul70. Handy's chief worry was that as he went into the President's dining car, he stepped on Fala, thus opening an important conference with flushed apologies.

16. Leahy, *I Was There,* 175; JCS 105th mtg, 16Aug43, 10:00 am, *ABC 334 JCS Mins (12–14–42), Sec 5.*

17. Mins CCS 108th mtg, 15Aug43, 2:30 pm, *US For Rels, Quebec, 1943,* 864–65.

18. Ibid, 864–66; Todd to OPD, 26Jul43, *OPD Exec 5, Item 11.*

19. Marshall had canvassed this possibility with the other Joint Chiefs of Staff before the meeting, when they agreed they had to have a firm decision. Mins CCS 108th mtg, 15Aug43, 2:30 pm, *US For Rels, Quebec, 1943,* 862–69; Mins JCS 104th mtg, 15Aug43, 5:00 pm, *ABC 334 JCS Mins (12–14–42), Sec 5.*

20. Bryant, *Turn of the Tide,* 577–78.

21. Ibid, 579; Mins CCS 109th mtg, 16-Aug43, *US For Rels, Quebec, 1943,* 870.

22. Garland and Smith, *Sicily,* 449; Martin Blumenson, *Sicily: Whose Victory?* 1969, 146–47.

23. Mins CCS 113th mtg, 20Aug43, *US For Rels, Quebec, 1943,* 904–11.

24. Mins CCS with Roosevelt and Churchill, 23Aug43, *US For Rels, Quebec, 1943,* 942.

25. Wedemeyer, *Wedemeyer Reports,* 245.

26. Mins JCS spec mtg, 9Sept43, *ABC 334 JCS Mins (2–14–42), Sec 5;* Winston S. Churchill, *Closing the Ring,* 134–37, has text of paper he gave Roosevelt. A copy of the paper circulated by Marshall to the Joint Chiefs is in *ABC 334 CCS Mins (1–23–42), Sec 5.*

27. An irreverent soul, apparently in the Operations Division, commented in the margin: "Foreordained in Algiers Conference."

28. Mins JCS spec mtg, 9Sept43, *ABC 334 JCS Mins (2–14–42), Sec 5.*

29. King to Marshall, 11Jun43, enc memo for JCS, Future Campaign Opns in the Pacific Ocean Areas (circulated as JCS 353), *OPD 381 Security, Sec 5, Case 163.*

30. JCS 353/1, Rpt by Joint Staff Planners, 14Jun43, ibid; Mins JPS 80th mtg, 13Jun43, *ABC 334 JPS Mins (2–13–42), Sec 4.*

31. Mins JCS 92d mtg, 15Jun43, *ABC 334 JCS Mins (2–14–42), Sec 4.* Leahy agreed with Marshall in keeping the timing of operations with the JCS.

32. Mins JPS 80th mtg, 13Jun43, *ABC 334 JPS Mins (2–13–42), Sec 4;* Marshall to MacArthur, 4656, 11Jun43, CM-OUT 4580; MacArthur to Marshall, C-3134, 12Jun43, CM-IN 7367, *OPD Msg File.*

33. Mins JCS 92d mtg, 15Jun43, *ABC 334 JCS Mins (2–14–42), Sec 4.*

34. Marshall (for the JCS) to MacArthur, 4769, 14Jun43, CM-OUT 6093 (15Jun), *OPD 381 Security, Sec 5, Case 163.* This telegram was drafted by the Joint War Plans Committee at the request of the Joint Staff Planners.

35. MacArthur to Marshall, C-3302, 20-Jun43, CM-IN 13149 (21Jun), *OPD Msg File.* Two days after this reply, Gen Arnold informed MacArthur that the Washington planners were considering the withdrawal of one heavy bomber group and one medium

bomber group from his area for the Gilberts-Marshalls operations, in addition to the Naval Air Forces reported available. Arnold asked what specific effect the loss of these groups would have on his air operations. Regretfully but not angrily, MacArthur answered that while two bomber groups would not be missed in an area employing masses of air strength, they made up a "very high proportion" of his total strength. He felt their withdrawal would "collapse the offensive effort in the Southwest Pacific Area." In the end MacArthur did not lose these groups and was given two additional fighter groups for his offensive. Both Marshall and Arnold were opposed to shifting any of his air strength to Nimitz and found the needed bombers in the United States. Arnold to MacArthur, 5011, 22Jun43, CM-OUT 9340, *OPD Msg File;* MacArthur to Arnold, C-3413, 24Jun43, CM-IN 15013, *OPD Msg Log;* Matloff, *Strategic Planning, 1943–1944,* 189.

36. King to Marshall, 14Jun43; Marshall to King, 23Jun43, *WDCSA South Pacific Area.*

37. JCS 386, Report by the Joint Strategic Survey Committee, 28Jun43, *ABC 384 Pacific (6-28-43);* Mins JCS 94th mtg, 29Jun43, *ABC 334 JCS Mins (2-11-42), Sec 4.*

38. Matloff, *Strategic Planning, 1943–1944,* 192.

39. King to Marshall, 22Jul43; Marshall to King, 29Jul43, with Memo for Record, 4Aug43, on action taken, *OPD 381 Security, Sec 6, Case 196.*

40. Morton, *Strategy and Command,* 511–12.

41. Matloff, *Strategic Planning, 1943–1944,* 208–209; Mins JPS 94th mtg, 12Aug43, *ABC 334 JPS Mins (2-13-42), Sec 4;* Mins CPS 72d mtg, 13Aug43, *ABC 334 CPS Mins (1-23-42), Sec 3;* CPS 83, 16-Aug43, *ABC 381 Japan (27Aug42), Sec 3.*

42. Bryant, *Turn of the Tide,* 572, 587.

43. Matloff, *Strategic Planning, 1943–1944,* 235.

44. Marshall to Stilwell, 3259, 27Aug43, CM-OUT 11436; Marshall to Stilwell, 3243, 26Aug43, CM-OUT 10767, *OPD Msg File;* CCS 319/5, Final Quadrant Rpt to President and Prime Minister, 24Aug43, *US For Rels, Washington and Quebec, 1943,* 1127–28 (Opns in China-Burma-India Theater, 1943–44); also see Mins CCS 107th mtg, 14Aug-43, 4:30 pm, and Mins CCS 113th mtg, 20Aug43; Mins CCS mtgs with President and Prime Minister, 19 and 23-Aug43 for discussions on CBI Theater, ibid, 856ff.

45. Christopher Sykes, *Orde Wingate: A Biography,* 538–42.

46. Marshall int, 29Oct56 (author's notes).

47. Sykes, *Orde Wingate,* 533–34, 545.

48. Churchill to Roosevelt, 320, 19Jun43, *OPD 384 CTO, Sec 1, Case 12.*

49. Marshall to JCS, 28Jun43, ibid; Matloff, *Strategic Planning, 1943–1944,* 202. Matloff points out 202, n 73, that Gen Marshall was willing to let US troops serve under Brig Orde Wingate and under Lt Gen William J. Slim, for whom he had great respect.

50. Roosevelt to Churchill, 311, 9Jul43, *OPD Exec 10, Item 25.*

51. Marshall int, 21Nov56.

52. Marshall draft for President to send Churchill, 7Jul43, *OPD Exec 10, Item 63A.* Sent to Churchill, 8Jul43. Douglas's own account shows no basis for the feeling; see Sholto Douglas, *Combat and Command: Memoirs of Lord Douglas.*

53. Churchill, *Closing the Ring,* 77–78, 89; Bryant, *Turn of the Tide,* 567. Churchill indicates that he realized the proposal to appoint a relatively junior officer such as Mountbatten was an unusual step, but "having carefully prepared the ground beforehand, I was not surprised when the President cordially agreed." Part of the preparation may be explained in this statement of Marshall's recollection of the selection: "Finally, Mr. Churchill, as I recall, said, well, who did I suggest and I said Mountbatten. That's the way Mountbatten got his command out there." Marshall int, 21Nov56.

54. Marshall to Stilwell, Radios 3243, 3259, 26 and 28Aug43, *Stilwell Radio File.*

55. Joseph W. Stilwell, *The Stilwell Papers,* 1Nov43, 236–37.

56. Wedemeyer, *Wedemeyer Reports,* 248–50.

57. In his war memoirs Churchill listed no specific name; Stimson recorded Roosevelt's statement that the Prime Minister offered the command to Mar-

shall and the President's own mention of Eisenhower as the Chief of Staff's possible successor. Churchill told Stimson at lunch on 22Aug that he had suggested Marshall for the Supreme Command. Churchill, *Closing the Ring*, 85; Stimson Diary, 22Aug43; Sherwood, *Roosevelt and Hopkins*, 615, 758.

58. Marshall to President, 11Aug43, Divisions for OVERLORD on 1May44, *Marshall Library Files*.

59. Bryant, *Turn of the Tide*, 579.

60. Alanbrooke int, 5May61. To the question of pressure on the Prime Minister from the President, Lord Alanbrooke replied: "He didn't give me the impression that the President raised the matter with him. He may have. But anyhow, he told me that was the conclusion he had come to, and there-

fore, he wished to go back on the promise that he had made." His suggestion that Churchill had to give up the cross-Channel command to get Roosevelt's consent to Mountbatten's appointment is incorrect, although the Prime Minister may have given that reason. The principle that a British officer should have the Southeast Asia Command had been accepted by the United States earlier. Mountbatten's appointment was completely acceptable to Marshall and Roosevelt. Neither is there evidence of a trade in regard to the Mediterranean Command, as Brooke suggested later in the interview quoted above.

61. Ibid.

62. Marshall int, 15Nov56; Stimson Diary, 22Aug43; Leahy, *I Was There*, 178.

XIV: A SEASON OF RUMORS

I drew heavily on Millett, *Organization and Role of the Army Service Forces;* Sherwood, *Roosevelt and Hopkins;* and the extensive newspaper clipping collection of the Marshall Library. I am especially indebted to Miss Eugenia Lejeune for the excellent compilation of material which she made for me on the Supreme Command question.

1. Stimson Diary, 29Sept43.

2. Washington *Evening Star*, 15Jan43; New York *Mirror*, 28Feb43; New York *Journal-American*, 28Feb43.

3. New York *World-Telegram*, 18 and 25May, 7Jun43; New York *Herald Tribune*, 8Jun43. See also clipping files on Supreme Command, *Marshall Library Files*.

4. *Army and Navy Journal*, 4Sept43.

5. Millett, *Organization and Role of the Army Service Forces*, chap 2.

6. Ibid, chap 24.

7. Somervell to Marshall, 12Sept43, *Hq ASF, CofS, 1943 (4)*.

8. Stimson Diary, 16, 17, 18, 21, 22Sept; 5, 6, 13, 29Oct; 6 and 8Nov43.

9. Stimson Diary, 6Oct43. Detailed discussions of reactions in Washington are in Gen W. D. Styer, ASF CofS, to Somervell, 2, 3, 14Oct43, *Hq ASF, CofS, 1942-43 (6)*.

10. Washington *Post*, 1Jun63.

11. For Hopkins's part of the story, see excellent account in Sherwood's *Roosevelt and Hopkins*, 759-61. Also see Millett, *Organization and Role of the Army Service Forces*, 408-16, and my own account in *Supreme Command*, 24-32.

12. Stimson Diary, 15Sept43.

13. Ibid, 20 and 21Sept43.

14. Newark *Star-Ledger*, 19Sept43; Washington *Times-Herald*, 19Sept43.

15. Walter Trohan, Washington *Times-Herald*, 21Sept43.

16. *Cong Record*, 78th Cong, 1st sess, 20-Sept43, LXXXIX, 7682.

17. Washington *Times-Herald*, 20Sept43.

18. Walter Lippmann, "General Marshall," New York *Herald Tribune*, 23Sept43.

19. Washington *Post*, 22Sept43.

20. Washington *Times-Herald*, 25Sept43.

21. *Cong Record*, 78th Cong, 1st sess, 27-Sept43, LXXXIX, 7829.

22. Stimson Diary, 28Sept43.

23. Somervell to Marshall, 24Oct43, *Hq ASF, CofS, 1943 (4)*.

24. Detroit *Free Press*, 23Sept43.

25. New York *Herald Tribune*, 22 and 23-Sept43; New York *Sun*, 1Oct43.

26. Washington *Times-Herald*, 26Sept, 19-Oct43.

27. Sherwood, *Roosevelt and Hopkins*, 761. Note is reproduced.

28. Stimson Diary, 28Sept43. Stimson recognized that the US was asking a tremendous prize and that Churchill's position was made worse by the gossip over Marshall's new role.

29. Stimson Diary, 29Sept43; Sherwood, *Roosevelt and Hopkins*, 764.
30. Marshall int, 15Nov56. Gen Marshall also said that "a Tucson publisher" (presumably William Mathews) may have influenced Pershing's decision.
31. Pershing to President, 16Sept43, *Marshall Library Files*. Reproduced in Mrs Marshall's *Together*, 156–57.
32. Roosevelt to Pershing, 20Sept43, *Marshall Library Files; F. D. R.: His Personal Letters*, II, 1444–45.
33. Stimson Diary, 16, 17, and 18Sept43.
34. Ibid, 28Sept43.
35. Undated memo for record by Handy, apparently Oct43, *OPD 384 TS (1942–44), Case 20*. Stimson Diary, 29Sept43, mentions matter being turned over to Handy.
36. CG AAF Arnold to Handy, 29Sept43, *OPD 384 TS (1942–44), Case 15*.
37. Lincoln to Gailey, 21Jan44; Handy to Marshall, 4Oct43, *OPD 384 TS (1942–44), Case 15*; Marshall to Handy, 8Nov43, *OPD Exec 10, Item 63c, Pt 2*.
38. Revised draft Handy to CofS, 5Oct43, *OPD 384 TS (1942–44), Case 15*. Handy suggested Marshall be permitted to make "detailed" strategic decisions— Marshall changed this to "minor"— but not retain his seat on the Combined Chiefs of Staff.
39. This feeling was not shared by Montgomery, who disliked the plan and apparently the man as well. His an-

tipathy became more pronounced when Morgan backed Eisenhower in his disagreements with Montgomery. So intense were the latter's feelings that Marshall said later that he was not certain that had he become Supreme Commander, he could have kept Morgan as Chief of Staff because of Montgomery's animus. For early career, see Lt Gen Sir Frederick Morgan, *Peace and War; A Soldier's Life*.
40. Morgan, *Overture to Overlord*, 208–10, contains description of trip through Md and Va.
41. Ralph Ingersoll, *Top Secret*, 15; Morgan, *Overture to Overlord*, 193–212; Morgan int, 2Apr46.
42. Marshall to King, 4Nov43, *Marshall Library Files*.
43. Morgan, *Overture to Overlord*, 201–202; Morgan int, 8Feb47.
44. Marshall to Devers, 24Sept43, *Marshall Library Files*.
45. Marshall to Stimson, 8Nov43, *Marshall Library Files*.
46. Marshall int, 15Nov56. This statement was confirmed by Justice Douglas in later years.
47. *Newsweek*, 6Dec43, 30–32; Marshall int, 28Sept56 (author's notes).
48. President to Prime Minister, 403, 30-Oct43; Prime Minister to President, 481, 31Oct43; draft answer to No 481, President to Prime Minister, 1Nov43, *OPD Exec 10, Item 63c*.

XV: MARSHALL'S DILEMMAS

I have drawn on the following volumes to a considerable extent: *The Private Papers of Senator Vandenberg;* Romanus and Sunderland, *Stilwell's Mission to China;* John R. Deane, *The Strange Alliance;* and Martin Blumenson, *From Salerno to Cassino.*

1. Earl F. Ziemke, *Stalingrad to Berlin: The German Defeat in the East*, chaps 7 and 8; B. H. Liddell Hart, *The History of the Second World War*, 490–92; Geoffrey Jukes, *Kursk: The Clash of Armor*.
2. Comment to Col W. M. Spencer, 30-Mar46, forwarded to author by Spencer, 17Aug67.
3. US War Dept General Staff, *Biennial Report of the Chief of Staff of United States Army, July 1, 1941 to June 30, 1943 to the Secretary of War*, 31–33, 44. Other statistics list Soviet armies as engaging four-fifths of the German forces.

4. Sir John Dill, New York *Times*, 9Sept-43. For newspaper comments see booklet prepared by The Analysis Branch, War Dept Bur of Pub Rels, 1Oct43, in *Marshall Library Files*.
5. Later Marshall said of this period: "My problem was not to be forced into the invasion command at the start. There were political necessities. Mr. Roosevelt had many Republican and Democratic opponents. I could get many things if I asked for them which he couldn't. I shouldn't be immodest about this, but more than one Democratic leader and Republican would ask if I wanted [a certain measure] or

if I were speaking for the President. . . . [Senate Democratic leader Alben] Barkley particularly would call for me." Marshall int, 28Sept56 (author's notes).

6. Lewis B. Sebring, Washington *Post*, 26Sept43; Jack Turcott, Washington *Times-Herald*, 22Sept43. General MacArthur was quoted as saying: "It makes little difference whether I or others wield the weapons just so the cause for which our beloved country fights is victorious. However subordinate may be my role, I hope to play it manfully." Dispatches reprinted in Washington *Post* and *Times-Herald*, 22Sept-43.

7. Turcott, Washington *Times-Herald*, 22Sept43.

8. Associated Press, "More Power Asked for MacArthur," Washington *Post*, 22Sept43; Washington *Times-Herald*, 22Sept43.

9. Washington *Times-Herald*, 23Sept43.

10. Frazier Hunt, *The Untold Story of Douglas MacArthur*, 311–12; Hadley Cantril, *Public Opinion, 1935–1946*, 630–31, 666.

11. Vandenberg to Willoughby, 17Aug43, Vandenberg, *Private Papers*, 80.

12. Vandenberg to Wood, 15Sept43; entry of 30Sept43; Vandenberg to Willoughby, 17Aug43, ibid, 81, 82, 80 (italics in original).

13. O'Donnell, Washington *Times-Herald*, 22Sept43.

14. New York *World-Telegram*, 25Sept43.

15. Chennault to President, 5Sept43, *Hopkins Papers*, Bk VII, cited Romanus and Sunderland, *Stilwell's Mission to China*, 374.

16. Soong for President, 15Sept43, *Hopkins Papers*, Bk VII, cited ibid, 375.

17. Roosevelt to Marshall, 27Sept43, *Hopkins Papers*, Bk VII, cited ibid, 375.

18. Stimson Diary, 18Oct43.

19. Ibid, 19Oct43.

20. Somervell to Gen Ward, 1May50, cited Romanus and Sunderland, *Stilwell's Mission to China*, 376; Rpt to CCS by SAC, South-East Asia, 1943–1945, 3–7.

21. Somervell to Marshall, 24Oct43, *ASF CG's File (1943) (4)*.

22. Somervell, who played a key role in settling the disagreement, kept General Marshall fully informed, writing him among other things that the climax of the last discussion was "a heated argument between Stilwell, Chennault, and Madame regarding a whore house—this floored me!" Somervell also faithfully carried out the instructions Marshall had given him before leaving Washington for China: to warn Stilwell in the name of the Chief of Staff against making wisecracks about Chiang Kai-shek. Somervell to Marshall, 24Oct43, *ASF CG's File, Folder Chief of Staff (1943) (4)*; Stilwell, *Stilwell Papers*, 232–35; Stimson Diary, 19, 20Oct and 1Nov43 on Washington reactions to all this.

23. Romanus and Sunderland, *Stilwell's Mission to China*, 379, n 78, note that Stilwell did not officially receive the title of Deputy Supreme Allied Commander.

24. Charles F. Romanus and Riley Sunderland, *Stilwell's Command Problems*, 22–29. Slim, one of the few British officers the Chinese held in regard, reciprocated Stilwell's views. Slim int, 24Apr61.

25. Stilwell, *Stilwell Papers*, 10Nov43, 239; Don Lohbeck, *Patrick J. Hurley*, 256, 262–64. Hurley was later highly critical of Stilwell, but his early attitude was quite friendly. Hurley's biographer noted mainly the criticism. Stilwell was obviously upset by the battle of nerves then in progress in Chungking, but reports by Somervell of his conversation with Mountbatten at this period indicate that "Vinegar Joe" was less than fair to his superior.

26. Stilwell, *Stilwell Papers*, 237–38.

27. Marshall to Hopkins 10Oct41, *SecWar Safe File, Folder Russia*.

28. Deane to Marshall, 29Oct43, *OPD Exec 5, Item 12*. Later, after he had become extremely frustrated with the Russians, Deane may have changed his views somewhat. However years later he declined to associate himself with the harsher accusations, political and personal, against the Lend-Lease representative. Deane int, 31Oct60.

29. Marshall int, 14Nov56 (author's notes).

30. For material on Standley-Faymonville problems, see Adm William H. Standley and Adm Arthur A. Ageton, *Admiral Ambassador to Russia*, chaps 18–21.

31. In Harriman to Marshall, 23Sept43, *OPD Exec 1, Item 21*, the ambassador outlined points on which they agreed.

This included the fact that no direct representative of G-2 would be appointed at that time and that instead intelligence information would be sought from the British and the Russians. Marshall, in a letter to Harriman, 25Sept43, *OPD 336, Russia 28,* said: "My views are in accord with yours." The Military Mission included the heads of the Supply Division (Brig Gen Sidney P. Spalding) and Air Division (Brig Gen Hoyt Vandenberg), and a Naval Division (under Commodore— later Rear Adm—C. E. Olsen). Deane, as Chief of the Military Mission, reported to the Joint Chiefs of Staff. Since Marshall acted as agent for the Joint Chiefs in European matters, messages were still channeled through the War Department. For details of arrangement see ActSecState to chargé in USSR, 1Oct43, *US For Rels, The British Commonwealth, Eastern Europe, The Far East, 1943,* III, 704–705; Harriman to ActSecState, 4Nov43, ibid, 587–89.

32. Marshall ltr of instruction to Deane, 1Oct43, *OPD Exec 5, Item 12.* For background of mission see Matloff, *Strategic Planning, 1943–1944,* chap 13, John R. Deane, *The Strange Alliance,* 11–12.

33. Harriman to Marshall, 2Nov43, CM-IN 1946, *OPD Msg File,* recalls the earlier agreement.

34. Deane, *Strange Alliance,* 49 (italics added); Joseph R. McCarthy, *America's Retreat from Victory: The Story of George Catlett Marshall,* 42. (According to the President of Devin-Adair, publisher of the McCarthy volume, the book was written not by McCarthy but by newsman Forrest Davis. Devin A. Garrity to author, 7Jul72.)

35. McCarthy, *America's Retreat from Victory,* 41.

36. Ltr of instruction to Deane from CofS, 1Oct43, *OPD Exec 5, Item 12, Tab 1.*

37. Deane to Marshall, 29Oct43, *OPD Exec 5, Item 15.*

38. JCS to Deane, 799, 29Oct43, CM-OUT 13427 (30Oct); Harriman to Marshall, 2Nov43, CM-IN 1946 (4Nov), *OPD Msg File.*

39. JCS to Deane, 826, 8Nov43, CM-OUT 2946; Hull to Handy, 1007, 20Nov43,

CM-OUT 8182; Marshall to Deane, 32, 18Nov43, CM-OUT 7202; OPD to Deane, 23, 15Nov43, CM-OUT 6032, *OPD Msg File.*

40. Deane to JCS, 24, 28Oct43, CM-IN 16983, *OPD Msg File.*

41. Marshall to Leahy, 28Oct43, *Marshall Library Files;* JCS to Deane, 792, 28-Oct43, CM-OUT 12663, *OPD Msg File.*

42. Stimson Diary, 28, 31Oct43, 4Nov43; Eisenhower to CCS, W-3325 (in two parts), 25Oct43, CM-IN 14919, CM-IN 15186, *OPD Msg File.*

43. Stimson Diary, 28Oct43.

44. Martin Blumenson, *Salerno to Cassino,* 73–157.

45. Butcher, *My Three Years with Eisenhower,* 423–25; Marshall to Eisenhower, 22Sept43, *Marshall Library Files.*

46. Bryant, *Triumph in the West,* 30–32.

47. Churchill to Roosevelt, 7Oct43; Roosevelt to Churchill, 8Oct43, *OPD Msg File;* Churchill to Roosevelt, 8Oct43; Roosevelt to Churchill, 9Oct43, *OPD Exec 10, Item 64.* Churchill, *Closing the Ring,* 212–15, gives texts of the exchange. Copies, including drafts of the American replies, which Marshall helped to formulate, are in above files. The last sentence of the passage, beginning with the word "Strategically," was not in the War Dept draft of President to PM, 9Oct43.

48. The denouement bitterly disappointed Churchill, who showed he was still deeply displeased with the Americans when he came to write his memoirs. Surprisingly General Brooke—who had said earlier that they should not undertake the Aegean operation with the commitments they had in Italy—wrote in his postwar gloss on his diary entry: "At very little cost Crete and Rhodes could have been rendered possible operations without affecting Italy, whereas as matters stood [the American refusal to allocate additional resources for the eastern Mediterranean], these were possible only at the expense of Italian operations and were consequently ruled out." Bryant, *Triumph in the West,* 30–33, 38; Michael Howard, *The Mediterranean Strategy in the Second World War,* 51.

XVI: AN EXERCISE IN SELF-DENIAL

I have drawn heavily on the following: *US For Rels, Cairo-Tehran, 1943;* Bryant, *Triumph in the West;* Arnold, *Global Mission;* Leahy, *I Was There;* King and Whitehill, *Fleet Admiral King.* Interviews include those with Gens Handy, McCarthy, Alanbrooke, and Adm King.

1. *US For Rels, Cairo-Tehran,* chap 1.
2. Harriman to President, 26Oct43, ibid, 43–44.
3. Marshall to Leahy, 25Oct43, *Marshall Library Files.*
4. Churchill to Roosevelt, 26Oct43; Churchill to Roosevelt, 27Oct43; *US For Rels, Cairo-Tehran,* 41–42, 47–48.
5. Churchill to Roosevelt, 11Nov43, Roosevelt to Churchill, 11Nov43, ibid, 79–80.
6. Stimson to Hopkins, 10Nov43. Included in Stimson Diary under entry for that day.
7. Ibid, 11Nov43.
8. Kennedy, *Business of War,* 307, 312–13.
9. Dill to Brooke, 16Oct43, cited Bryant, *Triumph in the West,* 49–50.
10. "The Americans at no point 'insisted on abandoning Mediterranean operations.' In the discussion at Quebec in August, to which General Brooke's entries seem particularly to refer, they had stood firmly by the agreement reached at Washington the previous May, that the forces allotted to General Eisenhower should not be increased and that seven divisions should be returned from his command to the United Kingdom—divisions which were in fact still available to him when the invasion of Italy began. The fact that the agreed Allied Grand Strategy had been entirely successful in achieving its objectives, by bringing about a collapse of the Axis position in the Mediterranean and compelling the German High Command to divert forces from other fronts, did not seem in Washington a valid reason for abandoning it." Howard, *Mediterranean Strategy,* 47–48.
11. Kennedy, *Business of War,* 305.
12. King and Whitehill, *Fleet Admiral King,* 500–501; Arnold, *Global Mission,* 453–54.
13. Log of President's trip, *US For Rels, Cairo-Tehran,* 270–90; King and Whitehill, *Fleet Admiral King,* 501. Sherwood, *Roosevelt and Hopkins,* 768,

has Hopkins's memo on the incident, part of which is reproduced in the text. See Arnold, *Global Mission,* 455. Despite these well-documented accounts, the incident is rediscovered periodically by the press and given banner headlines as one of the closely kept secrets of the war.
14. Eisenhower, *Crusade in Europe,* 196; King and Whitehill, *Fleet Admiral King,* 504.
15. The quotation is from Sherwood, *Roosevelt and Hopkins,* 770, but the general sense of the statement is in Eisenhower, *Crusade in Europe,* 197.
16. Stimson Diary, 3Dec43.
17. Log of President's trip, *US For Rels, Cairo-Tehran,* 290; Butcher, *My Three Years with Eisenhower,* 406, says incorrectly that Marshall and King went on Monday; Arnold, *Global Mission,* 458, gives same departure time as King and Whitehill, *Fleet Admiral King,* 504, but suggests that the President also flew at the same time. Actually the President went later on Sunday, arriving the following morning.
18. It has been suggested by Barbara Tuchman and others that Chiang Kai-shek was offended because Churchill and Roosevelt did not meet him. Tuchman, *Stilwell and the American Experience in China, 1911–1945,* 401. However Roosevelt did not arrive until the following morning. Bryant indicates that Chiang Kai-shek was there shortly before Churchill.
19. Marshall int, 29Oct56 (author's notes).
20. *US For Rels, Cairo-Tehran,* 312–13.
21. Ibid, 313–15; Churchill, *Closing the Ring,* 328–29.
22. *US For Rels, Cairo-Tehran,* 317.
23. Stilwell's version was accepted by King for inclusion in his memoirs. Arnold, *Global Mission,* 461; Stilwell, *Stilwell Papers,* 245; King and Whitehill, *Fleet Admiral King,* 511.
24. Arnold, *Global Mission,* 462.
25. *US For Rels, Cairo-Tehran,* 322–26.
26. Marshall int, 20Nov56.

27. Ibid, 13Nov56 (author's notes). General Marshall added that he "had many hectic scenes with the Prime Minister. He could be strong and loud. Churchill, however, once he accepted a point would not hold it against me. He would put his arms around me."

28. *US For Rels, Cairo-Tehran*, 364–65.

29. Ibid, 477–82.

30. Bryant, *Turn of the Tide*, 380.

31. *US For Rels, Cairo-Tehran*, 521.

32. Marshall int, 15Nov56.

33. *US For Rels, Cairo-Tehran*, 543–55, 558–64.

34. Ibid, 576. Gen Deane, as head of the US Military Mission to Moscow, informed the Russians of all postponements in dates. Yet one of the witnesses against William Remington during an investigation for subversion testified that the date of D day was one of the secret items the Russians bought from him.

35. Marshall int, 11Feb57; Marshall, in int, 25Jul49, with Lamson, Hamilton, Matthews, and Smith, said the Joint Chiefs were always fearful that Roosevelt might lightly commit them to operations in the Balkans. "When President Roosevelt began waving his cigarette holder, you never knew where you were going," he said.

36. Marshall int, 11Feb57 (italics added).

37. King and Whitehill, *Fleet Admiral King*, 520–21.

38. For accounts of the visit see ibid, 521–22, Arnold, *Global Mission*, 472.

39. *US For Rels, Cairo-Tehran*, 681. Words in brackets are thus in published text.

40. Ibid, 724–25, 815–16.

41. See editorial note, ibid, 725. Marshall's name is omitted from the list of those present, but the President's log, 658, from which the bulk of the information on this page is taken, lists the CofS among those attending.

42. JCS to President, 17Nov43 (1st memo), ibid, 195, 203–205.

43. JCS to President, 17Nov43 (2d memo), ibid, 209.

44. JCS to President, 17Nov43, Enc B to 1st memo, ibid, 206.

45. Ibid, 252–53.

46. Memo by US CsofS, CCS 408, 25Nov43, ibid, 405–406.

47. Memo by Churchill, 25Nov43; memo by Br CsofS, 26Nov43, ibid, 407–408, 424–26.

48. Col Stanley J. Grogan tel int, 1Sept69.

49. Marshall ltr to Sherwood, in Sherwood, *Roosevelt and Hopkins*, 803.

50. Ibid; Marshall int, 15Nov56.

51. This was the way Marshall wrote it in the draft he sent to Gen Eisenhower; the actual message to Stalin has "the Command of Overlord" rather than "command of Overlord operation."

52. Marshall to Eisenhower, 7Dec43, *Marshall Library Files*.

53. Marshall to Sexton, 22Nov43, *Marshall Library Files*.

54. Lt Gen Marshall S. Carter (then a colonel) recalls that he had asked Sutherland for a ride in his plane to the Pacific theater. Soon afterward so many of the U.S. participants at the conference made similar requests that a second plane had to be provided.

55. Sexton to Marshall, 20Nov43, *Marshall Library Files*.

56. Hunt, *Untold Story of Douglas MacArthur*, 313–14.

57. Walter Krueger, *From Down Under to Nippon*, 28–29; Frank McCarthy's recollections of trip.

58. For extended quotation, which must be used with care, see MacArthur, *Reminiscences*, 183.

59. Ibid, 184.

60. Bryant, *Triumph in the West*, 390.

61. Marshall to Allen Brown, 27Dec43; Marshall to Clifton Brown, 29Dec43, *Marshall Library Files*.

62. Ltrs McCarthy to author, 24Jan and 1Feb68; Gen T. T. Handy int, 9Jul70.

63. Stimson Diary, 17, 18, and 23Dec43.

XVII: ITALY VERSUS ANVIL

I have drawn on Martin Blumenson, *Anzio;* Churchill, *Closing the Ring;* Bryant, *Triumph in the West;* Mark Clark, *Calculated Risk;* and the correspondence between Allen Brown and Madge Brown (now Mrs John Pendleton). Interviews were held with Gens Morgan, Alanbrooke, McCarthy, Eisenhower and with Harvey Bundy and Miss Cora Thomas.

1. Marshall to Eisenhower, 29Dec43; "I had brought him home, over his strenuous objections, to force him to take a brief rest before he undertakes his heavy obligations in England," Marshall to Roosevelt, 4Jan44, *Marshall Library Files.*

2. Eisenhower, *Crusade in Europe,* 216–17.

3. Information furnished by McCarthy and Dr A. B. Sageser, Kansas State University.

4. Folder on Alibi Club; Marshall to Leon and Agnes Thompson, 10Jan43, thanking them for the dinner the preceding week, *Marshall Library Files.* On Alibi Club see article by Frank C. Waldrop, "Washington Clubs," *Washingtonian,* Apr68, 48–49.

5. Stimson Diary, 3Jan44.

6. Ibid, 3 and 12Jan44.

7. Smith to Eisenhower, W-9389, 5Jan44, *OPD Exec 17, Item 25.*

8. Eisenhower to Smith, 6513, 5Jan44, *OPD Exec 17, Item 25.*

9. CsofS to Prime Minister, 1354, 14Jan44, *SHAEF SGS 381, Overlord-Anvil, I.*

10. Eisenhower to Marshall, 17Jan44, *OPD Exec 9, Bk 14.*

11. Martin Blumenson, *Anzio: The Gamble That Failed;* Blumenson, "General Lucas at Anzio," in *Command Decisions,* ed Greenfield, 323–50.

12. Churchill, *Closing the Ring,* 430, 434, 440–41.

13. Marshall int, 13Nov56 (author's notes).

14. Churchill, *Closing the Ring,* 441.

15. Stimson Diary, 12Jan44; Smith to Eisenhower, W-9715, 9Jan44, *OPD Exec 17, Item 25.*

16. Bryant, *Triumph in the West,* 93–94.

17. Blumenson, *Anzio,* 58–60, 63–65, 86–95.

18. Churchill, *Closing the Ring,* 486–89.

19. Marshall to Devers, 18Feb44, *Marshall Library Files;* Blumenson, *Anzio,* 139; Mark W. Clark, *Calculated Risk,* 306.

20. Marshall to Eisenhower, 205, 1Mar44, *SHAEF Files.*

21. Eisenhower to Marshall, W-9856, 22-Jan44, *SHAEF Files.*

22. Eisenhower to Marshall, B-33, 23Jan44, *SHAEF SGS 381, Overlord-Anvil, I.*

23. Tel conv Morgan and Smith with Handy and Hull, 4Feb44, *SHAEF SGS 381, Overlord-Anvil, I;* Eisenhower to Marshall, W-10678, 6Feb44, *OPD Exec 10, Item 52A.*

24. Butcher, *My Three Years with Eisenhower,* 487.

25. Marshall to Eisenhower, 78, 7Feb44, *SHAEF SGS 381, Overlord-Anvil, I.*

26. He concluded by saying that it was not entirely a bad thing, inasmuch as it showed that the commander was on the job and was willing to fight for what he believed necessary to do the job, even though the staff in Washington might be irritated to distraction. Arnold, *Global Mission,* 429–30.

27. Eisenhower to Marshall, W-10786, 8Feb44, *SHAEF Files.*

28. Bundy int, 7Oct59. Stimson Diary, 16-Feb44, says: "Marshall has been particularly insistent upon the importance of this matter [recognition of Dill]." Stimson explained that Dill "was not only able but very fair-minded and tactful in his dealings with the Staff and has been a great factor in keeping the unity of Staff operations which has been so remarkable in campaigns thus far. Therefore we are trying to give him a boom in this country to show how important he is and to make the Prime Minister a little bit cautious about removing him."

29. Hull to Handy, 15Feb44, *OPD Exec 9, Bk 15, Paper 253;* Eisenhower to Marshall, W-11500, 19Feb44, *SHAEF Files.*

30. Leahy, *I Was There,* 223.

31. Dill wrote Brooke: "I have been in and out of Marshall's room lately trying to get him to see your point of view regarding ANVIL/OVERLORD and trying to get his point of view. I take it now that the United States Chiefs of Staff delegated their powers to Eisenhower

on this question, you will be satified."
Also see Bryant, *Triumph in the West*,
105.

32. JCS to Eisenhower, 151 and 153, 21-
Feb44, *OPD Exec 2, Item 11.*

33. SCAEF 6th mtg, 26Feb44, *SHAEF SGS
File, 337/11;* Eisenhower to Marshall,
B-245, 9Mar44, *OPD Msg File.*

34. Bryant, *Triumph in the West*, 108,
110-11.

35. The italics are Churchill's. Dill to
Marshall, 12Mar44, forwarding Church-
ill to Marshall, *OPD Exec 10, Item 66;*
Marshall to Eisenhower for Prime
Minister, 298, 15Mar44, *SHAEF Files.*

36. Marshall to Eisenhower, 314, 16Mar44,
SHAEF Files.

37. Marshall to Eisenhower, 25Mar44, CM-
OUT 14078, *OPD Exec 10, Item 52B.*

38. Bryant, *Triumph in the West*, 134.

39. Jt Staff Mission to War Cabinet, JSM
1613, 31Mar44, *OPD Exec 3, Item 16.*

40. Jt Staff Mission to Br CsofS, FMD 183,
1Apr44, *OPD Exec 3, Item 16.*

41. Handy signed Marshall to Eisenhower,
W-16455, 31Mar44, *SHAEF SGS 381,
Overlord-Anvil, I.*

42. Stimson Diary, 27Mar44.

43. Eisenhower to Marshall, S-50310, 12-
Apr44, *SHAEF Files.*

44. Churchill to Dill for Marshall, 021985,
16Apr44, *OPD Exec 3, Item 16,*
Churchill, *Closing the Ring*, 513-14.

45. Diary Office of CinC, 18Apr44.

46. Marshall to Eisenhower, W-14078, 25-
Mar44, *SHAEF Files.*

47. Ehrman, *Grand Strategy*, V, 260-63.

48. Devers to Marshall, B-12811, 31May44;
Bronze Star citation, cited Mrs Marshall, *Together*, 196.

49. Marshall to Allen Brown, 1Mar44,
Marshall Library Files.

50. Ibid, 11Mar44, *Marshall Library Files.*

51. Allen Brown to Madge Brown, 27Feb-
44, *Marshall Library Files.*

52. Ibid, 6Mar44, *Marshall Library Files.*

53. Ibid, 7Mar44, *Marshall Library Files.*

54. Ibid, 19Mar44, *Marshall Library Files.*

55. Ibid, 22 and 26Mar44, *Marshall Library Files.*

56. Marshall to Allen Brown, 24Mar44,
Marshall Library Files.

57. Allen Brown to Marshall, 10Apr44,
Marshall Library Files.

58. Marshall to Allen Brown, 18Apr44,
Marshall Library Files.

59. Ibid, 17May44, *Marshall Library Files.*

60. Mrs Marshall, *Together*, 195.

61. Miss Cora E. Thomas int, 10Mar61.

62. Mrs Marshall, *Together*, 195, said
"that morning" but General Marshall's
message to Allen's wife (Marshall to
Madge Brown, 30May44) says, "I have
just received a message from General
Clark . . . that Allen was killed in
his tank by a German sniper at 10
a.m. May 29th near Campolcone."
Copy furnished author by Allen's
widow.

XVIII: "MAN OF THE YEAR"

I have drawn on Palmer, Wiley, and Keast, *The Procurement and Training of Ground
Combat Troops;* Fairchild and Grossman, *The Army and Industrial Manpower;* Matloff, "90-Division Gamble," in *Command Decisions.*

1. *Time* also said: "The American people
do not, as a general rule, like or trust
the military. But they like and trust
General Marshall. This is no more
paradoxical than the fact that General
Marshall hates war. The secret is that
American democracy is the stuff Marshall is made of." *Time* credited him
with seven great contributions since
1939: (1) building the Army to its current strength from 200,000; (2) creating a training program and a schedule
of equipment unmatched anywhere;
(3) holding off hastily planned or ill-
advised military operations; (4) insisting on unity of command; (5) refusing

to send out green, ill-equipped troops;
(6) recognizing airpower early and
pushing the air program; and (7)
breaking "the traditionally supercili-
ous War Department enmity toward
innovations of equipment."

2. Freeman to Marshall, 30Dec42, with
attached editorial, "Man of the Year"
from the *Richmond News Leader, Marshall Library Files.*

3. Stimson Diary, 23Dec43.

4. Ibid, 31Dec43.

5. Ibid, 27, 29, 30, and 31Dec43.

6. Ibid, 31Dec43. Apparently Gen Marshall considered issuing a further statement on the strike. He received the

following from AsstSec McCloy on 5Jan: "For what it may be worth this is to let you know that I have given some thought and talked to a few people about the wisdom of your making a statement in re the strike situation, and my judgment is that, pending any further developments, it would be wiser to say nothing." *Marshall Library Files.*

7. William Frye, *Marshall: Citizen Soldier,* 351–52. Frye says Marshall erred on this occasion because he combined his usual objective off-the-record press briefing on the war with a red-hot statement on a current domestic problem.

8. Quoted in *Army and Navy Journal,* 15Jan44, 574. The *Journal* declared that the kindest thing that could be said about the labor organizations was that they failed to realize what they were doing. "Informed by General Marshall, it is to be believed they will now understand that strikes are in fact sabotage as serious as actual dynamiting of trains and of mills." Ibid, 8Jan44.

9. *Army and Navy Journal,* 15Jan44.

10. DeWeerd, *Selected Speeches and Statements,* 246–48. Original in *Marshall Library Files.*

11. Marshall to President, 27Jan44, *Marshall Library Files.*

12. Marshall to Smith, 21Feb44, *Marshall Library Files.*

13. Marshall to Lady Mary Burghley, 29-Mar44, *Marshall Library Files.*

14. Marshall [Pasco] to Bolté, 3Mar44, *Marshall Library Files.*

15. Ibid. While these were normal instructions, Marshall on occasion, particularly if he wanted to show troops to a guest of great importance, would accept honors.

16. Marshall [Pasco] to Lt Gen W. H. Simpson, 3Mar44, *Marshall Library Files.* He sometimes tried to do too much. One of the commanders involved believed that he did not leave sufficient time for all that he wanted to see. Bolté int, 28May58.

17. The final figure for the Army and Army Air Forces was set at approximately 8,300,000 in 1945.

18. Stimson Diary, 26Jan44. The 2d Cavalry Division was inactivated shortly after it went overseas in 1944, and its personnel was used to meet various shortages.

19. An unfortunate by-product of the whole affair was that someone leaked information on the War Department's intentions to the press. Opponents of the ASTP in the Pentagon suspected Col Herman Beukema, well-known professor of the social sciences at the U.S. Military Academy, director of the program. Secretary Stimson stuck loyally by the colonel, insisting that the investigators appointed by the Army were too severe and that he had confidence in him. Stimson Diary, 26-Jan and 18Feb44; Palmer, Wiley, and Keast, *Procurement and Training of Ground Combat Troops,* 38–39.

20. One million of these—in fifty ground divisions and supporting troops—were earmarked for shipment and would steadily be sent overseas. A quarter of a million were in Air Forces units being prepared for shipment out of the country. Larger groups were in training—three-quarters of a million fliers and nearly 100,000 instructors and assistants; a third of a million ground troops in replacement-training centers with 75,000 officers and men in charge of instruction. The remainder —and here he was later to seek replacements—were engaged in administration, maintenance, transportation, and supply. Although some surplus might be trimmed, there was little solution to his problems to be found in these men in uniform. Marshall to Stimson, 17Mar44, original to S/W before Cabinet meeting, 3/17/44, *Marshall Library Files.*

21. Marshall to UndSecWar Patterson, 17-Mar44, *Marshall Library Files.*

22. Marshall to Byrnes, 23Mar44, *Marshall Library Files.*

23. Stimson Diary, 22, 23, and 24Mar44.

24. Ibid, 29Mar44.

25. Ibid, 4Apr44.

26. Fairchild and Grossman, *Army and Industrial Manpower,* 236; *Time,* 24-Jan44.

27. Stimson Diary, 12Apr44. The quoted words represent Stimson's paraphrase of Marshall's statement.

28. Ibid, 20Apr44; Maurice Matloff, "The 90-Division Gamble," in *Command Decisions,* ed Greenfield, 366–81.

29. Howard to Marshall, 24Apr44, *Marshall Library Files.*

30. Marshall to Roberts, 6Apr44, *Marshall Library Files.*

31. Marshall to Devers, 7Apr44, *Marshall Library Files.*

32. McCarthy to Brig Gen Alexander D. Surles, 11May44, *WDCSA 680.2 (1944-45).*

33. Marshall to Hamilton Corbett, 26May44; Marshall to Mrs Erskine Wood, 10May44; Marshall to Wood, 10May44, *Marshall Library Files.* Note earlier visits of Marshall with Wood in my *George C. Marshall: Education of a General,* 312.

34. According to McCarthy, "General Marshall considered that in this action he had scored a sort of personal victory over the United States Navy and never stopped regaling Admiral King, the somewhat dour Chief of Naval Operations, with the story of how he improved the morale of the U.S. Air Forces at the expense of the Navy." McCarthy, memo to author, 18Jan61; William F. Haney to Marshall, 8Jun44, *Marshall Library Files.*

35. *Time,* 8May44, 11-12.

36. Stimson to Marshall, 10May44, in Diary, attached to entry of 11May44.

37. Stimson Diary, 11May44. See Matloff, "The 90-Division Gamble," in *Command Decisions,* ed Greenfield, 366-81.

38. Marshall to Devers, W-22650, 13Apr44, *OPD Msg File.*

39. Marshall to Eisenhower, W-22651, 13-Apr44, *OPD Msg File.*

40. Eisenhower to Marshall, 3Mar44, *OPD Exec 9, Bk 16;* Marshall to Eisenhower, 254, 9Mar44, *SHAEF Files.*

41. Marshall to Eisenhower, W-22651, 13-Apr44, *OPD Msg File.*

42. Butcher, *My Three Years with Eisenhower,* 17Apr44, 519.

43. Eisenhower to Marshall, 17Apr44, *Marshall Library Files.*

44. Stimson Diary, 25May44. Stimson remarked that Marshall deserved a lot of credit for the system, which other armies did not have. Marshall to Stimson, 6Jun44, quoting from Eaker to Arnold, *Marshall Library Files.*

45. Stimson Diary, 16 and 17May44; Matloff, *Strategic Planning, 1943-1944,* 410-12; Marvin A. Kreidberg and Merton G. Henry, *History of Military Mobilization in the United States Army, 1775-1945,* 628.

46. Marshall to Commanders, 22Mar44, *Marshall Library Files.*

47. Stimson Diary, 15Mar44.

48. Ibid, 12 and 17Apr44. The committee included key members of the Military and Naval Affairs and Appropriations committees. One of the junior members was Representative Lyndon B. Johnson of Texas. Marshall's part in the unification fight will be discussed more fully in a subsequent volume. See Vincent Davis, *Postwar Defense Policy and the U.S. Navy, 1943-1946,* chap 3; See also Demetrios Caraley, *The Politics of Military Unification: A Study of Conflict and the Policy Process,* 218, 250-52.

49. Stimson Diary, 3, 5, 8, and 9May44.

50. Ibid, 12 and 15May44.

51. Marshall to SecWar, 17Apr44, *Marshall Library Files.*

52. Leahy, *I Was There,* 221-22. Leahy says he discussed the measure with Vinson on 13Jan. For other details see memo from Maj Gen Miller G. White to Col William T. Sexton, 13Jan44, *Marshall Library Files.*

53. Marshall int, 14Feb57.

54. Harbord to Wadsworth, 9Feb44; Wadsworth to Harbord, 11Feb44; Harbord to Wadsworth, 14Feb44; Marshall to Wadsworth, 15Aug44, returning Harboard corres, *Marshall Library Files.* Harold Ross, editor of *The New Yorker,* passed on to Stephen Early, White House press secretary, letters from Harbord and asked for comment. Early in turn forwarded them to Marshall's office, where McCarthy—with assistance from Marshall—framed a suitable rebuttal. See Harbord file in *Marshall Library Files.*

55. Stimson Diary, 31Jan44.

56. Ibid, 1Feb44. In view of the fact that a Navy representative had said that Roosevelt had approved the Navy draft "in part," it may be argued that the President was accurate in his denial. Leahy's failure to mention the two-star advance may also be cited in Roosevelt's defense.

57. *Army and Navy Journal,* 4Mar44.

58. Stimson Diary, 18May44.

59. Ibid, 22May44.

60. *Look,* 16May44.

61. From account furnished the author by

Brig Gen Robert Cutler, War Department Coordinator for Soldier Voting in the Army and Air Corps, who was present. Cutler wrote the account on 30Jan61; *Marshall Library Files.* Substantially the same account appears in Robert Cutler, *No Time for Rest*, 228–29. In the book (published in 1965) he changes the number of governors to

forty-five. I have followed his earlier text. For King's participation and views, see King and Whitehill, *Fleet Admiral King*, 543.

62. Cutler, memo to author, 30Jan61, *Marshall Library Files.*

63. Memo containing suggested topics for CofS, unsigned [by member of staff], 5/26/44, *Marshall Library Files.*

XIX: OVERLORD AT LAST

I have drawn heavily on my notes collected in the period 1946–52 for the writing of *The Supreme Command* and my own recollections of the D-day period.

1. Marshall to Eisenhower, 5968, 25Aug-43, CM-OUT 10283, *OPD Msg File.*

2. Eisenhower to Marshall, 24Aug43, *OPD Exec 9, Bk 11.*

3. Eisenhower to Marshall, W-8367, 27-Aug43, *OPD Exec 3, Item 10.*

4. Eisenhower to Marshall, 6Sept43, *Marshall Library Files.*

5. Eisenhower to Marshall, 24Aug43, *OPD Exec 9, Bk 11.*

6. Eisenhower to Marshall, 6Sept44, *Marshall Library Files.* Stephen Ambrose, in a talk with the author, suggested that Bedell Smith may have told Marshall about the incidents when he was in Washington in October. If so, he failed to give Marshall details on Eisenhower's actions.

7. Pearson, not bound by the agreement, heard the story from other sources and decided to release it. In a mistaken effort to minimize the incidents Gen Smith denied that a reprimand had been given. His announcement brought a great outcry in the United States. Marshall's mail was soon filled · with angry letters demanding severe punishment or dismissal. Acting on the theory that the problem was one for Eisenhower to handle, Marshall took no action. Marshall to Eisenhower, 3233, 23Nov43, CM-OUT 8960, *OPD Exec 3, Item 11*, asks for full information and what Eisenhower had done. See folders in Marshall files on incident, including Eisenhower report and correspondence, pro and con; Ladislas Farago, *Patton: Ordeal and Triumph*, chaps 16 and 17; Garland and Smyth, *Sicily*, 426–31; Bradley, *Soldier's Story*, 160–62, 229, 357 and Eisenhower, *Crusade in Europe*, 179–81.

8. Eisenhower to Marshall, 20Sept43, *OPD Exec 3, Item 1c.*

9. Marshall to Eisenhower, 536, 21Oct43, *OPD Msg File.* It was the disruption of this plan to which Marshall referred in a letter to Roy Roberts mentioned earlier (359). Cf. Farago, *Patton*, 355, for the suggestion that Stimson had in mind Patton's transfer to the Fifth Army in connection with Alexander's plans for a dash northward. In the Cairo-Tehran conferences still in progress, both Stimson and Marshall had opposed any such ambitious plans on Alexander's part. There is no evidence that they considered such a role for Patton.

10. Eisenhower to Marshall, 24Aug43, *Marshall Library Files.*

11. Notes for CofS, on Eisenhower's stationery, 2Oct43, brought to Washington by Smith, *SHAEF Files* (italics in original).

12. Eisenhower to Marshall, 17Dec43, *OPD Exec 9, Bk 14.*

13. Ibid. See similar statement Smith to Hull, 138, 19Dec43, CM-IN 12388, *OPD Exec 17, Item 28.*

14. Marshall to Eisenhower, 5585, 23Dec-43, CM-OUT 8894, *OPD Exec 3, Pt 11.*

15. McNarney to Eisenhower, 5363, 21Dec-43, CM-OUT 7894, *OPD Exec 17, Item 28.*

16. Eisenhower to McNarney for Marshall, 187, 23Dec43, *Marshall Library Files.*

17. Eisenhower to Marshall, W-8550, 25-Dec43, CM-IN 16030, *OPD Exec 17, Item 28.*

18. Ibid.

19. Marshall to Eisenhower, 5810, 28Dec-43, CM-OUT 10107, *OPD Exec 17, Item 28.*

20. Eisenhower to Marshall, 8781, 29Dec-43, *OPD Exec 17, Item 28*. Marshall's earlier recommendation of Hodges had been reinforced by his statement to Eisenhower of 28Dec43: "Hodges is exactly same class of man as Bradley in practically every respect. Wonderful shot, great hunter, quiet, self-effacing, thorough understanding of ground fighting, DSC, etc., etc."

21. Marshall to Eisenhower, 5898, 29Dec-43, CM-OUT 10627, *OPD Exec 17, Item 28*.

22. Marshall to Eisenhower, R-8213, 17-Jan44; Wilson to Eisenhower, W-448, 18Jan44, CM-IN 11472, *OPD Msg File;* Eisenhower to Marshall, W-9745, 19-Jan44, *OPD Exec 17, Item 28*.

23. Marshall to Eisenhower, R-8213, 17-Jan44, *OPD Msg File;* Eisenhower to Marshall, W-9737, 18Jan44, CM-IN 11895, *OPD Exec 17, Item 28*.

24. Marshall to Eisenhower, R-8316, 19-Jan44, CM-OUT 7432, *OPD Exec 3, Pt 11;* Farago, *Patton*, 376, 382-83; Eisenhower to Marshall, W-9777, 20Jan-44, CM-IN 13079, *OPD Msg File;* Eisenhower to Marshall, 9737, 18Jan44, *OPD Exec 17, Item 28*.

25. As early as Jul41, McNair drew up for Marshall a list of officers he considered especially suited for higher command. Of the men who would later head the theaters, army groups, and armies, several—MacArthur, Krueger, Buckner, Stilwell, and Patton—already had important command assignments. Of the remainder a list of brig gens included Bradley, Gerow, Simpson, and Eichelberger, and a group of cols worthy of notice included Eisenhower, Patch, Clark, Handy, and J. Lawton Collins.

26. Of Huebner, for example, he said later: "Huebner I'd known as a first lieutenant in France in dugouts, trenches, etc., and I had a great fondness for and admiration for [him], particularly for his fighting qualities." Marshall int, 19Nov56.

27. Eisenhower to Marshall, W-8967, 31-Dec43, *OPD Exec 17, Item 28*.

28. Butcher, *My Three Years with Eisenhower*, 467.

29. Marshall to Eisenhower, 10Feb44, *WDCSA 381 (1944-45), Case 2;* Pogue, *Supreme Command*, 119.

30. Eisenhower to Marshall, 19Feb44; Bidwell to Brig Gen Frank N. Roberts, 21Feb44, *OPD Exec 9, Bk 15*.

31. Marshall to Eisenhower, 2Mar44, *OPD Exec 9, Bk 15*.

32. Eisenhower to Marshall, B-252, 10Mar-44, *SHAEF Files*.

33. Marshall int, 14Feb57.

34. Farago, *Patton*, 416ff.

35. Ibid, 417, contains the text that apparently was reported in British and U.S. newspapers. Although Eisenhower to Marshall, S-50908, 29Apr44, *OPD Exec 1, Item 28c*, said: "His actual words according to my reports were, 'Since it seems to be the destiny of America, Great Britain and Russia to rule the world, the better we know each other the better off we will be,'" he appears to have been misled by staff members of his own headquarters. According to Cmdr Butcher, Eisenhower's naval aide, "Our PRO [Press Relations Officer] has been busy on his own getting Russia included and to some extent has succeeded. . . ." Butcher, *My Three Years with Eisenhower*, 510-11. For the gist of Marshall's correspondence with Eisenhower, see Pogue, *Supreme Command*, 164-66, based on Eisenhower's personal file and Marshall's Executive Office File, made available to the author in the summer of 1946. *Papers of Eisenhower*, III, 1837-41, have the Eisenhower documents and summaries of other material.

36. Marshall to Eisenhower, WAR-28238, 26Apr44, *OPD Exec 1, Item 28c*.

37. Marshall to Eisenhower, WAR-29722, 29Apr44, *OPD Exec 1, Item 28c;* Farago, *Patton*, 417.

38. Ibid; Pogue, *Supreme Command*, 164-66; Marshall to Eisenhower, W-29722, 29Apr44, *OPD Exec 1, Item 28c*.

39. Marshall to Eisenhower, W-29722, 29-Apr44, *OPD Exec 1, Item 28c*.

40. Eisenhower to Marshall, S-50908, 29-Apr44, *OPD Exec 1, Item 28c*. Apparently Farago in his biography of Patton, 419-20, was misled by a long footnote in the author's *Supreme Command*, 165, n 17, into thinking that because a letter from Smith to Marshall is mentioned first that Smith actually wrote the severe letter cited above. This led him into an examination of reasons for Smith's animosity. In fact,

as Butcher's *My Three Years with Ei-senhower*, 531, points out, Smith had attempted to mollify Marshall. Smith's message of 27Apr44, S-50822, explaining to Marshall that Eisenhower was on a maneuver indicated that the Supreme Commander had been very reluctant to disclose Patton's presence in the United Kingdom for fear that he would create an incident. But Smith and the Press Relations Officer argued that newsmen would begin saying that they were trying to smuggle Patton in. *Papers of Eisenhower*, III, 1837–41, n 1838, makes clear that Smith was trying to play down Patton's indiscretion and that Eisenhower wrote the severe letter after returning to his headquarters.

41. Eisenhower to Patton, 29Apr44, *Marshall Library Files*.
42. Eisenhower to Marshall, S-50965, 30-Apr44, *OPD Exec 1, Item 28c*.
43. McNarney for Marshall to Eisenhower, W-30586, 1May44, *OPD Exec 1, Item 28c*.
44. Eisenhower to Marshall, S-51128, 3May44, *OPD Exec 1, Item 28c*.
45. Eisenhower to Patton, S-51129, 3May44; Stimson to Eisenhower, 5May44, *Eisenhower Personal File*.
46. Eisenhower to CCS, S-52026, 17May44, CM-IN 13179, *OPD Exec 6*.
47. Eisenhower to Marshall, 21May44, *OPD Exec 10, Item 57*. Incidents summarized in Pogue, *Supreme Command*, 163–64.

48. Stimson Diary, 24 and 31May; 1, 2, and 5Jun44. See later references 19 and 20Jun44.
49. Ibid, 1Jun44.
50. Diary Office of CinC, 23May44.
51. Eisenhower to Marshall, S-52951, 1Jun44; Eisenhower to Marshall, 031815, 3Jun44; Eisenhower to Marshall, S-53141, 4Jun44, *OPD Exec 6*; Eisenhower to CCS, SCAF 46, 5Jun44, *SHAEF Files*. See Pogue, *Supreme Command*, 166–70, based on interviews with most of the principals and on written accounts by two participants in the meeting, Air Marshal Sir James Robb and Gen Bull. See my own recollections and those of others of the D-day period in addresses given at Eisenhower Library, 6Jun69, in collection of addresses published by Eisenhower Foundation, *D-Day: The Normandy Invasion in Retrospect*.
52. Stimson Diary, 5Jun44.
53. See ibid, 6Jun44, for the Secretary's reaction.
54. Marshall to Madge Brown, 7Jun44, *Marshall Library Files*.
55. Mrs John W. Pendleton to author, 5Jan68. She had come to Washington just about the time that Clifton Brown, who had been sent back as a courier with Allen's effects, had attempted to call her in New York.
56. Eisenhower to Marshall, 90016, 6Jun44, *OPD Msg File*.
57. William D. Hassett, *Off the Record with F. D. R.: 1942–1945*, 249.

XX: OF DE GAULLE AND THE LJUBLJANA GAP

I have drawn on the *Reports by the Supreme Allied Commander, Mediterranean, to the Combined Chiefs of Staff on the Italian Campaign: Part I, 8 January 1944–10 May 1944; Part II, 10 May 1944–12 August 1944; Part III, 13 August 1944–12 December 1944;* and *Report by the Supreme Allied Commander, Mediterranean, to the Combined Chiefs of Staff on the Operations in Southern France, August 1944.*

1. Marshall to Roosevelt, S-53824, 15Jun44, CM-IN 11162, *SecWar Safe File, Folder French*.
2. McCarthy to author, 8Nov57 and 9Jul71; Marshall to Lee, 13Jun44, *Marshall Library Files*. For general details of trip see Arnold, *Global Mission*, 503–17; and King and Whitehill, *Fleet Admiral King*, 547–55.
3. The location, approximately a forty-minute drive outside London, had been selected by members of Gen Ei-

senhower's staff on the theory that the Germans might soon launch heavy bombing attacks on the British capital in retaliation for D day.
4. Arnold, *Global Mission*, 505.
5. See informal notes CCS 163d mtg, 11-Jun44, 2:15 pm, Stanwell Place, Middlesex, England, *OPD Exec 9, Bk 19*; Bryant, *Triumph in the West*, 157.
6. Informal notes, CCS 163d mtg, 11Jun44, *OPD Exec 9, Bk 19*; mins mtg held 11Jun44 at 2:15 pm Stanwell Place,

Middlesex, England, *ABC 334 CCS Mins (1-23-42), Sec 7.*

7. McCarthy to author, 8Nov67.

8. For the visit to the beach I have used Bradley, *Soldier's Story*, 289-91, in addition to accounts by Arnold, *Global Mission*, 504-507; King and Whitehill, *Fleet Admiral King*, 548-50; McCarthy to author, 8Nov67.

9. Churchill, *Triumph and Tragedy*, 13-14.

10. Marshall to Roosevelt, S-53824, 14Jun44, CM-IN 11162, *SecWar Safe File, Folder French.*

11. Arnold, *Global Mission*, 509-12, says that about seven rockets fell within five miles of them and one about a mile and a half away. He gives detailed descriptions of the weapons. Later in the war the more powerful and more sophisticated V-2 rocket was put into service.

12. President to Prime Minister cited in Smith signed Eisenhower to Marshall, S-51841, 14May44, *OPD Exec 10, Item 52d.*

13. Marshall to Roosevelt, 15May44; Smith to Marshall, S-51841, 15May44, CM-IN 10806, *OPD Security, Sec 4, Case 72.*

14. Eisenhower to Marshall, S-51959, 16-May44, *OPD Exec 10, Item 52d.*

15. Roosevelt to Marshall, 2Jun44, *Marshall Library Files.*

16. Pogue, *Supreme Command*, 142-50, based in part on ints with Gen de Gaulle, Brig Gen R. A. McClure, Lt Gen Sir Frederick Morgan, and Sir Robert Bruce Lockhart.

17. Marshall int, 29Oct56 (author's notes). Marshall spoke at the CCS mtg on 15-Jun of a somewhat difficult interview he had with Béthouart, apparently the previous day.

18. Stimson Diary, 16Jun44.

19. Marshall int, 13Nov56.

20. Roosevelt to Marshall, 14Jun44, *Marshall Library Files.* "Therefore," he continued with a dig at London, "there does not appear to be any objection to de Gaulle's visit to France as arranged by the British Government without consulting the United States."

21. de Gaulle, *War Memoirs*, II, 252-53; Anthony Eden, *The Reckoning: The Memoirs of Anthony Eden, Earl of Avon*, 526-27; Cordell Hull, *The Memoirs of Cordell Hull*, II, 1431-32; Churchill, *Closing the Ring*, 628-30.

22. Stimson Diary, 15Jun44. See also brief of tel conv Marshall to SecWar, 15Jun-44, *SecWar File.*

23. Stimson Diary, 22Jun44; Marshall int, 29Oct56. It is not clear just when and where this meeting took place. Marshall was at Chequers for dinner on the tenth but this was before he knew of de Gaulle's action. Apparently it was on 13 or 14Jun.

24. Marshall int, 13Nov56 (author's notes).

25. Stimson Diary, 14Jun44.

26. Ibid, 15Jun44.

27. See ibid, 15 and 20Jun44, on the role of SecNavy Forrestal and AsstSecWar McCloy, perhaps at Stimson's suggestion, in influencing the publications.

28. Ibid, 20Jun44.

29. Marshall to Dill, 28Jul44, *Marshall Library Files.* In int 29Oct56 Marshall said that when de Gaulle came here, "the President ordered me to meet him."

30. Washington *Times-Herald*, 20Jun44; New York *Herald Tribune*, 20Jun44.

31. Clark, *Calculated Risk*, 380-81; Marshall int, 5Oct56 (stenographic account).

32. Marshall to Mrs Madge Brown, 23Jun-44, *Marshall Library Files.*

33. Stimson Diary, 22Jun44.

34. Mins of special mtg with Marshall and Arnold at Advanced Hqs, SACMED, 17Jun44, SAC (44) Special, *ABC 384 Europe (5Aug43), Sec 9A.*

35. Wilson int, 20Apr61.

36. Wilson to Eisenhower, B-12995, 19-Jun44; comment on CCS to Wilson and Eisenhower, OZ 3116, 15Jun44, *OPD Exec 17, Item 20;* Eisenhower to Wilson, S-53967, 16Jun44, *SHAEF SGS 370.2/2*, Opns from Mediterranean in Support of Overlord, II.

37. Kennedy, *Business of War*, 334.

38. Eisenhower to Marshall, S-54239, 20-Jun44, CM-IN 16616, *OPD Exec 17, Item 20;* Marshall to Eisenhower, W-54372, 22Jun44, *OPD 381, 1942-44, Sec XVI, Case 405.*

39. Devers to Marshall, B-13019, 20Jun44, CM-IN 16360, *OPD Exec 17, Item 20.*

40. Macmillan, *Blast of War*, 416.

41. Handwritten note on Lt Col Frank S. Henry to Chief SS, 20Jun44, Opns to Assist OVERLORD with SS 240/17, *ABC 381 SS papers, 240/11-240/24 (7Jan43).*

42. Bryant, *Triumph in the West*, entry for 23Jun44, 166.

43. Kennedy, *Business of War*, entry for 22Jun44, 332 (italics in original).

44. Bryant, *Triumph in the West*, 165.

45. Eisenhower to CCS, S-54425, 23Jun44, CM-IN 19511, *OPD Exec 17, Item 20*. "France," he insisted, "is the decisive theater."

46. The landing in southern France, Marshall emphasized, was "the only operation which provides maximum support for OVERLORD, provides the required additional major port, puts the French forces in to France and opens the way for a greater number of U.S. divisions, utilizes air buildup in Corsica and concentrates maximum forces in the decisive theater." Marshall to Eisenhower, W-55794, 24Jun44, *OPD Exec 17, Item 20*.

47. Kennedy, *Business of War*, 334.

48. Contained with text of American reply in Eisenhower to Marshall, S-54760, 29Jun44, CM-IN 24126, *OPD Exec 17, Item 20;* part of text is in Ehrman, *Grand Strategy*, VI, 351–52.

49. Eisenhower to Marshall, S-54760, 29-Jun44, *OPD Exec 17, Item 20*.

50. Marshall to Eisenhower, W-58039, W-58040, W-58041, 29Jun44, *OPD Exec 17, Item 20*.

51. Prime Minister to President, 718, 28-Jun44, *OPD Exec 10, Item 63c*.

52. Corres of 28 and 29Jun44, between President and Prime Minister is given in Marshall to Eisenhower, W-58039, W-58040, W-58041, 29Jun44, *OPD Exec 17, Item 20*. Churchill, *Triumph and Tragedy*, 721–23, gives the full text of the 29Jun44 message from the President as he received it. It must be remembered that messages sent in code were supposed to be paraphrased when sent again. For this reason I have cited the body of the text as Churchill received it from Roosevelt, but have given the text of the final two paragraphs as they were added to the WD draft at the WH. This text and the matter of authorship are given in CKG [Col Charles K. Gailey] to Handy, 30Jun44, *OPD Exec 10, Item 71*.

53. Bryant, *Triumph in the West*, 167.

54. Eisenhower to Marshall, S-54849, 1Jul-44, CM-IN 411, *OPD Exec 17, Item 20*.

55. Butcher, *My Three Years with Eisenhower*, 10Jul44, 608.

56. Churchill to Ismay, 6Jul44, Churchill, *Triumph and Tragedy*, 691–92.

57. CCS to Wilson, COSMED, 139, 2Jul44, CM-IN 1613, *OPD Exec 10, Item 52c*.

58. Eisenhower to Marshall, S-56667, 2Aug-44, *OPD Msg File*.

59. Eisenhower to Marshall, FWD-12614, 5Aug44, *OPD Msg File*.

60. Eisenhower to Marshall, 11Aug44, *Marshall Library Files*, cited Butcher, *My Three Years with Eisenhower*, 639. Mtg was on 9Aug.

61. Eisenhower to Churchill, 11Aug44. On the fifteenth Churchill wrote: "Thank you for your most kind letter of August 11." *Eisenhower Personal File*.

62. Col Richard Park to SGS, 7Aug44, giving reply of Hopkins to Prime Minister; President to Prime Minister, 596, 7Aug44; PM to President, 8Aug44, *OPD Exec 10, Item 63c*.

63. Prime Minister to Eisenhower, 4519, 18Aug44, *Eisenhower Personal File;* see Ehrman, *Grand Strategy*, VI, 363–400; Eisenhower to Wilson pass to Churchill, CPA-90240, 24Aug44, *Eisenhower Personal File*.

64. See Maurice Matloff, "The Anvil Decision: Crossroads of Strategy," in *Command Decisions*, ed Greenfield, 383–400. On the importance of Marseille to Eisenhower's supply in fall and winter 1944–45, see Roland G. Ruppenthal, *Logistical Support of the Armies*, I, 124.

65. Marshall int, 29Oct56 (author's notes).

66. Ibid.

67. Ibid, 20Nov56.

68. Chester Wilmot, *The Struggle for Europe*, chap 23.

69. Moran, *Churchill*, entry of 4Aug44, 173.

70. Field Marshal Earl Alexander, *The Alexander Memoirs, 1940–1945*, ed John North, 115–17.

71. Alanbrooke int, 5May61. In a letter to Wilson, 2Aug44, cited in Bryant, *Triumph in the West*, 191, Brooke said: "It was a great pity that we were defeated over ANVIL in the end: Alex's talk about his advance on Vienna killed all our arguments dead. It is a pity because I do not see Alex advancing on Vienna this year unless he does it in the face of a crumbling Germany, and in that case he has am-

ple forces for the task and greater than he will be able to administer over snow-covered mountain passes. However, I do not feel that ANVIL can do much harm at this stage of the

war, and it may well prove of some use in introducing French forces to reinforce the Maquis."

72. Wilson int, 20Apr61.

73. Moran, *Churchill*, 184.

XXI: THE DRIVE TOWARD GERMANY

I have drawn on Eisenhower, *Crusade in Europe;* Montgomery, *Memoirs;* MacDonald, *Siegfried Line Campaign;* and Cole, *Lorraine Campaign.*

1. Butcher, *My Three Years with Eisenhower,* 66, 614–15.

2. Marshall int, 21Nov56.

3. Butcher, *My Three Years with Eisenhower,* 622.

4. Ibid, 630–31; Pogue, *Supreme Command,* 192–93.

5. Marshall to Eisenhower, W-73221, 31-Jul44, *OPD 311.23 TS (1942-44), Case 33;* Martin Blumenson, *Breakout and Pursuit,* 197–335.

6. Craven and Cate, *Army Air Forces in World War II,* III, 596; Lewis H. Brereton, *The Brereton Diaries: The War in the Air in the Pacific, Middle East and Europe, 30 October 1941-8 May 1945,* 309, 323; Eisenhower to Marshall, S-54239, 20Jun44, *SHAEF Files;* Marshall to Eisenhower, W-56294, 26-Jun44, *SHAEF G-3 Formation of FAAA 7281/1 Airborne;* Eisenhower to Marshall, S-55192, 8Jul44, *OPD Exec 10, Item 52c.*

7. Eisenhower to Marshall, CPA-90228, 17Aug44, *OPD Msg File.*

8. See ltr, Eisenhower to Arnold, 3Sept-44, n2, *Papers of Eisenhower,* IV, 2112–13. Charles B. MacDonald, "The Decision to Launch Operation Market-Garden," in *Command Decisions,* ed Greenfield, 329–41; Charles B. MacDonald, *The Siegfried Line Campaign,* 119–39. For criticism of the withdrawal of planes from transporting gasoline for ground troops in order to prepare for a drop at Tournai, see Liddell Hart, *History of the Second World War,* 563.

9. Stories cited in Butcher, *My Three Years with Eisenhower,* 648–49; Diary Office of CinC, 19Aug44.

10. Baldwin, New York *Times,* 17Aug44.

11. Marshall to Eisenhower, W-82265, 17-Aug44, *SHAEF Files.*

12. Eisenhower to Marshall, CPA-90230, 19Aug44, *SHAEF Files.* In his *Memoirs,* 228, Montgomery wrote: "I never

once had cause or reason to alter my master plan."

13. Eisenhower to Marshall, 24Aug44, *OPD Exec 9, Bk 22.*

14. Mrs Theodore Roosevelt, Jr, *Day Before Yesterday: The Reminiscences of Mrs. Theodore Roosevelt,* 450–51; Marshall ints, 28Sept56 and 11Apr57.

15. Stimson Diary, 21Aug44.

16. Marshall to Mrs Lesley J. McNair, 26-Jul44, *Marshall Library Files.*

17. Draft of Remarks for CofS at Ceremony Honoring Gen McNair—apparently 25May45, at Army War College —accepting plaque in honor of Gen McNair. The legend on the plaque read: "To commemorate the quiet thoroughness of this outstanding soldier"; *Marshall Library Files.*

18. Devers to Marshall, 1Jul44; Marshall to Devers, WX-66124, 16Jul44; Eisenhower to Marshall, 12Jul44, *Marshall Library Files;* Pogue, *Supreme Command,* 229.

19. Marshall int, 4Feb57. The Patton argument can be followed in Gen George S. Patton, *War as I Knew It;* Robert Allen, *Lucky Forward;* Ingersoll, *Top Secret;* Farago, *Patton;* and, more recently, in Liddell Hart, *History of the Second World War.* Montgomery's position is stated in his *Memoirs* and is supported by Alanbrooke in Bryant's *Triumph in the West.* The Eisenhower position on the broad-front versus narrow-front argument may be found in his *Crusade in Europe;* Stephen Ambrose, *Supreme Commander,* and his essay in *Papers of Eisenhower,* V, 39–48; Lt Gen Sir Francis de Guingand, *Operation Victory.* Also see Pogue, *Supreme Command,* and Ruppenthal, *Logistical Support of the Armies,* I. For a good statement on why Eisenhower could not deprive Bradley and Patton of their share in the ad-

vance, see Ehrman, *Grand Strategy,*
V, 380–81.

20. Butcher, *My Three Years with Eisenhower,* 638–39.

21. I have drawn on the convenient sum-
maries of Liddell Hart, *History of the
Second World War,* chap 32, and
Ziemke, *Stalingrad to Berlin.*

22. Fenard to Marshall, 23Aug44, *Marshall Library Files.*

23. Marshall to Fenard, 30Aug44, *Marshall Library Files.*

24. Pasco to Marshall, 19 and 22Aug44,
Sexton Papers. Arnold, *Global Mission,* 522–23. Gen and Mrs Marshall
had also visited former Amb and Mrs
Joseph Davies at their Adirondacks
lodge, Camp Topridge, in New York,
9–15Aug.

25. Pasco to Marshall, 19 and 21Aug44,
Sexton Papers.

26. Arnold, *Global Mission,* 523.

27. Ziemke, *Stalingrad to Berlin,* 340, 344–
45; Arnold, *Global Mission,* 524–25.

28. Marshall to Hopkins, 18Aug44, *Marshall Library Files.*

29. Mins CCS 172d mtg, 12Sept44, 12:00,
Octagon Conf Bk, Sept44, 191.

30. Ibid. See also Webster and Frankland,
*Strategic Air Offensive Against Ger-
many,* III, 65–68.

31. Lord Tedder, *With Prejudice,* 602–
606, 611–12.

32. Bryant, *Triumph in the West,* 219.

33. Mins CCS 172d mtg, 12Sept44, 12:00,
Octagon Conf Bk, 193.

34. Ibid, 195.

35. Mins CCS 1st Plenary Session, 13Sept-
44, 11:45 am, *Octagon Conf Bk,* 236–
37.

36. Bryant, *Triumph in the West,* 204.

XXII: ROADS TO TOKYO

For valuable sources see notes 19 and 21. I interviewed Adm Nimitz and Robert Sherrod for this chapter.

1. Marshall to MacArthur, 23Dec43, *Marshall Library Files.*

2. Marshall to MacArthur, 30Dec43; Adm
Richard S. Edwards to Marshall, 4Jan-
44, indicated that the carrier would be
available within a few days, *Marshall
Library Files.*

3. See sources cited Matloff, *Strategic
Planning, 1943–1944,* 456, n 12; and
MacArthur to Marshall, 2Feb44, CM-IN
1443, *OPD Msg File.*

4. Stimson Diary, 17Feb44.

5. MacArthur through Osborn to Stimson, 21Jan44, included with Stimson
Diary entry of 18Feb44. A copy of the
remarks MacArthur asked Osborn to
convey was given to Marshall by Osborn.

6. MacArthur to Marshall, 27Feb44, *Marshall Library Files.*

7. See similar episode in Pogue, *Ordeal
and Hope,* 378.

8. Marshall to MacArthur, 9Mar44, *Marshall Library Files.*

9. Marshall to MacArthur, 19Mar44, *Marshall Library Files.*

10. JCS to MacArthur and Nimitz, 12Mar-
44, CM-IN 5137, *OPD Msg File,* cited
Matloff, *Strategic Planning, 1943–1944,*
458–59.

11. Marshall to MacArthur, 8Jun44, *Marshall Library Files.*

12. MacArthur to Marshall, 18Jun44, *Marshall Library Files.*

13. Stimson Diary, 22Jun44.

14. Marshall to MacArthur, 24Jun44, *Marshall Library Files.*

15. Vandenberg, *Private Papers,* 83–84.

16. *Time,* 24Apr44.

17. Vandenberg, *Private Papers,* 85; *Time,*
24Apr44.

18. Vandenberg, *Private Papers,* 84–86.

19. For the basic account of the Marianas
story, see Samuel E. Morison, *New
Guinea and the Marianas;* Philip A.
Crowl, *Campaign in the Marianas;*
King and Whitehill, *Fleet Admiral
King;* Robert D. Heinl, *Soldiers of the
Sea: The U.S. Marine Corps, 1775–
1962.*

20. Morison, *New Guinea and the Marianas,* 339–40.

21. I have relied heavily on Crowl, *Campaign in the Marianas,* chap 10, for
treatment of this controversy. Crowl, a
naval officer in the Pacific in World
War II, was co-author with J. A. Isely
of *The U.S. Marines And Amphibious
Warfare.* His account is judicious and
well balanced and is considered fair by
the Navy, Army, and Marine Corps

historians. I am indebted to Robert
Sherrod for detailed newspaper coverage of the whole controversy and for
some of the principal items of correspondence. In defending his articles,
he got a number of pertinent documents from the Navy Department. The
original collection, now at Syracuse
University, was sent to me for copy-
ing at Sherrod's request. For his articles see "Saipan," *Life*, 28Aug44,
and "Command, The Generals Smith,"
Time, 18Sept44.

22. Nimitz to King, 27Oct44, *WDCSA
000.7, 1944–45*.
23. King to Marshall, 6Nov44, *WDCSA
000.7, 1944–45*.
24. Marshall to King, 22Nov44, *WDCSA
000.7, 1944–45*.
25. King to Marshall, 23Nov44, *WDCSA
000.7, 1944–45*.
26. Nimitz int, Nov60, said Marshall came
to see him a month or so after the
events on Saipan and declared that he
would never let soldiers serve again
under a Marine. Nimitz said that he
had never seen Marshall so exercised
While I do not question the possibility that Marshall may have had such
a feeling, it is a little difficult to resolve the time sequence. Although
Nimitz saw King on several occasions
in the summer and fall of 1944, when
King either met him in California or

flew out to the Pacific, it seems unlikely that he and Marshall saw each
other until early 1945, when Nimitz
appeared before the Joint Chiefs of
Staff in Washington. Marshall's only
visit to Nimitz's headquarters in the
Pacific was in Dec43 on his return
from the Cairo conference. It is worth
noting Nimitz's opinion of Marshall as
stated in 1960: "From the time I first
saw Marshall [in 1939], I thought he
was an able, distinguished man of
high moral integrity who would do
nothing he should not do. I never had
reason to change my mind."

27. Matloff, *Strategic Planning, 1943–1944*,
480–81.
28. See accounts by Leahy, *I Was There*,
246–49ff; King and Whitehill, *Fleet
Admiral King*, 566.
29. Nimitz int, Nov60.
30. MacArthur to King, with information
copy to Marshall, 5Aug44, *OPD 201,
MacArthur, (1942–44), Case 1*. Pasco
to Marshall, 15Aug44, ibid, said that
the copies had been brought from
Southwest Pacific by Col William L.
Ritchie for Marshall, King, and Leahy.
31. Marshall to MacArthur, 21Aug44;
Pasco to Marshall, 21Aug44; Mac-
Arthur to Marshall, 30Aug44, *OPD
384 TS (1942–44), Case 53*.
32. *Biennial Report of Chief of Staff of
US Army, July 1, 1943 to June 30,
1945 to the SecWar*, 71.

XXIII: SOLDIERS AS GOVERNORS

I have relied heavily on Coles and Weinberg, *Civil Affairs: Soldiers Become Governors;*
William Franklin, "Zonal Boundaries and Access to Berlin," *World Politics*, Oct 1963;
Matloff, *Strategic Planning for Coalition Warfare, 1943–1944; US For Rels, 1944*, I.

1. Coles and Weinberg, *Civil Affairs*.
2. Marshall int, 14Feb57.
3. Stimson Diary, 4Nov42.
4. Marshall int, 14Feb57. See ltr from
Maj Gen Julius Klein to author, 19-
Feb70, *Marshall Library Files*.
5. Marshall int, 14Feb57.
6. Stimson Diary, 6Nov42.
7. For background on this and other
early developments pertaining to the
school and CAD, see Coles and Weinberg, *Civil Affairs*, 3–69, and Cline,
Washington Command Post, 320–27.
8. Hilldring int, 30Mar59. The words
are Hilldring's summary of Marshall's
views.

9. Ibid. Only the statement that "we are
a priesthood" sounds unlike the language that Marshall used at other
times in speeches or testimony. Hilldring also quoted a story told him by
Roosevelt illustrating that MacArthur
in the 1930s shared this viewpoint.
The President said that when he first
asked MacArthur to take over the task
of organizing the Civilian Conservation Corps, Gen MacArthur replied
that he couldn't do it, since it was not
a task concerned with the defense of
the country. Roosevelt was at first irritated but he remarked to Hilldring
that on thinking it over that evening

he was pleased. "He said, I guess I must admit, as much as I was disturbed that morning, that if the Chief of Staff of the Army is so devoted to keeping the Army out of anything that smatters even slightly of a political activity and he feels this so strongly that he will defy the Commander-in-Chief, we've got something in the noodles of our professional soldiers that's good for the country. So I absolved MacArthur from culpability here. I didn't change my mind about wanting him to do it and insisting that he would do it, but I did get some vicarious satisfaction out of his behavior that morning. . . ." For MacArthur's views on the value to the Army of the CCC experience, see Pogue, Education of a General, 279.

10. Marshall to Stettinius, 13Jul44, Marshall Library Files. Marshall was an old friend of Stettinius and addressed this letter to "Ed." He also suggested that it might be best to keep the letter out of the records.

11. Stettinius to Marshall, 14Jul44, Marshall Library Files.

12. McCloy to Marshall, 15Jul44, Marshall Library Files.

13. For the best treatment of the question of zone boundaries, see William Franklin, "Zonal Boundaries and Access to Berlin," World Politics, Oct63, 1–31. See also Philip E. Mosely, "The Occupation of Germany: New Light on How the Zones Were Drawn," Foreign Affairs, Jul50, 580–604.

14. See folder in National Archives, OPD Exec 2, Item 11. The initial notes kept by the recorder are confusing. They indicate that Roosevelt said that Berlin was to be in the US zone. However this does not coincide with the map on which Roosevelt drew his lines and is contradicted by the instructions transmitted by the President. Moreover, within a few days Roosevelt had a chance to pass on the correctness of the instructions as recalled by Marshall. They appeared in a CCS paper, 320/4 (Rev), 4Dec43, incorporating Roosevelt's instructions as Marshall and Handy understood them, which the COSSAC staff was asked to examine. The map marked by Roosevelt was reprinted in Matloff's Strategic Planning, 1943–1944, 341, which ap-

peared in 1959, and reference is made to it, together with the pertinent papers regarding it, in US For Rels, Cairo-Tehran, 261, 786–87. It was reproduced, along with a sketch map—which corresponds with a later map put out by the State Department based on Boundaries referred to in CCS 320/4(Rev)—in 1966 in Cornelius Ryan's The Last Battle, facing 162. Cf similar sketch map in US For Rels 1944, I, facing 196, which also appeared in 1966. In his written account Ryan carefully handles the contradictory statements about whether the United States should or should not have Berlin. However his editors in their captions for the maps declared (162–63): "Roosevelt's desire to have Berlin for the United States was clearly evident from the lines he drew on the National Geographic map. . . ." The original Roosevelt map obviously shows no such thing. This statement is followed by another editorial comment: "Military minds prevailed and one of the plans that was substituted for FDR's was the one below—notice that Berlin is no longer included in the projected American zone. . . ." In fact it is similar to the State Department map, which attempted to indicate what Roosevelt had asked for. A crude sketch map, not reproduced, that accompanied Handy's instructions also shows Berlin east of the line. It seems likely that a hasty reading of this sketch, a crude overlay of the Roosevelt map, resulted in the inclusion of Cottbus, the exclusion of Berlin, and the failure to touch the Czech border. The later and neater sketch map follows the boundaries noted in Handy's memo of 19Nov and CCS 320/4(Rev), 4Dec43. Clearly if the United States Army changed Mr. Roosevelt's plans it was between 19Nov43 and 4Dec43, while the conference was in progress, and not weeks later in the Pentagon. A copy of the initial notes by the recorder, obviously not a stenographer, is included with the Handy memo and the short handwritten notes kept by Marshall. The initial record shows some blanks and some words, with question marks, that are almost nonsensical. In the final "official" version some of these blanks are filled in with what seem to be correct words; others are omitted entirely. It is this version that says Roosevelt wanted Berlin for the United States, although the map marked by the President does not do so and Marshall's instructions to Handy definitely say that Berlin is to be jointly occupied. Since the Handy version was available for Roosevelt's later scrutiny (in an official paper submitted the morning after Roosevelt had discussed the boundaries with Churchill), I am inclined to conclude that the Marshall version is correct.

15. Ryan, *Last Battle*, 149.
16. See *US For Rels, Cairo-Tehran*, 879–88, for pertinent information.
17. George F. Kennan, *Memoirs, 1925–1950*, 166–71.
18. Eisenhower, *Crusade in Europe*, 218–19; Eisenhower, *At Ease: Stories I Tell to Friends*, 267–68; Henry Luce, "To Ike, the Wall Rises between Opposing Ideas of Man," *Life*, 8Sept61, 46–49. In a conference with his policy advisers at the Brown Palace Hotel in Denver, Colorado, 29Jul52, Eisenhower mentioned pleading with President Roosevelt in Jan44 not to divide Germany. If the Russians insisted on having their area, he recommended that the Western Allies keep their part as a unit. This statement is in line with his *Crusade in Europe* statement. Copy of the conference remarks furnished author 13May71 by Dr Walter Judd, one of the advisers present. Cf article in *U.S. News & World Report*, 25Jan71, based on this transcript.
19. Eisenhower to Marshall, 15Feb44, *OPD Exec 9, Bk 15*.
20. Franklin, "Zonal Boundaries and Access to Berlin," *World Politics*, Oct63, 1–31; *US For Rels, Malta-Yalta*, 117–21, 127, 174, 956.
21. *US For Rels, Malta-Yalta*, 117–21, 127, 174, 956. At Yalta a decision was made to allocate a zone carved out of the areas assigned to the Western Allies. Marshall commented in 1956: "The occupation zones were an irritant to Churchill and a puzzle to me. . . . The boundaries were set in London. We thought the Russians would take Berlin before we could get there. Never entered our minds that we could get

to Berlin ahead of them." Marshall int, 14Nov56 (author's notes).
22. For excellent summary see Paul Y. Hammond, "Directives for the Occupation of Germany: The Washington Controversy," in *American Civil-Military Decisions; A Book of Case Studies*, ed Harold Stein, 311–464.
23. John Blum, ed, *From the Diaries of Henry Morgenthau, Jr.*, III, 328. Cantril, *Public Opinion, 1935–1946*, 1141. In Britain two-thirds of those expressing an opinion favored the permanent separation of the Ruhr, and more than half wanted Germany to be split into several states. A popular book of the period, *The Black Record of Germany, Past, Present, and Future*, by Sir Robert Vansittart, for many years Permanent Under Secretary of State for Foreign Affairs, called for "the defeat, demilitarisation, occupation, re-education of Germany" to create "a prosperous but not powerful Germany. . . . A full life and a full larder, but keep their arsenals empty." Preface, ix.
24. Pogue, *Supreme Command*, 353–58.
25. Blum, *Morgenthau Diaries*, III, 343–69.
26. Stimson Diary, 4Sept44.
27. Ibid, 5Sept44.
28. Ibid, 6Sept44.
29. Ibid, 7Sept44. Stimson in his Diary entry of 9Oct44 noted that the British ambassador, Lord Halifax, said that perhaps the best way to handle Nazi criminals was to shoot them without a trial.
30. Ibid, 9 and 11Sept44.
31. Ibid, 14Sept44.
32. Ibid, 16 and 17Sept44.
33. Eden, *Reckoning*, 552; Stimson Diary, 20Sept44.
34. Moran, *Churchill*, 193–95.
35. He also passed on Acheson's comment that Stimson's two memos were "remarkable examples of his rugged common sense and courage." Acheson to Marshall, 28May47; Marshall to Stimson, 30May47; note indicating Marshall wrote Stimson for permission to use them on 28Apr47, *Marshall Library Files*. The documents were made available to Marshall by Dr Rudolph Winnacker, Historian, Dept of Defense.

XXIV: VICTORY DEFERRED

I have interviews on this period with Gens Eisenhower, Bradley, Ridgway, Taylor, and Carter Clarke, Lady Mary Burghley, Lady Dill, Maj MacDonald-Buchanan.

1. See Pogue, *Ordeal and Hope,* app I.
2. Speech by Rep Forest A. Harness, *Cong Record,* 78th Cong, 2d sess, 11-Sept44, XC, pt 6, 7648–51. See also speech, ibid, 18Sept44, 7866–68.
3. *Pearl Harbor Attack Hearings,* 1132ff.
4. Ibid.
5. Marshall to Dewey, 27Sept44 (2d ltr), *Pearl Harbor Attack Hearings,* pt 3, 1132–33. Also see following pages for discussion of circumstances surrounding the letter. The second letter added: "A further most serious embarrassment is the fact that the British Government is involved concerning its most secret sources of information, regarding which only the Prime Minister, the Chiefs of Staff and a very limited number of other officials have knowledge." Marshall omitted from the last quoted paragraph the following: "I might add that the recent action of Congress in requiring Army and Navy investigations for action before certain dates has compelled me to bring back the Corps commander, General Gerow, whose troops are fighting at Trier, to testify here while the Germans are counterattacking his forces there. This, however, is a very minor matter compared to the loss of our code information."
6. Marshall testified in Dec45 that after the election, he sent Maj Gen Clayton Bissell, G-2, to Albany to show Dewey intercepted messages and the use made of them. He later invited him to the Pentagon to see other material, ibid, 1136–37.
7. Marshall to Truman, 22Sept45, *Marshall Library Files.*
8. Truman to Marshall, 24Sept45, *Marshall Library Files.*
9. *Life,* 17Dec45, 20, has edited text. See reprint of this version in Allen W. Dulles, *Great True Spy Stories,* 285–89.
10. Chester G. Starr, *From Salerno to the Alps,* 165, 305–306, 332; Ehrman, *Grand Strategy,* VI, 37–39.
11. Ehrman, *Grand Strategy,* VI, 47–48.
12. Ibid, 48–50; Leahy to President, 14-Oct44, sends draft of President to Prime Minister, replying to 793, *OPD Exec 10, Item 63c.*
13. James F. Byrnes, *All in One Lifetime,* 244. See folder Trips-France, 5–14Oct-44, *Marshall Library Files;* Handy int, 14Jul70.
14. Patton, *War as I Knew It,* 148.
15. Ltr Bradley to author, 6May68.
16. Montgomery, *Memoirs,* 254.
17. Marshall int, 15Nov56.
18. Lucian K. Truscott, *Command Missions: A Personal Story,* 439.
19. Jean de Lattre de Tassigny, *The History of the French First Army,* 194–95; Marshall int, 15Nov56; Handy int, 14-Jul70.
20. Marshall int, 15Nov56.
21. Ltr Maj Gen Paul Baade to Hist Div, 3Dec44, *After Action Reports 35th Div, Record Group 407, National Archives;* Baade to Marshall, 30Oct44; McCarthy to Pasco, 9, 11, and 12Oct-44; Marshall to CG 1st Army Hodges, 12Oct44; Marshall to CG V Corps Gerow, 12Oct44; Marshall to Eisenhower, 16Oct44, *Marshall Library Files;* Patton, *War as I Knew It,* 151.
22. Marshall to Mrs Patton, 25Oct44. This was actually in reply to Mrs Patton's letter of thanks for a telegram that Pasco had sent her at Marshall's request. See also Marshall to Mrs Eisenhower, 24Oct44, *Marshall Library Files.* As noted earlier, Marshall called few people by their first names. See my *Ordeal and Hope,* 476, n 50, where Eisenhower says he thinks he called him Ike only once.
23. Marshall to McCoy, 17Oct44, *Marshall Library Files.*
24. Marshall to Eisenhower, 16Oct44, *Marshall Library Files.* According to Stimson, Marshall considered Devers under some strain and not quite as much in command of his situation as Eisenhower clearly was. Marshall had spent a lot of time with Bradley, "whom he always thinks highly of." Stimson Diary, 16Oct44.
25. Stimson Diary, 3Nov44.
26. Marshall to Handy and Hull, 20Oct-

44, *OPD 381 TS (1942–44), Sec XVIII, Case 538/2;* Marshall to Eisenhower, W-50676, 22Oct44, *OPD 370.5 TS (1942–44), Sec XV, Case 520/8;* draft of directive to Eisenhower and others, SS 316, 20Oct44, *ABC 381 SS Papers (7Jan43), Nos. 314–326;* Pogue, *Supreme Command,* 307.

27. Eisenhower to Marshall, S-63616, 23-Oct44, *Papers of Eisenhower,* IV, 2247–49 (the long note to this cable summarizes in particular the discussions about air). For lengthy footnote on recommendations of planners, British Chief of Staff action, and Marshall's order to delay action, see Pogue, *Supreme Command,* 308, n 10.

28. Eisenhower to Marshall, S-63259, 21-Oct44, CM-IN 19569, *OPD Msg File.*

29. These involved ammunition for 8-inch guns and howitzers; 240-mm. howitzers; 155-mm. guns and howitzers; 105-mm. howitzers; and 81-mm. mortars.

30. Marshall to Eisenhower, W-50677, 22-Oct44, *Marshall Library Files.* To deal with this problem Eisenhower urged that Maj Gen Lucius Clay, then director of materiel for Gen Somervell's command, be sent temporarily to take charge of the port of Cherbourg.

31. Marshall to Eisenhower, WAR 51862, 25Oct44, *OPD Msg File;* Eisenhower to Marshall, S-63616, 23Oct44; Eisenhower to Marshall, S-64077, 26Oct44, *SHAEF Files.*

32. Eisenhower to Marshall, S-67807, 22-Nov44, *WDCSA 471 TS (1944–45), Case 4.*

33. Churchill to Roosevelt, 844, 6Dec44; Roosevelt to Churchill, 672, 9Dec44.

Leahy had forwarded the Churchill message to Marshall and King for response. A note on message 672 indicates that it was sent to Churchill as corrected by Marshall, *OPD Exec 10, Item 63c, Pt 2.*

34. Marshall to Stark, 8Dec44, *Marshall Library Files.*

35. Moran, *Churchill,* 189–90.

36. Stimson Diary, 4 and 9Nov44.

37. See Dill file in Marshall papers on last illness, funeral, and statue and Robert Woods Bliss correspondence.

38. Churchill to Marshall, OZ-6528, 5Nov-44, *Marshall Library Files.*

39. Marshall to Churchill, 7Nov44, *Marshall Library Files.*

40. Marshall to Lady Burghley, 16Dec44, *Marshall Library Files.*

41. Lady Dill to Marshall, 22Dec44 and 10Jan45, *Marshall Library Files.*

42. Marshall int, 11Feb57.

43. Stimson Diary, 13 and 14Sept44.

44. Although four five-star admirals were authorized, the Navy decided to postpone naming Adm Halsey for the moment. He was appointed Fleet Adm 4Dec45. Gen Bradley was made General of the Army as of 18Sept50.

45. Stimson Diary, 28Nov, 12 and 15Dec-44; *Cong Record,* 78th Cong, 2d sess, 15Dec44, XC, pt 7, 9527.

46. Stimson Diary, 13Nov44; *Cong Record,* 78th Cong, 2d sess, 5Dec44, XC, pt 7, HR 5493, 8837; 28Nov44, XC, pt 6, S 2192, 8501.

47. Marshall's G-2 Division reported to him on 12Dec44 the following regarding the strength of Allied armies on various fronts:

Western—	43 div	1,776,360 on	256 mile front (American)
	8 div	277,184 on	315 mile front (French)
	15 div	on	195 mile front (British and others)
Italian	6 div	on	70 mile front (American)
	15 div	on	113 mile front (British and others)
Dalmatian	9–10 div	30,000 on	340 mile front (Yugoslav partisans)
Russian	440 div	3,500,000 on	1450 mile front (Russians)
	12 div	140,000 on	100 mile front (Rumanians)
	7 div	21,000	(Yugoslavs)

DCofS G-2 Brig Gen John Weckerling to Marshall, 12Dec44, *Marshall Library Files.*

48. Pogue, *Supreme Command,* chap 20, 359–72.

49. Hugh M. Cole, *The Ardennes: Battle of the Bulge,* 80–102.

50. Stimson Diary, 18 and 19Dec44.

51. Marshall to Eisenhower, W-81088, 22-Dec44, *Marshall Library Files;* Marshall int, 14Nov56 (author's notes).

52. Of his talks with Marshall, Taylor wrote Ridgway on 17Jan45, "Everyone in Washington appeared pleased over

the conduct of Airborne troops in battle. However, General Marshall is emphatic in speaking about the 'timidity' of our planning. His idea of the proper Airborne operation is to seize an air head and then pour in large quantities of troops. He is plainly impressed with the use of Airborne troops in the

Southwest [Pacific]. I pointed out some of the difficulties in such an operation in Europe, but I am not sure he was listening. He damned without stint the Montgomery 'Carpet' in Holland."

53. Marshall to Eisenhower, W-84337, 30-Dec44, *Marshall Library Files.*

XXV: CRISIS IN MANPOWER

I relied heavily on Fairchild and Grossman, *Army and Industrial Manpower;* Lee, *Employment of Negro Troops;* Palmer and others, *Procurement and Training of Ground Combat Troops;* Tedder, *With Prejudice;* Churchill, *Triumph and Tragedy.* Interviews included those with Gens Lewis Hershey, Walter Bedell Smith, Ben Lear.

1. Stimson Diary, 21 and 28Dec44. See draft of statement for Stimson.
2. Philadelphia *Record,* 23Dec44.
3. Washington *Star,* 28Dec44.
4. Somervell to Marshall, n.d. but after 28Dec44, forwarding memo, n.d., no signature; note at top: "To accompany Mr. Stimson's weekly war review of last Thursday," BPR War Review by SecWar at Press Conference, 28Dec44, *Marshall Library Files.*
5. Ibid; note attached to Somervell to Marshall, n.d. but after 28Dec44, *Marshall Library Files.*
6. Somervell to Marshall, 30Dec44, *Marshall Library Files.*
7. WD press release, 12Dec44; Somervell to Marshall, 30Dec44, *Marshall Library Files.*
8. Stimson Diary, 15Jan45.
9. *Biennial Report of the Chief of Staff of the US Army, July 1, 1943 to June 30, 1945 to the Secretary of War,* 103–104.
10. Marshall concurred with Stimson on Wilbur's power and directness but feared that the appointment of "a [combat] soldier would antagonize Congress." Stimson Diary, 27Dec44.
11. Hershey made his case clear in Oct45, when he was shown a copy of Gen Marshall's final report containing the statement on "shortages in deliveries of inductees" cited above. The Selective Service head protested vigorously to the Chief of Staff. In addition to detailing Army changes in policy during the early part of 1943, he spelled out problems that arose later that year. He suggested that Army physical and mental standards had been set unreasonably high in the July–September

period, when 420,000 men out of 1,189,000 delivered by Selective Service to induction stations had been rejected. Of these 175,000 had been turned down for mental reasons unaccompanied by organic disability and "100,000 were neurotics of a type not identified normally in civilian life." In this case Hershey was alluding to the retention of Army peacetime standards, when conditions such as overweight and underweight, poor but correctible vision, tendency to bedwetting, and mental disturbances accounted for a significant number of rejections. Hershey to Marshall, n.d. but received in G-1 from Marshall, 1Oct45, *Marshall Library Files.* Hershey emphasized that sudden shifts in Army policy resulting from political pressures and momentary needs led to sudden stops in induction calls. He noted, for example, successful Air Forces efforts to reduce the recruitment from the states of Oregon, Washington, and California, when aircraft plants there needed men. Despite Hershey's complaints that part of Marshall's report gave a misleading picture, the Chief of Staff decided to let it stand. For the whole affair, see Hershey to Marshall, n.d. but received in G-1 from Marshall, 1Oct45; draft reply of 3Oct45 for Marshall's signature (not sent); advice of Surles to send no detailed reply, in Surles to Pasco, 5Oct45; and finally the reply, saying that "The fact they occurred and their effect on operations were sufficient for a factual recital of the military events as they happened," Marshall to Hershey, 8Oct45 (not sent), *Marshall Library Files.*

12. Stimson Diary, 31Dec44.

13. Ibid, 1 and 2Jan45.

14. It is difficult to arrive at an accurate figure for fighting and nonfighting men. Apparently Marshall and his staff in referring to supply personnel actually meant those at ports and bases. Every combat division had personnel engaged in housekeeping and supply activities. Lt Col John B. Morgan to Pasco, 2Jan45; Marshall to SecWar, 2Jan45; Pasco for Marshall to SecWar, 3Jan45; extract from SecWar's notes on mtg with President after cabinet mtg, 5Jan45, *Marshall Library Files.*

15. Pasco to Stimson, 5Jan45, *Marshall Library Files.* He ultimately had sixty-one.

16. Marshall int, 5Oct56, stenographic notes by Miss Mary L. Spilman; Stimson Diary, 4Jan45.

17. Stimson Diary, 27Dec44, 4Jan45.

18. Ibid, 4Jan45.

19. Marshall int, 5Oct56.

20. Stimson Diary, 9Jan45; Marshall int, 5Oct56.

21. Marshall int, 5Oct56.

22. Stimson Diary, 6Jan45; *Time,* 15Jan45. State of Union msg, *Cong Record,* 79th Cong, 1st sess, 6Jan45, XCI, pt 1, 91–96.

23. Fairchild and Grossman, *Army and Industrial Manpower,* 239.

24. Stimson Diary, 10Jan45.

25. Ibid, 19Jan45.

26. Ibid, 15Jan45.

27. Ltr President to Chmn House Mil Affs Comm, 17Jan45, enc Marshall and King to President, 16Jan45, in *Mobilization of Civilian Manpower, Hearings on H.R. 1119,* 79th Cong, 1st sess, 18-Jan45, 436–37; *Time,* 29Jan45; Stimson Diary, 16 and 17Jan45; Fairchild and Grossman, *Army and Industrial Manpower,* 240.

28. Stimson Diary, 23Jan45.

29. Ibid, 24Jan45.

30. Fairchild and Grossman, *Army and Industrial Manpower,* 240–41.

31. *Time,* 5 and 19Feb45.

32. Stimson Diary, 17Feb45.

33. Fairchild and Grossman, *Army and Industrial Manpower,* 241.

34. *Time,* 5Mar45; Stimson Diary, 22Feb-45.

35. Fairchild and Grossman, *Army and Industrial Manpower,* 244; see Stimson Diary entries for late February and March.

36. Marshall to Eisenhower, W-87829, 6Jan45, *Marshall Library Files.*

37. Marshall to Eisenhower, W-88777, 7Jan45, *Marshall Library Files.*

38. Eisenhower to Marshall, S-74291, 9Jan-45, *Marshall Library Files;* Marshall ints, 13Nov56 and 14Feb57; Lear int, 9May57.

39. Eisenhower to Marshall, S-74003, 7Jan-45, *SHAEF Files.*

40. Ulysses G. Lee, *Employment of Negro Troops,* 636–43.

41. Palmer, Wiley, and Keast, *Procurement and Training of Ground Combat Troops,* 14, 71–72, 202–203.

42. Reckord to Somervell, 15Jun43, *AG 353 (15Jun43).* "File Jul 26 1943" is stamped on the document.

43. ACofS G-3 Brig Gen Ray E. Porter to McNair, 13Jun43; AGF to CofS, 25Jun-43, *AG 353 (15Jun43).*

44. Marshall to McNair, 3Sept43, *AG 353.*

45. McNair to Marshall, 6Sept43, *AG 353.*

46. Eisenhower to Marshall, W-8706, 28-Dec43, CM-IN 17276, *OPD Msg File;* Palmer, Wiley, and Keast, *Procurement and Training of Ground Combat Troops,* 203–204.

47. Palmer, Wiley, and Keast, *Procurement and Training of Ground Combat Troops,* 204–19.

48. See attack on War Department by Sen Robert Taft, *Cong Record,* 79th Cong, 1st sess, 27Feb45, XCI, pt 2, 1475–77. See also memo by Brig Gen W. W. Irvin, 25Jan45; memo by Maj Gen I. H. Edwards, 3Mar45; Edwards to CofS 10Mar45.

49. Eisenhower to Marshall, 5Dec44, *OPD Exec 9, Bk 24;* Mil Mission Moscow Deane to JCS, M-22052, 17Dec44, CM-IN 16815, *OPD Msg File.*

50. Eisenhower to CCS, repeat to Br CsofS, SCAF 155, 21Dec44, *OPD Msg File.*

51. Marshall to Eisenhower, WX-82070, 25Dec44; *OPD 381 TS (1942–44), Sec XXI, Case 604;* CCS to Eisenhower, WARX-82144, 26Dec44, *OPD Msg File;* Pogue, *Supreme Command,* 406–407.

52. Marshall to Eisenhower, WX-82070, 25Dec44, *OPD 381 TS (1942–44), Sec XXI, Case 604.* Deane to Marshall, MX-22154, 25Dec44, *OPD Msg File,* makes clear that Stalin meant Devers's group

rather than Clark's in this last reference and that the reference was made only casually.

53. CCS to Eisenhower, FACS 119, 29Dec-44, *OPD Msg File.*

54. Tedder, *With Prejudice,* 642–43; Churchill, *Triumph and Tragedy,* 279.

55. Stalin to Churchill, 7Jan45; see also Churchill to Stalin, 9Jan45, *Triumph and Tragedy,* 279–80.

56. See Tedder, *With Prejudice,* 641–54; A. H. Birse, *Memoirs of an Interpreter,*

176–77; Tedder int, 13Feb47; Bull int, 27May59; Betts int, 18May50.

57. See my essay "The Struggle for a New Order," in *The Meaning of Yalta,* ed John L. Snell; Herbert Feis, *Churchill —Roosevelt—Stalin: The War They Waged, and The Peace They Sought,* 489–558; John S. D. Eisenhower, *The Bitter Woods,* 425; Marshal Georgei K. Zhukov, *Marshal Zhukov's Greatest Battles,* ed Harrison E. Salisbury, 267–90.

XXVI: THE GREAT MYTH

The most complete diplomatic and military records are contained in *US For Rels, Malta-Yalta.* My initial notes on the two conferences were taken from Marshall's own copy of the proceedings. Later, in 1955, I used galley proofs of the State Department volume, while writing three of the six chapters of *The Meaning of Yalta,* edited by John L. Snell, which contains many of my conclusions on the conference that space does not permit me to review here. Edward R. Stettinius, Jr, *Roosevelt and the Russians,* is based on the Secretary of State's papers and notes at the conference. James F. Byrnes, in *Speaking Frankly* and *All in One Lifetime,* provides his recollections. Gen Laurence Kuter, *Airman at Yalta,* gives the recollections of the chief airman in the American military delegation. Leahy's and King's memoirs contain pertinent information on their experiences. Athan G. Theoharis, *The Yalta Myths: An Issue in U.S. Politics, 1945–1955,* is an interesting study of public opinion and political discussion of the Yalta controversy. Diane S. Clemens's *Yalta* takes a revisionist view of the conference. I have interview material on this chapter from Gens Marshall, Hull, Kuter, Smith, Ismay, Deane, and McCarthy; Adms Leahy, King, and Cunningham; Field Marshal Alanbrooke; Marshal of the Royal Air Force Portal, and Amb Bohlen. I also talked with Gen Groves concerning the information available at that time about the atomic bomb. This chapter was read by Gen John E. Hull, Chief of the Operations Division in 1945, who was Gen Marshall's primary adviser on plans and operations at Yalta.

1. Frederick L. Allen, "Marshall, Arnold, King: Three Snapshots," *Harper's Magazine,* Feb45, 287.

2. The clock, pictures, a desk and table of the same design, and the flags are in the Marshall Library, Lexington, Va.

3. Allen, "Marshall, Arnold, King," *Harper's Magazine,* Feb45, 287.

4. Edward R. Stettinius, Jr, *Roosevelt and the Russians,* 33–35.

5. Groves to Marshall, 30Dec44, *US For Rels, Malta-Yalta,* 383–84.

6. Churchill to Roosevelt, 1Jan45, Churchill, *Triumph and Tragedy,* 338; *US For Rels, Malta-Yalta,* 460.

7. Marshall int, 20Nov56.

8. Eisenhower to Marshall, S-75090, 15-Jan45, *OPD Msg File* (italics in original). The basic memo was prepared by Brig Gen Arthur S. Nevins, Chief of the Operations Staff (G-3). Eisen-

hower in a memo to Nevins 14Jan45 indicated: "I have changed your memorandum, also, to discuss only the difference between an ineffectual Russian offensive and a strong and sustained one." In counting divisions he had estimated 61 United States divisions, including 4 airborne; 16 British, including 2 airborne, and 8 French divisions—85 divisions in all. "Finally, I have re-cast your language somewhat to make it a bit more optimistic. The fact is that 20, or even 10, additional divisions are not now in sight; consequently, there is no use asking for them. (Unless you consider that a total of 10 might finally be sent here from Italy.)" *Papers of Eisenhower,* IV, 2429–30. In his more detailed outline of 20Jan45 (Eisenhower to CCS, S-75871), Eisenhower again noted: "The enemy has now some eighty divisions on the Western Front, not all of them at full strength. Provided the Russian offensive is continued with vigour and the enemy maintains his front in Italy, this number is likely to dwindle. Should however the Russian offensive weaken and the Germans carry out a partial withdrawal from the Italian front there might be a diversion to my front of some ten or more divisions from Russia, and a dozen divisions from Italy. . . ." *SHAEF SGS 381*, Post Overlord Planning, 38, II. At the beginning of February he announced with delight to Bradley and Montgomery: "The Russian offensive has won great successes and the enemy has been forced to withdraw troops from the Western Front. It is of paramount importance therefore to close the Rhine north of Duesseldorf with all possible speed. . . ." Eisenhower to Bradley and Montgomery, 1Feb45, in *Papers of Eisenhower*, IV, 2465; cf Eisenhower, *Crusade in Europe*, 474–75.

9. Stimson Diary, 17Feb45.
10. Montgomery, *Memoirs*, 278–82.
11. Ibid, 286.
12. Eisenhower, "Notes on Conference with Gen G. C. Marshall, 28Jan45," Diary Office CinC; Montgomery, *Memoirs*, 289.
13. Diary Office CinC, 28Jan45.
14. Marshall int, 20Nov56.
15. Kuter, *Airman at Yalta*, 89–90.
16. The foregoing is based on *US For Rels, Malta-Yalta*, 464–65, 469–71, 473–76, 484–88.
17. Marshall int, 19Nov56.
18. Bryant, *Triumph in the West*, 301; Stimson Diary, 17Feb45.
19. *US For Rels, Malta-Yalta*, 532–33, 542–43; Moran, *Churchill*, 149–53, 207–208, 217–18.
20. *US For Rels, Malta-Yalta*, 544–45.
21. Kuter, *Airman at Yalta*, 3, 7–11, 14–17.
22. *US For Rels, Malta-Yalta*, President's log, 549–50; Kuter, *Airman at Yalta*, 110–16; King and Whitehill, *Fleet Admiral King*, 587–88.
23. Mark Twain, *Innocents Abroad* (Heritage Club ed), 293; *Time*, 19Feb45.
24. Robert K. Massie, *Nicholas and Alexandra*, 174–75. Admiral C. E. Olsen, "Full House at Yalta," *American Heritage*, Jan72, 21–25, 100–03, has detailed account of housekeeping ar-

rangements at Livadia Palace and two adjoining buildings where the American delegation (which he estimates at 270) was housed.
25. Kuter, *Airman at Yalta*, 122.
26. Massie, *Nicholas and Alexandra*, 521.
27. King and Whitehill, *Fleet Admiral King*, 588; Leahy, *I Was There*, 296–97; Stettinius, *Roosevelt and the Russians*, 81–84; Byrnes, *All in One Lifetime*, 259.
28. Ltr, Hull to author, 22Dec69.
29. Joseph R. McCarthy, *America's Retreat from Victory: The Story of George Catlett Marshall*, 61.
30. Marshall int, 4Feb57.
31. Pogue, *Ordeal and Hope*, 239.
32. For a convenient summary of much of the background material, see Def-Dept Bull, "The Entry of the Soviet Union into the War against Japan: Military Plans, 1941–1945," Sept55. See also essays by Forrest C. Pogue and by George A. Lensen in *Meaning of Yalta*, ed Snell.
33. CCS 300, Memo by JCS, Estimate of the Enemy Situation, 1943–44, 6Aug43, *US For Rels, Quebec, 1943*, 417–24. See Hopkins on unsigned memo, Sherwood, *Roosevelt and Hopkins*, 748–49. The views are much like others offered by Maj Gen James H. Burns, an assistant to Hopkins in Lend-Lease matters, and to some degree similar to views of Gen Embick.
34. Deane, *Strange Alliance*, 49–51 (italics added).
35. Hull, *Memoirs*, II, 413, 1309–10; Deane to JCS, 31Oct43, CM-IN 655; Harriman to Marshall, 2Nov43, CM-IN 1946, *OPD Msg File*.
36. Rpt by Comb Staff Planners, CCS 417, 2Dec43, *US For Rels, Cairo-Tehran*, 765.
37. Ibid, 770.
38. Memo by US CsofS, CCS 397 (rev), 3Dec43, ibid, 779.
39. Roosevelt rpt to Pacific War Council, 12Jan44, ibid, 868–70; alluded to in Harriman to Roosevelt, 15Dec44, *US For Rels, Malta-Yalta*, 378–79.
40. See also statement of Hollington Tong, 23Sept48; *US For Rels, Cairo-Tehran*, 891; *US Relations with China*, 558.
41. *US For Rels, Cairo-Tehran*, 566–67; William M. Franklin, "Yalta Viewed From Tehran," in *Some Pathways in Twentieth-Century History: Essays in*

Honor of Reginald Charles McGrane, ed Daniel R. Beaver.

42. *US For Rels, Cairo-Tehran,* 567–68.

43. Mins mtg of Pacific War Council, 12-Jan44, ibid, 868–69. Sec Hull's later surprise that Stalin had asked for concessions at Yalta, after his unequivocal promise in Moscow to fight Japan, should not be allowed to obscure the fact that the Russian leader spelled out in part for Roosevelt and Churchill what a more cynical SecState might well have realized was coming. Nor should it obscure the fact that they expected it.

44. DefDept Bull, "The Entry of the Soviet Union into the War against Japan." 28.

45. Decision amending JCS 924, 11Jul44, *ABC 384 Pacific (1–17–43), Sec 4.* Although these plans were ordered, "the invasion itself was never authorized," as Leahy has noted, *I Was There,* 245.

46. Unsigned memo Embick for JSSC to CofS, 30Sept44, *OPD 381, Sec XIX, Case 533.* This had been called for by Marshall at the beginning of the month.

47. Marshall to Embick, 3Oct44 (not sent), *OPD Exec 9, Bk 23.*

48. Harriman to Roosevelt, 24Sept44; President to Harriman, 4Oct44, *US For Rels, Malta-Yalta,* 5–7.

49. JCS to Deane, 28Sept44, CM-OUT 38050. Details in DefDept Bull 30.

50. Harriman to President, 17Oct44; Deane to JCS, 17Oct44, *US For Rels, Malta-Yalta,* 370–72. In Deane's message there is a detailed list of Russia's needs, totaling 1,056,000 tons. Included were 30,000 trucks, 400 C-47 aircraft, and 100 C-54 aircraft.

51. JCS 1176, Rpt by Jt Staff Planners, Russian Participation in the War against Japan, 23Nov44, DefDept Bull, 39–40 (italics added).

52. JCS 1176/6, Rpt by Jt Staff Planners, Russian Participation in the War against Japan, 18Jan45, as rev by JCS, 24Jan45; JCS to President, 23Jan45, "For the Joint Chiefs of Staff [George C. Marshall], Chief of Staff, US Army," in *US For Rels, Malta-Yalta,* 396, 388–94. Cf Anthony Kubek, *How the Far East Was Lost,* 117, which cites document—giving same source—as "General Marshall to President Roosevelt, January 23, 1945, Yalta Documents,

p. 396." In the text the author says that Marshall "submitted a memorandum to the President," without indicating that he was forwarding the document on behalf of the Joint Chiefs of Staff. Marshall acted on behalf of all the Chiefs, instead of Leahy's doing so, because Leahy had left that morning by ship with the President for Malta. Marshall and the other Chiefs left by plane two days later. Professor Kubek also insists that "A group of veteran intelligence officers, most of them regular Army colonels, prepared a document known as the Colonels' Report before our leaders went to Yalta." Ibid, 119. However the source he cites, *Military Situation in the Far East, Hearings,* 82d Cong, 2d sess, pt 4, 21Jun51, 2916–17 (held by the Senate committees on the Armed Services and on Foreign Relations), specifically gives an April date —which is referred to on 2914 and 2915 as 21Apr45 and on 2916 as 12Apr-45. According to the *Hearings,* 2916, Sen H. Alexander Smith asked, "Is that dated prior to the Yalta Conference?" and Sen Styles Bridges replied, "No; it was after Yalta but before Potsdam. . . ." The document itself has a fascinating and muddled history, which I shall discuss in my next volume.

53. Pasco note on Deane ltr to Marshall, 2Dec44, conveying views of Handy and Hull to Marshall; Marshall to Stimson, 21Dec44; Marshall to Deane, 2Jan45; Deane to Marshall, 3Jan45, *Marshall Library Files;* Pasco draft to Stimson, sent forward to President, 3Dec44; Marshall to Eisenhower, WAR-22163, 17Jan45, *OPD Exec 5, Item 19.*

54. Stettinius, *Roosevelt and the Russians,* 90–98.

55. *US For Rels, Malta-Yalta,* 564–66.

56. Stettinius says Alger Hiss and H. Freeman Matthews were there at the time, but the official minutes show that they came in after he had presented the agenda. Stettinius, *Roosevelt and the Russians,* 84; *US For Rels, Malta-Yalta,* 567.

57. *US For Rels, Malta-Yalta,* 564–67.

58. SecState to President, 2Feb45, ibid, 567. The memo that Stettinius says he presented and that presumably was discussed in the remainder of the meeting

is on 567–69 and Stettinius, *Roosevelt and the Russians*, 85–87. On the discussion see pages following. Harriman had made the President aware of these demands on 15Dec44.

59. *US For Rels, Malta-Yalta*, 379–83, 385–88, says Blakeslee and Borton memos were not included in the Briefing Book, and apparently not brought to FDR's attention.

60. King and Whitehill, *Fleet Admiral King*, 591–92. It seems likely that King confused this session with a meeting in the summer of 1945, when in fact he did say that southern Sakhalin was enough. By that time there was widespread doubt that Russian aid was essential. But by then the agreement with Stalin had been signed.

61. Leahy, *I Was There*, 317–18. Leahy also said (312): "I offered no objection to the decision to seek Russian assistance, although personally, I believed that the United States, single-handed if necessary, could defeat her within the time estimated." (This is an interpolated statement in the book and not in his diary for the date.) What he did say in his diary under 1Jan45 date (286) was that Japan was facing inevitable eventual defeat but that

there was "little prospect of obtaining from them an unconditional surrender within the year that was before us." His entry on 4Feb45, (298–300), mentions nothing of the concessions, although under 8Feb45, (307–11), he says that Harriman told him privately of talks between Roosevelt and Stalin on the latter's demands. As to the 10Feb plenary session, where he was the only member of the Joint Chiefs of Staff present, he says in his book (318): "It may come as a surprise to learn that the misnamed 'concessions' evoked little discussion and no argument when Stalin . . . formally announced that Russia would enter the war against Japan within two or three months with certain understandings. These . . . were substantially those that Ambassador Harriman had reported to me as agreed upon between Roosevelt and Stalin on February 8."

62. Marshall int, 4Feb57.

63. Kuter, *Airman at Yalta*, 128–30.

64. Marshall int, 4Feb57.

65. Cf Clemens, *Yalta*, chap 8; Franklin, "Yalta Viewed from Tehran," in *Some Pathways in Twentieth-Century History*, ed Beaver.

XXVII: THE FALTERING AXIS

For the Dresden episode I have drawn heavily on Craven and Cate, *The Army Air Forces in World War II*, III; Webster and Frankland, *The Strategic Air Offensive Against Germany*, III; David Irving, *The Destruction of Dresden*, (1963 and 1964); R. H. S. Crossman, "Apocalypse at Dresden," *Esquire*, Nov63; Joseph W. Angell, Jr, "Historical Analysis of the 14–15Feb45 Bombing of Dresden," USAF Historical Division Research Project (1953); Anthony Verrier, *The Bomber Offensive* (1968); and an excellent study, based on interviews and a fresh look at sources, by Melden Smith, "The Bombing of Dresden Reconsidered: A Study in Wartime Decision Making" (PhD diss, Boston University, 1971).

1. In Marshall int, 14Feb57, he said: "I never got caught in a review but once. . . ."

2. Clark, *Calculated Risk*, 423–26.

3. Marshall int, 15Feb57.

4. Clare Boothe Luce to Marshall, 6Jan45; Luce to SecWar, 6Jan45; Stimson to Luce, 12Jan45; Marshall to Pasco, 9Jan45, *Marshall Library Files; Cong Record, 79th Cong, 1st sess*, XCI, pt 1, 6Jan45, 91–96.

5. Col Wilton B. Persons to CofS, 8Mar45 with handwritten note by McCarthy; Marshall to Wilson, 8Mar45, *Marshall*

Library Files; New York *Times*, 6 and 22Mar; 4May45.

6. Clark, *Calculated Risk*, 425.

7. *US For Rels, Malta-Yalta*, 608.

8. This text is from MacArthur, *Reminiscences*, 249. Marshall to President, 5Feb45, *OPD Exec 17, Item 15*, sent above text, but he wrote "historic" instead of "historical" with notation: "I suggest you send some such message to MacArthur."

9. Lee, *Employment of Negro Troops*, 573, 576–78.

10. Marshall to Eisenhower, F-26834, 13-

Feb45, *SHAEF Files.* Summarizing a report by Marshall on the 92d Division, Stimson wrote in his Diary, 21-Feb45: "This is believed by the Army to be a very clear demonstration of the unreliability of Negro troops unless they are at least supported by white commissioned and noncommissioned officers. The 92d Division has been nursed and trained and strengthened more than any division we have and the men simply would not either stand fire or stay out nights fire or no fire. As Marshall remarked, the only place they could be counted on to stand would be in Iceland in summertime where there was daylight for 24 hours."

11. See Pogue, *Education of a General,* 260, and present vol, chap 5.

12. Lee, *Employment of Negro Troops,* 576–79.

13. FDR to SecState Stettinius, 4Dec44, *US For Rels, Malta-Yalta,* 174. "We are against reparations."

14. See *Meaning of Yalta,* ed Snell, 136–37.

15. Mins 1st Tripartite Military mtg, 5Feb45, *US For Rels, Malta-Yalta,* 595ff.

16. Ibid, 596. In connection with the above statement Marshall is first quoted as saying that the Allies lacked ground superiority. Later both he and Brooke spoke of "sufficient superiority."

17. Ibid, 597.

18. Ibid, 583.

19. For the analysis of the reasons for the decision on Dresden, I have relied on Webster and Frankland, *Strategic Air Offensive,* III, 43, 54–57, 100–102, 112–17.

20. *US For Rels, Malta-Yalta,* 583.

21. Ibid, 599–600; USSTAF MAIN-IN 15172, 1Feb45; USSTAF MAIN-IN 15873, 5Feb45, *USSTAF Historical Division Film, 519.523, RG 18,* National Archives.

22. Pertinent documents cited in Joseph W. Angell, Jr, "Historical Analysis of the 14–15Feb45 Bombing of Dresden," 13–14.

23. Loutzenheiser to Giles, 6Mar45, *AAF (AAG) 000.800 Germany, 1.*

24. Marshall to Stimson, Bombing of Dresden, 6Mar45, ibid, and *Marshall Library Files.*

25. Craven and Cate, *Army Air Forces in World War II,* III, 731 n84. Original memo by Stimson to Marshall, 6Mar-

45; McCarthy to Marshall, 6Mar45, with Marshall's "O.K."; McCarthy to CG, AAF, 6Mar45, *Marshall Library Files.*

26. McCarthy to Giles, 20Mar45; McCarthy to Kyle, 7Apr45, with reply by WHK[yle] in *Marshall Library Files;* USSTAF to CG, USAAF, Washington, n.d. but in reply to WAR 49485, 6Mar45, *USSTAF Historical Division Film, 519.523, RG 18,* National Archives.

27. Webster and Frankland, *Strategic Air Offensive Against Germany,* III, 112–13.

28. The figure of 35,000 is based on information uncovered after the appearance of David Irving's *The Destruction of Dresden* (1963 and 1964). Irving accepted a figure of 135,000 after the reported finding of a contemporary police report. See discussions by Angell, "Historical Analysis," and Melden Smith, "The Bombing of Dresden Reconsidered: A Study in Wartime Decision Making," both favoring the 35,000 figure. Smith cites letter by Irving to *London Times,* 7Jul66, in which he says that new information shows the 135,000 figure to be in error. Irving's letter quoted a German report by the Dresden area police chief, made about one month after the raids and furnished to Irving in 1966 by the East German authorities, which declared: "Casualties by March 10, 1945, 18,375 dead, 2,212 seriously injured, and 13,918 slightly injured had been registered, with 350,000 homeless and permanently evacuated." The total death toll, "primarily women and children," was expected to reach 25,000; fewer than 100 of the dead were servicemen.

29. Eisenhower, *Crusade in Europe,* 365–67, 474–76.

30. Luce, "To Ike, the Wall Rises Between Opposing Ideas of Man," *Life,* 8Sept61, 46–49; Albert L. Warner, "Our Secret Deal over Germany," *Saturday Evening Post,* 2Aug52, 30, 66.

31. *US For Rels, Malta-Yalta,* 464–66; Lt Gen Walter Bedell Smith, *My Three Years in Moscow,* 21–22.

32. Montgomery, *Memoirs,* 290–92. Montgomery says he repeated next to Churchill what he had said on 1Mar.

33. Marshall to Eisenhower, 6Mar45, *Marshall Library Files.*

34. Eisenhower to Marshall, FWD-17802, 12Mar45, *SHAEF Files;* Eisenhower to Marshall, 12Mar45, *Marshall Library Files.*

35. Eisenhower to CG 12th Army Gp and 6th Army Gp, 12Mar45, *Marshall Library Files.*

36. Marshall to Eisenhower, WX-57751, 23Mar45, *Marshall Library Files.*

37. Marshall to Eisenhower, W-59318, 27-Mar45, *Marshall Library Files.*

38. Eisenhower to Marshall, FWD-18258, 28Mar45, *SHAEF Files.*

39. Eisenhower to CCS, FWD-17645, 8Mar-45, *SHAEF Files.*

40. Eisenhower to Marshall, 26Mar45, *Marshall Library Files.*

41. Eisenhower to Mil Mission Moscow, Inf CCS, FWD-18264, SCAF 252, 28-Mar45, *SHAEF SGS 373.5, I.*

42. Marshall to Eisenhower, WAR 61337, forwarding Br CsofS views, 30Mar45, *OPD Msg File;* CCS 805/4, Memo by Rep of BrCsofS, 4Apr45, *ABC 384 Europe (5Aug43), Sec 1-D.*

43. Churchill to Br CsofS, 31Mar45, *Triumph and Tragedy,* 460–62.

44. Churchill to Eisenhower, 31Mar45, *SHAEF Files;* Prime Minister to Roosevelt, 1Apr45, Churchill, *Triumph and Tragedy,* 463–66.

45. Marshall to President, 2Apr45, Study of War Department on Probable Developments in German Reich, *OPD 381 TS (1945), Sec IV, Case 97/9.*

46. Ltr McCarthy to author, 7Feb70, *Marshall Library Files.*

47. Ltr Mrs Roosevelt to Marshall, 15Apr-45; McCarthy memo on funeral arrangements to Marshall, 13Apr45, *Marshall Library Files.*

48. Stimson Diary, 13Apr45.

49. Pasco to Marshall, 12Apr45.

50. Pasco to CofS, 14Apr45; Marshall to Wilby, 16Apr45, *Marshall Library Files.*

51. James M. Burns, *Roosevelt: The Soldier of Freedom,* 599–612, drew together a number of accounts for a moving description of the funeral. William Hassett said that two officers helped the pallbearers, but McCarthy and others were certain that Powder was involved. The exertions by Sgt Powder, who had suffered for some months with a heart condition, worried Gen Marshall, who instructed Col McCarthy to tell the sergeant that it would be "absolutely necessary in the future to make such arrangements as to preclude any physical exertion on his part other than walking. . . . Although his physical exertion yesterday was a matter of emergency, he should give careful advance thought in order to be prepared for such emergencies without taking over himself." McCarthy to Marshall, two memos about Powder, 16Apr45, *Marshall Library Files.*

52. In addition to Burns, see Stimson Diary, 15Apr45; King and Whitehill, *Fleet Admiral King,* 600; Hassett, *Off the Record with F. D. R.,* 343–45. On the evening of the funeral, Mrs. Roosevelt wrote to General Marshall: "My dear General, I want to tell you tonight how deeply I appreciate your kindness and thoughtfulness in all the arrangements made. My husband would have been grateful and I know it was all as he would have wished it. He always spoke of his trust in you and of his affection for you. With my gratitude and sincere thanks. Very sincerely yours, Eleanor Roosevelt." (Eleanor Roosevelt to Gen Marshall, April 15th, 15Apr45 handwritten letter in *Marshall Library Files.*)

XXVIII: END IN EUROPE

I have drawn on Dulles, *The Secret Surrender;* Stalin's correspondence with Roosevelt and Churchill; Churchill, *Triumph and Tragedy;* Bryant, *Triumph in the West;* Pogue, *The Supreme Command;* and Bradley, *A Soldier's Story.* Interviews include those with Gens Eisenhower, Ismay, Bradley, Hodges, Simpson, Deane, Bedell Smith; Air Marshals Portal and Tedder; Field Marshals Montgomery and Alanbrooke.

1. Stimson Diary, 2Apr45.

2. Ibid, 3Apr45.

3. Burns, *Roosevelt: The Soldier of Freedom,* 229–38.

4. Churchill to Eisenhower, 2Apr45, cited Churchill, *Triumph and Tragedy,* 467.

5. Ehrman, *Grand Strategy,* VI, 150.

6. Ibid, 150–51.

7. Stimson Diary, 11, 12, and 13Mar45. Allen W. Dulles, *The Secret Surrender*, 147–51, has a convenient chronology of the correspondence and action. See Toland, *Last 100 Days*, chap 13.

8. Stimson Diary, 17Mar45.

9. Molotov to British and American Governments, 23Mar45, Dulles, *Secret Surrender*, 149; *Correspondence between the Chairman of the Council of Ministers of the U.S.S.R. and the Presidents of the U.S.A. and the Prime Ministers of Great Britain During the Great Patriotic War of 1941–45*, II, 296–97. (Cited hereafter as *Stalin Correspondence*.) For the background of Molotov's announcement see *US For Rels, Europe, 1945*, V, 820–29.

10. Stalin to President, 29Mar45; Marshall to Leahy, 29Mar45, draft ltr for President to Stalin, *Marshall Library Files; Stalin Correspondence*, II, 200–201, 204–205.

11. Stalin to Roosevelt, 3Apr45, cited Churchill, *Triumph and Tragedy*, 446–47; *Stalin Correspondence*, II, 205–206.

12. Leahy to Marshall, 4Apr45, *Marshall Library Files.*

13. Marshall to Leahy, 4Apr45, with original draft President to Stalin, which contained Stimson's penciled suggestions. Filed with it is the copy of the msg, revised by Leahy and approved by the President, that was sent from the WH to Stalin, 222, 4Apr45, *Marshall Library Files*. See Dulles, *Secret Surrender*, 151, for statement that Justice Byrnes told him later that he had modified the stronger language of the original draft. See also *Stalin Correspondence*, II, 207–209.

14. Roosevelt to Stalin, 222, 4Apr45, *Marshall Library Files*. Churchill italicized the words of the last sentence in his *Triumph and Tragedy*, 448–49, saying that although he felt that Roosevelt had not drafted the entire message, "he might well have added this final stroke himself. It looked like an addition or summing up, and it seemed like Roosevelt himself in anger." Roosevelt's own considered reaction was shown more clearly on 12Apr45 in his last cable to the Prime Minister: "I would minimize the general Soviet problem as much as possible, because these problems, in one form or another, seem to arise every day, and

most of them straighten out, as in the case of the Berne meeting. We must be firm however, and our course thus far is correct." Cited Churchill, *Triumph and Tragedy*, 454. In the last cable message Roosevelt sent from Warm Springs on 12Apr45, according to Leahy, he wrote Harriman, "It is my desire to consider the Berne misunderstanding a minor incident." Leahy, *I Was There*, 336; see *Stalin Correspondence*, II, 214, for Roosevelt to Stalin, recd 13Apr45. Cf. Ryan, *Last Battle*, 164, on Mrs. Anna Rosenberg's recollections of Roosevelt's outburst against Stalin on March 24, 1944.

15. Churchill to Stalin, 6Apr45, cited Churchill, *Triumph and Tragedy*, 449–51.

16. Stalin to Roosevelt, 7Apr45, cited Churchill, *Triumph and Tragedy*, 451–52.

17. Marshall int, 11Feb57; Gen Antonov to Gen Deane, 30Mar45, *Stalin Correspondence*, II, 210–11.

18. Stalin to Churchill, 7Apr45; Churchill to Roosevelt, 11Apr45; Roosevelt to Churchill, 12Apr45, cited Churchill, *Triumph and Tragedy*, 451–54; *Stalin Correspondence*, I, 316–17.

19. Eisenhower to Marshall, 16Aug45, *Marshall Library Files.*

20. Memo by JCS, CCS 805/2, Plan of Campaign in Western Europe, 30Mar45, *ABC 384 Europe (5Aug43), Sec 1-D.*

21. Eisenhower to Marshall, FWD-18710, 7Apr45, *Marshall Library Files*. See earlier msgs, Eisenhower to Marshall, SHAEF 260, 31Mar45, *ABC Europe (5Aug43), Sec 1-D*. See Marshall to Stettinius, 13Jul44, cited above in chap 23, 459.

22. Marshall int, 11Feb57.

23. Kenneth Strong, *Intelligence at the Top*, 187–88. For a provocative study of the whole National Redoubt question see Rodney Minott, *The Fortress That Never Was.*

24. Leahy says in his memoirs that his notes indicate that the question was never brought formally before the CCS for action. Leahy, *I Was There*, 351.

25. Truman to Churchill, 21Apr45, cited Leahy, *I Was There*, 349–51.

26. According to Ryan, *Last Battle*, 321, Bradley conceded that his account in *Soldier's Story* created the erroneous impression that he gave his estimate

to Eisenhower in March and that he was speaking of the fight from that time on, when in fact his estimate was made after his first troops crossed the Elbe and referred to possible heavy losses in Berlin. It was easy to misread Bradley's account since the 100,000-casualty figure seemed more likely if it had been made in March after he had crossed the Rhine rather than in mid-April after the crossing of the Elbe. The price for taking Berlin was indisputably high. Harrison E. Salisbury, in his edition of *Marshal Zhukov's Greatest Battles*, says (288): "The cost of the final battle in Soviet casualties . . . was enormous: 305,000 from April 16 to May 8 in the First and Second Byelorussian and the First Ukrainian Fronts alone."

27. Montgomery to Eisenhower, M-568, 6Apr45; Eisenhower to Montgomery, 8Apr45; *Eisenhower Personal Files;* Montgomery to Eisenhower, M-1070, 9Apr45, *SHAEF Files.*

28. Stephen E. Ambrose, *Eisenhower and Berlin, 1945: The Decision to Halt at the Elbe,* gives the various arguments but concludes in favor of Eisenhower.

29. Eisenhower to Marshall, 15Apr45, *Marshall Library Files;* Bradley, *Soldier's Story,* 537–39.

30. Marshall int, 11Feb57.

31. WD memo, with covering note by Maj Gen Clayton L. Bissell, G-2, 22Mar45, *OPD 381, Sec IV.*

32. Eisenhower to CCS, SCAF 264, 5Apr-45, *SHAEF SGS 373.5, Bomb-Line, Liaison, and Co-ordination of Fronts, I.*

33. COS to JSM, COS (W) 748, 11Apr45, *SHAEF SGS 373.5, Bomb-Line, Liaison, and Co-ordination of Fronts, I.*

34. Lincoln to Hull, 13Apr45, CCS 805/7 and CCS 805/8, *OPD 381 TS, Sec V,* (italics in original); CCS to SHAEF, FACS 176, 12Apr45; Eisenhower to CCS, SCAF 274, 11Apr45; Eisenhower to Mil Mission Moscow, SCAF 275, 12-Apr45, *SHAEF SGS 373.5, Bomb-Line, Liaison, and Co-ordination of Fronts, I.*

35. CCS to Eisenhower, FACS 191, 21Apr-45; Eisenhower to CinC ExFor, Cmdrs 12th, 6th Army Gps, FWD 19624, 21-Apr45, *SHAEF SGS 373.5, Bomb-Line, Liaison, and Co-ordination of Fronts, I.*

36. Eisenhower to Mil Mission, Moscow, SCAF 298, 22Apr45; Eisenhower to Mil Mission, Moscow, SCAF 292, 21-

Apr45, *SHAEF SGS 373.5, Bomb-Line, Liaison, and Co-ordination of Fronts, I.*

37. Eisenhower to Mil Mission Moscow, SCAF 299, 23Apr45; Mil Mission Moscow to Eisenhower, MX-24032, 24Apr-45; Mil Mission Moscow to Eisenhower, MX 24055, 25Apr45, *SHAEF SGS 373.5, Bomb-Line, Liaison, and Co-ordination of Fronts, I.* The British, fearing that the Russians were trying to apply the line of the Elbe in the north as well as in the center of the SHAEF line, asked Eisenhower to make the distinction clear.

38. Marshall to Eisenhower, W-74256, 28-Apr45, *OPD 381 TS (1945), Sec V, Case 123.*

39. Eisenhower to Marshall, FWD 20225, 1May45, *SHAEF Files.*

40. Pogue, *Supreme Command,* 469. On Grew see *US For Rels, Europe, 1945,* IV, 448–53.

41. Marshall int, 11Feb57.

42. *US For Rels, Cairo-Tehran,* 255–56.

43. Stimson Diary, 25Aug44. In his notes for the conference, included with the entry, he had made his view stronger: "Let her [Russia] do the dirty work but don't father it." However Stimson was thinking mainly of punishment of Nazi officials; a few weeks later he strongly opposed the Morgenthau Plan as a policy that would bankrupt Germany or destroy her industry.

44. In fact, when Marshall had urged this arrangement on AsstSecWar McCloy, the latter was reminded of Clausewitz (see chap 23, 459–60).

45. *The Forrestal Diaries,* ed Walter Millis, 49–50; *US For Rels, Europe, 1945,* V, 252.

46. Stimson Diary, 23Apr45.

47. *US For Rels, Europe, 1945,* V, 253; cf Harry S. Truman, *Memoirs,* I, 77.

48. *US For Rels, Europe, 1945,* V, 253.

49. Stimson Diary, 23Apr45.

50. *US For Rels, Europe, 1945,* V, 254 (italics added).

51. See Truman's statements in *US For Rels, Europe, 1945,* V, 255; cf Gabriel Kolko, *The Politics of War: The World and United States Foreign Policy, 1943–1945,* 391, 395. Note also that Kolko, who had earlier said that "Leahy, the strongest advocate of a tough policy toward Russia, was on hand to provide the continuity and play on the same penchant for the

dramatic and the absurd," includes Leahy among the hard-liners at the conference of advisers, although Forrestal in his summary of the discussions distinctly thought that the Admiral took more or less the position of the SecWar. Certainly Leahy was not unreasonable in his statement. See Kolko, 381 and 395, and *Forrestal Diaries*, 49–50. The question arises whether a firm stand to indicate that the US was not weakening was the same as a determination to force a break if need be. Only Forrestal im-

plied that he was ready to go that far. See Kolko, 395.

52. *US For Rels, Europe, 1945*, V, 257–58.
53. Truman, *Memoirs*, I, 245.
54. Toland, *Last 100 Days*, 483–542; Dulles, *Secret Surrender*, 188–196.
55. Marshall to Eisenhower, W-78438, 7May45, *Marshall Library Files*.
56. Eisenhower to Marshall, FWD 20926, 8May45, *Marshall Library Files*.
57. Stark to Marshall, 30Mar45, *Marshall Library Files*.
58. Prime Minister to Wilson for Marshall, 30Mar45, *Marshall Library Files*.

Index

Lovett, Assistant Secretary of War for
Air Robert A., 68, 86
Lucas, Maj. Gen. John P., 331, 332,
333, 375
Luce, Rep. Clare Boothe, 177, 536, 537
Luce, Henry, 463, 547
Lunger, Mrs. Marjorie. *See* Payne, Sgt.
Marjorie

MacArthur, Gen. Douglas, x, 99, 104,
116, 125, 255, 453; and controversies,
163–66, 168, 169, 176, 440–42, 626,
638; and Marshall, 66, 77, 80, 89, 129,
176, 206, 323–24, 439, 441, 444, 538;
and Roosevelt, 169, 170, 440; and
U.S. strategy, 8, 160–61, 166, 167, 174,
252–53, 281, 440, 441–43, 451–52, 635;
political activities, 176–78, 277, 281–
284, 323, 337, 445–46, 627; and Vandenberg, 177, 178
McAuliffe, Maj. Gen. A. C., 486
McCarthy, Col. Frank, 17–18, 46, 52, 63,
64, 102, 122, 221, 352, 391, 505, 613
McCarthy, Sen. Joseph R., 268, 292,
522
McCloy, Assistant Secretary of War
John J., 68, 86, 123, 141, 142, 144,
145, 157, 182, 459, 460, 493, 623
McCormack, Rep. John, 108, 270, 282
McCormick, Robert R., 271
McIntire, Vice Adm. Ross T., 121
McIntyre, Marvin, 89
Macmillan, Harold, 181, 407, 408
McNair, Lt. Gen. Lesley J., x, 62, 71,
87, 117, 265, 354, 370, 427–28, 500
McNarney, Gen. Joseph T., xi, 68, 84,
367, 428, 564, 618
McNutt, Paul, 12, 13, 354, 356
Magruder, Brig. Gen. John, 63
Malta conference, 502, 506, 507, 513–
518, 548, 550, 607
Marianas, 447
Maris, Brig. Gen. Ward, 127
Marseille, 407, 415
Marshall, Gen. of the Army George C.:
and Allies, ix, 257–59, 275, 281, 285,

291–92, 300, 309–11, 550, 565–66, 657;
as Army's advocate, 14, 103, 130–35,
196–97, 269, 327–28, 348–49, 359, 365,
367–69, 495–97, 553–54, 557, 570–71,
583; and commissions, 110, 118, 121,
124–27; demobilization plans of, 94–
95, 574–75; and Dewey, 471–73; and
family, 43–48, 221–22, 346; and
field commanders, 39, 76–78, 115,
117–21, 128, 186, 191–92, 195, 224,
332–33, 373, 374–78, 382, 389, 396,
423, 428, 439, 442, 497–98, 512, 554,
647; and French, 229, 231, 232–34,
236, 399, 400–403, 491; and friends,
47–51; inspection trips of, 73–74,
322–24, 352–54, 359–60, 403–405,
474–78, 536–39; and interservice
rivalry, 42, 70, 89, 152–53, 168–70,
172–76, 206, 252, 324, 448–51, 626,
653; and Japanese relocation, 146–
147; and labor problems, 349–50,
360; and manpower needs, 12–13,
223, 354–58, 361–64, 490–91, 492,
499–502, 534, 539, 552; in Normandy,
390–92, 394–96; personal characteristics of, 3, 43, 52–54, 57, 59–60, 101,
133, 134–35, 322, 368, 505–506, 617;
and postwar Germany, 297, 455, 461,
467, 535, 577; and press, 56, 128, 359,
405, 421, 429, 552, 643; and role in
political decisions, x, 194, 315–16,
459, 530–31, 561, 572, 577–78, 580,
654; and staff, 40, 53, 56–68, 74, 75,
78–79, 115, 138, 195, 362–63, 370,
374–75; and strategy, 8, 16, 173, 195,
196, 241, 243, 253–54, 334–35, 340–41,
393, 406, 408–409, 415, 417, 419, 436,
443–44, 527–28; and Supreme Commander's appointment, xi, 228, 260,
262–64, 266–78, 281, 296, 299, 319–
321, 637; and unconditional-surrender formula, 33, 34, 222; and WAC,
56, 57, 106–109, 113
—at conferences: Algiers, 218–220;
Anfa, 19, 21–22, 24, 26, 27–29, 31, 36–
37, 229, 614; Malta, 507, 508, 513–
517; OCTAGON, 434–36; QUADRANT,